New Perspectives

Microsoft® 365®
Office 2021®

Advanced

Cengage

Australia • Brazil • Canada • Mexico • Singapore • United Kingdom • United States

**New Perspectives Series® Microsoft®
Office 365® & Office 2021® Advanced**
Jennifer Campbell, Patrick Carey, Ann Shaffer

SVP, Product: Erin Joyner

VP, Product: Thais Alencar

Product Director: Mark Santee

Senior Product Manager: Amy Savino

Product Assistant: Ciara Horne

Learning Designer: Zenya Molnar

Content Manager: Christina Nyren

Digital Delivery Quality Partner: Jim Vaughey

Developmental Editors: Robin Romer,
Michael Sanford, Mary Pat Shaffer

VP, Product Marketing: Jason Sakos

Director, Product Marketing: Danaë April

Executive Product Marketing Manager: Jill Staut

IP Analyst: Ann Hoffman

IP Project Manager: Anjali Kambli

Production Service: Lumina Datamatics, Inc.

Designer: Erin Griffin

Cover Image Source: Artur Debat/Getty Images

Mac Users: If you're working through this product using a Mac, some of the steps may vary. Additional information for Mac users is included with the Data files for this product.

Disclaimer: This text is intended for instructional purposes only; data is fictional and does not belong to any real persons or companies.

Disclaimer: The material in this text was written using Microsoft Windows 10 and Office 365 Professional Plus and was Quality Assurance tested before the publication date. As Microsoft continually updates the Windows 10 operating system and Office 365, your software experience may vary slightly from what is presented in the printed text.

Windows, Access, Excel, and PowerPoint are registered trademarks of Microsoft Corporation. Microsoft and the Office logo are either registered trademarks or trademarks of Microsoft Corporation in the United States and/or other countries. This product is an independent publication and is neither affiliated with, nor authorized, sponsored, or approved by, Microsoft Corporation.

Some of the product names and company names used in this book have been used for identification purposes only and may be trademarks or registered trademarks of Microsoft Corporation in the United States and/or other countries.

For product information and technology assistance, contact us at
**Cengage Customer & Sales Support, 1-800-354-9706 or
support.cengage.com.**

For permission to use material from this text or product, submit all
requests online at **www.copyright.com.**

Library of Congress Control Number: 2022938369

Student Edition ISBN: 978-0-357-67216-7
Looseleaf ISBN: 978-0-357-67217-4*
*Looseleaf available as part of a digital bundle

Cengage
200 Pier 4 Boulevard
Boston, MA 02210
USA

Cengage is a leading provider of customized learning solutions with employees residing in nearly 40 different countries and sales in more than 125 countries around the world. Find your local representative at **www.cengage.com.**

To learn more about Cengage platforms and services, register or access your online learning solution, or purchase materials for your course, visit **www.cengage.com.**

Notice to the Reader

Printed in the United States of America
Print Number: 01   Print Year: 2022

BRIEF CONTENTS

TABLE OF CONTENTS

EXCEL MODULES

**Module 9 Exploring Financial Tools
and Functions**
Analyzing a Business Plan . . . . **EX 9-1**

ACCESS MODULES

POWERPOINT MODULES

Getting to Know Microsoft Office Versions

Cengage is proud to bring you the next edition of Microsoft Office. This edition was designed to provide a robust learning experience that is not dependent upon a specific version of Office.

Microsoft supports several versions of Office:

- **Office 365:** A cloud-based subscription service that delivers Microsoft's most up-to-date, feature-rich, modern productivity tools direct to your device. There are variations of Office 365 for business, educational, and personal use. Office 365 offers extra online storage and cloud-connected features, as well as updates with the latest features, fixes, and security updates.

- **Office 2021:** Microsoft's "on-premises" version of the Office apps, available for both PCs and Macs, offered as a static, one-time purchase and outside of the subscription model.

- **Office Online:** A free, simplified version of Office web applications (Word, Excel, PowerPoint, and OneNote) that facilitates creating and editing files collaboratively.

Office 365 (the subscription model) and Office 2021 (the one-time purchase model) had only slight differences between them at the time this content was developed. Over time, Office 365's cloud interface will continuously update, offering new application features and functions, while Office 2021 will remain static. Therefore, your onscreen experience may differ from what you see in this product. For example, the more advanced features and functionalities covered in this product may not be available in Office Online or may have updated from what you see in Office 2021.

For more information on the differences between Office 365, Office 2021, and Office Online, please visit the Microsoft Support site.

Cengage is committed to providing high-quality learning solutions for you to gain the knowledge and skills that will empower you throughout your educational and professional careers.

Thank you for using our product, and we look forward to exploring the future of Microsoft Office with you!

Using SAM Projects and Textbook Projects

SAM Projects allow you to actively apply the skills you learned live in Microsoft Word, Excel, PowerPoint, or Access. Become a more productive student and use these skills throughout your career.

To complete SAM Textbook Projects, please follow these steps:

SAM Textbook Projects allow you to complete a project as you follow along with the steps in the textbook. As you read the module, look for icons that indicate when you should download **sam** ⬇ your SAM Start file(s) and when to upload **sam** ⬆ the final project file to SAM for grading.

Everything you need to complete this project is provided within SAM. You can launch the eBook directly from SAM, which will allow you to take notes, highlight, and create a custom study guide, or you can use a print textbook or your mobile app. Download IOS or Download Android.

To get started, launch your SAM Project assignment from SAM, MindTap, or a link within your LMS.

Step 1: Download Files

- Click the "Download All" button or the individual links to download your **Start File** and **Support File(s)** (when available). You <u>must</u> use the SAM Start file.

- Click the Instructions link to launch the eBook (or use the print textbook or mobile app).

- Disregard any steps in the textbook that ask you to create a new file or to use a file from a location outside of SAM.

- Look for the SAM Download icon **sam** ⬇ to begin working with your start file.

- Follow the module's step-by-step instructions until you reach the SAM Upload icon **sam** ⬆.

- Save and close the file.

Step 2: Save Work to SAM

- Ensure you rename your project file to match the Expected File Name.

- Upload your in-progress or completed file to SAM. You can download the file to continue working or submit it for grading in the next step.

Step 3: Submit for Grading

- Upload the completed file to SAM for immediate feedback and to view the available Reports.

  - The **Graded Summary Report** provides a detailed list of project steps, your score, and feedback to aid you in revising and re-submitting the project.

  - The **Study Guide Report** provides your score for each project step and links to the associated training and textbook pages.

- If additional attempts are allowed, use your reports to assist with revising and resubmitting your project.

- To re-submit the project, download the file saved in step 2.

- Edit, save, and close the file, then re-upload and submit it again.

For all other SAM Projects, please follow these steps:

To get started, launch your SAM Project assignment from SAM, MindTap, or a link within your LMS.

Step 1: Download Files

- Click the "Download All" button or the individual links to download your **Instruction File**, **Start File**, and **Support File(s)** (when available). You <u>must</u> use the SAM Start file.

- Open the Instruction file and follow the step-by-step instructions. Ensure you rename your project file to match the Expected File Name (change _1 to _2 at the end of the file name).

Step 2: Save Work to SAM

- Upload your in-progress or completed file to SAM. You can download the file to continue working or submit it for grading in the next step.

Step 3: Submit for Grading

- Upload the completed file to SAM for immediate feedback and to view available Reports.

  - The **Graded Summary Report** provides a detailed list of project steps, your score, and feedback to aid you in revising and resubmitting the project.

  - The **Study Guide Report** provides your score for each project step and links to the associated training and textbook pages.

- If additional attempts are allowed, use your reports to assist with revising and resubmitting your project.

- To re-submit the project, download the file saved in step 2.

- Edit, save, and close the file, then re-upload and submit it again.

For additional tips to successfully complete your SAM Projects, please view our Common Student Errors Infographic.

Customizing Word and Automating Your Work

Automating a Document for a Rock Climbing Gym

Objectives

Session 8.1
- Insert a shape
- Add text to a shape
- Apply ligatures and stylistic sets to text
- Compress photos
- Translate text
- Add a custom paragraph border
- Create a watermark

Session 8.2
- Edit building block properties
- Copy a building block to another document or template
- Copy a style to another document or template
- Add properties to a document
- Insert document properties into the document content
- Insert and customize fields

Session 8.3
- Learn about Trust Center settings
- Record and run macros
- Edit macros using Visual Basic
- Copy macros to another document or template
- Record an AutoMacro

Case | Alexander Griffin Rock Gym

Sam Nguyen manages Alexander Griffin Rock Gym, an indoor rock climbing gym in the student fitness center at Elliot Bay College in Seattle, Washington. All students and alumni who want to use the gym must sign a waiver acknowledging that they understand the potential risks. Sam has asked you to help him create the waiver as a Word template, which he'll place on the desktop of the computer at the front counter. Employees will be able to double-click the file to create new Word documents based on the template.

Sam wants you to add some additional content to the template, including the company name on a photo background; placeholders in Spanish, Chinese, and Vietnamese for the legal text; and a watermark and header indicating the template is a draft. He wants you to use a Quick Part and a style stored in another template and insert document properties in the template. He also wants you to add dialog boxes that will pop up, requesting the information that needs to be filled in when each new waiver document is created. In addition, Sam wants you to create a macro to insert the company slogan in a footer. Finally, he wants you to create an AutoMacro to highlight a reminder to request proof of age from each customer.

Starting Data Files

Word8	**Module**	**Review**
	NP_WD_8-1.dotx	NP_WD_8-3.dotx
	NP_WD_8-2.dotx	Support_WD_8_NewStyles.dotx
	Support_WD_8_Wall.jpg	Support_WD_8_People.jpg

Case1

NP_WD_8-4.dotx
Support_WD_8_RealtyStyles.dotx

Case2

NP_WD_8-5.dotx
Support_WD_8_Planting.jpg
Support_WD_8_Potomac.dotx

Session 8.1 Visual Overview:

The proofing language is the language used by the spell checker. You can set the proofing language for a document or for selected text.

The spell-check icon next to a language in the Language dialog box indicates that the language is installed on the computer.

Languages that appear above this line will be detected automatically.

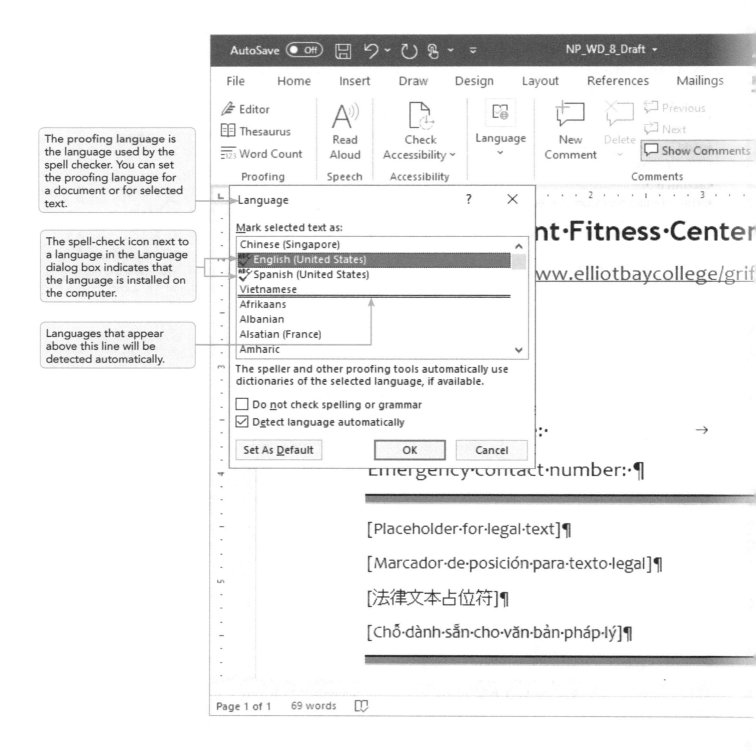

Translating Text

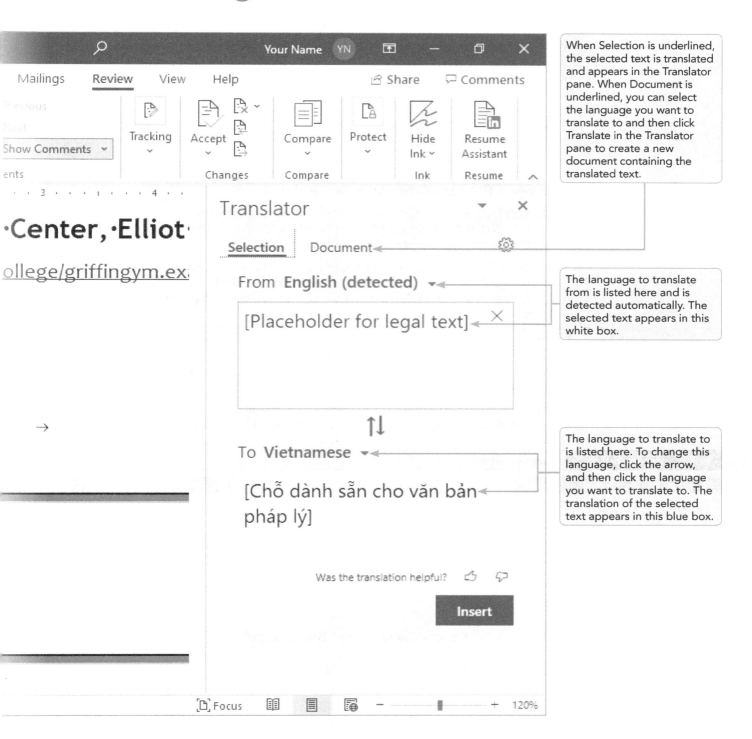

When Selection is underlined, the selected text is translated and appears in the Translator pane. When Document is underlined, you can select the language you want to translate to and then click Translate in the Translator pane to create a new document containing the translated text.

The language to translate from is listed here and is detected automatically. The selected text appears in this white box.

The language to translate to is listed here. To change this language, click the arrow, and then click the language you want to translate to. The translation of the selected text appears in this blue box.

Inserting a Shape

You can add a variety of shapes to a document, such as lines, rectangles, stars, and more. To draw a shape, click the Shapes button in the Illustrations group on the Insert tab, click a shape in the gallery, and then click and drag to draw the shape in the size you want. Like any object, you can resize a shape after you insert it.

Sam wants you to add a rectangle shape that contains the company name at the top of the template. He has already created a draft of the template with most of the text he wants to include, so you'll open that template and then add the shape to it. To modify a template, you must open it using the Open screen in Backstage view. If you double-click a file in a File Explorer window or open it via the New screen, a new document based on the template will be created.

To open the template and insert a shape:

1. **sam** ⬇ Using the Open command in Backstage view, open the template **NP_WD_8-1.dotx** located in the Word8 > Module folder included with your Data Files. The file name in the title bar is NP_WD_8-1.

   Trouble? If the file name in the title bar is Document1 (or some other number), close the document and then repeat Step 1, taking care to use the Open command in Backstage view so that you open the template rather than create a new document based on the template.

2. Save the file as a template named **NP_WD_8_Draft** in the location specified by your instructor.

3. If necessary, change the Zoom level to **120%**, and then display the rulers and nonprinting characters.

4. Click the **Insert** tab, and then in the Illustrations group, click the **Shapes** button. The Shapes gallery opens, as shown in Figure 8–1.

> Be sure to save the file as a template and not as a document, and verify that you are saving the template to the correct folder.

Figure 8–1	Shapes gallery

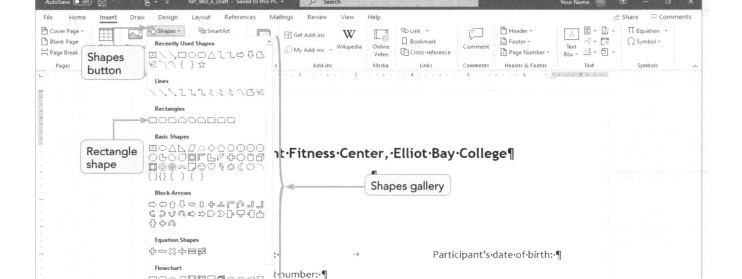

5. Under Rectangles, click the **Rectangle** shape. (Use the ScreenTip to identify the shape.) The gallery closes, and the pointer changes to the thin cross pointer $+$.

6. At the top of the document, click to insert a rectangle that is one inch square. The Shape Format tab appears on the ribbon.

7. Click the **Shape Format** tab. The measurements of the shape appear in the Shape Height and Shape Width boxes in the Size group.

8. Click in the **Shape Height** box to select the value in it, type **1.5**, and then press **ENTER**. The height of the shape changes to 1.5 inches. Unlike pictures, the aspect ratio for shapes is not locked, so the width of the shape doesn't change.

9. Click in the **Shape Width** box, type **8.5**, and then press **ENTER**. The rectangle is now the same width as the page.

10. In the Arrange group, click the **Align** button, and then click **Align Center**. The center of the shape aligns with the center of the page.

11. Click the **Align** button again, and then click **Align Top**. The top of the rectangle aligns with the top margin on the page. The rectangle is on top of the first three paragraphs in the document. You will fix this later.

You've already had a little experience with one type of shape—a text box is a shape specifically designed to contain text. However, you can add text to any shape you draw—just start typing while the shape is selected.

To add text to a shape and format it:

1. With the shape selected, type **Alexander Griffin Rock Gym**. (Do not type the period.) The text appears in the shape, centered horizontally.

2. On the Shape Format tab, in the Text group, click the **Align Text** button. On the menu, Middle is selected. Although the vertical alignment of the text in the shape is set to Middle, the text itself is not centered vertically because, like a regular paragraph in a document, the paragraph in the shape has eight points of space below it. See Figure 8–2.

Figure 8–2 **Paragraph center-aligned horizontally and vertically, with space after the paragraph**

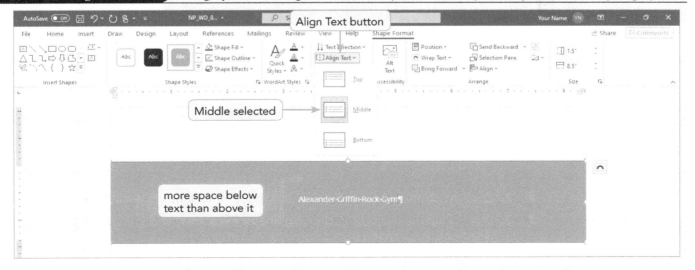

Tip

You can change the indent of text in a shape by clicking the Increase Indent or Decrease Indent button in the Paragraph group on the Home tab or by dragging the Left Indent marker on the ruler.

3. Click the **Layout** tab, and then in the Paragraph group, change the value in the After box to **0 pt**. The text in the shape moves down a little and is now centered vertically. If you wanted to change the horizontal alignment of text in a shape, you would use the alignment buttons in the Paragraph group on the Home tab.

4. Point to the rectangle border so that the pointer changes to the move pointer 🕀, and then click the border. The entire shape is selected. When you select the entire shape, text formatting is applied to all the text in the shape.

5. On the ribbon, click the **Home** tab.

6. In the Font group, click the **Font arrow**, scroll down the list, and then click **Trebuchet MS**.

7. In the Font group, click the **Font Size arrow**, and then click **28**.

8. In the Font group, click the **Bold** button ⑧. The text in the shape is now 28-point, bold Trebuchet MS.

Next, you need to change the shape's fill. When you draw a shape, it is filled with the Accent 1 color from the Theme Colors set. You can modify the fill of a shape by changing its color; by adding a gradient (shading in which one color blends into another or varies from one shade to another), a textured pattern, or a picture; or by removing it completely.

You can also modify the outline of a shape. The default outline is a darker shade of the Accent 1 theme color. You can change the outline by changing its color, width, and style, or you can remove it completely.

To change the shape's fill and remove the outline:

1. Click the **Shape Format** tab, and then in the Shape Styles group, click the **Shape Fill arrow**. The Shape Fill gallery opens. On the color palette, the Orange, Accent 1 color is selected. The default shape fill is the theme's Accent 1 color. See Figure 8–3.

Figure 8–3 **Shape Fill menu**

2. Click the **Brown, Accent 5** color. The shape fill changes to a shade of brown.

3. In the Shape Styles group, click the **Shape Fill arrow**, and then point to **Gradient**. A submenu opens. See Figure 8–4.

| Figure 8–4 | Gradient gallery on the Shape Fill menu |

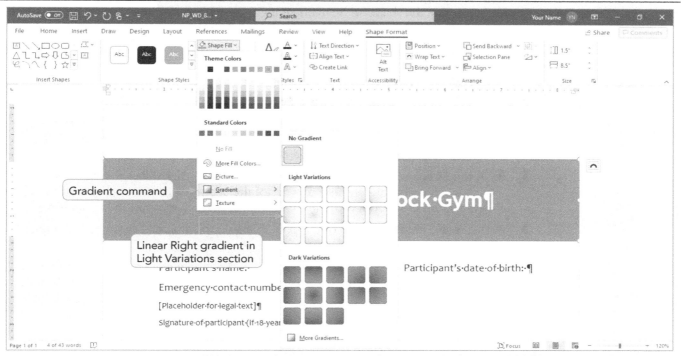

▶ **4.** In the Light Variations section, click the **Linear Right** gradient (the first gradient in the second row in the Light Variations section). The shape fill changes to a gradient in shades of brown, with the darker shade on the left fading to a lighter shade on the right. Now you'll remove the outline.

▶ **5.** In the Shape Styles group, click the **Shape Outline arrow**, and then click **No Outline**. The outline is removed.

Sam has decided he wants you to fill the shape with a photo to make it more dramatic. When a shape filled with a picture is selected, both the Picture Format tab and the Shape Format tab appear on the ribbon.

To fill a shape with a picture:

▶ **1.** On the Shape Format tab, in the Shape Styles group, click the **Shape Fill arrow**, and then click **Picture**. The Insert Pictures dialog box opens.

▶ **2.** Click **From a file**. The Insert Picture dialog box opens.

▶ **3.** Navigate to the **Word8 > Module** folder, click **Support_WD_8_Wall.jpg**, and then click **Insert**. The shape is filled with the photo.

When you fill a shape with a photo whose dimensions are different from the shape's dimensions, the photo is distorted to force it to fill the shape. In this case, the photo was distorted because it was stretched horizontally to fill the width of the shape and shrunk vertically to fit inside the shape.

You can fix this by using the Fill or Fit commands on the Crop menu. The Fill command matches the picture's height or width to the shape's height or width (whichever is longer) and crops the rest of picture. The Fit command fits the picture completely inside the shape while maintaining the aspect ratio of the picture. This means there will likely be empty space around the picture inside the shape.

To adjust the picture inside the shape:

1. On the ribbon, click the **Picture Format** tab.

2. In the Size group, click the **Crop arrow**, and then click **Fit**. The proportions of the picture are reset, and the entire picture fits inside the rectangle. This leaves empty space in the shape on either side of the picture.

3. In the Size group, click the **Crop arrow**, and then click **Fill**. The picture is enlarged to completely fill the width of the shape, and the top and bottom of the picture are cropped off. In the Size group, the Crop button is selected.

4. Move the pointer on top of the picture inside the shape. The pointer changes to the four-headed arrow pointer ⊹.

5. Press and hold the mouse button, and then drag the picture down until the top of the picture is aligned with the top of the shape. The Crop button is still selected.

6. In the Size group, click the **Crop** button. The Crop button is no longer selected, and the crop handles are removed from the shape.

The text on top of the picture is a little hard to read. To make the text more readable, you will change the transparency of the picture and change the color of the text.

To change the transparency of the picture and the color of the text:

1. On the Picture Format tab, in the Adjust group, click the **Transparency** button. A gallery of transparency percentages opens. If you wanted to customize the transparency, you could click Picture Transparency Options to open the Format Picture pane, where you could enter a custom transparency percentage. See Figure 8–5.

Figure 8–5   **Transparency gallery**

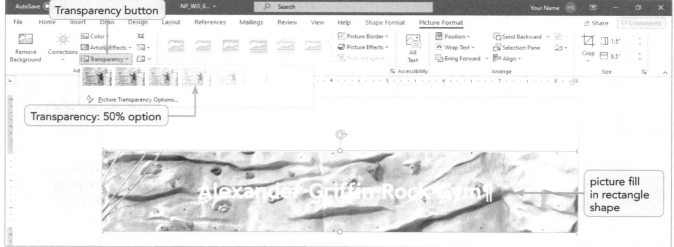

Sorbis/Shutterstock.com

▶ **2.** In the gallery, click the **Transparency: 50%** option. The picture inside the shape is 50 percent more transparent, and you can now see the text in the first paragraph behind the rectangle.

▶ **3.** Click the **Home** tab.

▶ **4.** In the Font group, click the **Font color arrow** [A ⌄], and then click the **Brown, Text 2, Darker 50%** color.

   Next, you need to move all the text in the document down so that the first line of text in the document is not underneath the rectangle.

▶ **5.** Click anywhere in the paragraph that begins with "Participant's name," and then press the ↑ key three times. The insertion point is in the first paragraph behind the rectangle.

▶ **6.** On the ribbon, click the **Layout** tab, and then in the Paragraph group, change the value in the Before box to **114 pt**. The first paragraph now has 114 points of space before it, shifting it below the rectangle.

▶ **7.** Save the changes to the template.

Applying Advanced Text Formatting

As with regular text, you can apply a variety of text effects and formatting to text that you add to a shape. In addition to the basic formatting options—such as font size, font color, and italic formatting—Word offers more advanced text formatting options, including ligatures and stylistic sets. A **ligature** is a connection between two characters. In some fonts, you can apply ligatures to visually connect characters such as the letter "f" and the letter "i." Some font designers also provide additional styles—called stylistic sets—for the characters within a font. Some of the style changes are obvious; others are very subtle. Ligatures and stylistic sets are not available for all fonts.

   Sam wants you to use ligatures in the company name in the rectangle shape to connect the second "f" and "i" in "Griffin." He also wants you to see if there are any stylistic sets available that will change the shape of any of the letters.

To change the ligature setting and stylistic set of the text in the shape:

▶ **1.** Click the rectangle shape's border to select the entire shape, and then on the ribbon, click the **Home** tab.

▶ **2.** In the Font group, click the **Text Effects and Typography** button [A ⌄], and then point to **Ligatures**. The Ligatures submenu opens. See Figure 8–6.

Figure 8–6	Ligatures submenu

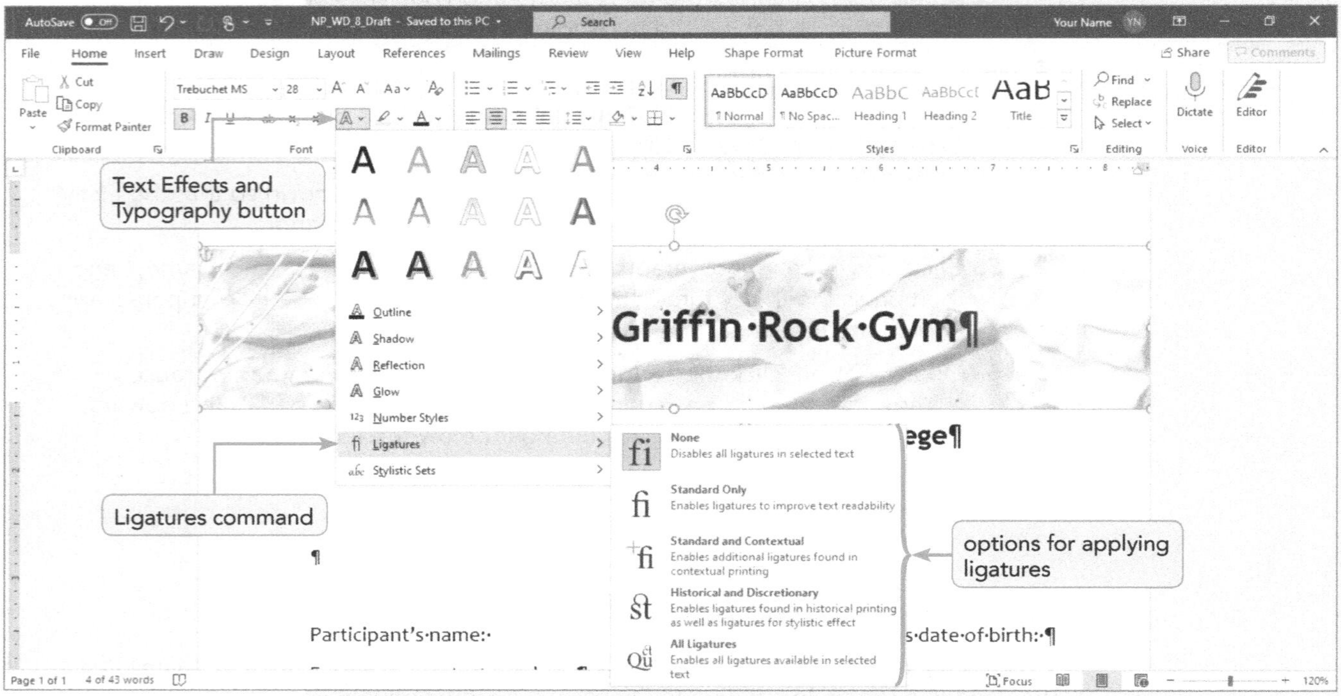

Sorbis/Shutterstock.com

▶ **3.** Click **Historical and Discretionary**. The second "f" and "i" in "Griffin" are now joined.

▶ **4.** In the Font group, click the **Text Effects and Typography** button, and then point to **Stylistic Sets**. The Stylistic Sets submenu opens. The default set is displayed at the top, with alternate sets provided by the font designer below. In the second stylistic set in the "Individual" section, the "A" has a crossbar that is lower than the default version, and the round part of the "R" is slightly larger. See Figure 8–7.

Figure 8–7	Stylistic Sets submenu

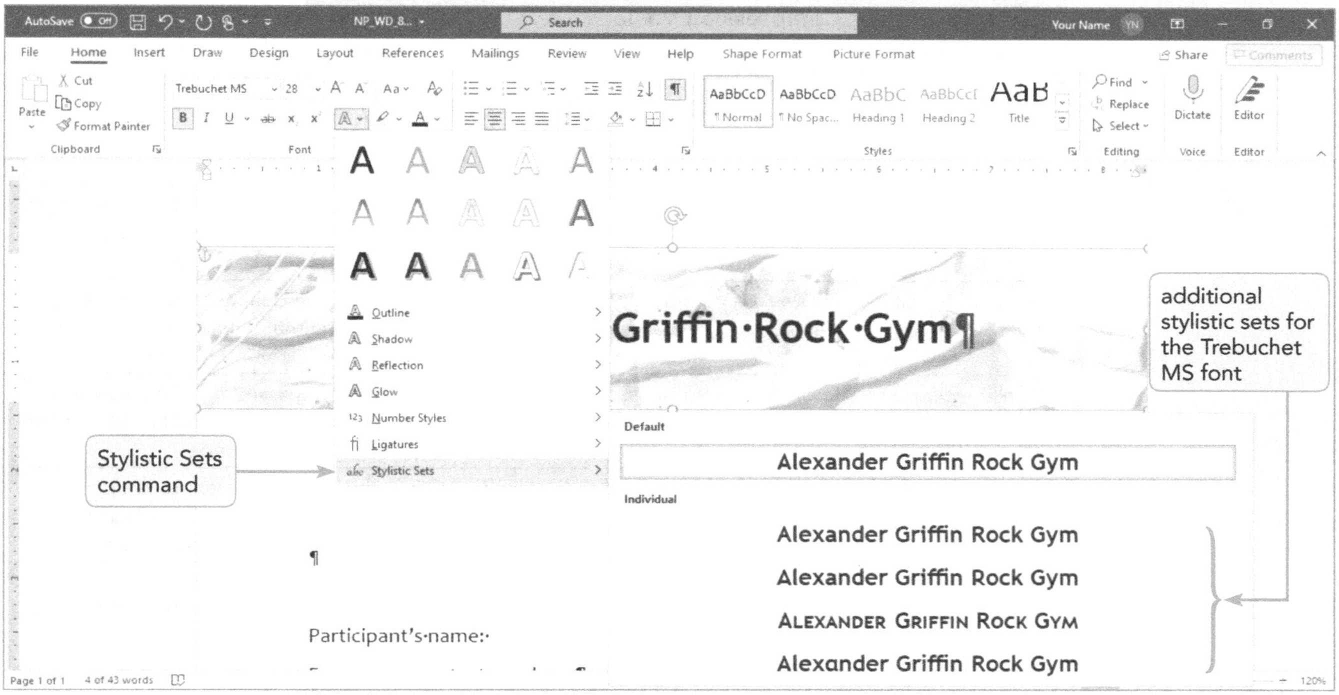

Sorbis/Shutterstock.com

5. Click the second style below "Individual." The style of the font changes, and the letters "A" and "R" change shape. You can see the change if you undo the action and then redo it.

6. On the Quick Access Toolbar, click the **Undo** button . The action of changing the stylistic set is undone, and the letter "A" is changed back to its original style.

7. On the Quick Access Toolbar, click the **Redo** button . The stylistic set is reapplied, and the letters "A" and "R" are again changed.

8. Save the changes to the template.

Compressing Pictures in a Document

Pictures added to Word documents are compressed by default to 220 pixels per inch (ppi). This setting, which can be changed in the Word Options dialog box, is applied automatically to all pictures in the document. You can change the default setting to High fidelity or to 330, 220, 150, or 96 ppi, or you can turn off the automatic compression feature. For some pictures, you can choose to compress them further after you insert them. See Figure 8–8 for a description of the compression options available.

Figure 8–8	Photo compression settings

Compression Setting	Compression Value	When to Use
High fidelity	Photos are compressed very minimally.	Use when a picture in a document will be viewed on a high-definition (HD) display, when photograph quality is of the highest concern, and when file size is not an issue.
HD (330 ppi)	Photos are compressed to 330 pixels per inch.	Use when the quality of the photograph needs to be maintained on HD displays and file size is of some concern.
Print (220 ppi)	Photos are compressed to 220 pixels per inch.	Use when the quality of the photograph needs to be maintained when printed. This is the default resolution.
Web (150 ppi)	Photos are compressed to 150 pixels per inch.	Use when a picture in a document will be viewed on a low-definition display or uploaded to a webpage.
E-mail (96 ppi)	Photos are compressed to 96 pixels per inch.	Use when it is important to keep the overall file size small, such as for documents that need to be emailed.
Use default resolution	Photos are compressed to the resolution specified on the Advanced tab in the Word Options dialog box. (The default setting is 220 ppi.)	Use when file size is not an issue, or when the quality of the photo display is more important than file size.
Do not compress images in file	Photos are not compressed at all.	Use when it is critical that photos remain at their original resolution.

Compressing photos reduces the size of the file, but it also reduces the quality of the photos. When you compress pictures, you remove pixels. If the picture is small, some compression won't matter; but if the picture is large or if you remove too many pixels, the difference in quality will be noticeable.

Before you change the compression of the photo in the shape, you'll verify the current default compression setting.

To check the picture compression setting for the NP_WD_8_Draft template:

1. On the ribbon, click the **File** tab, scroll down, and then in the navigation pane, click **Options**. The Word Options dialog box opens.

2. In the navigation pane, click **Advanced** to display the Advanced options, and then scroll down until you can see the Image Size and Quality section. See Figure 8–9.

Figure 8–9	Advanced options in the Word Options dialog box

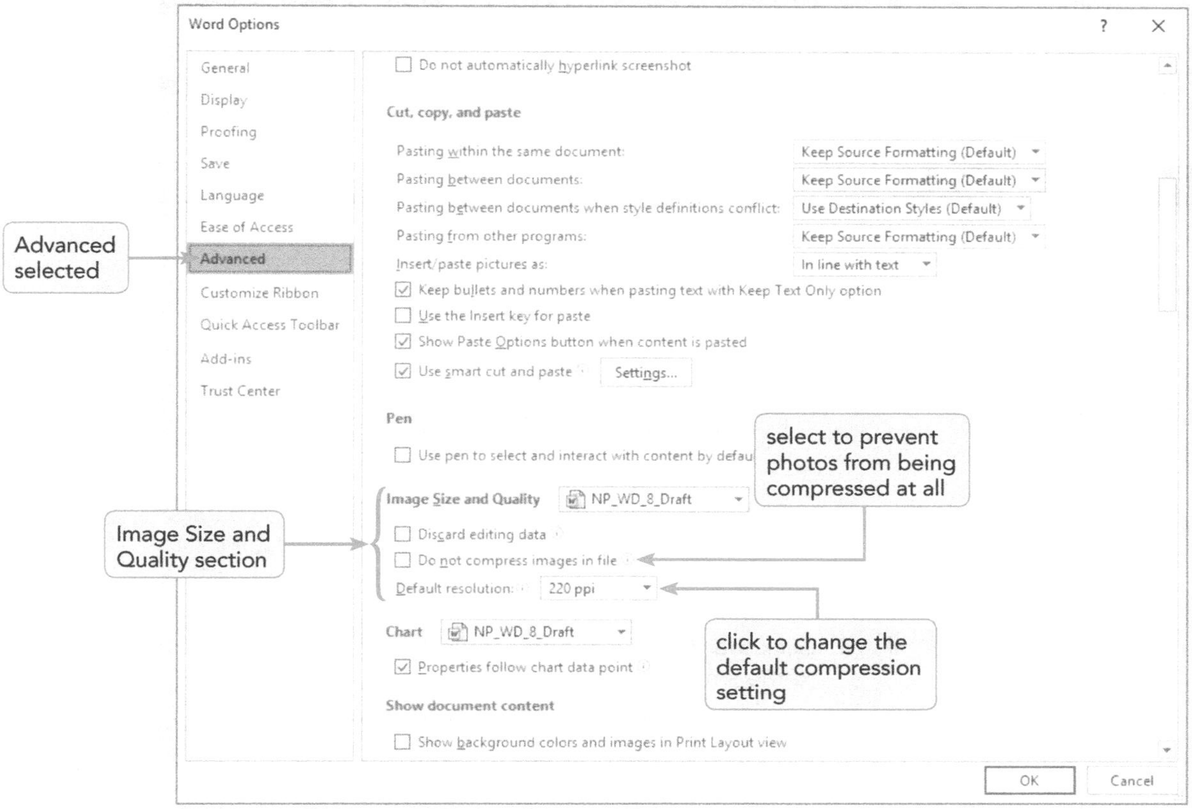

3. In the Image Size and Quality section, verify that the box next to "Default resolution" contains 220 ppi.

4. Click **Cancel** to close the dialog box without making any changes.

The waiver form will not be distributed for customers to take home—they will sign it and give it back to the employee who checks them in. However, Sam wants to be able to send the template via email to various people in the company for their approval. He also wants to be able to email the final form to customers so they can print and sign the form ahead of time. Therefore, he wants you to compress the photo to the smallest size possible.

Reference

Modifying Photo Compression Settings

- Click a photo to select it.
- On the ribbon, click the Picture Format tab.
- In the Adjust group, click the Compress Pictures button to open the Compress Pictures dialog box.
- Click the option button next to the resolution you want to use.
- To apply the new compression settings to all the photos in the file, click the Apply only to this picture check box to deselect it.
- To keep cropped areas of photos, click the Delete cropped areas of pictures check box to deselect it.
- Click OK.

To compress the photo further:

▶ **1.** With the entire shape selected, click the **Picture Format** tab.

▶ **2.** In the Adjust group, click the **Compress Pictures** button 🖼. The Compress Pictures dialog box opens. Under Resolution, the Use default resolution option button is selected. See Figure 8–10.

Figure 8–10   Compress Pictures dialog box

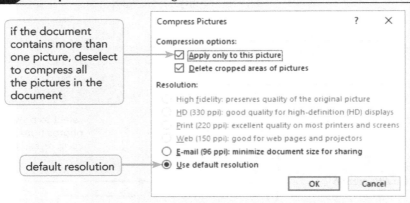

if the document contains more than one picture, deselect to compress all the pictures in the document

default resolution

▶ **3.** Click the **E-mail (96 ppi)** option button. This setting compresses the photos to the smallest possible size.

At the top of the dialog box, under Compression options, the Apply only to this picture check box is selected. This is the only photo in the document, so changing this setting will have no effect. The Delete cropped areas of pictures check box is also selected. To make the file size as small as possible, you will leave this check box selected as well.

▶ **4.** Click **OK**. The photo is compressed to 96 ppi, and the cropped areas are removed. You can verify this using the Crop button.

▶ **5.** In the Size group, click the **Crop** button. The crop handles appear around the picture, and the cropped portion of the picture below the shape is gone.

▶ **6.** In the Size group, click the **Crop** button to turn that option off.

Translating Text

You can use tools in Word to translate text into other languages. Keep in mind, however, that the translations generated by Word are not always perfect. After you translate all or part of a document, have an expert in the language review the translation and make any necessary corrections. See the Session 8.1 Visual Overview for more information about translating text.

Selecting an Option for Translating Text

You can use the Translate button in the Language group on the Review tab to translate selected text in a document or to translate the entire document. If you translate the entire document, a new document containing the translated text is created.

At Elliot Bay College, many students and alumni speak English as a second language. The first language for some students is Spanish, while other students speak Chinese or Vietnamese as a first language. Sam wants to provide the legal disclaimers in the waiver in Spanish, Chinese, and Vietnamese as well as in English. He has placeholder text in the document to indicate where the legal text of the waiver will be added. He wants you to add this same placeholder text in Spanish, Chinese, and Vietnamese to remind him to have the legal text translated after it is provided.

To translate selected text:

▶ **1.** Scroll down to position the paragraph that begins with "Participant's name" at the top of the document window.

▶ **2.** Select the entire line containing the text "[Placeholder for legal text]."

▶ **3.** Click the **Review** tab.

▶ **4.** In the Language group, click the **Translate** button, and then click **Translate Selection**. The Translator pane opens on the right. See Figure 8–11.

| Figure 8–11 | Translator pane |

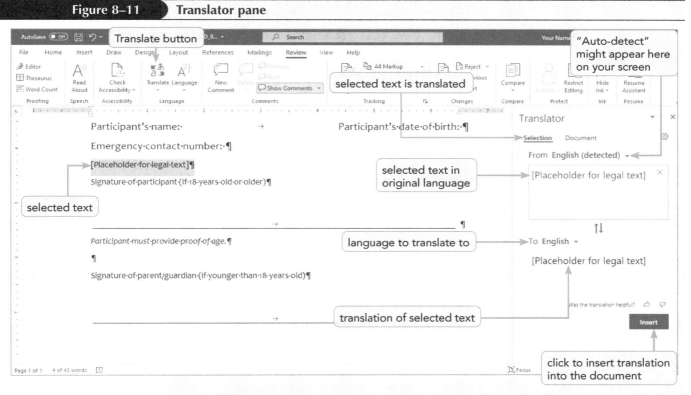

Trouble? If the Use Intelligent Services? dialog box appears, click Turn on.

At the top of the pane, Selection is underlined, which means only the selected text will be translated. You could click Document to translate the entire document instead. The selected text appears in the top white box, and the label above it identifies the language of the text you want to translate, in this case, English. The label above the bottom blue box identifies the language you want to translate the selected text to, in this case, English. The text in the blue box is the translation of the selected text.

Trouble? If English does not appear after "To" above the blue box, don't worry about it. Continue with Step 5.

▶ **5.** In the Translator pane, next to "To English," click the **arrow** ▼. An alphabetical list of languages appears. The bottom of the list is hidden.

▶ **6.** In the Translator pane, drag the scroll box down to the bottom of the scroll bar.

▶ **7.** Scroll the alphabetical list of languages, and then click **Spanish**. The Spanish translation of the selected text appears in the blue box.

▶ **8.** In the document, click at the end of the line "[Placeholder for legal text]," and then press **ENTER**.

▶ **9.** In the Translator pane, click **Insert**. The Spanish translation is pasted at the location of the insertion point.

▶ **10.** In the document, click at the end of the line that contains the Spanish translation, and then press **ENTER** to insert a new blank paragraph. In the Translator pane, the text you originally selected still appears in the white From box.

▶ **11.** In the Translator pane, next to "To Spanish," click the **arrow** ▼, scroll the list up, and then click **Chinese Simplified**. The Chinese translation of the selected text appears in the blue box.

▶ **12.** In the Translator pane, click **Insert**. The Chinese translation is pasted at the location of the insertion point in the document.

▶ **13.** Click in the blank paragraph below the Chinese translation.

▶ **14.** In the Translator pane, change the translation language to **Vietnamese**, and then click **Insert**. The Vietnamese translation appears in the document.

▶ **15.** At the top of the Translator pane, click the **Close** button ✕.

Changing the Proofing Language of Specific Words

The spell checker in Word can be very helpful, but when it flags words that are spelled correctly, the wavy red lines under the words can be distracting. In the waiver template, words in the two foreign phrases are flagged as misspelled. This is because the proofing language for the template is set to English.

You can change the proofing language for an entire document or template or for only specific words to any language supported by Microsoft 365. If the proofing language you specify is not installed on your computer, the words in that language will no longer be flagged as misspelled, but Word will not be able to determine if the foreign language words are spelled correctly. However, if you open the file on a computer that has that language installed, you can use the spell checker to check the words.

You will set the proofing languages for the paragraphs containing the three foreign phrases to the specific languages used.

To set the proofing language for the paragraphs containing text in other languages:

▶ **1.** Select the entire paragraph containing the Spanish translation of "Placeholder for legal text." The wavy red lines that indicate misspelled words appear below the words.

Trouble? If there are no wavy red lines below the Spanish words, continue with Step 2, but note that you will not see any differences after completing Step 5.

▶ **2.** On the Review tab, in the Language group, click the **Language** button, and then click **Set Proofing Language**. The Language dialog box opens. See Figure 8–12.

Figure 8–12 Language dialog box

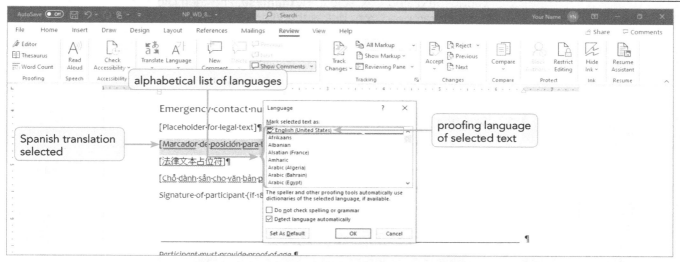

By default, the selected text is marked as English. The spell check icon next to English (United States) indicates that this language is installed. If there are any other languages above the line, it means that words typed in those languages should be detected automatically as long as the Detect language automatically check box is selected.

3. Make a note of any other languages that are listed below English on your screen and above the line. You will need to reset this list later.

4. Scroll down the alphabetical list until you see Spanish (United States). Notice that all the variations of Spanish have a spell-check icon next to them. Microsoft 365 sold in English-speaking countries comes with the English, Spanish, and French languages installed.

   Trouble? If there is no spell-check icon next to Spanish (United States), then that language is not installed on your computer. The proofing language will still be changed for the selected words; continue with Step 5.

5. Click **Spanish (United States)**, and then click **OK**. The wavy red lines under the selected words disappear.

   Trouble? If a yellow bar appears at the top of the document below the ribbon telling you that you are missing proofing tools, click the Close button ☒ at the right end of the yellow bar.

6. Select the entire paragraph containing the Chinese translation, click the **Language** button in the Language group, and then click **Set Proofing Language**. At the top of the list, "Spanish (United States)" now appears above the line with English.

7. Scroll the list until you can see Chinese (Singapore). The spell-check icon does not appear next to this language. This means the language is not installed on your computer.

8. Click **Chinese (Singapore)**, and then click **OK**. The dialog box closes, and the wavy red lines are removed from below the Chinese translation.

▶ **9.** Select the entire paragraph containing the Vietnamese translation, open the Language dialog box, select **Vietnamese**, and then click **OK**. The wavy red lines are removed from below the Vietnamese translation, and the yellow MISSING PROOFING TOOLS bar appears at the top of the document below the ribbon. The yellow bar tells you that Vietnamese is not being checked and asks if you want to download proofing tools. Sam will install the language later, so you will close the message bar.

▶ **10.** At the right end of the yellow bar, click the **Close** button ⊠.

▶ **11.** Save the changes to the template.

Now you will reset the languages list to the state it was in before you set the proofing languages for the foreign phrases.

To reset the proofing languages list:

▶ **1.** On the ribbon, click the **File** tab, and then in the navigation pane, click **Options**. The Word Options dialog box opens.

▶ **2.** In the navigation pane, click **Language**. Language options appear in the dialog box. See Figure 8–13.

Figure 8–13   **Language options in the Word Options dialog box**

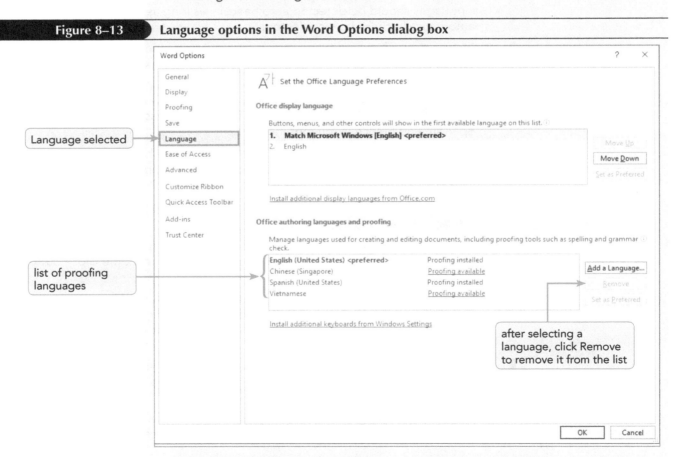

3. In the Office authoring languages and proofing section, click **Chinese (Singapore)** in the list. The buttons to the right of the list become available.

4. If Chinese (Singapore) was not listed in the Language dialog box (shown in Figure 8–12) before you set the proofing languages, click **Remove** to remove Chinese (Singapore) from the list; if Chinese (Singapore) was listed in the Language dialog box, do not click Remove.

5. If Spanish (United States) and Vietnamese were not listed in the Language dialog box before you set the proofing languages, remove them.

Tip

You can also open the Language tab in the Word Options dialog box by clicking the Language button in the Language group on the Review tab, and then clicking Language Preferences.

6. Click **OK**. The Word Options dialog box closes. If you removed any languages, the Microsoft Office Language Preferences Change dialog box opens with a message indicating you need to restart Office for your language changes to take effect. You don't need to restart Word right now. The change will take effect the next time you close and restart Word.

    Trouble? If you did not remove any of the three languages, the dialog box does not appear. Click anywhere in the document to deselect the text, and skip Step 7.

7. Click **OK**, and then click anywhere in the document to deselect the text.

8. Save the changes to the template.

Proskills

Written Communication: Utilizing Global Content Standards

The world is smaller than it ever has been. Many companies do business with companies in other countries or have international customers. If you work for a company that has international ties, you should evaluate the documents you create to make sure they contain information that is appropriate for and clear to an international audience. For example, when a date is written using numbers in the United States, the first number is the month and the second is the day of the month. In Europe, the order is reversed—the first number is the day of the month and the second is the month. It is important to know how your audience will interpret a date written as numbers. For example, August 12, 2025 would be written as 8/12/2025 in the United States, and as 12/8/2025 in Europe. A European reading the United States format and someone from the United States reading the European format could interpret the date as December 8, 2025. Customers and foreign companies with whom your company does business will appreciate your efforts to consider their needs.

Adding a Custom Paragraph Border

Borders can be used not only to draw attention to text but also to separate parts of a document so it is easier to read. You already know how to add a basic border around a paragraph. You can also create a custom border by changing the style, line weight (thickness), and color.

Reference

Adding a Custom Border

- Position the insertion point in the paragraph to which you want to add a custom border.
- On the ribbon, click the Home tab.
- In the Paragraph group, click the Borders arrow, and then click Borders and Shading to open the Borders tab in the Borders and Shading dialog box.
- In the Setting list, click the Custom button.
- In the Style list, click a border style.
- Click the Color arrow, and then click a border color.
- Click the Width arrow, and then click a border width.
- In the Preview area, click the sides of the paragraph around which you want the border to appear.
- Click OK.

Sam wants you to add a border to separate the top part of the waiver, which contains the customer data, and the part of the waiver that will contain the legal language cautioning climbers that they potentially could be injured.

To insert a custom border in the template:

1. Click anywhere in the paragraph containing "Emergency contact number." This is the last line of customer information. The next line will contain the legal paragraphs that need to be added to the waiver.

2. Click the **Home** tab.

3. In the Paragraph group, click the **Borders arrow** ⊞ ˅ , and then click **Borders and Shading**. The Borders and Shading dialog box opens with the Borders tab selected.

4. In the Style list, scroll to the bottom of the list, and then click the third style from the bottom. In the Preview area on the right, the border encompasses the entire paragraph. You need to change this using the Custom setting on the left side of the dialog box.

5. In the Setting list on the left, click the **Custom** button. Now you need to remove the borders from the top and sides of the paragraph.

6. In the Preview area, click the left border. The border you clicked is removed from the preview.

7. Click the top and right borders of the paragraph in the Preview area to remove those borders. Now you will change the thickness of the border.

8. Click the **Width** arrow, and then click **4 ½ pt**. The border at the bottom of the paragraph in the Preview area is still three points. You need to reapply it with the new width selected.

9. In the Preview area, click the border at the bottom of the paragraph. The border is now 4½ points wide. See Figure 8–14.

Figure 8–14 **Borders tab in the Borders and Shading dialog box**

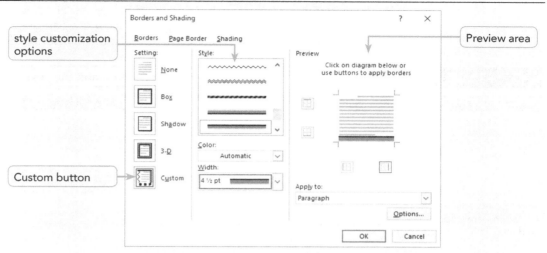

style customization options

Custom button

Preview area

▶ **10.** Click **OK**. The custom border you created appears below the "Emergency contact number" paragraph.

The border is closer to the paragraph above it than to the paragraph below it. You will adjust the space between the border and the paragraph you applied it to so that it appears centered between the two paragraphs.

To change the space between the border line and the text:

▶ **1.** Make sure the insertion point is still in the paragraph containing "Emergency contact number."

▶ **2.** On the Home tab, in the Paragraph group, click the **Borders arrow**, and then click **Borders and Shading**. The Borders and Shading dialog box opens.

▶ **3.** In the dialog box, click **Options**. The Border and Shading Options dialog box opens. See Figure 8–15.

Figure 8–15 **Border and Shading Options dialog box**

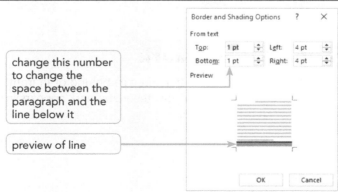

change this number to change the space between the paragraph and the line below it

preview of line

▶ **4.** Click in the **Bottom** box, and then change the value to **8 pt**.

▶ **5.** Click **OK**, and then click **OK** in the Borders and Shading dialog box. The border you added shifts eight points below the paragraph containing "Emergency contact number" and the line you inserted. See Figure 8–16.

Figure 8–16   **Paragraph with eight points of space between it and the custom border**

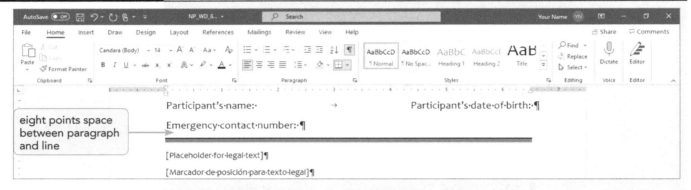

Sam tells you that he also wants the border to appear between the legal text and the section that will contain the signature of the participant. The border is part of the paragraph formatting, so you can use the Format Painter to copy it.

To use the Format Painter to copy the paragraph border:

▶ **1.** Select the paragraph containing "Emergency contact number."

▶ **2.** On the Home tab, in the Clipboard group, click the **Format Painter** button, and then click anywhere on the Vietnamese translation you inserted. The font and paragraph formatting of the "Emergency contact number" paragraph is applied to the paragraph containing the Vietnamese translation.

   Trouble? If the font size of the Vietnamese translation changed to 14 points, select the entire paragraph containing the Vietnamese translation, click the Font size arrow in the Font group on the Home tab, and then click 11.

▶ **3.** Click a blank area of the document, and then save the changes to the template.

Creating a Watermark

A **watermark** is text or a graphic that appears behind or in front of existing text on the printed pages of a document. Usually, the watermark appears in a light shade in the background of each printed page.

Reference

Creating a Custom Text Watermark

- On the ribbon, click the Design tab.
- In the Page Background group, click the Watermark button, and then click Custom Watermark to open the Printed Watermark dialog box.
- Click the Text watermark option button.
- Click the Text arrow, and then click an option in the list; or delete the text in the Text box, and then type the text you want to use as the watermark.
- If desired, click the Font arrow, and then click a font; click the Size arrow, and then click a font size; and click the Color arrow, and then click a color.
- If desired, deselect the Semitransparent check box to make the text darker.
- If desired, click the Horizontal option button to lay out the text horizontally rather than diagonally.
- Click OK.

Sam wants you to add a watermark identifying the waiver as a draft document. You'll do this next.

To add a watermark:

1. On the ribbon, click the **Design** tab, and then in the Page Background group, click the **Watermark** button. The Watermark gallery opens. The gallery is divided into sections: Confidential, Disclaimers, and Urgent. See Figure 8–17.

Figure 8–17 **Watermark gallery and menu**

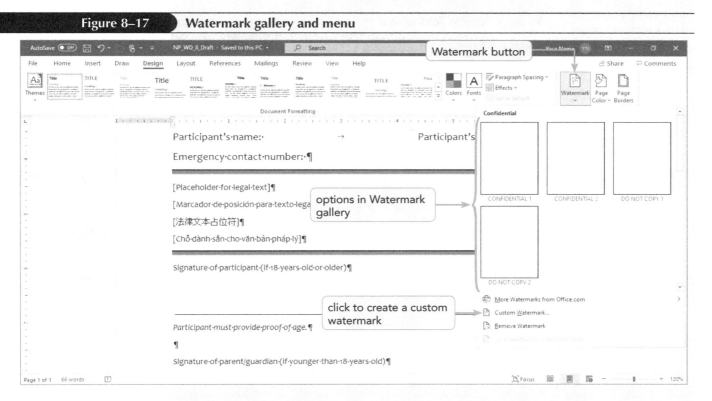

Although Draft is in the gallery both as a horizontal and a diagonal watermark, you will see what other options are available.

▶ **2.** Scroll to the bottom of the gallery to see the rest of the choices, and then below the gallery, click **Custom Watermark**. The Printed Watermark dialog box opens. The No watermark option button is selected, so none of the commands except the three option buttons are available to be selected. See Figure 8–18.

Figure 8–18   **Printed Watermark dialog box**

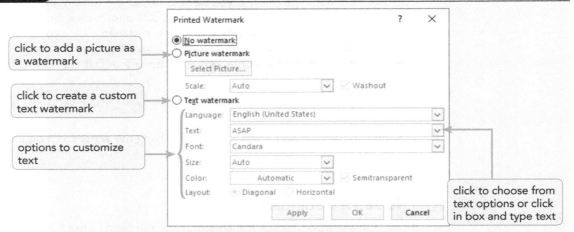

click to add a picture as a watermark	
click to create a custom text watermark	
options to customize text	

click to choose from text options or click in box and type text

Tip

To insert a picture as a watermark, click the Picture watermark option button, and then click Select Picture.

▶ **3.** Click the **Text watermark** option button. The commands below that option button become available.

▶ **4.** Click the **Text arrow** to open a list of text watermarks. There are more options in this list than there were in the gallery. You can select one of these or type your own in the Text box.

▶ **5.** Click **DRAFT**. You can customize text watermarks by changing the language, font, font size, font color, and transparency of the text. You can also change the direction of the text. With the default options, the text will be semitransparent, light gray, and slanted in a diagonal direction.

▶ **6.** Click **OK**. "DRAFT" appears in light gray, arranged horizontally, as a watermark in the template.

▶ **7.** Save the changes to the template.

In this session, you added a shape with formatted text, inserted a photo as the shape fill, compressed the photo, applied ligatures and stylistic sets to the text in the shape, translated text, and added a custom border and a watermark. In the next session, you'll edit the properties of a building block, copy a Quick Part and a style from one template to another, and add properties and fields to the template.

Insight

Customizing the Ribbon, Quick Access Toolbar, and Status Bar

You can modify the ribbon, the Quick Access Toolbar, and the status bar to suit your working style. To customize the ribbon and the Quick Access Toolbar, click the File tab on the ribbon, and then in the navigation pane, click Options to open the Word Options dialog box. Click Customize Ribbon or click Quick Access Toolbar in the navigation pane on the left. The dialog box changes to show two lists. The list on the left contains the commands available to either the ribbon or the Quick Access Toolbar. The list on the right contains the tabs on the ribbon or the buttons on the Quick Access Toolbar. By default, the list on the left displays the most popular commands. To see all the available commands, click the Choose commands from arrow above the list of commands on the left, and then click All Commands. To see all available macros, click the Choose commands from arrow, and then click Macros.

To add a button to the Quick Access Toolbar, click a command in the list on the left, and then click Add; to remove a button, click it in the Customize Quick Access Toolbar list on the right, and then click Remove. The process of customizing the ribbon is a little more complex. You cannot delete any buttons, groups, or tabs that are on the ribbon by default. To add a button, you need to create a new group on an existing tab or create a new tab and then create a group on that tab. To create a new tab, in the Customize the Ribbon list on the right, click the tab after which you want the new tab to appear, and then click New Tab. To create a new group, click the tab on which you want the group to appear, and then click New Group. With the new group selected, click commands in the list on the left, and then click Add. Rename the new tab or group by selecting it in the Customize the Ribbon list and then clicking Rename. If you want to reset the ribbon or the Quick Access Toolbar, click Reset in the dialog box, and then click Reset all customizations.

To customize the status bar, right-click a blank area of the status bar to open a menu of buttons you can add. Buttons with a checkmark next to them are already on the status bar. Click a button that does not have a checkmark next to it to add it to the status bar. Click a button that has a checkmark next to it to remove it from the status bar.

Sam is pleased with the final template. He thinks it will help his employees work more efficiently.

Review

Session 8.1 Quick Check

1. How do you add text to a shape that you draw?
2. What is a ligature?
3. What is the default compression for photos in a Word document?
4. What properties of a paragraph border can you change?
5. What is the proofing language?
6. What is a watermark?

Session 8.2 Visual Overview:

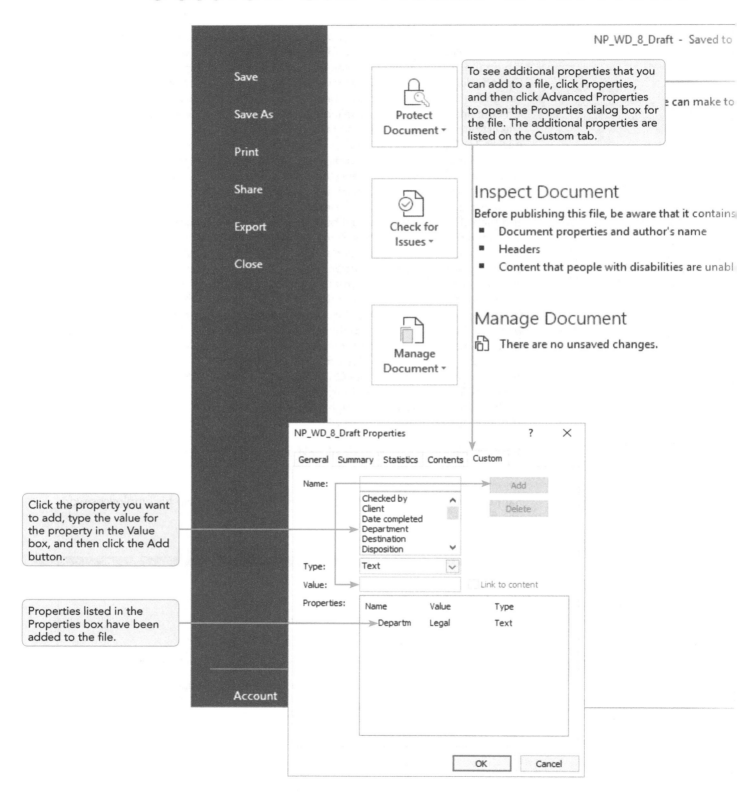

NP_WD_8_Draft - Saved to

Save

Save As

Print

Share

Export

Close

Account

Protect Document ▾

To see additional properties that you can add to a file, click Properties, and then click Advanced Properties to open the Properties dialog box for the file. The additional properties are listed on the Custom tab.

e can make to

Inspect Document

Before publishing this file, be aware that it contains

- Document properties and author's name
- Headers
- Content that people with disabilities are unabl

Check for Issues ▾

Manage Document

There are no unsaved changes.

Manage Document ▾

NP_WD_8_Draft Properties   ?   ✕

General   Summary   Statistics   Contents   Custom

Name: [   ]   Add

Checked by
Client
Date completed
Department
Destination
Disposition   Delete

Type: Text ▾

Value: [   ]   Link to content

Properties:

Name	Value	Type
Departm	Legal	Text

OK   Cancel

Click the property you want to add, type the value for the property in the Value box, and then click the Add button.

Properties listed in the Properties box have been added to the file.

File Properties

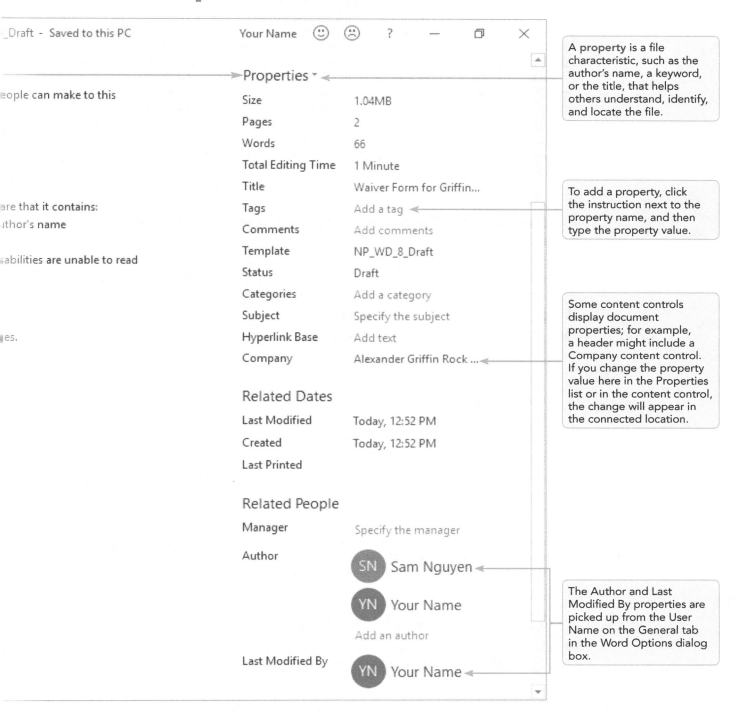

_Draft – Saved to this PC

Your Name ☺ ☹ ? — ▢ ✕

eople can make to this

are that it contains:
uthor's name

abilities are unable to read

es.

Properties ▾

Size	1.04MB
Pages	2
Words	66
Total Editing Time	1 Minute
Title	Waiver Form for Griffin…
Tags	Add a tag
Comments	Add comments
Template	NP_WD_8_Draft
Status	Draft
Categories	Add a category
Subject	Specify the subject
Hyperlink Base	Add text
Company	Alexander Griffin Rock …

Related Dates

Last Modified	Today, 12:52 PM
Created	Today, 12:52 PM
Last Printed	

Related People

Manager	Specify the manager
Author	SN Sam Nguyen
	YN Your Name
	Add an author
Last Modified By	YN Your Name

A property is a file characteristic, such as the author's name, a keyword, or the title, that helps others understand, identify, and locate the file.

To add a property, click the instruction next to the property name, and then type the property value.

Some content controls display document properties; for example, a header might include a Company content control. If you change the property value here in the Properties list or in the content control, the change will appear in the connected location.

The Author and Last Modified By properties are picked up from the User Name on the General tab in the Word Options dialog box.

Editing Building Block Properties

Building blocks, which are all of the preformatted content—including Quick Parts—that you can insert into a document via a Word gallery, are stored in templates. They can be stored in the Building Blocks template on a computer so that they are available to all documents on that computer, or they can be stored in a document template so that they are always available to people who use the template, no matter what computer they work on.

Previously, Sam created a template in which he stores styles and building blocks that are used frequently in company documents. He did this so he can keep all of this information in one place. One of the items in that template is a formatted Quick Part that contains the webpage address of the Rock Gym. Sam wants you to copy that Quick Part from his template to the NP_WD_8_Draft template, but first, you'll look at the Quick Parts gallery in the NP_WD_8_Draft template to confirm that the gallery currently does not contain any Quick Parts.

To examine the Quick Parts gallery in the NP_WD_8_Draft template:

1. If you took a break after the last session, use the Open command in Backstage view to open the **NP_WD_8_Draft** template. First, you'll examine the Quick Parts gallery in this template.

2. On the ribbon, click the **Insert** tab.

3. In the Text group, click the **Explore Quick Parts** button 🗈 ▾. If any Quick Parts were stored in this template, they would appear at the top of the Quick Parts menu; however, no Quick Parts are currently stored in the NP_WD_8_ Draft template.

   Trouble? If you see Quick Parts on the menu, they are stored in the Normal template or in the Building Blocks template, both of which are stored on your computer. You can ignore those Quick Parts.

4. Press **ESC** to close the Explore Quick Parts menu.

Like files, building blocks have properties. In Sam's template, the Rock Gym Webpage Address Quick Part is missing a Description property. You'll open the template Sam created and save a copy in the location where you are saving your files. Then you'll edit the Rock Gym Webpage Address Quick Part by adding a description so that the user understands what the Quick Part contains.

To edit the properties for the Quick Part:

1. Use the Open command in Backstage view to open the template **NP_WD_8-2.dotx** located in the Word8 > Module folder, and then save it as a template named **NP_WD_8_Styles** in the location specified by your instructor. This file appears to be empty.

2. On the ribbon, click the **Insert** tab, and then in the Text group, click the **Explore Quick Parts** button 🗈 ▾. A Quick Part containing the formatted web address of the Rock Gym webpage appears in the gallery above the Quick Parts menu.

3. Point to the **Rock Gym Webpage Address** Quick Part. Note that no ScreenTip appears.

4. Right-click the **Rock Gym Webpage Address** Quick Part, and then on the shortcut menu, click **Edit Properties**. The Modify Building Block dialog box opens. See Figure 8–19.

Figure 8–19 Modify Building Block dialog box

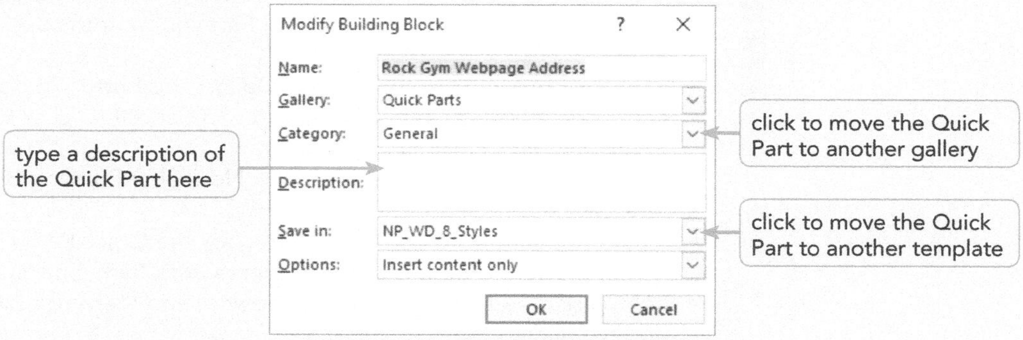

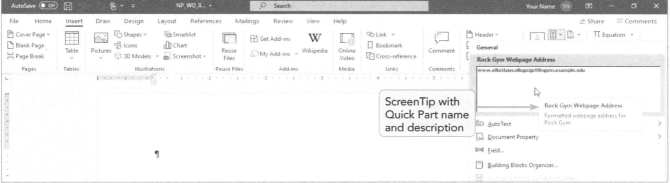

5. Click in the **Description** box, type **Formatted webpage address for Rock Gym**, and then click **OK**. A dialog box opens, asking if you want to redefine the building block entry.

6. Click **Yes**. Now you'll examine the description in the ScreenTip.

7. In the Text group, click the **Explore Quick Parts** button [icon], and then point to the **Rock Gym Webpage Address** Quick Part. A ScreenTip now appears containing the Quick Part name as well as the description you added. See Figure 8–20.

Figure 8–20 ScreenTip after adding the description to the Quick Part

8. Save the changes to the template.

Copying a Building Block to Another Document or Template

Now that you've edited the Rock Gym Webpage Address Quick Part stored in the NP_WD_8_Styles template, you'll copy it to the NP_WD_8_Draft template. To copy a building block from one custom template to another, you first change the location in which the building block is saved from the custom template to the Normal template or to the Building Blocks template. The Normal template is the template on which new, blank documents are based, and the Building Blocks template contains all the building blocks, such as the headers available on the Header button, that are available to all Word documents. From within the custom template, you edit the Save in property of the building block so it is saved to the custom template.

Reference

Copy a Quick Part to Another Template

- In the template containing the Quick Part you want to copy, click the Insert tab on the ribbon.
- In the Text group, click the Explore Quick Parts button to open the Quick Parts gallery.
- Right-click the Quick Part you want to copy, and then click Edit Properties to open the Modify Building Block dialog box.
- Click the Save in arrow, and then click Normal or Building Blocks.
- Click OK.
- In the template to which you want to copy the Quick Part, click the Insert tab, and then in the Text group, click the Explore Quick Parts button.
- Right-click the Quick Part you are copying, and then click Edit Properties to open the Modify Building Block dialog box.
- Click the Save in arrow, and then click the current template name.
- To keep a copy of the Quick Part in the original template, close that template without saving changes.

To copy a Quick Part between templates:

1. In the NP_WD_8_Styles template, open the Modify Building Block dialog box for the Rock Gym Webpage Address Quick Part again.

2. In the dialog box, click the **Save in arrow**. The list that opens contains the current template, NP_WD_8_Styles, and the Normal and Building Blocks templates. It does not include the NP_WD_8_Draft template even though that template is open. You'll store the Rock Gym Webpage Address Quick Part in the Building Blocks template.

3. Click **Building Blocks**, click **OK**, and then click **Yes** to confirm that you want to redefine the entry. Now you can access the Quick Part from within the NP_WD_8_Draft template.

   Next, you'll switch to the NP_WD_8_Draft template. Do not save the changes made to the NP_WD_8_Styles template.

4. On the ribbon, click the **View** tab.

5. In the Window group, click the **Switch Windows** button, and then click **NP_WD_8_Draft** to make it the active template.

6. Click the **Insert** tab if necessary, and then in the Text group, click the **Explore Quick Parts** button 🗐 ▾. The Rock Gym Webpage Address Quick Part now appears in the gallery because it was stored in the Building Blocks template.

7. Right-click the **Rock Gym Webpage Address** Quick Part, and then click **Edit Properties**. The Modify Building Block dialog box opens with Building Blocks listed in the Save in box. You need to change the Save in location to the NP_WD_8_Draft template.

8. Click the **Save in arrow**, click **NP_WD_8_Draft**, click **OK**, and then click **Yes** to confirm the change.

9. Switch back to the NP_WD_8_Styles template, and then open the Quick Parts gallery. The Rock Gym Webpage Address Quick Part no longer appears in the gallery. To keep the Rock Gym Webpage Address Quick Part in the NP_WD_8_Styles template, you will close the template without saving the changes to it.

10. In the title bar, click the **Close** button ✕. A dialog box opens asking if you want to save the changes to NP_WD_8_Styles.

▶ **11.** Click **Don't Save**. The NP_WD_8_Styles template closes, and the NP_WD_8_ Draft template is the active template. Because you did not save the change you made to the template, the Rock Gym Webpage Address Quick Part is still stored in the NP_WD_8_Styles template.

▶ **12.** Save the changes to the NP_WD_8_Draft template. Now the Rock Gym Webpage Address Quick Part is also saved with the NP_WD_8_Draft template.

Finally, you'll insert the Rock Gym Webpage Address Quick Part in the NP_WD_8_Draft template.

▶ **13.** At the top of the document, click in the empty paragraph below "Student Fitness Center, Elliot Bay College."

▶ **14.** On the Insert tab, in the Text group, click the **Explore Quick Parts** button 📄 ▾, and then click the **Rock Gym Webpage Address** Quick Part to insert it into the template. See Figure 8–21.

Figure 8–21	Rock Gym Webpage Address Quick Part inserted in NP_WD_8_Draft template

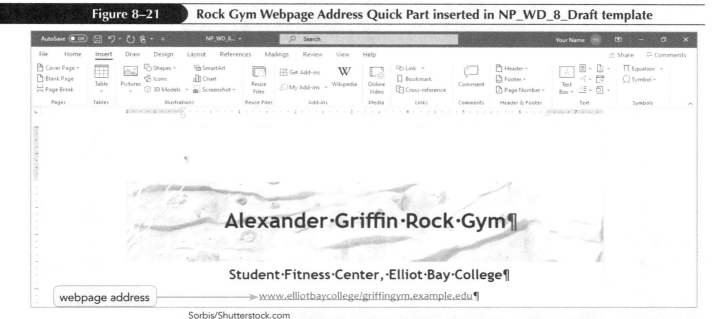

Sorbis/Shutterstock.com

▶ **15.** Save the changes to the template.

Insight

Creating Building Blocks in Other Galleries

Word has many predesigned building blocks for a wide variety of items, including cover pages, calendars, numbering, and text boxes. For example, when you click the Header or Footer button on the Insert tab, the preformatted options in the gallery are building blocks.

In addition to creating Quick Parts—building blocks stored in the Quick Parts gallery— you can create custom building blocks in any of the galleries that contain building blocks. For example, if you create a custom header, you can use the Save Selection to Quick Part Gallery command on the Quick Parts menu to open the Create New Building Block dialog box. In that dialog box, click the Gallery arrow and then click Headers to store the custom header in the Headers gallery instead of in the Quick Parts gallery.

Copying a Style to Another Document or Template

You can also copy styles from one document or template to another. To do this, you open the Styles pane, click the Manage Styles button to open the Manage Styles dialog box, and then click the Import/Export button to open the Organizer dialog box. In this dialog box, you can copy specific styles from one document or template to another.

Reference

Copying a Style to Another Document or Template

- On the ribbon, click the Home tab.
- In the Styles group, click the Styles Dialog Box Launcher.
- In the Styles pane, click the Manage Styles button to open the Edit tab in the Manage Styles dialog box.
- Click the Import/Export button to open the Styles tab in the Organizer dialog box.
- Below the In Normal list on the right, click Close File.
- Below the empty box on the right, click Open File, navigate to the location of the document or template to which or from which you want to copy a style, click the file, and then click Open.
- In the list containing the style you want to copy, click the style name.
- Click Copy.
- Click Close.

Sam wants you to create a new style from the formatted company name in the rectangle shape at the top of the NP_WD_8_Draft template. Then he would like you to copy this style to the NP_WD_8_Styles template.

To create a new style:

1. In the rectangle at the top of the NP_WD_8_Draft template, select **Alexander Griffin Rock Gym**.

2. On the ribbon, click the **Home** tab.

3. In the Styles group, click the **More** button 📄, and then click **Create a Style**. The Create New Style from Formatting dialog box opens. The default style name is selected in the Name box. See Figure 8–22.

Figure 8–22   Create New Style from Formatting dialog box

4. In the Name box, type **Company Name** and then click **OK**. The style is added to the template and to the Style gallery.

5. Save the changes to the template.

Now that you've created the Company Name style, you can copy it to the NP_WD_8_Styles template.

To copy a style from one template to another:

▶ **1.** On the Home tab, in the Styles group, click the **Styles Dialog Box Launcher**. The Styles pane opens.

▶ **2.** At the bottom of the Styles pane, click the **Manage Styles** button ⒜. The Manage Styles dialog box opens with the Edit tab selected. This dialog box lists all the styles available to the document. See Figure 8–23.

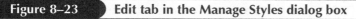

Figure 8–23   Edit tab in the Manage Styles dialog box

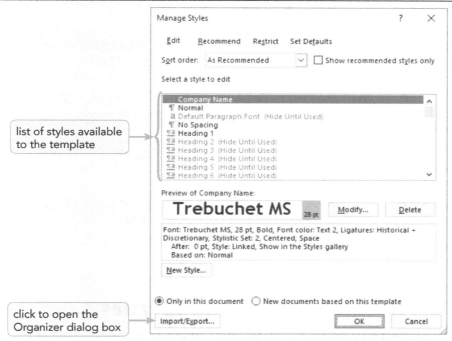

▶ **3.** At the bottom of the Manage Styles dialog box, click **Import/Export**. The Organizer dialog box opens with the Styles tab selected. See Figure 8–24.

Figure 8–24   Styles tab in the Organizer dialog box

The "In NP_WD_8_Draft" list on the left contains the list of styles stored in the NP_WD_8_Draft template. The "In Normal" list on the right contains the list of styles stored in the Normal template. You want to copy a style from the NP_WD_8_Draft template to the NP_WD_8_Styles template.

▶ **4.** Below the In Normal list, click **Close File**. The list of styles in the Normal template is removed, and the Close File command button changes to the Open File command button.

▶ **5.** Click **Open File** to open the Open dialog box.

▶ **6.** Navigate to the location where you are storing your files, click the **NP_WD_8_Styles** template, and then click **Open**. The list of styles stored in the NP_WD_8_Styles template appears in the list on the right side of the Organizer dialog box.

Tip

To change the list in the Open dialog box to include documents as well as templates, click All Word Templates next to File name in the dialog box, and then click All Word Documents.

You can copy from either list to the other list. If you select a style in the list on the right, the Copy command button changes to point to the list on the left. You need to copy the selected Company Name style in the In NP_WD_8_Draft list on the left to the In NP_WD_8_Styles list on the right.

▶ **7.** With the Company Name style selected in the In NP_WD_8_Draft list on the left, click **Copy**. The Company Name style is copied to the list of styles stored in the NP_WD_8_Styles template.

▶ **8.** Click **Close**. A dialog box opens telling you that you have modified content in NP_WD_8_Styles and asking if you want to save the changes to that template.

▶ **9.** Click **Save**. The copied style is saved to the NP_WD_8_Styles template even though that template is not currently open.

▶ **10.** In the Styles pane, click the **Close** button ✕.

Working with File Properties

File properties describe a file. You can use file properties, such as the file size, the number of pages, or the title, to organize documents or to search for files that have specific properties. See the Session 8.2 Visual Overview for more information about file properties.

Some content controls are linked to document properties so that the controls "pick up" and display the property information. For example, if you insert a header that includes a Title content control, that control is tied to the Title document property, and if you specified a Title document property for the document, it will be displayed in the Title content control in the header. The connection works both ways, so that if you change the title in a Title content control, the Title document property will be changed as well.

Adding Document Properties

To add properties, you need to display the Info screen in Backstage view. Sam wants you to add several properties. First, he wants you to add yourself as a document author. He also wants you to add a descriptive Title property, Status property, and Company property.

To add document properties:

▶ **1.** On the ribbon, click the **File** tab, click **Info**, and then scroll to the bottom of the screen. The Info screen in Backstage view is displayed. The document properties are listed on the right side of the screen. See Figure 8–25.

Figure 8–25   **Document properties on the Info screen**

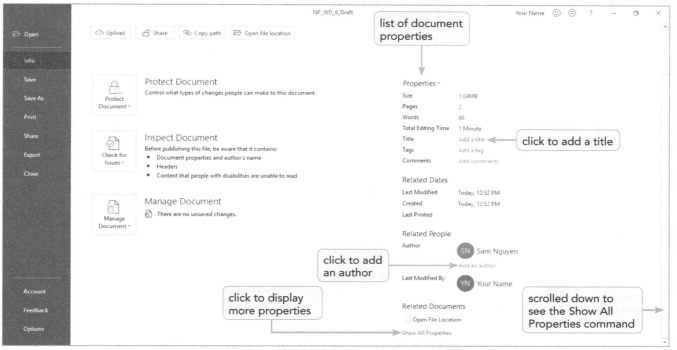

When a document is created, if you are signed in to your Microsoft account, the Author and Last Modified By properties are picked up from your Microsoft account username; if you are not signed in to your Microsoft account, the Author property is picked up from the User name box in the Word Options dialog box. Because Sam created the original document, his name is listed as the Author. You'll add yourself as an author.

▶ **2.** In the Related People section, click **Add an author**, type your name in the box that appears, and then click a blank area of the screen.

Trouble? If you pressed ENTER after typing your name and a dialog box opens, click a blank area of the screen.

▶ **3.** In the Properties section at the top of the right pane, next to Title, click **Add a title**, type **Waiver Form for Griffin Rock Gym** in the box that appears, and then click a blank area of the screen. The Title property is not the same as the file name. The Title property appears in any Title content controls in the template, such as in a header or footer that contains a Title content control.

Now you need to add the Status and Company properties. These properties are not currently visible.

▶ **4.** Scroll to display the bottom of the Info screen, and then click **Show All Properties**. The Properties list expands to include all of the common document properties, and you can now see the Status and Company properties.

▶ **5.** Next to Status, click **Add text**, and then type **Draft**.

▶ **6.** Next to Company, click **Specify the company**, type **Alexander Griffin Rock Gym**, and then click a blank area of the screen.

Trouble? If a company name appears in the box next to Company, delete it, and then type Alexander Griffin Rock Gym.

Sam also wants you to add a Department property identifying the Legal department as the department that will ultimately store the master version of the template. The Department property is not listed on the Info screen. To add this property, you need to open the Properties dialog box for the template and then add the property on the Custom tab.

To add a custom document property:

▶ **1.** At the top of the list of document properties, click the **Properties** button, and then click **Advanced Properties**. The NP_WD_8_Draft Properties dialog box opens with the Summary tab selected. The Title, Author, and Company boxes reflect the changes you made on the Info screen.

Trouble? If the Summary tab is not selected, click the Summary tab.

▶ **2.** Click the **Custom** tab. This tab lists additional properties you can add.

▶ **3.** In the Name list near the top of the dialog box, click **Department**. "Department" appears in the Name box above the list.

▶ **4.** Click in the **Value** box, type **Legal** and then click **Add**. "Department" and the value you gave it appear in the Properties list below the Value box.

▶ **5.** Click **OK**.

▶ **6.** On the Info screen, in the navigation pane, click **Save**. The changes to the template are saved, and Backstage view closes.

Tip

To create a new property, type its name in the Name box, select a type in the Type box, type a value in the Value box, and then click Add.

The properties you added will make it easy for Sam to organize and locate files based on these properties, and he won't have to insert text into content controls that are linked to these properties.

Inserting Document Properties into the Template

Sam wants you to add a header that contains the Status property. The watermark that identifies the document as a draft will remain in the template until it is finalized by the Legal department. He will update the Status property as he makes changes to the template before it is finalized.

Many of the standard document file properties are listed in a submenu on the Quick Parts menu, so you can insert them from there. When you insert a document property from the Quick Parts menu, you insert it as a content control.

To insert a document property as a content control into the template:

▶ **1.** On the ribbon, click the **Insert** tab.

▶ **2.** In the Header & Footer group, click the **Header** button, and then click **Edit Header**. The header area in the document becomes active, and the Header & Footer tab is the active tab.

▶ **3.** Click the **Insert** tab.

▶ **4.** In the Text group, click the **Explore Quick Parts** button 🖹▾, and then point to **Document Property**. A submenu listing some of the document properties opens. See Figure 8–26.

Figure 8–26 **Document Property submenu on the Quick Parts menu**

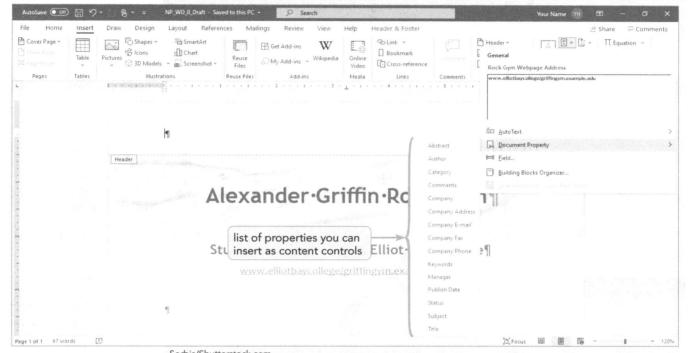

Sorbis/Shutterstock.com

▶ **5.** Click **Status**. A content control labeled Status appears in the header with "Draft" in it.

Now you will make sure that the property in the content control changes if you change it on the Info screen, and vice versa.

To update the Status property:

▶ **1.** On the ribbon, click the **File** tab, click **Info**, scroll down, and then click **Show All Properties**. The Status property is "Draft."

▶ **2.** Next to Status, click **Draft** to select the word, and then type **First Revision**.

▶ **3.** Scroll up if necessary, and then at the top of the navigation pane, click the **Back** button ⬅. In the header, the Status property in the content control is updated with the new property value.

▶ **4.** In the header, select **First Revision**, type **Draft**, and then double-click in the document. Header & Footer view closes.

▶ **5.** On the ribbon, click the **File** tab, click **Info**, scroll down, and then click **Show All Properties**. In the Properties list, examine the Status property. It should be "Draft," but the change to the property may not appear until you close and reopen the file. You'll do that next.

▶ **6.** In the navigation pane, click **Save**, and then close the **NP_WD_8_Draft** file without closing Word.

Trouble? If you clicked the Close button to close the document, a dialog box opens, asking if you want to save changes to "Building Blocks." Click Cancel.

▶ **7.** Use the Open command in Backstage view to open the **NP_WD_8_Draft** file, click the **File** tab, click **Info**, scroll down, click the **Show All Properties** link, and confirm that the Status property is "Draft."

▶ **8.** Scroll up if necessary, and then at the top of the navigation pane, click the **Back** button ⊖ to close Backstage view.

Sam also wants you to insert the Department property in the header, but that property does not appear on the Document Property submenu on the Quick Parts menu. To insert this custom property, you'll need to insert it as a field.

Automating Documents Using Fields

Using fields is a powerful method for automating a document. Recall that a field is a code that instructs Word to insert information that can change in a document. For example, when you insert the current date using the Insert Date and Time button in the Text group on the Insert tab and keep the Update automatically check box selected, you actually insert a field. Word provides many fields that you can include in documents. Figure 8–27 lists some of the most common fields.

Figure 8–27 **Common fields**

Field	Code (Example)	Action
Date	{DATE \@ "MMMM d, yyyy"}	Inserts the current date/time
Fill-in	{FILLIN "Your name?" * MERGEFORMAT}	Inserts information filled in by the user
NumPages	{NUMPAGES}	Inserts the total number of pages in the document
Page	{PAGES}	Inserts the current page number
Ref	{REF BookmarkName}	Inserts the contents of the specified bookmark

When you insert a field into a document, the corresponding field code includes the name of the field and an optional instruction, prompt, and switches, which are enclosed in braces { } (also called French brackets or curly brackets). An **instruction** is a word or phrase that specifies what the field should do, such as display a **prompt**, which is a phrase that tells the user how to proceed. A **switch** is a command that follows *, \#, \@, or \! and turns on or off certain features of the field. For example, a switch can specify how the result of the field is formatted. Figure 8–28 shows a field code that contains a field name, instructions, and a switch.

Figure 8–28 **Components of a field code**

{FILLIN "Product name:" \@ MERGEFORMAT}

open brace · field name · instructions (prompt) · switch · close brace

The field name, FILLIN, specifies that this field asks the user to supply (fill in) some information. The instruction is a prompt (Product name:) that tells the user what to type. The switch (\@ MERGEFORMAT) specifies that the field's result (the user fill-in information) should retain any formatting applied to the field even if the user fills in new information. All field codes must include braces and a field name, but not all field codes include instructions and switches.

Inserting a Custom Property Using the Field Dialog Box

One of the things you can insert as a field is a custom file property. The Department property is a custom property, so to insert it in the header, you need to use the Field dialog box. You'll do this now.

To insert a custom property as a field:

▶ **1.** Double-click in the header area. The header becomes active, and the insertion point is before the word "Draft."

▶ **2.** Press **TAB** twice to move the Draft property to the right margin in the header, and then press the ← key twice to move the insertion point back to the left margin.

▶ **3.** On the ribbon, click the **Insert** tab.

▶ **4.** In the Text group, click the **Explore Quick Parts** button, and then click **Field**. The Field dialog box opens.

▶ **5.** In the Please choose a field section, click the **Categories arrow**, and then click **Document Information**. The Field names list is filtered to include only fields in the Document Information category.

▶ **6.** In the Field names list, click **DocProperty**. The middle section of the dialog box changes to display options for the DocProperty field. See Figure 8–29.

Figure 8–29	Field dialog box with the DocProperty field selected

properties for selected field

click to filter the list to fields in a specific category

selected field

click to see the code for the selected field, including instructions and switches

Field

Please choose a field

Categories:
Document Information

Field names:
Author
Comments
DocProperty
FileName
FileSize
Info
Keywords
LastSavedBy
NumChars
NumPages
NumWords
Subject
Template
Title

Field properties

Property:
Author
Bytes
Category
Characters
CharactersWithSpaces
Comments
Company
CreateTime
Department
HyperlinkBase
Keywords
LastPrinted
LastSavedBy
LastSavedTime
Lines

Field options

No field options available for this field

☑ Preserve formatting during updates

Description:
Insert the value of the property chosen in Options

Field Codes   OK   Cancel

▶ **7.** In the Property list, click **Department**, and then click **OK**. "Legal," the Department property for the document, appears in the header.

Trouble? If the field code is displayed in the header instead of the word "Legal," press ALT+F9.

Now that you've inserted a field, you can examine its field code. You'll do this now.

To examine the field code:

▶ **1.** In the header, right-click **Legal**, and then on the shortcut menu, click **Toggle Field Codes**. The field code for the field you right-clicked appears instead of the content. The field code for the Department document property is { DOCPROPERTY Department * MERGEFORMAT }.

▶ **2.** Right-click **Draft**. The Toggle Field Codes command is not on this shortcut menu because this is a content control, not a field. (Although some content controls contain fields, this one does not.) Notice that this shortcut menu includes the command Remove Content Control.

▶ **3.** Right-click the Department field code at the left margin in the header, and then click **Toggle Field Codes**. The field code is hidden again, and only the contents of the field are displayed.

▶ **4.** Double-click anywhere in the document except in the header to close the header area.

Proskills

Teamwork: Using Properties and Fields

Templates are helpful when you work with a team of people who all need to create similar documents. If you want all users to insert specific document properties in the documents created from the template, displaying the properties in content controls or as fields in the template helps ensure that the needed information is not overlooked and is always inserted in each document. Keep this in mind if you need to create a template for use by a group.

Customizing the Date Field

You're already familiar with the Date field, which inserts the current date and time or inserts parts of the date and time in the format you select, such as the full name for the current month (for example, February) and the day, but not the year or any part of the time.

Fields are updated when you open a document, but sometimes they must be updated while you are working on a document to ensure they contain the most recent information. For example, if you insert the NumPages field, which identifies the total number of pages in a document, and then create additional pages in the document, you need to update the field. This is important if you plan to print the document before closing it.

Sam wants the NP_WD_8_Draft template to be updated with the current date whenever it is opened. You'll insert the Date field using the Insert Date and Time button on the ribbon, and then you'll examine the field codes for the Date field.

To insert the Date field and view the field codes:

▶ **1.** Click in the empty paragraph below the webpage address.

▶ **2.** On the ribbon, click the **Insert** tab, if necessary, and then in the Text group, click the **Insert Date and Time** button 🗓 to open the Date and Time dialog box.

▶ **3.** In the Available formats list, click the format located fifth from the bottom (the format in the style 5/25/2025 3:21:42 PM). You want the date to be inserted as a field that will be updated every time the template is opened.

▶ **4.** If the Update automatically check box is not selected, click the **Update automatically** check box to select it.

▶ **5.** Click **OK**. The current date and time to the second are inserted in the document.

▶ **6.** Click the date. Although this is a field, the borders of a content control appear around the date, and the title tab includes an Update command button.

▶ **7.** On the title tab of the content control, click **Update**. The time is updated to a few seconds later than when you inserted it.

▶ **8.** Right-click the date, and then click **Toggle Field Codes** on the shortcut menu. The field codes for the field you right-clicked are displayed instead of the content. The field code for the format you chose is { DATE \@ "M/d/yyyy h:mm:ss am/pm" }.

> **Tip**
>
> You can also press F9 to update the selected field.

The field code for the date specifies how the date is formatted. You could change the format of the date by editing the field code, or you could select another format in the Field dialog box.

The part of the field code that specifies how the date will appear consists of a string of letters. Most of it is easily decipherable. For example, if you look at the field code for the date currently displayed in the document, it is apparent that "d" (or "D") indicates the date, "y" (or "Y") indicates the year, and "s" indicates seconds. You also should be able to figure out that an uppercase "M" indicates the month, while a lowercase "m" indicates minutes. What is not obvious from this example is that an uppercase "H" and a lowercase "h" indicate different things. A lowercase "h" indicates the hour using the 12-hour format, and this format needs "am/pm" as part of the field code. An uppercase "H" indicates the hour using the 24-hour standard; this format does not need "am/pm" as part of the format.

Date field codes also indicate the number of digits used or whether the month is displayed as letters or numbers. The letters "yy" will display the year as two digits, while "yyyy" will display the year as four digits. Months are displayed as follows:

- "M" displays the month as a single digit for January through September, and two digits for October through December.
- "MM" displays the month as two digits for all months.
- "MMM" displays the month using its three-letter abbreviation.
- "MMMM" displays the month using the full word.

Reference

Editing a Field Code

- Right-click the field, click Toggle Field Codes, and then edit the field code.
or
- Right-click the field, and then click Edit Field on the shortcut menu to open the Field dialog box with the field selected in the Field names list.
- Click Field Codes.
- Edit the code in the Field codes box.
- Click OK.

Sam wants you to change the format of the Date field so it does not include the seconds and so that it displays the time using the 24-hour format rather than the 12-hour format and am/pm.

To edit the Date field format:

▶ 1. Right-click the date field code, and then click **Edit Field** on the shortcut menu. The Field dialog box opens. Date is selected in the Field names list on the left, and the format you chose is selected in the Date formats list in the middle.

▶ 2. At the bottom of the dialog box, click **Field Codes**. The right side of the dialog box changes to display the Advanced field properties section with the field code for the selected format listed in the Field codes box. The general format for the syntax of the Date field appears under the Field codes box. See Figure 8–30.

Figure 8–30	Field dialog box with the Date field codes displayed

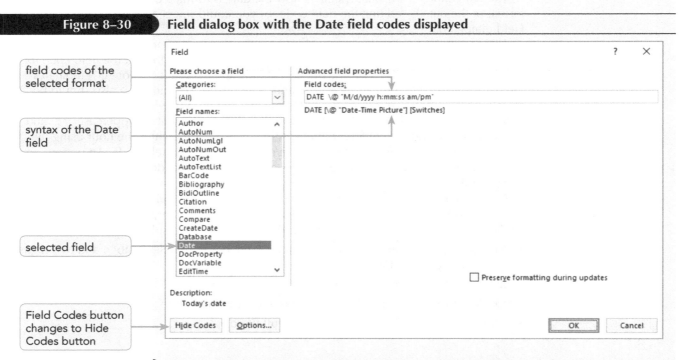

field codes of the selected format

syntax of the Date field

selected field

Field Codes button changes to Hide Codes button

▶ 3. In the Field codes box, click between "pm" and the double quotation marks, and press **BACKSPACE** nine times to delete ":ss am/pm" at the end of the field code.

▶ 4. Press the ← key three times to move the insertion point to between "h" and the colon, press **BACKSPACE** to delete the "h," and then type **H**.

▶ **5.** Click **OK**. The Field dialog box closes, and the date appears in the new format. Note that the field codes automatically toggled off.

▶ **6.** Right-click the date, and then click **Toggle Field Codes** on the shortcut menu. The field code is now { DATE \@ "M/d/yyyy H:mm" }.

▶ **7.** Toggle the field codes off, and then save the changes to the template.

Inserting a Fill-In Field

A Fill-in field is a field that causes a dialog box to open, prompting the user to enter information when a document is created from a template. When you insert a Fill-in field, you need to type the text that will prompt the user for the required information.

Reference

Inserting a Fill-In Field

- On the ribbon, click the Insert tab.
- In the Text group, click the Explore Quick Parts button, and then click Field.
- In the Field names list, click Fill-in.
- In the Field properties section, click in the Prompt box, and then type the text you want to appear in the dialog box that opens.
- Click the Preserve formatting during updates check box to deselect it.
- Click OK.
- Click Cancel in the dialog box that opens containing the prompt.

For each customer, Sam's employees will double-click the waiver template on the desktop to create a new document based on the template. To make sure all the information is entered in the template, Sam wants a dialog box to open requesting each piece of information. You'll add Fill-in fields to do this.

To insert a Fill-in field:

▶ **1.** Position the insertion point after the space following "Participant's name:".

▶ **2.** On the Insert tab, in the Text group, click the **Explore Quick Parts** button ▦▾, and then click **Field**. The Field dialog box opens.

▶ **3.** In the Please choose a field section, scroll the alphabetical Field names list, and then click **Fill-in**. The middle part of the dialog box changes to display a Prompt box, where you will type the text that will appear as an instruction in the dialog box that opens when the document is opened. See Figure 8–31.

Figure 8–31 Field dialog box with the Fill-in field selected

type text that will appear as the instruction text for the user

deselect to prevent the user from changing the format of the text entered

Trouble? If you don't see the Fill-in option in the list, click the Categories arrow, and then click (All).

4. In the Field properties section, click in the **Prompt** box, and then type **Enter participant's name:** (with a colon at the end).

5. Click the **Preserve formatting during updates** check box to deselect it. When this check box is checked, Word preserves any formatting that the user applies to the field. For example, if you change the format to bold, red formatting, and this check box is selected, the bold, red formatting will appear when you update the field. If you clear this check box, Word will update the field information but retain the original formatting.

6. Click **OK**. A Microsoft Word dialog box appears with the prompt you typed, "Enter participant's name:". See Figure 8–32.

Figure 8–32 Prompt box for the Fill-in field

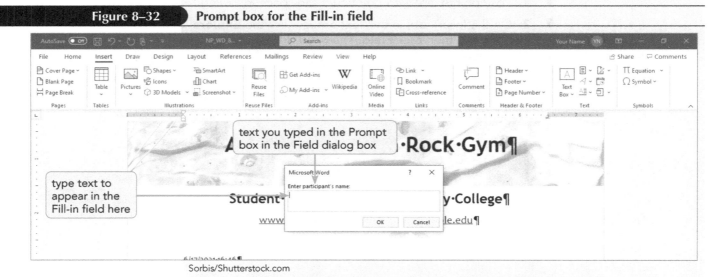

text you typed in the Prompt box in the Field dialog box

type text to appear in the Fill-in field here

Sorbis/Shutterstock.com

This is the dialog box that will appear when a document based on this template is first opened. Anything the user types in the box will appear at the location of the Fill-in field in the document. You want the field to be empty in the template so that the user can enter the climber's name each time a new document is created from the template, so you will close this dialog box without entering any text.

▶ **7.** Click **Cancel** to close the dialog box. It looks as if there is no change in the document. The insertion point is blinking after the space to the right of "Participant's name:".

▶ **8.** Right-click the space to the right of "Participant's name:", and then click **Toggle Field Codes** on the shortcut menu. The Fill-in field code is displayed. The Fill-in field code has no switch, but it does include the text you specified for the prompt. You can click anywhere in the field code to modify the prompt or to add a switch.

▶ **9.** Right-click the Fill-in field code, and then click **Toggle Field Codes** to hide the field codes.

Next, you'll insert Fill-in fields for the participant's date of birth and for an emergency contact number.

To create the Fill-in fields for the participant's date of birth and an emergency contact number:

▶ **1.** Position the insertion point after the space following "Participant's date of birth:".

▶ **2.** On the Insert tab, in the Text group, click the **Explore Quick Parts** button ▣▾, and then click **Field** to open the Field dialog box.

▶ **3.** Scroll down the Field names list, and then click **Fill-in**.

▶ **4.** In the Field properties section, click in the **Prompt** box, and then type **Enter participant's date of birth:** (including the colon).

▶ **5.** Click the **Preserve formatting during updates** check box to deselect it, and then click **OK**. The Field dialog box closes, and a dialog box opens containing the prompt to enter the participant's date of birth.

▶ **6.** Click **Cancel**.

▶ **7.** Position the insertion point after the space following "Emergency contact number:" and then insert a Fill-in field with the prompt text **Enter participant's emergency contact number:** (including the colon). (Do not preserve formatting during updates.)

▶ **8.** Save the changes to the template.

Make sure you save the changes to the template because you will be creating a document based on this template in the next set of steps.

Now that you've added the Fill-in fields, you need to test them to make sure they work as you expect when you open a document based on the NP_WD_8_Draft template. Recall that if you save a template to the Custom Office Templates folder, you can open a new document based on that template directly from the New screen in Backstage view. If a template is stored in a folder other than the Custom Office Templates folder, you need to double-click the document in the File Explorer folder window to create a new document based on that template.

To create a new document based on the template and add text to the Fill-in field:

▶ **1.** On the taskbar, click the **File Explorer** button ▢ . The File Explorer window opens.

▶ **2.** Navigate to the drive and folder where you are saving your files. The blue bar at the top of the NP_WD_8_Draft icon indicates that it is a template file.

▶ **3.** Point to the **NP_WD_8_Draft** template. The ScreenTip that appears indicates that the file is a Microsoft Word template.

Trouble? If no ScreenTip appears, the folder is in Content view. Click the View tab on the ribbon, and then in the Layout group, click any view except Content.

▶ **4.** Double-click the **NP_WD_8_Draft** template. A new document based on the template is created, and the prompt for the first Fill-in field appears, asking for the participant's name. The insertion point is in the prompt dialog box.

Trouble? If the prompt dialog box does not appear, close the document, save the changes to the NP_WD_8_Draft template, and then repeat Step 4.

▶ **5.** In the Enter participant's name box, type **John Doe** and then click **OK**. The dialog box closes, and the second Fill-in field prompt box appears, asking for the participant's date of birth.

▶ **6.** Type **8/22/2002**, and then click **OK**. The third Fill-in field prompt dialog box opens asking for the participant's emergency contact number. You will close this dialog box without entering any data.

▶ **7.** Click **OK**. The contents of the template appear in a new document with the information you typed in the prompt boxes after Participant's name and Participant's date of birth. You need to add the phone number.

▶ **8.** To the right of "Emergency contact number:", right-click after the space following the colon, and then on the shortcut menu, click **Update Field**. The dialog box requesting the contact number appears again.

▶ **9.** Type **(206) 555-0125**, and then click **OK**. The phone number appears in the document. Notice that the current date and time appear below the webpage address near the top of the document.

▶ **10.** Close the document without saving it. The NP_WD_8_Draft template is the active template again.

Trouble? If you are taking a break and closing Word, a dialog box appears asking if you want to save changes to "Building Blocks." Click Don't Save.

In addition to the fields you used, there are a few other fields, for which there are no content controls to insert the equivalent information, that are useful to know about. These fields are described in Figure 8–33. These fields are all available in the Field dialog box.

Figure 8–33	Useful fields

Field	Description of Inserted Text
FileName	Name of the saved file
FileSize	Size of the file on disk
NumPages	Total number of pages
SaveDate	Date the document was last saved
UserInitials	User initials on the General page in the Word Options dialog box
UserName	User name on the General page in the Word Options dialog box

In this session, you've edited the properties for building blocks, copied building blocks and styles, added and updated file properties, and inserted properties as a content control and as a field. You also created Fill-in fields to request information from the user. In the next session, you'll record and edit a macro, save the document in which the macro is stored, and then copy a macro from one template to another. You'll also record an AutoMacro that will run every time a document is created based on the template.

Review

Session 8.2 Quick Check

1. What is a property?
2. How do you copy a building block from one template to another?
3. How do you access document properties?
4. What are the two ways you can insert a document property?
5. How do you update a field?
6. What is a Fill-in field?

Session 8.3 Visual Overview:

Microsoft Visual Basic for Applications is a programming language provided within each app of the Microsoft 365 suite to help you extend the program's capabilities.

You can assign a macro to a button or shortcut key combination when you record it by clicking the appropriate button in the Record Macro dialog box.

Type a name for a macro you are recording in the Macro name box of the Record Macro dialog box.

You can change the storage location for a macro by clicking the Store macro in arrow and selecting the storage location.

Type a description for a macro you are recording in the Description box.

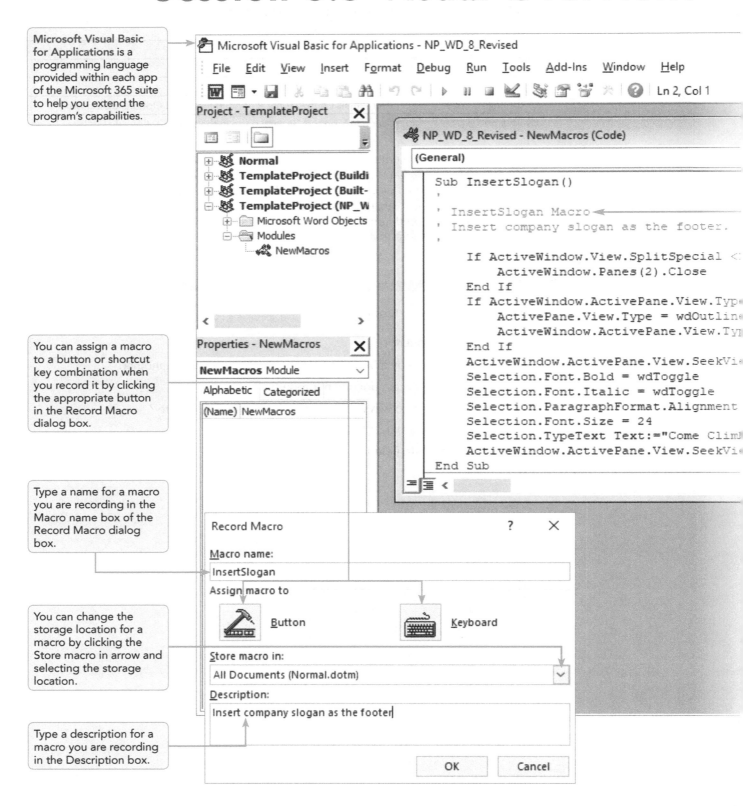

Microsoft Visual Basic for Applications - NP_WD_8_Revised

File   Edit   View   Insert   Format   Debug   Run   Tools   Add-Ins   Window   Help

Ln 2, Col 1

Project - TemplateProject

Normal
TemplateProject (Buildi
TemplateProject (Built-
TemplateProject (NP_W
  Microsoft Word Objects
  Modules
    NewMacros

Properties - NewMacros

NewMacros Module

Alphabetic   Categorized

(Name) NewMacros

NP_WD_8_Revised - NewMacros (Code)

(General)

```
Sub InsertSlogan()
'
' InsertSlogan Macro
' Insert company slogan as the footer.
'
    If ActiveWindow.View.SplitSpecial <
        ActiveWindow.Panes(2).Close
    End If
    If ActiveWindow.ActivePane.View.Typ
        ActivePane.View.Type = wdOutline
        ActiveWindow.ActivePane.View.Typ
    End If
    ActiveWindow.ActivePane.View.SeekVi
    Selection.Font.Bold = wdToggle
    Selection.Font.Italic = wdToggle
    Selection.ParagraphFormat.Alignment
    Selection.Font.Size = 24
    Selection.TypeText Text:="Come Clim
    ActiveWindow.ActivePane.View.SeekVi
End Sub
```

Record Macro   ?   ✕

Macro name:

InsertSlogan

Assign macro to

Button   Keyboard

Store macro in:

All Documents (Normal.dotm)

Description:

Insert company slogan as the footer

OK   Cancel

Working with Macros

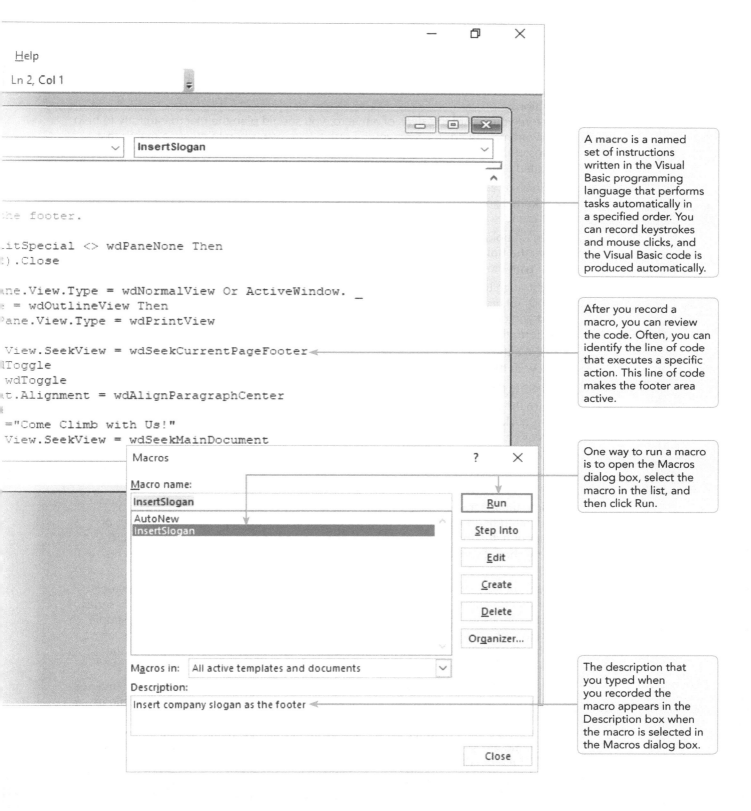

Help

Ln 2, Col 1

InsertSlogan

he footer.

itSpecial <> wdPaneNone Then
).Close

ne.View.Type = wdNormalView Or ActiveWindow. _
= wdOutlineView Then
Pane.View.Type = wdPrintView

View.SeekView = wdSeekCurrentPageFooter
Toggle
wdToggle
t.Alignment = wdAlignParagraphCenter

="Come Climb with Us!"
View.SeekView = wdSeekMainDocument

A macro is a named set of instructions written in the Visual Basic programming language that performs tasks automatically in a specified order. You can record keystrokes and mouse clicks, and the Visual Basic code is produced automatically.

After you record a macro, you can review the code. Often, you can identify the line of code that executes a specific action. This line of code makes the footer area active.

Macros   ?   ×

Macro name:

InsertSlogan

AutoNew
InsertSlogan

Macros in: All active templates and documents

Description:

Insert company slogan as the footer

Run
Step Into
Edit
Create
Delete
Organizer...

Close

One way to run a macro is to open the Macros dialog box, select the macro in the list, and then click Run.

The description that you typed when you recorded the macro appears in the Description box when the macro is selected in the Macros dialog box.

Planning a Macro

Macros can help automate repetitive tasks. See the Session 8.3 Visual Overview for more information about macros. Using macros to run frequently executed commands has two main advantages. Combining a number of keystrokes and mouse clicks into a macro saves time and helps you complete your work faster. Also, assuming you record a macro accurately—without typos or other mistakes—the keystrokes and mouse clicks will always play back error-free. A macro that inserts text or performs formatting operations will consistently insert the same text and perform the same formatting operations.

Before you record the steps of a macro, you should plan the macro carefully to help you avoid making errors when you record it. Sam wants you to create a macro that will insert the formatted company slogan into the footer of the document. To insert formatted text in the footer, you need to:

- Activate the footer area—To accomplish this, you'll click the Insert tab on the ribbon, click the Footer button in the Header & Footer group, and then click Edit Footer on the menu.

- Turn on bold formatting—To accomplish this, you'll click the Home tab, and then click the Bold button in the Font group. By turning on the character formatting before you type the text, you save yourself the step of selecting the text after you type it.

- Right-align the text—To accomplish this, you'll click the Align Right button in the Paragraph group on the Home tab. Because this is a paragraph formatting command and you don't need to do anything in order to select the current paragraph, you could perform this step before or after you type the text.

- Change the font size to 24 points—To accomplish this, you'll click the Font Size arrow in the Font group on the Home tab, and then click 24.

- Type the text—You'll type the slogan for the Rock Gym ("Come Climb with Us!").

- Close the footer area—To accomplish this, you'll click the Header & Footer tab, and then click the Close Header and Footer button in the Close group. You want to add this as part of the macro because after you insert the text in the footer, you're finished working in the footer area.

Now that you have a plan, you can set up the recording in the Macros dialog box. In the Macros dialog box, you need to do the following:

- Name the macro—A macro name must begin with a letter and can contain a maximum of 80 letters and numbers; the name can't contain spaces, periods, or other punctuation (although you can use the underscore character). The macro name should summarize its function. For example, if you record a macro to resize a picture, you could name the macro ResizePic.

- Describe the macro (optional)—A detailed description of a macro helps you recall its exact function. This is especially important if a macro performs a complex series of operations that can't be summarized in the macro name. For example, a simple macro name, such as PositionPicLeft, doesn't describe the picture features, such as borders and text wrapping. You could include that type of information in the description.

- Attach the macro to a template or document—Unless you specify otherwise, macros you create are attached to the global template, Normal.dotx, and are available in every Word document created on that computer. You can choose instead to attach a macro to another open template. When you do this, the macro is available whenever that template is open or when a new document is created based on that template, even if the template or new document is opened on another computer.

- Assign the macro to a toolbar button, menu, or keyboard shortcut (optional)—To make it a little easier to run a macro, you can assign a macro to a button that you add to the Quick Access Toolbar or to a keyboard shortcut.

One potential disadvantage to working with macros is that they are sometimes used to spread computer viruses. Therefore, on most computers, Word is set to prevent macros from running without your knowledge. However, the settings can be changed so that macros are prevented from running at all. You need to make sure that you will be able to run the macro that you are going to record. You'll do that next.

Examining Trust Center Settings

A macro virus is a virus written into a macro code. Because you can't tell if a macro has a virus when you open a document, Word has built-in security settings to protect your computer. The default setting is for macros to be disabled and for a yellow Security Warning bar to be displayed at the top of the document with a message stating this. See Figure 8–34. In this case, you can click the Enable Content button if you are sure the macros in the document are safe to run. If you enable content in a document and then save it, the document becomes a trusted document on your computer and the Security Warning bar will not appear the next time you open that document.

Figure 8–34	Security warning stating that macros have been disabled

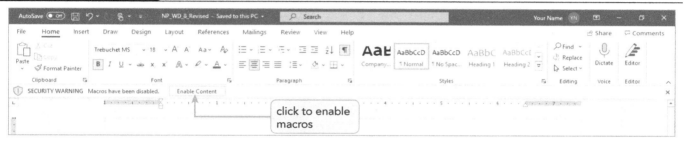

Another setting completely disables macros. When you try to run one, a dialog box appears, stating that macros are disabled and that you do not have the option to override this setting.

You'll check your macro security settings now.

To check macro security settings:

1. On the ribbon, click the **File** tab, scroll down, and then in the navigation pane, click **Options**. The Word Options dialog box opens.

2. In the navigation pane, click **Trust Center**. The dialog box changes to display links to articles about security and privacy on the Internet and the Trust Center Settings button.

3. Click **Trust Center Settings**. The Trust Center dialog box opens.

4. In the navigation pane, click **Macro Settings**, if necessary. The Trust Center shows the current macro settings. See Figure 8–35.

Figure 8–35	Trust Center dialog box displaying macro settings

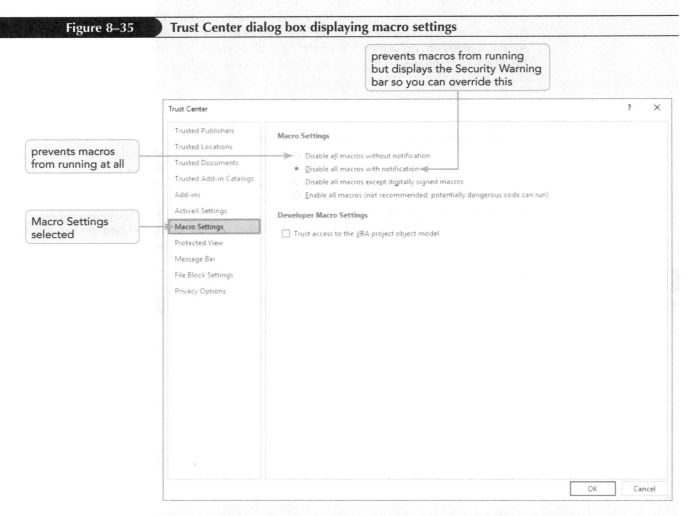

5. If the Disable all macros with notification option button is not selected, note which option is selected so you can reset this setting at the end of the module, and then click the **Disable all macros with notification** option button.

6. Click **OK**, and then click **OK** in the Word Options dialog box.

Recording a Macro

To record a macro, you turn on the macro recorder, perform keystrokes and mouse operations, and then turn off the macro recorder. When you play back the macro, Word performs the same sequence of keystrokes and mouse clicks. Note that you can't record mouse operations within the document window while you record a macro—for example, you can't select text with the mouse or drag and drop text—but you can use the mouse to select buttons and options on the ribbon.

You are ready to record the macro that inserts the slogan for the Rock Gym as a right-aligned footer.

Reference

Recording a Macro

- On the ribbon, click the View tab.
- In the Macros group, click the Macros arrow, and then click Record Macro; or on the status bar, click the Start Recording button.
- In the Record Macro dialog box, type a name for the macro in the Macro name box and type a description for the macro in the Description box.
- To save the macro in the current document or template, click the Store macro in arrow, and then select the document or template name.
- Use the Button or Keyboard button to assign the macro to a button or assign a shortcut key combination, respectively.
- Click OK to start recording the macro.
- Perform the mouse actions and keystrokes you want to record.
- On the ribbon, click the View tab. In the Macros group, click the Macros arrow, and then click Stop Recording; or on the status bar, click the Stop Recording button.

Before you record the macro, you'll name the macro, attach it to the template, add a description of the macro, and assign it to a shortcut key combination.

To prepare to record the InsertSlogan macro:

▶ **1.** If you took a break after the last session, use the Open command in Backstage view to open the **NP_WD_8_Draft.dotx** template.

▶ **2.** On the ribbon, click the **View** tab.

▶ **3.** In the Macros group, click the **Macros arrow**, and then click **Record Macro**. The Record Macro dialog box opens. The temporary name Macro1 is selected in the Macro name box. See Figure 8–36.

Figure 8–36	Record Macro dialog box

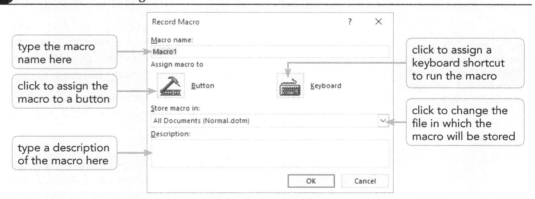

type the macro name here

click to assign the macro to a button

type a description of the macro here

click to assign a keyboard shortcut to run the macro

click to change the file in which the macro will be stored

▶ **4.** In the Macro name box, type **InsertSlogan**.

You want to attach the macro to the current template, not to the Normal template.

▶ **5.** Click the **Store macro in arrow**, and then click **Documents Based On NP_WD_8_Draft**.

▶ **6.** Click in the **Description** box, and then type **Insert company slogan as the footer** in the box. Next, you'll assign the macro to a shortcut key combination so you don't need to open the Macros dialog box to run it.

Be sure to switch the macro location to the template. Otherwise, the macro will be stored on your computer and will not be in your final template file.

▶ **7.** Click the **Keyboard** button. The Customize Keyboard dialog box opens. The macro is selected in the Commands list, and the insertion point is blinking in the Press new shortcut key box. See Figure 8–37.

Figure 8–37 Customize Keyboard dialog box

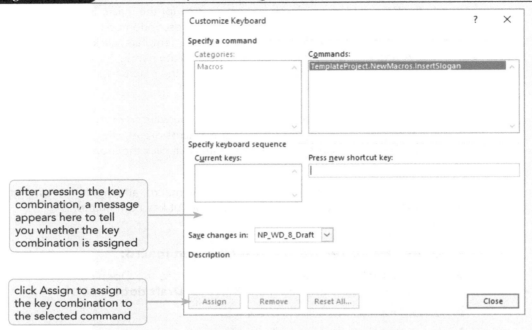

after pressing the key combination, a message appears here to tell you whether the key combination is assigned

click Assign to assign the key combination to the selected command

Tip

To add a shortcut key combination or button to an existing macro, click the File tab, click Options, click Customize Ribbon or Quick Access Toolbar, click Choose commands from, click Macros, select the macro in the list, and then click Customize next to Keyboard shortcuts or click the Add button.

▶ **8.** Press **ALT+CTRL+SHIFT+A**. A message appears below the Current keys box stating that this key combination is unassigned.

▶ **9.** Click **Assign**. The key combination you chose appears in the Current keys list. Now when you press ALT+CTRL+SHIFT+A, the macro you are about to record will run.

▶ **10.** Click **Close** in the Customize Keyboard dialog box. The dialog boxes close, and the pointer changes to the macro recording pointer ▯, indicating that you are recording a macro. On the status bar, the Stop Recording button ▯ appears in place of the Start Recording button ▯.

Trouble? If the Start Recording button was not on the status bar in the place where the Stop Recording button is now, it is not a problem.

From this point, Word records every keystroke and mouse operation you make until you stop the recording, so perform these steps carefully and complete them exactly as shown. If you make a mistake, you can stop recording and start over. It does not matter how long you take to perform the steps. When the macro is run, the steps will execute very quickly.

When you finished with all the steps, click the Stop Recording button ▯ on the status bar, or on the View tab, in the Macros group, click the Macros arrow, and then click Stop Recording.

To record the InsertSlogan macro:

Tip

You can pause the recording by clicking the Macros arrow in the Macros group on the View tab, and then clicking Pause Recording.

1. On the ribbon, click the **Insert** tab.

> **Trouble?** If you make a mistake while recording the macro, stop recording, and then repeat the "To prepare to record the InsertSlogan macro" steps. Click Yes when you are asked if you want to replace the existing macro, and then repeat this set of steps.

2. In the Header & Footer group, click the **Footer** button, and then click **Edit Footer**. The footer becomes active. The slogan needs to be formatted in bold.

3. On the ribbon, click the **Home** tab, and then in the Font group, click the **Bold** button B. Sam wants the slogan right-aligned.

4. In the Paragraph group, click the **Align Right** button ≣. The font size of the slogan needs to be 24 points.

5. In the Font group, click the **Font Size arrow**, and then click **24**.

6. Type **Come Climb with Us!**. After the text is inserted in the footer, you want the footer area to be inactive.

7. Click the **Header & Footer** tab, and then in the Close group, click the **Close Header and Footer** button. You are finished recording the steps of the macro.

8. On the ribbon, click the **View** tab.

9. In the Macros group, click the **Macros arrow**, and then click **Stop Recording**. The pointer changes back to the normal pointer, and the button on the status bar changes back to the Start Recording button 🔛.

Now that you've recorded a macro, you're ready to run it.

Running Macros

To **run** a macro means to cause the recorded or programmed steps of the macro to be executed. To run a macro, you can open the Macros dialog box, select the macro in the list, and then click Run. To open the Macros dialog box, you click the Macros button in the Macros group on the View tab. If you assigned the macro to a button when you recorded it, you can click the button to run the macro. Finally, if you assigned a keyboard shortcut to the macro when you recorded it, as you did when you recorded the InsertSlogan macro, you can press the shortcut keys you assigned.

To test the macro you created, you need to remove the footer and the formatting that was inserted when you recorded the macro. Note that you can't do this with the Remove Footer command on the Footer menu because that command deletes only the text; it does not remove the formatting. If you ran the macro with the formatting still applied in the footer, it would toggle the bold formatting command off. Instead, you will make the footer area active, remove the formatting, and then delete the footer text. After completing those steps, you can run the macro.

To run the InsertSlogan macro:

▶ **1.** Double-click in the footer area, and then select the entire line and the paragraph mark.

▶ **2.** Click the **Home** tab, and then in the Font group, click the **Clear All Formatting** button [A̲]. The formatting is removed, and the text is left-aligned.

▶ **3.** Press **DEL** to delete the text in the footer, and then double-click anywhere in the document to make the footer inactive.

▶ **4.** Press **ALT+CTRL+SHIFT+A**. The formatted footer is entered in the footer area, and the footer area becomes inactive. The macro works as it should. You can use the Undo button to see the list of tasks the macro performed.

▶ **5.** On the Quick Access Toolbar, click the **Undo arrow** 🔄. Notice that the top several actions all begin with "VBA-" ("VBA" refers to the Visual Basic programming language). These are the recorded actions that the macro performed. See Figure 8–38.

Figure 8–38   **Undo list after running the macro**

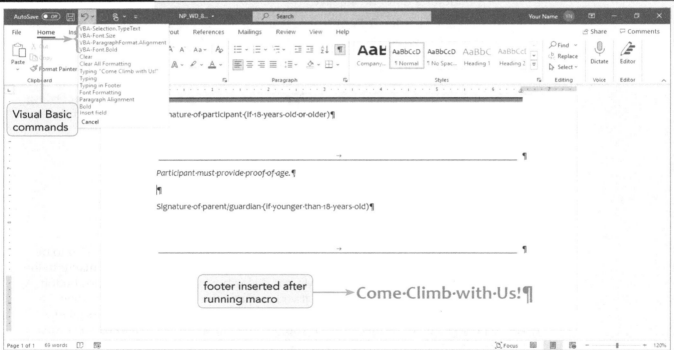

▶ **6.** Press **ESC** to close the Undo menu without selecting anything.

Sam decides he wants the slogan to be italicized and centered in the footer. You could record a new macro, but it's easier to edit the one you already recorded.

Editing a Macro Using the Visual Basic Window

When you record a macro, you are actually creating a Visual Basic program. Each action you performed while recording the macro created a line of code in Visual Basic. You can see the code by opening the Visual Basic window. You can usually examine the code and identify specific actions even if you don't have a thorough understanding of Visual Basic.

You'll open the Visual Basic window and examine it.

To open the Visual Basic window and examine the code for the InsertSlogan macro:

▶ **1.** On the ribbon, click the **View** tab, and then in the Macros group, click the **Macros** button. The Macros dialog box opens, listing the macro you recorded.

Trouble? If you see other macros listed in the Macros dialog box, they are probably stored in the Normal template on your computer. Continue with the next step.

▶ **2.** In the list of macros, click **InsertSlogan**, if necessary, and then click **Edit**. The Microsoft Visual Basic for Applications window opens with an open Code window displaying the InsertSlogan macro commands. See Figure 8–39.

Figure 8–39   **Visual Basic window with the code for the InsertSlogan macro**

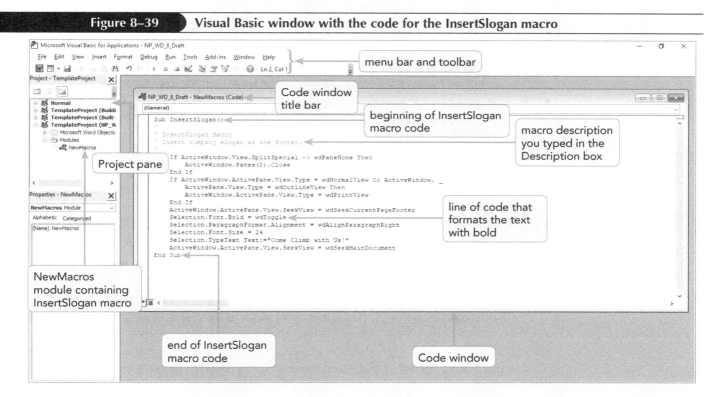

In addition to the Code window, the Visual Basic window includes a Project pane, which displays a list of all templates saved on the computer you are working on. Instead of a ribbon with tabs and buttons, the Visual Basic window contains a menu bar and a toolbar with buttons.

Trouble? If the Code window is not open, click View on the Visual Basic menu bar, and then click Code.

When you record a macro, it is stored in something called a module. Notice that the title bar of the Code window does not contain the macro name; it contains NewMacros—the name of the module—instead. As you can see in the first line in the Code window, the macro starts with "Sub" followed by the macro name, and the last line contains "End Sub." If you recorded a second macro in this template, the commands for that macro would be listed below the "End Sub" line, and the second macro would be enclosed between its own "Sub" and "End Sub" lines.

The line of code "Selection.Font.Bold = wdToggle" is the line that was recorded with you clicked the Bold button. The line "Selection.ParagraphFormat.Alignment = wdAlignParagraphRight" is the line that was recorded when you clicked the Align Right button. You'll edit the macro by adding a line of code similar to the line that formats the text as bold to format the slogan so it is also italicized. Then you will modify the line of code that contains the paragraph alignment instruction so that the text is centered.

To edit the InsertSlogan macro and test the revised macro:

▶ **1.** In the Code window, click at the end of the line "Selection.Font.Bold = wdToggle." To add the command to italicize the text, you type the same code on a new line, except you will replace the word "Bold" with "Italic."

▶ **2.** Press **ENTER**, type **Selection.Font.Italic = wdToggle** (do not type a period). Next, you will modify the line of code that right-aligns the text so that the text will be centered instead of right-aligned.

▶ **3.** Click at the end of the line "Selection.ParagraphFormat.Alignment = wdAlignParagraphRight."

▶ **4.** Press **BACKSPACE** five times, and then type **Center**. The line now reads "Selection.ParagraphFormat.Alignment = wdAlignParagraphCenter".

▶ **5.** In the title bar of the Visual Basic window, click the **Close** button ⊠. The Visual Basic window closes, and the NP_WD_8_Draft template is the active window. Changes you have made to the code are saved automatically with your Word document. Now you'll test the revised macro.

   Trouble? If the Visual Basic window is still open, you clicked the Close button in the Code window. Click the Close button in the title bar of the Visual Basic window.

▶ **6.** Clear the formatting from the footer text, delete the footer text, and then close the footer area. This time, you'll run the macro from the Macros dialog box.

▶ **7.** Click the **View** tab, and then in the Macros group, click the **Macros** button. The Macros dialog box opens with InsertSlogan listed.

▶ **8.** If necessary, click **InsertSlogan** to select it, and then click **Run**. The edited macro runs, and the footer is now centered and italicized as well as bold.

Now that you've recorded and tested the macro, you need to save the template with the macro.

Saving a Document with Macros

In order to save macros in a document, the document must be saved as a Macro-Enabled Document or a Macro-Enabled Template. If you try to save a document or a template that contains macros in the ordinary Word Document or Template file format, a warning dialog box appears, asking if you want to save the document as a "macro-free" document—in other words, without the macros. If you click Yes, the macro is not saved when you save the changes. If you click No, the Save As dialog box opens so that you can change the file type to one that is macro-enabled.

To save the template with the macro:

▶ **1.** On the Quick Access Toolbar, click the **Save** button 🖫. A dialog box opens, warning that the macro cannot be saved in a macro-free document and asking if you want to continue saving as a macro-free document. This is not what you want.

▶ **2.** Click **No**. The dialog box closes, and the Save As dialog box appears.

▶ **3.** Click the **Save as type arrow**. Notice that two file types are macro-enabled—a Word document and a Word template. You want to save this as a macro-enabled template.

▶ **4.** Click **Word Macro-Enabled Template**. The current folder, which is listed in the Address bar at the top of the dialog box, changes to the Custom Office Templates folder.

▶ **5.** Navigate to the location where you are storing your files.

▶ **6.** sam⬆ In the File name box, replace "Draft" with **Revised** so that the file name is NP_WD_8_Revised, and then click **Save**. The template is saved as a macro-enabled template.

> Be sure to navigate to the folder where you are storing your files. Otherwise, the template will be stored in the Custom Office Templates folder on your hard drive.

Copying Macros to Another Document or Template

You can copy macros from one document or template to another. To do this, you open the same Organizer dialog box you used when you copied the Company Name style to the NP_WD_8_Styles template. In this case, you'll use the Macros tab instead of the Styles tab.

When you copy recorded macros that are stored in the NewMacros module of a particular document or template, you actually copy the entire module. If a document or template contains multiple macros and you want to copy only one of them, first copy the NewMacros module. Then, in the document or template to which you copied the macro, open the Visual Basic window and delete the code for the macros you don't want; or open the Macros dialog box, select each macro that you don't want, and then click Delete.

Reference

Copying Macros to Another Document or Template

- On the ribbon, click the View tab.
- In the Macros group, click the Macros button to open the Macros dialog box.
- Click Organizer to open the Macro Project Items tab in the Organizer dialog box.
- Below the In Normal list on the right, click Close File.
- Below the empty box on the right, click Open File, navigate to the location of the document or template you want to copy macros to or from, click the file, and then click Open.
- In the list containing the macro you want to copy, click NewMacros.
- Click Copy.
- Click Close.

Sam wants you to copy the macro you recorded to the NP_WD_8_Styles template. You'll do this now.

To copy macros from the template to another template:

▶ **1.** On the ribbon, click the **View** tab, if necessary, and then in the Macros group, click the **Macros** button. The Macros dialog box opens.

▶ **2.** Click **Organizer**. The Organizer dialog box opens with the Macro Project Items tab selected. See Figure 8–40.

Figure 8–40 Macro Project Items tab in the Organizer dialog box

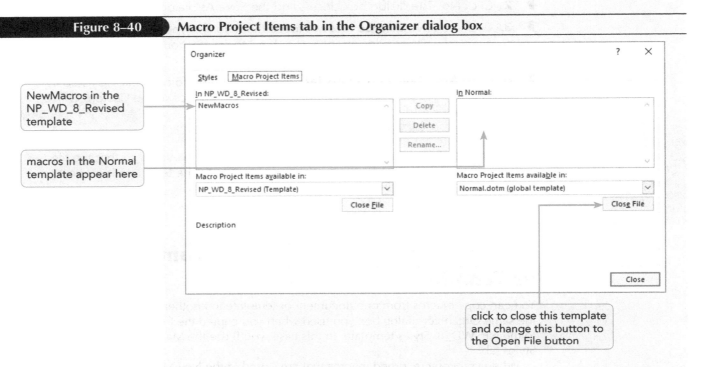

NewMacros in the NP_WD_8_Revised template

macros in the Normal template appear here

click to close this template and change this button to the Open File button

---

▶ **3.** Below the In Normal list on the right, click **Close File**. The command button changes to Open File.

▶ **4.** Click **Open File**, navigate to the location where you are storing your files, click the **NP_WD_8_Styles** template, and then click **Open**. In the Organizer dialog box, "To NP_WD_8_Styles" appears above the box on the right. The box is empty because that template does not contain any macros. In the In NP_WD_8_Revised list on the left, NewMacros is selected.

▶ **5.** Click **Copy**. NewMacros is copied to the To NP_WD_8_Styles list.

▶ **6.** Click **Close**. A dialog box opens, asking if you want to save the changes to "NP_WD_8_Styles."

▶ **7.** Click **Save**. A dialog box opens, asking if you want to continue saving the document as a macro-free document.

▶ **8.** Click **No**. The Save As dialog box opens.

▶ **9.** Click the **Save as type arrow**, and then click **Word Macro-Enabled Template**. The current folder changes to the Custom Office Templates folder.

▶ **10.** Navigate to the location where you are storing your files, change the file name to **NP_WD_8_StylesWithMacros**, and then click **Save**. The template is saved as a macro-enabled template named NP_WD_8_StylesWithMacros. Note that the NP_WD_8_Revised template is still the active template.

Insight

Copying Macros When the Destination File Already Contains a NewMacros Module

If you want to copy a macro or macros contained in a NewMacros module from one template to another template that already contains a NewMacros module, you need to copy the code in the Visual Basic window. To do this, open both the template containing the macro you want to copy and the destination template, and then open the Visual Basic window in either template. In the Project pane on the left, one of the projects listed includes the name of the template containing the macro, and one includes the name of the template to which you want to copy the macro. Under the Project whose name includes the current template's name, NewMacros is selected. Next to the Project whose name includes the other open document's name, click the plus sign to expand the list. In the expanded list, click the plus sign next to Modules so you can see NewMacros in that document. Right-click that instance of NewMacros, and then click View Code to open the NewMacros Code window for that document. In the Code window that contains the code you want to copy, drag to select all of the code from the Sub line through the End Sub line, click Edit on the menu bar, and then click Copy. Make the other Code window active, click below the last End Sub line in that window, click Edit on the menu bar, and then click Paste. Then you can close the Visual Basic window and save the template that contains the pasted code.

Recording an AutoMacro

An **AutoMacro** is a macro that runs automatically when you perform certain basic operations, including starting Word, creating a document, opening a document, closing a document, and closing Word. AutoMacros have special reserved names so that when you create a macro using one of them, the macro runs at the point determined by the code built into that AutoMacro. For example, if you use the reserved name AutoNew to create a macro and save it in a template, the macro will run automatically when you create a new document based on that template. Figure 8–41 lists the AutoMacros and describes when each runs.

Figure 8–41 AutoMacros available in Word

AutoMacro Name	When the AutoMacro Runs
AutoExec	Runs each time you start Word
AutoNew	Runs when you start a new document
AutoOpen	Runs each time you open an existing document
AutoClose	Runs each time you close a document
AutoExit	Runs each time you exit Word

Sam wants to remind his employees that they must ask for identification that proves the age of each customer. He asks you to record an AutoNew macro in the NP_WD_8_ Revised template so that whenever a new document is created from the template, the document will scroll to display the line "Participant must provide proof of age." in the window and highlight it in yellow. Although the line is easy to see in the document now, after the legal text is added, it will be either at the bottom of the first page or on the second page.

To create the AutoNew macro:

▶ **1.** On the ribbon, click the **View** tab, if necessary.

▶ **2.** In the Macros group, click the **Macros arrow**, and then click **Record Macro**. The Record Macro dialog box opens.

▶ **3.** In the Macro name box, type **AutoNew**. This macro name tells Word to run the macro when you begin a new document based on this template.

▶ **4.** Click the **Store macro in arrow**, and then click **Documents Based On NP_WD_8_Revised** so the macro runs only if a new document is opened from the NP_WD_8_Revised template.

▶ **5.** Click in the **Description** box, and then type **Highlight line stating that participant must provide proof of age** in the box. You won't assign this macro to a toolbar or a keyboard shortcut because it will run automatically when the new document is opened.

▶ **6.** Click **OK**.

You're now ready to record the commands of the AutoNew macro. The first thing you need to do is scroll to display "Participant must provide proof of age." in the window and select the text. If the template was finished—that is, if the legal language was already added—you could use the arrow keys to move the insertion point down, and then select the text. Because adding the legal text will change the number of lines and paragraphs between the beginning of the document and the phrase, you need to use the Find command instead.

▶ **7.** On the ribbon, click the **Home** tab.

Tip
Click Special in the expanded Find and Replace dialog box to add special characters to the Find what box or the Replace with box.

▶ **8.** In the Editing group, click the **Find arrow**, and then click **Advanced Find**. The Find and Replace dialog box opens with the Find tab selected. You're using the Advanced Find box because when you click Find Next, the text is selected, not just highlighted as it is when you use the Navigation pane.

▶ **9.** In the Find what box, type **Participant must provide proof of age.**, and then click **Find Next**. The phrase is highlighted in the document.

▶ **10.** Click **Cancel** to close the Find and Replace dialog box.

▶ **11.** In the Font group, click the **Text Highlight Color** button ⌗ to highlight the selected text with yellow, and then press the ← key to deselect the highlighted text. This completes the operations for the AutoNew macro.

▶ **12.** On the status bar, click the **Stop Recording** button ☐. You don't want to save the template with the highlighting, so you'll remove the highlighting before saving the template again.

▶ **13.** Select the yellow highlighted text "Participant must provide proof of age."

▶ **14.** In the Font group, click the **Text Highlight Color arrow** ⌗⌄ then click **No Color**.

▶ **15.** Save the changes to the template.

Now you need to test your template. Remember, to create a new document based on a template, you need to double-click it in a File Explorer window.

When you create a document based on a macro-enabled template, the macros are not saved in the new document even if you save the new document as a macro-enabled document. However, the macros will still be available from within the document if the template and the document remain in their original folders. If you move the document to another computer, the macros will no longer be available to the document.

To test the AutoNew macro in a new document based on the NP_WD_8_Revised template:

1. On the taskbar, click the **File Explorer** button [icon]. The File Explorer window opens.

2. Navigate to the drive and folder where you are saving your files. Double-click the **NP_WD_8_Revised** template. A new document based on the template is created, and the prompt for the first Fill-in field appears, asking for the participant's name.

3. Type your name, and then click **OK**. The dialog box asking for the participant's date of birth opens.

4. Type **8/22/2002** and then click **OK**. The dialog box asking for the contact number opens.

5. Type **(206) 555-0125** and then click **OK**. The dialog box closes and the content of the document is displayed. The AutoNew macro runs and the phrase "Participant must provide proof of age." is highlighted.

   Trouble? If a dialog box opens warning you that macros in this project are disabled, you closed Word since you created the AutoNew macro. Click OK in the dialog box, and then click the Enable Content button in the Security Warning bar at the top of the document.

6. Save the document as a regular Word document—that is, not macro-enabled—named **NP_WD_8_Test** in the location specified by your instructor, and then close the document.

7. If you needed to change the Macro Settings in the Trust Center dialog box, open the Word Options dialog box, click **Trust Center** in the navigation pane, click **Trust Center Settings**, click the option button next to the setting originally applied on your computer, and then click **OK** twice.

8. Close the **NP_WD_8_Revised** template and close Word. A dialog box opens, asking if you want to save changes to "Building Blocks." This appears because when you copied the Quick Part from the NP_WD_8_Styles template to the NP_WD_8_Draft template, you first copied it to the Building Blocks template and then removed it from the Building Blocks template. Because you did not actually change the Building Blocks template, it does not matter if you save the changes.

   Trouble? If you took a break after the previous session, this dialog box already appeared and will not appear again. Skip Step 9.

9. Click **Don't Save**. Word closes.

Review

Session 8.3 Quick Check

1. What is a macro?

2. What are two advantages of using a macro?

3. Briefly describe how to record a macro.

4. Why would you need to edit a macro?

5. How do you run a macro named MyMacro if it's not assigned to a button on the Quick Access Toolbar or to a shortcut key combination?

6. What are AutoMacros?

Practice

Review Assignments

Data Files needed for the Review Assignments: NP_WD_8-3.dotx, Support_WD_8_NewStyles.dotx, Support_WD_8_People.jpg

Students and alumni of Elliot Bay College can reserve the Rock Gym for special events, such as a birthday or graduation party. Sam Nguyen created another template that employees of the Rock Gym can use when they schedule an event. He wants you to add graphic elements and other elements, including file properties, and record macros to make filling out the form easier. Complete the following steps:

1. Open the template **NP_WD_8-3.dotx** located in the Word8 > Review folder included with your Data Files. Save the template as a macro-enabled template named **NP_WD_8_Form** in the location specified by your instructor. (*Hint*: After changing the file type to a macro-enabled template, make sure you navigate to the location where you are saving your files.)

2. Insert a rectangle shape that is the width of the document (8.5 inches wide) and 1.5 inches high. In the shape, type **Alexander Griffin Rock Gym**, press ENTER, and then type **Student/Alumni Event Registration**. Position the shape so it is aligned with the center of the page and with the top of the page.

3. Change the fill color of the shape to Brown, Accent 5, and then fill the shape with the Linear Down gradient in the Dark Variations section of the Gradient gallery. Remove the shape outline.

4. Copy the style named Company Name from the template **Support_WD_8_NewStyles.dotx**, located in the Word8 > Review folder, to the NP_WD_8_Form template, and then apply it to all of the text in the rectangle.

5. Change the text color of the text "Student/Alumni Event Registration" to Light Yellow, Background 2, and then change the stylistic set to the third set in the Individual list.

6. Add a custom paragraph border below the paragraph containing "Contact Number." Select the style that uses dashes separated by dots (the last style in the Styles list when you first open the Borders and Shading dialog box). Change the weight of the line to 1½ points. Increase the space between the bottom of the paragraph and the border to 8 points.

7. Insert another rectangle shape 2 inches high and 8.5 inches wide. Align the rectangle vertically with the bottom of the page and horizontally with the center of the page.

8. Remove the shape outline, and then fill the shape with the picture in the file **Support_WD_8_People.jpg**, located in the Word8 > Review folder. Adjust the picture so it is not distorted and so that the top of the picture aligns with the top of the rectangle.

9. Compress the photo in the rectangle to E-mail (96 ppi) and remove cropped areas.

10. Copy the Rock Gym Webpage Address Quick Part from the template named **Support_WD_8_NewStyles.dotx** located in the Word8 > Review folder to the NP_WD_8_Form template. Close the Support_WD_8_NewStyles template without saving changes.

11. Show all properties on the Info screen, and then add **Sam Nguyen** as the Manager property and **Events** as the Categories property.

12. Add the custom document property "Checked by" with your name as the value.

13. In the footer, type **Checked by**, press SPACEBAR, and then insert the custom property Checked by as a field. Press ENTER, type **Approved by**, press SPACEBAR, and then insert the Manager property as a content control.

14. In the paragraph containing "Current Date," after the Tab character, insert the Date field set to update automatically, and then edit the field codes so that the date and time appear in the format June 25, 2025 3:10 PM. (*Hint*: Update the field after you edit the field code.)

15. Add the following Fill-in fields, remembering to deselect the Preserve formatting during updates check box for each Fill-in field you create.
    a. After the Tab character next to "Event Date:" insert a Fill-in field with the prompt **Enter event date:**
    b. After the Tab character next to "Student/Alumnus Name:" insert a Fill-in field with the prompt **Enter student/alumnus name:**
    c. After the Tab character next to "Contact Number:" insert a Fill-in field with the prompt **Enter contact number:**

16. Translate the placeholder text "[Information about required deposit]" into Spanish, and then place the translation between square brackets in a paragraph below the English placeholder text. Translate the same text again into Chinese Simplified and Vietnamese, and place each translation in paragraphs below the Spanish translation.

17. Change the proofing language of the paragraphs in Spanish, Chinese, and Vietnamese to Spanish (United States), Chinese (Singapore), and Vietnamese, respectively. Then remove Spanish, Chinese (Singapore), and Vietnamese as proofing languages if they were not set as proofing languages before you did this step.

18. Add the text watermark SAMPLE arranged diagonally across the page.

19. Change your macro security settings, if necessary, so that macros are disabled with notification.

20. Record a macro named **InsertWebPageAddress** stored in documents based on NP_WD_8_Form. Type **Insert Rock Gym webpage address in header** as the Description. Assign the keyboard shortcut **ALT+CTRL+SHIFT+B** to the macro. When the macro starts recording, do the following:
    a. Click the Insert tab, click the Header button in the Header & Footer group, and then click Edit Header.
    b. Click the Insert tab. In the Text group, click the Explore Quick Parts button, and then click the Rock Gym Webpage Address Quick Part.
    c. Click the Home tab, and then in the Paragraph group, click the Align Right button.
    d. Click the Header & Footer tab, and then in the Close group, click the Close Header and Footer button.
    e. Stop recording.

21. Edit the InsertWebPageAddress macro so that the header is center-aligned. In the header, remove the formatting, delete the text, and then close the Header area. Test the macro by running it.

22. Create an **AutoNew** macro stored in the NP_WD_8_Form template with **Highlight deposit percentage** as the description. The steps for this macro are:
    a. Use the Advanced Find box to find 10%.
    b. In the Font group on the Home tab, click the Text Highlight Color button.
    c. Press the ↓ key.
    d. Stop recording.

23. Remove the highlight you added while recording the AutoNew macro, and save the changes to the template.

24. Open a File Explorer window, navigate to the location where you are saving your files, and then double-click the NP_WD_8_Form template. Add **June 4, 2025** as the date of the event, your name as the student/alumnus name, and **(206) 555-0103** as the contact number.

25. Save the document as a regular Word document—that is, not macro-enabled—named **NP_WD_8_FormTest** in the location specified by your instructor, and then close the document.

26. If you changed the security settings for macros, reset the security to its original level. Close the NP_WD_8_Form template, saving changes if prompted, and close Word. Do not save the changes to the Building Blocks template.

Apply

Case Problem 1

Data Files needed for this Case Problem: NP_WD_8-4.dotx, Support_WD_8_RealtyStyles.dotx

Franklin Realty Group   Deb Surma owns Franklin Realty in Franklin, Massachusetts. When clients interested in purchasing a home first contact the agency, agents fill out a Housing Preferences sheet. Deb created a template to collect this information, and she asks you to complete it by adding Fill-in fields and formatting. Complete the following steps:

1. Open the template **NP_WD_8-4.dotx** from the Word8 > Case1 folder included with your Data Files, and then save it as a macro-enabled template named **NP_WD_8_Realty** in the location specified by your instructor. (Make sure you navigate to the correct folder after changing the file type.) Change your macro security settings, if necessary, so that macros are disabled with notification.

2. Copy the Franklin Realty and Web Address Quick Parts from the template **Support_WD_8_RealtyStyles.dotx**, located in the Word8 > Case1 folder to the NP_WD_8_Realty template. Edit the properties of the Franklin Realty Quick Part to include **Letterhead** as the description. Edit the properties of the Web Address Quick Part to include **Website** as the description.

3. Insert the Franklin Realty Quick Part at the beginning of the document. Click after the phone number, press ENTER, and then insert the Web Address Quick Part. If there is a blank paragraph below the website address, delete it.

4. Insert a rectangle that is 1.3 inches high and 6.5 inches wide. Remove the fill from the rectangle. Change the color of the shape outline to White, Background 1, Darker 50%. Change the weight of the shape outline to 6 points. Apply the Round bevel effect to the shape (using the Shape Effects menu).

5. Align the rectangle with the center and the top of the page. Change the left indent of the paragraphs inserted with the Franklin Realty and Web Address Quick Parts to 0.25 inches, and then change the space before the paragraph containing "Franklin Realty Group" to 18 points.

6. Copy the style Form Heading from the template **Support_WD_8_RealtyStyles.dotx**, located in the Word8 > Case1 folder to the NP_WD_8_Realty template. Apply the style to the text Housing Preferences.

7. Add your name as an Author property. On the Info screen in Backstage view, right-click the Author property Deb Surma, and then click Remove Person. Insert the Author property as a content control next to "Agent."

8. In the blank paragraph above "Name," insert the current date as a field that gets updated automatically, and then modify the field as needed so the date appears in the format 3 Mar 2025.

9. Below the paragraph containing "Phone," add a double-line border that is 1½ points wide. Change the space between the line and the paragraph to 12 points.

10. Next to each of the paragraphs below the date, add the following Fill-in fields. Do not preserve formatting for any of them.
    a. Name: **Client name**
    b. Address: **Client address**
    c. Phone: **Client phone**
    d. Type: **House or Condo?**
    e. Number of bedrooms: **# of bedrooms**
    f. Garage: **Garage required?**
    g. Central air: **Central air required?**
    h. Finished basement: **Finished basement required?**
    i. Fireplace: **Fireplace required?**

11. Add the custom text watermark ORIGINAL diagonally on the page.

12. Record a macro named **InsertFooter** stored in documents based on NP_WD_8_Realty to insert **Franklin Realty Group** as a footer. Add **Insert Franklin Realty Group as a footer** as the description. Assign the keyboard shortcut **ALT+CTRL+SHIFT+C** to the macro. As part of the macro, center the footer, format the text as Arial, and apply the middle stylistic set in the Individual section. (*Hint*: You need to press and hold SHIFT, and then press an arrow key to select the text to format it.)

13. Save the template, and then create a new document based on the NP_WD_8_Realty template. Enter your name in the Client name Fill-in field, 123 Main St., Franklin, MA 02038 as the address, (508) 555-0198 as the phone number, and reasonable responses in the rest of the prompt boxes. Save the document as a document named **NP_WD_8_RealtyTest** in the location specified by your instructor.

14. Change the macro security settings back to the original setting, if necessary, and then close all open documents. Do not save changes to the Building Blocks template, and do not save changes to the Support_WD_RealtyStyles template.

Challenge

Case Problem 2

Data Files needed for this Case Problem: NP_WD_8-5.dotx, Support_WD_8_Planting.jpg, Support_WD_8_Potomac.dotx

Potomac Pro Groundskeeping   Scott Rivera is the owner of Potomac Pro Groundskeeping, a commercial landscaping company in Alexandria, Virginia. Scott wants to create a form listing the services his company offers for new customers. He wants to be able to give it to new customers so they can check off the services they want. Scott started creating the form, and he asked you to use the document he created to create a template for collecting customers' information. Complete the following steps:

1. Open the document **NP_WD_8-5.dotx**, located in the Word8 > Case2 folder included with your Data Files, and then save it as a macro-enabled template named **NP_WD_8_Landscaping** in the location specified by your instructor. Make sure you navigate to the correct folder after changing the file type.

2. Change the macro security settings, if necessary.

3. Copy the Quick Part named **Company Name** from the **Support_WD_8_Potomac.dotx** template to the NP_WD_8_Landscaping template. Close the Support_WD_8_Potomac template without saving changes. Insert the Company Name Quick Part in the first paragraph in the document.

4. Insert the Flowchart: Preparation shape (in the Flowchart section of the Shapes gallery), and then resize it so that it is 6.5 inches wide and 0.5 inch high. Align its center with the center of the page, and then position it so the green alignment guide indicates that the top of the shape aligns with the bottom of the paragraph containing the company name.

5. Apply the Subtle Effect – Blue, Accent 1 shape style in the second column of the Theme Styles section of the Shape Styles gallery, and then remove the shape outline.

6. In the shape, type **1430 Lincoln Avenue, Alexandria, VA 22314**. Change the font size to 12 points. Remove the space below this paragraph.

⊕ **Explore** 7. Display the Fill-in field code after "Company or Office Park." (*Hint*: Right-click to the right of the paragraph mark after the space following "Company or Office Park," and then click Toggle Field Codes.) Copy the field code, and then paste the copied code after the space following "Contact Name:" and after the space following "Street Address:". Edit the prompts in the pasted codes to match the text in each line.

⊕ **Explore** 8. Insert a Fill-in field after "City, State, Zip" with the prompt **City, State, Zip**, setting the default response to **Alexandria, VA 22314**. (*Hint*: Select the appropriate check box in the Field options section of the Field dialog box.)

9. Add a border above the paragraph containing "Services." Use the triple-line border that is just above the wavy line in the Style list and change its color to the Blue, Accent 1, Darker 25% color. Adjust the spacing between "Services" and the line to 8 points.

10. Select the "Sign a three-year contract for a 10% discount!" paragraph, and apply the second stylistic set in the Individual section.

✦ **Explore** 11. Insert the picture **Support_WD_8_Planting.jpg**, located in the Word8 > Case2 folder, as a picture watermark with the Washout effect.

12. Create an **AutoNew** macro that moves the insertion point to the end of the document by pressing CTRL+END, and then moves the insertion point up one line so that it is positioned after the space after "Lead Tech." Store the macro in the NP_WD_8_Landscaping template, and type **Position the insertion point after Lead Tech** as the Description.

13. Save the changes to the template.

✦ **Explore** 14. Translate the entire document into Spanish. Save the Spanish version as a macro-enabled template named **NP_WD_8_Spanish** in the location where you are saving your files. Note that the Fill-in field prompts will not be translated. If necessary, replace "Guardasedura" with "Groundskeeping" and "Alejandría" with "Alexandria."

15. Copy the macro you recorded from the NP_WD_8_Landscaping template to the NP_WD_8_Spanish template. Save the changes to the NP_WD_8_Spanish template.

16. Create a new document based on the NP_WD_8_Landscaping template. Enter **Riverside Industrial Park** as the office park name, your name as the customer name, enter **123 Main St.** as the street address, and then accept the default text for the city, state, and zip code. After the AutoNew macro runs, type **Scott** as the landscaper's name. Save the document as **NP_WD_8_LandscapingTest** in the location specified by your instructor.

17. Change the macro security settings back to the original setting, if necessary. Close all open documents. Do not save changes to the Building Blocks template.

Objectives

Session 9.1
- Plan and design an online form
- Split cells
- Rotate and align text
- Move gridlines
- Modify borders
- Change cell margins

Session 9.2
- Learn about content controls
- Insert content controls
- Modify the properties of content controls
- Modify placeholder text in content controls
- Test content controls

Session 9.3
- Learn about cell referencing in formulas
- Use a formula in a table
- Group content controls
- Restrict document editing for a form
- Fill in an online form

Creating Online Forms Using Advanced Table Techniques

Developing an Order Form

Case | SS Mississippi Star

Emi Nakata is the activities director on the SS *Mississippi Star*, a steamboat cruise ship that cruises the Mississippi River between Memphis, Tennessee and New Orleans, Louisiana. Several times a year, she plans themed cruises, such as cruises that provide a focus on art, dance, bird watching, genealogy, or cooking. She is currently planning a crafts cruise, and one of the activities that will be offered is painting pottery. Passengers who participate in this activity can pick up their finished pieces after they are dry, have them delivered to their cabins, or pay a fee to have the pieces shipped home. Emi asks you to create an online form to collect each participant's name and contact information as well as their preference for collecting the finished pottery pieces.

You'll start with a partially completed Word table that Emi created. First, you'll modify the structure and the format of the table. Next, you'll add different types of content controls and special fields to accept specific types of information, and you'll customize the placeholder text to help the user fill out the form. You'll also add a formula that will calculate the shipping fee if a passenger wants to ship their painted piece home. When the form is complete, you'll add a password to protect the form from being changed accidentally, and then you'll test the form by filling in sample information.

Starting Data Files

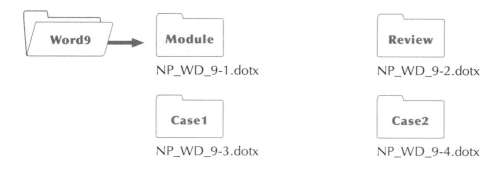

Word9 → Module
NP_WD_9-1.dotx

Review
NP_WD_9-2.dotx

Case1
NP_WD_9-3.dotx

Case2
NP_WD_9-4.dotx

Session 9.1 Visual Overview:

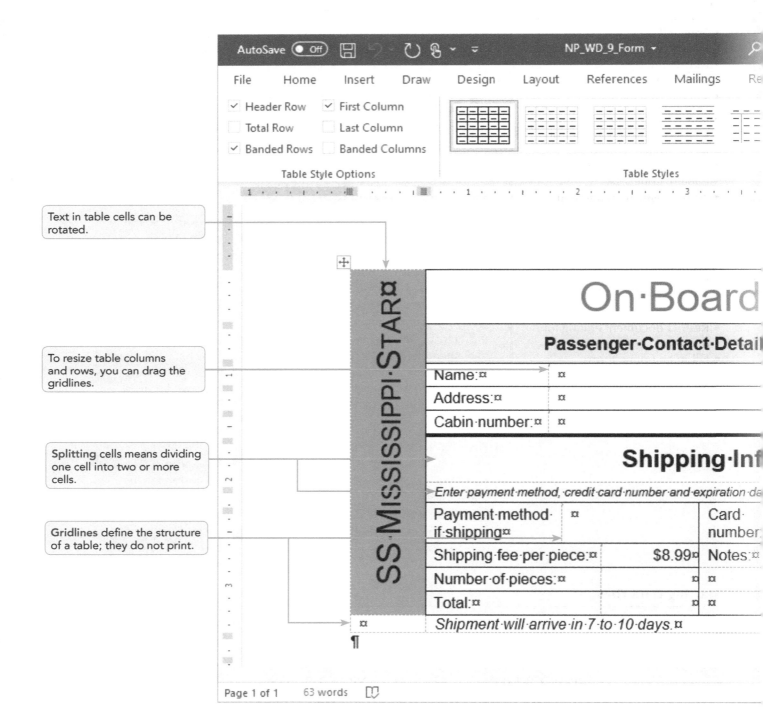

Text in table cells can be rotated.

To resize table columns and rows, you can drag the gridlines.

Splitting cells means dividing one cell into two or more cells.

Gridlines define the structure of a table; they do not print.

Custom Table

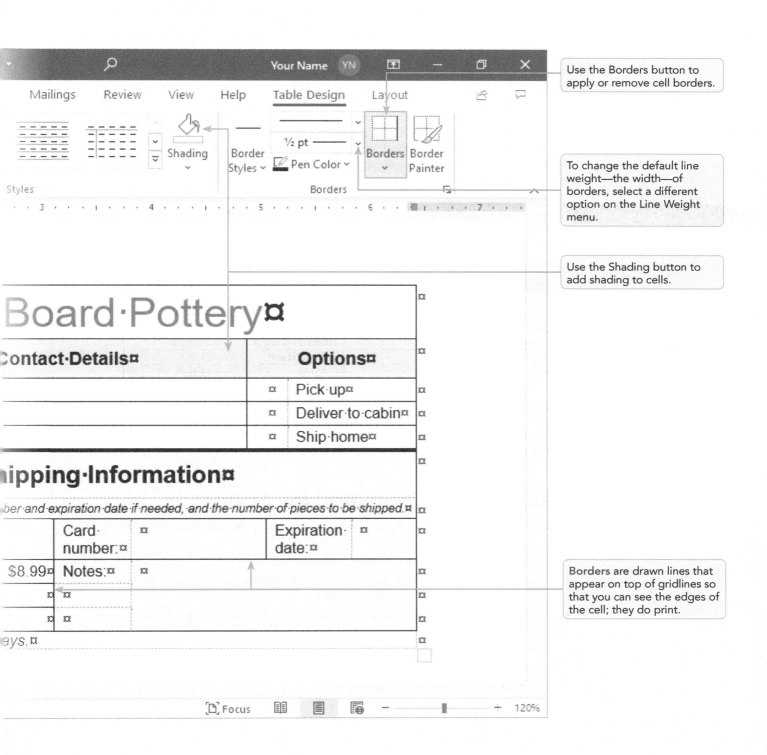

Use the Borders button to apply or remove cell borders.

To change the default line weight—the width—of borders, select a different option on the Line Weight menu.

Use the Shading button to add shading to cells.

Borders are drawn lines that appear on top of gridlines so that you can see the edges of the cell; they do print.

Creating and Using Online Forms

An online form is a document that contains labels and corresponding blank areas in which a user enters the information requested. When you create an online form using Word, it's a good idea to use a template file rather than a regular Word file so that users can't change the form itself when entering their information.

To create an online form, you need to add content controls. You have used content controls that display information about a document, such as the document title or the author name. When a content control is linked to information in a document, such as the document title, that information is inserted in the document wherever that control appears. When you insert a content control in a form, you create an area that can contain only the type of information that you specify, such as text or a date. You can also specify a format for the information stored in a control and create rules that determine what kind of information the control will accept. For example, Figure 9–1 shows a form with different types of information, including text, a date, and a value selected from a list.

Figure 9–1	Portion of an online form

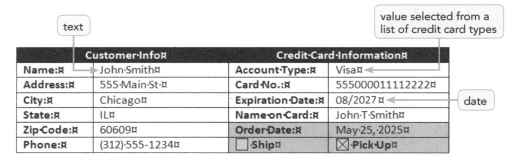

The fact that you can specify the type of information that appears in a control, thereby allowing only certain types of data, helps prevent users from entering incorrect information. Placeholder text in each control tells the user what information is required for that particular part of the form.

Planning and Designing the Form

The online form you'll create for Emi will consist of a Word table that will contain space for the following:

- The passenger's contact information and cabin number
- A section that lists the passenger's choice for getting the pottery home (pick up, deliver to the passenger's cabin, or ship to their home)
- A section that lists the shipping fee per piece and calculates the total and lists the passenger's payment choice
- A notes area

Figure 9–2 shows Emi's sketch for the online form. She wants you to use a table structure to keep the elements organized.

Figure 9–2   **Sketch of the structure of the online form**

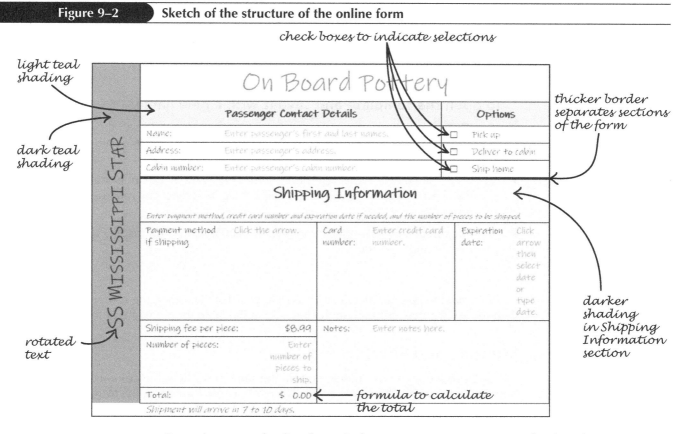

One advantage of online forms is that programmers can extract the data that users enter and export it to a database. If you need to design a form whose information will be extracted and exported to a database, include only one piece of data or information in each cell or content control. For example, the type of credit card, the credit card number, and the credit card expiration date would need to be stored in three separate content controls. This also applies to names and addresses. First and last names should be in separate content controls, and each part of an address—the street address, city, state, and zip code—should be in separate content controls.

The form in this module has been formatted so you can focus on all the components you can use to create a form without spending too much time executing the same skills. Therefore, in this form, there is only one container for the passenger's first and last names, and only one container for the passenger's address. Also note that most people have an email address and more than one phone number. Normally, containers for these pieces of information would need to be included in a form. Again, to keep the form simple for this module, this information is not collected.

Proskills

Decision Making: Using a Table as the Structure for a Form

Planning the layout of a form is important. If you skip this step, you could end up with a form that is so confusing that users miss important sections. You want the labels and areas in which the user enters the data to be clear. A table is an effective way to organize a form in a logical way. The rows and columns provide a natural organization for labels and areas where the user fills in information. You can add shading and formatting to specific cells to make certain parts of the table stand out or to divide the form into sections. Taking the time to plan and make decisions about how data should appear in a form will result in a form that is easier to build and straightforward for someone to fill out, and one that collects data that is useful and accurate.

Creating a Custom Table for a Form

Emi created the table for the form and saved it as a template. You'll customize the table based on Emi's design shown earlier in Figure 9–2.

To open the template and save it with a new name:

▶ 1. **sam⁺** ⬇ Use the Open command in Backstage view to open the template **NP_WD_9-1.dotx**, which is located in the Word9 > Module folder included with your Data Files.

▶ 2. Save the file as a Word template named **NP_WD_9_Form** in the location specified by your instructor. You will not be including any macros in this template.

▶ 3. If necessary, change the Zoom level to **120%**, and then display the rulers and nonprinting characters.

To format the table to match Emi's sketch, you'll start by merging some cells and then inserting a new column on the left side of the table for the name of the form.

Merging and Splitting Cells

As you have seen, you can merge cells in the same row, the same column, or the same rectangular block of rows and columns. To begin formatting the form, you need to merge some of the cells that contain headings so that they more clearly label the sections of the form.

To merge cells in the table:

▶ 1. In the first row, click in the cell containing "On Board Pottery," and then drag across the three blank cells to the right of that cell. The four cells in the first row are selected.

Tip

You can also click the Eraser button in the Draw group on the Layout tab, and then click a gridline between cells to merge the two cells.

▶ 2. On the ribbon, click the **Layout** contextual tab, and then in the Merge group, click the **Merge Cells** button. The four cells are merged into one cell.

▶ 3. In the second row, merge the cells containing "Passenger Contact Details" and the blank cell to its right, and then merge the cells containing "Options" and the blank cell to its right. The second row in the table now contains two merged cells.

▶ 4. In the last column, merge the empty cell to the right of the cell containing "Notes" with the two cells beneath it. Compare your screen to Figure 9–3.

Figure 9–3	Merged cells in the table

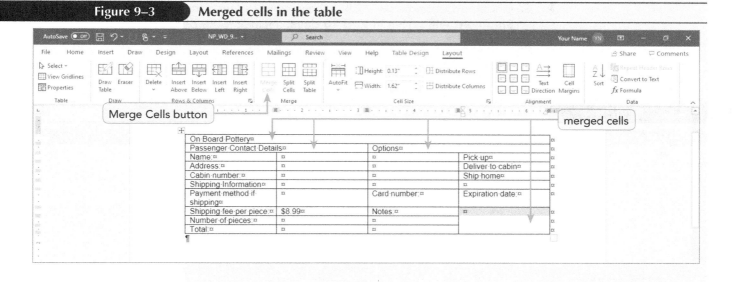

Emi's sketch shows the ship name to the left of the table, rotated so it reads from bottom to top on a shaded background without any borders. To add this to the form, you will insert a new blank column as the first column in the table, then you will merge the cells of the new column to form one long cell.

To insert a new column and merge the cells:

▶ **1.** In the first row, click in the "On Board Pottery" cell.

▶ **2.** On the Layout tab, in the Rows & Columns group, click the **Insert Left** button. A new column is inserted to the left of the current column, and all the cells in the new column are selected.

▶ **3.** In the Merge group, click the **Merge Cells** button. The new column now contains one merged cell.

▶ **4.** Type **SS Mississippi Star**.

In Emi's sketch, there is a note below the table. You need to add a new row at the bottom of the table to contain this note.

To add a new bottom row and merge the cells:

▶ **1.** Click in the first column in the cell containing "SS Mississippi Star," if necessary.

▶ **2.** On the Layout tab, in the Rows & Columns group, click the **Insert Below** button. A new second row is inserted. This is because the merged cell in the first column is considered to be in the first row.

▶ **3.** On the Quick Access Toolbar, click the **Undo** button 🔁. The new second row is removed.

▶ **4.** In the last row, click the "Total" cell, and then in the Rows & Columns group, click the **Insert Below** button. A new bottom row is added to the table.

▶ **5.** In the new bottom row, click in the second cell, and then type the following: **Shipment will arrive in 7 to 10 days.** (including the period).

▶ **6.** In the last row, merge the cells in the second, third, fourth, and fifth columns. The last row now contains two cells—one in the first column, and one merged cell that spans the second through fifth columns. See Figure 9–4.

Figure 9–4 **Table with new column and row**

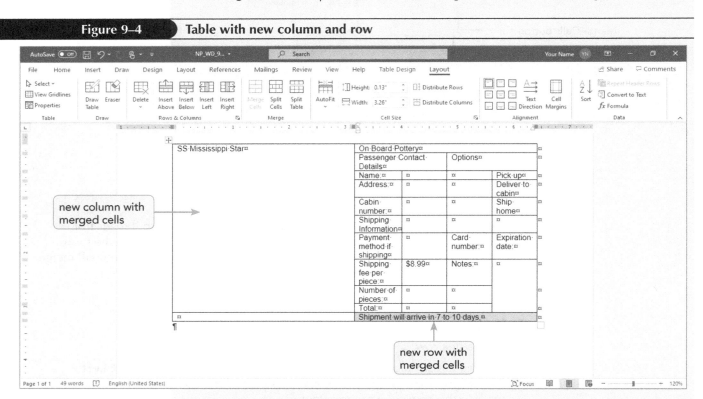

▶ **7.** Save the template.

You can also split cells. If you split cells vertically, you increase the number of columns in a row. If you split cells horizontally, you increase the number of rows in a column. If you select multiple adjacent cells, when you split them, you can specify whether you want to first merge the selected cells into one cell before the split, or whether you want each cell split individually.

Reference

Splitting Cells

- Select the cell or cells that you want to split.
- On the ribbon, click the Layout tab, and then in the Merge group, click the Split Cells button.
- In the Split Cells dialog box, check the Merge cells before split check box if you want the cell contents to merge into one cell before they split into more columns or rows; or uncheck the Merge cells before split check box if you want the cell contents to split into columns and rows without merging first.
- Set the number of columns and rows into which you want to split the current cell or cells.
- Click OK.

In Emi's sketch, there is a cell to the right of the cell containing "Card number," and there is a cell to the right of the cell containing "Expiration date." To create these cells, you will split each of those cells into two columns.

To split cells into two columns:

▶ **1.** In the seventh row in the table, select the last two cells in the row (the cells containing "Card number" and "Expiration date").

▶ **2.** On the Layout tab, in the Merge group, click the **Split Cells** button. The Split Cells dialog box opens. See Figure 9–5.

| Figure 9–5 | Split Cells dialog box |

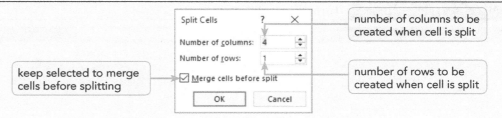

The values in the Number of columns and Number of rows boxes are based on the number of cells selected. Also, the Merge cells before split check box is selected. With these options, the two selected cells will be merged into one cell, and all of the text in the two cells will be combined into that one merged cell. Then the merged cell will be split into four columns, and the text in the selected cells will be distributed in the new cells. In this case, it would place the text in the first two cells created by the split. This is not what you want. Instead, you want each individual cell to split so that the text from each of the original selected cells appears in the left cell in each pair and a new cell is created to the right of each of the original two cells.

Tip

You can also click the Draw Table button in the Draw group on the Layout tab, and then drag to draw a gridline in a cell to split that cell.

▶ **3.** In the Split Cells dialog box, click the **Merge cells before split** check box to deselect it. The value in the Number of columns box changes to 2. Now each of the selected cells will be split into two columns and one row.

▶ **4.** Click **OK**. Each selected cell is split into two columns, with the text from each of the original selected cells appearing in the left cell in each pair.

In Emi's sketch, there is a row below the row containing "Shipping Information," but this row is not included in the Word table she created. You could insert a row using one of the Insert commands in the Rows & Columns group on the Layout tab. But because you need to merge the cell containing "Shipping Information" with the cells to its right, you'll use the Split Cells button to merge the cells in this row into one cell, and then split the merged row into two rows.

To split the "Shipping Information" cell into two rows:

▶ **1.** Select the cell containing "Shipping Information" and the three blank cells to its right.

Tip

To split a table into two or more tables, click in the row that you want to be the first row in the new table, and then on the Layout tab, in the Merge group, click the Split Table button.

2. On the Layout tab, in the Merge group, click the **Split Cells** button. This time, you will keep the Merge cells before split check box selected because you want the cells in the row to merge into one cell before splitting into two rows so that each row contains only one wide cell.

3. In the Number of columns box, type **1**, press **TAB** to move to the Number of rows box, type **2**, and then click **OK**. The selected cells merge into one cell, and then that cell is split into two rows.

4. Click in the new blank cell below "Shipping Information," and then type **Enter payment method, credit card number and expiration date if needed, and the number of pieces to be shipped.** (including the period). See Figure 9–6.

Figure 9–6   **Form after splitting cells**

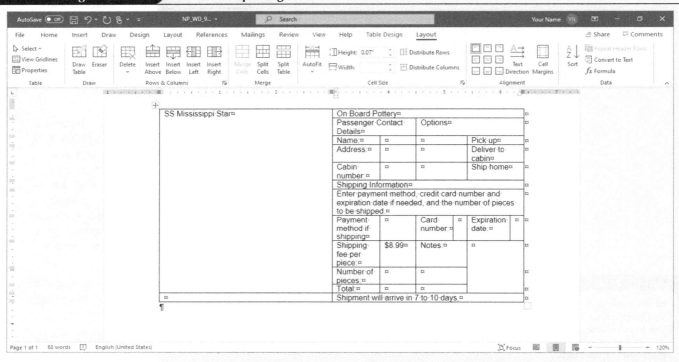

5. Save the template.

Rotating Text in a Cell

You can rotate text in a cell to read from the top to the bottom or from the bottom to the top. In Emi's sketch, the ship name in the first column reads from the bottom of the column up to the top. You'll do this next.

To rotate the text in the first column:

1. Click in the merged cell in the first column. You don't need to select any text because the command to rotate the text in the cell applies to all the text in the cell.

▶ **2.** On the Layout tab, in the Alignment group, click the **Text Direction** button. The text in the first column rotates so that it reads from top to bottom. Note that the icon on the Text Direction button changed to reflect this.

▶ **3.** Click the **Text Direction** button again. The text in the cell and the arrows on the button change to show the text reading from bottom to top. See Figure 9–7. If you clicked the button again, the text would read from left to right again.

| Figure 9–7 | Cell with rotated text |

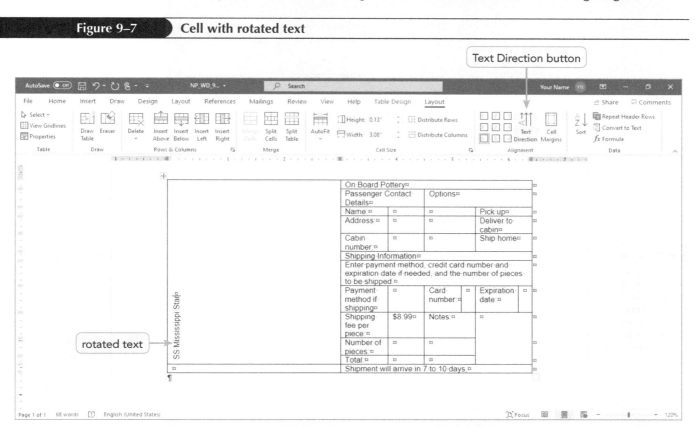

Moving Gridlines to Change Column Widths and Row Heights

Next, you need to adjust the cell sizes in the table. To match Emi's sketch, you need to format individual cells within a column to be different widths. The default setting for tables in Word is for the columns to automatically resize larger if needed to accommodate long text strings. For many tables, this works well. For this form, however, you need to be able to control the column widths. Therefore, before you change the column widths and row heights in the table, you need to change the table property that causes the columns to automatically resize to fit the text. After you do that, if you set column widths, they will stay the width you specify.

To turn off automatic resizing in the table's properties:

▶ **1.** On the Layout tab, in the Table group, click the **Properties** button. The Table Properties dialog box opens with the Table tab selected.

▶ **2.** Click **Options**. The Table Options dialog box opens. See Figure 9–8.

Figure 9–8   **Table Properties and Table Options dialog boxes**

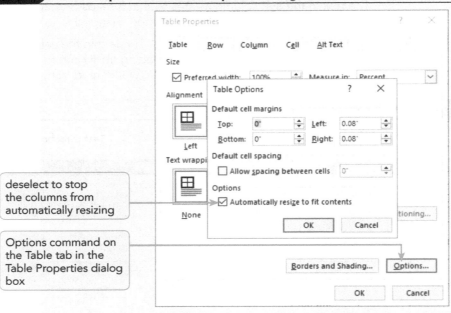

deselect to stop the columns from automatically resizing

Options command on the Table tab in the Table Properties dialog box

▶ **3.** Click the **Automatically resize to fit contents** check box to deselect it. This will stop the columns from automatically resizing.

▶ **4.** Click **OK**, and then click **OK** in the Table Properties dialog box.

You can resize columns and rows by specifying column widths and row heights in the boxes in the Cell Size group on the Layout tab; by changing the measurements on the Row and Column tabs in the Table Properties dialog box; or by dragging the gridlines in the table. To resize the width of individual cells, you first select the cell, and then type a measurement in the Width box in the Cell Size group on the Layout tab or drag the left or right gridline.

When you resize columns, rows, and cells by dragging the gridlines, you can see how the change in size affects the contents of the cells. Also, when you drag gridlines, the columns, rows, or cells on either side of the gridline you are dragging adjust so that the overall table width is not affected. If you change sizes by entering new values in the Height and Width boxes in the Cell Size group on the Layout tab, only the column or row whose measurement you changed is affected. This means that the table width or height changes because none of the other columns or rows adjust.

Now that you have created the basic table structure, you will adjust cell widths and heights to match Emi's sketch.

To change the width of columns:

▶ **1.** Click in the first column, if necessary. On the ruler, the Move Table Column marker ▦ between the first two columns is positioned at the 3-inch mark.

▶ **2.** On the Layout tab, in the Cell Size group, click in the **Width** box, type **0.7**, and then press **ENTER**. The first column is now only 0.7 inches wide, and the table no longer stretches horizontally from margin to margin. This is because only the width of the first column changed.

3. On the Quick Access Toolbar, click the **Undo** button. The width of the first column changes back to its original width of 3.08 inches.

4. Position the pointer on top of the gridline between the first two columns so that the pointer changes to the column resize pointer ╋╟╋.

5. Press and hold the mouse button, drag the gridline to the left until the Move Table Column marker ▦ is just to the right of the 0.5-inch mark on the ruler, and then release the mouse button. The measurement in the Width box in the Cell Size group on the Layout tab should be 0.69". As the width of the first column changed, the width of the second column adjusted so that the overall width of the table stayed the same. See Figure 9–9.

Figure 9–9 **Resized columns**

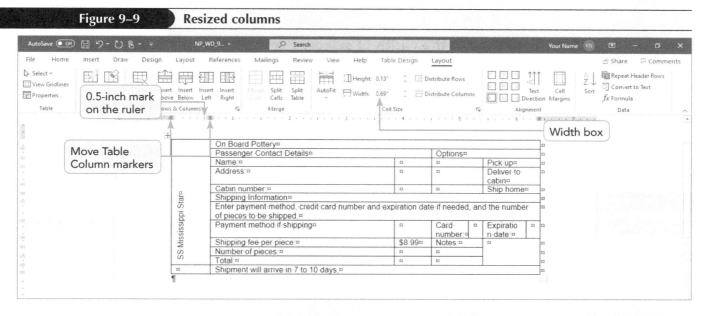

Trouble? If the measurement in the Width box in the Cell Size group on the Layout tab is not exactly 0.69", don't worry about it.

In Emi's sketch, the width of the cells in the Passenger Contact Details section is different than the width of the cells in the rows beneath it. To change the width of some of the cells in a column, you need to select those cells first. Then you can drag the gridline to the right of the selected cells.

To change the width of selected cells:

1. Click in the cell containing "Name," and then drag down through the next two cells below it. The three cells from the cell containing "Name" through the cell containing "Cabin number" are selected.

2. Position the pointer on top of the gridline to the right of the selected cells so that the pointer changes to the column resize pointer ╋╟╋.

3. Press and hold the mouse button, drag the gridline to the left until the gridline is just to the right of the cell marker in the "Cabin number" cell, and then release the mouse button. The Move Table Column marker ▦ is just to the left of the 1.625-inch mark on the ruler (the 1⅝-inch mark), and

the measurement in the Width box in the Cell Size group on the Layout tab should be 1.12".

Trouble? If the measurement in the Width box in the Cell Size group on the Layout tab is not exactly 1.12", don't worry about it.

If you press and hold ALT while you are dragging a gridline, the measurement between gridlines in the table appears on the ruler between the Move Table Column markers. You need to make several more adjustments to cell widths in the table so that the form will match Emi's sketch. You will press ALT while you are dragging so that your screen matches the figures in this text as closely as possible.

To change the width of selected cells to exact measurements:

▶ **1.** Select the three empty cells to the right of the "Name," "Address," and "Cabin number" cells.

▶ **2.** Press and hold **ALT**, position the pointer over the gridline on the right side of the selected cells so that it changes to ◀‖▶, press and hold the mouse button, and then drag the pointer to the right slightly. The ruler changes to indicate the exact widths between the Move Table Column markers. (Note that these widths are a little narrower than the cell width.) See Figure 9–10.

Figure 9–10	Moving a gridline while pressing ALT

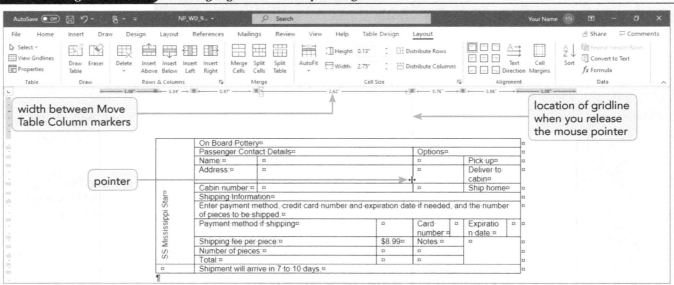

Trouble? When you press ALT, Key Tips—labels identifying the letter you can press on the keyboard to select a command on the ribbon—appear on the ribbon. You can ignore them while you are resizing the column.

Trouble? The exact measurement between the second and third Move Table Column markers on your screen might not match the measurement shown in Figure 9–10. Do not be concerned about this.

▶ **3.** Using the measurements on the ruler as a guide and keeping **ALT** pressed, drag the gridline to the right until the distance between the Move Table Column markers marking the borders of the selected cells is about 3", and then release the mouse button and **ALT**. The width of the selected cells and the cells to the right of the selected cells changes.

4. Select the three empty cells to the left of the cells containing "Pick up," "Deliver to cabin," and "Ship home," press and hold **ALT**, and then drag the gridline on the right side of the selected cells to the left until the distance between the Move Table Column markers marking the borders of the selected cells is about 0.2" and the width of the cells to the right of the selected cells is about 1". (Make sure "Deliver to cabin" stays on one line.)

5. Click in the cell containing "Passenger Contact Details."

6. On the Layout tab, in the Table group, click the **Select** button, and then click **Select Cell**. The cell containing "Passenger Contact Details" is selected.

7. Drag the gridline on the right side of the selected cell to the right so that it aligns with the gridline on the right of the three empty cells below it. If you press ALT while you are dragging, the measurement between the two Move Table Column markers marking the borders of the selected cell is about 4.11".

   Trouble? If you have trouble aligning the gridlines, press ALT while you drag.

   Trouble? If the widths of other cells below the "Passenger Contact Details" cell also change, you clicked in the "Passenger Contact Details" cell instead of selecting it. Undo the width change, and then repeat Steps 5 through 7, taking care to select the entire cell in Step 6 before dragging the gridline in Step 7.

8. Select the cell containing "Payment method if shipping," resize it so the measurement between the two Move Table Column markers marking the left and right edges of the selected cell is about 1.1", and then resize the cell to its right so the measurement between the two Move Table Column markers marking the gridlines of the selected cell is also about 1.1".

9. Resize the cell containing "Card number" so the measurement between the two Move Table Column markers marking the left and right edges of the selected cell is about 0.55", resize the cell to its right so the measurement between the two Move Table Column markers marking the left and right edges of the selected cell is about 1.1", and then resize the cell containing "Expiration date" so the measurement between the two Move Table Column markers marking the left and right edges of the selected cell is about 0.63".

10. Select the cell containing "Shipping fee per piece" and the two cells below it, and then resize the selected cells so the measurement between the two Move Table Column markers marking the left and right edges of the selected cells is about 1.45".

11. Select the three cells to the right of the cells containing "Shipping fee per piece," "Number of pieces," and "Total," and then resize the selected cells so the measurement between the two Move Table Column markers marking the left and right edges of the selected cells is about 0.75" and the right gridline of the selected cells aligns with the left gridline of the "Card number" cell in the row above the selected cells.

12. Select the cell containing "Notes" and the two empty cells below it, and then resize the selected cells so that the distance between the Move Table Column markers marking the left and right edges of the selected cells is about 0.55" and the right gridline aligns with the right gridline of the "Card number" cell. Compare your table to the one shown in Figure 9–11.

Figure 9–11   Table with resized columns

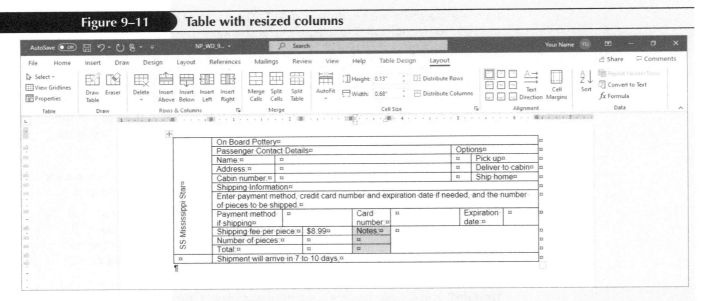

Trouble? If the measurement in the Width box in the Cell Size group on the Layout tab is not 0.69" for the first column, resize the first column so that the distance between the Move Table Column markers is 0.53". If the measurement in the Width box is not 1.12" for the cells containing "Name," "Address," and "Cabin number," select those three cells and resize them so that the measurement between the Move Table Column markers is 0.97".

You can also adjust the height of rows in a table. To visually separate the various sections of the form, you'll increase the height of the section heading rows.

To change the height of the section heading rows by moving the gridlines:

1. Click anywhere in the table, making sure that no text is selected, and then position the pointer over the bottom gridline of the row containing "Passenger Contact Details" and "Options" so that it changes to the row resize pointer ⇕.

2. Press and hold **ALT**, and then drag the bottom gridline down until the distance between the Adjust Table Row markers on the vertical ruler that mark the top and bottom edges of the row is about 0.3".

3. Drag the bottom gridline of the row containing "Shipping Information" down until the distance between the Adjust Table Row markers on the vertical ruler that mark the top and bottom edges of the row is about 0.4" and the row is approximately double its original height. See Figure 9–12.

Figure 9–12   **Rows resized in table**

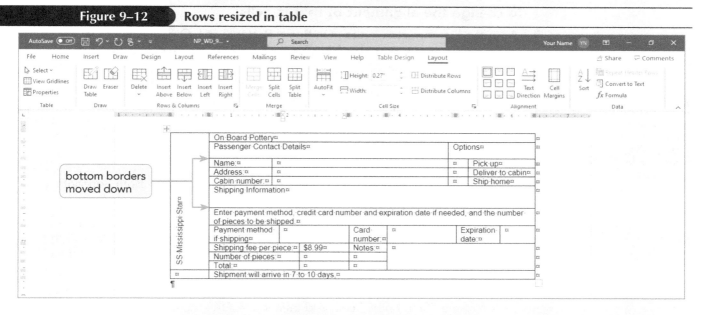

4. Save the template.

Insight

Using the AutoFit Command

The AutoFit button in the Cell Size group on the Layout tab offers some additional options for changing the width of table columns. When you first create a table, its columns are all the same width, and the table stretches from the left to the right margin. If you enter data that is wider than the cell you are typing in, the data wraps in the cell to the next line. (Note that if the word you type is long and does not contain any spaces, the column will widen as much as needed to fit the word until the columns to its right are 0.15 inches wide, at which point the text will wrap in the cell.) If you want the columns to resize wider to accommodate data, you can select the table, click the AutoFit button, and then click AutoFit Contents. When you do this, columns that contain data that is longer than the width of the column will resize wider, if possible, to accommodate the widest entry. If the widest entry in a column is narrower than the column, the AutoFit Contents command will resize that column narrower to just fit that data. If you have adjusted column widths, either manually or by using the AutoFit Contents command, so that the table no longer stretches from the left to the right margin, you can click the AutoFit button and then click AutoFit Window. This will resize all the columns proportionally so that the table stretches from the left to the right margin. This command is useful if you paste a table copied from another file and it is too wide to fit on the page.

Aligning Cell Content

Now that you've sized the rows and columns appropriately, you can align the text within cells. The text in the cells of a table is, by default, left-aligned and positioned at the top of the cell. On the Layout tab, in the Alignment group, there are nine buttons you can use to align text in a cell. You can align text at the left and right edges of a cell, and you can center-align it. You can also change the vertical alignment to position the text at the top, middle, or bottom of a cell.

To make the form more attractive and easier to read, you'll center the text for the section headings and change the alignment of the text in the first column.

To change the alignment of text in cells:

1. In the first row, click in the "On Board Pottery" cell. On the Layout tab, in the Alignment group, the Align Top Left button ⊟ is selected. Because this row is only tall enough to fit one line of text, you don't need to change the vertical alignment, but you do need to center it horizontally.

2. In the Alignment group, click the **Align Top Center** button ⊟.

3. Select the cells containing "Passenger Contact Details" and "Options." The text in these cells needs to be centered both horizontally and vertically.

4. In the Alignment group, click the **Align Center** button ⊟.

5. Align the text in the cell containing "Shipping Information" both horizontally and vertically.

The empty cells in the Options section will contain check boxes. The check boxes will look better if they are centered horizontally and vertically. And the labels in the cells next to them would look better if they were center-aligned vertically.

6. Click in the cell to the left of the "Pick up" cell, drag down to the cell to the left of the "Ship home" cell, and then in the Alignment group, click the **Align Center** button ⊟.

7. Click in the "Pick up" cell, drag down to the "Ship home" cell, and then in the Alignment group, click the **Align Center Left** button ⊟.

8. Select the cell containing "$8.99" and the two cells below it, and then in the Alignment group, click the **Align Top Right** button ⊟.

9. In the first column, click in the cell containing the rotated text. The nine alignment buttons in the Alignment group change so the lines are vertical instead of horizontal.

10. In the Alignment group, click the **Align Center** button ⊟. The text in the first column is center-aligned. See Figure 9–13.

Figure 9–13 **Table after changing the alignment of text in cells**

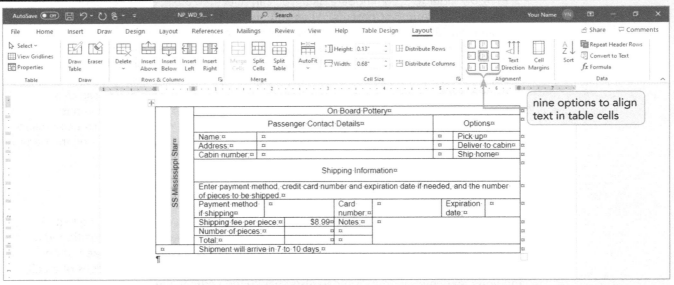

11. Save the template.

Removing Borders

A table is defined by its gridlines; borders are lines that appear on top of gridlines. Gridlines do not print, but borders do. You can display or hide gridlines while you are working; but even when hidden, the gridlines still define the table's structure. When you create a table, ½-point borders appear along all the gridlines by default.

To match Emi's sketch, you'll remove the borders between all the labels and the empty cells next to them. You'll begin by removing the right border of cells that contain the labels for the passenger information. You will do this by deselecting commands on the Borders menu.

To remove borders from cells using the commands on the Borders menu:

1. Under "Passenger Contact Details," select the cells containing "Name," "Address," and "Cabin number."

2. On the ribbon, click the **Table Design** tab.

3. In the Borders group, click the **Borders arrow** ⊞▾. The Borders menu opens. All of the border options in the Borders menu are selected except No Border and the two diagonal borders. See Figure 9–14.

Figure 9–14   Borders menu

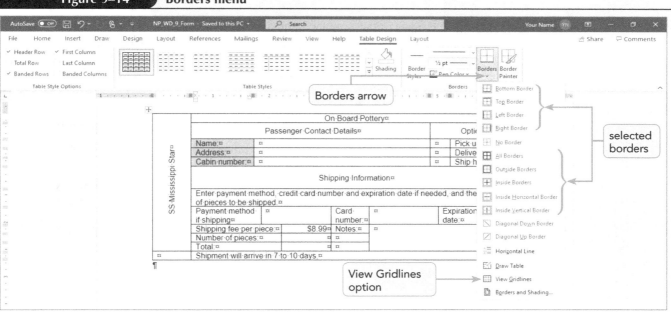

Trouble? If the Borders menu did not open, you clicked the Borders button instead of the arrow beneath it. Undo the change, and then repeat Step 3.

4. Click **Right Border**. The menu closes, and the right border is removed from the selected cells.

5. Deselect the cells. If gridlines are visible, a dotted line appears where the right border was; if gridlines are not visible, you don't see anything where the right border was.

6. Click in one of the cells whose right border you removed, and then click the **Borders arrow** ⊞▾ again. Note that now, not only is the Right Border option deselected, but all of the Borders options below it are deselected as well.

Tip

You can also click the View Gridlines button in the Table group on the Layout tab to display or hide gridlines.

7. If the View Gridlines command at the bottom of the Borders button menu is not selected, click **View Gridlines**; if it is selected, click a blank area of the document to close the Borders button menu without making any changes. Even though you removed the right border from these cells, the gridline that defines the structure of these cells is still there. See Figure 9–15.

Figure 9–15   **Table after a border between columns is removed**

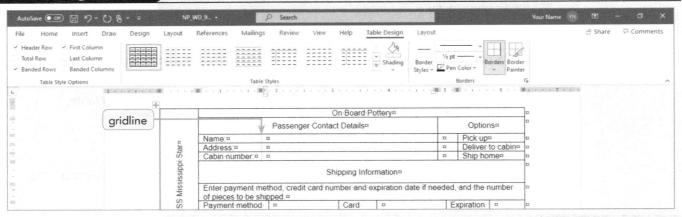

Sometimes it's hard to figure out exactly which commands on the Borders menu should be selected or deselected, so you might find it easier to use the Borders and Shading dialog box to modify or remove borders. You'll use this method to remove the borders to the left of the labels in the Options section.

To remove borders using the Borders and Shading dialog box:

1. Select the three cells containing labels under "Options" (from the cell containing "Pick up" through the cell containing "Ship home").

2. On the Table Design tab, in the Borders group, click the **Borders arrow** , and then click **Borders and Shading**. The Borders and Shading dialog box opens with the Borders tab on top. See Figure 9–16.

| **Figure 9–16** | Borders tab in the Borders and Shading dialog box |

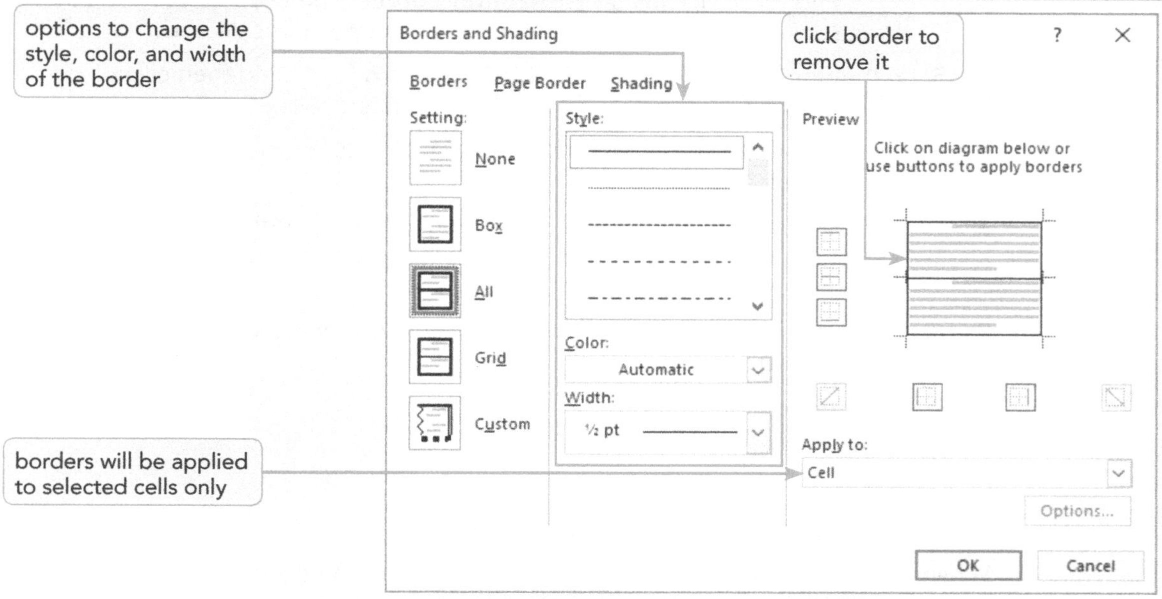

options to change the style, color, and width of the border

click border to remove it

borders will be applied to selected cells only

In the Apply to box at the bottom of the Preview section, note that "Cell" is selected. This means any changes you make will be applied to each of the selected cells. The Preview section illustrates the borders on the selected cells. In the Setting list, the All button is selected.

▶ **3.** In the Preview section, click the left border. The border disappears. Notice that in the Setting list, the All button is deselected, and the Custom button is now selected.

Trouble? If one of the other borders disappeared or if you added a vertical border, click that border to make it reappear or disappear, and then click the left border in the Preview section again.

▶ **4.** Click **OK**, and then click a blank area of the table to deselect the cells. The left border of the cells you had selected is removed.

Next, you need to remove the borders between the cells containing "Payment method if shipping," "Card number," and "Expiration date" and the empty cells to the left of each of those cells. You also need to remove the borders between the cells containing the labels related to shipping fees and the empty cells to the right. You'll also remove all the borders in the Notes section so it looks like one large section. Finally, you will remove the borders around the sentence in the last row and around the form name in the first column.

To remove additional borders:

▶ **1.** Remove the right border of the cells containing "Payment method if shipping," "Card number," and "Expiration date."

▶ **2.** Remove the right border of the cells containing "Shipping fee per piece," "Number of pieces," and "Total."

▶ **3.** Select the cell containing "Notes" and the two cells below it.

▶ **4.** On the Table Design tab, in the Borders group, click the **Borders arrow** ▦ ˅, and then click **Inside Horizontal Border**. The borders between the three selected cells are removed. Keep the three cells selected.

▶ **5.** In the Borders group, click the **Borders arrow** ▦ ˅, and then click **Right Border**. The right borders of the selected cells are removed.

▶ **6.** Remove the border between the cell containing "Shipping Information" and the cell beneath it.

▶ **7.** In the last row, select the two cells, remove the left, right, and bottom borders, and the border between the empty first cell and the cell containing "Shipment will arrive in 7 to 10 days."

▶ **8.** In the top cell in the first column (the cell containing the rotated text), remove the top, bottom, and left borders.

▶ **9.** Save the template.

Changing the Width of Borders

When you create a table, ½-point borders appear along all the gridlines by default. You can modify the borders so they are different widths, or line weights. You'll make the top border of the "Shipping Information" cell thicker than the rest of the borders in the table. To do this, you can use the Borders and Shading dialog box, or you can use the Border Painter button in the Borders group on the Table Design tab.

To draw a thicker border to separate the top of the form and the shipping information section:

▶ **1.** On the Table Design tab, click the **Line Weight arrow** | ½ pt ——— ˅ | and then click **3 pt**. Now, any borders you insert will be 3 points thick rather than the default ½ point. Notice that the Border Painter button in the Borders group is now selected, and the pointer is now the paintbrush pointer ✏.

▶ **2.** Drag the pointer along the top border of the cell containing "Shipping Information." The top border is now 3 points wide. See Figure 9–17.

Figure 9–17   **3-point border separates table sections**

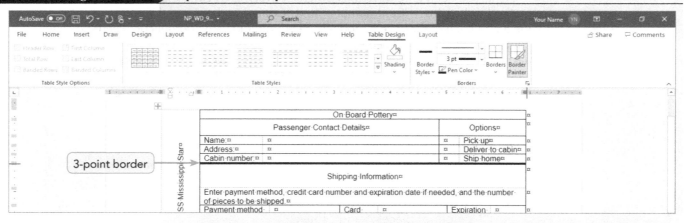

Trouble? If only part of the line above the cell containing "Shipping Information" is thicker, you clicked instead of dragging along the border. Drag along the remaining part of the border to finish drawing the thicker border.

▶ **3.** In the Borders group, click the **Border Painter** button. The button is deselected and the pointer changes back to its usual shape.

Changing Cell Margins

Cell margins are the distance between the contents of cells and the cells' gridlines. When you create a new table, the default top and bottom cell margins for all the cells are zero inches, and the default left and right cell margins are 0.08 inches.

The table for the form is very compact and seems a little tight. To fix this, you'll first change the top and bottom margins of all the cells in the table to 0.03 inches.

To change the cell margins for all the cells in the table:

▶ **1.** On the ribbon, click the **Layout** contextual tab.

▶ **2.** In the Table group, click the **Properties** button. The Table Properties dialog box opens with the Table tab selected.

▶ **3.** Click **Options**. The Table Options dialog box opens. The default cell margins for the cells in the table are at the top of the dialog box. See Figure 9–18.

| **Figure 9–18** | **Table Options dialog box** |

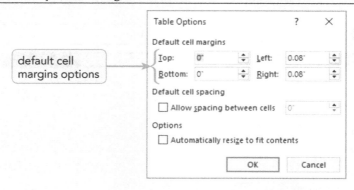

default cell margins options

▶ **4.** In the Default cell margins section, click the **Top** box up arrow three times. The value in the Top box changes to 0.03".

▶ **5.** Use the same method to change the value in the **Bottom** box to 0.03".

▶ **6.** Click **OK**, and then click **OK** in the Table Properties dialog box. The margins above and below each cell entry increase to 0.03".

Tip

To change the space between cells in a table, select the Allow spacing between cells check box, and change the value in the box.

Most of the table looks fine, but the cell containing "Shipping Information" and the cell below it don't need the wider top and bottom margins, nor do the cells in the bottom row. You'll change the top and bottom margins for those cells now.

To change cell margins for specific cells:

▶ **1.** Select the cell containing "Shipping Information" and the cell below it.

▶ **2.** On the Layout tab, in the Table group, click the **Properties** button. The Table Properties dialog box opens.

▶ **3.** Click the **Cell** tab, and then click **Options**. The Cell Options dialog box opens. It is similar to the Table Options dialog box. Because the Same as the whole table check box is selected, the margin boxes in the Cell margins section are not available.

▶ **4.** Click the **Same as the whole table** check box to deselect it. Now the margin boxes are available.

▶ **5.** Click the **Top** box down arrow three times to change the value to 0", and then click the **Bottom** box down arrow three times to change the value in that box to 0" as well.

▶ **6.** Click **OK**, and then click **OK** in the Table Properties dialog box. The top and bottom margins in the "Shipping Information" cell and the cell below it are changed back to 0 inches.

You also need to change the top and bottom margins in the cells in the last row back to 0 inches.

▶ **7.** Select the two cells in the last row in the table (the cell containing "Shipment will arrive in 7 to 10 days." and the cell to its left), and then in the Table group, click the **Properties** button. The Table Properties dialog box opens with the Cell tab selected.

▶ **8.** Click **Options**, click the **Same as the whole table** check box to deselect it, change the values in the Top and Bottom boxes to **0"**, and then click **OK** twice. Compare your screen to Figure 9–19.

Tip

To change a table to a floating object and wrap text around it, click the Properties button in the Table group on the Layout tab, and then in the Text wrapping section, click the Around button.

Figure 9–19	Table after changing the cell margins

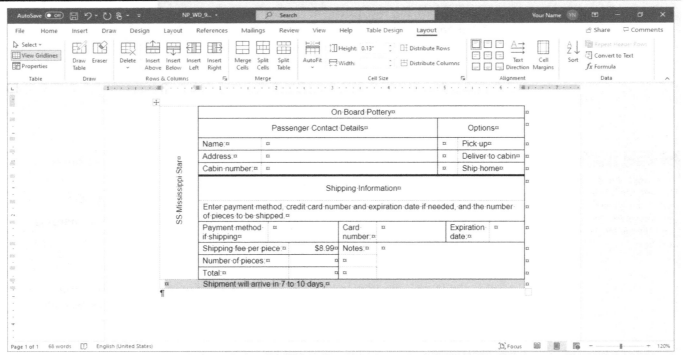

▶ **9.** Save the template.

Applying Custom Formatting to Text and Cells

To finish the form, you will add formatting to the table. First, you will change the font, font size, and font style of some of the text.

To change the font, font size, and font style of text in cells:

▶ **1.** In the first column, select **SS Mississippi Star**, and then on the ribbon, click the **Home** tab.

▶ **2.** In the Font group, click the **Font Size arrow**, and then click **22**.

Tip

To change the font of text in a table cell, select the text or the cell, click the Font arrow in the Font group on the Home tab, and then click the font you want to use.

▶ **3.** In the Font group, click the **Font Dialog Box Launcher**. The Font dialog box opens with the Font tab selected.

▶ **4.** In the Effects section, click the **Small caps** check box, and then click **OK**. The lowercase letters in the selected text are now small uppercase letters.

▶ **5.** In the first row, select **On Board Pottery**.

▶ **6.** In the Font group, click the **Font Size arrow**, and then click **28**.

▶ **7.** In the Font group, click the **Font Color arrow** A ▾ , and then click the **Teal, Accent 5, Darker 25%** color.

▶ **8.** In the second row, select the cells containing "Passenger Contact Details" and "Options," change the font size of the text in the selected cells to **12** points, and then in the Font group, click the **Bold** button B .

▶ **9.** Select the text **Shipping Information**, change the font size to **16** points, and then in the Font group, click the **Bold** B button.

▶ **10.** In the cell below the "Shipping Information" cell, select all of the text, change the font size to **8** points, and then in the Font group, click the **Italic** button I .

▶ **11.** In the last row, select **Shipment will arrive in 7 to 10 days.** and then in the Font group, click the **Italic** button I .

Now you will add colored shading to the cells containing "Passenger Contact Details" and "Options," and gray shading to the Shipping Information section.

To shade cells in the table:

▶ **1.** Select the cells containing "Passenger Contact Details" and "Options."

▶ **2.** On the Home tab, in the Paragraph group, click the **Shading arrow** ◇ ▾ and then click the **Teal, Accent 5, Lighter 60%** color.

Tip

You can also use the Shading button in the Table Styles group on the Table Design tab.

▶ **3.** In the cell containing "Shipping Information," click between the words "Shipping" and "Information," and then drag down to the second to last row. All the cells below the thick border are selected except the cells to the right of the "Card number," "Expiration date," and "Notes" cells and the cells in the bottom row.

▶ **4.** Press and hold **CTRL**, click in the empty cell to the right of the "Card number" cell, drag down to the merged cell to the right of the "Notes" cell, and then release **CTRL**. Now all the cells below the thick border are selected except the cells in the last row.

▶ **5.** In the Paragraph group, click the **Shading arrow** , and then click the **Gray, Accent 6, Lighter 80%** color. The selected cells are filled with the color you selected.

▶ **6.** Click in the merged cell in the first column (the cell containing "SS Mississippi Star"), and then change the shading color to the **Teal, Accent 5** color.

Now you will see what the table looks like without the gridlines being visible and without the hidden formatting marks.

▶ **7.** In the Paragraph group, click the **Show/Hide ¶** button ¶ to deselect it.

▶ **8.** On the ribbon, click the **Layout** contextual tab, and then in the Table group, click the **View Gridlines** button to deselect it. See Figure 9–20.

Figure 9–20   Final structure and design of the table

▶ **9.** In the Table group, click the **View Gridlines** button. The gridlines are again displayed.

▶ **10.** Click the **Home** tab, and then in the Paragraph group, click the **Show/Hide ¶** button ¶ to select it.

▶ **11.** Save the template.

You have created and formatted a custom table. In the next session, you will add content controls that passengers will use to enter their information.

Review

Session 9.1 Quick Check

1. What does it mean to split cells in a table?

2. How do you rotate text in a table cell?

3. What happens when you select a cell and then change its dimensions in the Height and Width boxes in the Cell Size group on the Layout tab?

4. What appears below the horizontal ruler when you press and hold ALT as you drag a column gridline?

5. How do you align text in a cell?

6. What are cell margins?

Session 9.2 Visual Overview:

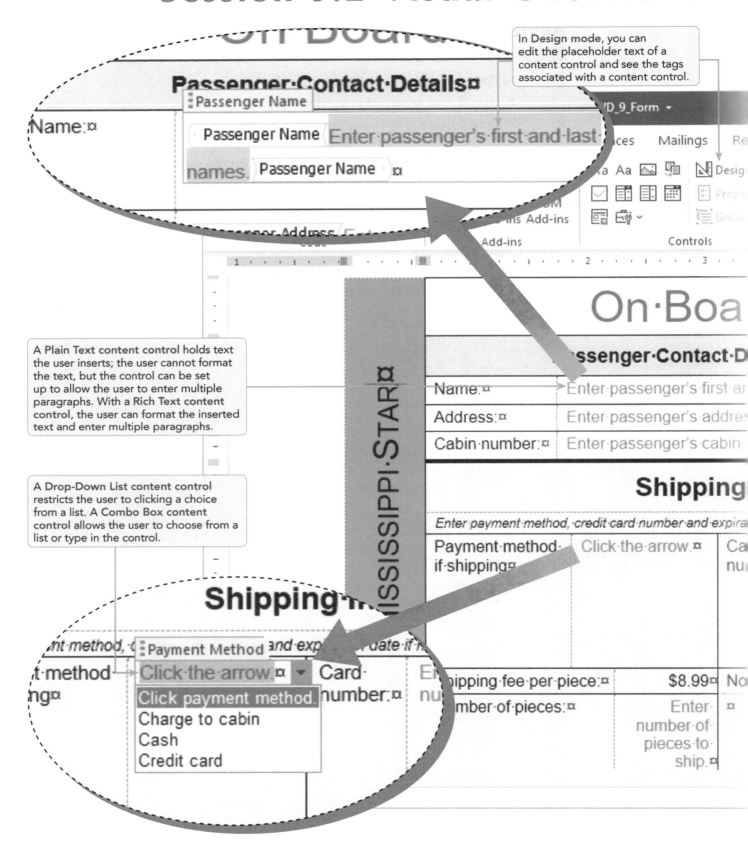

In Design mode, you can edit the placeholder text of a content control and see the tags associated with a content control.

A Plain Text content control holds text the user inserts; the user cannot format the text, but the control can be set up to allow the user to enter multiple paragraphs. With a Rich Text content control, the user can format the inserted text and enter multiple paragraphs.

A Drop-Down List content control restricts the user to clicking a choice from a list. A Combo Box content control allows the user to choose from a list or type in the control.

Passenger·Contact·Details¤

Passenger Name

Passenger Name   Enter·passenger's·first·and·last·names.   Passenger Name   ¤

MISSISSIPPI·STAR¤

On·Boa

ssenger·Contact·D

Name:¤   Enter·passenger's·first·an
Address:¤   Enter·passenger's·addres
Cabin·number:¤   Enter·passenger's·cabin

Shipping

Enter·payment·method, credit·card·number·and·expira

Payment·method· if·shipping¤   Click·the·arrow·¤   Ca nu

Shipping·fee·per·piece:¤ $8.99¤   No
Number·of·pieces:¤   Enter· number·of· pieces·to· ship.¤

Payment Method

Click·the·arrow·¤   ▼   Card· number:¤

Click payment method.
Charge to cabin
Cash
Credit card

Content Controls

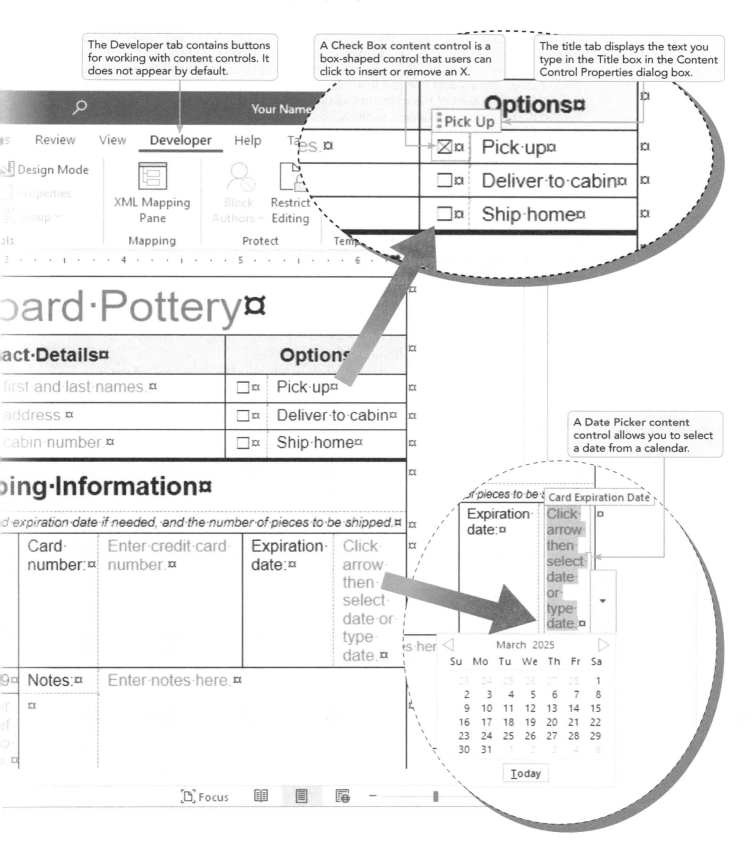

The Developer tab contains buttons for working with content controls. It does not appear by default.

A Check Box content control is a box-shaped control that users can click to insert or remove an X.

The title tab displays the text you type in the Title box in the Content Control Properties dialog box.

A Date Picker content control allows you to select a date from a calendar.

Understanding Content Controls

You have formatted the table to make it attractive and easy to read. Now you need to insert the most important elements of an online form—content controls. The content controls will help users enter information into the form quickly and efficiently. You have used content controls when you worked with headers, footers, and cover pages. In this session, you will learn how to insert your own content controls rather than just entering information into content controls that are already there.

Each content control has properties associated with it that you specify when you insert it. For all types of content controls, you can specify a title, which is displayed in a title tab at the top of the content control. You can also choose whether to allow the content control to be deleted and whether to allow users to edit the contents of the control after they have entered information. In addition, each type of content control has other properties that you can adjust that are specific to that control.

The options for inserting content controls are located on the Developer tab. You'll display the Developer tab now.

To display the Developer tab on the ribbon:

1. If you took a break after the last session, use the Open command in Backstage view to open the file **NP_WD_9_Form.dotx** from the location where you are saving your files.

2. On the ribbon, click the **File** tab, and then in the navigation pane, click **Options**. The Word Options dialog box opens.

3. In the navigation pane, click **Customize Ribbon**. The right pane of the dialog box changes to show two lists—one labeled Choose commands from, and one labeled Customize the Ribbon.

4. In the Customize the Ribbon list, click the **Developer** check box to select it, if necessary. See Figure 9–21.

Tip

You can also right-click a tab on the ribbon, and then click Customize the Ribbon on the shortcut menu.

Figure 9–21   **Word Options dialog box with Customize Ribbon selected**

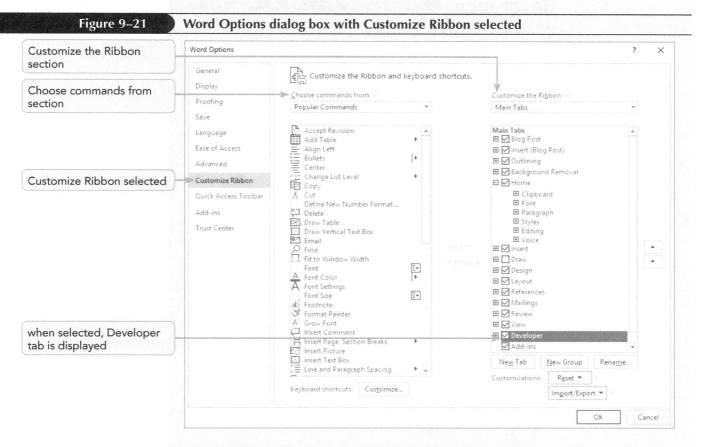

> **5.** Click **OK**. The dialog box closes, and the Developer tab is displayed on the ribbon to the right of the View tab.

Inserting Text Content Controls

To allow a user to input text in a form, you insert Plain Text or Rich Text content controls. Rich Text content controls allow the user to add multiple paragraphs of text and to format some or all of the text. Plain Text content controls are restricted to single paragraphs, although you can specifically allow users to insert manual line breaks. In addition, in a Plain Text content control, all of the text must be formatted identically; for example, if the user formats one word with bold, all of the text will be formatted with bold.

Reference

Inserting a Plain Text or a Rich Text Content Control

- On the ribbon, click the Developer tab, and then in the Controls group, click the Plain Text Content Control or the Rich Text Content Control button.
- In the Controls group, click the Properties button.
- In the Title box, type a control title.
- If you want the text entered in the content control to be formatted differently than the default format, click the Use a style to format text typed into the empty control check box, and then click the Style arrow and select a style, or click New Style to define a new style.
- Click the Content control cannot be deleted check box if you want to prevent users from deleting the content control.
- For a Plain Text content control, click the Allow carriage returns (multiple paragraphs) check box to allow the user to insert more than one paragraph.
- Click the Remove content control when contents are edited check box to delete the content control and leave only the text the user inserts.
- Click OK.
- If desired, switch to Design mode, and then replace the default placeholder text with specific instructions to the user.

You need to enter several Plain Text content controls in the form. First, you'll enter one in the cell to the right of the "Name" cell.

To insert a Plain Text content control and set its properties:

▶ 1. In the "Passenger Contact Details" section, click in the cell to the right of the cell containing "Name," and then on the ribbon, click the **Developer** tab.

▶ 2. In the Controls group, click the **Plain Text Content Control** button ⌊Aa⌋. A Plain Text content control is inserted in the cell. See Figure 9–22.

Figure 9–22   **Plain Text content control inserted**

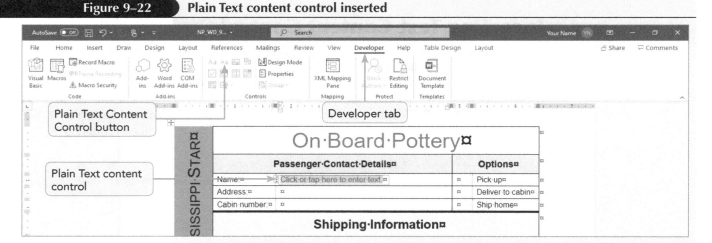

▶ 3. In the Controls group, click the **Properties** button. The Content Control Properties dialog box opens. The Title property identifies the content control. See Figure 9–23.

| Figure 9–23 | Content Control Properties dialog box for a Plain Text content control |

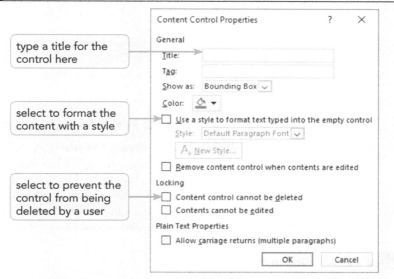

type a title for the control here

select to format the content with a style

select to prevent the control from being deleted by a user

Content Control Properties   ?   ✕

General

Title:

Tag:

Show as: Bounding Box ⌄

Color: 🖌 ▼

☐ Use a style to format text typed into the empty control

Style: Default Paragraph Font ⌄

A₊ New Style...

☐ Remove content control when contents are edited

Locking

☐ Content control cannot be deleted

☐ Contents cannot be edited

Plain Text Properties

☐ Allow carriage returns (multiple paragraphs)

OK   Cancel

Tip

If the user will need to enter multiple paragraphs in a Plain Text control, click the Allow carriage returns (multiple paragraphs) check box in the Content Control Properties dialog box.

4. Click in the Title box, and then type **Passenger Name**. This text will be displayed in the tab at the top of the control in the form. To make the passenger's name stand out, you will format it with the Strong style, which formats it as bold.

5. Click the **Use a style to format text typed into the empty control** check box, click the **Style arrow**, and then click **Strong**.

Next, you'll set a property in the control so users won't be able to delete the content control.

6. Click the **Content control cannot be deleted** check box, and then click **OK**. The title "Passenger Name" now appears on the title tab of the content control. See Figure 9–24.

| Figure 9–24 | Title tab on a content control after adding a Title property |

title tab

7. Click a blank area of the table to deselect the content control.

Usually, the user knows what information to enter into a control just by looking at the title. However, someone using the form for the first time might need instructions, and both new and experienced users sometimes need clarification regarding how to enter information. To assist the user, you can customize the placeholder text to provide specific instructions for each control.

Emi wants you to modify the placeholder text to make the form more clear. To change the placeholder text, you need to switch to Design mode. If you are not in Design mode, you will enter information into the control instead of editing the placeholder text.

To change the placeholder text in the Passenger Name content control:

▶ **1.** In the Controls group, click the **Design Mode** button. The button is selected, and tags appear at the beginning and end of the Plain Text content control that you inserted. Tags mark the location of the control in the document and are useful when you plan to use your form in another program. Because you didn't type anything in the Tag box in the Content Control Properties dialog box, the tag is the same as the Title property. See Figure 9–25.

Figure 9–25	Form in Design mode

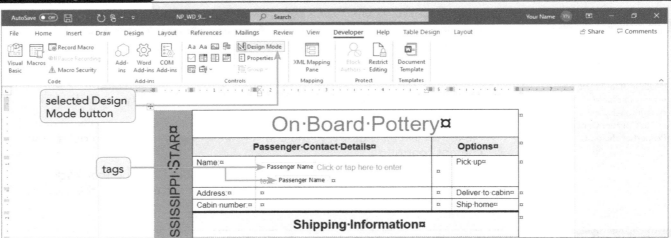

2. Select the placeholder text **Click or tap here to enter text** (but do not select the period), and then type **Enter passenger's first and last names**. The text you typed replaces the default placeholder text.

Trouble? If any of the text you type is black instead of gray, undo your change, carefully select just the current placeholder text without selecting the period, and then type the new placeholder text in Step 2.

You can remain in Design mode to add additional content controls. You need to add Plain Text content controls in the cells to the right of "Address," "Cabin number," "Card number," "Number of pieces," and "Notes."

To enter additional Plain Text content controls:

▶ **1.** Click in the cell to the right of the cell containing "Address," insert a Plain Text content control, and then in the Controls group, click the **Properties** button.

Tip

To delete a control, make sure the form is in Design mode, right-click the control, and then click Remove Content Control on the shortcut menu.

2. In the Title box, type **Passenger Address**.

3. Click the **Content control cannot be deleted** check box, and then click **OK**.

4. Select the placeholder text **Click or tap here to enter text** (but do not select the period), and then type **Enter passenger's address**.

   Trouble? If the replacement placeholder text that you type is black instead of gray, and if you don't see the Passenger Address tags, click the Undo button [↺] to undo the change you made. Click the Design Mode button in the Controls group to select it, and then repeat Step 4.

5. Click in the cell to the right of the "Cabin number" cell, insert a Plain Text content control, and then open the Content Control Properties dialog box.

6. Enter **Cabin Number** as the Title property, click the **Content control cannot be deleted** check box, click **OK**, and then replace the placeholder text with **Enter passenger's cabin number**.

7. In the cell to the right of the "Card number" cell, insert a Plain Text content control that cannot be deleted, add **Credit Card Number** as the Title property, and then replace the placeholder text with **Enter credit card number**.

8. In the cell to the right of the "Number of pieces" cell, insert a Plain Text content control that cannot be deleted, add **No. of Pieces** as the Title property, and then replace the placeholder text with **Enter number of pieces to ship**.

9. In the cell to the right of the "Notes" cell, insert a Plain Text content control that cannot be deleted, add **Notes** as the Title property, and then replace the placeholder text with **Enter notes here**.

10. Save the changes to the template.

All the text content controls are now inserted in the form. It's a good idea to test content controls after you insert them. First, you need to turn Design mode off.

To turn off Design mode and test two of the Plain Text content controls:

1. In the Controls group, click the **Design Mode** button to deselect it.

2. Click in the cell containing the Passenger Name content control (the cell to the right of the cell containing "Name" in the "Passenger Contact Details" section). The content control is selected, and you see the title tab with the name of the content control on it.

3. Type **Jane Doe**. The text you typed replaces the placeholder text, and it is formatted with the Strong style as you specified in the Properties dialog box when you inserted this content control.

4. Click in the cell to the right of the cell containing "Address." The placeholder text in this cell is selected, and the title tab containing "Passenger Address" is displayed.

5. Type **123 Main Street**. The name replaces the placeholder text. This text is not formatted with a style.

   Now that you have tested the two content controls, you need to delete the text you typed to reset the content controls so they display the placeholder text.

▶ **6.** On the Quick Access Toolbar, click the **Undo** button ↻. The text you typed in the Address content control is removed. You can also use the BACKSPACE and DEL keys to delete text in content controls.

> **Trouble?** If all the text in the Passenger Address content control was not removed, click the Undo button ↻ as many times as needed to delete all of the address you typed.

▶ **7.** Click in the cell containing "Jane Doe," and then press **BACKSPACE** and **DEL** as needed to delete the name.

▶ **8.** Click in any other cell in the table. The placeholder text reappears in the Passenger Name content control.

Inserting Date Picker Content Controls

To create a content control that contains a date, you use the Date Picker content control. When you insert a Date Picker content control, you can specify what the date will look like in the completed form. To do this, you select a format from a list or create your own format using the same pattern of letters you used when you modified the Date field. For example, the format d-MMM-yy displays the date January 7, 2025, as 7-Jan-25, and the format dddd, MMMM dd, yyyy displays the date as Wednesday, January 07, 2025.

Reference

Inserting a Date Picker Content Control

- On the ribbon, click the Developer tab, and then in the Controls group, click the Date Picker Content Control button.
- In the Controls group, click the Properties button.
- In the Title box, type the control title.
- Click the Content control cannot be deleted check box if you want to prevent the user from deleting the content control.
- In the Display the date like this list, click a format for the date, or replace the letters that indicate the format in the box as needed.
- Click OK.
- If desired, switch to Design mode, and then replace the default placeholder text with specific instructions to the user.

For the cell that will contain the expiration date for the passenger's credit card, Emi wants you to insert a content control that allows only a date to be entered. To do this, you will use a Date Picker content control.

To insert a Date Picker content control in the form:

▶ **1.** Click in the cell to the right of the cell containing "Expiration date," and then in the Controls group, click the **Date Picker Content Control** button 📅. A Date Picker content control is entered in the cell.

▶ **2.** In the Controls group, click the **Properties** button. The Content Control Properties dialog box for a Date Picker control opens. The top of this dialog box is the same as the Content Control Properties dialog box for a Text control. See Figure 9–26.

Figure 9–26   **Content Control Properties dialog box for a Date Picker content control**

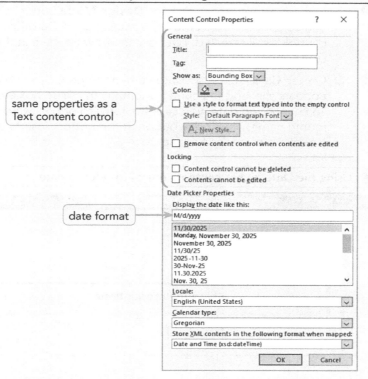

same properties as a Text content control

date format

3. In the Title box, type **Card Expiration Date**, and then click the **Content control cannot be deleted** check box.

   Now you need to select the format of the date. Credit card expiration dates include only the month and year; for example, if a card expires in June 2027, it would appear as 06/2027. In the list in the Date Picker Properties section of the dialog box, the first date format is selected, and in the "Display the date like this" box, the format is M/d/yyyy.

4. Click in the **Display the date like this** box, press ← if necessary to position the insertion point before "M," and then type **M**. Now months that are expressed with a single digit will have a zero before the month number.

5. Press → once to position the insertion point before the first forward slash, and then press **DEL** twice to delete "/d". The format is now MM/yyyy.

6. Click **OK**. Now you need to change the placeholder text.

7. In the Controls group, click the **Design Mode** button to switch to Design mode, and then replace the placeholder text with **Click arrow then select date or type date**.

8. Save the template.

Now you will test the Date Picker content control that you entered. First, you must turn off Design mode.

To test the Card Expiration Date content control:

▶ **1.** In the Controls group, click the **Design Mode** button to exit Design mode. The content control in the cell containing the Card Expiration Date content control is still selected, but now an arrow appears at the right edge of the control.

▶ **2.** On the Card Expiration Date content control, click the **arrow**. A calendar appears showing the current month with a blue box around the current date. To change the date, you click the forward or backward arrows next to the month name. The Today button at the bottom inserts the current date and closes the calendar. See Figure 9–27.

| Figure 9–27 | Using the Date Picker content control to select a date |

▶ **3.** At the top of the calendar, click ▷ several times to scroll to any month in the future, and then click **1**. The calendar closes, and the month and the year you chose appear in the cell in the format you specified when you inserted the content control—in this case, a two-digit number for the month and a four-digit number for the year. For example, if you clicked a date in February 2026, it will appear as 02/2026. Because this format shows only the month and year, you can click any date in the month.

▶ **4.** On the Quick Access Toolbar, click the **Undo** button ↺. The date you selected is removed from the content control.

▶ **5.** Type **Feb 2026**, and then click any other cell in the table. The date you typed appears as 02/2026.

▶ **6.** On the Quick Access Toolbar, click the **Undo** button ↺. The date you typed is removed from the content control.

Inserting List Content Controls

When the information required in a form is limited to specific entries, you can use content controls that offer the user a list of choices. You create the list, and the user clicks one of the choices in the list. This type of content control makes it possible for the user to complete a form faster and without making any spelling errors. Word offers three types of list content controls—Drop-Down List, Combo Box, and Building Block Gallery.

Drop-Down List content controls restrict the user to clicking a choice from a list. When you insert the control, you add items to the list and arrange them in an order that suits you. When users complete the form, they are allowed to choose only one item from the list. They cannot type anything else in the control.

Reference

Inserting a Drop-Down List or Combo Box Content Control

- On the ribbon, click the Developer tab, and then in the Controls group, click the Drop-Down List Content Control or the Combo Box Content Control button.
- In the Controls group, click the Properties button.
- In the Title box, type the control title.
- Click the Content control cannot be deleted check box if you want to prevent the user from deleting the content control.
- Click Add to open the Add Choice dialog box. In the Display Name box, type an entry for the list, and then click OK. Repeat for each entry you want to include in the list.
- To change the wording of an entry, click the entry in the list, and then click the Modify button. In the Modify Choice dialog box, edit the text in the Display Name box, and then click OK.
- To move an entry up or down in the list, click it, and then click Move Up or Move Down.
- To remove an entry from the list, click it, and then click the Remove button.
- Click OK.
- If desired, switch to Design mode, and then replace the default placeholder text with specific instructions to the user.

If a passenger wants to ship their painted piece home, they need to pay the shipping fee. They can have it charged to their cabin, pay in cash, or use a credit card. You need to insert a Drop-Down List content control that includes these choices in the drop-down list.

To insert a Drop-Down List content control for the payment method:

▶ **1.** Click in the blank cell to the right of "Payment method if shipping."

▶ **2.** In the Controls group, click the **Drop-Down List Content Control** button ▦ and then click the **Properties** button. The Content Control Properties dialog box for a Drop-Down List appears. See Figure 9–28.

Figure 9–28 Content Control Properties dialog box for a Drop-Down List content control

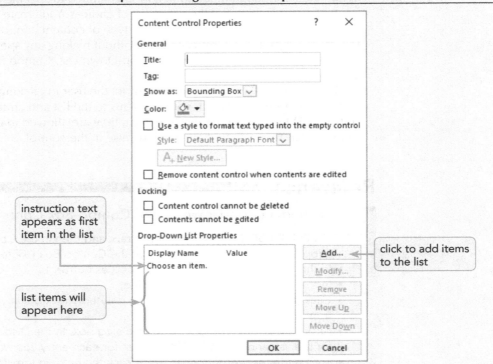

instruction text appears as first item in the list

list items will appear here

click to add items to the list

> **3.** In the Title box, type **Payment Method**, and then click the **Content control cannot be deleted** check box. Now you need to add the items that will appear in the drop-down list below the instruction text.

> **4.** Click **Add**. The Add Choice dialog box opens. The insertion point is in the Display Name box.

> **5.** Type **Cash**. As you typed in the Display Name box, the same text appeared in the Value box. You can connect a form to an Access database; and if you do, the contents of the Value field are entered into the database. You can ignore this for now.

> **6.** Click **OK**. The Add Choice dialog box closes, and "Cash" appears as the first item in the list below "Choose an item."

> **7.** Add **Charge to cabin** and **Credit card** to the list. You want to move "Charge to cabin" up so it is the first item in the list below the "Choose an item" instruction text.

> **8.** In the list, click **Charge to cabin**, and then click **Move Up**. "Charge to cabin" is now the first item in the list below the instruction text. Now you need to modify the instruction text.

> **9.** In the list, click **Choose an item.** and then click **Modify**. The Modify Choice dialog box opens. It's identical to the Add Choice dialog box.

> **10.** Replace the text in the Display Name box with **Click payment method.** and then click **OK**. See Figure 9–29.

Figure 9–29   **List items added and reordered**

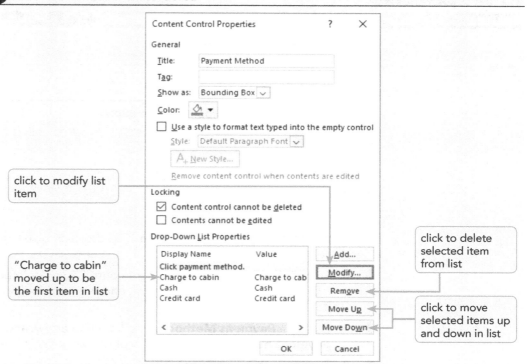

> **11.** Click **OK** to close the Content Control Properties dialog box.

> **12.** Turn on Design mode, and then replace the placeholder text in the Payment Method content control with **Click the arrow**.

> **13.** Save the changes to the template.

Now you'll test the Drop-Down List content control. Remember, you need to turn Design mode off before you can use the content controls.

To test the Drop-Down List content control:

> **1.** Turn off Design mode, and then click the **Payment Method** content control arrow. The list of choices you typed in the Content Control Properties dialog box appears. See Figure 9–30.

Figure 9–30 Drop-Down List content control list displayed

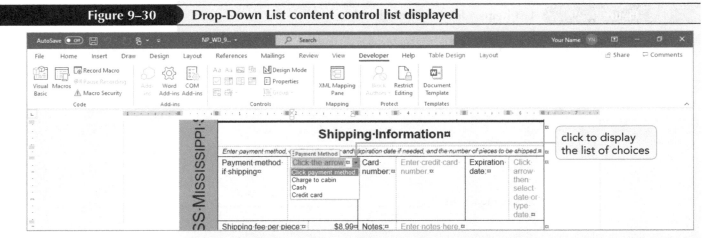

2. In the list, click **Charge to cabin**. The choice you selected appears in the content control.

3. Press **DEL**. The text in the content control is not deleted. This is because it is a Drop-Down List content control, and the user's only option is to choose an item in the list.

4. Click the **Payment Method** content control arrow, and then click **Click payment method.** The instructional text appears in the control again.

5. Type any letter or number. Nothing happens for the same reason nothing happened when you tried to delete your choice.

A Combo Box content control is similar to a Drop-Down List content control in that it offers the user a list of choices. But a Combo Box content control also allows users to type their own response if it doesn't appear in the list provided. For example, if a business created an online form for their customers, the list for the Combo Box content control that contains the customer's city could include the city the business is in as well as a few neighboring cities and towns. If most of the business's customers live in one of the cities in the list, this would make it easier and quicker for those customers to select their city names. However, occasionally customers from other cities may want to purchase something. Unlike a Drop-Down List content control, the Combo Box content control would allow those customers to type the name of their city in the control.

Building Block Gallery content controls are also similar to Drop-Down List content controls. However, instead of creating the list of choices a user can click, you select AutoText, Equations, Tables, Quick Parts, or a custom gallery of building blocks. When the user clicks the arrow on the content control, they can select an item in the gallery you chose.

Inserting Check Box Content Controls

Many of the dialog boxes you have used in Word and in other programs include check boxes that you click to select and deselect items. Similarly, a Check Box content control is a box-shaped control that users can click to insert or remove an "X." You might include check box content controls in an online survey form for questions such as, "Which of the following items do you plan to purchase in the next six months?"

Reference

Inserting a Check Box Content Control

- On the ribbon, click the Developer tab, and then in the Controls group, click the Check Box Content Control button.
- In the Controls group, click the Properties button.
- In the Title box, type the control title.
- Click the Content control cannot be deleted check box if you want to prevent users from deleting the content control.
- Click OK.

You need to add Check Box content controls in the three empty cells in the Options section.

To insert Check Box content controls:

▶ **1.** Click in the cell to the left of the "Pick up" cell, and then on the ribbon, click the **Developer** tab, if necessary.

▶ **2.** In the Controls group, click the **Check Box Content Control** button ☑. A Check Box content control is inserted in the cell. See Figure 9–31.

Figure 9–31 ▶ **Check Box content control inserted in the form**

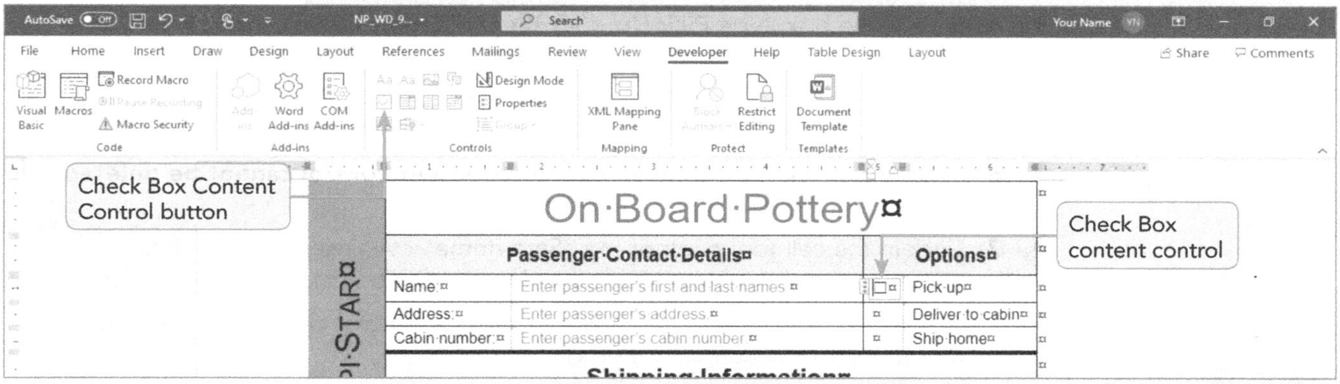

▶ **3.** In the Controls group, click the **Properties** button to open the Content Control Properties dialog box for a Check Box content control. See Figure 9–32.

Figure 9–32 Content Control Properties dialog box for a Check Box content control

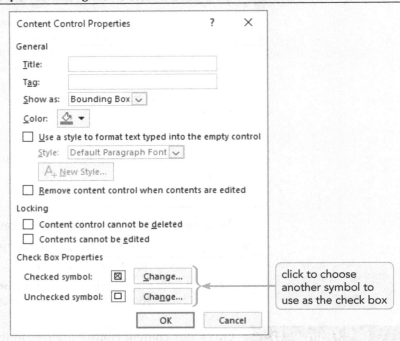

4. In the Title box, type **Pick Up**, click the **Content control cannot be deleted** check box to select it, and then click **OK**.

5. Click in the cell to the left of the "Deliver to cabin" cell, insert a Check Box content control, and then open the Content Control Properties dialog box.

6. In the Title box, type **Deliver**, click the **Content control cannot be deleted** check box to select it, and then click **OK**.

7. Click in the cell to the left of the "Ship home" cell, insert a Check Box content control, and then open the Content Control Properties dialog box.

8. In the Title box, type **Ship**, click the **Content control cannot be deleted** check box to select it, and then click **OK**.

9. Save the changes to the template.

Make sure you save the changes to the template so that you have a final version of the template before continuing with the next section.

Now you need to test the Check Box content controls. To select (place an "X" in) or deselect (remove the "X" from) a Check Box content control, you can click it, or while the content control is active, press SPACEBAR.

To test the Check Box content controls:

1. Make sure Design mode is turned off.

2. Click the **Pick Up** check box. The box is selected, as indicated by the "X" inside it.

3. Press **TAB** twice. The Deliver Check Box content control is selected.

4. Press **SPACEBAR**. The check box is selected.

5. Click the **Pick Up** check box to remove the "X," and then click the **Deliver** check box to remove the "X."

Insight

Repeating Section Content Controls

A Repeating Section content control is a content control that allows you to duplicate the contents of the content control by clicking a plus sign that is displayed when the content control is active. For example, suppose you create a table to list your home inventory for insurance purposes. You could add a Text content control in the first column to name the item, a Picture content control in the second column so you can add a picture of the item, and a Date Picker content control in the third column to indicate when the item was purchased. You select all three content controls, and then insert a Repeating Section content control. When you click the plus sign button displayed below and to the right of the active Repeating Section content control, another row is created in the table containing the same content controls as in the first row. Note that if you use the Group command, you can no longer click the plus sign button to duplicate the content of a Repeating Section content control; however, if you use the Restrict Editing command, you can. You'll learn about the Group and Restrict Editing commands in Session 9.3.

The form is almost complete. In the next session, you'll finish the form by inserting a formula in the cell next to "Total" to calculate the total fee, and then you will restrict editing in the form so that users can enter information only in the appropriate cells.

Review

Session 9.2 Quick Check

1. What tab must be displayed on the ribbon in order to access content controls?
2. What is the difference between a Rich Text content control and a Plain Text content control?
3. How do you provide the user with instructions for using a content control?
4. What button must be selected in the Controls group on the Developer tab in order to edit the placeholder text of a content control?
5. What is the difference between a Combo Box content control and a Drop-Down List content control?
6. What is a Check Box content control?

Session 9.3 Visual Overview:

When you protect a form, it must not be in Design mode.

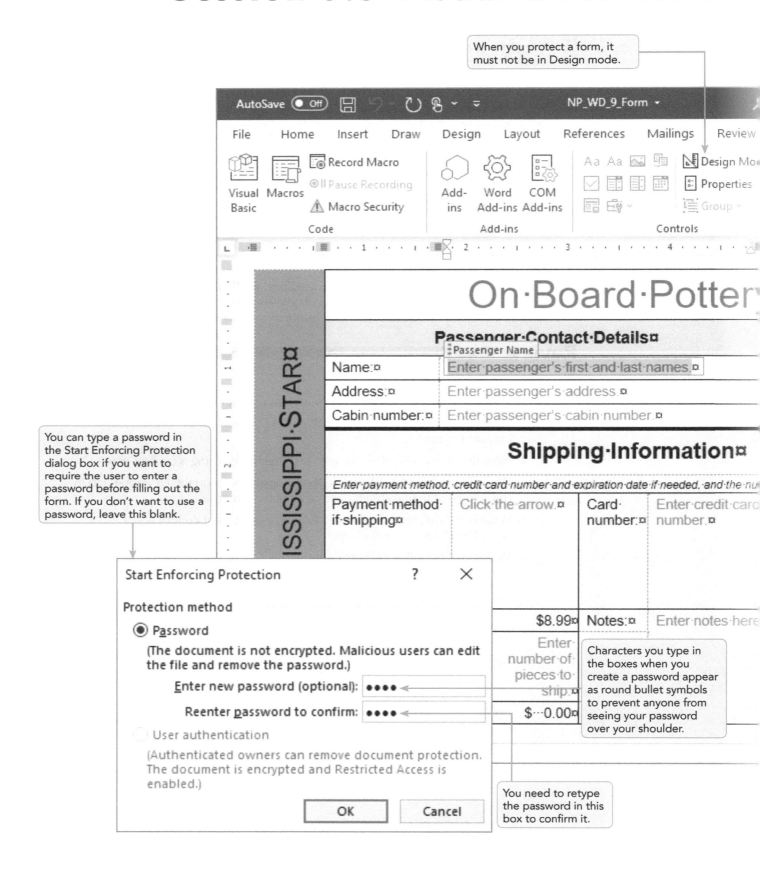

You can type a password in the Start Enforcing Protection dialog box if you want to require the user to enter a password before filling out the form. If you don't want to use a password, leave this blank.

Start Enforcing Protection ? ✕

Protection method

⦿ P̲assword

(The document is not encrypted. Malicious users can edit the file and remove the password.)

E̲nter new password (optional): ●●●●

Reenter p̲assword to confirm: ●●●●

Characters you type in the boxes when you create a password appear as round bullet symbols to prevent anyone from seeing your password over your shoulder.

◯ User authentication

(Authenticated owners can remove document protection. The document is encrypted and Restricted Access is enabled.)

You need to retype the password in this box to confirm it.

OK   Cancel

Protecting a Document

When the Restrict Editing button is selected, the Restrict Editing pane appears.

Select this option to make the list in this section available.

Click this arrow to see a list of options for restricting editing. This option restricts the document to filling in forms, that is, to interacting with content controls and fields.

When you are ready to begin protecting the document, click this button.

Using Formulas in a Table

A **formula** is a mathematical statement that calculates a value. You can add formulas to cells in tables to calculate values based on the values in other cells in the table. For example, in the form you are creating, the cell to the right of the "Total" cell needs to contain a formula that multiplies the shipping fee per piece by the number of pieces to be shipped. Before you insert a formula in a table, you need to understand how cells are referenced in a table.

Referencing Table Cells

In order to use a formula in a cell, you need to refer to specific cells in the table. As you have seen when working with embedded Excel worksheet objects, cells in a table are referenced by a letter that corresponds to the column and a number that corresponds to the row. The first column is column A, the second column is column B, and so on; likewise, the first row is row 1, the second row is row 2, and so on. This means the cell in the first column and the first row is cell A1, the cell in the first column and the second row is cell A2, and the cell in the second column and the first row is cell B1.

It can be difficult to identify a cell's reference in a table containing merged and split cells because each row might have a different number of columns and each column might have a different number of rows. To identify the column letter in any row, count from the left to right in each row. In the table you created, row 1 contains two columns—columns A and B—with the ship name "SS Mississippi Star" in column A and the "On Board Pottery" in column B. Row 2 contains three columns. As in row 1, column A contains the ship name, but column B contains "Passenger Contact Details," and column C contains "Options." This is because although the merged cell containing the ship name is cell A1, it is also the first cell in all of the rows it is next to, making the column containing the cell with "Passenger Contact Details" column B.

Counting rows in a table with merged and split cells is a little trickier. In all of the columns in the table you created, even column A, there are 12 rows—the total number of rows in the table. This means that even though it appears as if there are only two rows in column A, the cell without borders in the last row in column A (the cell to the left of the cell containing the footnote) is cell A12 because there are 12 rows in the table and this cell appears next to the other cells in row 12.

Now that you understand how to reference cells, you need to understand formulas.

Understanding Formulas

When you insert a formula in a table, you use the Formula button in the Data group on the Layout tab. Formulas in a table always start with an equal sign. For example,

$$= 1 + 2$$

is a formula that calculates the sum of 1 plus 2, which is 3. The formula

$$= 2 * 3$$

multiplies 2 by 3 to produce a result of 6. In this formula, the numbers 2 and 3 are **constants**—values that don't change.

Formulas can also include **variables**, which are symbols for values that can change. For example, if you want to add the values that appear in cells A1 and A2 in a Word table, you could write the formula as follows:

$$= A1 + A2$$

This formula looks in the referenced cells (cells A1 and A2) and uses the contents to calculate the result of the formula. So if cell A1 contains 1 and cell A2 contains 2, the result of adding these two numbers—3—is displayed. If you change the values in the referenced cells—for example, if you change the value in cell A1 to 4—then the result of the formula will change without you needing to modify the formula, in this example, to 6.

Formulas can also contain functions. A **function** is a named operation that replaces the action of an arithmetic expression; basically, it's a shorthand way of writing a formula. Word provides 18 functions that you can use in tables. One of the most commonly used functions is the SUM function, which adds numbers. Most functions have **arguments**, which are values that the function needs in order to calculate its result. Arguments appear between parentheses immediately after the name of the function. For example, the SUM function to add the values in cells A1 and A2 would be written as follows:

$$= SUM(A1,A2)$$

In this example, cells A1 and A2 are the arguments. Because tables are grids, and functions such as SUM are frequently used at the bottom of a column or the end of a row, you can use LEFT, RIGHT, ABOVE, and BELOW as the argument, and SUM will add the contents of all the cells in the specified direction.

Inserting a Formula in a Table Cell

A formula in a table cell is a field that can be updated when you change the data used in the formula calculation. Like any field, when you insert a formula in a table cell, you can specify how the result will be formatted in the document. To do this, you choose a pattern of digits and symbols, such as $#,###,### or 00.00, that describes how the number will look. Figure 9–33 lists the most commonly used symbols for describing a number format.

Figure 9–33   **Symbols that describe number formats**

Symbol	Purpose	Example
0 (Zero)	Displays a digit in place of the zero in the field result. If the result doesn't include a digit in that place, the field displays a zero.	"00.0" displays "05.0" "0" displays an integer of any number of digits
#	Displays a digit in place of the # only if the result requires it. If the result doesn't include a digit in that place, the field displays a space.	"$##.00"displays "$ 5.00"
. (decimal point)	Determines the decimal point position.	See examples above.
, (comma)	Separates a series of three digits.	"$#,###,###" displays "$3,450,000"
- (hyphen)	Includes a minus sign if the number is negative or a space if the number is positive.	"-0" displays an integer as " 5" or "-5"
; (semicolon)	Separates the format of positive and negative numbers.	"$##0.00;-$##0.00" displays "$ 55.50" if positive, "-$ 55.50" if negative
(parentheses around negative number)	Puts parentheses around a negative result.	"$##0.00;($##0.00)" displays "$ 55.50" if positive, "($ 55.50)" if negative
$, %, etc.	Displays a special character in the result.	"0.0%" displays "5.0%"

You need to insert a formula in the cell to the right of the cell containing "Total" to multiply the shipping fee per piece by the number of pieces. This cell is in the third column—column C—and is in the second-to-last row of the table, row 11. To calculate the total, you will multiply the value in the cell to the right of the "Shipping fee per piece" cell—cell C9—and the value in the cell to the right of the "Number of pieces" cell—cell C10.

You will insert the formula now.

To insert a formula for the total fee:

▶ **1.** If you took a break after the last session, use the Open command in Backstage view to open the file **NP_WD_9_Form.dotx** from the location where you are saving your files.

▶ **2.** Click in the cell to the right of the cell containing "Total." This is the cell that will contain the formula to multiply the shipping fee per piece by the number of pieces being shipped.

▶ **3.** On the ribbon, click the **Layout** contextual tab, and then in the Data group, click the **Formula** button. The Formula dialog box opens. The SUM function appears in the Formula box with the argument ABOVE, and the insertion point is blinking after "ABOVE." See Figure 9–34.

Figure 9–34 Formula dialog box

▶ **4.** Press **BACKSPACE** as many times as needed to delete SUM(ABOVE), but do not delete the equal sign.

Trouble? If you deleted the equal sign, type =.

▶ **5.** Click the **Paste function arrow**. The list that appears contains the functions available to use in Word documents. You need the function that multiplies values.

▶ **6.** Scroll down the alphabetical list, and then click **PRODUCT**. In the Formula box, =PRODUCT() appears with the insertion point between the parentheses. You need to insert the arguments so that the function multiplies the value in cell C9 by the value in cell C10.

▶ **7.** Type **C9,C10**. The function is now =PRODUCT(C9,C10).

▶ **8.** Click the **Number format** arrow, and then click **$#,##0.00;($#,##0.00)** to set the number format as a dollar amount. This style formats positive numbers so the dollar sign appears before the number, a comma is used to separate thousands, and two decimal places are used to show cents. Negative numbers are formatted the same way except they will appear between parentheses. If you wanted to, you could edit the format. For example, you could delete ".00" so that the result appears as a whole dollar amount.

▶ **9.** Click **OK**. The dialog box closes. The result of the calculation—"$ 0.00"— appears in the cell to the right of the "Total" cell. The result is $0 because there is no value in the cell that is supposed to contain the number of pieces so the formula is multiplying 8.99 by zero.

▶ **10.** Change the Zoom level to **100%**, and then compare your screen to the final form shown in Figure 9–35.

Figure 9–35   Final form

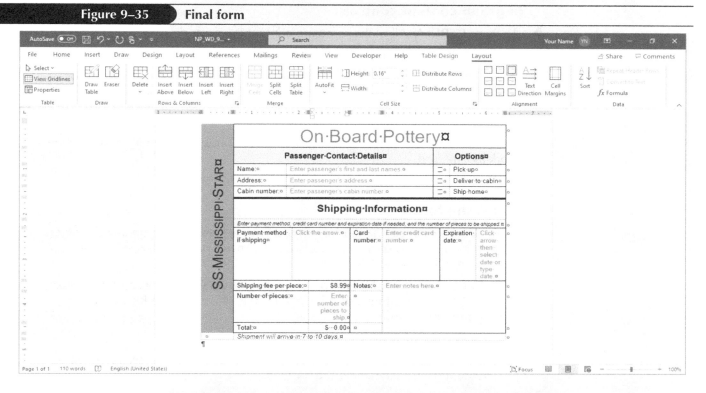

> **11.** Change the Zoom level back to **120%**, and then save the changes to the template.

Now you need to test the formula. Recall that fields update when the document is opened, when you click the Update Field command on the shortcut menu, or when you press F9.

To test the formula:

> **1.** Click the **No. of Pieces** content control, and then type **3**. Now you need to update the formula field.

> **2.** Right-click the field in the cell to the right of the "Total" cell, and then on the shortcut menu, click **Update Field**. The value in the field updates to $ 26.97. The formula works correctly.

> **3.** On the Quick Access Toolbar, click the **Undo** button twice to remove the 3 in the cell to the right of the "Number of pieces" cell. The actions you took while testing the formula are undone.

Grouping Content Controls

When you create an online form, you need to prevent users from modifying the form except for being able to enter values in content controls. To do this, select the labels and content controls to which you want to apply the command, and then use the Group command in the Controls group on the Developer tab. You will do this now.

To group content controls:

▶ **1.** Press **CTRL+A**. All of the template content is selected.

▶ **2.** On the ribbon, click the **Developer** tab.

▶ **3.** In the Controls group, click the **Group** button, and then click **Group**. Now nothing in the form can be modified except the content controls.

Now you'll test some of the content controls in the protected form to make sure they still work as expected.

To test the form:

▶ **1.** Click in the cell containing "On Board Pottery," and then type any character. Nothing happens because the Group command prevents any part of the form from being modified except content controls.

▶ **2.** Click the **Passenger Name** content control, type your name, and then press **TAB**. The next content control to the right is selected—the Pick Up Check Box content control.

▶ **3.** Click the **Pick Up** check box to select it.

▶ **4.** Click the **No. of Pieces** content control, and then type **2**. Now you need to update the field containing the formula.

▶ **5.** Right-click the field to the right of the cell containing "Total." The Update Field command is on the shortcut menu, but it is not available to be clicked—it is grayed out.

▶ **6.** On the Quick Access Toolbar, click the **Undo arrow** ↺ ▾, and then in the menu, click the entry **Typing** followed by your name. All the changes you made to the form while testing it are undone.

Trouble? If all the changes to the form are not undone, click the Undo button ↺ again.

Because the Group command prevents anything in the form from being changed except for content controls, the Update field command is not available on the shortcut form. Therefore, you need to use another method to protect the content that you don't want users to be able to change. First, you'll ungroup the form.

To ungroup the content controls:

▶ **1.** Click anywhere in the table.

▶ **2.** On the Developer tab, in the Controls group, click the **Group** button.

▶ **3.** Click **Ungroup**.

Restricting Document Editing

As you have seen, the Group command applies restrictions for editing the document so that users can enter data only in content controls and are prevented from making changes to the text or structure of the form. However, because the form you are working on includes a formula field that needs to be updated after you enter values in content controls, you need to set editing restrictions by using the Restrict Editing command.

When you use the Restrict Editing command, you can specify that the document is read-only, meaning a user can open and view it but cannot make any changes to it. You can also give restricted access to users for either making tracked changes or adding comments. Finally, for a form, you want users to be able to enter content in the content controls and to update fields, so you can give them limited access to fill in the form. Refer to the Session 9.3 Visual Overview for more information about setting editing restrictions.

One advantage to using the Restrict Editing command instead of the Group command is that you can set a password to prevent users from turning the restriction off. When you create a password, you should create one that you can easily remember but that others cannot easily guess. If you forget the password, there is no way to recover it, and you will not be able to remove the editing restriction.

Because a form that has editing restrictions allows the user to enter data only in content controls, make sure you do not select the "Remove content control when contents are edited" property for content controls you insert. If you do, as soon as the user types one character in a control, the control will be deleted, and the user will not be able to enter any more data.

Reference

Restricting Editing for Filling in a Form

- On the ribbon, click the Developer tab, and then in the Protect group, click the Restrict Editing button.
- In the Restrict Editing pane, click the "Allow only this type of editing in the document" check box to select it, click the arrow, and then click Filling in forms.
- Click Yes, Start Enforcing Protection. If the button is grayed out (not available), click the Design Mode button in the Controls group on the Developer tab to turn off Design mode.
- In the Start Enforcing Protection dialog box, type a password in the Enter new password (optional) box, type the same password in the Reenter password to confirm box, and then click OK; or, if you do not want to use a password, just click OK.
- To turn off protection, click Stop Protection at the bottom of the pane.
- If you used a password, type it in the Password box in the Unprotect Document dialog box, and then click OK.

You'll restrict editing in the form so that the only thing users can do is enter data in the content controls.

To restrict editing for filling in a form:

▶ **1.** On the ribbon, click the **Developer** tab, and then make sure Design mode is turned off. You cannot restrict editing when the form is in Design mode.

▶ **2.** In the Protect group, click the **Restrict Editing** button. The Restrict Editing pane opens to the right of the document window. See Figure 9–36.

Figure 9–36   **Restrict Editing pane**

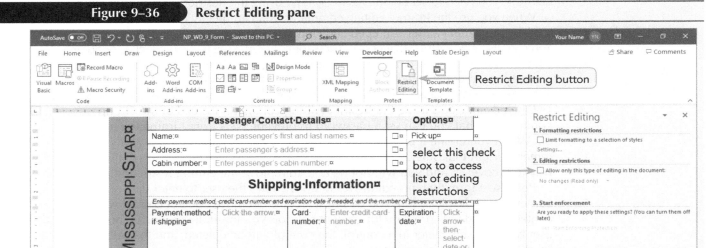

3. In the "2. Editing restrictions" section, click the **Allow only this type of editing in the document** check box to select it. The box below that check box becomes available and displays "No changes (Read only)."

4. Click the section 2 **arrow** to display a list of ways you can choose to restrict editing, and then click **Filling in forms**.

5. In the "3. Start enforcement" section, click **Yes, Start Enforcing Protection**. The Start Enforcing Protection dialog box opens.

   In the next steps, be very careful to type the password exactly as shown or you will not be able to open it later.

6. Click in the **Enter new password (optional)** box, and then type **Form** as the password. The characters you type appear as round bullet symbols. Passwords are case sensitive, so "Form" is not the same as "form." Note that this password is not a strong password—it would be easy for someone to guess, and it does not contain numbers or symbols in addition to letters. However, for the purposes of testing the form, it's fine.

7. Press **TAB** to move the insertion point to the Reenter password to confirm box, type **Form**, and then click **OK**. The Restrict Editing pane changes to inform you that the document is protected from unintentional editing, and the Stop Protection command button appears at the bottom of the pane. Because you can't edit the form now, most of the buttons on the ribbon are unavailable (grayed out). See Figure 9–37.

Figure 9–37 | **Form after restricting editing**

Trouble? If a dialog box appears telling you that the passwords don't match, click OK, delete the dots in both password boxes, and then repeat Steps 6 and 7.

▶ **8. sam**⬆ Save the changes to the template.

If you ever want to remove the password, display the Restrict Editing pane, and then click Stop Protection. If a password is set, the Unprotect Document dialog box opens with a Password box. Type the password in the Password box, and then click OK. The Restrict Editing pane changes to display the options for setting restrictions again.

Filling in the Online Form

So far, you have been acting as the form designer and creator. Now it's time to try out the form from the user's point of view to make sure there are no unexpected glitches. You can do this by filling in the form just as a user would.

Because the form template is not saved in the Custom Office Templates folder, you need to double-click the form template in a File Explorer window.

To open a new form from the template:

▶ **1.** On the taskbar, click the **File Explorer** button 🔲. The File Explorer window opens.

▶ **2.** Navigate to the drive and folder where you are saving your files, and then double-click the **NP_WD_9_Form** template. A new document based on the template is created, and the first content control—the Passenger Name content control—is selected.

Now you will enter information in the form.

To enter information in the form:

▶ **1.** With the Passenger Name content control selected, type your first and last names, and then press **TAB**. The text you typed appears in the cell and is formatted in bold because of the Properties settings you entered earlier, and the Passenger Address content control is now selected. This is an example of why you should always test the final form. When you were creating the form and you pressed TAB after entering data in the Passenger Name content control, the Pick Up Check Box content control was selected. By testing the form in a new document, you will have the same experience as a person using the form will have.

▶ **2.** In the Passenger Address content control, type **123 Main St., Natchez, MS 39120**, and then press **TAB**. The Cabin Number content control is selected.

▶ **3.** In the Cabin Number content control, type **401**, and then press **TAB**. The Payment Method content control is selected.

▶ **4.** Click the **Payment Method** content control arrow, click **Credit card**, and then press **TAB**. The Credit Card Number content control is selected.

▶ **5.** In the Credit Card Number content control, type **1234 5678 9012**, and then press **TAB**. The Card Expiration Date content control is selected.

▶ **6.** Click the Card Expiration Date **arrow**, scroll to June of the current year, and then click any date. The calendar closes, the date is displayed in the format 06/2025, and the insertion point is before "06" in the date.

▶ **7.** Press → seven times to position the insertion point after the year, press **BACKSPACE** twice, and then type **26**. The expiration date is now 06/2026.

▶ **8.** Press **TAB**. The Notes content control is selected.

▶ **9.** Type **Leave on back porch.** and then press **TAB**. The No. of Pieces content control is selected.

▶ **10.** In the No. of Pieces content control, type **4**. Now you need to update the field containing the formula.

▶ **11.** Right-click the field in the cell to the right of the "Total" cell to open the shortcut menu. The Update Field command is again on this menu, and because the form is restricted, it is the only command available.

▶ **12.** Click **Update Field**. "$ 35.96"—the result of multiplying the shipping fee by the number of pieces—is displayed in the cell.

The check boxes in the Options section were never selected as you pressed TAB to move around the form.

13. To the left of the "Ship home" cell, click the check box. An "X" appears in the check box. After you click the check box, the Payment Method content control becomes selected. Compare your screen to Figure 9–38.

Figure 9–38 **Form completed in a new document**

As you saw, pressing TAB to move from one content control to another did not work as expected. There is no way to fix this when a protected form contains content controls unless you create fairly complex macros in the Visual Basic window. If the online form will be filled out by employees, you can train them in the best way to fill out the form. If the online form will be filled out by new users each time, such as by new customers, you should take the order in which the content controls are selected when you press TAB into consideration when you create the form. For example, in the NP_WD_9_Form template, you could move the Options section so it is between the Passenger Contact Details and Shipping Information sections. Then the user's eye will be drawn to the check boxes even if they press TAB after entering the cabin number. Likewise, the Notes section could be placed below the rows that contain the fees and total calculation. You could also add an instruction reminding the user to right-click the Total field to update the result.

To save the test form and remove the Developer tab from the ribbon:

▶ 1. Click the File tab on the ribbon, click **Save**, navigate to the location where you are saving your files, replace the text in the File name box with **NP_WD_9_Test**, and then click **Save**.

You're ready to show the completed template and test form to Emi. Before you do, you'll remove the Developer tab from the ribbon.

▶ 2. If the Developer tab was not displayed when you started working with content controls, hide it by right-clicking any tab on the ribbon, clicking **Customize the Ribbon**, clicking the **Developer** check box in the Customize the Ribbon list, and then clicking **OK**.

▶ 3. Close the **NP_WD_9_Test** document.

▶ 4. Close the **NP_WD_9_Form** template.

Proskills

Problem Solving: Organizing a Form

The form you created in this module contains information organized in a logical way for the person who needs to create and store the form. However, as you saw when you entered the information in the form, it is not set up in the most logical way for a user who presses TAB to move from one control or field to the next. When you design a form, keep TAB behavior in mind and try to come up with a design that works for both the person entering the data and the person reading the form. For example, for this form, you could fill all the cells that the user needs to fill out with a color to draw the user's attention to those cells. You could also consider redesigning the table so that pressing TAB moves the user through the form in a more logical order—such as taking the user through the personal contact information fields before moving on to the credit card information fields. If you keep the end user—the person who will be filling out the form—in mind, you will be able to create a form that is easy to fill out without missing any of the content controls.

Emi is pleased with the appearance of the form you created and with how well it works. She's sure it will make the process of gathering information from passengers more efficient.

Review

Session 9.3 Quick Check

1. In a table, how do you reference the cell in the third column and the first row?

2. What is a formula?

3. What is always the first character in a formula in a Word table?

4. What is a variable?

5. What is an argument?

6. How does the number 34 appear if the format is specified as $##0;($##0)?

7. What happens when you use the Group command on a form that contains content controls?

Practice

Review Assignments

Data Files needed for the Review Assignments: NP_WD_9-2.dotx

For theme cruises for people interested in writing, Emi Nakata arranges for successful published authors to give lectures. She also schedules a private reception after the lecture for interested passengers. Although the cost of the lecture is included in the cruise fee, passengers who want to attend the private reception need to register and pay a $75 fee. Emi asked you to create an online form that she can use to register passengers for the reception. She added most of the information she wants to include in a table. You need to format the table, insert content controls and a formula, and test the form. Complete the following steps:

1. Open the template **NP_WD_9-2.dotx** from the Word9 > Review folder included with your Data Files, and then save it in the location specified by your instructor as a template named **NP_WD_9_Reception**.

2. In the first row, select all five cells, and then split the selected cells into one column and two rows, merging the cells before you split them. Move the text "Private Reception" into the cell in the new second row.

3. Select all the cells to the right of the cells containing "Name," "Address," "Phone," and "Email." (A total of 12 cells should be selected.) Split the selected cells into one column and four rows, merging the cells before you split them.

4. Merge the following cells:
   a. in the last row, the cell containing text and the next two cells to its right (The cell in the last column of that row should not be merged.)
   b. in the first column, the cell containing "Contact Info" and the three cells below it
   c. in the first column, the cell containing "Reception Details" and the next two cells below it (The cell in the bottom row of the first column should not be merged with the "Reception Details" cell.)

5. Select the cells containing "Reception Date," "Author Name," and "Reception Location," and then split each cell into two cells in the same row. (*Hint*: Do not merge the cells before splitting.) There should be an empty cell to the right of each of the cells you selected.

6. Split the cell containing "Food Allergies" into one column and two rows. Then split the cell in the new row below the "Food Allergies" cell into four columns.

7. Select the empty cell above the "Allergy notes" cell, and then split that cell into four columns and two rows.

8. Select the "Allergy notes" cell and the cell below it, and then split those cells into two columns and one row. (Merge the cells before splitting so that the result is two cells.)

9. Rotate the text in the merged cells containing "Contact Info" and "Reception Details" so the text reads up from the bottom.

10. In the first row, change the size of "SS Mississippi Star" to 28 points and change the font color to Teal, Accent 5, Darker 25%.

11. In the second row, shade the cell containing "Private Reception" with the Teal, Accent 5, Darker 25% color, and change the font color to White, Background 1. Change the font size to 28 points, and then add bold and small caps formatting.

12. In the first column, change the size of the text in the two merged cells to 10 points, change the font color to Teal, Accent 5, Darker 50%, and format it as bold.

13. Format the text in the cells containing "Name," "Address," "Phone," "Email," "Reception Date," "Author Name," "Reception Location," "Reception Fee," "No. of Tickets," "Total," "Food Allergies," and "Allergy notes" as bold. Then change the size of the text "Allergy notes" to 10 points.

14. Shade the cell containing "Food Allergies" and all of the cells below it with the Dark Purple, Text 2, Lighter 80% color.

15. In the last row, italicize the text "Tickets will not be issued until payment is processed."

16. In the Food Allergies section, in the three cells in column G below the cell containing "Food Allergies," enter the following: **Peanuts**, **Tree nuts**, and **Dairy**. In the three cells in column I (the last column), enter the following: **Shellfish**, **Gluten**, and **Other**.

17. Center the content of the cells containing "SS Mississippi Star," "Private Reception," "Contact Info," "Reception Details," and "Food Allergies" both horizontally and vertically.

18. Center the content of the cells containing "Reception Date," "Author Name," and "Reception Location" and the empty cells to their right vertically (but leave these cells left-aligned horizontally.)

19. Center the content of the cells containing "Reception Fee," "No. of Tickets," and "Total" vertically (but leave these cells left-aligned horizontally). Then center the content of the cells to the right of each of these cells vertically, and change the horizontal alignment of those cells so the contents are right-aligned.

20. Center the content of the cells containing the types of food allergies vertically, but leave them left-aligned horizontally. Center the content of the cells to the left of the six types of food allergies both vertically and horizontally.

21. Turn off the option to automatically resize the table to fit its contents, and then change the top and bottom cell margins for all the cells in the table to **0.02"**. Change the top and bottom cell margins for the cells in the first and second rows back to **0"**.

22. Resize the columns so the distance between the Move Table Column markers matches the measurements shown in Figure 9–39. Make sure you resize the columns in the order they are listed. (*Hint*: Note that the table has nine columns—column A through column I—and 12 rows. The cell containing "Reception Date" is in cell B7, and the cell containing "Author Name" is in cell B9 because in the "Food Allergies" section there are extra rows.)

Figure 9–39 **Column measurements for the table in the NP_WD_9_Reception form**

Cells	Measurement
"Contact Info," "Reception Details," and the blank cell below them (cells A3, A7, and A12)	0.3"
Cells in column B from the cell containing "Name" through the cell containing "Reception Location" (cells B3 through B11)	0.8"
Cells to the right of the cells containing "Reception Date," "Author Name," and "Reception Location" (cells C7, C9, and C11)	2.3"
"Reception Fee," "No. of Tickets," and "Total" (cells D7, D9, and D11)	0.8"
Cells to the right of the cells containing "Reception Fee," "No. of Tickets," and "Total" (cells E7, E9, and E11)	0.4"
Cell containing "Tickets will not be issued until payment is processed" (cell B12)—make sure the right border of this cell aligns with the right border of cells E7, E9, and E11)	4.75"
Three cells in the first column below "Food Allergies" (cells F8, F9, and F10)	0.5"
Three cells in the second column below "Food Allergies" (cells G8, G9, and G10)	1"
Three cells in the third column below "Food Allergies" (cells H8, H9, and H10)	0.5"
"Allergy Notes" (cell F11)	0.5"

23. Add a 3-point border between row 6 and row 7.

24. Change the Line Weight box in the Borders group on the Table Design tab back to ½ point, and then remove the borders from the right side of the following cells:
    - B3 ("Name") through B11 ("Reception Location")
    - D7 ("Reception Fee") through D11 ("Total")
    - F11 ("Allergy notes")

25. Remove the border from the left side of the cells containing "Peanuts," "Tree nuts," "Dairy," "Shellfish," "Gluten," and "Other."

26. Remove the top, left, and right borders from cell A1 (the cell containing "SS Mississippi Star").

27. In the last row, remove the border between the first and second cells.

28. Display the Developer tab, if necessary, and then insert Plain Text content controls in the cells to the right of the cells listed in Figure 9–40. Use the contents of the cell to the left of the content control as the title of the control. Do not allow the controls to be deleted. Revise the placeholder text as indicated in Figure 9–40.

Figure 9–40   Placeholder text for the Plain Text content controls in the NP_WD_9_Reception form

Cell	Placeholder Text
Name	**Enter passenger name.**
Address	**Enter passenger address.**
Phone	**Enter passenger phone number.**
Email	**Enter passenger email address.**
Author Name	**Enter author name.**
No. of Tickets	**Enter number of tickets.**
Allergy notes	**Enter additional information about food allergies.**

29. Change the properties of the Name content control (cell C3) so that it uses the Strong style.

30. Insert a Date Picker content control in the cell to the right of "Reception Date" (cell C7) with the title of **Reception Date**. Do not allow the control to be deleted, and use M/d/yy as the date format. Change the placeholder text to **Click arrow, scroll to month, and click date.** (including the period).

31. Insert a Drop-Down List content control in the cell to the right of "Reception Location" (cell C11). Use **Reception Location** as the title, do not allow the control to be deleted, and add **Mark Twain Lounge**, **Ragtime Club**, and **Delta Grille** as the choices. Reorder these options so that they are in alphabetical order. Change the instruction text at the top of the list and the placeholder text to **Select reception location.** (including the period).

32. Insert a Check Box content control in each of the cells to the left of the six types of food allergies. Use the text in the cell to the right of each check box as the title, and do not allow them to be deleted.

33. Insert a formula in cell E11 (the cell to the right of the cell containing "Total") to multiply the contents of the cell to the right of "Reception Fee" by the contents of the cell to the right of "No. of Tickets." Change the format to show currency with no decimal places. (*Hint:* Remove the decimal point and the two zeros after the decimal point both inside and outside the parentheses.)

34. Restrict editing in the template for filling in a form with the password **Reception**.

35. Save the changes to the template. Hide the Developer tab if it was hidden at the beginning of the Review Assignments.

36. Open a new document based on the NP_WD_9_Reception template. (*Hint*: Remember to double-click the template in a File Explorer window.) Fill in the form using the passenger data **John Doe**, **123 Main St.**, **Hannibal**, **MO 63401**, **(573) 555-0188** as the phone number, **j.doe@ example.com** as the email address, **August 15, 2025** as the reception date, **Jane Smith** as the author name, Mark Twain Lounge as the reception location, and **3** as the number of tickets, and select Tree nuts as a food allergy. Insert your name in the cell to the right of "Notes." Remember to update the formula field in the cell that calculates the total fee.

37. Save the completed form as **NP_WD_9_ReceptionTest** in the location specified by your instructor. Close all open documents.

Apply

Case Problem 1

Data File needed for this Case Problem: NP_WD_9-3.dotx

Las Cruces College   Incoming freshmen at Las Cruces College in Las Cruces, New Mexico, fill out dorm preference forms that indicate their preference for a room style (single, double, and so on) and their personal living style (messy/neat, early riser/late bedtime, and so on). Maura Sheehan, the college's director of admissions, has asked you to create an online form that incoming freshmen can fill out when they attend orientation in the late spring. Complete the following steps:

1. Open the file **NP_WD_9-3.dotx**, located in the Word9 > Case1 folder. Save the file as a template named **NP_WD_9_Dorm** in the location specified by your instructor.

2. Select the table and then change the option so that the table does not automatically resize to fit contents.

3. Select all of the cells in the first row, and then split them into one column and two rows. Move "Dorm Preferences" into the second row. Format the text in the first row with 24-point Copperplate Gothic Bold. Change the size of the text in the second row to 16 points. Change the alignment of the text in the first and second rows to Top Center.

4. Remove all the borders around the merged cell in the first row. Remove all the borders around the merged cell in the second row except for the bottom border.

5. In the fourth and sixth rows, merge all the cells. Shade the merged cells in the fourth and sixth rows with the Black, Text 1 color, and then change the alignment of the text in each row to Top Center.

6. In the fifth row (which contains cells with the text "First Choice," "Second Choice," "Third Choice," and "Fourth Choice"), select all four cells, and then split the cells into two rows, keeping the text in the fifth row (the cells in the new sixth row will be empty). Center-align the contents of all of the cells in the fifth row and in the new sixth row both horizontally and vertically. Remove the border between rows 5 and 6. If necessary, change the height of rows 5 and 6 to 0.32" in the Height box in the Cell Size group on the Layout tab.

7. Merge cells A8 through A11, and then shade the merged cell with the Light Gray, Accent 2, Lighter 80% color. Merge cells C8 through C11, and then shade the merged cell with the Light Gray, Accent 1, Darker 25% color.

8. In merged cell A8, type **Sleep Habits**. In merged cell C8, type **Neatness**. Change the font size of the text in cell A8 and cell C8 to 16 points. Rotate the text in merged cell A8 and in merged cell C8 so it reads from the bottom up, and then center the text in both cells horizontally and vertically.

9. Shade cell B8 (the cell containing "Select all that apply.") with the Light Gray, Accent 2, Lighter 80% color. Shade cell D8 (the cell containing "How neat are you? Select only one.") with the Light Gray, Accent 1, Darker 25% color.

10. Split cells B9 (the cell containing "Bed before 11 p.m."), B10 (the cell containing "Early riser"), B11 (the cell containing "Late riser"), and B12 (the empty cell in the last row) into two columns so that the text is in column B and there is an empty cell to the right of each of those cells (cell B12 will not contain any text). Center the contents of cells B9, B10, and B11 vertically and keep them left-aligned. Center the contents of the empty cells C9, C10, and C11 both horizontally and vertically.

11. Split cells E9 (the cell containing "Very neat"), E10 (the cell containing "Somewhat neat"), E11 (the cell containing "Not neat"), and E12 (the empty cell in the last row) into two columns so that the text is in column E and there is an empty cell to the right of each of those cells (cell E12 will not contain any text). Center the contents of cells E9, E10, and E11 vertically and keep them left-aligned. Center the contents of the empty cells F9, F10, and F11 both horizontally and vertically.

12. Remove all the borders around cells A8, B8, D8, E8, and all the cells in row 12. Select cells B9 through C11, and then remove all the borders except for the inside horizontal borders. Select cells E9 through F11, and then remove all the borders except for the inside horizontal borders and the right border.

13. The distances between the Move Table Column markers of the cells in the table are listed in Figure 9–41. Remember to adjust the widths from left to right. The widths of the cells in your table should be adjusted to be as close as possible to the widths listed in Figure 9–41.

Figure 9–41   **Column measurements for the table in the NP_WD_9_Dorm form**

Cell	Measurement
A3 (the cell containing "Name")	0.5"
B3 (the cell to the right of the cell containing "Name")	2.9"
C3 (the cell containing "Student ID Number") (*Hint*: Make sure "Student ID Number" fits on one line.)	1.3"
A8 and A12 (the cell containing "Sleep Habits" and the empty cell below it)	0.3"
B9 through B12 (the cell containing "Bed before 11 p.m." through the empty cell below the cell containing "Late riser")	1.5"
B8 (the cell containing "Select all that apply") and C8 through C12 (the cell to the right of the cell containing "Bed before 11 p.m." through the empty cell in the last row in column C) (*Hint*: Click in cell B8 to the right of "Select all that apply." and then drag straight down to cell C12. Note that cell B8 will be wider than cells C8 through C12 even after you make this adjustment.)	0.25"
D8 and D12 (the cell containing "Neatness" and the empty cell below it)	0.3"
E9 through E12 (the cell containing "Very neat" through the empty below the cell containing "Not neat")	2.9"

14. Merge cells A12 through C12 (the first three cells in the last row), and then shade the merged cell with the Light Gray, Accent 2, Lighter 80% color. Merge cells D12 through F12 (the last three cells in the last row), and then shade the merged cell with the Light Gray, Accent 1, Darker 25% color.

15. In cells B10, B11, E9, E10, and E11, select the text below the first line, italicize it, and then change the font size of the italicized text to nine points.

16. Insert a Plain Text content control in cell B3 (the cell to the right of the cell containing "Name") with the title **Student Name** and formatted with the Strong style. Do not allow the control to be deleted. Change the placeholder text to **Enter your name.** (including the period).

17. Insert a Plain Text content control in cell D3 (the cell to the right of the cell containing "Student ID Number") with the title **Student ID**. Do not allow the control to be deleted. Change the placeholder text to **Enter your student ID number.** (including the period).

18. Insert a Drop-Down List content control in cell A6 (the cell below the cell containing "First Choice"). The Title property is **Room Style**. The choices in the list are **Single**, **Double**, **Triple**, and **Suite (6 to 8 people)**. Change the first option in the list (the instruction text) to **Select a dorm room style.** (including the period). Change the placeholder text to **Click arrow.** (including the period). Insert this same content control in cells B6, C6, and D6.

19. Insert Check Box content controls in cells C9, C10, C11, F9, F10, and F11. Do not add a Title property to these controls. Do not allow the controls to be deleted.

20. Turn on Design mode, group all of the content to protect the form's structure, and then turn off Design mode.

21. Save the changes to the form.

22. Create a new document based on the NP_WD_9_Dorm template. Add your name as the student name, type **12-3456** as the Student ID number, select a different option in each of the dorm style choice lists, and then follow the instructions to select options in the bottom section.

23. Save the new document as **NP_WD_9_DormTest** in the location specified by your instructor. Close all open documents.

Challenge

Case Problem 2

Data File needed for this Case Problem: NP_WD_9-4.dotx

Charleston Office Supply Center   Carlos Gomez is the senior manager at Charleston Office Supply Center in Charleston, South Carolina. The store sells office supplies to businesses in and around Charleston. They offer same-day delivery on most items. The store was established less than a year ago, and the owners have asked Carlos to try to streamline their ordering system. Carlos asks you to help him create an online form, which will need to contain several formulas. Carlos realizes that Excel would be a better tool to use; however, Excel is not installed on the computers his staff will be using to input the orders, so for now, the staff will use a Word form. Complete the following steps:

1. Open the template **NP_WD_9-4.dotx** from the Word9 > Case2 folder included with your Data Files, and then save it as a template to the location specified by your instructor with the name **NP_WD_9_Order**.

2. Merge the four cells in the first row, and then split the merged cell into two rows. Move the text "Order Form" to the cell in the second row, and then remove the blank paragraph below "Charleston Office Supply Center," if necessary.

3. In the first row, format the text as 28-point Franklin Gothic Demi Cond, and change its color to Brown, Accent 3, Darker 50%. Center the text horizontally, and then remove all the cell borders.

4. In the second row, shade the cell with the Brown, Accent 3, Darker 25% color, change the size of the text to 20 points, and change the text color to White, Background 1. Center the text horizontally.

5. In the third row, shade the cells with the Brown, Accent 3, Lighter 80% color.

6. Select cells D3 through D9 (the cell in row 3 containing "Total" through the last cell in column D), and then drag the left border to change the width of these cells so that the distance between the Move Table Column markers on the ruler is about 1".

7. Select cells C3 through C9 (the cell containing "Price" through the last cell in column C), and then drag the left border to change the width of these cells so that the distance between the Move Table Column markers on the ruler is about 0.9".

8. Select cells B3 and B4 (the cell containing "Quantity" and the blank cell below it), and then drag the left border to change the width of these cells so that the distance between the Move Table Column markers on the ruler is about 0.8".

9. Merge cells A6 and B6 (the cell containing "Notes" and the cell to its right). Then merge the six cells below this merged cell. Remove the border between the "Notes" cell and the merged cell below it. (*Hint*: If you can't remove the border between the cells, try removing the border below the "Notes" cell or the border above the blank cell below the "Notes" cell.)

10. Shade cells B6 through C8 (the block of six cells from the cell containing "Subtotal" to the cell to the right of the cell containing "Tax") with the Brown, Accent 3, Lighter 60% color.

11. Shade cells B9 and C9 (the cells in the bottom row containing "Total" and the cell to its right) with the Black, Text 1 color. (Note that the text changes to white automatically.) Apply bold formatting to these cells.

12. In the fourth row, right-align cell D4 (the cell below the "Total" cell in column D), and then right-align cell C4 (the cell below the cell containing "Price"). Right-align cells C6 (the cells to the right of "Subtotal") through C9 (the cell to the right of "Total").

13. Format the border to the left of the cells containing "Subtotal," "Delivery," "Tax," and the "Total" cell in the last row so it is 3 points wide.

14. Select the four cells in row 5, and then shade the cells with the Black, Text 1 color. Then, with the four cells still selected, change the font size of these cells to 2 points.

15. Insert Plain Text content controls in the cells listed in Figure 9–42. Do not allow the controls to be deleted.

Figure 9–42   **Plain Text content controls for the NP_WD_9_Order form**

Cell	Title	Placeholder Text
A4 (the cell below the cell containing "Item")	Item	Type item name.
B4 (the cell below the cell containing "Quantity")	Quantity	Enter quantity.
C4 (the cell below the cell containing "Price")	Price per Item	Enter price per item.
A7 (the merged cell below the cell containing "Notes"	Notes	Enter notes if needed.
C7 (the cell to the right of the cell containing "Delivery")	Delivery	Refer to delivery fee chart.

16. In cell D4 (the cell below the cell containing "Total"), insert a formula that multiplies the value in cell B4 (the cell below "Quantity") by the value in cell C4 (the cell below "Price"). Format the number using the format that shows a dollar sign.

⊕ **Explore** 17. Select the entire fourth row in the table (the row containing the content controls and the formula), and then add a Repeating Section Content Control.

18. In the cell to the right of the cell containing "Subtotal," insert a formula that uses the SUM function to add the values in the cells above the cell using "ABOVE" as the argument. Format the number using the format that shows a dollar sign.

⊕ **Explore** 19. Select the cell containing the formula field to the right of the cell containing "Subtotal," and then create a bookmark named **Subtotal**. Then, in the cell to the right of the cell containing "Tax," insert a formula that multiplies the sales tax in Charleston, South Carolina (9%) by the value stored in the field bookmarked by the Subtotal bookmark. (*Hint*: To calculate the sales tax, you need to multiply by 0.09.) Format the number using the format that shows a dollar sign.

Explore 20. Select the cell to the right of the cell containing "Delivery," and then create a bookmark named **Delivery**. Select the cell containing the formula field to the right of the cell containing "Tax," and then create a bookmark named **Tax**.

Explore 21. In the last row, in the cell to the right of the cell containing "Total," insert a formula using the SUM function to add the values stored in the locations bookmarked by the Subtotal, Delivery, and Tax bookmarks. (*Hint*: Use the bookmark names as the arguments for the SUM function.) Format the number using the format that shows a dollar sign. (Note that the empty row with the font size of 2 points is required to prevent the bookmarks from changing when you use the Repeating Section Content Control in Step 24.)

22. Save the changes to the template, and then create a new document based on the template. Save the new document as a document named **NP_WD_9_OrderTest** in the location specified by your instructor.

Explore 23. Add the data listed in Figure 9–43. (*Hint*: Click the Plus Sign button to the right of the row to use the Repeating Section content control to create a new row with the same content controls.)

Figure 9–43 Data for the NP_WD_9_OrderTest document

Item	Quantity	Price per Item
Metal 5-shelf bookcase	5	$275.45
24 × 42 cubicle panels	20	$145.25
Heavy-duty cross-cut shredder	10	$120.00

24. Change the alignment of the entries in the Price cells in the two new rows so that it matches the formatting in the original row.

25. Update the fields in the Total column for the three items. Note that the total price is correct only in the first row.

Explore 26. Edit the formulas in the Total column in the two new rows so that they correctly use the values in their rows to calculate the total. (*Hint*: Toggle the field codes on, and then edit the row references in the field codes.) If necessary, update the fields to recalculate the totals.

27. In the cell to the right of the "Delivery" cell, enter **$50.00**.

28. Update the fields in the cells to the right of "Subtotal" and "Tax" and in the black-shaded cell to the right of "Total."

29. Add your name in the Notes content control, save the NP_WD_9_OrderTest document and close it, and then close the NP_WD_9_Order template.

Module **10**

Managing Long Documents

Creating a Survey Report for a Personal Chef Association

Objectives

Session 10.1
- Work in Outline view
- Create a master document
- Insert and create subdocuments
- Unlink a subdocument
- Reopen a master document

Session 10.2
- Add numbers to headings
- Add numbered captions
- Create cross-references
- Insert an endnote
- Create a chart in a document
- Restrict editing in a document
- Check for hidden data
- Check for accessibility

Session 10.3
- Evaluate section and page breaks
- Apply different page number formats in document sections
- Create odd and even pages
- Insert a style reference
- Insert nonbreaking hyphens and spaces
- Create and update an index
- Create a table of figures
- Update fields before printing
- Check compatibility with earlier versions of Word
- Encrypt and mark a document as final

Case | World Association of Personal Chefs

The World Association of Personal Chefs (WAPC), an organization with headquarters in New York City, provides networking opportunities and educational services for professional personal chefs. Every year, the WAPC holds a meeting that includes seminars, a vendor showcase for new products in an exposition hall, and networking opportunities in the evenings. The Annual Meeting Committee hired Marketfield Research Associates to conduct a survey of the meeting participants, presenters, and corporate patrons to find out if they were satisfied with the meeting this year and to collect suggestions for next year's meeting. Bailey Lawrence, chair of the Annual Meeting Committee, has asked for your help creating a report on the survey results. The report will include front matter (title page, table of contents, and list of figures) and an index as well as numbered figures and cross-references. The report must be set up to print on both sides of the paper, and it will require different formats and footers for even and odd pages. When you are finished with the report, you will safeguard it against unauthorized edits by encrypting it, and then you will mark the report as final.

Starting Data Files

Module

NP_WD_10-1.docx
Support_WD_10_Patrons.docx
Support_WD_10_Presenters.docx

Review

NP_WD_10-2.docx
Support_WD_10_Alonzo.docx
Support_WD_10_Marie.docx

Case1

NP_WD_10-3.docx
Support_WD_10_Background.docx
Support_WD_10_Market.docx
Support_WD_10_Summary.docx

Case2

(none)

Session 10.1 Visual Overview:

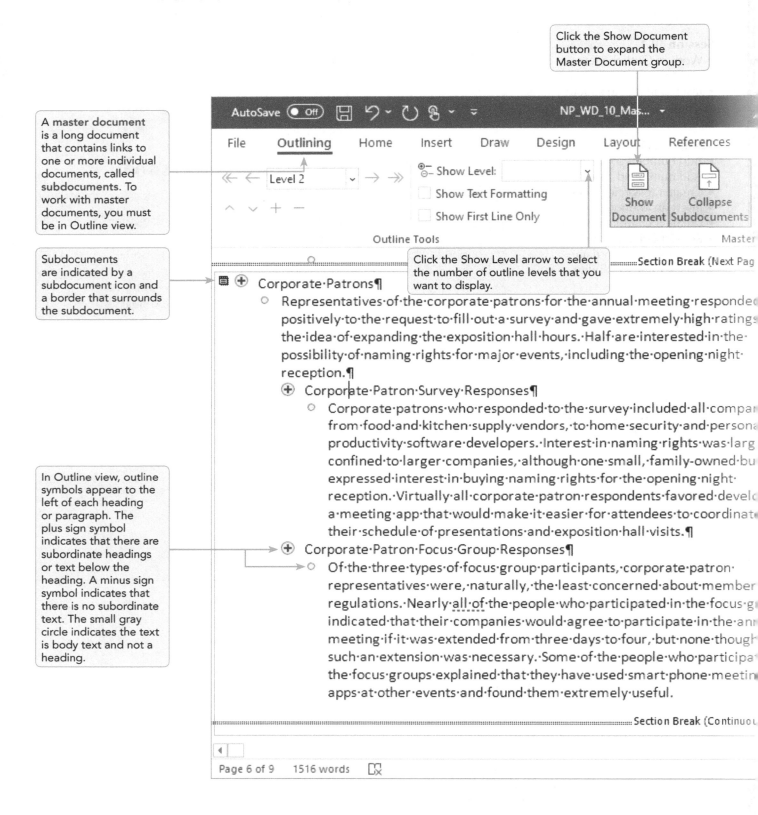

Click the Show Document button to expand the Master Document group.

A master document is a long document that contains links to one or more individual documents, called subdocuments. To work with master documents, you must be in Outline view.

Subdocuments are indicated by a subdocument icon and a border that surrounds the subdocument.

Click the Show Level arrow to select the number of outline levels that you want to display.

In Outline view, outline symbols appear to the left of each heading or paragraph. The plus sign symbol indicates that there are subordinate headings or text below the heading. A minus sign symbol indicates that there is no subordinate text. The small gray circle indicates the text is body text and not a heading.

Corporate·Patrons¶

  Representatives·of·the·corporate·patrons·for·the·annual·meeting·responded positively·to·the·request·to·fill·out·a·survey·and·gave·extremely·high·ratings the·idea·of·expanding·the·exposition·hall·hours.·Half·are·interested·in·the· possibility·of·naming·rights·for·major·events,·including·the·opening·night· reception.¶

   Corporate·Patron·Survey·Responses¶

   Corporate·patrons·who·responded·to·the·survey·included·all·compar from·food·and·kitchen·supply·vendors,·to·home·security·and·persona productivity·software·developers.·Interest·in·naming·rights·was·larg confined·to·larger·companies,·although·one·small,·family-owned·bu expressed·interest·in·buying·naming·rights·for·the·opening·night· reception.·Virtually·all·corporate·patron·respondents·favored·devel a·meeting·app·that·would·make·it·easier·for·attendees·to·coordinat their·schedule·of·presentations·and·exposition·hall·visits.¶

   Corporate·Patron·Focus·Group·Responses¶

   Of·the·three·types·of·focus·group·participants,·corporate·patron· representatives·were,·naturally,·the·least·concerned·about·member regulations.·Nearly·all·of·the·people·who·participated·in·the·focus·g indicated·that·their·companies·would·agree·to·participate·in·the·ann meeting·if·it·was·extended·from·three·days·to·four,·but·none·though such·an·extension·was·necessary.·Some·of·the·people·who·participa the·focus·groups·explained·that·they·have·used·smart·phone·meetin apps·at·other·events·and·found·them·extremely·useful.

Section Break (Continuou

Page 6 of 9   1516 words

Master Documents

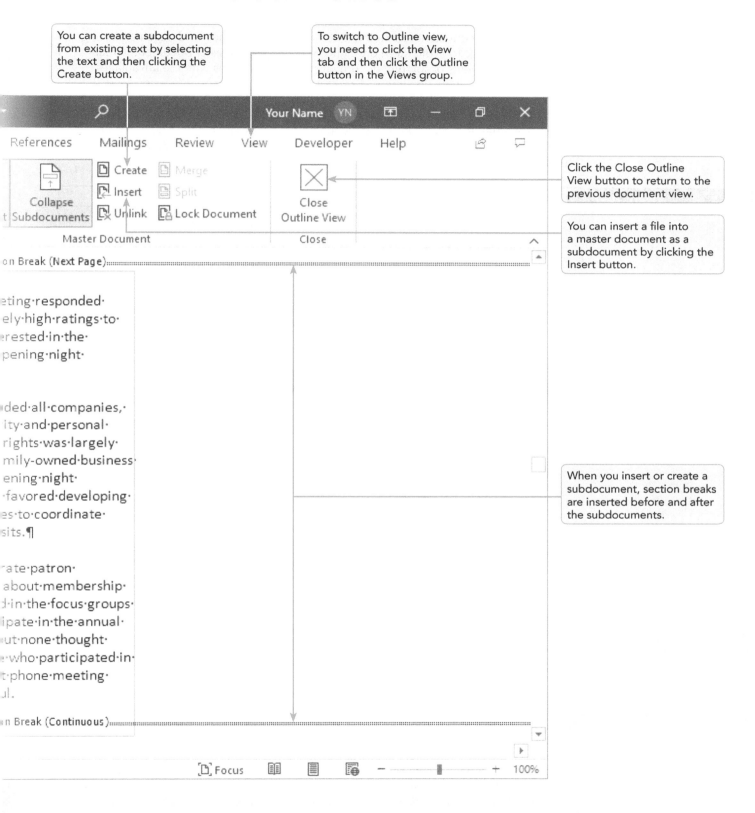

You can create a subdocument from existing text by selecting the text and then clicking the Create button.

To switch to Outline view, you need to click the View tab and then click the Outline button in the Views group.

Click the Close Outline View button to return to the previous document view.

You can insert a file into a master document as a subdocument by clicking the Insert button.

When you insert or create a subdocument, section breaks are inserted before and after the subdocuments.

Working with Master Documents

Manipulating pages in a long document can be cumbersome and time consuming. On the other hand, splitting a long document into several shorter documents makes it hard to maintain consistent formatting and to ensure that section and page numbering are always correct. To avoid these problems, you can use a master document, which combines the benefits of splitting documents into separate files with the advantages of working with a single document. A master document is also helpful when several people are simultaneously working on different parts of the same document. Each team member can submit a separate document; you can then quickly organize these individual documents into a single, complete document by creating a master document. Figure 10–1 illustrates the relationship between master documents and subdocuments.

Figure 10–1	Master document and subdocument

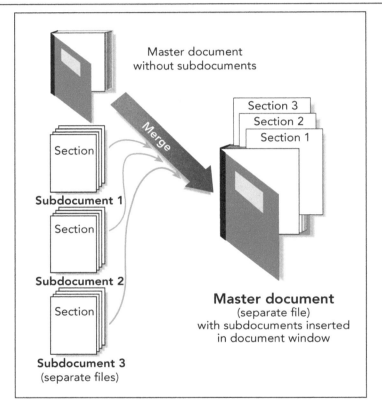

Working with a master document has several advantages:

- **Consistent formatting across elements**—You can set up styles, headers, footers, and other formatting elements in only the master document; any subdocuments you create or insert will have the same formatting.
- **Accurate numbering**—You can number the master document, including all subdocuments, with consecutive page numbers, heading numbers, and figure numbers. If you rearrange, delete, or add material, Word updates the numbers to reflect your changes.
- **Accurate cross-referencing**—You can refer to figures or tables in subdocuments, and Word will keep the cross-references updated.
- **Complete table of contents and index**—You can easily compile a table of contents and create an index for a master document.
- **Faster editing**—You can edit the master document all at once, or you can edit each subdocument individually. Any changes in the master document automatically take effect and are saved in the subdocument files and vice versa.

Working in Outline View

To create a master document, you need to work in Outline view. When you apply a heading style to a paragraph, you also apply an outline level that matches the heading level. The top-level heading (the Heading 1 style) is Level 1, with subheadings (Heading 2, Heading 3, etc.) labeled as Level 2, Level 3, and so on. Paragraphs that are not formatted as headings have Body Text as the outline level.

Creating an Outline in Outline View

The document outline is created when you apply the built-in heading styles to paragraphs. You can also create an outline in Outline view by applying outline levels to paragraphs.

Reference

Creating an Outline in Outline View

- On the View tab, in the Views group, click the Outline button.
- Type the first Level 1 heading, and then press ENTER.
- To demote a heading, click the Demote button in the Outline Tools group on the Outlining tab, or press TAB.
- To promote a heading, click the Promote button in the Outline Tools group on the Outlining tab, or press SHIFT+TAB.
- To change text to body text, click the Demote to Body Text button in the Outline Tools group on the Outlining tab.

Bailey asks you to create the outline for her report. You'll start working on this in Outline view.

To create an outline in Outline view:

1. Start Word, create a new, blank document, and then save it as **NP_WD_10_Draft** in the location specified by your instructor.

2. Display nonprinting characters.

3. On the ribbon, click the **View** tab, and then in the Views group, click the **Outline** button. The document switches to Outline view, and a new tab, Outlining, appears on the ribbon and is selected. The outline level of the current paragraph is Level 1. See Figure 10–2.

Figure 10–2	Outline view

4. Change the Zoom level to **120%**.

5. Type **Overview** and then press **ENTER**. The text you typed is formatted with the Heading 1 style.

6. Type **Corporate Patrons** and then press **ENTER**. You want the next two headings to be Level 2 headings.

7. In the Outline Tools group, click the **Demote** button →. The second paragraph indents, the outline symbol next to the second line changes to a plus sign, and the Outline Level button in the Outline Tools group changes to indicate that this paragraph is now Level 2.

8. Type **Corporate Patron Survey Responses**, press **ENTER**, type **Corporate Patron Focus Groups**, and then press **ENTER** again.

9. In the Outline Tools group, click the **Promote** button ← to add a Level 1 heading, and then type **Participants**.

Next, Bailey wants you to add body text under the "Overview" heading. To do this, you'll need to add a new paragraph and then demote it to body text.

To add body text to an outline:

1. In the first line of the outline, click after "Overview," and then press **ENTER**. A new paragraph is created at Level 1.

2. In the Outline Tools group, click the **Demote to Body Text** button ⇒. The paragraph is indented, and the outline symbol changes to a small gray circle, which indicates body text. The outline symbol next to the first line changes to a plus sign.

3. Type **Report on the survey conducted by Marketfield Research Associates** (do not type a period). See Figure 10–3.

Figure 10–3   **Text in Outline view**

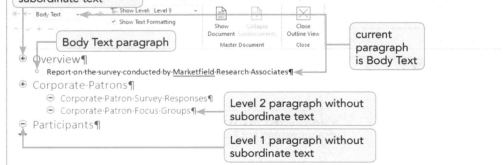

Trouble? If the text on your screen is all black and the same size, click the Show Text Formatting check box in the Outline Tools group to select it.

4. Save your changes, and then close the document (but do not close Word).

Changing the Outline Level of a Heading

Bailey added new content to the document, created a custom style for headings in the front and end matter, and added a table of contents. She asks you to continue editing it.

To open the report and view the headings with the custom styles:

▶ 1. **sam** ⬇ Open the document **NP_WD_10-1.docx**, located in the Word10 > Module folder included with your Data Files, type your name on the title page in the blank paragraph below "Marie Choi," and then save it as **NP_WD_10_Master** in the location specified by your instructor.

▶ 2. If necessary, change the Zoom level to **120%**.

▶ 3. Scroll down to page 3, and then select **List of Figures**. On the Home tab, in the Styles group, the custom Front/End Matter Heading style is selected. (It appears as "Front/End…" in the Style gallery.)

▶ 4. Scroll up to page 2, and then select **Contents** in the paragraph with the red shading. This paragraph also has the Front/End Matter Heading style applied.

When you use the Table of Contents command to create a table of contents, the outline level of each heading determines whether the heading is included. Paragraphs that have an outline level of Body Text are not included in the table of contents. In the NP_WD_10_Master document, the heading "Contents" is included as the first entry in the table of contents, but it shouldn't be. The "Contents" heading is formatted with the custom Front/End Matter Heading style that Bailey created. To prevent the "Contents" heading from being included in the table of contents, you need to create a new style with an outline level of Body Text.

To create a style based on a heading with the Body Text outline level:

▶ 1. On the Home tab, in the Styles group, click the **More** button ⊽, and then click **Create a Style**. The small Create New Style from Formatting dialog box opens with the text in the Name box selected.

▶ 2. Type **Contents Heading** in the Name box, and then click **Modify**. The large Create New Style from Formatting dialog box opens. You need to change the outline level.

▶ 3. At the bottom of the dialog box, click **Format**, and then click **Paragraph**. The Paragraph dialog box opens with the Indents and Spacing tab selected. In the General section, Level 1 appears in the Outline level box. You need to change the outline level to Body Text.

▶ 4. Click the **Outline level** arrow, click **Body Text**, and then click **OK** in each open dialog box. The new Contents Heading style appears as the first style in the Style gallery. Because you changed the outline level to Body Text, the heading formatted with the Contents Heading style will not be included in the table of contents. You need to update the table of contents to see this change.

▶ 5. Click anywhere in the table of contents below the "Contents" heading, click the **References** tab, and then in the Table of Contents group, click the **Update Table** button. The Update Table of Contents dialog box opens.

▶ 6. Click the **Update entire table** option button, and then click **OK**. The table of contents is updated, and the "Contents" heading is no longer included as an entry in it.

Reorganizing a Document in Outline View

Outline view has several symbols and buttons that you use when viewing and reorganizing your document. Refer to the Session 10.1 Visual Overview for information on these symbols and buttons. To select an entire section, you click the outline symbol next to that section's heading. To move a section after you select it, you can drag it or click the Move Up or Move Down button on the Outlining tab, which is visible only in Outline view. You can also use buttons on the Outlining tab to change the level of a heading. For instance, you might want to change a Level 1 heading to a Level 2 heading or change a Level 3 heading to a Level 1 heading.

Bailey wants you to reorganize the document somewhat. You will do this in Outline view. First, you need to examine the document in Outline view.

To view the document in Outline view:

▶ **1.** Switch to Outline view, and then change the Zoom level to **120%**, if necessary. The entire document is displayed. However, you cannot see the Level 1 headings, including the "List of Figures" heading, and you cannot see the "Contents" heading. This is because the text color of these headings is White, Background 1 and the Show Text Formatting check box in the Outline Tools group is selected.

▶ **2.** In the Outline Tools group, click the **Show Text Formatting** check box to deselect it, if necessary. The Level 1 headings and the "Contents" heading are now visible.

▶ **3.** If necessary, deselect the **Show First Line Only** check box in the Outline Tools group.

▶ **4.** In the Outline Tools group, click the **Show Level** arrow, and then click **Level 2**. The document changes to hide all the text at the Body Text level and display only the headings at Level 1 and Level 2. There are no Level 3 headings in the document. Note that the first heading in the document is the "List of Figures" heading. This is because the "Contents" heading has the outline level of Body Text.

▶ **5.** Click anywhere in the **Overview** heading, and then in the Outline Tools group, click the **Expand** button ⊞. The "Overview" heading expands to show the next available level. In this case, because there are no Level 3 headings, the body text is displayed.

▶ **6.** In the Outline Tools group, click the **Collapse** button ⊟ to collapse the "Overview" heading and show only Level 1 and Level 2 headings.

You can easily move sections in the document while working in Outline view. When you move a heading in Outline view, you also move the entire section; that is, you move the heading and its subordinate text. Note that it is customary to refer to a part of a document that begins with a heading as a "section." Don't confuse this use of the word "section" with a Word section—as in a part of a document that is identified by section breaks.

Bailey wants the Survey Overview section to be the first section in the Overview section. She also wants the Executive Summary section to appear before the Participants section. You'll move these sections next.

To move sections in the outline:

▶ **1.** Next to the Level 2 heading "Survey Overview," click the **plus sign** outline symbol ⊕. The heading is selected.

> **2.** Position the pointer over the Survey Overview **plus sign** outline symbol ⊕, press and hold the mouse button, and then drag up without releasing the mouse button. As you drag, a horizontal line appears, indicating the position of the heading as you drag. See Figure 10–4.

Figure 10–4	Moving a heading to a new location in the outline

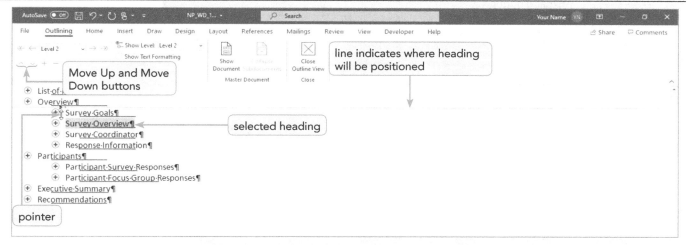

> **3.** When the horizontal line is above the "Survey Goals" heading, release the mouse button. "Survey Overview" now appears above "Survey Goals" and is the first Level 2 heading below the Level 1 heading "Overview."
>
> **4.** Next to "Participants," click the **plus sign** outline symbol ⊕. The heading next to the symbol that you clicked as well as its subordinate headings are selected.
>
> **5.** Drag the "Participants" heading and its subordinate headings down below the "Executive Summary" heading.
>
> **6.** Drag the "Executive Summary" heading above the "Overview" heading.
>
> **7.** On the Outlining tab, in the Outline Tools group, click the **Show Level** arrow, and then click **All Levels**. The headings expand to display the body text beneath them.
>
> **8.** Scroll so that the "Executive Summary" heading is at the top of the window. See Figure 10–5.

Tip

You can also click the Move Up and Move Down buttons in the Outline Tools group to move selected headings in an outline.

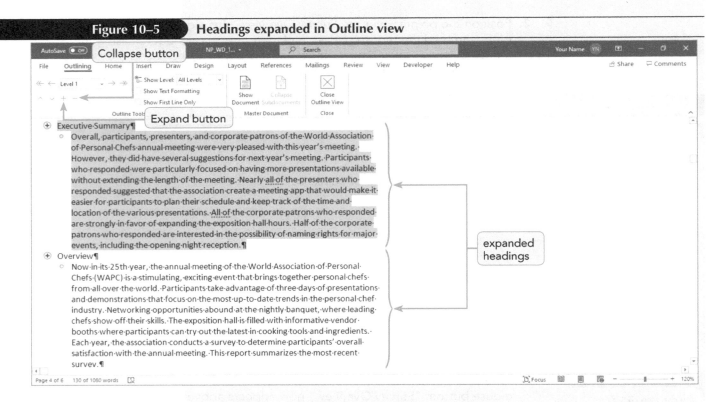

Figure 10–5 **Headings expanded in Outline view**

9. Save the changes to the document.

Creating a Master Document

To create a master document, you can convert parts of the document into subdocuments, or you can insert existing files as subdocuments. As soon as a document contains subdocuments, it becomes a master document. You can open, edit, and print subdocuments individually; or you can open, edit, and print the entire master document as a single unit. When you save a master document, Word saves each subdocument as a separate file. A master document contains links to its subdocuments rather than the text of the subdocuments themselves. You can display the content of subdocuments in the master document, however, and edit them from within the master document if you want.

To convert part of a document into a subdocument, you need to select the text you want to convert into the subdocument in Outline view. The first paragraph selected must have an outline level (in other words, it cannot be Body Text). To create a master document by using existing files as subdocuments, you insert the files as subdocuments, which creates a link between the master document and the inserted files. Inserting subdocuments into a master document is different from inserting Word files into a document. Inserted Word files become part of the document in which they're inserted, whereas subdocument files remain separate from the master document in which they're inserted.

Sometimes a lock icon 🔒 appears near the subdocument icon 🖳 to indicate that the subdocument is locked. You can't edit locked subdocuments, and commands on the ribbon are unavailable when the insertion point is positioned in a locked subdocument. The lock feature is important when more than one person is working on a master document because it allows only one person at a time to edit a subdocument.

Bailey's master document is the file NP_WD_10_Master. She wants you to create subdocuments from two of the sections currently in the NP_WD_10_Master document, and she wants you to insert two subdocuments created by colleagues.

Proskills

Teamwork: Leading a Workgroup

In networking terminology, a group of colleagues who have access to the same network server and work together on a common project is called a **workgroup**. The person who oversees a workgroup must build trust among the team members, figure out how best to facilitate communication among the team members, and give the team members a chance to get to know one another. Often a workgroup is charged with creating a document, and each member is responsible for writing at least one part of the document. If you are the leader of this type of workgroup, it's your job to make sure that each team member has the correct document templates and access to the same styles so that when you combine the subdocuments to create the final master document, it will have a consistent style and formatting.

Creating a Subdocument

When you create a subdocument from text in a master document, a new file containing the text of the subdocument is created in the same folder that contains the master document. The name of the new file is the first paragraph formatted with a heading style. The text of the new subdocument is no longer saved in the master document file; instead a link to the subdocument is added to the master document. As shown in the Session 10.1 Visual Overview, the subdocument appears in a box marked with a subdocument icon.

Bailey wants you to convert the "Participants" and "Recommendations" sections into subdocuments.

To create a subdocument by converting text in the master document:

▶ **1.** Scroll down until you can see the "Participants" heading, and then click the Participants **plus sign** outline symbol ⊕. The "Participants" heading and its subordinate text and headings are selected. This is the text you will convert to a subdocument.

▶ **2.** On the Outlining tab, in the Master Document group, click the **Show Document** button to select it. The Master Document group expands to display six additional buttons that you can use to create and work with master documents. See Figure 10–6.

Figure 10–6	Master Document group expanded on Outlining tab

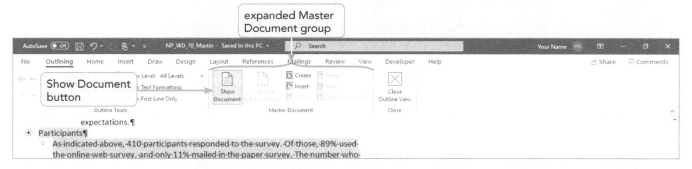

▶ **3.** On the Outlining tab, in the Master Document group, click the **Create** button. A border appears around the "Participants" section, continuous section breaks appear before and after the section, and the Subdocument icon appears to the left of the "Participants" heading.

4. Scroll down, and then next to the "Recommendations" heading, click the **plus sign** outline symbol ⊕.

5. In the Master Document group, click the **Create** button. The Recommendations section is now a subdocument.

6. Save the NP_WD_10_Master file with the new subdocuments. When you save your changes, new files named "Participants" and "Recommendations" are created. You can see this in the Open dialog box.

7. Click the **File** tab, and then in the navigation pane, click **Open**.

8. Click **Browse**, and then navigate to the location where you are storing your files, if necessary. You see the two subdocuments that you created from within the master document—Participants and Recommendations. See Figure 10–7.

Figure 10–7   **Subdocuments in the master document listed in the Open dialog box**

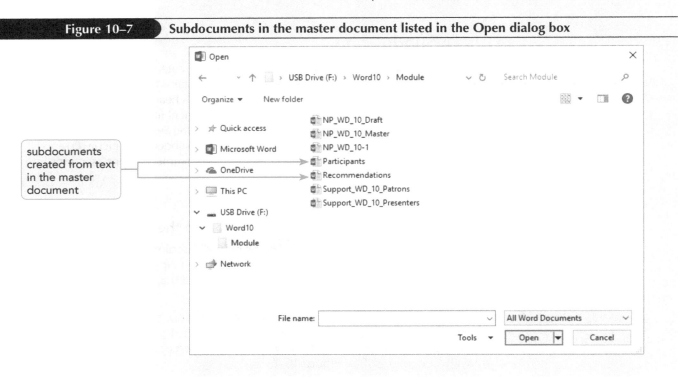

subdocuments created from text in the master document

Inserting Subdocuments

When you insert a subdocument into a master document, the subdocument appears in the master document at the location of the insertion point. Similar to a subdocument created from text in a master document, the inserted subdocument is stored in the subdocument file, and a link is created in the master document to the subdocument.

Alonzo Garza created a document describing corporate patrons who responded to the survey, and Marie Choi created a document about presenters. Bailey asks you to insert these documents into the master document. Before you do this, however, you'll make a backup copy of each of these files.

To make a backup copy of the subdocuments:

1. Make sure the Open dialog box is still open, navigate to the **Word10 > Module** folder if necessary, and then open the file **Support_WD_10_Presenters.docx**.

2. Save the file Support_WD_10_Presenters as **NP_WD_10_Presenters** in the location specified by your instructor, and then close this file.

3. Open the file **Support_WD_10_Patrons.docx**, located in the Word10 > Module folder, save it as **NP_WD_10_Patrons** in the location specified by your instructor, and then close this file. The master document NP_WD_10_Master appears in the window in Outline view.

Now you can insert the copies of the two subdocuments into the master document. You'll start with Alonzo's document, which is the NP_WD_10_Patrons document.

To insert subdocuments into the master document:

1. Scroll so you can see the Level 1 heading "Participants," and then click in the empty Body Text paragraph above the section break. This is where you'll insert the first subdocument.

   Trouble? If you can't click in the blank Body Text paragraph, click in the "Participants" paragraph, and then press the ↑ key.

2. In the expanded Master Document group, click the **Insert** button. The Insert Subdocument dialog box, which is similar to the Open dialog box, opens.

3. If necessary, navigate to the location where you are storing your files.

4. Click the file **NP_WD_10_Patrons.docx**, and then click **Open**. The file is inserted as a subdocument at the location of the insertion point (just above the section break above the heading "Participants"). Note that like the created subdocuments, the inserted subdocument has a Continuous section break after it. However, it has a Next Page section break before it.

5. Change the Zoom level to **90%**, scroll so that you can see the entire Corporate Patrons section and the beginning of the Participants section, and then compare your screen to Figure 10–8.

Figure 10–8	Inserted subdocument

> **Trouble?** If there is only one Continuous section break below the inserted subdocument, click the Undo button ↺ on the Quick Access Toolbar, and then repeat Steps 1 through 4, making sure in Step 1 to click in the empty blank Body Text paragraph above the section break.

▶ **6.** Change the Zoom level back to **120%**, and then scroll down so you can see the "Recommendations" heading.

▶ **7.** Click in the blank Body Text paragraph above the "Recommendations" heading. This is where you'll insert the document created by Marie Choi, NP_WD_10_Presenters, as a subdocument.

▶ **8.** At the insertion point, insert the document **NP_WD_10_Presenters** as a subdocument. The document is inserted as a subdocument with a Next Page section break before it and a Continuous section break after it.

Next, you will save the master document with the subdocuments.

▶ **9.** On the Quick Access Toolbar, click the **Save** button 🖫. The NP_WD_10_ Master file is now saved as a master document with four subdocuments.

Examining Subdocument Links

The master document NP_WD_10_Master now contains four subdocuments—or, more precisely, links to four subdocuments. Even though you can manipulate the subdocuments in the master document, the text of these subdocuments is stored in the NP_WD_10_Patrons, Participants, NP_WD_10_Presenters, and Recommendations files, and not in the NP_WD_10_Master file. When the subdocuments are displayed or expanded, you can see the text of the subdocuments. When the subdocuments are collapsed, you see only the hyperlink to the subdocuments. When the link to a subdocument is displayed, the lock icon 🔒 appears next to the subdocument icon 🗎. This means you cannot modify the link text.

Note that because the subdocuments are linked to the master document, you should not rename or move the subdocument files. If you do, the link between the master and subdocuments will be broken.

You will examine the links now.

To view the subdocument links:

▶ **1.** In the Master Document group, click the **Collapse Subdocuments** button. The button you clicked changes to the Expand Subdocuments button, and the document scrolls to the beginning.

▶ **2.** Scroll down until you see the links at the end of the document. See Figure 10–9.

Figure 10–9   Links to subdocuments

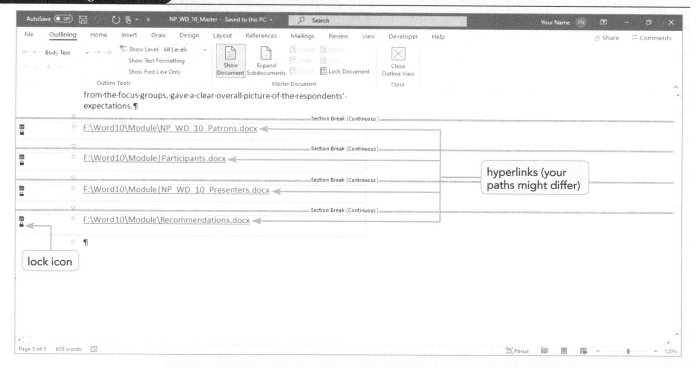

3. In the Master Document group, click the **Expand Subdocuments** button. The button changes back to the Collapse Subdocuments button, and the document scrolls back to the beginning.

4. Scroll down so that you can see that the text of the subdocuments appears in the master document again.

Insight

Splitting and Merging Subdocuments

If one subdocument becomes too long and unwieldy, or if you want two people to work on what is currently one subdocument, you can split the subdocument by dividing it into two subdocument files. On the other hand, if your master document contains adjacent subdocuments that are fairly short and simple with few graphics or tables, it's sometimes helpful to merge the subdocuments. When you merge subdocuments, Word inserts the contents of the second subdocument into the first one. Then when you save the master document, the first subdocument file contains the contents of both subdocuments. The second subdocument file remains on your disk but is no longer used by the master document. You could delete this file without affecting your master document.

To split a subdocument, select the heading you want to split into its own subdocument by clicking the plus sign next to the heading, and then in the Master Document group on the Outlining tab, click the Split button. To merge two adjacent subdocuments, click the subdocument icon next to the first subdocument, press and hold SHIFT, click the subdocument icon next to the second subdocument, and then release SHIFT. Then, in the Master Document group on the Outlining tab, click the Merge button.

Unlinking a Subdocument

You can unlink a subdocument and incorporate the content into the master document. This decreases the number of subdocuments but increases the size of the master document. The removed subdocument file still exists, but the master document file can no longer access it. You can delete this unused subdocument file without affecting the master document.

Bailey decides that the short Recommendations subdocument doesn't need to be a subdocument. She asks you to unlink this content so it is stored in the master document rather than in the subdocument.

To unlink the Recommendations subdocument:

▶ **1.** Next to the Level 1 heading "Recommendations," click the **subdocument** icon 🖳 to select the entire Recommendations subdocument.

▶ **2.** On the Outlining tab, in the Master Document group, click the **Unlink** button. The Recommendations subdocument is unlinked from the master document, and the text of the subdocument becomes part of the master document again.

▶ **3.** Save the changes to the master document.

▶ **4.** Close the NP_WD_10_Master document, but do not close Word.

Reopening a Master Document

When you open a master document that has one or more subdocuments, Word doesn't open the subdocuments or display their text in the master document. Instead, the hyperlinks to the subdocuments appear in the master document. In order to see the text of the subdocuments in the master document, you must expand them in Outline view.

You'll reopen the master document and expand the subdocuments now.

To reopen the NP_WD_10_Master master document and expand the subdocuments:

▶ **1.** Open the **NP_WD_10_Master** document.

▶ **2.** Scroll to page 5. The master document opened with the three subdocuments collapsed to their links. Notice on the status bar that the document is currently six pages long.

Trouble? If, instead of dark orange underlined hyperlinks, you see code that begins with "{HYPERLINK ...," press ALT+F9 to hide the field codes and display the actual hyperlinks.

Now that you have opened the master document, you need to expand the subdocuments. As with all the master document commands, you must be in Outline view to expand subdocuments.

To expand subdocuments:

▶ **1.** Switch to Outline view.

▶ **2.** On the Outlining tab, in the Master Document group, click the **Show Document** button, and then, if necessary, scroll down so that you can see the three subdocument links above the "Recommendations" heading. Notice that the lock icon 🔒 appears next to each subdocument link. Collapsed subdocuments are always locked.

▶ **3.** In the Master Document group, click the **Expand Subdocuments** button, and then scroll down until you can see that the text of the subdocuments replaced the links.

You have learned how to manipulate subdocuments within a master document. In the next session, you'll add numbers to the headings in the document, add numbered captions to objects in the document, and add cross-references to those captions. Then you will insert an endnote, create a chart in the document, restrict editing so that all changes are tracked with the Track Changes feature, check the document for hidden information, and check the document for accessibility.

Insight

Splitting a Window

To examine two sections of a document at the same time, you can use the Split Window command or the New Window command. To split a window, click the View tab, and then in the Window group, click the Split button. This adds a double horizontal line across the screen, splitting the screen into two windows. You can then scroll in either window to view any part of the document. The other window will not scroll, allowing you to view a different part of the document in the second window. In the Window group on the View tab, the Split button changes to the Remove Split button. To remove the split, you click the Remove Split button.

When you split a window, there is still only one ribbon at the top of the screen. Another way to examine two parts of a document at once is to click the New Window button in the Window group on the View tab. When you do this, a second copy of the document is opened in a new window. The ribbon is displayed at the top of both windows. To view the open Word windows one on top of another, click the Arrange All button in the Window group on the View tab.

Review

Session 10.1 Quick Check

1. What is a master document?

2. What is a subdocument?

3. What are three advantages of using a master document to manage long documents, rather than working with separate, smaller documents?

4. Describe the two ways to create a master document.

5. What happens after you create a subdocument from text in a master document and you save the new master document?

6. Is the text of a subdocument stored in the master document?

7. Describe how to remove a subdocument from a master document.

Session 10.2 Visual Overview:

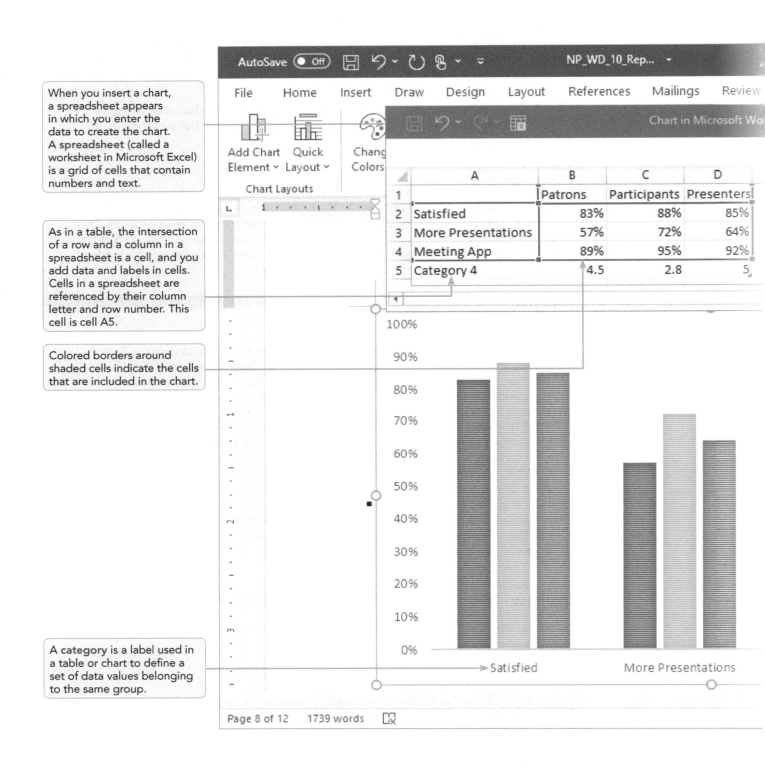

When you insert a chart, a spreadsheet appears in which you enter the data to create the chart. A spreadsheet (called a worksheet in Microsoft Excel) is a grid of cells that contain numbers and text.

As in a table, the intersection of a row and a column in a spreadsheet is a cell, and you add data and labels in cells. Cells in a spreadsheet are referenced by their column letter and row number. This cell is cell A5.

Colored borders around shaded cells indicate the cells that are included in the chart.

A category is a label used in a table or chart to define a set of data values belonging to the same group.

Creating a Chart

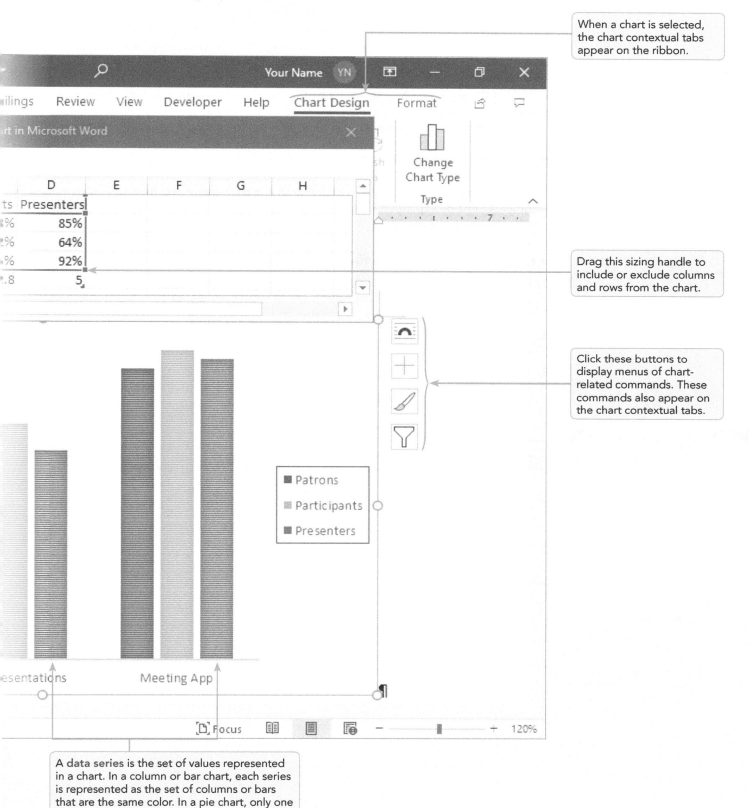

When a chart is selected, the chart contextual tabs appear on the ribbon.

Drag this sizing handle to include or exclude columns and rows from the chart.

Click these buttons to display menus of chart-related commands. These commands also appear on the chart contextual tabs.

A data series is the set of values represented in a chart. In a column or bar chart, each series is represented as the set of columns or bars that are the same color. In a pie chart, only one data series is represented.

Adding Numbers to Headings

Bailey wants you to give each heading a number—for example, "1. Executive Summary" and "2. Overview." You could manually insert the numbers before each heading, but if you had to add, reorder, or delete a heading, you would need to manually change all the numbers. Instead, you can number the parts of a document by automatically numbering the paragraphs that have an outline level. This feature has several advantages:

- **Automatic sequential numbering**—The heading numbers are maintained in consecutive order, even if you add, delete, or move a section.
- **Numbering across subdocuments**—The same-level headings in subdocuments in the master document are numbered consecutively.
- **Consistent style**—The heading numbers in subdocuments have the number style specified in the master document.

Note that when you use automatic numbering in a master document, the subdocuments must be expanded in order for the headings to be numbered properly.

To number headings automatically in the master document:

1. If you took a break after the previous session, open the **NP_WD_10_Master** document from the folder where you are saving your files, switch to Outline view, and then expand the subdocuments.

2. Scroll so that the heading "List of Figures" is at the top of the window, and then click anywhere in the heading "Executive Summary."

3. On the ribbon, click the **Home** tab, and then in the Paragraph group, click the **Multilevel List** button. The Multilevel List menu opens. The List Library contains four list styles that can be used with headings. See Figure 10–10.

Figure 10–10 **Multilevel list styles**

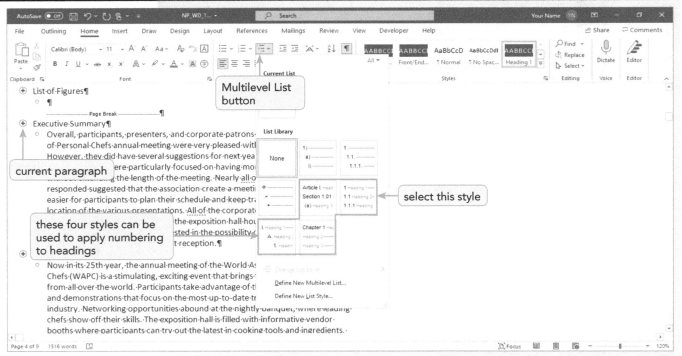

Bailey wants to use the numbering style that shows a number followed by "Heading 1." This style is sometimes called the legal paragraph numbering style.

4. Click the last style in the second row of the List Library. The numbers are applied to the document headings, and a sample of the numbering style is now included as part of the heading styles in the Style gallery.

Each Level 1 heading from the insertion point to the end of the document (that is, each heading formatted in the Heading 1 style) has a single number. The numbers assigned to the Level 2 headings consist of the number of the Level 1 heading just above it, followed by a period, and then a sequential number. The "List of Figures" heading is also numbered. This is because the "List of Figures" heading is formatted with a custom style named Front/End Matter Heading that is based on the Heading 1 style. See Figure 10–11.

Figure 10–11   **Master document in Outline view showing numbered headings**

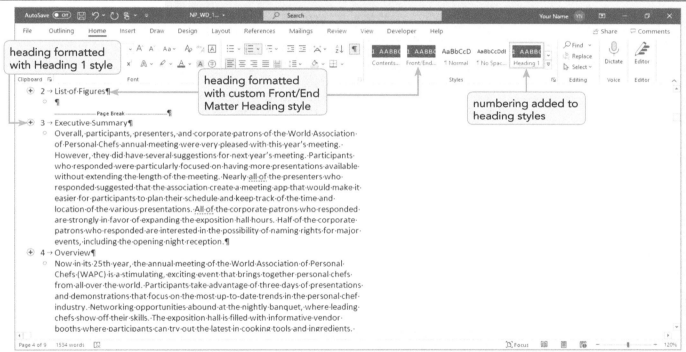

Bailey wants you to customize the numbering format so that each number is followed by a period.

5. Click the **Multilevel List** button, and then click **Define New Multilevel List**. The Define new Multilevel list dialog box opens. See Figure 10–12.

Figure 10–12	Define new Multilevel list dialog box

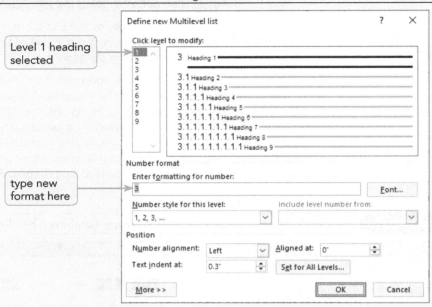

Level 1 heading selected

type new format here

You want to change the default setting "1" for Heading 1 styles to "1." (with a period following the number) and change the default setting for Heading 2 styles to "1.1." (with a period following the second number).

6. In the Click level to modify list, make sure 1 is selected. In the Enter formatting for number box, the number 3 appears because the current paragraph in the document is numbered 3.

7. In the Enter formatting for number box, click to the right of the number 3, and then type a period.

8. In the Click level to modify list, click **2**.

9. In the Enter formatting for number box, click to the right of 3.1, and then type a period after the 1.

10. Click **OK**. The numbers next to the headings change to include periods after each number. Notice the Heading 1 and Heading 2 styles in the Style gallery in the Styles group on the Home tab have been updated to reflect the new number style.

Tip

To restart or continue numbering in a numbered list or to set the starting value, select the list, click the Numbering arrow, click Set Numbering Value, and then select the options you want.

The numbering you defined in the Define new Multilevel list dialog box is applied to paragraphs using a built-in heading style, such as Heading 1 and Heading 2. This includes the "Contents" heading because the Contents Heading style that you created is based on the List of Figures style, which is based on the Heading 1 style.

Bailey does not want either the "Contents" or "List of Figures" headings to be numbered with the rest of the headings in the document because they are not really part of the document outline; they are part of the front matter. To fix this, you will modify the style definition of the Front/End Matter Heading and the Contents Heading styles to remove the numbering from these headings.

To modify the style definitions:

▶ **1.** On the Home tab, in the Styles group, right-click the **Contents Heading** style (it appears as Contents… in the Style gallery), and then click **Modify** on the shortcut menu. The Modify Style dialog box opens.

▶ **2.** Click the **Format** button, and then click **Numbering**. The Numbering and Bullets dialog box opens with the Numbering tab selected.

▶ **3.** Click the **None** style to select it, if necessary.

▶ **4.** Click **OK**, and then click **OK** in the Modify Style dialog box. The Contents Heading style has been modified so that it does not include a number. You can see this in the Style gallery on the Home tab.

▶ **5.** Repeat Steps 1 through 4 for the Front/End Matter Heading style (it appears as Front/End… in the Style gallery). In the gallery, the Front/End Matter Heading style no longer has a number before the style name.

▶ **6.** Click the **Outlining** tab.

▶ **7.** In the Outline Tools group, click the **Show Level** arrow, click **Level 2**, and then scroll to see the top of the document. The "List of Figures" heading is no longer numbered. See Figure 10–13.

Figure 10–13 **Numbering removed from the contents and List of Figures headings**

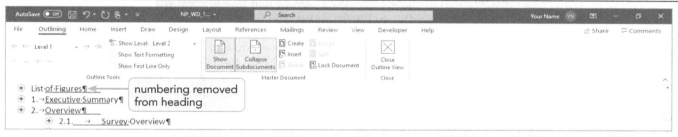

Make sure you save the changes so you have a final version of the master document.

▶ **8.** Save the changes to the document.

Note that as you edit a document that contains numbered headings, heading numbers might sometimes disappear from some headings. If that happens, select the affected heading, and then apply the correct heading style from the Style gallery.

You can continue to work with the master document, but Bailey tells you that she has all the updated documents from her team members, so you will unlink all of the subdocuments.

To unlink all of the subdocuments:

▶ **1.** Save the document as **NP_WD_10_Report** in the location specified by your instructor.

▶ **2.** Next to the heading "3. Corporate Patrons," click the **subdocument** icon ▦.

▶ **3.** In the Master Document group, click the **Unlink** button. The subdocument is unlinked from the master document, and the text of the subdocument becomes part of the master document.

▶ **4.** Unlink the subdocument whose first heading is "4. Participants," and then unlink the subdocument whose first heading is "5. Presenters."

▶ **5.** On the Outlining tab, in the Close group, click the **Close Outline View** button.

▶ **6.** Save the changes to the document.

Inserting Numbered Captions

A figure is any kind of illustration, such as a photograph, chart, map, or graph. You can add captions below figures using automatic figure numbering. A **caption** consists of a label, such as "Figure," "Fig.," or "Table," and a number, and usually a description of the figure. When you create captions using the Insert Caption command, the caption is numbered automatically using the Seq field, which inserts an automatic sequence number. For example, the first figure is numbered Figure 1, the second is numbered Figure 2, and so on. If you later insert a figure before an existing figure, move a figure, or reorder the parts of the document, the figure numbers in the captions renumber automatically.

When you add a caption to an inline object, the caption is inserted as text in a new paragraph. When you add a caption to a floating object, it is created inside a text box without a border, and the text wrap on the text box containing the caption is the same as text wrap on the figure it is connected to; that is, if the text wrap on a floating object is Square, the text wrap on the text box containing the caption will be Square as well.

When creating a caption, you can choose to number the captions sequentially as they appear in the document (1, 2, 3, etc.), or you can include the number of the first heading above the caption that is formatted with the Heading 1 style. For example, you could use 1-1 for the first caption under the heading "1. Executive Summary," 1-2 for the second caption under the heading "1. Executive Summary," and so on. The captions for figures in the "2. Overview" section would then be numbered 2-1, 2-2, and so on. This type of numbering is sometimes called double-numbering.

Reference

Creating Captions

- Select the table or figure to which you want to apply a caption.
- On the References tab, in the Captions group, click the Insert Caption button.
- Click the Label arrow, and then click the type of object to which you're applying the caption (for example, figure or table), or click the New Label button, type a new label, and then click OK.
- Click the Position arrow, and then click the option to specify whether you want the caption to appear above or below the figure.
- To use double-numbering that includes the number of the preceding Heading 1 heading, click the Numbering button, select the Include chapter number check box in the Caption Numbering dialog box, and then click OK.
- Click after the number in the Caption box, and then type a caption.
- Click OK.

Bailey included figures to illustrate key points in the report. In section "2.3. Survey Coordinator," she inserted a picture of Anthony Santana, the president of Marketfield Research Associates. Also, in section "6. Recommendations," she added a SmartArt graphic illustrating the survey's conclusions. Bailey wants to include captions for each figure so that she can refer to them in the text.

To create a numbered caption:

▶ **1.** Scroll until you can see the heading "2.3. Survey Coordinator" and the photo of Anthony Santana on page 5. The picture is below the heading "2.3. Survey Coordinator."

▶ **2.** Click the photo of Anthony to select it. This photo is a floating object with Square text wrapping.

▶ **3.** On the ribbon, click the **References** tab, and then in the Captions group, click the **Insert Caption** button. The Caption dialog box opens. The insertion point is blinking to the right of "Figure 1" in the Caption box. See Figure 10–14.

Figure 10–14	Caption dialog box

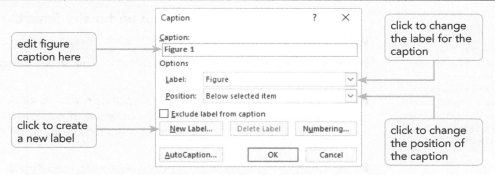

▶ **4.** In the Caption box, type **:** (a colon), press **SPACEBAR**, and then type **Anthony Santana**.

▶ **5.** In the Caption dialog box, click the **New Label** button. The New Label dialog box opens with the insertion point in the Label box.

▶ **6.** Type **Fig.** (including the period), and then click **OK**. The label in the Caption and Label boxes changes to "Fig."

▶ **7.** Click **OK**. The numbered caption is inserted below the figure as a floating text box without a border and with Square text wrapping. See Figure 10–15.

Figure 10–15	Photo with a caption in a floating text box

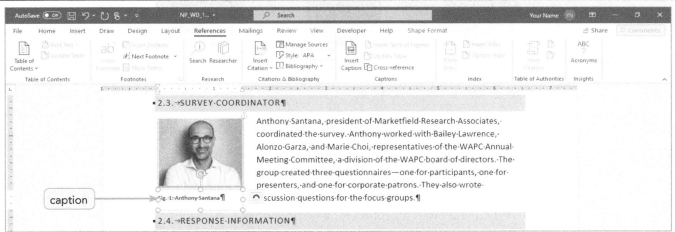

Rido/Shutterstock.com

You can see that the figure number in the caption is a field by displaying the field code.

▶ **8.** In the figure caption, right-click **1**, and then click **Toggle Field Codes** on the shortcut menu. The field code for the number 1 in the caption appears.

▶ **9.** Right-click the field code, and then click **Toggle Field Codes** to display the number instead of the field code.

Now, using the same procedure, you'll insert another numbered caption under the SmartArt graphic illustrating the survey's conclusions.

Tip

To change the colors of SmartArt shapes, use the Change Colors button in the SmartArt Styles group on the SmartArt Design tab. To apply styles or other effects, use the styles in the SmartArt Styles group on the SmartArt Design tab or the buttons in the Shape Styles group on the Format tab.

To insert a numbered caption under the SmartArt graphic:

▶ **1.** Scroll so that you can see the SmartArt graphic at the top of page 9.

▶ **2.** Click the SmartArt graphic to select it. The SmartArt graphic is an inline object.

▶ **3.** On the References tab, in the Captions group, click the **Insert Caption** button. The Caption dialog box opens with Fig. 2 in the Caption box because this will be the second object in the document identified with the label "Fig."

▶ **4.** Change the caption in the Caption box to read **Fig. 2: Survey conclusions** and then click **OK**. The caption is inserted below the SmartArt graphic in a new paragraph. Compare your screen to Figure 10–16.

Figure 10–16   SmartArt graphic with a caption in a new paragraph

▶ **5.** Save the changes to the document.

If you need to modify a caption after it has been inserted, you can edit it as you would any other text in the document.

When you insert a caption for a floating object, the caption is anchored to the same paragraph as the object. This means that if that paragraph moves, both the object and the caption move with it. When you insert a caption for an inline object, the formatting of the paragraph that contains the object changes so that the Keep with next option on the Line and Page Breaks tab in the Paragraph dialog box becomes selected.

Now that you have inserted figure captions for each illustration in the document, you will refer to each of them in the text. For that, you'll use cross-references.

Creating Cross-References

A **cross-reference** is a notation within a document that refers to a figure or table caption, to a heading, or to a footnote or an endnote. If you use the Cross-reference command to insert the reference to a caption and then the figures or tables are reordered, the cross-references will update also. This is because when you insert a cross-reference using the Cross-reference command in Word, a hidden bookmark is created to the item you are referencing and the Ref field is inserted to display the bookmarked item.

Reference

Creating Cross-References

- Move the insertion point to the location where you want to insert the cross-reference.
- Type the text preceding the cross-reference, such as "See" and a space.
- On the References tab, in the Captions group, click the Cross-reference button.
- In the Cross-reference dialog box, click the Reference type arrow, and then select the type of item you want to reference.
- Click the Insert reference to arrow, and then select the amount of information from the reference to be displayed in the cross-reference.
- In the For which list, click the item you want to reference.
- Click Insert to insert the cross-reference.
- Click Close to close the dialog box.

Bailey wants the figures in the report referenced within the text, so you'll insert cross-references to the two figures.

To insert a cross-reference to Figure 1:

▶ **1.** Scroll to page 5 so that you can see the heading "2.3. Survey Coordinator."

▶ **2.** In the paragraph below the "2.3. Survey Coordinator" heading, in the first line, click between "Santana" and the comma. This is where you will insert the first cross-reference.

▶ **3.** Press **SPACEBAR**, type **(see** and then press **SPACEBAR** again. The beginning of the edited sentence is now "Anthony Santana (see , president of...." Now you're ready to insert the automatically numbered cross-reference.

▶ **4.** On the References tab, in the Captions group, click the **Cross-reference** button. The Cross-reference dialog box opens. See Figure 10–17.

Figure 10–17   **Cross-reference dialog box showing numbered items**

numbered items (headings) in document displayed because Numbered item is selected as the Reference type

click to change the type of item to be referenced

Cross-reference   ?   ×

Reference type: Insert reference to:
Numbered item   ∨   Paragraph number   ∨
☑ Insert as hyperlink   ☐ Include above/below
   Separate numbers with [   ]
For which numbered item:
1. Executive Summary
2. Overview
  2.1. Survey Overview
  2.2. Survey Goals
  2.3. Survey Coordinator
  2.4. Response Information
3. Corporate Patrons
  3.1. Corporate Patrons Survey Responses
  3.2. Corporate Patrons Focus Group
4. Participants
  4.1. Participant Survey Responses
  4.2. Participant Focus Group Responses

                            Insert   Cancel

▶ **5.** Click the **Reference type** arrow, scroll down, and then click **Fig**. The bottom part of the dialog box changes to display the two figure captions in the document, and the Insert reference to box changes to Entire caption. The Insert as hyperlink check box is selected by default. This means you can press and hold CTRL, and then click the cross-reference in the document to jump to the item referenced. See Figure 10–18.

Figure 10–18   **Cross-reference dialog box showing captions for the label "Fig."**

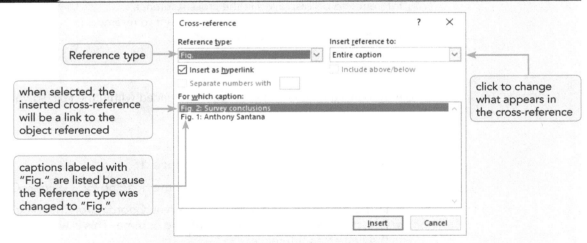

Reference type

Cross-reference   ?   ×

Reference type: Insert reference to:
Fig.   ∨   Entire caption   ∨
☑ Insert as hyperlink   ☐ Include above/below

when selected, the inserted cross-reference will be a link to the object referenced

   Separate numbers with [   ]
For which caption:
Fig. 2: Survey conclusions
Fig. 1: Anthony Santana

click to change what appears in the cross-reference

captions labeled with "Fig." are listed because the Reference type was changed to "Fig."

                            Insert   Cancel

You want the reference to the figure to list only the label "Fig." and the figure number, not the entire caption.

▶ **6.** Click the **Insert reference to** arrow, and then click **Only label and number**.

▶ **7.** In the For which caption list, click **Fig. 1: Anthony Santana**, and then click **Insert**. The cross-reference is inserted in the document. In the dialog box, Cancel changes to Close.

▶ **8.** Click **Close**, and then type **)** after the cross-reference in the document to close the parentheses. The phrase "(see Fig. 1)" appears in the report, so that the beginning of the sentence is "Anthony Santana (see Fig. 1), president of...."

> **Trouble?** If "Fig. 2" appears as the reference instead of "Fig. 1," you clicked the wrong item in the For which caption list in the Cross-reference dialog box. Delete the reference, and then repeat Steps 4 through 7, taking care to click Fig. 1: Anthony Santana in the list.

▶ **9.** In the first line below the heading "2.3. Survey Coordinator," point to **Fig. 1**. A ScreenTip appears telling you that you can press CTRL and click to use the link.

▶ **10.** Press and hold **CTRL**, and then click. The Fig. 1 label and figure number under the photo of Anthony Santana is selected.

The power of all automatic numbering features in Word—heading numbering, caption numbering, and cross-references—becomes evident when you edit a long document with many figures. Now you'll add cross-references to the other figure.

To insert another cross-reference:

Tip

To move SmartArt shapes, select a shape and then use one of the buttons in the Create Graphic group on the SmartArt Design tab or open the text pane, and move the items in the bulleted list.

▶ **1.** Scroll to the bottom of page 8, and in the last paragraph on the page (the paragraph below the "Recommendations" heading), click after the last sentence.

▶ **2.** Press **SPACEBAR**, type **(See** and then press **SPACEBAR**.

▶ **3.** In the Captions group, click the **Cross-reference** button. The Cross-reference dialog box opens, displaying the settings you used last. Fig. is selected in the Reference type box, and Only label and number is selected in the Insert reference to box. Fig. 2 is selected in the For which caption list because it is the first option in the list.

▶ **4.** Click **Insert**, and then click **Close**. The cross-reference to Fig. 2 is inserted.

▶ **5.** Type **.)** (a period followed by a closing parenthesis).

▶ **6.** Save the changes to the document.

Inserting an Endnote

As you know, an endnote is an explanatory comment or reference that appears at the end of a document. You know to look for an endnote if a reference marker appears next to text.

Bailey needs you to insert two endnotes in the report.

To insert endnotes:

▶ **1.** On page 8, in the last paragraph, position the insertion point after the period at the end of the second to last sentence (after "Therefore, we strongly recommend investigating vendors for such an app.").

Tip

To see the "i" more clearly, increase the Zoom level.

▶ **2.** On the References tab, in the Footnotes group, click the **Insert Endnote** button. The document scrolls to the end, and the insertion point appears next to "i" below a horizontal line at the end of the document. The "i" is inside a dotted-line rectangle and is hard to see.

▶ **3.** Type **The Committee recommends hiring First Labs to develop the app.** (including the period). See Figure 10–19.

Figure 10–19 Endnote inserted at the end of the document

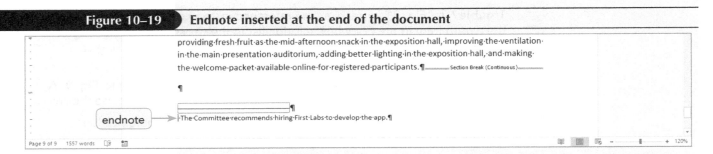

4. Double-click the endnote number **i**. The document scrolls to page 8, and the endnote reference mark is selected.

   Trouble? If you have difficulty double-clicking the endnote number, scroll to page 8 so that you can see the endnote reference mark, and then continue with Step 5.

5. Move the pointer on top of the endnote reference mark on page 8. The pointer changes to the reference mark pointer ⌷, and the text of the endnote you typed appears in a ScreenTip above the reference mark.

6. Go to page 5, and then in the paragraph below the "2.3. Survey Coordinator" heading, place the insertion point after the period after the second to last sentence (after "The group created three questionnaires—one for participants, one for presenters, and one for corporate patrons.").

7. In the Footnotes group, click the **Insert Endnote** button. The document scrolls to the end, and a new endnote numbered "i" is inserted above the existing endnote. The new endnote appears first because its reference appears earlier in the document. The existing endnote was renumbered "ii".

8. Type **The questionnaires are available online at www.wapc.example. com/questionnaires.** and then press **SPACEBAR**. The webpage address you typed changes to a link after you press SPACEBAR.

Inserting a Chart

The terms "chart" and "graph" often are used interchangeably; however, they have distinct meanings. A **chart** is a graphic that represents data using bars, columns, dots, lines, or other symbols to make the data easier to understand and to make it easier to see the relationships among the data. A **graph** shows the relationship between variables along two axes or reference lines. Although charts show relationships, they don't use a coordinate system like graphs do.

Despite these differences in the definitions, in Word, a chart is any visual depiction of data in a spreadsheet, even if the result is more properly referred to as a graph (such as a line graph). Refer to the Session 10.2 Visual Overview for more information about creating charts in Word.

As you know, you can insert a chart created in Microsoft Excel into any Word document. However, you can also create a chart from within a Word document by clicking the Chart button in the Illustrations group on the Insert tab. Doing so will open a window containing a spreadsheet with sample data, and a sample chart will appear in the document. You can then edit the sample data in the spreadsheet so that your data will be represented in the chart in the document.

Reference

Creating a Chart

- On the Insert tab, in the Illustrations group, click the Chart button to open the Insert Chart dialog box.
- In the list on the left, click the desired chart type.
- In the row of styles, click the desired chart style.
- Click OK.
- In the spreadsheet that opens, enter the data that you want to plot.
- In the spreadsheet window, click the Close button.

Bailey would like you to add a chart in section "2.1. Survey Overview" to illustrate some of the survey responses.

To create a chart in the survey document:

▶ **1.** Scroll to the middle of page 5 so that the last line of the paragraph above the yellow highlighted placeholder text [INSERT CHART] is at the top of the document window, and then delete [**INSERT CHART**] (but do not delete the paragraph mark).

▶ **2.** On the ribbon, click the **Insert** tab, and then in the Illustrations group, click the **Chart** button. The Insert Chart dialog box opens. See Figure 10–20.

Figure 10–20   **Insert chart dialog box**

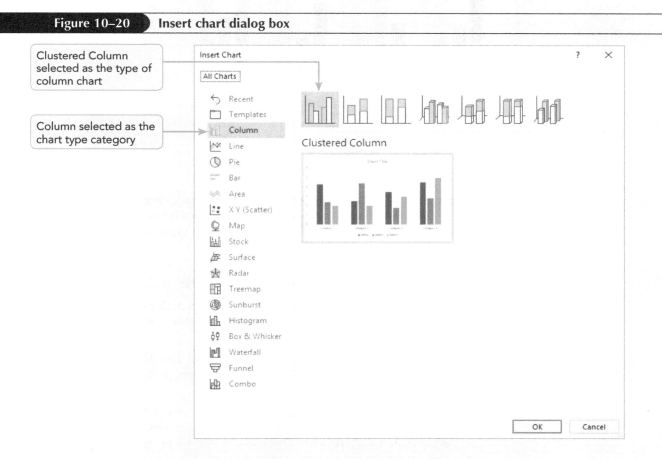

Clustered Column selected as the type of column chart

Column selected as the chart type category

Column is selected in the list of chart type categories on the left, and Clustered Column is selected in the row of column chart types at the top and is shown in the preview area. You want to create a column chart, so you do not need to make any changes.

▶ **3.** Click **OK**. A sample column chart is inserted in the document, and a small spreadsheet (sometimes called a datasheet) opens above the chart. The colored borders around the cells in the spreadsheet indicate which cells of data are included in the chart. See Figure 10–21.

Figure 10–21	Spreadsheet containing sample data for a column chart

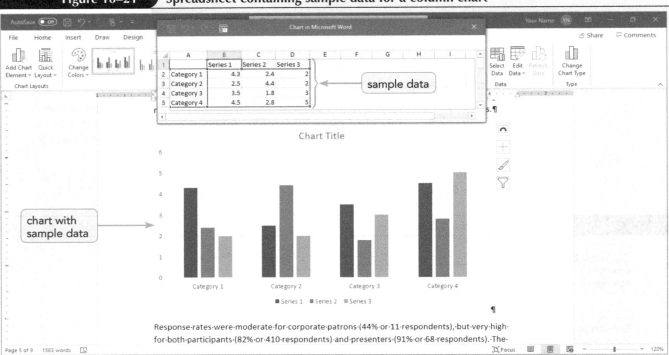

To create the chart for Bailey's report, you must edit the sample data in the spreadsheet. When you work with a worksheet, the selected cell is the **active cell**. Data you enter appears in the active cell. The active cell has a green border around it.

To enter row and column labels in the chart:

▶ **1.** In the spreadsheet, click cell **A2**. This is now the active cell. The first category will show the percentage of respondents who answered yes, they were satisfied with this year's meeting.

▶ **2.** Type **Satisfied**, and then press **ENTER**. The name of the first category in the chart changes to reflect the new row label that you just typed, and cell A3 is now the active cell.

▶ **3.** In cell A3, type **More Presentations**, and then press **ENTER**. This category will show the percentage of respondents who answered yes, they would like more presentations next year. The name of the second category in the chart changes to reflect the new row label that you just typed, and cell A4 is now the active cell. In cell A3, you can no longer see all of the text that you typed.

The column is not wide enough to display all of the text when the cells to its right contain data.

▶ **4.** In cell A4, type **Meeting App**, and then press **ENTER**. This category will show the percentage of respondents who answered yes, they would like a meeting app to make it easier for participants to plan their schedule and keep track of the time and location of the presentations.

▶ **5.** Click cell **B1**, type **Patrons**, and then press **TAB**. The active cell is now cell C1, and the chart legend changes to reflect the new column label.

▶ **6.** In cell C1, type **Participants**, and then press **TAB**.

▶ **7.** In cell D1, type **Presenters**, and then press **ENTER**. Cell B2 is the active cell.

Next, you will widen columns A and C so that you can see the row and column labels.

▶ **8.** Move the pointer on top of the column border between the column A and column B headings—that is, between the boxes containing the column headings A and B—so that the pointer changes to the resize column width pointer ↔, and then double-click. Column A widens to fit the widest entry in the column—the text in cell A3.

▶ **9.** Move the pointer on top of the column border between the column C and column D headings, and then double-click. Column C widens to fit the widest entry in the column—the text in cell C1. See Figure 10–22.

Figure 10–22   **Row and column labels replaced**

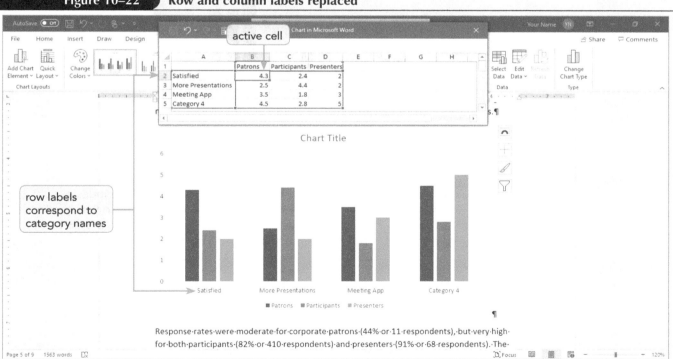

Now you need to enter the data for your chart. You will enter data in cells B2 through D4.

To enter data in the spreadsheet:

▶ **1.** In cell B2, type **83%**, press **ENTER**, type **57%** in cell B3, press **ENTER**, type **89%** in cell B4, and then press **ENTER**. The column chart in the document changes to reflect the new data.

▶ **2.** Click cell **C2**, type **88%**, press **ENTER**, type **72%**, press **ENTER**, type **95%**, and then press **ENTER**.

▶ **3.** Click cell **D2**, type **85%**, press **ENTER**, type **64%**, press **ENTER**, type **92%**, and then press **ENTER**. Compare your screen to Figure 10–23.

| Figure 10–23 | Data entered into the spreadsheet |

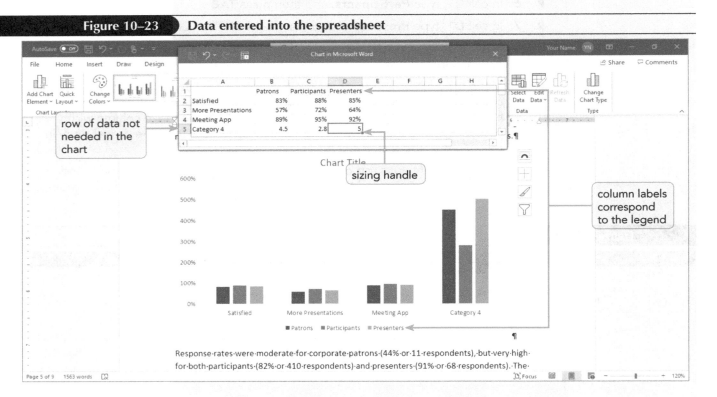

You have entered all the data for the chart. However, the chart still includes a category titled Category 4. There are only three categories in this chart, so you need to exclude the last row of data in the spreadsheet. When you remove it, the largest value on the vertical axis will be 100%, and the chart will be much clearer.

To remove the data in row 5 from the chart:

▶ **1.** Move the pointer on top of the small blue sizing handle at the lower-right corner of cell D5 so that the pointer changes to ↖.

▶ **2.** Drag the sizing handle up to the bottom of cell D4. The colored border shading indicating which cells will be included in the chart changes to show that row 5 is no longer included. The column chart now includes only three categories, and the highest value on the vertical axis is 100%. See Figure 10–24.

Figure 10–24   Chart after excluding row 5

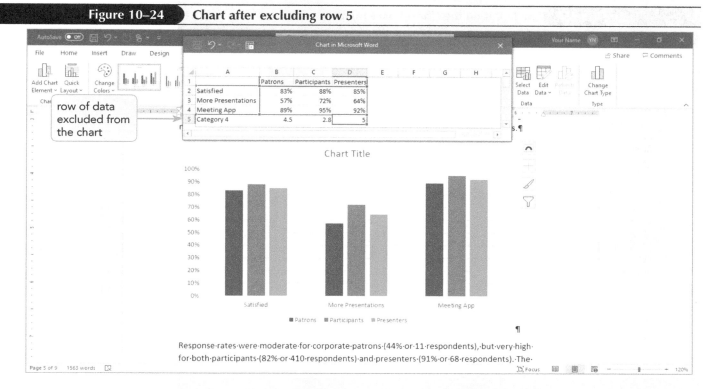

> **3.** In the spreadsheet title bar, click the **Close** button ✕ to close the spreadsheet. The new chart is selected in the document, and two chart contextual tabs appear on the ribbon.

Once the chart is in the document, you can modify it by changing or formatting the various elements of the chart. For example, you can apply a chart style to your chart to change its look. You can also edit or remove the title of a chart. Bailey wants you to modify the chart by applying a style, deleting the title, and repositioning the legend.

To change the chart style:

> **1.** To the right of the chart, click the **Chart Styles** button ▱. In the menu that opens, the Style tab is selected. This tab lists the same chart styles that appear in the Chart Styles group on the Chart Design tab on the ribbon. See Figure 10–25.

Figure 10–25   Style tab on the Chart Styles menu

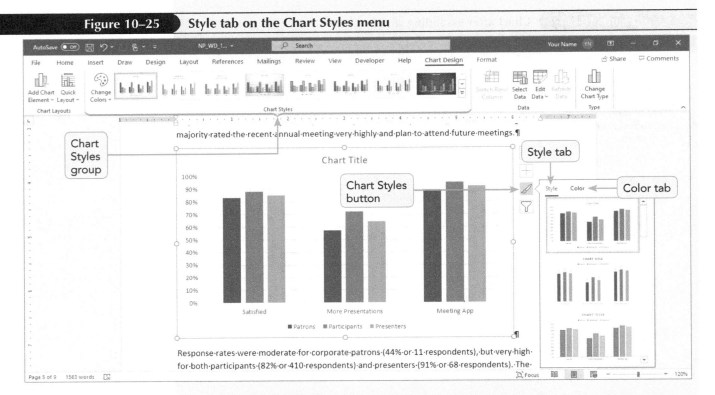

2. On the menu, click the **Style 3** style. The columns in the chart now have faint horizontal stripes, and the legend appears at the top of the chart.

3. On the menu, click the **Color** tab. A list of color palettes for the chart appears.

4. Click the **Colorful Palette 2** palette. The third column in each category changes to gray.

You don't need a chart title because this chart will have a numbered figure caption, so you will remove it. You will also reposition the legend so it appears on the right side of the chart rather than above it.

To remove the chart title and reposition the legend:

1. To the right of the chart, click the **Chart Elements** button ⊞. The Chart Elements menu opens to the left of the chart. See Figure 10–26.

Figure 10–26   Chart Elements menu

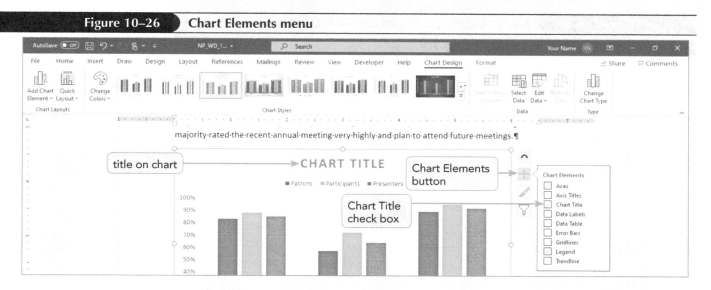

2. On the menu, click the **Chart Title** check box to remove the checkmark. The chart title is removed from the chart.

3. On the menu, point to **Legend**. A small arrow ▶ appears.

4. Click the **arrow** ▶ to open the Legend submenu. See Figure 10–27.

Figure 10–27   Legend submenu on the Chart Elements menu

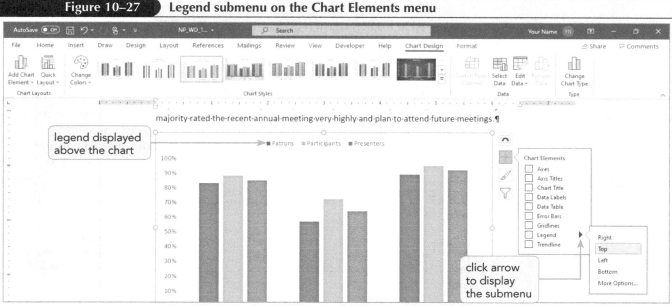

5. In the submenu, click **Right**. The legend now appears to the right of the chart.

6. At the bottom of the Legend submenu, click **More Options**. The Format Legend pane opens with the Legend Options button 📊 selected on the Legend Options tab.

7. Click the **Fill & Line** button 🖌, and then click **Border** to expand the list of border options. See Figure 10–28.

Figure 10–28   **Format Legend pane with the Fill & Line button selected on the Legend Options tab**

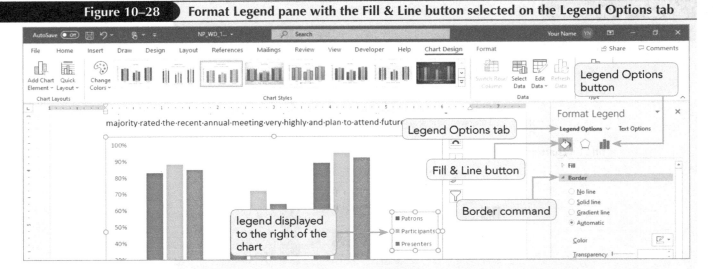

8. Click the **Solid line** option button. A solid line border is added around the legend in the chart.

9. At the top of the Format Legend pane, click the **Close** button ⊠, and then click a blank area of the chart to deselect the legend, but keep the chart selected. Now you can see the border that you added around the legend.

Finally, you need to insert a caption under the chart. Recall that this chart was inserted between the photo of Anthony Santana and the SmartArt graphic.

To insert a figure caption under the chart:

1. On the ribbon, click the **References** tab, and then in the Captions group, click the **Insert Caption** button. The Caption dialog box opens, and Fig. 2 appears in the Caption box. This is because you are inserting this caption before the previously numbered Fig. 2. The old Fig. 2 is renumbered as Fig. 3.

   Trouble? If Figure 2 appears in the Caption box, click the Label arrow, and then click Fig.

2. Change the figure caption to **Fig. 2: Chart showing percentage of respondents who said "yes" to questions** and then click **OK**. Because the chart is an inline object, the caption appears in a new paragraph below the chart.

3. Scroll to page 9 to see that the caption under the SmartArt graphic has been renumbered as Fig. 3.

4. Scroll up to see the last sentence on page 8. The cross-reference to Fig. 3 did not update.

5. In the last sentence on page 8, right-click the cross-reference, and then on the shortcut menu, click **Update Field**. The cross-reference is updated so it is "(See Fig. 3.)."

The cross-reference fields in a document update automatically when you close and then reopen the file. You could also press CTRL+A to select all of the text in the document, and then press F9 to update all fields in the selected text.

Now you need to insert a cross-reference to the chart.

To insert a cross-reference to the chart:

▶ **1.** Scroll so that the "2.4. Response Information" heading on page 5 is at the top of the document window, and then click after the last sentence in the paragraph below the heading (which ends with "…and plan to attend future meetings.").

▶ **2.** Press **SPACEBAR**, type **The chart shown in** and then press **SPACEBAR**.

▶ **3.** On the References tab, in the Captions group, click the **Cross-reference** button. The Cross-reference dialog box opens. Fig. is selected as the Reference type, Only label and number appears in the Insert reference to box, and Fig. 2 is selected in the For which caption list.

▶ **4.** Click **Insert**, and then click **Close**. The cross-reference to Fig. 2 is inserted.

▶ **5.** Press **SPACEBAR**, and then type **illustrates the percentage of respondents who responded "yes" to the questions asking if they were satisfied with this year's meeting, if they want more presentations offered next year, and if they want a meeting app.** (including the period).

▶ **6.** Save the changes to the document.

Next, you'll help Bailey control the kinds of changes the other members of the board of directors can make to the report.

Insight

Inserting Equations

If you need to add a complex mathematical equation to a document, you can use the Equation button in the Symbols group on the Insert tab. Click the Equation arrow, and then click one of the common equations on the menu to insert that equation. If the equation you want to enter is not listed in the menu, click the Equation button to insert an equation text box, and then type the equation, using the buttons in the Symbols group on the Equation Design tab to insert mathematical symbols, such as the square root sign ($\sqrt{\ }$). You can also click buttons in the Structures group on the Equation Design tab to insert mathematical structures such as fractions ($\frac{3}{4}$ or ¾) or the integral sign, which is used in calculus ($\int$).

You can also click the Ink Equation button in the Tools group on the Equation Design tab to open the Math Input Control window. Using a stylus or your finger if you have a touchscreen device or using the pointer, drag to write the equation in the window. When you are finished, click Insert to close the window and insert the equation you drew in the equation text box in the document.

Restricting Editing to Allow Only Tracked Changes or Comments

Because Bailey has already done a fair amount of work on the document, she'd like to retain some control over the kinds of changes the other writers make to it. Therefore, she decides to restrict editing in the document. As you know, you can set editing restrictions for a document. In addition to restricting users to only filling in content controls and form fields, you can prevent users from making formatting changes. When specifying formatting restrictions, you can limit formatting changes in the document to a specific list of styles. You can also prevent users from changing the theme or changing the Quick Style Set. You can force all changes to be tracked, or you can restrict users so that the only type of change they can make is to add comments.

When specifying editing restrictions, you can choose from the following options:

- **Tracked changes**—Allows users to make any editing changes as well as any of the formatting changes allowed by the formatting restrictions, but all changes are marked with revision marks
- **Comments**—Allows users to insert comments, but not to make any other changes
- **Filling in forms**—Allows users to fill in forms only
- **No changes (Read only)**—Allows users to read the document but not to make changes

You can also allow people you specify to edit parts or all of a document. After you select the check box to allow only a specific type of editing in the document, an Exceptions section appears in the Restrict Editing pane. Here, you can click the More users link and then select users who are allowed to edit the document.

When you apply editing restrictions to a document, you can choose to require a password in order to turn off the editing restrictions. If you are restricting editing in a document because you are concerned that someone might make unauthorized changes to the document, then you should definitely use a password. However, if you are restricting editing in a document that will be shared among a small group of colleagues, and you are using the feature only to ensure that all changes are tracked with revision marks, then a password typically isn't necessary.

It is important that you create passwords you can remember or record them in a secure location. If you protect a document with a password and then forget the password, there is no way to retrieve it.

Reference

Restricting Editing in a Document

- On the Review tab, in the Protect group, click the Restrict Editing button to open the Restrict Editing pane.
- To restrict formatting changes to text formatted with specific styles, select the Limit formatting to a selection of styles check box in the Formatting restrictions section, click Settings to open the Formatting Restrictions dialog box, deselect any style you want to prevent users from changing, and then click OK.
- To prevent users from changing the theme, click Settings in the Formatting restrictions section, select the Block Theme or Scheme switching check box, and then click OK.
- To prevent users from changing the style set, click Settings in the Formatting restrictions section, select the Block Quick Style Set switching check box, and then click OK.
- To specify editing restrictions, select the Allow only this type of editing in the document check box in the Editing restrictions section, click the arrow, and then click the editing restriction you want to apply.
- To allow specific people to edit part of the document, select the Allow only this type of editing in the document check box in the Editing restrictions section, select the part you want to allow them to edit, click the More users link in the Editing restrictions section, type the user's email address, click OK, and then select the check box next to the user's email address.
- In the Start enforcement section, click the Yes, Start Enforcing Protection button.
- If desired, in the Start Enforcing Protection dialog box, type a password in the Enter new password (optional) box and in the Reenter password to confirm box.
- Click OK.

Because Bailey wants to be able to see exactly what changes the other team members make to the report, she decides to protect the document by applying the Tracked changes editing restriction. You already have some experience working with the Track Changes feature, which marks additions, deletions, moved text, and formatting changes with revision marks.

Note that if you apply editing restrictions to a master document, those restrictions are not applied to the separate subdocument files. For example, if you restrict editing in a master document so that all changes are tracked, revision marks will appear in any expanded subdocuments. However, if you open the subdocuments in separate document windows, you can edit the subdocuments without tracking the revisions.

In addition to protecting the document using tracked changes, Bailey wants to apply one formatting restriction—in particular, she wants to block any user from changing the document theme. You're ready to protect the NP_WD_10_Report document.

To apply formatting and editing restrictions to the document:

▶ **1.** On the ribbon, click the **Review** tab, and then in the Protect group, click the **Restrict Editing** button. The Restrict Editing pane opens. Bailey wants to block users from changing the document theme.

▶ **2.** In the 1. Formatting restrictions section, click the **Settings** link to open the Formatting Restrictions dialog box. See Figure 10–29.

| Figure 10–29 | Restrict Editing pane and the Formatting Restrictions dialog box |

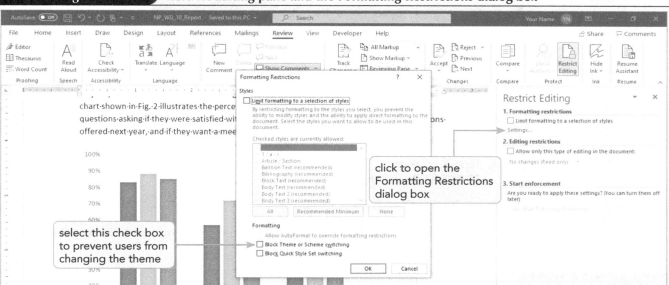

If you wanted to prevent others from modifying styles or applying direct formatting to the document, you would select the "Limit formatting to a selection of styles" check box, and then modify the Checked styles are currently allowed list so that only the styles users may modify are selected.

▶ **3.** Near the bottom of the dialog box, click the **Block Theme or Scheme switching** check box to select it, and then click **OK**. The Formatting Restrictions dialog box closes.

▶ **4.** In the Editing restrictions section of the Restrict Editing pane, click the **Allow only this type of editing in the document** check box.

Tip

To allow people you specify to edit parts or all of a document, select the Allow only this type of editing in the document check box, select the text they will be allowed to edit, select the check box below 2. Editing restrictions, click More users, type the person's email address in the dialog box, and then select that person's email address in the pane.

5. In the Editing restrictions section, click the **arrow**—which, by default, is set to No changes (Read only). In addition to the Filling in forms command that you used when you restricted an online form so that users could change only content controls, Tracked changes and Comments appear as options.

6. Click **Tracked changes**.

7. In the Start enforcement section, click the **Yes, Start Enforcing Protection** button. The Start Enforcing Protection dialog box opens. You will not set a password.

8. Click **OK**. The Restrict Editing pane changes to include the Stop Protection button.

9. In the Restrict Editing pane, click the **Close** button ☒.

Bailey asks you to revise the Executive Summary section. Because you restricted editing, your changes will be tracked.

To edit the document with restrictions:

1. On the Review tab, in the Tracking group, click the **Display for Review** arrow, and then click **All Markup**, if necessary.

2. Scroll to the top of page 4 so that you can see the heading "1. Executive Summary" and the paragraph below it. Bailey wants you to edit the beginning of the second sentence in the paragraph so it starts with "They did, however, have several suggestions…."

3. In the second sentence below the heading "1. Executive Summary," select **However**, the comma after it, and the space after the comma, and then press **DEL** twice. Because the document is protected for tracked changes, Word marks the selected text and the first character of the next word—the "t" in "they"—for deletion and adds a revision line in the margin.

4. Type **T**, click after "did" in the second line, type **,** (a comma), press **SPACEBAR**, and then type **however,** (including the comma).

5. On the ribbon, click the **Design** tab. In the Document Formatting group, the Themes button as well as the Colors, Fonts, and Effects buttons are unavailable because you blocked users from changing the document theme. See Figure 10–30.

Figure 10–30 **Restricted document after deleting text**

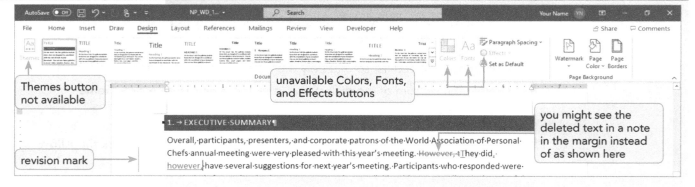

You'll now see what the document would look like if you accepted the revision—that is, if no revision marks appeared in the document.

To review the document with the revision accepted:

▶ **1.** On the ribbon, click the **Review** tab.

▶ **2.** In the Tracking group, click the **Display for Review** arrow, and then click **No Markup**. The revision marks are removed, and the document appears as it would if you had accepted the revisions.

It's helpful to use the No Markup setting to display the document as if all the revision marks have been accepted or rejected, without actually accepting or rejecting the revision marks. However, after you review the document using the No Markup setting, it's easy to forget to go back and accept or reject the revision marks. If you do forget, you might then accidentally send out a document that contains revision marks. Such a mistake could make you look unprofessional, or, even worse—depending on the nature of your revisions—inadvertently reveal sensitive information. To make sure a document doesn't contain any revision marks, or any other types of information that you don't want to reveal to readers of your document, you can use the Document Inspector. Before you do, you'll turn off the editing restrictions.

To turn off the editing and formatting restrictions:

▶ **1.** On the Review tab, in the Protect group, click the **Restrict Editing** button. The Restrict Editing pane opens.

▶ **2.** At the bottom of the pane, click the **Stop Protection** button. Because there is no password assigned, the Restrict Editing pane changes to show the restriction options, and the restrictions are immediately turned off. However, you still need to remove the formatting restrictions.

▶ **3.** In the 1. Formatting restrictions section, click the **Settings** link to open the Formatting Restrictions dialog box, click the **Block Theme or Scheme switching** check box to deselect it, and then click **OK** to close the dialog box.

▶ **4.** Close the Restrict Editing pane, and then save the changes to the document.

Proskills

Decision Making: Choosing When to Restrict Editing in a Document

It's not convenient or useful to restrict editing in every document you create. But if you plan to send a document to colleagues for their comments, you should take the time to restrict editing in the document first so that your colleagues' changes are tracked with revision marks. Otherwise, you might encounter surprises in documents after they are published, mailed, or emailed. For example, a colleague might introduce an error by changing an important sales figure using outdated sales information, and then forget to tell you about the change. You can prevent this by protecting your shared documents using tracked changes.

Checking a Document with the Document Inspector

The **Document Inspector** examines a document for hidden properties, personal information, and comments and revision marks. If it finds any, it gives you the opportunity to remove them. When you remove revision marks with the Document Inspector, all changes are accepted as if you had used the Accept button in the Changes group on the Review tab.

You can also use the Document Inspector to check a document for personal information stored in the document properties, headers, or footers. In addition, it can search for hidden text (text that is hidden from display using the Hidden check box on the Font tab of the Font dialog box) and for special types of data that can be stored along with the document.

At this point, the document still contains your marked edit to the second sentence in the paragraph below the Executive Summary heading, although you can't see the revision marks. You'll use the Document Inspector now to check for revision marks and other hidden information. To access the Document Inspector, you need to display the Info screen in Backstage view.

To check the document using the Document Inspector:

▶ **1.** On the ribbon, click the **File** tab and then click **Info** to display the Info screen in Backstage view.

▶ **2.** Click the **Check for Issues** button, and then click **Inspect Document**. The Document Inspector dialog box opens. See Figure 10–31.

Figure 10–31   **Document Inspector dialog box**

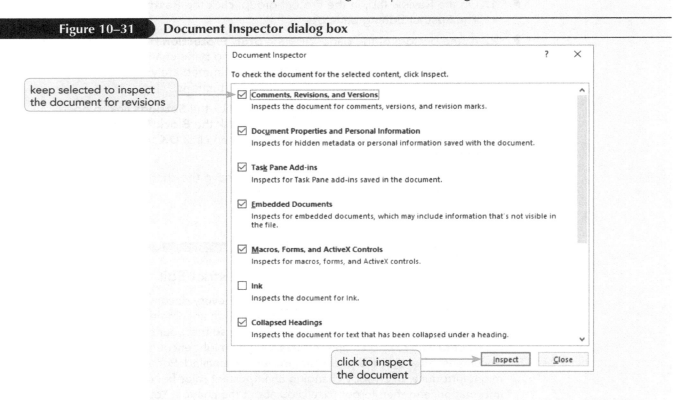

keep selected to inspect the document for revisions

click to inspect the document

Trouble? If a dialog box opens indicating that the file has not been saved, click Yes.

▶ **3.** Click **Inspect**. The Document Inspector dialog box changes to indicate that revision marks, document properties, embedded documents, and custom XML data were found in the document. See Figure 10–32.

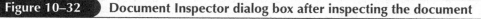

Figure 10–32   **Document Inspector dialog box after inspecting the document**

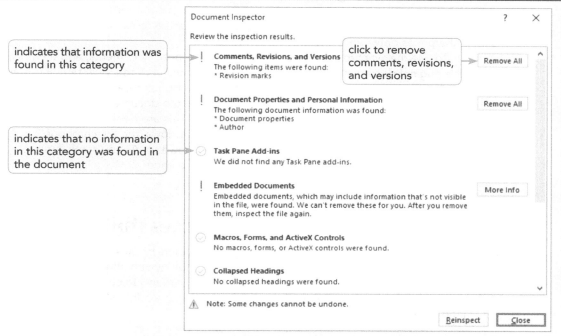

You need to remove the revision marks.

▶ **4.** In the Comments, Revisions, and Versions section at the top of the dialog box, click **Remove All**. The top section changes to show that all items in that category were successfully removed.

▶ **5.** Click **Close**. The Document Inspector dialog box closes.

▶ **6.** At the top of the navigation pane, click the **Back** button ⊖ to close Backstage view. Next, you'll verify that the revision marks were removed.

Trouble? If Backstage view is already closed, skip Step 6.

▶ **7.** On the Review tab, in the Tracking group, click the **Display for Review** arrow (which currently displays "No Markup"), and then click **All Markup**. If the document contained the revision marks to mark the changes you made to the paragraph below the "1. Executive Summary" heading on page 4, you would see them now. Because you used the Document Inspector to remove all revision marks, the changes you made have been accepted.

▶ **8.** Save the changes to the document.

Insight

Using Synchronous Scrolling

One of the difficult aspects of collaborating on a document with other people is keeping track of which copy of the file is the correct one, and making sure that all the intended edits are entered into the correct file. If confusion arises, you can open up both documents, display them side by side, and then scroll through both documents at the same time. Scrolling through two documents at once—a process known as **synchronous scrolling**—allows you to quickly assess the overall structure of two documents. If this side-by-side comparison suggests numerous differences between the documents, you can then use the Compare feature to examine, in detail, the differences between the two documents.

To use the synchronous scrolling feature, open both documents, and then display the original document in the window. On the ribbon, click the View tab, and then in the Window group, click the View Side by Side button. If three or more documents are open, a dialog box opens so that you can choose the document you want to display next to the original document. If only two documents are open, the second document appears next to the original document. In both windows, the Synchronous Scrolling button is selected in the Window group on the View tab. As you scroll in either document, the other document scrolls at the same pace.

Checking Documents for Accessibility

People with certain disabilities are able to use computers because of technology that makes them accessible. For example, assistive technology can allow people who cannot use their arms or hands to use foot, head, or eye movements to control the pointer. One of the most common assistive technologies is the screen reader, which identifies objects on the screen and produces audio output of the text.

Graphics and tables cause problems for users of screen readers unless they have alt text. When a screen reader encounters an object in a Word document that has alt text, it announces that an object is on the page, and then it reads the alt text. You already know how to add alt text to pictures. Other types of graphics, such as shapes, SmartArt graphics, and charts need alt text as well. You can add alt text to shapes or a SmartArt graphic by clicking the Alt Text button in the Accessibility group on the Shape Format tab or the Format tab for SmartArt. To add alt text to objects that do not have an Alt Text button on their contextual Format tab, you can right-click the object, and then on the shortcut menu, click Edit Alt Text.

To help you to identify parts of the document that might be problematic for people who must use assistive technologies such as a screen reader, you can use the Accessibility Checker. The Accessibility Checker classifies potential problems into three categories—errors, warnings, and tips. Content flagged as an error is content that is difficult or impossible for people with certain disabilities to access. Content flagged with a warning is content that may be difficult for many people with certain disabilities to access. Content flagged with a tip isn't necessarily impossible for people with disabilities to access, but by presenting it in a different way, you could likely make it easier to access.

You will use the Accessibility Checker to see what adjustments you should consider in order to make the document accessible.

To check the document for accessibility issues:

▶ **1.** On the ribbon, click the **File** tab, and then click Info in the navigation pane to display the Info screen in Backstage view.

▶ **2.** Click the **Check for Issues** button, and then click **Check Accessibility**. Backstage view closes, and the Accessibility pane is displayed to the right of the document window. Two objects are listed in the Missing alternative text section, and two objects are listed in the Image or objects not inline section.

Trouble? If the objects are not listed in the Accessibility pane, click a section heading or its expand arrow to display the objects.

Trouble? If you see a Convert button in the Accessibility pane, click it.

▶ **3.** In the Accessibility pane, click the object that starts with **Chart**. A number follows "Chart" in the item name in the pane. The document scrolls to the column chart that you inserted. See Figure 10–33. Note that the chart in Figure 10-33 is highlighted in gray, but yours might not be highlighted.

| Figure 10–33 | Chart selected in the Errors section of the Accessibility pane |

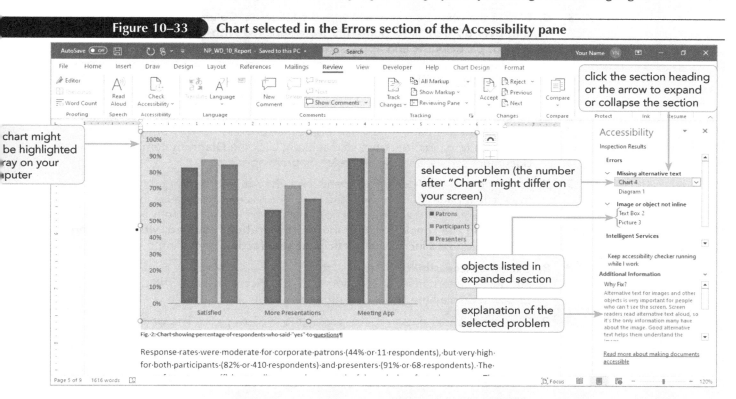

At the bottom of the Accessibility pane, an explanation of the problem and suggestions for how to fix it are displayed. In this case, you can add alt text to the chart to describe it.

▶ **4.** In the document, point to a blank area of the chart so that the "Chart Area" ScreenTip appears, right-click the chart, and then on the shortcut menu, click **Edit Alt Text**. The Alt Text pane opens. You can either add text in the white box that describes the object or click the Mark as decorative check box to indicate to screen readers that this object should be ignored. See Figure 10–34.

Figure 10–34 Alt text options in the Alt Text pane

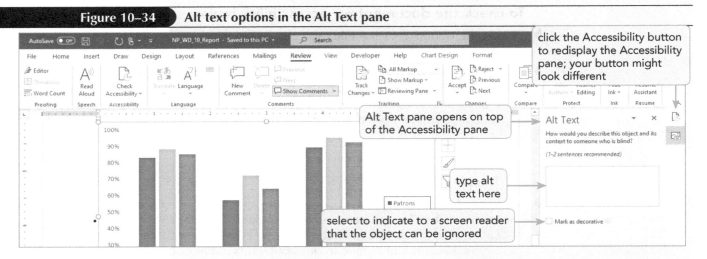

click the Accessibility button to redisplay the Accessibility pane; your button might look different

Alt Text pane opens on top of the Accessibility pane

type alt text here

select to indicate to a screen reader that the object can be ignored

▶ **5.** Click in the white box, and then type the following: **Column chart showing that over 80% of all respondents were satisfied with this year's meeting; 72% of participants and approximately 60% of corporate patrons and presenters want more presentations next year; and almost everyone wants a meeting app with 89% of corporate patrons, 92% of presenters, and 95% of participants responding "yes" to that question.** (including the period).

▶ **6.** To the right of the Alt Text pane, click the **Accessibility** button to display the Accessibility pane. The Chart object has been removed from the Errors list. In the Missing alternative text section, click the **Diagram** item. The document scrolls, and the SmartArt diagram appears.

▶ **7.** To the right of the Accessibility pane, click the **Alt Text** button to display the Alt Text pane. Click in the white box, which is empty because the selected SmartArt diagram does not have alt text yet, and then type **Diagram illustrating the conclusion that more presentations coupled with a meeting app should yield increased participant satisfaction.** (including the period).

▶ **8.** Click the **Accessibility** button to display the Accessibility pane. In the Suggested alternative text section, click the **Picture** object. The document scrolls to display the photo of Anthony.

▶ **9.** Click the Alt Text button to display the Alt Text pane. The white box contains the description that was automatically generated when the picture was inserted. Although the description is correct, a more specific description would be more helpful. Select all of the text in the white box, and then type **Photo of Anthony Santana**. (Do not type the period.) The text you typed replaces the selected text.

▶ **10.** Close the Alt Text pane. In the Accessibility pane, the Suggested alternative text section no longer appears.

Floating objects in a document might not be accessible to people with vision disabilities. To address this concern, you could change floating objects to inline objects. In the Accessibility pane, the Picture object is selected. The photo of Anthony Santana is a floating object.

▶ **11.** In the Accessibility pane, click the **Text Box** object. The caption under the photo of Anthony is selected. Bailey tells you that it is fine to leave these two objects as floating objects because they are not critical to understanding the document contents.

▶ **12.** Close the Accessibility pane, and then save the document.

In this session, you added advanced elements to a document, including automatically numbered headings, figure captions, cross-references, and endnotes. You also created a chart from within the document, and then you applied editing restrictions to the document. Finally, you checked the document for hidden information using the Document Inspector and checked it to make sure it is accessible to all readers. In the next session, you'll add different footers on odd and even pages and insert a reference to text formatted with a style on a page in a footer. You will also create an index and a table of figures. Finally, you will check the document for compatibility with earlier versions of Word, encrypt it, and mark it as final.

Review

Session 10.2 Quick Check

1. Explain how to add automatic numbering to section titles in a master document.

2. What button do you use to insert a figure caption?

3. Suppose you want to include the text "(See Figure 3)" in a report, and you want to make sure the figure number is automatically renumbered, if necessary, to reflect additions or deletions of figures in the document. What should you do?

4. What happens when you insert a chart using the Chart button in the Illustrations group on the Insert tab?

5. What kind of editing restrictions can you specify when protecting a document?

6. What types of formatting restrictions can you specify?

7. What does the Document Inspector find?

8. What is alt text?

Session 10.3 Visual Overview:

An index is an alphabetical list of entries—that is, words, phrases, and categories (or subjects)—accompanied by the page numbers on which they appear in a printed document. Click the References tab to access the commands for creating an index.

AutoSave ⬤ Off ⟲ ↺ ⟳ 🖰 ▾ ⮯   NP_WD_10_Rep... ▾

File   Home   Insert   Draw   Design   Layout   **References**   Mailings   Re

Table of Contents ▾   📄 Add Text ▾   📄! Update Table   ab¹   aḃ¹ ▾   Insert Footnote 🔲   ⓘ Search   Researcher   Insert Citation ▾   🔳 Manage Sourc   📝 Style: APA   📖 Bibliography ▾

Footnotes ⟲   Research   Citations & Bibliography

Mark Index Entry   ?   ✕

Index

Main entry: overview   Heading:

Subentry: Heading:

Options

◯ Cross-reference: See

◯ Current page

◉ Page range ◀

Bookmark: OverviewBookmark ◀

Page number format

☐ Bold

☐ Italic

This dialog box stays open so that you can mark multiple index

To mark a range of pages as an index entry, select the text, create a bookmark for the selected text, and then select the bookmark in the Page range section as the item to be marked.

Mark Index Entry   ?   ✕

Index

Main entry: WAPC ◀   Heading:

Subentry: Heading:

Options

◯ Cross-reference: See

◉ Current page ◀

◯ Page range

Bookmark:

The default is for the Current page option button to be selected.

Page number format

☐ Bold

☐ Italic

To mark all instances of a word for the index, click the Mark All button.

This dialog box stays open so that you can mark multiple index entries.

[Mark]   [Mark All]   [Cancel]

1. → EXECUTIVE·SUMMARY¶

Overall,·participants·{·XE·"respondents:participan "·········enters"·}·and·corporate·patro /orld·Association·of·Personal· eeting,·annual"·\t·"*See*·annual ey·did,·however,·have·severa

Participants·who·responded·were·particularly·fo available·without·extending·the·length·of·the·m "respondents:presenters"·}·who·responded·sugg meeting·app·that·would·make·it·easier·for·partic to·plan·their·sch

When you mark an index entry, an XE field code is inserted.

presentations.·Al·of·the·corporate·patrons·{·XE·" responded·are·strongly·in·favor·of·expanding·the hours.·Half·of·the·corporate·patrons·{·XE·"respo responded·are·interested·in·the·possibility·of·na the·opening·night·reception.¶

2. → OVERVIEW¶

Now·in·its·25th·year,·the·annual·meeting·{·XE·"ar Association·of·Personal·Chefs·(WAPC·{·XE·"WAPC

Indexing a Document

To mark text for inclusion in the index, click the Mark Entry button on the References tab or press ALT+SHIFT+X. The Mark Index Entry dialog box can stay open while you continue to select text and mark index entries.

To compile an index, you click the Insert Index button. The index is inserted as a field.

Mailings   Review   View   Developer   Help   ⬈ Share   ⬚ Comments

Your Name   YN

🔍

📷 Manage Sources
📄 Style: APA ˅
🗐 Bibliography ˅

Insert Caption

Mark Entry

Mark Citation

ABC
?
Acronyms

ns & Bibliography   Captions   Index   Table of Authorities

· 3 · · · 4 · · · 5 · · ·

Mark Index Entry   ?   ✕

Index

Main entry: meeting, annual   Heading:

Subentry: Heading:

Options

◉ Cross-reference: *See* annual meeting

○ Current page

○ Page range

Bookmark: ˅

Page number format

☐ Bold

☐ Italic

This dialog box stays open so that you can mark multiple index entries.

ents:participants"·}·presenters{·XE·

orporate·patrons{·

n·of·Personal·Chef

A cross-reference index entry is a phrase that tells readers to look at a different index entry to find the information they seek.

ual·

t·"*See*·annual·mee   with·this·

,·have·several·suggestions·for·next·year's·meeting.·

particularly·focused·on·having·more·presentations·

ngth·of·the·meeting.·Nearly·all·of·the·presenters{·XE·

sponded·suggested·that·the·association·create·a·

asier·for·participants{·XE·"respondents:participants"·}·

ack·of·the·time·and·location··of·the·various·

patrons{·XE·"respondent   yho·

expanding·the·exposition

ns{·XE·"respondents:corporate·patrons··}·who·

ssibility·of·naming·rights·for·major·events,·including·

Main index entries can have subentries that are divisions or subcategories of a main entry.

Mark Index Entry   ?   ✕

Index

Main entry: respondents   Heading:

Subentry: participants   Heading:

Options

○ Cross-reference: *See*

◉ Current page

○ Page range

Bookmark: ˅

Page number format

☐ Bold

☐ Italic

This dialog box stays open so that you can mark multiple index entries.

Mark   Mark All   Cancel

eeting{·XE·"annual·meeting"·}·of·the·World·

PC{·XE·"WAPC"·}·is·a·stimulating,·exciting·event·that·

🗔 Focus   📖   ▤   🗔   —

Evaluating Section and Page Breaks in a Document

Tip

If you need to add line numbers to a document, on the Layout tab, in the Page Setup group, click the Line Numbers button, and then select an option on the menu.

When you inserted subdocuments in the master document, section breaks were also inserted. Formatting instructions are embedded in a section break. Therefore, if the subdocuments contain formatting that conflicts with formatting in the master document, the entire master document could become corrupt. Also, the Next Page section breaks sometimes create a page break where you don't want one. To avoid bad page breaks and sections with conflicting formatting, you will delete the section breaks now.

To view the page and section breaks in the report:

Tip

If you want to scroll from side to side instead of vertically, click the Side to Side button in the Page Movement group on the View tab.

1. If you took a break after the previous session, open the document **NP_WD_10_Report**.

2. Press **CTRL+HOME** to move the insertion point to the beginning of the document, if necessary, and then scroll through the document, noting the manual page breaks after the text on page 1, after the table of contents on page 2, and after the empty paragraph below "List of Figures" on page 3. Then note the Next Page section breaks on pages 5 and 7, the two Continuous section breaks on page 6, the Continuous section break just before the Next Page section break on page 7, the two Continuous section breaks on page 8, and the Continuous section break on page 9. (The label for the Continuous section break on page 7 is hidden, and you can see only the dashed lines that represent the break at the end of the paragraph above the Next Page section break.)

You need to remove the unnecessary section breaks so that the page breaks are in the correct locations and so you do not get any unexpected results from formatting instructions that are embedded in the continuous section breaks. When you remove a section break, the section following that break assumes the formatting of the section before it. Therefore, you should remove section breaks starting from the end of a document.

To remove section breaks in the document:

1. On page 9, click between the paragraph mark and the Continuous section break, and then press **DEL**. The section break is deleted.

2. Scroll up to the middle of page 8.

3. Above the "6. Recommendations" heading, click in the Continuous section break that spans the width of the page, and then press **DEL**.

4. At the end of the paragraph above the heading "6. Recommendations," click between the period and the Continuous section break, press **ENTER** to insert a paragraph mark, and then press **DEL**.

5. Scroll up to the middle of page 7.

6. Above the "5. Presenters" heading, click in the Continuous section break that spans the width of the page, and then press **DEL**.

7. At the end of the paragraph above the heading "5. Presenters," click between the paragraph mark and the Continuous section break, and then press **DEL**.

8. Scroll up to the middle of page 6, and then delete the section break above the heading "4. Participants."

▶ **9.** At the end of the paragraph above the heading "4. Participants," click between the period and the Continuous section break, press **ENTER** to insert a paragraph mark, and then delete the section break at the end of the paragraph above the heading "4. Participants."

▶ **10.** Scroll up to the bottom of page 5, and then delete the section break at the end of the last paragraph. All of the section breaks have been deleted.

▶ **11.** Save the changes to the document.

Applying Different Page Number Formats in Sections

Most books, reports, and other long documents use a different page-numbering scheme for the front matter—the pages preceding the main document, including material such as the title page and table of contents—than for the body of the report. Front matter is usually numbered with lowercase Roman numerals (i, ii, iii, etc.), whereas the pages in the body of the report are numbered with Arabic numerals (1, 2, 3, etc.).

Creating Sections for Different Page-Numbering Schemes

Bailey wants to use a different page-numbering scheme for the front matter of the NP_WD_10_Report document. She also wants to add footers to the document that include the page numbers. You need to create three sections in the document so that you can start the page numbering in the front matter at page i, and start the page numbering in the body of the report at page 1.

To create three sections in the document:

▶ **1.** Scroll to display page 1, and then click the manual page break. You will delete the page break, and then insert a Next Page section break so that the title page is in section 1 and the rest of the report is in section 2.

▶ **2.** Press **DEL**. The manual page break is deleted, and the heading "Contents" and the entire table of contents move up to the current page.

▶ **3.** On the ribbon, click the **Layout** tab.

▶ **4.** In the Page Setup group, click the **Breaks** button, and then under Section Breaks, click **Next Page**. A new page following a section break is created. The insertion point is in a blank paragraph on page 2. You need to delete this blank paragraph.

▶ **5.** Press **DEL**. The blank paragraph is deleted.

▶ **6.** Scroll up to see the list of names on page 1. It doesn't look like there is a section break after your name. You can verify that the section break is there by switching to Draft view.

▶ **7.** On the ribbon, click the **View** tab, and then in the Views group, click the **Draft** button. The document is displayed in Draft view, and you can see the Next Page section break below your name and above the "Contents" heading.

▶ **8.** In the Views group, click the **Print Layout** button.

Now you need to change the page break after the "List of Figures" heading on page 3 to a Next Page section break.

▶ **9.** Scroll to page 3, click the manual page break, and then press **DEL**. The manual page break is deleted, and the "1. Executive Summary" heading and the text that follows it moves up to the current page.

▶ **10.** Position the insertion point in front of "Executive." You will not be able to click in front of the "1" because it is formatted as a numbered list.

▶ **11.** Insert a Next Page section break. Now the title page is in section 1, the front matter is in section 2, and the body of the report is in section 3.

Centering Text Vertically on a Page

Next, you'll format the title page so that the text is centered vertically on the page, and then you'll set up the page numbers for the front matter.

To center the title page text vertically on the page:

▶ **1.** Press **CTRL+HOME** to position the insertion point on page 1 (the title page).

▶ **2.** On the Layout tab, in the Page Setup group, click the **Page Setup Dialog Box Launcher** ⬚. The Page Setup dialog box opens.

▶ **3.** Click the **Layout** tab. Notice that "This section" appears in the Apply to box in the Preview section of the dialog box. This means that the options you select on this tab will affect only the text in this section (which consists only of the title page). See Figure 10–35.

Figure 10–35   **Layout tab in the Page Setup dialog box**

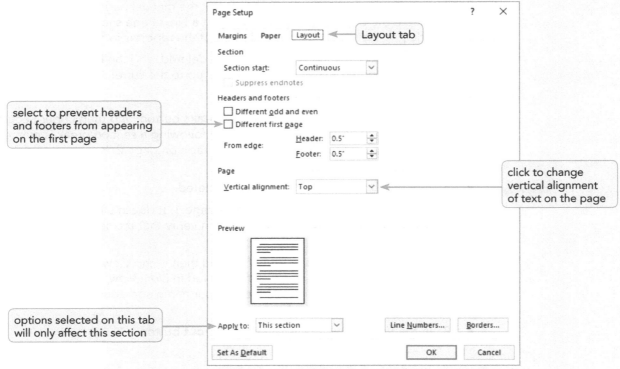

> **4.** Click the **Vertical alignment** arrow, and then click **Center**. This specifies that the text on the title page—the only page in this section—will be centered vertically on the page.

> **5.** Click **OK** to close the dialog box.

> **6.** On the ribbon, click the **View** tab, and then in the Zoom group, click the **One Page** button. You can see that the text on the title page is centered vertically on the page.

> **7.** Switch the Zoom level back to **120%**.

Setting Up Page Numbers in Different Sections

Now you're ready to set up the page numbering for the document. First, you will add page numbers to the front matter. You'll start by inserting a page number using one of the default page number styles. Then you will format the page numbers as lowercase Roman numerals (i, ii, iii, etc.). The title page typically is not counted as a page in the front matter, so you will also specify that the page number on the first page of the front matter—the page containing the table of contents—starts at page i.

To set up page numbers for the front matter:

> **1.** Scroll to page 2, and then position the insertion point to the left of the "Contents" heading.

> **2.** On the ribbon, click the **Insert** tab.

> **3.** In the Header & Footer group, click the **Page Number** button, point to **Bottom of Page**, and then click **Plain Number 3**. The document switches to Header and Footer view, the Header & Footer tab is displayed, and a page number field is inserted in the footer at the right margin on page 2. This page number was inserted in the footer on all the pages in the document—in other words, in all three sections.

> **4.** In the Header & Footer group, click the **Page Number** button, and then click **Format Page Numbers**. The Page Number Format dialog box opens. See Figure 10–36.

Figure 10–36   **Page Number Format dialog box**

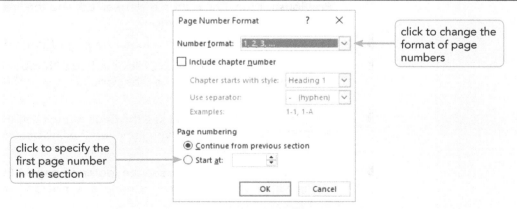

You need to change the format of the page numbers in this section to lowercase Roman numerals.

▶ **5.** Click the **Number format** arrow, scroll down, and then click **i, ii, iii, …** .

▶ **6.** In the Page numbering section, click the **Start at** option button. The Roman numeral one (i) is displayed in the Start at box.

▶ **7.** Click **OK** to close the Page Number Format dialog box. The page number field in the footer on the Contents page displays the page number "i." Note on the status bar that this is still considered to be page 2 in the document. See Figure 10–37.

| Figure 10–37 | Page numbered i on page 2 of the document |

page number 2 of 8 on the status bar

Footer -Section 2-

Same as Previous

page number i

Page 2 of 8   1615 words

▶ **8.** Scroll up so that you can see the footer on page 1 (the title page). The page number in this footer is 1. That's because the options in the Page Number Format dialog box are applied to only the current section, and the insertion point was in the footer in section 2 (the section containing the front matter) when you opened the Page Number Format dialog box.

Bailey does not want a page number to appear on the title page. Recall that when you add information in a header or footer in a document with sections, the headers and footers are linked between sections. You can break this link to enable the creation of a different header or footer in different sections.

To break the link between footers in different sections and remove the footer from the title page:

▶ **1.** Make sure the insertion point is still in the footer on page 2 (numbered page i in the footer).

▶ **2.** On the Header & Footer tab, in the Navigation group, click the **Link to Previous** button. The button is deselected, and the link between the footers in sections 1 and 2 is removed.

▶ **3.** Scroll up, and then click in the footer on page 1 (the title page).

▶ **4.** In the Header & Footer group, click the **Page Number** button, and then click **Remove Page Numbers**. The page number in the footer on page 1 is removed.

▶ **5.** Scroll down so that you can see the page number on the page containing the table of contents. Because you removed the link between the sections, this page number is still there.

▶ **6.** Scroll down so that you can see the footer on page 4 (as indicated on the status bar) in the document. This page is numbered 3 in the footer.

Page 4 in the document is numbered page 3 because the footer in this section—section 3—is still linked to the footer in section 2, and you started the page numbering at i (1) in that section. You do want the page numbers in the body of the report to use Arabic numerals (1, 2, 3), but you need to change the formatting so that the numbering in this section starts at page 1. To do this, you'll unlink the sections, and then start the numbering in section 3 with 1.

To set up the page numbers for section 3 to begin with 1:

▶ **1.** Click in the footer on page 4 of the document (currently numbered 3). This is the first page of the body of the report.

▶ **2.** On the Header & Footer tab, in the Navigation group, click the **Link to Previous** button to deselect it.

▶ **3.** In the Header & Footer group, click the **Page Number** button, and then click **Format Page Numbers** to open the Page Number Format dialog box. In the Number format list, "1, 2, 3, …" is selected. You need to indicate that you want this section to begin with page number 1.

▶ **4.** Click the **Start at** option button in the Page numbering section to select it. The Arabic numeral one (1) appears in the Start at box.

▶ **5.** Click **OK** to close the dialog box, and then scroll down to view the footers in the rest of the document. The page numbering in section 3 starts with page 1 on the page containing the heading "1. Executive Summary" and proceeds consecutively through the document to page 5.

▶ **6.** Close Header and Footer view, and then save the changes to the document.

Changing the Footer and Page Layout for Odd and Even Pages

Most professionally produced books and reports are printed on both sides of the paper and then bound. The blank space on the inside of each page, where the pages are bound together, is called the **gutter**. When you open a bound book or report, odd-numbered pages appear on the right, and even-numbered pages appear on the left. Often, the headers and footers for odd-numbered pages contain text that is different from the headers or footers for the even-numbered pages.

Bailey wants to follow these standards in the NP_WD_10_Report document. Specifically, she wants you to use the page layouts shown in Figure 10–38.

Figure 10-38   Page setup for odd and even pages

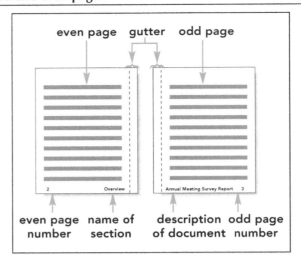

To do this, you'll use the following guidelines:

- Set the gutter to one-half inch. This will cause the text on odd pages to shift to the right (one-half inch in this case), leaving a wider margin on the left, and the text on even pages to shift to the left (again, one-half inch), leaving a wider margin on the right. When the even and odd pages are printed back-to-back, the gutters line up on the same edge of the paper, thus leaving room for the binding.
- Change the location for page numbers so it's different on odd and even pages. In a page layout that distinguishes between odd and even pages, the page numbers are usually printed near the outside edge of the page rather than near the gutter to make them easier to see in a bound copy. On odd pages, the page numbers appear on the right; on even pages, the numbers appear on the left.
- Enter different text for the footers on odd and even pages. In many books, the section title is in the header or footer of odd pages, and the book or chapter title is in the header or footer of even pages. Sometimes this text is shifted toward the gutter (just as page numbers are shifted toward the outer edge). Bailey wants the odd-page footers to contain the text "Annual Meeting Survey Report") and the even-page footers to include the section title (for example, "Overview") closer to the gutter.

First, you'll increase the size of the gutter to allow enough room to bind the report without obscuring any text. To make this change, you'll use the Page Setup dialog box.

To specify a gutter margin in the document:

▶ **1.** On the second page of the document (numbered page i, with the heading "Contents"), position the insertion point before the heading "Contents." On the status bar, note that the total number of pages in the document is 8, and the current page is page 2.

▶ **2.** On the ribbon, click the **Layout** tab, and then in the Page Setup group, click the **Page Setup Dialog Box Launcher** ⊑ to open the Page Setup dialog box.

▶ **3.** Click the **Margins** tab, and then change the setting in the Gutter box to **0.5"**.

▶ **4.** Near the bottom of the dialog box, click the **Apply to** arrow. You can choose to apply the settings in this dialog box to the current section, to the whole document, or from this point forward.

▶ **5.** Click **This point forward**. Now, the gutter margin will be applied to the remainder of the report—all the pages except the title page.

▶ **6.** Click **OK**. The Page Setup dialog box closes, and the gutter margin increases to one-half inch.

Because the document is not yet set up for odd and even pages, the gutter margin is the left margin on all of the pages. On the status bar, notice that the document now contains nine pages. This is because the increase in the left margin pushed some text onto subsequent pages.

When you set up a document to be printed on odd and even pages, headers and footers on the current page remain, but they are removed from every other page. So if the current page is an odd page, the headers and footers on all the odd pages remain but are removed from all of the even pages. You will set up the document to print on odd and even pages now.

To change the page setup for printing odd and even pages:

▶ **1.** Make sure the insertion point is still before the "C" in the "Contents" heading.

▶ **2.** Open the Page Setup dialog box again, and then click the **Layout** tab.

▶ **3.** In the Headers and footers section, click the **Different odd and even** check box. Now the footers on the odd pages of the document will differ from those on the even pages.

   You want this change applied to both the current section—section 2, which contains the front matter—and the next section—section 3, which contains the body of the report. Because you positioned the insertion point on the page containing the table of contents, you can change the Apply to setting so that the odd-even formatting is applied from this point forward.

▶ **4.** At the bottom of the dialog box, click the **Apply to** arrow, click **This point forward**, and then click **OK**. On the status bar, the number of total pages in the document is now 10. On the current page, which is now page 3 according to the status bar and therefore an odd page, the gutter margin is still on the left.

▶ **5.** Scroll so that you can see the footer on page i (page 3 on the status bar) and the top of page ii (page 4 on the status bar), and then click anywhere on page 4. The indicator on the status bar shows that this page is page 4, which is an even page. Because it is an even page, the gutter margin is on the right. Note that the footer on page i, an odd page, has not changed.

▶ **6.** Scroll down so that you can see the footer on page ii (page 4). The footer you created no longer appears on this page, an even page.

When you applied the setting for odd and even pages, an additional page was added to the document. You'll examine the document to see what happened.

To view the document in Multiple Page view:

▌ **1.** On the ribbon, click the **View** tab, and then in the Zoom group, click the **Multiple Pages** button. The Zoom level changes so that you can see three pages across the screen at a time.

▌ **2.** Click anywhere on the title page. The page number indicator on the status bar shows that the insertion point is on page 1 of 10.

▌ **3.** Click anywhere on the Contents page. The page number indicator on the status bar shows that the insertion point is on page 3 of 10.

The first page of a document formatted for odd and even pages is always an odd page—a right page. However, you numbered the second page in the document—the Content page—as page i, which is also an odd page. A document cannot have two odd-numbered pages in a row. To fix this, an additional blank page is automatically added between the title page and the Contents page. The total page count on the status bar includes this hidden blank page.

The blank page after the title page is part of the document. When you print the document, your printer will include a blank page after the title page. Also, if you save the document as a PDF file, a blank page will appear after the title page. This is exactly what you want in a document that will be printed on both sides of each page—the blank page ensures that the back of the title page remains blank. If the document did not include this blank page, then the Contents page would be printed on the back of the title page, turning the Contents page (which is set up to be an odd page) into an even page. The remaining odd and even pages would also be reversed.

Now that you have specified that odd and even pages will be set up differently, you can add footer text and format page numbering differently in the odd and even footers.

To format footers differently for odd and even pages:

▌ **1.** Change the Zoom level back to **120%**, and then on the ribbon, click the **Insert** tab.

▌ **2.** In the Header & Footer group, click the **Footer** button, and then click **Edit Footer**. The label "Odd Page Footer -Section 2-" appears on the left side of the footer area. In the right margin, the footer contains the page number "i." The insertion point is to the left of the page number. This is the odd page footer in the second section of the document. Because this is an odd page, you'll leave the page number at the right and insert the document name at the left.

▌ **3.** Type **Annual Meeting Survey Report**, and then press **TAB** twice. As you press TAB, the text you typed shifts to the left margin.

▌ **4.** On the Header & Footer tab, in the Navigation group, click the **Next** button. The footer on the next page, labeled "Even Page Footer -Section 2-," appears on the left side of the footer area, and the insertion point is at the left margin in the footer.

▌ **5.** In the Header & Footer group, click the **Page Number** button, point to **Bottom of Page**, and then click **Plain Number 1**. A page number field appears above the blank paragraph in the footer, displaying the page number "ii."

Now you need to add "Annual Meeting Survey Report" to the odd pages in section 3 because you unlinked the sections earlier.

▶   **6.** In the Navigation group, click the **Next** button. The insertion point appears to the left of the page number field in the next section footer. The label in this footer is "Odd Page Footer -Section 3-." Note that in the Navigation group, the Link to Previous button is not selected.

▶   **7.** Type **Annual Meeting Survey Report**, and then press **TAB** twice.

▶   **8.** In the Navigation group, click the **Next** button. The even page footer on page 6 (numbered page 2) of the document appears. This is the first even page in Section 3. In the Navigation group, the Link to Previous button is still selected. Even though you removed the link between sections 2 and 3, after you applied formatting for odd and even pages, a link was reestablished between the even pages. Therefore, when you added the page numbers to the even pages, they were added to the even pages in section 3 as well.

▶   **9.** Close Header and Footer view.

After you have finished setting up a long document, you should scroll through to make sure the page breaks are in logical places.

To review the document and adjust page breaks:

▶   **1.** Press **CTRL+HOME**, and then scroll down the document examining the page breaks until you see the bottom of page 5 (numbered page 1) and the top of page 6. The bulleted list that starts at the bottom of page 5 contains only three items, and the automatic page break moved the last bulleted item to the next page. It would be better if this short list appeared on one page.

▶   **2.** In the heading "2.2. Survey Goals," position the insertion point before "Survey."

▶   **3.** Click the **Insert** tab, and then in the Pages group, click the **Page Break** button. The heading "2.2. Survey Goals" moves to page 6.

▶   **4.** Continue scrolling through the document to examine the page breaks. The rest of the page breaks are fine.

▶   **5.** Save the changes to the document.

Inserting a Style Reference into a Footer

Often in long reports, the section title appears in the footer on even pages. For example, on an even page that includes the heading "4. Participants," you would insert the heading "Participants" in the footer. Rather than manually entering a heading in each footer, you can insert the StyleRef field in the footer to pick up the first heading of whatever heading level you specify that appears on the page. The StyleRef field inserts text formatted with the style you specify. Like many of the Word features you've used in this module, style references are useful because they allow Word to update information automatically in one part of a document to reflect changes made in another part of a document.

Bailey wants you to format the footer on each even page so it includes the first Level 1 heading on the page. When you do this, if an even page does not contain a Level 1 heading, the most recent Level 1 heading from a prior page will be inserted. To do this, you'll insert a style reference to the Heading 1 style.

To insert a style reference to the section title into the footer:

▶ **1.** Scroll up to page 6 (numbered page 2), and then click anywhere on page 6.

▶ **2.** On the Insert tab, in the Header & Footer group, click the **Footer** button, and then click **Edit Footer**. The insertion point appears to the left of the page number on page 6.

▶ **3.** Press the → key to move the insertion point to the right of the page number field, and then press **TAB** twice to position the insertion point at the right margin in the footer.

▶ **4.** On the ribbon, click the **Insert** tab. Recall that to insert a field, you must use the command on the Quick Parts menu.

▶ **5.** In the Text group, click the **Explore Quick Parts** button 📄 ▾, and then click **Field** to open the Field dialog box.

▶ **6.** Click the **Categories** arrow, and then click **Links and References**.

▶ **7.** In the Field names box, click **StyleRef**. Next, you'll indicate the style to which the StyleRef field code should refer.

▶ **8.** In the Style name box, click **Heading 1** (the style applied to the main headings in the document). See Figure 10–39.

Figure 10–39 Field dialog box after selecting the StyleRef field and the Heading 1 style

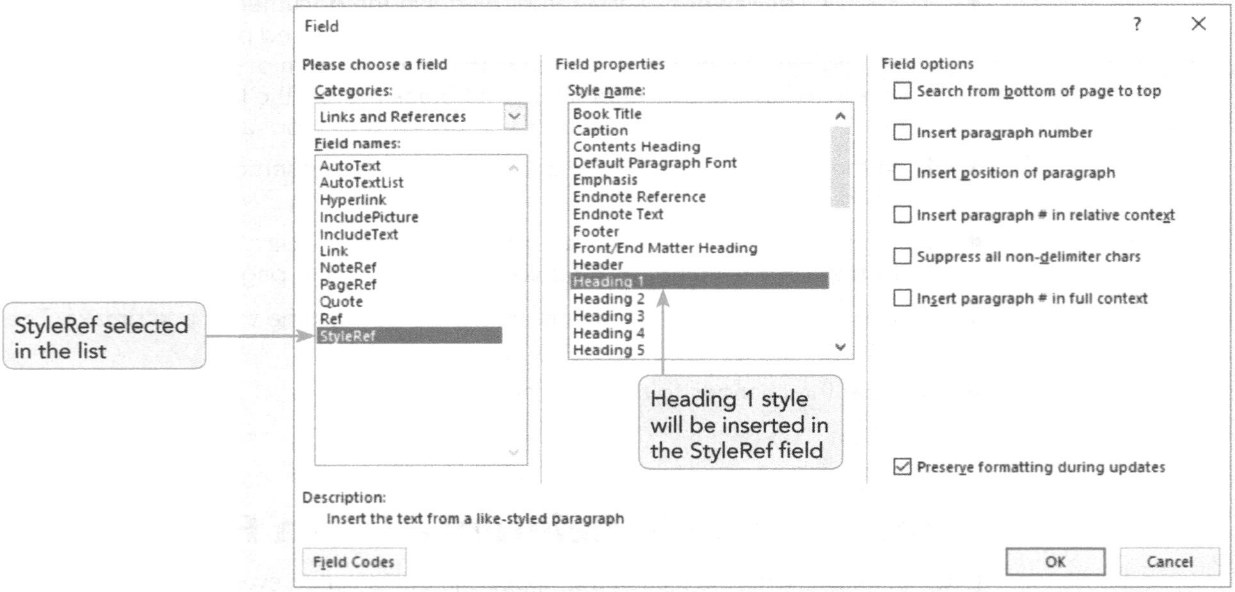

StyleRef selected in the list

Heading 1 style will be inserted in the StyleRef field

▶ **9.** Click **OK**. The Field dialog box closes. The heading "Overview" appears in the footer on page 6 (numbered page 2). Although this heading does not appear on page 2, it is the most recent heading before this page that is formatted with the Heading 1 style.

▶ **10.** Scroll up to see the three Level 2 headings on page 6, and then scroll up until you see the "2. Overview" heading on page 5.

▶ **11.** Scroll down to view the middle of page 8 (numbered page 4), which is the next even-numbered page. The heading "4. Participants" appears in the middle of this page.

▶ **12.** Scroll to view the bottom of page 8. The footer contains the heading "Participants."

▶ **13.** Scroll up so that you can see the footer on page 4 (numbered page ii). It contains the "Executive Summary" heading, which is the first heading on page 5 that is formatted with the Heading 1 style. This appears because neither page 4 nor any of the pages before page 4 contain text formatted with the Heading 1 style.

▶ **14.** Scroll down so that you can see the footer on page 6 (numbered page 2), and then click in the footer, if necessary.

▶ **15.** On the ribbon, click the **Header & Footer** tab, and then in the Navigation group, click the **Link to Previous** button to deselect it.

▶ **16.** Scroll back up so that you can see the footer on page 4 (numbered page ii), right-click **Executive Summary** in the footer, and then on the shortcut menu, click **Edit Field**. The Field dialog box opens showing the current settings for this field.

▶ **17.** In the Style name list, click the **Front/End Matter Heading** style, and then click **OK**. The text on the right side of the footer changes to "List of Figures," which is the heading on this page that is formatted with the Front/End Matter Heading style.

▶ **18.** Close Header and Footer view, and then save the changes to the document.

The report is now set up so Bailey can print the document on both sides of the page and bind it at the gutter margin, like a book.

Inserting Nonbreaking Hyphens and Spaces

In addition to page breaks, you should also look through your document for awkward line breaks. For example, the paragraph below the heading "2.1. Survey Overview" on page 5 of the document contains the hyphenated word "e-survey," and it is split onto two lines, which makes it a little difficult to read. Although this isn't a serious problem, readers might be confused to see "e-" at the end of a line. To prevent Word from breaking a hyphenated word over two lines, you need to use a **nonbreaking hyphen**, also called a **hard hyphen**, which is a hyphen that does not allow the word or phrase containing it to break between two lines. To insert a nonbreaking hyphen, you use the Special Characters tab in the Symbol dialog box. By contrast, a **breaking hyphen**, or **soft hyphen**, is a hyphen that allows the word containing it to appear on different lines. To insert a soft hyphen, you press the hyphen key on your keyboard.

To insert nonbreaking hyphens in "e-survey":

▶ **1.** Scroll to the bottom of page 5 in the document (numbered page 1).

▶ **2.** In the paragraph under the heading "2.1. Survey Overview," at the end of the second line, click after "e-".

▶ **3.** Press **BACKSPACE** to delete the breaking hyphen. The "e" becomes joined to "survey," and the word "esurvey" appears on the next line. Now you'll insert the nonbreaking hyphen.

▶ **4.** On the ribbon, click the **Insert** tab.

> **5.** In the Symbols group, click the **Symbol** button, and then click **More Symbols**. The Symbol dialog box opens with the Symbols tab selected.

> **6.** Click the **Special Characters** tab. A list of special symbols appears. See Figure 10–40.

| **Figure 10–40** | Special Characters tab in the Symbol dialog box |

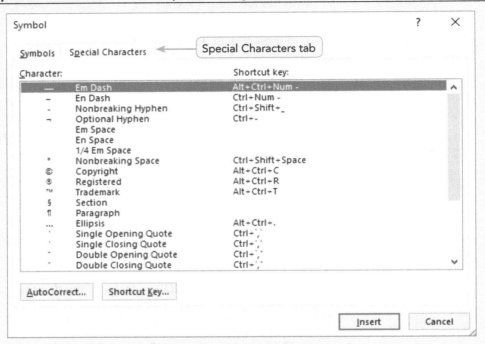

> **Tip**
>
> You can also press CTRL+SHIFT+_ to insert a nonbreaking hyphen.

> **7.** Click **Nonbreaking Hyphen**, click **Insert** to insert the hyphen into the document at the location of the insertion point, and then click **Close**. The Symbol dialog box closes, and the word "e-survey" now contains a nonbreaking hyphen.

Another important special character is the nonbreaking space. A **nonbreaking space** is a space that does not allow the words on either side of it to break over two lines. For example, the phrase "10 KB" (where KB stands for kilobytes, as in a 10 KB file) might be hard to read or distracting if the "10" appears at the end of one line and "KB" appears at the beginning of the next line. To avoid this problem, you can insert a nonbreaking space between the "10" and the "KB."

In the paragraph you just revised, the word "March" now appears at the end of one line and the year "2025" appears at the beginning of the next line. It would be better to keep these words together on one line.

To insert a nonbreaking space:

> **1.** In the paragraph under the heading "2.1. Survey Overview," click at the end of the fourth line (after the space after "March"), and then press **BACKSPACE**. The space after "March" is deleted, and "March2025" appears at the beginning of the next line.

> **2.** On the Insert tab, in the Symbols group, click the **Symbol** button, and then click **More Symbols**.

Tip

You can also press CTRL+SHIFT+SPACEBAR to insert a nonbreaking space.

3. In the Symbol dialog box, click the **Special Characters** tab.

4. In the Character list, click **Nonbreaking Space**, click **Insert**, and then click **Close**. A nonbreaking space appears between "March" and "2025" at the beginning of the second to last line. The nonbreaking space is indicated with a small, open circle.

5. Save the changes to the document.

Creating an Index

Bailey wants you to create an index to help readers locate information in the report. Refer to the Session 10.3 Visual Overview for more information about indexes. To create an index, you first mark the words and phrases in the document that you want to appear as entries in the index. Then you compile the index to create the list of terms you marked along with the pages on which the marked terms appear.

Marking Index Entries

When you mark an index entry, you select the word or phrase you want to appear in the index, and then use the Mark Index Entry dialog box to refine the entry. When you mark an index entry in your document, Word inserts a field code that appears if you display nonprinting characters.

When you mark entries, you can mark only the selected term as an entry or you can mark all instances of the selected term throughout the document as entries. To create a useful index, you need to think carefully about the terms or concepts a user might want to find in the document. Then you need to decide if you want the index to list the page number of one instance of that term, the page numbers of a few individual instances, or all the page numbers on which the term appears. To mark just the selected instance of a term as an index entry, you click Mark in the Mark Index Entry dialog box. To mark all instances of the selected term in the document as index entries, you click Mark All in the Mark Index Entry dialog box.

To create the index for the NP_WD_10_Report, you'll start by marking the main entries for the index.

Reference

Marking Index Entries and Subentries

- Select the word or phrase you want to mark as an index entry.
- On the References tab, in the Index group, click the Mark Entry button to open the Mark Index Entry dialog box; or press ALT+SHIFT+X to open the Mark Index Entry dialog box.
- If necessary, edit the entry in the Main entry box, and then, if desired, type an entry in the Subentry box.
- In the Options section, make sure the Current page option button is selected.
- Click Mark to mark this occurrence, or click Mark All to mark every occurrence in the document.
- Click Close.

To start creating the index, you'll mark "WAPC" at the point where it appears in parentheses after the full name of the organization as an index entry. You don't need to mark every instance of "WAPC" as entries because someone who looks up this term probably wants to know what it stands for.

To mark one instance of the main index entry "WAPC":

1. On page 5 (page 1 in the footer), in the paragraph below the heading "2. Overview," in the first sentence, select **WAPC**. You will add the selected term to the index.

2. On the ribbon, click the **References** tab, and then in the Index group, click the **Mark Entry** button. The Mark Index Entry dialog box opens. The term you selected, "WAPC," appears in the Main entry box, and the Current page option button is selected in the Options section of the dialog box. This ensures that the current page of this entry will appear in the index.

3. Click **Mark**. In the document, the field code {XE "WAPC"} appears next to the selected term "WAPC." See Figure 10–41.

Figure 10–41 "WAPC" marked as an index entry

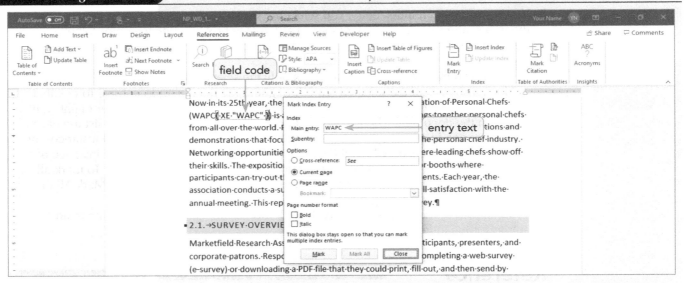

Trouble? If you can't see the field code that was inserted, drag the dialog box by its title bar to reposition it.

Next, you'll mark the phrases "focus group" and "exposition hall" as index entries. You want to mark every instance of these phrases as entries because someone who looks these terms up in the index would want to see where they are referenced.

Note that you do not need to close the Mark Index Entry dialog box to work in the document.

To mark additional index entries in the report:

▶ **1.** Click anywhere in the document, and then in the paragraph below the heading "2. Overview," in the sixth line, select **exposition hall**.

▶ **2.** Click in a blank area of the Mark Index Entry dialog box. The text in the Main entry box changes to "exposition hall."

▶ **3.** Click **Mark All** in the Mark Index Entry dialog box. Word searches the document for every occurrence of "exposition hall" and marks the first occurrence of the phrase in each paragraph. In the document, you can see that Word has inserted the field code {XE "exposition hall"} next to the selected phrase.

▶ **4.** Click in the document, and then press CTRL+END to move to the end of the document. In the last paragraph, the first instance of "exposition hall" is marked as an index entry, but the second instance of the phrase in the paragraph is not.

Marking Subentries

A high-quality index contains subentries as well as main entries. Subentries are indented in a list below the main entry. For the survey report, Bailey wants "respondents" to be a main entry with subentries of "corporate patrons," "participants," and "presenters," and she wants every instance marked.

To create subentries in an index:

▶ **1.** Scroll back to page 5 (page 1 in the footer) so that you can see the heading "2.1. Survey Overview" and the last five lines of the paragraph above this heading.

▶ **2.** In the first sentence of the paragraph below the heading "2.1. Survey Overview," select **participants**.

▶ **3.** Click in a blank area of the Mark Index Entry dialog box. The word "participants" appears in the Main entry box.

▶ **4.** Select the text in the Main entry box, press **DEL**, and then type **respondents**.

▶ **5.** Click in the **Subentry** box, type **participants**, and then click **Mark All**. All instances of "participants" are marked as subentries under the main entry "respondents." In the XE field code that was inserted, notice the main entry "respondents" appears, followed by a colon and then the subentry. In the paragraph above the heading, both instances of "participants" are marked as subentries. For subentries, when you mark all instances, every instance in the document is marked, not just the first instance in each paragraph. See Figure 10–42.

Figure 10–42 Subentry "participants" marked

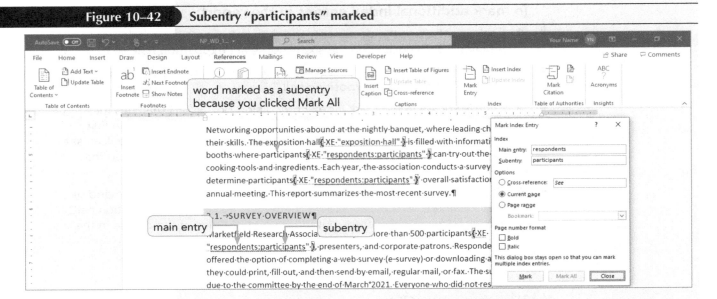

Now you need to mark "presenters" and "corporate patrons" as subentries for "respondents."

6. Click in the document, and then in the first sentence in the first paragraph below the heading "2.1. Survey Overview," select **presenters**.

7. Click in a blank area in the Main Index Entry dialog box, and then replace the text in the Main entry box with **respondents**.

8. Click in the **Subentry** box, type **presenters**, and then click **Mark All**.

9. In the document, in the first sentence in the first paragraph below the heading "2.1. Survey Overview," select **corporate patrons**.

10. Mark all instances of **corporate patrons** as a subentry in the index to **respondents**.

You also need to mark all instances of the word "respondents" so that page numbers will appear next to that entry.

11. Scroll to page 7 in the document (marked page 3 in the footer), and then in the paragraph below the heading "2.4. Response Information," in the second line, select **respondents**.

12. Mark all instance of "respondents" as a main entry in the index.

Creating Cross-Reference Index Entries

You create cross-reference index entries to tell readers to look at a different index entry to find the information they seek. For example, in the NP_WD_10_Report document, the phrase "annual meeting" is frequently used. However, someone searching for this concept in the index might search instead for the phrase "meeting, annual." You can create an index entry for "meeting, annual" and insert a cross-reference to the main entry "annual meeting."

Reference

Creating a Cross-Reference Index Entry

- Select the word or phrase you want to cross-reference. If that word is not already marked as a main entry, mark all instances of that word as a main entry.
- On the References tab, in the Index group, click the Mark Entry button to open the Mark Index Entry dialog box; or press ALT+SHIFT+X to open the Mark Index Entry dialog box.
- Delete any text in the Main entry box, and then type the term you want to be listed as a main entry.
- In the Options section, click the Cross-reference option button, and then after "See," type the main entry you want to reference.
- Click Mark.
- Click Close.

You will mark every instance of "annual meeting" as a main entry, and then create a cross-reference to the main entry "annual meeting" next to the entry "meeting, annual."

To create a cross-reference index entry:

▶ **1.** Scroll to the top of page 5 to display the paragraph below the heading "1. Executive Summary," and then in that paragraph, in the third line, select **annual meeting**.

▶ **2.** Mark all instances of the phrase "annual meeting" as a main entry in the index.

▶ **3.** In the Mark Index Entry dialog box, edit the entry in the Main entry box so it is **meeting, annual**.

▶ **4.** In the Options section of the dialog box, click the **Cross-reference** option button. The insertion point appears to the right of the word "See" in the Cross-reference box.

▶ **5.** Type **annual meeting** and then click **Mark**. You can't click Mark All because a cross-reference entry appears only once in the index and doesn't include a page number. In the document, a field code for the "meeting, annual" entry appears before or after the field code for the main entry "annual meeting." See Figure 10–43.

Figure 10–43	Cross-reference entry created

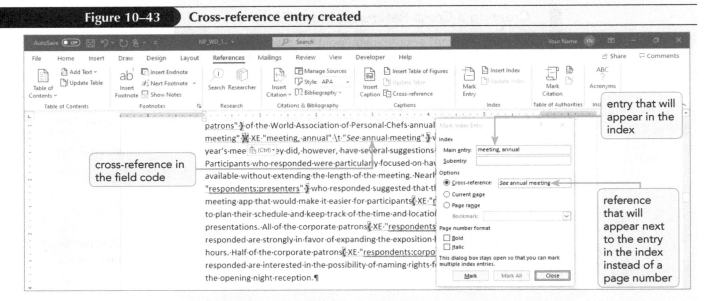

Trouble? The cross-reference field code might appear before the field code marking "annual meeting" as a main index entry. This will not cause any problems with the index.

▶ **6.** In the Mark Index Entry dialog box, click **Close**.

Creating an Index Entry for a Page Range

In addition to main entries and subentries that list individual pages, sometimes you'll want to include an index entry that refers to a range of pages. For example, you could create an entry for the "Overview" heading and refer users to the range of pages that contain all of the information under this heading. To do this, you first create a bookmark marking the page range you want to index, and then you create an index entry to this bookmark.

Reference

Creating a Page Range Index Entry

- Select all the text over a range of pages that you want to mark as an index entry.
- On the Insert tab, in the Links group, click the Bookmark button.
- Type the name of the bookmark, and then click the Add button.
- On the References tab, in the Index group, click the Mark Entry button to open the Mark Index Entry dialog box; or press ALT+SHIFT+X to open the Mark Index Entry dialog box.
- Click the Page range option button, click the Bookmark arrow, and then click the bookmark name for the range of pages.
- Click Mark.
- Click Close.

You need to create an index entry for the section "Overview." This entry will span a range of pages.

To create an index entry with a reference to a range of pages:

1. Switch to Outline view, and then, if necessary, scroll so that you can see the heading "2. Overview."

   Trouble? If the Level 1 headings aren't visible, click the Show Text Formatting check box in the Outline Tools group on the Outlining tab to deselect it.

2. Next to "2. Overview," click the **plus sign** symbol ⊕. The entire "2. Overview" section is selected, including its subsections.

3. On the ribbon, click the **Insert** tab, and then in the Links group, click the **Bookmark** button. The Bookmark dialog box opens.

4. Type **OverviewBookmark** as the bookmark name, and then click **Add**. A bookmark to the selected text is created.

5. Close Outline view, click the **References** tab, and then in the Index group, click the **Mark Entry** button. The Mark Index Entry dialog box opens and "Overview" appears in the Main entry box. Because the text is black and selected in the Main entry box, it is hard to read on the orange background.

6. Edit the text in the Main entry box so it is all lowercase.

7. Click the **Page range** option button, click the **Bookmark** arrow, and then click **OverviewBookmark**.

8. Click **Mark** to mark this index entry. The document scrolls to show the last sentence in the selected page range and the index field code that indicates that this is the end of the page range.

9. Click in the document, and then scroll up one line so you can see the whole index entry. See Figure 10–44.

Figure 10–44   Page range entry created

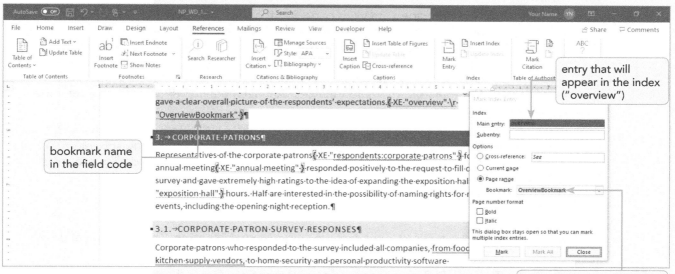

10. In the Mark Index Entry dialog box, click **Close**.

11. Save the changes to the document.

Using the AutoMark Feature

When you use the Mark All command, only the exact spelling and capitalization that you select is marked throughout the document. So when you marked all instances of "respondents," the word "Respondents" was not marked. (However, if a word includes an apostrophe, the word is marked; for example, *respondents'* would be marked.) One way to handle this is to create an AutoMark file, also called a concordance file. An AutoMark file contains a two-column table listing all the variations of a word that you want marked as the entry in the index in the left column, and the way the main entry should appear in the index in the right column. Then you reference the AutoMark file, and every instance of the words listed in the first column are marked as index entries.

If you want, you can create an AutoMark file as an alternative to using the Mark Index Entry dialog box to mark all instances of terms as index entries. Then after you mark the terms in the document using the AutoMark file, you can review the document and mark additional terms using the Mark Index Entry dialog box.

Reference

Using the AutoMark Feature

- Create a new document, and then insert a two-column table.
- In the left column, type a variation of the main index entry.
- In the right column, type the main index entry.
- Save the document.
- In the document containing the index, on the References tab, in the Index group, click the Insert Index button to open the Index dialog box.
- Click the AutoMark button to open the Open Index AutoMark File dialog box, navigate to the location of the AutoMark file, click it, and then click Open.

To create an AutoMark file:

1. Scroll to page 7 (marked page 3 in the footer) so that you can see the headings "2.3. Survey Coordinator" and "2.4. Response Information" and the paragraphs below those headings. In the paragraph below the heading "2.4. Response Information," the phrase "annual meeting" is marked as an index entry. However, in the paragraph below the heading "2.3. Survey Coordinator," in the fourth line, "Annual Meeting" is not marked as an index entry.

2. Scroll to the bottom of page 5 (marked page 1 in the footer) so that you can see the last paragraph on the page. In the third line, "Respondents" is not marked as an index entry even though you had marked all instances of "respondents."

3. Create a new, blank document, and then create a table consisting of two columns and two rows.

4. In the first cell in the first row, type **Annual Meeting**. This is the variation of the index entry.

5. Press **TAB**, and then type **annual meeting**. This is the marked index entry. The word "annual" was autocorrected so that the first letter is uppercase.

6. Point to **Annual** so that the **AutoCorrect Options** box ▭ appears.

7. Point to the **AutoCorrect Options** box ▭ so that it changes to the **AutoCorrect Options** button � ▾, and then click the **AutoCorrect Options** button ▭ ▾. A menu appears.

8. On the menu, click **Stop Auto-capitalizing First Letter of Table Cells**. The menu closes, and the word you typed is changed back to all lowercase. The insertion point is still in the second cell in the first row.

9. Click in the first cell in the second row, type **Respondents**, and then press **TAB**. The insertion point moves to the second cell in the second row.

10. Type **respondents**.

11. Save the document as **NP_WD_10_AutoMark** in the location specified by your instructor, and then close the file. The NP_WD_10_Report file is the current document.

Now that you have created your AutoMark file, you need to access it from within the NP_WD_10_Report document. You can't do this from the Mark Index Entry dialog box; you need to use the Index dialog box.

To access the AutoMark file and mark the AutoMark entries:

1. On the ribbon, click the **References** tab, and then in the Index group, click the **Insert Index** button. The Index dialog box opens with the Index tab selected.

2. Click **AutoMark**. The Open Index AutoMark File dialog box opens. It is similar to the Open dialog box.

3. Navigate to the location where you saved the NP_WD_10_AutoMark file, click **NP_WD_10_AutoMark** to select it, and then click **Open**. All words in the document that match the words in the first column in the table in the AutoMark file are marked as main entries, using "annual meeting" and "respondents" as the entries. On page 5 (marked page 1 in the footer), in the paragraph below the heading "2.1. Survey Overview," an index field code appears next to "Respondents," marking the word with the entry "respondents."

4. Scroll to page 7 (marked page 3 in the footer) so that you can see the heading "2.3. Survey Coordinator" and the paragraph below it. In the fourth line of the paragraph, an index field code appears next to "Annual Meeting," marking it with the entry "annual meeting."

5. Press **CTRL+HOME** to move to the beginning of the document. Because the AutoMark file marked every instance of "Annual Meeting" as an index entry, that phrase was marked on the document title page. However, that instance of the phrase should not be included in the index, so you will delete the field code.

6. Above the list of names on the title page, select **{ XE "annual meeting" }**, and then press **DEL**. Now when you create the index, that instance of "annual meeting" will not be included.

Compiling an Index

After you mark all the desired index entries, subentries, cross-references, page-range references, and AutoMark entries, you're ready to **compile** the index—that is, you're ready to generate the index using the marked entries. Most often, indexes appear at the end of books, reports, or long documents.

Reference

Compiling an Index

- Move the insertion point to the location where you want to insert the index.
- Hide the field codes.
- On the References tab, in the Index group, click the Insert Index button.
- Select the desired options for controlling the appearance of the index.
- Click OK.

You'll compile the index on a new page at the end of the document. You need to create that new page. First, you need to hide the field codes. If the field codes are displayed when you compile the index, words are moved and may appear on different pages.

To create a new page for the index:

1. Scroll so that you can see the bottom of page 5 (marked page 1 in the footer) and the top of page 6 (marked page 2 in the footer). The index entry field codes on page 5 (marked page 1 in the footer) have caused some of the last paragraph on page 5 to appear on page 6, and the page break you inserted after this paragraph means that the rest of page 6 is blank. Also note on the status bar that there are now 11 pages in the document.

2. Click the **Home** tab on the ribbon, and then, in the Paragraph group, click the **Show/Hide** button ¶ to hide nonprinting characters and the field codes. With the field codes hidden, the entire paragraph at the bottom of page 5 now fits on that page, and page 6 is now filled with text. Also, there are now 10 pages in the document.

3. Press **CTRL+END**. The insertion point moves to the last paragraph in the document, which is the empty paragraph above the endnotes on page 10 (marked page 6 in the footer). This is an even page in the document.

4. Insert a Next Page section break, and then scroll to the new page in the document. The empty paragraph and the endnotes were moved to the new page. On the status bar, the new page is page 11. In the footer, the new page is page 1.

5. At the top of page 11, with the insertion point in the blank paragraph at the top of the new page, type **Index**, and then press **ENTER**.

6. Format **Index** with the Front/End Matter Heading style.

   At the bottom of page 11, the footer contains the wrong page number.

7. Scroll to the bottom of page 11, and then double-click in the footer area. The Header & Footer tab appears and is selected.

Tip

If two odd pages or two even pages in a row are created when you insert a Next Page section break, undo the action, click the Breaks button in the Page Setup group on the Layout tab, and then click Even Page or Odd Page on the menu to create a new page of the type you specified.

▶ **8.** In the Header & Footer group, click the **Page Number** button, and then click **Format Page Numbers**. The Page Number Format dialog box opens.

▶ **9.** In the Page numbering section, click the **Continue from previous section** option button, and then click **OK**. The dialog box closes, and the page number in the footer changes to 7.

▶ **10.** On the Header & Footer tab, in the Close group, click the **Close Header and Footer** button.

An index is usually the last item in a document. However, your document contains endnotes that appear at the end of the document. When you created the new page, the endnotes moved to that page as well. You need to change the location of the endnotes so that they appear at the end of the previous section.

To change the location of the endnotes:

▶ **1.** Scroll to page 10 (marked page 6 in the footer), and then click anywhere in the last paragraph on the page.

▶ **2.** On the ribbon, click the **References** tab, and then in the Footnotes group, click the **Dialog Box Launcher** ⬚. The Footnotes and Endnotes dialog box opens. The Endnotes option button is selected, and End of document appears in the Endnotes box.

  Trouble? If the Endnotes option button is not selected, click it.

▶ **3.** Click the **Endnotes** arrow, and then click **End of section**.

▶ **4.** At the bottom of the dialog box, click **Apply**. The endnotes now appear at the end of the current section, after the last paragraph on page 10.

Now you are ready to compile the index.

To compile the index:

▶ **1.** Press **CTRL+END**. The insertion point appears in the blank paragraph below the "Index" heading on page 11.

▶ **2.** On the ribbon, click the **References** tab, and then in the Index group, click the **Insert Index** button. The Index dialog box opens with the Index tab selected. In the Formats box, From template appears, indicating that the index will be formatted using the document's template styles, and in the Columns box, 2 appears, indicating that the index will be arranged in two columns. See Figure 10–45.

Figure 10–45 Index dialog box

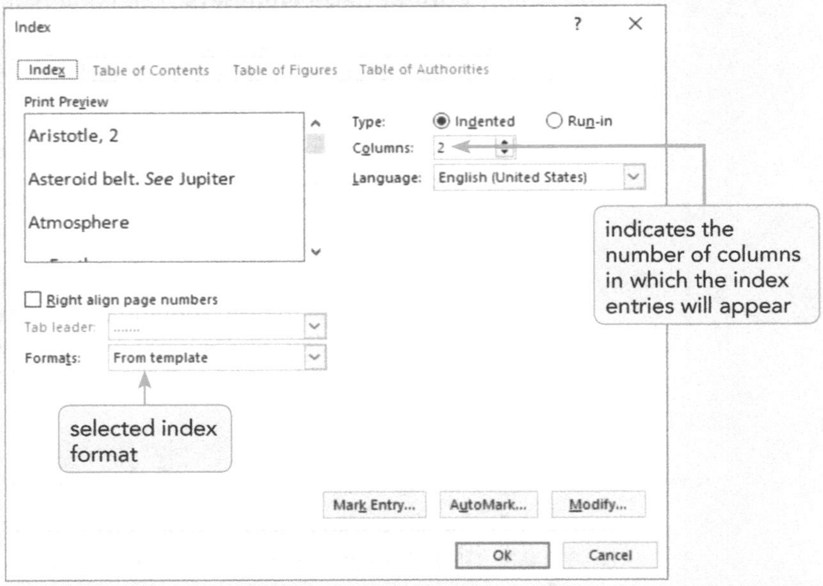

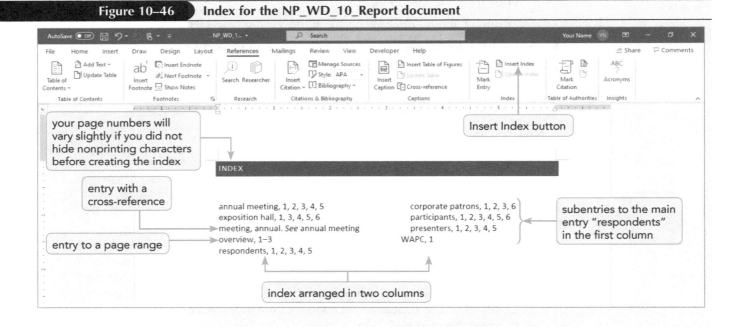

3. Click **OK**. The dialog box closes, and the index is compiled. See Figure 10–46.

Figure 10–46 Index for the NP_WD_10_Report document

The column break in the Index is not in the best position. The main entry "respondents" should be in the same column as its subentries. You will update the index in the next section, so you will wait to see what effect the update has on the index before you fix this issue.

Updating an Index

After an index is compiled, you can still make changes to it, including adding new entries. To update an index, you click the Update Index button in the Index group on the References tab. This is similar to updating a table of contents. Likewise, if you created a table of figures or a table of authorities, you could click the appropriate Update button in the Captions or Table of Authorities group on the References tab.

Bailey asks you to add one more entry to the index. You'll mark the entry and then update the index to include the new entry.

To create a new index entry and then update the index:

▶ **1.** Scroll up to page 6 (page 2 in the footer), in the paragraph below the "2.3. Survey Coordinator" heading, in the first line, select the phrase **Marketfield Research Associates**.

▶ **2.** On the References tab, in the Index group, click the **Mark Entry** button, and then in the Mark Index Entry dialog box, click **Mark All**. The phrase is marked as an index entry, and the nonprinting characters and the field codes are toggled back on. Now you need to update the index.

▶ **3.** Close the Mark Index Entry dialog box, and then hide the nonprinting characters so that the page numbers will be correct.

▶ **4.** Press **CTRL+END**, and then click anywhere in the index. The entire index field is selected.

▶ **5.** On the ribbon, click the **References** tab, and then in the Index group, click the **Update Index** button. The entry "Marketfield Research Associates" is added to the index. Notice that the "respondents" entry shifted to the second column, so you no longer need to add a column break to the index.

> **Tip**
>
> You can also right-click the index field, and then click Update Field on the shortcut menu to update the index.

Your index is short but representative of the type of entries that would appear in a full index. Of course, to create a proper index, you would need to carefully examine each page to identify important terms or phrases that should be marked as index entries.

You have made many changes to the document, so you need to update the table of contents.

To update the table of contents:

▶ **1.** Go to page 3 in the document so that you can see the table of contents, and then click anywhere in the table of contents. The entire table of contents field is selected.

▶ **2.** On the References tab, in the Table of Contents group, click the **Update Table** button. The Update Table of Contents dialog box opens.

▶ **3.** Click the **Update entire table** option button, and then click **OK**. The table of contents is updated to include the numbered headings, the "Index" heading, and the updated page numbers.

Creating a Table of Figures

A table of figures is a list of the captions for all the pictures, charts, graphs, slides, or other illustrations in a document, along with the page number for each. As with a table of contents, the entries in a table of figures are links to the captions to which they refer. You can click an entry in a table of figures to jump to that caption in the document.

To create a table of figures:

1. Scroll to page 4 in the document, display nonprinting characters, position the insertion point in the blank paragraph below the heading "List of Figures," and then hide nonprinting characters again.

2. On the ribbon, click the **References** tab if necessary, and then in the Captions group, click the **Insert Table of Figures** button. The Table of Figures dialog box opens with the Table of Figures tab selected. See Figure 10–47.

Figure 10–47 Table of Figures dialog box

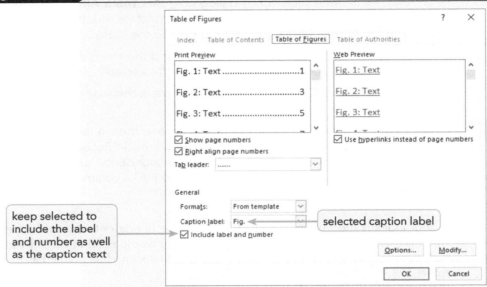

Notice that Fig. appears in the Caption label box. This is the correct label for the figures in this document. Below the Caption label box, the Include label and number check box is selected. This must be selected in order for the label "Fig." and the figure number to be listed as well as the caption text.

Trouble? If Fig. does not appear in the Caption label box, click the Caption label arrow, and then click Fig.

3. Click **OK**. The table of figures is generated, as shown in Figure 10–48.

Figure 10–48 Table of figures in the document

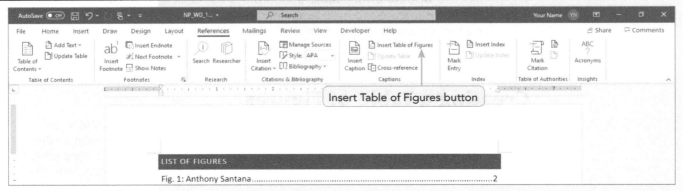

4. Save the document.

Insight

Creating a Table of Authorities

Besides tables of contents and lists of figures, Word can also generate other lists. When creating legal documents, you may have to create a table of authorities, which is a list of references to cases, statutes, or rules. Similar to other Word-generated lists, a table of authorities includes the page numbers on which the references appear. To create a table of authorities, first mark all the citations (references) by clicking the References tab, click the Mark Citation button in the Table of Authorities group to display the Mark Citation dialog box, select the appropriate category (Cases, Statutes, Rules, Treatises, and so forth), and then click Mark or Mark All. Then you can generate the table of authorities by clicking the Insert Table of Authorities button in the Table of Authorities group on the References tab. To update a table of authorities after adding more citations to a document, click the Update Table button in the Table of Authorities group on the References tab.

Updating Fields Before Printing

> **Tip**
>
> To print only one section in a document, on the Print screen in Backstage view, click in the Pages box, and then type the letter "s" followed by the section number.

Many of the elements you have added to the NP_WD_10_Report document, such as the cross-references and the table of contents, include fields. As you know, you should always update fields in a document before printing to ensure you are printing the most current information in the document. Instead of manually updating the fields, you can set Word to automatically update fields before printing. By default, the option to update fields before printing is turned off.

Bailey wants you to print the document. Before you do, you'll set the option to update the fields before printing.

Note: If your instructor does not want you to print the document, read, but do not execute the following steps.

To change the options to update fields before printing and print the document:

1. On the ribbon, click the **File** tab, scroll down, and then in the navigation pane, click **Options**. The Word Options dialog box opens.

2. In the navigation pane, click **Display**, and then click the **Update fields before printing** check box under "Printing options" to select it, if necessary.

   Trouble? If the Update fields before printing check box is already selected, do not click it.

3. Click **OK** to close the dialog box. Now you will print the document. Because the fields will be updated, you need to make sure the nonprinting characters are hidden so the index is updated correctly.

> **Tip**
>
> If you are going to print on paper that is a size other than 8½" x 11", click the Size button in the Page Setup group on the Layout tab or click the Letter button on the Print screen in Backstage view.

4. Hide nonprinting characters, click the **File** tab, and then in the navigation pane, click **Print**. The Print screen appears in Backstage view.

5. Click the **Print** button. The Update Table of Contents dialog box opens, prompting you to update the table of contents. The Update page numbers only option button is selected.

6. Click **OK**. The dialog box closes, and the Update Table of Figures dialog box opens with the Update page numbers only option button selected.

▶ **7.** Click **OK**. The dialog box closes, and the document prints. Next, you should turn off Update fields before printing so you leave Word in the same state you found it when you started this module.

▶ **8.** Click the **File** tab, scroll down, and then in the navigation pane, click **Options** to open the Word Options dialog box.

▶ **9.** In the navigation pane, click **Display**.

▶ **10.** If the Update fields before printing check box was not selected prior to you completing this set of steps, click the **Update fields before printing** check box to deselect it.

Trouble? If the Update fields before printing check box was already selected prior to you completing this set of steps, do not click it to deselect it.

▶ **11.** Click **OK**.

Checking Compatibility

Bailey plans to send the final version of the survey report to the other board members. Because they do not all have the most recent version of Word, she asks you to check the document for features that are not compatible with earlier versions of Word.

To check compatibility with earlier versions of Word:

▶ **1.** On the ribbon, click the **File** tab and then click **Info**. The Info screen opens in Backstage view.

▶ **2.** Click the **Check for Issues** button, and then click **Check Compatibility**. The Microsoft Word Compatibility Checker dialog box opens. Several issues were found. See Figure 10–49.

Figure 10–49   **Microsoft Word Compatibility Checker dialog box**

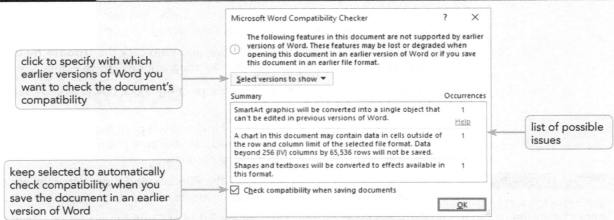

You'll inform Bailey of these incompatibilities so she can decide if she wants to save the document in an earlier format.

▶ **3.** If the **Check compatibility when saving documents** check box is not selected, click it. Now the Compatibility Checker will run automatically if you try to save the document in an earlier version of Word.

▶ **4.** Click **OK**.

Encrypting a Document

To **encrypt** a file is to modify the data structure to make the information unreadable to anyone who does not have the password. When you encrypt a Word document, you assign a password to the file. When you create passwords, keep in mind that they are case sensitive; this means that "PASSWORD" is different from "password." Also, you must remember your password. If you forget the password you assign to a document, you won't be able to open it.

Reference

Encrypting a Document

- Click the File tab and then click Info to open the Info screen in Backstage view.
- Click the Protect Document button, and then click Encrypt with Password.
- In the Encrypt Document dialog box, type a password in the Password box, and then click OK to open the Confirm Password dialog box.
- Retype the password in the Reenter password box.
- Click OK.

Bailey asks you to encrypt the report to prevent any unauthorized readers from opening it.

To encrypt the document:

▶ 1. On the ribbon, click the **File** tab and then click **Info.** The Info screen opens in Backstage view.

▶ 2. Click the **Protect Document** button, and then click **Encrypt with Password**. The Encrypt Document dialog box opens. Here, you'll type a password.

Tip

To remove the password, delete the password in the Encrypt Document dialog box, and then click OK.

▶ 3. Type **Report** in the Password box. The characters appear as black dots to prevent anyone from reading the password over your shoulder.

▶ 4. Click **OK**. The Confirm Password dialog box opens.

▶ 5. Type **Report** again, and then click **OK**. The dialog box closes, and a message appears next to the Protect Document button on the Info screen, indicating that a password is required to open this document.

Now, when you save the file, it will be in an encrypted format so that it can't be opened except by someone who knows the password. (Usually, you would use a stronger password than "Report." But for the purpose here, you'll keep it simple.)

Proskills

Decision Making: Creating Strong Passwords You Can Easily Remember

In a world where sharing digital information electronically is an everyday occurrence, a password used to encrypt a document is just one more password to remember. When deciding on a password, you should consider a strong password that consists of at least eight characters using a combination of uppercase and lowercase letters, numbers, and symbols. However, this type of password can be difficult to remember, especially if you have to remember multiple passwords. Some people use the same password for everything. This is not a good idea because if someone ever discovered your password, they would have access to all of the data or information protected by that password. Instead, you should come up with a plan for creating passwords. For example, you could choose a short word that you can easily remember for one part of the password. The second part of the password could be the name of the file, website, or account, but instead of typing it directly, type it backwards, or use the characters in the row above or below the characters that would spell out the name. Or you could split the name of the website and put your short word in the middle of the name. Other possibilities are to combine your standard short word and the website or account name, but replace certain letters with symbols—for example, replace every letter "E" with "#," or memorize a short phrase from a poem or story and use it with some of the substitutions described above. Establishing a process for creating a password means that you will be able to create strong passwords for all of your accounts that you can easily remember.

Making a Document Read-Only

You can make a document **read-only**, which means that others can read but not modify the document. There are two ways to make a document read-only. You can mark the document as final, or you can set the document to always open as read-only. If you mark a document as final, the next time the file is opened, it will be read-only. If you turn off the read-only status, make changes, and then save and close the file, it will no longer be marked as final. If a document is set to always open as read-only and you turn off the read-only status to make changes, the next time the document is opened, it will still be marked as read-only.

Bailey asks you to try both ways of making the document read-only.

To mark the document as final and to always open as read-only:

▶ **1.** On the Info screen in Backstage view, click the **Protect Document** button, and then click **Mark as Final**. A dialog box opens indicating that the document will be marked as final and saved.

▶ **2.** Click **OK**. The dialog box closes and another dialog box opens, telling you that the document was marked as final.

▶ **3.** Click **OK**. The dialog box closes, a message is added next to the Protect Document button telling you that the document has been marked as final, and "[Read-Only]" appears next to the document title in the title bar.

▶ **4.** In the navigation pane, click the **Back** button ⊕ to exit Backstage view. The ribbon is collapsed, a yellow MARKED AS FINAL bar appears below the collapsed ribbon, the Marked as Final icon appears on the status bar, and "Read-Only" appears in the title bar. See Figure 10–50.

Figure 10–50   **Document marked as final**

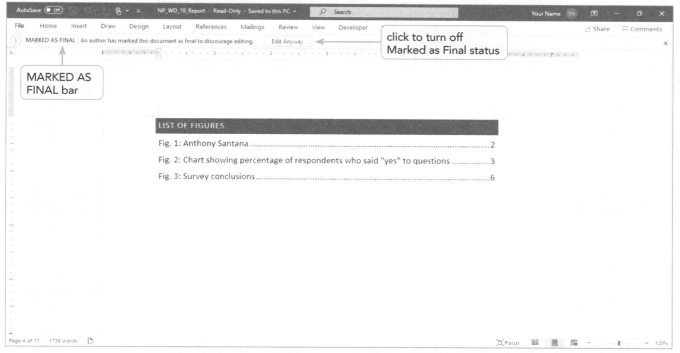

MARKED AS FINAL bar

click to turn off
Marked as Final status

LIST OF FIGURES

5. Close the NP_WD_10_Report file, and then reopen it. The Password dialog box appears.

6. In the Password box, type **Report**, and then click **OK**. The document opens, and the yellow MARKED AS FINAL bar appears.

7. In the MARKED AS FINAL bar, click **Edit Anyway**. The bar disappears, and the ribbon is displayed.

8. Save the document, close it, and then reopen it, typing **Report** in the Password box when asked. The yellow MARKED AS FINAL bar does not appear.

9. Click the **File** tab, click **Info**, click the **Protect Document** button, and then click **Always Open Read-Only**. Additional text added next to the Protect Document button name tells you that the document has been set to read-only.

10. In the navigation pane, click **Save**.

11. Close and then reopen the document. After you enter the password, a dialog box opens telling you that the author would like you to open this as read-only and asking if you want to open as read-only. If you click Yes, the document will open with the yellow bar at the top again. If you click No, the document will open without the yellow bar at the top and you will be able to edit it.

12. Click **No**. The document opens. The yellow bar is not at the top and the ribbon is available.

13. Save the changes to the document, close it, and then reopen it. The same dialog box appears asking if you want to open the document as read-only. The Always open as read-only status stays applied to the file unless you change it on the Info screen in Backstage view.

14. **sam** ⬆ Click **Cancel**. The document does not open.

Insight

Adding a Digital Signature to a Document File

A **digital signature** is an electronic attachment not visible in the file that verifies the authenticity of the author or the version of the file by comparing the digital signature to a digital certificate. A **digital certificate** is a code attached to a file that verifies the identity of the creator of the file. When you digitally sign a document, the file is marked as read-only. If anyone removes the read-only status to make changes to the document, the signature is marked as invalid because it is no longer the same document the signatory signed. You can obtain a digital certificate from a certification authority.

To add a digital signature to a document, click the Protect Document button on the Info screen in Backstage view, click Add a Digital Signature, and then click OK. If the Get a Digital ID dialog box opens, telling you that you don't have a digital ID and asking if you would like to get one from a Microsoft Partner, that means no digital certificate is stored on the computer you are using. If you click Yes, your browser starts, and a webpage opens listing certificate authorities from whom you can purchase a digital certificate. Note that you cannot add a digital signature to a master document; you must unlink all the subdocuments first.

If you or your company has access to a Rights Management Server or you are using Office 365 with RMS Online, you can restrict access to a document so that others can read it but not make any changes to it or copy or print it. To do this, click the Protect Document button, and then use the Restrict Access command.

You have completed the survey report for Bailey. The skills you learned in this module will be extremely useful as you create long documents for school and in the workplace.

Review

Session 10.3 Quick Check

1. What type of page numbers are typically used in front matter?

2. What happens when you change the "Start at" page number in a section?

3. Explain what a gutter margin is.

4. How do you insert a heading in a footer using a field code?

5. Why would you use a nonbreaking hyphen or a nonbreaking space in a document?

6. What are the four types of entries you can create using the Mark Index Entry dialog box?

7. What is an AutoMark file?

8. When a document is marked as final, can it be edited?

Practice

Review Assignments

Data Files needed for the Review Assignments: NP_WD_10-2.docx, Support_WD_10_Alonzo.docx, Support_WD_10_Marie.docx

The annual meeting of the World Association of Personal Chefs (WAPC), which brings together personal chefs from all over the world, has traditionally been held at midrange resorts in order to encourage the highest possible attendance. Although the results of the survey the WAPC Annual Meeting Committee conducted indicated that most participants, presenters, and corporate patrons were satisfied with the most recent annual meeting, the committee members are considering switching to biennial meetings at more upscale locations. The committee hired Marketfield Research Associates to conduct another survey to find out if WAPC members would rather attend a meeting only every other year (biennially) but at more upscale resorts—and therefore at a higher cost—or if they would prefer to continue to attend annual meetings at a more moderate cost per meeting. Bailey Lawrence, along with Alonzo Garza and Marie Choi, created the documents that will become the master document and the subdocuments for the report on the new survey. It's your job to compile the report as a master document and then perform the necessary revisions, such as creating an index. Complete the following steps:

1. Start Word, create a new, blank document, switch to Outline view, and then save the document as **NP_WD_10_Report2** in the location specified by your instructor.

2. Type the following as Level 1 and Level 2 headings as an outline.

   Recommendations
   Background
     Survey Background
     Response Rates
   Summary
   Corporate Patrons
   Participants
   Presenters

3. Move the Level 1 heading "Background" with its subordinate text below the "Summary" heading, and then move the Level 1 heading "Recommendations" below the Level 1 heading "Presenters."

4. Insert the following as body text under the Level 1 heading "Recommendations" (including the period): **The WAPC Annual Meeting Committee recommends switching to biennial meetings held for four days.** Save your changes, and then close the document.

5. Open the document **NP_WD_10-2.docx** from the Word10 > Review folder included with your Data Files. Add your name in the blank paragraph below the name "Marie Choi" on the title page, and then save it as **NP_WD_10_Master2** in the location specified by your instructor.

6. On page 1, select the "Table of Contents" heading, and then create a new style named **TOC** that is based on the current formatting of that heading but has Body Text as an outline level.

7. Convert the sections beginning with the headings "Survey of Corporate Patrons," "Survey of Participants," and "Survey of Presenters" into individual subdocuments. Save your changes to the master document so that the subdocuments are saved as individual files.

8. Open the file **Support_WD_10_Alonzo.docx**, which is located in the Word10 > Review folder, save it as **NP_WD_10_Alonzo** in the same folder that contains the file NP_WD_10_Master2, and then close the file NP_WD_10_Alonzo. In the NP_WD_10_Master2 document, insert the **NP_WD_10_Alonzo** file as a subdocument in the Body Text paragraph above the "Survey of Corporate Patrons" heading.

9. Open the file **Support_WD_10_Marie.docx**, which is located in the Word10 > Review folder, save it as **NP_WD_10_Marie** in the same folder that contains the file NP_WD_10_Master2, and then close the file NP_WD_10_Marie. At the end of the NP_WD_10_Master2 document, in the last blank paragraph, insert the **NP_WD_10_Marie** file as a subdocument. Save the master document.

10. In Outline view, use the Show Level button to display the first two levels of headings. Position the insertion point in the "Survey of Corporate Patrons" heading, and then add automatic numbering to all the section headings using the same style on the Multilevel List menu that you used in the module steps. Change the style of the Level 2 headings (headings formatted with the Heading 2 style) so the period is replaced with a dash (hyphen). Modify the formatting of the Front/End Matter Heading style and the TOC style so that the headings with those styles applied are not numbered.

11. Save the changes to the document.

12. Make sure you saved the changes to the document, and then save the document as **NP_WD_10_Biennial** in the location specified by your instructor.

13. In the NP_WD_10_Biennial document, unlink all five subdocuments. Save the changes to the document.

14. Starting from the end of the document, delete all the section breaks in the document (do not delete the manual page break after the paragraph after the "Table of Contents" heading), and delete the blank paragraph above the heading "5 Survey of Presenters" and the blank paragraph above the heading "3 Survey of Corporate Patrons." Add Next Page section breaks before the headings "Table of Contents" and "1 Executive Summary."

15. On page 5, replace the yellow highlighted placeholder text "[Chart 1]," "[Chart 2]," and "[Chart 3]" with pie charts. For each chart, do not change the text in cell B1, type **Responded** in cell A2, and type **Did not respond** in cell A3. After adding the following data, remove rows 4 and 5 in the spreadsheet from the chart:

Chart 1:

Responded **23%**

Did not respond **77%**

Chart 2:

Responded **80%**

Did not respond **20%**

Chart 3:

Responded **94%**

Did not respond **6%**

16. For each chart, make the following format changes:

a. Remove the chart title.

b. Change the style to Style 7, and change the color scheme to Colorful Palette 3.

c. Change the position of the legend so it is on the right side of the chart.

d. Resize each chart object so it is 2.5" high and 4.5" wide (using the Shape Height and Shape Width boxes in the Size group on the Format tab).

e. Center each chart horizontally in the paragraph.

17. Insert **Figure 1: Percentage of corporate patron respondents** as a caption below the first pie chart. Insert **Figure 2: Percentage of participant respondents** as a caption below the second pie chart. Insert **Figure 3: Percentage of presenter respondents** as a caption below the third pie chart.

18. In the paragraph below the heading "2-2 Response Information," replace the yellow highlighted placeholders for the cross-references with cross-references to the pie charts using only the figure label and number.

19. In the paragraph below the heading "2 Overview," insert an endnote after the last period in the paragraph. Type **WAPC members Brad Welke and Jana Saadi assisted as well.** (including the period).

20. Restrict editing in the document by not allowing users to change the theme and allowing only changes marked with tracked changes. Do not require a password.

21. In the paragraph below the heading "1 Executive Summary," in the last sentence, change the "50%" to **60%**.

22. Remove the editing restrictions so that users are allowed to make changes without having them tracked. Do not remove the restriction for changing the theme.

23. Use the Document Inspector to remove comments, revisions, and versions.

24. Use the Accessibility Checker to identify the elements that could cause problems for people who use assistive devices. Add the following alt text to the three charts:

    Figure 1 **Chart illustrating that only 23% of corporate patrons responded to the survey**

    Figure 2 **Chart illustrating that 80% of participants responded to the survey**

    Figure 3 **Chart illustrating that 94% of presenters responded to the survey**

25. Center the title page between its top and bottom margins.

26. In the front matter, insert lowercase Roman numeral page numbers right-aligned in the footer, with page i starting on the Table of Contents page. Remove the link to the first section (the title page), and then remove the page number on the title page.

27. Insert Arabic numerals as page numbers right-aligned in the footer on the rest of the pages of the report, with page 1 starting on the page containing the heading "1 Executive Summary."

28. Set up all the pages except the title page so that they have a 0.5" gutter.

29. Set up all the pages except the title page so odd and even pages have different formatting.

30. Set up footers so that the odd-page footers include the document title **Biennial Meeting Feasibility Survey** at the left margin and the page number at the right margin. In the section of the document numbered with Arabic numerals, set up even-page footers so that the page number is at the left margin and a style reference to the Heading 1 style is at the right margin. In the section of the document numbered with Roman numerals, set up even-page footers so that the page number is at the left margin and a style reference to the Front/End Matter Heading style is at the right margin. (*Hint*: Review the even-page footers to make sure the even-page footers in the section containing the Arabic page numbers include a reference to the Heading 1 style, and that the even-page footer in the section containing the Roman numeral page numbers include a reference to the Front/End Matter style. Break the link between the previous sections if needed.)

31. At the end of the document (before the end note), insert a new, blank paragraph, and then insert a Next Page section break. Type **Index** in the blank paragraph on the new last page, and then press ENTER. Format "Index" with the Front/End Matter Heading style, and then modify the footer on this page so that the page number is correct and so that the field references the Front/End Matter Heading style.

32. Change the location of the endnotes so that they appear at the end of the section before the section that contains the "Index" heading.

33. In the paragraph below the heading "6 Recommendations," change the hyphen at the end of the second line between "two" and "day" to a nonbreaking hyphen. (*Hint*: If the hyphen between "two" and "day" does not appear at the end of the line, check to make sure the gutter margin of all of the sections except for the section containing the title page is still set to 0.5".) In the paragraph below the heading "2-2 Response Information," at the end of the second line, change the space between "(see" and the cross-reference to Figure 2 to a nonbreaking space.

34. Review the document for bad page breaks, and then insert a page break before the heading "4-2 Participant Focus Group Responses." Select the page break you inserted, and apply the Normal style to that paragraph.

35. Create the following index entries:

    a. Mark the first instance of "WAPC" in the body of the report. (Do not mark this text on the title page.)

    b. Mark every occurrence of "participants," "corporate patrons," and "presenters" as subentries to the main entry "respondents." Then mark every occurrence of "respondents."

    c. Mark every instance of "upscale" as a main index entry. Create "opulent" as a cross-reference index entry to the main entry "upscale."

d. Bookmark the section "2 Overview" (including the two subsections) with a bookmark named **OverviewSection**, and then mark the bookmark as a page range index entry under the main entry "overview." (*Hint*: Make sure you change the text in the Main entry box so that it is "overview" and not "Overview.")

e. Create an AutoMark file named **NP_WD_10_NewAutoMark** that contains the entries shown in Figure 10–51, and then mark the AutoMark entries.

Figure 10–51   Data for NP_WD_10_NewAutoMark file

participant	participants
Participants	participants
Participant	participants
corporate patron	corporate patrons
Corporate patrons	corporate patrons
Corporate patron	corporate patrons
presenter	presenters
Presenters	presenters
Presenter	presenters

36. Move the insertion point to the end of the document, below the heading "Index." Hide nonprinting characters, and then generate the index.

37. Mark every instance of "biennial" as a main index entry. Hide nonprinting characters, and then update the index. (*Hint*: Click the Layout tab, click the Breaks button in the Page Setup group, and then click Column.)

38. Display nonprinting characters, click before the blank paragraph mark below the heading "List of Figures" in the front matter, and then press ENTER. (*Hint*: If the paragraph containing the section break is formatted with the Heading 1 style, undo the last action, position the insertion point before the paragraph mark, and then press ENTER.) Hide the nonprinting characters, and then in the first empty paragraph below the "List of Figures," insert a table of figures.

39. With the nonprinting characters hidden, insert a table of contents below the "Table of Contents" heading in the front matter using the Custom Table of Contents command on the Table of Contents menu.

40. Encrypt the document using the password **Biennial**. If requested, update the fields before printing, and then print the document. If you changed the Printing option in the Word Options dialog box to update the fields before printing, change it back.

41. Mark the document as Always open read-only, save it, and then close it.

Apply

Case Problem 1

Data Files needed for this Case Problem: NP_WD_10-3.docx, Support_WD_10_Background.docx, Support_WD_10_Market.docx, Support_WD_10_Summary.docx

Bradford Estate   Bradford Estate was established in 1727 on 85 acres in Westerly, Rhode Island. The estate, located on the coastline, was the summer residence of various families for more than 250 years. The mansion contains 16 rooms and was completed in 1754. The estate has been neglected for the past 50 years, and last year, the nonprofit group The Friends of Bradford Estate was established to prepare a plan to modernize the facilities and market the estate as a viable location for small conferences and events. Members of the group have written drafts of the various parts of the business plan for the estate in preparation for requesting a loan. They asked you to help put the final document together and format it. Complete the following steps:

1. Open the document **NP_WD_10-3.docx** from the Word10 > Case1 folder included with your Data Files, and then save it as **NP_WD_10_Plan** in the location specified by your instructor.

2. On the title page (page 1), in the blank paragraph below "Prepared By," type your name.

3. On page 1, in the blank paragraph above the "List of Tables" heading, type **Contents**, and then press ENTER. Apply the Headings style to the "Contents" paragraph, and then create a new style named **Contents** based on the custom Headings style, but with an outline level set to Body Text.

4. Open the files **Support_WD_10_Background.docx**, **Support_WD_10_Market.docx**, and **Support_WD_10_Summary.docx**, which are located in the Word10 > Case1 folder, and then save them as **NP_WD_10_Background**, **NP_WD_10_Market**, and **NP_WD_10_Summary**, respectively, in the same folder in which you saved NP_WD_10_Plan. Close these three files.

5. In the NP_WD_10_Plan document, in the blank paragraph above the heading "Index," insert the files **NP_WD_10_Summary**, **NP_WD_10_Background**, and **NP_WD_10_Market**, in that order, as subdocuments.

6. Show Level 1 headings in Outline view, and then add automatic numbering to all headings formatted with the Heading 1 style using the style in the first column in the last row on the Multilevel List menu. Modify the heading numbers by replacing the period after the heading number for level 1 with) (a close parenthesis). Remove the numbering from the custom Contents and Headings style definitions.

7. Save the changes to the master document, and then save the document as **NP_WD_10_PlanFinal** in the location specified by your instructor.

8. Unlink the three subdocuments, and then save the document again.

9. Delete the Continuous section break on page 6. Delete the two Continuous section breaks on page 4. Delete the two Continuous section breaks on page 2, and then restore the "II) Background" heading by placing the insertion point before the word "Background" at the end of the third paragraph on the page, pressing ENTER, and then applying the Heading 1 style to the "Background" paragraph. Finally, delete the Continuous section break below the "List of Tables" heading on page 1.

10. On page 4, replace the placeholder text "[INSERT COLUMN CHART]" with a column chart based on the data in the table above it. Do not type the column headers in cells A1 and B1. (*Hint*: When the spreadsheet opens, click in the document behind it, and then scroll the document so that you can see the table.)

11. Remove the chart title and the legend, change the color scheme to Colorful Palette 4, and then use the Shape Height and Shape Width boxes in the Size group on the Format tab to change the dimensions of the chart object to 2.8" high and 5" wide. Center the chart horizontally on the page.

12. Add captions to the two tables in the document using the label "Table." Do not add any descriptive text to the table captions. Make sure the numbering format is 1, 2, 3,… and the caption appears above the table. (Note that table captions appear above tables by default.) Center the paragraph containing the captions horizontally on the page.

13. Add a caption to the chart using the label "Figure." After the space following the figure number in the caption, add **Projected number of events in 2026** as the descriptive text.

14. Add cross-references where indicated to the two tables and to the chart, using only the label and number.

15. Insert Next Page section breaks before the "Contents," "I) Summary," and "Index" headings. Insert an ordinary page break before the "List of Tables" heading. Insert another ordinary page break on page 5 before the second paragraph after the "IV) Market Analysis" heading so that paragraph and the bulleted list after it move to the next page.

16. Center the text on the title page between its top and bottom margins.

17. Set up the pages (except the title page) as odd and even pages, with a 0.5" gutter.

18. Insert page numbers in the front matter using lowercase Roman numerals center-aligned at the top of the page, with page i starting on the "Contents" page, and then remove the page number on the title page. (You might need to reinsert the page numbers in the front matter after changing the format.) Start Arabic numeral page numbering with page 1 on the page containing the "I) Summary" heading (page 5 on the status bar). If necessary, correct the page number on the last page (the page with the "Index" heading) so it continues from the previous section.

19. On page i (page 3 on the status bar), unlink the footer from the previous section, type **Bradford Estate Business Plan**, and then center it horizontally in the footer.

20. On page 2 (page 6 on the status bar), insert a style reference in the footer so that the Heading 1 text appears. Center the text in the footer.

21. On page 2 (page 6 on the status bar), unlink the even page footers from the previous section. Then in the footer of page ii (page 4 on the status bar), edit the field in the footer so that the text formatted with the Headings style appears.

22. In the third bulleted item below the heading "IV) Market Analysis," replace the hyphen in "25-mile" with a nonbreaking hyphen.

23. In the first paragraph below the heading "V) Market Size," replace the space between "$210" and "million" with a nonbreaking space.

24. Mark every occurrence of "events" as a main entry in the index.

25. Create a cross-reference index entry for the word "bookings" to the main entry "events."

26. In Outline view, click the plus sign symbol next to "IV) Market Analysis," press and hold SHIFT, click the plus sign symbol next to "VI) Projected Bookings," and then bookmark the selected three sections with a bookmark named **Market**. Mark the bookmark as a page range index entry under the main entry **market**.

27. Create an AutoMark file named **NP_WD_10_PlanAutoMark** stored in the location specified by your instructor. Add the terms **event**, **Events**, and **Event** as entries in the left column of the table, and add **events** as the main entry in all three rows in the right column, and then mark those entries using the AutoMark file.

28. Position the insertion point in the paragraph below the "Index" heading, and then compile the index using the default settings. Remember to hide nonprinting characters before compiling the index.

29. Insert the table of contents using the Custom Table of Contents command. Remember to hide nonprinting characters before creating the table of contents.

30. Below the "List of Tables" heading in the front matter, before the paragraph mark, insert a list of all the tables. (*Hint*: In the Table of Figures dialog box, change the option in the Caption label box.)

31. Mark the document as final, and then close it.

Create

Case Problem 2

There are no Data Files needed for this Case Problem.

Preparing a Group Report   Your instructor will divide your class into workgroups of three to six students and will appoint a workgroup leader or have each workgroup select one. Each workgroup will collaborate to prepare a document that explains how specific Word features can be useful in the workplace. The group can decide if each member of the group needs to provide a description of a separate feature or if group members are allowed to collaborate. The final document needs to contain a description of at least three different features of Word along with explanations of their uses in the workplace. Complete the following steps:

1. Conduct a planning meeting to discuss how the workgroup will accomplish its goals, and how it can make all the sections consistent in style and format.

2. Create an outline for the document. The first heading should be **Introduction**, and this should be followed by a paragraph that describes the report.

3. Plan the document's overall formatting. Choose an appropriate theme. Decide if you want to use the default heading styles or modify the heading styles. Also, decide how you want to format figures, including how you want text to wrap around these elements. You will use two-sided printing, so plan the headers and footers accordingly.

4. Create a new document to be used as the master document for the report, and then save it as **NP_WD_10_Features** in the location specified by your instructor. Create a title page, and then set up headings for the table of contents and the index. Add the "Introduction" heading and paragraph. On the title page, if you are completing one document as a group, on the title page, type **Prepared by:** and then add each group member's name in a list sorted in alphabetical order by the group members' last names. If each member of the group is completing a separate document, type **Prepared by:** followed by your name, and then type **Group Members:** and add each group member's name in a list sorted in alphabetical order by the group members' last names (including your own name).

5. Each feature should appear in its own section on a new page. Each feature description should include at least one screenshot. (*Hint*: Use the Screen Clipping command on the Screenshot menu in the Illustrations group on the Insert tab.) Do not include captions or cross-references at this point. Format each section according to the formatting plan created in Step 3, and then protect each section for tracked changes (without a password).

6. Each group member should review the documents written by the other members of the group. Make at least one edit per document (the changes should be marked with revision marks), and then pass each document file along to the next group member so that all of the group's changes are made in a single copy of each document file. When everyone is finished, each workgroup member should have a copy of his or her document file that contains edits from all the members of the workgroup.

7. Retrieve the file for your section, unprotect the document, and then accept or reject the edits made by the other workgroup members. Discuss each section with the other group members as necessary until you all agree on the final status of all the sections.

8. Insert the prepared documents as subdocuments, and then format the document consistently according to the formatting plan you agreed on in Step 3. Add figure captions and cross-references.

9. Save the changes to the master document. Then, save the file as **NP_WD_10_FinalReport** in the location specified by your instructor, and unlink the subdocuments.

10. In the NP_WD_10_FinalReport document, remove the section breaks inserted when the subdocuments were inserted or created, and then add Next Page, Odd Page, or Even Page section breaks as needed so that you can set up different headers, footers, and page numbering for the title page, the front matter, and the body of the document.

11. Set up the document so the pages are formatted as odd and even pages. Create appropriate headers or footers for the odd and even pages. Make sure you include page numbers, the document title, and section names in the headers and/or footers.

12. Insert the table of contents.

13. Mark appropriate index entries (make sure you have at least eight entries in the index), and then compile the index.

14. Review the document on the Print screen in Backstage view, and then make any necessary changes to ensure that your document looks polished and professional. Save the changes to the document.

15. Change the setting to update fields before printing, and then print the document. Print on both sides of the document pages, if possible.

16. Change the setting to update fields before printing back to its original setting, if necessary, and then close the document.

Objectives

Session 9.1
- Work with financial functions to analyze loans and investments
- Create an amortization schedule
- Calculate interest and principal payments for a loan or investment

Session 9.2
- Perform calculations for an income statement
- Interpolate and extrapolate a series of values
- Calculate a depreciation schedule

Session 9.3
- Determine a payback period
- Calculate a net present value
- Calculate an internal rate of return
- Trace a formula error to its source

Exploring Financial Tools and Functions

Analyzing a Business Plan

Case | Holoease

Asli Kaplan is a financial analyst for Holoease, a startup tech company based in Athens, Georgia, that is introducing a new product: holographic printers for companies, small businesses, and individuals. Because of technological breakthroughs, the Holoease line of printers is more affordable and easier-to-use than previous models produced by other companies. The problem that still needs to be overcome is financial.

To obtain the capital that Holoease will need to start production, Asli must create a business plan that details the financial challenges the company will face and the likely return investors can expect within the next five years of operation. Asli needs your help in projecting future revenue, expenses, and cash flow. To do those calculations, you will rely on the Excel library of financial tools and functions.

EXCEL

Starting Data Files

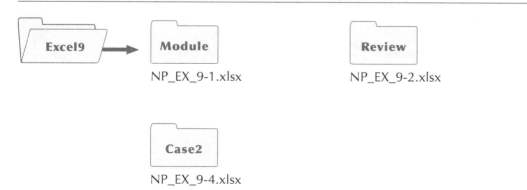

Excel9 → Module
NP_EX_9-1.xlsx

Review
NP_EX_9-2.xlsx

Case1
NP_EX_9-3.xlsx

Case2
NP_EX_9-4.xlsx

Session 9.1 Visual Overview:

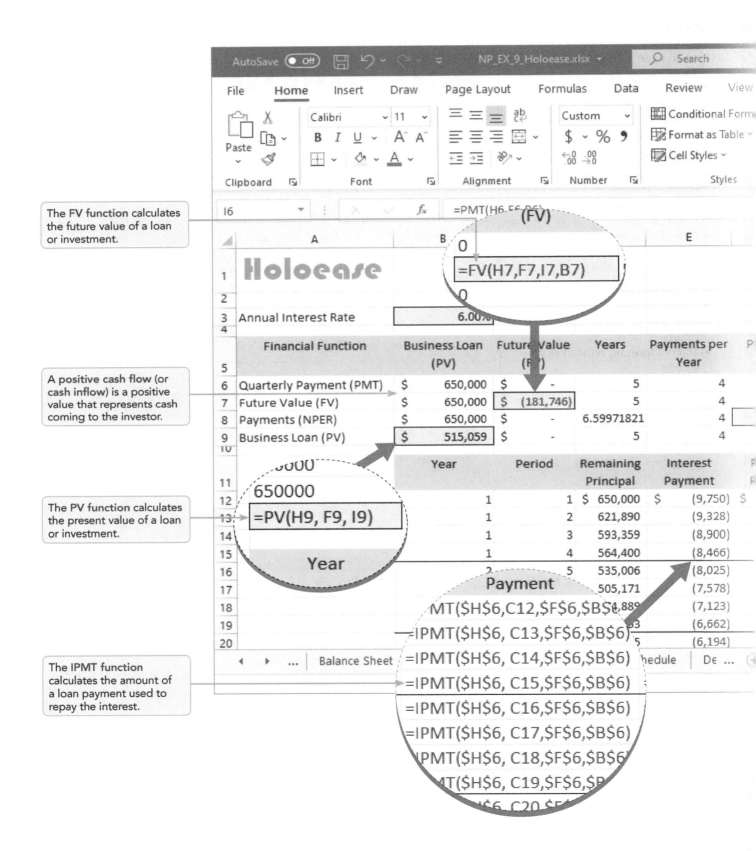

The FV function calculates the future value of a loan or investment.

A positive cash flow (or cash inflow) is a positive value that represents cash coming to the investor.

The PV function calculates the present value of a loan or investment.

The IPMT function calculates the amount of a loan payment used to repay the interest.

NP_EX_9_Holoease.xlsx

I6   =PMT(H6...

(FV)

0

=FV(H7,F7,I7,B7)

0

Holoease

Annual Interest Rate	6.00%	

Financial Function	Business Loan (PV)	Future Value (FV)	Years	Payments per Year
Quarterly Payment (PMT)	$ 650,000	$ -	5	4
Future Value (FV)	$ 650,000	$ (181,746)	5	4
Payments (NPER)	$ 650,000	$ -	6.59971821	4
Business Loan (PV)	$ 515,059	$ -	5	4

650000

=PV(H9, F9, I9)

Year

Payment

Year	Period	Remaining Principal	Interest Payment
1	1	$ 650,000	$ (9,750)
1	2	621,890	(9,328)
1	3	593,359	(8,900)
1	4	564,400	(8,466)
2	5	535,006	(8,025)
		505,171	(7,578)
		4,889	(7,123)
		3	(6,662)
		5	(6,194)

MT($H$6,C12,$F$6,$B$6...
=IPMT($H$6, C13,$F$6,$B$6)
=IPMT($H$6, C14,$F$6,$B$6)
=IPMT($H$6, C15,$F$6,$B$6)
=IPMT($H$6, C16,$F$6,$B$6)
=IPMT($H$6, C17,$F$6,$B$6)
IPMT($H$6, C18,$F$6,$B$6
MT($H$6, C19,$F$6,$B
$6, C20 $F

Balance Sheet   hedule   De ...

Loan and Investment Functions

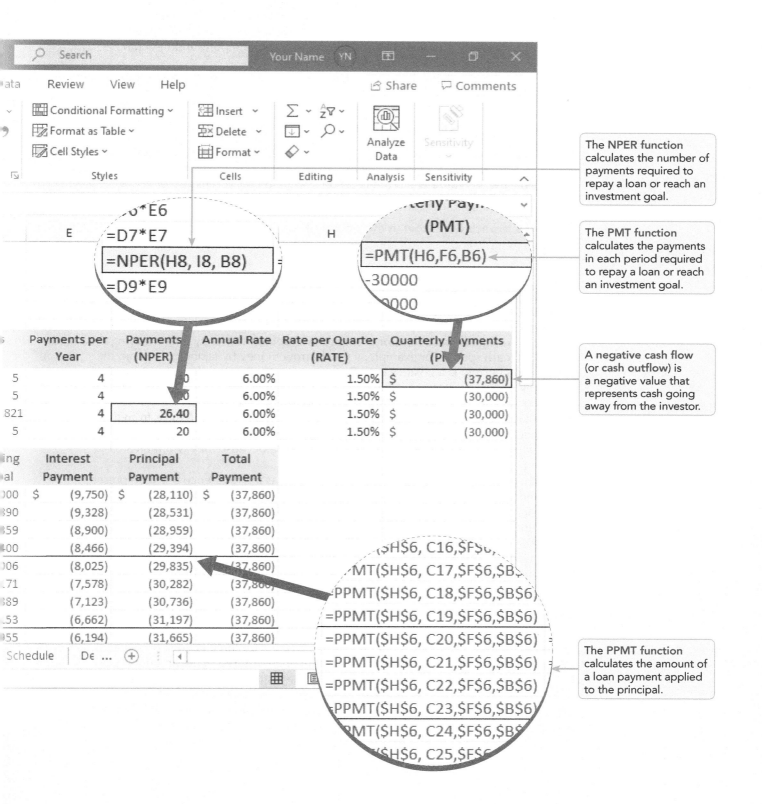

The NPER function calculates the number of payments required to repay a loan or reach an investment goal.

The PMT function calculates the payments in each period required to repay a loan or reach an investment goal.

A negative cash flow (or cash outflow) is a negative value that represents cash going away from the investor.

The PPMT function calculates the amount of a loan payment applied to the principal.

Introducing Financial Functions

In this module, you will learn the Excel skills you need to calculate important financial results used in business planning and analysis. In the process, you'll explore how to evaluate the financial aspects of a business proposal to finance a tech startup company. Be aware that this will be a simplified treatment of a very complicated financial problem that usually involves dozens of pages of financial reports and in-depth discussions with a team of accountants and lawyers.

You will start by opening the workbook that Asli created for the Holoease business plan.

To open the Holoease workbook:

▶ **1.** **sam**↓ Open the **NP_EX_9-1.xlsx** workbook located in the **Excel9 > Module** folder included with your Data Files, and then save the workbook as **NP_EX_9_Holoease** in the location specified by your instructor.

▶ **2.** In the Documentation worksheet, enter your name and the date.

▶ **3.** Go to each worksheet in the workbook and review its contents.

This module focuses on **financial functions**, which are the Excel functions used for analyzing loans, investments, and financial metrics. Many financial functions deal with **cash flow**, which is direction of money to and from an individual or group. A positive cash flow, or cash inflow, represents money that is coming to an individual (cash received). A negative cash flow, or cash outflow, represents money that is leaving the individual (cash spent). For example, if you borrow money by taking out a loan, the amount you borrow is a positive cash flow to you but a negative cash flow from the lender. When you start to repay the loan, the repayments are negative cash flows away from you back to the lender. On the other hand, money you invest is a negative cash flow because you are spending money on the investment, but any returns from that investment back to you are positive cash flows. Pay close attention to when positive and negative currency values are used in this module because they will indicate the direction of the cash flow.

Another important concept in financial functions is the difference between present value and future value. As the names imply, **present value** refers to the current value of a loan or investment, whereas **future value** references that loan or investment's value at a future date. For example, if you take out a loan for $50,000, its present value is $50,000, and if you repay the entire loan, its future value is $0.

Asli wants to estimate the costs associated with business loans to the company. To do that, you will use the Excel financial functions associated with loans and investments.

Calculating Borrowing Costs

The cost of a loan to an individual or business is based on three factors: principal, interest, and time. **Principal** is the amount of the loan. **Interest** is the amount added to the principal by the lender. You can think of interest as a "user fee" because the borrower is paying for the right to use the lender's money. Generally, interest is expressed as an annual percentage rate, or APR. For example, an 8% APR means that the annual interest rate on the loan is 8% of the amount owed to the lender.

An annual interest rate is divided by the number of payments per year (often monthly or quarterly). So, if the 8% annual interest rate is paid monthly, the resulting monthly interest rate is 1/12 of 8%, or about 0.67% per month. If payments are made quarterly, then the interest rate per quarter would be 1/4 of 8%, or 2% per quarter.

The third factor in calculating the loan cost is the time required to repay the loan, which is specified as the number of payment periods. The number of payment periods is based on the length of the loan multiplied by the number of payments per year. For example, a 10-year loan that is paid monthly has 120 payment periods. If that same 10-year loan is repaid quarterly, it has 40 payment periods.

Excel calculates five values associated with loans and investments:

- The required payment for each period of the loan or investment (PMT)
- The future value of the loan or investment (FV)
- The total number of payments (NPER)
- The present value of the loan or investment (PV)
- The interest rate of the loan or investment (RATE)

Knowing four of these values, you can use a financial function to calculate the fifth. You will start by exploring how to calculate the payment required for each period.

Calculating Payments with the PMT Function

To determine the size of payments made periodically to either repay a loan or reach an investment goal, use the PMT or payment function

> PMT(***Rate, Nper, Pv,*** [***Fv***=0], [***Type***=0])

where ***Rate*** is the interest rate per period, ***Nper*** is the total number of payment periods, ***Pv*** is the present value of the loan or investment, and ***Fv*** is the future value of the loan or investment after all the scheduled payments have been made. The ***Fv*** argument is optional and has a default value of 0. Finally, the optional ***Type*** value specifies whether payments are made at the end of each period (***Type***=0) or at the beginning (***Type***=1). The default is to assume that payments are made at the end of each period.

For example, if Asli's company borrows $500,000 at 6% annual interest to be repaid quarterly over a five-year period, the ***Rate*** value would be 6%/4, or 1.5%, because the 6% annual interest rate is divided into four quarters. The ***Nper*** value is 4×5 (four payments per year for five years), resulting in 20 payments over the five-year period. The PMT function for this loan would be entered as

> PMT(6%/4, 4*5, 500000)

returning the negative cash flow value –$29,122.87, indicating that the company must pay almost $30,000 each quarter to entirely repay the $500,000 loan in five years at 6% annual interest. Note that you enter the loan amount ($500,000) as a positive cash flow value because it represents money to the company. Also note that a default value of 0 is assumed for the ***Fv*** argument because the loan will be completely repaid and thus have a future value of 0. If you were to use the PMT function to calculate payments made toward an investment, you would use a negative ***Pv*** value and Excel would return a positive value since the investment is money being returned to you.

Reference

Working with Loans and Investments

- To calculate the size of the monthly or quarterly payments required to repay a loan or meet an investment goal, use PMT function

    PMT(*Rate, Nper, Pv,* [*Fv*=0], [*Type*=0])

    where *Rate* is the interest rate per period, *Nper* is the total number of payment periods, *Pv* is the present value, *Fv* is the future value, and *Type* specifies whether payments are made at the end of each period (*Type*=0) or at the beginning (*Type*=1).
- To calculate the future value of a loan or an investment, use the FV function

    FV(*Rate, Nper, Pmt,* [*Pv*=0], [*Type*=0])

- To calculate the number of payments required to repay a loan or meet an investment goal, use the NPER function

    NPER(*Rate, Pmt, Pv,* [*Fv*=0], [*Type*=0])

- To calculate the present value of a loan or an investment, use the PV function

    PV(*Rate, Nper, Pmt,* [*Fv*=0], [*Type*=0])

- To calculate the interest rate on a loan or an investment, use the RATE function

    RATE(*Nper, Pmt, Pv,* [*Fv*=0], [*Type*=0], [*Guess*=0.1])

    where the optional *Guess* argument provides an initial guess of the interest rate value.

Holoease plans to take out a business loan of $650,000 to cover some of the costs for the first few years of business. Asli wants you to calculate the quarterly payment on a $650,000 loan at 6% annual interest to be completely repaid in five years. A good practice is to enter the loan conditions into separate cells rather than including them in the PMT function. This makes the loan conditions visible and allows them to be changed in a what-if analysis. You will enter the loan conditions in the workbook Asli created, and then use the PMT function to calculate the quarterly payment.

To calculate a quarterly payment with the PMT function:

▶ 1. Go to the **Loan Analysis** worksheet. Asli has already entered and formatted much of the content in this worksheet.

▶ 2. In cell **B4**, enter **6%** as the annual interest rate of the loan.

▶ 3. In cell **B7**, enter **$650,000** as the amount of the business loan.

▶ 4. In cell **C7**, enter **0** for the future value of the loan because the loan will be completely repaid by the company.

▶ 5. In cell **D7**, enter **5** as the length of the loan in years.

▶ 6. In cell **E7**, enter **4** as the number of payments per year, which is quarterly.

▶ 7. In cell **F7**, enter the formula **=D7*E7** to calculate the total number of loan payments. In this case, four loan payments per year for five years is 20.

▶ 8. In cell **G7**, enter the formula **=$B$4** to display the annual interest rate specified in cell B4.

▶ 9. In cell **H7**, enter the formula **=G7/E7** to calculate the interest rate for each payment. In this case, the annual interest rate divided by quarterly payments returns 1.5% as the interest rate per quarter.

Be sure to use the interest rate for that payment period rather than the annual interest rate to apply the PMT function correctly.

▶ **10.** In cell **I7**, enter the formula **=PMT(H7,F7,B7)** to calculate the payment due each quarter based on the rate value in cell H7, the number of payments specified in cell F7, and the amount of the loan in cell B7. The formula returns ($37,860), a negative value that indicates the company will need to make payments of $37,860 each quarter to pay off the loan in five years. See Figure 9–1.

Figure 9–1   **Quarterly payment required to repay a loan**

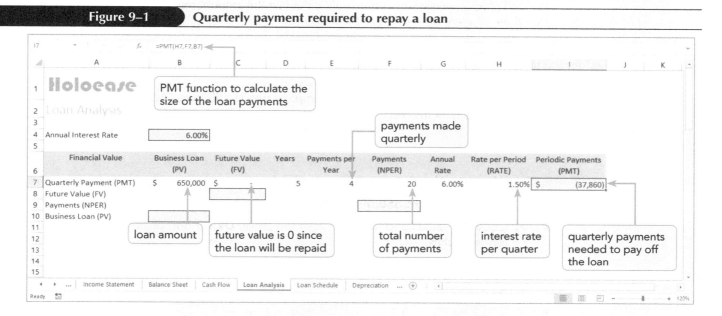

The $37,860 quarterly payments are higher than Asli anticipated. Asli was hoping for payments closer to $30,000 and asks you to determine how much of the loan would be unpaid after five years with quarterly payments of $30,000. You can calculate the amount left on the loan using the FV function.

Calculating a Future Value with the FV Function

So far, you have used the default value of 0 for the future value because the intent was to completely repay the loan. However, when a loan will not be completely repaid, you use the FV function to calculate the loan's future value after a specified number of periods. The future value will be the amount that still needs to be repaid to the lender. The syntax of the FV function is

```
FV(Rate, Nper, Pmt, [Pv=0], [Type=0])
```

where the **Rate**, **Nper**, **Pmt**, and **Type** values still represent the interest rate per period, the number of payments, the payment each period, and when the payment is due (beginning or end of the period). The **Pv** argument is optional and represents the present value of the loan or investment, which is assumed to be 0 by default.

The FV function is often used with investments to calculate the future value of a series of payments. For example, if you deposit $100 per month in a new savings account that has a starting balance of $0 and pays 1% interest annually, the FV function to calculate the future value of that investment after 10 years or 120 months is

```
FV(1%/12, 10*12, -100)
```

which returns $12,614.99. The extra $614.99 above the total amount of $12,000 you deposited is the interest earned from the money during that 10-year period. Note that the payment value is –100 because it represents the monthly deposit (negative cash flow), and the value returned by the FV function is positive because it represents money returned to the investor (positive cash flow). The *Pv* value in this example is assumed to be 0 because no money was in the savings account before the first deposit.

When used with a loan, a positive payment value is included as the present value of the loan. For example, if you borrow $10,000 at 4% annual interest and repay the loan at a rate of $250 per month, you would calculate the amount remaining on the loan after three years or 36 months as the future value

```
FV(4%/12, 12*3, -250, 10000)
```

which returns ($1,727.33), a negative value indicating that you still owe more than $1,700 on the loan at the end of three years.

Asli wants to know how much the company would still owe after five years if the quarterly payments were $30,000. You will use the FV function to calculate this future value.

To calculate the future value of the loan:

▶ **1.** In cell **B8**, enter **$650,000** as the size of the loan.

▶ **2.** Copy the values and formulas from the range **D7:H7** and paste them in the range **D8:H8**.

▶ **3.** In cell **I8**, enter **–$30,000** as the size of the quarterly payments. Again, the value is negative because it represents money that the company will spend (negative cash flow).

▶ **4.** In cell **C8**, enter the formula **=FV(H8, F8, I8, B8)** to calculate the future value of the loan based on the rate value in cell H8, the number of payments specified in cell F8, the quarterly payments specified in cell I8, and the present value of the loan entered in cell B8. The formula returns ($181,746), a negative value that indicates the company will still owe the lender more than $180,000 at the end of the five-year period. See Figure 9–2.

Figure 9–2   Future value of a loan

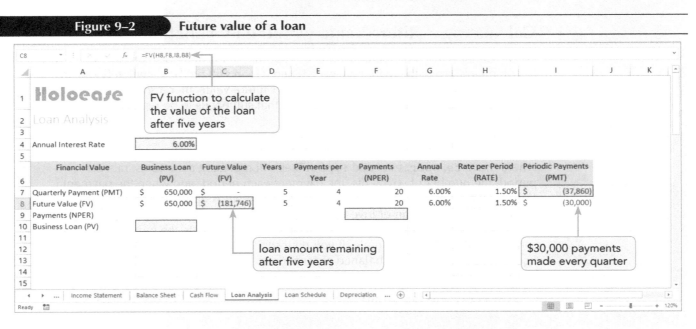

At 6% annual interest, about 27% of the original $650,000 loan will still need to be repaid at the end of five years if the quarterly payments are limited to $30,000.

Insight

Calculating Inflation with the FV Function

You can use the FV function to calculate future costs, adjusting for the effects of inflation. To project a future value of an item, use

```
FV(Rate, Years, 0, Present)
```

where *Rate* is the annual inflation rate, *Years* is the number of years in the future for which you want to project the cost of the item, and *Present* is the present-day cost. For example, if an item currently costs $15,000 and the inflation rate is 2.3%, the cost of the item in eight years is calculated using

```
FV(2.3%, 8, 0, 15000)
```

which returns –$17,992.70. The negative value is based on how Excel handles the FV function with positive and negative cash flows. For the purposes of predicting an inflated value, you can ignore the minus sign and use a value of $17,992.70 as the future cost of the item. Notice that you enter 0 for the value of the *Pmt* argument because you are not making payments toward inflation.

The FV function can also be used to express today's dollars in terms of yesterday's dollars by entering a negative value for the *Years* value. For example, the following function uses a value of –8 for years

```
FV(2.3%, -8, 0, 15000)
```

returning the value –$12,505.07, indicating that at an annual inflation rate of 2.3%, $15,000 today is equivalent to about $12,500 eight years ago.

Because a significant amount of the original loan would still be unpaid after five years, Asli wants to know how much more time would be required to repay the $650,000 loan assuming quarterly payments of $30,000. You can calculate the length of the payment period using the NPER function.

Calculating the Payment Period with the NPER Function

The NPER function calculates the number of payments required either to repay a loan or to reach an investment goal. The syntax of the NPER function is

```
NPER(Rate, Pmt, Pv, [Fv=0], [Type=0])
```

where the *Rate*, *Pmt*, *Pv*, *Fv*, and *Type* arguments are the same as described with the PMT and FV functions. For example, the following function calculates the number of $20 monthly payments needed to repay a $1,000 loan at 4% annual interest:

```
NPER(4%/12, -20, 1000)
```

The formula returns 54.7875773, indicating that the loan and the interest will be completely repaid in about 55 months.

To use the NPER function for investments, you define a future value of the investment along with the investment's present value and the periodic payments made to the investment. If you placed $200 per month in an account that pays 3% interest compounded monthly, the following function calculates the number of payments required to reach $5,000:

```
NPER(3%/12, -200, 0, 5000)
```

The formula returns 24.28, which is just over two years. Note that the *Pv* value is set to 0 based on the assumption that no money was in the account before the first deposit.

Tip

The NPER function returns the number of payments, not necessarily the number of years.

You will use the NPER function to calculate how long it will take to repay a $650,000 loan at 6% interest with quarterly payments of $30,000.

To calculate the number of payments for the loan:

▶ **1.** Copy the present and future values of the loan in the range **B7:C7** and paste them into the range **B9:C9**.

▶ **2.** In cell **E9**, enter **4** to specify that payments are made quarterly.

▶ **3.** Copy the annual interest rate, rate per quarter, and size of the quarterly payments values and formulas in the range **G8:I8** and paste them in the range **G9:I9**.

Tip

If the NPER function returns #NUM!, the loan cannot be repaid because the payments for each period are less than the interest due.

▶ **4.** In cell **F9**, enter the formula **=NPER(H9, I9, B9)** to calculate the required number of payments based on the interest rate per quarter in cell H9, the quarterly payments value in cell I9, and the present value of the loan in cell B9. The formula returns 26.40, indicating that about 27 payments are required to fully repay the loan.

▶ **5.** In cell **D9**, enter the formula **=F9/E9** to divide the total number of payments by the number of payments per year, which determines the number of years needed to repay the loan. The formula returns 6.599718, indicating that the loan will be repaid in about 6.6 years.

▶ **6.** Select cell **F9**. See Figure 9–3.

Figure 9–3   **Payments required to repay the loan**

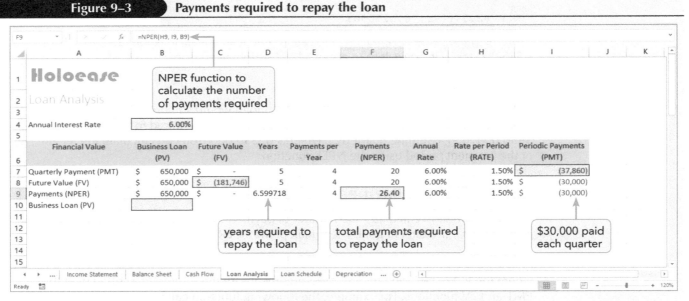

The company doesn't want to take more than six years to repay a business loan, so Asli suggests that you calculate the size of the loan that could be repaid within five years at $30,000 per quarter.

Calculating the Present Value with the PV Function

The PV function calculates the present value of a loan or an investment. For a loan, the present value would be the current size of the loan. For an investment, the present value is the amount of money initially placed in the investment account. The syntax of the PV function is

```
PV(Rate, Nper, Pmt, [Fv=0], [Type=0])
```

where the **Rate**, **Nper**, **Pmt**, **Fv**, and **Type** arguments have the same meanings they had for the other financial functions. You can use the PV function to calculate the loan amount that you can afford given a set number of payments and an annual interest rate. For example, if you make $100 monthly payments at 4% annual interest for four years (or 48 months), the function to calculate the largest loan you can afford is

```
PV(4%/12, 48, -100)
```

which returns $4,428.88. Note that because you are paying $100 per month for 48 months, the total amount paid back to the lender is $4,800. The $371.12 difference between the total amount paid and the loan amount represents the cost of the loan in terms of the total amount of interest paid.

You can also use the PV function with investments to calculate the initial payment required to reach a savings goal. For example, if you add $100 per month to a college savings account that grows at 4% annual interest and you want the account to reach a future value of $25,000 in 10 years (or 120 months), the following function returns the size of the initial payment:

```
PV(4%/12, 120, -100, 25000)
```

The function returns –$6,892.13, indicating you must start with almost $6,900 in the account to reach the $25,000 savings goal at the end of 10 years. You will use the PV function to determine the largest loan that Holoease can afford if the company pays back the loan with quarterly payments of $32,000 made over a five-year period at 6% annual interest.

To apply the PV function to calculate the loan size:

▶ **1.** Copy the loan condition values and formulas in the range **C7:H7** and paste them in the range **C10:H10**.

▶ **2.** In cell **I10**, enter **–$32,000** as the quarterly payment amount.

▶ **3.** In cell **B10**, enter **=PV(H10, F10, I10)** to calculate the size of the loan based on the interest rate per quarter value in cell H10, the number of payments specified in cell F10, and the size of the quarterly payments in cell I10. The formula results specify a loan amount of $549,396. See Figure 9–4.

Figure 9–4   **Present value of the loan**

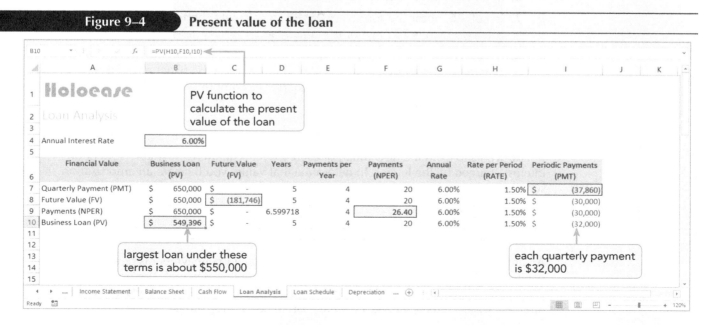

Asli will recommend a loan amount of $550,000 to be repaid at 6% interest in quarterly payments over the first five years of the company's operation. You will enter this loan amount in the Startup worksheet, which contains the company's startup costs and assets.

To enter the loan amount:

▶ 1. Go to the **Startup** worksheet.

▶ 2. In cell **B26**, enter **550,000** as the loan amount.

▶ 3. Review the Startup worksheet, noting the expenses and assets for starting up the company as well as other sources of funding. You will use some of these values later.

Asli wants you to provide more detailed information about the proposed business loan in the Loan Schedule worksheet. You'll start by entering the terms of the loan and calculate the exact value of each loan payment.

To calculate the size of the loan payments:

▶ 1. Go to the **Loan Schedule** worksheet.

▶ 2. In cell **A5**, type **=** to begin the formula, go to the **Startup** worksheet, click cell **B26**, and then press **TAB**. The formula **=Startup!B26** entered in cell A5 displays the loan amount of $550,000 from cell B26 in the Startup worksheet.

▶ 3. In cell **B5**, enter **6.00%** as the annual interest rate.

▶ 4. In cell **C5**, enter **4** as the number of payments per year because the company plans to make quarterly payments.

▶ 5. In cell **D5**, enter the formula **=B5/C5** to calculate the interest rate per quarter. The formula returns 1.50% as the interest rate.

▶ 6. In cell **E5**, enter **5** to indicate that the loan will be repaid in five years.

▶ 7. In cell **F5**, enter the formula **=C5*E5** to calculate the total number of payments, which is 20 payments in this case.

▶ 8. In cell **G5**, enter the formula **=PMT(D5, F5, A5)** to calculate the size of each payment. The formula returns –$32,035, which is the exact amount the company will have to spend per quarter to completely repay the $550,000 loan in five years.

Asli wants to examine how much of each $32,035 quarterly payment is spent on interest charged by the lender. To determine that value, you'll create an amortization schedule.

Creating an Amortization Schedule

An amortization schedule specifies how much of each loan payment is devoted to paying interest and how much is devoted to repaying the principal. The principal is the amount of the loan that is still unpaid. In most loans, the initial payments are usually directed toward interest charges. As more of the loan is repaid, the percentage of each payment devoted to interest decreases (because the interest is being applied to a smaller and smaller principal) until the last few payments are almost entirely devoted to repaying the principal. Figure 9–5 shows a typical relationship between the amount paid toward interest and the amount paid toward the principal plotted against the number of payments.

Figure 9–5   **Interest and principal payments**

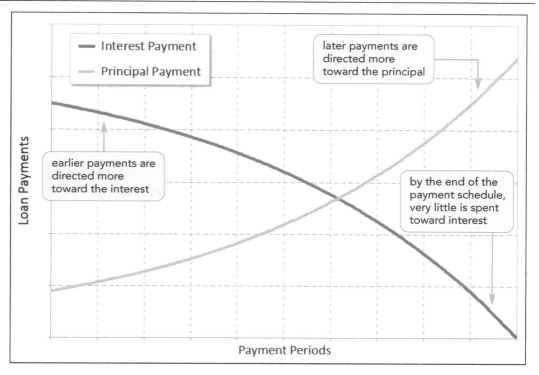

Calculating Interest and Principal Payments

To calculate the amount of a loan payment devoted to interest and to principal, use the IPMT and PPMT functions. The IPMT function returns the amount that each payment is directed toward paying the interest on the loan. It has the syntax

```
IPMT(Rate, Per, Nper, Pv, [Fv=0], [Type=0])
```

where the **Rate**, **Nper**, **Pv**, **Fv**, and **Type** arguments have the same meaning as they do for the PMT and other financial functions. The **Per** argument indicates the payment period for which the interest is due. For example, the following function calculates how much interest is due in the third payment of the company's $550,000 loan at 6% interest paid quarterly over five years:

```
IPMT(6%/4, 3, 20, 550000)
```

returning a value of –$7,531.09, indicating that the company will owe about $7,500 in interest in the third payment. The PPMT function calculates the amount used to repay the principal and has a similar syntax:

```
PPMT(Rate, Per, Nper, Pv, [Fv=0], [Type=0])
```

The function to calculate the amount of the third payment that is devoted to principal is

```
PPMT(6%/4, 3, 20, 550000)
```

returning a value –$24,504.06. Note that the sum of the interest payment and the principal payment is –$32,035.15, which is the quarterly payment amount returned by the PMT function in cell G5 of the Loan Schedule worksheet. The total amount paid to the bank each quarter doesn't change—the only change is how that amount is allocated between interest and principal.

Asli asks you to use the IPMT and PPMT functions to complete an amortization schedule for the proposed loan. The Loan Schedule worksheet already contains the table in which you'll enter the formulas to track the changing amounts spent on principal and interest over the next five years.

To create the amortization schedule for the company's loan:

▶ **1.** In cell **C9**, enter the formula **=A5** to display the initial principal of the loan.

Tip

Use absolute references to apply the same loan conditions to every payment period when you copy the formulas to the rest of the amortization schedule.

▶ **2.** In cell **D9**, enter the formula **=IPMT($D$5, B9, $F$5, $A$5)** to calculate the interest due for the first payment, with $D$5, $F$5, and $A$5 referencing the loan conditions specified in row 5 of the worksheet, and cell B9 referencing the number of the period. The formula returns the value –$8,250, which is the amount of interest due in the first payment.

▶ **3.** In cell **E9**, enter the formula **=PPMT($D$5, B9, $F$5, $A$5)** to calculate the portion of the payment applied to the principal in the first period. Excel returns the value –$23,785, which is the amount of the first payment directed toward reducing the principal.

▶ **4.** In cell **F9**, enter the formula **=D9+E9** to calculate the total payment for the first period of the loan. The formula returns –$32,035, matching the quarterly payment value in cell G5. See Figure 9–6.

Figure 9–6   **Initial payment in the amortization schedule**

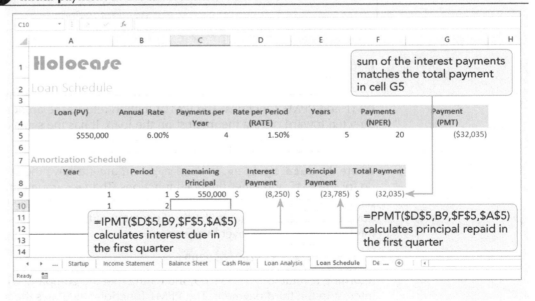

The formulas for the rest of the amortization schedule are like those used for the first quarter except that the remaining principal in column C must be reduced by the amount paid toward the principal from the previous quarter.

To complete the amortization schedule:

▶ **1.** In cell **C10**, enter the formula **=C9+E9** to add the remaining principal at the start of the first quarter to the first quarter principal payment. The remaining principal at the start of the second quarter is $526,215.

▶ **2.** Copy the formulas in the range **D9:F9** and paste them in the range **D10:F10** to calculate the interest, principal, and total payment for the second quarter. The interest paid drops to –$7,893 because the interest is charged on a smaller principal, while the amount paid toward the principal increases to –$24,142. The total payment remains $32,035, a valuable check that the formulas are correct.

▶ **3.** Use the fill handle to extend the formulas in the range **C10:F10** to the range **C11:F28**. The formulas are copied into the rest of the rows of the amortization schedule to calculate the remaining principal, interest payment, principal payment, and total payment for each of the remaining 18 quarters of the loan.

▶ **4.** Click the **Auto Fill Options** button ⊞, and then click the **Fill Without Formatting** option button. The formulas are entered without overwriting the existing worksheet formatting. Notice that in the last quarterly payment at the end of the fifth year, only $473 of the $32,035 payment is used to pay the interest on the loan. The remaining $31,562 is used to pay off the principal.

▶ **5.** In cell **C29**, enter the formula **=C28+E28** to calculate the final balance of the loan after the final payment. The final balance is $0.00, verifying that the loan is completely repaid at the end of the five-year period. See Figure 9–7.

Figure 9–7   **Completed amortization schedule**

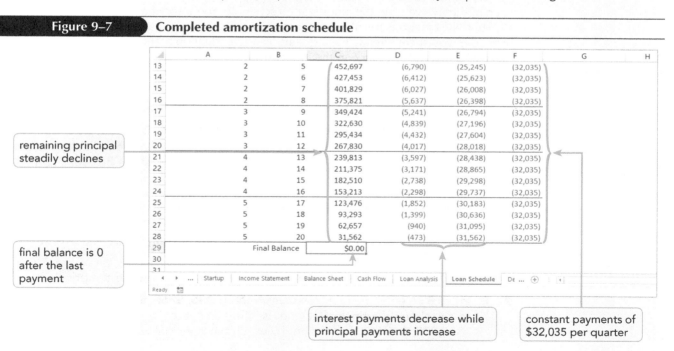

remaining principal steadily declines

final balance is 0 after the last payment

interest payments decrease while principal payments increase

constant payments of $32,035 per quarter

	A	B	C	D	E	F	G	H
13	2	5	452,697	(6,790)	(25,245)	(32,035)		
14	2	6	427,453	(6,412)	(25,623)	(32,035)		
15	2	7	401,829	(6,027)	(26,008)	(32,035)		
16	2	8	375,821	(5,637)	(26,398)	(32,035)		
17	3	9	349,424	(5,241)	(26,794)	(32,035)		
18	3	10	322,630	(4,839)	(27,196)	(32,035)		
19	3	11	295,434	(4,432)	(27,604)	(32,035)		
20	3	12	267,830	(4,017)	(28,018)	(32,035)		
21	4	13	239,813	(3,597)	(28,438)	(32,035)		
22	4	14	211,375	(3,171)	(28,865)	(32,035)		
23	4	15	182,510	(2,738)	(29,298)	(32,035)		
24	4	16	153,213	(2,298)	(29,737)	(32,035)		
25	5	17	123,476	(1,852)	(30,183)	(32,035)		
26	5	18	93,293	(1,399)	(30,636)	(32,035)		
27	5	19	62,657	(940)	(31,095)	(32,035)		
28	5	20	31,562	(473)	(31,562)	(32,035)		
29		Final Balance	$0.00					
30								
31								

◀ ▶ … Startup | Income Statement | Balance Sheet | Cash Flow | Loan Analysis | Loan Schedule | De … ⊕ ◀

Ready

Asli finds it helpful to see how much interest the company is paying each quarter. However, many financial statements also show the amount paid toward interest and principal over the whole year because this information is used when creating annual budgets and calculating taxes.

Calculating Cumulative Interest and Principal Payments

Cumulative totals of interest and principal payments can be calculated using the CUMIPMT and CUMPRINC functions. The **CUMIPMT function** calculates the sum of several interest payments and has the syntax

```
CUMIPMT(Rate, Nper, Pv, Start, End, Type)
```

where **Start** is the starting payment period for the interval you want to sum and **End** is the ending payment period. This function does not specify a future value because the assumption is that loans are always completely repaid. Also, note that the **Type** argument is not optional. You must specify whether the payments are made at the end of the period (**Type**=0) or at the start (**Type**=1). For example, to calculate the total interest paid in the second year of the company's loan (at the end of quarters 5 through 8), you would enter the function

```
CUMIPMT(6%/4, 20, 550000, 5, 8, 0)
```

which returns –$24,867.01 as the total spent on interest in the second year of the loan.

To calculate the cumulative total of payments made toward the principal, you use the **CUMPRINC function**, which has a similar syntax:

```
CUMPRINC(Rate, Nper, Pv, Start, End, Type)
```

The following function calculates the total amount spent on reducing the principal of the loan during the fifth to eighth quarters

```
CUMPRINC(6%/4, 20, 550000, 5, 8, 0)
```

returning a value of –$103,273.61, indicating that the amount remaining on the loan is reduced by more than $100,000 during the second year.

Asli wants you to add the total interest and principal payments for the loan for each of the five years in the amortization schedule. You'll use the CUMIPMT and CUMPRINC functions to calculate these values. The table at the bottom of the Loan Schedule worksheet already has the starting and ending quarters for each year of the loan, which you'll reference in the functions.

To calculate the cumulative interest and principal payments:

▶ 1. In cell **B36**, enter the formula **=CUMIPMT($D$5, $F$5, $A$5, B34, B35, 0)** to calculate the cumulative interest payments for the first year. The formula returns –$30,838, which is the amount spent on interest the first year. Notice that the formula uses absolute references to cells D5, F5, and A5 for the *Rate*, *Nper*, and *Pv* arguments so that these arguments always reference the loan conditions at the top of the worksheet, which don't change throughout the loan schedule. The references to cells B34 and B35 for the start and end arguments are relative because they change based on the period over which the payments are made.

   Next you'll calculate the cumulative payments made toward the principal.

▶ 2. In cell **B37**, enter the formula **=CUMPRINC($D$5, $F$5, $A$5, B34, B35, 0)** to calculate the principal payments in the first year. The formula returns –$97,303, which is the amount by which the principal will be reduced the first year.

▶ 3. Copy the formulas in the range **B36:B37** and paste them in the range **C36:F37** to calculate the cumulative interest and principal payments for each of the next four years.

▶ 4. Click cell **F37**. See Figure 9–8.

| Figure 9-8 | Annual cumulative interest and principal payments |

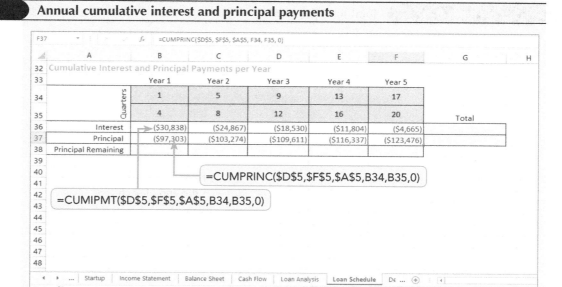

Each year, more money is spent reducing the principal. For example, in Year 5, the company will spend $4,665 on interest payments and will reduce the loan principal by $123,476. Next you will calculate the total paid on interest and principal through the five years of the loan and the principal remaining at the end of each year.

To complete the cumulative payment table:

1. Select the range **G36:G37**.

2. On the Home tab, in the Editing group, click the **AutoSum** button to calculate the total interest and principal payments over the five years of the loan, which are $90,703 and $550,000, respectively.

   Finally, you will calculate the principal remaining at the end of each of the five years of the loan.

3. In cell **B38**, enter the formula **=$A$5+B37** to add the cumulative principal payment to the initial amount of the loan in cell A5. The formula returns $452,697, which is the amount of the loan remaining to be paid after the first year.

4. In cell **C38**, enter the formula **=B38+C37** to calculate the remaining principal at the end of Year 2 by adding the Year 1 principal to the Year 2 principal payments. The formula returns $349,424.

5. Copy the formula in cell **C38** and paste it in the range **D38:F38** to calculate the remaining principal at the end of each of the next three years. Note that at end of the fifth year, the principal remaining is zero since the entire loan is paid off.

6. Select cell **A31** to deselect the table. Figure 9-9 shows the final table of cumulative interest and principal payments.

Figure 9-9 **Total loan payments**

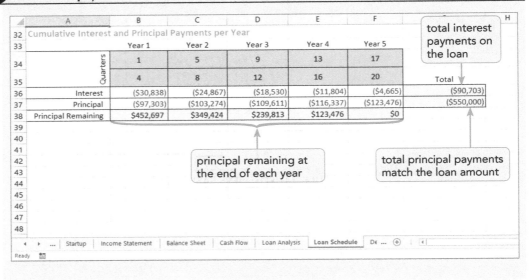

Cumulative Interest and Principal Payments per Year							Total
		Year 1	Year 2	Year 3	Year 4	Year 5	total interest payments on the loan
Quarters	1	5	9	13	17		
	4	8	12	16	20		Total
Interest	($30,838)	($24,867)	($18,530)	($11,804)	($4,665)		($90,703)
Principal	($97,303)	($103,274)	($109,611)	($116,337)	($123,476)		($550,000)
Principal Remaining	$452,697	$349,424	$239,813	$123,476	$0		

principal remaining at the end of each year

total principal payments match the loan amount

Startup | Income Statement | Balance Sheet | Cash Flow | Loan Analysis | **Loan Schedule** | De ...

The Loan Schedule worksheet shows that the company will spend more than $90,000 in interest payments to finance this loan. Calculating the total principal payment lets you verify that the loan conditions are set up correctly. If the total payment on the principal does not match the initial amount of the loan, there must be a mistake in the calculations used in the loan schedule.

Proskills

Written Communication: Writing a Financial Workbook

A properly written financial workbook should communicate key pieces of information in a way that is concise and quickly grasped. It should also be editable to allow exploration of what-if scenarios that analyze the impact of different assumptions on the financial bottom line. To help ensure that any financial workbook you create meets these goals, keep in mind the following principles:

- Place all important financial variables at or near the top of a worksheet so that they are visible to others. For example, place the interest rate you use in calculations in a clearly labeled worksheet cell.

- Use defined names with the financial variables to make it easier to apply them in formulas and functions.

- Clearly identify the direction of the cash flow in all your financial calculations by expressing the cash value as negative or positive. Using the wrong sign will turn the calculation of a loan payment into an investment deposit or vice versa.

- Place argument values in worksheet cells where they can be viewed and changed. Never place these values directly into a financial formula.

- When values are used in more than one calculation, enter them in a cell that you can reference in all formulas rather than repeating the same value throughout the workbook.

- Use the same unit of time for all the arguments in a financial function. For example, when using the PMT function to calculate monthly loan payments, the interest rate and the number of payments should be based on the interest rate per month and the total months to repay the loan.

A financial workbook that is easy to read and understand is more useful to yourself and others when making business decisions.

You have finished analyzing the conditions for the company's business loan. In the next session, you'll make projections about the company's future earnings by developing projection of the company's income statement over the next five years.

Review

Session 9.1 Quick Check

1. Explain the difference between positive and negative cash flow. If you borrow $20,000 from a bank, is that a positive or negative cash flow? Explain your answer.

2. What is the formula to calculate how much a savings account would be worth if the initial balance is $1,000 with monthly deposits of $75 for 10 years at 4.3% annual interest compounded monthly? What is the formula result?

3. You want a savings account to grow from $1,000 to $5,000 within two years. Assume the bank provides a 3.2% annual interest rate compounded monthly. What is the formula to calculate how much you must deposit each month to meet your savings goal? What is the formula result?

4. A business takes out a loan for $250,000 at 4.8% interest compounded monthly. If the business can afford to make monthly payments of only $1,500 on the loan, what is the formula to calculate the number of months required to repay the loan completely? What is the formula result?

5. Rerun your calculations from Question 4 assuming that the business can afford only a $1,000 monthly payment. What is the revised formula and resulting value? How do you explain the result?

6. A business takes out a 10-year loan for $250,000 at 5.3% interest compounded monthly. What is the formula to calculate the monthly payment and what is the resulting value?

7. For the loan conditions specified in Question 6, provide formulas to calculate the amount of the first payment used for interest and the amount of the first payment used to repay the principal. What are the resulting values?

8. For the loan conditions specified in Question 6, what are the formulas to calculate how much interest the business will pay in the first year and how much the business will repay toward the principal? What are the resulting values?

9. For the loan conditions in Question 6, calculate the total cost of the loan in terms of the total interest paid through the 10 years of the loan.

Session 9.2 Visual Overview:

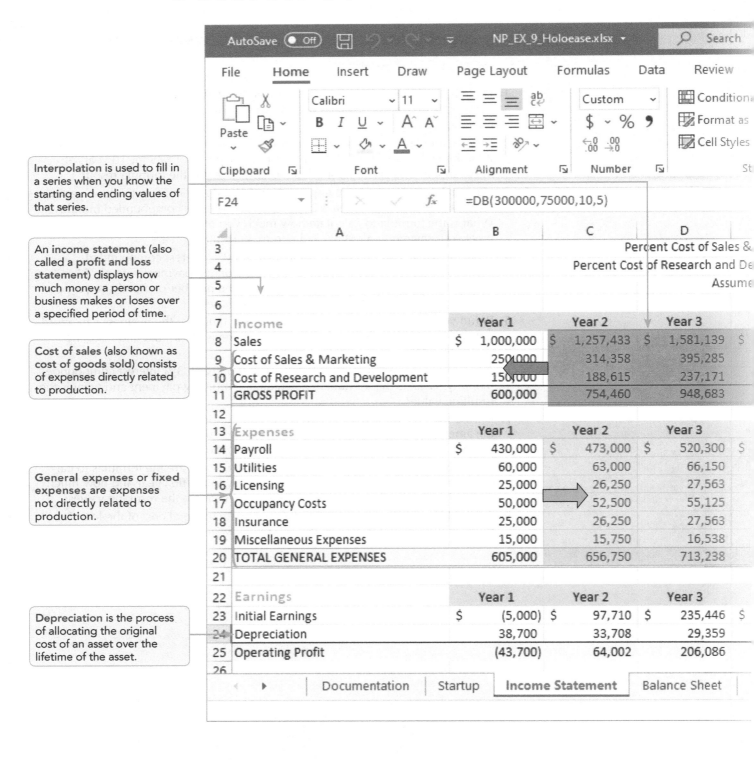

Interpolation is used to fill in a series when you know the starting and ending values of that series.

An income statement (also called a profit and loss statement) displays how much money a person or business makes or loses over a specified period of time.

Cost of sales (also known as cost of goods sold) consists of expenses directly related to production.

General expenses or fixed expenses are expenses not directly related to production.

Depreciation is the process of allocating the original cost of an asset over the lifetime of the asset.

AutoSave ● Off — NP_EX_9_Holoease.xlsx — Search

File | Home | Insert | Draw | Page Layout | Formulas | Data | Review

F24 — fx =DB(300000,75000,10,5)

	A	B	C	D
3				Percent Cost of Sales &
4				Percent Cost of Research and De
5				Assume
6				
7	Income	Year 1	Year 2	Year 3
8	Sales	$ 1,000,000	$ 1,257,433	$ 1,581,139
9	Cost of Sales & Marketing	250,000	314,358	395,285
10	Cost of Research and Development	150,000	188,615	237,171
11	GROSS PROFIT	600,000	754,460	948,683
12				
13	Expenses	Year 1	Year 2	Year 3
14	Payroll	$ 430,000	$ 473,000	$ 520,300
15	Utilities	60,000	63,000	66,150
16	Licensing	25,000	26,250	27,563
17	Occupancy Costs	50,000	52,500	55,125
18	Insurance	25,000	26,250	27,563
19	Miscellaneous Expenses	15,000	15,750	16,538
20	TOTAL GENERAL EXPENSES	605,000	656,750	713,238
21				
22	Earnings	Year 1	Year 2	Year 3
23	Initial Earnings	$ (5,000)	$ 97,710	$ 235,446
24	Depreciation	38,700	33,708	29,359
25	Operating Profit	(43,700)	64,002	206,086
26				

Documentation | Startup | **Income Statement** | Balance Sheet

Income Statements and Depreciation

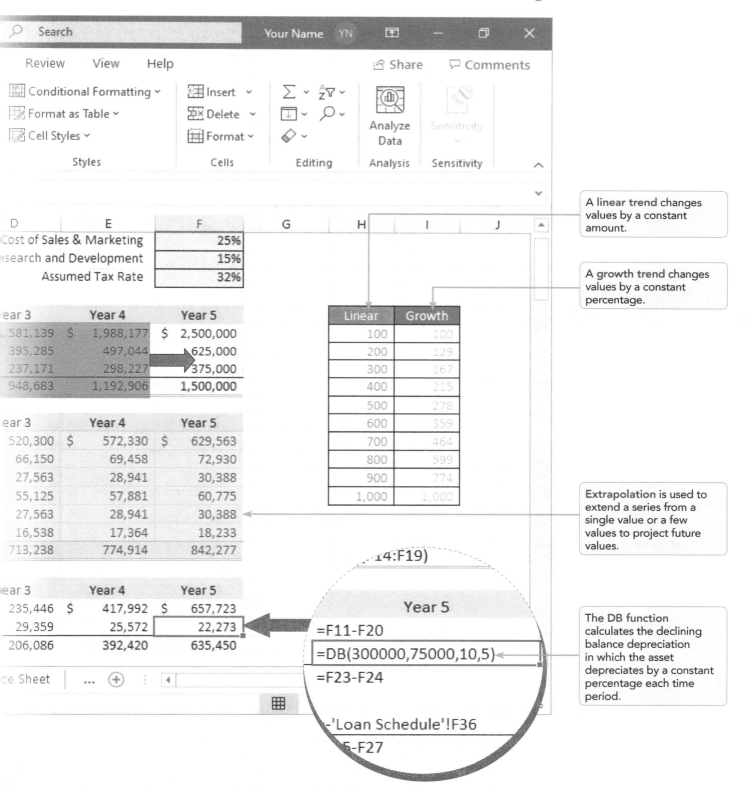

A linear trend changes values by a constant amount.

A growth trend changes values by a constant percentage.

Extrapolation is used to extend a series from a single value or a few values to project future values.

The DB function calculates the declining balance depreciation in which the asset depreciates by a constant percentage each time period.

	Linear	Growth
	100	100
	200	129
	300	167
	400	215
	500	278
	600	359
	700	464
	800	599
	900	774
	1,000	1,000

Cost of Sales & Marketing   25%
Research and Development   15%
Assumed Tax Rate   32%

D	E	F
Year 3	**Year 4**	**Year 5**
1,581,139 $	1,988,177 $	2,500,000
395,285	497,044	625,000
237,171	298,227	375,000
948,683	1,192,906	1,500,000

Year 3	**Year 4**	**Year 5**
520,300 $	572,330 $	629,563
66,150	69,458	72,930
27,563	28,941	30,388
55,125	57,881	60,775
27,563	28,941	30,388
16,538	17,364	18,233
713,238	774,914	842,277

Year 3	**Year 4**	**Year 5**
235,446 $	417,992 $	657,723
29,359	25,572	22,273
206,086	392,420	635,450

14:F19)

Year 5

=F11-F20
=DB(300000,75000,10,5)
=F23-F24

-'Loan Schedule'!F36
5-F27

Projecting Future Income and Expenses

A key part of any business plan is a projection of the company's future income and expenses in an income, or profit and loss, statement. Income statements are usually created monthly, semiannually, or annually.

Asli created the Income Statement worksheet to project the company's income and expenses for its first five years of operation. The income statement is divided into three main sections. The Income section projects the company's income from sales of its line of holographic printers as well as the cost of sales, marketing, and development for those printers. The Expenses section projects the general expenses incurred by company operations regardless of the number of printers it manufactures and sells. The Earnings section estimates the company's net profit and tax liability. You'll review this worksheet now.

To view the Income Statement worksheet:

▶ **1.** If you took a break after the previous session, make sure the NP_EX_9_Holoease workbook is open.

▶ **2.** Go to the **Income Statement** worksheet, and review the three main sections—Income, Expenses, and Earnings. See Figure 9–10.

| Figure 9–10 | Income Statement worksheet |

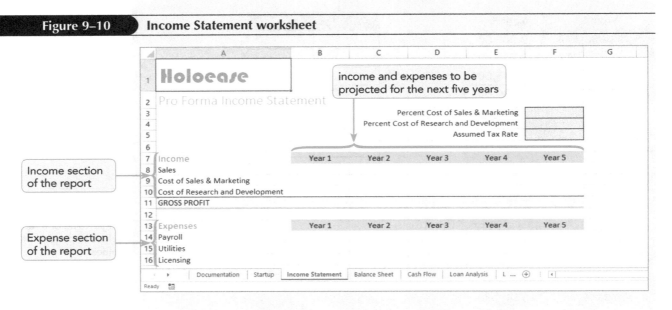

To project the financial future of the company, you will have to decide how the company will grow and expand. With Excel, you can project either a linear trend or a growth trend.

Exploring Linear and Growth Trends

Assuming that Holoease will be successful and grow over the next five years, Asli foresees two possibilities: (1) Revenue will grow by a constant amount from one year to the next; or (2) Revenue will grow by a constant percentage each year. The first scenario, in which revenue changes by a constant amount, is an example of a linear trend. When plotted, a linear trend appears as a straight line. The second possibility, in which revenue changes by a constant percentage rather than a constant amount, is an example of a growth trend. For example, each value in a growth trend might be 15%

higher than the previous year's value. When plotted, a growth trend appears as a curve with the greatest numerical differences occurring near the end of the series.

Figure 9–11 shows a linear trend and a growth trend for revenue that starts at $1,000,000 in Year 1 increasing to $2,500,000 by Year 5. The growth trend lags behind the linear trend in the early stages but reaches the same revenue value at the end of the time period.

Figure 9–11   **Linear and growth trends**

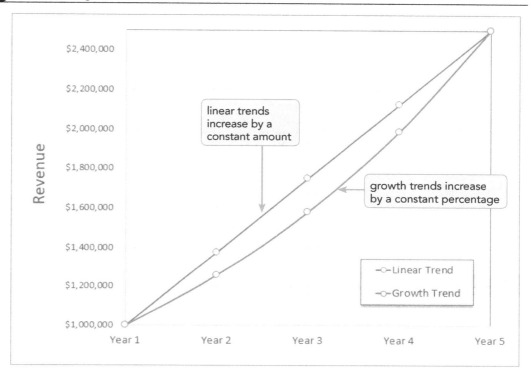

To fill in the data from a linear trend or a growth trend, you can use interpolation.

Interpolating from a Starting Value to an Ending Value

Interpolation is the process that estimates values that fall between a starting point and an ending point. You can use AutoFill to interpolate values for both linear and growth trends. Asli wants you to estimate revenues for each of the company's first five years, assuming that the company's revenue will grow from $1,000,000 in Year 1 to $2,500,000 in Year 5. Asli first wants to determine how much revenue will be generated each year if the revenue grows by a constant amount. You'll interpolate the company's revenue for Year 2 through Year 4 using a linear trend.

To project future revenue based on a linear trend:

▶ **1.** In cell **B8**, enter **$1,000,000** as the Year 1 revenue.

▶ **2.** In cell **F8**, enter **$2,500,000** as the Year 5 revenue.

▶ **3.** Select the range **B8:F8**, which includes the starting and ending revenue values.

▶ **4.** On the Home tab, in the Editing group, click the **Fill** button, and then click **Series**. The Series dialog box opens.

▶ **5.** Verify that the **Rows** option button in the Series section and the **Linear** option button in the Type section are selected. Excel will fill the series within the same rows using a linear trend.

▶ **6.** Click the **Trend** check box to insert a checkmark and apply a trend that interpolates between the starting and ending values in the selected range. See Figure 9–12.

Figure 9–12   **Series dialog box for interpolation**

▶ **7.** Click **OK**. The values inserted in the range C8:E8 show the company's projected revenue based on a linear trend. See Figure 9–13.

Figure 9–13   **Linear trend values**

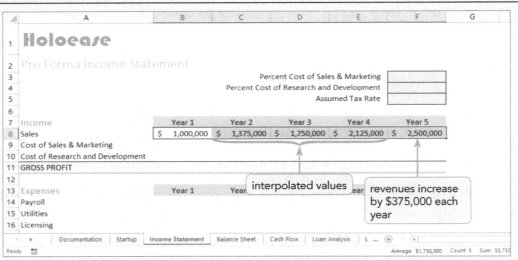

The linear trend projects an increase in the company's revenue of $375,000 per year. Next, you'll fill in the revenue values in Year 2 through Year 4 assuming a growth trend. To interpolate the growth trend correctly, you first must remove the Year 2 through Year 4 values, leaving those cells blank.

To project future revenue assuming a growth trend:

You must leave the middle cells in the range blank to interpolate new values.

▶ **1.** Select the range **C8:E8**, and then press **DELETE** on your keyboard to clear the contents of those cells.

▶ **2.** Select the range **B8:F8**.

3. On the Home tab, in the Editing group, click the **Fill** button, and then click **Series**. The Series dialog box opens.

4. In the Type section, click the **Growth** option button, and then click the **Trend** check box to select it, applying a growth trend to the interpolated values.

5. Click **OK**. The Year 1 through Year 5 revenue projections are now based on a growth trend. See Figure 9–14.

Figure 9–14	Growth trend values

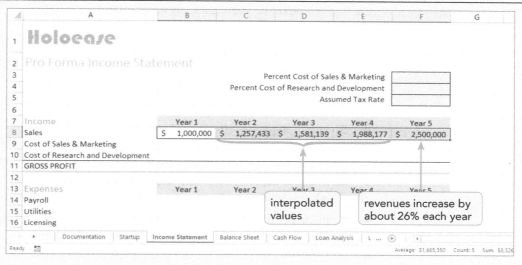

In a growth trend, the values change by a constant percentage each year. You can determine the percentage change by dividing one year's revenue value by the previous year's revenue. For the projected revenue values, the values grow at a constant rate of about 25.74% per year. The largest revenue increase occurs at the end of the five-year period. For example, revenue grows by $257,433 from Year 1 to Year 2, but by $511,823 from Year 4 to Year 5.

Insight

Interpolating and Extrapolating in Charts

You can add interpolated values to any scatter chart by adding a trendline to the chart. To add a trendline, select the chart, click the Chart Elements button for the chart, and then click the Trendline check box. Excel supports trendlines for exponential (or growth) trends, linear (straight line) trends, logarithmic trends, polynomial trends, power trends, and moving averages. All these options can be found in the Format Trendline pane of the chart.

Trendlines can be extrapolated forward or backward from the points in the scatter chart by setting the forecast options in the Format Trendline pane. Again, these extrapolated values can be based on a wide variety of functions including linear and exponential functions. For more information, you can display the equation of the trendline on the chart itself.

Calculating the Cost of Goods Sold

The next part of the worksheet displays the cost of sales, also known as the cost of goods sold. Holoease needs to purchase the raw material to create the printers, and it also must invest time into the development and upgrade of the software used to generate the holographic images. Asli has estimated for every dollar of sales revenue, the company will need to spend 25 cents on sales and marketing and 15 cents on research and development. As the company's revenue increases, these costs will also increase. The difference between the company's sales revenue and the cost of goods sold is the company's **gross profit**.

Asli wants you to project the cost of goods sold and the company's gross profit for each of the next five years using those estimates.

To project the cost of goods sold and the gross profit:

▶ **1.** In cell **F3**, enter **25%** as the percentage cost of sales and marketing.

▶ **2.** In cell **F4**, enter **15%** as the percentage cost of research and development.

▶ **3.** In cell **B9**, enter the formula **=B8*$F$3** to multiply the Year 1 revenue by the cost of goods percentage for sales and marketing. Excel returns a value of 250,000, which is the estimated cost of sales and marketing for Year 1.

▶ **4.** In cell **B10**, enter the formula **=B8*$F$4**. Excel returns a value of 150,000, which is the estimated cost of research and development in Year 1.

▶ **5.** In cell **B11**, enter the formula **=B8–(B9+B10)**. Excel returns a value of 600,000, which is the estimated gross profit in Year 1.

▶ **6.** Copy the formulas in the range **B9:B11** and paste them in the range **C9:F11** to calculate the cost of goods sold and the gross profit for Year 2 through Year 5. See Figure 9–15.

Figure 9–15   **Cost of goods sold and gross profit**

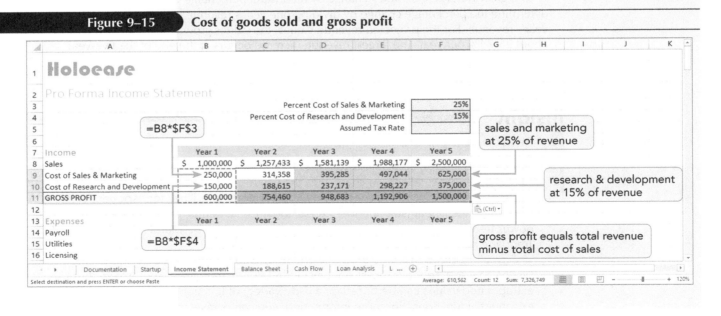

Based on these calculations, the company's gross profit is projected to increase from $600,000 in Year 1 to $1,500,000 in Year 5.

Reference

Interpolating and Extrapolating a Series

To interpolate a series of values between starting and ending values:
- Select the range with the first cell containing the starting value, blank cells for middle values, and the last cell containing the ending value.
- On the Home tab, in the Editing group, click the Fill button, and then click Series.
- Select whether the series is organized in rows or columns, select the type of series to interpolate, and then check the Trend check box.
- Click OK.

To extrapolate a series from a starting value:
- Select a range with the first cell containing the starting value followed by blank cells to store the extrapolated values.
- On the Home tab, in the Editing group, click the Fill button, and then click Series.
- Select whether the series is organized in rows or columns, select the type of series to extrapolate, and then enter the step value in the Step value box.
- Click OK.

The next section of the income statement contains the projected general expenses for the company. These expenses are not directly related to production. For example, the company must purchase insurance, provide for general maintenance, and pay for office space, regardless of the number of products it sells. You'll add the Year 1 general expenses to the Income Statement worksheet.

To enter the Year 1 expenses:

▶ 1. In the range **B14:B19**, enter the following general expense values: **$430,000** in cell B14 for payroll, **60,000** in cell B15 for utilities, **25,000** in cell B16 for licensing, **50,000** in cell B17 for occupancy costs, **25,000** in cell B18 for insurance, and **15,000** in cell B19 for miscellaneous expenses.

▶ 2. In cell **B20**, enter the formula **=SUM(B14:B19)** to calculate the total expenses for Year 1. The formula returns the value 605,000.

The total expenses for the first year will be $5,000 greater than the gross profit, so the company will lose money, whether this is true for the remaining four years depends in part on how fast expenses will grow relative to gross profit.

Extrapolating from a Series of Values

Extrapolation differs from interpolation in that only a starting value is provided; the succeeding values are estimated by assuming that the values follow a trend. As with interpolation, Excel can extrapolate a data series based on either a linear trend or a growth trend. With a linear trend, the data values are assumed to change by a constant amount. With a growth trend, they are assumed to change by a constant percentage. To extrapolate a data series, you must provide a step value representing the amount by which each value is changed as the series is extended. You do not have to specify a stopping value.

Asli estimates that the company's payroll will increase by 10% per year. The other costs will increase by 5% per year. These increases are equivalent to multiplying each year's expenses by 1.10 and 1.05, respectively. Rather than writing this formula into the worksheet, you'll extrapolate the expenses using the Fill command.

To extrapolate the Year 1 expenses:

▸ **1.** Select the range **B14:F14** containing the cells in which the Year 1 through Year 5 payroll expenses will be entered.

▸ **2.** On the Home tab, in the Editing group, click the **Fill** button, and then click **Series**. The Series dialog box opens.

▸ **3.** In the Type section, click the **Growth** option button, and then type **1.10** in the Step value box. See Figure 9–16.

Figure 9–16   **Series dialog box for extrapolation**

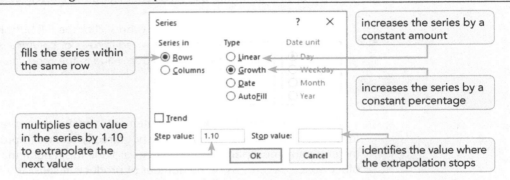

- fills the series within the same row
- multiplies each value in the series by 1.10 to extrapolate the next value
- increases the series by a constant amount
- increases the series by a constant percentage
- identifies the value where the extrapolation stops

▸ **4.** Click **OK**. The payroll expenses are extrapolated into Year 2 through Year 5, culminated in a Year 5 payroll of $629,563.

Next, you will extrapolate the other general expenses assuming a growth rate of 5%.

▸ **5.** Select the range **B15:F19**. Do not select the row containing the total general expenses.

▸ **6.** In the Editing group, click the **Fill** button, and then click **Series**. The Series dialog box opens.

▸ **7.** Click the **Growth** option button, and then type **1.05** in the Step value box to increase the expenses by 5% per year.

▸ **8.** Click **OK**. The expense values from Year 1 are extrapolated into the Year 2 through Year 5 columns. For example, the expense for utilities increases to $72,930 in Year 5.

▸ **9.** Copy the formula in cell **B20** and paste it in the range **C20:F20** to calculate the total general expenses for the company for each of the five years.

Tip

To extrapolate a decreasing trend, use a negative step value for a decreasing linear trend, and a step value between 0 and 1 for a decreasing growth trend.

The calculations show that the projected general expenses will rise from $605,000 in Year 1 to $842,277 by the end of Year 5. Next, you want to calculate the company's earnings during each of the next five years. The initial earnings estimate is equal to the company's gross profit minus the total general expenses.

To calculate the company's initial earnings:

▸ **1.** In cell **B23**, enter the formula **=B11–B20** to subtract the total general expenses from the gross profit for Year 1. The estimate of earnings for the first year is a loss of $5,000.

▸ **2.** Copy the formula in cell **B23** and paste it in the range **C23:F23** to project yearly earnings through Year 5. See Figure 9–17.

| Figure 9-17 | Projected general expenses and earnings |

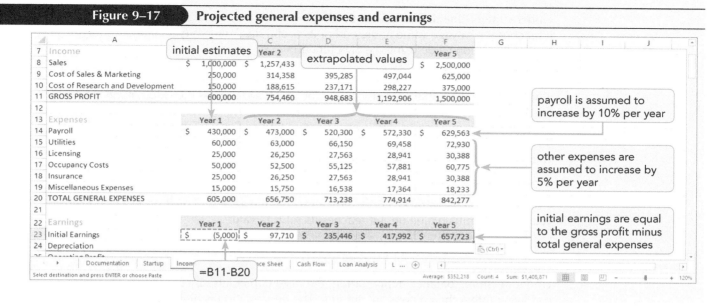

The calculations project that the company's annual earnings will increase from $5,000 loss in Year 1 to a net gain of $657,723 in Year 5.

Calculating Depreciation of Assets

The financial status of a company is not determined solely by its revenue, expenses, or annual earnings. Its wealth is also tied up in noncash assets such as equipment, land, buildings, and vehicles. These assets are known as **tangible assets** because they are long-lasting material assets not intended for sale but for use only by the company. Not all material assets are tangible assets. For example, assets such as the ingredients a restaurant uses when preparing its dishes are not considered tangible assets because although they are used in the cooking process, they are sold indirectly to the consumer in the form of a finished meal. However, items such as the cooking stove, refrigeration units, deep fryers, and so forth are tangible assets for that restaurant.

Tangible assets wear down over time and lose their value and thus reduce the company's overall worth. Tax laws allow companies to deduct this loss from reported earnings on the company's income statement, reducing the company's tax liability. The loss of the asset's original value doesn't usually happen all at once but is instead spread out over several years in a process known as depreciation. For example, an asset whose original value is $200,000 might be depreciated to $50,000 after 10 years of use. Different types of tangible assets have different rates of depreciation. Some items depreciate faster than others, which maintain their value for longer periods. In general, to calculate the depreciation of an asset, you need to know the following:

• The asset's original cost
• The length of the asset's useful life
• The asset's salvage value, which is the asset's value at the end of its useful life
• The rate at which the asset is depreciated over time

There are several ways to depreciate an asset. This module focuses on straight-line depreciation and declining balance depreciation.

Straight-Line Depreciation

Under **straight-line depreciation**, an asset loses value by equal amounts each year until it reaches the salvage value at the end of its useful life. You can calculate the straight-line depreciation value using the SLN function

```
SLN(cost, salvage, life)
```

where **cost** is the initial cost or value of the asset, **salvage** is the value of the asset at the end of its useful life, and **life** is the number of periods over which the asset will be depreciated. In most cases, life is expressed in terms of years. For example, to calculate the yearly depreciation of an asset with an initial value of $200,000 and a salvage value of $50,000 after 10 years, use the function

```
SLN(200000, 50000, 10)
```

which returns a value of $15,000, indicating that the asset will decline $15,000 every year from its initial value until it reaches its salvage value.

Declining Balance Depreciation

Under **declining balance depreciation**, the asset depreciates by a constant percentage each year rather than a constant amount. The depreciation is highest early in the asset's lifetime and steadily decreases as the asset itself loses value. Figure 9–18 compares the yearly straight-line and declining balance depreciation over a 10-year lifetime as an asset declines from its initial value of $300,000 down to $75,000.

Figure 9–18	**Straight-line and declining-balance depreciation**

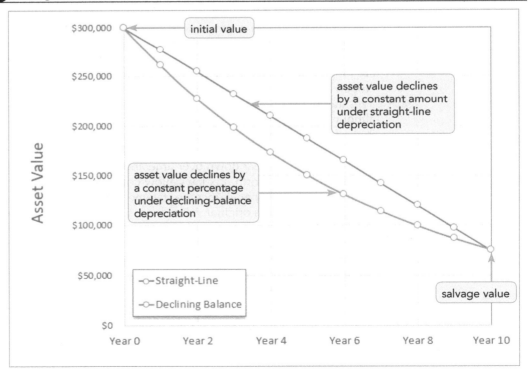

An asset shows a greater initial decline under declining balance depreciation than under straight-line depreciation. Declining balance depreciation is another example of a negative growth trend in which the asset decreases in value by a constant percentage rather than by a constant amount, as is the case with straight-line depreciation.

You can calculate the declining balance depreciation with the DB function

DB(**cost, salvage, life, period,** [month=12])

where **cost, salvage,** and **life** are again the initial value, salvage value, and lifetime of the asset, respectively, and **period** is the period for which you want to calculate the depreciation. If you are calculating depreciation on a yearly basis, then period would contain the year value of the depreciation. For example, to calculate the fourth year of depreciation of a $200,000 asset that declines to a salvage value of $50,000 after 10 years, you would use the function

DB(200000, 50000, 10, 4)

which returns $17,048.03, indicating that the asset declines in value more than $17,000 during its fourth year of use. By contrast, the asset's depreciation in its fifth year is

DB(200000, 50000, 10, 5)

which returns $14,848.83. The depreciation is smaller in the fifth year because the asset has a lower value later into its useful life.

The DB function also supports an optional month argument, which is needed when the asset is used for only part of the first year. For example, if you are depreciating the $200,000 asset after using it for only two months in Year 1, you would calculate its depreciation in the fifth year as

DB(200000, 50000, 10, 5, 2)

which returns $16,681.50. The depreciated value is higher because the asset has not been subjected to wear and tear for a full five years, making it more valuable going into Year 5.

Asli estimates that Holoease will have $300,000 in tangible assets at its startup. The useful life of these assets is estimated at 10 years with a salvage value of $75,000. You will add this information to the company's startup figures and then apply it to the Depreciation worksheet.

To specify the values of the tangible assets:

▶ **1.** Go to the **Startup** worksheet.

▶ **2.** In cell **B13**, enter **300,000** as the value of the long-term assets.

▶ **3.** Go to the **Depreciation** worksheet.

▶ **4.** In cell **B4**, type **=** to begin the formula, go to the **Startup** worksheet, click cell **B13**, and then press **ENTER**. The formula =Startup!B13 is entered in cell B4, displaying the $300,000 long-term assets value from the Startup worksheet.

▶ **5.** In cell **B5**, enter **$75,000** as the asset's estimated salvage value.

▶ **6.** In cell **B6**, enter **10** as the useful life of the asset.

Next, you'll calculate the depreciation of the company equipment using straight-line depreciation.

To calculate the straight-line depreciation:

▶ **1.** In cell **B10**, enter the formula **=SLN($B$4, $B$5, $B$6)** to calculate the straight-line depreciation in Year 1 based on the cost value in cell B4, the salvage value in cell B5, and the life value in cell B6. The formula returns a depreciation value of $22,500, indicating the asset will decline in value by $22,500 in Year 1.

▶ **2.** Copy the formula in cell **B10** and paste it in the range **C10:F10** to calculate the straight-line depreciation for the remaining years. Because the straight-line depreciation is a constant amount every year, the formula returns a depreciation value of $22,500 for Year 2 through Year 5.

Next, you will calculate the cumulative depreciation of the asset from Year 1 through Year 5.

▶ **3.** In cell **B11**, enter the formula **=B10** to display the depreciation for the first year.

▶ **4.** In cell **C11**, enter the formula **=B11+C10** to add the Year 2 depreciation to the depreciation from Year 1. The total depreciation through the first two years is $45,000.

▶ **5.** Copy the formula in cell **C11** and paste it in the range **D11:F11** to calculate cumulative depreciation through the first five years. By Year 5, the asset's value will have declined by $112,500.

▶ **6.** In cell **B12**, enter the formula **=$B$4–B11** to calculate the depreciated asset's value after the first year. The asset's value is $277,500.

▶ **7.** Copy the formula in cell **B12** and paste it in the range **C12:F12**. By Year 5, the asset's value has been reduced to $187,500.

▶ **8.** Click cell **B10** to deselect the copied range. See Figure 9–19.

Figure 9–19	**Straight-line depreciation of the asset**

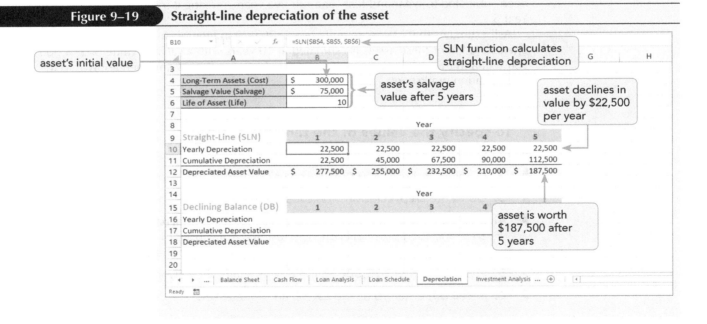

Asli also wants to explore the depreciation of the company's tangible assets under the declining balance depreciation method.

To calculate the declining balance depreciation:

▶ **1.** In cell **B16**, enter the formula **=DB($B$4, $B$5, $B$6, B15)** to calculate the declining balance depreciation for Year 1 based on the initial cost of the asset in cell B4, the salvage value in cell B5, the life of the asset in cell B6, and the current period (or year) in cell B15. The formula returns 38,700, which is the amount that the assets will depreciate in Year 1.

▶ **2.** Copy the formula in cell **B16** and paste it in the range **C16:F16** to calculate the depreciation in each of the remaining four years. The depreciation amount decreases each year under the declining balance schedule, dropping to $22,273 in Year 5.

▶ **3.** Copy the formulas in the range **B11:F12** and paste it in the range **B17:F18** to calculate the cumulative depreciation and depreciated value of the asset.

▶ **4.** Click cell **B16** to deselect the copied range. See Figure 9–20.

Figure 9–20	Declining-balance depreciation of the asset

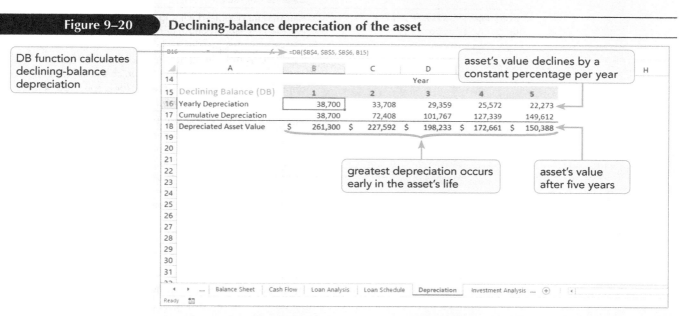

Based on the declining balance depreciation method, the value of the asset declines to $150,388 by the end of Year 5, which is lower than the Year 5 value under the straight-line depreciation model. Figure 9–21 describes several other depreciation functions that can be used to satisfy specialized accounting needs.

Figure 9–21	Excel depreciation functions

Function	Description
SLN(cost, salvage, life)	Returns the straight-line depreciation in which the asset declines by a constant amount each year, where *cost* is the initial cost of the asset, *salvage* is the salvage value, and *life* is the useful lifetime of the asset.
DB(cost, salvage, life, period, [month])	Returns the declining balance depreciation in which the asset declines by a constant percentage each year, where *period* is the year of the depreciation and *month* is an optional argument that defines the number of months that the asset was owned during Year 1.
SYD(cost, salvage, life, period)	Returns the sum-of-years' digit depreciation that results in a more accelerated depreciation than straight-line depreciation, but a less accelerated depreciation than declining balance depreciation.
DDB(cost, salvage, life, period, [factor=2])	Returns the double-declining balance depreciation that doubles the depreciation under the straight-line method and applies that accelerated rate to the original asset value minus the cumulative depreciation. The *factor* argument specifies the factor by which the straight-line depreciation is multiplied. If no factor is specified, a factor of 2 (for doubling) is assumed.
VDB(cost, salvage, life, start, end, [factor=2], [no_switch=FALSE])	Returns a variable declining depreciation for any specified period using any specified depreciation method, where *start* is the starting period of the depreciation, *end* is the ending period, *factor* is the rate at which the depreciation declines, and *no_switch* specifies whether to switch to the straight-line method when the depreciation falls below the estimate given by the declining balance method.

Adding Depreciation to an Income Statement

Depreciation is part of a company's income statement because even though the company is not losing actual revenue, it is losing value as its tangible assets depreciate, which reduces its tax liability. Asli wants to add the declining balance depreciation figures from the Depreciation worksheet to the projected income statement to project the company's operating profit, which represents the company's profits before taxes.

To add depreciation to the income statement:

▶ 1. Go to the **Income Statement** worksheet.

▶ 2. In cell **B24**, type **=** to begin the formula, go to the **Depreciation** worksheet, click cell **B16**, and then press **ENTER**. The formula =Depreciation!B16 is entered and displays the depreciation value 38,700 for Year 1.

▶ 3. Copy the formula in cell **B24** and paste it in the range **C24:F24** to show the annual depreciation for Year 2 through Year 5.

▶ 4. In cell **B25**, enter the formula **=B23–B24** to subtract the depreciation from the company's initial earnings. The projection shows a loss in operating profit for the company in the first year of $43,700.

▶ 5. Copy the formula in cell **B25** and paste it in the range **C25:F25** to calculate the operating profit for Year 2 through Year 5.

Even when depreciation of its assets is included, the company's operating profit increases throughout the five-year period, culminating in a Year 5 operating profit of $635,450.

Proskills

Decision Making: Choosing a Depreciation Schedule

How do you decide which method of depreciation is the most appropriate? The answer depends on the type of asset being depreciated. Tax laws allow different depreciation methods for different kinds of assets and different situations. In general, you want to choose the depreciation method that most accurately describes the true value of the asset and its impact on the company's financial status.

In tax statements, depreciation appears as an expense that is subtracted from the company's earnings. So, if you accelerate the depreciation of an asset in the early years of its use, you might be underestimating the company's profits, making it appear that the company is less profitable than it is. On the other hand, depreciating an asset slowly could make it appear that the company is more profitable than it really is. For this reason, the choice of a depreciation method is best made in consultation with an accountant who is fully aware of the financial issues and tax laws.

Adding Taxes and Interest Expenses to an Income Statement

Interest expenses are also part of a company's income statement. You have already projected the annual interest payments the company will have to make on its $550,000 loan (shown earlier in row 36 of Figure 9–9). Rather than reenter these values, you can reference the calculated values from that worksheet in the income statement. Because those values were displayed as negative numbers, you'll change the sign to match the format of the Income Statement worksheet in which those interest expenses are entered as positive values.

To include the interest expense in the income statement:

▶ 1. In cell **B27**, type **=−** (an equal sign followed by a minus sign) to begin the formula.

▶ 2. Go to the **Loan Schedule** worksheet, click cell **B36**, which contains the total interest payments in Year 1, and then press **ENTER**. The formula = −'Loan Schedule'!B36 is entered in the cell, returning the value 30,838.

▶ 3. In cell **B28**, enter the formula **=B25−B27** to subtract the interest expense from the operating profit for Year 1. Excel returns a value of −74,538, indicating that the company will lose almost $75,000 pretax for the first year.

▶ 4. Copy the formulas in the range **B27:B28** and paste them in the range **C27:F28** to calculate the interest payments and pretax profits for the remaining years.

Despite losing almost $75,000 in the first year, by the fifth year when interest payments are included, the company's projected pretax profit is $630,785.

Finally, you need to account for the taxes that the company will pay on the money it makes. Asli estimates that the company will be subject, in general, to a 32% tax rate on its pretax income. You will add this tax rate to the Income Statement worksheet and then calculate the company's tax liability. The company will pay taxes only if it makes money, so you will use an IF function to test whether the pretax income is positive before calculating taxes. If the pretax profit is negative, the tax will be zero.

To calculate the company's tax liability:

▶ **1.** In cell **F5** of the Income Statement worksheet, enter **32%** as the assumed tax rate.

▶ **2.** In cell **B30**, enter the formula **=IF(B28>0, B28*$F$5, 0)** to test whether the pretax income in Year 1 is greater than 0. If it is, then the pretax income will be multiplied by the tax rate in cell F5; otherwise, the formula will return 0. Because the company will show a net loss in its first year of operation, the formula should return a value of 0.

▶ **3.** In cell **B31**, enter the formula **=B28–B30** to subtract the taxes owed for Year 1 from the pretax income.

▶ **4.** Copy the formulas in the range **B30:B31** and paste them in the range **C30:F31** to calculate the tax liability and after-tax profit for the remaining years. After accounting for taxes, Holoease will show an after-tax profit of $428,934 by the end of its fifth year.

▶ **5.** Click cell **B30** to deselect the copied formulas. See Figure 9–22.

Figure 9–22   **Revised income statement**

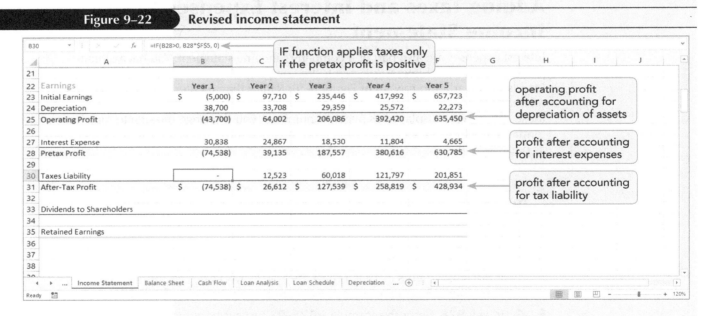

▶ **6.** Save the workbook.

With the initial financial planning laid out, the company needs to attract some investors. In the next session, you will evaluate the return on investment that the company will be able to offer investors and the impact it will have on the company's profitability.

Review

Session 9.2 Quick Check

1. The first value in a linear trend is 50 and the fifth value is 475. What are the values of the second, third, and fourth items?

2. The first value in a growth trend is 50 and the fifth value is 475. What are the values of the second, third, and fourth items?

3. By what percentage do the values in Question 3 grow?

4. The first value in a series is 100. Extrapolate the next four values assuming a linear trend with a step size of 125.

5. The first value in a series is 100. Extrapolate the next four values if each value grows by 18% over the previous value.

6. A new business buys $20,000 worth of computer equipment. If the useful life of the equipment is 10 years with a salvage value of $3,000, provide the formula to determine the depreciation during the first year assuming straight-line depreciation. What is the formula result?

7. Provide the value of the asset in Year 1 through Year 5 using the depreciation schedule in Question 6.

8. Assume a declining balance depreciation for the computer equipment described in Question 6 and provide the formula and result to determine the depreciation in the first year.

9. Provide the value of the asset in Year 1 through Year 5 using the declining balance depreciation schedule in Question 8.

Session 9.3 Visual Overview:

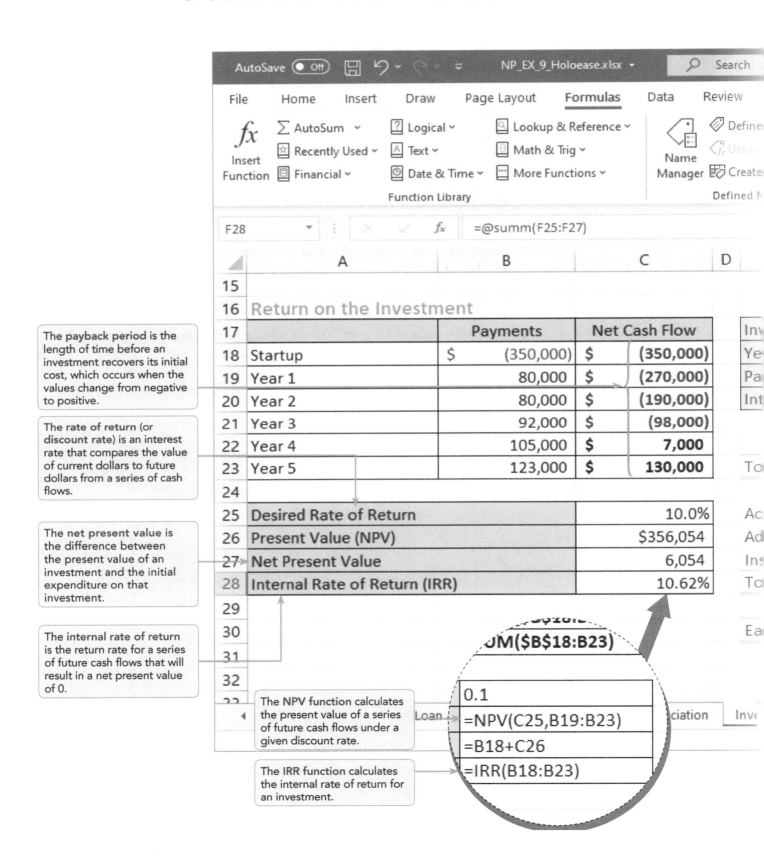

The payback period is the length of time before an investment recovers its initial cost, which occurs when the values change from negative to positive.

The rate of return (or discount rate) is an interest rate that compares the value of current dollars to future dollars from a series of cash flows.

The net present value is the difference between the present value of an investment and the initial expenditure on that investment.

The internal rate of return is the return rate for a series of future cash flows that will result in a net present value of 0.

AutoSave ● Off   NP_EX_9_Holoease.xlsx ▾   Search

File   Home   Insert   Draw   Page Layout   **Formulas**   Data   Review

fx Insert Function   Σ AutoSum ▾   Recently Used ▾   Financial ▾   Logical ▾   Text ▾   Date & Time ▾   Lookup & Reference ▾   Math & Trig ▾   More Functions ▾   Name Manager

Function Library   Defined N

F28   *fx*   =@summ(F25:F27)

Return on the Investment (row 16)

	Payments	Net Cash Flow
Startup	$ (350,000)	$ (350,000)
Year 1	80,000	$ (270,000)
Year 2	80,000	$ (190,000)
Year 3	92,000	$ (98,000)
Year 4	105,000	$ 7,000
Year 5	123,000	$ 130,000
Desired Rate of Return		10.0%
Present Value (NPV)		$356,054
Net Present Value		6,054
Internal Rate of Return (IRR)		10.62%

The NPV function calculates the present value of a series of future cash flows under a given discount rate.

The IRR function calculates the internal rate of return for an investment.

UM($B$18:B23)

0.1
=NPV(C25,B19:B23)
=B18+C26
=IRR(B18:B23)

NPV and IRR Functions and Auditing

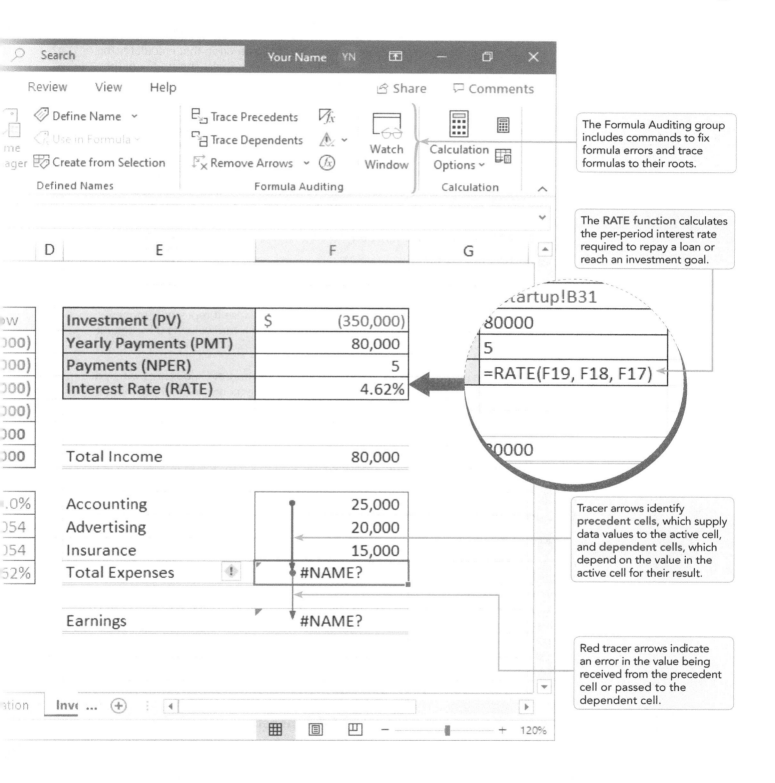

The Formula Auditing group includes commands to fix formula errors and trace formulas to their roots.

The RATE function calculates the per-period interest rate required to repay a loan or reach an investment goal.

Investment (PV)	$	(350,000)
Yearly Payments (PMT)		80,000
Payments (NPER)		5
Interest Rate (RATE)		4.62%

Startup!B31
80000
5
=RATE(F19, F18, F17)

Total Income   80,000

80000

Accounting	25,000
Advertising	20,000
Insurance	15,000
Total Expenses	#NAME?

Earnings   #NAME?

Tracer arrows identify precedent cells, which supply data values to the active cell, and dependent cells, which depend on the value in the active cell for their result.

Red tracer arrows indicate an error in the value being received from the precedent cell or passed to the dependent cell.

Calculating Interest Rates with the RATE Function

When you evaluated potential loans in the first session, you may have noticed that the *Pmt*, *Fv*, *Nper*, and *Pv* arguments are matched by the PMT, FV, NPER, and PV functions. The *Rate* argument also has a matching RATE function that calculates the interest rate based on the values of the other financial arguments. The syntax of the RATE function is

```
RATE(Nper, Pmt, Pv, [Fv=0], [Type=0], [Guess=0.1])
```

where *Nper* is the number of payments, *Pmt* is the amount of each payment, *Pv* is the loan or investment's present value, *Fv* is the future value, and *Type* defines when the payments are made. The optional *Guess* argument is used when the RATE function cannot calculate the interest rate value and needs an initial guess to arrive at a solution.

The RATE function is used primarily to calculate the return from investments. For example, if you put $14,000 in an investment and then receive $150 per month for the next 10 years (or 120 months) for a total of $18,000, you can calculate the interest rate from that investment using the function

```
RATE(120, 150, -14000)
```

<table>
<tr><td>

Tip

Always multiply the RATE function results by the number of payments per year. For monthly payments, multiply the rate value by 12.

</td></tr>
</table>

which returns an interest rate of 0.43% per month or 5.2% annually. Note that the payment values of $150 are positive because the payments are coming to you (positive cash flow), but the present value –14,000 is negative because it represents money initially spent in the investment (negative cash flow). The future value is 0 by default because once the initial investment has been completely paid back to you, there are no funds left.

With loans, the positive and negative signs of the *Pmt* and *Pv* values are switched. For example, if you borrow $14,000 and repay it with payments of $150 per month over the next 10 years, you can calculate the monthly interest rate as

```
RATE(120, -150, 14000)
```

which again returns 0.43% per month or 5.2% annually. Notice that the payment value is negative, and the present value is positive because this transaction is a loan to you.

Not every combination of payments and present value will result in a viable interest rate. If you calculate the interest rate for a $14,000 loan that is repaid with payments of $100 per month for 120 months, the function

```
RATE(120, -100, 14000)
```

returns an interest rate of –0.25% per month or –3.0% annually. The interest rate is negative because you cannot repay a $14,000 loan within 10 years by paying only $100 per month. The total payments would amount to only $12,000.

Holoease needs $350,000 in startup capital from a group of investors. The company is considering repaying the group $80,000 per year for the first five years of the company's operation for a total return of $400,000. Asli wants to know the annual interest rate that this repayment schedule would represent to the investors. You will use the RATE function to find out.

To calculate the interest rate of the investment:

▶ **1.** If you took a break after the previous session, make sure the NP_EX_9_Holoease workbook is open.

▶ **2.** Go to the **Startup** worksheet, and then in cell **B31**, enter **350,000** as the amount contributed by investors.

▶ **3.** Go to the **Investment Analysis** worksheet, which you'll use to analyze the value of investing in the company.

▶ **4.** In cell **B6**, type **=–** (an equal sign followed by a minus sign), go to the **Startup** worksheet, click cell **B31**, and then press **ENTER**. The formula =–Startup!B31 is entered in the cell.

The formula displays the negative value $(350,000) in the cell. You want to use a negative value because you are examining this investment from the point of view of the group of investors, who are making an initial startup payment of $350,000 to the company (a negative cash flow).

▶ **5.** In cell **B7**, enter **80,000** as the annual payment. The value is positive because this money is being repaid to the investors each year (a positive cash flow from their point of view).

▶ **6.** In cell **B8**, enter **5** as the total number of payments made to the investors.

▶ **7.** In cell **B9**, enter the formula **=RATE(B8, B7, B6)** to calculate the interest rate of this repayment schedule based on the number of payments in cell B8, the size of each payment in cell B7, and the present value of the investment in cell B6. See Figure 9–23.

Figure 9–23 **Interest rate of the investment**

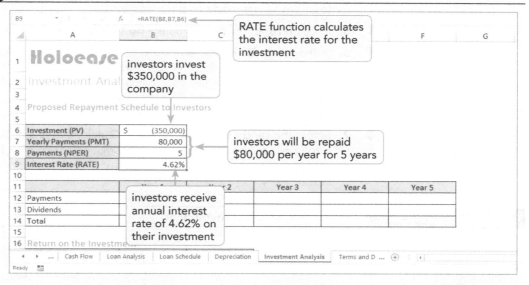

Based on these calculations, the annual interest rate to the investors for this repayment schedule is 4.62%. One way to interpret this value is that it is like to placing $350,000 in a savings account that pays 4.62% annual interest. Is this a good investment? There are several ways of making that determination. One way is the payback period.

Viewing the Payback Period of an Investment

The payback period is the length of time required for an investment to recover its initial cost. For example, a $400,000 investment that returns $25,000 per year would take 16 years to repay the initial cost of the investment.

The company doesn't believe it can attract investors if all it can promise is a 4.62% annual interest rate. Another possibility is to augment the $80,000 per year with dividends taken from the company's annual profits. Because the company will not show much profit initially, leaving less cash to pay dividends, Asli is examining the following schedule of dividend payments: Year 1—$0; Year 2—$0; Year 3—$12,000;

Year 4—$25,000; and Year 5—$43,000 for a total of $80,000 spread over the company's first five years, resulting in a grand total of $480,000 repaid to investors for their $350,000 initial investment.

Asli wants you to add these dividends to the repayment of the investors' original $350,000 investment and then calculate the payback period.

To determine the payback period for the investment:

▶ 1. In cell **B12**, enter the formula **=$B$7** to reference the annual loan repayment to the investors.

▶ 2. Copy the formula in cell **B12** and paste it in the range **C12:F12** to apply the same $80,000 loan repayment to each year.

▶ 3. In the range **B13:F13**, enter the following dividends: **0** in cell B13, **0** in cell C13, **12,000** in cell D13, **25,000** in cell E13, and **43,000** in cell F13.

▶ 4. Select the range **B14:F14**, and then use AutoSum to calculate the total reimbursement to the investor group for each of the first five years. The total values range from $80,000 in Year 1 to $123,000 in Year 5.

Next, you'll add these totals to the initial investment to view the cumulative total payments made to the investors.

▶ 5. In cell **B18**, enter the formula **=B6** to reference the initial investment value.

▶ 6. In the range **B19:B23**, enter the following formulas to reference the annual payments made to the investors: **=B14** in cell B19 for the Year 1 repayment, **=C14** in cell B20 for the Year 2 repayment, **=D14** in cell B21 for the Year 3 repayment, **=E14** in cell B22 for the Year 4 repayment, and **=F14** in cell B23 for the Year 5 repayment.

▶ 7. Select the range **B18:B23**, click the **Quick Analysis** button 📊, click **Totals**, scroll right to the end of the Totals tools, and then click **Running Total** to calculate a column of running totals for the net cash flow to investors. See Figure 9–24.

Figure 9–24	Payback period of the investment

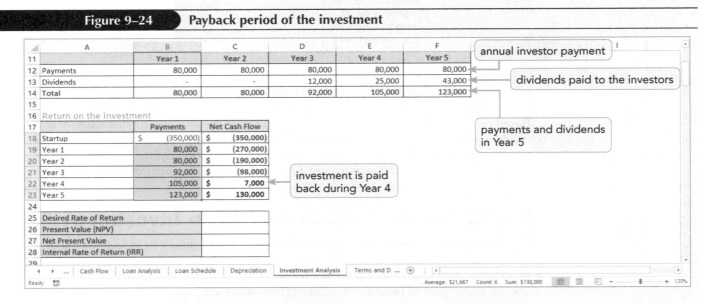

Based on these calculations, the investors will be repaid for their investments during the fourth year (when the value of the cumulative net cash flow changes to positive). By the end of the fifth year, investors will see a profit of $130,000 on their original investments.

Calculating Net Present Value

The payback period is a quick method of assessing the long-term value of an investment. The major drawback of the payback period is that it does not consider the time value of money. To understand why, you must explore how time impacts financial decisions.

The Time Value of Money

The **time value of money** is based on the observation that money received today is often worth more than the same amount received later because you can always invest the money you receive today and earn interest on that investment. The time value of money can be expressed by what represents a fair exchange between current dollars and future dollars.

For example, is it better to get $100 today or $105 one year from now? The answer depends on what you could do with that $100 during the year. If you could invest it in an account that pays 6% interest per year, the $100 would turn into $106 in one year, making it better to receive the $100 now and invest it; but, if you could earn only 4% interest on the $100, it would be better to wait a year and receive the $105.

The interest rate you assume for the present value of your investment is known as the rate of return, or the discount rate. The rate of return defines the time value of money and provides a method of comparing present value to future value.

You can use the PV function to calculate the time value of money under different rates of return. For example, the following PV function calculates the present value of receiving $100 per year for the next five years at a 6% annual rate of return:

```
PV(6%, 5, 100)
```

The function returns a negative value of –$421.24, indicating that it would be a fair exchange to spend $421.24 today to receive $100 per year for each of the next five years. In other words, $421.24 today is worth the same as $500 spread out over $100 annual payments if the discount rate is 6%.

For investments that pay off at the end without any intermediate payments, enter 0 for the payment value and enter the amount returned by the investment as the future value. So, to calculate the present value of receiving $500 at the end of five years at a 6% rate of return, enter the PV function

```
PV(6%, 5, 0, 500)
```

which returns –$373.63, indicating that it would be a fair exchange to spend $373.63 today to receive $500 five years from now.

You also can use the FV function to estimate how much a dollar amount today is worth in terms of future dollars. For example, to determine the future value of $100 in two years when the rate of return is 5%, enter

```
FV(5%, 2, 0, -100)
```

which returns a value of $110.25. The positive cash flow indicates that spending $100 today is a fair exchange for receiving $110.25 two years from now.

Using the NPV Function

The PV function assumes that all future payments are equal. If the future payments are not equal, you must use the NPV function to determine the present value of the investment. The syntax of the NPV function is

```
NPV(Rate, value1, [value2, value3,…])
```

where **Rate** is the rate of return, and **value1**, **value2**, **value3**, and so on are the values of future payments. The NPV function assumes payments occur at the end of each payment period and the payment periods are evenly spaced.

For example, to calculate the present value of a three-year investment that pays $100 at the end of the first year, $200 at the end of the second year, and $500 at the end of the third year with a 6% annual rate of return, you would apply the NPV function

```
NPV(6%, 100, 200, 500)
```

which returns a value of $692.15, indicating that this repayment schedule is equivalent to receiving $692.15 today if the discount rate is 6%.

Unlike the PV function, which returns a negative value for the investment's present value, the NPV function returns a positive value. This occurs because the PV function returns a cash flow value that indicates how much you need to invest now (a negative cash flow) to receive money later (a positive cash flow); whereas the NPV function calculates the value of those payments in today's dollars based on your chosen rate of return.

You can receive surprising results examining the time value of money. Consider an investment that has a 6% rate of return with these transactions: Year 1—investor receives $250; Year 2—investor receives $150; Year 3—investor receives $100; Year 4—investor pays $150; and Year 5—investor pays $400.

At first glance, this seems to be a bad investment. The investor receives $500 in the first three years but spends $550 in the last two years, for a net loss of $50. However, that analysis doesn't consider the time value of money. When the present value of this transaction is calculated using the NPV function

```
NPV(6%, 250, 150, 100, -150, -400)
```

the present value of the investment is $35.59, a positive result. The investment is profitable because the investor receives the money early and pays it back later using dollars of lesser value.

Choosing a Rate of Return

Whether an investment is profitable or not often depends on what value is used for the rate of return. The rate of return is related to the concept of risk—the possibility that the entire transaction will fail, resulting in a loss of the initial investment. Investments with higher risks generally should have higher rates of return. If an investor places $350,000 in a simple bank account (a low-risk venture), the investor would not expect a high rate of return; on the other hand, investing the $350,000 in a startup company like Holoease is riskier and merits a higher rate of return.

After discussing the issue with financial analysts, the company has settled on a 10% rate of return, meaning that Holoease will return to the investors at least as much as they would get if they had invested $350,000 in an account paying 10% annual interest over five years. You'll use that rate of return in the NPV function as you calculate the present value of the proposal that Asli will make to the group of investors.

To calculate the present value of the investment:

▶ **1.** In cell **C25**, enter **10.0%** as the desired rate of return.

▶ **2.** In cell **C26**, enter **=NPV(C25, B19:B23)** to calculate the present value of the investment based on the rate value in cell C25 and the return paid to the investors for Year 1 through Year 5 in the range B19:B23. The formula returns $356,054 which is the present value of the investment to the investor group. You will add this present value to the cost initial investment in order to calculate the net present value.

Be sure to add the initial case flow value to the value return by the NPV function to get the net present value.

▶ **3.** In cell **C27**, enter **=B18+C26** to add the initial investment to the present value of the investment over the next five years. The net present value is $6,054.

▶ **4.** Select cell **C26**. See Figure 9–25.

Figure 9-25	Net present value of the investment

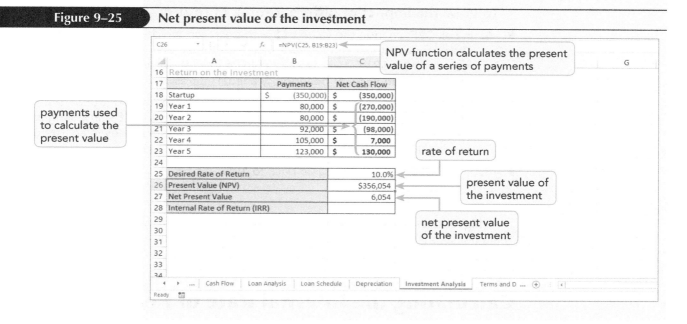

According to these results, the $350,000 investment in the company is worth $6,054 more than placing the same amount in a different investment paying 10% annual interest. Of course, that assumes Holoease will be as profitable as Asli hopes and will be able to honor the terms of the investor agreement over the next five years.

Insight

Understanding Net Present Value and the NPV Function

Net present value is the difference between the present value of a series of future cash flows and the current value of the initial investment. One source of confusion for Excel users is that despite its name, the NPV function does not actually return the net present value of an investment. Instead, it returns the investment's present value based on the returns that the investment will provide in the future.

To calculate the net present value in Excel, the initial cost of the investment must be added to the present value of the returns from the investment using the formula

```
=initial investment + NPV value
```

where *initial investment* is the initial cost of the investment and *NPV value* is the value of the NPV function applied to future returns. The initial investment is assumed to have a negative cash flow because that investment is being purchased, and it is assumed to be based on current, not future, dollars.

The exception to this formula occurs when the initial investment also takes place in the future. For example, if the initial investment takes place in one year and the returns occur annually after that, then the NPV function will return the net present value without having to be adjusted because the initial investment is also paid with discounted dollars.

In any financial analysis, it is a good idea to test other values for comparison. You will rerun the analysis using return rates of 8% and 12%.

To view the impact of different rates of return:

▶ **1.** In cell **C25**, change the value to **8%** to decrease the desired rate of return. The net present value in cell C27 increases to $26,584 indicating that investment is about $27,000 more profitable (in current dollars) than what could be achieved by an account bearing 8% annual interest.

▶ **2.** In cell **C25**, change the value to **12%**, increasing the desired rate of return. The net present value of the investment declines to –$12,789. Investing in the company would be less profitable than putting the money in an account bearing 12% interest by almost $13,000 in current dollars.

▶ **3.** In cell **C25**, change the value back to **10%**.

At higher rates of return, the net present value of the company investment decreases. That's not surprising because the investment is compared against other investments offering higher return rates.

Calculating the Internal Rate of Return

Your analysis of net present value under different return rates illustrates an important principle: At some return rate, the net present value of an investment switches from positive (profitable) to negative (unprofitable). Figure 9–26 shows the change in net present value for the Holoease investment under different rates of return.

Figure 9–26 Net present value and internal rate of return

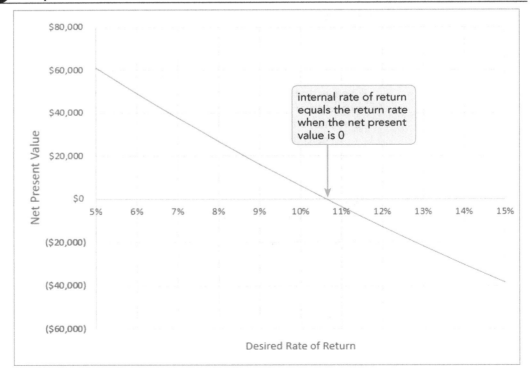

The point at which the net present value of an investment equals 0 is called the internal rate of return (IRR) of the investment. The internal rate of return is another popular measure of the value of an investment because it provides a basis of

comparison between investments. Investments with higher internal rates of return are preferred to those with lower IRRs.

Using the IRR Function

The IRR function calculates the internal rate of return for an investment. Its syntax is

    IRR(**values**, [*guess*=0.1])

where **values** are the cash flow values from the investment, and *guess* is an optional argument in which you provide a guess for the IRR value. A guess is needed for financial transactions that have several possible internal rates of return. This can occur when the investment switches between negative and positive cash flows several times during its lifetime. For those types of transactions, an initial guess helps Excel locate the final value for the IRR. Without the guess, Excel might not be able to calculate the IRR. If you don't include a guess, Excel will use an initial guess of 10% for the IRR and proceed from there to determine the answer.

For example, the internal rate of return for a $500 investment that pays $100 in the first year, $150 in the second and third years, and $200 in the fourth year is calculated using the IRR function

Tip
You must enclose values you enter directly in the IRR function in curly braces. This is not necessary if the values are expressed as cell references.

    IRR({-500, 100, 150, 150, 200})

which returns a value of 6.96% indicating that the return for this investment is equally profitable as an account that pays 6.96% annual interest.

The order of payments affects the internal rate of return. In the above example, the total amount of money paid back on the investment is $600. However, if the payments were made in the opposite order—$200, $150, $150, and $100—the internal rate of return would be calculated as

    IRR({-500, 200, 150, 150, 100})

which returns a value of 8.64%. The increased rate of return is due to the larger payments made earlier with dollars of greater value.

The list of values in the IRR function must include at least one positive cash flow and one negative cash flow, and the order of the values must reflect the order in which the payments are made and the payoffs are received. Like the NPV function, the IRR function assumes that the payments and payoffs occur at evenly spaced intervals. Unlike the NPV function, you include the initial cost of the investment in the values list.

Reference

Calculating the Value of an Investment

- To calculate the net present value when the initial investment is made immediately, use the NPV function with the discount rate and the series of cash returns from the investment. Add the cost of the initial investment (negative cash flow) to the value returned by the NPV function.
- To calculate the net present value when the initial investment is made at the end of the first payment period, use the NPV function with the discount rate and the series of cash returns from the investment. Include the initial cost of the investment as the first value in the series.
- To calculate the internal rate of return, use the IRR function with the cost of the initial investment as the first cash flow value in the series. For investments that have several positive and negative cash flow values, include a guess to aid Excel in finding a reasonable internal rate of return value.

You will calculate the internal rate of return that can be quoted to the investor group for Holoease.

To calculate the internal rate of return for the investment:

▷ **1.** In cell **C28**, enter the formula **=IRR(B18:B23)** to calculate the internal rate of return, where the range B18:B23 contains the initial investment and the returns that investors can expect. The internal rate of return is 10.62%.

▷ **2.** Select cell **C28**. See Figure 9–27.

Figure 9–27 ▷ **Internal rate of return**

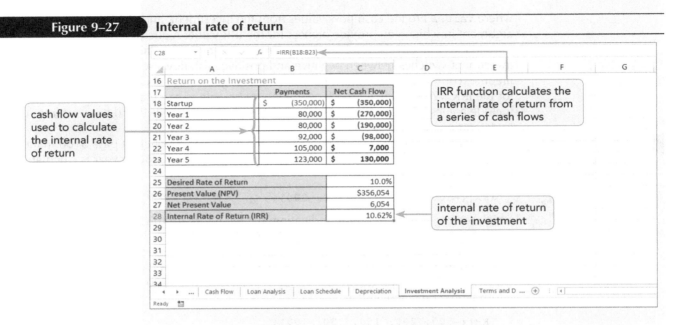

cash flow values used to calculate the internal rate of return

IRR function calculates the internal rate of return from a series of cash flows

internal rate of return of the investment

Based on the IRR calculation, Asli can tell potential investors that they will receive a 10.62% return on their investments if the financial projections for the company are met.

Proskills

Decision Making: Using NPV and IRR to Compare Investments

Investors will always have several investment options. In comparing two investments, investors usually want to select the investment with the higher net present value or the higher internal rate of return. However, if investors rely solely on the net present value, they can receive contradictory results depending on the value specified for the desired rate of return.

For example, consider the following two returns from an initial investment of $1,000. Option 1 has a higher net present value when discount rates are greater than 9%, while Option 2 has a higher net present value when the discount rate is 9% or less.

Option	Investment	Year 1	Year 2	Year 3	Year 4
Option 1	–$1,000	$350	$350	$350	$350
Option 2	–$1,000	$0	$0	$0	$1,600

Using the internal rate of return instead of the net present value can also lead to contradictory results. This often occurs when an investment switches several times between positive and negative cash flows during its history. In those situations, more than one internal rate of return value could fit the data.

To choose between two or more investments, it is a good idea to graph the net present value for each investment against different possible rates of return. By comparing the graphs, you can reach a decision about which investment is the most profitable and under what conditions.

Exploring the XNPV and XIRR Functions

Both the NPV and IRR functions assume that the cash flows occur at evenly spaced intervals such as annual payments in which the cash receipts from an investment are returned at the end of the fiscal year. For cash flows that appear at unevenly spaced intervals, Excel provides the XNPV and XIRR functions.

The **XNPV function**, which calculates the net present value of a series of cash flows at specified dates, has the syntax

XNPV(**Rate, Values, Dates**)

where **Rate** is the desired rate of return, **Values** is the list of cash flows, and **Dates** are the dates associated with each cash flow. The series of values must contain at least one positive and one negative value. The cash flow values are discounted starting after the first date in the list, with the first value not discounted at all. Figure 9–28 shows an investment in which the initial deposit of $300,000 on September 8, 2021 is repaid with eight payments totaling $340,000 spaced at irregular intervals over the next two years. The net present value of this investment is $7,267.04 based on a 7.2% rate of return. Note that the net present value is not $40,000 (the difference between the initial deposit and the total payments) because the investment is paid back over time with dollars of lesser value.

| Figure 9–28 | Net present value calculated over irregular intervals |

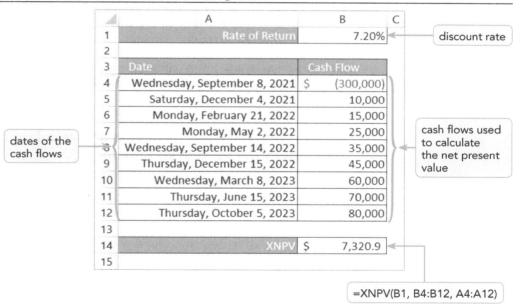

=XNPV(B1, B4:B12, A4:A12)

Likewise, the following **XIRR function** calculates the internal rate of return for a series of cash flows made at specified dates

XIRR(**Values, Dates,** [*Guess*=0.1])

where **Values** is the list of cash flow values, **Dates** are the dates of each cash flow, and *Guess* is an optional argument that guesses at the internal rate of return when you have a complicated set of cash flows with multiple possible return rates. Figure 9–29 shows the internal rate of return for the transaction presented in Figure 9–28. This investment's internal rate of return is 9.01%.

Figure 9–29 Internal rate of return calculated over irregular intervals

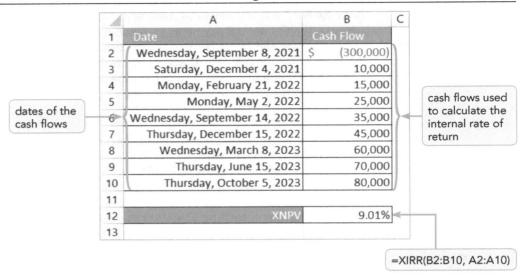

In the Holoease business plan, all payments to the investors are to be made at regular intervals, at the end of the upcoming fiscal years, so you do not need to use either the XNPV or the XIRR function.

To complete the projected income statement for the company, Asli wants you to estimate the company's retained earnings, which is the money that the company will earn each year after accounting for depreciation, interest expenses, taxes, and dividends to shareholders. You will enter the dividend payments and calculate the retained earnings in the Income Statement worksheet.

To enter the dividend payments and calculate the retained earnings in the income statement:

▶ **1.** Go to the **Income Statement** worksheet.

▶ **2.** In cell **B33**, type **=** to begin the formula, go to the **Investment Analysis** worksheet, click cell **B13,** and then press **ENTER** to insert the formula ='Investment Analysis'!B13 into the cell. No value appears in the cell because there are no dividends in the first year.

▶ **3.** In cell **B35**, enter the formula **=B31–B33** to subtract the dividends from the after-tax profit, returning the Year 1 retained earnings. At the end of Year 1, the company has a net loss of $74,538.

Next, you will calculate the net earnings for the remaining four years.

▶ **4.** Copy the range **B33:B35** and paste it in the range **C33:F35**.

▶ **5.** Click cell **F35** to deselect the copied range. Figure 9–30 shows the projected retained earnings for Holoease from Year 1 through Year 5.

| Figure 9–30 | Final income statement |

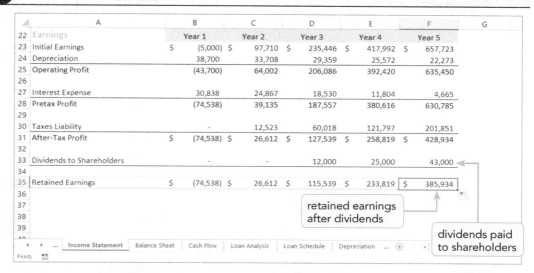

⊿	A	B	C	D	E	F	G
22	Earnings	Year 1	Year 2	Year 3	Year 4	Year 5	
23	Initial Earnings	$ (5,000) $	97,710 $	235,446 $	417,992 $	657,723	
24	Depreciation	38,700	33,708	29,359	25,572	22,273	
25	Operating Profit	(43,700)	64,002	206,086	392,420	635,450	
26							
27	Interest Expense	30,838	24,867	18,530	11,804	4,665	
28	Pretax Profit	(74,538)	39,135	187,557	380,616	630,785	
29							
30	Taxes Liability	-	12,523	60,018	121,797	201,851	
31	After-Tax Profit	$ (74,538) $	26,612 $	127,539 $	258,819 $	428,934	
32							
33	Dividends to Shareholders	-	-	12,000	25,000	43,000	
34							
35	Retained Earnings	$ (74,538) $	26,612 $	115,539 $	233,819	$ 385,934	

retained earnings after dividends

dividends paid to shareholders

Income Statement | Balance Sheet | Cash Flow | Loan Analysis | Loan Schedule | Depreciation ...

Ready

Based on Asli's projections, the annual retained earnings of the company will grow to $385,934 by Year 5 after accounting for all expenses, depreciation, interest payments, taxes, and owed dividends. At the end of the fifth year, the company has completely repaid its $550,000 startup loan and its investors.

Auditing a Workbook

In designing this workbook, Asli created several worksheets with interconnected values and formulas. The initial financial conditions entered in the Startup worksheet impact the company's loan repayment schedule. The values in the Depreciation worksheet are used in the Income Statement to access the company's yearly pretax profits. The dividends in the Investment Analysis worksheet are used to calculate the annual retained earnings. This interconnectedness gives Asli the ability to view the impact of changing one or more financial assumption on a wide variety of financial statements.

Two of these statements are stored in the Balance Sheet and the Cash Flow worksheets. The Balance Sheet worksheet projects what the company will own in both cash and tangible assets and what it will owe to banks and investors for each of the next five years. The Cash Flow worksheet projects the cash the company will have on hand through in its first five years of operation. You will view the contents of these worksheets now.

To review the Balance Sheet and Cash Flow worksheets:

▶ **1.** Go to the **Balance Sheet** worksheet. Many cells display the #NAME? error value. See Figure 9–31.

| Figure 9–31 | Error values in the Balance Sheet worksheet |

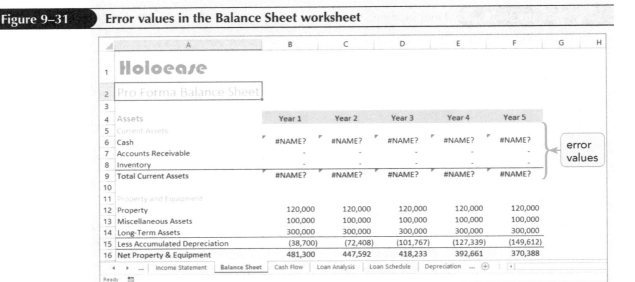

> ▶ **2.** Go to the **Cash Flow** worksheet and scroll to the bottom of the worksheet. Note that several other cells also display the #NAME? error value.

The downside of a workbook with many interconnected worksheets and formulas is that an error in one cell can propagate throughout the entire workbook. Does the error displayed in the Balance Sheet originate in that worksheet or is it somewhere else? Asli wants you to locate the source of the #NAME error. To do that, you will use auditing tools.

Tracing an Error

One of most useful tools in fixing an error-filled workbook is the Trace Error tool. In tracing an error value to its source, you need to work with dependent and precedent cells. A dependent cell is one whose value depends on the values of other cells in the workbook. A precedent cell is one whose value is used by other cells. For example, if cell C15 contains the formula =C13+C14, then cell C15 is a dependent cell because it relies on cells C13 and C14 for its value. This makes cells C13 and C14 precedent cells. Any error values in cell C13 or cell C14 would propagate to cell C15. A cell can be both a dependent and precedent. For example, if cell C15 is used by another cell in the workbook, then it becomes the precedent to that cell.

To locate the source of an error value, you select any cell containing the error value and trace that error back through the line of precedent cells. If any of the precedent cells displays an error value, you need to trace that cell's precedents and so on until you reach an error cell that has no precedents. That cell is the source of the error. After correcting the error, if other errors still exist, repeat this process until you have removed all the errors from the workbook.

Reference

Tracing Error Values

- Select the cell containing an error value.
- On the Formulas tab, in the Formula Auditing group, click the Error Checking arrow, and then click Trace Error.
- Follow the tracer arrows to a precedent cell containing an error value.
- If the tracer arrow is connected to a worksheet icon, double-click the tracer arrow, and open the cell references in the worksheet.
- Continue to trace the error value to its precedent cells until you locate a cell containing an error value that has no precedent cells with errors.

You will use the auditing tools to trace the #NAME? error values in the Balance Sheet worksheet back to their source or sources, and then correct the errors.

To trace the errors in the Balance Sheet worksheet:

▶ **1.** Go to the **Balance Sheet** worksheet, and then click cell **F9**. You'll start tracing the error from this cell.

▶ **2.** On the ribbon, click the **Formulas** tab.

▶ **3.** In the Formula Auditing group, click the **Error Checking arrow**, and then click **Trace Error**. A tracer arrow is attached to cell F9. See Figure 9–32.

| Figure 9–32 | Error value being traced |

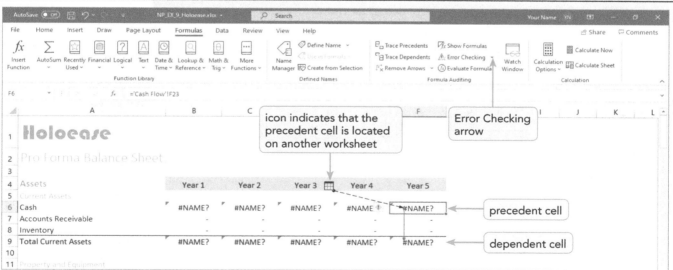

The tracer arrow provides a visual clue to the source of the error. A blue tracer arrow indicates that no error has been received or passed. A red tracer arrow indicates that an error has been received from the precedent cell or passed to the dependent cell. In this case, a red tracer arrow points from cell F6 to cell F9, indicating that cell F6 is the source of the error in cell F9. However, cell F6 also has a precedent cell. A black dashed tracer arrow points from a worksheet icon , indicating that the precedent cell for the value in cell F6 is in another worksheet in the workbook. You'll follow the tracer arrow to that sheet.

To continue tracing the error to its source:

▶ **1.** Double-click the **tracer arrow** that connects the worksheet icon ▦ to cell F6. The Go To dialog box opens, listing a reference to cell F23 in the Cash Flow worksheet.

▶ **2.** In the Go to box, click the reference to cell **F23**, and then click **OK**. Cell F23 in the Cash Flow worksheet is now the active cell.

▶ **3.** On the Formulas tab, in the Formula Auditing group, click the **Error Checking arrow**, and then click **Trace Error** to trace the source of the error in cell F23.

The tracer arrows pass through several cells in row 23 before going to cell B23 and settling on cell B20. Cell B20 has a single precedent indicated by the blue arrow and the blue box, which surrounds the range that is the precedent to the formula in cell B20. Because blue is used to identify precedent cells that are error free, the source of the error must be in cell B20 of the Cash Flow worksheet, which is selected.

▶ **4.** Review the formula for cell B20 in the formula bar. Notice that the function name in the formula is entered incorrectly as SUMM, which is why the #NAME? error code appears in cell B20. See Figure 9–33.

Figure 9–33	Source of the error value

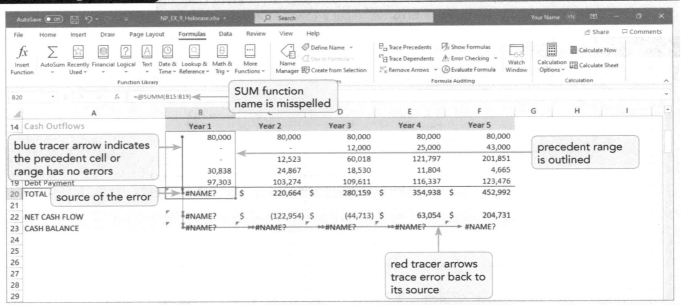

▶ **5.** In cell **B20**, change the formula to **=SUM(B15:B19)**, and then press **ENTER**. After you edit the formula, the #NAME? error values disappear from the worksheet. If a dialog box opens asking if you want to see an explanation of @, press **Enter**. If a dialog opens saying this formula is not supported by older Excel versions, press **Enter** to insert the formula.

Tip

To restore tracer arrows that have disappeared, retrace the formulas in the workbook.

▶ **6.** On the Formulas tab, in the Formula Auditing group, click the **Remove Arrows** button if necessary to remove all the tracer arrows from the worksheet.

▶ **7.** Return to the **Balance Sheet** worksheet and verify that no error values appear on that sheet.

▶ **8.** Click the **Remove Arrows button**, if necessary, to remove the tracer arrows from the worksheet.

Trouble? If the tracer arrows already disappeared from your workbook, it's not a problem. Excel removes tracer arrows automatically after a few seconds.

You can use the auditing tools to track any cell formula whether or not it contains an error. To trace the precedents of the active cell, click the Trace Precedents button in the Formula Auditing group on the Formulas tab (or press CTRL+[). To locate cells that are dependent upon the active cell, click the Trace Dependents button (or press CTRL+]).

Evaluating a Formula

Another way to explore the relationship between cells in a workbook is by evaluating formulas using the Evaluate Formula tool. From the Evaluate Formula dialog box, you can display the value of different parts of the formula or display other formulas in the cell references in the formula to discover the source of the formula's value. This is helpful for subtle worksheet errors that are not easily seen and fixed.

On a balance sheet, the value of the company's total assets should equal the value of the total liabilities and equity. Checking that these totals match is a basic step in auditing any financial report. In the Balance Sheet worksheet, the total assets in row 18 are equal to the total liabilities and equity in row 34 for Year 1 through Year 4. However, in Year 5 these values do not match. The company's Year 5 total assets shown in cell F18 are $637,366, but the Year 5 total liabilities and equity shown in cell F34 is $760,841. Because the values differ, an error must occur somewhere in the workbook. You'll use the Evaluate Formula tool to evaluate the formula in cell F34 to locate the source of the error.

To evaluate the formula in cell F34 of the Balance Sheet worksheet:

▶ **1.** Select cell **F34**, which contains the total liabilities and equity value for Year 5.

▶ **2.** On the Formulas tab, in the Formula Auditing group, click the **Evaluate Formula** button. The Evaluate Formula dialog box opens with the formula in cell F34 displayed. See Figure 9–34.

Figure 9–34   **Evaluate Formula dialog box**

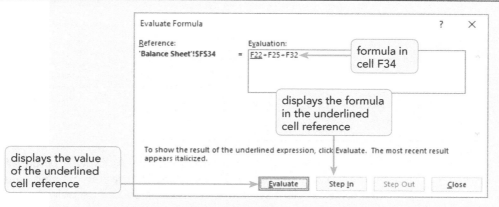

From this dialog box, you can evaluate each component of the formula in cell F34. To display the value of the underlined cell reference, click Evaluate. If the underlined part of the formula is a reference to another formula located elsewhere in the workbook, click Step In to display the other formula. Likewise, click Step Out to hide the nested formula.

▶ **3.** Click **Evaluate**. The selected cell reference F22 is replaced with the current liabilities for Year 5 (0). Cell F25 is now the underlined reference.

▶ **4.** Click **Step In** to view the formula in cell F25. Below the original formula, the formula ='Loan Schedule'!E38 appears, indicating that cell F25 gets its value from cell E38 in the Loan Schedule worksheet. See Figure 9–35.

Figure 9–35	Stepping into a formula

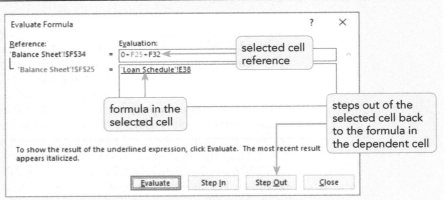

▶ **5.** Click **Step In** to evaluate the formula in cell E38 of the Loan Schedule worksheet. See Figure 9–36.

Figure 9–36	Source of the error found

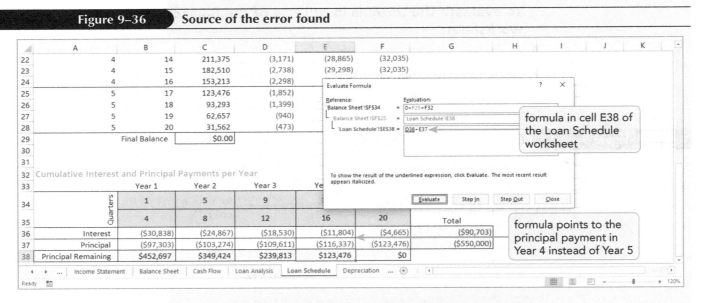

You've located the source of the problem. As shown in Figure 9–36, cell E38 in the Loan Schedule worksheet is the Principal Remaining value for Year 4 of the loan payment schedule. However, it should be pointing to cell F38, which contains the Year 5 value, because you are examining liabilities and assets for Year 5.

▶ **6.** Click **Step Out** to hide the nested formula and redisplay the Balance Sheet worksheet.

▶ **7.** Click **Close** to close the Evaluate Formula dialog box and return to the Balance Sheet worksheet with cell F25 selected.

▶ **8.** In cell **F25**, change the formula to **='Loan Schedule'!F38** to change the cell reference from cell E38 to cell F38. The total liabilities and equity value in cell F34 changes to $637,366 matching the total assets value in cell F18. The balance sheet is in balance again.

Using the Watch Window

Workbooks can contain dozens of worksheets with interconnected formulas. When you change a value in one worksheet, you may want to view the impact of that change on cell values in other worksheets. Moving among worksheets can be slow and clumsy if the values you want to follow are spread across many worksheets. Rather than jumping to different worksheets, you can create a **Watch Window**, which is a window that displays values of cells located throughout the workbook. When you change a cell's value, a Watch Window allows you to view the impact of the change on widely scattered dependent cells. The window also displays the workbook, worksheet, defined name, cell value, and formula of each cell being watched.

Asli wants to know the financial impact of a government tax rate increase from 32% to 38%. You'll create a Watch Window to display the company's Year 5 retained earnings, the Year 5 net worth value, and the Year 5 cash balance value.

To use the Watch Window to display values from multiple cells:

▶ **1.** Go to the **Income Statement** worksheet and scroll to the top of the sheet.

▶ **2.** On the Formulas tab, in the Formula Auditing group, click the **Watch Window** button. The Watch Window opens.

▶ **3.** Click **Add Watch**. The Add Watch dialog box opens.

▶ **4.** Click cell **F35** in the Income Statement worksheet, and then click **Add**. The Year 5 retained earnings value in cell F35 of the Income Statement worksheet is added to the Watch Window.

▶ **5.** Click **Add Watch**, go to the **Balance Sheet** worksheet, click cell **F36**, and then click **Add**. The Year 5 net worth value from cell F36 of the Balance Sheet worksheet is added to the Watch Window.

Tip

You can assign defined names to watched cells to make the Watch Window easier to interpret.

▶ **6.** Click **Add Watch**, go to the **Cash Flow** worksheet, click cell **F23**, and then click **Add**. The Year 5 cash balance in cell F23 of the Cash Flow worksheet is added to the Watch Window.

Now you can see the impact on these three values when the tax rate changes from 32% to 38%.

To modify the tax rate value:

▶ **1.** In the Income Statement worksheet, click cell **F5**. This cell contains the assumed tax rate.

▶ **2.** Change the assumed tax rate value from 32% to **38%**. The Watch Window shows the impact of increasing the tax rate. See Figure 9–37.

Figure 9–37   Watch Window under 38% tax rates

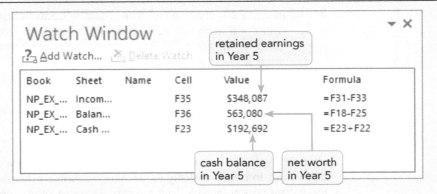

From the Watch Window, you can observe the effect of the revised tax rate by the end of the company's first five years. The Year 5 retained earnings amount in the Income Statement worksheet drops about $40,000 from $385,934 to $348,087; the Year 5 net worth value in the Balance Sheet worksheet falls about $75,000 from $637,366 to $563,080. Finally, the Year 5 balance in the Cash Flow worksheet also drops about $75,000 from $266,978 to $192,692. With operating margins so tight in the tech field, those losses are a great concern. Asli will study this more closely and perhaps revise the business plan to deal with this possibility. You will restore the tax rate to its original values.

To restore the tax rate:

▶ **1.** In cell **F5**, change the tax rate value back to **32%**.

▶ **2.** Close the Watch Window.

▶ **3.** sam↑ Save the workbook, and then close it.

You have completed the initial financial analysis of Asli's business plan for Holoease. This is, of course, a preliminary rough estimate of the factors and issues involved with providing a 5-year projection of the company's financial future. More in-depth analysis in consultation with financial analysts, lawyers, and other interested parties, will still be required before going forward.

Review

Session 9.3 Quick Check

1. If you take out a loan for $200,000 that must be repaid in 10 years with quarterly payments of $7,200, what is the formula to calculate the annual interest rate of the loan? What is the result?

2. If the annual rate of return is 5%, is $95 today worth more than, less than, or the same as $100 a year from now? Show the formula and formula results you used to answer this question.

3. You receive $50 at the end of Year 1 from an investment, $75 at the end of Year 2, and $100 at the end of Year 3. If the rate of return is 6%, what is the present value of this investment? Show the formula and formula results you used to answer this question.

4. You spend $350 on an investment that pays $75 per year for the next six years. If you make the investment immediately, what is the net present value of the investment? Assume a 6% rate of return. Show the formula and formula results you used to answer this question.

5. Suppose that instead of spending $350 immediately on an investment, you spend $350 one year from now and then receive $75 per year for the next six years after that. What is the net present value assuming a 6% rate of return? Show the formula and formula results you used to answer this question.

6. Calculate the internal rate of return for the investment in Question 4. If another investment is available that pays a 7.3% rate of return, should you take it? Show the formula and formula results you used to answer this question.

7. When tracing an error with the auditing tools, what do red tracer arrows indicate?

8. What is the purpose of the Watch Window?

Practice

Review Assignments

Data File needed for the Review Assignments: NP_EX_9-2.xlsx

After consulting with financial analysts and accountants, Asli has some new figures for the Holoease business plan. The company can get slightly better conditions on the business loan, which means that Holoease needs less money from investors to fund the company. Asli has also modified the depreciation schedule for the business's tangible assets. Asli wants you to make the necessary changes in the workbook to calculate the company's financial data for the next five years. Complete the following:

1. Open the **NP_EX_9-2.xlsx** workbook located in the Excel9 > Review folder included with your Data Files. If a dialog box opens, asking whether you want to update links, click Don't Update. Save the workbook as **NP_EX_9_Plan** in the location specified by your instructor.

2. In the Documentation sheet, enter your name and the date.

3. In the Loan Scenarios worksheet, in cell B4, enter **5.75%** as the annual interest rate that the company will secure for a business loan of $750,000.

4. Complete the calculations for the Loan Scenarios worksheet, which includes the constants you will need:

   a. In cell I7, use the PMT function to calculate the size of the quarterly payments for the $750,000 loan. Use cell H7 for the Rate argument, cell F7 for the Nper argument, and cell B7 for the Pv argument.

   b. In cell C8, use the FV function to calculate the future value of the loan assuming that quarterly payments are limited to $22,000. Use cell H8 for the Rate argument, cell F8 for Nper argument, cell I8 for the Pmt argument, and cell B8 for the Pv argument.

   c. In cell F9, use the NPER function to calculate the total number of payments required to repay a $750,000 loan with quarterly payments of $22,000. Use cell H9 for the Rate argument, cell I9 for the Pmt argument, cell B9 for the Pv argument, and cell C9 for the Fv argument.

   d. In cell D9, calculate the payback period in years by dividing the value in cell F9 by the value in cell E9.

   e. In cell B10, use the PV function to calculate the present value of the loan the company can afford if quarterly payments are limited to $22,000 over a 10-year period. Use cell H10 for the Rate argument, cell F10 for Nper argument, and cell I10 for the Pmt argument.

5. In the Startup Plan worksheet, in cell B25, enter **660,000** as the size of the loan that Holoease will take out to fund its startup costs.

6. Create an amortization schedule for the business loan in the Amortization Schedule worksheet. In cell G5, calculate the payment per quarter by using the PMT function with cell D5 as the Rate argument, cell F5 as the Nper argument, and cell A5 as the Pv argument.

7. Calculate the quarterly payments made to interest and principal:

   a. In cell D9, use the IPMT function to calculate the interest payment for the first quarter. In cell E9, use PPMT function to calculate the principal payment for the first quarter. Use cell $D$5 for the Rate argument, cell B9 for the Per argument, cell $F$5 for the Nper argument, and cell $A$5 for the Pv argument.

   b. AutoFill the formulas in the range D9:E9 to the range D10:E48 to calculate the payments for the remaining quarters. Fill the formulas without formatting.

   c. Verify that the loan is completely repaid by checking that the value in cell C49 is equal to $0.00.

8. Complete the Amortization Schedule worksheet by calculating the cumulative interest and principal payments per year:

   a. In cell B55, use the CUMPRINC function to calculate the principal paid for the first year. In cell B56, use the CUMIPMT function to calculate the interest paid for the first year. Use cell $D$5 used for the Rate argument, cell $F$5 for the Nper argument, cell $A$5 for the Pv argument, cell B53 for the Start argument, cell B54 for the End argument, and 0 for the Type argument.

   b. Copy the range B55:B56 and paste it in the range C55:F56.

9. Project future income statements under this new business plan. In the Profit and Loss worksheet, in the range C8:E8, project the company's revenue for the next five years by interpolating the Year 2 through Year 4 revenue assuming a growth trend. The costs of marketing and R&D as well as gross profit will be calculated for you.

10. In the range C14:F14, extrapolate the Year 2 through Year 5 payroll expenses by assuming the payroll will grow by 12% per year. In C15:F17, extrapolate the other expenses by assuming they grow by 5% per year from the initial Year 1 values. The range C18:F18 automatically calculates the total expenses for Year 2 through Year 5.

11. Calculate depreciation of the company's tangible assets. In the Startup Plan worksheet, in cell B12, enter **350,000** as current value of the long-term tangible assets.

12. Asli estimates that the long-term tangible assets will depreciate to a salvage value of $50,000 in 15 years. In the Depreciation worksheet, in the range B10:F10, calculate the yearly straight-line depreciation of the long-term assets using the SLN function with absolute references to the Cost, Salvage, and Life values in the range B4:B6.

13. In the range B16:F16, use the DB function to calculate the yearly declining balance of the assets using absolute references to the Cost, Salvage, and Life values in the range B4:B6 and relative references to the Period values in the cells B15 through F15.

14. In the Profit and Loss worksheet, in the range B22:F22, enter formulas to reference the declining balance depreciation values in the range B16:F16 of the Depreciation worksheet.

15. In the range B25:F25, enter formulas to reference the cumulative interest payments in the range B56:F56 of the Amortization Schedule worksheet. Enter the interest expenses as positive values by changing the sign of the interest value.

16. In the range B28:F28, use an IF function to calculate the company's taxes for each year. If the company's pretax profit in row 26 is negative, set the tax to 0; otherwise, multiply the assumed tax rate in cell F5 by the pretax profit.

17. Calculate the value of the company to potential investors. In the Startup Plan worksheet, in cell B30, enter **$250,000** as the amount the company hopes to attract from investors.

18. Calculate the rate of return if the investor group is paid $55,000 per year for the next five years on the $250,000 investment. In the Investment worksheet, in cell B9, use the RATE function to calculate the interest of the proposed repayment schedule using the corresponding values in the range B6:B8.

19. The company will also offer investors dividends on their investment. In cell B13, enter **$0** for the Year 1 dividend. In cells C13 and D13, enter **$6,000** as the Year 2 and Year 3 dividends. In cells E13 and F13, enter **$25,000** for the Year 4 and Year 5 dividends.

20. In the range C18:C23, calculate the payback period of the investment by calculating a running total of the values in the range B18:B23.

21. Determine the profitability of the investment to the investors:

   a. In cell C25, enter **12%** as the desired rate of return for the investors.

   b. In cell C26, use the NPV function to calculate the present value of the investment using the desired rate of return in cell C25 and the payments in the range B19:B23.

   c. In cell C27, calculate the net present value by adding to the cost of the initial investment in cell B18 to the present value in cell C26.

   d. In cell C28, use the IRR function to calculate the internal rate of return for this investment using the cash flow values in the range B18:B23.

22. In the Profit and Loss worksheet, in the range B31:F31, enter formulas to reference the yearly dividend values paid to the shareholders in the range B13:F13 of the Investment worksheet.

23. An error is somewhere in the workbook. Starting with cell F18 in the Balance sheet, trace the #REF error in the workbook back to its source, and correct it.

24. Save the workbook, and then close it.

Apply

Case Problem 1

Data File needed for this Case Problem: NP_EX_9-3.xlsx

Eagle Manufacturing   Jim Helt is a financial manager at Eagle Manufacturing, a steel manufacturer specializing in construction projects ranging from support structures used in large buildings and highways to decorative railings for new homes and apartments. For each piece of industrial equipment the company needs, Jim must evaluate whether it is better to purchase the equipment or to lease the equipment for several years before replacing it with newer models. Currently, Jim must choose between buying a large-capacity hydraulic steel metal press for $35,000 or leasing that machinery for three years for $500 a month. You'll use the Excel financial functions to compare the cost of buying versus leasing. Complete the following:

1. Open the **NP_EX_9-3.xlsx** workbook located in the Excel9 > Case1 folder included with your Data Files. Save the workbook as **NP_EX_9_Eagle** in the location specified by your instructor.

2. In the Documentation worksheet, enter your name and the date.

3. In the Buy vs. Lease worksheet, in cell B4, enter **$35,000** as the purchase price of the sheet metal press.

4. The sheet metal press has a salvage value of $15,000 after 120 months, or 10 years. In the range B5:B6, enter the salvage value and the salvage time (in months).

5. If the company does opt to buy the sheet metal press, the company will purchase a service maintenance contract that will cover maintenance costs for the next three years. In cell B9, enter **$950** as the cost of this contract.

6. If the company buys the sheet metal press it will also have to pay sales tax on the purchase. In cell B10, enter **3.25%** as the sales tax rate. In cell B11, enter a formula to calculate the amount of sales tax by multiplying the sales tax rate by the current price of the equipment.

7. If the company decides to buy the sheet metal press, Jim believes that it can be sold after three years for 90% of its depreciated value. In cell B12, enter **90%** as the resale percentage.

8. If the company decides to lease this equipment, Eagle Manufacturing will have to pay a $2,500 security deposit and a monthly payment of $500. Enter these values in the range B15:B16.

9. The table in columns D through G will be used to track the monthly cost of buying versus leasing over the next 36 months. In cell E4, enter a formula that shows the current price of the equipment entered in cell B4.

10. Calculate the value of the equipment as it depreciates each year as follows:

    a. In cell E5, calculate the difference between the value in cell E4 and the depreciation of the sheet metal press in the first month of use using the DB function. Use cells $B$4, $B$5, and $B$6 for the Cost, Salvage, and Life arguments and use cell D5 for the Period argument.

    b. Use AutoFill to fill the formula in cell E5 through the range E6:E40. Fill the formulas without formatting.

11. In cell F4, enter as a negative cash flow the initial cost of purchasing the sheet metal press by adding the cost of the equipment in cell B4, the cost of the service contract in cell B9, and the cost of the sales tax in cell B11.

12. For Month 1 through Month 36, the company will not have to make any payments on the sheet metal press. Enter **0** as the cash flow values in the range F5:F40.

13. After Month 36, the company will sell sheet metal price at a reduced value. In cell F41, enter as a positive cash flow the final depreciated value of the equipment in cell E40 multiplied by the resale percentage in cell B12.

14. If the company chooses to lease the sheet metal press it must first pay the security deposit. In cell G4, enter as a negative cash flow the cost of the security deposit on the digital equipment entered in cell B15.

15. Every month Eagle Manufacturing must pay the leasing fee. In the range G5:G40, enter as a negative cash flow the monthly lease payment from cell B16.

16. After the term of the lease is over, the company will return the sheet metal press and receive the security deposit back. In cell G41, enter the value of the security deposit from cell B15 as a positive cash flow.

17. To assess the time value of money, Jim will assume a **5.25%** discount rate. Enter this value into cell B19. To express this as a monthly percentage, in cell B20, enter a formula to divide the value of cell B19 by 12.

18. Calculate the net present value of buying the sheet metal press. In cell B21, add the initial investment in cell F4 to the present value of owning and then reselling the equipment after three years. To determine the present value of owning the equipment, use the NPV function with the monthly discount rate in cell B20 as the rate of return and the values in the F5:F41 as the cash flows for owning and using the equipment.

19. Calculate the cost leasing the sheet metal press in current dollars. In cell B22, calculate the net present value by adding the initial cost of the security deposit in cell G4 to the value returned by the NPV function for the discount rate in cell B20 and the cash flows in the range G5:G41.

20. Determine whether buying is less expensive than leasing. In cell B23, enter an IF function that displays the text **BUY** if the net present value of buying the equipment is greater than the net present value of leasing the equipment; otherwise display the text **LEASE**.

21. Save the workbook.

22. The decision to buy versus lease is closely related to the time value of money. If the discount rate is high, then Eagle Manufacturing will be selling the sheet metal press in three years for dollars of substantially reduced value. Redo your analysis by changing the discount rate in cell B19 to **6.50%**.

23. Save the workbook as **NP_EX_9_Eagle2** in the location specified by your instructor, and then close it.

Challenge

Case Problem 2

Data File needed for this Case Problem: NP_EX_9-4.xlsx

Midwest Copper   Linda Rubin is a project analyst at Midwest Copper, a mining company in northern Minnesota. The company is considering investing in a copper mine near Spirit River. Linda wants you to help develop a financial workbook that analyzes the cost of opening the mine, running it for 25 years, and then cleaning up the mine site after its useful life is over. Complete the following:

1. Open the **NP_EX_9-4.xlsx** workbook located in the Excel9 > Case2 folder included with your Data Files. Save the workbook as **NP_EX_9_Mine** in the location specified by your instructor.

2. In the Documentation worksheet, enter your name and the date.

3. In the Project Analysis worksheet, enter the following initial assumptions for the project:
   a. In cell B5, enter **$12.30** as the startup costs for the project (in millions).
   b. In cell B6, enter **32.0%** as operation costs as a percentage of the mine's revenue.
   c. In cell B7, enter **$13.25** as the cleanup cost in current dollars (in millions).
   d. In cell B8, enter **25** as the years of operation of the proposed copper mine.
   e. In cell B9, enter **3.4%** as the projected annual inflation rate over the course of the mine's existence.

⊕ **Explore** 4. In cell B12, use the FV function to calculate the cleanup cost in 25 years, using the inflation rate in cell B9, the number of years in cell B8, a payment value of 0, and the present value of the cleanup cost in cell B7. Change the sign of the result so it appears as a positive value.

5. In cell G6, enter the startup cost of the mine using the value in cell B5.

6. Enter the following projected annual income values that the mine will generate:
   a. In cell E7, enter **$0.75** as the projected earnings for Year 1 (in millions).
   b. In cell E16, enter **$18.00** as the projected earnings for Year 10 (in millions).
   c. In cell E26, enter **$4.00** as the projected earnings for Year 20 (in millions).
   d. In cell E31, enter **$1.00** as the projected earnings for Year 25 (in millions).

7. Fill in the missing income values in column E:

   a. Interpolate the rising income values between cells E7 and E16 assuming a growth trend.

   b. Interpolate the declining income values between cells E16 and E26 assuming a growth trend.

   c. Interpolate the declining income values between cells E26 and E31 assuming a linear trend.

8. In the range F7:F31, calculate the annual operational costs of the mine by multiplying the income value for each year by the operational cost percentage in cell B6.

9. Linda estimates the copper mine will have $1.80 million in fixed costs in Year 1. Enter **$1.80** in cell G7.

10. Linda projects that fixed costs will initially grow at a rate of 4% per year. Extrapolate the Year 1 fixed cost value through Year 20 in the range G8:G26.

11. From Year 21 to Year 25, Linda projects that fixed costs will decline by 10% per year (so that each year's fixed cost is 90% of the previous year). Extrapolate the Year 21 fixed-cost values through Year 25 in the range G27:G31 using a growth value of **0.9**.

12. In cell G32, enter the cleanup cost using the value in cell B12.

13. In the range H6:H32, calculate the copper mine's gross profit by subtracting the sum of the annual cost of goods and fixed costs from the mine's annual income. AutoFill the values without formatting.

14. In the range I6:I32, calculate the running total of gross profit for each year.

15. Create a line chart of the range D5:D32,I5:I32 to show the cumulative profit of the mine. Move and resize the chart to cover the range K5:Q20. The payback period is indicated where the line chart crosses the horizontal axis.

16. In cell B13, calculate the total income from the copper mine by adding all the values in column E. In cell B14, calculate the total cost of the mine by adding all the values in columns F and G. Note that by the raw totals, the mine appears to lose money because the total expenses are greater than the total income.

⊕ **Explore** 17. Because the cash flow from the mine changes between positive and negative several times during its 25-year projected history, there are different possible internal rates of return. Calculate two possible rates of return from the copper mine:

   a. In cell A17, enter **1.0%** as your guess for the rate of return. In cell B17, calculate the internal rate of return using the profit values in the range H6:H32 and your guess in cell A17.

   b. In cell A18, enter **10.0%** as your guess for the rate of return. In cell B18, calculate the internal rate of return using the cash flow values in the range H6:H32 and your guess in cell A18.

18. Supplement your calculations of the internal rate of return with calculations of the net present value of the copper mine investment under different discount rates:

   a. In the range A21:A39, enter the discount rates from 1% to 10% in steps of 0.5%.

   b. In the range B21:B39, add the value of cell $H$6 to the present value of the cash flows in the range $H$7:$H$32 using the NPV function with the corresponding discount rate in column A.

19. Create a scatter chart with smooth lines of the data in the range A20:B39. Move and resize the chart to cover the range K22:Q32. Note that the chart crosses the horizontal axis twice indicating that there are two possible rates of return.

20. Save the workbook, and then close it.

Objectives

Session 10.1
- Retrieve data with the Query Editor
- Create and edit a query
- Chart trends and forecast future values

Session 10.2
- Add data to the Excel Data Model
- Manage table relations in Power Pivot
- Create PivotTables drawing data from several connected tables

Session 10.3
- Drill through a hierarchy of fields
- Create maps with the map chart type
- Create map presentations with 3D Maps

Analyzing Data with Business Intelligence Tools

Presenting Sales and Revenue Data

Case | Cup and Platter

Dmitry Kovan is an account manager at Cup and Platter, a consumer retail chain that specializes in home furnishings and kitchen products. Dmitry is developing a sales report that analyzes sales data on select products and product categories sold on the company's website and five Cup and Platter stores located in Brooklyn, Chicago, Indianapolis, Philadelphia, and Washington, D.C. The report needs to analyze consumer preferences and project future sales revenue based on thousands of sales transactions. This large volume of data will be retrieved from a variety of data sources, including text files and external databases. You will help Dmitry by accessing and analyzing the data using Excel data tools.

Starting Data Files

Excel10 →

Module

NP_EX_10-1.xlsx
Support_EX_10_Data.accdb
Support_EX_10_History.csv
Support_EX_10_TwoYear.csv

Review

NP_EX_10-2.xlsx
Support_EX_10_Sales01.csv
Support_EX_10_Sales02.csv
Support_EX_10_Sales03.accdb

Case1

NP_EX_10-3.xlsx
Support_EX_10_Yogurt.accdb

Case2

NP_EX_10-4.xlsx.
Support_EX_10_Turkeys.csv
Support_EX_10_Migration.csv

Session 10.1 Visual Overview:

The Power Query Editor is an Office tool used to write queries.

A query is a request for information from a data source. This query retrieves information from the Year, Business Year, and Revenue ($mil) fields.

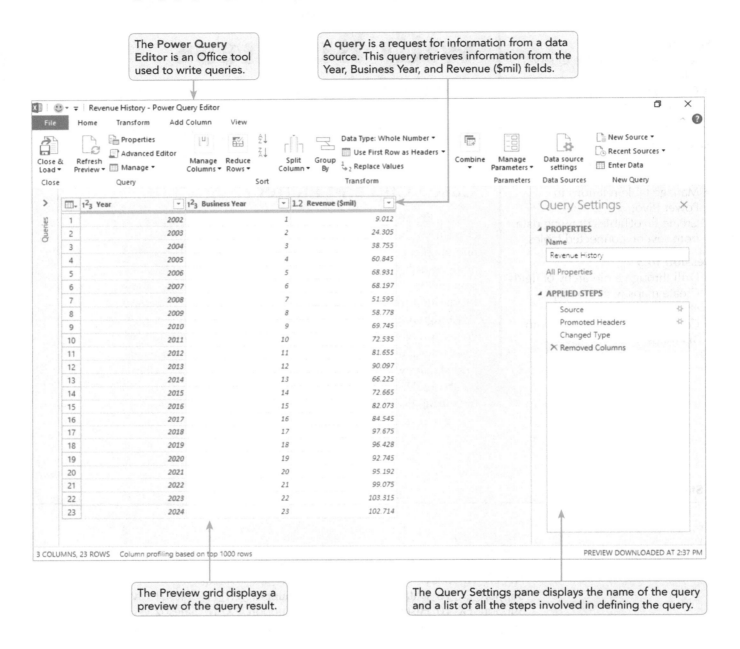

The Preview grid displays a preview of the query result.

The Query Settings pane displays the name of the query and a list of all the steps involved in defining the query.

Queries and Trendlines

To create a query, you click commands in the Get & Transform Data group on the Data tab and select the data source.

To create a worksheet containing forecasted values, including values that follow a seasonal pattern, you click the Forecast Sheet button.

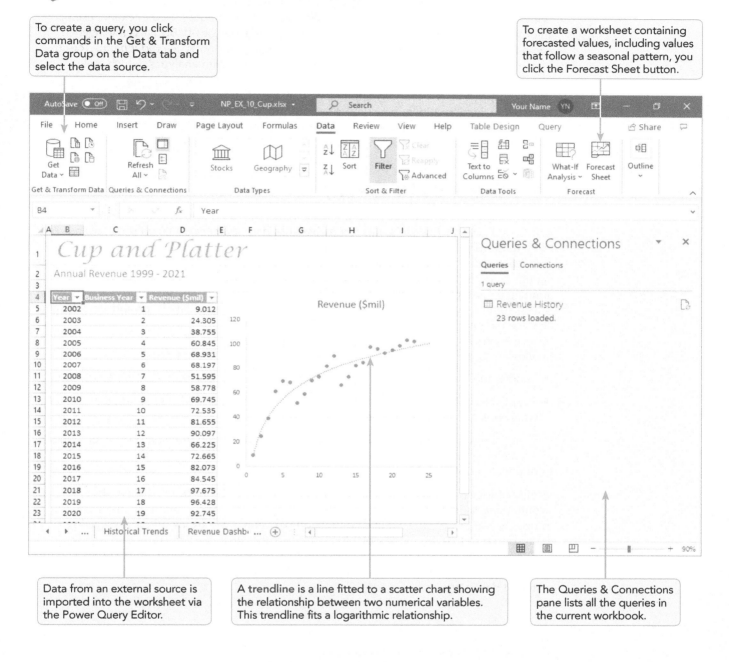

Data from an external source is imported into the worksheet via the Power Query Editor.

A trendline is a line fitted to a scatter chart showing the relationship between two numerical variables. This trendline fits a logarithmic relationship.

The Queries & Connections pane lists all the queries in the current workbook.

Introducing Business Intelligence

With so much information available, data analysts must find the useful information hidden within a mass of data values and sources. The tools and techniques used to extract useful information from data is referred to as **Business Intelligence** (or **BI**). Business Intelligence seeks to answer questions of fact, such as *What happened?* and *When did it happen?* and *Where did it happen?* Business Intelligence is often paired with **analytics**, which seeks answers to strategic planning questions, such as *Why did it happen?* and *How can we make it happen again?* Properly applied, Business Intelligence accelerates and improves decision making, resulting in a competitive advantage in the marketplace.

In this module, you'll learn the tools you need to turn Excel into an effective Business Intelligence platform. That process starts with data queries.

Writing a Data Query

Data being analyzed is often located in an external file or data source. To access that data for use in Excel, you create a data query. Because data sources often contain thousands or even millions of records, a query will typically include commands to reduce the data to a manageable size. This lets you import only those items of interest to you. For example, a human resources manager might construct a query to retrieve company salary records, limiting the search to employees from a particular department who were hired within a specified time interval. Queries can also be used to create new data fields and records so that the data imported into Excel is "cleaned up" and ready for study.

In the process of creating a query, you establish a connection between the Excel workbook and the data source. A connection does one of the following:

- Imports the data once, creating a "snapshot" of the data at a specific moment in time

- Establishes a "live connection" that will be updated periodically, ensuring that the workbook contains the most current data

- Establishes a connection but leaves the data residing within the data source, creating a smaller, more manageable workbook and avoiding the confusion of creating duplicate copies of the data across multiple locations

A climatologist might be interested only in temperature values from past epochs and would need to import that data only once. On the other hand, a financial analyst would probably want to establish a live connection between a workbook and a stock market data source so that the workbook always reflects the most current values and trends.

Dmitry wants you to report on Cup and Platter's annual revenue from its 23-year history. You will use Power Query to import the company's financial history from an external data source.

Using Power Query

Power Query is a BI tool that writes queries for almost any kind of data source, from text files to websites to large data structures. With Power Query, you can specify which parts of the data you want to import and how that data should be formatted. You can even modify the structure of the data prior to bringing it into Excel.

Text files are the simplest and one of the most widely used data storage formats, containing only text and numbers without any internal coding, formulas, or graphics. The data are usually organized in columns separated by a character known as a **delimiter**. The most commonly used delimiters are commas and tabs. Text files with comma delimiters are known as **Comma Separated Values (CSV) files**.

Figure 10–1 shows some lines from the CSV text file Dmitry wants you to use. The data are arranged in five columns separated by commas. The column titles, shown in the first line of the figure, are Year, Business Year, Revenue ($mil), Units Sold, and Notes. The remaining lines of the file contain the annual sales figures and commentary for the 23 years of sales data.

Figure 10–1	Data arranged in a CSV file

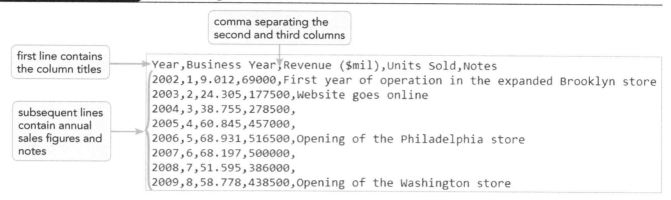

first line contains the column titles

comma separating the second and third columns

subsequent lines contain annual sales figures and notes

```
Year,Business Year,Revenue ($mil),Units Sold,Notes
2002,1,9.012,69000,First year of operation in the expanded Brooklyn store
2003,2,24.305,177500,Website goes online
2004,3,38.755,278500,
2005,4,60.845,457000,
2006,5,68.931,516500,Opening of the Philadelphia store
2007,6,68.197,500000,
2008,7,51.595,386000,
2009,8,58.778,438500,Opening of the Washington store
```

You want to be careful saving financial data in a CSV file because commas within currency totals will be interpreted as column separators. If your data requires commas, use a text file in which a tab character separates one column from another.

Reference

Constructing a Query

- On the Data tab, in the Get & Transform Data group, click the Get Data button.
- On the Get Data menu, select a data source category, click the type of file or the data source, and then import the data source file.
- Click Transform Data, and then in the Power Query Editor, click toolbar commands to transform the data from the data source.
- In the Query Settings pane, edit the steps in the query.
- On the Home tab, in the Close group, click the Close & Load arrow, and then click Close & Load To.
- In the Load To dialog box, select how to load the data, and then click Load.

You will create a query to retrieve the data values from the CSV file shown in Figure 10–1.

To create a query to the revenue history data:

▶ 1. **sam** ⬇ Open the **NP_EX_10-1.xlsx** workbook located in the **Excel10 > Module** folder included with your Data Files, and then save the workbook as **NP_EX_10_Cup** in the location specified by your instructor.

▶ 2. In the Documentation worksheet, enter your name and the date.

▶ 3. Go to the **Company History** worksheet. You will place the revenue data that Dmitry has compiled in this worksheet.

Tip

You can also open CSV files directly in Excel using the Open command in Backstage view.

▶ 4. On the ribbon, click the **Data** tab, and then in the Get & Transform Data group, click the **From Text/CSV** button. The Import Data dialog box opens.

▶ **5.** Navigate to the **Excel10 > Module** folder included with your Data Files, if necessary, click the **Support_EX_10_History.csv** file, and then click **Import**. A preview of the data from the CSV file appears. See Figure 10–2.

Figure 10–2   **Preview of queried data**

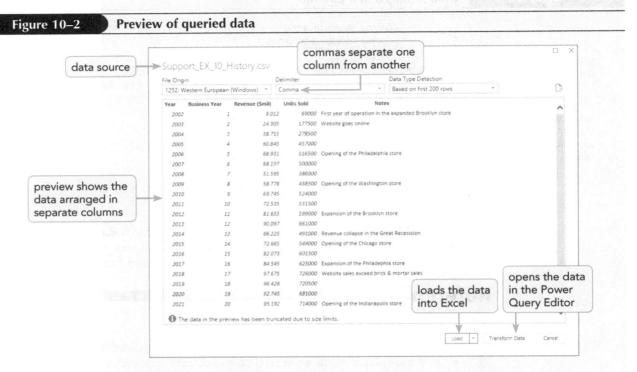

▶ **6.** Click **Edit** or **Transform Data**. The Power Query Editor window for this data source opens. See Figure 10–3.

Figure 10–3   **Power Query Editor window**

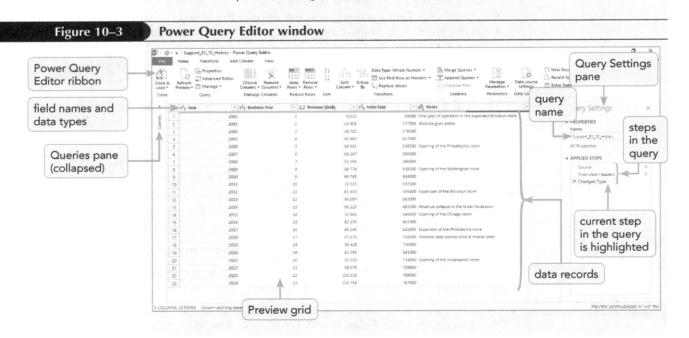

Power Query assigns each query a name. The default is the name of the data source, which in this case is the Support_EX_10_History file. You will change the name of the query to Revenue History.

To set the query name:

▶ **1.** Click the **Name** box located near the top of the Query Settings pane.

▶ **2.** Select the default name assigned to the query, and then press **DELETE**.

▶ **3.** Type **Revenue History** as the query name, and then press **ENTER**. The query is renamed.

A query is entered as a list of commands appearing in the APPLIED STEPS box of the Query Settings pane. Power Query entered three commands to import the data from the CSV file. To better understand what Power Query is doing, you will view the impact of each step on the data query by viewing the status of the data in the Preview grid.

To view the first three steps of the query:

▶ **1.** In the Query Settings pane, in the APPLIED STEPS box, click **Source**. The Source step establishes the connection to the Support_EX_10_History.csv file. The Preview grid displays the appearance of the data after this step but before the next step. At this point in the query process, the default column names are Column1 through Column5, and all fields are treated as containing only text values, as indicated by A^B_C.

▶ **2.** In the APPLIED STEPS box, click **Promoted Headers**. In this step, Power Query uses the first line in the CSV file as a header row and assigns field names to the five columns of data.

▶ **3.** In the APPLIED STEPS box, click **Changed Type**. The Changed Type step applies data types to the values in the five columns, with the Year, Business Year, and Unit Sold fields defined as containing whole numbers 1^2_3, the Revenue ($mil) field as containing decimal numbers 1.2, and the Notes field as containing text A^B_C.

You can modify a query step by selecting the step in the APPLIED STEPS box and clicking the Gear icon ⚙ to the right of the step title. You can also delete a step by clicking the Delete button ✕ that appears to the left of the selected step title. Be aware, however, that editing or deleting a query step might cause subsequent steps to fail.

Insight

M: The Language of Power Query

All steps in Power Query are written in the language **M**, which is a **mashup query language** that extracts and transforms data from a data source. Each expression in M is applied as a function that creates or acts upon the connection to the data source. For example, the following Csv.Document() function from the M language retrieves the contents of the revenue.csv file located in the Excel folder of the user's MAIN computer, using a comma symbol as the delimiter to separate one column of data from the next:

```
=Csv.Document(File.Contents("\\MAIN\Excel\Revenue.csv"),
[Delimiter=",",Encoding=1252])
```

As you progress in your understanding of Power Query, you may find it more efficient to write your own commands in M rather than letting the Power Query Editor do it for you. You can view and edit all the M commands in a query by clicking the Advanced Editor button in the Query group on the Home tab of the Power Query Editor window.

Retrieving Data into an Excel Table

Once the data is in the form you want, you can load the data into your Excel workbook. Queried data can be imported into an Excel table, PivotTable, or PivotChart. You can also just create a connection to the data source and load the actual data later. Dmitry wants you to load the financial history data into an Excel table on the Company History worksheet. You'll import the data now.

To load the query data into an Excel table:

Be sure to click the Close & Load arrow so you can choose where to place the imported data.

▶ **1.** On the Home tab, in the Close group, click the **Close & Load arrow**, and then click **Close & Load To**. The Import Data dialog box opens.

Trouble? If Excel loaded the data into a new worksheet, you clicked the Close & Load button. Cut and paste the Excel table into cell A3 in the Company History worksheet and then read but do not perform Steps 2 through 4.

▶ **2.** Verify that the **Table** option button is selected, and then click the **Existing worksheet** option button.

▶ **3.** If necessary, click cell **B4** to enter the expression =$B$4 in the cell reference box.

▶ **4.** Click **OK**. After a few seconds, the data is loaded into a new table on the Company History worksheet. See Figure 10–4.

| Figure 10–4 | Queried data loaded into an Excel table |

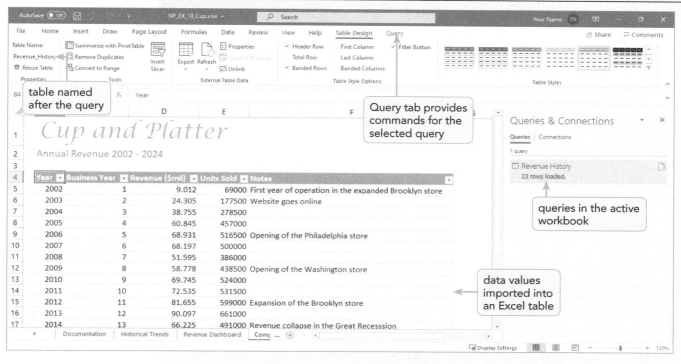

Excel assigns the new table the same name as the query that generated it. When the Revenue_History table is selected, the ribbon includes the Table Design tab and the Query tab, which contains commands for editing the selected query. The Queries & Connections pane also appears, listing all the queries in the active workbook.

Editing a Query

Dmitry wants you to edit the Revenue History query, removing the Units Sold and Notes columns so the table focuses only the revenue data. To edit a query, point to that query in the Queries & Connections pane. A dialog box opens, displaying information about the selected query and options for modifying the query. You'll edit the Revenue History query now.

To edit the existing Revenue History query:

▶ 1. In the Queries & Connections pane, point to **Revenue History**. A dialog box appears with information about the query. See Figure 10–5.

Figure 10–5   **Revenue History dialog box**

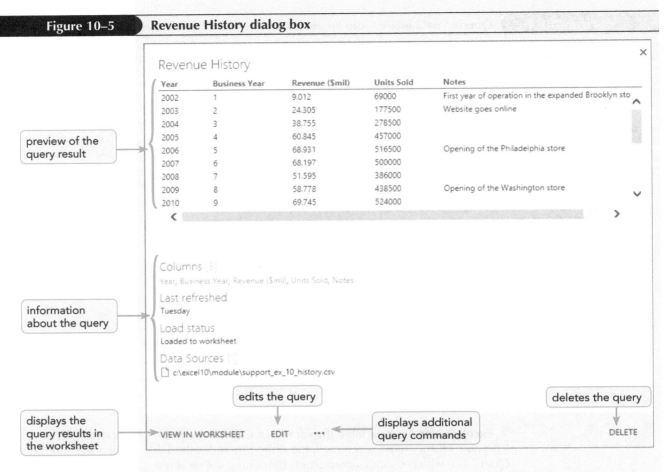

2. At the bottom of the box, click **EDIT**. The Power Query Editor window for the Revenue History query opens.

3. Click the **Units Sold** column header, hold down **CTRL**, click the **Notes** column header to select both columns, and then release the CTRL key.

4. On the Home tab, in the Manage Columns group, click the **Remove Columns** button. The Units Sold and Notes columns are removed from the query, leaving only the Year, Business Year, and Revenue ($mil) columns.

5. On the Home tab, in the Close group, click the **Close & Load** button. The edited query is loaded, and the Revenue History table now shows only the first three columns from the data source.

Note that removing columns from a query does not affect the data in the data source. It affects only the data that was imported into Excel.

Refreshing Query Data

Tip

To load a query to a different location, click the Load To button in the Load group on the Query tab, and specify a new location in the Import Data dialog box.

Loading data from a query into Excel creates a snapshot of that data. If the values in the data source change, the connection can be refreshed to show the most current information. You can refresh a query by clicking the Refresh button in the Load group on the Query tab.

To automatically refresh a data query, click the Refresh All arrow in the Queries & Connections group on the Data tab, and then click Connection Properties. The Query Properties dialog box opens to the Usage tab. From that tab, you can view controls for the connection to the query's data source. You can have Excel automatically refresh external data on a periodic schedule or whenever the workbook is opened. In this way, you can ensure the workbook contains timely and accurate information.

Insight

Excel Tables as Data Sources

An Excel table or a data range can be a data source for other Excel workbooks. To create a query to an Excel table or data range, select the table or data range, and then click the From Table/Range button in the Get & Transform Data group on the Data tab.

One advantage of using Power Query for tables and data ranges is that you then have access to all the unique tools and commands in Power Query. You can filter, reorder, and transform the table or data range for use in the current workbook or in other workbooks. However, like all queries, any changes you make to the data in the query do not impact the content or structure of the table or data range itself.

Transforming Data with Queries

A data source is often not organized in the way you need it for your report. As you have seen, you can use Power Query to remove columns from the data source. Power Query also includes tools to create new columns, group data values, and calculate summary statistics. This capability is particularly useful for large datasets in which the analyst is interested in only overall measures and not individual values.

Dmitry has another CSV file with two years of daily revenue totals for Cup and Platter. Dmitry wants a query that totals this data by month. You will use Power Query to group and summarize the data from the CSV file. First, you'll access the data source.

To write a query to access the Two Year Revenue data source:

▶ **1.** Go to the **Recent History** worksheet.

▶ **2.** On the Data tab, in the Get & Transform Data group, click the **From Text/ CSV** button. The Import Data dialog box opens.

▶ **3.** If necessary, navigate to the **Excel10 > Module** folder included with your Data Files, click the **Support_EX_10_TwoYear.csv** file, and then click **Import**. The preview box for the CSV file opens.

▶ **4.** Click **Edit** or **Transform Data** to open the Power Query Editor.

▶ **5.** In the Query Settings pane, in the Name box, change the name of the query from Support_EX_10_TwoYear to **Recent History**. See Figure 10–6.

| Figure 10–6 | Initial preview of the Recent History query |

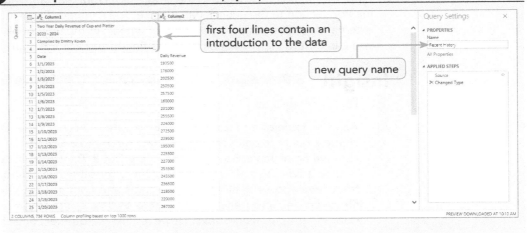

It is not uncommon for text files to include a few lines of descriptive text prior to the data. However, the inclusion of an introduction means that Power Query cannot automatically set up the data query. You must do that manually. You will indicate that the data begins on the fifth row of the file and then establish the data types of column headers for the two data fields in the CSV file.

To set up the data query:

▶ **1.** On the Home tab, in the Reduce Rows group, click the **Remove Rows** button, and then click **Remove Top Rows**. The Remove Top Rows dialog box opens.

> **Tip**
>
> You can use the Remove Rows command to also remove bottom rows, duplicate rows, and blank rows from the data.

▶ **2.** In the Number of rows box, type **4** and then click **OK**. The first four rows are removed from the data.

▶ **3.** On the Home tab, in the Transform group, click the **Use First Row as Headers** button. The top row is used as the column headers for the two data columns.

Excel creates the Date and Daily Revenue fields, assigning the Date data type 📅 to the Date field and the Whole Number data type 1²₃ to the Daily Revenue field. Next, you will add a new column to the data query.

Adding a New Column

Dmitry wants to know the monthly revenue totals, not the daily revenue totals shown in the data file. Because revenue figures are tallied at the end of each month, you will add a new column named Month displaying the date of the last day in each month—that is, 1/31/2024 for January, 2/29/2024 for February, and so forth.

To create a new column with the end-of-month dates:

1. If necessary, click the **Date** column heading to select that column.

2. On the ribbon, click the **Add Column** tab, and then in the From Date & Time group, click the **Date** button. A menu opens with date options.

3. On the menu, point to **Month**, and then click **End of Month**. The End of Month column is added to the data.

4. Double-click the **End of Month** column heading to select the current column name, type **Month** as the new column name, and then press **ENTER**. The column is renamed and resized. See Figure 10–7.

Figure 10–7	Month column added to the data query

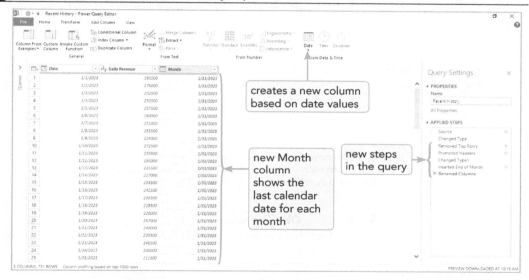

You will complete the query by grouping revenue values within the same month.

Grouping Values in a Query

You can group the data in a query by the values within one or more of its columns. When you create a grouping, Power Query adds a new column that summarizes the numeric values within each group by calculating statistics such as the sum, average, median, minimum, maximum, or count of those values.

Dmitry wants the query to return the total revenue within each month. You will group the query by the values in the Month column and create a new column containing the sum of the Revenue field.

To calculate the monthly revenues:

1. On the ribbon, click the **Transform** tab, and then in the Table group, click the **Group By** button. The Group By dialog box opens.

2. If necessary, click the **Group by** box, and then click **Month** to group the values by the dates in the Month column.

  3. In the New column name box, double-click **Count**, and then type **Monthly Revenue** as the name of the new column to be added to the query, and then press **TAB**.

  4. In the Operation box, select **Sum** to apply the sum function to the column, and then press **TAB**.

  5. In the Column box, select **Daily Revenue** as the column to sum within the Month group. See Figure 10–8.

Figure 10–8   **Group By dialog box**

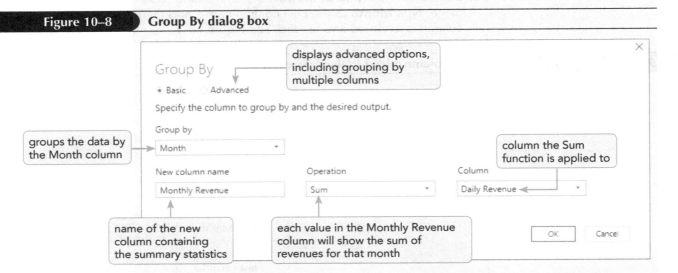

  6. Click **OK**. The values in the data query are grouped in a new column named Monthly Revenue. The Daily Revenue column is removed from this new grouping.

You can now load queried data into an Excel table.

To close and load the Monthly Revenue query:

  1. On the ribbon, click the **Home** tab. In the Close group, click the **Close & Load arrow**, and then click **Close & Load To**. The Import Data dialog box opens.

  2. Verify that the **Table** option button is selected.

  3. Click the **Existing worksheet** option button, and then click cell **B4** in the Recent History worksheet to load the Excel table containing the query data into that location.

  4. Click **OK**. The 24 monthly revenue values appear in an Excel table in the Recent History worksheet.

  5. Select the range **C5:C28**, and then format the selected cells with the **Currency** number format with no decimal places. See Figure 10–9.

Figure 10–9   Imported monthly revenue values

▶ **6.** Close the Queries & Connections pane.

The contents of the Recent_History table provides Dmitry with valuable insight into how Cup and Platter's sales vary throughout the year. For example, the lowest revenue total occurred in February 2023 in which Cup and Platter gained $4,481,000 in revenue (cell C6). The highest occurred in December 2024 in which the total revenue was $18,007,500 (cell C28). Can these numbers provide information for projecting revenue totals in future months? You will do that analysis shortly.

Insight

Moving a Query's Data Source

The connection between a workbook and a data source is lost when one or the other is moved to a new location. If the files are no longer stored in the original location, the data can no longer be refreshed. To update the path between the workbook and the data source, do the following:

1. Open the query in the Power Query.
2. Double-click the Source step from the list of query steps in the APPLIED STEPS box.
3. Specify the new location of the data source in the File path box.
4. Click OK to save the query with the new location of the data source.

After saving the query, you can refresh the query within Excel and verify that it can again connect to the data source without error.

Charting Trends

Recognizing trends and projecting future values is an important goal of Business Intelligence. One way of identifying a trend is with a trendline added to a chart.

Reference

Adding and Editing a Trendline

To add a trendline:
- Create a scatter chart of the data.
- Select the chart, click the Chart Elements button, click the Trendline arrow, and then select the type of trendline.

To edit a trendline:
- Double-click the trendline in the scatter chart to open the Format Trendline pane.
- Select the option button for the type of trendline to fit to the data.
- Enter the number of future values in the Forward box to project future values along the same trend.
- Click the Display Equation on chart check box to display the equation of the trendline.
- Click the Display R-squared value on chart check box to display the R^2 value that indicates how well the trendline fits the data.

Dmitry wants you to create a scatter chart showing the company's annual revenue from the past 23 years with trendline indicating the general pattern of revenue growth. Dmitry is interested in learning whether revenues have grown by a constant amount each year or are showing signs of leveling off.

To create a scatter chart of the company's annual revenue:

1. Go to the **Company History** worksheet, and then select the range **C4:D27**.

2. Click the **Insert** tab. In the Charts group, click the **Insert Scatter (X, Y) or Bubble Chart** button, and then click **Scatter** (the first chart in the gallery). A scatter chart plotting Revenue vs. Business Year appears in the worksheet.

3. Move the chart to the **Historical Trends** worksheet, and then move and resize it to cover the range **B4:H16**.

4. Add the title **Annual Revenue ($mil)** to the vertical axis and the title **Business Year** to the horizontal axis.

5. Change the chart title to **Trend in Annual Revenue**.

6. Click the **Chart Elements** button, and then click the **Trendline** check box. A straight line is added to the chart showing a general upward trend in the revenue figures over the past 23 years. See Figure 10–10.

Figure 10–10   **Linear trendline added to a scatter chart**

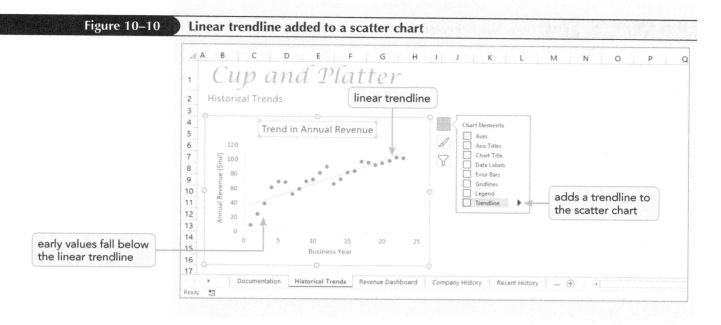

Excel scatter charts support the following trendline types:

- **Linear** for straight-line trends that increase or decrease by a constant amount (the default)
- **Exponential** for data values that rise or fall at increasingly higher rates
- **Logarithmic** for trends that increase or decrease quickly and then level out
- **Moving Average** to smooth out data by charting the average of consecutive data points
- **Polynomial** for trends that fluctuate between peaks and valleys
- **Power** for trends that increase or decrease by a constant multiple

Tip

Power and Exponential trendlines cannot be used if the data contains zero or negative values.

The straight line in the chart you created for Dmitry is for a linear trend, based on the assumption that revenue increases by a constant amount each year. However, the linear trendline overestimates the revenue in the early years. Dmitry thinks that a logarithmic trendline would be more appropriate because revenues grew rapidly at the beginning and then leveled off in later years. Dmitry also wants the logarithmic trendline extended two years into the future so that the company can estimate future revenue.

To change the trendline to logarithmic and project future values:

1. With the chart still selected, click the **Chart Elements** button ⊞, and then click the **Trendline** check box. The linear trendline disappears from the chart.

2. Click the **Trendline arrow** to display a menu of trendline options, and then click **More Options**. The Format Trendline pane opens.

3. In the Trendline Options section, click the **Logarithmic** option button. The logarithmic trendline appears on the chart.

4. Scroll down the Format Trendline pane to the Forecast options, type **2** in the Forward box, and then press **ENTER**. The trendline extends to forecast the company's annual revenue for the next two periods, or years. See Figure 10–11.

Figure 10–11   **Revenue estimated using a logarithmic trend**

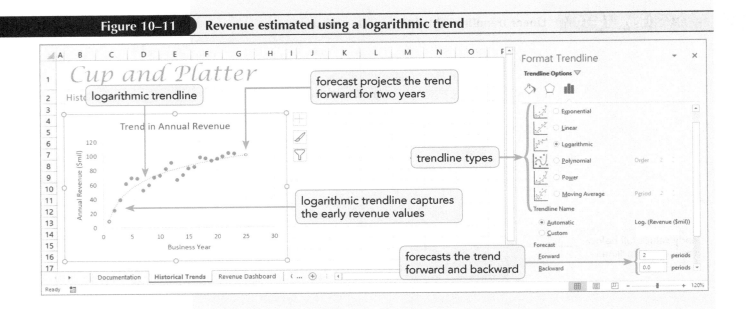

The logarithmic trendline follows the general growth of the company's annual revenue better than the linear trend though slightly underestimate revenues of the past three years. Dmitry will use the logarithmic trendline going forward, which indicates that the company's annual revenue should be at or above $100 million for each of the next two years.

Insight

Judging a Trendline with R^2

How well a trendline fits the data can be evaluated using the **R^2 statistic**, which measures what percentage of the variability in the data can be explained by the trend-line. The R^2 statistic is expressed as a decimal between 0 and 1 where an R^2 value such as 0.85 indicates that 85% of the variability of the data can be accounted for by the trendline. R^2 values close to 1 indicate much of the data can be fitted by the trendline. On the other hand, R^2 values close to 0 indicate there is little evidence of a trend in the data based on the fitted line. You can display the R^2 value for an Excel trendline by clicking the Display R-squared value on chart check box in the Format Trendline pane.

Creating a Forecast Sheet

Forecast sheets are another Excel tool used for displaying trends and projecting future values. One advantage of forecast sheets is that they can be used to analyze **seasonal data** in which the values follow a periodic pattern during the calendar year.

Reference

Creating a Forecast Sheet and Setting the Forecast Options

- Select the data range containing the date values and numeric values to be forecasted.
- On the Data tab, in the Forecast group, click the Forecast Sheet button.
- In the Create Forecast Worksheet dialog box, click Options.
- To add a seasonal trend to the forecasts, in the Seasonality group, click the Set Manually option, and then enter the number of periods in one season.
- To set the confidence interval for the forecasted values, enter a value in the Confidence Interval input box.
- To set the extent of the forecast, enter the ending date in the Forecast End box.
- Click Create.

Dmitry wants to create a forecast sheet to track the seasonal changes in monthly revenue and project next year's monthly revenue.

To generate a forecast sheet of the monthly revenue:

1. Go the **Recent History** worksheet, and select the range **B4:C28**.

2. On the ribbon, click the **Data** tab, and then in the Forecast group, click the **Forecast Sheet** button. The Create Forecast Worksheet dialog box opens, showing a preview of the forecasted values. See Figure 10–12.

Figure 10–12 **Create Forecast Worksheet dialog box**

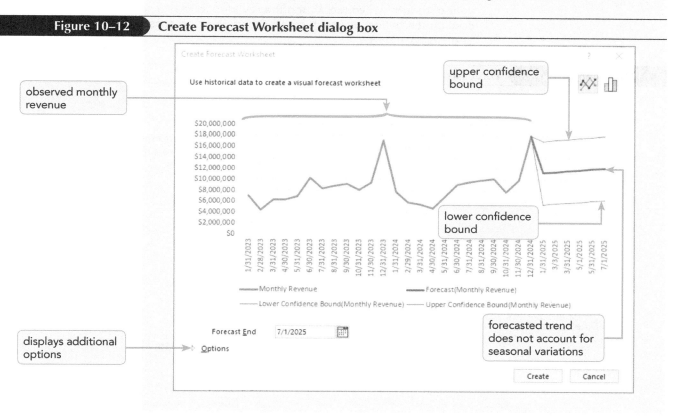

Tip

To change the confidence interval percentage, click Options in the Create Forecast Worksheet dialog box, and then enter a new value in the Confidence Interval box.

Excel uses two years of monthly revenue figures to project the revenue trend up to July 1, 2025. The trend is bracketed by upper and lower **confidence bounds**, which provide a measure of the uncertainty of the forecast by indicating within what range the forecasted values will lie. The default is to create 95% confidence bound for a region in which one is 95% confident that the actual values will appear. Thus, if the 95% confidence bound for a forecasted revenue ranges from $10 million to $15 million, you would be 95% confident that the eventual revenue will be not less than $10 million and not greater than $15 million. The fact that the upper and lower bounds are so far apart in Figure 10–12 indicates a large measure of uncertainty in the projected monthly revenue.

However, Dmitry notes that revenue follows a seasonal pattern with the highest sales totals occurring in November and December and low sales in January through March. The forecasted values have not picked up this trend. You will revise the forecast to account for seasonal variability.

To create a seasonal forecast of the monthly revenue:

1. In the lower-left corner of the Create Forecast Worksheet dialog box, click **Options**. The dialog box expands to display the forecast options.

Tip

You need at least two complete years of data to project a seasonal trend for the next year.

2. In the Seasonality group, click the **Set Manually** option button, and then enter **12** in the Set Manually box. This specifies a seasonal pattern that will repeat itself every 12 months.

3. In the Forecast End box, change the date to **12/31/2025** to forecast a year of monthly revenue. When the revenue follows a seasonal pattern, the confidence bands are much smaller than when no seasonality was assumed. See Figure 10–13.

Figure 10–13   Forecasts with a seasonal trend

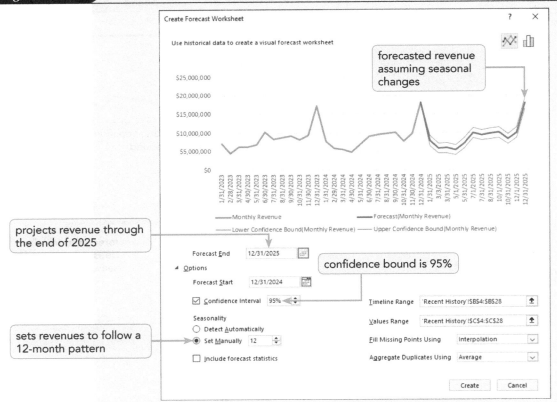

4. Click **Create**. A new worksheet containing the forecasted values is added to the workbook. The forecasted values have been placed within an Excel table.

5. If the Forecast Sheet dialog box opens, read the message, and then click **Got it!**

6. Rename the forecast worksheet as **Monthly Revenue Forecasts** and then move the sheet directly before the Data Sources worksheet near the end of the workbook.

7. Click the **Table Design** tab, and then in the Properties group, click the **Table Name** box and change the table name to **Forecast_Table**.

8. Scroll down to the bottom of the worksheet to view the projected revenue totals. See Figure 10–14.

Figure 10–14 ▶ **Forecast worksheet**

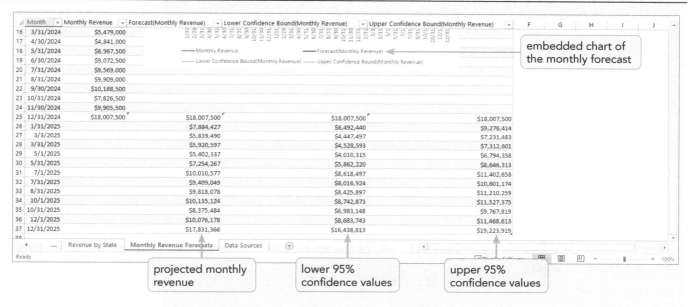

From the forecasted values, Dmitry projects the December 2025 revenue to be about $17.83 million (cell C37) and is 95% confident that the revenue will be at least about $16.438 million (cell D37) but not more than about $19.223 million (cell E37).

You will complete this part of the report by moving the forecast chart into the Historical Trends worksheet.

To move the monthly revenue chart:

1. Move the embedded chart on the Monthly Revenue Forecasts worksheet to the **Historical Trends** worksheet.

2. Move and resize the chart to cover the range **J4:R16**.

3. Remove the chart legend.

4. Add the chart title **Trend in Monthly Revenue**.

▶ **5.** Add the axis titles **Monthly Revenue** and **Date** to the vertical and horizontal axes.

▶ **6.** Close any open worksheet panes. See Figure 10–15.

Figure 10–15   **Annual and monthly revenue trends**

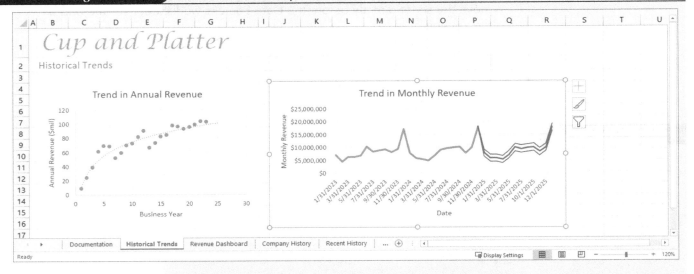

▶ **7.** Save the workbook.

Dmitry will include both charts in a report projecting future revenue for the company.

Proskills

Teamwork: Maintaining Data Security

Data security is essential for any business to maintain the integrity of its data and retain the trust of its colleagues and customers. It is critical to secure data to prevent lapses in security. If your workbooks are connected to external data sources, keep in mind the following tips:

- **Apply data security controls.** Make sure your data files are set up with password controls to prohibit unauthorized access.
- **Keep software updated.** Be sure to diligently update the software that stores your data with the latest security patches.
- **Closely monitor data copying.** Have only one source of your data. When multiple copies of the data exist, data security, consistency, and integrity are compromised.
- **Encrypt your data.** Use data encryption to prevent hackers from gaining unauthorized access to sensitive information.

Maintaining data security requires that everyone with access to your data files knows how to retrieve and process that data appropriately. In the end, your data will be only as secure as the work habits of the people who access it.

You have completed the revenue estimates and projections using data retrieved with the Power Query Editor. In the next session, you'll perform analyses that involve combining data from several data sources within a single PivotTable and PivotChart.

Review

Session 10.1 Quick Check

1. What is Business Intelligence?
2. What is a query?
3. What is a delimiter?
4. What is a CSV file?
5. How do you undo an action in the Power Query Editor?
6. What trendline should you add to a chart for data that increases or decreases quickly and then levels out?
7. What does a 95% confidence bound tell you about forecasted values?

Session 10.2 Visual Overview:

The Power Pivot add-in provides access to the **Data Model**, which is a database attached to an Excel workbook.

A database is a highly structured collection of data values organized into separate tables. This database has five tables.

You can click the Diagram View button in Power Pivot to view the structure and relationships of the tables in the Data Model.

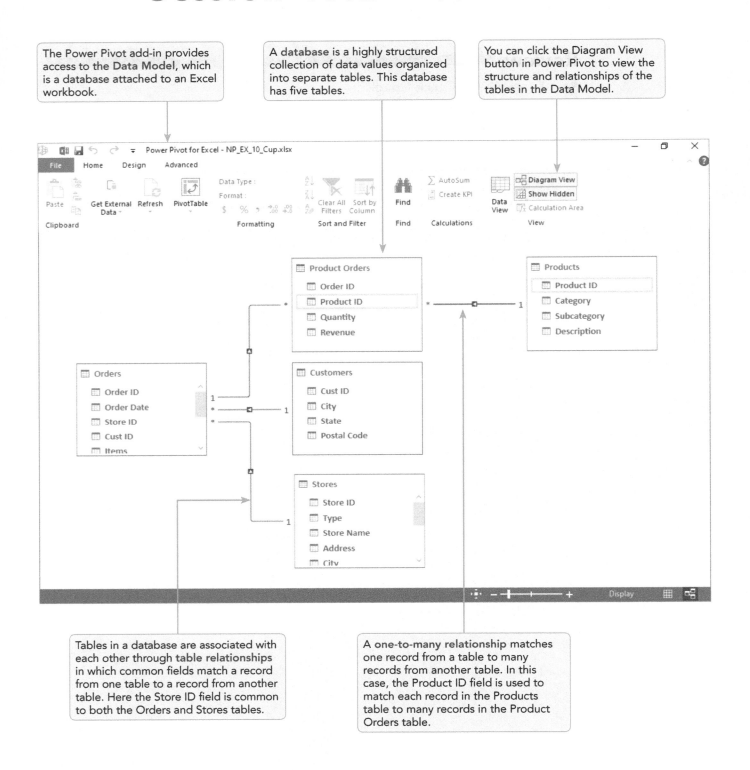

Tables in a database are associated with each other through table relationships in which common fields match a record from one table to a record from another table. Here the Store ID field is common to both the Orders and Stores tables.

A one-to-many relationship matches one record from a table to many records from another table. In this case, the Product ID field is used to match each record in the Products table to many records in the Product Orders table.

Power Pivot and the Data Model

You click the Manage button to manage the contents of the Data Model.

When the Power Pivot add-in is activated, the Power Pivot tab appears on the ribbon.

PivotTables can retrieve data from multiple fields in different tables in the Data Model.

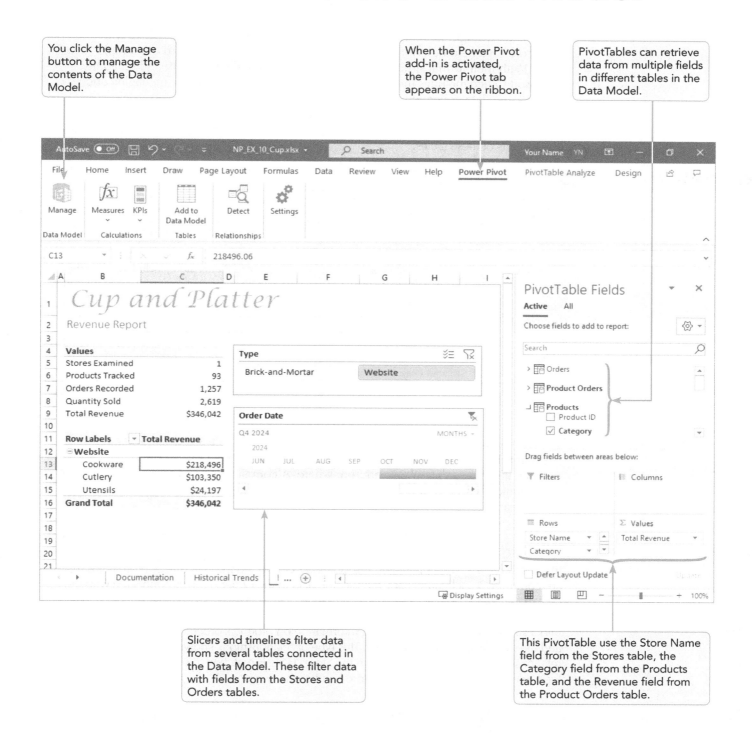

Slicers and timelines filter data from several tables connected in the Data Model. These filter data with fields from the Stores and Orders tables.

This PivotTable use the Store Name field from the Stores table, the Category field from the Products table, and the Revenue field from the Product Orders table.

Introducing Databases

In this session, you will use Excel to retrieve data from a database. A database is a structured collection of data values, often organized into tables with each table focusing on a single subject. Database tables are very similar to Excel tables with each column a field describing a characteristic and each row a record of multiple fields. With their formal structure, databases help insure data integrity and reliability. Microsoft Office includes the Microsoft Access database program for managing and storing large data collections.

Dmitry has an Access database file containing five tables describing different aspects of the sales transactions between Cup and Platter and its customers. Figure 10–16 summarizes the contents of these tables.

| Figure 10–16 | Cup and Platter database tables |

Table	Contains
Customers	Data on customers that have bought items from Cup and Platter, including the general location of the customer
Orders	Data on customer orders made at a Cup and Platter store, including when the order was made, the ID of the store, the ID of the customer who made the order, the total quantity of items, and the costs associated with the order
Product Orders	Sales data on specific products purchased from Cup and Platter, the quantity purchased, and the ID of the order in which the purchase occurred
Products	Product information on specific products offered by Cup and Platter including the product category, subcategory, and a general description of the product
Stores	Data on five Cup and Platter stores located across the country and the company website

By extracting information from all five tables, Dmitry can learn what products customers have been purchasing, how many they purchased and for how much, as well as when they were purchased and from where. A complete inventory of Cup and Platter sales would involve millions of records, so, for the purpose of this analysis, you'll limit your research to 93 selected products sold over the past two years.

Relational Databases

In a database with multiple tables, the tables are connected through one or more fields that are common to each table. For example, the data in the Orders table is connected with the data in the Stores table through the common field StoreID. As shown in Figure 10–17, by matching the values of the StoreID field, information from both tables can be combined into a single data structure providing information on products ordered at Cup and Platter and the store that handled the order. This type of relationship is known as a one-to-many relationship because one record from the Stores table is matched to several records from the Orders table (because a single store handles many orders).

Figure 10–17   **Tables related by a common field**

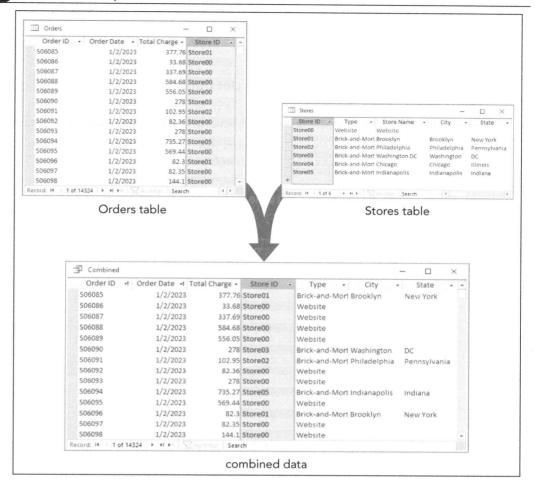

Orders table   Stores table

combined data

Another type of relationship is the **one-to-one relationship** in which one record from the first table can be matched to only one record from the second table. If the Cup and Platter database had a table with information about the head manager of each store, it would have a one-to-one relationship with the Stores table because each store would have only one head manager.

Databases in which tables can be joined through the use of common fields are known as **relational databases**. Because the tables can be joined through common fields, it is unnecessary to duplicate the same piece of information in multiple tables. Information about Cup and Platter stores needs to be entered in only one table and then connected to other tables via a table relationship. Removing duplication makes it easier to manage large datasets and improves data quality and integrity.

Querying an Access Database

Power Query supports almost all the popular database applications, including Microsoft Access, SQL Server, Oracle, IBM DB2, and MySQL. You then use the Query Editor to create a query that extracts data from any one table within those databases, or you can create a query that extracts data from several tables. You will access the tables stored in the Cup and Platter Access database file.

To create a query to an Access database table:

▶ **1.** If you took a break after the previous session, make sure the NP_EX_10_Cup workbook is open.

▶ **2.** On the ribbon, click the **Data** tab, and then in the Get & Transform Data group, click the **Get Data** button. A menu of data options appears.

▶ **3.** On the menu, point to **From Database** to display a list of database sources, and then click **From Microsoft Access Database**. The Import Data dialog box opens.

▶ **4.** Select the **Support_EX_10_Data.accdb** file located in the **Excel10 > Module** folder, and then click **Import**. The Navigator dialog box shows a list of the tables in the database.

▶ **5.** Click **Customers** in the table list to preview the Customer table contents. See Figure 10–18.

Figure 10–18	Navigator dialog box

The Customers table has four fields. The Cust ID field uniquely identifies a Cup and Platter customer, and the City, State, and Postal Code fields specify the customer's location. Though not shown in the dialog box, the Customers table has 7,734 records. With so many records, Dmitry doesn't want to create a large Excel table to hold all the customer data. An alternative is to use the Excel Data Model.

Exploring the Data Model

The Data Model is a database attached to an Excel workbook that provides many of the tools found in database programs such as Microsoft Access. Because the Data Model is part of the workbook, its contents are immediately available to PivotTables, PivotCharts, and other Excel tools. One advantage of storing data in the Data Model rather than in a worksheet is that data stored in the Data Model are compressed, resulting in a smaller file size. Compressing the data also means that queries run faster, and PivotTables load quicker. The drawback is that Data Model contents are not visible in the workbook. To view them, you must use Power Pivot, an Excel add-in for managing the Data Model contents.

Data are placed into the Data Model using the same Power Query application used for retrieving data from CSV files and other data sources. Once placed in the Data Model, Excel establishes a connection between the Data Model contents and the workbook. Essentially, it's like having a connection to an external data source even though the Data Model is saved within the workbook file.

You will load the contents of the Customers table into the Data Model.

To load the Customers table into the Data Model:

1. With the Navigator dialog box still open and the Customers table still selected, click the **Load arrow**, and then click **Load To**. The Import Data dialog box opens.

Be sure to only create a connection; don't load the data into an Excel table, PivotTable, or PivotChart.

2. Click the **Only Create Connection** option button. This option establishes a connection between the Data Model contents and the workbook without loading the data in to an Excel table, PivotTable, or PivotChart.

3. Click the **Add this data to the Data Model** check box. See Figure 10–19.

Figure 10–19   **Import Data dialog box to load data into the Data Model**

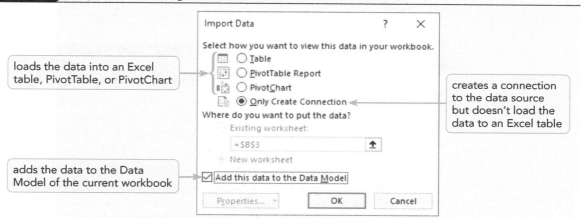

loads the data into an Excel table, PivotTable, or PivotChart

adds the data to the Data Model of the current workbook

creates a connection to the data source but doesn't load the data to an Excel table

4. Click **OK** to establish the connection to the Data Model. When the data loading is complete, the Customers query appears in the Queries & Connection pane indicating that 7,734 rows have been loaded.

Trouble? If you see an Excel table containing the Items Purchased data, delete the table and the query, repeat the previous set of steps to recreate the query, and then repeat Steps 1 through 4, making sure to load the table only to the Data Model and not to an Excel table.

You will add the remaining tables from the database to the workbook's Data Model. Because the data have been structured within the Access database, you will not need to edit the data contents with Power Query. You'll load the remaining four tables in the Data Model.

To load the remaining database tables:

1. On the Data tab, in the Get & Transform Data group, click the **Get Data** button, point to **From Database**, and then click **From Microsoft Access Database** to select the database source. The Import Data dialog box opens.

2. Select the **Support_EX_10_Data.accdb** file, and then click **Import**. The Navigator dialog box opens.

> 3. Click the **Select multiple items** check box so you can select more than one table from the database. Check boxes appear before each table name.

> 4. Click the **Orders**, **Product Orders**, **Products**, and **Stores** check boxes to select those tables. As you select a check box, a preview of that table's contents appears in the Navigator dialog box.

> 5. Click the **Load arrow**, and then click **Load To**. The Import Data dialog box opens.

> 6. Make sure the **Only Create Connection** option button and the **Add this data to the Data Model** check box are selected to load the tables without placing them in Excel tables, PivotTables, or PivotCharts.

> 7. Click **OK** to load the four tables into the Data Model.

After several seconds, the four tables will be listed as queries in the Queries & Connections pane. There are 14,324 rows are loaded from the Orders table, 21,418 rows from the Product Orders table, 93 rows from the Products table, and 6 rows from the Stores table. Later, Dmitry might perform a more complete analysis involving the entire sales lineup, but even this sample of a few products results in a large dataset to manage.

Proskills

Written Communication: Designing a Database

Databases are great tools to organize information, track statistics, and generate reports. When used with Excel, a properly designed database can provide valuable information and help you make informed financial decisions. Whether you are creating a database in the Data Model or Microsoft Access, keep in mind the following guidelines:

- **Split data into multiple tables.** Keep each table focused on a specific topical area. Link the tables through one or more common fields.
- **Avoid redundant data.** Key pieces of information, such as a customer's address or phone number, should be entered in only one place in your database.
- **Use understandable field names.** Avoid using acronyms or abbreviations that may be unclear or confusing.
- **Maintain consistency in data entry.** Include validation rules to ensure that rules such as abbreviating titles (for example, Mr. instead of Mister) are always followed.
- **Test the database on a small subset of data before entering all the data.** The more errors you eliminate early, the sooner your database will be ready for use.

A badly designed or improperly used database will end up creating more problems rather than solving them.

With all the tables loaded into the Data Model, you can view their contents with Power Pivot.

Transforming Data with Power Pivot

Tip

Excel tables can be added to the Data Model by selecting the table and clicking the Add to Data Model button in the Tables group on the Power Pivot tab.

Power Pivot is a BI tool built into Excel used for managing data from multiple sources in a single data structure. With Power Pivot you can define table relationships, reorganize and regroup your data, and create new columns from calculations on existing fields. Many of the skills used with Excel tables and data ranges can also be applied to the tables in Power Pivot, but Power Pivot offers even more commands and options to manage your data.

Because Power Pivot is an add-in, you must install it before using it to work with the contents of the Data Model. You can have Excel install the Power Pivot add-in by attempting to view the contents of the Data Model. If Power Pivot is not already installed, Excel will install it for you.

To install Power Pivot:

▶ **1.** On the Data tab, in the Data Tools group, click the **Manage Data Model** or **Go to the Power Pivot Window** button. If Power Pivot is not installed, a dialog box opens, prompting you to enable the Data Analysis add-ins.

▶ **2.** If prompted, click **Enable**. If it is not already present, the Power Pivot tab appears on the ribbon, and the Power Pivot window opens showing the contents of the Data Model.

▶ **3.** If necessary, maximize the window to fill the entire screen. See Figure 10–20.

Figure 10–20	Power Pivot window

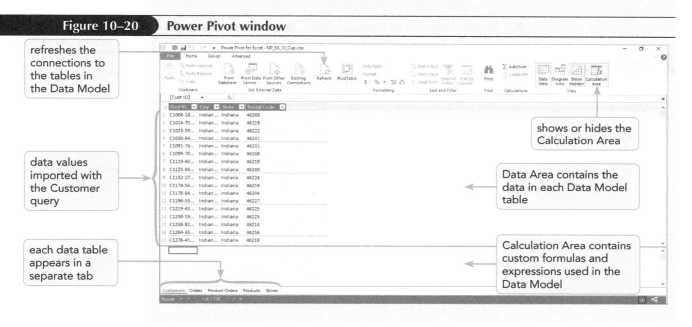

refreshes the connections to the tables in the Data Model

data values imported with the Customer query

each data table appears in a separate tab

shows or hides the Calculation Area

Data Area contains the data in each Data Model table

Calculation Area contains custom formulas and expressions used in the Data Model

The Power Pivot window places each table in the Data Model on a separate tab. The Data Area displays the contents of each table. Below the table grid is the Calculation Area used for writing customized functions and expressions.

To view the contents of the Data Model:

▶ **1.** Use the top vertical scroll bar to scroll up and down the rows of the Customers tab to view other customer records.

▶ **2.** Click the **Orders** tab to view the contents of the Orders table.

▶ **3.** Click the **Product Orders** tab to review records from the Product Orders table.

▶ **4.** Click the **Products** tab to view information about select products sold by Cup and Platter.

▶ **5.** Click the **Stores** tab to view information and the five brick-and-mortar Cup and Platter stores as well as the company's website.

▶ **6.** Return to the **Customers** tab.

Exploring the Data Model in Diagram View

So far, you have looked at the Data Model in **Data view**, which shows the contents of each table in a separate tab. You can also examine the Data Model in **Diagram view**, which lists the fields within each table. Diagram view is useful when you want to work with the general structure of the Data Model. From Diagram view, you can quickly define the relationships that connect the tables. You will switch to Diagram view now.

To switch to Diagram view and arrange the tables:

▶ **1.** On the Home tab, in the View group, click the **Diagram View** button. Power Pivot displays each table in a separate box with the table name and a list of fields. Power Pivot initially lines up all the tables horizontally in the Diagram view window.

▶ **2.** If necessary, use the scroll bars to scroll through Diagram view to review all of the table contents.

▶ **3.** Drag the tables by their table names to arrange them as shown in Figure 10–21.

Figure 10–21	Power Pivot in Diagram view

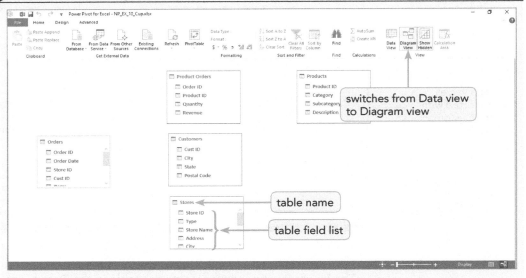

Managing Table Relationships

Table relationships are defined in Diagram View by dragging a common field between two tables. In a one-to-many relationship one of the tables acts as a lookup table for the other. For example, the Stores table acts as a lookup table for the Orders table, providing specific information about the store in which the purchase was made. Diagram View indicates the existence of a relationship by a line connecting the two tables.

Dmitry wants you to establish the following relations between the five tables:

- Orders table to the Customers table through the Cust ID field, matching every order with a customer
- Orders table to the Stores table through the Store ID field, matching every order with a store

- Orders table to the Product Orders table through the Order ID field, matching every order with products purchased on that order
- Product Orders table to the Products table through the Product ID field, matching every product order with information about that product

You'll establish these relationships between the tables in the Data Model now.

To define table relationships in Diagram View:

1. Click the **Orders** table to select it.

2. Drag the **Store ID** field from the Orders table and drop it onto the Store ID field in the Stores table. Power Pivot connects the two tables with a line. A "1" appears where the line connects to the Stores table and a "*" appears next to connection to the Orders table, indicating that this is a one-to-many relationship in which one store can be matched to many orders.

3. Drag the **Cust ID** field from the Orders table and drop it onto the Cust ID field in the Customers table. Power Pivot establishes another one-to-many relationship between the Orders table (many) and the Customers table (one) because one customer can be matched to several orders.

4. Drag the **Order ID** field from the Orders table and drop it onto the Order ID field in the Product Orders table. This establishes another one-to-many relationship. In this case, the Orders table is the "one" and the Product Orders table is the "many" because a single order might include several products.

5. Drag the **Product ID** field from the Product Orders table and drop it onto the Product ID field in the Products table, creating a one-to-many relationship between the two tables. See Figure 10–22.

| Figure 10–22 | Table relationships defined in Power Pivot |

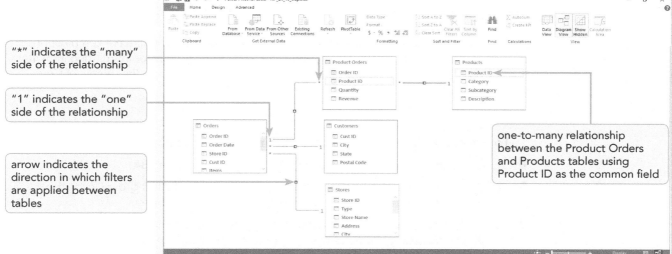

"*" indicates the "many" side of the relationship

"1" indicates the "one" side of the relationship

arrow indicates the direction in which filters are applied between tables

one-to-many relationship between the Product Orders and Products tables using Product ID as the common field

Arrows in the connecting lines indicate the direction in which filters propagate between tables. The arrow in the Stores and Orders table relation in Figure 10–22 points from Stores to Orders so that filtering the Stores table (perhaps to show records from a single store) also filters records in the Orders table. However, the reverse is not possible: Filtering the Orders table will not affect the Stores table. The arrow points in one direction only.

You can determine how a filter will affect other tables in the Data Model by following the arrows. The Orders table is connected to the Product Orders table, so that any filtering done to the Stores table will also pass through the Orders table to the Product Orders table. In this way, filters applied to one table will propagate through the Data Model wherever there exists a connected path pointing from one table to the next.

You will close Power Pivot now and return to the Excel workbook.

Tip

You can also define table relationships in an Excel workbook by clicking the Relationships button in the Data Tools group on the Data tab.

To return to the Excel workbook:

▶ **1.** Close the Power Pivot window. Power Pivot saves the table relationships you've defined.

▶ **2.** If a Security Warning bar appears indicating that external connections have been disabled, click **Enable Content**, and then click **Yes** to enable the connections to the Access database and the Data Model.

▶ **3.** Close the Queries & Connections pane.

With the table relationships defined, you are ready to analyze the Cup and Platter sales data, pulling information from any of the five tables in the Data Model.

Creating a PivotTable from the Data Model

Any of the tables in the Data Model can be analyzed in a PivotTable or PivotChart. A single PivotTable or PivotChart might draw information from multiple tables if the tables are connected via a series of table relationships.

Dmitry wants you to create a dashboard to view revenue totals for different combinations of stores, products, customer locations, and dates. The first PivotTable for this dashboard will provide a general summary of the items that Dmitry has compiled from the sample of Cup and Platter products.

To create a PivotTable based on the Data Model:

▶ **1.** Go to the **Revenue Dashboard** worksheet and click cell **B4**.

▶ **2.** On the ribbon, click the **Insert** tab, and then in the Tables group, click the **PivotTable** button. The Create PivotTable dialog box opens.

▶ **3.** Verify that the **Use this workbook's Data Model** option button is selected, that the **Existing Worksheet** option button is selected, and that **'Revenue Dashboard'!$B$4** appears in the Location box. See Figure 10–23.

Figure 10–23	Create PivotTable dialog box

Data Model selected as the PivotTable data source

Create PivotTable   ?   ✕

Choose the data that you want to analyze
- ○ Select a table or range
    - Table/Range: _____   ⬆
- ○ Use an external data source
    - [Choose Connection...]
    - Connection name:
- ◉ Use this workbook's Data Model

Choose where you want the PivotTable report to be placed
- ○ New Worksheet
- ◉ Existing Worksheet
    - Location: 'Revenue Dashboard'!$B$4

inserts a PivotTable in cell B4 of the Revenue Dashboard worksheet

Choose whether you want to analyze multiple tables
- ☐ Add this data to the Data Model

[OK]   [Cancel]

▶ **4.** Click **OK** to insert the PivotTable. The five tables from the Data Model are listed in the PivotTable Fields pane along with the three Excel tables also present in the workbook.

▶ **5.** On the PivotTable Analyze tab, in the PivotTable group, click the **PivotTable Name** box and enter **Summary** as the PivotTable name.

▶ **6.** In the PivotTable group, click the **Options** button. The PivotTable Options dialog box opens.

▶ **7.** Click the **Autofit columns widths on update** check box to deselect it. This prevents the column widths in the PivotTable from resizing.

▶ **8.** Click **OK**.

Dmitry wants you to add summary calculations to the PivotTable showing the number of stores examined, the number of products tracked, the number of customer orders placed, the total number of items ordered, and finally the total revenue generated. You will start with the count of the number of stores, the number of products, and the number of orders.

To display the summary calculations:

▶ **1.** In the PivotTable Fields pane, scroll down the list of tables, and then click the **Stores** table. The list of fields in the table appears.

▶ **2.** Drag the **Store ID** field into the Values area box, change the label "Count of Store ID" to **Stores Examined**, and then display the field using the Number format with no decimal places and a thousands separator.

▶ **3.** Repeat Steps 1 and 2 for the **Product ID** field in the Products table, placing the Product ID field after the Stores Examined field and changing the label name to **Products Tracked**.

▶ **4.** Repeat Steps 1 and 2 for the **Order ID** field from the Orders table, placing Order ID field after the Products Tracked field and changing the label name to **Orders Recorded**.

▶ **5.** Drag the **ΣValues** icon from the Columns area box to the Rows area box. The summary statistics are displayed in a single column on different rows. The report tracks 6 stores, 93 products, and 14,324 orders.

Next, you'll add a count of the total quantity of items sold and the total revenue generated for the company to the PivotTable.

To complete the PivotTable:

▶ **1.** Click the **Product Orders** table in the table list to view its contents, and then drag the **Quantity** field into the Values area box, placing it below the Orders Recorded value field.

Trouble? To drag the Quantity field to the bottom of the entries in the Values area box, you might need to scroll down the area box first.

▶ **2.** Change the label name from "Sum of Quantity" to **Quantity Sold** and display the field value in the Number format with a thousands separator and no decimal places. The value 29,979 appears in cell C8.

▶ **3.** Drag the **Revenue** field from Product Orders table in to the Values area box after the Quantity Sold value field.

▶ **4.** Change the name of the field from "Sum of Revenue" to **Total Revenue** and display the value in the Currency format with no decimal places. See Figure 10–24.

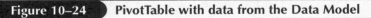

Figure 10–24   PivotTable with data from the Data Model

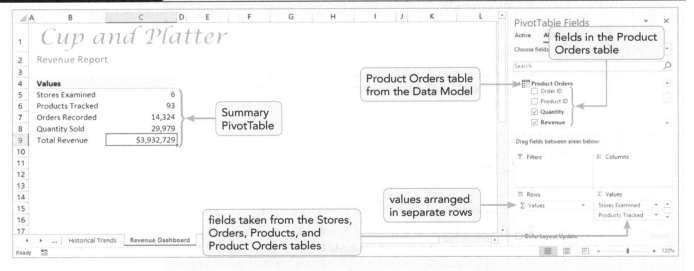

Tabulating Across Fields from Multiple Tables

PivotTables can also tabulate values from different tables so that the row and columns of the table involves categories from different tables in the Data Model. You'll add another PivotTable to the worksheet showing the revenue totals organized by store and product category.

To show revenue by store and product category:

▶ **1.** Click cell **B11**, click the **Insert** tab on the ribbon, and then in the Tables group, click the **PivotTable** button. The Create PivotTable dialog box opens.

▶ **2.** Click **OK** to insert the PivotTable. The PivotTable Fields pane opens.

▶ **3.** On the PivotTable Analyze tab, in the PivotTable group, click the **PivotTable Name** box and change the PivotTable name to **Product by Store**.

▶ **4.** In the PivotTable group, click the **Options** button. The PivotTable Options dialog box opens.

▶ **5.** Click the **Autofit column widths on update** check box to deselect it, and then click **OK**.

▶ **6.** In the PivotTable Fields pane, click the **Stores** table from the list of tables, and then drag the **Store Name** field into the Rows area box.

▶ **7.** Click the **Products** table, and then drag the **Category** field into the Rows area box directly below the Store Name field.

▶ **8.** Click the **Product Orders** table, and then drag the **Revenue** field into the Values area box.

▶ **9.** Change the field name from "Sum of Revenue" to **Total Revenue** and display the values in Currency format with no decimal places. See Figure 10–25.

| Figure 10–25 | Total revenue displayed by store and product category |

Trouble? If your PivotTable is showing blanks for the Store or Category fields, check your table relations in Power Pivot, verifying that you are connecting the tables through a common field.

From the PivotTable report, Dmitry learns that Cup and Platter gets more of its revenue from its cookware products, followed by cutlery, and then utensils. Cup and Platter sells most of its wares online. For example, the website brought in about $1.29 million in cookware sales (cell C33) compared to the brick-and-mortar stores, which brought in about $168,000 at the Washington D.C. store (cell C29) and almost $282,000 at the Brooklyn store (cell C13). The other product categories show a similar range of revenue figures.

Applying Slicers and Timelines from the Data Model

Slicers and timelines can be applied across multiple tables if the tables are connected through a common field. Dmitry wants you to add a slicer to the dashboard that filters the PivotTables by company website and brick-and-mortar stores.

To add a slicer to the dashboard:

1. With the Product by Store PivotTable still selected, click the **Insert** tab on the ribbon, and then in the Filters group, click the **Slicer** button. The Insert Slicers dialog box opens.

2. On the Active tab, scroll down to the Stores table, and then click the **Type** check box. See Figure 10–26.

Figure 10–26   Insert Slicers dialog box

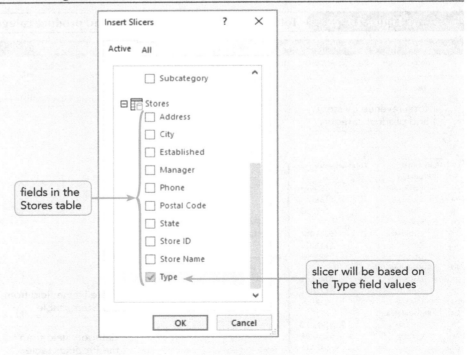

3. Click **OK** to insert the slicer.

4. Move and resize the slicer to cover the range **E4:I7**.

5. On the Slicer tab, in the Buttons group, change the Columns box to **2** columns. See Figure 10–27.

Figure 10–27   Type slicer from the Stores table

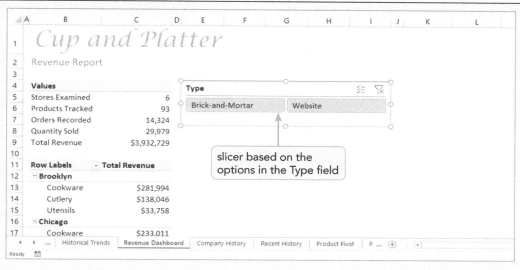

Dmitry also wants to filter the sales values by date. You will add a timeline slicer to the dashboard, basing it on the Order Date field from the Orders table.

To add the Order Date timeline to the dashboard:

1. On the ribbon, click the **Insert** tab, and then in the Filters group, click the **Timeline** button. The Existing Connections dialog box opens.

2. Click the **Data Model** tab, and then click **Open** to access the Data Model tables. The Insert Timelines dialog box opens.

3. Go to the **Orders** table, and then click the **Order Date** check box.

4. Click **OK** to insert the timeline.

5. Move and resize the slicer to cover the range **E9:I16**. See Figure 10–28.

Figure 10–28   Order Date timeline from the Orders table

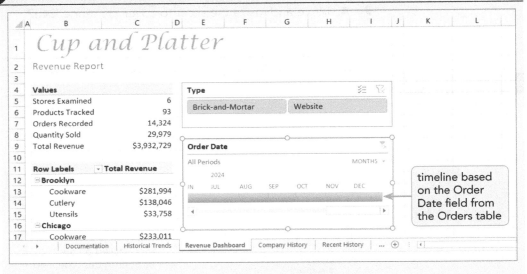

timeline based
on the Order
Date field from
the Orders table

Next, you'll connect the slicer and the timeline to the two PivotTables on the dashboard. Then you'll use them to display revenue figures for the website in the fourth quarter of 2024.

To connect the slicer and timeline to the PivotTables:

1. With the timeline still selected, on the ribbon, click the **Timeline** tab.

2. In the Timeline group, click the **Report Connections** button. The Report Connections (Order Date) dialog box opens.

3. Click the **Product by Store** and **Summary** check boxes to apply the timeline to both PivotTables in the dashboard, and then click **OK**.

4. Click the **Type** slicer to select it, click the **Slicer** tab on the ribbon, and then in the Slicer group, click the **Report Connections** button. The Report Connections (Type) dialog box opens.

5. Click the **Summary** check box, and then verify that the check boxes for both PivotTables are selected.

6. Click **OK**.

7. In the Type slicer, click **Website** to filter the dashboard, showing results only from the company website.

8. In the Order Date timeline, click **OCT** from 2024, and then drag over **NOV** and **DEC** to filter the dashboard for orders placed in Q4 2024, from October through December 2024. See Figure 10–29.

Tip

You can also select the 4th quarter of 2024 by changing the time scale of the timeline to QUARTERS and clicking Q4 from 2024.

Figure 10–29   **Dashboard filtered by store type and order date**

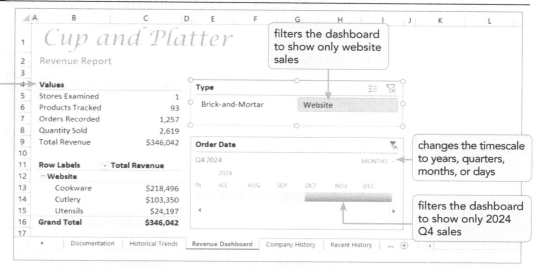

summary statistics from orders placed on the website in 4th quarter of 2024

filters the dashboard to show only website sales

changes the timescale to years, quarters, months, or days

filters the dashboard to show only 2024 Q4 sales

▶ **9.** Click the **Clear Filter** button ☒ in the slicer and timeline to show results from all the records in the Data Model.

▶ **10.** Save the workbook.

Based on the filters applied through the Type slicer and the Order Date timeline, Dmitry learns that in the 4th quarter of 2024, the website generated about $346,000 in revenue from the 93 selected products with about $218,000 coming from cookware sales, $103,000 from cutlery sales, and $24,000 from sales of cooking utensils. The fact that filtering field values from one table affected the summary statistics of fields in the other tables is a consequence of the relationships you set up in Figure 10–22.

In this session, you loaded data from an Access database into the Data Model and then analyzed data from fields spread across multiple tables in a PivotTable. In the next session, you'll continue to explore Business Intelligence tools by learning how to organize fields into a hierarchy and how to display data in geographic maps.

Review

Session 10.2 Quick Check

1. What is a relational database?

2. What is a one-to-many relationship?

3. What is the advantage of placing large tables in the Data Model rather than in an Excel table that is visible in the workbook?

4. What is Power Pivot?

5. Describe how to create a table relationship in Power Pivot Diagram view.

6. In Diagram view, what does the arrow on the line connecting two tables indicate?

7. What is the advantage of using table relationships when creating a PivotTable report?

Session 10.3 Visual Overview:

Quick Explore is a feature of PivotTables and PivotCharts for drilling into a hierarchy or to explore the impact of other fields on your data outcomes.

A hierarchy is an organization of fields that start with the most general and go down to the most specific; the Product List hierarchy includes three fields.

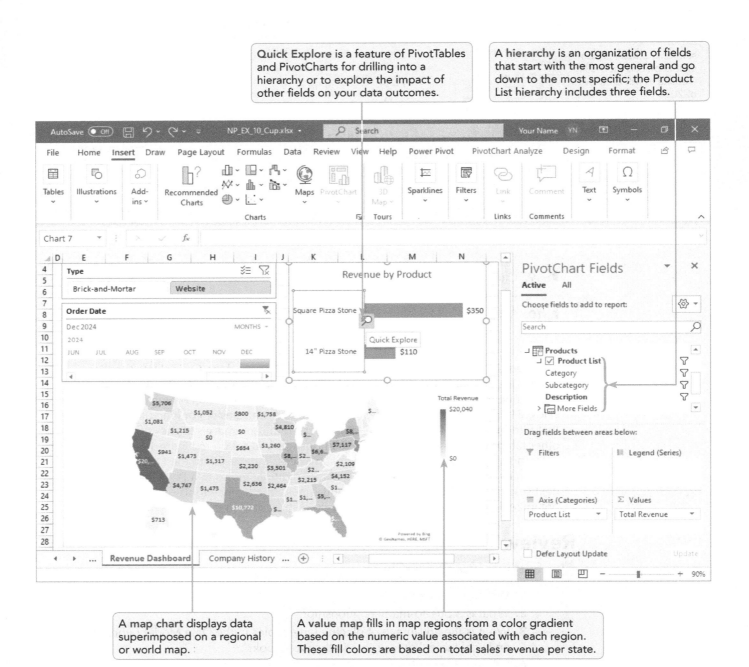

A map chart displays data superimposed on a regional or world map.

A value map fills in map regions from a color gradient based on the numeric value associated with each region. These fill colors are based on total sales revenue per state.

Hierarchies and Maps

3D Maps is an Excel tool that presents data geographically on a virtual 3-D globe.

The height of each column is based on the value of the Revenue field.

Map data is placed in layers, which are superimposed on the map.

The location of each marker is determined by the customer's postal code.

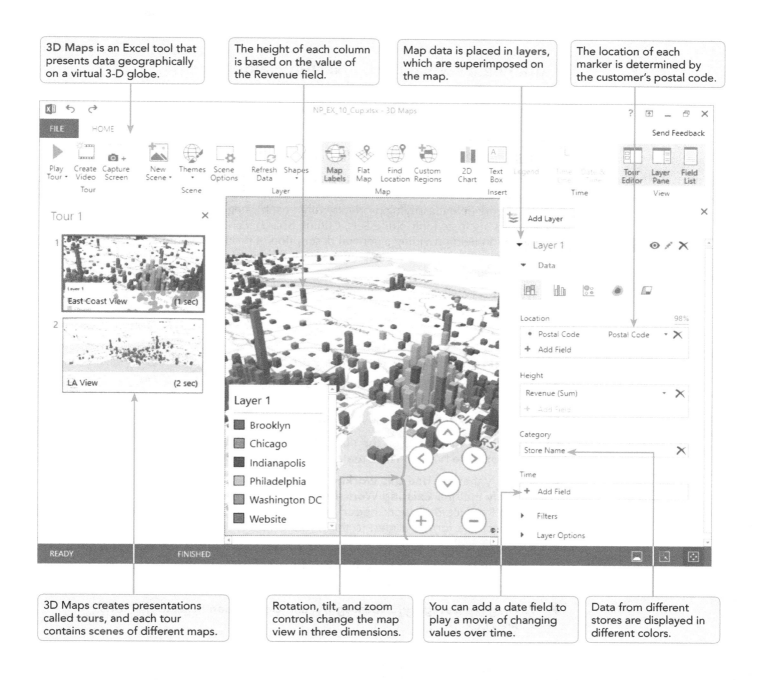

3D Maps creates presentations called tours, and each tour contains scenes of different maps.

Rotation, tilt, and zoom controls change the map view in three dimensions.

You can add a date field to play a movie of changing values over time.

Data from different stores are displayed in different colors.

Working with Outlines and Hierarchies

Often in data analysis, you want to drill into the data, going from a general overview down to a more detailed view. Timelines provide this feature by allowing you to examine data across years, quarters, months, and down to individual days. You can do the same thing with PivotTable fields by nesting more specific fields inside of general ones.

Outlining a PivotTable by Nested Fields

When you nest fields within a PivotTable row or column, Excel adds outline buttons to expand your view of the data at a greater level of detail or collapse to get a more general view. Dmitry wants you to create a PivotTable that includes this feature for the types of products sold by Cup and Platter.

The Products table contains the following fields describing Cup and Platter products:

- Category field specifying the general product category (Cookware, Cutlery, and Utensils)
- Subcategory field classifying products within each category so that a category like Cutlery is organized into Knife Sets, Cutting Boards, Paring Knives, and so forth
- Description field providing a general description of products within each Subcategory, such as the 7-piece knife sets and 8-piece knife sets sold within the Knife Sets subcategory

You'll create a PivotTable that calculates total revenue broken down by the Category, Subcategory, and Description fields.

To insert the Product Revenue PivotTable:

1. If you took a break after the previous session, make sure the NP_EX_10_Cup workbook is open.

2. Go to the **Product Pivot** worksheet.

3. Click the **Insert** tab on the ribbon, and then in the Tables group, click the **PivotTable** button. The Create PivotTable dialog box opens.

4. Verify that the **Use this workbook's Data Model** option button is selected, verify that the **Existing Worksheet** option button is selected, click cell **B4** in the Product Pivot worksheet if necessary to select it, and then click **OK**. The PivotTable form is added to the worksheet.

5. On the PivotTable Analyze tab, in the PivotTable group, click the **PivotTable Name** box, and enter **Product Revenue** as the PivotTable name.

6. In the PivotTable Fields pane, click the **Products** table to open it.

7. Drag the **Category**, **Subcategory**, and **Description** fields to the Rows area box.

8. In the PivotTable Fields pane, click the **Product Orders** table to open it, and then drag the **Revenue** field to the Values area box.

9. Change the value field name from "Sum of Revenue" to **Total Revenue** and change the number format to Currency with no decimal places. See Figure 10–30.

| Figure 10–30 | Total Revenue by product fields |

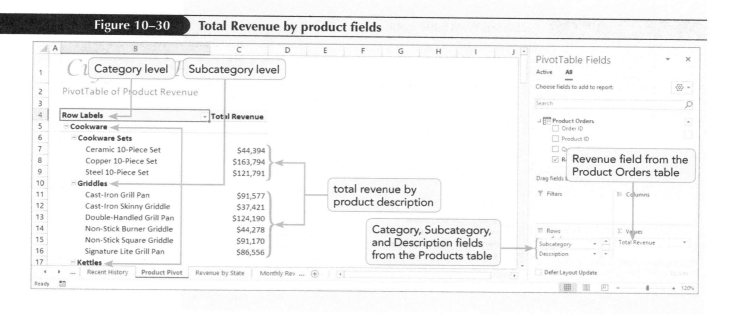

The PivotTable opens in an expanded view, showing total revenue across the lowest field level, which in this case is the Description field. You can collapse the fields to show data at the highest level, which is the Category field for these tabulations. You can also expand and collapse individual items within each field to view some with more detail and others with less detail. You'll expand and collapse the fields in the row area of the PivotTable now.

To collapse and expand the categories in the PivotTable:

1. In front of Cookware Sets, click the **Collapse Outline** button ⊟. The Cookware Sets subcategory collapses and the PivotTable shows $329,979 as the total revenue for all cooking sets.

2. In front of Cookware, click the **Collapse Outline** button ⊟. The Cookware category collapses and the PivotTable shows $2,503,562 as the total revenue for all cookware.

3. On the PivotTable Analyze tab, in the Active Field group, click the **Collapse Field** button ⊣≡. The entire PivotTable collapses to display revenue totals at the Category level. See Figure 10–31.

Figure 10–31   Collapsed PivotTable outline

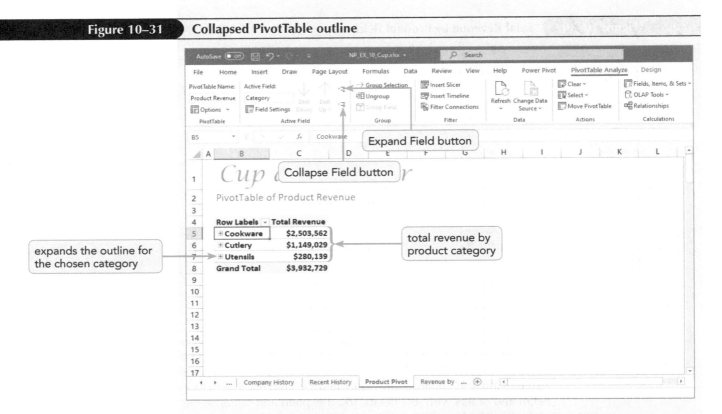

▶ **4.** In the Active Field group, click the **Expand Field** button to expand all
field levels so that the PivotTable again shows total revenue by product
description.

In this way, you can display revenue totals at any level of specificity. However, a
PivotTable outline can be unwieldy if the table contains a lot of categories or nested
levels. If you're interested only in the total revenue generated by, say, pizza stone sales,
you would have to go down several field levels and in the process the table would
show results for other categories you're not interested in. To limit the view to only those
categories of interest, you can create a hierarchy.

Drilling Down a Field Hierarchy

A hierarchy is named set of fields organized from the most general down to the most
specific. Unlike outlines involving multiple fields nested within one another, a hierarchy
displays only one field level at a time. To switch the PivotTable view from one field level
to the next lower level, you drill down into the hierarchy. Thus, you can drill down into
a hierarchy of product fields, displaying revenue totals from all product categories and
then revenue from all cookware products and, finally, revenue from all types of pressure
cookers. To go from the most specific field to the most general, you **drill up** the hierarchy;
going up from pressure cooker sales to cookware sales to sales of all products.

Reference

Creating a Hierarchy of Fields

- View the Data Model in Diagram view in the Power Pivot window.
- Click the Create Hierarchy button in the table box to create a hierarchy for the table.
- Specify a name for the hierarchy.
- Drag fields into the hierarchy, arranged in order from the most general down to the most specific.

Hierarchies are defined within Power Pivot, becoming part of the data structure of their tables. Once defined, a hierarchy is treated as any other PivotTable field and can be moved to different sections of the PivotTable. Dmitry wants you to create a hierarchy named "Product List" containing the Category, Subcategory, and Description fields from the Products table. You'll return to Power Pivot now to create this hierarchy.

To create a hierarchy of the fields in the Products table:

▶ **1.** On the ribbon, click the **Power Pivot** tab, and then in the Data Model group, click the **Manage** button. The Power Pivot window opens.

▶ **2.** On the Home tab, in the View group, click the **Diagram View** button, if necessary, to switch Power Pivot to Diagram view.

▶ **3.** Point to the bottom border of the **Products** table box until the pointer changes to a double arrow pointer ↕, and then drag the bottom border until the table box is twice as high.

▶ **4.** Point to the upper-right corner of the table box, and then click the **Create Hierarchy** button ⊞. A new entry named "Hierachy1" appears in the Products field list.

▶ **5.** With the name selected, type **Product List** as the hierarchy name, and then press **ENTER**.

▶ **6.** Click the **Category** field, hold down **SHIFT** and click the **Description** field to select the Category, Subcategory, and Description fields, and then release SHIFT.

▶ **7.** Drag the select fields on top of the Product List hierarchy, placing the three fields into that hierarchy. See Figure 10–32.

Figure 10–32   **Fields in the Product List hierarchy**

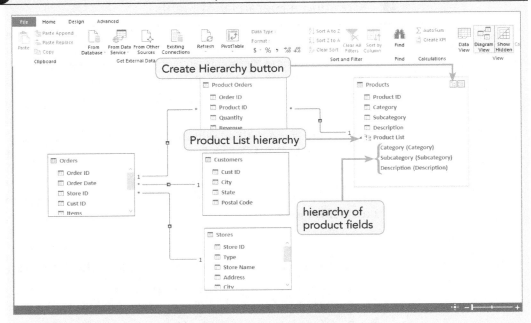

▶ **8.** Close Power Pivot to return to the Excel workbook.

The Product List hierarchy is now part of the Products table and appears within the PivotTable Fields pane. You will replace the Category, Subcategory, and Description fields displayed in the PivotTable row with the Product List hierarchy, which contains all those fields.

To add the Product List hierarchy to the PivotTable:

▶ **1.** Drag the **Category**, **Subcategory**, and **Description** fields out of the Rows area box, removing them from the PivotTable.

▶ **2.** If necessary, click the **Products** table in the PivotTable Fields pane to display its contents.

▶ **3.** Drag the **Product List** hierarchy from the field list and drop it into the Rows area box to add it to the PivotTable. The PivotTable displays the total revenue broken down by the Category field. The Expand Outline button ⊞ appears to the left of each product category (Cookware, Cutlery, and Utensils).

Though it looks like nothing has changed in the PivotTable, you can now drill down into the Product List hierarchy, viewing the revenue totals within each category, subcategory, and description group. Dmitry wants you to use the Product List hierarchy to show the total revenue from sales of Cup and Platter's line of pressure cookers.

To drill down and up the Product List hierarchy:

▶ **1.** Click cell **B5**, containing the Cookware label. You want to drill down this product category.

Tip

To view the PivotTable data in outline form, click the Expand buttons in front of the column or row labels.

▶ **2.** On the ribbon, click the **PivotTable Analyze** tab, and then in the Active Field group, click the **Drill Down** button. The column labels change, displaying the subcategories within the Cookware category, starting with Cookware Sets and ending with Woks.

▶ **3.** In cell B10, click the **Pressure Cookers** label, and then click the **Drill Down** button to view revenue totals of the pressure cooker line. Cup and Platter sells three pressure cookers with revenues ranging from about $69,000 to $164,000. See Figure 10–33.

Figure 10–33	PivotTable drilled down the Product List hierarchy

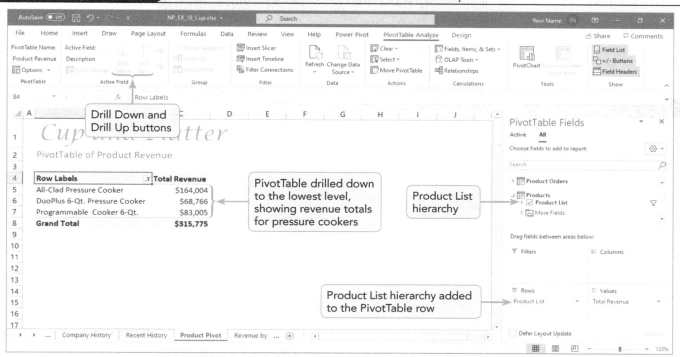

Next, you'll drill up the Product List hierarchy moving from the most specific categories to the most general.

▶ **4.** Click cell **B5** to select the "All-Clad Pressure Cooker" label.

▶ **5.** Click the **Drill Up** button twice to go up the hierarchy and back to the level containing the Category field. At each step in the process the labels in the PivotTable row are replaced with categories of the next highest level in the Product List hierarchy.

Using a hierarchy creates a simpler and cleaner PivotTable that focuses your attention on those details of most interest to you. However, you can always use the Expand Outline and Collapse Outline buttons to view the table outline.

Dmitry wants you to add this product revenue information to the dashboard as a clustered bar chart. You'll create the PivotChart based on this table and add it to the Revenue Dashboard worksheet.

To create a PivotChart of product revenue:

▶ **1.** With the PivotTable still selected, click the **PivotTable Analyze** tab on the ribbon, and then in the Tools group, click the **PivotChart** button. The Insert Chart dialog box opens.

▶ **2.** On the All Charts tab, click **Bar** as the chart type, click **Clustered Bar** as the chart subtype, and then click **OK**. The bar chart is added to the worksheet.

▶ **3.** Move the chart to the **Revenue Dashboard** worksheet, and then move and resize it to cover the range **K4:N16**.

▶ **4.** Change the chart title to **Revenue by Product**, add data labels to the chart showing revenue totals for each category, and remove the chart legend and chart gridlines.

▶ **5.** Click the **Chart Elements** button ⊞, click the **Axes arrow**, and then click the **Primary Horizontal** check box to remove the horizontal axis from the chart.

▶ **6.** On the PivotChart Analyze tab, in the Show/Hide group, click the **Field List** and **Field Buttons** buttons to deselect them. The field list and buttons no longer appear on the chart and the worksheet. See Figure 10–34.

Figure 10–34   Revenue by Product PivotChart

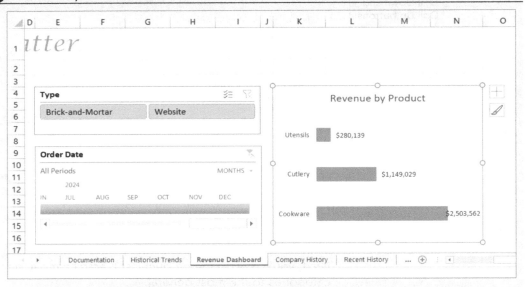

Finally, you'll connect the Product Revenue PivotTable to both the slicer and the timeline on this worksheet.

▶ **7.** Click the **Type** slicer to select it, click the **Slicer** tab on the ribbon, and then in the Slicer group, click the **Report Connections** button. The Report Connections (Type) dialog box opens.

▶ **8.** Click the **Product Revenue** check box to add it to the list of connected PivotTables for the slicer, and then click **OK**.

▶ **9.** Click the **Order Date** timeline, click the **Timeline** tab, and then in the Timeline group, click the **Report Connections** button. The Report Connections (Type) dialog box opens.

▶ **10.** Click the **Product Revenue** check box to add it to the list of connected PivotTables for the timeline, and then click **OK**.

▶ **11.** In the Type slicer, click **Website**, and then in the Order Date timeline, click **Dec 2024**. The PivotChart filters to show the website revenue for December 2024, matching the results shown in the range B13:C14. Almost $11,000 of the revenue comes from sales of utensils, more than $50,000 from cutlery, and more than $100,000 from cookware.

The process of drilling down and drilling up through a hierarchy can be done with PivotCharts using the Quick Explore Tool.

Viewing Data with the Quick Explore Tool

The Quick Explore Tool is a feature of PivotTables and PivotCharts used to drill into data at any level of specificity or to explore the impact of other fields on your analysis. As with PivotTables, drilling down or up a PivotChart replaces the categories from one field with those of another. You'll use the Quick Explore tool to drill down the Revenue by Product PivotChart to view sales data on Cup and Platter cooking thermometers.

To drill down the Revenue by Product PivotChart using the Quick Explore tool:

▶ **1.** Click the **Utensils** category in the Revenue by Product PivotChart. The Quick Explore button 🔎 appears below the label.

Trouble? If the Quick Explore button does not appear, right-click the Utensils category and click Quick Explore on the shortcut menu in Step 2.

▶ **2.** Click the **Quick Explore** button 🔎. The Explore box appears with options to drill down the Products table to the Subcategory field or to choose a different field to display in the PivotChart. See Figure 10–35.

| Figure 10–35 | Quick Explore button |

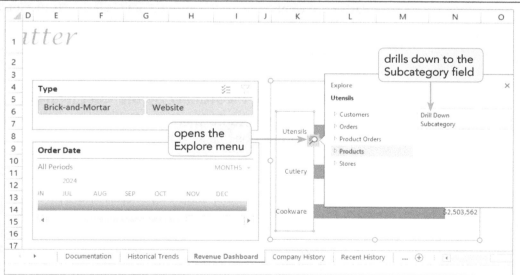

Tip

You can drill up the PivotChart by clicking Drill Up Category in the Explore box.

3. In the Explore box, click **Drill Down Subcategory**. The horizontal axis labels are replaced with Subcategory values ranging from Zesters to Colanders.

4. In the PivotChart, click the **Thermometers** subcategory, click the **Quick Explore** button 🔍 that appears, and then click **Drill Down Description** in the Explore box. The PivotChart displays revenue totals for three types of cooking thermometers. See Figure 10–36.

Figure 10–36   **Cooking thermometer sales**

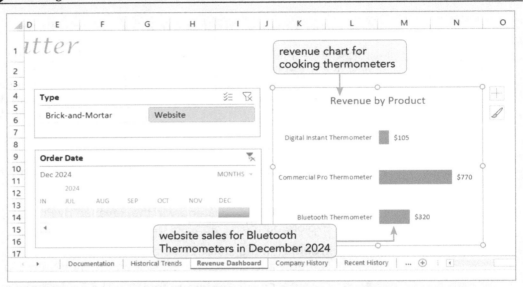

Drilling into the data, Dmitry learns that in December 2024, website sales were $320 in Bluetooth Cooking Thermometers, $770 in Commercial Pro Thermometers, and $105 in Digital Instant Thermometers. A customer support specialist using Dmitry's dashboard wants to know the location of the customers making these purchases. You'll use Quick Explore to display revenue from Bluetooth Thermometers by the State field from the Customers table.

To display the PivotChart by the Cust ID field:

1. Click the **Bluetooth Thermometer** category, and then click the **Quick Explore** button 🔍.

   Trouble? If the Quick Explore button does not appear, right-click the Blue Thermometer category and then click Quick Explore on the shortcut menu.

2. In the list of tables, double-click **Customers** to view the field list. You can drill to any field within the field list.

3. In the field list, click **State**, and then click **Drill to State**. Drilling to a new field changes the structure of the PivotChart. A dialog box opens to confirm that you want to replace the data in the Product Pivot PivotTable.

4. Click **OK**. The $320 in website sales of Bluetooth Thermometers in December 2024 was divided between $240 in Florida and $80 in Arizona. See Figure 10–37.

| Figure 10-37 | Bluetooth thermometer revenue by state |

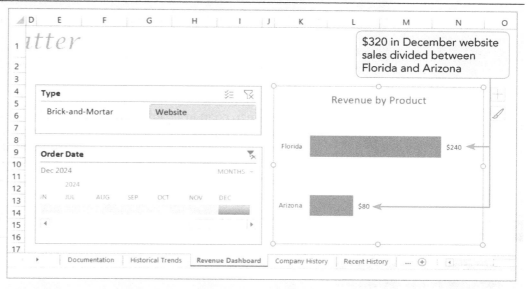

5. On the ribbon, click the **PivotChart Analyze** tab, and then in the Show/Hide group, click the **Field List** button. The PivotTable Fields pane opens. As you can see from the Filters area box, the PivotChart shows data from the Product List hierarchy.

6. Drag the **State** field out of the Axis (Categories) box to remove it, and then move the **Product List** hierarchy from the Filters box to the Axis (Categories) box. The PivotChart is restored to its original structure, showing total revenue charted against product category.

7. Close the PivotChart Fields pane.

8. Clear the filters from both the Type slicer and Order Date timeline to show revenue from all store types and all order dates.

The Quick Analysis Tool is useful for displaying important pieces of information such as who bought what products, when, and where. However, because it can change the PivotTable structure, you should be prepared to reorganize the PivotTable and PivotChart layouts when you are done using it.

Viewing Data with Map Charts

Location is another important aspect of data analysis. Financial analysts at Cup and Platter want to know what products are generating revenue for the company. The Advertising department wants to know who is buying those products so that it can target advertising dollars to specific regions and the country. The Shipping department wants customer location data to better predict shipping expenses. If the company opens another brick-and-mortar store, it can use location data to place the new store in a region filled with customers already supportive of the Cup and Platter brand.

Reference

Creating a Map Chart

- Create a data source with the first column or columns containing region names from countries down to states and counties.
- Enter data values in the last column of the data source.
- On the Insert tab, in the Charts group, click the Maps button.

You can create a map chart to plot data by location. Map chart data must be organized with the first column or columns indicating the map location and the last column containing the values to be charted. Excel supports two types of map charts. In a **value map**, regions are filled with a color gradient based on the numeric value associated with each region. In a **category map**, regions belonging to the same category share the same color. See Figure 10–38.

Figure 10–38	Value and category maps

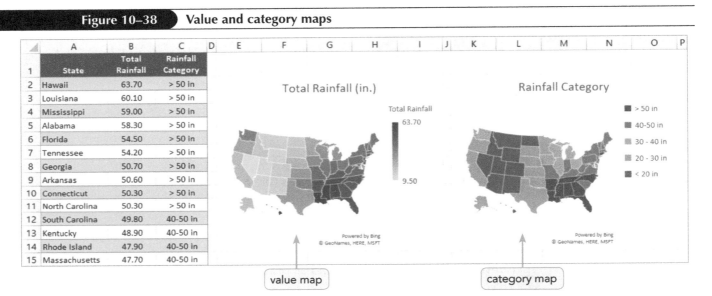

	State	Total Rainfall	Rainfall Category
2	Hawaii	63.70	> 50 in
3	Louisiana	60.10	> 50 in
4	Mississippi	59.00	> 50 in
5	Alabama	58.30	> 50 in
6	Florida	54.50	> 50 in
7	Tennessee	54.20	> 50 in
8	Georgia	50.70	> 50 in
9	Arkansas	50.60	> 50 in
10	Connecticut	50.30	> 50 in
11	North Carolina	50.30	> 50 in
12	South Carolina	49.80	40-50 in
13	Kentucky	48.90	40-50 in
14	Rhode Island	47.90	40-50 in
15	Massachusetts	47.70	40-50 in

value map   category map

Colors are always applied at the region level, filling in entire counties, states, or countries.

Creating a Value Map Chart

Dmitry wants you to add a value map to the dashboard showing revenue totals from each state. One challenge in creating a map chart based on data in the Data Model is that map is not a PivotChart type. To get around that problem, you'll first create a PivotTable of revenue broken down by state and then copy those PivotTable values into a data range, which *can* be mapped.

To create a PivotTable of revenue by state:

1. Go to the **Revenue by State** worksheet.

2. On the Insert tab, in the Tables group, click the **PivotTable** button.

3. In cell **B4** of the Revenue by State worksheet, insert a PivotTable using the workbook's Data Model.

4. Rename the PivotTable as **State Revenue**.

▶ **5.** Drag the **State** field from the Customers table into the Rows area box.

▶ **6.** Drag the **Revenue** field from the Product Orders table into the Values area box.

Next, you will copy the contents of the PivotTable to a data range using Paste Link so that any changes to the PivotTable values will be reflected in the data range.

To create a PivotTable of revenue by state:

▶ **1.** Select the range **B4:C55**, and then on the Home tab, in the Clipboard group, click the **Copy** button.

▶ **2.** Click cell **E4**, and then in the Clipboard group, click the **Paste arrow** and click **Paste Special**. The Paste Special dialog box opens.

Be sure to use Paste Link so that the data range always updates as the PivotTable updates.

▶ **3.** In the Paste Special dialog box, click the **Paste Link** button. The pasted PivotTable is linked to the original PivotTable.

▶ **4.** In cell **E4**, enter **State** as the column label, and then in cell **F4**, enter **Total Revenue** as the label.

▶ **5.** Select the range **F5:F55** and format the selection as **Currency** with no decimal places. See Figure 10–39.

Figure 10–39 PivotTable data pasted using Paste Link

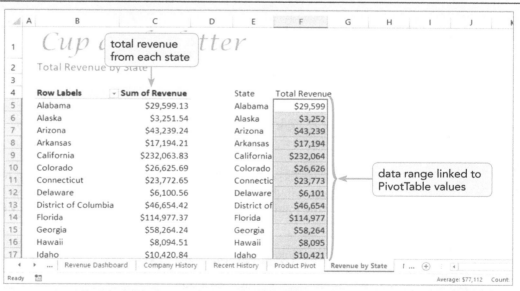

You can use this Paste Link technique with other chart types that are not supported by PivotCharts. For example, you can link PivotTable results to a data range for use in creating a histogram or scatter chart.

Be careful about the effect of filters. Some states might not be represented under some filters and thus would not be listed in the PivotTable. For example, a filter that limits the PivotTable to sales from the Chicago store might not show any revenue from customers who live outside the state of Illinois. However, Dmitry wants all states represented in the data, even if their revenue is zero. You can set the PivotTable options so that the PivotTable always displays every state, even when there is no data for that state.

To display all state categories:

▶ **1.** Right-click cell **B4**, and then click **PivotTable Options** on the shortcut menu. The PivotTable Options dialog box opens.

▶ **2.** Click the **Display** tab.

▶ **3.** Click the **Show items with no data on rows** and **Show items with no data on columns** check boxes so that the PivotTable always shows all rows and categories even when there is no data. See Figure 10–40.

Figure 10–40	PivotTable Options dialog box

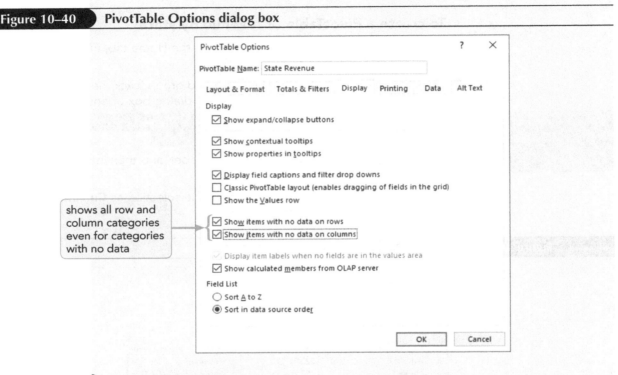

shows all row and column categories even for categories with no data

▶ **4.** Click **OK**.

The PivotTable now will always show data for all 50 states, no matter how it is filtered, as will the data range linked to that PivotTable. You will now create a map chart of the total revenue data using the values in the range E4:F55.

To map total revenue by state:

▶ **1.** Select the range **E4:F55**.

▶ **2.** On the ribbon, click the **Insert** tab, and then in the Charts group, click the **Recommended Charts** button. The Insert Chart dialog box opens.

▶ **3.** Verify that the **Filled Map** chart type is selected, and then click **OK**. The map chart is inserted into the workbook.

Trouble? If you are prompted to send your data to Bing to create the map chart, click I Accept or OK to retrieve location data from Bing.

Tip

If you don't see a revenue value, point to the state to view its revenue total.

4. Move the chart to the **Revenue Dashboard** worksheet, and then move and resize the chart to cover the range **E18:N32**.

5. Remove the chart title, and then add data labels to chart that will display total revenue superimposed over the state regions. See Figure 10–41.

Figure 10–41 **Revenue totals on the value map chart**

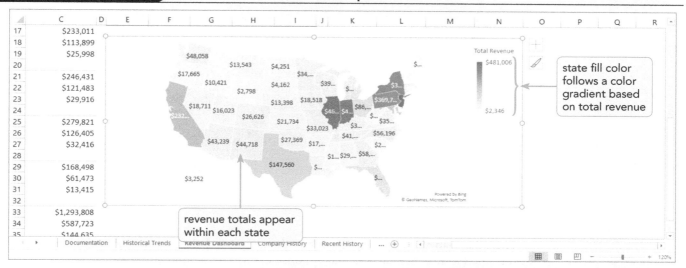

revenue totals appear within each state

state fill color follows a color gradient based on total revenue

The darkest colors are found in or near the locations of Cup and Platter stores (Brooklyn, Chicago, Indianapolis, Philadelphia, and Washington D.C.). Dmitry wants to filter the map chart so that it shows only the state revenue totals for website sales from December 2024. You'll connect the slicer and timeline to the State Revenue PivotTable and then use them to filter the map.

To connect the map chart to the slicer and timeline filters:

1. Scroll up the worksheet and click the **Type** slicer to select it.

2. On the Slicer tab, in the Slicer group, click the **Report Connections** button, add the **State Revenue** PivotTable to the list of connected tables, and then click **OK**.

3. Click the **Order Date** timeline to select it.

4. On the Timeline tab, in the Timeline group, click the **Report Connections** button, connect the timeline to the **State Revenue** PivotTable, and then click **OK**.

5. On the Type slicer, click the **Website** button, and then on the Order Date timeline, click **DEC 2024**.

6. Verify that the map chart shows revenue totals only for orders placed on the company website during December 2024. See Figure 10–42.

| Figure 10–42 | Revenue totals from the website in December 2024 |

From the map chart, Dmitry learns that the largest website sales occur in California, Texas, and Florida. As Cup and Platter considers where to build a new store, those states would be logical places for the location.

Proskills

Problem Solving: Specifying a Map Location

The map chart uses location names from the search site Bing to determine where to place data values. However, this can result in misplacing map locations when several regions share the same name. Does "Georgia" mean the state of Georgia within the United States or the county of Georgia located north of Turkey? Does "Norfolk" refer to the county in Massachusetts or the county in England? There are 31 different counties named "Washington" alone. Bing will use the context of other regions in your data list to decide on a location, but it can make mistakes.

To avoid confusion, include several columns in your data source: one to specify the country, another to specify the state, and a third to specify the county (if needed). You can also include a detailed region name such as "Georgia, United States" rather than "Georgia" to indicate that the location is a state within the United States and not an Eastern European country. Finally, avoid abbreviations when possible. Spell out state names like Indiana rather than using the two-letter abbreviation IN. Many regions share the same abbreviation. If your data is not mapped correctly, try different combinations of names and locations to correct the problem.

Formatting a Map Chart

Excel supports several formatting options specific to map charts. To access the map formatting options, right-click any of the map regions and click Format Data Series on the shortcut menu. In the Format Data Series pane, you can set the map projection; define the scope of the mapped area; add labels identifying counties, states, and countries; and define the fill colors used by the map.

The default map format uses a map projection that preserves the relative size of regions on the globe with the map area set just large enough to incorporate all regions listed in the data. Figure 10–43 shows a map chart using the Mercator map projection with the map area set to the entire world, adding labels as country names where they would fit.

Figure 10–43   Map chart formatting options

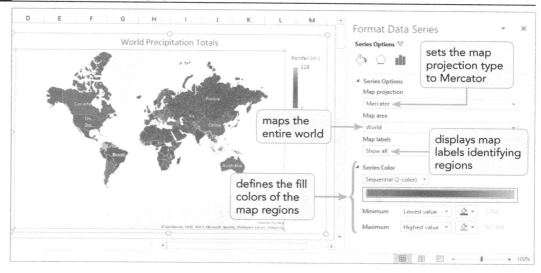

Map charts have several limitations: They cannot be used directly with PivotTables. They can plot only high-level regions like counties, states, and countries, but not map points like cities, postal codes, or latitude and longitude. They cannot be zoomed in to smaller regional areas.

Dmitry wants to focus a revenue map on one region of the country such as the southwestern United States. Because of the map chart limitations, you'll need to use 3D maps.

Insight

Using Linked Data Types

When analyzing geographic data, you will often want to include information about the regions being studied. For example, if you are reporting total sales revenue by state, it might be helpful to compare the revenue totals to state populations. **Linked data types** are data types linked to resources on the Internet. At the time of this writing, Excel supports two linked data types: Stocks for stock market information and Geography for geographic data. Microsoft plans to add more linked data types as it refines this Excel feature.

To retrieve data from a Linked Data Type, enter your stock symbols or map names into a worksheet, select the range containing those values, and then on the Data tab, in the Data Types group, click the Stocks or Geography linked data type. If Excel finds a match between your data and its online resources, it will convert your data to a Stocks or Geography data type. When you select your data, the Insert Data command appears, which you can use to choose the relevant stock market or geographic information you want to download from the Internet and add to your worksheet.

The linked data type feature is not available with every version of Excel, so check Excel Help to determine whether you have access to this feature.

Visualizing Data with 3D Maps

3D Maps is an Excel tool for creating map presentations. The presentations are not displayed within the workbook but instead open in a separate window with a different set of ribbon tabs and commands. Map presentations are called tours, and each tour contains one or more map scenes that can be played as a movie with one map scene transitioning into another. For example, Dmitry could create a tour with a first scene displaying sales data from one region of the country and a second scene displaying sales data from a different region. A tour can be shown to colleagues and clients as part of a presentation or saved as a video file.

You'll open 3D Maps so you can create a tour for Dmitry.

To open 3D Maps:

▶ **1.** In the Revenue Dashboard worksheet, click cell **A1** to deselect any charts or slicers currently selected.

▶ **2.** On the ribbon, click the **Insert** tab, and then in the Tours group, click the **3D Map** button.

▶ **3.** If necessary, click the **Tour 1** map in the Launch 3D Maps dialog box. The 3D Maps window opens. See Figure 10–44.

Figure 10–44   **3D Map window**

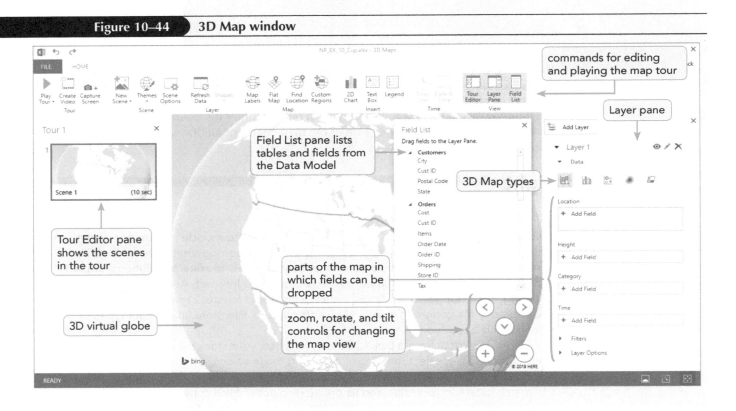

The 3D map window is organized into four sections: The Tour Editor pane lists the map scenes in the current tour. A map of the data is displayed in 3D view. The Field List pane shows tables and fields from the current workbook and Data Model. The Layer pane defines where and how data will be used in the map. A single map can contain multiple overlapping layers. You add data to a map scene by dragging fields onto area boxes in the Layer pane.

Tip

To rotate and tilt the map, press SHIFT+arrow in the direction you want the map to move. To zoom the map, press SHIFT+ + to zoom in and SHIFT+– to zoom out.

Superimposed on the map are controls for changing the map view. The Zoom in control ⊕ focuses on specific regions in the map. The Zoom out control ⊖ gives a wider view of the map. The Tilt up control ⊼ tilts the map and the Tilt down control ⊻ tilts the map down. The Rotate Left control ⧀ and the Rotate Right control ⧁ rotates the map from side to side. You can also use your mouse pointer to drag the virtual 3D globe into a new view of the data.

Dmitry wants a map showing the location of Cup and Platter customers by their postal code. You'll create this map scene using the Postal Code field from the Customers table.

To map the location of Cup and Platter customers:

▶ **1.** In the Tour Editor pane, click the **Close** button ☒ to make more screen space for the 3D map you will create.

▶ **2.** In the Field List box, drag the **Postal Code** field from the Customers table into the Location box in the Layer pane. Markers appear on the map at every location of a Cup and Platter customer.

  Trouble? If you don't see all the markers plotted on the map, be patient. Depending on your connection speed, it might take several seconds for all the markers to be plotted on the map.

▶ **3.** Click the **Zoom out** control ⊖ (or press **SHIFT+–**) until the entire continental United States is in view.

▶ **4.** Drag the globe to the left, moving your view.

▶ **5.** On the Home tab, in the Map group, click the **Map Labels** button. Descriptive labels appear on the map. See Figure 10–45.

Figure 10–45 **Customers mapped by postal code**

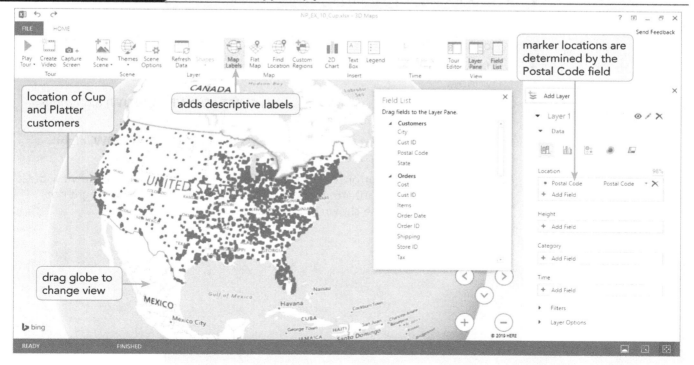

Once you have the general view of the map, you can set how you want the data displayed.

Choosing a Map Style

There are five ways of plotting data on a 3D map: The Stacked Column map ▥ displays data values as column markers divided into categories. The Clustered Column map ▥ displays data values as column markers with separate columns for each category value. The Bubble map ▥ displays markers as bubbles with bubble sizes determined by the values of a numeric field. The Heat map ◉ displays markers with colors of increasing intensity determined by the values of a numeric field. Finally, the Region map ▱ fills in regions such as states and countries with colors determined by the values of a numeric or categorical field.

Dmitry wants you to create a Clustered Column map with the column heights determined by the Revenue field and the categories determined by the Store Name field. You'll modify the map now.

To create the Clustered Column map:

▶ **1.** At the top of the Layer pane, click the **Clustered Column** icon ▥.

▶ **2.** Drag the **Revenue** field from the Product Orders table and drop it in the Height box in the Layer pane. The columns heights change to reflect how much money each customer spent.

▶ **3.** Drag the **Store Name** field from the Stores table and drop it in the Category box in the Layer pane. The columns change colors to reflect which location each customer purchased from.

▶ **4.** In the Field List pane, click the **Close** button ✖ to view more of the 3D map.

▶ **5.** Click the **Layer 1** legend box to select it, and then drag the lower-right sizing handle to reduce the size of the box to display all the locations in one column without excess space on the right. More screen space is now available to view the map.

▶ **6.** Use your mouse to move Washington D.C. into the center of the Map window.

▶ **7.** Click the **Tilt down** button ⊙ (or press **SHIFT+DOWN ARROW**) eight times to view the map at a lower angle.

▶ **8.** Click the **Rotate Right** button ⊙ (or press **SHIFT+RIGHT ARROW**) eight times to show a view of the data above the Eastern seaboard.

▶ **9.** Click the **Zoom in** button ⊕ (or press **SHIFT++**) twice to magnify the view of the map. See Figure 10–46. Note that the rendering of your map might not exactly match the one shown in the figure.

| Figure 10–46 | Clustered column map from above the Eastern seaboard |

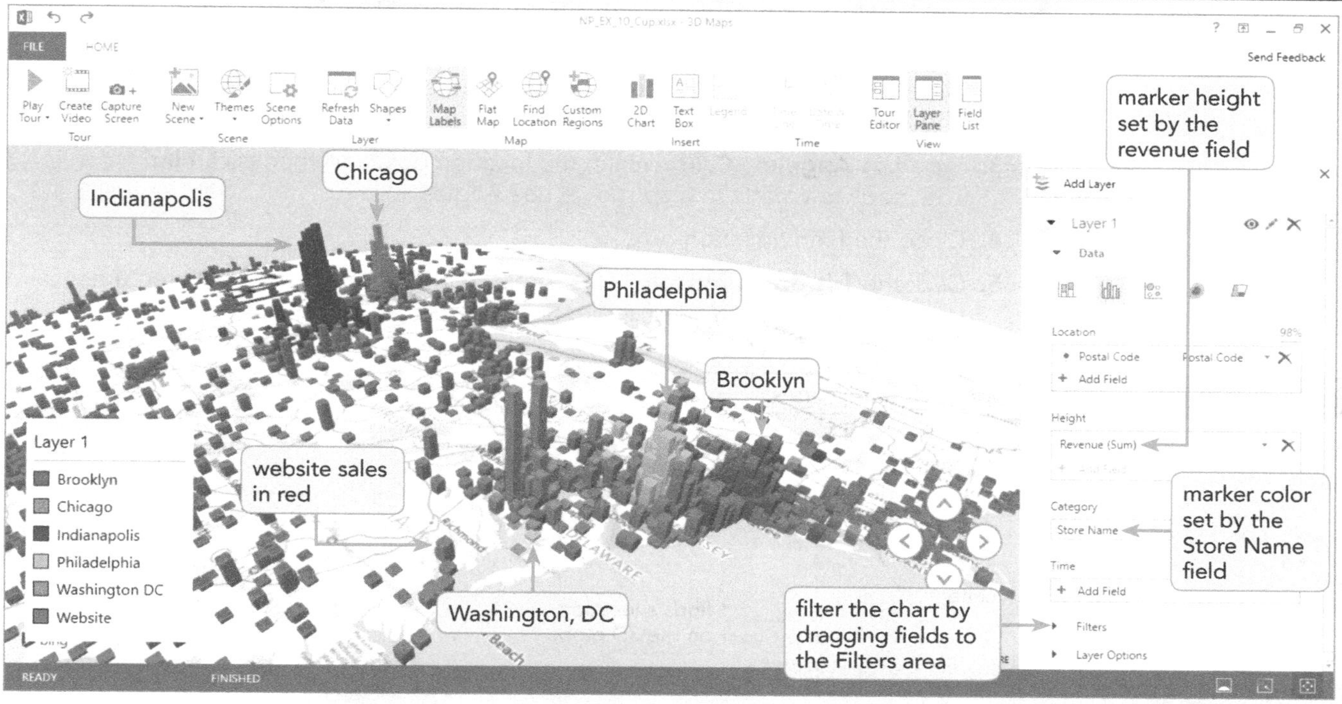

Cup and Platter is considering opening a new store in Los Angeles. As part of a presentation on this proposal, Dmitry wants another scene showing total revenue from potential store customers already living in the Los Angeles area.

Insight

Using Dates and Times in 3D Maps

If your data contains a date and time field like the date of a customer order, you can add that field to the Time box in the Layer pane. Adding a date/time field creates a play button on the map that you can use to view how the mapped data changes over time. For example, Dmitry could use the Order Date field to view changing revenue totals throughout the year in different regions of the country.

Creating New Scenes

New scenes can be created using an empty world map as the background—as you did when creating the first scene in this tour—or you can copy a current scene as the starting point for the next map. You can also create customized scenes with backgrounds of your choosing. For this new scene, you will copy the current scene and then change the view to show revenue in the Los Angeles area.

To add a new scene showing Los Angeles revenue to the tour:

▶ **1.** On the Home tab, in the Scene group, click the **New Scene** button. A second scene is added to the tour using the settings of the first scene.

▶ **2.** On the Home tab, in the Map group, click the **Find Location** button. The Find Location dialog box opens.

▶ **3.** Type **Los Angeles, California** in the location box, and then click **Find**. The map view shifts to a spot over Los Angles.

▶ **4.** Close the Find Location box.

▶ **5.** Click the **Tilt down button** ⊙ (or press **SHIFT+DOWN ARROW**) ten times to view the map at a lower angle. See Figure 10–47.

Figure 10–47   **Tour with two scenes**

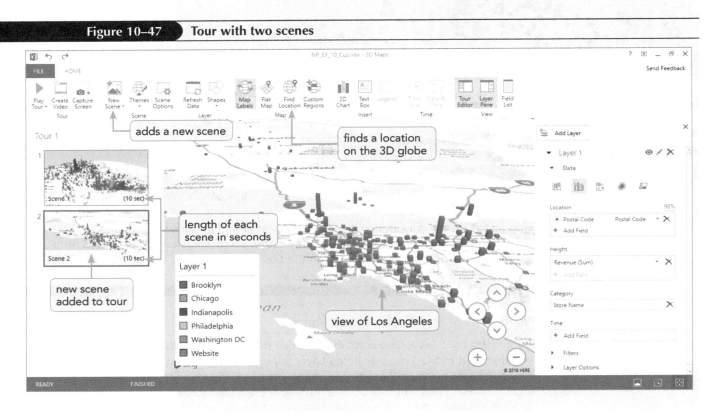

You will complete this tour by adding the transition timing between Scene 1 and Scene 2.

Setting Scene Options

Each scene in a tour has a duration measured in the seconds. The default duration is 10 seconds, but you can change the duration by modifying the scene options. You can also change the length of time required to transition from one scene to the next. During the transition, the 3D maps tool gradually changes the values and styles associated with one scene to match the values associated with the next scene. For example, with the two scenes you created, the transition will gradually change from a view of the United

States along the East Coast to a new view along the West Coast. You can enhance the transition with the following effects:

- Circle and Figure 8 effects add a repetitive circular motion to transition
- Dolly and Rotate Globe effects move the map clockwise in a straight line
- Push In effect zooms in on the scene
- Fly Over effect moves the map from top to bottom mimicking a camera flying over the object

You'll set the scene options of the two scenes in the tour.

To set the scene options:

1. With the second scene still selected in the Tour Editor, on the Home tab, in the Scene group, click the **Scene Options** button. The Scene Options dialog box opens. Because the second scene is selected, the changes you make in the Scene Options box affect that scene.

2. In the Scene duration (sec) box, change the value to **2** so that the second scene lasts two seconds.

3. In the Scene Name box, type **LA View** to rename the scene.

4. In the Transition duration (sec) box, change the value to **4** so that the length of transition from Scene 1 to Scene 2 is 4 seconds.

5. Click the **Effect** button, and then click **Push In**. The Push In effect is added to the transition. Do not make any change to the effect speed. See Figure 10–48.

Tip

Transition durations are always measured from the previous scene; no transition is applied to the first scene in the tour.

Figure 10–48   **Scene Options dialog box**

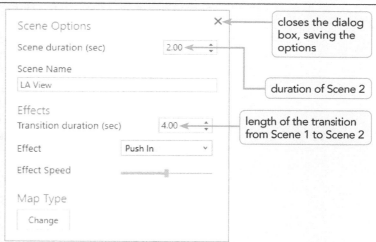

Scene Options   × ← closes the dialog box, saving the options

Scene duration (sec)   2.00 ← duration of Scene 2

Scene Name

LA View

Effects

Transition duration (sec)   4.00 ← length of the transition from Scene 1 to Scene 2

Effect   Push In

Effect Speed

Map Type

Change

6. In the Tour Editor pane, click **Scene 1** to select it. Now you can set options for the first scene.

7. Change the Scene duration to **1** second, change the Scene Name to **Northeast View**, and then close the Scene Options dialog box. The Scene 1 options are saved and applied.

Playing a Tour

Playing a tour presents all the scenes of the tour in order using the scene options you set. You will play the tour to view a presentation of revenue totals from across the United States on a 3D map.

To play the tour:

▶ 1. On the Home tab, in the Tour group, click the **Play Tour** button. The tour plays with the camera moving from the Northeast to Los Angeles over the United States. By default, tours are played in full screen view.

▶ 2. Press **ESC** to return to the 3D Maps window.

▶ 3. In 3D Maps window, click the **Close** button ☒. All changes are saved automatically, and you are returned to the workbook.

▶ 4. **sam**⬆ Save the workbook, and then close it.

Tip

To revise the tour and add new scenes, click the 3D Maps button in the Tours group on the Insert tab.

Dmitry appreciates the tour you've created and will use it in a report on Cup and Platter revenue and the prospects of opening a new store in the Los Angeles area.

Insight

Getting Ideas for Analysis

If you want ideas on how to present the information in a dataset, you can use the Excel Analyze Data tool, which examines data and uncovers trends and associations that you might want to highlight. To use the Analyze Data tool, place your data in an Excel table or data range, and then on the Home tab, in the Analysis group, click the Analyze Data button.

The Analyze Data tool takes your data and previews several charts in an Analyze Data (Ideas) pane, highlighting possibly interesting trends and factors you might want to include in your analysis. Some of the things the Ideas tool looks for are:

- **Ranks.** Do certain data categories result in outcomes significantly larger than others? For example, are there stores that are high sellers? The Analyze Data tool will preview charts that highlight those stores for further analysis.
- **Trends.** Are there trends in the data? Are sales increasing, decreasing, or showing seasonal variability? The Analyze Data tool will preview scatter charts with trendlines that highlight important trends.
- **Outliers.** Does the data contain unusual values or outliers? Is there a store that is significantly underperforming or a product that is exceeding expected sales? The Analyze Data tool will suggest charts that focus on those unusual outcomes.
- **Majority Categories.** Is there a single factor that contributes to most of the outcomes? Are most of the sales associated with one store or one product line? The Analyze Data tool will preview charts that showcase those important factors in your data.

Once you've reviewed the suggested charts from the Analyze Data (Ideas) pane, you can select and insert those charts directly into your workbook to be used in any reports or dashboards you create. Remember, the Analyze Data tool should be the beginning of your analysis, providing you with insights and motivation to further pursue the stories hidden in your data.

You've completed analyzing the large amount of data Dmitry had on the Cup and Platter company sales. In the process, you've retrieved data from a variety of data sources, combined data from different sources in a single report, and presented that data using tables, charts, maps, and tours. This just touches on the power of Power Query, Power Pivot, and 3D maps. If you explore these BI tools in greater depth, you'll find they are powerful tools with many useful features.

Review

Session 10.3 Quick Check

1. What is a hierarchy? How do you create a hierarchy?
2. What is the advantage of a hierarchy over an outline in a PivotTable design?
3. What are the two types of map charts?
4. Name three limitations of map charts.
5. What is a map tour?
6. Which 3D map type should you use to display locations with higher-sale totals in colors of greater intensity?
7. What is the Analyze Data tool?

Practice

Review Assignments

Data Files needed for the Review Assignments: NP_EX_10-2.xlsx, Support_EX_10_Sales01.csv, Support_EX_10_Sales02.csv, Support_EX_10_Sales03.accdb

Dmitry has another set of sales data for you to analyze. This time, you will look at the short- and long-term trends in sales from Cup and Platter's website. This data has been stored in a pair of CSV files. Dmitry has also compiled sample data on revenue generated from electric items, bakeware, and dinnerware. You will use that data to generate a revenue report and display the data on a map chart and 3D Maps tour. Complete the following:

1. Open the **NP_EX_10-2.xlsx** workbook located in the Excel10 > Review folder included with your Data Files. Save the workbook as **NP_EX_10_StoresReport** in the location specified by your instructor.

2. In the Documentation sheet, enter your name and the date.

3. Dmitry wants to view how website sales have increased over the year. Create a query to retrieve data from the **Support_EX_10_Sales01.csv** file. Use Power Query to remove the first four rows of the text file and use the titles in the fifth row as column headers. Load the three columns of data into an Excel table in cell B4 of the Website History worksheet.

4. Create a scatter chart of the data stored the range C4:D26. Move the chart to the Summary Report worksheet in the range B4:H16. Add a polynomial trendline of order 2 to the chart. (Use the Format Trendline pane and choose the Polynomial option.) Forecast the trendline forward 2 periods (or years).

5. Dmitry wants to view monthly website sales from the past two years. Create a query to retrieve data from the **Support_EX_10_Sales02.csv** file. Load the data as an Excel table to cell B4 in the Recent Website Sales worksheet. Format the data in the range C5:C28 as currency with no decimal places.

6. Using the data in the range B4:C28 of the Recent Website Sales worksheet, create a Forecast sheet, forecasting website revenue through 12/31/2025. Assume a seasonality in the data of 12 periods (or months). Name the Forecast sheet as **Forecasts**.

7. Move the forecast chart to the Summary Report worksheet in the range B18:H29. Remove the chart legend and add the chart title **Two-Year Forecast**.

8. Dmitry has a sampling of product sales from three Cup and Platter classes. Create a query that retrieves the Customers, Customer Orders, Items, Item Sales, and Stores tables from the **Support_EX_10_Sales03.accdb** Access database. Create a connection to the database file and add the tables in the Excel Data Model. Do not load any tables in an Excel table, PivotTable, or PivotChart.

9. Go to Power Pivot and create the following table relations between the five database tables:
   • Connect the Customer Orders and Customers tables through the Cust ID field.
   • Connect the Customer Orders and Stores tables through Store ID field.
   • Connect the Customer Orders and Item Sales tables through the Order ID field.
   • Connect the Item Sales and Items tables through the Item ID field.

10. Add a hierarchy to the Items table named **Item Tree** and add the Class, Subclass, and Group fields to it in that order.

11. Close Power Pivot and return to the workbook. In the Items Pivot worksheet, in cell B4, insert a PivotTable from the Data Model. Rename the table as **Items Pivot**. Add the Item Tree hierarchy from the Items table to the Rows area box, add the Type field from the Stores table to Columns area box, and add the Revenue field from the Item Sales table to the Values area box (displaying the revenue sum).

12. Create a clustered bar PivotChart from the Items Pivot PivotTable. Move the chart to the Summary Report worksheet in the range J11:P29. Remove the field buttons, primary horizontal axis, and gridlines from the chart. Move the chart legend to the bottom of the chart area. Add data labels to the chart.

13. Dmitry wants to examine revenue from coffee maker sales. Use the Quick Explore tool to drill down the bar chart categories through the Electrics class and the Coffee Makers subclass down to the group level, displaying total revenue of three coffee maker types.

14. Dmitry wants to view sales by state. In the State Revenue worksheet, add a PivotTable from the Data Model to cell B4. Name the PivotTable as **State Revenue**. Place the State field from the Customers table in the Rows area and the Revenue field from the Item Sales table in the Values area. In the PivotTable Options dialog box, on the Display tab, click the check boxes to show items with no data on the rows and columns.

15. Copy the data in the range B5:C55. Use Paste Link to paste references to the data values in the range E5:F55. Format the values in the range F5:F55 as currency. Enter **State** in cell E4 and enter **Revenue** in cell F4.

16. Create a Map chart of the data in the range E4:F55. Move the map to the Summary Report worksheet in the range R11:X29. Remove the chart title, add data labels to the chart, and then move the legend to the bottom of the chart area.

17. In the Summary Report worksheet, create a timeline using the Date field from the Customer Orders table. Place the timeline across the range J4:X10. Create connections between the timeline and the Items Pivot and State Revenue PivotTables. Use the timeline to filter the PivotTables to show data only from July 2024 through December 2024.

18. Dmitry wants a 3D Map presentation of this data. Insert a 3D Map. In scene 1, place the Postal Code field from the Customers table in the Location area, the Revenue field from the Items Sales table in the Height area, and the Store Name field from the Stores table in the Category area. Add map labels to the map.

19. Change the view of the globe to a location above Minnesota, looking down and to the east.

20. Create a second scene of this data positioned above Cuba looking northwest.

21. Change the durations of Scene 1 and Scene 2 to 1 second and play the tour verifying that your viewpoint moves across the United States from northwest of Chicago around to south of Florida.

22. Return to the workbook, save the workbook, and then close it.

Apply

Case Problem 1

Data Files needed for this Case Problem: NP_EX_10-3.xlsx, Support_EX_10_Yogurt.accdb

Umai Frozen Yogurt   Joan Amari is a sales executive for Umai Frozen Yogurt, a chain of frozen yogurt stores. Joan is responsible for overseeing 20 franchises in California. Joan wants to compare average customers per day at the franchises over the past three years and determine whether factors such as location, date, and weather play a significant role in the volume of customer traffic. She has data that contains over 21,000 records from the daily sales in the 20 stores from the past three years. Complete the following:

1. Open the **NP_EX_10-3.xlsx** workbook located in the Excel10 > Case1 folder included with your Data Files. Save the workbook as **NP_EX_10_Umai** in the location specified by your instructor.

2. In the Documentation sheet, enter your name and the date.

3. Use Power Query to access the **Support_EX_10_Yogurt.accdb** Access database, creating a connection to the Sales and Stores tables into the workbook's Data Model. You do not have to edit the query for these tables.

4. Open Power Pivot to view the Data Model in Diagram View. Create a relationship between the Sales and Stores table through the Store ID field.

5. In the Sales table, create a hierarchy named **Calendar** containing the Year, Month, and Weekday fields in that order.

6. Joan wants to analyze the number of customers served by the Umai Frozen Yogurt. Return to the workbook, and then insert a PivotTable in cell B4 of the Customer Calendar worksheet using the Data Model. Name the PivotTable **Customer Calendar**. Place the Calendar hierarchy from the Sales table in the Rows area of the PivotTable. Place the Customers field from the Sales table in the Values area. Change the field settings of the Sum of Customers value field to display the average of the Customers field with no decimal places.

7. Create a Line PivotChart from the PivotTable data. Move the PivotChart into the Sales Report worksheet, covering the range B14:I29. Remove the field buttons and the legend from the chart. Change the chart title to **Average Customers per Day**. Add data labels to the chart showing the value of each data marker.

8. Joan wants to know whether days of intense rainfall cause a decline in customer traffic. In the Rain Table worksheet, in cell B4, insert a PivotTable using the Data Model. Rename the PivotTable as **Rain Table**. Place the Rainy field from the Sales table in the Rows area. Display the average of the Customers field from the Sales table in the Values area. Display the average in the Number format with no decimal places.

9. Create a Clustered Column PivotChart of the Rain Table PivotTable. Move the PivotChart to cover the range K4:Q15 of the Sales Report worksheet. Remove the legend and the field buttons from the PivotChart. Change the chart title to **Average Customers per Day during Rainfall**. Add data labels to the chart.

10. Joan wants to examine the relationship between temperature and customer sales. In the Temperature Table worksheet, in cell B4, insert a PivotTable using the Data Model. Rename the PivotTable as **Temperature Table**. Place the Month field from the Sales table in the Rows area of the table. Display the average of the High Temp and Customers fields in the Values area of the table, in that order, to display the average high temperature and customers per month.

11. Joan wants to create a scatter chart of the relationship between average high temperature and average number of customers. Because PivotCharts cannot be created as scatter charts, you need to prepare the data to create a scatter chart of the relationship between average high temperature and average number of customers. Copy the range C4:D16 and use Paste Link to paste a link to the copied cells in the range F4:G16. Change the text in cell F4 to **Temperature** and change the text in cell G4 to **Customers**. Format the values in the range F5:G16 in the Number format with no decimal places.

12. Create a scatter chart of the data in the range F4:G16. Move the chart to the range K17:Q29 of the Sales Report worksheet. Change the chart title to **Customers vs. Temperature**. Add the axis titles to the chart, using **Average Customers per Day** for the Primary Vertical axis and **Average Temperature** for the Primary Horizontal axis. Change the scale of the vertical axis to go from 50 to 350. Change the scale of the Temperature axis to go from 50 to 110. Add a linear trendline to the chart.

13. Joan wants to view the charts on the Sales Report worksheet filtered by city. In the range B4:I12 of the Sales Report worksheet, insert a slicer using the City field from the Stores table. Lay out the slicer buttons in 4 columns and 5 rows. Connect the slicer to the three PiovtTables in the workbook.

14. Joan wants to show monthly results for the Malibu store from 2024. In the Sales Report worksheet, use the City slicer to show results for the Malibu store. In the Average Customers per Day chart, drill down into the 2024 Year category to the level of month.

15. As part of a presentation, Joan wants a map showing the locations of the stores with the highest average customers per day. Click cell A1 in the Sales Report worksheet, and then open a 3D Maps tour. Do the following to create a map showing the locations of the stores with the highest average customers per day:

   a. Place the City field from the Stores table in the Location box.

   b. Place the Customers field from the Sales table in the Height box. In the Height box, point to Customers (Sum), click the arrow, and then click Average on the menu to display the Customers (Average) instead of Customers (Sum).

   c. Change the map style to a heat map.

   d. Zoom into the state of California map to better view the average intensity of customer traffic in the 20 cites.

   e. Display the map labels.

16. Close the 3D Map tour, save the workbook, and then close it.

Challenge

Case Problem 2

Data Files needed for this Case Problem: NP_EX_10-4.xlsx, Support_EX_10_Turkeys.csv, Support_EX_10_Migration.csv

Department of Ornithology Karen Hatch is a professor in the Department of Ornithology at the University of West Hilton in Florida. Professor Hatch is examining the migratory habits of turkey vultures and has compiled tracking data on seven birds. Professor Hatch wants you to complete a workbook that displays the turkey's migratory pattern and analyzes the relationship between each bird's physical characteristics and the total distance they traveled. Complete the following:

1. Open the **NP_EX_10-4.xlsx** workbook located in the Excel10 > Case2 folder included with your Data Files. Save the workbook as **NP_EX_10_Ornithology** in the location specified by your instructor.

2. In the Documentation sheet, enter your name and the date.

3. Use Power Query to access the **Support_EX_10_Turkeys.csv** file, opening the file in the Power Query Editor, and then doing the following:

   a. Rename the query as **Turkeys**.

   b. Remove the summary text in the first three rows of the query.

   c. Use the text in the new first row as column headers.

   d. Remove the Species, Tracking Type, and Tracker columns from the query.

   e. Close and load the query to establish a connection to the Turkeys query and load it into the Data Model. Do not load the data into an Excel table, PivotTable, or PivotChart.

4. Use Power Query to access the **Support_EX_10_Migration.csv** file, and then edit the query as follows:

   a. Rename the query as **Migration**.

   b. Remove the first three rows from the query and use the new first row as column headers.

   c. Select the DateTime column; on the Add Column tab, in the From Date & Time group, click the Date button; and then click Date Only to create a new column named Date that contains only the date from the DateTime column.

   d. Remove the DateTime column from the query.

   e. Select the Date column and create a new column showing the End of Month date. Rename the column as **YearMonth**.

   f. Close and load the query to establish a connection to the Migration query and load it into the Data Model. Do not load the data into an Excel table, PivotTable, or PivotChart.

5. Use Power Pivot to create a relation between the Turkeys and Migration tables through the Tag field.

6. Karen wants to track the monthly distance traveled by each turkey vulture throughout the years. In the Migration Pivot worksheet, in cell B4, insert a PivotTable to track the monthly distance and average speed by each turkey vulture throughout the years.

   a. Rename the PivotTable as **Migration Pivot**.

   b. Move the Distance field from the Migration table to the Values area to calculate the sum of the Distance field. Rename the value field **Miles Traveled**.

   c. Move the YearMonth field to the Rows area. Remove the YearMonth (Year), YearMonth (Quarter), and YearMonth (Month) fields generated by Excel, leaving only the YearMonth field.

7. Karen wants a scatter chart of the data in the PivotTable. Copy the data in the range B4:C16 and paste a link to those copied cells in the range E4:F16 to set up the data for a scatter chart. Format the data in the range E5:E16 using the Short Date format. Format the Miles Traveled data in the range F5:F16 using the Number format with a thousands separator and no decimal places.

⊕ **Explore**   8. Create a scatter chart with smooth lines using the data in the range E4:F16. Complete the scatter chart as follows:

    a. Move the chart to cover the range B12:H27 on the Migration Dashboard worksheet.

    b. Change the chart title to **Turkey Vulture Monthly Migration**.

    c. Add the axis title **Miles Traveled** to the vertical axis and **Date** to the horizontal axis.

    d. Select the data labels on the horizontal axis and use the Orientation button in the Alignment group on the Home tab to angle the date text counterclockwise to fit within the chart area space.

  9. In the range B6:H10, add a slicer for the Tag field from the Turkeys table. Lay out the slicer in 4 columns and connect it to the Migration Pivot PivotTable. Filter the chart to show the migration results from tag B45664.

10. Karen wants to investigate whether a relationship exists between migration distance and the bird's weight. In the Weight Analysis worksheet, in cell B4 insert a PivotTable with the Weight field from the Turkeys table in the Rows area and the sum of the Distance field from the Migration table in the Values area. You'll use this to investigate whether a relationship exists between migration distance and the bird's weight.

11. Copy the data in the range B4:C12 and paste a link in the range E4:F12. Display the values in the range F5:F12 as numbers with a thousands separator and no decimal places. Create a scatter chart of the data in the range E4:F12. Add a linear trendline to the chart and change the chart title to **Miles Traveled vs. Weight (oz)**. Move the chart to the range J4:O11 in the Migration Dashboard worksheet.

12. Karen wants to see whether length is related to migration distance. In the Length Analysis worksheet, repeat Steps 10 and 11 comparing the migration distance to the bird's length. Place the chart in the range J12:O19 of the Migration Dashboard worksheet and change the chart title to **Miles Traveled vs. Length (in)**.

13. In the Wingspan Analysis worksheet, repeat Steps 10 and 11 to compare migration distance to the bird's wingspan. Place the chart in the range J20:O27 of the Migration Dashboard worksheet with the chart title **Miles Traveled vs. Wingspan (in)**. Set the scale of vertical axis to go from 0 to 20,000 in 5,000 unit increments to match the other charts on the dashboard.

14. Karen wants to display the route that the eight turkey vultures followed. Insert a 3D Map, and then do the following:

    a. Add map labels to the 3D globe.

    b. Drag the Latitude and Longitude fields from the Migration table to the Location area to show the path of the migration.

    c. Drag the Speed field from the Migration table to the Height area so that the height of the data markers is proportional to the bird's speed.

    d. Drag the Tag field from the Turkeys table to the Category area to identify each bird's migration route.

    e. Resize the Layer 1 box so that you can see all of the legend entries.

⊕ **Explore**   15. Do the following to see the turkey vulture migration in action:

    a. Drag the Date field from the Migration table to the Time area.

    b. Above and to the right of the Time area box, click the Clock button and click "Data shows for an instant" to have each marker replaced by the subsequent location of the bird in its migration.

    c. Click the Play button below the map to view the migration of the eight birds in action.

16. Close the 3D Map window, save the workbook, and then close it.

EXCEL

Objectives

Session 11.1
- Change a PivotTable layout
- Display and hide PivotTable grand totals and subtotals
- Sort PivotTable contents
- Filter PivotTable contents
- Group items within a PivotTable field

Session 11.2
- Apply calculations to a PivotTable
- Create PivotTable conditional formats
- Manage the PivotTable cache
- Create calculated items and calculated fields

Session 11.3
- Analyze PivotTables based on the Data Model
- Create a table measure using DAX
- Retrieve PivotTable data with the GETPIVOTDATA function
- Explore Excel Database functions

Exploring PivotTable Design

Summarizing Sales and Revenue Data

Case | QC Inn

Anna Fischer is a regional manager for QC Inn, a nationwide chain of affordable motels for vacationing families and business travelers. Anna is preparing the year-end report for 24 QC Inn franchises located in the Nebraska/South Dakota region. Anna's report will explore how revenue and occupancy rates have changed over the past two years and highlight those motels and regions that are performing below or above expectations. To create this report, you'll help Anna summarize daily motel data with a variety of PivotTable designs.

Starting Data Files

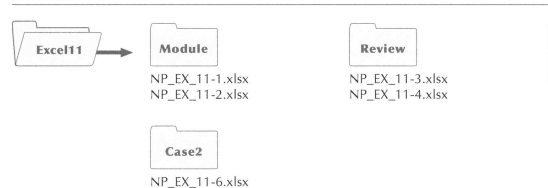

Excel11 →

Module
NP_EX_11-1.xlsx
NP_EX_11-2.xlsx

Review
NP_EX_11-3.xlsx
NP_EX_11-4.xlsx

Case1
NP_EX_11-5.xlsx

Case2
NP_EX_11-6.xlsx

Session 11.1 Visual Overview:

A PivotTable Outline layout places all fields in separate columns and subtotal rows at the top of each group.

A PivotTable Compact layout places all fields from the Rows area in one column and subtotal rows at the top of each group.

You can group a PivotTable by dates. In this PivotTable, the occupancy rates calculate on a weekly basis.

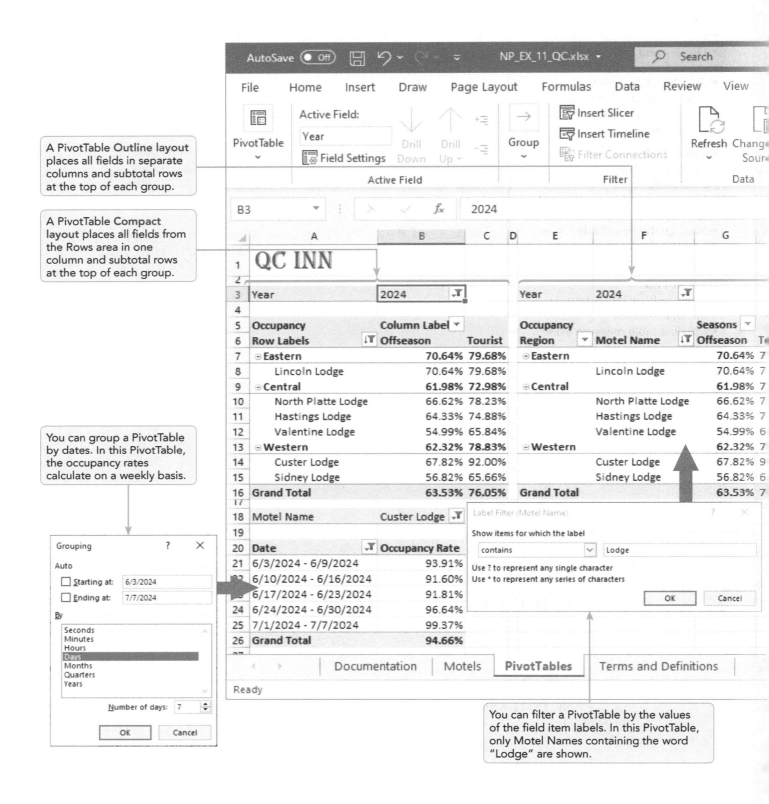

You can filter a PivotTable by the values of the field item labels. In this PivotTable, only Motel Names containing the word "Lodge" are shown.

Layouts, Sorting, Filtering, and Grouping

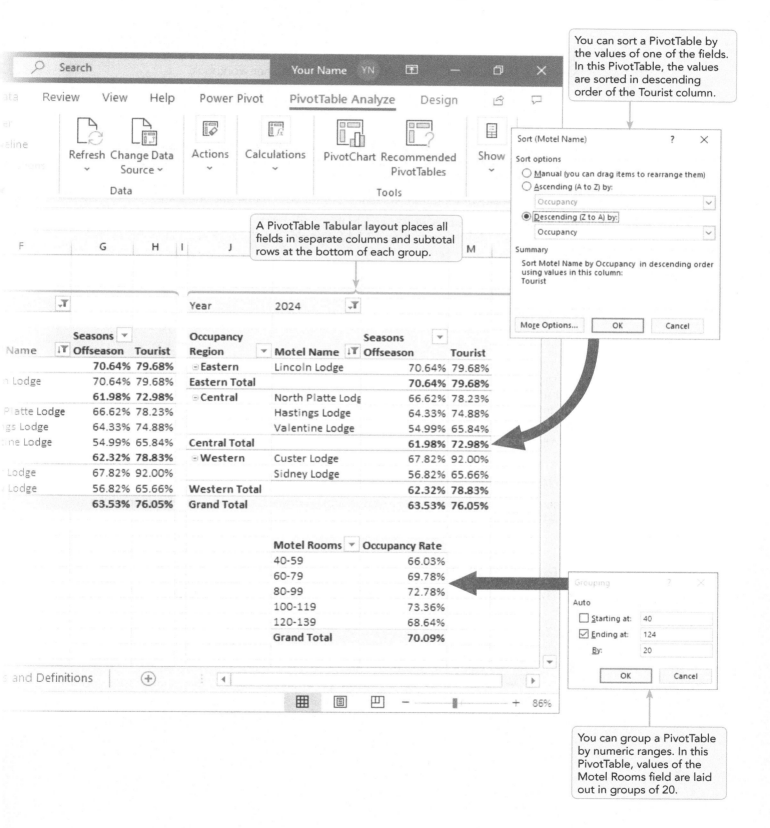

You can sort a PivotTable by the values of one of the fields. In this PivotTable, the values are sorted in descending order of the Tourist column.

A PivotTable Tabular layout places all fields in separate columns and subtotal rows at the bottom of each group.

Sort (Motel Name)   ?   ×

Sort options
- ○ Manual (you can drag items to rearrange them)
- ○ Ascending (A to Z) by:
  Occupancy
- ⦿ Descending (Z to A) by:
  Occupancy

Summary

Sort Motel Name by Occupancy in descending order using values in this column:
Tourist

More Options...   OK   Cancel

	Seasons	
Name	Offseason	Tourist
	70.64%	79.68%
Lodge	70.64%	79.68%
	61.98%	72.98%
Platte Lodge	66.62%	78.23%
gs Lodge	64.33%	74.88%
ine Lodge	54.99%	65.84%
	62.32%	78.83%
Lodge	67.82%	92.00%
Lodge	56.82%	65.66%
	63.53%	76.05%

Year   2024

Occupancy		Seasons	
Region	Motel Name	Offseason	Tourist
⊟ Eastern	Lincoln Lodge	70.64%	79.68%
Eastern Total		70.64%	79.68%
⊟ Central	North Platte Lodge	66.62%	78.23%
	Hastings Lodge	64.33%	74.88%
	Valentine Lodge	54.99%	65.84%
Central Total		61.98%	72.98%
⊟ Western	Custer Lodge	67.82%	92.00%
	Sidney Lodge	56.82%	65.66%
Western Total		62.32%	78.83%
Grand Total		63.53%	76.05%

Motel Rooms	Occupancy Rate
40-59	66.03%
60-79	69.78%
80-99	72.78%
100-119	73.36%
120-139	68.64%
Grand Total	70.09%

Grouping   ?   ×

Auto
- ☐ Starting at: 40
- ☑ Ending at: 124
- By: 20

OK   Cancel

You can group a PivotTable by numeric ranges. In this PivotTable, values of the Motel Rooms field are laid out in groups of 20.

Laying Out a PivotTable

PivotTables are perhaps the most indispensable tool Excel provides for summarizing and analyzing data. In this module, you will explore PivotTable designs and features to present data in a wide variety of formats and learn how to augment PivotTables with a wide range of summary calculations. Anna has already created an Excel workbook detailing daily usage numbers from the past two years at 24 QC Inn motels located in Nebraska and South Dakota. You'll start by reviewing her workbook.

To view Anna's workbook:

▶ 1. **sam** ⬇ Open the **NP_EX_11-1.xlsx** workbook located in the **Excel11 > Module** folder included with your Data Files, and then save the workbook as **NP_EX_11_QC** in the location specified by your instructor.

▶ 2. In the Documentation worksheet, enter your name and the date.

▶ 3. Go to the **Motels** worksheet. In this worksheet, Anna created an Excel table named Motels containing 17,544 records of daily stays at QC Inn motels from the past two years.

▶ 4. Review the fields in this table. Information on the fields is also included in the Terms and Definitions worksheet at the end of the workbook.

▶ 5. Review the other worksheets in the workbook. Note that some worksheets already include PivotTable report areas, which you will use in your report.

Anna wants to examine revenue totals and occupancy rates across motels, months, and seasons. She also wants to compare values from one year to the next. She'll use this information to identify which motels are succeeding in their location and which may be in trouble. You will start your analysis by examining how motel revenue varies between locations in the Nebraska/South Dakota sales territory.

Working with Grand Totals and Subtotals

Anna wants you to show motel revenue broken down by year and the location of the motel. You'll create a PivotTable containing motel and revenue data.

To create the PivotTable of motel revenue:

▶ 1. Go to the **Revenue vs Location** worksheet, and then make sure cell **B4** is selected to make the PivotTable report area active.

▶ 2. Drag the **Year** field to the Columns area, drag the **Region** and **Motel Name** to the Rows area, and then drag the **Revenue** field to the Values area.

▶ 3. Use the Value Field Settings dialog box to change the value field for Revenue from "Sum of Revenue" to **Total Revenue** and change the number format of the revenue values to Currency. See Figure 11–1.

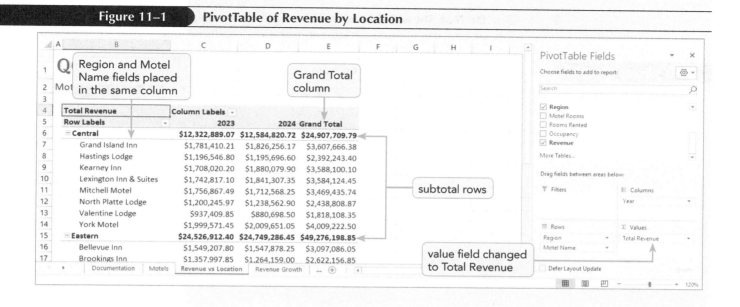

Figure 11–1   PivotTable of Revenue by Location

PivotTables, by default, include grand totals across all columns and rows. The grand totals in column E in this table provide the total revenue from 2023 and 2024 for each of the 24 motels and the grand totals in row 33 display the totals across all motels for each year. Based on this information, Anna can report that the chain had almost $100 million in total revenue (cell E33) with revenue totals slightly higher in 2024 than in 2023. Many individual motels saw their revenues increase. For example, the Grand Island Inn increased its annual revenue from $1.781 million in 2023 to $1.826 million in 2024 for a total of $3.608 million across the two years (row 7). Some motels saw revenue declines. The Valentine Lodge (row 13) saw its revenue decline from about $937,400 to about $880,700 for a two-year grand total of almost $1,818 million.

Subtotals appear for each of the three geographic regions. The motels in the Central region had about $24.9 million in revenue from the past two years (cell E6), while the Eastern and Western regions had two-year revenue totals of about $49.3 million (cell E15) and $25.2 million (cell E26), respectively.

If the grand totals and subtotals are not of interest, you can remove those totals from the report.

To remove the grand totals and subtotals from the PivotTable:

▶ 1. On the ribbon, click the **Design** tab to view commands for setting the appearance of your PivotTable, and then in the Layout group, click the **Grand Totals** button. A menu of options appears. You can turn off grand totals for the PivotTable rows and columns, keep the grand total values on for either rows or columns, or keep grand totals on for both (the default).

▶ 2. Click **Off for Rows and Columns**. The Grand Totals disappear from column E and row 33.

▶ 3. In the Layout group, click the **Subtotals** button. You have the option of removing all subtotal calculations or moving the location of the subtotal rows to either the top of each group or the bottom.

▶ **4.** Click **Do Not Show Subtotals** to remove the subtotals from the PivotTable. The subtotal calculations disappear from the PivotTable. See Figure 11–2.

Figure 11–2   **Grand total and subtotals removed from the PivotTable**

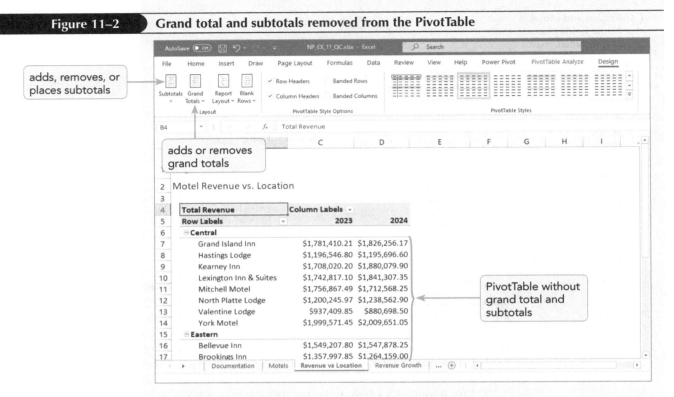

▶ **5.** Click the **Subtotals** button, and then click **Show All Subtotals at Top of Group** to restore the subtotal values.

You will next explore how to change the layout of a PivotTable report.

Insight

Displaying Multiple Subtotal Functions

The PivotTable default is to base subtotals on the same summary function that is applied to the individual table rows. So, a subtotal row will use the SUM function if the value field is summarized with sums and the AVERAGE function if the PivotTable shows averages of the value field. If you want to show the results of more than one summary function, you can add multiple subtotal rows with different calculations to a PivotTable. First, open the Field Settings dialog box for the field over which the summary statistics are calculated. In the Field Settings dialog box, go to the Subtotal & Filters tab, and then click the Custom option button. Select one or more functions from the list of summary functions, which includes Sum, Count, Average, Max, Min, and Product. Click OK to close the Field Settings dialog box. The PivotTable will now show multiple summary statistics in each subtotal row.

Changing the PivotTable Layout

You can lay out PivotTables in one of three ways: Compact (the default shown in Figure 11–1), Outline, and Tabular. The three layouts differ mainly in how they arrange multiple fields placed in the Rows area and where they display subtotal rows. Figure 11–3 summarizes these differences.

Figure 11–3	PivotTable layout options

Layout	Fields in the Rows Area	Subtotals
Compact	Placed together in the first column, separated by outlining buttons	Placed at the top of each row group
Outline	Placed in separate columns	Placed at the top of each row group
Tabular	Placed in separate columns	Placed at the bottom of each row group

Tip

Subtotals for a Tabular layout can only be placed at the bottom of a row group.

An advantage of the Compact layout is that it reduces PivotTable width by placing all fields from the Rows area in one column. The Outline and Tabular layouts are best if you want to use values from the PivotTable in a subsequent analysis by placing each field value in its own PivotTable cell. You can also repeat field values in the Outline and Tabular layouts so that every row shows a field value.

Reference

Choosing a PivotTable Layout

- On the Design tab, in the Layout group, click the Report Layout button.
- Choose the Compact form to place all fields in the Rows area within a single column; choose the Outline or Tabular forms to place the fields in separate columns.
- To repeat item labels within a field, click the Report Layout button, and then click Repeat All Item Labels.

You'll change the layout of the Revenue PivotTable to the Tabular form and repeat the field values within each row.

To display a PivotTable in Tabular layout:

1. On the Design tab, in the Layout group, click the **Report Layout** button, and then click **Show in Tabular Form**. The PivotTable changes to the Tabular layout.

2. In the Layout group, click the **Report Layout** button again, and then click **Repeat All Item Labels**. The name of the region is repeated for each row.

3. In the Layout group, click the **Blank Rows** button, and then click **Insert Blank Line After Each Item**. The PivotTable is easier to read now that each row group is separated with a blank row. See Figure 11–4.

Figure 11–4	PivotTable in a Tabular layout

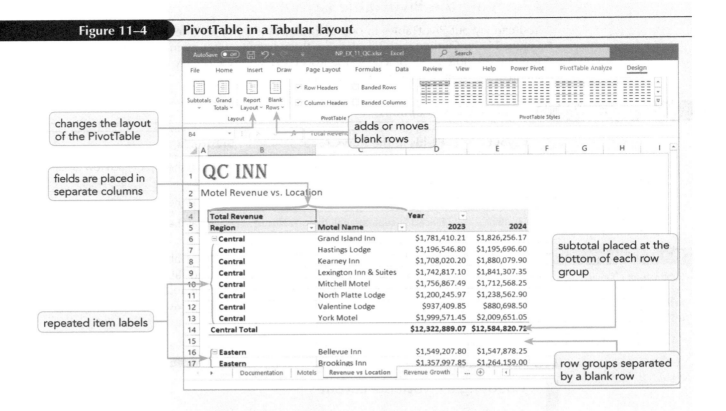

Anna finds the Tabular layout more readable for this data and more useful in the Revenue report.

Proskills

Written Communication: Setting Default PivotTable Options

Some professions have design standards that all reports must follow. The default Compact layout might not be one that you need use. Rather than changing the PivotTable layout every time you create a report, you can set your own preferred layout options.

To define your PivotTable defaults, click Options in Backstage view to open the Options dialog box. In the Options dialog box, click the Data tab, and then click the Edit Default Layout button in the Data options section to make changes to the default layout of PivotTables. In the Edit Default Layout dialog box, specify whether to show subtotals and, if so, where they should be placed, whether to show grand totals for PivotTable rows and/or columns, and finally whether new PivotTables should be created using the Compact, Outline, or Tabular layouts. To save time, you can select a cell from an existing PivotTable and then click Import to use all the layout choices from that PivotTable as the defaults going forward. To set defaults for PivotTable options other than layouts, click the PivotTable Options button in the Edit Default Layout dialog box. In the PivotTable Options dialog box, you can set all the other PivotTable options for any new PivotTables you create.

By defining your own PivotTable options, you can reduce the time required to create a finished report and make your reports more consistent in design and appearance.

Sorting a PivotTable

Tip

Month names are automatically sorted in calendar order (Jan, Feb, Mar, and so on); weekday names are sorted in day order (Sun, Mon, Tue, and so on).

PivotTables labels are automatically sorted in alphabetical order if they contain text or chronological order if they contain date/time values. Thus, both the region names and the motel names within region shown in Figure 11–4 are sorted alphabetically. Anna wants to change that order so that the regions are listed in geographic order going east to west and then within each region, the busiest motels are listed first.

Manually Sorting a Field

To change the order of the field items, you can use your mouse to drag and drop the item labels in your preferred order. A quicker approach is to select each item label and retype its name. The items will then be automatically resorted to match the names you enter. You'll use the typing approach to reorder the Region field, arranging the items in the order of Eastern, Central, and then Western.

To manually sort the Region field:

▶ 1. Click cell **B6** containing the text Central.

▶ 2. Type **Eastern** to specify the first item you want to appear in the field, and then press **ENTER**. The Central and Eastern categories switch position. The motels in the Eastern region are listed first in the table, starting with the Bellevue Inn. The motels for the Central and Western regions follow.

   Trouble? If the category is renamed but not reordered, you probably mistyped the category name. Undo that action, and then repeat Steps 1 and 2, being sure to type the name of the category correctly.

Excel remembers your chosen order so that if you recreate this PivotTable or create another PivotTable with the Region field, you will not have to reorder the items again.

Reference

Sorting PivotTables

- To manually sort the items within a PivotTable field, drag the field items or type the item labels in the order you prefer.
- To sort the items in ascending or descending order, click the Filter button next to the field name, and then click Sort A to Z or Sort Z to A on the menu.
- To sort a field based on values from another field in the PivotTable, click the Filter button next to the field name, click More Sort Options, select the field the sorting is based on, specify the sorting options, and then click OK.

Sorting by Value

You can have Excel automatically sort a field by clicking the Filter button next to the field name and selecting a sorting option from the menu. Anna wants you to sort the motels within each region so that the motels with the highest revenue appear at the top of the list. You will sort the values of the Motel Name field in descending order of the 2024 revenue.

To sort the motel names in descending order of revenue:

▶ **1.** Click the **Filter button** in cell C5 of the PivotTable to open the filter menu.

▶ **2.** Click **More Sort Options**. The Sort (Motel Name) dialog box opens.

▶ **3.** Click the **Descending (Z to A) by** option button, click the **Descending (Z to A) by** box, and then click **Total Revenue**. See Figure 11–5.

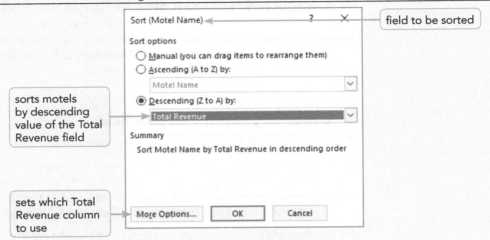

sorts motels by descending value of the Total Revenue field

sets which Total Revenue column to use

You can sort the motels by the 2023 revenue total, the 2024 total, or the grand total across both years. The default is to use the grand total, even if that grand total doesn't appear in the PivotTable. Anna wants the motels within each region sorted in descending order of the 2024 revenues.

▶ **4.** Click **More Options**. The More Sort Options (Motel Name) dialog box opens.

▶ **5.** Click the **Values in selected column** option button, and then press **TAB** to select the cell reference.

Make sure you select a cell from the column containing the values used for sorting.

▶ **6.** Click cell **E6** to replace the cell reference. This will sort the motel names by the 2021 revenue values in column E. See Figure 11–6.

Figure 11–6   More Sort Options (Motel Name) dialog box

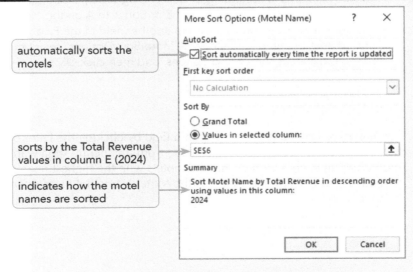

automatically sorts the motels

sorts by the Total Revenue values in column E (2024)

indicates how the motel names are sorted

> **7.** Click **OK** in each dialog box to return to the workbook. The motel names within each region are sorted in descending order of the 2024 revenue totals. See Figure 11–7.

Figure 11–7   **Motels sorted by 2024 revenue**

	A	B	C	D	E	F	G	H	I
4		**Total Revenue**		**Year**					
5		**Region**	**Motel Name**	**2023**	**2024**				
6		− **Eastern**	Omaha Inn & Suites	$3,431,356.10	$3,594,563.80				
7		**Eastern**	Lincoln Inn & Suites	$3,137,369.85	$3,210,499.85				
8		**Eastern**	Omaha Motel	$2,963,896.05	$3,189,714.80				
9		**Eastern**	Sioux Falls Inn & Suites	$2,871,411.20	$3,121,485.65				
10		**Eastern**	Lincoln Lodge	$2,271,586.40	$2,362,802.25				
11		**Eastern**	Sioux Falls Inn	$2,317,386.05	$2,309,047.45				
12		**Eastern**	Lincoln Motel	$2,675,656.55	$2,203,789.00		motels in each		
13		**Eastern**	Omaha Inn	$1,951,044.55	$1,945,346.40		region sorted		
14		**Eastern**	Bellevue Inn	$1,549,207.80	$1,547,878.25		in descending		
15		**Eastern**	Brookings Inn	$1,357,997.85	$1,264,159.00		order by 2024		
16		**Eastern Total**		**$24,526,912.40**	**$24,749,286.45**		revenue		
17									
18		− **Central**	York Motel	$1,999,571.45	$2,009,651.05				
19		**Central**	Kearney Inn	$1,708,020.20	$1,880,079.90				
20		**Central**	Lexington Inn & Suites	$1,742,817.10	$1,841,307.35				
21		**Central**	Grand Island Inn	$1,781,410.21	$1,826,256.17				
22		**Central**	Mitchell Motel	$1,756,867.49	$1,712,568.25				

Documentation | Motels | Revenue vs Location | Revenue Growth | ... | ⊕
Ready

The PivotTable now effectively shows the information that Anna needs for the report. The top-selling motel in the Eastern region for 2024 is the Omaha Inn & Suites with $3.594 million in revenue, followed by the Lincoln Inn & Suites and then the Omaha Motel with $3.210 million and $3.189 million, respectively. The top-selling motel for the Central region is the York Motel with over $2 million in 2024 revenue (cell E18), and the top-selling motel for the Western region is the Rapid City Inn with about $3.585 million in 2024 revenue (cell E28).

Insight

Sorting PivotTables by a Custom List

PivotTables can be automatically sorted alphabetically, by numeric value, or by date, in ascending or descending order. However, in some situations, you will want PivotTables automatically sorted based on a custom list. For example, Anna might want to always list motels based geographic location, going from east to west.

To create a custom list, click Options in Backstage view to open the Excel Options dialog box. Click the Advanced tab, scroll down to the General section, and then click the Edit Custom Lists button. The Custom Lists dialog box opens, from which you can create lists of items in any order to use with your PivotTables.

If later you want to prevent Excel from automatically sorting based on custom lists, go to the PivotTable Analyze tab, and then in the PivotTable group, click the Options button. In the PivotTable Options dialog box, on the Totals & Filters tab, deselect the Use Custom Lists when sorting check box, and then click OK.

The motels in the QC Inn chain are often built with different clientele in mind. For example, the line of Inn & Suites motels, such as the Omaha Inn & Suites, provides more spacious rooms and meeting facilities, perfect for the needs of business travelers and conferences. The success of those motels is of special interest to Anna, who wants to limit the PivotTable to those motels. You can narrow the scope of a PivotTable report using filters.

Filtering a PivotTable

Excel provides several ways of filtering PivotTables. You can add fields to the Filters area to give users the ability to select field values from a drop-down list. You can also connect slicers or timelines to the PivotTable. Finally, you can apply filters directly to the fields within the PivotTable. The four types of filters that can be applied directly to PivotTable fields are:

- **Manual filters**, which select values from check boxes listing all of the unique field values
- **Date filters**, which select data based on specific dates or date ranges
- **Label filters**, which select data based on the labels of the items in the field
- **Value filters**, which filter data based on values of a numeric field elsewhere in the PivotTable

Anna wants the Revenue table to show only those motels of the Inn & Suites line that had more than $3 million in revenue during 2024. To modify the report, you will first use a manual filter to narrow the focus of the PivotTable to 2024 revenue totals.

To apply a manual filter to the PivotTable:

▶ **1.** Click the **Filter button** in cell D4 next to the Year label.

▶ **2.** Click the **2023** check box to deselect it, leaving only the 2024 check box selected.

▶ **3.** Click **OK**. The 2023 revenue column is removed from the PivotTable, leaving only the 2024 revenue totals displayed in column D.

Tip

You can reduce the filter values by entering a search string in the Search box directly above the list of field item values.

Manual filters are a quick way to filter data. However, if data contains a lot of field values, the list of filter values will be extremely long. Another approach is to use the Label filter in which you limit the field to only those labels whose value matches specified criteria. You will narrow the PivotTable so that it only shows results from motels with the word "Suites" in their name. You'll filter the PivotTable now.

To apply a Label filter to the PivotTable:

▶ **1.** Click the **Filter button** in cell C5 next to the Motel Name label.

▶ **2.** Click **Label Filters** on the menu. A list of criteria that can be applied to the labels of the selected field appears.

▶ **3.** Click **Contains** from the list of filter options. The Label Filter (Motel Name) dialog box opens with "contains" already selected in the left box and the insertion point in the input box on the right.

▶ **4.** In the input box, type **Suites** to limit the PivotTable to only those motels with the word "Suites" in their name. See Figure 11–8.

Figure 11–8   **Label Filter (Motel Name) dialog box**

▶ **5.** Click **OK**.

The PivotTable is filtered to show 2024 revenue from five Inn & Suites motels located in Omaha, Lincoln, Sioux Falls, Lexington, and Deadwood. Note that Label filters can also be applied to labels that have numeric values. For example, a field specifying the number of rooms in the motel could be filtered to show only those motels with more than 100 rooms or between 50 and 75 rooms. Label filters, whether used with text strings or numeric values, always apply the filter to the field associated with the filter button. To filter a field based on the values from another field in the PivotTable, use a Value filter.

Anna wants to filter this PivotTable to show only those Inn & Suites motels with 2024 revenues of $3 million or greater. However, there is a problem. By default, only one filter can be applied to a field at a time: You can apply a Label filter or a Value filter to the Motel Name field, but not both. To apply multiple filters to a single field, you must first modify the PivotTable properties.

To allow multiple filters within the same field:

▶ **1.** Make sure the Revenue Location PivotTable is still selected.

▶ **2.** On the ribbon, click the **PivotTable Analyze** tab, and then, in the PivotTable group, click the **Options** button. The PivotTable Options dialog box opens.

▶ **3.** Click the **Totals & Filters** tab to view options for totals and filters.

▶ **4.** In the Filters section, click the **Allow multiple filters per field** check box. See Figure 11–9.

| Figure 11–9 | PivotTable Options dialog box |

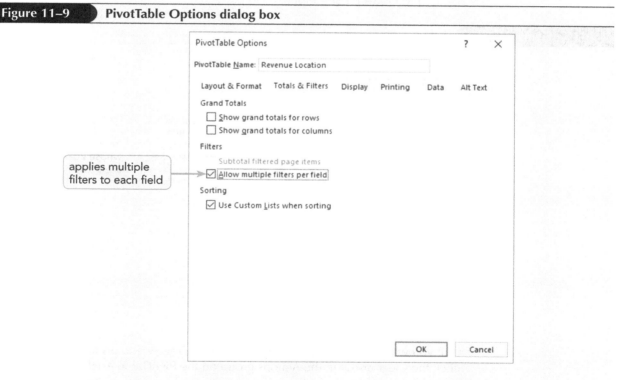

▶ **5.** Click **OK** to return to the workbook.

Next, you'll add a second filter that limits the PivotTable to only those motels with a total of revenue of $3 million or more.

To apply a Value filter to the PivotTable:

▶ **1.** Click the **Filter button** in cell C5 next to the Motel Name label.

▶ **2.** On the menu, click **Values Filters**. A submenu of filter options that can be applied to numeric values appears.

▶ **3.** Click **Greater Than Or Equal To**. The Value Filter (Motel Name) dialog box opens with Total Revenue already chosen as the numeric field that "is greater than or equal to" a specified value.

▶ **4.** In the input box on the right, type **3,000,000** to limit the PivotTable to those Inn & Suites motels with a total 2024 revenue of $3 million or greater. See Figure 11–10.

Figure 11–10 **Value Filter (Motel Name) dialog box**

5. Click **OK**. The Value filter is applied to the table. Three motels satisfy all the filter criteria. See Figure 11–11.

Figure 11–11 **Filtered revenue totals**

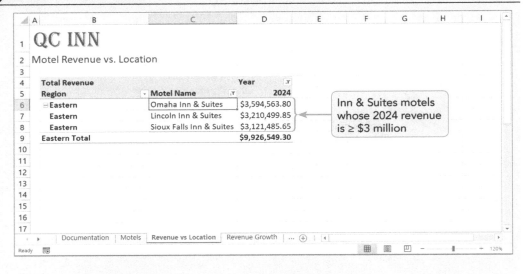

If you want to remove all the filters to display revenue totals for all motels, you can click the Clear arrow in the Actions group on the PivotTable Analyze tab, and then click Clear Filters.

Insight

Generating Multiple PivotTables with Show Report Filter Pages

You can create multiple copies of a PivotTable with the **Show Report Filters Pages** tool. To apply the tool, first place a field in the Filters area of the PivotTable. Then, rather than using the Filter button to switch the PivotTable between values of the filter, do the following:

1. Click the PivotTable Analyze tab.
2. In the PivotTable group, click the Options arrow, and then click Show Report Filter Pages.
3. In the Show Report Filter Pages dialog box, select the field from which to generate the filter pages.
4. Click OK.

Excel will generate new worksheets with each sheet containing a copy of the original PivotTable, filtered to show a different field value and the sheets automatically named for their field value. The PivotTables are not linked to the original table so any changes you make to the original PivotTable will not be reflected in the copies. The Show Report Filter Pages tool is a great way of quickly generating reports for specific stores, regions, or time periods in data.

Grouping PivotTable Fields

Total revenue is one metric to gauge the success or failure of a motel. Another is the average occupancy rate, which measures the percentage of available rooms being rented on average per night. A motel might not return a lot in revenue because of the size of its market, yet still be successful if it constantly rents out most of its rooms. On the other hand, a motel in a large market might be underutilized even if it is bringing in a large amount of revenue.

Anna is interested in exploring how occupancy rates in the Nebraska/South Dakota motels vary throughout the year. You'll create a new PivotTable report to calculate the average occupancy rate for each of the 24 motels from January through December in 2024.

To report on average occupancy rates:

▶ **1.** Go to the **Seasonal Occupancy** worksheet.

▶ **2.** Drag the **Year** field into the Filters area, drag the **Month** field into the Columns area, drag the **Motel Name** field into the Rows area, and drag the **Occupancy** field into the Values area. By default, Excel displays the sum of the occupancy rates, but Anna wants to analyze the average occupancy rate.

▶ **3.** Modify the Value Field Settings for the Sum of Occupancy so that the PivotTable displays the average occupancy as percentages with two decimal places and change the name from "Sum of Occupancy" to **Occupancy Rate**. The PivotTable now shows the average occupancy rate.

▶ **4.** On the ribbon, click the **Design** tab. In the Layout group, click the **Report Layout** button, and then click **Show in Tabular Form** to apply the Tabular layout to the PivotTable.

▶ **5.** On the Design tab, in the Layout group, click the **Grand Totals** button, and then click **On for Columns Only** to display the average occupancy rate for each month but not across all months. Anna wants to focus on occupancy rates for 2024.

▶ **6.** Click the **Filter button** in cell C4, **2024** on the submenu, and then click **OK** to display the occupancy rates for only 2024. See Figure 11–12.

Figure 11–12   Occupancy rates by month and motel for 2024

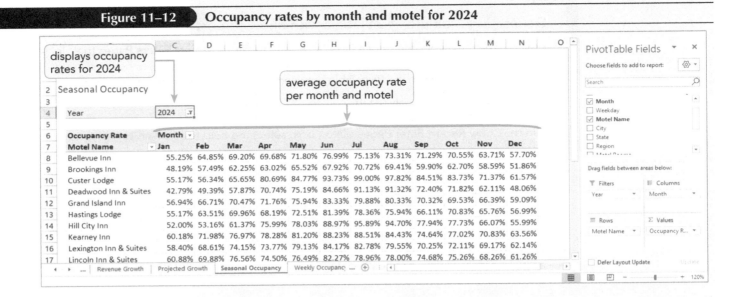

The size of this PivotTable is 12 columns by 24 rows, not including the grand total row. As a PivotTable grows, the sheer number of cells of data can be overwhelming. In those cases, you can reduce the PivotTable size by grouping common categories. For example, a PivotTable containing monthly sales data might be better understood if the months were grouped into quarters.

However, with the motel business, Anna is not really interested in quarterly reports as much as the comparison between the tourist season and the offseason. For motels in the Nebraska/South Dakota sales territory, tourist season lasts from May through September. Anna wants those months grouped together. The remaining months should be grouped together to constitute the motel's off season.

Reference

Grouping PivotTable Fields

- To manually group items within a PivotTable field, select individual items, and then on the PivotTable Analyze tab, in the Group group, click the Group Selection button, and then enter a name for the group in the Active Field box.
- To group a date field, select the field, and then on the PivotTable Analyze tab, in the Group group, click the Group Selection button, and then in the Grouping dialog box, specify starting and ending dates for the field and select the levels from Seconds up to Years in which the dates should be grouped.
- To group a numeric field, select the field, and then on the PivotTable Analyze tab, in the Group group, click the Group Selection button, and then in the Grouping dialog box, specify the numeric intervals on which the groups are based.

Manual Grouping

One way of creating a PivotTable group is through a **manual group** in which items within a field are combined to create a new group that appears as a new field within the PivotTable. You will use manual grouping to create a group of tourist season months and a group of offseason months.

To create a manual group:

▸ 1. Click cell **C7** containing the Jan label, hold down **SHIFT**, click cell **F7**, and then release SHIFT to select the range C7:F7.

▸ 2. Hold down **CTRL** and click cells **L7**, **M7**, and **N7**, and then release CTRL. The nonadjacent range C7:F7,L7:N7 is selected.

▸ 3. On the ribbon, click the **PivotTable Analyze** tab, and then in the Group group, click the **Group Selection** button. A new grouped field named Month2 is added to the PivotTable.

▸ 4. On the PivotTable Analyze tab, in the Active Field group, click the Active Field box, and then change the name from Month2 to **Season**.

▸ 5. Drag the **Month** field out of the Columns area. Only the Season field remains in the Columns area of the PivotTable.

Next, you will group the five remaining months, which make up the tourist season for the motels.

▸ 6. Click cell **D7**, hold down **SHIFT** and click cell **H7**, and then release SHIFT. The range D7:H7 is selected.

▸ 7. In the Group group, click the **Group Selection** button to group these months together. There are two group categories named Group1 and Group2.

▸ 8. Click cell **C7** and enter **Offseason** as the label for Group1, and then click cell **D7** and enter **Tourist Season** as the label for Group2. These categories now have more descriptive names.

▸ 9. Increase the width of column D to display the complete text of the field item label. See Figure 11–13.

Figure 11–13	Occupancy rates by season for 2024

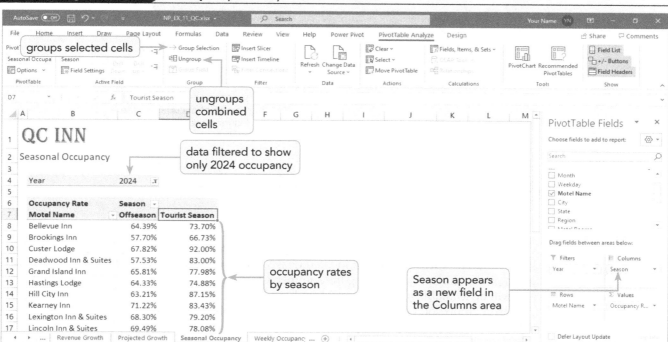

Not surprisingly, the occupancy rates during tourist season are higher than offseason. For example, the Bellevue Inn rents out on average 64.39% of its rooms each night during the offseason, a figure that rises to 73.70% during tourist season (row 8). Other motels show even greater improvement. The Deadwood Inn & Suites jumps from a 57.53% occupancy rate in the offseason to 83.00% during tourist season—an increase of more than 25% (row 11).

Anna wants a better view of the top-performing motels, so you will sort the PivotTable in descending order of occupancy rate during the tourist season.

To sort in descending order of the tourist season occupancy:

▶ **1.** Click the **Filter button** in cell B7 next to the Motel Name label.

▶ **2.** Click **More Sort Options** from the menu. The Sort (Motel Name) dialog box opens.

▶ **3.** Click the **Descending (Z to A) by** option button, and then select **Occupancy Rate** from the accompanying box.

▶ **4.** Click the **More Options** button. The More Sort Options (Motel Name) dialog box opens.

▶ **5.** Click the **Values in selected column** option button, press **TAB**, and then click cell **D8**.

▶ **6.** Click **OK** in each dialog box to return to the workbook. See Figure 11–14.

Figure 11–14   Sorted occupancy rates

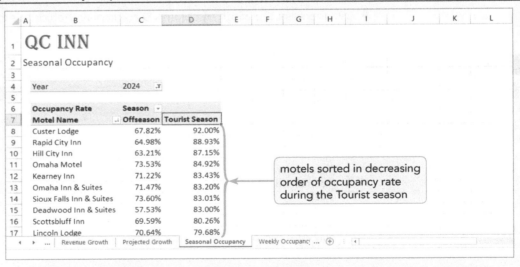

	Motel Name	Offseason	Tourist Season
8	Custer Lodge	67.82%	92.00%
9	Rapid City Inn	64.98%	88.93%
10	Hill City Inn	63.21%	87.15%
11	Omaha Motel	73.53%	84.92%
12	Kearney Inn	71.22%	83.43%
13	Omaha Inn & Suites	71.47%	83.20%
14	Sioux Falls Inn & Suites	73.60%	83.01%
15	Deadwood Inn & Suites	57.53%	83.00%
16	Scottsbluff Inn	69.59%	80.26%
17	Lincoln Lodge	70.64%	79.68%

motels sorted in decreasing order of occupancy rate during the Tourist season

The busiest motel in the tourist season is Custer Lodge with an average daily occupancy rate during tourist season of 92%. In fact, the top three motels—Custer Lodge, Rapid City Inn, and Hill City Inn—are all located near Mount Rushmore and the Black Hills, which are prime tourism spots during the summer. Once you have manually created a group, it will be available to other PivotTables based on the same data source. For example, the Season group you created can be used again with other PivotTables in this workbook.

Grouping by Dates

Even within a season, Anna knows that some weeks are busier than others. She wants you to break down the data by date. You'll begin creating the PivotTable to do that now.

To create a PivotTable of occupancy rate vs. date:

▶ **1.** Go to the **Weekly Occupancy** worksheet.

▶ **2.** Drag the **Occupancy** field to the Values area and drag the **Motel Name** field to the Filters area.

▶ **3.** Change the summary function for the Occupancy field from calculating the sum to calculating the average.

▶ **4.** Change the number format to display the averages as a percentage to two decimal places, and then change the Value field name to **Occupancy Rate**. The overall occupancy rate for all the motels is 70.09%.

▶ **5.** Drag the **Date** field to the Rows area. Excel creates an outline of nested fields, grouping the dates by year, quarter, and month. You want to view the nested fields.

▶ **6.** Click the **Design** tab. In the Layout group, click the **Report Layout** button, and then click **Show in Tabular Form**. Three columns labeled Years, Quarters, and Date appear.

▶ **7.** Click the **expand outline** button ⊞ in cell B8 to expand the 2024 Year field into its subgroups consisting of quarters.

▶ **8.** Click the **expand outline** button ⊞ in cell C8 to expand the Qtr1 field into its subgroups consisting of the months of Jan through Mar. See Figure 11–15.

Figure 11–15   Occupancy rates by year, quarters, and months

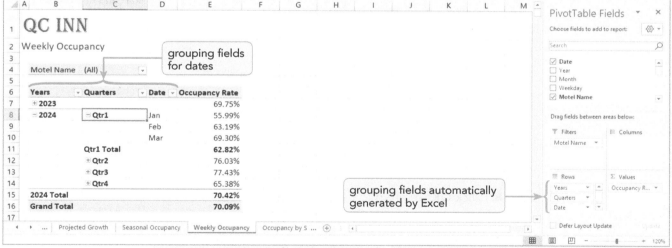

Tip

To remove automatic date groups, click any date field in the grouping and then click the Ungroup button in the Group group on the PivotTable Analyze tab.

When Excel encounters a date field that spans more than one year, it automatically groups the date values into quarters, months, and years. The grouping ends at the month level, so under the current grouping there is no way to view individual dates unless you regroup the data.

To group the dates in a different way, you can modify the group selection using the Grouping dialog box. You can regroup the dates to span any time interval from years down to seconds. You will use the Grouping dialog box to group the dates to show weekly occupancy rates during the summer of 2024 between Memorial Day and Labor Day.

To group the occupancy data by weeks:

▶ **1.** Click cell **B8** to select it.

▶ **2.** On the ribbon, click the **PivotTable Analyze** tab, and in the Group group, click the **Group Selection** button. The Grouping dialog box opens.

   Currently, the dialog box covers dates starting with 1/1/2023 through 1/1/2025. The Months, Quarters, and Years options are selected to group the date values from months, quarters, and years.

▶ **3.** In the Starting at input box, change the starting date to **5/27/2024**, which is Memorial Day in 2024.

▶ **4.** Press **TAB** twice, and change the ending date to **9/2/2024**, which is Labor Day in 2024.

▶ **5.** In the By box, click **Days** to select it and add it as a date grouping level.

▶ **6.** In the By box, click **Months**, **Quarters**, and **Years** to deselect and remove them as grouping levels.

▶ **7.** In the Number of days box, enter **7** so that you group the Date by 7-day weeks. See Figure 11–16.

Figure 11–16   **Grouping dialog box**

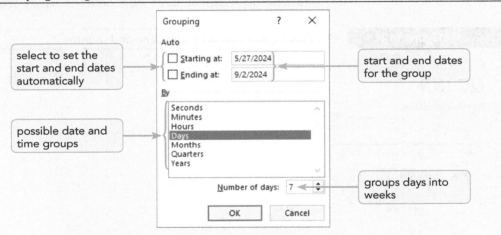

▶ **8.** Click **OK** to return to the workbook.

The occupancy rates are grouped into weeks from 5/27/2024 through 9/2/2024. Dates before 5/27/2024 or after 9/2/2024 constitute their own groups. You'll use a Date filter now to filter out those date ranges, focusing the PivotTable on the weeks during the summer of 2024. Then you'll view the weekly occupancy rates for select motels.

To apply a Date filter for dates:

▶ **1.** Click the **Filter button** in cell B6.

▶ **2.** On the Filter menu, click **Date Filters** to display a list of date filters that can be applied to the field.

▶ **3.** Click **Between**. The Date Filter (Date) dialog box opens.

▶ **4.** Enter **5/27/2024** in the first calendar box and then enter **9/2/2024** in the second calendar box. See Figure 11–17.

Figure 11–17   Date Filter dialog box

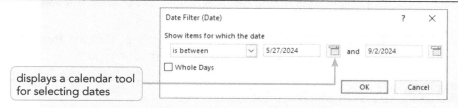

displays a calendar tool for selecting dates

> **5.** Click **OK** to return to the workbook.

> **6.** Click the **Filter button** in cell C4, click **Omaha Inn & Suites**, and then click **OK** to view the average weekly occupancy rate for that motel. See Figure 11–18.

Figure 11–18   Omaha Inn & Suites weekly occupancy rates

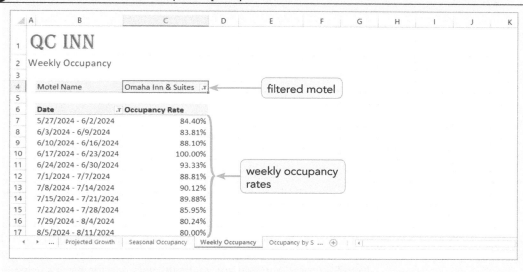

The weekly average occupancy rate for Omaha Inn & Suites consistently stays between 80% and 90%, except for the week of 6/17/2024 to 6/23/2024 during which the motel was filled. Upon further investigation, Anna learns that during that week Omaha was hosting the annual College World Series, which brought a lot of college baseball fans into the area, occupying many of the motels in Omaha.

Using the PivotTable, Anna can study the weekly occupancy rates for the other 23 motels in the Nebraska/South Dakota sales territory, learning when those motels were at their most busy during the summer of 2024.

Grouping by Numeric Fields

Anna wants to explore whether occupancy rates are related to the size of the motel. Are larger motels less likely to have high occupancy rates or are they large because they attract more customers and thus rarely have vacancies? To answer that question, you will create another PivotTable comparing average occupancy to motel size, where size is measured by the number motel rooms.

To apply a Label filter for dates:

> **1.** Go to the **Occupancy by Size** worksheet.

> **2.** Drag the **Occupancy** field to the Values area, and then drag the **Motel Rooms** field to the Rows area.

3. Change the Sum of Occupancy to display the average occupancy rate as percentages to two decimal places and change the Value field name to **Occupancy Rate**.

4. Click the **Design** tab. In the Layout group, click the **Report Layout** button, and then click **Show in Tabular Form**. See Figure 11–19.

Figure 11–19 Occupancy by motel size

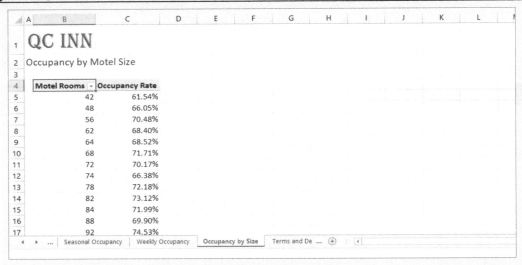

The PivotTable shows occupancy rates for motels with 42 rooms up to 124 rooms. With so many possible sizes, it's difficult to get a clear picture of the relationship between size and occupancy. To create a simpler PivotTable, you can group the values of the Motel Rooms field with each group category spanning an interval of motel sizes.

Anna wants you to list the motels in 20-room intervals, starting with motels containing 40 to 59 rooms. You will automatically generate the groups using the Grouping dialog box.

To group by number:

1. Click cell **B4** containing the Motel Rooms label to select it.

2. Click the **PivotTable Analyze** tab, and then in the Group group, click the **Group Field** button. The Grouping dialog box opens.

3. In the Starting at input box, enter the value **40**.

4. Press **TAB** three times, and then in the By input box, enter **20** as the group size. See Figure 11–20.

Figure 11–20 Grouping dialog box

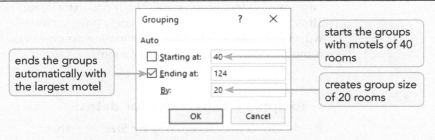

5. Click **OK** to return to the workbook. See Figure 11–21.

Figure 11–21	Motels grouped by size

Grouping motel rooms in groups of 20 gives a clearer picture of the relationship between motel size and occupancy. The lowest occupancy rates occur for the smallest and largest hotels with rates below 70%, and the mid-sized motels with 80 to 119 rooms typically fill about 73% of their rooms. It appears the motels that are most difficult to fill are either small (and presumably found in smaller markets) or large (and might be in more competitive markets).

The groups you create either manually or through the Grouping dialog box are retained with the PivotTable and available to all future PivotTables that share the same data source. Note that groups created through manual selection are stored as new fields, whereas groups created automatically or through the Grouping dialog box replace the PivotTable field that they group. That means that once you group the Date field by weeks, all future uses of the Date field will be grouped in that fashion.

You've finished your initial analysis of the motel data for the QC Inn chain, learning what factors have contributed to successful motels as well as when and where those motels will be the busiest. In the next session, you'll use PivotTables to perform other calculations on this motel data.

Review

Session 11.1 Quick Check

1. How does the Compact layout differ from the Tabular layout?
2. What are two ways of manually sorting a PivotTable field?
3. When sorting a PivotTable by values in a field, how are the field values sorted by default?
4. When would you use a Label filter in a PivotTable?
5. When would you use a Value filter in a PivotTable?
6. How do you allow a PivotTable field to include both a Date filter and a Value filter?
7. When a PivotTable field is manually grouped, how does Excel treat the grouped items?
8. What does Excel do to date fields that are added to a PivotTable?

Session 11.2 Visual Overview:

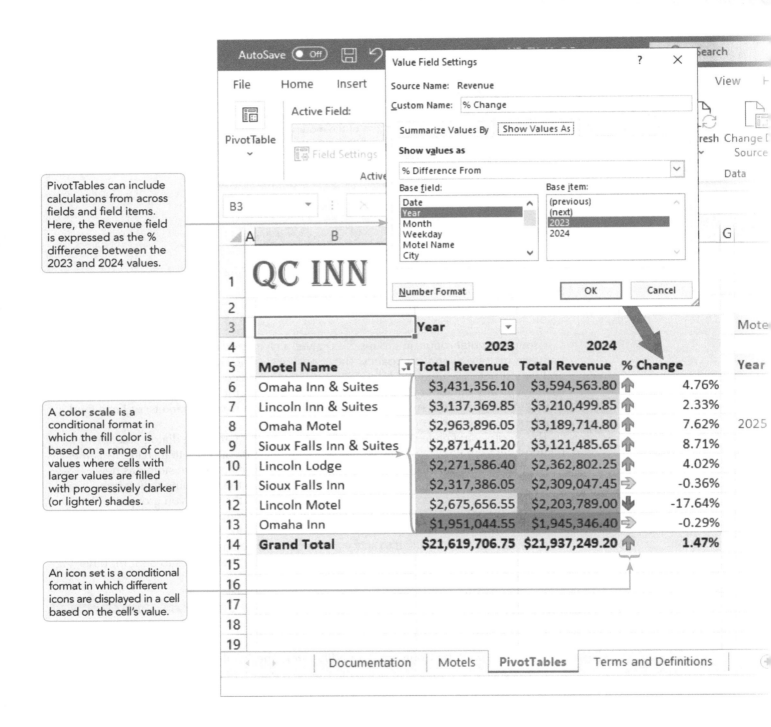

PivotTables can include calculations from across fields and field items. Here, the Revenue field is expressed as the % difference between the 2023 and 2024 values.

A color scale is a conditional format in which the fill color is based on a range of cell values where cells with larger values are filled with progressively darker (or lighter) shades.

An icon set is a conditional format in which different icons are displayed in a cell based on the cell's value.

Conditional Formats and Calculations

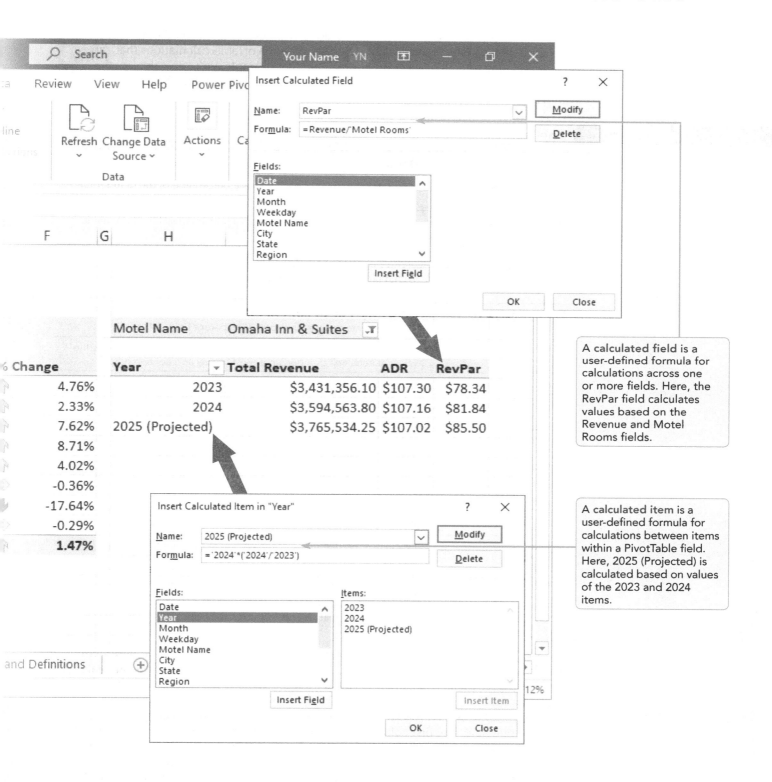

A calculated field is a user-defined formula for calculations across one or more fields. Here, the RevPar field calculates values based on the Revenue and Motel Rooms fields.

A calculated item is a user-defined formula for calculations between items within a PivotTable field. Here, 2025 (Projected) is calculated based on values of the 2023 and 2024 items.

Insert Calculated Field

Name: RevPar

Formula: =Revenue/`Motel Rooms`

Fields:
- Date
- Year
- Month
- Weekday
- Motel Name
- City
- State
- Region

Motel Name   Omaha Inn & Suites

Year	Total Revenue	ADR	RevPar
2023	$3,431,356.10	$107.30	$78.34
2024	$3,594,563.80	$107.16	$81.84
2025 (Projected)	$3,765,534.25	$107.02	$85.50

Insert Calculated Item in "Year"

Name: 2025 (Projected)

Formula: =`2024`*(`2024`/`2023`)

Fields:
- Date
- Year
- Month
- Weekday
- Motel Name
- City
- State
- Region

Items:
- 2023
- 2024
- 2025 (Projected)

% Change
- 4.76%
- 2.33%
- 7.62%
- 8.71%
- 4.02%
- -0.36%
- -17.64%
- -0.29%
- **1.47%**

Calculations with PivotTables

PivotTables support the following statistical functions to summarize data within each PivotTable field: Sum, Count, Average, Max, Min, Product, CountNumbers, StdDev, StdDevP, Var, and Varp. Each calculation is done without reference to other fields or items in the PivotTable. Figure 11–22 describes other PivotTable calculations that can be used to compare fields or items within a field. For example, you can calculate the difference between one field and another or calculate a running total of the items within a field.

Figure 11–22 **PivotTable calculations**

Calculation	Description
% of Grand Total	Calculates the value of each cell as a percentage of the grand total across all cells
% of Column Total	Calculates the value of each cell as a percentage of the total of its column
% of Row Total	Calculates the value of each cell as a percentage of the total of its row
% of Parent Row Total	With multiple fields in the Rows area, calculates the value of each cell as a percentage of the total of its parent field
% of Parent Column Total	With multiple fields in the Columns area, calculates the value of each cell as a percentage of the total of its parent field
% of Parent Total	With multiple fields in the Rows and/or Columns area, calculates the value of each cell as a percentage of its row and column parent
Running Total In	Calculates a running total within the cell's row or column
% Running Total In	Calculates a running total as a percentage within the cell's row or column
Rank Smallest to Largest	Calculates the rank of the cell within the cell's row or column with the smallest cell given a rank of "1"
Rank Largest to Smallest	Calculates the rank of the cell within the cell's row or column with the largest cell given a rank of "1"
% of	Calculates the percent of the cell value relative to another item in the PivotTable
Difference from	Calculates the difference of the cell value from another item in the PivotTable
% Difference From	Calculates the percent difference of the cell value from another item in the PivotTable
Index	Calculates the relative importance of the cell within the PivotTable

To apply these calculations, you will often have to identify a **base field** or **base item**, which is a field or item used as the basis for comparison. For example, if you calculate monthly revenue totals relative to the January total, January is the base item for the calculation.

Figure 11–23 shows a PivotTable in which different calculations are applied to the same Revenue field. The first column shows the rank of the total revenue for each motel from the largest to smallest within each region. The second column calculates the sum of the revenue for each motel. And, the third column calculates each motel's revenue as a percentage of its region and each region as a percentage of the grand total. This table provides a clear picture of how revenue totals are related across motels and regions.

Figure 11–23   Calculated ranks and percentage of parent row totals

Region	Motel Name	Rank Largest to Smallest	Sum	% of Parent Row Total
⊟ Central	Grand Island Inn	2	$903,704.57	33.35%
	Kearney Inn	1	$931,528.45	34.38%
	Lexington Inn & Suites	3	$874,507.60	32.27%
Central Total			**$2,709,740.62**	**16.27%**
⊟ Eastern	Bellevue Inn	6	$791,470.90	9.34%
	Brookings Inn	7	$603,661.10	7.12%
	Lincoln Inn & Suites	3	$1,545,787.85	18.24%
	Omaha Inn	5	$980,493.10	11.57%
	Omaha Inn & Suites	1	$1,814,091.40	21.41%
	Sioux Falls Inn	4	$1,175,380.70	13.87%
	Sioux Falls Inn & Suites	2	$1,562,503.15	18.44%
Eastern Total			**$8,473,388.20**	**50.88%**
⊟ Western	Deadwood Inn & Suites	3	$1,072,043.35	19.59%
	Hill City Inn	2	$1,426,482.70	26.07%
	Rapid City Inn	1	$2,023,142.29	36.98%
	Scottsbluff Inn	4	$949,639.80	17.36%
Western Total			**$5,471,308.14**	**32.85%**
Grand Total			**$16,654,436.96**	**100.00%**

subtotals show the percent of each region's total revenue compared to the grand total

revenue rank within each region

total revenue by motel

percent of total revenue within or across regions

Figure 11–24 shows a PivotTable with 2024 monthly revenue totals for the Rapid City Inn. The columns show the total revenue per month, a running total of monthly revenue, the difference in revenue from one month and the next, and the monthly revenue as a percentage of June's total revenue.

Figure 11–24   Monthly revenue calculations

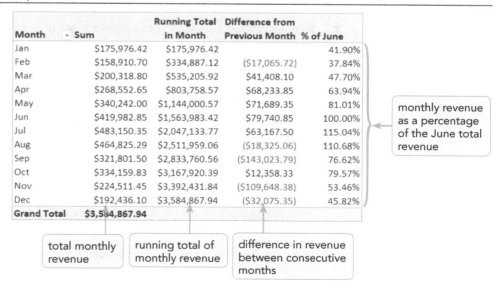

Month	Sum	Running Total in Month	Difference from Previous Month	% of June
Jan	$175,976.42	$175,976.42		41.90%
Feb	$158,910.70	$334,887.12	($17,065.72)	37.84%
Mar	$200,318.80	$535,205.92	$41,408.10	47.70%
Apr	$268,552.65	$803,758.57	$68,233.85	63.94%
May	$340,242.00	$1,144,000.57	$71,689.35	81.01%
Jun	$419,982.85	$1,563,983.42	$79,740.85	100.00%
Jul	$483,150.35	$2,047,133.77	$63,167.50	115.04%
Aug	$464,825.29	$2,511,959.06	($18,325.06)	110.68%
Sep	$321,801.50	$2,833,760.56	($143,023.79)	76.62%
Oct	$334,159.83	$3,167,920.39	$12,358.33	79.57%
Nov	$224,511.45	$3,392,431.84	($109,648.38)	53.46%
Dec	$192,436.10	$3,584,867.94	($32,075.35)	45.82%
Grand Total	**$3,584,867.94**			

monthly revenue as a percentage of the June total revenue

total monthly revenue

running total of monthly revenue

difference in revenue between consecutive months

Each column provides a different insight into the motel's monthly revenue. The running total shows how quickly revenue is generated through the year and can aid in developing the motel's budget. The column showing the differences from one month to the next is useful for planning future expenditures. A hotel manager can quickly see that expenses will have to be cut in September to make up for a $143,000 drop in revenue that month.

Reference

Calculating Values for a PivotTable Field

- Open the Value Field Settings dialog box for the field and click the Show Values As tab.
- To show ranks of items within a field, choose Rank Smallest to Largest or Rank Largest to Smallest.
- To calculate a running total of items within a field, choose Running Total In or % Running Total In.
- To calculate the change from one field item to another, choose Difference From or % Difference From.
- To calculate percentages of PivotTable totals, choose % of Column Total, % of Row Total, or % of Grand Total.
- To calculate percentages of a parent item in the table, choose % Of, % of Parent Column Total, % of Parent Row Total, or % Parent Total.
- Click OK.

Calculating Ranks

In the previous session, you created a PivotTable showing weekly occupancy during the summer of 2024. You will supplement this table now by ranking those weeks in order from most busy to least busy.

To rank items within a field:

1. If you took a break after the previous session, make sure the NP_EX_11_QC workbook is open.

2. Go to the **Weekly Occupancy** worksheet.

3. Drag the **Occupancy** field into the Values area box directly below the Occupancy Rate value.

4. Click cell **D6** to select it, click the **PivotTable Analyze** tab on the ribbon, and then in the Active Field group, click the **Field Settings** button. The Value Field Settings dialog box opens.

5. Click the **Show Values As** tab.

6. In the Show values as box, select **Rank Largest to Smallest** and then verify that **Date** is selected as the Base field because all ranks are determined relative to the occupancy rates within the Date field.

7. In the Custom name box, enter **Rank** as the name. See Figure 11–25.

Figure 11–25 **Ranks for the occupancy field calculation**

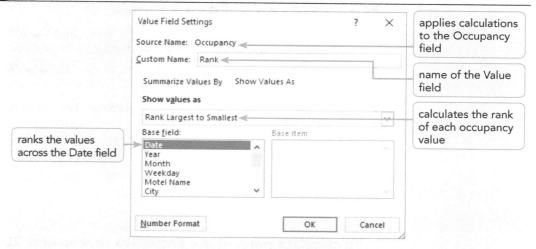

8. Click **OK**. A rank of each week is added to the PivotTable. See Figure 11–26.

Figure 11–26 **Ranks of the weekly occupancy rates**

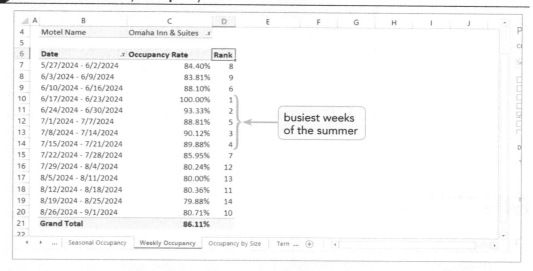

Adding the ranks makes it more evident that the highest occupancy occurs during the middle of the summer starting with the week of 6/17/2024 and going through the end of the week of 7/21/2024.

Calculating Percent Differences

Anna has collected two years of data to identify which motels are increasing their business and which are losing customers. You will create a PivotTable that compares annual revenue by year and motel and display the percentage growth of each motel's revenue from 2023 to 2024. First, you'll create the PivotTable of Total Revenue vs. Motel Name.

To create the Total Revenue vs. Motel Name PivotTable:

▸ **1.** Go to the **Revenue Growth** worksheet.

▸ **2.** Drag the **Year** field into the Columns area, drag the **Motel Name** into the Rows area, and drag the **Revenue** field into the Values area.

▸ **3.** Change Value field name "Sum of Revenue" to **Total Revenue** and display the revenue totals as currency.

▸ **4.** Change the PivotTable layout to a Tabular layout and turn on grand totals for the columns only.

Next, you will add a new column displaying the percentage growth in revenue for each motel.

To calculate percentage growth in revenue for 2024:

▸ **1.** Drag the **Revenue** field into the Values area directly below the Total Revenue value field. The new value field as "Sum of Revenue" is added to the PivotTable.

▸ **2.** Open the Value Field Settings dialog box for the "Sum of Revenue" value field.

▸ **3.** Change name from Sum of Revenue to **% Change**.

▸ **4.** Click the **Show Values As** tab.

▸ **5.** In the Show Values as box, click **% Difference From**.

▸ **6.** In the Base field box, click **Year** because you want to calculate percentage differences across years.

▸ **7.** In the Base item box, click **2023**, if necessary, to base all percentages relative to the 2023 revenue totals. See Figure 11–27.

Figure 11–27   Percent differences calculations

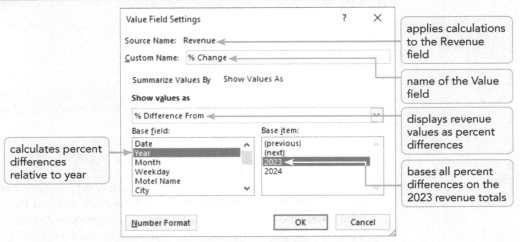

Tip

A hidden column is not removed from the worksheet, but instead is given a width of 0 pixels, effectively hiding it from the user.

8. Click **OK** to calculate the percent change from 2023 revenues to 2024. Two new columns appear on the PivotTable. Column F shows the percent change in revenue from 2023 to 2024 for each motel. Column D does the same calculation, but the column is blank because there is no percent change in 2023 revenue totals from themselves. To avoid confusing the reader, you will hide this column.

9. Right-click the **column D** heading, and then click **Hide** on the shortcut menu. Column D is hidden in the workbook. See Figure 11–28.

Figure 11–28   Monthly revenue calculations

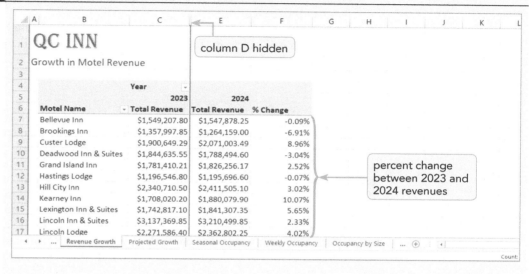

Overall, the motels in the QC Inn chain saw a revenue increase of 1.72% (cell F31), but this result was not uniform across motels. The revenue of the Lincoln Motel decreased by 17.64% (cell F18), while the annual revenue of Custer Lodge increased by 8.96% (cell F9). With so many numbers and calculations, the PivotTable can be difficult to read. You can correct that problem by adding a conditional format.

Displaying PivotTables with Conditional Formats

PivotTables do a great job of summarizing large amounts of data, but sometimes it can be overwhelming to wade through all those numbers. One way of making PivotTables more accessible is with a conditional format that highlights key values, painting a visual picture of the data. You can apply a conditional format to the following parts of a PivotTable:

- **Selected Cells.** The conditional format is applied directly to cells selected from the PivotTable.
- **All Cells Showing a Field Value.** The conditional format is associated with a specific field, wherever that field is located within the PivotTable.
- **All Cells Showing Multiple Field Values.** The conditional format is applied to cells where multiple fields intersect, such as the cells representing revenue totals from motels in each month.

The conditional format is applied within a PivotTable structure. If you alter the table's layout, the conditional format adapts to the new layout, following the new location of the field values wherever they end up.

You will explore two conditional formats that are well suited to PivotTables: icon sets and color scales.

Reference

Creating Icon Sets and Color Scales

- To display a conditional format with icon sets or color scales, select the data range or PivotTable, and then on the Home tab, in the Styles group, click the Conditional Formatting button.
- Click New Rule on the Conditional Formatting menu.
- For PivotTables, select which part of the PivotTable the rule should be applied to.
- For icon sets, select Icon Sets in the Format Style box and specify the value or percent ranges for each icon.
- For color scales, select 2-Color Scale or 3-Color Scale in the Format Style box and specify the color scale for the values in the data range or PivotTable field.
- Click OK.

Creating an Icon Set

An icon set is a conditional format in which different icons are displayed in a cell based on the cell's value. Icon sets are useful for highlighting extreme values or trends in your data.

Anna thinks the PivotTable you just created would benefit from icon sets that show an up arrow if a motel's revenue increased between 2023 and 2024, a down arrow for declining revenue, and a sideways arrow if the revenue stayed mostly the same. Anna wants the up arrow displayed when the revenue increases by more than 1% and the down arrow displayed when the revenue decreases by 1%. The other values should display the sideways arrow. For percentage values, you must enter decimals numbers in the conditional format dialog box. You will create this conditional format now.

To create the icon set conditional format:

1. Click cell **F7** to select a cell in the % Change column.

2. On the ribbon, click the **Home** tab. In the Styles group, click the **Conditional Formatting** button, and then click **New Rule**. The New Formatting Rule dialog box opens.

3. Click the **All cells showing "% Change" values** option button. This applies the conditional format to every cell in the % Change column, including the cell displaying the grand total across all motels.

4. In the Edit the Rule Description section, click the **Format Style arrow**, and then click **Icon Sets**.

> **Tip**
>
> To change or remove an icon in an icon set click the drop-down list arrow next to the icon image.

5. Click the **Icon Style arrow**, and then click the three-arrow icon set with the red arrow pointing down, the yellow arrow pointing sideways, and a green arrow pointing up.

6. Click the upper **Type** box, select **Number** and then enter **0.01** in the Value box. The up arrow will appear for motels that gained more than 1% in revenue.

7. Click the lower **Type** box, select **Number**, and then enter **–0.01**. The down arrow will appear for motels that lost more than 1% in revenue. See Figure 11–29.

Figure 11–29   New Formatting Rule dialog box

applies only to selected cells in the PivotTable

applies to all cells with a motel name and a year

applies to all cells in the % Change column

percentages entered as decimals

appears when % change is ≥1%

appears when % change is between 1% and −1%

appears when % change is < −1%

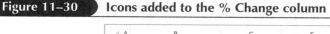

8. Click **OK** to apply the icons to all the values in the % Change column. See Figure 11–30.

Figure 11–30   Icons added to the % Change column

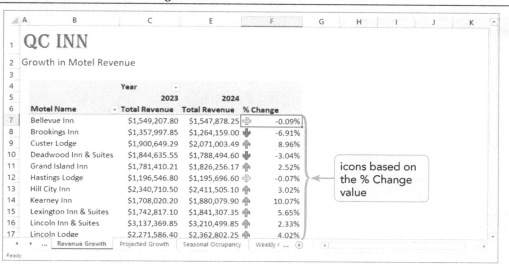

Trouble? If your icons are different, you probably mistyped something in the Conditional Formatting Rules Manager. Click the Conditional Formatting button, click Modify Rules, select the conditional format for the Icon Set, click Edit Rule, check the settings in your dialog box against those shown in Figure 11–29, correct any mistakes, and then click OK.

The arrow icons make it much easier to identify motels whose revenue increased significantly and those that saw a significant drop in revenue. Green up arrows figure prominently throughout the worksheet so it is quickly apparent that most motels in the QC Inn chain have shown a significant increase in revenue over the previous year.

Working with Color Scales

A color scale is a conditional format in which the fill color is based on a range of cell values where cells with larger values are filled with progressively darker (or lighter) shades. The varying shades in the color scale quickly identify the extreme values of the PivotTable field and highlight important trends in the data.

Anna wants the PivotTable to show the seasonal occupancy rates with a color scale that goes from red (low occupancy) through yellow and up to green (high occupancy). As with icon sets, you can apply the color scale to selected cells or cells based on their field values.

To apply a color scale to seasonal occupancy rates:

▶ **1.** Go to the **Seasonal Occupancy** worksheet and click cell **D8** to select it.

▶ **2.** On the Home tab, in the Styles group, click the **Conditional Formatting** button, and then click **New Rule**. The New Formatting Rule dialog box opens.

▶ **3.** Click the **All cells showing 'Occupancy Rate' values for 'Motel Name' and 'Season'** to apply the conditional format to cells at the intersection of the Motel Name and Season field values.

▶ **4.** In the Format Style box, click **3-Color Scale** to choose a color gradient going from red up to green. See Figure 11–31.

Figure 11–31 **New formatting rule for a color scale**

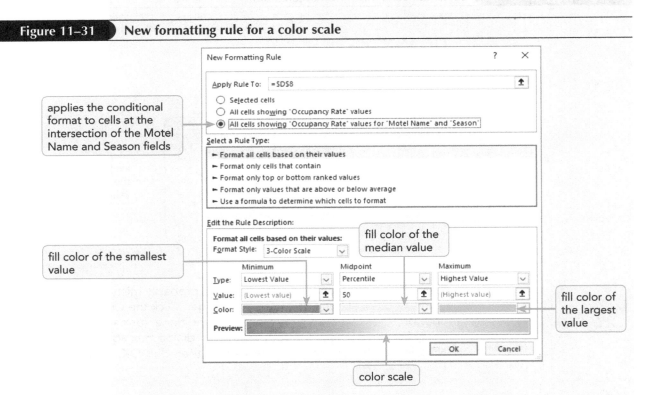

applies the conditional format to cells at the intersection of the Motel Name and Season fields

fill color of the smallest value

fill color of the median value

fill color of the largest value

color scale

▶ **5.** Click **OK**. A color scale is added to all the seasonal occupancy rates in the PivotTable. See Figure 11–32.

Figure 11–32   Color scales applied to the seasonal occupancy rates

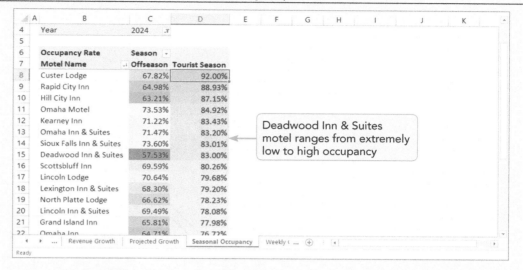

The color scale highlights trends in the data that might have gone unnoticed. Of interest to Anna is the performance of the Deadwood Inn & Suites motel, which goes from an extremely low occupancy rate during the offseason to a very high rate during tourist season. Anna might use this information to suggest to the motel manager ways that the Deadwood Inn & Suites could improve its profile in the offseason to take advantage of a potentially larger customer base.

Exploring the PivotTable Cache

The information used to create a PivotTable is stored within a data structure called the **PivotTable cache**. The cache contains an exact copy of the PivotTable's data source optimized for size and speed, which makes PivotTables very responsive to changes in content and layout. When you modify a PivotTable layout, Excel retrieves the data from the cache, not the original data source. In fact, if the data has been finalized and will not change, you could even delete the data source and work entirely from the information stored in the cache. (*Be sure you no longer need the data source before doing that!*) The existence of the cache is also why you must refresh your PivotTables whenever the data changes. Refreshing the PivotTable regenerates the cache so that it reflects the most recent version of the data source.

Sharing a Cache Between PivotTables

The price of speed and responsiveness is an increased file size because the same data is duplicated in both the workbook and the cache. Excel mitigates this problem by having all PivotTables operate from the same cache. This means that all PivotTables share the same fields and groups because that information is part of the cache. See Figure 11–33.

Figure 11–33	PivotTable cache shared by multiple PivotTables

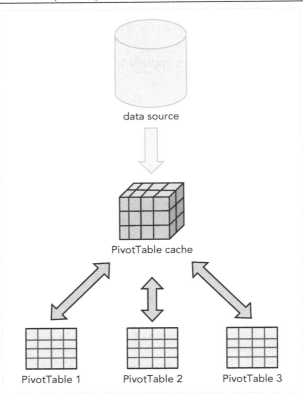

A consequence of sharing the same cache is that anything you do in one PivotTable becomes part of the cache and is instantly applied to the other PivotTables. For example, if you group the Date field by weeks in one table, the Date field will be grouped by weeks for every other PivotTable. You can't show weekly revenue figures in one PivotTable and then monthly revenue totals in a different PivotTable. If you regroup the dates in the second PivotTable to show monthly totals, the first table will be automatically regrouped to match.

One solution to this problem is to create separate caches for different PivotTables so that you can change the structure and contents of one PivotTable without affecting the others. Both caches connect to the same data source, so that the impact of refreshing the data source will still be reflected in both caches but changing one cache has no impact on the other. A separate cache will increase the size of your workbook file, but it will give you more flexibility in designing your PivotTables. See Figure 11–34.

Figure 11–34	Multiple PivotTable caches

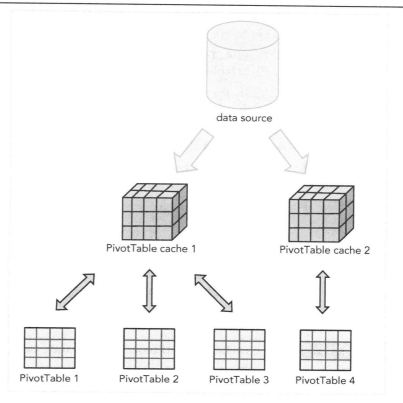

Creating a New Cache

To create a separate cache, you will use a tool that was available in older versions of Excel. Prior to Excel 2016, PivotTables were created using a tool called the **PivotTable Wizard**. Part of the PivotTable Wizard in versions of Excel 2007 and earlier was an option to create a PivotTable from an existing cache or to create a new cache. The PivotTable Wizard is still available, though not directly accessible from the ribbon.

Reference

Creating a PivotTable from a New Cache

- Press ALT+D and then press P to open the PivotTable Wizard.
- Specify the type of data and the type of report to create in Step 1 of the wizard.
- Specify the data source in Step 2 of the wizard.
- Click No to create the report using a new PivotTable cache.
- Specify the location of the PivotTable report in Step 3 of the wizard.
- Click Finish to insert the PivotTable report.

Anna wants you to create a new PivotTable that will project future performance of the motels in the QC Inn chain. Because the structure of this PivotTable will be different from the PivotTables you've already created, you will use a separate cache for it. You'll create this PivotTable using the PivotTable Wizard.

To create a PivotTable from a new cache:

▶ 1. Go to the **Projected Growth** worksheet and click cell **B6** to select it, if necessary.

▶ 2. Press **ALT+D** and then press **P** to launch the PivotTable Wizard. The PivotTable and PivotChart Wizard dialog box opens to the Step 1 of 3.

▶ 3. Verify that the **Microsoft Excel list or database** option button is selected as the data source and the **PivotTable** option button is selected as the type of report.

▶ 4. Click **Next**. The second step dialog box appears.

▶ 5. In the Range box, type **Motels** (the name assigned to the Excel table containing the motel data) as the data source of the PivotTable, and then click **Next**.

▶ 6. Click **No** when Excel prompts you to use an existing cache for the new PivotTable. This puts the new PivotTable you are creating in its own, separate cache. The Step 3 dialog box appears.

> You must click No or else Excel will not base the new PivotTable on its own separate cache.

▶ 7. Verify that the **Existing worksheet** option button is selected and the expression **=$B$6** appears in the range box.

▶ 8. Click **Finish** to create the new PivotTable report.

▶ 9. Change the name of the PivotTable to **Projected Growth**. See Figure 11–35.

| Figure 11–35 | New PivotTable report based on a separate cache |

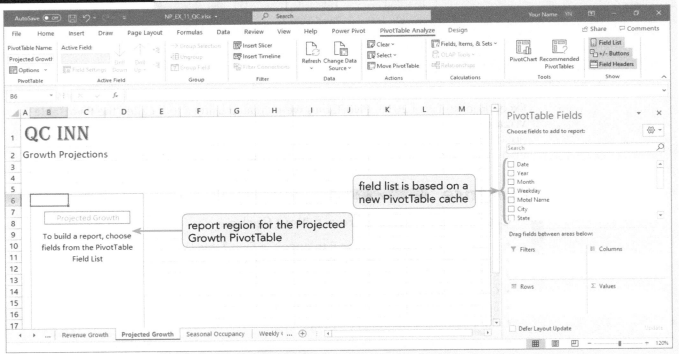

With the Projected Growth PivotTable generated from a new cache, you are ready to create a PivotTable projecting future revenue. That table will involve using calculated items and calculated fields.

Insight

Counting Your Caches

In a workbook with multiple PivotTables and multiple caches, you might want to know exactly how many caches are in use. Excel does not provide a direct way to get that information, but you can view it using the Excel programming language, Visual Basic for Applications (VBA). To view the total number of caches in your workbook at any given time, do the following:

1. Press ALT+F11 to open the Visual Basic Editor window.
2. Press CTRL+G to open a window in which you can immediately enter VBA commands.
3. Type `?ActiveWorkbook.PivotCaches.Count` and press ENTER. Excel returns a count of caches in the workbook.
4. Press ALT+Q to close the Visual Basic editor and return to the workbook.

Each PivotTable cache is given an index number. The first PivotTable cache is given an index of 1, the second an index of 2, and so forth. To identify the index number of the cache used for a specific PivotTable, select any cell in the PivotTable and then press ALT+F11, press CTRL+G, and enter the command `?ActiveCell.PivotTable.CacheIndex`. Excel will return the index number of the cache. Press ALT+Q to close the editor and return to your PivotTable.

Working with Calculated Items and Calculated Fields

PivotTables are not limited to the list of calculations supplied by Excel. You can enter your own formulas to create calculated items and calculated fields. First, you'll explore how to create a calculated item.

Creating a Calculated Item

A **calculated item** is a user-defined formula for calculations between items within a PivotTable field. For example, within the Motel Name field, you could create a calculated item that calculates the difference between the revenue of one group of motels and another. A calculated item appears as a new item within the field and can be moved, sorted, and filtered just like any other items. However, because it's a calculated item, any changes to the data are automatically reflected in its value.

Calculated items are part of the PivotTable cache. This means that a calculated item in one PivotTable is available to all PivotTables using the same cache. Be aware that calculated items cannot be shared between PivotTables that use different caches.

Reference

Creating a Calculated Item or Calculated Field

- Select any cell in a PivotTable field.
- On the PivotTable Analyze tab, in the Calculations group, click the Fields, Items, & Sets button.
- Click Calculated Item or click Calculated Field.
- Enter a name for the calculated item or field.
- In the Formula box, for a calculated item enter a formula that performs calculations on items within a field or for a calculated field, enter a formula that performs calculations between fields in the PivotTable's data source.
- Click OK.

You will create a PivotTable now that shows the revenue generated for each year and motel. Then, you will create a calculated item that projects next year's values.

To create a PivotTable of 2023 and 2024 performance:

▶ **1.** With the Projected Growth PivotTable still selected, drag the **Motel Name** field to the Filters area box, drag the **Year** field to the Rows area box, and then drag the **Revenue** field to the Values area box.

▶ **2.** Change Value field name from "Sum of Revenue" to **Total Revenue** and display the revenue totals as currency.

▶ **3.** Change the PivotTable layout to a Tabular layout and remove all grand totals from the table. See Figure 11–36.

| Figure 11–36 | Revenue by Year and Motel Name |

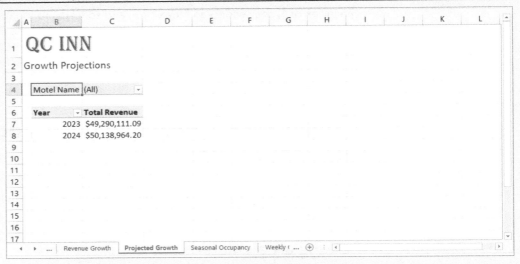

To project next year's revenue based on the 2023 and 2024 values, Anna assumes that revenues will increase at the same rate they increased between 2023 and 2024. The formula to calculate the 2025 revenue is:

$$2025\ revenue = (2024\ revenue) \times \frac{2024\ revenue}{2023\ revenue}$$

You'll create a calculated item based on this formula and add it to the PivotTable.

To create a calculated item that calculates the 2025 revenue:

▶ **1.** Click cell **B6** to select a cell in the Year column.

▶ **2.** On the ribbon, click the **PivotTable Analyze** tab. In the Calculations group, click the **Fields, Items, & Sets** button, and then click **Calculated Item**. The Insert Calculated Item in "Year" dialog box opens.

▶ **3.** Type **2025 (Projected)** in the Name box to change the name from Formula1, and then press **TAB** to go the Formula box.

▶ **4.** Type **=** to begin the formula, click **2024** in the Items box, and then click **Insert Item**.

5. Type ***(** to continue the formula, click **2024** in the Items box, and then click **Insert Item**.

6. Type **/** for the division operator, click **2023** in the Items box, click **Insert Item**, and then type **)** to finish the formula. The complete formula `='2024'*('2024'/'2023')` is entered the Formulas box. See Figure 11–37.

Figure 11–37   Insert Calculated Item in "Year" dialog box

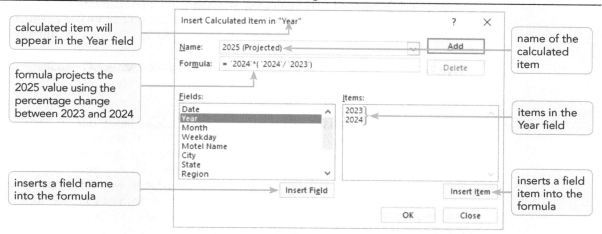

7. Click **OK**. The 2025 (Projected) formula is entered as a calculated item into the PivotTable and projected total revenue for all motels is displayed in cell C9. See Figure 11–38.

Figure 11–38   Projection of 2025 total revenue

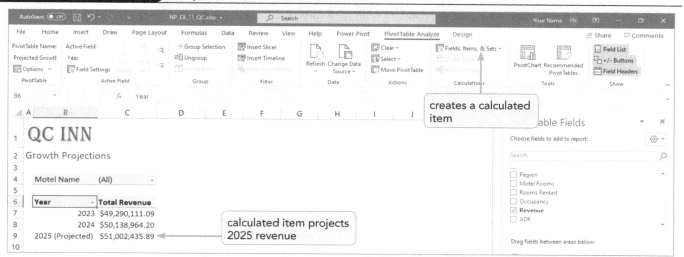

Next, you'll view projected revenues for individual motels within the QC Inn chain.

8. Click the **Filter** button in cell C4, select **Rapid City Inn** from the list of motels, and then click **OK**. The 2025 revenue for this motel is calculated in cell C9 as $3,752,993.55, which is a projected increase of about $168,000.

9. Click the **Filter** button in cell C4, click **Lincoln Motel** in the motel list, and then click **OK** to view the projected income for the Lincoln Motel.

If 2025 continues the trend shown in 2024, this motel's revenue will drop to $1,815,138.03, which is a decrease of almost $390,000.

▶ **10.** Click the **Filter** button in cell C4, select **(All)** to remove the filter, and then click **OK**. The PivotTable again shows projected revenue across all motels.

Note that in the formula for the calculated item, you never specified that the revenue field should be used in the calculation. Calculated items can be applied to any numeric field from the PivotTable. The only exception is that you cannot use calculated items for fields summarized with the average, standard deviation, or variance functions.

Insight

Calculated Items and Grouping

A PivotTable can have calculated items and grouped fields, but not both. The structure of the PivotTable cache does not allow for it. This is true even if the calculated item is placed within one field and the grouping is done on an entirely separate field. If you need to use both calculated items and grouped fields in a report, the best option is to create separate PivotTable caches: one for PivotTables with calculated items and one for PivotTables containing grouped fields. If necessary, you can then copy and paste the PivotTable values into a single comprehensive report showing both features.

Creating a Calculated Field

Where a calculated item performs calculations on items within a field, a **calculated field** is a user-defined formula for calculations across one or more fields. For example, a calculated field could multiply the value of a Rooms Rented field and a Price per Room field to return the total income generated from all the room rentals. Calculated fields are added to the list of PivotTable fields, appearing as just another set of fields. The effect would be the same as if you added them as calculated columns to the original data source.

Anna wants to evaluate the motel's financial performance. In addition to total revenue and the occupancy rate, the motel industry also compares motels by their average daily rate and their revenue per available room. Average daily rate (ADR) measures the revenue the motel earns per room rented and is calculated with the formula:

$$ADR = \frac{Revenue}{Rooms\ Rented}$$

The ADR value tells a financial analyst how much the motel is receiving from each room it rents and is a good indicator of the average room price.

Revenue per available room (RevPar) measures revenue per the total number of rooms in the motel (including the vacant rooms) and is calculated with the formula:

$$RevPar = \frac{Revenue}{Motel\ Rooms}$$

The RevPar value tells an analyst how the average price per room is affected by vacancies. A motel might have a very high ADR value if its rooms are expensive but a low RevPar value if it can't fill those rooms. Such a situation might lead a motel owner to reduce prices to attract more business and increase total revenue even though the revenue per rented room is lower.

The Motels data source doesn't include an ADR or RevPar field. Anna wants you to add these to the PivotTable as calculated fields, showing values for 2023 and 2024 and projecting those values into 2025. You will start by creating a calculated field to calculate ADR.

To create a calculated field for ADR:

1. On the PivotTable Analyze tab, in the Calculations group, click **Fields, Items, & Sets**, and then click **Calculated Field**. The Insert Calculated Field dialog box opens.

2. Enter **ADR** in the Name box, and then press **TAB**.

3. In the Formula box, type **=** to begin the formula, click **Revenue** in the Fields list, and then click **Insert Field**.

4. Type **/** for the division operator, click **Rooms Rented** in the Fields list, and then click **Insert Field**. The formula =Revenue/'Rooms Rented' appears in the Formula box. See Figure 11–39.

Tip

Fields do not have to be displayed in the PivotTable to be accessible to a calculated field formula.

Figure 11–39   Insert Calculated Field dialog box

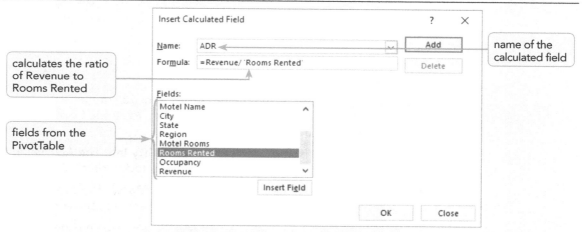

Insert Calculated Field   ? ✕

Name: ADR   ⟵ name of the calculated field   Add

Formula: =Revenue/ 'Rooms Rented'   Delete

calculates the ratio of Revenue to Rooms Rented

Fields:
Motel Name
City
State
Region
Motel Rooms
Rooms Rented
Occupancy
Revenue

fields from the PivotTable

Insert Field

OK   Close

5. Click **OK**. The Sum of ADR is added to the PivotTable with ADR calculations based on all the motels in the data source.

6. Click cell **D6** to select it, and then in the Active Field group, change the value of the Active Field box from Sum of ADR to **ADR** followed by a blank space to avoid conflict with the calculated field name. See Figure 11–40.

Figure 11–40   **Calculated ADR values**

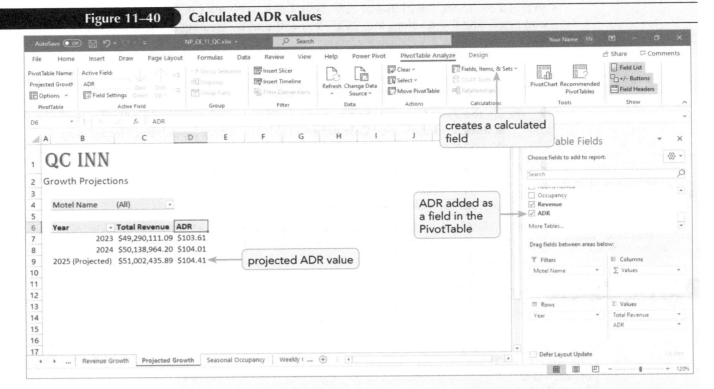

The average price of a rented room across all motels is currently about $104 and rising slightly in the upcoming year. You'll see how individual motels compare to this.

 ▶ **7.** In the Motel Name filter, select **Rapid City Inn**. The ADR value for a rented room at the motel is nearly $111, projected to drop slightly in 2025.

 ▶ **8.** In the Motel Name filter, select **Lincoln Motel**. The average price of a rented room at that motel is about $86, projected to drop slightly as well in 2025.

 ▶ **9.** In the Motel Name filter, select **(All)** to once again show the ADR values from across all motels in the QC Inn chain.

You'll use the same process to add RevPar as a calculated field to the PivotTable.

To create a calculated field for RevPar:

 ▶ **1.** On the PivotTable Analyze tab, in the Calculations group, click the **Fields, Items, & Sets** button, and then click **Calculated Field**. The Insert Calculated Field dialog box opens.

 ▶ **2.** In the Name box Enter **RevPar** as the field name, and then press **TAB**.

 ▶ **3.** In the Formula box, enter **=Revenue/'Motel Rooms'** as the formula, using the Fields box and the Insert Field button.

▶ **4.** Click **OK** to create the calculated field and return to the workbook.

▶ **5.** Click cell **E6** and change the value the Active Fields box from Sum of RevPar to **RevPar** followed by a blank space. See Figure 11–41.

Figure 11–41 **Calculated RevPar values**

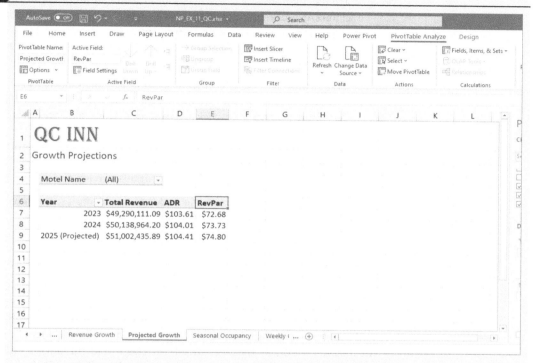

For all motels in the QC Inn chain, the revenue per room is projected to increase from $73.73 in 2024 to $74.80 in 2025. Again, you'll compare this to individual motels.

▶ **6.** In the Motel Name filter, select **Rapid City Inn**. The RevPar value for that motel is $83.01 in the current year and is projected to rise by more than $3 to $86.66, indicating that the motel is becoming more profitable to the chain.

▶ **7.** In the Motel Name filter, select **Lincoln Motel**. RevPar values for that motel have steadily declined from $59.12 in 2023 to $48.56 in 2024 and projected to drop further to $39.89 in 2025.

▶ **8.** In the Motel Name filter, select **(All)** to return to the RevPar values for all motels in the chain.

▶ **9.** Save the workbook, and then close it.

The RevPar numbers for the Lincoln Motel are particularly concerning to Anna. The low RevPar score indicates that the motel might be having problems getting business and that the motel might want to lower its prices to attract more customers and fill more rooms. The other alternatives are to attract more customers through customer incentives and reward programs, upgrading the facilities, and flexible pricing models that will take advantage of periods of high customer demand.

Insight

Setting the Solve Order for Calculated Items

The value shown in a PivotTable cell might be the result of applying several calculated items and fields. If you find that a cell is displaying an unexpected or wrong value, it could be a problem with the order of calculations. Excel has rules that determine which calculations are done first. But in some situations, performing the calculations in different orders produces different results. For example, doubling a cell's value and then adding 10 produces a different result than adding 10 to the cell's value and then doubling it. You can correct this problem by changing the default order.

To define the order in which calculations are applied within a PivotTable, do the following:

1. Select the PivotTable you want to reorder calculations for.
2. On the PivotTable Analyze tab, in the Calculations group, click the Fields, Items & Sets button, and then click Solve Order. The Calculated Item Solve Order dialog box opens.
3. Modify the order of the calculations by selecting a calculation formula and clicking the Move Up or Move Down buttons.
4. Click Close when the formulas are in the correct order.

Note that when you change the order of the formulas, the new order will be applied to all calculated items in that PivotTable.

Behind the Math of Calculated Items and Fields

The formulas for calculated items and fields can accept any worksheet function that uses numbers as arguments and returns a numeric value, such as the AVERAGE, SUM, or COUNT functions. However, calculated items and calculated formulas cannot use text functions nor can they reference data outside of the PivotTable. You could not, for instance, include the VLOOKUP function in formula for a calculated item or field because it will reference data outside of the PivotTable. Only data residing within another PivotTable field or entered explicitly as a constant is available.

The other important factor to consider is that calculated fields are always based on sums of fields. For example, the ADR calculations shown in Figure 11–40 are the equivalent of taking the sum of the revenue from all the motels and dividing that sum by the total number of rented rooms. But because calculated fields are limited to sums, you could not, for example, create a calculated field from an average value, such as the average occupancy rate.

The fact that calculated fields are limited only to sums can lead to incorrect results. Figure 11–42 shows a PivotTable that multiplies the value of the Rooms Rented field by the value of the Price per Room field to create the Total Income calculated field.

Figure 11–42   **Calculated formulas applied to grand totals**

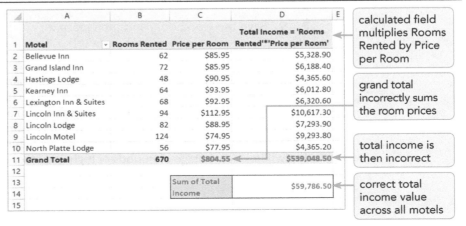

	A	B	C	D	E	
1	Motel	Rooms Rented	Price per Room	Total Income = 'Rooms Rented'*'Price per Room'		calculated field multiplies Rooms Rented by Price per Room
2	Bellevue Inn	62	$85.95	$5,328.90		
3	Grand Island Inn	72	$85.95	$6,188.40		
4	Hastings Lodge	48	$90.95	$4,365.60		
5	Kearney Inn	64	$93.95	$6,012.80		grand total incorrectly sums the room prices
6	Lexington Inn & Suites	68	$92.95	$6,320.60		
7	Lincoln Inn & Suites	94	$112.95	$10,617.30		
8	Lincoln Lodge	82	$88.95	$7,293.90		
9	Lincoln Motel	124	$74.95	$9,293.80		
10	North Platte Lodge	56	$77.95	$4,365.20		total income is then incorrect
11	**Grand Total**	**670**	**$804.55**	**$539,048.50**		
12						
13			Sum of Total Income	$59,786.50		correct total income value across all motels
14						
15						

The total income calculations are fine and reasonable for individual motels but make no sense when applied to the grand total because you would not sum the price of individual rooms to calculate total income across all rooms. You always want to confirm that the values a calculated field is summing should, in fact, be summed. It many cases, you will want to avoid displaying subtotals and grand totals for tables that involve calculated fields. Another way to solve this problem is to create a calculated measure, which you'll do in the next session.

 Proskills

Written Communication: Documenting PivotTables

As PivotTables grow in size and complexity, it is helpful to document your work for others. You should always give PivotTable fields and calculations clear and descriptive names. Choose formats that are appropriate for the type of data you are displaying and apply conditional formats if possible to highlight key features in your tables.

You should document any customized calculations used in a PivotTable somewhere in the workbook. You can create the documentation sheet, or you can have Excel create a list of calculated items and fields by doing the following:

1. Select the PivotTable whose calculated items and fields you want to document.
2. On the PivotTable Analyze tab, in the Calculations group, click the Fields, Items, & Sets button, and then click List Formulas.

Excel will create a new worksheet describing all the calculated items and fields, including the name of the items and the fields, the formulas involved, and the solution order. This is a static list, so if you add to or edit your calculated items and fields, you must regenerate the list of formulas.

You have finished designing PivotTables for the data in the Motels table. In the next session, you will explore design issues involved with creating PivotTables from data stored in an Excel Data Model.

Review

Session 11.2 Quick Check

1. How do you display the rank (smallest to largest) of a PivotTable field?
2. Conditional formats can be applied to which parts of a PivotTable?
3. What is the PivotTable cache?
4. If motels are grouped by size in one PivotTable, how are they displayed in other PivotTables sharing the same cache?
5. How do you create a PivotTable with its own cache?
6. What is the difference between a calculated item and a calculated field?
7. How is the value of a calculated field summarized within a PivotTable?
8. What is a potential mistake you could make with calculated fields?

Session 11.3 Visual Overview:

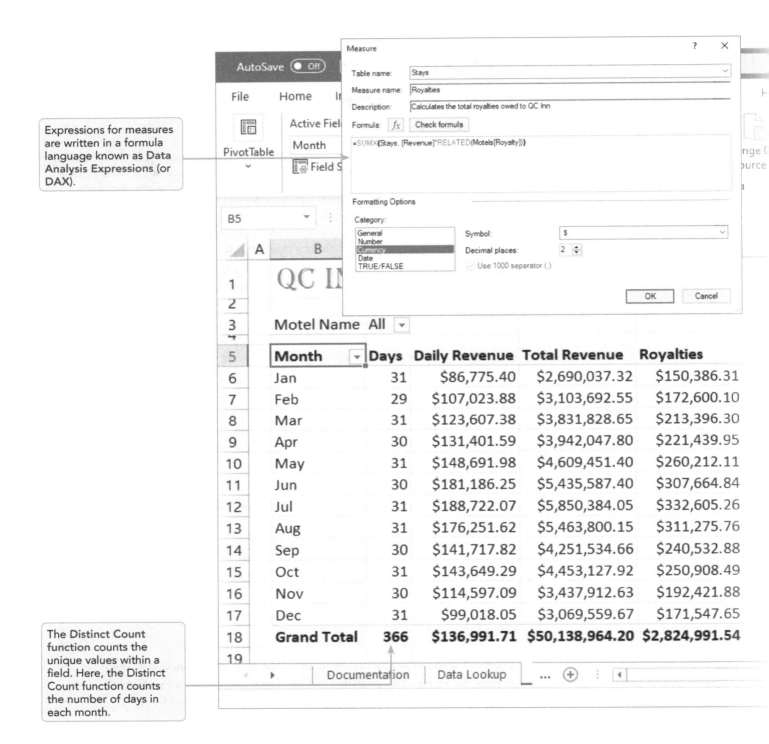

Expressions for measures are written in a formula language known as Data Analysis Expressions (or DAX).

The Distinct Count function counts the unique values within a field. Here, the Distinct Count function counts the number of days in each month.

Measure

Table name: Stays

Measure name: Royalties

Description: Calculates the total royalties owed to QC Inn

Formula: fx Check formula

=SUMX(Stays, [Revenue]*RELATED(Motels[Royalty]))

Formatting Options

Category:
General
Number
Currency
Date
TRUE/FALSE

Symbol: $
Decimal places: 2
Use 1000 separator (,)

OK   Cancel

B5

Motel Name All

Month	Days	Daily Revenue	Total Revenue	Royalties
Jan	31	$86,775.40	$2,690,037.32	$150,386.31
Feb	29	$107,023.88	$3,103,692.55	$172,600.10
Mar	31	$123,607.38	$3,831,828.65	$213,396.30
Apr	30	$131,401.59	$3,942,047.80	$221,439.95
May	31	$148,691.98	$4,609,451.40	$260,212.11
Jun	30	$181,186.25	$5,435,587.40	$307,664.84
Jul	31	$188,722.07	$5,850,384.05	$332,605.26
Aug	31	$176,251.62	$5,463,800.15	$311,275.76
Sep	30	$141,717.82	$4,251,534.66	$240,532.88
Oct	31	$143,649.29	$4,453,127.92	$250,908.49
Nov	30	$114,597.09	$3,437,912.63	$192,421.88
Dec	31	$99,018.05	$3,069,559.67	$171,547.65
Grand Total	**366**	**$136,991.71**	**$50,138,964.20**	**$2,824,991.54**

Documentation   Data Lookup

PivotTable Measures

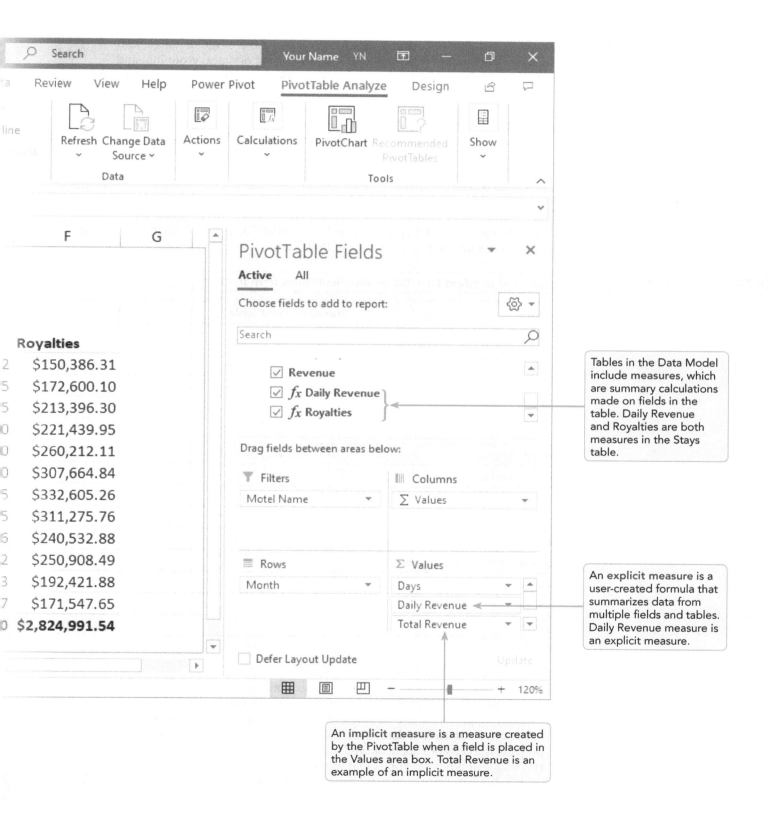

Tables in the Data Model include measures, which are summary calculations made on fields in the table. Daily Revenue and Royalties are both measures in the Stays table.

An explicit measure is a user-created formula that summarizes data from multiple fields and tables. Daily Revenue measure is an explicit measure.

An implicit measure is a measure created by the PivotTable when a field is placed in the Values area box. Total Revenue is an example of an implicit measure.

Introducing PivotTable Design Under the Data Model

So far, you have worked with PivotTables that summarized data from an Excel table. This kind of PivotTable is referred to as a **standard PivotTable** because it relies on a data source within the workbook, such as an Excel table or a data range, and includes many standard tools such as automatic sorting of dates, grouping, and calculated items and fields. However, the downside to placing all the data into one table or range is that you had to duplicate a lot of information. For example, the Motels table required the name of the motel, its size, and its location to be included in every record in the table. Such redundancy makes data susceptible to errors and is inefficient. From a data management perspective, it's much better to put the motel-specific information in one table and the daily customer visits information in another table, and then connect the two tables with a common field using Power Pivot under the Excel Data Model.

Standard PivotTables and PivotTables created from the Data Model do not support the same features. For example, you can create group field items in a standard PivotTable, but you can't with a PivotTable based on the Data Model. Figure 11–43 lists features that are supported by each type of PivotTable.

Figure 11–43   Features of standard PivotTables and PivotTables from the Data Model

Feature	Standard PivotTable	Data Model PivotTable
Product function	✔	
Count Numbers function	✔	
Distinct Count function		✔
Show Report Filter Pages tool	✔	
Drill into a PivotTable cell	✔	✔ (first 1000 rows)
Calculated items	✔	
Calculated fields	✔	
Grouping	✔	
Show Items with No Data option	✔	
Hierarchies		✔
Including filtered items in totals		✔
Connect multiple tables		✔
Calculated measures		✔
DAX functions		✔
Named sets		✔

The two PivotTable types are complementary: Sometimes you will use standard PivotTables and other times the Data Model. Standard PivotTables are quick to set up but do not support the more advanced features available through Power Pivot. Therefore, you might use standard PivotTables for quick analyses and Power Pivot for large projects with custom applications.

Anna created another workbook that uses data stored in the Data Model. You will use that workbook to learn how to work with PivotTables in that format. You'll open the workbook now.

To open the Data Model workbook:

▶ **1.** Open the **NP_EX_11–2.xlsx** workbook located in the **Excel11 > Module** folder included with your Data Files, and then save the workbook as **NP_EX_11_Inn** in the location specified by your instructor.

▶ **2.** In the Documentation worksheet, enter your name and the date.

▶ **3.** On the ribbon, click the **Power Pivot** tab, and then in the Data Model group, click the **Manage** button. Power Pivot opens.

▶ **4.** On the Home tab, in the View group, click the **Diagram View** button to display the relationship between the Motels and Stays tables.

▶ **5.** Close Power Pivot and return to the workbook.

The Motels table contains information about the 24 QC Inn motels in Nebraska and South Dakota. The Stays table describes daily stays at the motels during 2024. The Motels and Stays tables are connected via the common field Motel ID in a one-to-many relationship.

Insight

Named Sets and the Data Model

In a standard PivotTable, the combination of fields is repeated for every PivotTable level. For example, you can't choose to display one set of months for one year in your PivotTable and a different set of months for a different year. You must display the same set of months for both years.

PivotTables based on the Data Model allow for **named sets** to define which fields are displayed within each part of the PivotTable. The named set feature allows for asymmetric PivotTables in which the list of fields can differ within the same PivotTable. This means you could display one set of financial calculations for one year and a different set for another year.

To create a named set, on the PivotTable Analyze tab, in the Calculations group, click the Field, Items, & Sets button. You can then choose to define sets based on items in the PivotTable rows or PivotTable columns. Named sets are very useful in removing extraneous or irrelevant data from a final PivotTable report.

Calculating Distinct Counts

A distinct count is a count of the unique values from a field, which is different from the COUNT function which counts both unique values and duplicates. The DISTINCT COUNT function is available in PivotTables created from the Data Model.

You will use distinct counts in a PivotTable that analyzes daily sales across all the motels in the Nebraska/South Dakota sales territory. You'll begin creating this PivotTable by calculating the number of days within each month that the motels were open.

To begin creating the PivotTable:

▶ **1.** Go to the **Daily Revenue** worksheet. A PivotTable report area named "Daily Revenue" has already been set up in this worksheet.

▶ **2.** Drag the **Month** field from the Stays table into the Rows area box, drag the **Date** field from the Stays table into the Values area box, and then drag the **Motel Name** field from the Motels table into the Filters area box.

▶ **3.** Change the format of the Count of Date field to a number value with no decimal places.

   With Data Model PivotTables, month names are not automatically sorted in chronological order. You'll apply the custom sort list that Excel provides for sorting by month.

▶ **4.** Click the **Filter** button in cell B6, and then click **More Sort Options**. The Sort (Month) dialog box opens.

▶ **5.** Click the **Ascending (A to Z) by** option button and verify that **Month** appears in the box.

▶ **6.** Click **More Options**. The More Sort Options (Month) dialog box opens.

▶ **7.** Click the **Sort automatically every time the report is updated** check box to deselect it.

▶ **8.** Click the **First key sort order** box and click the **Jan, Feb, Mar...** custom list.

▶ **9.** Click **OK** in each dialog box to return to the workbook. Figure 11–44 shows the current PivotTable.

Figure 11–44   **PivotTable of Count of Date**

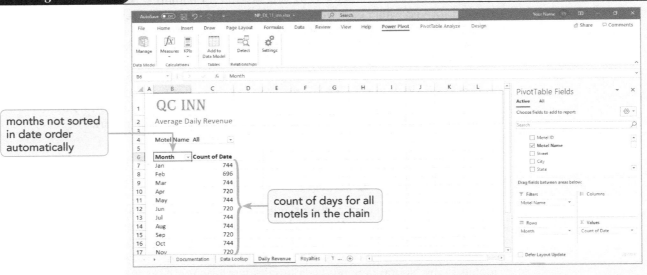

The PivotTable shows a count of days from every motel within every month. For example, the day count in January is 744 because there are 31 days in January multiplied by 24 motels, which equals 744 days. However, because Anna wants to count the number of days across all motels and doesn't want to count the same day more than once, you will replace the COUNT function in the PivotTable with the DISTINCTCOUNT function.

To calculate the distinct count of days:

▶ **1.** Click cell **C6** containing the Count of Date label to select it.

▶ **2.** On the ribbon, click the **PivotTable Analyze** tab, and then in the Active Field group, click the **Field Settings** button. The Value Field Settings dialog box opens.

▶ **3.** Scroll down the list of summary functions and select **Distinct Count**.

▶ **4.** In the Custom Name box, change the label from "Distinct Count of Date" to **Days**.

▶ **5.** Click **OK** to return to the workbook. The number of days in each month is now shown in column C.

You will use the distinct count of the days to determine the average number of customers per day at all of the QC Inn motels in the Nebraska/South Dakota sales territory. You can do this calculation by creating a measure.

Creating a Measure

Because PivotTables based on the Power Pivot Data Model do not support calculated fields, you must define a measure, which is a calculation that summarizes data from a Data Model table. PivotTables use two types of measures: implicit and explicit.

An implicit measure is a measure created by the PivotTable when a field is placed in the Values area box. For example, placing the Revenue field in the Values area creates the implicit measure "Sum of Revenue" to calculate a total revenue for each cell in the PivotTable. Implicit measures are limited to the standard summary functions: SUM, COUNT, MIN, MAX, AVG, and DISTINCTCOUNT and can be used only within a PivotTable or PivotChart.

An explicit measure is a user-created formula that summarizes data from multiple fields and tables. Measures become part of a data table's structure and are available to PivotTables, PivotCharts, and any application that can access the Data Model.

A crucial point to understand is that a measure provides the formula for summarizing data, but the data is determined by the PivotTable. Just like an implicit measure that calculates an average can be applied across different cells within a PivotTable, an explicit measure acts the same way. In writing a measure, you are telling Excel how to calculate a value; the PivotTable determines where it's applied.

Introducing DAX

An explicit measure is written in the formula language Data Analysis Expressions, or more commonly known as DAX. It's beyond the scope of this module to go deeply into the syntax of DAX. However, DAX uses many of the same functions used with Excel worksheets and Excel tables, so you can apply what you've learned about those topics to get started in writing your own measures in DAX.

For example, a reference to the Rooms Rented field would be written as `[Rooms Rented]`. To create a measure that calculates the sum of the Rooms Rented field, apply the formula `=SUM([Rooms Rented])`. If you need to specify the table, insert the table name prior to the field name, as in the expression `=SUM(Stays[Rooms Rented])` which calculates the sum of the Room Rented field from the Stays table.

Reference

Adding a Measure to a Data Model table

- On the Power Pivot tab, in the Calculations group, click the Measures button, and then click New Measure.
- In the Measures dialog box, specify the table that will contain the measure and the name of the measure.
- Enter the DAX formula for the measure.
- Specify the output format of the measure.
- Click OK to apply the measure to the table.

DAX is a powerful language. As you develop your Excel skills, knowledge of DAX and its uses will be essential for creating powerful and sophisticated Excel reports and applications. In this session, you'll just get started.

Adding a Measure to a Table

Measures are always associated with a table in the Data Model, and they become part of that table's definition. Anna wants you to create a measure for the Stays table that calculates the average number of motel rooms rented each day across the QC Inn chain. To calculate that value, you will divide the sum of the Rooms Rented field by a distinct count of the number of days. The measure formula written in DAX is:

```
=SUM([Rooms Rented])/DISTINCTCOUNT([Date])
```

You will create this measure the Measure dialog box.

To create a measure calculating the daily average motel rooms rented:

1. On the ribbon, click the **Power Pivot** tab. In the Calculations group, click the **Measures** button, and then click **New Measure**. The Measure dialog box opens.

2. Click the **Table Name arrow**, and then click **Stays** to add this measure to the Stays table.

> You must select the Stays table so that the measure is associated with the correct table in the Data Model.

3. Press **TAB**, and then type **Daily Rentals** in the Measure name box.

4. Press **TAB**, and then type **Average rooms rented daily at QC Inn motels** in the Description box.

5. Click after the = symbol in the Formula box, and then type **SUM(** to begin the formula. Note that as you type, Excel provides a list of functions, tables, and fields you can insert into the formula.

6. Double-click **[Rooms Rented]** from the field list to insert this field into the formula, and then type **)** to complete the SUM function.

Tip

> You can check for errors in a formula by clicking the Check formula button.

7. Type **/DISTINCTCOUNT(** as the next part of the formula, double-click **[Date]** in the fields list, and then type **)** to complete the formula. The formula `=SUM([Rooms Rented])/DISTINCTCOUNT([Date])` appears in the Formula box.

8. Click **Number** in the Category box and change the number of decimals displayed by the measure to **0**. See Figure 11–45.

Figure 11–45 Measure dialog box

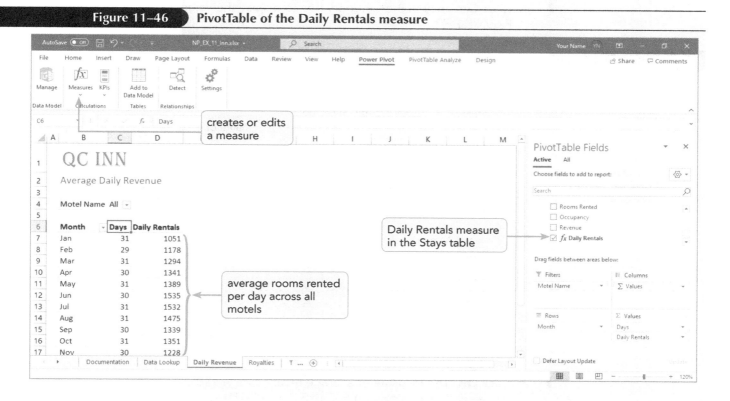

measure created in the Stays table

name of measure

checks the formula for errors

Table name: Stays

Measure name: Daily Rentals

Description: Average rooms rented daily at QC Inn motels

Formula: fx | Check formula |

=SUM([Rooms Rented])/DISTINCTCOUNT([Date])

calculates average rooms rented per day across all motels

format of calculated values

Category:
General
Number
Currency
Date
TRUE/FALSE

Format: Decimal Number

Decimal places: 0

☐ Use 1000 separator (.)

| OK | Cancel |

▶ **9.** Click **OK** to create the Daily Rentals measure. As shown in Figure 11–46, the measure is added as a new column to the PivotTable.

Figure 11–46 PivotTable of the Daily Rentals measure

creates or edits a measure

Daily Rentals measure in the Stays table

QC INN

Average Daily Revenue

Motel Name All

Month	Days	Daily Rentals
Jan	31	1051
Feb	29	1178
Mar	31	1294
Apr	30	1341
May	31	1389
Jun	30	1535
Jul	31	1532
Aug	31	1475
Sep	30	1339
Oct	31	1351
Nov	30	1228

average rooms rented per day across all motels

Based on the Daily Rentals measure, you learn that on a typical day in January 2024 that 1,051 rooms are rented from all the motels in the Nebraska/South Dakota sales territory. That number rises by almost 500 to 1,535 on a typical day in June. Overall in 2024, the Nebraska/South Dakota sales territory was hosting about 1,317 customers per day (cell D19).

Tip

Measures become part
of the table structure and
are available to any new
PivotTable that uses that
table.

Notice that the Daily Rentals measure is added to the list of items in the Stays table. The icon f_x indicates that Daily Rentals is a measure and not a table field. The measure is automatically added to the Values field, using the label name you specified in the Measure dialog box.

Next, you will create a measure named Daily Revenue that calculates the total revenue generated per day from the motels in the Nebraska/South Dakota sales territory.

To create the Daily Revenue measure:

▶ 1. On the Power Pivot tab, in the Calculations group, click the **Measures** button, and then click **New Measure**. The Measure dialog box opens.

▶ 2. Verify that **Stays** is selected in the Table name box, enter **Daily Revenue** in the Measure name box, and then enter **Average revenue collected daily at QC Inn motels** in the Description box.

▶ 3. Click after the = symbol in the Formula box and type **SUM(** to begin the formula.

▶ 4. Double-click **[Revenue]** in the field list, and then type **)** to complete the SUM function.

▶ 5. Type **/DISTINCTCOUNT(** to continue the formula, double-click **[Date]** in the fields list, and then type **)** to complete the formula. The formula =SUM([Revenue])/DISTINCTCOUNT([Date]) appears in the Formula box.

▶ 6. Click **Currency** in the Category box to display the values as currency. See Figure 11–47.

Figure 11–47	Daily Revenue measure

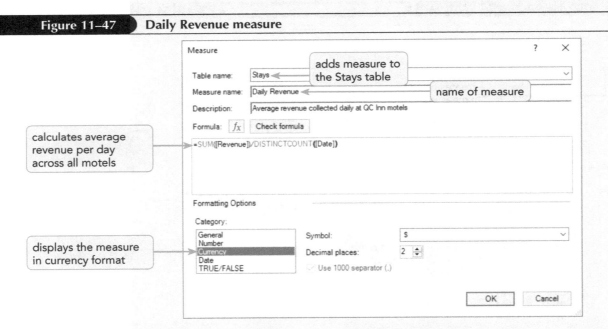

▶ 7. Click **OK**. The measure of average revenue collected daily from across all motels is shown in column E. See Figure 11–48.

| Figure 11–48 | Average daily revenue across all motels |

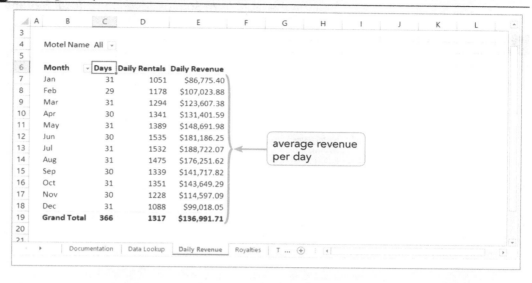

In January 2024, the Nebraska/South Dakota sales territory took in more than $86,000 on an average day. In July, at the height of the tourist season, the typical daily revenue collected for the territory was almost $189,000. To view average daily rentals and revenues for other combinations of motels and dates, Anna has only to change the structure of the PivotTable. The Daily Rentals and Daily Revenue measures will automatically recalculate for each cell in the new PivotTable.

The revenues collected by the 24 motels do not all go to QC Inn because the company franchises its motels. Instead, the company receives a percentage, or royalty, of the revenue in exchange for administrative help, infrastructure, advertising, and the right to use the QC Inn name.

Anna wants to track the total royalties collected from the Nebraska/South Dakota motels in the past year. To do that calculation, you will create a measure using data from multiple tables.

> **Tip**
>
> To view average daily revenues at specific motels, select the motel name from the PivotTable filter.

Calculating Measures Across Tables and Rows

The great power of DAX and Power Pivot becomes apparent when you need to combine data from multiple tables in a wide variety of ways. In this case, you want to combine data from two tables: the Revenue field from the Stays table that records the amount of revenue collected by each motel and the Royalty field from the Motels table that provides each motel's royalty rate. Motel franchises in the QC Inn chain will pay royalties from 4% of revenue up to 7% based on the contract between the franchise owner and the company.

Anna wants a PivotTable that shows the revenue and royalties for each motel. You will start creating this PivotTable now by inserting a column of total revenue.

To create a PivotTable of total revenue:

▶ **1.** Go to the **Royalties** worksheet.

▶ **2.** In the PivotTable Fields pane, click **All** to see all of the tables in the Data Model.

▶ **3.** Drag the **Motel Name** field from the Motels table into the Rows area box.

▶ **4.** Drag the **Revenue** field from the Stays table into the Values area, and then change the label from Sum of Revenue to **Total Revenue**. See Figure 11–49.

Figure 11–49   **PivotTable of total revenue by motel**

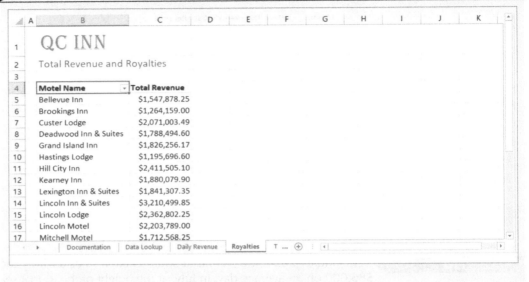

To calculate the total royalties owed to the company, you'll multiply the revenue collected by the motel's royalty rate. For example, if a motel collects $10,000 in revenue at a 6% royalty rate, it will owe the chain ($10,000) x (6%) = $600. Anna wants to use this calculation to sum the total royalties QC Inn collects from its franchised motels.

The RELATED Function

For every royalty calculation, you need to use the value of the Royalty field for the motel. You can look up a value from a table in the Data Model using the RELATED function

RELATED(*Table[field]*)

where **Table[*field*]** is the table and **_field_** is the field to retrieve the data from. So, to retrieve the value of the Royalty field in the Motels table, the expression is:

RELATED(Motels[Royalty])

Tip

You must have defined a table relation to use the RELATED function.

▶The RELATED function acts like a lookup table, but there's no lookup value. So how does the formula know where to find the correct royalty rate? The answer is that the relation between the Stays table and Motels table has already been defined in the Data Model. If you know the motel that generated the revenue, the table relation tells which record in the Motels table to use for the royalty rate.

The SUMX Function

Royalties are calculated by multiplying revenue by the value of the royalty field. At first, you might try the following formula that multiplies the sum of the Revenue field in the Stays table by the value of the Royalty field in the Motels table:

=SUM(Stays[Revenue])*RELATED(Motels[Royalty])

But this formula would not work. Nothing in the expression `SUM(Stays[Revenue])` indicates which revenue figures are being summed. You could be summing revenues from one motel or from several motels, each with a different royalty rate. Remember that the measure provides the formula, but the PivotTable supplies the data. There's no way to match the sum of the revenues to a single royalty rate.

Instead, you want to calculate the royalty owed each time revenue is collected by a motel and then add those royalties to get the total royalties paid to the company. That kind of sum, which proceeds through a table row-by-row, is calculated using the following SUMX function:

`SUMX(table, expression)`

where *table* is the table to go through row-by-row, and *expression* is an expression to calculate on each row of the table. SUMX then returns the sum of all those individual calculations. So, the expression

`[Revenue]*RELATED(Motels[Royalty])`

calculates the royalty on a single transaction, which you can then nest within the following SUMX function to sum all the calculations for every record in the Stays table:

`SUMX(Stays, [Revenue]*RELATED(Motels[Royalty]))`

This measure can then be added to a PivotTable to calculate total royalties for any combination of motels or dates within the year. You'll add this formula as a measure named Royalties to the PivotTable in the Royalties worksheet.

To create the Royalties measure:

▶ **1.** On the ribbon, click the **Power Pivot** tab. In the Calculations group, click the **Measures** button, and then click **New Measure**. The Measure dialog box opens.

▶ **2.** Verify that **Stays** is selected in the Table name box.

▶ **3.** Change the name of the measure to **Royalties** and enter the description **Calculates the total royalties owed to QC Inn** in the Description box.

▶ **4.** In the Formula box after the = symbol, type **SUMX(Stays, [Revenue]*RELATED(Motels[Royalty]))** to enter the formula. Remember, you can avoid typing mistakes by selecting table names, field names, and function names from the box that appears within the Formula box.

▶ **5.** Click **Check formula** to confirm the expression you entered contains no syntax errors.

   Trouble? If Excel reports an error, you probably mistyped the formula. Common errors include missing parentheses or square brackets around the field names. Check your formula against the formula in Step 4, correct any mistakes, and then repeat Step 5. If you are still having problems entering the formula correctly, you can copy the expression from the Terms and Definitions worksheet.

▶ **6.** In the Category box, click **Currency** to display the Royalties measure as currency. See Figure 11-50.

Figure 11–50 Royalties measure

Measure   ?   ×

Table name: Stays

Measure name: Royalties

Description: Calculates the total royalties owed to QC Inn

Formula: fx Check formula

=SUMX(Stays, [Revenue]*RELATED(Motels[Royalty]))

sums royalty values over each record in the Stays table

calculates royalty due for each revenue value

✓ No errors in formula.

Formatting Options

Category:

General
Number
Currency
Date
TRUE/FALSE

Symbol: $

Decimal places: 2

Use 1000 separator (,)

displays total royalties as currency

OK   Cancel

▶ 7. Click **OK**. The Royalties measure is added to the PivotTable.

▶ 8. Click the **Filter button** in cell B4, and then click **More Sort Options**. The Sort (Motel Name) dialog box opens.

▶ 9. Click the **Descending (Z to A)** option button, and then select **Royalties** in the box.

▶ 10. Click **OK** to return to the PivotTable. The PivotTable is sorted in descending order of royalties. See Figure 11–51.

Figure 11–51 PivotTable of revenue and royalties

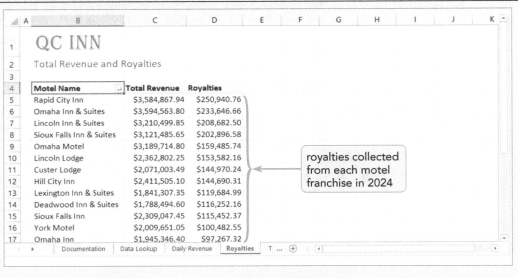

Motel Name	Total Revenue	Royalties
Rapid City Inn	$3,584,867.94	$250,940.76
Omaha Inn & Suites	$3,594,563.80	$233,646.66
Lincoln Inn & Suites	$3,210,499.85	$208,682.50
Sioux Falls Inn & Suites	$3,121,485.65	$202,896.58
Omaha Motel	$3,189,714.80	$159,485.74
Lincoln Lodge	$2,362,802.25	$153,582.16
Custer Lodge	$2,071,003.49	$144,970.24
Hill City Inn	$2,411,505.10	$144,690.31
Lexington Inn & Suites	$1,841,307.35	$119,684.99
Deadwood Inn & Suites	$1,788,494.60	$116,252.16
Sioux Falls Inn	$2,309,047.45	$115,452.37
York Motel	$2,009,651.05	$100,482.55
Omaha Inn	$1,945,346.40	$97,267.32

QC INN

Total Revenue and Royalties

royalties collected from each motel franchise in 2024

Documentation   Data Lookup   Daily Revenue   Royalties   T ...

The most royalties were collected from the Rapid City Inn with more than $250,000 in royalties from a total revenue of $3.585 million. The smallest royalty amount came from the Valentine Lodge with more than $35,000 in royalties from more than $880,000 in revenue (row 28). Altogether from the Nebraska/South Dakota sales territory, about $2.825 million in royalties were collected from more than $50 million in total revenue (row 29).

Insight

Exploring the X Functions in DAX

SUMX is one of the summary X functions in DAX. The others are AVERAGEX, COUNTX, MINX, MAXX, and PRODUCTX. As with SUMX, each X function evaluates an expression row-by-row within a table, applying the summary function to the row-by-row values. For example, the following AVERAGEX function goes through every record in the Stays table, calculates the rooms rented divided by the total number of rooms in the motel for each record, and then returns the average of those ratios:

```
=AVERAGEX(Stays, [Rooms Rented]/RELATED(Motels[Total Rooms]))
```

Similarly, the following COUNTX function counts up the number of days in which every room was rented:

```
=COUNTX(Stays,IF([Rooms Rented]=RELATED(Motels[Total Rooms]),1))
```

The measure goes through every record in the Stays table using the IF function to test whether the number of rooms rented equals the number of rooms in the motel. If they are equal, the value 1 is returned; otherwise, no numeric value is given. The COUNTX function then counts the number of records containing a numeric value which is the same as counting the number of days the motel was full.

DAX is a powerful language for constructing formulas using data from multiple tables, and the X functions are one of its more useful tools.

Retrieving PivotTable Data with GETPIVOTDATA

The reports you helped Anna create were limited to the 24 motels in Nebraska and South Dakota, but there are over 6,000 QC Inn motels in more than 35 countries and territories. A PivotTable providing summaries on each motel would be large and unwieldy. One solution to that problem is to treat a PivotTable itself as a data source and extract information from it for use in a report using the **GETPIVOTDATA function**. The syntax of the function is:

```
GETPIVOTDATA(data_field, pivot_table, [field1, item1,
field2, item2,...])
```

where *data_field* is the data you want to retrieve from the PivotTable, *pivot_table* is a reference to any cell within the PivotTable, and the *field1*, *item1*, *field2*, *item2*, and so on are optional field/item pairs that indicate the location the cell within the PivotTable. Each field or item value is a text string and must be enclosed within quotation marks.

Note that it doesn't matter how the PivotTable is structured. You can switch rows and columns, add subtotals, add grand totals, and so forth. As long as you specify a data field, a cell (any cell) within the PivotTable, and a list of fields and field items, the GETPIVOTDATA function can locate the value in the PivotTable.

The GETPIVOTDATA function works with both standard PivotTables and PivotTables created under the Data Model. Figure 11–52 shows an example of the GETPIVOTDATA function used with a standard PivotTable.

Figure 11–52 **GETPIVOTDATA function for a standard PivotTable**

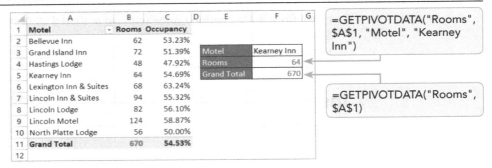

The first GETPIVOTDATA function

```
=GETPIVOTDATA("Rooms", $A$1, "Motel", "Kearney Inn")
```

returns the value of the Rooms field where Motel equals "Kearney Inn". In Figure 11–52, this is cell B5 in the PivotTable. If the field/item pairs are omitted as in the following function, the GETPIVOTDATA function returns the grand total of the Rooms field:

```
=GETPIVOTDATA("Rooms", $A$1)
```

With PivotTables based on the Data Model, the GETPIVOTDATA function is more complicated, expressing the fields and items of the PivotTable in terms of measures. For example, the GETPIVOTDATA function for retrieving the number of rooms from the Kearney motel in Figure 11–52 is

```
=GETPIVOTDATA("[Measures].[Sum of Rooms]",$A$1,"[Motel_
Data].[Motel]", "[Motel_Data].[Motel].&[Kearney Inn]")
```

and the GETPIVOTDATA function for retrieving the grand total of rooms across all motels is:

```
=GETPIVOTDATA("[Measures].[Sum of Rooms]",$A$1)
```

Fortunately, you don't have to write these formulas yourself. If you reference a PivotTable cell, Excel will automatically generate the GETPIVOTDATA function for you.

Reference

Inserting the GETPIVOTDATA function

- Click the cell in which you wish to place the GETPIVOTDATA function.
- Type = and then click the PivotTable cell. Excel enters a reference to the PivotTable cell using the GETPIVOTDATA function.
- Press ENTER to insert the formula.

Anna included a Data Lookup worksheet in which you will use the GETPIVOTDATA function to retrieve data from the Royalties PivotTable. You'll enter the GETPIVOTDATA functions now by referencing cells within the PivotTable.

To insert the GETPIVOTDATA function:

▶ **1.** Go to the **Data Lookup** worksheet.

▶ **2.** Click cell **C5** and type **=** to begin the formula.

> **3.** Click the **Royalties** sheet tab, click cell **C5** containing the total revenue for the Rapid City Inn, and then press **ENTER**. The GETPIVOTDATA function in cell C5 references the cell value from the PivotTable.

Next, you'll retrieve the value of the Royalties measure for the Rapid City Inn.

> **4.** Click cell **C6**, type **=** to begin the formula, click cell the **Royalties** sheet tab, click cell **D5**, and then press **ENTER**.

> **5.** Select the range **C5:C6** containing the GETPIVOTDATA functions. See Figure 11–53.

Figure 11–53   **Values referenced from the Royalties PivotTable**

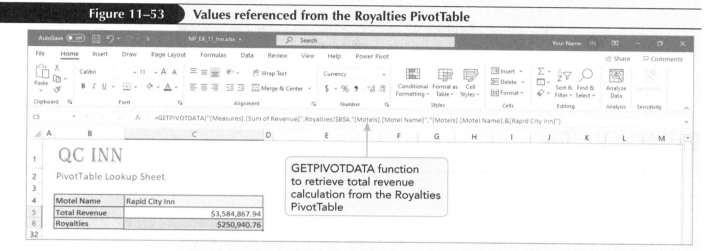

In Excel, the default behavior is to generate a GETPIVOTDATA function whenever you link to a cell within a PivotTable. If that's not what you want, you can change the default behavior: Select the PivotTable. On the PivotTable Analyze tab, in the PivotTable group, click the Options arrow, and then deselect the Generate GetPivotData option. After that, Excel will use familiar worksheet references to cells within a PivotTable in place of the GETPIVOTDATA function.

Anna wants the GETPIVOTDATA function to retrieve revenue and royalty values for any of the 24 motels. You will modify the GETPIVOTDATA functions now, replacing the explicit reference to the Rapid City Inn with a reference to whatever motel is named in cell C4.

To view PivotTable data for any motel:

> **1.** With the range C5:C6 still selected, press **CTRL+H**. The Find and Replace dialog box opens.

> **2.** Type **Rapid City Inn** in the Find what box.

> **3.** Press **TAB**, and then type **"&C4&"** in the Replace with box. See Figure 11–54.

Figure 11–54 Find and Replace dialog box

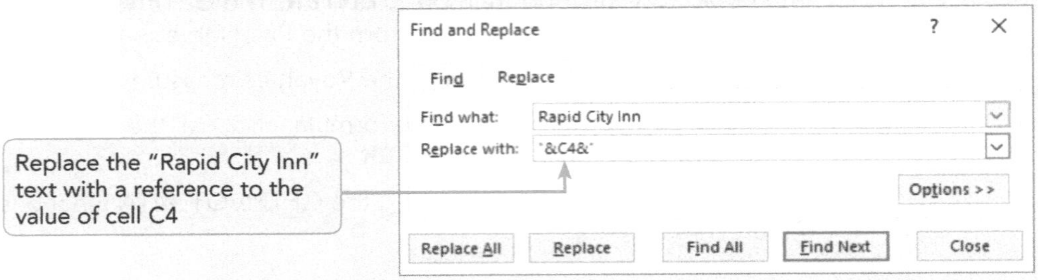

Replace the "Rapid City Inn" text with a reference to the value of cell C4

▶ **4.** Click **Replace All** to replace the text in the two selected cells. Excel reports that two replacements were made.

▶ **5.** Click **OK**, and then click **Close** to return to the workbook.

▶ **6.** In cell **C4**, enter **Hill City Inn** as the motel name. The worksheet updates to show the total revenue and royalties for the motel. See Figure 11–55.

Figure 11–55 PivotTable data for the Hill City Inn

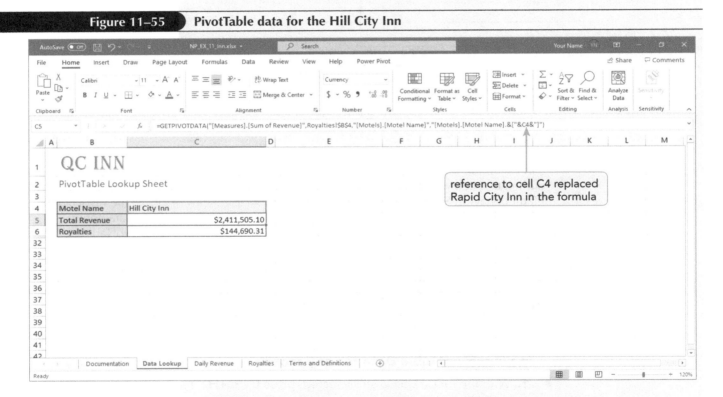

reference to cell C4 replaced Rapid City Inn in the formula

▶ **7.** 📌 Save the workbook, and then close it.

Anna can build upon this example to create a dashboard with PivotTable lookups. One of the great appeals of the GETPIVOTDATA function is that it gives you the flexibility to display PivotTable results in customized layouts and report styles.

Proskills

Problem Solving: Retrieving Measures from OLAP Cubes

Under the Data Model, you don't need a PivotTable to display PivotTable results. This is because the Data Model stores data in a multidimensional array of fields and measures known as a **Data Cube**. A Data Cube is part of an **Online Analytic Processing (OLAP)** database that is designed for the efficient reporting a large datasets. Rather than calculating and re-calculating a dataset that might have millions of records, an OLAP database has all those measures pre-stored for quick retrieval.

The Data Model is based on a Data Cube model, which is why you can store large datasets in the Data Model and have PivotTables quickly retrieve and display measures without having to wait for Excel to recalculate the PivotTable values.

You calculate measures directly from the Data Model without even needing a PivotTable by using the CUBEVALUE function

=CUBEVALUE(*connection*, [*expression1*, *expression2*, …])

where *connection* is the connection to an OLAP database like the Data Model and *expression1*, *expression2*, and so on are OLAP expressions that define how those measures should be filtered and retrieved. For example, the following formula retrieves the Sum of Revenue measure for the York Motel from the Data Model:

```
=CUBEVALUE("ThisWorkbookDataModel",
    "[Measures].[Sum of Revenue]",
    "[Motels].[Motel Name][York Motel]"
```

By adding more expressions to the CUBEVALUE function, you can filter the Sum of Revenue measure to cover any motel or combination of motels within any date interval you choose. The CUBEVALUE function is one of 7 CUBE functions supported by Excel.

Exploring Database Functions

Another way to summarize data from an Excel table or data range without using PivotTables is with a **Database function** (or **Dfunction**). Database functions calculate summary statistics including AVERAGE, COUNT, MAX, MIN, and SUM using criteria specified in a range. The general form of a Database function is

Dfunction(*database*, *field*, *criteria*)

where *database* specifies the data range containing the data including the column names, *field* is the name of a column from the data range or table, and *criteria* is a range containing filter criteria to apply to the database function. Figure 11–56 lists some of the Database functions used to calculate summary statistics from a database.

Figure 11–56 Database functions

Function	Description
DAVERAGE(*database, field, criteria*)	Calculates the average of the values in the *field* column under criteria specified in the *criteria* range
DCOUNT(*database, field, criteria*)	Counts the numeric values in the *field* column for cells matching the *criteria*
DCOUNTA(*database, field, criteria*)	Counts the nonblank cells in the *field* column for cells matching the *criteria*
DMAX(*database, field, criteria*)	Returns the maximum value of the *field* column for cells matching the *criteria*
DMIN(*database, field, criteria*)	Returns the minimum value of the *field* column for cells matching the *criteria*
DSUM(*database, field, criteria*)	Calculates the sum of the *field* column for cells matching the *criteria*
DSTDEV(*database, field, criteria*)	Calculates the standard deviation of the *field* column for cells matching the *criteria*
DGET(*database, field, criteria*)	Returns the first cell from *field* column matching the *criteria*

Figure 11–57 shows an example of the DAVERAGE, DSUM, and DMAX Database functions used to calculate the average, sum, and maximum value of revenue collected during August of 2024.

Figure 11–57 Summary statistics calculated with database functions

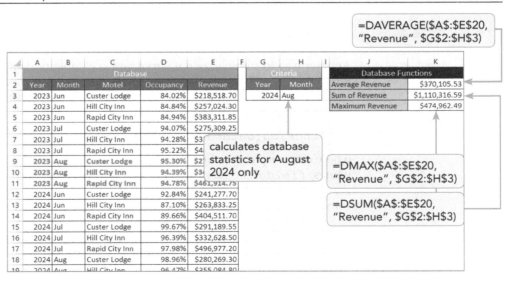

The criteria range operates the same way for the Database functions as it did for Advanced Filter criteria in that:

1. Field names are listed in the first row of the table and must exactly match the field names used from the database. Field names can be repeated in the same row for multiple criteria.
2. Criteria for each field are listed in subsequent rows of criteria range.
3. Criteria within the same row are combined using the AND logical operator.
4. Criteria in different rows are combined using the OR logical operator.

Figure 11–58 shows a criteria range with two rows so that the matching rows from the database contain either Hill City Inn revenue for 2023 or Custer Lodge Revenue for 2024.

| Figure 11–58 | Database calculations with multiple criteria |

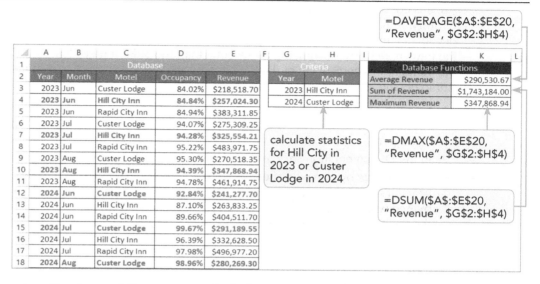

As with advanced filters, you can include operations in the criteria cells. An expression such as "> 300000" could be used to filter results to include only those rows in which revenues were greater than $300,000. If you want a quick way of calculating databases statistics, the Excel Database functions might be a good choice.

You've completed your initial work on the motel data for QC Inn. Anna will want to continue using these PivotTables to explore the data in preparation for the annual report.

Review

Session 11.3 Quick Check

1. What is a standard PivotTable?
2. What function should you use to count the number of unique values within a field?
3. What is the difference between an implicit measure and an explicit measure?
4. Write a DAX formula to calculate the average of the Revenue field values in the Stays table.
5. What DAX function do you use to retrieve a value from a Data Model table based on the table relation?
6. What is the difference between the SUM and SUMX functions?
7. What function do you use to retrieve values from a PivotTable?
8. What function do you use to retrieve calculated values from the Data Model without the use of a PivotTable?
9. What are the three arguments of an Excel Database function?

Practice

Review Assignments

Data Files needed for the Review Assignments: NP_EX_11-3.xlsx, NP_EX_11-4.xlsx

Anna is continuing to explore the motel data for the franchises in the Nebraska/South Dakota sales territory. Anna wants you to report on occupancy rates during a typical week to learn how much occupancy increases between the weekdays and the weekends. Anna is also interested in whether the new motels are showing higher revenue than the older motels. Finally, Anna wants to report the number and percentage of days in which each motel was completely filled during the year. Complete the following:

1. Open the **NP_EX_11-3.xlsx** workbook located in the Excel11 > Review folder included with your Data Files. Save the workbook as **NP_EX_11_Days** in the location specified by your instructor.

2. In the Documentation sheet, enter your name and the date.

3. The Revenue by Age worksheet shows average revenue compared to the age of each motel in years. It's difficult to spot any relationship between the two using individual ages. In the Revenue by Age worksheet, click cell A4, and then use the Group Field command in the Group group on the PivotTable Analyze tab to simplify the PivotTable by grouping the values in the Motel Age column in six 5-year groups going from 0 to 30 to see whether new motels have higher average revenue.

4. Compare motel performance on weekends vs. weekdays. In the Weekend Rates worksheet, manually group the Mon, Tue, Wed, and Thu items in the Weekday field of the PivotTable. Remove the Weekday field from the Columns area and rename Group1 as **Weekdays**. Manually group the Sun, Fri, and Sat items and change the name of that group from Group2 to **Weekends**. Click cell C4, and then use the Active Field box in the Active Field group on the PivotTable Analyze tab to change the name of the grouped field from Weekday2 to **Days**.

5. Enhance the appearance of the PivotTable with color. Click cell D6, click the Conditional Formatting button in the Styles group on the Home tab, and then click the New Rule command. For all cells showing Occupancy Rate values, format the values with a 3-color scale going from red (low occupancy) through yellow and up to green (high occupancy).

6. Explore how occupancy rates change from one day to the next within a typical week. In the Daily Occupancy worksheet, a PivotTable shows the average occupancy by day but organized with the groups you created in Step 4. Remove the Weekday2 group from the Rows area of the PivotTable. Click cell D5, and then click the Field Settings button in the Active Field group on the PivotTable Analyze tab. On the Show Values As tab, select the Difference From calculation with Weekday as the Base field and (previous) as the Base item. Change the Custom Name of the field to **Change in Rate**.

7. Use conditional formatting to indicate whether occupancy rates are going up, down, or remaining steady from one day to the next. Create a new conditional formatting rule that uses the red-yellow-green arrow icon set to highlight all cells showing change in rate values for weekdays. If the cell number is greater than or equal to 0.002 display a green up arrow. If the number is less than –0.002, display a red down arrow; otherwise, display a yellow sideways arrow. Note that Sunday will not have an icon because it's the first day of the week.

8. Examine how Revenue per Available Room or RevPar values change during the week. Go to the Daily RevPar worksheet and press ALT+D and then P to open the PivotTable Wizard. Use the data in the Motels table and select No in Step 2 to create a PivotTable from a new cache. Place the PivotTable report in cell B6 of the RevPar worksheet and rename the PivotTable **RevPar Pivot**. Place the Motel Name field in the Filters area and Weekday in the Rows area.

9. Click cell B6, click the Fields, Items, & Sets button in the Calculations group on the PivotTable Analyze tab, and then select Calculated Field. Create a calculated field named **RevPar** equal to the Revenue field divided by the Motel Rooms field. Change the label of value field from Sum of RevPar to **RevPar** followed by a blank space.

10. Summarize the RevPar values by weekdays and weekends. Click cell B6, click the Fields, Items, & Sets button in the Calculations group on the PivotTable Analyze tab, select Calculated Item, and then add the following calculated items:

   a. The **Weekday Average** calculated item using the formula =AVERAGE(Mon, Tue, Wed, Thu).

   b. The **Weekend Average** calculated item using the formula =AVERAGE(Sun, Fri, Sat).

11. Save the workbook, and then close it.

12. Open the **NP_EX_11-4.xlsx** workbook located in the Excel10 > Review folder included with your Data Files. Save the workbook as **NP_EX_11_Vacancy** in the location specified by your instructor. You'll use this workbook to examine how often the QC Inns motels have no vacancies.

13. In the Documentation sheet, enter your name and the date.

14. Go to the Vacancy Table worksheet. Click the Measures button in the Calculations group on the Power Pivot tab to add a new measure to the Stays table named **Days Filled**. Insert the description **Count of days with no vacancies** to indicate that this measure will calculate the number of days in which a motel was completely filled. Enter the following DAX formula:

   `=SUMX(Stays, IF([Rooms Rented]=RELATED(Motels[Total Rooms]),1,0))`

   (You can also copy this formula from the Terms and Definitions worksheet and paste it into the Measures dialog box. Be sure to type an equal sign (=) before the expression.) In the Formatting Options section, display the measure as a decimal number with no decimal places.

15. Add a second measure to the Stays table named **Percent Filled** with the description **Percent of days with no vacancies** that calculates the percent of days in which the motel was completely filled using the DAX formula and displays the value as a percentage number to two decimal places:

   `=[Days Filled]/[Count of Date]`

16. Make sure that both the Days Filled and the Percent Filled measures are added to the PivotTable. Note that motels will not be filled up except in the busiest of seasons.

17. Change the report layout to a tabular form.

18. Because the table is large and cumbersome, you'll set up a lookup worksheet to retrieve the vacancy data from the PivotTable. Go to the Vacancy Lookup worksheet, click cell C6, type = and then click cell E5 in the Vacancy Table worksheet to insert the GETPIVOTDATA function for that cell. Do the same with cell C7 to insert the GETPIVOTDATA function from cell F5 in the Vacancy Table worksheet.

19. Select the range C6:C7 and use the Find and Replace command to replace all occurrences within the selection of Bellevue Inn with "&C4&" (include the quotation marks). With the range C6:C7 still selected, use the Find and Replace command to replace all occurrences of Jan with "&C5&" (include the quotation marks).

20. Test the vacancy lookup by entering **Custer Lodge** in cell C4 and **Aug** in cell C5 to return the number and percentage of days in August with no vacancies at the Custer Lodge.

21. Save the workbook, and then close it.

Apply

Case Problem 1

Data File needed for this Case Problem: NP_EX_11-5.xlsx

Alcmaeon   Selene Marados is an account executive with Alcmaeon, a tech company that specializes in custom software for hospitals and clinics. Selene wants to create a report on software sales to hospitals and clinics in the previous year. Selene has stored sales data in a workbook containing a Data Model with four tables: an Agents table containing information about the sales staff, a Hospitals table containing data on the hospitals and clinics that purchase software licenses from Alcmaeon, a Products table containing data on the software products sold by the company, and a Sales table that contains information on each sales transaction. You will use these tables to generate an analysis of the sales data.

Sales agents working at Alcmaeon are paid a base salary plus a commission based on the percentage of revenue they generate beyond $350,000. Commission rates can vary from 4% to 6%. Selene wants the report to include the total compensation paid to the sales staff from the base salary and their commissions. Complete the following:

1. Open the **NP_EX_11-5.xlsx** workbook located in the Excel11 > Case1 folder included with your Data Files. Save the workbook as **NP_EX_11_Alcmaeon** in the location specified by your instructor.

2. In the Documentation sheet, enter your name and the date.

3. In the Revenue Report worksheet, in cell B4, create a PivotTable named **Revenue by Month**. Place the Date field from the Sales table in the Rows area. After Excel automatically groups the dates, remove the Date field from the Rows area, leaving only the Date (Month) field showing the names of the months. Change the PivotTable report layout to tabular form and do not display any grand totals in either the rows or the columns.

4. Place the Revenue field from the Sales table into the Values area four times and do the following to display sales revenue in different ways in your table:
   a. In the first column, Sum of Revenue, display the rank of the revenue values from largest to smallest and change the field label to **Rank**.
   b. In the second column, Sum of Revenue2, change the field label to **Total Revenue**.
   c. In the third column, Sum of Revenue3, track the increase in revenue over the year by displaying the running total. Change the field label to **Running Total**.
   d. In the last column, Sum of Revenue4, display the revenue values as % Running Total in Date (Month). Change the field label to **Percentage**.

5. Examine how sales vary by region and agent. Go to the Region Report worksheet and create a PivotTable in cell B4 named **Revenue by Region**. Place the Sales Region and the Name fields from the Agents table in the Rows area. Place the Revenue field from the Sales table in the Values area and change the field label from Sum of Revenue to **Total Revenue**. Change the layout to Outline form and add subtotals to the top of each region group.

6. Show the percentage of revenue generated by each agent and each region by placing the Revenue field a second time the Values area, displaying its values as a percent of the parent row total. Change the field label name to **Percent**.

7. To better view the top selling agents and regions, sort the items in the Sales Region column in descending order of the Percent field, and then sort the items in the Name field also in descending order of Percent.

8. Determine how many hospitals bought a software license during the past years and from which agents. In the Hospital Sales worksheet, in cell B4, create a PivotTable named **Clients**. Set the report layout to tabular form, showing grand totals for both rows and columns. Place the Name field from the Agents table in the Rows area and place the Date (Month) field from the Sales table in the Columns area.

9. Place the Hospital field from the Sales table in the Values area. Show how many clients each agent had during the year by displaying the distinct count of the Hospital field. Change the field label to **Clients**.

10. In the PivotTable Options dialog box for the PivotTable, on the Layout & Format tab, enter **0** as the value to show for empty cells.

11. Calculate each agent's total compensation from the past year. In the Sales Commissions worksheet, create a PivotTable in cell B4 named **Commissions**. Set the PivotTable layout to tabular form with no grand totals.

12. Place the Name field from the Agents table in the Rows area. Place the Base Salary field from the Agents table in the Values area. Change the field label to **Base Salary** followed by a blank space. Place the Commission field from the Agents table in the Values area. Change the field label to **Commission Rate**.

13. Place the Revenue field from the Sales table in the Values area. Change the field label to **Revenue Generated**.

14. Create a measure named **Earned Commission** in the Sales table with the description **Commission earned by revenue generated above a minimum amount** that calculates the amount of commission earned by a sales agent for revenue generated above a minimum level. Use the following DAX formula and format values returned by the measure as currency with no decimal places:

    `=(SUM([Revenue]) - SUM(Agents[Sales Minimum]))*SUM(Agents[Commission])`

    (You can copy this formula from the Tables and Measures worksheet if you have trouble entering it; be sure to insert an equal sign to start the formula and match all closing and opening parentheses.)

15. Create a measure named **Total Compensation** with the description **Total compensation from base salary and earned commission** that calculates the total compensation for each sales agent by adding the base salary and the earned commission. Use the following DAX formula and display total compensation in currency with no decimal places:

    `=SUM(Agents[Base Salary])+[Earned Commission]`

16. Make sure that the Earned Commission and Total Compensation measures are added to the PivotTable.

17. Sort the agent names in descending order of the Total Compensation column.

18. Save the workbook, and then close it.

Challenge

Case Problem 2

Data File needed for this Case Problem: NP_EX_11-6.xlsx

Computer Discount Essentials   Jamere Carter manages inventory for Computer Discount Essentials. Part of Jamere's job is to monitor the stocking levels in the company's warehouses to ensure that merchandise is restocked well before the warehouse runs out. Jamere stores inventory data in an Excel workbook with two tables in the Data Model: The Products table describes all the warehouse merchandise, including each item's initial stocking level and the level below which the item must be restocked. The Transactions table contains a daily record of transactions at the warehouse including items shipped out and items restocked. Jamere wants you to create a report on the current state of the warehouse, flagging those items that need immediate restocking and calculating the total value of all items in stock. Complete the following:

1. Open the **NP_EX_11-6.xlsx** workbook located in the Excel11 > Case2 folder included with your Data Files. Save the workbook as **NP_EX_11_CDE** in the location specified by your instructor.

2. In the Documentation sheet, enter your name and the date.

3. In the Inventory Report worksheet, in cell B7, insert a PivotTable named **Inventory Pivot**. Set the PivotTable layout to the tabular form with no grand totals. Set the layout to repeat all item labels.

4. Place the Category, SKU, and Description fields from the Products table in the Rows area.

5. Display the initial quantity of each item stocked in the warehouse by placing the Initial QTY field from the Products table in the Values area and change the field label from Sum of Initial QTY to **Starting QTY**.

6. Display the change in the item quantities over the past year by placing the Change field from the Inventory in the Values area and change the field label from Sum of Change to **Change in QTY**.

7. Determine the current quantity of each item left in the warehouse by adding a measure to the Products table named **Current QTY** with the description **Current quantity in stock**. Enter the DAX formula `=[Sum of Initial QTY]+[Sum of Change]`. Add the measure to the PivotTable, if needed.

8. Determine the value of the items in inventory by creating a measure for the Products table named **Inventory Value** with the description **Total value of the items in the inventory**. Enter the DAX formula `=SUMX(Products, [Unit Value]*[Current QTY])` and display the value as currency to two decimal places. Add the measure to the PivotTable, if needed.

9. Determine which items need to be restocked by creating a measure for the Products table named **Restock Order** with the description **Quantity of item to reorder**. Insert the following DAX formula that uses the SUMX and IF functions to calculate the amount of items that Jamere will have to order to bring the inventory up to the proper level:

    `=SUMX(Products, IF([Current QTY]<[Restock Level], [Restock Amount], 0))`

    Note that if an item is above the restocking level, this measure will return a value of zero (because no restocking is required). If you are having problems entering the formula, you can copy and paste the measure formula from the Data Summary worksheet.

⊕ **Explore** 10. Click cell I8 and add a conditional format icon set to all cells in the PivotTable showing Restock Order values. If the numeric value of a cell is greater than zero, indicating that the item needs restocking, display a red flag; for all other values do not display any icon. (*Hint*: You can select individual icons by clicking the drop-down list box next to each icon image in the New Formatting Rule dialog box.)

⊕ **Explore** 11. Jamere wants the total value of all items in the inventory displayed above the PivotTable. Because this total is not part of the PivotTable, you need to retrieve the measure directly from the Data Model using the CUBEVALUE function. In cell H5, enter the following formula to calculate the total value of all items in the warehouse by retrieving the Inventory Value measure:

    `=CUBEVALUE("ThisWorkbookDataModel","[Measures].[Inventory Value]")`

12. Resize the column widths of the PivotTable so that all values and labels can be read.

13. Jamere wants a table listing the names of the items by warehouse row and bin. In the Warehouse Grid worksheet, create a PivotTable in cell B4 named **Warehouse**, set the layout to the tabular form, and do not display any grand totals for the table.

14. Place the Warehouse Row field from the Products table in the Rows area and place the Storage Bin field from the Products table in the Columns area.

⊕ **Explore** 15. With DAX you can create measures that return text strings in place of numeric values by using the CONCATENATEX function. Display all the items stored in a warehouse row and bin in a comma-separated list by adding the following **Item List** measure to the Products table. Include the description **List of items from the warehouse inventory** and enter the measure formula:

    `=CONCATENATEX(Products, [Description], ", ")`

    Add the measure to the Values area of the PivotTable, if needed. Confirm that each cell in the PivotTable displays items stored in the matching storage bin and warehouse row.

16. Wrap the text in the cells containing the item lists within each cell. Resize the PivotTable column and row widths to fit the contents.

17. Save the workbook, and then close it.

Module 12

Developing an Excel Application

Creating a Data Entry App

Objectives

Session 12.1
- Create a WordArt graphic
- Plot data with a funnel chart
- Hide error values with the IFERROR function

Session 12.2
- Validate data entry
- Hide worksheet rows and columns
- Hide worksheets
- Protect worksheets and workbooks from edits
- Unlock worksheet cells to allow edits

Session 12.3
- Display the Developer tab
- Record and run a macro
- Assign a macro to a graphic or macro button
- Edit macro code in an editor

Case | Primrose Community Clinic

Jenya Rattan is a project coordinator for Primrose Community Clinic, a private nonprofit clinic in Toledo, Ohio. Currently, Jenya is directing fundraising efforts for a multimillion-dollar expansion of the clinic. Jenya is using Excel to monitor the fundraising efforts and generate reports for the clinic administrators and trustees. Jenya wants you to help develop an Excel application for entering donor information and reporting on fundraising progress.

Starting Data Files

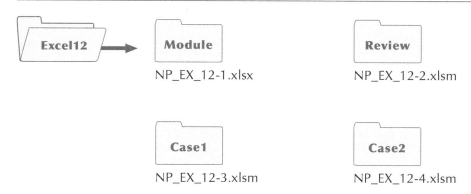

Excel12 →	Module	Review
	NP_EX_12-1.xlsx	NP_EX_12-2.xlsm
	Case1	Case2
	NP_EX_12-3.xlsm	NP_EX_12-4.xlsm

Session 12.1 Visual Overview:

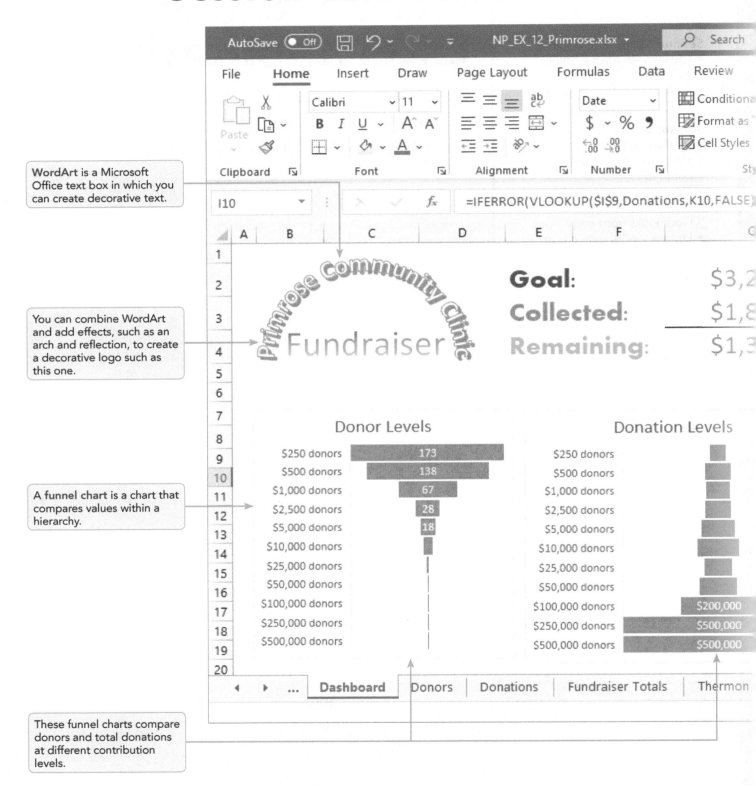

WordArt is a Microsoft Office text box in which you can create decorative text.

You can combine WordArt and add effects, such as an arch and reflection, to create a decorative logo such as this one.

A funnel chart is a chart that compares values within a hierarchy.

These funnel charts compare donors and total donations at different contribution levels.

WordArt and Funnel Charts

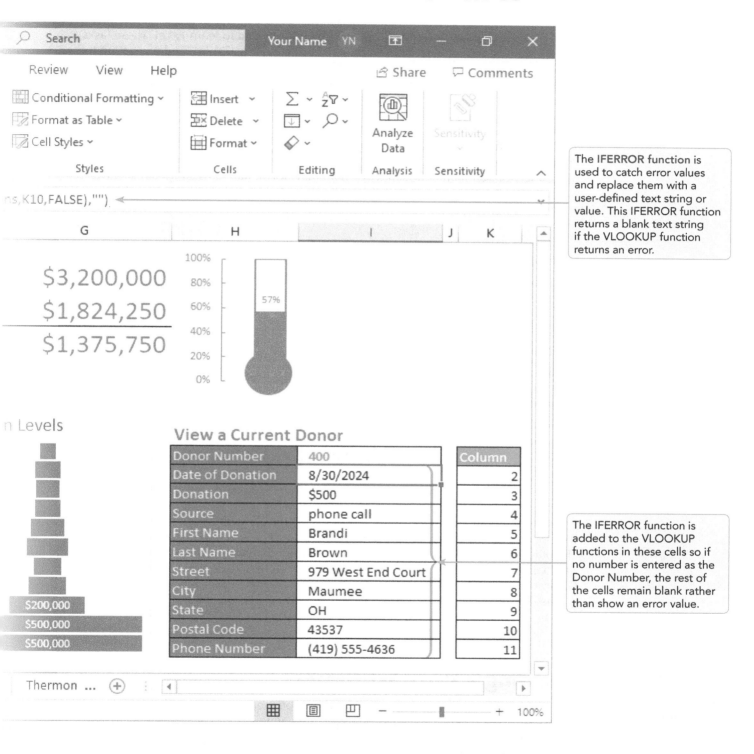

The **IFERROR** function is used to catch error values and replace them with a user-defined text string or value. This IFERROR function returns a blank text string if the VLOOKUP function returns an error.

The IFERROR function is added to the VLOOKUP functions in these cells so if no number is entered as the Donor Number, the rest of the cells remain blank rather than show an error value.

Planning an Excel Application

An **Excel application** is a workbook written or tailored to meet specific needs. Most applications include a customized interface to assist users, who are usually not Excel experts, to quickly and easily perform tasks without having to learn Excel. These tasks could include entering data, updating charts, updating PivotTables, and navigating the workbook contents. Because these workbooks usually contain formulas and data that should not be changed by users, many Excel applications lock or protect parts of the workbook. The goal of any Excel application is to present a product that allows users to focus on completing a few tasks while maintaining the accuracy and integrity of the data.

Jenya has started creating an Excel application for tracking donations made to the Primrose Community Clinic and entering new donors. The application will be used by a variety of staff members, some of whom may not be familiar with Excel, so Jenya wants the application to be as easy-to-use as possible. You'll open Jenya's workbook and view the current state of the application.

To view Jenya's workbook:

▶ **1. sam** ↓ Open the **NP_EX_12-1.xlsx** workbook located in the **Excel12 > Module** folder included with your Data Files, and then save the workbook as **NP_EX_12_Primrose** in the location specified by your instructor.

▶ **2.** In the Documentation worksheet, enter your name and the date.

▶ **3.** Go to each of the other worksheets in the workbook and review their contents. Note that some worksheets already have PivotTable report areas created for you.

▶ **4.** Go to the **Dashboard** worksheet when you are finished reviewing workbook contents.

Jenya wants you to focus on three worksheets: The Dashboard worksheet summarizing the fundraising effort, the Donors worksheet for entering information about new donors or retrieving information about current donors, and the Donations worksheet containing the Donations table listing all donations made to the clinic since the campaign began. The other worksheets provide the calculations for the charts and tables presented in the dashboard but will not be of interest to other staff members at the Primrose Community Clinic.

The dashboard is missing a few pieces that Jenya wants you to add. The first is a graphic of the Primrose Community Clinic name. You can create such a graphic using WordArt.

Creating a WordArt Graphic

WordArt is a Microsoft Office text box in which you create decorative text. WordArt can make a dashboard come alive with interesting graphics and attractive images. You begin by picking a WordArt style from the gallery and then adding decorative effects using tools on the ribbon.

You'll create a WordArt graphic containing the text "Primrose Community Clinic" to include on the dashboard.

To create a WordArt graphic for the dashboard:

▶ **1.** On the ribbon, click the **Insert** tab. In the Text group, click the **Text arrow** if necessary to display the menu of text objects, and then click the **WordArt** button. A gallery of WordArt styles appears. Each style is represented by the letter A.

▶ **2.** Click the WordArt style in the third row and fourth column of the gallery. White text with a dark orange border shadow containing the text "Your text here" appears in the workbook.

▶ **3.** Type **Primrose Community Clinic** to replace the default text with the name of the clinic.

▶ **4.** Use your mouse to select all the text in the WordArt box.

▶ **5.** On the ribbon, click the **Home** tab. In the Font group, click the **Font Size arrow**, and then click **28** as the font size. The WordArt reduces in size.

▶ **6.** Point to the WordArt border, and then use the Move pointer ✥ to drag the WordArt text box so the upper-left corner of the WordArt graphic is in cell A1. See Figure 12–1.

Figure 12–1	WordArt added to the dashboard

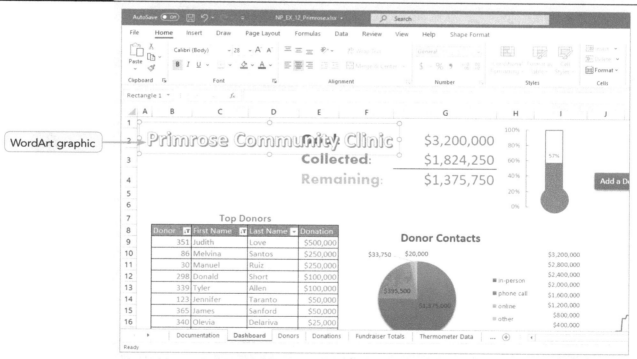

The WordArt graphic overlaps other content on the dashboard. You can fix that by formatting it. Among the decorative effects that you can apply to WordArt are drop shadows, glowing edges, reflections, and 3D rotations. You will apply a text effect that places the WordArt text in a semicircular arch.

To transform the WordArt text:

▶ **1.** With the WordArt graphic still selected, click the **Shape Format** tab on the ribbon, and then in the WordArt Styles group, click the **Text Effects** button. A menu of effects appears.

▶ **2.** On the Text Effects menu, point to **Transform**. The Transform gallery with different ways to transform the WordArt opens.

▶ **3.** In the Follow Path section, click the first option to apply the Arch transformation. You can change the height and width of the arch.

▶ **4.** In the Size group, enter **2** in the Shape Height box, press **TAB**, and then enter **2** in the Shape Width box. The text in the WordArt graphic is spread over a bigger arch.

▶ **5.** Drag the WordArt graphic so that the entire graphic is visible at the top of the worksheet. See Figure 12–2.

Figure 12–2   **Transformed WordArt graphic**

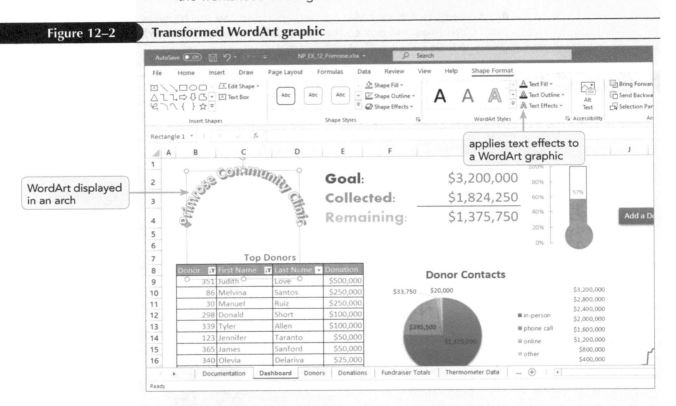

Jenya wants you to include a second WordArt graphic that contains the word "Fundraiser" in the dashboard. You will place this second WordArt below the arch you just created.

To insert the Fundraiser WordArt object:

▶ **1.** On the ribbon, click the **Insert** tab. In the Text group, click the **Text arrow** to view the menu of text objects if necessary, click the **WordArt** button, and then click the WordArt style in the second row and second column of the gallery. A WordArt text box in a blue font with reflected text is inserted in the worksheet.

▶ **2.** Type **Fundraiser** to replace the selected text, and then select **Fundraiser** in the WordArt text box.

▶ **3.** On the ribbon, click the **Home** tab. In the Font group, click the **Font Size arrow**, and then click **24**. The font size of the WordArt is reduced.

▶ **4.** Move the Fundraiser WordArt so it is centered directly under the WordArt arch you created in the previous set of steps. See Figure 12–3.

Figure 12–3	Reflected WordArt graphic

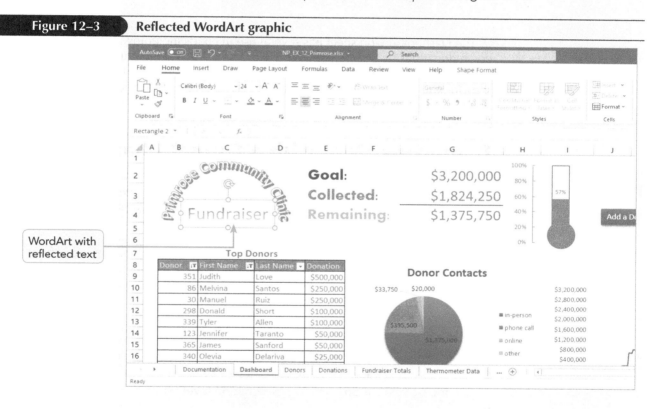

You can modify other parts of the WordArt style using commands and tools on the Shape Format tab. If you want to remove all the decorative features from a WordArt graphic, go to the Shape Format tab, click the WordArt gallery in the WordArt Styles group, and then click Clear WordArt.

Insight

Enhancing your Application with SmartArt

Another way of adding eye-catching graphics to application dashboards is with SmartArt. **SmartArt graphics** are professionally designed business graphics to create illustrations of flow charts, organization charts, cycle charts, and other diagrams. To create a SmartArt graphic, go to the Insert tab, and then in the Illustrations group, click the SmartArt button. The Choose a SmartArt Graphic dialog box opens from which you can choose a SmartArt diagram. The SmartArt graphics are organized into the following diagram categories: List, Process, Cycle, Hierarchy, Relationship, and Pyramid. You can also load SmartArt graphics from an external picture file or from the Microsoft Office website. Once you insert a SmartArt graphic, you can enter text labels to describe the graphic and format it with tools available on the ribbon. As with WordArt, SmartArt graphics support special formatting effects including drop shadows, reflections, glow edges, and 3D rotations.

The Dashboard worksheet has several useful charts including a pie chart that breaks down donations by type of donor contacts and a line chart that tracks the growth of the campaign fund since its inception. Jenya wants the dashboard to also include a chart showing the number of donors at different levels of donation. You can display this kind of information with a funnel chart.

Displaying Data with a Funnel Chart

Tip

Funnel charts are often used to track stages in a production process from initial stages through a completion stage.

A funnel chart is a chart that compares values within a hierarchy. Funnel charts get their name because they often appear in the shape of a funnel with the lowest level forming a wide top and the highest levels representing a progressively narrowing bottom. Fundraising donations often follow a funnel shape because many donors contribute small amounts, but few donors contribute large amounts.

Jenya wants a funnel chart that counts donors at different donation levels from $250 up to $500,000. The donation data you will use for the funnel chart is already in the Donor Sources worksheet. You will use that data to generate a funnel chart for the Dashboard worksheet.

To create a funnel chart of donors:

▶ 1. Go to the **Donor Sources** worksheet and select the range **B4:C15** containing the number of donors at each donation level.

▶ 2. On the ribbon, click the **Insert** tab, and then in the Charts group, click the **Recommended Charts** button. The Insert Chart dialog box opens.

▶ 3. Click the **All Charts** tab, and then in the list of chart types, click **Funnel**. There is one funnel chart available.

▶ 4. Click **OK**. The funnel chart is added to the workbook.

▶ 5. Move and resize the funnel chart to the **Dashboard** worksheet to cover the range **F20:H32**.

▶ 6. Change the chart title to **Donor Levels**.

▶ 7. On the Chart Design tab, in the Chart Styles group, click the **Change Colors** button, and then click **Colorful Palette 3**. See Figure 12–4.

| Figure 12–4 | Formatted funnel chart |

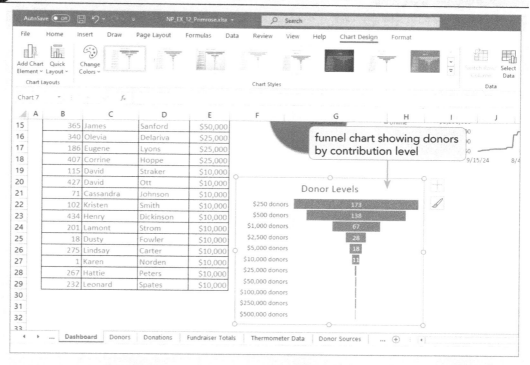

The funnel chart shows the drop-off in donors at higher contribution levels. So far, the campaign has 445 donors with 173 donors contributing at the $250 level, 138 donors at the $500 level, and only a handful donors at the highest levels.

Although few individuals have contributed large amounts to the campaign, the ones who did contributed a lot. Many fundraising efforts follow the 80/20 rule in which 80% of the total donations come from 20% of the donors. Jenya wants a second funnel chart that compares the total amount of contributions given by donors of different levels from $250 up to $500,000. You will create that funnel chart now.

To create a funnel chart of donations:

1. Go to the **Donation Sources** worksheet and select the range **B4:C15** containing the number of donations at each donation level.

2. On the ribbon, click the **Insert** tab, and then in the Charts group, click the **Recommended Charts** button. The Insert Chart dialog box opens.

3. On the Recommended Charts tab, click the **Funnel** chart type, and then click **OK**. The funnel chart of donations at different contribution levels is added to the worksheet.

4. Move and resize the funnel chart to the **Dashboard** worksheet to cover the range **I20:N32**.

5. Change the chart title to **Donation Levels**.

6. On the Chart Design tab, in the Chart Styles group, click the **Change Colors** button, and then click **Colorful Palette 3**. This funnel chart is formatted to match the Donor Levels funnel chart you created. See Figure 12–5.

Figure 12–5	Funnel chart of total donations by contribution level

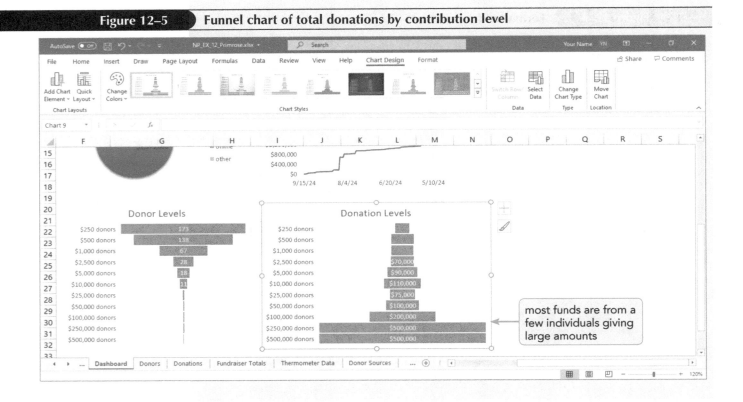

By breaking down donations by donor level, Jenya confirms that although most donors contribute at the lowest level, most of the total money raised comes from a few individuals contributing a lot. These charts illustrate that the success of the fundraising campaign depends in part on finding a few wealthy individuals willing to donate a great amount to the cause.

Insight

Creating a Thermometer Chart

Thermometer charts are fun charts to track progress toward a goal. The Dashboard worksheet includes one to show progress toward reaching the clinic's fundraising goal. Excel does not include a thermometer chart type, but you can create one by using a column chart and then reformatting it. To create a thermometer chart, do the following:

1. Enter the goal and progress toward a goal in a two-by-two table as follows:
Progress	Goal
57%	100%
2. Create a clustered column chart from the data range, and then on the Chart Design tab, in the Data group, click the Switch Row/Column button.
3. Double-click the Progress marker in the column chart to open the Format Data Series pane.
4. In the Series Option section, plot the Progress series on a secondary axis.
5. Set the range for both the primary and secondary axes to go from 0 to 1.

At this point, the two columns of the column chart are superimposed on each other. You can then edit the fill colors and line colors to create the thermometer effect. To make the chart look more like a thermometer, you can place a round shape filled with the progress color at the base of the column.

Because individual donors can have such a large impact on the success of the campaign, Jenya wants the Primrose Community Clinic staffers to be able to easily retrieve information on specific donors. You will add that feature next.

Hiding Error Values with the IFERROR Function

One challenge of creating an Excel application is ensuring that users are not distracted by error values that might appear in a cell. For example, an application might include the following formula to calculate the average value in the range A1:A50:

`=AVERAGE(A1:A50)`

However, if the range A1:A50 does not yet contain data, the formula will return the error value #DIV/0!. This error message can be confusing to users who are less familiar with Excel. To prevent this potential confusion, you can enclose formulas within the IFERROR function

`=IFERROR(value, value_if_error)`

where **value** is the value returned by a formula with no errors and **value_if_error** specifies a value if the formula does contain an error. Continuing the earlier example, the following formula returns the average of the data in the range A1:A50, but if no data has been entered in the range, it returns an empty text string:

`=IFERROR(AVERAGE(A1:A50), "")`

Jenya stores information about current donors in the Donations worksheet. The Donors worksheet already includes formulas to retrieve donor information based on a donor number. However, if no donor number is provided or an invalid donor number is included, the formulas will return the #N/A value. Jenya wants the VLOOKUP formulas to return an empty text string in place of an error value. You'll revise those formulas now.

> **Tip**
>
> In place of an empty text string, you can enter a text message that describes the error in more detail.

To add the IFERROR function to the VLOOKUP formulas:

▶ **1.** Go to **Donors** worksheet and select cell **E5**. In the range F6:F15, the VLOOKUP function retrieves corresponding information for the donor number entered in cell F5. The information is retrieved from the Donations table on the Donations worksheet using column index numbers specified in the range H6:H15. Currently, the table shows the information for the first donor—Karen Norden who donated $10,000.

▶ **2.** Delete the value in cell **F5**. The error value #N/A appears in the range F6:F15 because there is no longer a donor number to look up.

    Because Jenya does not want #N/A values appearing in the application, you'll revise the formula in cell F6 by enclosing the VLOOKUP function within an IFERROR function.

▶ **3.** Double-click cell **F6** to select it and enter Edit mode.

▶ **4.** Click directly after = to place the insertion point between the equal sign and VLOOKUP, and then type **IFERROR(** to begin the IFERROR function.

▶ **5.** Press **END** on your keyboard to move the insertion point to the end of the formula.

Be sure to type a comma before typing the *value_ if_error* to separate the arguments in the IFERROR function.

▶ **6.** Type **,"")** to complete the formula, and then press **ENTER**. The formula **=IFERROR(VLOOKUP($F$5,Donations,H6,FALSE),"")** is entered in cell F6. A blank text string appears instead of the #N/A value.

▶ **7.** Click cell **F6** and drag the fill handle down over the range **F7:F15** to copy the formula into the remaining cells in the range.

▶ **8.** Click the **Auto Fill Options button**, and then click **Fill Without Formatting** to retain the formats currently used in those cells. No error values appear on the worksheet even when a donor number is not entered. See Figure 12–6.

Figure 12–6 | **Error values hidden with the IFERROR function**

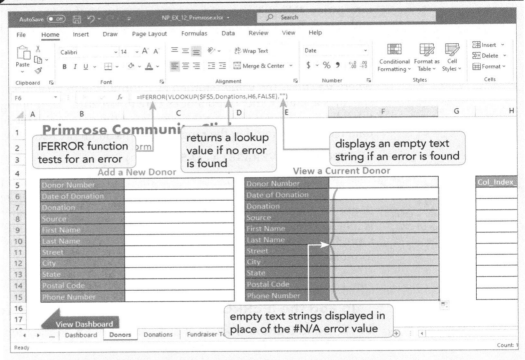

▶ **9.** In cell **F5**, enter **400** to look up information about the 400th donor. Information on Brandi Brown, who contributed $500 on August 30, 2024, appears.

▶ **10.** Save the workbook.

The IFERROR function eliminates distracting error values. However, remember to add this function only at the end of application development. When you first start building an application, you want to see all error values, so you can find and fix any mistakes in formulas or data.

Proskills

Written Communication: Handling Error Values

The IFERROR function is one of many functions supplied by Excel to catch errors. Another useful error function is the ISERROR function, which returns a value of TRUE if *value* is an error value and FALSE if it isn't:

    ISERROR(value)

For example, the following expression tests whether cell B10 contains an error value:

    ISERROR(B10)

The advantage of the ISERROR function is that you can enter the formula in one cell, such as B10, and then place an informative message about any errors in cell B10 within an adjacent cell. The following formula nests an ISERROR function within an IF function to display one message if cell B10 is in error and a different message if it is not:

    =IF(ISERROR(B10), "Input Error", "Input Valid")

The ISERROR function returns TRUE for any error value. To test for specific errors or specific data values, use the ISBLANK, ISNA, ISNUMBER, ISREF, ISLOGICAL, ISNONTEXT, or ISTEXT functions. For example, the ISNA function tests whether a cell is displaying the #N/A error value; the ISNUMBER function tests whether a cell contains a numeric value, and so forth. You can learn more about Excel error functions by viewing Excel Help.

Remember that an Excel application is designed for users who are not Excel experts, so you want to take advantage of the Excel error functions to catch errors for them. The end-user should focus on the task at hand, not on interpreting error values generated by the application.

You've completed your initial work on adding new graphics and charts to Jenya's application and you've used the IFERROR function to improve the appearance of the donor lookup. In the next session, you'll add features for entering new donor information that automatically notify the user when incorrect data is entered.

Review

Session 12.1 Quick Check

1. What is WordArt?
2. What is a funnel chart?
3. Convert the formula =B1/B10 into a formula that calculates this value only if there is no error and otherwise displays the message "Error Found".
4. Why would you use the IFERROR function?
5. What Excel function can be used to test whether a cell contains a numeric value?

Session 12.2 Visual Overview:

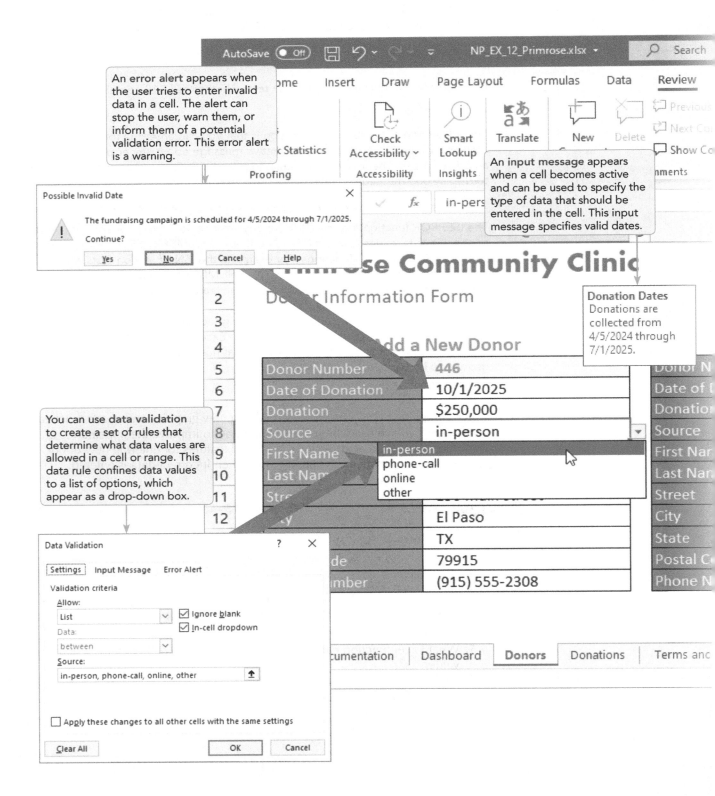

An error alert appears when the user tries to enter invalid data in a cell. The alert can stop the user, warn them, or inform them of a potential validation error. This error alert is a warning.

An input message appears when a cell becomes active and can be used to specify the type of data that should be entered in the cell. This input message specifies valid dates.

Possible Invalid Date

The fundraisng campaign is scheduled for 4/5/2024 through 7/1/2025.

Continue?

Yes   No   Cancel   Help

Donation Dates
Donations are collected from 4/5/2024 through 7/1/2025.

You can use data validation to create a set of rules that determine what data values are allowed in a cell or range. This data rule confines data values to a list of options, which appear as a drop-down box.

Primrose Community Clinic

Donor Information Form

Add a New Donor

Donor Number	446
Date of Donation	10/1/2025
Donation	$250,000
Source	in-person
First Name	
Last Name	
Street	
City	El Paso
State	TX
Postal Code	79915
Phone Number	(915) 555-2308

in-person
phone-call
online
other

Data Validation   ? ×

Settings | Input Message | Error Alert

Validation criteria

Allow:
List   ☑ Ignore blank
Data: ☑ In-cell dropdown
between
Source:
in-person, phone-call, online, other

☐ Apply these changes to all other cells with the same settings

Clear All   OK   Cancel

Documentation | Dashboard | **Donors** | Donations | Terms and

Data Validation and Workbook Protection

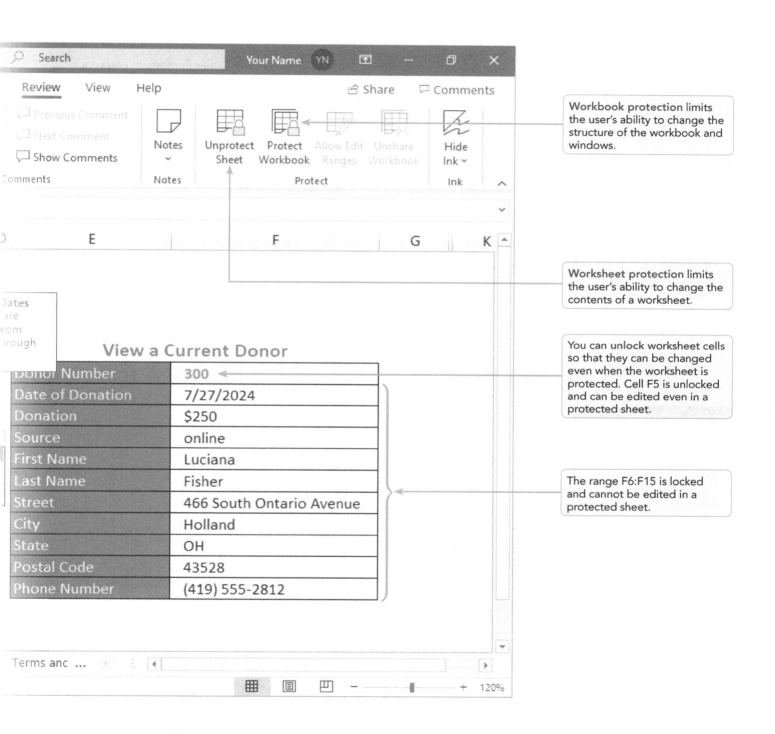

Workbook protection limits the user's ability to change the structure of the workbook and windows.

Worksheet protection limits the user's ability to change the contents of a worksheet.

You can unlock worksheet cells so that they can be changed even when the worksheet is protected. Cell F5 is unlocked and can be edited even in a protected sheet.

The range F6:F15 is locked and cannot be edited in a protected sheet.

View a Current Donor

Donor Number	300
Date of Donation	7/27/2024
Donation	$250
Source	online
First Name	Luciana
Last Name	Fisher
Street	466 South Ontario Avenue
City	Holland
State	OH
Postal Code	43528
Phone Number	(419) 555-2812

Validating Data Entry

Excel applications are intended to be used by people with all levels of Excel experience. However, anyone can mistakenly enter wrong data, change formulas, or delete important results. There may also be parts of the workbook you don't want users to even see. To avoid inadvertent changes to the application, you can restrict what users can do within an Excel application.

Whenever possible, you should have Excel calculate values rather than relying on user input. You can apply this rule to Jenya's application, which includes a worksheet form to enter information on new donors and donations. Jenya wants the user to enter the amount of the donation, the donor's contact information, and a donor ID number. The donor IDs are sequential—the first donor in the list is donor ID number 1, the second is donor ID number 2, and so forth. Thus, any new donor will always be assigned an ID that is 1 greater than the largest donor number currently in the donations list. Rather than have users enter that number manually, you'll insert a formula to automatically calculate the ID number based on the numbers already in the donations table.

To enter a formula to calculate the next donor number:

▶ 1. If you took a break after the previous session, make sure the NP_EX_12_Primrose workbook is open, and the Donors worksheet is the active sheet.

▶ 2. In cell **C5**, enter `=MAX(Donations[Donor Number])+1` as the formula to calculate the next donor ID with a value that is one greater than the maximum value of the Donor Number field from the Donations table. The cell displays 446 as the ID for the next donor to be added to the donations list. See Figure 12-7.

Figure 12-7	Formula automatically enters the donor number

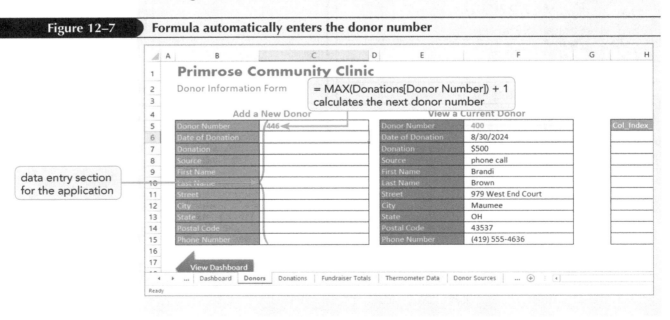

The rest of the fields in the range C6:C15 will contain values that must be entered by the user. You can also restrict the allowable data values for those cells by creating a **validation rule** that defines what data values are allowed and what are not.

Reference

Validating Data

- On the Data tab, in the Data Tools group, click the Data Validation button.
- Click the Settings tab.
- Click the Allow arrow, click the type of data allowed in the cell, and then enter the validation criteria for that data.
- Click the Input Message tab, and then enter a title and text for the input message.
- Click the Error Alert tab, and then, if necessary, click the Show error alert after invalid data is entered check box to insert a checkmark.
- Select an alert style, and then enter the title and text for the error alert message.
- Click OK.

Validating Dates

Tip

Only one validation rule can be assigned to a cell or data range.

Every validation rule is based on **validation criteria** specifying values allowed within a worksheet cell or range. For example, a date value might be limited to a range of dates or a numeric value might be limited to fall between a specified minimum and maximum value. Text values might be confined to a predefined list of possible entries. Figure 12–8 summarizes the types of criteria that Excel supports for validation rules.

Figure 12–8   **Validation criteria**

Type	Description
Any value	Any number, text, or date; removes any existing data validation
Whole Number	Integers only; you can specify the range of acceptable integers
Decimal	Any type of number; you can specify the range of acceptable numbers
List	Any value in a range or entered in the Data Validation dialog box separated by commas
Date	Dates only; you can specify the range of acceptable dates
Time	Times only; you can specify the range of acceptable times
Text Length	Text limited to a specified number of characters
Custom	Values based on the results of a logical formula

In cell C6, users will enter the date in which a new donation is made. The fundraising campaign is scheduled for 4/5/2024 through 7/1/2025, so any date must fall within that interval. You will create a validation rule for cell C6 that limits the cell value to dates between 4/5/2024 and 7/1/2025.

To create a validation rule for dates:

1. If necessary, click cell **C6** to select it.

Tip

To apply the same validation rule to multiple cells, select the range and then create the validation rule using the Data Validation dialog box.

2. On the ribbon, click the **Data** tab, and then in the Data Tools group, click the **Data Validation** button 🖳. The Data Validation dialog box opens.

3. If it is not already selected, click the **Settings** tab to display the criteria for the validation rule.

4. Click the **Allow** box, and then click **Date** to specify that dates are allowed in the cell.

▶ **5.** In the Data box, verify that **between** is selected as the comparison for the date criteria.

▶ **6.** In the Start date box, enter **4/5/2024** and in the End date box, enter **7/1/2025**. See Figure 12–9.

| Figure 12–9 | Data Validation dialog box |

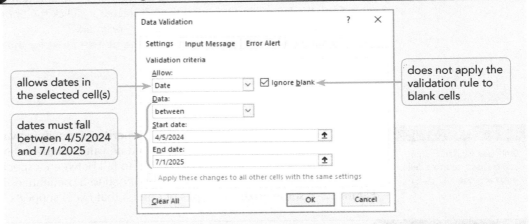

allows dates in the selected cell(s)

dates must fall between 4/5/2024 and 7/1/2025

does not apply the validation rule to blank cells

▶ **7.** Click **OK** to apply the validation rule to the cell.

To confirm that Excel will not allow invalid dates in the cell, you will try to enter a date that is *not* between 4/5/2024 and 7/1/2025.

To test the date validation rule:

Tip

Validation rules are tested only when the user exits Edit mode.

▶ **1.** In cell **C6**, type the date **8/1/2025** and press **ENTER**. A message dialog box opens, indicating that the cell value doesn't match the data validation restrictions defined for this cell.

▶ **2.** Click **Cancel** to close the dialog box and return to the cell with no specified date.

▶ **3.** In cell **C6**, type **9/18/2024** and press **ENTER**. Because this date satisfies the validation rule, no error message appears, and the date is accepted.

The default error message doesn't explain why the data was invalid. You can provide specific information to the user with a custom error message.

Creating a Validation Error Message

Excel provides three ways of responding to invalid data. In decreasing order of strictness, they are:

1. **Stop**—The user is stopped, and no data entry is allowed in the cell unless it satisfies the validation rule (the default).
2. **Warning**—The user is warned, and data is allowed in the cell only after it is confirmed by the user as being correct.
3. **Information**—The user is informed that possibly invalid data is being entered and is given the opportunity to cancel the data entry.

With each error response, you can create a custom message explaining in more detail why the data was invalid and what the user should do to correct the problem.

Jenya wants the rule for donation dates to display a warning because it is possible that some donations will fall outside of the campaign period. This gives users the ability to still insert a date value that falls outside the stated date range. You will create the warning message now.

To create the warning error message:

▶ **1.** Click cell **C6** to select it, and then on the Data tab, in the Data Tools group, click the **Data Validation** button. The Data Validation dialog box opens.

▶ **2.** Click the **Error Alert** tab. You'll create the warning message on this tab.

▶ **3.** Verify that the **Show error alert after invalid data is entered** check box is selected.

▶ **4.** Click the **Style** box, and then click **Warning** to set the type of error alert.

▶ **5.** Click the **Title** box, and then type **Possible Invalid Date** as the title for the error message.

▶ **6.** Click the **Error message** box, and then type **The fundraising campaign is scheduled for 4/5/2024 through 7/1/2025.** (including the period). See Figure 12–10.

Tip

If you don't want users to be constantly reminded about the validation rule, deselect the Show error alert after invalid data is entered check box.

Figure 12–10 Warning error alert message

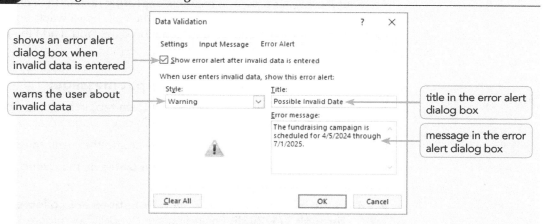

shows an error alert dialog box when invalid data is entered

warns the user about invalid data

title in the error alert dialog box

message in the error alert dialog box

▶ **7.** Click **OK**.

▶ **8.** Click cell **C6**, type **8/1/2025** as the donation date, and then press **ENTER**. The warning message you created appears. See Figure 12–11.

Figure 12–11   **Warning alert for an invalid date**

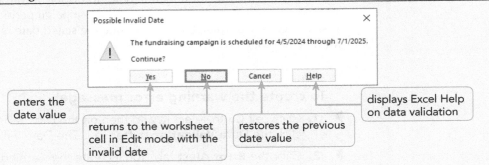

Possible Invalid Date

⚠ The fundraising campaign is scheduled for 4/5/2024 through 7/1/2025.

Continue?

Yes   No   Cancel   Help

- enters the date value
- returns to the worksheet cell in Edit mode with the invalid date
- restores the previous date value
- displays Excel Help on data validation

> **9.** Click **Cancel** to stop the attempt at entering a potentially invalid data and return to cell C6, restoring the previous valid date of 9/18/2024.

Rather than constantly notifying users of attempts of entering invalid data, you can make an application more user-friendly by providing the validation rules in advance with an input message.

Creating an Input Message

An input message is a pop-up message appearing next to the cell that gives information about the type of data that is expected in the cell. Jenya wants you to add an input message to cell C6 indicating valid donation dates. You'll add the input message now.

To create the donation dates input message:

> **1.** With cell C6 still selected, on the Data tab, in the Data Tools group, click the **Data Validation** button 📇. The Data Validation dialog box opens.

> **2.** Click the **Input Message** tab. You create the input message on this tab.

> **3.** Click the **Title** box, type **Donation Dates** as the dialog box title, and then press **TAB**.

> **4.** In the Input message box, type **Donations are collected from 4/5/2024 through 7/1/2025.** (including the period). See Figure 12–12.

Figure 12–12   **Custom input message**

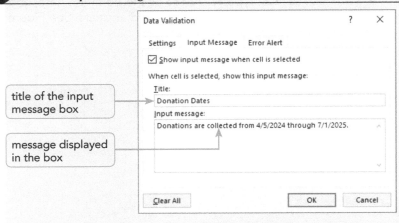

Data Validation   ?   ×

Settings   Input Message   Error Alert

☑ Show input message when cell is selected

When cell is selected, show this input message:

Title:
- title of the input message box → Donation Dates

Input message:
- message displayed in the box → Donations are collected from 4/5/2024 through 7/1/2025.

Clear All   OK   Cancel

▶ **5.** Click **OK**. Now when cell C6 is selected, an input message appears next to the cell. See Figure 12–13.

Figure 12–13 | **Input message box**

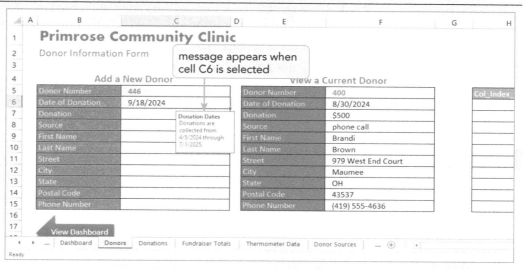

Jenya is confident that with the input message and validation rule, it is unlikely that invalid dates will be entered in cell C6. If at any time you need to remove the validation rule, error message, or input message from a cell or range, you can reopen the Data Validation dialog box and click the Clear Rules button.

Insight

Validating Against Past and Future Dates

Some applications, such as those that track sales or shipping data, limit the data to dates occurring before or after the current date. You can validate those dates using the TODAY function. To allow only dates before or on the current date, do the following:

1. Open the Data Validation dialog box.
2. Click the Allow box, and then click Choose Date.
3. Click the Data box, and then click "less than or equal to".
4. In the End date box, enter =TODAY().
5. Click OK.

Any date value that is less than or equal to the current date will be accepted. To allow only dates on or after the current date, change the value in the Data box to "greater than or equal to" and enter =TODAY() in the Start date box.

Validating Against a List

Another type of validation rule limits data values to a predefined list of accepted choices. Such lists appear within the cells as a drop-down list box from which the user can select a value, removing the need for typing. The list can be based on cells within the worksheet or entered directly into the Data Validation dialog box as a comma-separated list.

In this application, Jenya is tracking donations made in specific amounts from $250 up to $500,000. The donation categories are listed in the range J5:J15 of the Donors worksheet. You'll create a validation rule for cell C7 that limits its possible values to those listed in that range.

To validate the donation amounts against a list of values:

▶ **1.** Click cell **C7**, and then on the Data tab, in the Data Tools group, click the **Data Validation** button. The Data Validation dialog box opens.

▶ **2.** Click the **Settings** tab.

▶ **3.** Click the **Allow** box, and then click **List**.

> **Tip**
>
> To reference cells from another worksheet, use a named range in the expression.

▶ **4.** Press **TAB** to move the insertion point to the Source box, and then select the range **J5:J15**. The range reference =$J$5:$J$15 appears in the Source box. See Figure 12–14.

Figure 12–14 ▶ **List box validation**

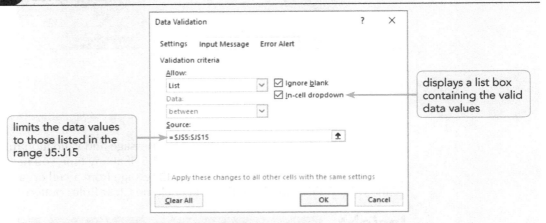

> limits the data values to those listed in the range J5:J15

> displays a list box containing the valid data values

▶ **5.** Click **OK** to return to the worksheet.

▶ **6.** Click the **arrow** button that appears next to cell C7 to display the list box of values, then scroll down and point to **$250,000**. See Figure 12–15.

Figure 12–15 ▶ **List box values**

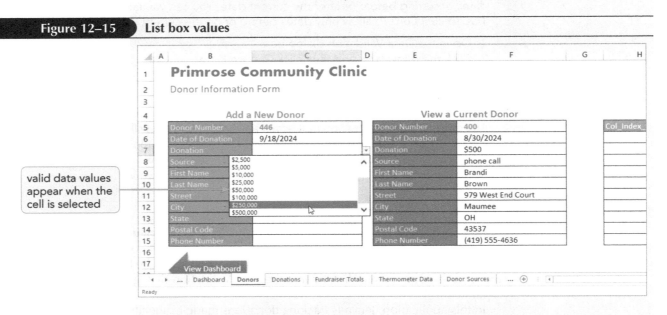

> valid data values appear when the cell is selected

▶ **7.** Click **$250,000**. The selected donation amount is entered in the cell.

In cell C8, users will enter the source of donation. The four possible values are in-person, phone call, online, or other. You'll enter a validation rule for cell C8 to limit values to these four choices by entering them as a comma-separated list in the Data Validation dialog box.

To validate donation source against a comma-separated list of values:

▶ **1.** Click cell **C8**, and then on the Data tab, in the Data Tools group, click the **Data Validation** button 📇. The Data Validation dialog box opens.

▶ **2.** On the Settings tab, click the **Allow** box, and then click **List**.

▶ **3.** Press **TAB** to move the insertion point to the Source box, and then type **in-person, phone call, online, other** (including the commas between each donation source). See Figure 12–16.

Figure 12–16	Comma-separated data values

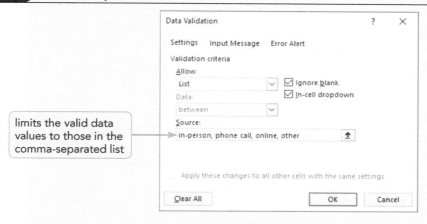

limits the valid data values to those in the comma-separated list

▶ **4.** Click **OK**.

▶ **5.** Click the **arrow** button next to cell C8, and then click **in-person**. The data source is added to the cell.

The only validation rule for the contact information in the range C9:C15 is that they should not be left blank. You can test for empty cells using a custom validation rule.

Creating a Custom Validation Rule

A custom validation rule is based on a logical expression that evaluates something as either TRUE (valid) or FALSE (invalid). For example, the expression `A10 = B10` returns a value of TRUE if cell A10 is equal to cell B10 and FALSE if it is not. The expression can include a reference to the cell for which you are validating, testing whether that cell's value satisfies the conditions of the logical expression.

The logical expression can include any of the Excel functions that evaluate as TRUE or FALSE. That means that the formula `=ISNUMBER(A10)` when applied to cell A10 will validate that cell only if it contains a number. You can combine logical expressions using an AND or an OR function to allow for multiple validation tests within the same cell. For example, the formula `=AND(A10 = B10, ISNUMBER(A10))` passes validation only when cell A10 is equal to cell B10 *and* is a number.

Jenya wants users to be informed that they have entered a blank value for a cell that should have a value. You will use the expression `=NOT(ISBLANK(C9))` to test whether

Tip

The expression for a custom validation rule can only return a logical (TRUE/FALSE) value.

the value in cell C9 is blank or not. If the cell is not blank, the expression returns the value TRUE (valid); otherwise, it returns the value FALSE (invalid). You'll apply this custom validation rule to all of the cells in the range C9:C15 and add an error alert.

To create a custom validation rule for the range C9:C15:

▶ **1.** Select the range **C9:C15**, and then on the Data tab, in the Data Tools group, click the **Data Validation** button [image]. The Data Validation dialog box opens.

▶ **2.** On the Settings tab, click the **Allow** box, and then click **Custom**.

▶ **3.** Click the **Ignore blank** check box to deselect it. This ensures that Excel does *not* ignore blank cells.

> Be sure to include the equal sign so Excel recognizes the custom validation rule as a formula.

▶ **4.** In the Formula box, type **=NOT(ISBLANK(C9))** to test whether the value in cell C9 is blank. See Figure 12–17.

Figure 12–17   **Custom validation rule**

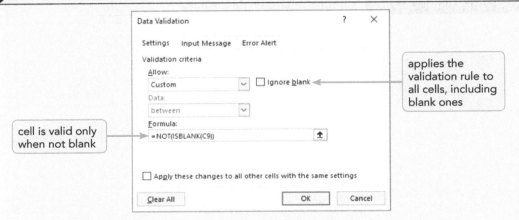

cell is valid only when not blank → Formula: =NOT(ISBLANK(C9))

applies the validation rule to all cells, including blank ones → Ignore blank

▶ **5.** Click the **Error Alert** tab, click the **Style** box, and then click **Information** to select the error alert style.

▶ **6.** Press **TAB**, type **Missing Data** in the Title box, press **TAB**, and then type **Do you mean to leave this cell blank?** in the Error message box.

▶ **7.** Click **OK** to apply the validation rule to the selected range.

▶ **8.** Double-click cell **C9** to enter Edit mode, and then without typing any content, press **ENTER**. The Missing Data dialog box opens, asking whether you intend to leave the cell blank.

▶ **9.** Click **OK** to leave cell C9 blank, return to the workbook, and select cell C10.

▶ **10.** Repeat Steps 8 and 9 for cell C10 to confirm that the validation rule also applies to this cell.

▶ **11.** In the range **C9:C15**, enter the remaining new donor information, as follows: **Kevin** in cell C9, **Nielsen** in cell C10, **100 Main Street** in cell C11, **El Paso** in cell C12, **TX** in cell C13, **79915** in cell C14, and **(915) 555-2308** in cell C15.

Every cell in the range C9:C15 obeys the same validation rule. Because you used a relative reference for the formula, the reference changes as the rule is applied throughout the range. For example, in cell C10, the expression is **=NOT(ISBLANK(C10))** and so forth. If you don't want a reference to change, use an absolute cell reference or a defined name in your formula.

Insight

Validating for Uniqueness

Some entries require unique data. For example, if you are entering ID numbers into a workbook, you will need to ensure that those ID numbers are unique and not duplicated. You can use a custom validation rule to test for uniqueness by using the COUNTIF function in the form

=COUNTIF(*range*, *cell*) = 0

where *range* is the *range* containing a list of data values and *cell* is the cell that should not have a value already entered in that list. For example, the following formula tests whether the value in cell B2 has already been entered in the range D1:D100:

=COUNTIF($D$1:$D$100, B2) = 0

If the cell you are validating is also part of the range containing the data values, the formula has this slightly different form which tests whether the cell value occurs exactly once in the selected range:

=COUNTIF(*range*, *cell*) = 1

The following formula validates the value in cell D1 against the entire range D1:D100.

=COUNTIF($D$1:$D$100, D1) = 1

If you apply this validation rule to all the cells in the range D1:D100, every cell will be validated for uniqueness within the range. If the range D1:D100 contains ID numbers, each ID must be unique to pass validation.

With custom validation rules and Excel functions, you can create a wide variety of powerful validation criteria in which cell values are validated against values in other cells or calculations of the values in other cells.

Validating Data Already in the Workbook

A validation rule is applied only during data entry when the cell is in Edit mode. Validation rules are not applied to cells already containing data. To check data already in the workbook you can use the Circle Invalid Data command, which does not remove invalid data but does circle it so that you can edit or remove on your own.

To validate data already entered in the workbook, do the following:

1. Enter a validation rule for the range of cells you want to validate.
2. On the Data tab, in the Data Tools group, click the Data Validation arrow, and then click Circle Invalid Data. Red circles surround each cell containing invalid data.
3. To remove the validation circles, edit the cell(s) to make them valid or click the Data Validation arrow and click Clear Validation Circles.

To ensure the integrity of your data, you should use the Circle Invalid Data command on any data table in which you plan to perform an analysis.

Hiding Workbook Content

Excel workbooks often contain content you don't want users to see. You can hide worksheet rows and columns or entire worksheets from the user. Sometimes this is done to prevent users from seeing sensitive material. But more often, it's done to remove distractions such as data that is not important to your users or to keep users from mistakenly editing content that should not be edited. Hiding a row, column, or worksheet does not impact any formula in the workbook. Hidden formulas work the same as visible ones.

Jenya wants you to hide the content of cells H through J in the Donors worksheet because their content is not of interest to the users entering or retrieving donor data.

To hide worksheet columns H through J:

▶ **1.** Select the column headers for column **H** through column **J**.

▶ **2.** Right-click the selected columns, and then click **Hide** on the shortcut menu. The columns are hidden.

▶ **3.** Look at the column headers and notice that they jump from G to K.

Jenya created several worksheets that contain the data used for generating the charts and PivotTables that appear on the Dashboard worksheet. She wants you to hide these sheets from users.

To hide worksheets in the workbook:

▶ **1.** Click the **Fundraiser Totals** sheet tab to select it.

▶ **2.** Use the Sheet Scrolling buttons in the lower-left corner of the workbook window to scroll to the last sheet in the workbook.

▶ **3.** Press **SHIFT**, click the **Donation History** sheet tab, and then release **SHIFT**. The Fundraiser Tools worksheet through the Donation History worksheet are now part of a worksheet group.

▶ **4.** Right-click the worksheet group, and then click **Hide** on the shortcut menu. The worksheet group is hidden, leaving only the Documentation, Dashboard, Donors, Donations, and Terms and Definitions worksheets still visible.

You can make a hidden worksheet visible again. Right-click any sheet tab in the workbook, click Unhide on the shortcut menu, click the name of the hidden worksheet you want, and then click OK to make the selected worksheet reappear. To unhide multiple worksheets, hold the CTRL key as you click each sheet name in the list of hidden worksheets.

Protecting Workbook Contents

A final way of restricting the actions of users in an application is to protect a worksheet or an entire workbook from unauthorized changes. Once a worksheet or workbook is protected, it can be altered only by users who know the password that opens the sheet for editing.

Protecting a Worksheet

When you set up worksheet protection, you specify which actions users are allowed in the protected sheet. The default is to allow users to only select cells, but you can also give users the ability to perform other tasks such as formatting cells, inserting rows and columns, editing scenarios, sorting data, and deleting rows and columns. As long as the worksheet is protected, those limitations are in place. They are removed only after the sheet is no longer protected.

Reference

Protecting a Worksheet

To unlock cells that users can access in a protected worksheet:
- Select the range to unlock so that users can enter data in them.
- On the Home tab, in the Cells group, click the Format button, and then click Format Cells (or press CTRL+1).
- In the Format Cells dialog box, click the Protection tab.
- Click the Locked check box to remove the checkmark.
- Click OK.

To protect a worksheet:
- On the Review tab, in the Protect group, click the Protect Sheet button.
- Enter a password (optional).
- Select all the actions you want to allow users to take when the worksheet is protected.
- Click OK.

Jenya wants you to protect the worksheets in the workbook that appear after the Documentation sheet. You'll protect each of the four sheets now.

To protect a worksheet:

1. Click the **Dashboard** sheet tab.

2. On the ribbon, click the **Review** tab, and then in the Protect group, click the **Protect Sheet** button. The Protect Sheet dialog box opens. See Figure 12–18.

Figure 12–18	Protect Sheet dialog box

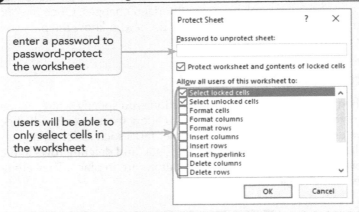

enter a password to password-protect the worksheet

users will be able to only select cells in the worksheet

In the Protect Sheet dialog box, you can specify a password that must be entered before the sheet can be unprotected. You can also go through a checklist of tasks that users are allowed to do within the protected sheet. The default is to allow users to select worksheet cells.

▶ **3.** Click **OK** to protect the sheet without a password and without allowing users to do anything other than selecting cells.

▶ **4.** For each of the three remaining worksheets in the workbook, go to the worksheet, click any cell in the worksheet, and then repeat Steps 2 and 3.

▶ **5.** Go to the **Donors** worksheet and click cell **C6**. You will verify that you cannot enter data into this protected sheet.

▶ **6.** Try to enter a value into the cell. An error message dialog box opens indicating that you cannot make changes on a protected sheet.

▶ **7.** Click **OK**.

Tip

Passwords are case-sensitive. The password "admin" is different from "ADMIN".

If you don't include a password in the Protect Sheet dialog box, any user will be able to unprotect the sheet by clicking the Unprotect Sheet button in the Protect group on the Review tab. If you do include a password, *don't lose it*. Without the password, you won't be able to unprotect the sheet.

Protecting a Workbook

Worksheet protection applies only to the contents of a worksheet, not to the worksheet itself. To keep a worksheet from being modified, you need to protect the workbook. You can protect both the structure and the windows of a workbook. Protecting the structure prevents users from renaming, deleting, hiding, or inserting worksheets. Protecting the windows prevents users from moving, resizing, closing, or hiding parts of the Excel window. The default is to protect only the structure of the workbook, not the windows used to display it.

Reference

Protecting a Workbook

- On the Review tab, in the Protect group, click the Protect Workbook button.
- Click the check boxes to indicate whether you want to protect the workbook's structure, windows, or both.
- Enter a password (optional).
- Click OK.

You can also add a password to the workbook protection. However, the same guidelines apply as for protecting worksheets. Add a password only if you are concerned that others might unprotect the workbook and modify it. If you add a password, keep in mind that it is case-sensitive, and you cannot unprotect the workbook without it.

Jenya asks that you protect the workbook itself so that users cannot inadvertently hide or delete a worksheet.

To protect Jenya's workbook:

▶ **1.** On the Review tab, in the Protect group, click the **Protect Workbook** button. The Protect Structure and Windows dialog box opens. See Figure 12–19.

| Figure 12–19 | Protect Structure and Windows dialog box |

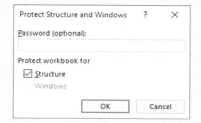

▶ **2.** Make sure the **Structure** check box is checked and the **Password** box is blank. The Windows check box is unavailable and unchecked.

▶ **3.** Click **OK** to protect the workbook without specifying a password.

▶ **4.** Right-click the **Donors** sheet tab, and then on the shortcut menu, notice that the Insert, Delete, Rename, Move or Copy, Tab Color, Hide, and Unhide commands are gray. This indicates that these options for modifying worksheets are no longer available in the protected workbook.

▶ **5.** Press **ESC** to close the shortcut menu.

Unprotecting a Worksheet and a Workbook

You can always unprotect a protected worksheet to make additional edits to its content. If you assigned a password when you protected the worksheet, you must enter that password to remove worksheet protection. Likewise, you can unprotect a protected workbook to make changes to its structure, such as if you need to insert a new worksheet or rename an existing worksheet. Once you make the changes you need to the worksheet content and workbook structure, you can then reapply worksheet and workbook protection.

Jenya has edits she wants you to make to the Donors worksheet. You will unprotect that worksheet to make the changes. You can leave the other worksheets protected.

To turn off protection for the Donors worksheet:

1. On the Review tab, in the Protect group, click the **Unprotect Sheet** button. The name of the button changes to Protect Sheet and the Donors worksheet is once again available for editing.

> **Tip**
>
> To remove workbook protection, click the Protect Workbook button in the Protect group on the Review tab.

Locking and Unlocking Cells

Most applications don't require that you protect everything. Usually, you want to allow users to edit some cells but not others. In particular, you don't want users to be able to edit cells containing formulas that are important to actions of the application. You can determine which cells users can edit with the locked property.

Every cell in the workbook contains a **locked property** that determines whether changes can be made to that cell. The locked property is unused until the worksheet is protected. Once a worksheet is protected, only those cells that are unlocked can be edited. See Figure 12–20.

| Figure 12–20 | Locked and unlocked cells |

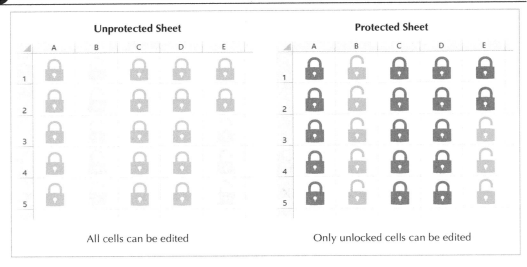

The default is to lock every cell in a worksheet. Once the sheet is protected, *all* cell contents are protected. However, you can unlock some cells to make them editable even with a protected worksheet.

Insight

Highlighting Unlocked Cells

You cannot tell from the worksheet which cells are locked or unlocked until you protect the sheet and attempt to edit cells. However, you can highlight all the unlocked cells with conditional formatting and the CELL function. The **CELL function** is used to retrieve information about a cell and has the syntax:

CELL(*info_type*, *reference*)

where ***info_type*** is the name of information about the cell and ***reference*** is the cell reference. For example, the following formula determines whether cell A1 is locked:

=CELL("protect", A1)

The formula returns a value of 1 for locked cells and 0 for unlocked cells. You can use this formula in a conditional format to highlight unlocked cells in the worksheet. Do the following:

1. Unprotect the worksheet and select all cells in the sheet.
2. On the Home tab, in the Styles group, click the Conditional Formatting button, and then click New Rule.
3. In the New Formatting Rule dialog box, click Use a formula to determine which cells to format.
4. In the Format values where this formula is true box, enter the formula =CELL("protect", A1)=0.
5. Click Format to select a format for cells that are unlocked, and then click OK.
6. Click OK to apply the conditional format.

Every unlocked cell in the selected range will be formatted with the conditional format you chose.

Jenya wants users to be able to edit the cells in the range C6:C15 and cell F5. You'll change the lock property of those cells now.

To unlock the cells in the range C6:C15,F5:

1. Select the nonadjacent range **C6:C15,F5**.

2. On the ribbon, click the **Home** tab. In the Cells group, click the **Format** button, and then click **Format Cells** (or press **CTRL+1**). The Format Cells dialog box opens.

3. Click the **Protection** tab to view protection options for the selected cells.

4. Click the **Locked** check box to remove the checkmark. See Figure 12–21.

Figure 12–21   **Protection tab in the Format Cells dialog box**

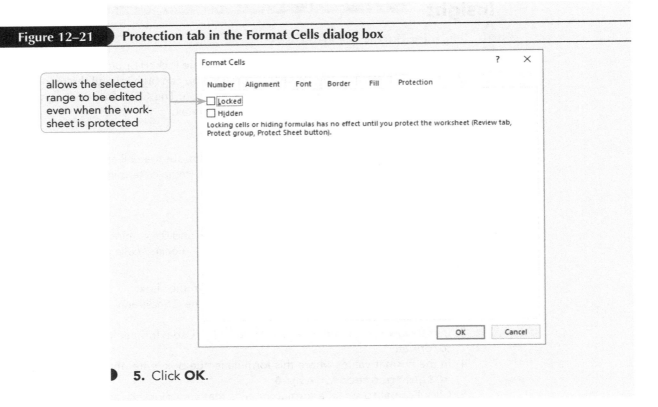

allows the selected
range to be edited
even when the work-
sheet is protected

5. Click **OK**.

Next, you will protect the Donors worksheet again and confirm you can edit the unlocked cells even when the sheet is protected.

To protect the Donors worksheet:

1. On the ribbon, click the **Review** tab, and then in the Protect group, click the **Protect Sheet** button. The Protect Sheet dialog box opens.

2. Click **OK** to apply protection to the worksheet.

3. Click cell **F5**, type **300** as the donor number, and then press **ENTER**. The worksheet displays data for Luciana Fisher who donated $250 to the campaign on 7/27/2024. You were able to edit a cell that was unlocked.

4. Double-click cell **F6** to attempt to go into Edit mode. A dialog box opens, alerting you that the cell is protected. You cannot edit a cell that was not unlocked.

5. Click **OK** to close the dialog box.

6. Double-click cell **C11**, change Kevin Nielsen's street address from 100 Main Street to **150 Main Street**, and then press **ENTER**. You can edit this unlocked cell.

7. Save the workbook.

The only cells that users can edit in the Donors worksheet are the cells you want them to edit. Any cell containing a formula or a design element is locked and cannot be edited.

Proskills

Teamwork: Assigning Ranges to Users

A workbook might be shared among several colleagues. But you might want to assign each colleague a different range to edit. The technique of unlocking cells does not distinguish between one user and another. The cells in a workbook are locked or unlocked for every user.

You can fine-tune access to the contents of a workbook using the Allow Edit Ranges button in the Protect group on the Review tab. This tool lets you define who can edit which ranges when the worksheet is protected. You can even create different passwords for each range. Thus, workers in one department can edit one range of data and while workers in another department are limited to a different range.

Editable ranges are a useful tool when you have several groups of employees accessing and editing the workbook. You can then control who has access to existing data and who has the clearance to enter new data.

You've restricted access to Jenya's Excel workbook by controlling what kind of data users can enter, what parts of the workbook are visible to them, and what parts of the workbook can be edited. In the next session, you will finish Jenya's application by creating a macro to insert new donors into the Donations table.

Review

Session 12.2 Quick Check

1. What are three responses to invalid data?
2. Why would you create an input message for a cell?
3. What are two ways of specifying a validation list?
4. Provide a custom validation expression that validates the data only if cell C10 is less than or equal cell D10.
5. When do you use the Circle Invalid Data command?
6. Can you rename a protected worksheet? Explain why or why not.
7. What is a locked cell? When does locking a cell take effect?

Session 12.3 Visual Overview:

The Macros button opens the Macro dialog box, which you use to run or edit macros.

The Record Macro button opens the Record Macro dialog box, which you use to start recording a macro.

The macro security settings control the security level for workbooks containing macros.

In the Record Macro dialog box, you specify a name, shortcut key, location, and description of a macro.

The macro recorder records Excel commands and stores them in a macro.

A macro button runs the assigned macro when clicked.

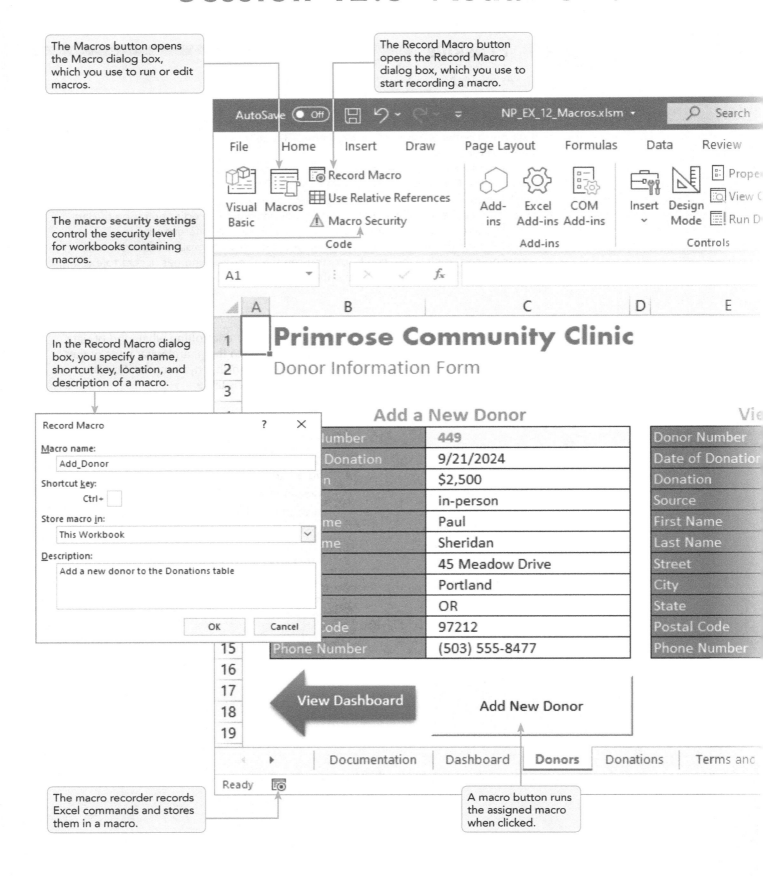

Macros and Visual Basic for Applications

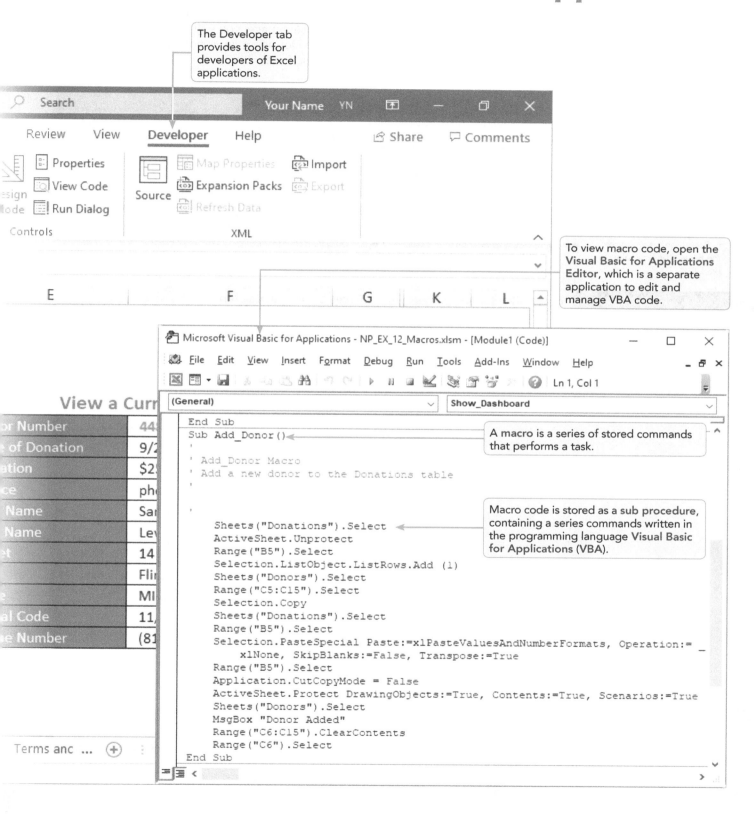

The Developer tab provides tools for developers of Excel applications.

To view macro code, open the Visual Basic for Applications Editor, which is a separate application to edit and manage VBA code.

A macro is a series of stored commands that performs a task.

Macro code is stored as a sub procedure, containing a series commands written in the programming language Visual Basic for Applications (VBA).

```
End Sub
Sub Add_Donor()
'
' Add_Donor Macro
' Add a new donor to the Donations table
'
'
    Sheets("Donations").Select
    ActiveSheet.Unprotect
    Range("B5").Select
    Selection.ListObject.ListRows.Add (1)
    Sheets("Donors").Select
    Range("C5:C15").Select
    Selection.Copy
    Sheets("Donations").Select
    Range("B5").Select
    Selection.PasteSpecial Paste:=xlPasteValuesAndNumberFormats, Operation:= _
        xlNone, SkipBlanks:=False, Transpose:=True
    Range("B5").Select
    Application.CutCopyMode = False
    ActiveSheet.Protect DrawingObjects:=True, Contents:=True, Scenarios:=True
    Sheets("Donors").Select
    MsgBox "Donor Added"
    Range("C6:C15").ClearContents
    Range("C6").Select
End Sub
```

Loading the Excel Developer Tab

Jenya wants you to complete the Excel application by creating a customized interface that allows users to navigate the workbook, add new donors, and update the dashboard without using the Excel menu. In developing this interface, you will need access to Excel developer tools on the Developer tab. The Developer tab is not displayed by default, so you will first have to add the tab to the Excel ribbon.

To add the Developer tab to the ribbon:

▶ 1. If you took a break after the previous session, make sure the NP_EX_12_Primrose workbook is open.

▶ 2. Look for the **Developer** tab on the ribbon. If you do not see it, continue with Step 3; otherwise, read but do not perform the rest of these steps.

Tip

You can also click Options in Backstage view to open the Excel Options dialog box.

▶ 3. Right-click a blank spot on the ribbon, and then click **Customize the Ribbon** on the shortcut menu. The Excel Options dialog box opens.

▶ 4. In the right pane, click the **Developer** check box to select it. See Figure 12–22.

Figure 12–22 Customize Ribbon category in the Excel Options dialog box

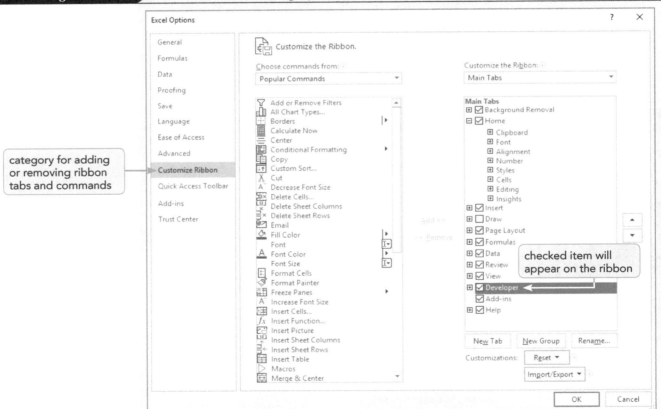

▶ 5. Click **OK**. The dialog box closes, and the Developer tab is added to the ribbon.

Now that you've added the Developer tab, you can start working on the next phase in developing an Excel application: creating a macro.

Automating Tasks with Macros

A macro is a collection of commands that accomplish a task. The tasks could be short and straightforward such as switching between one workbook and another, or they can be long and involved such as adding a new record to an Excel table and refreshing the reports that rely on that table. Macros save time by replacing a long sequence of commands with a single command.

Macros are stored as lines of program code, usually attached to the workbook. When you run a macro, Excel accesses the stored code, executing every command in the macro. There are two ways to generate macro code: You can type the code directly into a program editor, or you can record the actions to accomplish the task and have Excel write the macro code for you based on the recording. The best way to start learning about macros is through the recording process.

Recording a Macro

The macro recorder works like any other kind of recorder: You start the recorder, perform whatever tasks you wish, and then stop the recorder. All of your actions are recorded as macro code for later playback.

Reference

Recording a Macro

- Save the workbook before you start the recording.
- On the Developer tab, in the Code group, click the Record Macro button.
- Enter a name for the macro.
- Specify a shortcut key (optional).
- Specify the location to store the macro.
- Enter a description of the macro (optional).
- Click OK to start the macro recorder.
- Perform the tasks you want to automate.
- Click the Stop Recording button.

Jenya wants users of the workbook to be able to quickly access the contents of the dashboard. To accomplish that task, you will record a macro to switch to the Dashboard worksheet from anywhere in the workbook. You'll begin the macro recorder now.

To start the macro recorder:

> **1.** Save the workbook.

> **2.** Go to the **Documentation** worksheet. This is the starting point of the macro.

> **3.** On the ribbon, click the **Developer** tab.

> **4.** In the Code group, click the **Record Macro** button. The Record Macro dialog box opens.

> **5.** Type **Show_Dashboard** in the Macro name box, and then press **TAB** twice to go to the Store macro in box.

> **6.** If it is not already selected, select **This Workbook** from the Store macro in box to store the macro in the current workbook, and then press **TAB** to go to the Description box.

> **7.** Type **Display the contents of the Dashboard** in the Description box. See Figure 12–23.

Always save your workbook before beginning a recording. If you make a mistake in the recording, you can close the file without saving your changes and try again.

| Figure 12–23 | Record Macro dialog box |

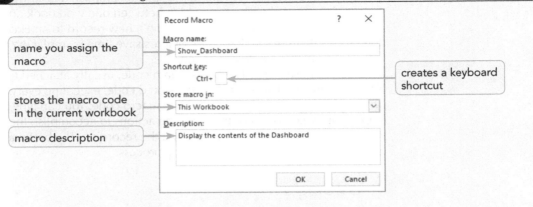

You are ready to begin recording your actions. From this point on, every command you perform will be recorded as part of the Show_Dashboard macro. In any macro recording, you want to be very careful and precise in following the steps because every command you perform will be recorded in the order you perform them in. You'll start recording the macro now.

To record the macro:

▶ **1.** Click **OK** to begin the recorder.

▶ **2.** Click the **Dashboard** sheet tab to make Dashboard the active sheet in the workbook.

▶ **3.** Click cell **A1** to make it the active cell in the worksheet. Note that even if cell A1 is already the active cell, you still select it to ensure that is always the active cell when a user switches to the dashboard.

▶ **4.** On the Developer tab, in the Code group, click the **Stop Recording** button. The macro recording is turned off and no additional tasks will be added to the macro code.

Be sure to turn off the macro recorder when you are done. Otherwise, the recorder will add every additional task to the macro code.

The Show_Dashboard macro that you recorded is stored in the current document.

Insight

Creating a Macro Library with the Personal Macro Workbook

Excel has three options for storing macro code: in the current workbook where the macro was recorded, in a new workbook, or in the Personal Macro workbook. The **Personal Macro workbook** is a hidden workbook named Personal.xlsb that opens whenever you start Excel. Every macro in the Personal Macro workbook is accessible to any open workbook, making the Personal Macro workbook an ideal location for a macro library.

The Personal.xlsb file is stored in the Excel XLSTART folder. If you want to share your macro library, you can send colleagues a copy of the workbook or you can make that workbook available on a shared server. An IT department might have such a macro library stored on a shared server with macros tailored to specific needs of its organization or company.

Running a Macro

After recording a macro, you should run it to verify that it works as intended. In running the macro, Excel runs the same commands in the same order that they were recorded, including any mistakes you may have made during the recording!

Reference

Running a Macro

- Press the shortcut key assigned to the macro.
or
- On the Developer tab, in the Code group, click the Macros button.
- Select the macro from the list of macros.
- Click Run.

You will test the Show_Dashboard macro by running it.

To run the Show_Dashboard macro:

▶ **1.** Go to the **Donors** worksheet as the starting point for running the macro. The macro should work from any worksheet.

▶ **2.** On the Developer tab, in the Code group, click the **Macros** button (or press **ALT+F8**). The Macro dialog box opens. See Figure 12–24.

Figure 12–24 ▶ **Macro dialog box**

▶ **3.** Verify the **Show_Dashboard** macro is selected, and then click **Run**. The Dashboard worksheet becomes the active sheet with cell A1 selected.

Trouble? If the macro does not go to the Dashboard worksheet, you probably made a mistake in recording the actions. Close the workbook without saving, and then reopen the workbook and repeat both set of steps in the previous section to record the macro again.

The Show_Dashboard macro will work from any sheet in the workbook, jumping the user to cell A1 in the Dashboard worksheet. Before creating other macros, you should save your workbook and the macro you recorded so you don't lose your work if you make mistakes in recording other macros.

Saving and Opening a Macro-Enabled Workbook

Workbooks that contain macros pose a security risk for Excel because macros could contain viruses or malicious software. The default Excel file format does not support macros. If you want to save a workbook containing macros, you must save it in the macro-enabled workbook format, preserving both your data and the macro code attached to the workbook. You will save the NP_EX_12_Primrose workbook as a macro-enabled workbook.

To save Jenya's workbook as a macro-enabled workbook:

▶ **1.** On the ribbon, click the **File** tab, and then in the navigation bar, click **Save As**.

▶ **2.** Type **NP_EX_12_Macros** in the File name box.

▶ **3.** Click **Save as type** box below the file name box, and then click **Excel Macro-Enabled Workbook (*.xlsm)** so you can save the macro you just recorded with your workbook.

▶ **4.** Click **Save**. Excel saves the file NP_EX_12_Macros.xlsm to the same folder containing the NP_EX_12_Primrose.xlsx file.

▶ **5.** Close the workbook.

Next you will reopen the workbook file. When Excel encounters a macro-enabled workbook, it prompts you, for security reasons, to enable the macros in the workbook. If you don't enable the macros, they remain part of the workbook, but you cannot run them. This extra step is done to prevent you from mistakenly opening a third-party workbook containing malicious code. You'll reopen the NP_EX_12_Macros workbook now, enabling the macros it contains.

To open the macro-enabled NP_EX_12_Macros workbook:

▶ **1.** Open the **NP_EX_12_Macros** workbook. A Message Bar with a security warning that the workbook contains macros that have been disabled appears below the ribbon. See Figure 12–25.

Figure 12–25	Security Warning for a macro-enabled workbook

macros are disabled until you enable them

▶ **2.** Click **Enable Content** to enable the macros in your workbook. The workbook opens.

After you enable content from a macro-enabled workbook, Excel adds the file to a list of trusted documents. As a trusted document, the security warning will not reappear as long as the workbook name or file location remains unchanged.

Assigning Macros to Shapes and Buttons

Macros can be assigned to graphic objects and command buttons so that you and others can quickly run macros by clicking those objects. You do not need the Developer tab to run your macro once it's been recorded.

Assigning a Macro to a Shape

Any object within a workbook that can be clicked can be turned into an object that runs a macro. Assigning a macro to a graphic object simplifies an application for users because they only have to click objects within the workbook, not interact with the Excel ribbon or buttons.

Jenya created an arrow shape containing the text "View Dashboard" on the Donors worksheet. You will assign the Show_Dashboard macro to this object.

To assign a macro to a graphic:

▶ 1. Go to the **Donors** worksheet.

▶ 2. On the ribbon, click the **Review** tab, and then in the Protect group, click the **Unprotect Sheet** button. You can now make modifications to the worksheet.

▶ 3. Right-click the **View Dashboard** arrow graphic in rows 17 through 19, and then click **Assign Macro** on the shortcut menu. The Assign Macro dialog box opens.

▶ 4. In the list of macros, click **Show_Dashboard** to select it, and then click **OK**. The macro is assigned to the graphic.

▶ 5. Click cell **A1** to deselect the arrow graphic.

▶ 6. On the Review tab, in the Protect group, click the **Protect Sheet** button. The Protect Sheet dialog box opens.

▶ 7. Click **OK** to again protect the contents of the worksheet. Now you'll test the macro.

▶ 8. Click the **View Dashboard** graphic. Cell A1 in the Dashboard worksheet becomes the active cell.

The dashboard also includes a graphic arrow for displaying the contents of the Donors worksheet. You'll create a new macro named Show_Donors_Sheet to show the contents of that sheet.

To record a macro to show the Donors worksheet:

▶ 1. Save the workbook so that if you make a mistake you can restart the process of creating the Show_Donors_Sheet macro.

▶ 2. On the ribbon, click the **Developer** tab, and then in the Code group, click the **Record Macro** button. The Record Macro dialog box opens.

▶ **3.** Type **Show_Donors_Sheet** in the Macro name box, type **Go to the Donors worksheet** in the Description box, and then verify that **This Workbook** appears in the Store macro in box.

▶ **4.** Click **OK** to begin the recorder.

▶ **5.** Click the **Donors** sheet tab, and then click cell **A1** to select it (even if it is already selected).

▶ **6.** Click the **Stop Recording** button to stop the macro recorder and create the Show_Donors_Sheet macro.

Next, you will assign the macro to the Add a Donor graphic arrow on the dashboard.

To assign the Show_Donors_Sheet macro to a graphic object:

▶ **1.** Go to the **Dashboard** worksheet.

▶ **2.** On the ribbon, click the **Review** tab, and then in the Protect group, click the **Unprotect Sheet** button so you can edit the contents of the worksheet.

▶ **3.** Right-click the **Add a Donor** arrow in the upper-right corner of the dashboard, and then click **Assign Macro**. The Assign Macro dialog box opens.

▶ **4.** In the macros list, click **Show_Donors_Sheet** to select it, and then click **OK**.

▶ **5.** Click cell **A1** to deselect the arrow graphic.

▶ **6.** In the Protect group, click the **Protect Sheet** button to open the Protect Sheet dialog box, and then click **OK**. The worksheet is once again protected.

▶ **7.** Click the **Add a Donor** arrow and verify that cell A1 in the Donors worksheet becomes the active cell.

Trouble? If the macro fails or reports an error, close the workbook without saving changes, then reopen the workbook, and then repeat the previous two sets of steps to record the macro again.

By using graphic arrows, users can quickly switch between viewing the dashboard and viewing the worksheet containing information on specific donors.

Insight

Assigning Keyboard Shortcuts to Macros

Another way to quickly run a macro is with a keyboard shortcut. You can assign a short-cut key to run the macro within the Record Macro dialog box by selecting CTRL plus a letter or selecting CTRL+SHIFT plus a letter. If you use a shortcut key combination that is already assigned to a default Excel shortcut, the new shortcut you create over-rides the default Excel shortcut for the workbook. For example, using CTRL+p to run a macro overrides the default keyboard shortcut for opening the Print screen (CTRL+P).

Some users find macro shortcut keys a quick way to run a macro. Others dislike them because they can sometimes override the original function of the shortcut key, confusing users who use the built-in Excel keyboard shortcuts. The keyboard short-cut exists as long as the macro-enabled workbook is opened. Once you close the workbook, the keyboard shortcut for the macro disappears and any Excel commands assigned to the keyboard combination return.

Another way to assign a macro to a worksheet object is to assign it to a form button.

Assigning a Macro to a Button

Tip

You can create a customized menu interface for an Excel application by inserting form controls from the Developer tab.

The Developer tab includes options for creating **form controls**, which are form elements used for entering data and running commands. You can create form controls for input boxes, check boxes, spinners, and list boxes among other choices. The controls can also be linked to worksheet cells so that a user can set or change a cell value by clicking a form control.

You'll examine one type of form control called a macro button that can be clicked to run a macro. The first macro button will be used with a macro that adds a new donor to the Donations table based on information from the Donors worksheet. You'll start the process of recording the Add_Donor macro.

To begin creating the Add_Donor macro:

▶ **1.** Save the workbook so that if you make a mistake you can restart the process of creating the Add_Donor macro.

▶ **2.** On the ribbon, click the **Developer** tab, and then in the Code group, click the **Record Macro** button. The Record Macro dialog box opens.

▶ **3.** Verify that **This Workbook** appears in the Store macro in box.

▶ **4.** Type **Add_Donor** in the Macro name box, and then type **Add a new donor to the Donations table** in the Description box.

▶ **5.** Click **OK** to start the recorder.

After this point every command you enter will be recorded. Note that this macro contains several steps, so take it slow and perform every action precisely as described. Do not omit or add anything. It's often a good idea to practice any set of steps before doing them with the macro recorder. If you do practice the steps, be sure to reset the workbook back to its original conditions before you start the actual recording.

Caution! If at any time you make a mistake as you perform these steps, you can stop the recording, close the workbook without saving changes, and then reopen the workbook and try again starting from the previous set of steps. Another option is to stop the macro, click the Macros button from Code group on the Developer tab, select Add_Donor from the list of macros, click Delete to remove the macro, and repeat the previous set of steps to begin creating the macro again. If you choose this method, make sure that you have reset the workbook to its original condition prior to recording the macro.

To add a new donor to the donations table:

▶ **1.** Click the **Donations** sheet tab to display the contents of the donations table.

▶ **2.** On the ribbon, click the **Review** tab, and then in the Protect group, click the **Unprotect Sheet** button to enable you to edit the worksheet.

▶ **3.** Click cell **B5** to select it.

▶ **4.** On the ribbon, click the **Home** tab, and then in the Cells group, click the **Insert** button to insert a new record at the top of the Donations table.

▶ **5.** Click the **Donors** sheet tab to return to the Donors worksheet.

6. Select the range **C5:C15**, and then in the Clipboard group, click the **Copy** button.

7. Click the **Donations** sheet tab.

8. In the Clipboard group, click the **Paste arrow**, and then click **Paste Special** to open the Paste Special dialog box.

9. In the Paste section, click the **Values and number formats** option button, and then at the bottom of the dialog box, click the **Transpose** check box. See Figure 12–26.

Figure 12–26	Paste Special dialog box

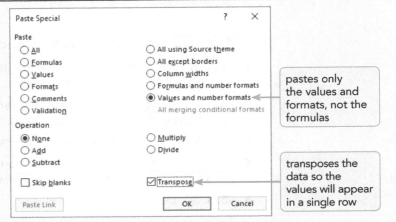

10. Click **OK** to paste the copied values into the top row of the Donations table. See Figure 12–27.

Figure 12–27	New donor added to the Donations table

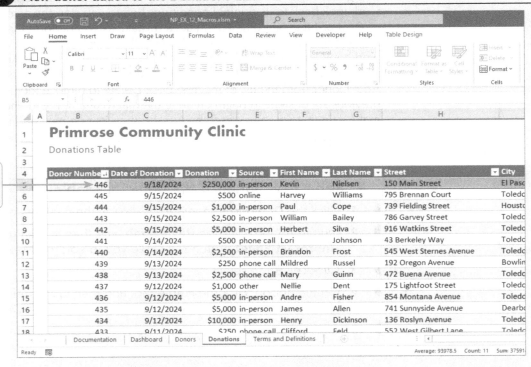

▶ **11.** On the ribbon, click the **Review** tab, and then in the Protect group, click the **Protect Sheet** button to open the Protect Sheet dialog box.

▶ **12.** Click **OK** to again protect the worksheet contents.

▶ **13.** Click the **Donors** sheet tab to return to the Donors worksheet.

▶ **14.** Click cell **C5** to make it the active cell in the worksheet.

▶ **15.** On the ribbon, click the **Developer** tab, and then in the Code group, click the **Stop Recording** button. You have completed recording the macro.

With the Add_Donor macro recorded and saved, you will assign it to a macro button you place on the Donors worksheet.

To create a macro button for the Add_Donor macro:

▶ **1.** On the ribbon, click **Review** tab, and then in the Protect group, click the **Unprotect Sheet** button so that you can add a form control to the worksheet contents.

▶ **2.** On the ribbon, click the **Developer** tab, and then in the Controls group, click the **Insert** button. A gallery of Form Controls appears with a variety of objects that can be placed in the worksheet. See Figure 12–28.

| Figure 12–28 | Gallery of Form Controls and ActiveX Controls |

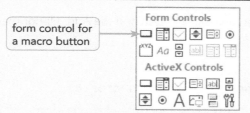

▶ **3.** Click the **Button (Form Control)** icon in the first row and first column of the Form Controls section and then point to cell **C17**.

▶ **4.** Click and drag the pointer over the range **C17:C18** and then release the mouse button. The Assign Macro dialog box opens.

▶ **5.** Click **Add_Donor** in the list of macros to assign to the button, and then click **OK**. A new button appears on the worksheet.

▶ **6.** With the button still selected in the worksheet, type **Add New Donor** as the button label. See Figure 12–29.

Figure 12–29 Button to run the Add_Donor macro

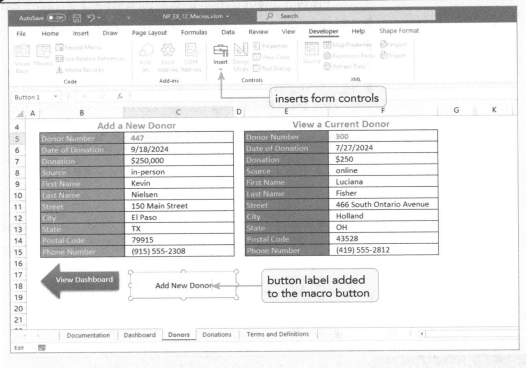

You will test the macro button and the Add_Donor macro now by adding a new donor to the Donations table.

To test the Add_Donor macro:

1. Click cell **C6** to deselect the macro button.

2. On the ribbon, click the **Review** tab, in the Protect group, click the **Protect Sheet** button to open the Protect Sheet dialog box, and then click **OK** to again protect the worksheet contents.

3. In the range **C6:C15**, enter the following data: **9/19/2024** in cell C6, **$10,000** in cell C7, **other** in cell C8, **Laura** in cell C9, **Raymond** in cell C10, **8 Elm Drive** in cell C11, **Columbus** in cell C12, **OH** in cell C13, **43229** in cell C14, and **(614) 555-4856** in cell C15.

4. Click the **Add New Donor** button. Excel runs the Add_Donor macro, adding the data to the Donations table and returning the Donors worksheet.

5. Go to the **Donations** sheet to verify that Laura Raymond's donation was added to the table. See Figure 12–30.

Figure 12–30   Laura Raymond donation added using a macro

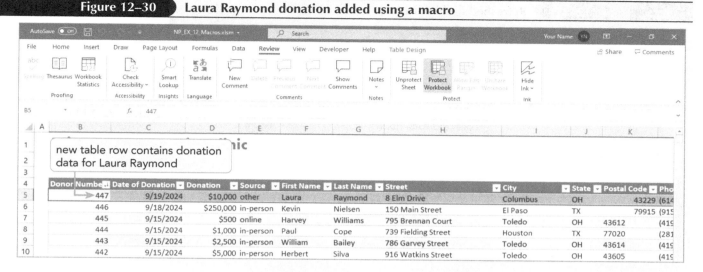

Trouble? If the macro fails or returns an error message, close the workbook without saving changes. Reopen the workbook and repeat each set of steps in this section, beginning with creating the Add_Donor macro. If you still cannot get the macro to work, ask your instructor or technical support person for help.

The donations from the two new donors you added to the Donations table will not be reflected in the statistics shown on the dashboard until you refresh the PivotTable cache. Jenya wants you to create a final macro that updates the PivotTable cache so that the dashboard displays the most current information on the fundraising campaign.

To create the Refresh_Dashboard macro:

1. Go to the **Dashboard** worksheet.

2. Save the workbook so that if you make a mistake you can restart the process of creating the Refresh_Dashboard macro.

3. On the ribbon, click the **Developer** tab, and then in the Code group click the **Record Macro** button. The Record Macro dialog box opens.

4. Enter **Refresh_Dashboard** as the macro name. Verify that **This Workbook** is selected in the Store macro in box. Enter **Refresh the PivotTable cache for the dashboard** in the Description box, and then click **OK** to begin recording.

5. On the ribbon, click the **Review** tab, and then in the Protect group, click the **Unprotect Sheet** button to allow edits in the worksheet.

6. On the ribbon, click the **Data** tab, and then in the Queries & Connections group, click the **Refresh All** button. Excel updates the dashboard to show the impact of the two new donors on the campaign. See Figure 12–31.

Figure 12–31   Refreshed dashboard

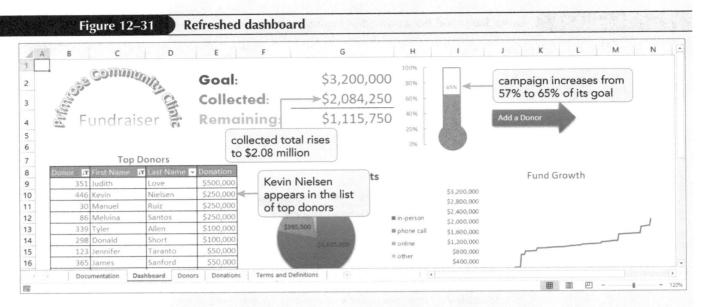

7. On the ribbon, click the **Review** tab, in the Protect group, click the **Protect Sheet** button, and then click the **OK** button in the dialog box to protect the worksheet.

8. On the ribbon, click the **Developer** tab, and then in the Code group, click **Stop Recording**. The Refresh_Dashboard macro is complete.

Jenya wants you to add a macro button to the Dashboard worksheet to run the Refresh_Dashboard macro.

To create a macro button for the Refresh_Dashboard macro:

1. On the ribbon, click the **Review** tab, and then in the Protect group, click the **Unprotect Sheet** button to enable you to add a button to the worksheet.

2. On the ribbon, click the **Developer** tab. In the Controls group, click the **Insert** button, and then click **Button (Form Control)** in the first row and column of the Format Controls section of the gallery.

3. Drag the pointer over the range **J2:L3** of the Dashboard worksheet to create a button. The Assign Macro dialog box opens.

4. Click **Refresh_Dashboard** in the macro list, and then click **OK**. The macro is assigned to the selected button.

5. With the macro button still selected, type **Refresh Dashboard** as the new button label. See Figure 12–32.

Figure 12–32   Refresh Dashboard macro button

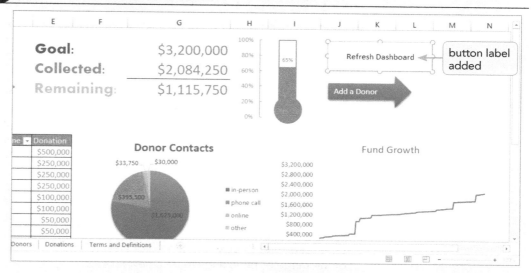

6. Click cell **A1** to deselect the button.

7. On the ribbon, click the **Review** tab, in the Protect group, click the **Protect Sheet** button, and then click **OK** in the dialog box to again protect the worksheet.

8. In the Dashboard worksheet, click the **Refresh Dashboard** button. The contents of the worksheet are refreshed.

Trouble? If the macro returns an error message, close the workbook without saving changes. Reopen the workbook and repeat the previous set of steps to create the Refresh_Dashboard macro and then repeat this set of steps to create the macro button.

You've now created four macros to make it easier for users of Jenya's workbook to enter new donor information and update the contents of the dashboard. However, to put the finishing touches on the application, you will view and edit the content of the macro code you generated with the macro recorder.

Insight

Data Entry with a Data Form

Another way of automating the data entry process is with an **Excel data form**, which is a dialog box containing the field names from the table or data range along with input boxes for entering new data. To create a data form from an Excel table or data range, do the following:

1. Make sure each column in the structured range of data or the Excel table has column headers. These headers become the labels for each field on the form.
2. Make sure the Form button is on the Quick Access Toolbar. If not, click the Customize Quick Access Toolbar button, and then click More Commands. In the Quick Access Toolbar options, click the Choose commands from box, click Commands Not in the Ribbon, click the Form button in the box, click the Add button, and then click OK.
3. Select the range or table for which you want to create the data form.
4. On the Quick Access Toolbar, click the Form button. The data form opens with the selected fields ready for data entry.
5. Enter data in each box, and then click New to add the complete record to the end of the range or table and create a new record.
6. Click Close to close the data form.

Data forms can be helpful when people who are unfamiliar with Excel need to enter data. They can also be useful when a worksheet is very wide and requires repeated horizontal scrolling.

Working with the VBA Editor

Macro code is written in a programming language called Visual Basic for Applications (VBA), which is the programming language used by all Microsoft Office apps. Once you know the basics of VBA in one Office program, you can apply much of what you learn to create applications for the other programs in the Office suite.

Opening the VBA Editor

The content of a macro code can be accessed in the Visual Basic for Applications editor. The editor is a separate application that works with Excel and other Office programs to fix, edit, and manage VBA code. You'll open the editor now to view the code of the Add_Donor macro.

To view the code of the Add_Donor macro:

▶ 1. On the ribbon, click the **Developer** tab, and then in the Code group, click the **Macros** button.

▶ 2. With **Add_Donor** highlighted in the list of macros, click the **Edit** button. The Visual Basic for Applications editor opens showing the code of the Add_Donor macro. See Figure 12–33.

Figure 12–33   VBA Editor window

Trouble? Depending on how your computer is configured, the layout and contents of your window might differ from that shown in Figure 12–33. If all the windows of the VBA editor are not shown, you can display them by selecting the name of the window on the View menu.

The VBA Editor opens with the four windows: The Project Explorer window displays a treelike diagram consisting of every open workbook. The Properties window shows the properties associated with the selected object in the Project Explorer window. The Code window contains the VBA code, including the code of every recorded macro. The Immediate window lets you enter and run VBA commands. In this session, you will work with the contents of the Code window.

Understanding Sub Procedures

In VBA, macros are stored in blocks of code called sub procedures, which have the general syntax

```
Sub procedure(arguments)
 'comments
 commands
```

Tip

Every comment line must begin with the ' character.

where **procedure** is the name of the sub procedure, **arguments** are any arguments used in the sub procedure, **comments** are descriptive comments about the sub procedure, and **commands** are the command run by the sub procedure. Even without knowing VBA syntax, you can often interpret what each command does by examining the code used in the command. Figure 12–34 describes the content of the Show_Dashboard sub procedure.

Figure 12–34 Sub procedure for the Show_Dashboard macro

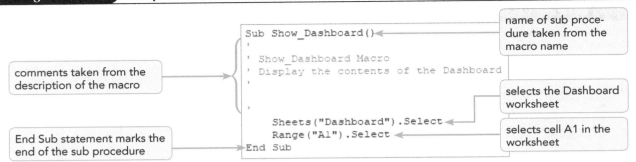

Both the name of the sub procedure and the description are taken from the macro name and macro description entered in the Record Macro dialog box (refer back to Figure 12–23). This sub procedure has only two commands. The first command selects the Dashboard worksheet, and the second command selects cell A1 within that worksheet.

Sub procedures are organized in a folder called a **module**. A VBA project could have multiple modules, and multiple sub procedures within each module. The first module is named Module1, the second is called Module2, and so forth. Modules are primarily a way of grouping related macros.

Editing a Macro with the VBA Editor

Learning the syntax of VBA is beyond the scope of this text, but you can do some simple tasks to add to the code that was generated by the macro recorder. To enter a VBA command, you write the text of the command in the Code window. As you type a command, the editor will provide pop-up windows to assist you in writing error-free code.

Reference

Editing a Macro

- On the Developer tab, in the Code group, click the Macros button, select the macro in the Macro name list, and then click Edit; or on the Developer tab, in the Code group, click the Visual Basic button.
- Use the Visual Basic Editor to edit the macro code.
- On the menu bar, click File, and then click Close and Return to Microsoft Excel.

Jenya wants you to modify the Add_Donor macro so that it displays a message box when a donor has been successfully added to the Donations worksheet. You can display a message box using the VBA command

```
MsgBox message
```

where **message** is the text of the message to display in the box. The following VBA command creates a message box with the text "Donor added":

```
MsgBox "Donor added"
```

Jenya also wants you to clear the data in the range C6:C15 of the Donors worksheet after a donor has been successfully added to the Donations table, in preparation for adding information on the next donor. You can clear the contents of a range using the VBA command

```
Range(range).ClearContents
```

where *range* is the cell range whose contents should be cleared. To clear the contents of the cells in the range C6:C15, you use the VBA command:

```
Range("C6:C15").ClearContents
```

You'll add both commands to the Add_Donor sub procedure now.

To edit the Add_Donor sub procedure:

▶ 1. Scroll down the contents of the Code window until you see the Add_Donor sub procedure. The sub procedure contains a sequence of commands to insert new donor data in the first row of the Donations table.

   Trouble? If you don't see the Add_Donor sub procedure in the Code window, it might have been stored in a different module. Double-click a different module in the Project Explorer window to locate the sub procedure.

▶ 2. Scroll down and click at the end of the `Sheets("Donors").Select` line.

▶ 3. Press **ENTER** to insert a new line.

▶ 4. Type `MsgBox "Donor added"` to create the Donor added message box, and then press **ENTER** to insert a command to display a message box.

▶ 5. Type `Range("C6:C15").ClearContents` to clear the contents of the cells in the range C6:C15. (Do not select the similarly named `ClearComments` in your code, which only clears comments attached to the selected range.) As you type the command, you can select different parts of the command by selecting the command value and pressing TAB. See Figure 12–35.

Figure 12–35	Edited sub procedure

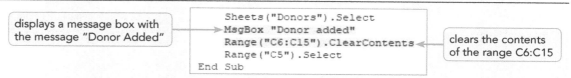

```
                          Sheets("Donors").Select
displays a message box with    MsgBox "Donor added"
the message "Donor Added"      Range("C6:C15").ClearContents      clears the contents
                          Range("C5").Select                      of the range C6:C15
                      End Sub
```

▶ 6. On the menu bar, click **File**, and then click **Close and Return to Microsoft Excel** (or press **CTRL +Q**).

You'll test the revised macro by adding a donor to the Donations list using the Add_Donor macro.

To add a new donor to the Donations list:

▶ 1. Go to the **Donors** worksheet.

▶ 2. In the range **C6:C15**, enter the following data: **9/20/2024** in cell C6, **$250** in cell C7, **phone call** in cell C8, **Sandra** in cell C9, **Lewis** in cell C10, **14 Upton Court** in cell C11, **Flint** in cell C12, **MI** in cell C13, **48532** in cell C14, and **(810) 555-1008** in cell C15.

▶ 3. Click the **Add New Donor** macro button. The donor information is added as a new row in the Donations table. A dialog box with the message "Donor Added" appears.

▶ **4.** Click **OK** to close the dialog box and continue the macro. The data in the range C6:C15 is cleared and the form is ready for information on another donor.

▶ **5.** Go to the **Donations** worksheet and confirm that the Sandra Lewis has been inserted as a new donor in the table. See Figure 12–36.

Figure 12–36   **New donor added to the Donations table**

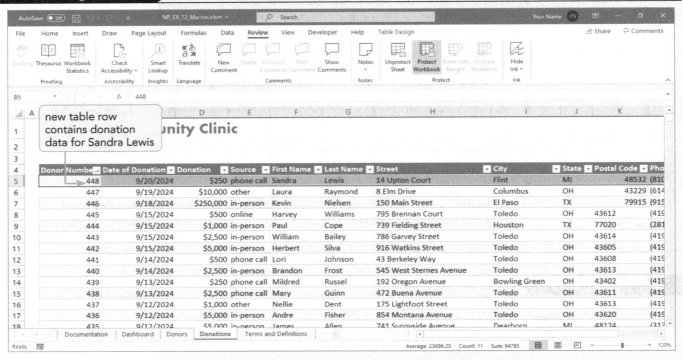

▶ **6.** Go to the **Dashboard** worksheet, and then click the **Refresh Dashboard** button to update the dashboard with Sandra Lewis' contribution. The amount contributed to the campaign has increased to $2,084,500, which is still 65% of the way to the fundraising goal.

You've finished creating and editing macros. Because you no longer need the Developer tab, you will remove this tab from the ribbon.

To remove the Developer tab from the ribbon:

▶ **1.** Right-click an empty area of the ribbon, and then click **Customize the Ribbon** on the shortcut menu.

▶ **2.** In the Main Tabs box on the right, click the **Developer** check box to deselect the Developer tab.

▶ **3.** Click **OK** to apply the changes to the ribbon. The Developer tab no longer appears on the ribbon.

▶ **4.** **sam**⬆ Save the workbook, and then close it.

Jenya is pleased with your work on the Excel application for managing donations to the Primrose Community Clinic. The changes you made to the workbook will enable staffers at the clinic to enter fundraising data without data entry errors and to monitor the progress of the campaign.

 Proskills

Decision Making: Planning and Recording a Macro

Planning and practice help to ensure you create an error-free macro. First, decide what you want to accomplish. Then, consider the best way to achieve those results. Next, practice the keystrokes and mouse actions before you begin recording. This may seem like extra work, but it reduces the chance of error when you actually record the macro. As you set up a macro, consider the following:

- Choose a descriptive name that identifies the macro's purpose.
- Weigh the benefits of selecting a shortcut key against its drawbacks. Although a shortcut key is another way to run a macro, you are limited to one-letter shortcuts, which don't identify the shortcut's purpose. Your macro shortcut key might override another shortcut key provided by Microsoft Office.
- Store the macro with the current workbook unless the macro can be used with other workbooks.
- Include a description that provides an overview of the macro and perhaps your name and contact information.

Good decision making includes thinking about what to do and what not to do as you progress to your goals. This is true when developing a macro as well.

Protecting Against Macro Viruses

If you plan on distributing an Excel application to a wider audience, you need to consider how Excel manages security to ward off viruses. A **virus** is a computer program designed to copy itself into other programs with the intention of causing mischief or harm. When unsuspecting users open these infected workbooks, Excel automatically runs the attached virus-infected macro. **Macro viruses** are a type of virus that uses a program's own macro programming language to distribute the virus. Macro viruses can be destructive and can modify or delete files that may not be recoverable. Excel provides several security levels for managing exposure to macro viruses.

Macro Security Settings

The macro security settings control how Excel manages a macro-enabled workbook. For example, one user may choose to run macros only if they are "digitally signed" by a developer who is on a list of trusted sources. Another user might want to see a notification when a workbook contains macros, which the user can then choose to enable or disable. Excel has four levels of macro security settings, as described in Figure 12–37.

Figure 12–37   Macro security settings

Setting	Description
Disable all macros without notification	All macros in all workbooks are disabled and no security alerts about macros are displayed. Use this setting if you don't want macros to run.
Disable all macros with notification	All macros in all workbooks are disabled, but security alerts appear when the workbook contains a macro. Use this default setting to choose on a case-by-case basis whether to run a macro.
Disable all macros except digitally signed macros	The same as the "Disable all macros with notification" setting except any macro signed by a trusted publisher runs if you have already trusted the publisher. Otherwise, security alerts appear when a workbook contains a macro.
Enable all macros	All macros in all workbooks run. Use this setting temporarily in such cases as when developing an application that contains macros. This setting is not recommended for regular use.

You set macro security for all Microsoft Office programs in a central location called the **Trust Center**. To access the Trust Center:

1. On the ribbon, click the File tab, and then in the navigation bar, click Options to open the Excel Options dialog box.

2. Click Trust Center in the list of option categories.

3. Click the Trust Center Settings button to view or change specific security settings.

Figure 12–38 shows the Trust Center dialog box opened to the settings for handling macro-enabled workbooks. By default, all potentially dangerous content in a macro-enabled workbook is blocked and the user is notified that some content is disabled. You can place files you consider trustworthy in a location defined as trustworthy. Any workbook opened from a trusted location is considered safe and will not be blocked.

Figure 12–38   Macro Settings in the Trust Center

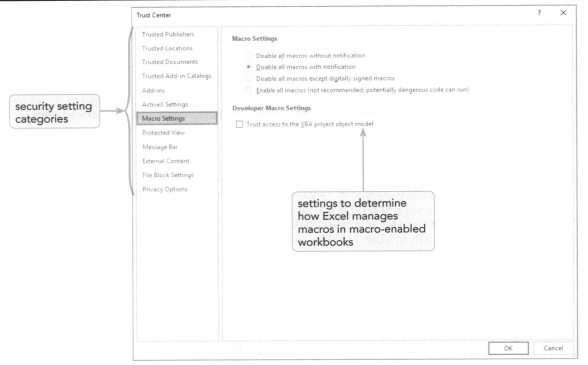

Adding a Digital Signature to a Workbook

Another way to mark a trusted workbook is to assign it a **digital signature**, which marks the workbook as coming from a trusted author. Digital signatures are added as the last step before distributing a workbook to a wide audience of users. Before you can add a digital signature to a workbook, you need to obtain a digital ID (also called a digital certificate) that proves your identity. Digital certificates are typically issued by a certificate authority. After you have a digital certificate, do the following to digitally sign your workbook:

1. On the ribbon, click the File tab, and then, in the navigation bar, click Info.
2. On the Info screen, click the Protect Workbook button, and then click Add a Digital Signature.
3. If the Get a Digital ID dialog box opens, asking if you would like to get a digital ID from a Microsoft Partner, click Yes. Your browser opens to a website with information about digital signature providers and available digital IDs.
4. Select a provider and follow the steps to obtain a digital ID from that provider.

By digitally signing your workbooks, you can assure others that the workbook has not been altered since its creation by the document's author. A digital signature is removed any time the workbook is saved, ensuring that no one (including the original workbook author) can modify the document without removing the digital signature. In this way, a chain of custody is established from document creation to document distribution, ensuring that no third party has altered your Excel application.

Review

Session 12.3 Quick Check

1. What is the Developer tab?
2. What is the Personal Macro workbook?
3. What is the one thing you should do before starting the macro recorder?
4. What is a macro-enabled workbook?
5. How do you assign a macro to a graphic shape or form button?
6. What is VBA?
7. What is a sub procedure?
8. What VBA command would you enter to clear the contents of the data in the range A1:A50?
9. What VBA command would you enter to display a message box with the message "End of Project"?

Practice

Review Assignments

Data File needed for the Review Assignments: NP_EX_12-2.xlsm

Jenya needs to create another Excel application for the Primrose Community Clinic that tracks payments on the pledges made by donors. You will help complete the application by creating a macro that adds donor payments to a table of payments and then updates a dashboard to reflect the current payment status. To maintain data integrity, you will validate the payment information entered by the user and restrict access to parts of the workbook. Complete the following:

1. Open the macro-enabled workbook **NP_EX_12-2.xlsm** located in the Excel12 > Review folder included with your Data Files. Save the workbook as **NP_EX_12_Payments** in the location specified by your instructor.

2. In the Documentation worksheet, enter your name and the date.

3. In the Documentation worksheet, insert a WordArt object from the first row and third column of the WordArt gallery. Change the text to **Primrose Community Clinic**. Select the entire text and change the font size to 28 points. Move the WordArt graphic to the upper-left corner of the worksheet.

4. In the Fully Paid Donations worksheet, insert a funnel chart of the data in the range B4:C15. Move the funnel chart to the Summary worksheet, and resize it to cover the range H8:M20. Change the chart title to **Fully Paid Donors by Donation Level**.

5. In the Payment Form worksheet (which displays the total amount pledged, paid, and owed by donors), use an IFERROR function in cells F4 and F6 to display a blank text string if the formulas in those cells return an error.

6. Hide the Pledge Tables through Fully Paid Donations worksheets.

7. On the Review tab, in the Protect group, use the Protect Workbook button to protect the structure of the workbook. Do not specify a password for the protected workbook.

8. In the Payment Form worksheet, use data validation to add a validation list to cell C4 using the data in the range H4:H451 of the Payment Form worksheet as the source.

9. Create a validation rule for cell C5 to allow date values greater than or equal to 9/20/2024. Add an input message to the cell with the title **Payment Date** and the input message **Enter a date of 9/20/2024 or later**. If an invalid date is entered, display only a warning alert with the title **Invalid Date** and the message **Confirm the date of the payment**.

10. Create a validation rule for cell C6 to allow only decimal numbers between 1 and 500,000.

11. Hide column H in the Payment Form worksheet.

12. Select the range C4:C6, and then use the Protection tab in the Format Cells dialog box to unlock the data in that range.

13. For each of the six visible worksheets, click the Protect Sheet button in the Protect group on the Review tab and protect the sheets, allowing users only to select locked and unlocked cells. Do not specify a password.

14. In the Payment Form worksheet, in the range C4:C6, enter the following data: **18** in cell C4, **9/25/2024** in cell C5, and **$6,750** in cell C6.

15. Display the Developer tab on the ribbon.

16. Save the workbook, and then record a macro in this workbook named **Add_Payment** with the description **Add a new payment to the Payments table**. Record the following steps in the macro:

    a. Go to the Payments worksheet, and then on the Review tab, in Protect group, click the Unprotect Sheet button.

    b. Click B5, and then on the Home tab, in the Cells group, click the Insert button to insert a new row into the table.

    c. Go to the Payment Form worksheet, select range from cell C6 up to cell C4, and then copy the selected data.

    d. Go to the Payments worksheet, and on the Home tab, in the Clipboard group, click the Paste arrow, and then click Paste Special.

  e. In the Paste Special dialog box, select the Values and number formats option button and the Transpose check box, and then click OK to paste the payment date into row 5 of the worksheet.

  f. Go to the Summary worksheet, and then on the Review tab, in the Protect group, click the Unprotect Sheet button.

  g. On the Data tab, in the Queries and Connections group, click the Refresh All button.

  h. On the Review tab, in the Protect group, click the Protect Sheet button and allow users to only select lock and unlocked cells.

  i. Go to the Payments worksheet, and then on the Review tab, in the Protect group, click the Protect Sheet button and allow users to only select lock and unlocked cells.

  j. Go to the Payment Form worksheet, and then click cell C4.

  k. Stop the macro recorder.

17. On the Developer tab, in the Code group, click the Macros button, and then click Edit to edit the VBA code for the Add_Payment macro, adding the following new lines of code directly after the command `Range("C4").Select` line near the end of the sub procedure:

```
MsgBox "Payment Entered"
Range("C4:C6").ClearContents
```

18. Close the VBA editor and return to the workbook.

19. Unprotect the Payment Form worksheet, insert a macro button over the range B8:C9, assign the Add_Payment macro to the button, and then enter **Add Payment** as the button label.

20. Protect the Payment Form worksheet again, allowing users only to select locked and unlocked cells.

21. In the range C4:C6, enter the following data: **30** in cell C4, **9/26/2024** in cell C5, and **$10,000** in cell C6.

22. Click the Add Payment macro button to add the data in the Payments table and refresh the contents of the Summary worksheet, and then click OK to close the Payment Entered dialog box.

23. In cell C4, enter **30** and then confirm that $8,750 is still owed on the donor's pledge.

24. In the Summary worksheet, verify that the total amount owed on the pledges is now $828,380.

25. Save the workbook and then close it.

Apply

Case Problem 1

Data File needed for this Case Problem: NP_EX_12-3.xlsm

Invent Software David Wright is a hiring manager for the Human Resources (HR) department at Invent Software, a growing company that creates software for inventory management. David is using Excel to track the hiring process from initial job postings through interviews to job offers and wants your help in developing an application to automate the process of reporting key hiring metrics. He also wants it to include safeguards to help prevent user error. David already created part of the application and needs you to finish it. Complete the following:

1. Open the **NP_EX_12-3.xlsm** workbook located in the Excel12 > Case1 folder included with your Data Files. Save the workbook as **NP_EX_12_Invent** in the location specified by your instructor.

2. In the Documentation worksheet, enter your name and the date.

3. In the Dashboard worksheet, create the following WordArt object:

  a. Insert the WordArt object showing text in a black font with a hard red drop shadow located in the third row and second column of the WordArt gallery.

  b. Change the default text to **Invent Software**.

  c. Move the WordArt object to the upper-left corner of the worksheet.

  d. Apply an 18-point golden glow text effect to the WordArt object, choosing the effect in the fourth row and first column of the gallery of glow effects.

4. Insert a funnel chart of the data in the range F8:G13. Move and resize the chart to cover the range J6:K15. Change the chart title to **Application History**.

5. In cell F19, create a list validation based on the data in the range O8:O18. In cell G19, create a list validation based on the data in the range Q8:Q13. The application will now be able to retrieve data on applicants that match specified search criteria.

6. Use the arrow buttons in cells F19 and G19 to select the values **Accountant** and **Onsite Interview**.

7. In the Dashboard worksheet, hide the contents of columns O through Q.

8. Hide the Applicants, Application PivotTable, and Terms and Definitions worksheets.

9. Protect the workbook. Do not specify a password for the document.

10. In the Dashboard worksheet, unlock cells F19 and G19, and then protect the worksheet to allow only selecting locked and unlocked cells. Do not specify a password for the protected sheet.

11. Save the workbook, and then use the macro recorder to create a macro for this workbook named **Lookup_Applicants** with the description **Retrieve application data using an advanced filter**.

12. Start the recorder, and perform the following tasks to create the macro:
    a. Unprotect the worksheet.
    b. Click the Data tab, and then in the Sort & Filter group, click the Advanced button.
    c. In the Advanced Filter dialog box, click the Copy to another location option button, enter **Applicants[#All]** in the List range box to retrieve data from the Applicants table, verify that **$F$18:$G$19** is displayed in the Criteria range box, and **$F$21:$M$21** is displayed in the Copy to box. Click click OK to apply the advanced filter.
    d. Protect the worksheet.
    e. Stop the recorder.

13. Unprotect the worksheet and create a macro button in the range H17:H19 to run the Lookup_Applicants macro. Change the label of the button to **Retrieve Records**. Protect the worksheet again, allowing users to only select locked and unlocked cells. Do not specify a password.

14. Use VBA to modify the code so the application displays a message indicating the number of records found using the advanced filter. In the Visual Basic for Applications editor, directly before the End Sub statement in the Lookup_Applicants sub procedure, add the following commands:

```
recNum = Application.WorksheetFunction.Count(Range("K:K"))
MsgBox recNum & " record(s) found"
```

15. Close the editor and return to the workbook.

16. Choose Website Designer from the slicer to display a funnel chart of the application history for the Website Designer position.

17. Select Website Designer and Onsite Interview from cells F19 and G19, and then click the Retrieve Records button to retrieve the 24 records of applicants who got only as far as the onsite interview stage.

18. Save the workbook, and then close it.

Challenge

Case Problem 2

Data File needed for this Case Problem: NP_EX_12-4.xlsm

Milwaukee Cheese   Roberta Olson is a dispatch manager for Milwaukee Cheese, a large cheese and dairy supply company operating in the Midwest. One of Roberta's jobs is to provide the shipping assignments to the company drivers among 27 Wisconsin cities. It is company policy that no driver logs more than 350 miles in a single day driving from one distribution center to the next. You will help Roberta develop an Excel application for entering driving assignments that fulfill company policy.

Roberta's worksheet includes a Driving Form worksheet in which you will enter commands to store each leg of a driving itinerary. The legs will then be stored in the Itinerary table of the Driving Itinerary worksheet. The distances between the 27 cities are stored in the Distance Table worksheet. Distances will be automatically calculated for you.

In this application, you will combine validation tests within a single cell using a custom validation formula. For a driving leg to be valid it should start and end in one of the 27 cities, and the total driving distance should not exceed 350 miles. Complete the following:

1. Open the **NP_EX_12-4.xlsm** workbook located in the Excel12 > Case2 folder included with your Data Files. Save the workbook as **NP_EX_12_Cheese** in the location specified by your instructor.

2. In the Documentation worksheet, enter your name and the date.

3. In the Driving Form worksheet, you will enter individual legs of a driving itinerary. The mileage between starting and ending cities is calculated in cell F6. Currently that cell displays an error value because no cities have been specified in cells D6 and E6. Revise the formula in cell F6 so that it displays a blank text string in place of an error value.

4. This form will use the AutoComplete feature to fill in the city names in cells D6 and E6. There is no need to display the city names in rows 7 through 33 for AutoComplete to work. Hide rows 7 through 33 in the worksheet so that content doesn't distract the user.

5. Unlock cells D6 and E6.

⊕ **Explore** 6. The data in cells D6 and E6 have two validation rules: The city names must be included in the list of cities. The total of the driving mileage in cell F6 and the value stored in the dist range name should be less than or equal to 350. In the range D6:E6, create a custom validation rule using the following formula:
   =AND(COUNTIF(cities,D6)=1,SUM($F$6,dist)<=350)

7. If the validation rule is violated, display a warning box with the title **Invalid Data** and the message **You either mistyped the city name or adding this leg will result in a total driving distance exceeding 350 miles.** (including the period).

8. Hide the Distance Table worksheet.

9. Protect the workbook. Do not specify a password.

10. Protect the contents of the Driving Form and Driving Itinerary worksheets, allowing users to only select locked and unlocked cells. Save the workbook.

11. In the Driving Form worksheet, enter **Milwaukee** as the starting city of the first leg in cell D6, and then enter **West Allis** as the ending city in cell E6. Verify that the distance between the two cities is 7 miles.

12. Save the workbook.

13. Use the macro recorder to create a macro for this workbook named **Add_Leg** with the description **Add a leg to the driving itinerary**.

14. Start the recorder, and then perform the following tasks:
    a. Go to the Driving Itinerary worksheet and unprotect the sheet.
    b. Press F5 and go to the travel_end cell.
    c. Insert a new sheet row above the travel_end cell. (*Hint*: On the Home tab, in the Cells group, click the Insert arrow, and then click Insert Sheet Rows.)
    d. Go to the Driving Form worksheet and copy the values in the range C6:F6.
    e. Return to the Driving Itinerary worksheet and use the Paste Special command to paste the values and number formats into the active cell of the worksheet.
    f. Protect the Driving Itinerary worksheet.
    g. Press F5 and go to the travel_end cell again.
    h. Unprotect the Driving Form worksheet.
    i. Copy the value in cell E6 and paste that value into cell D6.
    j. Click cell E6, and then press DEL to clear the contents of the cell.
    k. Protect the Driving Form worksheet.
    l. Stop the recorder.

15. Unprotect the Driving Form worksheet and insert a macro button in the range D35:E37 to play the Add_Leg macro. Change the label of the macro button to **Add Leg to the Itinerary**. Protect the Driving Form worksheet again.

16. Use the data form to enter the following legs into the driving itinerary: West Allis to Madison, and then Madison to La Crosse.

17. Verify that when you try to enter a fourth driving leg of La Crosse to Marshfield, the application warns you that you are about to exceed the allowed driving distance. Do not enter Marshfield as the last leg of the trip. Instead enter Eau Claire as the last leg.

⊕ **Explore** 18. When a macro switches between worksheets, the quick jump from one sheet to another can be distracting. To correct this problem, edit the Add_Leg sub procedure in the Visual Basic for Applications editor.

    a. Directly after the initial comment section at the top of the sub procedure insert the following command to turn off screen updating while the macro is running:

```
Application.ScreenUpdating = False
```

    b. Directly before the closing End Sub command at the bottom of the sub procedure, insert the following command to turn screen updating back on:

```
Application.ScreenUpdating = True
```

19. Close the editor and then return to the workbook.

20. Save the workbook, and then close it.

ACCESS

OBJECTIVES

Session 9.1
- Create an action query to create a table
- Create an action query to append data
- Construct an action query to delete data
- Build an action query to update data

Session 9.2
- Define many-to-many relationships between tables
- Define one-to-one relationships between tables
- Understand join types
- Create a query using a self-join
- View and create indexes for tables

Using Action Queries and Advanced Table Relationships

Enhancing User Interaction with the Health Database

Case | *Lakewood Community Health Services*

Lakewood Community Health Services is a nonprofit health clinic located in Atlanta, Georgia. It provides a range of medical services to patients of all ages. The clinic specializes in chronic disease management, cardiac care, and geriatrics. Donna Taylor, the office manager for Lakewood Community Health Services, oversees a small staff and is responsible for maintaining records for the clinic's patients.

The Lakewood staff developed the Health database of patient, visit, billing, employee, and treatment data, and the employees use **Microsoft Access 2019** (or simply **Access**), to manage it. Donna has been enhancing the Health database containing tables, queries, forms, and reports that she and other staff members use to track patients and their visits. Donna has asked you to continue enhancing the database by creating some advanced queries and integrating more tables into the database.

STARTING DATA FILES

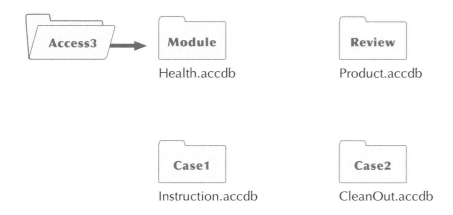

Access3 → Module
Health.accdb

Review
Product.accdb

Case1
Instruction.accdb

Case2
CleanOut.accdb

Session 9.1 Visual Overview:

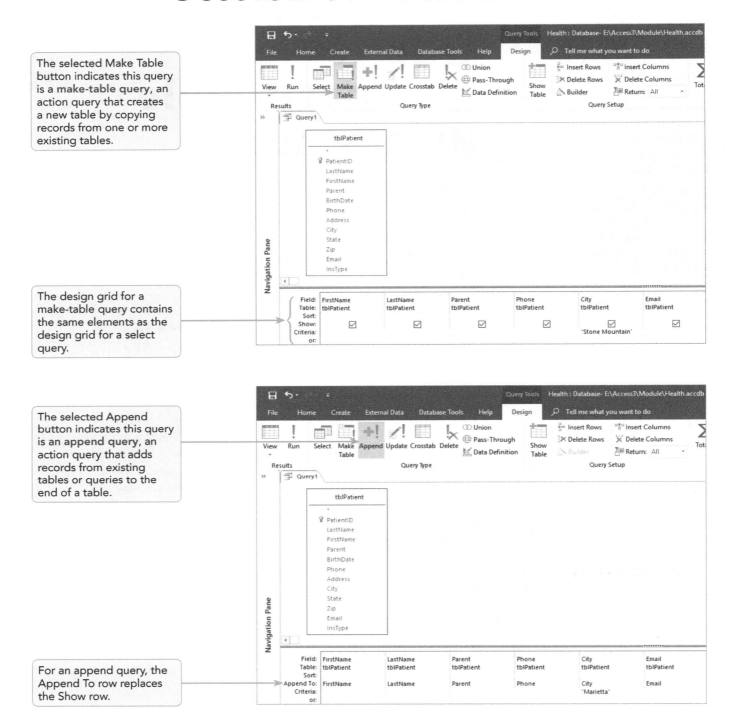

The selected Make Table button indicates this query is a make-table query, an action query that creates a new table by copying records from one or more existing tables.

The design grid for a make-table query contains the same elements as the design grid for a select query.

The selected Append button indicates this query is an append query, an action query that adds records from existing tables or queries to the end of a table.

For an append query, the Append To row replaces the Show row.

Action Queries

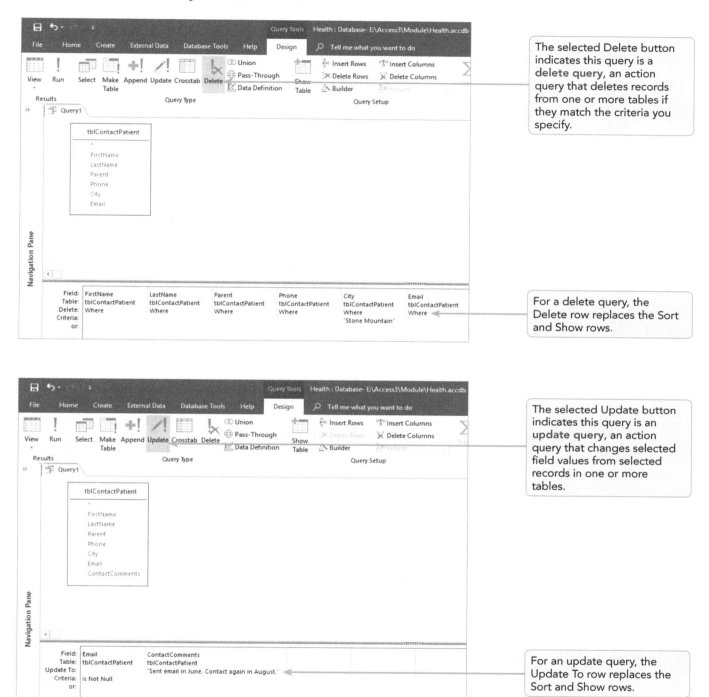

The selected Delete button indicates this query is a **delete query**, an action query that deletes records from one or more tables if they match the criteria you specify.

For a delete query, the Delete row replaces the Sort and Show rows.

The selected Update button indicates this query is an **update query**, an action query that changes selected field values from selected records in one or more tables.

For an update query, the Update To row replaces the Sort and Show rows.

Action Queries

Queries can do more than display answers to the questions you ask; they can also perform actions on the data in the tables in your database. An **action query** is a query that adds, changes, or deletes multiple table records at a time. For example, Donna could use an action query to delete all paid invoices from the previous year. As shown in the Visual Overview for Session 9.1, Access provides four types of action queries: the make-table query, the append query, the delete query, and the update query. Action queries can modify many records in a table at one time. Even though enforcing referential integrity can help to avoid accidental loss of data, you should first create a select query that chooses the records you need to update. After you confirm that the query selects the correct records, you can convert it to the appropriate action query.

A make-table query creates a new table by copying records from one or more existing tables. The new table can be an exact copy of the records in an existing table, a subset of the fields and records in an existing table, or a combination of the fields and records from two or more tables. The query does not delete the selected fields and records from the existing tables, although in some situations taking this additional step makes sense for database management. One common use of a make-table query is to move records to a history table. A **history table** contains data that is no longer needed for current processing but that you might need to reference in the future. For instance, Donna could use a make-table query to create a table of records for patients that have not visited the clinic for more than five years, and then remove those records from the source tables. The new table created by a make-table query reflects data at a point in time; future changes made to the original (existing) tables are not reflected in the new table. You need to run the make-table query periodically if you want the newly created table to contain current data.

An append query adds records from existing tables or queries to the end of another table. For an append query, you choose the fields you want to append from one or more tables or queries; the selected data remains in the original tables. Append queries are most often used to append records to history tables.

A delete query deletes a group of records from one or more tables if the records match the criteria you specify. You choose which records you want to delete by entering selection criteria. Deleting records removes them permanently from the database after the database is compacted.

INSIGHT

Appending to History Tables

Tables containing data about cleared checks, former employees, inactive customers, and obsolete products are examples of history tables. Because the records you append to a history table are no longer needed for current processing in the original table, you can delete the records from the original table after you append the records to the history table. Before deleting the data from the original table, be sure to verify that you appended the correct records. When you delete data, the deletion is permanent.

An update query changes selected field values from selected records in one or more tables. You choose the fields and records you want to change by entering the selection criteria and the update rules. Donna could use an update query to add text in the comment field of every patient record that contains an email address to note that an email message had been sent to these patients. Update queries are particularly valuable in performing multiple updates to large tables.

Creating a Make-Table Query

Donna wants to contact all patients who live in Stone Mountain to remind them about the importance of annual flu vaccinations. She asks you to create a new temporary table containing the FirstName, LastName, Parent, Phone, City, and Email fields from the tblPatient table for all patients whose City field value is Stone Mountain. She only wants to keep this table for this phone call campaign. After the campaign, she will not need the table anymore. She wants to create a temporary table instead of a query so she can modify it by adding notes that she will take when she calls the patients who live in Stone Mountain. By creating a new temporary table, Donna doesn't need to worry about disrupting or changing the data in any existing tables or in any objects based on the tables. After Donna is satisfied that all patients have been called and she's gathered their feedback, she can delete the temporary table.

INSIGHT

Making Temporary Tables

Duplicating data in a database is frowned upon. When a database has multiple copies of data and a change is made, the data could have errors if some instances of the data are changed and others are not changed. However, sometimes it is useful to create a temporary table for a specific purpose. When the table is no longer needed, it is deleted. For instance, the manager of a small appliance store might want to notify all customers who purchased a toaster more than two years ago that a new model is now available. The manager could create a temporary table containing the First Name, Last Name, and Phone Number for each of these customers, and add a field for comments so the staff can indicate when they called each customer and whether they left a message or spoke to the customer directly. It would not make sense to track this information in the database because it does not directly relate to the customers' purchases. When the telephone campaign is finished, the table could be deleted.

You can create the new temporary table for Donna by using a make-table query that uses fields from the tblPatient table in the Health database. When you run a make-table query, you create a new table. The records in the new table are based on the records in the query's underlying tables. The fields in the new table will have the data type and field size of the fields in the query's underlying tables. The new table will not preserve the primary key designation or field properties such as the format or lookup properties.

REFERENCE

Creating a Make-Table Query

- Create a select query with the necessary fields and selection criteria.
- On the Query Tools Design tab, click the Run button in the Results group to preview the results.
- Switch to Design view to make any necessary changes to the query, and then, when the query is correct, click the Make Table button located in the Query Type group on the Query Tools Design tab.
- In the Make Table dialog box, type the new table name in the Table Name box, making sure the Current Database option button is selected to include the new table in the current database; or, click the Another Database option button, enter the database name in the File Name box, and then click the OK button.
- Click the Run button, and then click the Yes button to confirm the creation of the new table.

You'll create the new temporary table now using a make-table query. You'll base the make-table query on the tblPatient table.

To create and run the select query based on the tblPatient table:

▶ **1.** **sam** ⬇ Start Access, and then open the **Health** database from the **Access3 > Module** folder included with your Data Files.

Trouble? If you don't have the starting Data Files, you need to get them before you can proceed. Your instructor will either give you the Data Files or ask you to obtain them from a specified location (such as a network drive). If you have any questions about the Data Files, see your instructor or technical support person for assistance.

Trouble? If the security warning is displayed below the ribbon, click the Enable Content button.

▶ **2.** Make sure the Navigation Pane is closed, click the **Create** tab, and then, in the Queries group, click the **Query Design** button. The Show Table dialog box opens on top of the Query window in Design view.

▶ **3.** Add the **tblPatient** field list to the Query window, and then close the Show Table dialog box.

▶ **4.** Resize the tblPatient field list to display all its fields, and then add the **FirstName**, **LastName**, **Parent**, **Phone**, **City**, and **Email** fields to the design grid in that order.

Next, you'll enter the City field's selection criterion of Stone Mountain.

▶ **5.** In the design grid, click the **City Criteria** box, type **Stone Mountain**, and then press **TAB**. The condition changes to "Stone Mountain". See Figure 9–1.

Figure 9–1 | **Select query on which make-table query will be based**

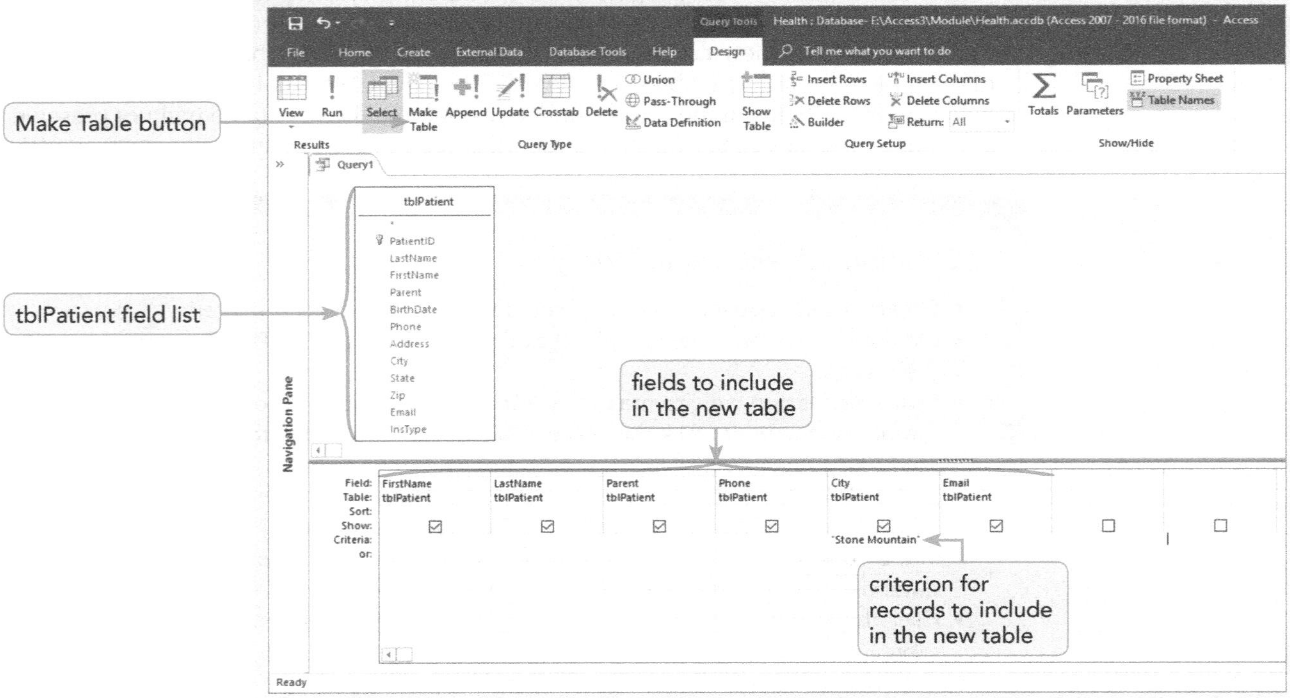

Make Table button

tblPatient field list

fields to include in the new table

criterion for records to include in the new table

You've completed the select query, so now you can run it to make sure the recordset contains the data Donna needs.

▶ **6.** Run the query. The query recordset shows the seven records for Stone Mountain patients.

Now that you have verified that the records selected contain the city Stone Mountain, you can be confident these are the same records that the make-table query will select. Next, you'll change the query to a make-table query.

To change the query type, and then run and save the make-table query:

▶ **1.** Switch to Design view, and then on the Query Tools Design tab, in the Query Type group, click the **Make Table** button. The Make Table dialog box opens. You use the dialog box to enter a name for the new table and designate the database to be used to store the table. See Figure 9–2.

Figure 9–2   **Make Table dialog box**

option to create the new table in the Health database

option to create the new table in another database

enter the new table name here

Be sure to select the Current Database option button; otherwise, Access will require you to specify the name of another data file in which to place the table.

▶ **2.** In the Table Name box, type **tblContactPatient**, make sure the **Current Database** option button is selected, ensuring the new table will be added to the Health database, and then click **OK**.

Now that you have created and tested the query, you can run it to create the tblContactPatient table. After you run the query, you can save it, and then view the new table. Because you have not saved the query yet, the name on the tab is Query1.

▶ **3.** Run the query. A dialog box opens, indicating that you are about to paste seven rows into a new table. Because you are running an action query that alters the contents of the database, you have the opportunity to cancel the operation, if necessary, or to confirm it.

▶ **4.** Click **Yes**. The dialog box closes, and the make-table query creates the tblContactPatient table. The query is still displayed in Design view.

▶ **5.** Save the query as **qryContactPatientMakeTable**, close the query, and then open the Navigation Pane. The qryContactPatientMakeTable query appears in the Queries list with a special icon indicating that it is a make-table query. See Figure 9–3.

| Figure 9–3 | Query type icons in the Navigation Pane |

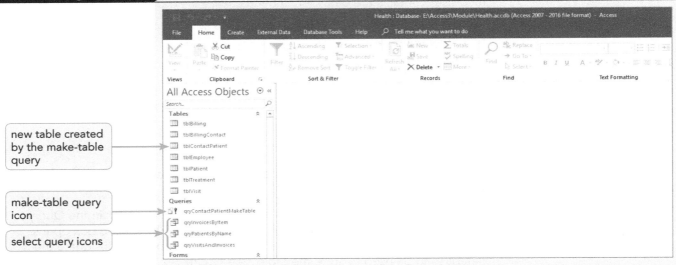

new table created by the make-table query

make-table query icon

select query icons

You can now open the tblContactPatient table to view the results of the make-table query.

Trouble? You may have to increase the width of the Navigation Pane to see the entire name of the query.

6. Open the **tblContactPatient** table in Datasheet view, resize all datasheet columns to their best fit, and then click the first row's **FirstName** field value to deselect all values. See Figure 9–4.

| Figure 9–4 | tblContactPatient table datasheet |

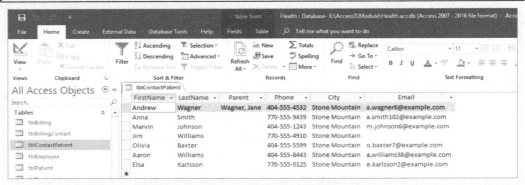

The tblContactPatient table includes the FirstName, LastName, Parent, Phone, City, and Email fields for patients who live in Stone Mountain. Make-table queries do not transfer Caption property settings to the created tables, so the FirstName and LastName column headings do not contain spaces. The tblContactPatient table also does not include formatting for the phone number. Other field properties that do not transfer include Decimal Places, Default Value, Format, Input Mask, Validation Rule, and Validation Text.

7. Save your datasheet changes, close the table, and then close the Navigation Pane.

Donna can now make any necessary changes to the tblContactPatient table records when she contacts patients without affecting the tblPatient table in the Health database.

PROSKILLS

Decision Making: Determining When to Delete Objects

A database evolves to meet the needs of its users, and eventually some database objects are no longer needed. A table, query, or report created for a special event, for instance, would no longer be useful after that event is over. Likewise, a database might contain a form created to enter data that is no longer relevant. Periodically, you should evaluate the objects in your database and consider whether they are still providing useful information. If some are not, you may want to delete such tables, queries, forms, and reports. If the database is a large one and serves a large user base, you will want to gain input from all users before deciding to delete objects.

Creating an Append Query

Donna has decided to expand the list of patients that she will contact to include the patients who live in Marietta. She asks you to add these new records to the tblContactPatient table. You could make this change by modifying the selection criterion in the qryContactPatientMakeTable query to select owners with City field values of Marietta. If you ran this modified query, however, you would overwrite the existing tblContactPatient table with a new table. If Donna had made any changes to the existing tblContactPatient table records, creating a new table would overwrite these changes as well.

Instead, you will create the qryContactPatientAppend query as a select query to select only owners whose city is Marietta, and then you'll change the query to an append query. An append query adds records from existing tables or queries to the end of another table. When you run this new query, the selected records will be appended to (added to the bottom of) the records in the existing tblContactPatient table.

REFERENCE

Creating an Append Query

- Create a select query with the necessary fields and selection criteria.
- On the Query Tools Design tab, click the Run button in the Results group to preview the results.
- Switch to Design view to make any necessary changes to the query, and then, when the query is correct, click the Append button located in the Query Type group on the Query Tools Design tab.
- In the Append dialog box, select the table name in the Table Name box, making sure the Current Database option button is selected to include the new table in the current database; or click the Another Database option button, enter the database name in the File Name box, and then click the OK button.
- Click the Run button, and then click the Yes button to confirm appending the records to the table.

You can now create the append query you'll use to include the additional patient data Donna wants in the tblContactPatient table.

To create the append query:

▶ **1.** Click the **Create** tab, and then, in the Queries group, click the **Query Design** button. The Show Table dialog box opens on top of the Query window in Design view.

▶ **2.** Add the **tblPatient** field list to the Query window, and then close the Show Tables dialog box.

▶ **3.** Resize the tblPatient field list to display all its fields, then add the **FirstName**, **LastName**, **Parent**, **Phone**, **City**, and **Email** fields to the design grid in that order. The selected fields match the fields in the table to which the records will be appended.

Next, you'll enter the selection criterion of Marietta for the City field.

▶ **4.** In the design grid, click the **City Criteria** box, type **Marietta**, and then press **TAB**. See Figure 9–5.

Figure 9–5 Changing the selection criterion

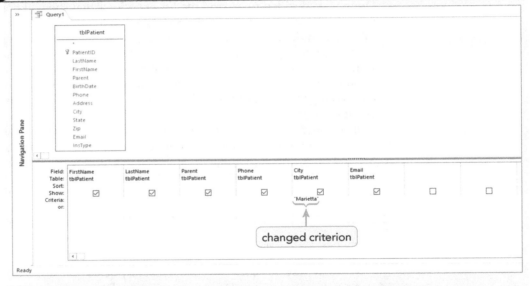

Before you can run the query to append the records to the tblContactPatient table, you have to change the query type to an append query. It is always a good idea to test an action query before you run it, so you will first run this select query to make sure it selects the correct records. Then you will change the query type to an append query and run it to append the new records to the tblContactPatient table.

▶ **5.** On the Query Tools Design tab, in the Query Type group, click the **Select** button to select it (if necessary).

▶ **6.** Run the query. The query recordset shows the five records for patients who live in Marietta.

These five records are the additional records you will append to the tblContactPatient table. Now that you've verified that the results shown in the query are correct, you can change the query type to an append query.

7. Switch to Design view, and then on the Query Tools Design tab, in the Query Type group, click the **Append** button. The Append dialog box opens. You use this dialog box to select the name of the table to which you want to append the data and to designate the database to be used to store the table.

8. In the Table Name box, click the arrow, click **tblContactPatient**, ensure that the **Current Database** option button is selected, and then click **OK**. The Append To row replaces the Show row in the design grid.

The Append To row in the design grid identifies the fields that the query will append to the designated table. The FirstName, LastName, Parent, Phone, City, and Email fields are selected and will be appended to the tblContactPatient table, which already contains these same six fields for patients.

You'll run and save the append query now.

To run and save the append query:

1. Run the query. A dialog box opens, warning that you are about to append five rows.

2. Click **Yes** to acknowledge the warning. The dialog box closes, and the append query adds the five records to the tblContactPatient table. The Query window is still displayed in Design view.

3. Save the query as **qryContactPatientAppend**, and then close the query.

Next, you'll open the tblContactPatient table to make sure that the five records were appended to the table.

4. Open the Navigation Pane, open the **tblContactPatient** table datasheet, resize the fields to their best fit, and then click the first row's **FirstName** field value to deselect all values. See Figure 9–6.

Figure 9–6   **tblContactPatient table datasheet after appending records**

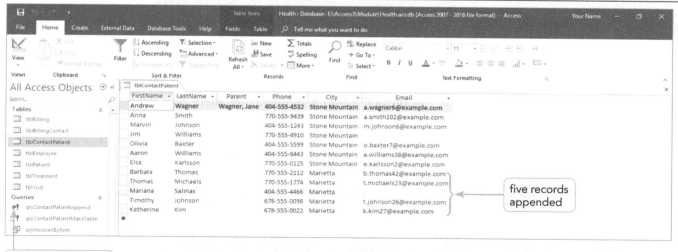

The new records have been added to the tblContactPatient table. Because the tblContactPatient table does not have a primary key, the new records appear at the end of the table.

▶ **5.** Save your datasheet changes, close the table, and then close the Navigation Pane.

Donna has contacted all the patients in the tblContactPatient table who are located in the city of Stone Mountain. She asks you to delete these records from the tblContactPatient table so that it contains only those records for patients she has not yet contacted.

Creating a Delete Query

You can either delete records in a table individually or create a delete query to remove a group of them all at once. When using a delete query, you specify one or more criteria that identify the records you want to delete. For example, to delete the records Donna no longer needs from the tblContactPatient table, you can create a delete query to delete the patient records in the table whose city is Stone Mountain.

Creating a Delete Query

- Create a select query with the necessary fields and selection criteria.
- On the Query Tools Design tab, click the Run button in the Results group to preview the results.
- Switch to Design view to make any necessary changes to the query, and then, when the query is correct, click the Delete button located in the Query Type group on the Query Tools Design tab.
- Click the Run button, and then click the Yes button to confirm deleting the records.

You will create the delete query next.

To create the delete query:

▶ **1.** Click the **Create** tab, and then, in the Queries group, click the **Query Design** button. The Show Table dialog box opens on top of the Query window.

▶ **2.** Add the **tblContactPatient** field list to the Query window, and then close the Show Table dialog box.

▶ **3.** Resize the tblContactPatient field list if necessary to display all its fields, and then add all the fields in order from the tblContactPatient field list to the design grid.

▶ **4.** In the design grid, click the **City Criteria** box, type **Stone Mountain**, and then press **TAB**. The criterion changes to "Stone Mountain". Only the records with a City field value of Stone Mountain will be selected when you run the query.

▶ **5.** Run the query. The query recordset shows the seven records with City field values of Stone Mountain. The select query is correct. See Figure 9–7.

Figure 9–7   **Seven records to be deleted**

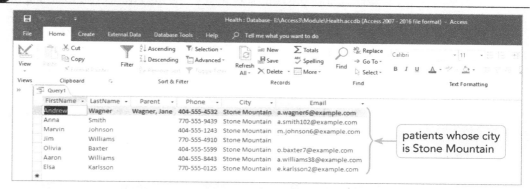

Trouble? If your query did not select the correct seven records, switch to Design view, correct the selection criterion, and then run the query again.

Now that you have verified that the query selects the correct records, you can change the query to a delete query.

▶ 6. Switch to Design view, and then on the Query Tools Design tab, in the Query Type group, click the **Delete** button. In the design grid, the Delete row replaces the Sort and Show rows.

▶ 7. Run the query. A dialog box opens, warning that you are about to delete seven rows from the table.

TIP

Once records have been deleted from a table using a delete query, they cannot be restored using the Undo command.

▶ 8. Click **Yes** to acknowledge the warning. The dialog box closes, and the seven records are deleted from the tblContactPatient table. The Query window is still displayed in Design view.

▶ 9. Save the query as **qryContactPatientDelete**, and then close the query. Next, you'll open the tblContactPatient table to verify that the records have been deleted.

▶ 10. Open the Navigation Pane, and then open the **tblContactPatient** table in Datasheet view. The table contains five records, and the Stone Mountain records were correctly deleted. See Figure 9–8.

Figure 9–8   **tblContactPatient table after deleting seven records**

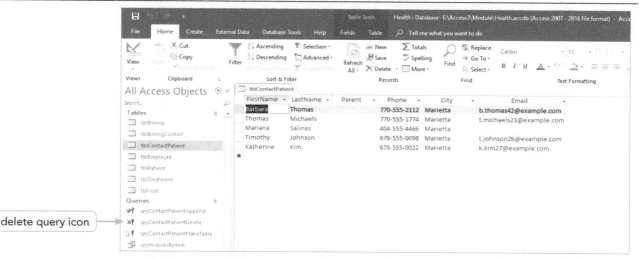

Donna wants you to make some structural changes to the tblContactPatient table. First she wants you to add a field named ContactComments where she can keep notes about the calls she makes. She also wants you to add appropriate captions to the FirstName and LastName fields. You can add the field and captions to the tblContactPatient table without affecting the other objects in the Health database, including the tblPatient table, because the tblContactPatient table was created as a temporary table to serve a specific, one-time purpose.

To add the new ContactComments field to the tblContactPatient table and add field captions:

▶ **1.** Switch to Design view.

You'll set the data type for the new field to Long Text, so that Donna is not limited to 255 characters of data in the field, as she would when using the Short Text data type.

▶ **2.** Click the **Field Name** box below the Email field, type **ContactComments**, press **TAB**, type the letter **l**, and then press **TAB** to select the Long Text data type.

▶ **3.** Press **F6** to position the insertion point in the Format box in the Field Properties pane, press **TAB**, and then type **Contact Comments** in the Caption box. You've completed adding the ContactComments field to the table. See Figure 9–9.

| Figure 9–9 | ContactComments field added to the tblContactPatient table |

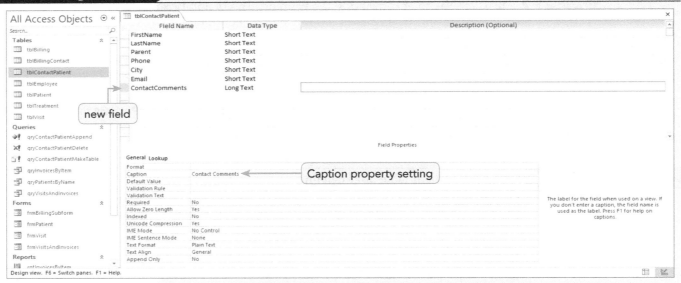

▶ **4.** Add the caption **First Name** to the FirstName field, and then add the caption **Last Name** to the LastName field.

▶ **5.** Save your changes to the table structure, switch to Datasheet view, and then resize the columns to their best fit. Notice that the captions and new field are displayed.

▶ **6.** Save your changes to the table layout, close the table, and then close the Navigation Pane.

Donna has sent an email message to each patient who has an email address in the Email field, and she wants to update the ContactComments field in the tblContactPatient table with the same comments for all records with an email address in the Email field. To accomplish this for Donna, you'll create an update query.

Creating an Update Query

Recall that an update query changes selected field values and records in one or more tables. An update query is useful when a group of records in a table all require the same change to data in the same field. For example, in the tblContactPatient table, Donna wants to enter the same comment in the ContactComments field for those patients who have an email address. She could type the comments in the ContactComments field for one of the records and then copy and paste the comments to the other records. However, performing these steps takes time and could result in incorrectly updating a record or neglecting to update one of the records. Instead, using an update query allows Donna to make this change to the table records quickly and accurately.

REFERENCE

Creating an Update Query

- Create a select query with the necessary fields and selection criteria.
- On the Query Tools Design tab, click the Run button in the Results group to preview the results.
- Switch to Design view to make any necessary changes to the query, and then, when the query is correct, click the Update button located in the Query Type group on the Query Tools Design tab.
- Type the updated values in the Update To boxes for the fields you want to update.
- Click the Run button, and then click the Yes button to confirm changing the records.

Now you can create an update query to update the ContactComments field in the tblContactPatient table for records that contain an email address in the Email field.

To create the update query:

▶ 1. Click the **Create** tab, and then in the Queries group, click the **Query Design** button to open the Show Table dialog box on top of the Query window.

▶ 2. Add the **tblContactPatient** field list to the Query window, close the Show Table dialog box, and then resize the tblContactPatient field list to display all its fields.

   You will select the Email and ContactComments fields for the query results. The Email field lets you select records for patients who have an email address listed in this field. The ContactComments field is the field Donna needs to update.

▶ 3. Add the **Email** and **ContactComments** fields, in that order, to the design grid.

▶ 4. In the design grid, click the **Email Criteria** box, type **Is Not Null**, and then press **TAB**. The query will select a record only if the Email field contains a value—in other words, if the field is not null.

▶ 5. Run the query. The query recordset displays four records, each containing an Email value. The select query is correct.

   Now that you have verified that the query selects the correct records, you can change it to an update query.

> **6.** Switch to Design view, and then on the Query Tools Design tab, in the Query Type group, click the **Update** button. In the design grid, the Update To row replaces the Sort and Show rows.

You specify how you want to change a field value for the selected records by entering an expression in the field's Update To box. An expression is a calculation resulting in a single value. You can type a simple expression directly into the Update To box.

> **7.** In the design grid, click the **ContactComments Update To** box, type **"Sent email in June. Contact again in August."** (be sure to type the quotation marks), and then drag the right border of the ContactComments column to the right to display the entire expression value. See Figure 9–10.

Figure 9–10   **Update query for the tblContactPatient table**

> **8.** Run the query. A dialog box opens, warning that you are about to update four rows in the tblContactPatient table.

TIP

For text expressions that contain quotation marks, you need to type the quotation marks twice. For example, to enter the expression A "text" expression, type "A ""text"" expression".

> **9.** Click the **Yes** button. The dialog box closes, and the query updates the ContactComments field values for patients who have an email address in the Email field. The Query window is still displayed in Design view.

You are finished updating the tblContactPatient table, so you'll save and close the query.

> **10.** Save the query as **qryContactPatientUpdate** and then close the query.

Now you can view the tblContactPatient table to see the results of the update operation.

To view the updated tblContactPatient table:

> **1.** Open the Navigation Pane, open the **tblContactPatient** table in Datasheet view, and then resize the Contact Comments column to its best fit. The ContactComments field values for patients who have email addresses have been updated correctly. See Figure 9–11.

| Figure 9–11 | tblContactPatient table with updated ContactComments field values |

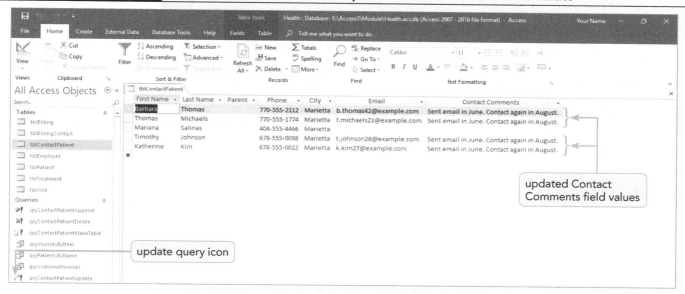

▶ **2.** Save the table datasheet changes and close the table.

▶ **3.** If you are not continuing on to the next session, close the Health database.

INSIGHT

Deleting Action Queries

You usually create an action query and run it for a special purpose. In most cases, you need to run the query only once. If you create and run an action query and then save it, you might accidentally run it again. Doing so would update tables in unintended ways. Therefore, after you've run an action query, you shouldn't save it in your database. Deleting an action query at this point prevents users from running it by mistake.

Donna can now use action queries in her future work with the Health database. In the next session, you'll learn about the different types of relationships you can create between tables, and you'll view and create indexes to increase a database's efficiency.

REVIEW

Session 9.1 Quick Check

1. What is an action query?

2. What precautions should you take before running an action query?

3. What is the difference between a make-table query and an append query?

4. What does a delete query do?

5. What does an update query do?

6. How does the design grid change when you create an update query?

Session 9.2 Visual Overview:

For a many-to-many relationship, you must create a third table, known as a **relationship table**, and form one-to-many relationships between the two original primary tables and the relationship table. The tblTreatment table exists only because the tblBilling and tblEmployee tables have a many-to-many relationship.

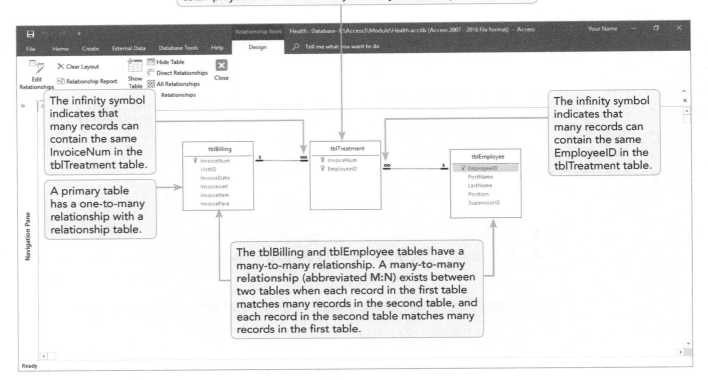

The infinity symbol indicates that many records can contain the same InvoiceNum in the tblTreatment table.

A primary table has a one-to-many relationship with a relationship table.

The infinity symbol indicates that many records can contain the same EmployeeID in the tblTreatment table.

The tblBilling and tblEmployee tables have a many-to-many relationship. A **many-to-many relationship** (abbreviated M:N) exists between two tables when each record in the first table matches many records in the second table, and each record in the second table matches many records in the first table.

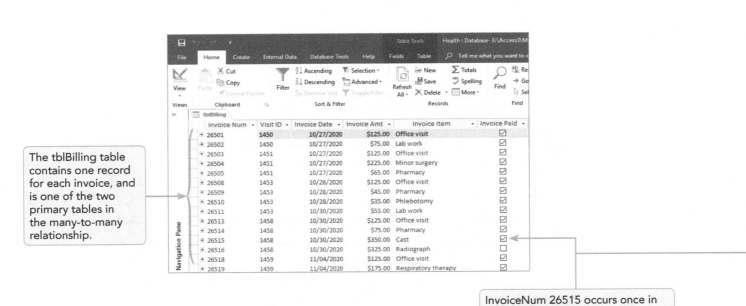

The tblBilling table contains one record for each invoice, and is one of the two primary tables in the many-to-many relationship.

InvoiceNum 26515 occurs once in the tblBilling table but twice in the tblTreatment table.

Many-to-Many Relationship

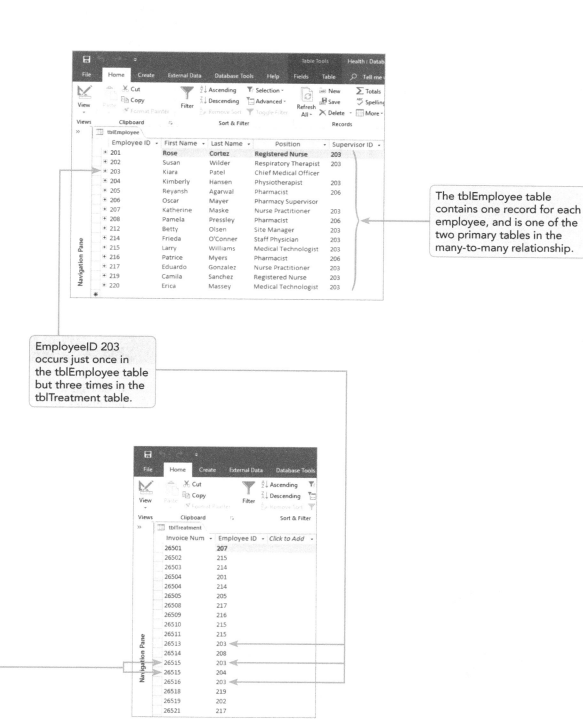

The tblEmployee table contains one record for each employee, and is one of the two primary tables in the many-to-many relationship.

EmployeeID 203 occurs just once in the tblEmployee table but three times in the tblTreatment table.

Understanding Types of Table Relationships

As you know, a one-to-many relationship (abbreviated as 1:M) exists between two tables when each record in the primary table matches zero, one, or more records in the related table, and when each record in the related table matches at most one record in the primary table. For example, Figure 9–12 shows a one-to-many relationship between portions of the tblPatient and tblVisit tables. It also shows a sample query based on the two tables. (Most examples in this session use portions of tables for illustrative purposes.) For instance, patient 13273 has one visit, patient 13275 has two visits, and patient 13276 has three visits.

Figure 9–12	One-to-many relationship and sample query

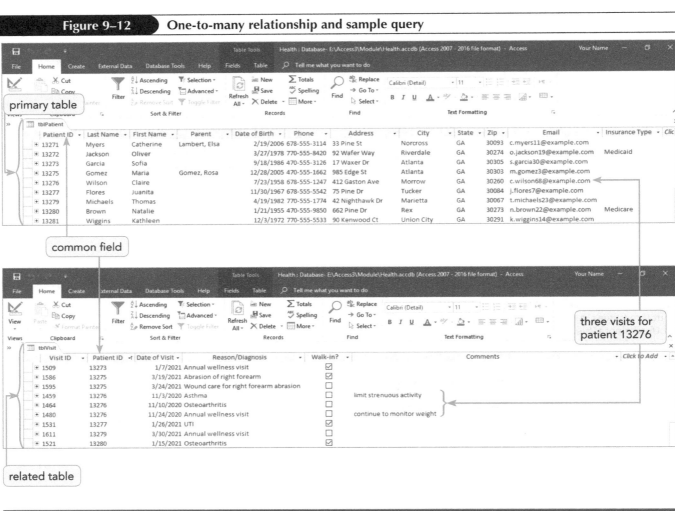

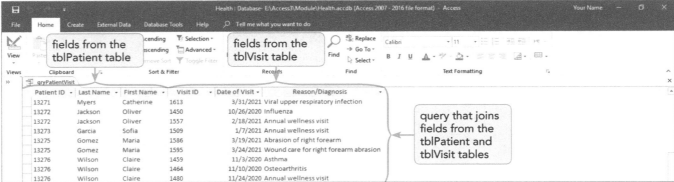

You use the common field—the PatientID field—to form the one-to-many relationship between the tblPatient and tblVisit tables. When you join the two tables based on PatientID field values, you can extract data from them as if they were one larger table. For example, you can join the tblPatient and tblVisit tables to create the qryPatientVisit query shown in Figure 9–12. In the qryPatientVisit query, the Patient ID, Last Name, and First Name columns are from the tblPatient table, and the Visit ID, Date of Visit, and Reason/Diagnosis columns are from the tblVisit table.

In addition to one-to-many relationships between tables, you can also relate tables through many-to-many and one-to-one relationships.

Many-to-Many Relationships

In the Health database, an invoice can represent treatment performed by many employees, and each employee can provide treatment on many invoiced patients, so the tblBilling and tblEmployee tables have a many-to-many relationship, as shown in the Session 9.2 Visual Overview.

When you have a many-to-many relationship (abbreviated as M:N) between two tables, you must create a third table, known as a relationship table, and form one-to-many relationships between the two original primary tables and the relationship table. For instance, the tblTreatment table, shown in the Session 9.2 Visual Overview, exists only because the tblBilling and tblEmployee tables have a many-to-many relationship. Each record in the tblTreatment table contains two foreign keys. The EmployeeID field is a foreign key that allows you to join the tblEmployee table to the tblTreatment table. The InvoiceNum field is a foreign key that allows you to join the tblBilling table to the tblTreatment table. The primary key of the tblTreatment table is a composite key, consisting of the combination of the EmployeeID and InvoiceNum fields. Each pair of values in this primary key is unique.

Unlike a one-to-many or one-to-one relationship, a many-to-many relationship is not represented by a single line between two tables in the Relationships window. Rather, a many-to-many relationship is represented by the two one-to-many relationships between the primary tables and the relationship table. For instance, Visual Overview 9.2 shows a one-to-many relationship line between the tblBilling and tblTreatment tables and another one-to-many relationship line between the tblEmployee and tblTreatment tables. Because the tblTreatment table is a relationship table, these two relationships together represent a many-to-many relationship.

You can see the one-to-many relationship between each primary table and the relationship table by examining the records. For example, the thirteenth record in the tblTreatment table represents a surgery for InvoiceNum 26515 that was performed by Kiara Patel, who has EmployeeID 203. EmployeeID 203 appears in many records in the tblTreatment table that represent treatment Kiara Patel billed on many other invoices including 26513 and 26516. Also, InvoiceNum 26515 appears in two tblTreatment table records, each for a different employee: Kimberly Hansen and Kiara Patel.

Decision Making: Identifying Many-to-Many Relationships

Although one-to-many relationships are the most common type of table relationship, many-to-many relationships occur frequently, and most databases have one or more many-to-many relationships. When developing a database, you need to decide when the relationship between two tables should be many-to-many rather than one-to-many. You can recognize when this relationship is appropriate by thinking about how all the pieces of data interrelate, as demonstrated by the following examples:

- In a college database, a student takes more than one class, and each class has more than one student enrolled; a course has many prerequisites and can be the prerequisite to many courses.
- In a pharmacy database, a medication is prescribed to many customers, and a customer can take many medications.
- In an airline database, a flight has many passengers, and a passenger can take many flights.
- In a publisher database, an author can write many books, and a book can have multiple authors.
- In a manufacturing database, a manufactured product consists of many parts, and a part can be a component in many manufactured products.
- In a film database, a movie has many actors, and each actor appears in many movies.

Common one-to-many relationships can turn into many-to-many relationships when circumstances change. For example, a department in an organization has many employees, and an employee usually works in a single department. However, an instructor can have a joint appointment to two college departments, and some companies hire employees and split their time between two departments. You must carefully analyze each situation and design your table relationships to handle the specific requirements for today and for the future.

When you join tables that have a many-to-many relationship, you can extract data from them as if they were one larger table. For example, you can join the tblBilling and tblEmployee tables to create a qryTreatment query. As shown in the Session 9.2 Visual Overview, in the tblTreatment table, the EmployeeID field joins the tblEmployee and tblTreatment tables, and the InvoiceNum field joins the tblBilling and tblTreatment tables.

One-to-One Relationships

A **one-to-one relationship** (abbreviated as **1:1**) exists between two tables when each record in the first table matches at most one record in the second table, and each record in the second table matches at most one record in the first table. Most relationships between tables are either one-to-many or many-to-many; the primary use for one-to-one relationships is as entity subtypes. An **entity subtype** is a table whose primary key is a foreign key to a second table and whose fields are additional fields for the second table.

For most patients, the Address, City, State, and Zip fields in the tblPatient table identify both the patient's location and billing address, which is where Lakewood Community Health Services sends the patient's invoices. In a few cases, however, a friend or relative pays the medical bills, so the billing name and address are different from the patient's name and address. You can handle these two sets of names and addresses in two ways. One way is to add the BillingCompany, BillingAddress, BillingCity, BillingState, and BillingZip fields to the tblPatient table. For each patient with an additional billing name and address, you store the appropriate values in these billing fields. For those patients who do not have additional billing information, you leave these billing fields null.

Another way to handle the two sets of addresses is to create an entity subtype, which in this case could be a table named tblBillingContact. In the tblBillingContact table, the PatientID field, which is the primary key, is also a foreign key to the tblPatient table. A record appears in the tblBillingContact table only for those patients who have different mailing and billing names and addresses. All billing data appears only in the tblBillingContact table. The tblPatient table and the tblBillingContact table, which is an entity subtype, have a one-to-one relationship, as shown in Figure 9–13.

| Figure 9–13 | tblPatient and tblBillingContact tables with a 1:1 relationship |

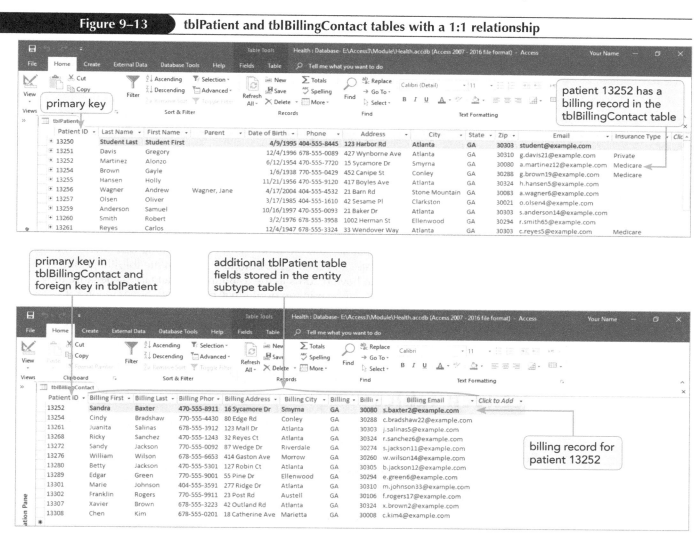

When you define a one-to-one relationship between tables, you can extract data from them as if they were one larger table. For example, you can define a relationship between the tblPatient and tblBillingContact tables to create the qryBillingContactData query shown in Figure 9–14.

Figure 9–14   **Query results produced by joining tables having a 1:1 relationship**

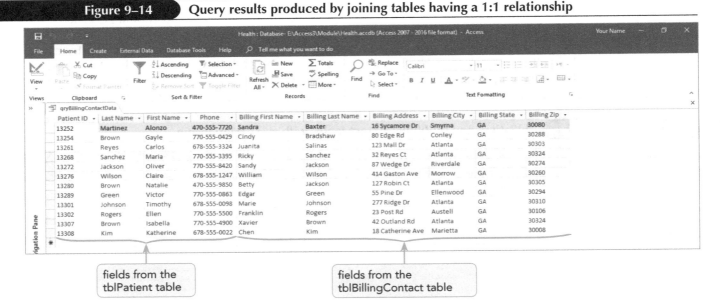

fields from the
tblPatient table

fields from the
tblBillingContact table

The relationship between the tblPatient and tblBillingContact tables is based upon the common PatientID field. In the query, the Patient ID, Last Name, First Name, and Phone columns are from the tblPatient table; and the Billing First Name, Billing Last Name, Billing Address, Billing City, Billing State, and Billing Zip columns are from the tblBillingContact table. Only the 12 patients who have records in the tblBillingContact table—because they have different billing addresses—appear in the qryBillingContactData query recordset.

Next, you'll define a many-to-many relationship between the tblBilling and tblEmployee tables and a one-to-one relationship between the tblPatient and tblBillingContact tables.

Defining M:N and 1:1 Relationships Between Tables

Similar to the way you define one-to-many relationships, you define many-to-many and one-to-one relationships in the Relationships window. First, you'll open the Relationships window and define the many-to-many relationship between the tblBilling and tblEmployee tables, using the tblTreatment table as the relationship table. You'll start by defining a one-to-many relationship between the tblBilling and tblTreatment tables, with tblBilling as the primary table, tblTreatment as the related table, and InvoiceNum as the common field (the primary key in the tblBilling table and a foreign key in the tblTreatment table). Next, you'll define a one-to-many relationship between the tblEmployee and tblTreatment tables, with tblEmployee as the primary table, tblTreatment as the related table, and EmployeeID as the common field (the primary key in the tblEmployee table and a foreign key in the tblTreatment table).

To define a many-to-many relationship between the tblBilling and tblEmployee tables:

▶ **1.** If you took a break after the previous session, make sure that the Health database is open.

▶ **2.** Close the Navigation Pane (if necessary), click the **Database Tools** tab, and then in the Relationships group, click the **Relationships** button to open the Relationships window.

3. On the Relationship Tools Design tab, in the Relationships group, click the **Show Table** button to open the Show Table dialog box.

4. Add the **tblTreatment**, **tblBillingContact**, and **tblEmployee** field lists to the Relationships window, and then close the Show Table dialog box.

5. Resize the tblBillingContact field list and the tblPatient field list, so that all field names are visible, and then drag the field list title bars of the field lists for the tblBillingContact, tblBilling, tblEmployee, and tblTreatment tables to arrange them as shown in Figure 9–15.

| Figure 9–15 | After adding three table field lists to the Relationships window |

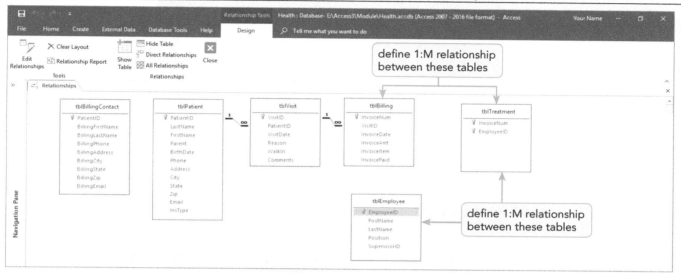

First, you'll define the one-to-many relationship between the tblBilling and tblTreatment tables.

6. In the tblBilling field list, click **InvoiceNum**, and then drag it to **InvoiceNum** in the tblTreatment field list. When you release the mouse button, the Edit Relationships dialog box opens.

The primary table, related table, and common field appear at the top of the dialog box. The Relationship Type box at the bottom of the dialog box lists One-To-Many. You'll enforce referential integrity and cascade updates to related fields, but you won't cascade deletions to related records because you want to preserve the Billing contact information in case it will be used again later.

7. Click the **Enforce Referential Integrity** check box, and then click the **Cascade Update Related Fields** check box. You have now selected all the necessary relationship options.

8. Click the **Create** button to close the dialog box and define the one-to-many relationship between the two tables. The completed relationship appears in the Relationships window.

9. Repeat Steps 6 through 8 to define the one-to-many relationship between the primary tblEmployee table and the related tblTreatment table, using EmployeeID as the common field. See Figure 9–16.

Now you'll define a one-to-one relationship between the tblPatient and tblBillingContact tables. Not all patients have billing contact information, so it will be important to create the relationship by dragging from the tblPatient table to the tblBillingContact table to preserve referential integrity.

To define a one-to-one relationship between the tblPatient and tblBillingContact tables:

> Be sure to drag from the tblPatient to the tblBillingContact table and not the reverse.

> **1.** In the tblPatient field list, click **PatientID**, and then drag it to **PatientID** in the tblBillingContact field list. When you release the mouse button, the Edit Relationships dialog box opens.
>
>   The primary table, related table, and common field appear at the top of the dialog box. The Relationship Type box at the bottom of the dialog box lists One-To-One.
>
>   **Trouble?** If an error message appears indicating a violation of referential integrity, you mistakenly dragged the PatientID field from the tblBillingContact table to the tblPatient table. Click the Cancel button and try again, dragging from the tblPatient table to the tblBillingContact table.

> **2.** Click the **Enforce Referential Integrity** check box, click the **Cascade Update Related Fields** check box, and then click the **Create** button to define the one-to-one relationship between the two tables and close the dialog box. The completed relationship appears in the Relationships window. See Figure 9–17.

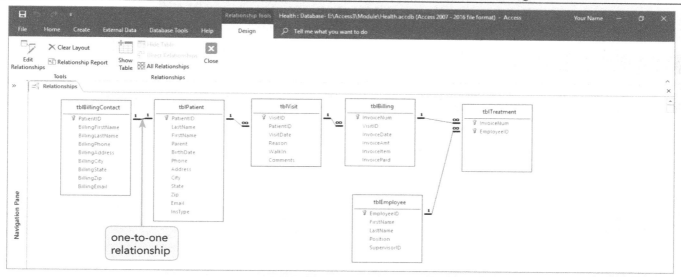

| Figure 9–17 | 1:1 relationship defined between the tblPatient and tblBillingContact tables |

Each side of the relationship has the digit 1 at its end of the join line to indicate a one-to-one relationship between the two tables.

▶ **3.** Save your relationship changes.

The tblEmployee table contains data about the employees at Lakewood Community Health Services who provide patient care. Donna asks you to create a select query to display the employees in the tblEmployee table and their supervisors. The select query you'll create will require a special join using the tblEmployee table.

Understanding Join Types

The design of the Health database includes a one-to-many relationship between the tblPatient and tblVisit tables using PatientID as the common field, which allows you to join the two tables to create a query based on data from both tables. While the term *join* is sometimes used to refer to any relationship between tables in a database, **join** is also a technical database term that describes how data from the tables in a relationship is selected and returned. The most common type of join is referred to as an inner join, which is the type of join you have used in your work with the database for Lakewood Community Health Services thus far. Two other types of joins are the outer join and the self-join.

Inner and Outer Joins

An **inner join** selects records from two tables only when the records have the same value in the common field that links the tables. For example, in a database containing a table of student information and a table of class information, an inner join would return all student records that have a matching class record and all class records that have a matching student record. In the Health database, PatientID is the common field for the tblPatient and tblBillingContact tables. As shown in Figure 9–18, the results of a query based on an inner join of these two tables would return only those records that have a matching ID value. The record in the tblPatient table with a Patient ID column value of 13250 is not included in the query recordset because it fails to match a record with the same Patient ID column value in the tblBillingContact table.

(That patient does not have a different billing address.) Because primary key values can't be null, records with null foreign key values do not appear in a query recordset based on an inner join. You usually use an inner join whenever you perform a query based on more than one table; it is the default join you have used to this point. You can specify or change the join type of a relationship in the Join Properties dialog box.

Figure 9–18	Example of an inner join

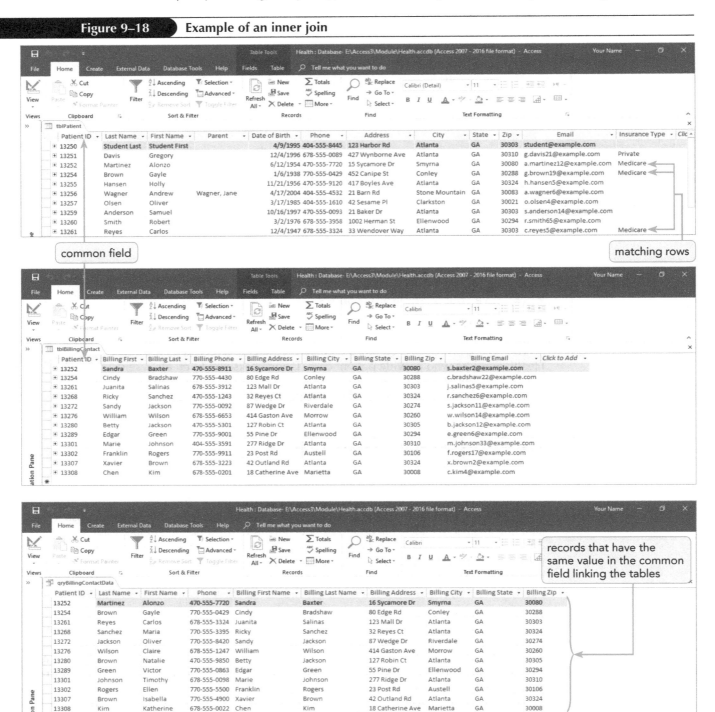

An **outer join** selects *all* records from one table along with only those records from a second table that have matching common field values. For example, in a database containing a student table and a class table, you could create two different outer joins between these two tables. One outer join would return the records for all students whether or not the students are enrolled in classes, and another outer join between these two tables would return all classes whether or not any students are enrolled in them. In the Health database, you would use this kind of join if you wanted to see, for example, all records from the tblPatient table and any matching records from the tblBillingContact table. Figure 9–19 shows an outer join for the tblPatient and tblBillingContact tables. All records from the tblPatient table appear in the query recordset, along with only matching records from the tblBillingContact table. Notice that the record from the tblPatient table for Patient ID 13250 appears in the query recordset even though it does not match a record in the tblBillingContact table.

Figure 9–19   **Example of an outer join**

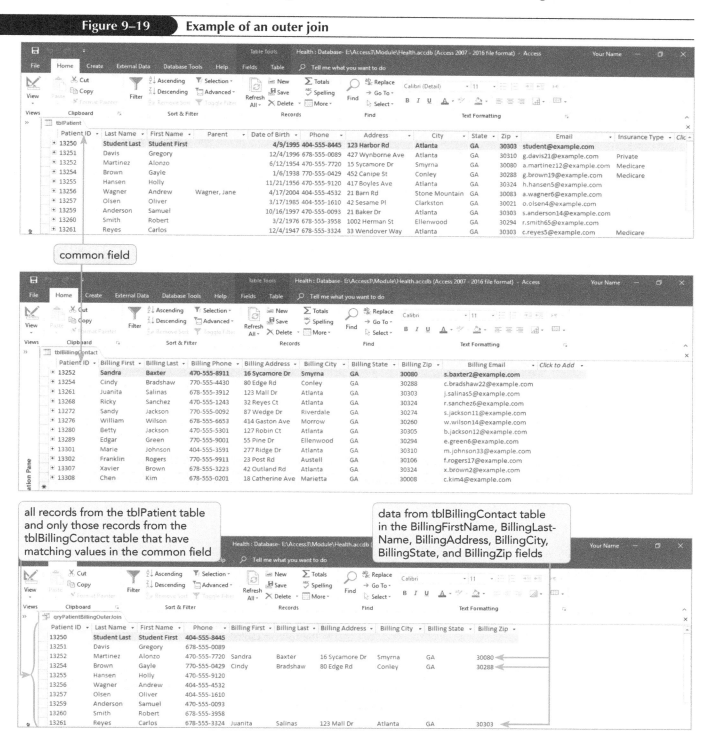

common field

all records from the tblPatient table and only those records from the tblBillingContact table that have matching values in the common field

data from tblBillingContact table in the BillingFirstName, BillingLast-Name, BillingAddress, BillingCity, BillingState, and BillingZip fields

Another example of an outer join using the tblPatient and tblVisit tables is shown in Figure 9–20. All records from the tblVisit table appear in the query recordset. If any tblVisit records had a Patient ID that did not match a Patient ID in the tblPatient table, these records would not be in the query recordset. For example, the Patient ID 13313 record from the tblPatient table does not appear in the query recordset because it does not match a record in the tblVisit table.

Figure 9–20   **Another example of an outer join**

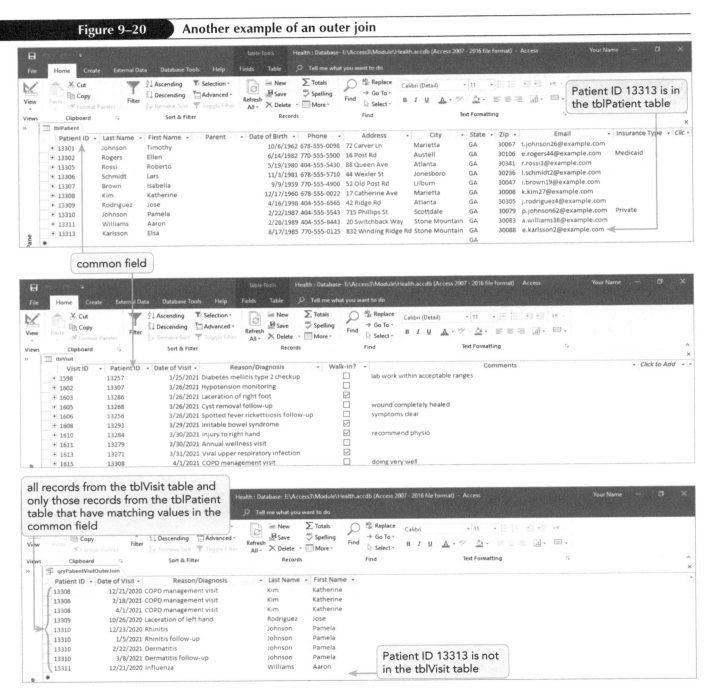

Any relationship you create in Access is by default an inner join, but you can change the join type between two tables to be an outer join in the Join Properties dialog box. You'll view the join type between the tblPatient and tblVisit tables and examine the options for changing the join type.

To view the join type between the tblPatient and tblVisit tables:

1. Right-click the **join line** between the tblPatient and tblVisit tables, and then click **Edit Relationship** on the shortcut menu to open the Edit Relationships dialog box.

   Trouble? If the Edit Relationship dialog box does not open, click the join line, and then on the Relationship Tools Design tab, in the Tools group, click the Edit Relationships button.

2. Click the **Join Type** button in the dialog box to open the Join Properties dialog box. See Figure 9–21.

Figure 9–21   Join Properties dialog box

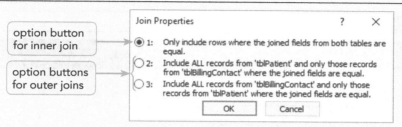

In the Join Properties dialog box, the first option button is selected, indicating that the join type between the tblPatient and tblVisit tables is an inner join. You would click the second or third option button to establish an outer join between the two tables. You'd select the second option if you wanted to select all records from the tblPatient table and any matching records from the tblVisit table based on the PatientID common field. You'd select the third option if you wanted to select all records from the tblVisit table and any matching records from the tblPatient table based on the PatientID common field.

When you change the join type for a relationship between two tables in the Relationships window, every new object created based on the two related tables uses the join type you selected in the Join Properties dialog box. Existing queries, reports, or forms based on the two related tables continue to use the join type that was in effect at the time you created these items.

Donna wants to continue to use an inner join for all queries based on the related tblPatient and tblVisit tables.

3. Click the **Cancel** button to close the Join Properties dialog box without making any changes, and then click the **Cancel** button to close the Edit Relationships dialog box without making any changes.

4. Close the Relationships window, and then if you are prompted to save changes, click **No** to ensure that you don't change the relationship type.

Self-Joins

A table can also be joined with itself; this join is called a **self-join**. A self-join can be either an inner or outer join. For example, the tblEmployee table lists all employees, and for each employee who has a supervisor, the SupervisorID is included. The SupervisorID is the EmployeeID of the supervisor. It doesn't make sense to have separate SupervisorID and Employee ID fields. Imagine a situation with multiple supervisors, and each supervisor also has a supervisor. Separate tables for supervisors would be very confusing. The supervisors are also employees, and thus the EmployeeID for a supervisor is entered in the SupervisorID field. This is a case where a self-join would be used. The tblEmployee table would be joined to itself so the SupervisorID field could be related to the EmployeeID field to display the name of the supervisor for each employee. You would use a self-join to relate the SupervisorID field to the EmployeeID field to determine the name of the supervisor if you wanted to see records from the tblEmployee table together with information about each employee's supervisor. Figure 9–22 shows a self-join for the tblEmployee table. In this case, the self-join is an inner join because records appear in the query results only if the SupervisorID field value matches an EmployeeID field value. To create this self-join, you would add two copies of the tblEmployee field list to the Query window in Design view and then join the SupervisorID field of one tblEmployee field list to the EmployeeID field of the other tblEmployee field list.

Figure 9–22   Example of self-join

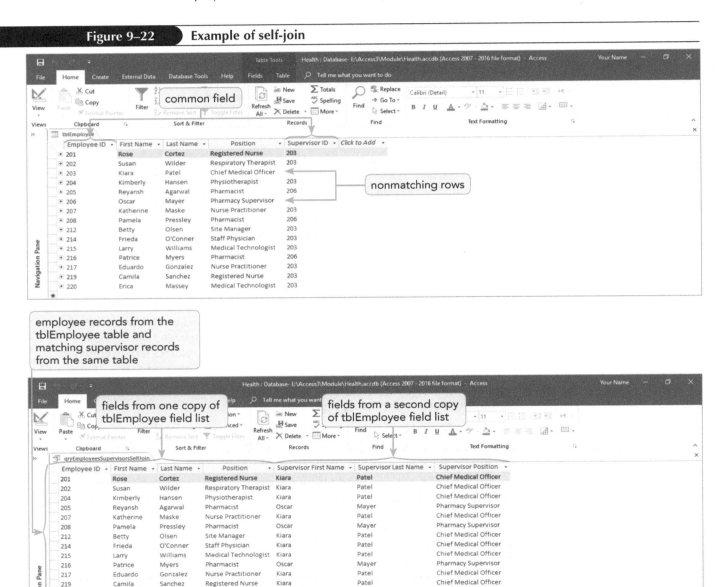

In Figure 9–22, the query results show the record for each employee in the tblEmployee table with a value in the SupervisorID field, and the detail for each record includes information about the supervisor for that employee. The supervisor information also comes from the tblEmployee table through the SupervisorID field. The join for the query is an inner join, so only employees with nonnull SupervisorID field values appear in the query recordset.

You need to create a query to display the employees and their supervisors in the tblEmployee table. This query requires a self-join. To create the self-join, you need to add two copies of the tblEmployee field list to the Query window in Design view and then add a join line from the EmployeeID field in one field list to the SupervisorID field in the other. The SupervisorID field is a foreign key that matches the primary key field EmployeeID. You can then create a query to display employee information with the related supervisor information.

REFERENCE

Creating a Query Using a Self-Join

- Click the Create tab on the ribbon.
- In the Queries group, click the Query Design button.
- In the Show Table dialog box, double-click the table for the self-join, double-click the table a second time, and then click the Close button.
- Click and drag the primary key field from one field list to the foreign key field in the other field list.
- Right-click the join line between the two tables, and then click Join Properties to open the Join Properties dialog box.
- Click the first option button to select an inner join, or click the second option button or the third option button to select an outer join, and then click the OK button.
- Select the fields, specify the selection criteria, select the sort options, and set other properties as appropriate for the query.

Now you'll create the query using a self-join to display supervisor information with the relevant employee records.

To create the query using a self-join:

1. Click the **Create** tab, and then in the Queries group, click the **Query Design** button. The Show Table dialog box opens on top of the Query window in Design view.

2. Double-click **tblEmployee** to add the tblEmployee field list to the Query window.

3. Double-click **tblEmployee** again to add a second copy of the tblEmployee field list to the Query window, and then close the Show Table dialog box. The left field list is identified as tblEmployee, and the right field list is identified as tblEmployee_1 to distinguish the two copies of the table.

   You will now create a join between the two copies of the tblEmployee field list by linking the EmployeeID field in the tblEmployee field list to the SupervisorID field in the tblEmployee_1 field list. The SupervisorID field is a foreign key that matches the primary key field, EmployeeID.

4. In the tblEmployee field list, click the **EmployeeID** field, and then drag it to the **SupervisorID** field in the tblEmployee_1 field list. A join line is created between the two fields. You can verify that this is an inner join query by opening the Join Properties dialog box.

5. Right-click the join line between the two field lists, and then click **Join Properties** on the shortcut menu to open the Join Properties dialog box. See Figure 9–23.

Figure 9–23	Join Properties dialog box

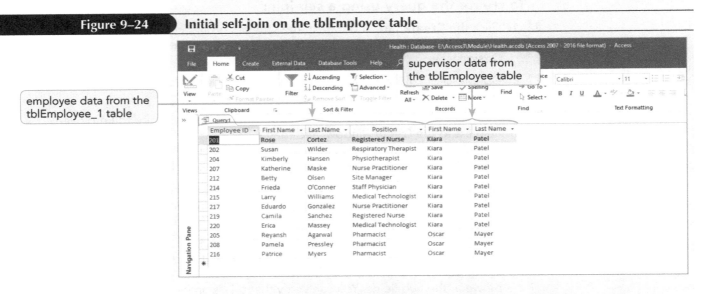

The first option button is selected, indicating that this is an inner join. Because the inner join is correct, you can close the dialog box and then add the necessary fields in the design grid.

Your query will use each employee's SupervisorID value to retrieve data associated with the supervisor's corresponding EmployeeID value. To accomplish this, you choose the employee-related records from the tblEmployee_1 field list, which is connected to the other field list using the SupervisorID field.

▶ 6. Click the **Cancel** button, and then from the tblEmployee_1 field list, add the **EmployeeID**, **FirstName**, **LastName**, and **Position** fields to the design grid.

▶ 7. From the tblEmployee field list, add the **FirstName** and **LastName** fields to the design grid.

The tblEmployee field list is connected to the other field list using the EmployeeID field, so the FirstName and LastName fields will display the first and last names of the supervisor for each record in the tblEmployee_1 field list.

▶ 8. Run the query. The query recordset displays six fields and 13 records. See Figure 9–24.

Figure 9–24	Initial self-join on the tblEmployee table

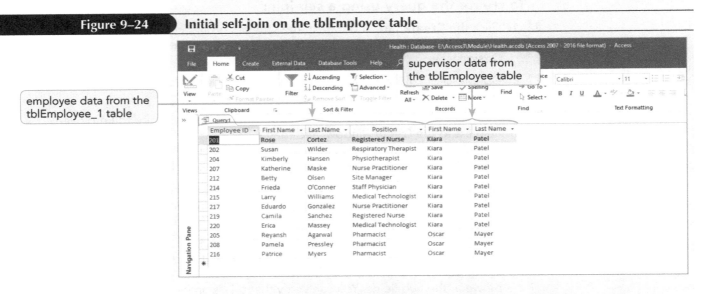

The query recordset displays all employees and their supervisors with the exception of the records for Kiara Patel and Oscar Mayer because their records contain null SupervisorID field values. (They are supervisors of the other employees and do not have assigned supervisors.) Remember that an inner join doesn't display records from the second table unless it contains a matching value in the common field. In the tblEmployee_1 table, the SupervisorID field values for Kiara Patel and Oscar Mayer are null, so the inner join doesn't select their records in the tblEmployee table.

Trouble? If your query results do not match Figure 9–24, switch to Design view and review the preceding steps to make any necessary corrections to your query design. Then run the query again.

Two columns in the query recordset are titled "First Name," and two columns are titled "Last Name." Donna asks you to rename the two rightmost columns so that the contents of the query recordset will be more clear. After you set the Caption property for the two rightmost fields, the column names in the query recordset will be, from left to right, Employee ID, First Name, Last Name, Position, Supervisor First Name, and Supervisor Last Name. You'll also sort the query in ascending order by EmployeeID.

To set the Caption property for two query fields and sort the query:

▶ **1.** Switch to Design view.

▶ **2.** Click the **Field** box for the fifth column.

▶ **3.** On the Query Tools Design tab, in the Show/Hide group, click the **Property Sheet** button, and then set the Caption property to **Supervisor First Name**.

▶ **4.** Click the **Field** box for the sixth column, and then set the Caption property to **Supervisor Last Name**.

▶ **5.** Close the Property Sheet, click the right side of the EmployeeID Sort box to display the sort order options, and then click **Ascending**.

▶ **6.** Save the query as **qryEmployeesSupervisors**, run the query, resize all columns to their best fit, and then click the first row's Employee ID field value to deselect all values. The query recordset displays the new captions for the fifth and sixth columns. See Figure 9–25.

| Figure 9–25 | Final self-join on the tblEmployee table |

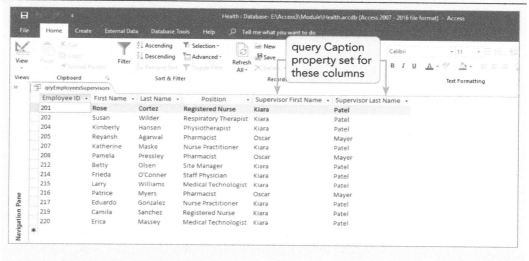

▶ **7.** Save and close the query.

Donna wonders if her staff's work will take longer as the Health database grows with the addition of more table records. Specifically, she wants to know if queries will take longer to run. Using indexes will help make her queries run faster.

Using Indexes for Table Fields

Suppose you need to find all the pages in a book that discuss a specific topic. The fastest, most accurate way to perform your search is to look up the topic in the book's index. In a similar fashion, you can create indexes for fields in a table, so that Access can quickly locate all the records in a table that contain specific values for one or more fields. An **index** is a list that relates field values to the records that contain those field values.

In Access, an index is automatically created for a table's primary key. When you view a table in datasheet view, the records are always in primary key order, even though they may not have been entered in that order. This is due to the automatically created index for the primary key. For example, the tblBilling table in the Health database includes an index for the InvoiceNum field, which is the table's primary key. Conceptually, as shown in Figure 9–26, each record in the tblBilling table is identified by its record number, and the InvoiceNum index has two columns. The first column contains a record number in the tblBilling table, and the second column contains the InvoiceNum value for that record number. For instance, InvoiceNum 26503 in the index has a record number value of 3; and record number 3 in the tblBilling table contains the data for InvoiceNum 26503.

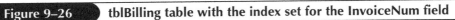

| Figure 9–26 | **tblBilling table with the index set for the InvoiceNum field** |

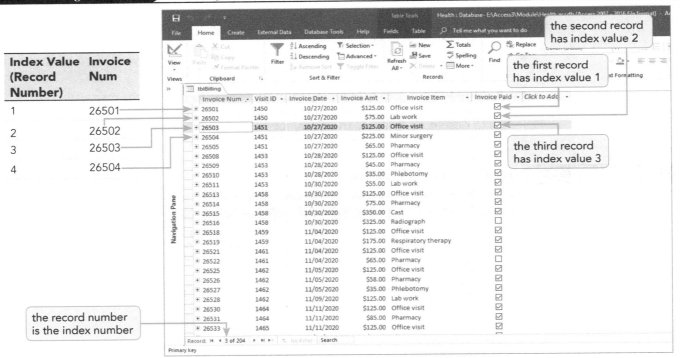

Because InvoiceNum values in the tblBilling table are unique, each row in the InvoiceNum index has a single record number. An index for a non-primary-key field, however, may contain multiple record numbers in a row. Figure 9–27 illustrates a VisitID index for the tblBilling table. Because VisitID is a foreign key in the tblBilling table (a visit can have many invoices), each VisitID entry in the index can be associated with many record numbers in the tblBilling table. For instance, VisitID 1450 in the index has record number values of 1 and 2, and record numbers 3, 4, and 5 in the tblBilling table contain the invoice data for VisitID 1451.

Figure 9–27   **tblBilling table with index for the VisitID field**

If you were to create an index for the VisitID field in the tblBilling table, queries that use VisitID as a sort field or as a selection criterion would run faster.

INSIGHT

Benefits and Limitations of Indexes

With small tables, the increased speed associated with indexes is not readily apparent. In practice, tables with hundreds of thousands or millions of records are common. In such cases, the increase in speed is dramatic. In fact, without indexes, many database operations in large tables would not be practical because they would take too long to complete. Why the speed difference in these cases? Sorting or selecting records from a large table without an index requires numerous accesses to storage media to retrieve table records because the entire table can't fit in computer memory. In contrast, indexes are usually small enough to fit completely in computer memory, and records can be sorted and selected based on indexes with minimal need to access storage media. Because accessing storage media is generally slower than performing operations in computer memory, using indexes in large tables is faster.

The speed advantage of using an index must be weighed against two disadvantages: The index adds storage requirements to the database, and it takes time to update the index as you add and delete records. Except for primary key indexes, you can add and delete indexes at any time. Thus, you can add an index if you think searching and querying would be faster as the number of records in the database increases. You can also delete an existing index if you later deem it to be unnecessary.

You can view the existing indexes for a table by opening the table in Design view.

View a Table's Indexes

- Open the table in Design view.
- To view an index for a single field, click the field, and then view the Indexed property in the Field Properties pane.
- To view all the indexes for a table or to view an index consisting of multiple fields, click the Indexes button in the Show/Hide group on the Table Tools Design tab.

You'll view the indexes for the tblTreatment table.

To view the indexes for the tblTreatment table:

1. Open the Navigation Pane, and then open the **tblTreatment** table in Design view.

2. On the Table Tools Design tab, in the Show/Hide group, click the **Indexes** button to open the Indexes: tblTreatment dialog box. Click **PrimaryKey** in the Index Name column, and then drag the dialog box to the position shown in Figure 9–28.

Figure 9–28 Indexes for the tblTreatment table

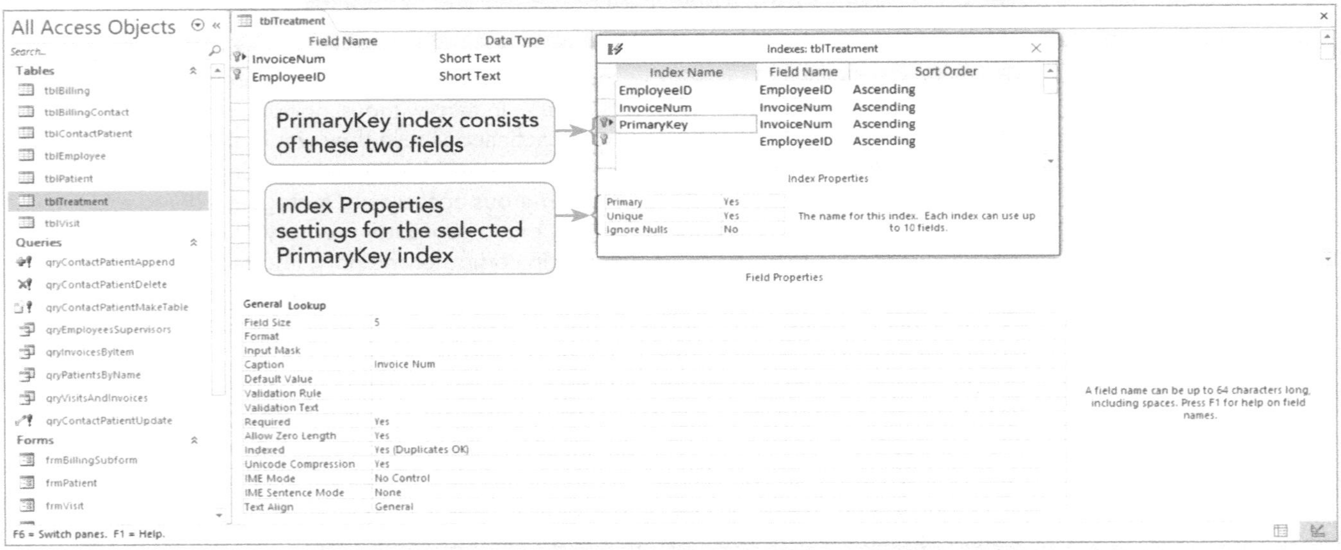

In the Indexes: tblTreatment dialog box, the properties in the Index Properties section apply to the selected PrimaryKey index, which consists of the table's composite key of the InvoiceNum and EmployeeID fields. Because EmployeeID in the fourth row of the dialog box does not have an Index Name property value, both InvoiceNum and EmployeeID make up the PrimaryKey index. The PrimaryKey index was generated automatically when the table was created, and the InvoiceNum and EmployeeID fields were designated as the table's composite key. The properties for the PrimaryKey index indicate that this index is the primary key index (Primary property setting of Yes) and that values in this index must be unique (Unique property setting of Yes)—that is, each InvoiceNum and EmployeeID pair of field values must be unique. The Ignore Nulls property setting of No means that records with null values for the InvoiceNum field or EmployeeID field are included in the index, but this setting is ignored because the Yes setting for the Primary property doesn't allow either field to have a null value.

▶   **3.** Close the Indexes: tblTreatment dialog box, and then close the table.

INSIGHT

Default Automatic Indexes

In addition to the automatically created primary key index, an index is also automatically created for any field name that contains the following letter sequences: "code", "ID", "key", or "num". You can add, change, and delete from this list of letter sequences to manage the automatic indexes created in a database. To do so, click the File tab to open Backstage view, click Options in the navigation bar to open the Access Options dialog box, and then click Object Designers in the left pane. In the Table design view section, the AutoIndex on Import/Create box displays, by default, ID;key;code;num. Modify the entries in the AutoIndex on Import/Create box if you want a different list of letter sequences to be used in automatically created indexes for the fields in your tables.

Over the past few weeks, Donna's staff has been monitoring the performance of the Health database by timing how long it takes to run queries. She wants her staff to let her know if the performance changes over the next several days as a result of creating an index for the City field in the tblPatient table. Many queries use the City field as a sort field or selection criterion, and adding an index might speed up those queries.

Creating an Index

You can create an index for a single field using the Indexes dialog box or by setting the Indexed property for the field in Design view. However, for a multiple-field index, you must create the index in the Indexes dialog box.

REFERENCE

Creating an Index

- Open the table in Design view.
- To create an index for a single field, click the field, and then set the Indexed property in the Field Properties pane.
- To create an index consisting of multiple fields, click the Indexes button located on the Table Tools Design tab in the Show/Hide group to open the Indexes dialog box.
- Enter a name for the index in the first Index Name box, and select the first field in the Field Name box.
- In the second Index Name box, leave the name blank, and select the second field in the Field Name box.
- Set additional field names in each row as needed, leaving the Index Name box blank for each row except the first one, set other properties as necessary for the index, and then close the Indexes dialog box.

Next, you'll create an index for the City field in the tblPatient table by setting the field's Indexed property.

To create an index for the City field in the tblPatient table:

▶ **1.** Open the **tblPatient** table in Design view, and then close the Navigation Pane.

▶ **2.** On the Table Tools Design tab, in the Show/Hide group, click the Indexes button to open the Indexes: tblPatient dialog box, and then position the dialog box as shown in Figure 9-29.

Figure 9-29 Indexes list for the tblPatient table

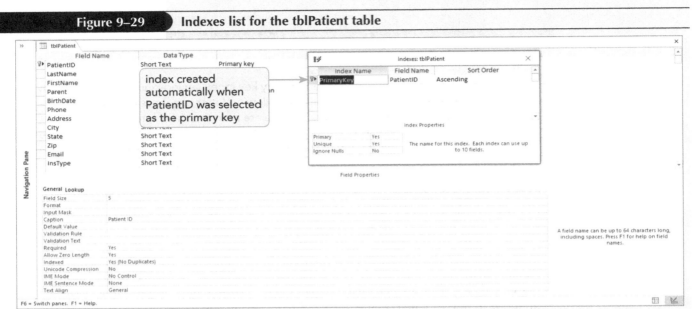

An index was created for the PatientID field because it is the primary key. The PatientID index would have been created even if the field wasn't the primary key because the field name has an ID suffix. No other indexes exist for the tblPatient table. You'll create an index for the City field that allows duplicates because the same City field value can appear in many records in the tblPatient table.

▶ **3.** Click **City** in the Field Name column to make it the current field.

The Indexed property in the Field Properties pane for the City field is currently set to No, indicating there is not an index on the City field.

▶ **4.** Click the right side of the **Indexed** box in the Field Properties pane, and then click **Yes (Duplicates OK)**. An index for the City field is created with duplicate values allowed. Setting the Indexed property automatically created the City index in the Indexes: tblPatient dialog box. See Figure 9-30.

Figure 9–30   **City index added to the tblPatient table**

5. Close the dialog box, save your table design changes, and then switch to Datasheet view.

6. Change the first record in the table so the Last Name and First Name columns contain your last and first names, respectively.

7. **sam** ↑ Close the table, make a backup copy of the Health database, compact and repair the database, and then close it.

The work you completed with table relationships, table and query joins, and indexes will make it much easier for Donna and her staff to enter, retrieve, and view information in the Health database.

Session 9.2 Quick Check

REVIEW

1. What are the three types of relationships you can define between tables?

2. What is an entity subtype?

3. What is the difference between an inner join and an outer join?

4. Describe the results of two different outer joins that you could create between a members table and a classes table in a database for a fitness club.

5. What is a self-join?

6. What is an index?

7. In Access, an index is generated automatically for a table's ___ key.

PRACTICE

Review Assignments

Data File needed for the Review Assignments: Product.accdb

The Product database contains data about Lakewood Community Health Services suppliers and their products, as well as data about the invoices from the suppliers and the payments made by Lakewood Community Health Services to the suppliers. The database also contains queries, forms, and reports. Donna wants you to define relationships between the tables and to create some new queries for her. Complete the following steps:

1. Open the **Product** database located in the Access3 > Review folder provided with your Data Files, and then click the Enable Content button next to the security warning, if necessary.

2. Modify the first record in the tblSupplier table datasheet so the Contact First Name and Contact Last Name columns contain your first and last names, and the Company Comments field contains your city and state. Close the table.

3. Define a many-to-many relationship between the tblInvoice and tblPayment tables, using the tblInvoicePayment table as the relationship table. Define a one-to-one relationship between the primary tblSupplier table and the related tblSupplierCreditLine table. Select the referential integrity option and the cascade updates option for the relationships.

4. Create a make-table query based on the tblProduct table, selecting the ProductID, SupplierID, ProductName, Price, TempControl, and Sterile fields, and selecting only those records for products that require a temperature-controlled environment. Use **tblProductSpecialEnviron** as the new table name, store the table in the current database, and then run the query. Save this query as **qryMakeSpecialEnviron** and close the query.

5. Open the tblProductSpecialEnviron table, and then adjust the column widths to their best fit. Format the TempControlled and Sterile fields to Yes/No. (*Hint*: In Design View, select the field name, and then select the Format property to Yes/No.) Save and close the tblProductSpecialEnviron table.

6. Create an append query based on the tblProduct table, selecting the ProductID, SupplierID, ProductName, Price, TempControl, and Sterile fields, and selecting only those records for products that are sterile and do not require a temperature-controlled environment. Append the records to the tblProductSpecialEnviron table, run the query, save it as **qryAppendSterile**, and then close the query. Open the tblProductSpecialEnviron table, and then verify that the records have been added. Close the table.

7. Create a delete query that deletes all records in the tblProductSpecialEnviron table in which the Price is less than $20.00. Run the query, save it as **qryDeletePriceLess20**, and then close the query. Open the tblProductSpecialEnviron table, verify that the table now contains 30 records, and then close the table.

8. Create a query using a self-join that selects all products in the tblProduct table that are included in another product. To do so, add two copies of the tblProduct field list to the query design window, and then create a relationship between the ProductID field in the first list and the IncludedIn field in the second list. The query results should display the ProductID and ProductName fields for the included items. (*Hint*: These should come from the second field list.) The query should also assign the captions **Collection Product ID** and **Collection Product Name** as appropriate to the fields. In Design view, sort the records in ascending order by the Collection Product ID column. Resize all columns in the datasheet to best fit, save the query as **qryProductCollection**, and then close the query

9. Open the tblProductSpecialEnviron table in Design view, specify the primary key, add an index that allows duplicates for the SupplierID field, and then save and close the table.

10. Make a backup copy of the database, compact and repair the database, and then close it.

Case Problem 1

Data File needed for this Case Problem: Instruction.accdb

Great Giraffe Jeremiah Garver is the operations manager at Great Giraffe, a career school in Denver, Colorado. Great Giraffe offers part-time and full-time courses in areas of study that are in high demand by industries in the area, including data science, digital marketing, and bookkeeping. Jeremiah created the Instruction database to track and view information about the students, faculty, and courses his business offers. The database also contains queries, forms, and reports. Jeremiah wants you to define relationships between the tables and to create some new queries for him. Complete the following steps:

1. Open the **Instruction** database located in the Access3 > Case1 folder provided with your Data Files, and then click the Enable Content button next to the security warning, if necessary.

2. Modify the first record in the tblFaculty table datasheet so the First Name and Last Name columns contain your first and last names. Close the table.

3. Define a many-to-many relationship between the tblCourse and tblFaculty tables, using the tblTeaching table as the relationship table. Define a one-to-one relationship between the primary tblStudent table and the related tblScholarship table. Select the referential integrity option and the cascade updates option for the relationships.

4. Create a make-table query based on the qryAllPaymentPlanStudents query, selecting all fields from the query and only those records where the City field value is **Denver**. Use **tblCityPaymentPlan** as the new table name, store the table in the current database, and then run the query. Save the query as **qryMakeCityPaymentPlan**, and close the query. Open the tblCityPaymentPlan table and verify the City value is Denver for all records. Close the tblCityPaymentPlan table.

5. Create an append query based on the qryAllPaymentPlanStudents query that selects all fields for only those records where the City field value is **Littleton**. Append the records to the tblCityPaymentPlan table and run the query. Save the query as **qryAppendLittleton**, and then close the query. Open the tblCityPaymentPlan table and verify that the City column includes values of both Denver and Littleton. Close the tblCityPaymentPlan table.

6. Create an update query to select all records in the tblCityPaymentPlan table where the value in the City field value is **Littleton**, and set the remaining balance to 0. Run the query, save it as **qryUpdateLittletonToZero**, and then close the query. Open the tblCityPaymentPlan table and verify balances for the Littleton students have been reduced to $0. Close the tblCityPaymentPlan table.

7. Create a delete query that deletes all records in the tblCityPaymentPlan table in which the BalanceDue field value is greater **$1500**. Run the query, save it as **qryDeleteMoreThan1500**, and then close the query. Open the tblCityPaymentPlan table, resize all columns to their best fit, and then verify there are no records whose BalanceDue field is greater than $1500. Save your layout changes, and then close the tblCityPaymentPlan table.

8. Create a query using a self-join that lists all faculty that have supervisors. To do so, add two copies of the tblFaculty field list to the query design window, and then create a relationship between the FacultyID field in the first list and the SupervisorID field in the second list. The query results should display the FacultyID, FacultyFirst, and FacultyLast fields. (*Hint*: These should come from the second field list.) The query should also assign the captions **Faculty ID**, **Faculty First Name**, and **Faculty Last Name**, respectively, to these fields. The query results should also include the following fields for the supervisor of each faculty member: FacultyFirst, FacultyLast, and Position. (*Hint*: These should come from the first field list.) The query should also assign the captions **Supervisor First Name**, **Supervisor Last Name**, and **Supervisor Position**, respectively, to these fields. Sort the records in ascending order by the Faculty ID column. Resize all columns in the datasheet to best fit, save the query as **qryFacultySupervisors**, and then close the query.

9. Open the tblCityPaymentPlan table in Design view, add an index that allows duplicates for the City field, and then save and close the table.

10. Make a backup copy of the database, compact and repair the database, and then close it.

CHALLENGE

Case Problem 2

Data File needed for this Case Problem: CleanOut.accdb

Drain Adopter Tandrea Austin manages the Drain Adopter program for the Department of Water and Power in Bellingham, Washington. The program recruits volunteers to regularly monitor and clear storm drains near their homes to ensure the drains are clear and unobstructed when large rainstorms are predicted. Tandrea created the CleanUp database to track, maintain, and analyze data about the drains and volunteers in the Drain Adopter program. Tandrea asks you to define table relationships and create some new queries for her. Complete the following steps:

1. Open the **CleanOut** database located in the Access3 > Case2 folder provided with your Data Files, and then click the Enable Content button next to the security warning, if necessary.
2. Change the first record in the tblEmployee table datasheet so the First Name and Last Name columns contain your first and last names. Close the table.
3. Define a many-to-many relationship between the tblDrain and tblEmployee tables, using the tblSpotCheck table as the related table. Define a one-to-one relationship between the primary tblVolunteer table and the related tblAlternateVolunteer table. Select the referential integrity option and the cascade updates option for the relationships.
4. Create a make-table query based on the qryFirstVolunteers query, selecting all fields from the query and only those records where the Trained field value is **Yes**. Use **tblSpecialVolunteers** as the new table name, store the table in the current database, and then run the query. Save the query as **qryMakeSpecialVolunteers**, and close the query. Open the tblSpecialVolunteers table, and verify the records are all from the first three months of 2021 and the value for the Trained field is Yes (-1) for all records. Close the tblSpecialVolunteers table.
5. **Explore** 5. Create an append query based on the tblVolunteer table that selects the VolunteerID, FirstName, Zip, Email, SignupDate, and Trained fields for only those records where the value of the SignupDate field is between April 1, 2021 and May 31, 2021. Append the records to the tblSpecialVolunteers table and run the query. (*Note*: You are pulling data from one table and appending it to another table.) Save the query as **qryAppendAprilMay**, and then close the query. Open the tblSpecialVolunteers table and verify that the SignupDate column now contains only dates for the first five months of 2021. Close the tblSpecialVolunteers table.
6. Create an update query to select all records in the tblSpecialVolunteers table where the value of the Trained field is **No** and update it to **Yes**. Run the query, save it as **qryUpdateTrained**, and then close the query.
7. **Explore** 7. Open the tblSpecialVolunteers table and change the format of the Trained field to a Yes/No display format. Verify the Trained field for all records is now set to Yes. Resize all columns to their best fit, and then close and save the tblSpecialVolunteers table.
8. Create a delete query that deletes all records in the tblSpecialVolunteers table in which the SignupDate field is between March 1, 2021 and May 31, 2021. Run the query, save it as **qryDeleteMarchAprilMay**, and then close the query. Open the tblSpecialVolunteers table, resize all columns to their best fit (if necessary), and then verify that all records have SignupDate field value in either January 2021 or February 2021. Save your layout changes, and then close the tblSpecialVolunteers table.
9. **Explore** 9. Create a select query with an outer join between the tblVolunteer and tblAlternateVolunteer tables, selecting all records from the tblVolunteer table and any matching records from the tblAlternateVolunteer table. Display the VolunteerID, FirstName and LastName fields from the tblVolunteer table and the AltFirstName and AltLastName fields from the tblAlternateVolunteer table. (*Hint*: You will need to modify the Join Properties for the relationship between the tblVolunteer and tblAlternateVolunteer tables.) Save the query as **qryVolunteerAltOuterJoin**, and then run and close the query. Your output of the query should consist of all records from the tblVolunteer table, and only those records from the tblAlternateVolunteer table that have a match in the tblVolunteer table.
10. Make a backup copy of the database, compact and repair the database, and then close it.

ACCESS

Automating Tasks with Macros

Creating a User Interface for the Health Database

Case | *Lakewood Community Health Services*

Donna Taylor recently hired new staff at Lakewood Community Health Services. The new staff members have limited experience working with databases, so Donna consults with Mista Kristiansen, the database developer for the clinic, about providing training to the new staff. In addition, Mista suggests implementing some advanced Access features to automate and control how users interact with the Health database. One of these features helps to create a custom user interface that will make it easier for inexperienced users to access the database and minimize the chance that an unauthorized user could change the design of any database object.

To meet the needs of the less experienced users, she would like the interface to display specific forms and reports and all the queries in the database, so that users can select objects they want to work with from the interface. For more advanced users, Mista would like a form with buttons users can click to perform common tasks. In this module, you will automate tasks in the Health database by creating and editing macros. You will also modify the user interface for the database by creating buttons that are linked to macros and by creating a navigation form.

STARTING DATA FILES

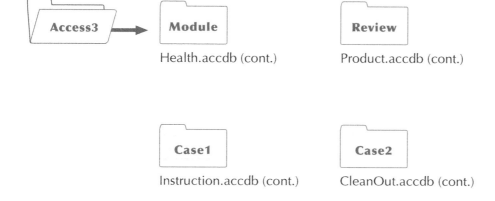

Access3 → Module
Health.accdb (cont.)

Review
Product.accdb (cont.)

Case1
Instruction.accdb (cont.)

Case2
CleanOut.accdb (cont.)

Session 10.1 Visual Overview:

Click the Single Step button to single step, which executes one macro action at a time, pausing between actions.

The Action Catalog button is a toggle to open and close the Action Catalog pane.

Click the Run button to run the macro.

A macro is a recorded sequence of commands or keystrokes that can be saved and then executed, or run, in a single action by the user.

The mcr prefix tag identifies the object as a macro.

The instruction that initiates each individual command or keystroke within a macro is called an action.

The OpenForm action opens a specified form in a specified view.

A piece of data that an action requires is known as an argument.

A comment is a text description for the benefit of database developers and has no effect on the macro. A comment starts with /* and contains a description of one or more tasks.

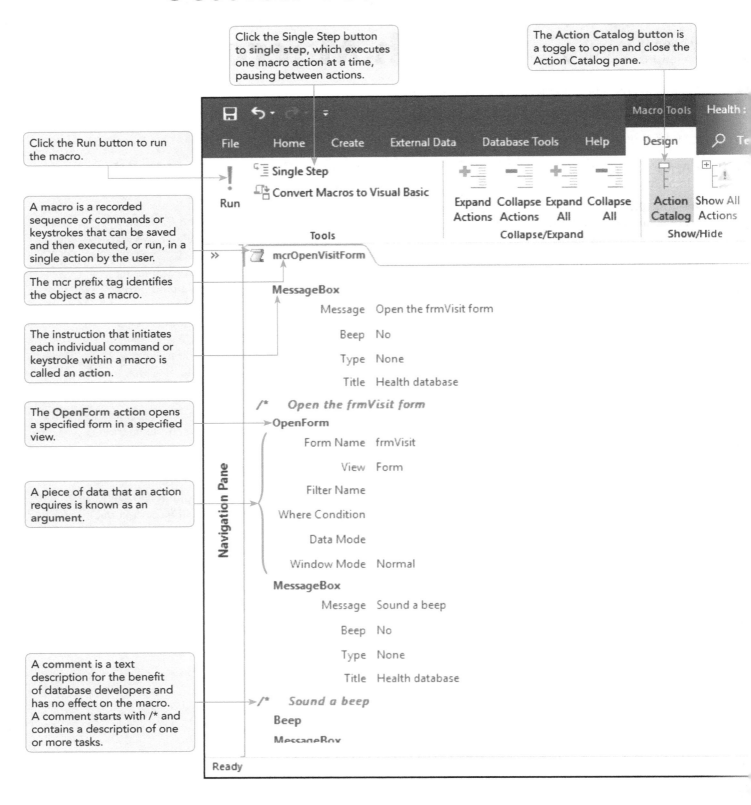

Macro Tools	Health :
File Home Create External Data Database Tools Help Design	Te

Single Step
Convert Macros to Visual Basic
Run
Tools

Expand Actions   Collapse Actions   Expand All   Collapse All   Action Catalog   Show All Actions
Collapse/Expand   Show/Hide

Navigation Pane

mcrOpenVisitForm

MessageBox
Message   Open the frmVisit form
Beep   No
Type   None
Title   Health database

/*   *Open the frmVisit form*
OpenForm
Form Name   frmVisit
View   Form
Filter Name
Where Condition
Data Mode
Window Mode   Normal

MessageBox
Message   Sound a beep
Beep   No
Type   None
Title   Health database

/*   *Sound a beep*
Beep
MessageBox

Ready

The Macro Designer Window

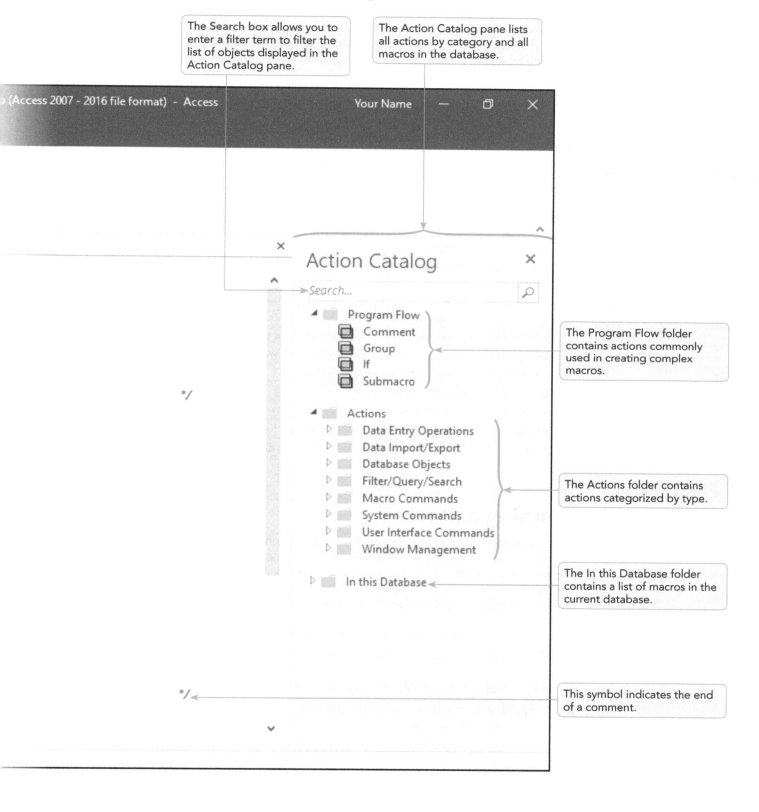

The Search box allows you to enter a filter term to filter the list of objects displayed in the Action Catalog pane.

The Action Catalog pane lists all actions by category and all macros in the database.

(Access 2007 - 2016 file format) - Access

Your Name

Action Catalog

Search...

▲ ▦ Program Flow
　　▣ Comment
　　▣ Group
　　▣ If
　　▣ Submacro

The Program Flow folder contains actions commonly used in creating complex macros.

▲ ▦ Actions
　▷ ▦ Data Entry Operations
　▷ ▦ Data Import/Export
　▷ ▦ Database Objects
　▷ ▦ Filter/Query/Search
　▷ ▦ Macro Commands
　▷ ▦ System Commands
　▷ ▦ User Interface Commands
　▷ ▦ Window Management

The Actions folder contains actions categorized by type.

▷ ▦ In this Database

The In this Database folder contains a list of macros in the current database.

This symbol indicates the end of a comment.

Introduction to Macros

Mista plans to automate some tasks in the Health database, initially by using macros. A **macro** is a recorded sequence of commands or keystrokes that can be saved and then executed, or run, in a single action by the user. The instruction that initiates each individual command or keystroke within the macro is called an action. Macros automate repetitive tasks, such as opening forms, tables, and reports; printing selected form records; and running queries.

Access provides more than 80 common actions you can include in database macros. Each of these actions has a designated name you reference to include its instruction in a macro. Figure 10–1 lists the names and corresponding instructions for Access actions commonly used in macro development.

Figure 10–1 **Frequently used Access actions**

Action	Description
ApplyFilter	Applies a filter to a table, form, or report to restrict or sort the records in the recordset
Beep	Produces a beep tone through the computer's speakers
CloseWindow	Closes the specified window, or the active window if none is specified
FindRecord	Finds the first record (or the next record, if the action is used again) that meets the specified criteria
GoToControl	Moves the focus to a specified field or control on the active datasheet or form
MessageBox	Displays a message box containing a warning or informational message
OpenForm	Opens a form in the specified view
QuitAccess	Exits Microsoft Access
RunMacro	Runs a macro
SelectObject	Selects a specified object so you can run an action that applies to the object
SendKeys	Sends keystrokes to Microsoft Access or another active program

Running a Macro

Mista created a macro with multiple actions to demonstrate to Donna how using macros will make working with the Health database easier for the newer staff members. Mista's macro is named mcrOpenVisitForm, and it performs multiple actions using the frmVisit form. You can reference and run a macro from within a form or report, or you can run a macro by right-clicking its name in the Macros section of the Navigation Pane.

You will run the mcrOpenVisitForm macro from the Navigation Pane.

To run the mcrOpenVisitForm macro:

▶ 1. **sam** ⬇ Start Access, and then open the **Health** database you worked with in the previous module.

   Trouble? If the security warning is displayed below the ribbon, click the Enable Content button.

▶ 2. Make sure the Navigation Pane is open, scroll down the Navigation Pane (if necessary) to view the Macros section, right-click **mcrOpenVisitForm**, and then click **Run** on the shortcut menu. A message box opens. See Figure 10–2.

Figure 10–2 | **Message box opened by the first action in the mcrOpenVisitForm macro**

Health database

Open the frmVisit form

OK

Opening the message box is the first action Mista added to the mcrOpenVisitForm macro. As in other computer applications, a **message box** in Access is a special dialog box that contains a message and a **command button**, but no options. A command button is a button that performs an action when a user clicks it. The message box that Mista created specifies that the next macro action will open the frmVisit form. When the user clicks the OK button, the message box will close, and the macro will resume with the next action. Mista added this message box and other message boxes to the macro so that she could demonstrate to Donna how macros can execute multiple actions to complete multistep tasks. With macros you create for working databases, you don't include message boxes between steps as Mista did in her macro.

▶ **3.** Click **OK**. The next two actions in the mcrOpenVisitForm macro are performed: the frmVisit form opens, and the second message box opens. See Figure 10–3.

Figure 10–3 | **Second and third actions in the mcrOpenVisitForm macro**

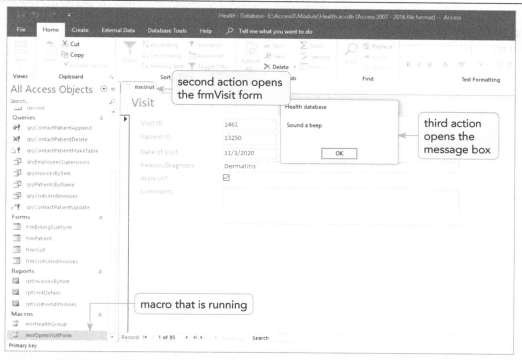

▶ **4.** Click **OK**. A beep sounds, and the third message box opens. These are the fourth and fifth actions in the mcrOpenVisitForm macro.

Trouble? If your computer doesn't have speakers or if your audio is turned down or muted, you won't hear the beep. If you do hear the beep, it might not sound like a beep at all, depending on your computer and its settings.

▶ 5. Click **OK**, and then drag the message box from its title bar to the right so you can view the values displayed in the form. The frmVisit form now displays record 17 for VisitID 1549. The sixth action in the mcrOpenVisitForm is displaying record 17, and the seventh action is displaying the message box with the message "Close the form."

▶ 6. Click **OK**. The frmVisit form closes, and the mcrOpenVisitForm macro ends.

Now that you have run Mista's sample macro to view it as a user would, you will view the code, or instructions, for the macro and examine its components.

Viewing a Macro in the Macro Designer

You create, view, and edit a macro using the **Macro Designer**, which is a development environment built into Access. To open the Macro Designer, you'll open the macro in Design view.

To open Macro Designer and view the mcrOpenVisitForm macro:

▶ 1. Right-click **mcrOpenVisitForm** in the Navigation Pane, click **Design View** on the shortcut menu, and then close the Navigation Pane. The Macro Designer displays the mcrOpenVisitForm macro. See Figure 10–4.

| Figure 10–4 | Macro Designer showing the mcrOpenVisitForm macro |

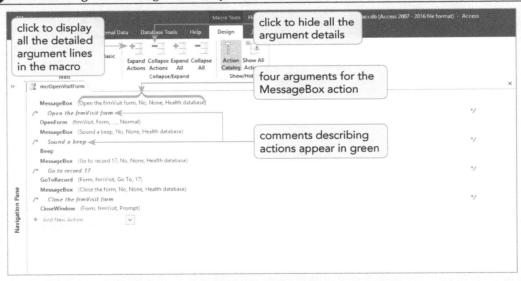

The Macro Designer lists the actions included in the macro. In addition to actions, a macro can also include arguments and comments, as described in the Session 10.1 Visual Overview. You can change the view of the Macro Designer to display more detail.

2. On the Macro Tools Design tab, in the Collapse/Expand group, click the **Expand All** button to display all the details for the actions, arguments, and comments that make up the mcrOpenVisitForm macro.

   If you rest the mouse pointer on the MessageBox action or on any argument line, a ScreenTip displays a brief explanation of the action or argument. You can also use Help to learn about specific actions and their arguments and about macros in general.

3. Move the mouse pointer over the **MessageBox** action at the top of the Macro Designer. The mouse pointer changes to the hand pointer 🖑, and a ScreenTip appears, describing the action and common ways to use the action.

4. Click **MessageBox**. The arguments for the message are displayed in a shaded box.

After a macro has been created, you can modify it in the Macro Designer. You can add or delete actions, and modify the arguments for an action. Mista asks you to add actions to the mcrOpenVisitForm macro. Before doing so, you need to understand how arguments are used in macros.

Using Arguments in a Macro

Some actions require information. For instance, if an action is going to open a form, the action needs to know the name of the form to open. A piece of data that is required by an action is known as an argument. An action can have more than one argument; multiple arguments are separated by commas.

The mcrOpenVisitForm macro contains a MessageBox action as the first action. The name of the MessageBox action is followed by the four arguments needed by the action—Message, Beep, Type, and Title:

- The Message argument contains the text that appears in the message box when it is displayed.
- The Beep argument is either Yes or No to specify whether a beep sounds when the message box opens.
- The Type argument determines which icon, if any, appears in the message box to signify the critical level of the message. The icon choices are None (no icon), Critical ⊗, Warning? ?, Warning! ⚠, and Information ①.
- The Title argument contains the word(s) that will appear in the message box title bar.

Adding Actions to a Macro

You can modify a macro by adding or deleting actions in the Macro Designer. When you add an action, you use the Add New Action box at the bottom of the Macro Designer window. After entering the appropriate arguments, you use the Move up and Move down buttons for the action to position it within the macro.

You'll add two actions, the MessageBox and FindRecord actions, to the mcrOpenVisitForm macro between the GoToRecord action and the last MessageBox action. You'll start by adding the MessageBox action and then moving it up to the correct position within the macro.

To add the MessageBox action to the mcrOpenVisitForm macro and position it in the macro:

▶ **1.** On the Macro Tools Design tab, in the Collapse/Expand group, click the **Collapse Actions** button to hide all the detailed argument lines in the macro. Only the lines for the actions and comments are now displayed in the Macro Designer.

Below the last action in the macro is the Add New Action box, which you use to add actions to the end of the macro.

▶ **2.** Click the **Add New Action** arrow to display the list of actions, scroll down the list (if necessary), and then click **MessageBox**. The list closes, a new MessageBox action is added to the end of the macro with its four arguments displayed, and two arguments are set with default values. See Figure 10–5.

Figure 10-5 | **MessageBox action added to mcrOpenVisitForm**

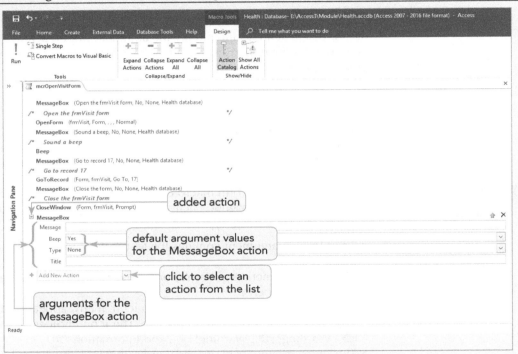

You'll enter values for the Message and Title arguments, change the Beep argument value from Yes to No, and retain the default Type argument value of None.

▶ **3.** Click in the **Message** box, type **Find visit 1586**, and then press **TAB**. The contents of the Beep box are now selected.

▶ **4.** Click the **Beep** arrow, click **No** in the list, press **TAB** twice, and then type **Health database** in the Title box. See Figure 10–6.

Figure 10–6   **Argument values added to MessageBox action**

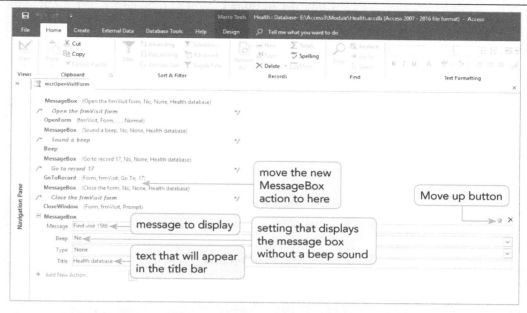

This MessageBox action is currently the last action in the mcrOpenVisitForm macro. However, it should be the seventh action in the macro, so that it takes place after the GoToRecord action that moves to record 17 and before the MessageBox action with the message "Close the form." You need to move the new MessageBox action three positions up in the macro.

5. In the upper-right corner of the shaded MessageBox action box, click the **Move up** button 🔼 three times to move the action to its correct position below the GoToRecord action. See Figure 10–7.

Figure 10–7   **New MessageBox action after being moved up**

▶ **6.** On the Macro Tools Design tab, in the Collapse/Expand group, click the **Collapse Actions** button to hide all the argument lines in the MessageBox action.

Next you'll add the FindRecord action to the macro to find the record for VisitID 1586. You use the **FindRecord action** to find the first record, or the next record if the action is used again, that meets the criteria specified by the FindRecord arguments.

You could add the FindRecord action to the bottom of the macro and move it up three positions as you did for the MessageBox action. Instead, you'll search for the action in the Action Catalog pane and then drag it to its correct position in the macro.

To add the FindRecord action to the mcrOpenVisitForm macro:

▶ **1.** In the Action Catalog pane, click the **Search** box, and then type **find**. A filtered list of actions containing the search term "find" is displayed.

▶ **2.** Drag the **FindRecord** action from the Action Catalog pane to the Macro Designer window and position it immediately below the newly added MessageBox action until a red line appears just below the MessageBox action. See Figure 10–8.

| Figure 10–8 | Dragging the FindRecord action to the macro |

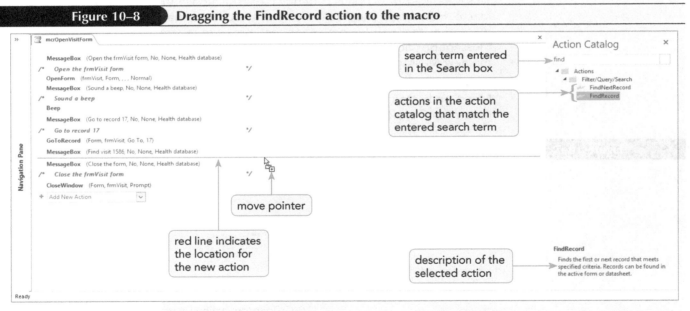

▶ **3.** Release the mouse button to add the FindRecord action to the macro. The FindRecord action has seven arguments.

> **Trouble?** If you drag the wrong action or drag the action to the wrong location, delete the action by clicking its Delete button ⊠ to the right of the Move up and Move down buttons, and then repeat Steps 2 and 3.

To find the record for VisitID 1586, you need to set the Find What argument to a value of 1586. You'll accept the defaults for the other action arguments.

▶ **4.** Click in the **Find What** box, type **1586**, and then next to FindRecord, click the **Collapse** button ⊟ to hide all the argument boxes for the action.

Finally, you'll add a comment above the FindRecord action to document the FindRecord action.

▶ **5.** In the Action Catalog pane, click the **blank square** on the right end of the Search box to clear the contents of the Search box. The Action Catalog pane again displays the categories of available actions.

▶ **6.** In the Program Flow section of the Action Catalog pane, drag **Comment** to the macro, and position it immediately above the FindRecord action. A Comment box is displayed, with move buttons and a Delete button to its right.

▶ **7.** Click in the **Comment** box, type **Find visit 1586**, and then click a blank area of the Macro Designer to close the Comment box. See Figure 10–9.

Figure 10–9 | **Actions and comment added to the mcrOpenVisitForm macro**

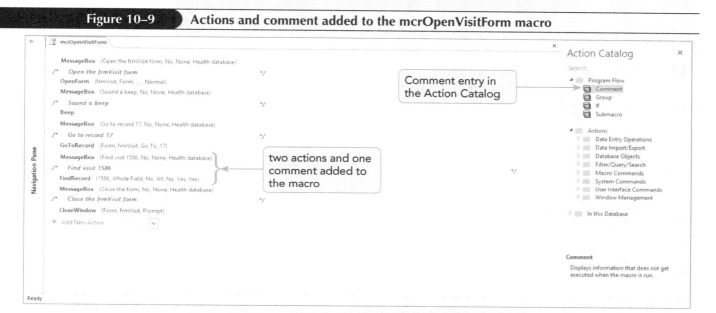

▶ **8.** On the Quick Access Toolbar, click the **Save** button 🖫 to save your macro design changes.

After you create or change a macro, you should test it. You can use single step mode to make sure the individual actions in a macro are executed in the proper order and that the arguments for a given action are correctly set.

PROSKILLS

Teamwork: Using Comments to Share Information

When working with a team to develop and maintain a database, you'll be regularly reading and making changes to macros that other team members wrote; in addition, other team members will be changing and extending macros that you created. Therefore, it's important to use comments to document the macros you write. Including a comment before each related set of actions to explain its purpose can help other team members understand the structure of your macro. In addition, including comments makes it easier for everyone on the team to find and fix any errors, because they can compare the explanation of what a section of a macro should do, as given in the comment, with the actions that follow.

Single Stepping a Macro

When you create a complicated macro with many actions, you'll often find it useful to run through the macro one step at a time. In Access, you can do this using single step mode. In **single step mode**, a macro is executed one action at a time, with a pause between actions. Using single step mode is also referred to as single stepping, and allows you to confirm you have listed actions in the right order and with the correct arguments. If you have problems with a macro, you can use single step mode to find the causes of the problems and to determine appropriate corrections. The Single Step button in the Tools group on the Macro Tools Design tab is a toggle you use to turn single step mode on and off. Once you turn on single step mode, it stays on for all macros until you turn it off.

REFERENCE

Single Stepping a Macro

- On the Macro Tools Design tab in the Macro Designer, click the Single Step button in the Tools group.
- In the Tools group, click the Run button.
- In the Macro Single Step dialog box, click the Step button to execute the next action.
- To stop the macro, click the Stop All Macros button.
- To execute all remaining actions in the macro and turn off single step mode, click the Continue button.

Now that you have added actions to the mcrOpenVisitForm macro, you'll single step through it to ensure the actions are in the correct order and the arguments are correctly set.

To single step through the macro:

▶ 1. On the Macro Tools Design tab, in the Tools group, click the **Single Step** button to turn on single step mode. The button appears selected, indicating that single step mode is on.

▶ 2. In the Tools group, click the **Run** button. The Macro Single Step dialog box opens. See Figure 10–10.

Figure 10–10   **Macro Single Step dialog box**

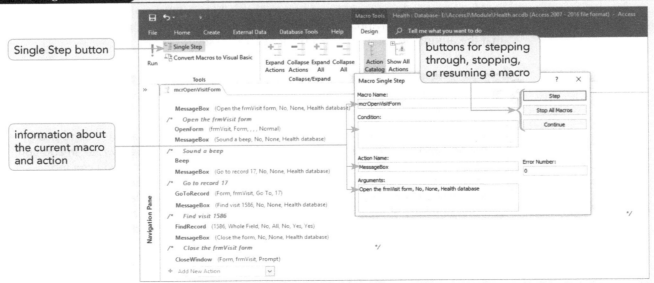

Trouble? If the first message box opens instead of the Macro Single Step dialog box, you turned off single stepping in Step 1 when you clicked the Single Step button. Click the OK button to run the complete macro, and then repeat Steps 1 and 2.

When you single step through a macro, the Macro Single Step dialog box opens before performing each action. This dialog box shows the macro's name and the action's condition, name, and arguments. The action will be executed or not executed, depending on whether the condition is true or false. From this dialog box, you can step through the macro one action at a time, stop the macro and return to the Macro Designer, or continue by executing all remaining actions without pausing. If you click the Continue button, you also turn off single step mode.

▶ 3. Click **Step**. The first action in the macro (MessageBox) runs. Because the MessageBox action pauses the macro, the Macro Single Step dialog box remains hidden until you click the OK button in the message box.

▶ 4. Click **OK** to close the message box. The Macro Single Step dialog box shows the macro's second action (OpenForm).

▶ 5. Click **Step**. The second action in the macro runs, opening the frmVisit form, and shows the macro's third action (MessageBox) in the Macro Single Step dialog box.

▶ 6. Continue clicking **Step** and **OK** until the "Find visit 1586" message box opens, making sure you read the Macro Single Step dialog box carefully and observe the actions that occur. At this point, record 17 is the current record in the frmVisit form.

▶ 7. Click **OK**, and then click **Step**. The FindRecord action runs, record 33 for VisitID 1586 is now the current record in the frmVisit form, and the Macro Single Step dialog box shows the macro's last MessageBox action.

▶ 8. Click **Step**, click **OK**, and then click **Step**. The Macro Single Step dialog box closes automatically after the last macro action is completed; the last macro action closes the frmVisit form.

You've finished checking Mista's macro and can turn off the single step feature.

▶ 9. Click the **Macro Tools Design** tab, in the Tools group, click the **Single Step** button to turn off single step feature, and then click the **Close 'mcrOpenVisitForm'** button ⊠ to close the macro.

Next, you will review another macro Mista created for the frmVisit form.

Using a Command Button with an Attached Macro

Mista created a macro that she associated with a command button on the frmVisit form that you just opened using the mcrOpenVisitForm macro. A command button is a control that runs a macro when you click it. To add a command button to a form, you open the form in Design view and use the Button tool in the Controls group on the Form Design Tools Design tab. After adding the command button to the form, and while still in Design view, you attach a macro to the command button. Then, when a user clicks the command button, the macro's actions are executed.

You'll use the Open Patient Table command button on the frmVisit form to see how a command button works.

To use the Open Patient Table command button:

▶ 1. Open the Navigation Pane, open the **frmVisit** form in Form view, click **1461** in the Visit ID box to deselect all values, and then close the Navigation Pane. The first visit with VisitID 1461 and PatientID 13250 is displayed. See Figure 10–11.

Figure 10–11   Open Patient Table command button on the frmVisit form

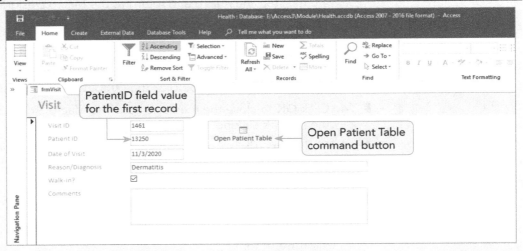

▶ 2. Click the **Open Patient Table** command button. The frmVisit form remains open, and the tblPatient table opens. The tblPatient table is the active object. See Figure 10–12.

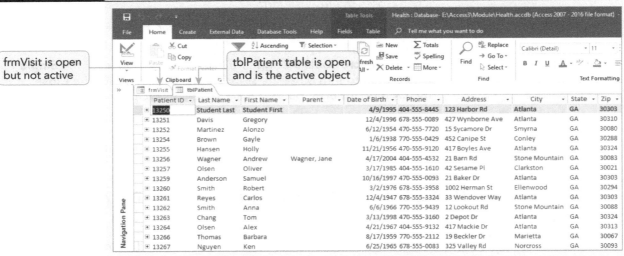

Clicking the Open Patient Table command button triggered an attached macro that opened the tblPatient table. The tblPatient table will remain open until it is closed manually or by another macro.

▶ 3. Close the **tblPatient** table. The frmVisit form is now the active object.

Understanding Events

Clicking the Open Patient Table command button is an event, and the opening of the tblPatient table is controlled by setting an event property. An **event** is something that happens to a database object, such as a user clicking a check box or a form being loaded. You can connect an action to a specific event so the action occurs in response to that event. For example, an event occurs when you click a command button on a form, when you use the mouse to position the pointer on a form, or when you press a key to choose an option. In your work with Access, you've initiated hundreds of events on forms, controls, records, and reports without any special effort. For example, events you've triggered in forms include Open, which occurs when you open a form; Activate, which occurs when the form becomes the active window; and Close, which occurs when you close a form and the form is removed from the screen. Each event has an associated event property. An **event property** specifies how an object responds when an event occurs. For example, each form has OnOpen, OnActivate, and OnClose event properties associated with the Open, Activate, and Close events, respectively.

Event properties appear in the Property Sheet when you create forms and reports. Unlike most properties you've used previously in the Property Sheet, event properties do not have an initial value. If an event property contains no value, it means the event property has not been set. In this case, no special action results when the associated event occurs. For example, if the OnOpen event property of a form is not set and you open the form, then the Open event occurs (the form opens), and no special action occurs beyond the opening of the form. You can set an event property value to a macro name, and the named macro will run when the event occurs. For example, you could write a macro that automatically selects a particular field in a form when you open it. You can also create a group of statements using Visual Basic for Applications (VBA) code and set the event property value to the name of that group of statements. The group of statements, or **procedure**, is then executed when the event occurs. Such a procedure is called an **event procedure**. You will learn more about VBA code and procedures in the next module.

When you clicked the Open Patient Table command button on the frmVisit form, the Click event occurred and triggered an attached macro. This happened because the Open Patient Table command button contains an OnClick event property setting, which you will examine next.

To view the OnClick event property setting for the Open Patient Table command button:

TIP

The Event tab in the Property Sheet lists the names of the event properties with spaces, even though you type each event property name without a space.

1. Switch to Design view, right-click the **Open Patient Table** command button control, click **Properties** on the shortcut menu to open the Property Sheet (if necessary), and then click the **Event** tab (if necessary).

2. Right-click the **On Click** box, click **Zoom** on the shortcut menu to open the Zoom dialog box, and then click to the right of the selected text to deselect it. See Figure 10–13.

   Event property values are often longer than the boxes in the Property Sheet can display at once. Working with them in the Zoom dialog box ensures you can always see the entire value.

Figure 10–13	Macro attached to the OnClick event property

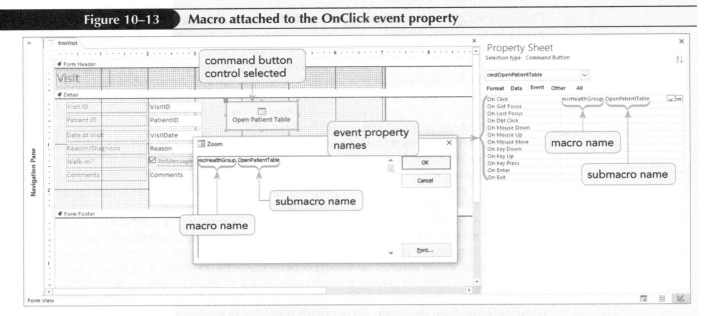

Trouble? The position of the Zoom dialog box may be slightly different from the figure. You may move the Zoom dialog box to align with the figure for clarity.

The OnClick event property value shown in the Zoom dialog box is mcrHealthGroup. OpenPatientTable. This is an example of a reference to a submacro in a macro.

Understanding Submacros

If you need to create several related macros, you can create them as submacros in a single macro instead of creating them as separate macros. A **submacro** is a complete macro with a Submacro header within a macro. Submacros are especially useful in a large database that contains many objects as they allow you to limit the number of objects by consolidating related macros. Because you can specify a submacro to run in response to an event, using submacros gives you more options than simply creating a large macro that performs many actions. For example, if a form's design uses command buttons to open a form with a related record and to print the related record displayed in the form, you can create one macro for the form that contains two submacros— one submacro to open the form, and a second submacro to print the related record. Because you created the macro specifically for the form object, you can store all the submacros you need in a single macro.

When you reference a submacro in an event property value, a period separates the macro name from the submacro name. For the OnClick event property value shown in Figure 10–13, for example, mcrHealthGroup is the macro name and OpenPatientTable is the submacro name. When you click the Open Patient Table command button on the frmVisit form, the actions contained in the OpenPatientTable submacro are processed. This submacro is located in the mcrHealthGroup macro.

You'll now close the Zoom dialog box, and then you'll open the Macro Designer from the Property Sheet.

To open the mcrHealthGroup macro in the Macro Designer:

▶ **1.** Click **Cancel** in the Zoom dialog box to close it. In the Property Sheet for the selected Open Patient Table command button, the On Click box contains an arrow and a Build button. The command button is named cmdOpenPatientTable; *cmd* is a prefix tag to identify a command button control. See Figure 10–14.

Figure 10–14	Property Sheet Event tab for the Open Patient Table command button

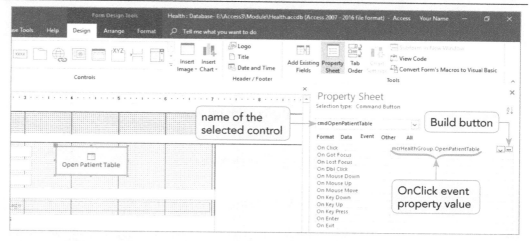

You click the On Click arrow if you want to change the current macro to a different macro, and you click the Build button if you want to use the Macro Designer to view or change the existing macro. The Build button is also called the **Macro Builder** when you use it to work with macros.

▶ **2.** Click the **Build** button ⊡ on the right end of the On Click box. The Macro Designer opens and displays the mcrHealthGroup macro and the OpenPatientTable submacro. See Figure 10–15.

Figure 10–15	Macro Designer displaying the mcrHealthGroup macro and its submacro

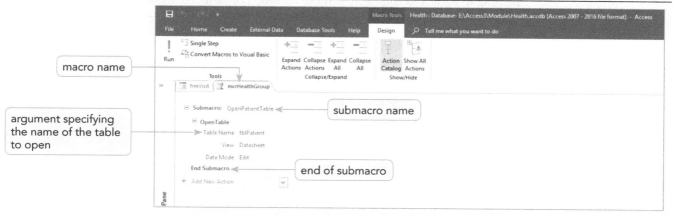

The mcrHealthGroup macro consists of one submacro that starts with the Submacro statement and ends with the End Submacro statement. These statements are not actions; they are control statements to identify the beginning and end of a submacro. If a macro contains several submacros, each submacro starts with a Submacro statement and ends with an End Submacro statement.

The OpenPatientTable submacro consists of a single action, OpenTable, which opens the tblPatient table. The OpenTable action arguments are as follows:

- The **Table Name argument** specifies the name of a table that will open when the macro is run.
- The **View argument** specifies the view in which the object will open. For tables, you can specify Datasheet, Design, Print Preview, PivotTable, or PivotChart.
- The **Data Mode argument** specifies the table's data entry options. Allowable settings for this argument are Add (users can add new records but can't change or delete existing records), Edit (users can change and delete existing records and can add new records), and Read Only (users can only view records). If you don't select an argument value, Edit is the default setting.

Now that you've seen a macro attached to a command button, Mista asks you to add a command button to the frmVisit form and then attach a new macro to the command button. Users can then click the command button to print the current record in the frmVisit form. Mista created the mcrHealthGroup macro to group together all the submacros in the Health database. You'll add a submacro to the mcrHealthGroup macro to print the current record.

Adding a Submacro

To print the contents of a form's current record, normally you have to click the File tab to display Backstage view, click Print in the navigation bar, click Print in the list of options, click Selected Record(s), and then click the OK button—a process that takes five steps and several seconds. As an alternative, you can create a command button on the form, create a macro that prints the contents of a form's current record, and then attach the macro to the command button on the form. Instead of following multiple steps to print the form's current record, a user could simply click the command button.

First, you'll add a submacro to the mcrHealthGroup macro. You'll use the SelectObject and RunMenuCommand actions for the new submacro. The **SelectObject action** selects a specified object so that you can run an action that applies to the object. The **RunMenuCommand action** selects and runs a command on the ribbon. The specific argument you'll use with the RunMenuCommand action is the **PrintSelection argument**, which prints the selected form record. Because macros and submacros are database objects, you'll follow the naming conventions for database objects when naming macros and submacros. These naming conventions include using descriptive object names so that the object's function is obvious, capitalizing the first letter of each word in the name, and excluding spaces from the name. Therefore, you'll name the submacro PrintSelectedRecord when you add the submacro to the mcrHealthGroup macro.

Adding a Submacro

REFERENCE

- Open the macro in the Macro Designer.
- Click the Add New Action arrow, click Submacro, and then type the submacro name in the Submacro box.
- Click the Add New Action arrow above the End Submacro statement, click the action you want to use, and then set the action's arguments.
- If the submacro consists of more than one action, repeat the previous step for each action.
- Add comments as needed to the submacro to document the submacro's function or provide other information.
- Save the macro.

You'll now add the PrintSelectedRecord submacro to the mcrHealthGroup macro.

To add the PrintSelectedRecord submacro to the mcrHealthGroup macro:

1. Click the **Collapse** icon ⊟ to the left of Submacro OpenPatientTable to collapse the actions and arguments for the submacro.

2. Click the **Add New Action** arrow to display the list of actions and control statements, and then click **Submacro**. A submacro box appears with the default name selected in it, which is Sub followed by one or more numbers. You will replace the default name with a more appropriate name for the submacro.

3. Type **PrintSelectedRecord** in the Submacro box. The Submacro and End Submacro statements are added to the macro, and another Add New Action box is displayed between these two statements. See Figure 10–16.

Figure 10–16	New submacro added

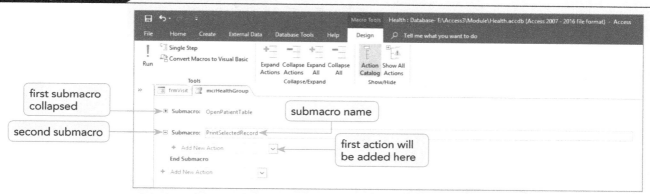

You need to select the SelectObject action and set its arguments.

4. Between the Submacro and End Submacro statements, click the **Add New Action** arrow, scroll down the list, and then click **SelectObject**. The **SelectObject action** is added to the PrintSelectedRecord submacro. This action has three arguments. The first argument, Object Type, specifies the type of database object to select. The second argument, Object Name, specifies the name of the object to open. The third argument, In Database Window, specifies whether to open the object in the database window (Yes) or not (No). You would open a table, form, or report in the database window if it is not already open. If the table, form, or report is already open, you would select No as the value for the Database Window argument.

You need to open a form named frmVisit, so you'll set these arguments first.

5. Click the **Object Type** arrow, click **Form**, click the **Object Name** arrow, and then click **frmVisit**. Because the form will be open when you run the macro, you'll leave the In Database Window argument set to No.

You'll next select the RunMenuCommand action and set its arguments. The RunMenuCommand action lets you add a command available on the ribbon to a submacro. The Command argument in this submacro lets you select the command. In this case, the Command argument is named PrintSelection.

6. Below the SelectObject action, click the **Add New Action** arrow, scroll down the list, and then click **RunMenuCommand**. The RunMenuCommand action

box appears with the Command box, in which you specify the Command argument.

▶ 7. Click the **Command** arrow, scroll down the list, and then click **PrintSelection**. You've completed the second action. You'll add another SelectObject action to the submacro to make the frmVisit form the active object after the selected record prints.

▶ 8. Below the RunMenuCommand action, click the **Add New Action** arrow, scroll down the list, click **SelectObject**, set the Object Type argument to **Form**, and then set the Object Name argument to **frmVisit**. You've finished adding the three actions to the PrintSelectedRecord submacro. See Figure 10–17.

Figure 10–17   Three actions added to the PrintSelectedRecord submacro

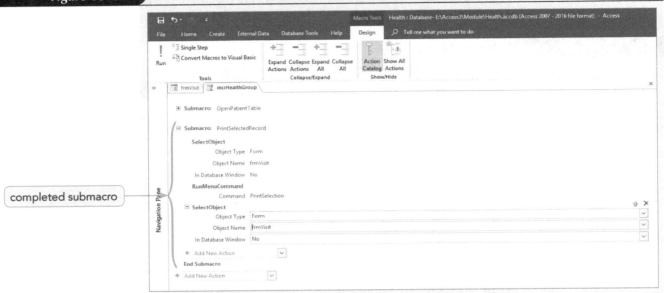

▶ 9. Save your macro design changes, and then close the mcrHealthGroup macro. The frmVisit form is the active object.

Next, you'll add a command button to the frmVisit form. After you attach the PrintSelectedRecord macro to the command button control, you'll be able to click the command button to print the current frmVisit form record.

INSIGHT

Using Submacros, Subforms, Subqueries, and Subreports

You can create a small macro and embed it in another macro as a submacro. Likewise, you can create a small form and embed it in another form as a subform, create a small query and embed it in another query as a subquery, and create a small report and embed it in another report as a subreport. The techniques for each of these object types are quite different.

- To embed a macro as a submacro, you use the Macro Designer and add a submacro as a new action.
- To embed a subform, you view the main form in Design view and add the subform using the wizard, or you drag the subform to the main form.
- To embed a query as a subquery, you use SQL view to copy the SQL for the sub-query, and then you paste it in the SQL statement for the main query.
- To embed a report as a subreport, you use the Subreport Wizard, or you drag the report to the main report in Design view.

Although the techniques are different, the underlying logic is the same. An embedded object works with the data that is used by the main object. That is, a subform uses the related data from the main form, a subreport uses the related data from the main report, a subquery uses the related data from the main query, and a submacro is executed as an action of the main macro.

Adding a Command Button to a Form

In Design view for a form, you use the Button tool in the Controls group on the Form Design Tools Design tab to add a command button control to a form. If the Use Control Wizards tool is selected when you click the Button tool, the Command Button Wizard guides you through the process of adding the command button control. You'll explore adding the command button control directly to the frmVisit form without using the wizard, and then you'll set the command button control's properties using its Property Sheet.

To add a command button control to the frmVisit form:

▶ **1.** Close the Property Sheet, and then click the **Form Design Tools Design** tab.

▶ **2.** In the Controls group, click the **More** button ⬇, and then make sure the **Use Control Wizards** tool 🔲 is not selected.

   Trouble? If the Use Control Wizards tool has an orange background, click it to disable the control wizards, and then continue with Step 3.

▶ **3.** In the Controls group, click the **Button** tool 🔲.

▶ **4.** Position the pointer's plus symbol (+) to the right of the Open Patient Table button in the Details section, and then click the mouse button. A second command button is added to the form. See Figure 10–18.

| Figure 10–18 | New command button added to the frmVisit form |

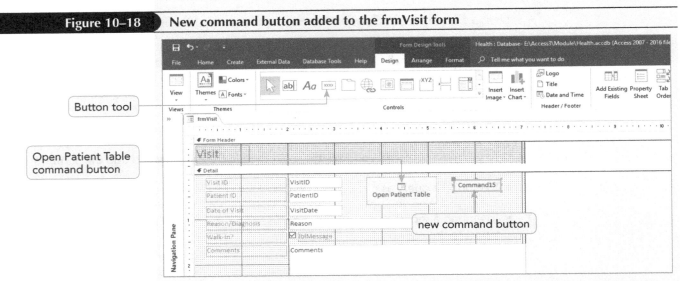

Trouble? If the Command Button Wizard dialog box opens, click the Cancel button to close it. On the Form Design Tools Design tab in the Controls group, click the More button, click the Use Control Wizards tool to deselect it, and then repeat Steps 3 and 4.

Trouble? The command button on your screen might show a different number in its label, depending on how you completed the previous steps. This difference will not affect the command button or macro.

You can now attach the PrintSelectedRecord submacro to the command button.

Attaching a Submacro to a Command Button

So far you've created the PrintSelectedRecord submacro and added the command button to the frmVisit form. Now you'll attach the submacro to the command button control's OnClick property so that the submacro is executed when the command button is clicked.

To attach the PrintSelectedRecord submacro to the command button control:

1. Make sure the new command button control is selected.

2. Open the **Property Sheet**, and then, if necessary, click the **Event** tab in the Property Sheet.

TIP

You can drag the left edge of the Property Sheet to the left to display more of the macro and submacro names if needed.

3. Click the **On Click** arrow to display the macros list, and then click **mcrHealthGroup.PrintSelectedRecord**.

You can change the text that appears on the command button (also known as the command button's label or caption) by changing its Caption property. You can also replace the text with a picture by setting its Picture property, or you can include both text and a picture. Mista wants you to place a picture of a printer on the command button and to display text on the command button.

4. In the Property Sheet, click the **Format** tab, click the **Picture** box, and then click the **Build** button ⋯ that appears on the right side of the Picture box. The Picture Builder dialog box opens. See Figure 10–19.

Figure 10–19 | **Picture Builder dialog box**

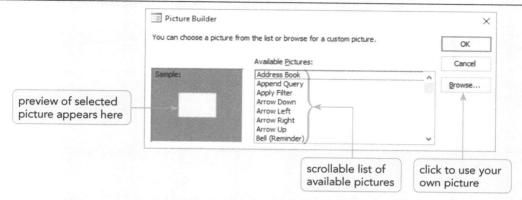

preview of selected picture appears here

scrollable list of available pictures

click to use your own picture

The Picture Builder dialog box contains an alphabetical list of pictures supplied with Access. You can scroll the list and select one of the pictures, or you can click the Browse button to select your own picture. When you select a picture, a sample is displayed on the command button in the Sample box.

5. Scroll the Available Pictures box, and then click **Printer**. A picture of a printer is displayed on the command button in the Sample box.

6. Click **OK**. The Picture Builder dialog box closes, and the printer picture is displayed on the command button in the form.

7. Change the Caption property to **Print Selected Record**, and then press **TAB**.

The **Picture Caption Arrangement property** specifies how a command button's Caption property value is arranged in relation to the picture placed on the command button. The choices are No Picture Caption, General, Top, Bottom, Left, and Right.

8. Click the **Picture Caption Arrangement** arrow, and then click **Bottom**. The caption will appear below the printer picture. However, the command button is not tall enough or wide enough to display the picture and caption, so you'll resize it.

9. Use the middle-bottom sizing handle and the middle-right sizing handle to increase the width and height of the command button so it is approximately the same size as the Open Patient Table button and looks like the one shown in Figure 10–20.

Figure 10-20   **Command button with picture and caption**

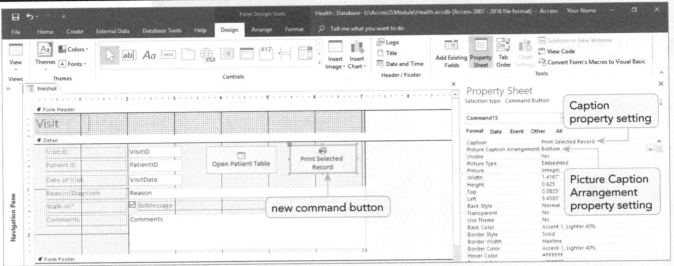

Trouble? If the background color of your button does not match the Open Patient Table button, in the Property Sheet, on the Format tab, click the Use Theme box, click the Use Theme arrow, and then click No.

Next, you'll save the frmVisit form and test the command button.

In this session, you have learned how to create and use macros in a form to automate tasks. In the next session, you'll create a navigation system that will limit access to the database objects while still allowing users to run queries and view forms and reports. You'll create a form that contains a list box to display specific forms, reports, and queries in the Health database, use a SQL statement to select the values for the list box, and then add command buttons to the form.

To save the form and test the command button:

1. Close the Property Sheet, save your form design changes, and then switch to Form view.

2. Navigate to the last visit record, for VisitID 1493.

3. Click the **Print Selected Record** command button on the form to open the Print dialog box. Notice that the submacro correctly set the print range to print the selected record.

TIP

If the Print dialog box contains a Print to File check box, you can print to a file instead of printing on paper.

4. Click **OK** to print the last visit record. The submacro returns control to the frmVisit form after the record is printed.

5. Close the form.

6. If you are not continuing on to the next session, close the Health database.

REVIEW

Session 10.1 Quick Check

1. What is a macro?
2. What is the Macro Designer?
3. What does the MessageBox action do?
4. What are you trying to accomplish when you single step through a macro?
5. What is an event property?
6. How do you add a picture to a command button?

Session 10.2 Visual Overview:

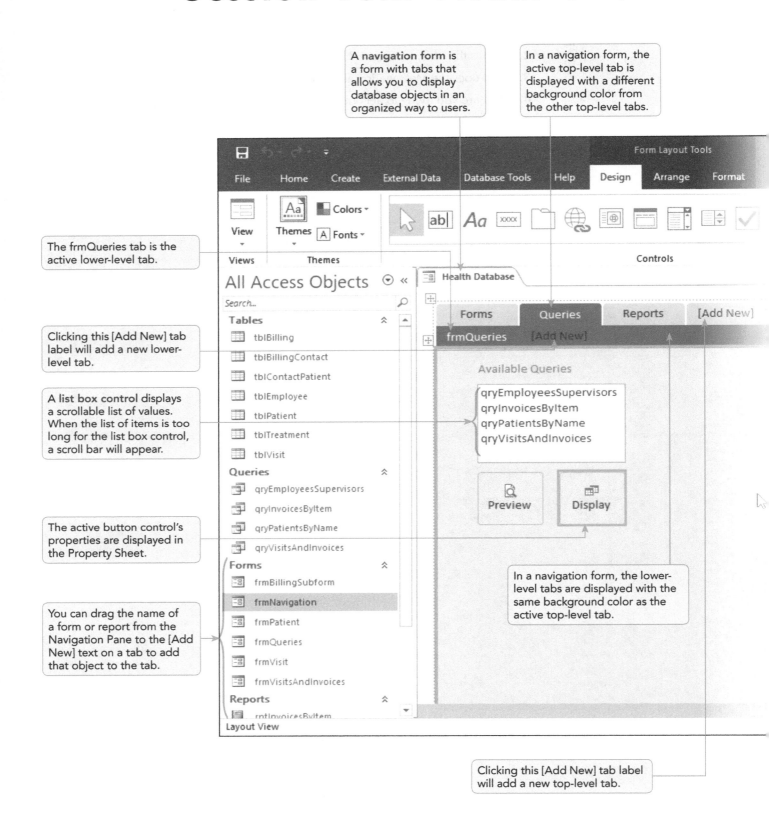

A navigation form is a form with tabs that allows you to display database objects in an organized way to users.

In a navigation form, the active top-level tab is displayed with a different background color from the other top-level tabs.

The frmQueries tab is the active lower-level tab.

Clicking this [Add New] tab label will add a new lower-level tab.

A list box control displays a scrollable list of values. When the list of items is too long for the list box control, a scroll bar will appear.

The active button control's properties are displayed in the Property Sheet.

You can drag the name of a form or report from the Navigation Pane to the [Add New] text on a tab to add that object to the tab.

In a navigation form, the lower-level tabs are displayed with the same background color as the active top-level tab.

Clicking this [Add New] tab label will add a new top-level tab.

A Navigation Form

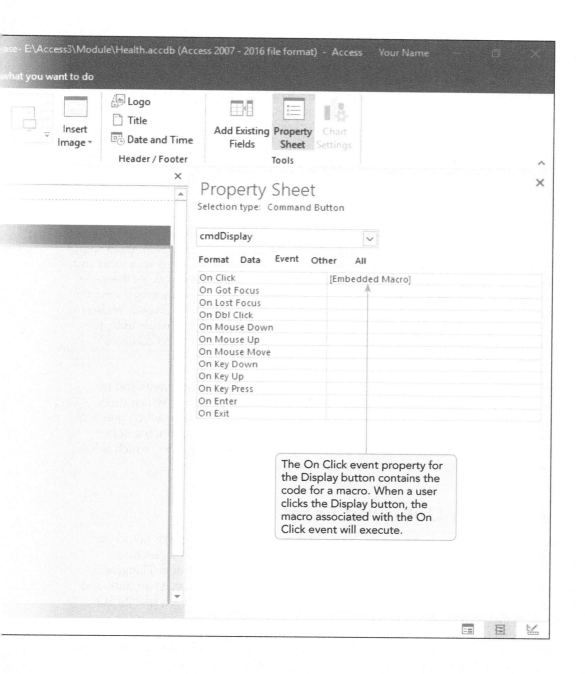

The On Click event property for the Display button contains the code for a macro. When a user clicks the Display button, the macro associated with the On Click event will execute.

Designing a User Interface

A **user interface** is what you see and use when you communicate with a computer application. Mista wants to provide a simple user interface for the Health database to assist beginning users as they become familiar with and start using the database objects.

PROSKILLS

Problem Solving: Restricting Access to Database Objects and Prohibiting Design Changes

It's important to ensure that data is as accurate as possible. Many database users do not have much experience with database applications and could inadvertently corrupt data. However, database users need to be able to add, change, and delete data. If they make updates using forms and special queries, such as action queries, users can manipulate only the data on forms and queries, without accessing the rest of the data in the tables upon which the forms and queries are built. To minimize the risk of users inadvertently corrupting data, users should be restricted to updating only the data they need. For this reason, a database administrator might create forms and special queries for the purpose of restricting the users' ability to access only authorized data. Users also need to review and print information from a database using reports, forms, and queries. Similarly, users should not be allowed to change the design of any database object or the design of the user interface. You can create a user interface that meets all these needs and restrictions. When users open a database, you can present them with a form that allows them to choose among the available forms, reports, and queries and to navigate from one object to another object as they perform their work. At the same time, you can limit users to this controlled user interface, thereby preventing them from changing any aspect of the design of the database. By considering the needs of users and by using the features and tools provided by the DBMS, you can enable users to work productively with a database and ensure the integrity of the stored data.

Before she creates the user interface for the Health database, Mista wants you to create a form to display a list of the database queries in a list box, from which users can select and run a query. The list will include only select queries, not action queries, because you want to prevent inexperienced users from selecting and running action queries. Mista's technique enables users to choose and run select queries, which select records from tables but do not affect the records in a table.

Creating an Unbound Form

When the form controls in a form do not need data from a table or query, you create an unbound form. The data displayed in an unbound form can be provided by a Structured Query Language (SQL) statement. Recall that SQL is a standard language used in querying, updating, and managing relational databases. To create an unbound form, you create a blank form, add one or more form controls, and then specify SQL statements that provide the form data.

All the objects you've created and used so far are standard objects in which users need to navigate from record to record, or from page to page in the case of reports, and to perform other operations such as copying data and closing the object. For unbound forms, users do not need to perform any of these operations, so when you create an unbound form, you can remove these features from the form.

The Health database contains several queries, and more queries might be added in the future. To allow users to choose from the available queries, Mista wants you to create a form that will display the queries in a list box. The Session 10.2 Visual Overview shows a preview of the frmQueries form you'll create as part of a navigation form. To create the frmQueries form, you'll begin by creating a blank form. You'll add a list box control and two command buttons to the form, and you'll enter a SQL statement that will provide the contents of the list box.

The Health database contains a few action queries. First, you'll delete any action queries that are in the Health database, then you'll create the frmQueries form.

Next, you'll create the frmQueries form.

To delete the action queries in the Health database:

1. If you took a break after the previous session, make sure that the Health database is open and the Navigation Pane is displayed.

2. If you want to keep the action queries you created, make a copy of the Health database.

> **TIP**
>
> You can also use this shortcut menu to delete a table, form, report, or macro from the database.

3. In the Navigation Pane, right-click **qryContactPatientAppend**, and then click **Delete** on the shortcut menu. A dialog box opens that prompts you to confirm that you want to delete the query.

4. In the dialog box, click the **Yes** button to confirm that you want to delete the query. The qryContactPatientAppend query is deleted from the database.

5. Repeat Steps 3 and 4 to delete the following queries from the database: **qryContactPatientDelete**, **qryContactPatientMakeTable**, and **qryContactPatientUpdate**.

6. Close the Navigation Pane.

Next, you'll create the frmQueries form.

To create and save the frmQueries form:

1. Click the **Create** tab, and then in the Forms group, click the **Blank Form** button. A blank form opens in the Form window in Layout view, and the Field List pane is displayed.

2. Close the Field List pane, and then switch to Design view.

3. Save the form with the name **frmQueries**.

> **TIP**
>
> Some developers prefer to set form properties after they've created all the form controls.

Some Access form properties are especially helpful in designing a user interface; for Mista's form, you'll use properties that let you disable the display of the Close button, the navigation buttons, the record selector, and the right-click shortcut menu. In addition, to match Mista's design, you need to set the Caption property to "Queries," which is the value that appears on the object tab when you open the form. Figure 10–21 shows the form property settings you will use to create the frmQueries form for Mista.

Figure 10–21 **Frequently used Access actions**

Property	Setting	Function
Caption	Queries	Value that appears on the form's object tab when the form is open
Close Button	No	Disables the display of the Close button on the form's object tab
Navigation Buttons	No	Disables the display of navigation buttons at the bottom of the form
Record Selectors	No	Disables the display of a record selector on the left side of the form
Shortcut Menu	No	Disables the display of the shortcut menu when a user right-clicks the form

Next you'll use the Property Sheet to set the form properties shown in Figure 10–21.

To set the properties for the unbound frmQueries form:

▶ **1.** Right-click the form selector, ▪ and then click **Properties** on the shortcut menu to open the form's Property Sheet.

▶ **2.** If necessary, click the **Format** tab in the Property Sheet to display the format properties for the form.

You can now set the Caption property for the form. As you know, the Caption property value will appear on the tab when the form is displayed.

▶ **3.** Click the **Caption** box, and then type **Queries**.

Next, you'll set the Record Selectors property. Because the form does not display any records, there's no need to include a record selector.

▶ **4.** In the Record Selectors box, double-click **Yes** to change the property setting from Yes to No.

Next you'll set the remaining form properties.

▶ **5.** Scrolling as necessary, set the Navigation Buttons property to **No**, and set the Close Button property to **No**.

▶ **6.** Click the **Other** tab in the Property Sheet to display the Other page of the Property Sheet, and then set the Shortcut Menu property to **No**.

▶ **7.** Close the Property Sheet, and then save your form design changes.

Now that you have set the form's properties, you can add a list box control to the form.

Adding a List Box Control to a Form

You can add a list box control to a form using the Control Wizards tool, or you can set the properties for the list box control individually in the control's Property Sheet.

The label associated with the list box control that you will add to the frmQueries form will identify the list box for the user. The list box control will include queries in the Health database that users can preview or view. A user will be able to click the name of a query to select it and then click one of the command buttons to preview or view the query. Double-clicking a query name in the list box will also open the query datasheet.

You will not use the Control Wizards tool to create the list box control because you'll be using a SQL statement to provide the query names for the list box control.

Adding a List Box Control to a Form

- Switch to Design view, if necessary.
- If necessary, on the Form Design Tools Design tab, in the Controls group, click the More button, and then click the Use Control Wizards tool to select or deselect it, depending on whether you want to use the wizard.
- On the Form Design Tools Design tab, in the Controls group, click the More button, and then click the List Box tool.
- Position the pointer's plus symbol (+) where you want to place the upper-left corner of the list box control, and then click the mouse button.
- If you use the List Box Control Wizard, complete the dialog boxes to choose the source of the list, select the fields to appear in the list box, select a sort order, size the columns, and select the label; or if you do not use the List Box Wizard, set the Row Source property and size the list box control.

Now you'll add the list box control to the form.

To add the list box control to the form and position its label:

1. Click the **Form Design Tools Design** tab, in the Controls group, click the **More** button ⏷, and then make sure the **Use Control Wizards** ⬛ tool is not selected.

2. In the Controls gallery, click the **List Box** tool ⬛. You may have to scroll to locate it.

3. Position the pointer's plus symbol (+) approximately 0.5 inches from the top and 0.5 inches from the left edge of the Details section, and then click the mouse button. A list box control and attached label control appear in the form. See Figure 10–22.

   Trouble? If your list box control is sized or positioned differently, resize it or move it until it matches the list box control shown in Figure 10–22.

Figure 10–22   **Form with the list box control and label control**

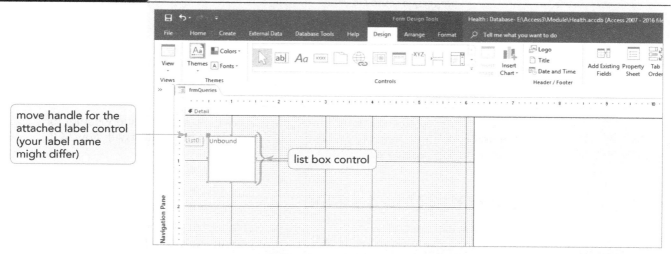

move handle for the attached label control (your label name might differ)

list box control

Next you'll move the attached label control from its current position to above the list box control.

▶ **4.** Click the label control to select it, position the mouse pointer on the move handle in the upper-left corner of the label control, and then drag it to position it two grid dots above the list box control and aligned with the left edge of the list box control.

You can now set the Caption property for the label control.

▶ **5.** Open the Property Sheet, and then click the **Format** tab, if necessary.

▶ **6.** Set the label control's Caption property value to **Available Queries**.

▶ **7.** Resize the label control by dragging its right border to the right until it is wide enough to display all of the caption text.

▶ **8.** Close the Property Sheet. Now you'll save the form and check your progress by switching to Form view.

▶ **9.** Save your form design changes, and then switch to Form view. See Figure 10–23.

Figure 10–23	frmQueries form displayed in Form view

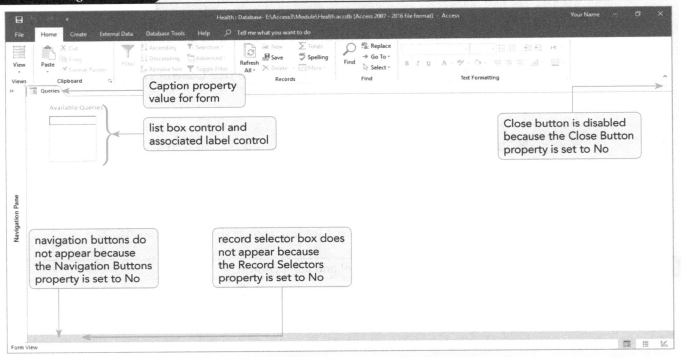

Next you need to enter the SQL statement that will provide the query names for the list box control. Before you do so, you need to become familiar with how SQL statements are structured.

Introduction to SQL

Much of what is accomplished in Access behind the scenes is done with SQL. Whenever you create a query, for example, Access constructs an equivalent SQL statement. When you save a query, Access also saves the SQL statement version of the query.

In viewing the SQL statements, you'll recognize some of the query statement names. This is not a coincidence. SQL has five statement types: select, update, delete, insert, and create. These correspond with the Access queries Select, Update, Delete, Append, and Make Table. For example, the following SQL statement selects records in the tblPatient table, selecting the fields PatientID, LastName, FirstName, and City where the city is Atlanta:

SELECT tblPatient.PatientID, tblPatient.LastName, tblPatient.FirstName, tblPatient.City FROM tblPatient
    WHERE ((((tblPatient.City)="Atlanta"));

INSIGHT

Using SQL

Instead of using an application with a graphical user interface like Access, which allows you to perform database tasks by clicking buttons and completing dialog boxes, a database administrator in a large organization uses a relational DBMS such as mySQL or Oracle and uses SQL statements to query, update, delete, and make tables. Every full-featured relational DBMS has its own version of the current standard SQL. If you learn SQL for one relational DBMS, it's a relatively easy task to begin using SQL for other relational DBMSs. When you work with two or more relational DBMSs, which is the case in most companies, you'll learn that few differences exist among the various SQL versions.

Viewing a SQL Statement for a Query

When you are working in Design view or viewing a query recordset, you can see the SQL statement that is equivalent to your query by switching to SQL view.

You'll start learning about SQL by examining the SQL statements that are equivalent to two existing queries: qryPatientsByName and qryVisitsAndInvoices.

To view the SQL statement for the qryPatientsByName query:

▶ **1.** Open the Navigation Pane, open the **qryPatientsByName** query datasheet, and then close the Navigation Pane. The query displays 52 records from the tblPatient table. The columns displayed are Patient, Patient ID, Last Name, First Name, Parent, Date of Birth, Phone, Address, City, State, Zip, and Email.

▶ **2.** Right-click the **qryPatientsByName** object tab to open the shortcut menu, click **SQL View** to display the query in SQL view, and then click a blank area of the window to deselect the SQL statement. See Figure 10–24.

Figure 10–24	SQL view for the qryPatientsByName query

SQL statement

Thus far, you have been able to complete all Access database tasks using the options on the ribbon, in dialog boxes, and in the Property Sheet. If you learn SQL so you can use it efficiently, you will be able to enter your own SQL statements in SQL view. If you work with more complicated databases, you might find that you need the extra power of the SQL language to implement your database strategies fully.

SQL uses the **SELECT statement** to define what data it retrieves from a database and how it presents the data. A SELECT statement like the one shown in Figure 10–24 must follow these rules:

TIP

The first clause of a SQL statement begins with SELECT, CREATE, UPDATE, DELETE, or INSERT.

- The basic form of a SQL SELECT statement includes four sections, known as clauses. Each clause starts with a different keyword: SELECT, FROM, WHERE, and ORDER BY. After the SELECT keyword, you list the fields you want to display. After FROM, you list the tables used in the query. After WHERE, you list the selection criteria. After ORDER BY, you list the sort fields.
- If a field name includes a space or a special symbol, you enclose the field name in brackets. Because the Health database does not use field names with spaces or special symbols, you don't have to enclose its field names in brackets. However, if your database had a field name such as *Contract Type*, then you would use [Contract Type] in a SQL statement. Some database administrators prefer to enclose every field name in square brackets to make it easier to identify field names in SQL statements.
- You precede a field name with the name of its table by connecting the table name to the field name with a period. For example, you would enter the PatientID field in the tblVisit table as *tblVisit.PatientID*.
- You use commas to separate values in a list of field names or a list of table names, and you end the SELECT statement with a semicolon.

The SQL statement shown in Figure 10–24 selects the Patient, Patient ID, Last Name, First Name, Parent, Date of Birth, Phone, Address, City, State, Zip, and Email fields from the tblPatient table; the records are sorted in ascending order by the Patient ID field. The SQL statement does not contain a WHERE clause, so the recordset includes all records from the tblPatient table when the query is run.

You can enter or change SQL statements directly in SQL view. If you enter a SQL statement and then switch to Design view, you will see its equivalent in the design grid.

Next, you'll examine the SQL statement for the qryVisitsAndInvoices query.

To view the SQL statement for the qryVisitsAndInvoices query:

▶ **1.** Close the qryPatientsByName query, open the Navigation Pane, open the **qryVisitsAndInvoices** query in Design view, and then close the Navigation Pane. The query selects data from the tblVisit and tblBilling tables and does not sort the records. The fields included in the query design are PatientID, VisitID, InvoiceAmt, VisitDate, and Reason.

▶ **2.** On the Query Tools Design tab, in the Results group, click the **View** button arrow, click **SQL View** to change to SQL view, and then click a blank area of the window to deselect the SQL statement. See Figure 10–25.

Figure 10–25 **SQL view for the qryVisitsAndInvoices query**

SELECT tblVisit.PatientID, tblVisit.VisitID, tblBilling.InvoiceAmt, tblVisit.VisitDate, tblVisit.Reason
FROM tblVisit INNER JOIN tblBilling ON tblVisit.VisitID = tblBilling.VisitID;

SQL statement

The SELECT statement for this query is similar to the one shown in Figure 10–24, except that it includes an INNER JOIN clause. The INNER JOIN clause selects records from the two tables only when the records have the same value in the common fields that link the tables. The general syntax for a SQL statement with an inner join is the following:

SELECT *field list* FROM *Table1* INNER JOIN *Table2* ON *Table1.Field1* = *Table2.Field2*;

Access uses the ON clause instead of the standard SQL WHERE clause.

▶ **3.** Close the query. The frmQueries form in Form view is now the active object.

The SQL SELECT statements mirror the query options you viewed in Design view. In effect, every choice you make in Design view is reflected as part of the SQL SELECT statement. Viewing the SQL statements generated from queries that you design is an effective way to begin learning SQL.

You now can enter the SQL statement that will provide the query names for the list box control.

Using a SQL Statement for a List Box Control

You'll use a SQL SELECT statement to retrieve the list of query names from one of the Access system tables. **System tables** are special tables maintained by Access that store information about the characteristics of a database and about the structure of the objects in the database. Although system tables do not appear in the Navigation Pane, you can retrieve information from them using SELECT statements. One of the system tables, the **MSysObjects table**, keeps track of the names, types, and other characteristics of every object in a database. The Name and Type fields are the two MSysObjects table fields you'll use in the SELECT statement. The Type field value contains a numeric value that corresponds to an object type. Figure 10–26 shows the numbers that correspond to some commonly used objects. For instance, a table is a type 1 object, and a query is a type 5 object. If the Type value of an MSObject is 5, then the MSObject referred to must be a query. The values may seem cryptic, but think of them as values that Microsoft developers have assigned to these objects so they can use a number instead of a name.

| Figure 10–26 | MSysObjects table Type field values |

Object Type	Type Field Value in MSysObjects Table
Table	1
Query	5
Form	−32768
Report	−32764
Macro	−32766
Module	−32761

TIP

SQL is not case sensitive, but typing SQL keywords in uppercase is an industry convention and makes the statements more readable.

Access creates special system queries to handle many tasks for you; each of these queries has a name that begins with the tilde (~) character. When a form contains a list box control, combo box control, or subform control, Access creates a system query to manage the functionality of these controls. For instance, when the frmVisit form was created, Access created a hidden system query called ~sq_ffrmVisit. You cannot see these system queries because users should not be able to run them or manipulate them.

The purpose of the system queries is to manage the functionality of the form controls. You want to exclude the special system queries from the list box control you've created for the user interface. Because every system query name begins with the ~ character, you'll use the Left function in your SELECT statement to identify the query names that begin with ~ and exclude those from the list of queries to appear in the list box control. The **Left function** provides the first character(s) in a text string. The format of the Left function is *Left*(text string, number of characters). You'll test the first character of the name of each query to determine if it is the ~ character. If the first character is not the ~ character, you'll include the query name in the list box control. You'll use *Left([Name], 1)* to retrieve the first character of the Name field, and you'll use the not equal operator (<>). To include only those queries whose names do not begin with the ~ character, you'll use the expression *Left([Name], 1)<>"~"*. Access interprets this expression as "the first character of the Name field does not equal the ~ character." The complete SELECT statement that you will use to select the list of query names is as follows:

SELECT [Name] FROM MSysObjects WHERE [Type]=5 And Left([Name],1)<>"~" ORDER BY [Name];

Recall that the Row Source property for a control specifies the data source, such as a table, a query, or a SQL statement. You'll enter the SELECT statement as the value for the Row Source property for the list box control you created.

To set the Row Source property for the list box control:

▶ **1.** Switch to Design view, right-click the **list box** control to open the shortcut menu, click **Properties** to open the Property Sheet, and then click the **Data** tab (if necessary).

▶ **2.** Right-click the **Row Source** box to open the shortcut menu, and then click **Zoom**. The Zoom dialog box opens.

Be sure to type the semicolon at the end of the SELECT statement.

▶ **3.** In the Zoom dialog box, type **SELECT [Name] FROM MSysObjects WHERE [Type]=5 And Left([Name],1)<>"~" ORDER BY [Name];** as shown in Figure 10–27.

Figure 10–27 **SELECT statement for the list box control**

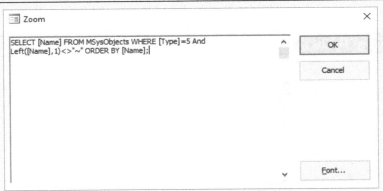

▶ **4.** Click the **OK** button to close the Zoom dialog box.

▶ **5.** Close the Property Sheet, save your form design changes, and then switch to Form view. The queries in the database (excluding system queries) now appear in alphabetical order in the list box control. See Figure 10–28.

Figure 10–28 | **List box control displaying query names**

query names retrieved by a SQL statement from the MSysObjects table

Trouble? If a syntax error message appears, click the OK button, switch to Design view, right-click the list box control, click Properties, right-click the Row Source box, and then click Zoom. Correct the SELECT statement so it's the same as the statement shown in Step 3, click the OK button, and then repeat Step 5.

6. Switch to Layout view, and then resize the list box by dragging its right border to the right until the query names are fully displayed.

Next you will add the two command button controls to the form that are specified in Mista's design: Preview and Display. The Preview command button will allow users to view the query in Print Preview, and the Display command button will allow users to view the query as a datasheet. When a user clicks either command button, the query that opens is the query the user has selected in the list box. For the Print Preview button, you'll attach a macro to the command button's On Click property that will display the selected query in Print Preview. Similarly, you'll attach a macro to the Display command button that will display the selected query as a datasheet. You'll add both command button controls and appropriate macros to the form. First, you'll add the Preview command button to the form.

To add the Preview command button control to the form:

1. Switch to Design view, click the **Form Design Tools Design** tab, and then increase the width of the form to 4" and the length of the form to 4" (if necessary).

2. In the Controls group, click the **More** button ⬇, make sure the Use Control Wizards tool 🖉 is deselected, and then in the Controls group, click the **Button** tool ▭.

3. Position the pointer's plus symbol (+) below and aligned with the left edge of the list box control in the Details section, and then click the mouse button.

   A command button control is added to the form.

4. If necessary, open the Property Sheet for the command button control.

   You can now change the default text that appears on the command button to the word "Preview" and add the Print Preview picture. When you add the picture, the button will be too small to display both the picture and the caption. You'll fix that in subsequent steps.

▶ **5.** In the Property Sheet, click the **Format** tab (if necessary), set the Caption property to **Preview**, click the **Picture** box, and then click the **Build** button ⊡ on the right end of the Picture box. The Picture Builder dialog box opens.

▶ **6.** Scroll the Available Pictures box, and then click **Preview**. A Print Preview picture appears on the command button in the Sample box.

▶ **7.** Click **OK** to close the Picture Builder dialog box and to place the Print Preview picture on the command button.

▶ **8.** Click the **Picture Caption Arrangement** box, click its **arrow**, and then click **Bottom**.

Mista wants you to change the background color of the command button. You'll change the color and then resize the button control to display the caption as well.

▶ **9.** On the Property Sheet, click the **Back Color** box, click its **Build** button ⊡, in the Theme Colors section, click **Green, Accent 6, Lighter 60%** (third color down in the last column), and then close the Property Sheet.

▶ **10.** Use the bottom-right sizing handle and the middle-right sizing handle to change the size of the command button control to match the size shown in Figure 10–29. The width of the button should be less than half the width of the list box control because you'll be adding another button control of the same size to the right. See Figure 10–29.

Figure 10–29 **Preview command button added to the form**

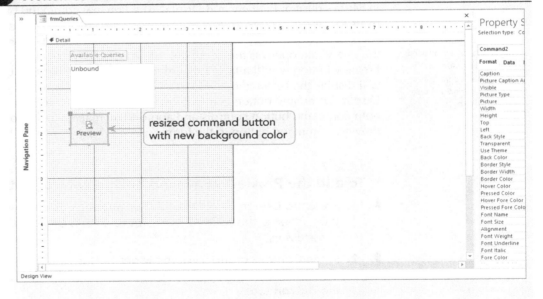

Instead of repeating the steps to add the command button control for viewing a query recordset, you'll copy the Preview command button control and paste it in the Detail section. This will also ensure the button controls are the same dimensions. After moving the copied button control into position, you can change its properties to control the text and picture that will appear on it.

To add the Display command button control to the form:

1. Right-click the **Preview** command button control, and then click **Copy** on the shortcut menu.

2. Right-click a blank area of the grid, and then click **Paste** on the shortcut menu. A copy of the command button is added in the upper-left corner of the Detail section.

3. Move the new command button into position to the right of the original command button, aligning the bottom edges of the two buttons and aligning the right edge of the new button with the right edge of the list box. See Figure 10–30.

Figure 10–30   Command button control duplicated and repositioned

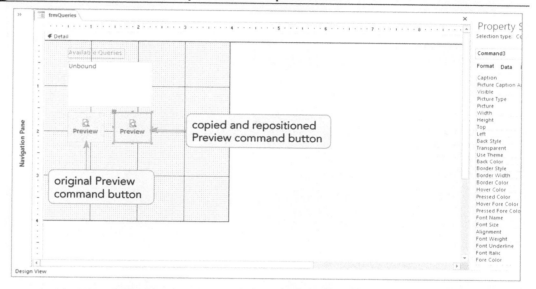

4. Open the Property Sheet for the new command button (if necessary), set the Caption property to **Display**, click the **Picture property Build button** [...], and then in the Picture Builder dialog box, set the Picture property to **MS Access Query**.

5. Save your form design changes.

Before creating the macros for the form and for the command button controls to open the query selected by the user, you'll set the Name property for the list box control. The naming convention for a list box control is to use the three-letter prefix LST in lowercase (lst). You'll enter the name lstQueryList for the list box control. You'll also set the background color of the Detail section and the list box control.

To set the Name property for the list box and to set background colors:

1. Click the list box control to make it the active control.

Be sure to type the first character as a lowercase L, not as a number 1.

2. In the Property Sheet, click the **All** tab, select the value in the **Name** box, and then type **lstQueryList**.

▶ **3.** Click the **Back Color** box, click its **Build** button ⋯ , and then in the Theme Colors section of the color palette, click the **White, Background 1** color (row 1, column 1).

▶ **4.** Click the **Detail** section bar, and then set the section's Back Color property to **White, Background 1, Darker 15%** (row 3, column 1 in the Theme Colors section of the color palette).

▶ **5.** Save your form design changes, and then switch to Form view to display the completed frmQueries form. See Figure 10–31.

Figure 10–31	Completed list box control

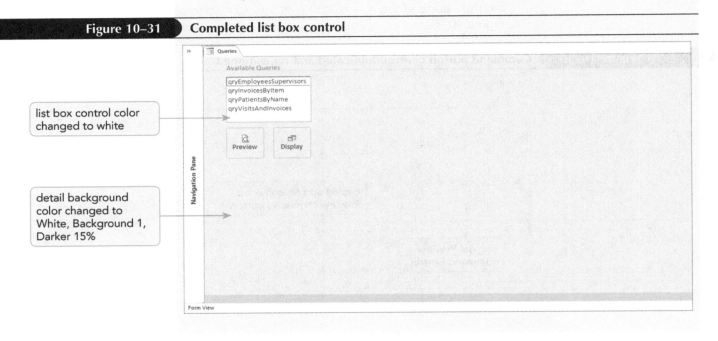

You now can create the macros for the frmQueries form.

Creating Multiple Macros for a Form

Mista wants to highlight the first query name in the list box control when the frmQueries form first opens. You can accomplish this by placing the focus on the first query name. When an item has the focus, it may be selected and appear highlighted, or a flashing insertion point may be visible in the control. In general, it is a good practice to ensure a form element has the focus when the form opens so that if a user presses ENTER, the default behavior of the element with the focus is executed. If no form controls have the focus when a form opens and a user presses ENTER, an error message might be displayed, which could confuse or frustrate users. To avoid this situation, you'll place the focus on the first query name in the lstQueryList list box control when the form opens.

When a user double-clicks a query name in the list box or selects a query name and then clicks the Display command button, the selected query should open in Datasheet view. When a user selects a query name in the list box and then clicks the Preview command button, the selected query should open in Print Preview. You'll create and attach four different macros to the objects on your form to enable these behaviors. You'll start by creating and attaching a macro to the On Load property for the form to place the focus on the first query name in the list box control and highlight it when the form opens.

The **Load event** occurs when a form or report opens. When you attach a macro to the Load event through the On Load property for the form, the actions in the macro are processed each time the form opens. You'll create a macro containing two actions. First, you'll use the GoToControl action to move the focus to the list box control. This action does not set the focus to any specific query name in the list box control, so you'll use the SendKeys action to send the DOWN ARROW keystroke to the list box control. The SendKeys action will result in the first query name in the list box being highlighted. The end result of these two actions will be that when a user opens the frmQueries form, the first query name will have the focus.

To create the macro for the On Load property:

▶ **1.** Switch to Design view, and then, in the Property Sheet, click the **Event** tab.

▶ **2.** Click the **On Load** box, and then click its **Build** button ⊡. The Choose Builder dialog box opens and includes three options for setting the property value. See Figure 10–32.

Figure 10–32   **Choose Builder dialog box**

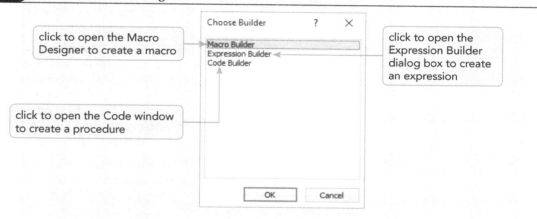

You'll attach a macro to the event property.

▶ **3.** Make sure **Macro Builder** is selected, and then click **OK** to open the Macro Designer.

▶ **4.** Click the **Add New Action** arrow to display the list of actions, and then click **GoToControl**. The list closes, and a new GoToControl action is added with one argument.

▶ **5.** In the Control Name box, type **lst** and then double-click the **lstQueryList** AutoComplete option. This is the Name property setting for the list box control.

   Trouble? If you do not see the lstQueryList AutoComplete value, you most likely typed the number 1 as the first character instead of a lowercase L. Delete the characters you have typed and retype the correct beginning characters.

   The second and final action you need to add is the SendKeys action. The SendKeys action doesn't appear in the Add New Action list. You'll verify this and then use the Show All Actions button to display the SendKeys action.

▶ **6.** Click the **Add New Action** arrow, scroll down the list, notice that the SendKeys action doesn't appear in the list, and then click the **Add New Action** arrow to close the list.

▶ **7.** On the Macro Tools Design tab, in the Show/Hide group, position the mouse pointer over the **Show All Actions** button to display the button's ScreenTip. See Figure 10–33.

Figure 10–33 Macro for the On Load property of the form

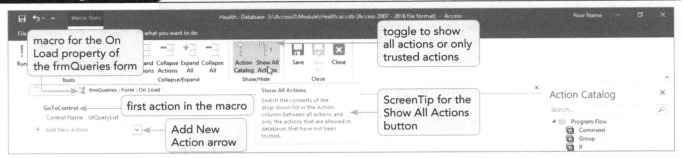

By default, only trusted actions are displayed in the Add New Action list, but you can display all actions by clicking the Show All Actions button. The actions that are categorized as unsafe actions (not trusted) are not displayed in the list by default; this includes the SendKeys action. This action is considered unsafe because an inexperienced developer could use the SendKeys action to send keystrokes to the database application that could delete data, for instance. Because you need to use the SendKeys action and you understand the risks, you'll display all actions so you can select it from the menu.

8. In the Show/Hide group, click the **Show All Actions** button to toggle it on, click the **Add New Action** arrow, scroll the list, and then click **SendKeys**. The list closes, and a SendKeys action is added to the macro with two arguments. You'll use the Keystrokes value of {Down}, which represents the DOWN ARROW keystroke, and a Wait value of No, which prevents the macro from pausing when it runs. (If the macro pauses, the DOWN ARROW keystroke might not be received right away, and the first query in the list box control may not receive the focus.)

   Trouble? If SendKeys isn't in the list, check the Show All Actions button; if it has a white background, it is toggled off. Click it again, click the Add New Action arrow, and then select the SendKeys action.

9. In the Keystrokes box, type **{Down}** to complete the macro. See Figure 10–34.

Figure 10–34 Completed macro for the On Load property of the form

10. Position the mouse pointer over the icon to the left of the SendKeys action. The icon's ScreenTip of "Unsafe Action" identifies that the action isn't a trusted action.

11. Save the macro, and then close the Macro Designer to return to the frmQueries form in Design view.

Now you'll create the macros for the Preview and Display command button controls.

To create the macros for the command button controls:

1. Click the **Preview** command button control.

2. In the Property Sheet, click the **On Click** box (if necessary), click its **Build** button ⋯ to open the Choose Builder dialog box, and then click the **OK** button to open the Macro Designer.

   When users click the Preview command button, the query selected in the list box control should open in Print Preview.

3. Click the **Add New Action** arrow, scroll the list, and then click **OpenQuery**. The list closes, and a new OpenQuery action is added with three arguments.

   You'll enter the expression =[lstQueryList] in the Query Name box to indicate the query to open is equal to the name of the query selected in the lstQueryList list box control.

4. In the Query Name box, type an equal sign (**=**). The Query Name arrow to the right of the Query Name box changes to the Expression Builder button.

5. Click the **Expression Builder** button ⬡ to open the Expression Builder dialog box, double-click **lstQueryList** in the Expression Categories list, and then click **OK** to close the dialog box. The expression = [lstQueryList] is now displayed in the Query Name box.

6. Click the **View** arrow, and then click **Print Preview** to complete the macro. See Figure 10–35.

Figure 10–35	Completed macro for the Preview command button

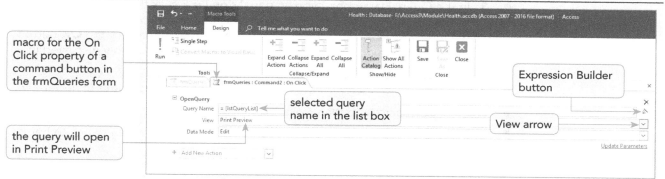

macro for the On Click property of a command button in the frmQueries form

the query will open in Print Preview

selected query name in the list box

Expression Builder button

View arrow

Because you did not set the Name property for the command buttons, the object tab displays the default name of Command2 (your name might be different).

7. Save the macro, and then close the Macro Designer.

   Next you'll create the macro for the Display command button.

8. Repeat Steps 2 to 5 for the Display command button.

9. Set the View property for the OpenQuery action to **Datasheet** (if necessary). See Figure 10–36.

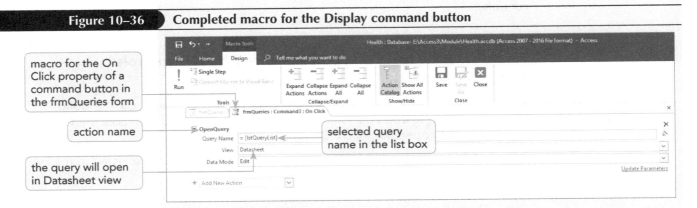

Figure 10–36   Completed macro for the Display command button

macro for the On Click property of a command button in the frmQueries form

action name

the query will open in Datasheet view

selected query name in the list box

▶ **10.** Save the macro, and then close the Macro Designer.

Next you'll add a macro that will open a query in Datasheet view if the user double-clicks a query name in the list box control.

To create the macro for the list box control:

▶ **1.** Click the **list box** control, in the Property Sheet, click the **On Dbl Click** box, click its **Build** button 〔...〕 to open the Choose Builder dialog box, and then click the **OK** button to open the Macro Designer.

▶ **2.** Click the **Add New Action** arrow, scroll the list, and then click **OpenQuery**. The list closes, and a new OpenQuery action is added with three arguments.

▶ **3.** In the Query Name box, type an equal sign (**=**), click the **Expression Builder** button 〔⌁〕 to open the Expression Builder dialog box, double-click **lstQueryList** in the Expression Categories list, and then click the **OK** button to close the dialog box. The expression *=[lstQueryList]* is now displayed in the Query Name box.

▶ **4.** Set the View property for the OpenQuery action to **Datasheet** (if necessary).

▶ **5.** Save the macro, and then close the Macro Designer.

▶ **6.** Close the Property Sheet, save your form changes, and then switch to Form view.

You have finished creating the macros for the form. Next, you will test the list box control and the command button controls.

After creating a custom form, you should test the form in Form view. For the frmQueries form, you need to double-click a query name in the list box to make sure the query datasheet opens. You also need to scroll the list box, click a query name, and then click the Display command button to make sure the query datasheet opens and click the Preview command button to make sure the query opens in Print Preview.

To test the form's controls:

▶ **1.** Double-click the first query name in the list box to verify that the correct query datasheet opens, and then close the query to make the frmQueries form the active object.

▶ **2.** Repeat Step 1 for each of the other query names in the list box.

▶ **3.** Click a query name in the list box, click the **Preview** command button to verify that the correct query opens in Print Preview, and then close the Print Preview window to make the frmQueries form the active object.

Note that the Preview command button turns blue when the mouse pointer is positioned on it and when it is clicked. This formatting is applied to the button automatically.

▶ **4.** Repeat Step 3 for the other query names in the list box.

▶ **5.** Click a query name in the list box, click the **Display** command button to verify that the correct query datasheet opens, and then close the query to make the frmQueries form the active object.

▶ **6.** Repeat Step 5 for the other query names in the list box.

Because the frmQueries form's Close button is disabled, you need to switch to Design view, which still has an enabled Close button, to close the form, or you can close the form by using the shortcut menu for the form object's tab.

▶ **7.** Right-click the **Queries** tab, and then click **Close** on the shortcut menu.

You've completed the custom frmQueries form. The frmQueries form is an example of a form designed to allow a user to easily choose a select query and view the records, without having to know how to run a query from the Navigation Pane. Next, Mista wants you to create the navigation form for the Health database. You'll incorporate the frmQueries form into this overall navigation system.

Creating a Navigation Form

The frmVisit form is a great example of navigation using a single form. You can set properties in Access to display only a single form if that's sufficient to provide the functionality users need and to restrict them from being able to accidentally use other database objects or to corrupt data. If users need access to several queries, forms, reports, or other database objects, though, another option is to build a separate navigation form. A navigation form is a form with tabs that allows you to present database objects in an organized way to users.

A database generally uses either one or more single, independent forms or a navigation form. The choice to use one or the other generally depends on the designer's assessment of the abilities of people using the database. If the users have little experience with databases, a navigation form approach might be better. If they have more experience, a few well-designed forms that the users can select themselves might be a better approach.

Mista wants to restrict the access users have to the Health database to just the queries that will be displayed in the frmQueries form and to selected forms and reports. To control how users interact with the database, she wants you to create a navigation form that provides users access to only those database objects. Six predefined layouts for a navigation form are available in Access, with the layouts differing in the placement of tabs and subtabs. Of the several navigation form styles available, Mista wants you to use the Horizontal Tabs, 2 Levels layout.

To create the navigation form:

▶ **1.** On the ribbon, click the **Create** tab.

▶ **2.** In the Forms group, click the **Navigation** button. The Navigation gallery opens. See Figure 10–37.

Figure 10–37   **The Navigation gallery**

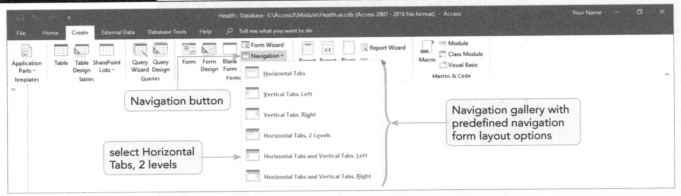

▶ **3.** Click **Horizontal Tabs, 2 Levels** in the gallery, and then close the Field List pane. The navigation form with the default title of Navigation Form opens in Layout view. See Figure 10–38.

Figure 10–38   **Initial navigation form**

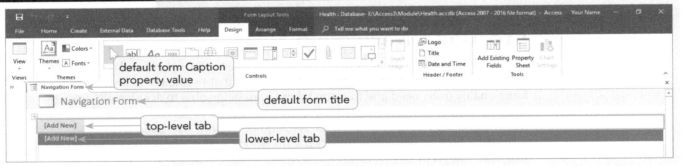

Because the navigation form won't display data from the database, it will be an unbound form. You'll enter the labels "Forms," "Reports," and "Queries" for the top-level tabs. You'll then drag the forms and reports that Mista wants to include in the navigation form from the Navigation Pane to the lower-level tabs. The Session 10.2 Visual Overview shows a preview of the completed top-level tabs as well as a lower-level tab. You won't add the frmVisit form to the navigation form because the frmVisit form was created as a manual navigation form for a more advanced user. The macros for previewing and displaying the records would not function in the navigation form because they become submacros of the frmVisit subform of the frmNavigation form. The macros would have to be rewritten to work in a navigation form. If you wanted to have this functionality in a navigation form, you would create a new version of the frmVisit form that is designed to work as a subform of a navigation form. The frmVisit form you created is designed to work as a stand-alone form, not as a subform. However, the simple select queries, simple forms, and reports all work well as subforms in a navigation form.

To add names and objects to the navigation form:

1. Click the top **[Add New]** tab, type **Forms**, and then press **ENTER**. The name on the first tab changes to Forms, and a second tab appears to its right.

   Trouble? If you type the first letter and it does not appear in the tab, click the tab again to switch to editing mode.

   Trouble? If you need to correct or change a tab name, click the name, edit the name, and then press ENTER.

2. Click the **[Add New]** tab to the right of the Forms tab, type **Queries**, and then press **ENTER**.

3. Click the **[Add New]** tab to the right of the Queries tab, type **Reports**, and then press **ENTER**. You have created the top-level tabs and named them Forms, Queries, and Reports. To create the lower-level tabs that will display these respective objects, you will drag some form and report objects from the Navigation Pane to the lower-level tabs. As you drag the objects, their names are added to the tabs.

TIP

You can drag only forms and reports, not queries, to tabs in a navigation form.

4. Open the Navigation Pane, click the **Forms** tab in the navigation form, and then drag the **frmVisitsAndInvoices** form from the Navigation Pane to the lower-level [Add New] tab. The frmVisitsAndInvoices form opens in the first tab below the Forms tab, and the tab displays the form's name.

   Trouble? If you drag the wrong object to a tab, right-click the tab, click Delete on the shortcut menu, and then drag the correct object to the tab.

   Trouble? You can rearrange the order of objects on the lower-level tabs by dragging the name of an object from its current tab to a new tab.

5. Drag the **frmPatient** form from the Navigation Pane to the next [Add New] tab to the right of the frmVisitsAndInvoices tab. You've added the two forms Mista wants users to work with in the Health database. See Figure 10–39.

Figure 10–39   Navigation form after adding two forms to lower-level tabs

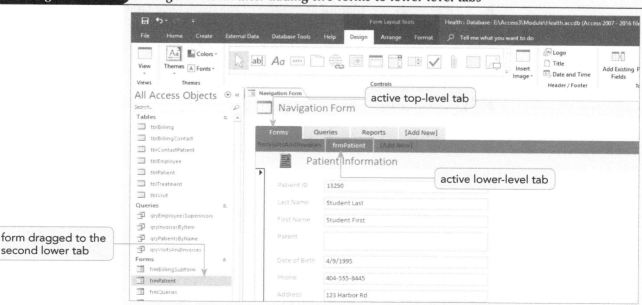

▶ **6.** Click the Queries tab at the top of the navigation form, and then drag the **frmQueries** form from the Navigation Pane to the [Add New] tab below the Queries tab. Although you can't drag queries to a navigation form, in this case you're instead dragging the form you created that users can use to view and print queries.

▶ **7.** Click the **Reports** tab at the top of the navigation form, and then drag from the Navigation Pane to the lower-level tabs, in order, the **rptVisitDetails** report, the **rptVisitsAndInvoices** report, and the **rptInvoicesByItem** report. Notice that each report opens as you drag it to the form.

▶ **8.** Close the Navigation Pane. You've finished adding objects to the navigation form. See Figure 10–40.

Figure 10–40 **Reports added to the navigation form**

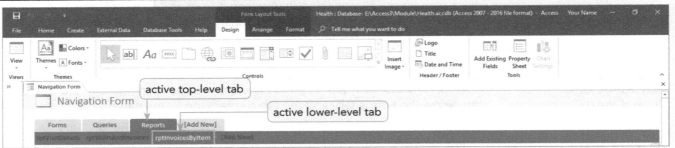

Mista asks you to delete the picture at the top of the navigation form, delete the form title, set the form's Caption property to "Health Database," and then save the form.

To finalize the navigation form:

▶ **1.** Right-click the **picture** at the top of the form, click **Delete** on the shortcut menu, right-click the **form title**, and then click **Delete** on the shortcut menu.

▶ **2.** Save the form as **frmNavigation**, and then switch to Design view.

▶ **3.** Open the Property Sheet for the form, and then set the Caption property to **Health Database**.

▶ **4.** Switch to Form view. See Figure 10–41.

Figure 10–41	Completed navigation form

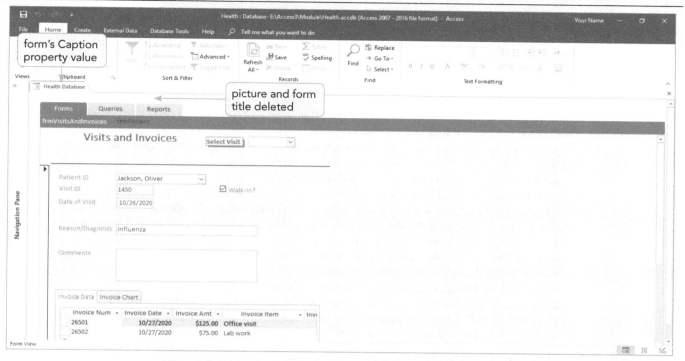

5. Navigate through the navigation form by clicking each top-level tab and its lower-level tabs.

When you click the Queries tab, you may notice that the first query is not selected. This is because the frmQueries form is a subform of the frmNavigation form, and the Load event occurs on the frmNavigation form but does not occur on its subforms. When you load the frmQueries form itself, the Load event occurs on the frmQueries form. You'll need to click a query in the Available Queries list box before you click one of the command buttons on the form.

6. **sam** ⬆ Save and close the form, make a backup copy of the database, compact and repair the database, and then close it.

> **TIP**
>
> When you click the Forms tab's lower-level tabs, you need to click a blank area of the form to place the focus in the first field in the record.

Mista is happy with the two user interfaces you created for the Health database. She can direct experienced users to the database objects, including the frmVisit form that has some advanced features. She can load the frmNavigation form for users who are less experienced.

Session 10.2 Quick Check

REVIEW

1. What is a list box control?

2. What are system tables?

3. What are the five SQL statement types, and which query types do they correspond to?

4. When does the Load event occur?

5. What is a navigation form?

PRACTICE

Review Assignments

Data File needed for the Review Assignments: Product.accdb (cont. from Module 9)

Mista wants you to create a user interface for the Product database. To help with this request, complete the following steps:

1. Open the **Product** database you worked with in the previous module. Delete the action queries qryAppendSterile, qryDeletePriceLess20, and qryMakeSpecialEnviron. If you want to keep the action queries, first save a copy of the Product database as **Product_M9**, and then delete the action queries from the Product database.

2. Design and create a blank form named **frmQueries** that has the following components and characteristics:
   a. Set the form's Caption property to **Product Queries**.
   b. Add a list box control (approximately 0.5 inches from the top of the form and 0.5 inches from the left border of the form) with a Name property value of **lstQueryList** that displays all the query names contained in the Product database, excluding those that start with a "~" character. To place the query names in the list box control, use a SQL SELECT statement to retrieve the query names from the MSysObjects table, and display the queries in alphabetical order. (*Hint*: Use the same SQL select query that you used in the module.) Widen the list box control to approximately 2.5 inches.
   c. In the attached label control, change the caption to **Queries Available**, formatted with a 12-point, bold Calibri font, position the label above the list box control, and increase the width of the label control to fit the text.
   d. Add two command buttons below the list box control. The left command button should display the Preview icon above the word **Preview**, and the right command button should display the MS Access Query icon above the word **Display**. Resize the buttons to the same size so that they both show their icon and text.
   e. Create a macro for the form that moves the focus to the first query name in the list box control when the form loads.
   f. Create a macro that causes the query datasheet to display the selected query, and then configure the form so the macro runs when a user double-clicks a query name in the list box.
   g. Create a macro that causes the query datasheet to display the selected query, and then configure the form so the macro runs when a user selects a query name in the list box and clicks the right command button (the Display button).
   h. Create a macro for the left command button (Preview button) that opens the selected query in Print Preview.
   i. Set the background color of the Detail section to Green 3 in the Standard Colors section. Set the background color of the list box and the two command buttons to Green 2.
   j. Disable the form's shortcut menu, record selectors, Close button, and navigation buttons.
   k. Test the form.

3. Create a navigation form named **frmNavigation**, using the Horizontal Tabs, 2 Levels layout that includes the following tab names and objects:
   a. Use **Forms** as the name for the far left, top-level tab and place the following forms below it as lower-level tabs, in order: frmSupplier and frmSuppliersWithProducts. Expand the second lower-level tabs to show each entire form name.
   b. Use **Queries** as the name for the second tab, and place the frmQueries form below it on a lower-level tab.
   c. Use **Reports** as the name for the third tab, and place the following reports below it as lower-level tabs, in order: rptSupplier and rptSupplierProducts. Expand the second lower-level tabs to show each entire report name.
   d. Delete the navigation form's picture and title and set the form's caption to **Product**.
   e. Test the navigation form, remembering to first select a query in the list on the Queries tab before testing the command buttons.

4. Make a backup copy of the database, compact and repair the database, and then close it.

Case Problem 1

APPLY

Data File needed for this Case Problem: Instruction.accdb *(cont. from Module 9)*

Great Giraffe Jeremiah wants you to create a user interface for the Instruction database. To help with this request, complete the following steps:

1. Open the **Instruction** database you worked with in the previous module. Delete the action queries qryAppendLittleton, qryDeleteMoreThan1500, qryMakeCityPaymentPlan, and qryUpdateLittletonToZero. If you want to keep the action queries, first save a copy of the Instruction database as **Instruction_M9**, and then delete the action queries from the Instruction database.

2. Design and create a form named **frmQueries** that has the following components and characteristics:

   a. Set the form's Caption property to **Instruction Queries**.

   b. Add a list box control (approximately 1 inch from the top of the form and 1 inch from the left border of the form) with a Name property value of **lstQueryList** that displays all the query names contained in the Instruction database, excluding those that start with a "~" character. To place the query names in the list box control, use a SQL SELECT statement to retrieve the query names from the MSysObjects table, and display the queries in reverse alphabetical order (descending order). (*Hint*: Use the same SQL select query that you used in the module.) Widen the list box control to approximately 2.25 inches.

   c. In the attached label control, change the caption to **Available Queries**, formatted with a 12-point, bold, italic Calibri font, position the label above the list box control, and increase the width of the label control to fit the text.

   d. Add two command buttons below the list box control. The left command button should display the Preview icon *below* the word **Preview**, and the right command button should display the MS Access Query icon *below* the word **Display**.

   e. Create a macro for the form that moves the focus to the first query name in the list box control when the form loads.

   f. Create a macro that causes the query datasheet to display the selected query, and then configure the form so the macro runs when a user double-clicks a query name in the list box.

   g. Create a macro that causes the query datasheet to display the selected query, and then configure the form so the macro runs when a user selects a query name in the list box and clicks the right command button (the Display button).

   h. Create a macro for the left command button (Preview button) that opens the selected query in Print Preview.

   i. Set the background color of the Detail section to Light Blue 3 in the Standard Colors section. Set the background color of the list box and the two command buttons to Light Blue 2.

   j. Disable the form's shortcut menu, record selectors, and navigation buttons, but do not disable the Close button.

   k. Test the form.

3. Create a navigation form named **frmNavigation** using the Horizontal Tabs, 2 Levels layout that includes the following tab names and objects:

   a. Use **Forms** as the name for the far left, top-level tab and place the following forms below it as lower-level tabs, in order: frmCourseData, frmStudentInfo, and frmStudentsByCourse. Expand the second lower-level tabs to show each entire form name.

   b. Use **Queries** as the name for the second tab, and place the frmQueries form below it on a lower-level tab.

   c. Use **Reports** as the name for the third tab, and place the following reports below it as lower-level tabs, in order: rptCourseRosters and rptStudentList. Expand the second lower-level tabs to show each entire report name.

    d. Delete the navigation form's picture and title and set the form's caption to **Instruction Information**.

    e. Test the navigation form, remembering to first select a query in the list on the Queries tab before testing the command buttons.

4. Make a backup copy of the database, compact and repair the database, and then close it.

Case Problem 2

Data File needed for this Case Problem: CleanOut.accdb *(cont. from Module 9)*

Drain Adopter   Tandrea wants you to create a user interface for the CleanOut database. To help with this request, complete the following steps:

1. Open the **CleanOut** database you worked with in the previous module. Delete the action queries qryAppendAprilMay, qryDeleteMarchAprilMay, qryMakeSpecialVolunteers, and qryUpdateTrained. If you want to keep the action queries, first save a copy of the Instruction database as **CleanOut_M9**, and then delete the action queries from the CleanOut database.

2. Design and create a form named **frmQueries** that has the following components and characteristics:

    a. Set the form's Caption property to **CleanOut Queries**.

    ⊕ **Explore** b. Add a list box control (approximately 0.75 inches from the top of the form and 0.75 inches from the left border of the form) with a Name property value of **lstQueryList** that displays all the query names contained in the CleanOut database, excluding those that start with a "~" character. To place the query names in the list box control, use a SQL SELECT statement to retrieve the query names from the MSysObjects table, and display the queries in reverse alphabetical order (descending order). (*Hint*: By default SQL sorts data in ascending order. To sort the data in descending order you would place the keyword DESC at the end of the ORDER BY clause just prior to the semicolon in the SQL statement.) Widen the list box control to approximately 2.25 inches.

    In the attached label control, change the caption to **Available Queries**, formatted with a 12-point, bold, italic, underlined Calibri font, position the label above the list box control, and increase the width of the label control to fit the text.

    ⊕ **Explore** c. Add two command buttons below the list box control. The left command button should display the Preview icon to the left of the word **Preview**, and the right command button should display the MS Access Query icon to the left of the word **Display**.

    ⊕ **Explore** d. Create a macro for the form that moves the focus to the third query name in the list box control when the form loads, not the first entry. (*Hint*: You used the SendKeys action once to give the focus to the first name in the list box, so performing the action twice more should move the focus down two additional entries).

    e. Create a macro that causes the query datasheet to display the selected query, and then configure the form so the macro runs when a user double-clicks a query name in the list box.

    f. Create a macro that causes the query datasheet to display the selected query, and then configure the form so the macro runs when a user selects a query name in the list box and clicks the right command button (the Display button).

    g. Create a macro for the left command button (Preview button) that opens the selected query in Print Preview.

    h. Set the background color of the Detail section to Aqua Blue 3 in the Standard Colors section. Set the background color of the list box to Aqua Blue 2.

    i. Disable the form's shortcut menu, record selectors, and navigation buttons, but do not disable the Close button.

    j. Test the form.

⊕ **Explore** 3. Create a navigation form named **frmNavigation** using the Horizontal Tabs and Vertical Tabs, Left layout that includes the following tab names and objects. (*Hint*: The categories

CHALLENGE

of Forms, Queries, and Reports are the horizontal values across the top of the form, with lower-level values beginning in the vertical slots.)

a. Use **Forms** as the name for the far left, top-level horizontal tab and place the following forms below it as lower-level vertical tabs, in order: frmVolunteerData, frmVolunteerMasterData, and frmVolunteersAndDrains. Expand the vertical lower-level tabs to show each entire form name.

b. Use **Queries** as the name for the second horizontal tab, and place the frmQueries form below it on a vertical lower-level tab.

c. Use **Reports** as the name for the third horizontal tab, and place the following reports below it as vertical lower-level tabs, in order: rptVolunteerList and rptVolunteersAndDrains. Expand the vertical lower-level tabs to show each entire report name.

d. Delete the navigation form's picture and title and set the form's caption to **CleanOut Information**.

e. Test the navigation form, remembering to first select a query in the list on the Queries tab before testing the command buttons.

4. Make a backup copy of the database, compact and repair the database, and then close it.

OBJECTIVES

Session 11.1
- Describe user-defined functions, Sub procedures, and modules
- Review and modify an existing Sub procedure in an event procedure
- Create a function in a standard module
- Test a procedure in the Immediate window

Session 11.2
- Create event procedures
- Compile and test functions, Sub procedures, and event procedures
- Create a field validation procedure

Using and Writing Visual Basic for Applications Code

Creating VBA Code for the Health Database

Case | *Lakewood Community Health Services*

Donna Taylor is pleased with your progress in developing the user interface for the Health database. She realizes that many different people will be entering information in the Health database. Whenever users enter data manually, they introduce the potential for typographical errors. Donna wants you to modify the frmVisit, frmPatient, and frmVisitsAndInvoices forms to make data entry easier and to highlight important information on them. To make these modifications, you will write Visual Basic for Applications code.

ACCESS

STARTING DATA FILES

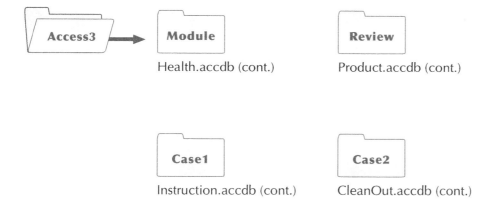

Access3 → Module
Health.accdb (cont.)

Review
Product.accdb (cont.)

Case1
Instruction.accdb (cont.)

Case2
CleanOut.accdb (cont.)

Session 11.1 Visual Overview:

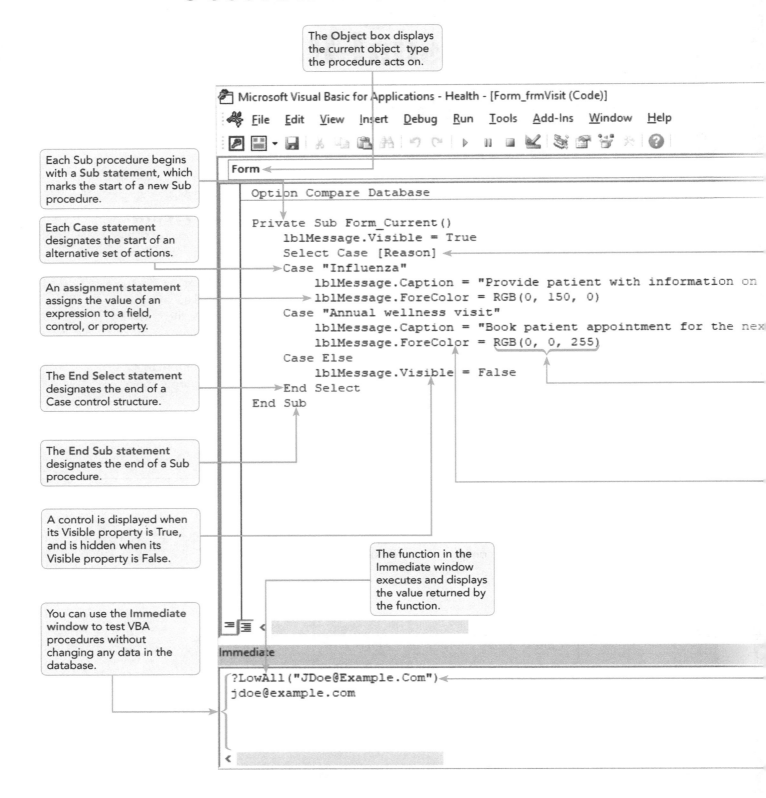

The **Object box** displays the current object type the procedure acts on.

Each Sub procedure begins with a Sub statement, which marks the start of a new Sub procedure.

Each Case statement designates the start of an alternative set of actions.

An assignment statement assigns the value of an expression to a field, control, or property.

The End Select statement designates the end of a Case control structure.

The End Sub statement designates the end of a Sub procedure.

A control is displayed when its Visible property is True, and is hidden when its Visible property is False.

You can use the Immediate window to test VBA procedures without changing any data in the database.

The function in the Immediate window executes and displays the value returned by the function.

```
Microsoft Visual Basic for Applications - Health - [Form_frmVisit (Code)]

File   Edit   View   Insert   Debug   Run   Tools   Add-Ins   Window   Help

Form

    Option Compare Database

    Private Sub Form_Current()
        lblMessage.Visible = True
        Select Case [Reason]
        Case "Influenza"
            lblMessage.Caption = "Provide patient with information on
            lblMessage.ForeColor = RGB(0, 150, 0)
        Case "Annual wellness visit"
            lblMessage.Caption = "Book patient appointment for the nex
            lblMessage.ForeColor = RGB(0, 0, 255)
        Case Else
            lblMessage.Visible = False
        End Select
    End Sub
```

```
Immediate

?LowAll("JDoe@Example.Com")
jdoe@example.com
```

VBA Code Window

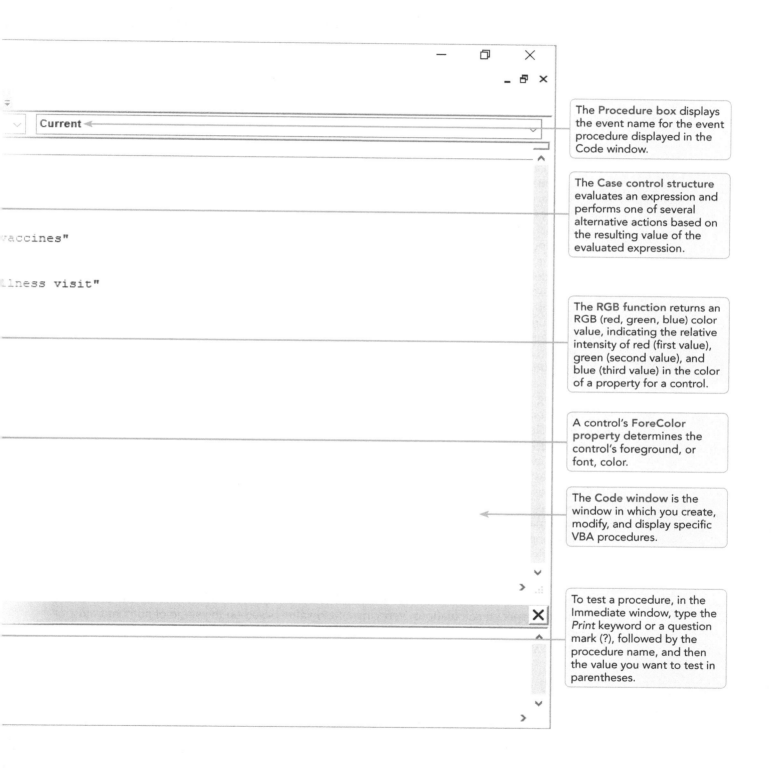

The Procedure box displays the event name for the event procedure displayed in the Code window.

The Case control structure evaluates an expression and performs one of several alternative actions based on the resulting value of the evaluated expression.

The RGB function returns an RGB (red, green, blue) color value, indicating the relative intensity of red (first value), green (second value), and blue (third value) in the color of a property for a control.

A control's ForeColor property determines the control's foreground, or font, color.

The Code window is the window in which you create, modify, and display specific VBA procedures.

To test a procedure, in the Immediate window, type the *Print* keyword or a question mark (?), followed by the procedure name, and then the value you want to test in parentheses.

Introduction to Visual Basic for Applications

Your next task in developing the Health database is to add a procedure to ensure proper capitalization of data entered using the frmPatient form. Donna wants the email addresses in the database to have a uniform case rather than the inconsistency that inevitably happens when users type their own data. She wants to make sure that all values entered in this form's Email field will be stored in the tblPatient table using lowercase letters. She asks you to modify the form so that it will automatically convert any uppercase letters entered in the Email field to lowercase. One method to accomplish this is to use an input mask to convert all letters to lowercase when the data is entered. An alternate method is to use Visual Basic for Applications to convert the letters to lowercase when the data is entered. This method could be used as the foundation for a more complex method to validate an email address. An input mask can restrict characters during data entry, but Visual Basic for Applications could also check to see if the email address contains the @ symbol and a valid suffix such as .com, which an input mask cannot do.

Visual Basic for Applications (VBA) is the programming language provided with Access and other Office programs. VBA has a common syntax and a set of common features for all Microsoft Office programs, but it also has features that are unique for each Microsoft Office program due to each program's distinct structure and components. For example, because Access has fields, tables, queries, forms, other objects, tab controls, subforms, and other controls that are unique to it, VBA for Access includes features that support these particular components. In contrast, because Microsoft Excel does not have these same Access components, VBA for Excel does not support them, but it does support cells, ranges, and worksheets—three of the basic structures of Excel. The fundamental VBA skills you learn for one of the Microsoft Office programs transfer to any other Microsoft Office program, but to become proficient with VBA in another program, you first need to master its unique aspects.

When you use a programming language, such as VBA, you write a set of instructions to direct the computer to perform specific operations in a specific order, similar to writing a set of instructions for a recipe or an instruction manual. The Visual Overview for Session 11.1 shows the VBA Code window with instructions for Access to use in the frmVisit form. The process of writing instructions in a programming language is called **coding**. You write the VBA instructions, each of which is called a **statement**, to respond to an event that occurs with an object or a form control in a database. A language such as VBA is, therefore, is called an **event-driven language**, because an event in the database triggers a set of instructions. It is also called an **object-oriented language**, because each set of instructions operates on objects in the database. Your experience with macros, which are also event-driven and object-oriented, should facilitate your learning of VBA. Although you must use macros if you need to assign actions to a specific keyboard key or key combination, you can use VBA for everything else you normally accomplish with macros. VBA provides advantages over using macros, such as better error-handling features and easier updating capabilities. You can also use VBA in situations that macros do not handle, such as creating your own set of statements to perform special calculations, verifying a field value based on the value of another field or set of fields, or dynamically changing the color of a form control when a user enters or views a specific field value.

Understanding Procedures

As you learned in the previous module when working with macros, an event is something that happens to a database object, such as a user clicking a check box or a form being loaded. You can connect an action to a specific event so the action occurs in response to that event. Each event has an associated event property, which specifies how an object responds when an event occurs. In the previous module, you set event property values to macro names, and Access executed the macros when those events occurred. You can also create a group of statements, known as a procedure, using VBA code and set an event property value to the name of that procedure. Access then executes the procedure when the event occurs. As you know, such a procedure is called an event procedure. Access has over 60 events and associated event properties. Figure 11–1 describes some frequently used Access events. Each event (such as the AfterUpdate event) has an associated event property (AfterUpdate) and event procedure (ContractNum_AfterUpdate for the AfterUpdate event procedure for the ContractNum control).

Figure 11–1   **Frequently used Access events**

Event	Description
AfterUpdate	Occurs after changed data in a control or a record is updated
BeforeUpdate	Occurs before changed data in a control or a record is updated
Click	Occurs when a user presses and then releases a mouse button over a control in a form
Current	Occurs when the focus moves to a record, making it the current record, or when a form is refreshed or requeried
DblClick	Occurs when a user presses and releases the left mouse button twice over a control in a form within the double-click time limit
Delete	Occurs when a user performs some action, such as pressing the Delete key, to delete a record, but before the record is actually deleted
GotFocus	Occurs when a form or a form control receives the focus
Load	Occurs when a form is opened and its records are displayed
MouseDown	Occurs when a user presses a mouse button
NoData	Occurs after Access formats a report for printing that has no data (the report is bound to an empty recordset), but before the report is printed; you use this event to cancel the printing of a blank report
Open	Occurs when a form is opened, but before the first record is displayed; for reports, the event occurs before a report is previewed or printed

The two types of VBA procedures are Function procedures and Sub procedures. A **user-defined function**, or **function procedure**, performs operations, returns a value, accepts input values, and can be used in expressions (recall that an expression is a calculation resulting in a single value). For example, some of the Health database queries use built-in Access functions, such as Sum, Count, and Avg, to calculate a sum, a record count, or an average. To meet Donna's request, you will create a function named LowAll by entering the appropriate VBA statements. The LowAll function will accept the value entered in a field value box—in this case, the Email field—as an input value, convert all characters in the field value to lowercase, and then return the changed field value to be stored in the database and displayed in the field value box.

A **Sub procedure** executes instructions and accepts input values but does not return a value and cannot be used in expressions. Most Access procedures are Sub procedures because you need the procedures to perform a series of actions or operations in response to an event. Later in this module, you will create a Sub procedure that displays a message in the frmVisitsAndInvoices form only when the visit date is earlier than a specified date.

Understanding Modules

You store a group of related procedures together in an object called a **module**. Figure 11–2 shows the structure of a typical module.

| Figure 11-2 | Structure of a VBA module and its procedures |

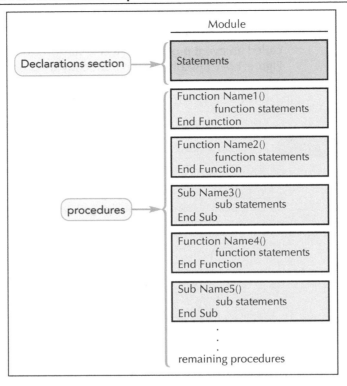

Each module starts with a **Declarations section**, which contains statements that apply to all procedures in the module. One or more procedures, which follow the Declarations section and which can be a mixture of functions and Sub procedures, constitute the rest of the module. The two basic types of modules are standard modules and class modules.

A **standard module** is a database object that is stored in memory with other database objects (queries, forms, and so on) when you open the database. You can use the procedures in a database's standard modules from anywhere in the database—even from procedures in other modules. All standard modules are listed in the Modules section of the Navigation Pane. A procedure that more than one object can use is called a **public procedure**. For example, the LowAll procedure that you will create converts all letters in the value passed to it to lowercase. Although you are creating this procedure specifically to work with Email field values, you will place it in a standard module and make it public. You could then use the LowAll procedure for any object in the database.

A **class module** is usually associated with a particular form or report. When you create the first event procedure for a form or report, an associated form or report class module is also created. When you add additional event procedures to the form or report, they are automatically added to the class module for that form or report. Each event procedure in a class module is a **local procedure**, or a **private procedure**, which means that only the form or report for which the class module was created can use the event procedure.

Using an Existing VBA Procedure

Before creating the LowAll procedure for Donna, you'll use an existing procedure that Donna created in the class module for the frmVisit form. The Lakewood Community Health Services team would like to provide information about annual flu vaccines for patients who come to the clinic for influenza. They would also like to book the next annual wellness visit for all patients who come to the clinic for an annual wellness visit. To remind the staff to provide information and book the next wellness visit, Donna created a local procedure stored in the class module of the frmVisit form that displays the message about annual flu vaccines in red text in a box to the right of the Walk-in? check box, and displays the message reminding the user to book the next annual wellness visit in blue text. For patients with any other reason for visiting the clinic, the class module makes the box invisible.

You'll navigate through the records using the frmVisit form to observe the effects of the procedure.

To navigate a form that uses a VBA procedure:

1. **sam** ↓ Start Access, and then open the **Health** database you worked with in the previous two modules.

2. Open the Navigation Pane (if necessary), open the **frmVisit** form in Form view, and then close the Navigation Pane. Navigate to the third record, VisitID 1585, by clicking the **Next record** button ▶ twice. The value "Book patient appointment for the next annual wellness visit" is displayed in a blue font to the right of the Walk-in? check box because the Reason field value is "Annual wellness visit." See Figure 11–3.

| Figure 11–3 | Using an existing VBA procedure |

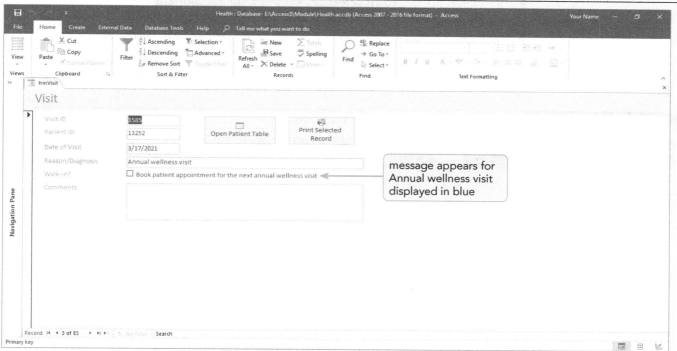

3. Click the **Next record** button ▶ three times to move to the sixth record. The frmVisit form displays record 6 for VisitID 1590. There is no value displayed to the right of the Walk-in? check box because the Reason field is neither "Annual wellness visit" nor "Influenza."

4. Navigate to record 18 for VisitID 1483. Because the Reason value for this visit is "Influenza," the text "Provide patient with information on annual flu vaccines" is displayed in a red font to the right of the Walk-in? check box.

Donna asks you to change the red color for the display of "Provide patient with information on annual flu vaccines" to green so that it doesn't appear to be an urgent warning.

Examining a VBA Event Procedure

The VBA procedure that controls the display of the message and its color for each record is in the class module for the frmVisit form. The statements in the procedure are processed when you open the frmVisit form and also when the focus leaves one record and moves to another. The event called the **Current event** occurs when the focus shifts to the next record loaded in a form, making it the current record. This also happens when the form loads and when the form is refreshed. The **Current property** contains a reference to a macro, VBA code, or some other expression that runs when the Current event occurs.

To change the color of the text "Provide patient with information on annual flu vaccines" from red to green, you'll modify the event procedure for the form's OnCurrent property. First, you'll switch to Design view, and then you'll display the event procedure.

TIP

Pay attention to the property names as you move from the Property Sheet to VBA. The names are interrelated, yet the syntax is different in each environment.

To display the event procedure for the form's OnCurrent property:

▶ **1.** Switch to Design view.

▶ **2.** Right-click the **form selector** ■ to display the shortcut menu, and then (if necessary) click **Properties** to open the Property Sheet for the form.

▶ **3.** Click the **Event** tab (if necessary) to display the Event page, click the **On Current** box, and then (if necessary) drag the left border of the Property Sheet to the left until the On Current property value is visible. See Figure 11–4.

Figure 11–4 **Event properties for the frmVisit form**

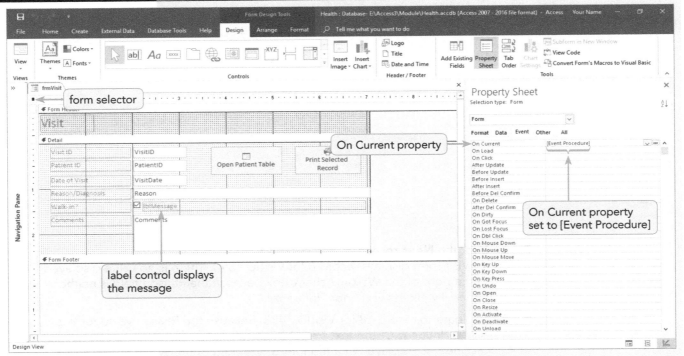

The On Current property is set to [Event Procedure], indicating that a VBA procedure is called when the Current event occurs. You'll click the Build button to display the procedure.

▶ **4.** In the On Current box, click the **Build** button . The Code window opens in the Visual Basic window. See Figure 11–5.

Figure 11–5   **Code window in the Visual Basic window**

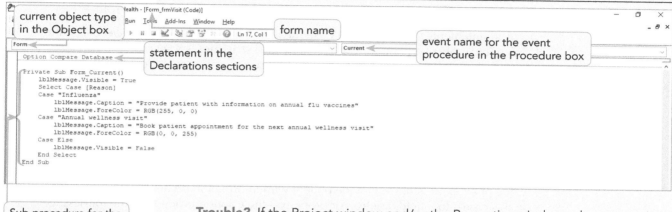

Sub procedure for the form's Current event

Trouble? If the Project window and/or the Properties windows also appear in your Visual Basic window, click their Close buttons to close them.

Trouble? If the Code window isn't maximized within the VBA window, click the Maximize button.

The program you use to create and modify VBA code is called the **Visual Basic Editor** (**VBE** or **editor** for short), and the **Visual Basic window** is the program window that opens when you use VBE. As shown in the Session 11.1 Visual Overview, the Code window is the window in which you create, modify, and display specific VBA procedures. You can have as many Code windows open as you have modules in the database. In the Code window, the Object box in the upper-left of the window indicates the current object type (Form), and the Procedure box in the upper-right of the window indicates the event name (Current) for the event procedure you are viewing.

All event procedures are Sub procedures. A horizontal line visually separates each procedure in the Code window. Each Sub procedure begins with a Sub statement and ends with an End Sub statement. The Sub statement includes the scope of the procedure (private or public), the name of the procedure (for example, Form_Current, which means the Current event for the form control), and opening and closing parentheses. The **scope** of a procedure indicates where the procedure is available. If its scope is public, the procedure is available in all objects in the database. If its scope is private, the procedure is available only in the object in which it is created. Event procedures are private by default. For instance, the event procedure in the OnCurrent property in the frmVisit form is private, and other forms do not have access to this procedure code.

Notice the Option Compare statement in the Declarations section above the horizontal line. The Option Compare statement designates the technique used to compare and sort text data. The default method "Database," as shown in Figure 11–5, means letters are compared and sorted in alphabetical order, using the language settings specified for Access on your computer.

The remaining statements in the Form_Current procedure shown in Figure 11–5 use only two controls in the form: The Reason field from the tblVisit table; and lblMessage, which is a label control that displays "Provide patient with information on annual flu vaccines" or "Book patient appointment for the next annual wellness visit" when it's visible. Based on the Reason field value, the statements in the procedure do the following:

- When the Reason field value is "Influenza," set the Caption property for the lblMessage control to "Provide patient with information on annual flu vaccines" and set its font color to red.
- When the Reason field value is "Annual wellness visit," set the Caption property for the lblMessage control to "Book patient appointment for the next annual wellness visit" and set its font color to blue.
- When the Reason field has any other value, hide the lblMessage control.

The statements from the *Select Case [Reason]* statement to the *End Select* statement are an example of a control structure. A **control structure** is a set of VBA statements that work together as a unit. The Case control structure is a conditional control structure. A **conditional control structure** evaluates an expression—the value of the Reason field, in this case—and then performs one of several alternative actions based on the resulting value (or condition) of the evaluated expression. Each Case statement, such as *Case "Influenza"* and *Case Else*, designates the start of an alternative set of actions.

Statements such as *lblMessage.Caption = "Provide patient with information on annual flu vaccines"* are assignment statements. An assignment statement assigns the value of an expression—"Provide patient with information on annual flu vaccines", in this case—to a field, control, or property—the Caption property of the lblMessage control, in this case.

Because a property is associated with a control, you use the general form of *ControlName.PropertyName* to specify a property for a control. An assignment statement such as *lblMessage.ForeColor = RGB(255, 0, 0)*, for example, assigns a value to the ForeColor property of the lblMessage control. A control's ForeColor property determines the control's foreground, or font, color. The expression in this assignment statement uses a built-in VBA function named RGB. The RGB function returns an RGB (red, green, blue) color value, indicating the relative intensity of red (first value), green (second value), and blue (third value) in the color of a property for a control. Figure 11–6 displays a list of some common colors and the red, green, and blue values for the RGB function that produces those colors. Each color component value must be in the range 0 through 255. Instead of using the RGB function for the eight colors shown in Figure 11–6, you can use one of the VBA constants (vbBlack, vbBlue, vbCyan, vbGreen, vbMagenta, vbRed, vbWhite, or vbYellow). A **VBA constant** is a predefined memory location that is initialized to a value that doesn't change. For example, *lblMessage.ForeColor = vbRed* and *lblMessage.ForeColor = RGB(255, 0, 0)* would set the color of the lblMessage control to red. You must use the RGB function when you want colors that differ from the eight colors shown in Figure 11–6.

| Figure 11–6 | RGB function values for some common colors |

Color	Red Value	Green Value	Blue Value	VBA Constant
Black	0	0	0	vbBlack
Blue	0	0	255	vbBlue
Cyan	0	255	255	vbCyan
Green	0	255	0	vbGreen
Magenta	255	0	255	vbMagenta
Red	255	0	0	vbRed
White	255	255	255	vbWhite
Yellow	255	255	0	vbYellow

INSIGHT

Assigning a Color Value

A color value can be assigned to a control property using a variety of methods. A color value could be one of the following:

- A built-in VB constant such as vbRed, vbWhite, or vbBlack.
- A set of red, green, and blue values, each ranging from 0 to 255, specified in the RGB function. For instance, RGB(0,255,0) represents the color green.
- A hexadecimal value that represents color intensities of red, green, and blue. For instance, 00FF00 represents the color green. The first two characters represent red, the second two characters represent green, and the last two characters represent blue. Similar to the RGB function, these triplets represent the intensity of each color, mixed to form the resulting color.
- A ColorIndex property value, which uses a color code specific to VBA. For instance, the color green has a ColorIndex value of 4.
- A Microsoft Access color code, which is a code specific to Access. For instance, the color green has the Microsoft Access color code 32768.

With all those choices, which one should you use? The most common are the built-in VB constants, RGB function, and hexadecimal values. The RGB function and hexadecimal values are also used in web design and VB.NET programming, so you may find these techniques especially useful if you modify webpage code as well.

The Visible property determines whether or not a control is displayed. A control is displayed when its Visible property is True, and the control is hidden when its Visible property is False. The *lblMessage.Visible = True* statement, which is processed before the *Select Case [Reason]* statement, displays the lblMessage control. Because Donna doesn't want the lblMessage control to appear for reasons other than Influenza and Annual wellness visit, the *lblMessage.Visible = False* statement hides the lblMessage control when the Reason field value doesn't equal one of the two reasons.

Modifying an Event Procedure

Donna wants you to change the red color for the display of the message "Provide patient with information on annual flu vaccines" to green. This requires changing the red RGB function value of (255, 0, 0) to the green value (0, 150, 0). To make this change, you'll modify the first set of RGB function values in the event procedure. Then you'll close the Visual Basic window and save and test your modifications.

To modify, save, and test the event procedure:

▶ **1.** In the line lblMessage.Forecolor = RGB(255, 0, 0), double-click **255** to select it, and then type **0** to replace the selected value. The RGB function is now RGB(0, 0, 0).

▶ **2.** In the same line of code, double-click the next **0**, and then type **150**. The RGB function is now RGB(0, 150, 0), which is a value that will produce a medium shade of green. See Figure 11–7.

Figure 11–7   **Modified RGB values**

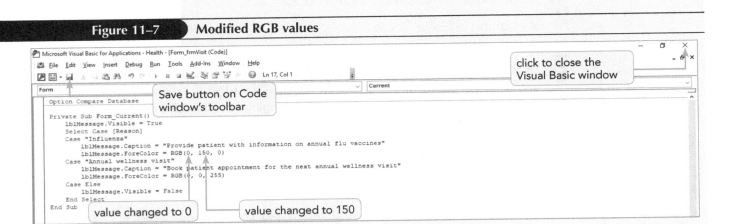

value changed to 0

value changed to 150

▶ 3. On the Code window's toolbar, click the **Save** button 🔲 to save your changes.

▶ 4. On the Visual Basic window's title bar, click the **Close** button ☒ to close it and return to the Form window in Design view.

▶ 5. Close the Property Sheet, save your form design changes, and then switch to Form view.

▶ 6. Navigate to record 18 for the VisitID 1483. The text "Provide patient with information on annual flu vaccines" is displayed in green to the right of the Walk-in? check box. Your modification to the event procedure was completed successfully. See Figure 11–8.

Figure 11–8   **Forecolor changed in frmVisit form**

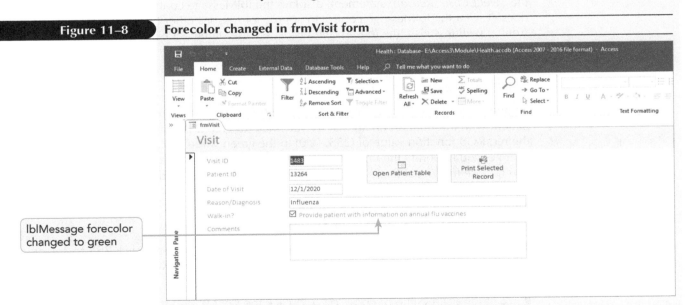

lblMessage forecolor changed to green

▶ 7. Close the frmVisit form.

Now that you have viewed and modified an event procedure, you'll create a function in a standard module.

Creating Functions in a Standard Module

Donna wants you to create a VBA procedure for the frmPatient form that will automatically convert the values entered in the Email field to lowercase. For example, if a user enters "JDoe@Example.Com" as the email address, the procedure will automatically convert it to "jdoe@example.com". Donna feels that this function will make data more uniform in the database. Additionally, she might want to add code later that ensures the entry is a valid email address, and this VBA procedure could serve as a foundation for further validation code.

Any user input in the Email field is a **string**, which is one or more characters that could include alphabetic characters, numbers, spaces, and punctuation. To accomplish the change Donna wants, you will first create a simple function, named LowAll, that accepts a string input value and converts that string to lowercase. You will create the function by typing the required statements in the Code window. Then you will create an event procedure that calls the LowAll function whenever a user enters a value in the Email field using the frmPatient form.

Whenever a user enters or changes a field value in a control or in a form and then changes the focus to another control or record, the **AfterUpdate event** is automatically triggered, which, by default, simply accepts the new or changed entry. However, you can set the AfterUpdate event property of a control to a specific event procedure in order to have something else happen when a user enters or changes the field value. In this case, you need to set the Email field's AfterUpdate event property to [Event Procedure] and then code an event procedure to call the LowAll function. Calling the LowAll function will cause the entry in the Email field to be converted to lowercase letters before storing it in the database.

You could add the LowAll function to the class module for the frmPatient form. However, adding the function to the class module for the frmPatient form would make it a private function; that is, you could not use it in other forms or database objects. Because Donna and her staff might use the LowAll function in other forms in the Health database, you'll instead place the LowAll function in a new standard module named basHealthProcedures (*bas* is a standard prefix for modules). Generally, when you enter a procedure in a standard module, it is public, and you can use it in event procedures for any object in the database.

To create a new standard module, you'll begin by opening the Code window.

To create a new standard module:

▶ **1.** On the ribbon, click the **Create** tab.

▶ **2.** In the Macros & Code group, click the **Module** button. A new Code window opens in the Visual Basic window. See Figure 11–9.

| Figure 11–9 | New standard module in the Code window |

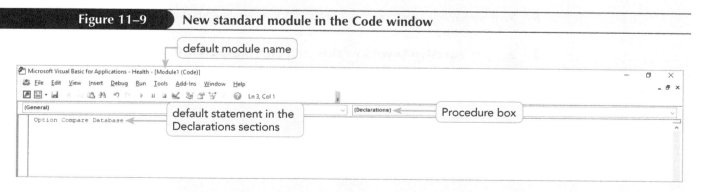

Trouble? If other windows appear in your Visual Basic window, click their Close buttons to close them.

In the Code window for the new standard module, the Procedure box indicates the Declarations section as the current procedure in the module. The Option Compare statement is automatically included in the Declarations section of a new module. The LowAll function is a simple function that does not require additional statements in the Declarations section.

Creating a Function

Each function begins with a **Function statement** and ends with an **End Function statement**. Each procedure in the Code window is separated by a horizontal line. You can view a procedure's statements by selecting the procedure name from the Procedure box.

You'll start the LowAll function with the statement *Function LowAll(FValue)*. LowAll is the function name, and FValue is used as a placeholder for the input value in the function definition. When a user enters a value for the Email field in the frmPatient form, that value will be passed to the LowAll function and substituted for FValue in the function definition. A placeholder like FValue is called a **parameter**. The value passed to the function and used in place of the parameter when the function is executed is called an **argument**. In other words, the value passed to the function is the argument, which is assigned to the parameter named FValue.

INSIGHT

VBA Naming Rules

Each VBA function name, Sub procedure name, argument name, and any other name you create must conform to the following rules:
- It must begin with a letter.
- It cannot exceed 255 characters.
- It can include letters, numbers, and the underscore character (_). You cannot use a space or any punctuation characters.
- It cannot contain keywords—such as Function, Sub, Case, and Option—that VBA uses as part of its language.
- It must be unique, that is, you can't declare the same name twice within the same procedure.

Next you'll enter the LowAll function in the Code window.

To enter the LowAll function in the Code window:

▶ **1.** If necessary, position the insertion point two lines below the Option Compare statement.

▶ **2.** Type **Function LowAll(FValue)** and then press **ENTER**. The editor displays a horizontal line that visually separates the new function from the Declarations section and adds the End Function statement. See Figure 11–10.

Figure 11-10   Function entered in the Code window

The LowAll function will consist of a single executable assignment statement that you will place between the Function and End Function statements. The assignment statement you'll enter is *LowAll = LCase(FValue)*. The value of the expression, which is LCase(FValue), will be assigned to the function, which is LowAll.

The expression in the assignment statement uses a built-in Access function named LCase. The **LCase function** accepts a single string argument as input, converts the value of the argument to lowercase letters, and then returns the converted value. The assignment statement assigns the converted value to the LowAll function. Figure 11-11 illustrates this process.

Figure 11-11   Evaluation of the assignment statement

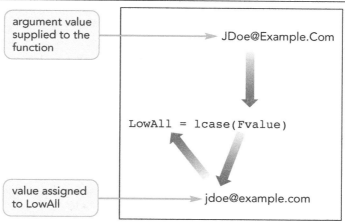

Before entering the assignment statement, you will add a comment line to explain the procedure's purpose. You can include comments anywhere in a VBA procedure to describe what the procedure does or what a statement does. You begin a comment with the word Rem (for "Remark") or with a single quotation mark ('). VBA ignores anything following the word Rem or the single quotation mark on a single line.

PROSKILLS

Written Communication: Guidelines for Writing VBA Code

It is standard to use proper case in writing VB statements, that is, the first character of each keyword is capitalized, as in the statement End If. In addition, you should use comments in a VBA procedure to explain the purpose of the procedure and to clarify any complicated programming logic used. Comments can be used to identify the name of the original creator of a procedure, the purpose of the procedure, and a history of changes made to the procedure, including who made each change and for what purpose.

Although VBA does not require statements to be indented in procedures, experienced programmers indent statements to make procedures easier to read and maintain. Pressing TAB once indents a line four spaces to the right, and pressing SHIFT+TAB or BACKSPACE once moves the insertion point four spaces to the left. Commenting and indenting your procedures will help you recall the logic of the procedures you created months or years ago and will help others understand your work.

To add a comment and statement to the LowAll function:

1. Click in the blank line between the Function and End Function statements (if necessary) to position the insertion point, and then press **TAB**.

   You will add the comment in this blank line. The single quotation mark is a comment marker, and it indicates that the text that follows is a comment and will not be executed.

2. Type **'Convert all letters of a field value to lowercase**, and then press **ENTER**.

   Notice that the editor displays the comment in green and moves the insertion point to a new indented line. After entering the comment line, you can enter the assignment statement, which is the executable statement in the function that performs the actual conversion of the argument to lowercase.

3. Type **LowAll = LCase(**

   The editor displays a Quick Info banner with a reminder that LCase accepts a single string argument. See Figure 11–12.

Figure 11–12 ▶ **LowAll function entered in the Code window**

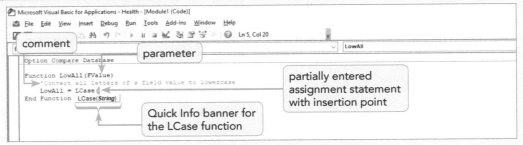

Trouble? If the Quick Info banner is not displayed, click Tools on the menu bar, click Options, click the Editor tab (if necessary), click the Auto Quick Info check box to select it, and then click the OK button.

You'll now finish typing the assignment statement.

> **4.** Type **FValue)** to finish the assignment statement. The editor scans each statement for errors when you press ENTER or move the insertion point to another line. Because the function is complete and you want the editor to scan the line you just entered for errors, you must move the insertion point to another line.

> **5.** Press **DOWN ARROW** to move the insertion point to the next line. See Figure 11–13.

Figure 11–13	Complete LowAll statement in the Code window

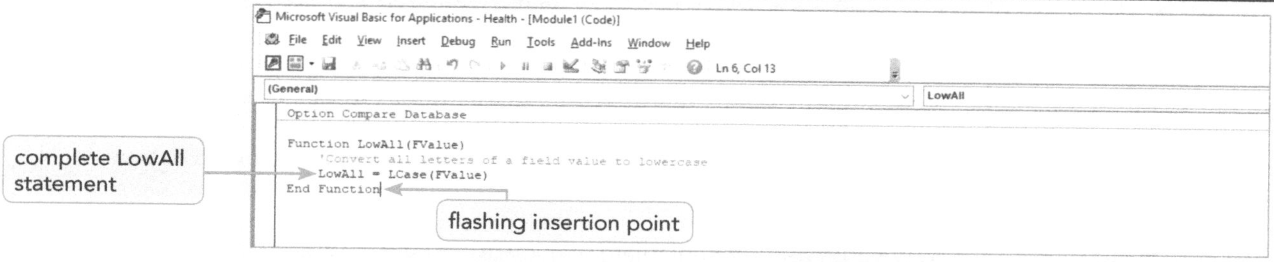

complete LowAll statement

flashing insertion point

You have finished entering the function in the module, so you'll save it before continuing with your work. When you click the Save button in the Visual Basic window, the editor saves the module and its procedures. If you are entering a long procedure, it's a good idea to save your work periodically.

To save the module:

> **1.** On the Code window toolbar, click the **Save** button 🖫 to open the Save As dialog box.

> **2.** In the Module Name box, type **basHealthProcedures**, and then press **ENTER**. The Save As dialog box closes, the editor saves the module, and the new module name appears in editor the title bar.

After creating a module, you should test its procedures.

Testing a Procedure in the Immediate Window

When you finish entering a VBA statement, the editor checks the statement to make sure its syntax is correct. Even though you may have entered all procedure statements with the correct syntax, however, the procedure may still contain logic errors. A **logic error** occurs when a procedure produces incorrect results. For example, the LowAll function would have a logic error if you typed JDoe@Example.Com and the function changed it to JDOE@EXAMPLE.COM or anything other than the correct result of jdoe@example.com. Even the simplest procedure can contain logic errors. Be sure to test each procedure thoroughly to ensure that it does exactly what you expect it to do in all situations.

When working in the Code window, you can use the **Immediate window** to test VBA procedures without changing any data in the database. The Immediate window allows you to run individual lines of VBA code for **debugging**, or testing. In the Immediate window, you can enter different values to test the procedure you just entered. To test a procedure, you type the *Print* keyword or a question mark (?), followed by the procedure name, and then the value you want to test in parentheses. For example, to test the LowAll function in the Immediate window using the test word JDoe@Example.Com, you type *?LowAll("JDoe@Example.Com")* and then press ENTER. The editor executes the function and displays the value returned by the function (you expect it to return jdoe@example.com). Note that you must enclose a string of characters within quotation marks in the test statement.

REFERENCE

Testing a Procedure in the Immediate Window

- In the Code window, click View on the menu bar, and then click Immediate Window to open the Immediate window.
- Type a question mark (?), the procedure name, and the procedure's arguments in parentheses. If an argument contains a string of characters, enclose the argument in quotation marks.
- Press ENTER, and verify that the result displayed is the expected output.

Now you'll use the Immediate window to test the LowAll function.

To test the LowAll function in the Immediate window:

1. Click **View** on the menu bar, and then click **Immediate Window**. The editor opens the Immediate window below the Code window and places the insertion point inside the window.

2. Type **?LowAll("JDoe@Example.Com")** and then press **ENTER**. The editor executes the function and displays the function result, jdoe@example.com, on the next line. See Figure 11–14.

Figure 11–14 **LowAll function executed in the Immediate window**

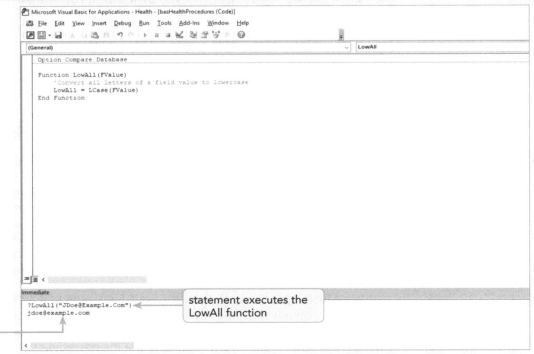

result of executing the function

statement executes the LowAll function

Trouble? If a dialog box displays an error message, click the OK button in the dialog box, correct the error in the Immediate window, and then press ENTER. If the function does not produce the correct output (jdoe@example.com), compare your code to Figure 11-13, correct the LowAll function statements in the Code window as necessary, save your changes, click a blank line in the Immediate window, and then repeat Step 2.

To test the LowAll function further, you could enter several other test values, retyping the entire statement each time. Instead, you'll select the current test value, type another value, and then press ENTER.

▶ **3.** Delete the email address **JDoe@Example.Com** in the first line of the Immediate window.

▶ **4.** Type **JDOE@EXAMPLE.COM**, move the insertion point to the end of the line, and then press **ENTER**. The editor executes the function and displays the function result, jdoe@example.com, on a new line.

▶ **5.** On the Immediate window's title bar, click the **Close** button ☒.

▶ **6.** On the Visual Basic window's title bar, click the **Close** button ☒.

▶ **7.** If you are not continuing on to the next session, close the Health database.

INSIGHT

Converting a Macro to Visual Basic

Creating a macro can be a bit more user-friendly than learning VBA code. Some people may find it easier to create a macro and then convert it to VBA. They may find that they have a database with several macros but have learned some VBA and would like to convert the macros to VBA so they can copy them and use them in other databases, or keep as much code as possible in a standard module.

To convert a macro to VBA, you open the macro you'd like to convert, then use the Convert Macros to Visual Basic button in the Tools group on the Macro Tools Design tab.

Your initial test of the LowAll function in the standard module is successful. In the next session, you'll modify the frmPatient form to execute the LowAll function for the Email field in that form.

REVIEW

Session 11.1 Quick Check

1. Why is Visual Basic for Applications called an event-driven, object-oriented language?

2. What is an event procedure?

3. What are the differences between a user-defined function and a Sub procedure?

4. Describe the two different types of modules.

5. The _____ of a procedure is either private or public.

6. What is the Immediate window used for?

Session 11.2 Visual Overview:

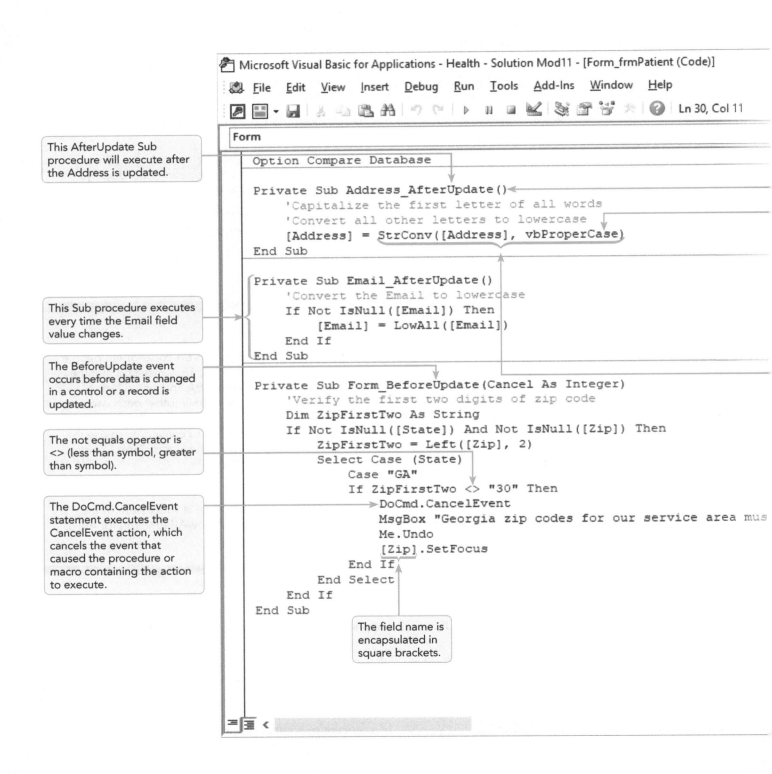

Microsoft Visual Basic for Applications - Health - Solution Mod11 - [Form_frmPatient (Code)]

File   Edit   View   Insert   Debug   Run   Tools   Add-Ins   Window   Help

Ln 30, Col 11

Form

> This AfterUpdate Sub procedure will execute after the Address is updated.

```
Option Compare Database

Private Sub Address_AfterUpdate()
    'Capitalize the first letter of all words
    'Convert all other letters to lowercase
    [Address] = StrConv([Address], vbProperCase)
End Sub

Private Sub Email_AfterUpdate()
    'Convert the Email to lowercase
    If Not IsNull([Email]) Then
        [Email] = LowAll([Email])
    End If
End Sub

Private Sub Form_BeforeUpdate(Cancel As Integer)
    'Verify the first two digits of zip code
    Dim ZipFirstTwo As String
    If Not IsNull([State]) And Not IsNull([Zip]) Then
        ZipFirstTwo = Left([Zip], 2)
        Select Case (State)
            Case "GA"
            If ZipFirstTwo <> "30" Then
                DoCmd.CancelEvent
                MsgBox "Georgia zip codes for our service area mus
                Me.Undo
                [Zip].SetFocus
            End If
        End Select
    End If
End Sub
```

> This Sub procedure executes every time the Email field value changes.

> The BeforeUpdate event occurs before data is changed in a control or a record is updated.

> The not equals operator is <> (less than symbol, greater than symbol).

> The DoCmd.CancelEvent statement executes the CancelEvent action, which cancels the event that caused the procedure or macro containing the action to execute.

> The field name is encapsulated in square brackets.

Example of an Event Procedure

BeforeUpdate

Whenever a user enters or changes a field value in a control or in a form and changes the focus to another control or record, Access automatically triggers the AfterUpdate event.

The vbProperCase constant is a VBA constant that specifies the conversion of the first letter in every word in a string to uppercase letters and the conversion of all other letters to lowercase letters.

The StrConv function converts the letters in a string to a form indicated in the second argument in the function.

30"

Understanding How an Event Procedure Processes Commands

As stated in the previous session, when you add a procedure to a form or report, a class module for that form or report is created automatically, and the procedure is added to that class module. When you create an event procedure, the procedure runs only when a specific event occurs.

Now that you have created the LowAll function as a public procedure in the standard module named basHealthProcedures, you can create an event procedure for the frmPatient form to call the LowAll function for the Email field's AfterUpdate event. Whenever a user enters or changes an Email field value, the AfterUpdate event occurs, so by calling the LowAll function for the Email field's AfterUpdate event, you'll ensure that your event procedure will run whenever this field has a new or changed value.

What exactly happens when a procedure is called? There is an interaction between the calling statement and the function statements. Figure 11–15 shows the process for the LowAll procedure.

Figure 11–15 Process of executing a function

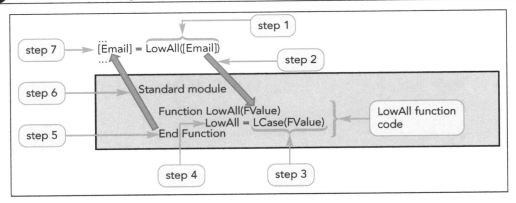

The steps in Figure 11–15 are numbered in the order in which they occur as the statement and the function are processed. These steps are as follows:

- **Step 1:** The call to the function LowAll passes the value of the argument [Email] to the function. This is the value of the Email field that is entered or changed by the user.
- **Step 2:** The function LowAll begins, and the parameter FValue receives the value of [Email].
- **Step 3:** FValue is changed to lowercase.
- **Step 4:** The result of the function is assigned to the name of the function (LowAll). This is how the result will be returned from the function when the function completes.
- **Step 5:** The function LowAll ends.
- **Step 6:** The value of LowAll is returned to the point of the call to the function.
- **Step 7:** The value of [Email] is set equal to the returned value of LowAll.

Although it might look complicated, the general function process is simple. The statement contains a **function call**, which is a statement that contains the name of the function plus any parameters required by the function. When the statement is executed, the function call is performed, the function is executed, a single value is returned to the original statement, and the statement's execution is completed. You should study the steps in Figure 11–15 and trace their sequence until you understand the complete process.

Once you understand the steps in which the event procedure will process, you should consider how to construct the event procedure in the Visual Basic (VB) Editor.

All event procedures are Sub procedures. The VB editor automatically adds the Sub and End Sub statements to an event procedure. All you need to do is place the statements between the Sub and End Sub statements. Figure 11–16 shows the completed event procedure in the Code window.

Figure 11–16   **AfterUpdate event procedure for the Email field**

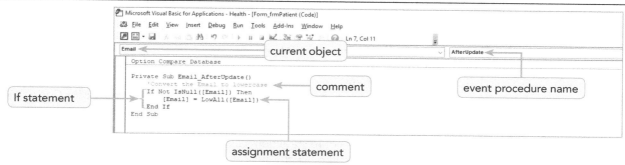

TIP

If the name of a control contains spaces or special characters, the underscores are substituted for them in the event procedure name.

In reviewing the completed event procedure in Figure 11–16, notice the following. Each event procedure is named in a standard way, using the name of the control, an underscore (_), and the event name. No parameters are passed to an event procedure, so nothing is placed in the parentheses following the name of the Sub procedure.

A user might delete an existing Email field value so that it contains no value, or becomes null. In this case, calling the function accomplishes nothing. The procedure is designed to call the LowAll function only when a user changes the Email field to a value that is not null. The If statement screens out the null values. In its simplest form, an **If statement** executes one of two groups of statements based on a condition, similar to common English usage. For example, consider the English statements, "If the door is unlocked, I'll open it and walk through it. Otherwise, I'll knock on the door and wait until someone unlocks it." In these sentences, the two groups of statements come before and after the "otherwise," depending on the condition, "if the door is unlocked." The first group of statements consists of the clause "I'll open it and walk through it." This clause is called the **true-statement group** because it's what happens if the condition ("the door is unlocked") is true. The second group of statements contains "I'll knock on the door and wait until someone unlocks it." This clause is called the **false-statement group** because it is what happens if the condition is false. VBA uses the keyword *If* to precede the condition. The keyword *Then* precedes the true-statement group, and the keyword *Else* precedes the false-statement group. The general syntax of a VBA If statement is:

```
If condition Then
    true-statement group
[Else
    false-statement group]
End If
```

The true-statement group executes when the condition is true, and the false-statement group when the condition is false. In this statement's syntax, the bracketed portions are optional. Therefore, you must omit the *Else* and its related false-statement group when you want a group of statements to execute only when the condition is true.

TIP

Notice that the Email field name is enclosed in brackets, even though brackets are optional for field names and control names that do not contain spaces and special characters.

In Figure 11–16, the If statement uses the VBA **IsNull function**, which returns a value of True when the Email field value is null and False when it is not null. The *Not* in the If statement is the same logical operator you've used previously to negate an expression. So, the statement *[Email] = LowAll([Email])* executes only when the Email field value is not null.

Adding an Event Procedure

To add an event procedure to a control in a form or report, you need to open the form or report in Design view. In this case, you need to add an event procedure to the frmPatient form, specifically to the Email field's AfterUpdate event property.

REFERENCE

Adding an Event Procedure to a Form or Report

- Open the form or report in Design view, select the control whose event property you want to set, open the Property Sheet for the control, and then click the Event tab in the Property Sheet.
- Click the appropriate event property box, click its Build button, click Code Builder in the Choose Builder dialog box, and then click the OK button to open the Code window in the VB editor.
- Enter the Sub procedure statements in the Code window.
- Compile the procedure, fix any statement errors, and then save the event procedure.

Next you'll add the event procedure to the frmPatient form.

To add the event procedure to the frmPatient form:

▶ **1.** If you took a break after the previous session, make sure that the Health database is open.

▶ **2.** Open the Navigation Pane (if necessary), open the **frmPatient** form in Design view, and then close the Navigation Pane.

▶ **3.** Right-click the **Email** field value box to select it and to display the shortcut menu, click **Properties** to open the Property Sheet, and then, if necessary, click the **Event** tab in the Property Sheet. You need to set the AfterUpdate property for the Email field value box.

Trouble? If you do not see any events on the Event tab, you might have clicked the Email label control instead of the field value box. Right-click the Email field value box.

▶ **4.** Click the **After Update** box, click its **Build** button ⬚ to open the Choose Builder dialog box, click **Code Builder**, and then click **OK**. The Code window opens in the Visual Basic window. See Figure 11–17.

Figure 11–17　Starting a new event procedure in the Code window

▶ **5.** Enter the statements shown in Figure 11–18, using TAB to indent the lines as shown in the figure (if necessary), pressing ENTER at the end of each line, and pressing BACKSPACE to move one tab stop to the left.

▶ **6.** Compare your screen with Figure 11–18, and make any necessary corrections by selecting the errors and typing the corrections.

| Figure 11–18 | Completed event procedure |

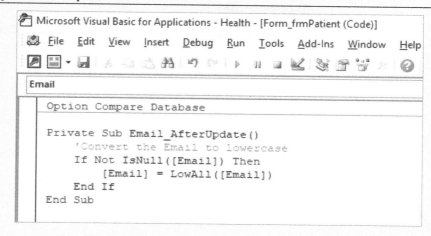

Before saving the event procedure, you'll compile the module.

Compiling Modules

The VBA programming language is not the computer's native language. Although you can learn VBA and become fluent in it, computers cannot understand or learn VBA. For a computer to understand the statements in your VBA modules, the statements must be translated into a form that the computer processor can use. The process of translating modules from VBA to a form your computer processor understands is called **compilation**; you say that you **compile** the module when you translate it.

You can compile a procedure at any time as you enter it by clicking the Compile command on the Debug menu in the Visual Basic window. The procedure and all other procedures in all modules in the database are then compiled. Also, when you run a procedure for the first time, the procedure is compiled automatically, and a dialog box will open if any syntax errors exist in the procedure, in which case the computer cannot translate the procedure statements. If no errors are detected, the procedure translates.

INSIGHT

The Importance of Compiling Procedures

It's best to compile and save your modules after you've made changes to them, to make sure they don't contain syntax errors. If you don't compile a procedure when you first create it or after you've changed it, the procedure will be compiled when the first user opens the form or report that uses the procedure. The user could encounter a syntax error and be unable to use the form or report. You don't want users to experience these types of problems, so you should compile and fully test all procedures as you create them.

You'll now compile the procedures in the Health database and save the class module for the frmPatient form.

To compile the procedures in the Health database and save the class module:

▶ **1.** Click **Debug** on the menu bar, and then click **Compile Health**. The modules in the database are compiled. Because you have no syntax errors, the VBA statements translate.

   Trouble? If any error messages appear, correct the errors in the Code window and repeat Step 1.

▶ **2.** Save your module changes, close the Visual Basic window, and then close the Property Sheet.

You have created the function and the event procedure and have set the event property. Next, you'll test the event procedure in the frmPatient form to make sure it works correctly.

Testing an Event Procedure

You need to display the frmPatient form in Form view to test the Email field's event procedure by entering a few different test Email field values in the first record of the form. Moving the focus to another control in the form or to another record triggers the AfterUpdate event for the Email field and executes the attached event procedure. Because the LowAll function is attached only to the frmPatient form, the automatic conversion to lowercase of Email field values is not in effect when you enter them in the tblPatient table or in any other object in the Health database.

To test the event procedure:

▶ **1.** Switch to Form view, and navigate to record 2, Patient ID 13251.

▶ **2.** Select the **Email** field value (g.davis21@example.com), type **G.DAVIS21@ EXAMPLE.COM** in the Email text box, and click the Zip text box control to enter the data. Access executes the AfterUpdate event procedure for the Email field and changes the Email field value to "g.davis21@example.com." See Figure 11–19.

Figure 11–19 **frmPatient form after executing the event procedure**

lowercase Email Address field value

▶ **3.** Repeat Step 2 again, this time entering **G.Davis21@Example.com** in the Email box. The correct value of g.davis21@example.com is displayed in the Email box.

Donna is happy with the functionality you've added to the Email box. Next she wants you to create a more complex function for the Zip field in the frmPatient form.

Adding a Second Procedure to a Class Module

Donna has found her staff makes frequent errors when entering Georgia zip codes, whose first two digits are always 30 in the primary area that Lakewood Community Health Services serves. She asks you to create a procedure that will verify that Georgia zip codes are in the correct range (beginning with 30) when her staff updates the Zip field in the frmPatient form. One option is to use a form validation rule, but Donna would like to be able to add complexity later, to validate other zip codes because patients from other areas in Georgia and other states may visit the clinic. Also, Donna would like to be able to use this VBA code in other databases. If the validation property is used in the tblPatient table instead of using VBA, then this validation rule would have to be re-created in another database. Instead, by creating an event procedure, Donna will be able to copy the VBA code and paste it into another VBA window in another database.

You'll build a simple procedure that can be modified later to add more complexity. For this procedure, you will use an event procedure attached to the BeforeUpdate event for the frmPatient form. The BeforeUpdate event occurs before changed data in a control or a record is updated. You'll use the form's BeforeUpdate event for this new procedure because you want to find data-entry errors for Georgia zip codes and alert users to the errors before the database is updated.

Designing the Field Validation Procedure

Figure 11–20 shows the procedure that you will create to verify Georgia zip codes for the area that the Lakewood Community Health Services primarily serves. You've already seen several of the statements in this procedure in your work with the LowAll function and with the form's Current event.

Figure 11–20	Zip validation procedure

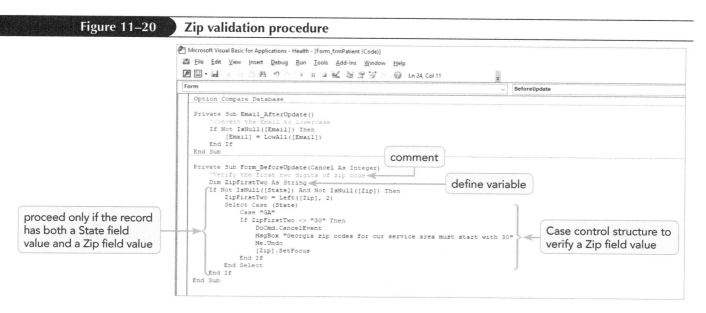

The Sub and End Sub statements begin and end the Sub procedure. As specified in the Sub statement, the Sub procedure executes when the form's BeforeUpdate event occurs. Within parentheses in the Sub statement, *Cancel As Integer* defines Cancel as a parameter with the Integer data type. VBA has data types that are different from the Access data types you've used to define table fields, but each Access data type is equivalent to one of the VBA data types. For example, the Access Number data type with an Integer field size is the same as the VBA Integer data type, and the Access Short Text data type is the same as the VBA String data type. Figure 11–21 shows the primary VBA data types.

Figure 11–21	Primary VBA data types

Data Type	Stores
Boolean	True/False values
Byte	Integer values from 0 to 255
Currency	Currency values from –922,337,203,685,477.5808 to 922,337,203,685,477.5807
Date	Date and time values from 1 January 100 to 31 December 9999
Decimal	Non-integer values with 0 to 28 decimal places
Double	Non-integer values from $-1.79769313486231*10^{308}$ to $-4.94065645841247*11^{-324}$ for negative values, from $4.94065645841247*11^{-324}$ to $1.79769313486232*10^{308}$ for positive values, and 0
Integer	Integer values from –32,768 to 32,767
Long	Integer values from –2,147,483,648 to 2,147,483,647
Object	Any object reference
Single	Non-integer values from $-3.402823*10^{38}$ to $-1.401298*11^{-45}$ for negative values, from $1.401298*11^{-45}$ to $3.402823*10^{38}$ for positive values, and 0
String	Text values up to 2 billion characters in length
Variant	Any numeric or string data type

When an event occurs, the default behavior for the event is performed. For some events, such as the BeforeUpdate event, the event procedure or macro executes before performing the default behavior. Thus, if something is wrong and the default behavior should not occur, you can cancel the default behavior in the event procedure or macro. For this reason, the Cancel parameter is automatically included for the BeforeUpdate event.

The second procedure statement, which starts with a single quotation mark, is a comment. The third statement, *Dim ZipFirstTwo As String*, declares the String variable named ZipFirstTwo that the Sub procedure uses. A **variable** is a named location in computer memory that can contain a value. If you use a variable in a module, you must explicitly declare it in the Declarations section or in the procedure where the variable is used. You use the **Dim statement** to declare variables and their associated data types in a procedure. The Sub procedure will assign the first two digits of a zip code (the Zip field) to the ZipFirstTwo variable and then use the variable when verifying that a Georgia zip code the clinic primarily serves begins in the correct range. Because the zip code could contain a value that begins with zero (0), the ZipFirstTwo variable uses the String data type instead of a numeric data type. The first two characters of any zip code for the Georgia area primarily served by the clinic are represented as the string value "30".

The procedure should not attempt to verify records that contain null field values for the State field and the Zip field. To screen out these conditions, the procedure uses the fourth procedure statement, *If Not IsNull([State]) And Not IsNull([Zip]) Then*, which pairs with the last *End If* statement. The *If* statement determines whether both the State and Zip fields are nonnull. If both conditions are true (both fields contain values), then the next statement in the procedure executes. If either condition is false, then the paired End If statement executes, and the following End Sub statement ends the procedure without the execution of any other statement.

The fifth procedure statement, *ZipFirstTwo = Left([Zip], 2)*, uses a built-in VBA function, the Left function, to assign the first two characters of the Zip field value to the ZipFirstTwo variable. The Left function returns a string containing a specified number of characters from the left side of a specified string. In this case, the Left function returns the leftmost two characters of the Zip field value.

You encountered the Case control structure previously in the frmVisit form's Current event procedure. For the BeforeUpdate event procedure, the *Select Case [State]* statement evaluates the State field value. For a State field value equal to GA (indicating the record should have a GA zip code), the next If statement is executed. For all other State field values, nothing further in the procedure is executed; the default behavior is performed, and control returns back to the form for further processing. The procedure uses the Case control structure because although Donna wants the procedure to verify the first two characters of only Georgia zip codes for now, she might want to expand the procedure in the future to verify the first two digits of zip codes for other areas of Georgia and other states as Lakewood Community Health Services expands its services.

Because valid Georgia zip codes in the area the clinic serves begin with "30", invalid values for the Zip field will not be equal to "30". The not equals operator in VBA is <> (less than symbol followed by the greater than symbol). The next VBA statement, *If ZipFirstTwo <> "30" Then*, is true only for invalid Georgia zip codes. When the If statement is true, the next four statements are executed. When the If statement is false, nothing further in the procedure is executed, the default behavior performs, and control returns back to the form for further processing.

The first of the four VBA statements that executes for invalid Georgia zip codes is the DoCmd statement. The DoCmd statement executes an action in a procedure. The *DoCmd.CancelEvent* statement executes the CancelEvent action. The CancelEvent action cancels the event that caused the procedure or macro containing the action to execute. In this case, the BeforeUpdate event cancels and does not update the database with the changes to the current record. In addition, subsequent events—those that would have occurred if the BeforeUpdate event had been executed—are canceled. For example, in addition to the form's BeforeUpdate event being triggered when you move to a different record, the following events are also triggered when you move to a different record, in the order listed: BeforeUpdate event for the form, AfterUpdate event for the form, Exit event for the control with the focus, LostFocus event for the control with the focus, RecordExit event for the form, and Current event for the form. When the CancelEvent action is executed, all these events are canceled, and the focus remains with the record being edited.

TIP

The macro MessageBox action is the same as the VBA MsgBox statement.

The second of the four VBA statements that are executed for invalid Georgia zip codes is the MsgBox statement. The *MsgBox "Georgia zip codes for our service area must start with 30"* statement displays its message in a message box that remains on the screen until the user clicks the OK button. The message box appears on top of the frmPatient form so the user can view the changed field values in the current record.

For invalid Georgia zip codes, after the user clicks the OK button in the message box, the *Me.Undo* statement is executed. The Me keyword refers to the current object—in this case, the frmPatient form. Undo is a method that clears all changes made to the current record in the frmPatient form, so that the field values in the record return to the way they were before the user made the current changes. A **method** is an action that operates on specific objects or controls.

Finally, for invalid Georgia zip codes, the *[Zip].SetFocus* statement is executed. SetFocus is a method that moves the focus to the specified object or control. In this case, the focus is moved to the Zip field in the current record in the frmPatient form.

Adding a Field Value Event Procedure

You can now add an event procedure for the frmPatient form's BeforeUpdate event property that will execute whenever field values in a record are entered or updated.

To add the event procedure for the frmPatient form's BeforeUpdate event property:

▶ **1.** Switch to Design view, open the **Property Sheet** for the frmPatient form, and then if necessary, click the **Event** tab in the Property Sheet.

▶ **2.** Click the **Before Update** box, click the **Before Update** arrow, click [**Event Procedure**], and then click the **Build** button ⬚. The Code window, which contains new Private Sub and End Sub statements, opens in the Visual Basic window. Horizontal lines separate the Option Compare statement from the new procedure and from the AfterUpdate event procedure you entered earlier.

> When entering "30", be sure to enter the number zero, not the letter O.

▶ **3.** Press **TAB**, and then type the Sub procedure statements exactly as shown in Figure 11–22. Press **ENTER** after you enter each statement, press **TAB** to indent lines as necessary, and press **BACKSPACE** to move the insertion point one tab stop to the left. When you are finished, your screen should look like Figure 11–22.

Figure 11–22	Event procedure for the frmOwner form's BeforeUpdate event

existing event procedure for the Email controls's AfterUpdate event property

new event procedure for the frmOwner form

type these 14 statements

▶ **4.** On the menu bar, click **Debug**, and then click **Compile Health** to compile all the modules in the Health database.

> **Trouble?** If a message box appears identifying an error, click the OK button in the message box, compare your Code window with the one shown in Figure 11–22, make any necessary corrections, and then repeat Step 4 to scan the statements for errors again and to compile the module.

▶ **5.** Save your class module changes.

▶ **6.** Close the Visual Basic window to return to the Form window, and then close the Property Sheet.

You can now test the BeforeUpdate event procedure. To do so, you'll switch to Form view and enter valid and invalid Zip field values in the frmPatient form.

To test the form's BeforeUpdate event procedure:

1. Switch to Form view with the form displaying record 1. The first two digits of the Zip field value, 30, represent a valid Georgia zip code for the service area.

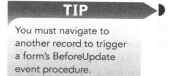

TIP

You must navigate to another record to trigger a form's BeforeUpdate event procedure.

2. Select **30303** in the Zip box, type **12345**, press **TAB** to move to the Email box, and then click the **Next record** button ► to move to the next record. The BeforeUpdate event procedure for the frmPatient form executes and determines that the Georgia zip code's first two digits are incorrect and displays the message box you included in the procedure. See Figure 11–23.

Figure 11–23   **After the frmPatient form's BeforeUpdate event procedure detects an error**

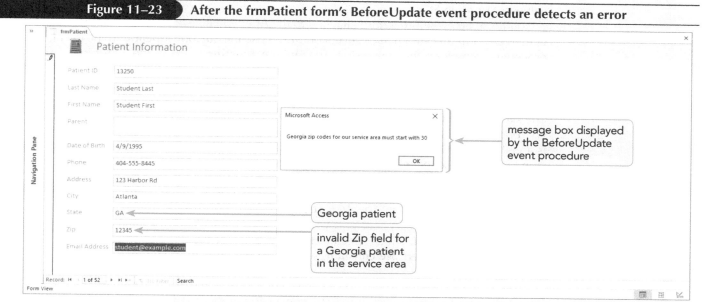

While the message box is displayed, the updated Zip field value of 12345 remains on screen for you to review.

3. Click **OK**. The message box closes, the Undo method changes the Zip field value to 30303 (its original value), and the SetFocus method moves the focus to the Zip box.

4. With the Zip field value set to **30303**, navigate to the next record. The form's BeforeUpdate event procedure verifies that the zip code is a valid value for a Georgia patient in the service area, and the focus moves to the Zip box for the next record.

5. Navigate back to record 1, change the State field value to **SC**, change the Zip field value to **12345**, and then click the **Next record** button ► to move to the next record. The form's BeforeUpdate event procedure checks zip codes only when the State field value is "GA" (Georgia), so even though the zip code 12345 is not valid for South Carolina (abbreviated SC), the focus moves to the Zip box in the next record anyway.

Next, you'll change the first record's State field value to GA and the Zip field value to 30303, which are the original values for the record.

6. Navigate to the first record, change the State field value to **GA**, and then change the Zip field value to **30303**.

Donna is impressed with the zip code validation you've added to the frmPatient form. She has one additional procedure she wants you to create for the form.

Adding an Event Procedure to Change the Case of a Field Value

Donna wants to make it quicker for users to enter an address when using the frmPatient form, so she asks you to create a procedure that will automatically convert the case of letters entered in the Address field. This procedure will capitalize the first letter of each word in the field and change all other letters to lowercase. For example, if a user enters "12 mAin sT" as the Address field value, the event procedure will correct the field value to "12 Main St".

You'll use an event procedure attached to the AfterUpdate event for the Address field to perform this automatic conversion. You'll use the StrConv function in the event procedure to perform the conversion. The **StrConv function** converts the letters in a string to all uppercase letters or to all lowercase letters, or converts the first letter of every word in the string to uppercase letters and all other letters to lowercase letters, which is a pattern known as proper case. The StrConv function ignores numbers. The statement you'll use in the event procedure is *[Address] = StrConv([Address], vbProperCase)*. The StrConv function's second argument, the **vbProperCase constant**, is a VBA constant that specifies the conversion of the first letter in every word in a string to uppercase letters and the conversion of all other letters to lowercase letters. Recall that the LowAll function you created earlier in this tutorial used the statement *LowAll = LCase(FValue)* to convert every character in a string to lowercase. You could also have used the statement *LowAll = StrConv(FValue, vbLowerCase)* to accomplish the same result. Other VBA constants you can use with the StrConv function are the **vbUpperCase constant**, which specifies the conversion of the string to all uppercase letters, and the **vbLowerCase constant**, which specifies the conversion of the string to all lowercase letters.

Next, you'll create the AfterUpdate event procedure for the Address field in the frmPatient form to perform the automatic conversion of entered and updated Address field values.

To add the event procedure for the Address field's AfterUpdate event:

▶ **1.** Switch to Design view.

▶ **2.** Right-click the **Address** field value box to display the shortcut menu, and then click **Properties** to open the Property Sheet for the control.

▶ **3.** If necessary, click the **Event** tab in the Property Sheet.

▶ **4.** Click the **After Update** box, click the **After Update** arrow, click **[Event Procedure]**, and then click the **Build** button ⌐…⌐. The Code window, which contains new Private Sub and End Sub statements, opens in the Visual Basic window. The Code window also contains two other event procedures defined in the form's class module: one event procedure for the form's BeforeUpdate event, and another event procedure for the Email field's AfterUpdate event.

▶ **5.** Press **TAB**, and then type the Sub procedure statements exactly as shown in Figure 11–24.

| Figure 11–24 | Event procedure for the Address control's AfterUpdate event |

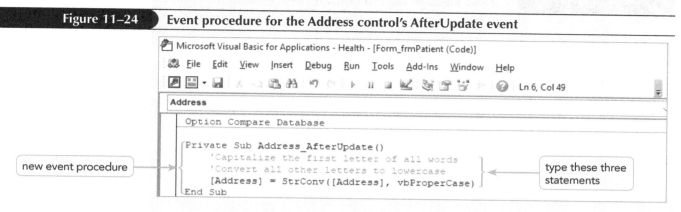

6. Click **Debug** on the menu bar, click **Compile Health**, save your class module changes, close the Visual Basic window, and then close the Property Sheet.

You can now test the event procedure. To do so, you'll view the frmPatient form in Form view and test the Address field's event procedure by entering different Address field values.

To test the new event procedure for the Address field:

1. Switch to Form view. You'll test the new event procedure by entering Address field values in record 1.

2. Select the current value in Address box, type **123 harbor rd** and then press **ENTER**. The AfterUpdate event procedure for the Address field executes and changes the Address field value to "123 Harbor Rd".

3. Repeat Step 2 two more times, entering **123 harBOR rD** (correctly changed to "12 Harbor Rd"), and then entering **123 HARBOR RD** (correctly changed to "123 Harbor Rd").

4. Close the form.

Hiding a Control and Changing a Control's Color

Donna wants you to add a message to the frmVisitsAndInvoices form that will remind her staff when a visit record should be considered for archiving from the tblVisit table. Specifically, when the visit date is prior to the year 2021, Donna wants the VisitDate field value displayed in red; all other VisitDate field values should be displayed in black. She also wants to display a message to the right of the VisitDate box in red only when the visit is a candidate for archiving. The red font will help to draw attention to these visit records. Figure 11–25 shows a preview of the formatting she's requesting.

Figure 11–25   **Archive message and red VisitDate field value in frmVisitsAndInvoices form**

In the frmVisitsAndInvoices form, you will add a label to the right of the VisitDate field value box that will display the text "Archive if paid?" in red. Because Donna wants the text to appear only when the VisitDate field has a value earlier than 1/1/2021, you will change the label's Visible property during execution. You will also change the foreground color of the value in the VisitDate field value box to red when the VisitDate field value is earlier than 1/1/2021 and to black for all other dates.

Because the change to the Visible property takes place during execution, you will add code to the Current event procedure in the frmVisitsAndInvoices form. To set a property in a VBA statement, you enter the object name followed by a period and the property name. For example, if the label name for the message is lblArchiveMsg, then the statement *lblArchiveMsg.Visible = False* hides the label on the form.

PROSKILLS

Problem Solving: Using Sample Code from Other Sources

Creating your first few VBA procedures from scratch can be a daunting task. To get started, you should take advantage of the available resources that discuss various ways of designing and programming commonly encountered situations. These resources include the sample databases available from Microsoft, Access VBA books, periodicals, websites that provide sample code, and Access Help. These resources contain sample procedures and code segments, often with commentary about what the procedures and statements accomplish and why. However, when you create a procedure, you are responsible for knowing what it does, how it does it, when to use it, how to enhance it in the future, and how to fix it when problems occur. If you simply copy statements from another source without thoroughly understanding them, you won't be able to enhance or fix the procedure in the future. In addition, you might overlook better ways to accomplish the same thing—better because the procedure would run faster or would be easier to enhance. In some cases, the samples you find might be flawed, so that they won't work properly for you. The time you spend researching and completely understanding sample code will pay dividends in your learning experience to create VBA procedures.

First, you'll add a label to the frmVisitsAndInvoices form that will display a message in red for each value that has a VisitDate field value earlier than 1/1/2021. For all other dates, the label will be hidden.

To add the label to the frmVisitsAndInvoices form:

▶ **1.** Open the Navigation Pane, open the **frmVisitsAndInvoices** form in Design view, and then close the Navigation Pane.

▶ **2.** On the Form Design Tools Design tab, in the Controls group, click the **Label** tool $\boxed{Aa}$.

▶ **3.** In the Detail section, position the plus symbol of the Label tool pointer two grid dots to the right of the VisitDate field value box, and then click the mouse button.

▶ **4.** Type **Archive if paid?** and then press **ENTER**. The new label control appears in the form and displays the Error Checking Options button. See Figure 11–26.

Figure 11–26	Label control added to the form

Trouble? If you do not see the Error Checking Options button, error checking is disabled in Access. Click the File tab, click Options in the navigation bar, click Object Designers, scroll down the page, click the Enable error checking check box to add a checkmark to it, click the OK button, click a blank area in the form, and then click the "Archive if paid?" label control. Continue with Step 5.

▶ **5.** Position the pointer on the **Error Checking Options** button $\boxed{!}$. The message "This is a new label and is not associated with a control" appears. Because the new label should not be associated with a control, you'll choose to ignore this error.

▶ **6.** Click the **Error Checking Options** arrow $\boxed{!}$, and then click **Ignore Error**. The Error Checking Options button disappears.

▶ **7.** Press and hold **SHIFT**, click the **VisitDate** field value box to select this control and its label control, release **SHIFT**, right-click one of the selected controls, point to **Align**, and then click **Top** to top-align the selected controls.

Trouble? If the Error Checking Options button appears, click the Error Checking Options button arrow, and then click Dismiss Error.

You'll now set the label control's Name and ForeColor properties, and you'll add the Current event procedure to the frmVisitsAndInvoices form.

To set the label's properties and add the Current event procedure to the form:

▶ 1. Deselect all controls, right-click the **Archive if paid?** label control to display the shortcut menu, and then click **Properties** to open the Property Sheet.

▶ 2. Click the **All** tab (if necessary), and then set the Name property for the Archive if paid? label control to **lblArchiveMsg**.

You can now set the ForeColor property for the label so that the message is displayed in red.

▶ 3. Click the **Fore Color** box, and then click its **Build** button ⋯ to display the color gallery.

▶ 4. Click the **Red** color (row 7, column 2 in the Standard Colors palette), and then press **ENTER**. The ForeColor property value is set to the code for red (#ED1C24), and in the form it now appears in red.

Next you will enter the event procedure for the form's Current event. This event procedure will execute whenever the frmVisitsAndInvoices form is opened or the focus moves from one record to another.

▶ 5. Select the form, scroll down the Property Sheet to the On Current box, click the **On Current** box, click the **On Current** arrow, click [**Event Procedure**], and then click the **Build** button ⋯ to open the Code window in the Visual Basic window, displaying the Sub and End Sub statements.

▶ 6. Press **TAB**, and then type the Sub procedure statements exactly as shown in Figure 11-27.

Figure 11-27 Current event procedure for the frmVisitsAndInvoices form

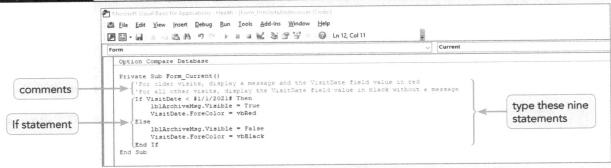

The form's Current procedure uses an If statement to determine whether the current value of the VisitDate field is less than 1/1/2021. If the current value of the VisitDate field is less than 1/1/2021, the procedure sets the lblArchiveMsg control's Visible property to True (which means the "Archive if paid?" message will appear in the frmVisitsAndInvoices form), and it sets the VisitDate control's ForeColor property to vbRed (red). If the current value of the VisitDate field is greater than or equal to 1/1/2021, the procedure sets the lblArchiveMsg control's Visible property to False, hiding the message in the form, and sets the VisitDate control's ForeColor property to vbBlack.

▶ 7. Click **Debug** on the menu bar, and then click **Compile Health** to compile all the modules in the Health database.

▶ 8. Save your class module changes, close the Visual Basic window, and then close the Property Sheet.

You'll now test the frmVisitsAndInvoices form's Current event procedure.

To test the Current event procedure for the frmVisitsAndInvoices form:

▶ **1.** Switch to Form view. The first record for VisitID 1450 is displayed in the form with the Date of Visit date prior to 1/1/2021. The "Archive if paid?" message appears in red, as does the VisitDate field value of 10/26/2020.

   Trouble? If a dialog box is displayed indicating a runtime error, the event procedure could not execute. Click the Debug button in the dialog box to open the event procedure in the Code window with the line containing the error highlighted. Check the statements carefully against those shown in Figure 11–27. Make the necessary changes so they match the figure exactly, compile the module, save the module, and then close the Code window. Then repeat Step 1.

▶ **2.** Navigate to the last record to display record 85 for Visit ID 1623, for which the visit date is 4/5/2021. The "Archive if paid?" message is not displayed, and the VisitDate field value is displayed in black.

▶ **3.** **sam** ⬆ Close the form, make a backup copy of the database, compact and repair the database, and then close it.

Donna is pleased with the modifications you have made to the forms using Visual Basic code. The forms will be easier for her staff to use and help to minimize errors.

REVIEW

Session 11.2 Quick Check

1. The VBA ___ statement executes one of two groups of statements based on a condition.
2. What happens when you compile a module?
3. What is the purpose of the Dim statement?
4. The ___ function returns a value of true if the field value is empty and false if the field value is not empty.
5. What is the purpose of the DoCmd statement?
6. What is a method?
7. What is a VBA constant?
8. You can use the UCase function or the ___ function to convert a string to all uppercase letters.
9. What does the Visible property determine?
10. What does the ForeColor property determine?

Review Assignments

PRACTICE

Data File needed for the Review Assignments: Product.accdb (*cont. from Module 10*)

Donna asks you to continue your work on the Product database by enhancing the usability of the frmSuppliersWithProducts form and the frmSupplier form. To help with this request, complete the following steps:

1. Open the **Product** database you worked with in the previous two modules.
2. In the frmSuppliersWithProducts form, create an event procedure on the AfterUpdate event for the Address field to convert Address field values to proper case—capitalize the first letter of each word, and convert all other letters to lowercase. When adding event procedures or user-defined functions, remember to always document your code as you did in the main module. Test the procedure, and then close the form.
3. Create an event procedure on the Current event for the frmSuppliersWithProducts form to do the following:
   a. Display the InitialContact field value in red when the date is December 1, 2020, or later, and in black for earlier dates.
   b. Display the message **Newer Supplier** below the InitialContact box in red text. Display the message only when the InitialContact field value is December 1, 2020, or later. Use **lblSupplierMsg** as the name of the new label control to contain the message.
   c. Test the procedure, and then save and close the form.
4. Create a user-defined function called **CapAll** that will accept one argument called **FValue**, convert it to uppercase, and return the uppercase value back to the instruction that called it. (*Hint*: Use the UCase function to convert characters to uppercase.) Store this user-defined function in a standard module called **basProductProcedures**.
5. In the frmSupplier form, create an event procedure on the AfterUpdate event for the State field that will convert the characters to uppercase only if the field value box is not empty. Call the CapAll function to perform the character conversion. Test the procedure, and then close the form.
6. Make a backup copy of the database, compact and repair the Product database, and then close the database.

Case Problem 1

APPLY

Data File needed for this Case Problem: Instruction.accdb (*cont. from Module 10*)

Great Giraffe   Jeremiah asks you to continue your work on the Instruction database by enhancing the usability of some of the forms. To help with this request, complete the following steps:

1. Open the **Instruction** database you worked with in the previous two modules.
2. Create a user-defined function called **CapAll** that will accept one argument called **FValue**, convert it to uppercase, and return the uppercase value back to the instruction that called it. (*Hint*: Use the UCase function to convert characters to uppercase.) When adding event procedures or user-defined functions, remember to always document your code as you did in the main module. Store this user-defined function in a standard module called **basInstructionProcedures**.
3. In the frmStudentsByCourse form, create an event procedure on the AfterUpdate event for the InstanceID field that will convert the characters to uppercase only if the field value box is not empty. Call the CapAll function to perform the character conversion. Test the procedure, and then close the form.
4. In the frmStudentsByCourse form, create an event procedure on the AfterUpdate event for the Title field to convert Title field values to proper case—capitalize the first letter of each word, and convert all other letters to lowercase. Test the procedure, and then close the form.

5. Create an event procedure on the Current event for the frmCourseData form to do the following:
   a. Display the HoursPerWeek field value in red when the value equals 40, and in black otherwise.
   b. Display the message **Full Week** to the right of the HoursPerWeek box in red text. Display the message only when the HoursPerWeek field value equals 40. Use **lblFullWeekMsg** as the name of the new label control to contain the message.
   c. Test the procedure, and then save and close the form.
6. Make a backup copy of the database, compact and repair the database, and then close it.

Case Problem 2

Data File needed for this Case Problem: CleanOut.accdb *(cont. from Module 10)*

Drain Adopter   Tandrea asks you to continue your work on the CleanOut database by enhancing the usability of some of the forms. To help with this request, complete the following steps:

1. Open the **CleanOut** database you worked with in the previous two modules.
2. In the frmVolunteerMasterData form, create an event procedure for the AfterUpdate event on the Street field to convert Street field values to proper case—capitalize the first letter of each word, and convert all other letters to lowercase. Test the procedure, and then close the form. When adding event procedures or user-defined functions, remember to always document your code as you did in the main module.

Explore 3. In the frmVolunteerMasterData form, create an event procedure for the form's BeforeUpdate event to verify the Zip field values by doing the following:
   a. For a State field value of WA in the city of Bellingham, WA, the first four digits of the Zip field value must equal 9822. If the Zip field value is invalid, display an appropriate message, cancel the event, undo the change, and move the focus to the Zip field.
   b. No special action is required for other Zip field values.
   c. Test the procedure, and then save your form changes.

Explore 4. In the frmVolunteerData form, create an event procedure for the form's Current event to do the following:
   a. Display the SignupDate field value in a bold, blue text when the value is in the first three months of the year 2021, and in normal, black text for all other values. (*Hint*: Use the FontBold property set with the value True for bold or False for not bold, and use the color vbBlue for blue.)
   b. Display the message **First Adopters** to the right of the SignupDate box in a label control called **lblFirstAdoptersMsg**, in bold, blue text only when the SignupDate field value is in the first three months of the year 2021. (*Hint*: Use the Font Weight property to make the label bold, and use the Blue from the standard colors.)
   c. Test the procedure, and then save your form changes.
5. Make a backup copy of the database, compact and repair the database, and then close it.

CHALLENGE

MODULE **12**

OBJECTIVES

Session 12.1
- Filter By Form and apply an advanced filter/sort
- Save a filter as a query and apply the saved query as a filter
- Create a subquery
- Create a multivalued field

Session 12.2
- Create an Attachment field
- Use an AutoNumber field
- Save a database as a previous version
- Analyze a database's performance
- Link a database to a table in another database
- Update linked tables
- Split a database
- Encrypt a database with a password
- Set database properties and startup options

ACCESS

Managing and Securing a Database

Administering the Health Database

Case | *Lakewood Community Health Services*

Donna Taylor will be offering training sessions for staff members to learn how to use the Health database. Before she begins these training sessions, she asks for your help in finalizing the database. Your remaining work will apply advanced Access features for filtering, creating subqueries, and using advanced field types in tables, such as multivalued fields and Attachment fields. In addition, you will learn about database management, database security, and maximizing the database's overall performance. You'll also set database startup options as a final step in the development of the Health database.

STARTING DATA FILES

Access3 → **Module**

Health.accdb (cont.)
Support_AC_12_KimberlyHansen-BachelorDegree.docx
Support_AC_12_KimberlyHansen-Expenses.xlsx
Support_AC_12_KimberlyHansen-MasterDegree.pdf
Support_AC_12_Referral.accdb

Review

Product.accdb (cont.)
Support_AC_12_Ads.accdb
Support_AC_12_Autoclave.xlsx
Support_AC_12_Autoclave_Specification_Sheet.pdf

Case1

Instruction.accdb (cont.)
Support_AC_12_Allen.txt
Support_AC_12_RoomOptions.accdb

Case2

CleanOut.accdb (cont.)
Support_AC_12_BEN36NE_111820.txt
Support_AC_12_Trucks.accdb

Session 12.1 Visual Overview:

The Degree field is defined as a multivalued field. A multivalued field is a lookup field that allows you to store more than one value in a field in each record.

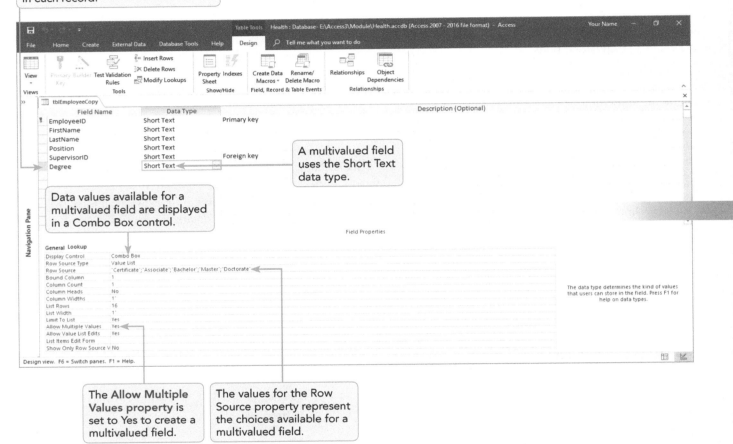

A multivalued field uses the Short Text data type.

Data values available for a multivalued field are displayed in a Combo Box control.

The Allow Multiple Values property is set to Yes to create a multivalued field.

The values for the Row Source property represent the choices available for a multivalued field.

Multivalued Fields and Subqueries

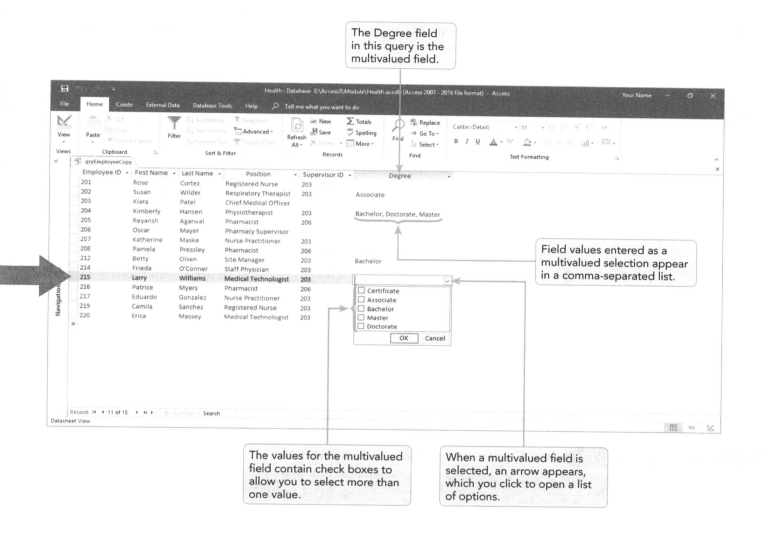

The Degree field in this query is the multivalued field.

Field values entered as a multivalued selection appear in a comma-separated list.

The values for the multivalued field contain check boxes to allow you to select more than one value.

When a multivalued field is selected, an arrow appears, which you click to open a list of options.

Additional Filtering Options

As you know, you can use a filter to temporarily display specified records from a table or form. In previous modules, you used AutoFilter and Filter By Selection. Two additional filtering features in Access are Filter By Form and Advanced Filter/Sort.

Recall that Filter By Form filters records that match multiple selection criteria using the same Access logical and comparison operators used in queries. After applying one of these filter tools, you can use the Sort Ascending or Sort Descending buttons in the Sort & Filter group on the Home tab to rearrange the records, if necessary.

Advanced Filter/Sort lets you specify multiple selection criteria and set a sort order for selected records in the Filter window, in the same way you specify record selection criteria and sort orders for a query in Design view.

Donna needs to know which patients visited Lakewood Community Health Services in November 2020, as well as which patients in Atlanta and Marietta have private health insurance. She'd like to access this information from the Health database quickly, without creating a query. Although Donna has used filters with a query datasheet and a form, she's never used a filter with a table datasheet. You'll use a filter to display all clinic visits with November 2020 visit dates in the tblVisit table datasheet.

To filter records in the tblVisit table datasheet:

▶ 1. Start Access, and then open the Health.accdb database you worked with in the previous three modules.

   Trouble? If the security warning is displayed below the ribbon, click the Enable Content button.

▶ 2. Open the Navigation Pane (if necessary), open the **tblVisit** table in Datasheet view, and then close the Navigation Pane.

▶ 3. Click the **arrow** on the Date of Visit column heading to open the AutoFilter menu, point to **Date Filters** to open a submenu of context-sensitive options, and then point to **All Dates In Period** to open a submenu. See Figure 12–1.

Figure 12–1	AutoFilter menu and submenus for a date field

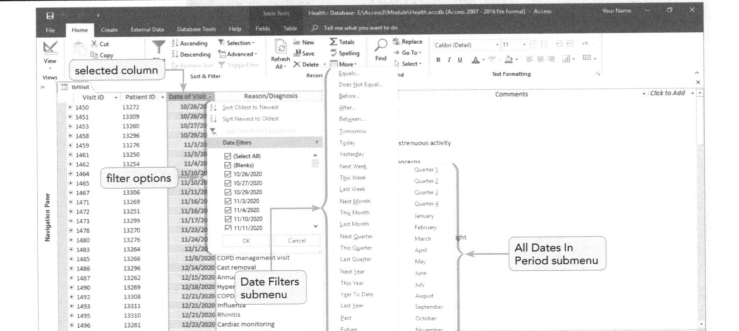

The Date of Visit menu displays all the values that appear in the Date of Visit column; you use the Date of Visit menu when you want to select specific values for the filter. The Date Filters submenu displays filter options that apply to a Date field, and the All Dates In Period submenu displays additional filter options for a Date field.

▶ **4.** In the All Dates In Period submenu, click **November**. Only the 11 records with November visit dates are displayed in the datasheet. If you save a table with an applied filter, the filter is saved, and you can reapply the filter anytime you open the table datasheet.

▶ **5.** Save and close the tblVisit table.

▶ **6.** Open the Navigation Pane, open the **tblVisit** table datasheet to display all 85 records, and then on the Home tab, in the Sort & Filter group, click the **Toggle Filter** button. The VisitDate filter is applied, displaying the 11 records with November visit dates.

▶ **7.** Close the tblVisit table.

Next, you'll use Filter By Form to produce the other results Donna wants—the list of patients from Atlanta or Marietta who have private health insurance.

Filter By Form

You use the Filter By Form filter option when you need to filter data in a table or form on multiple criteria. When you select the Filter By Form option from the Advanced button menu in the Sort & Filter group, a blank datasheet opens that includes all the fields in the table, and this blank datasheet has two tabs—the Look for tab and the Or tab. In the blank datasheet on the Look for tab, you specify multiple selection criteria by entering conditions in the appropriate field value boxes. If you enter criteria in more than one field, you create the equivalent of an And condition—any record that matches all criteria will be selected. To create an Or condition, you enter the criteria for the first part of the condition in the field on the Look for tab's datasheet and then click the Or tab at the bottom of the datasheet window to display a new blank datasheet. You enter the criteria for the second part of the condition on the Or tab's blank datasheet. Any record that matches all criteria on the Look for datasheet or all criteria on the Or datasheet will be selected.

REFERENCE

Selecting Records Using Filter By Form

- Open the table or query datasheet or the form in Form view.
- On the Home tab, in the Sort & Filter group, click the Advanced button, and then click Filter By Form.
- Enter a simple selection criterion or an And condition in the Look for tab or form, using the boxes for the appropriate fields.
- If you need to specify an Or condition, click the Or tab, and then enter the Or condition in the second datasheet or form. Continue to enter Or conditions on separate datasheets or forms by using the Or tab.
- On the Home tab, in the Sort & Filter group, click the Toggle Filter button.

Donna wants to display records for only those patients in Atlanta and Marietta with private health insurance. To accomplish this, the multiple selection criteria you will enter are: Atlanta *and* Private *or* Marietta *and* Private.

To select the records using Filter By Form:

▶ **1.** Open the **tblPatient** table to display the 52 records in the recordset, and then close the Navigation Pane.

▶ **2.** On the Home tab, in the Sort & Filter group, click the **Advanced** button, click **Filter By Form** to display a blank datasheet that has two tabs: the Look for tab and the Or tab. The Look for tab is the active tab. See Figure 12–2.

Figure 12–2 **Blank form for Filter By Form option**

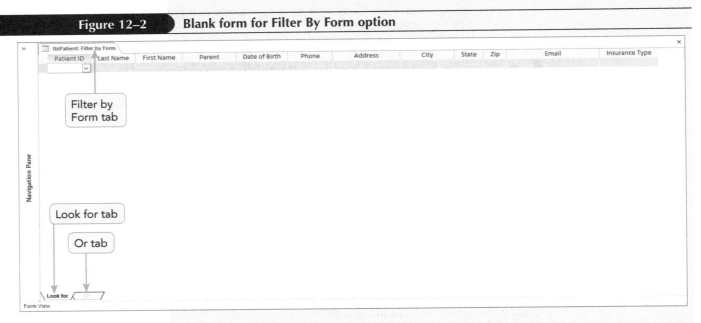

For a criterion, you can select a value from the list of values in a field value box, or you can use a comparison operator (such as <, >=, <>, and Like) and a value, similar to conditions you enter in the query design grid.

▶ **3.** Click the **City** box, click the **City** arrow, and then click **Atlanta**. The criterion "Atlanta" appears in the City box.

▶ **4.** Click the **Insurance Type** box, click the **Insurance Type** arrow, and then click **Private**. Access adds the criterion "Private" to the Insurance Type box.

Before you add other options to the filter, you'll verify that the filter is working.

▶ **5.** In the Sort & Filter group, click the **Toggle Filter** button. The records that contain Atlanta for the city and Private for the Insurance Type are displayed.

The results contain three records. Now you'll return to the Filter by Form window to continue creating the filter.

▶ **6.** On the Home tab, in the Sort & Filter group, click the **Advanced** button, and then click **Filter By Form** to return to the filter.

You've specified the logical operator (And) for the condition "Atlanta" And "Private". To add the rest of the criteria, you need to display the Or blank datasheet.

TIP

Notice that a third tab, also labeled "Or", is now available in case you need to specify another Or condition.

7. Click the **Or** tab to display a second blank datasheet. The insertion point is in the City box.

8. Click the **City** arrow to display the list, and then click **Marietta**.

9. Click the **Insurance Type** box, click the **Insurance Type** arrow, and then click **Private**. The filter is now set for the second And condition of "Marietta" And "Private". See Figure 12–3.

Figure 12–3   **Completed filter using Filter By Form option**

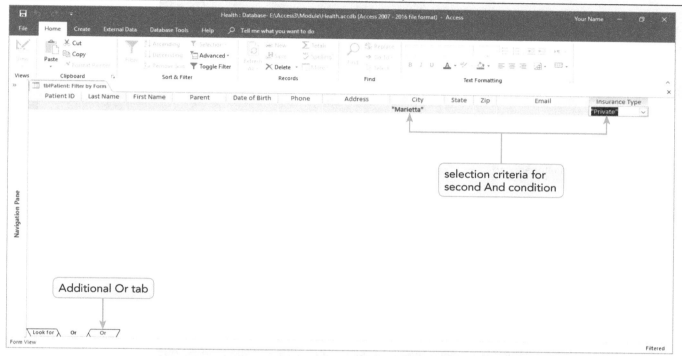

Combined with the Look for conditions, you now have the Or conditions and the complete Filter By Form conditions. Much like building queries, all data that is on the same line in the criteria must be satisfied in order for the record to satisfy the criteria.

10. In the Sort & Filter group, click the **Toggle Filter** button, and then scroll to the right until both the City and Insurance Type columns are visible (if necessary). The filter displays the five records that match the selection criteria and displays "Filtered" in the navigation bar. See Figure 12–4.

Figure 12-4   **Records that match the Filter By Form criteria**

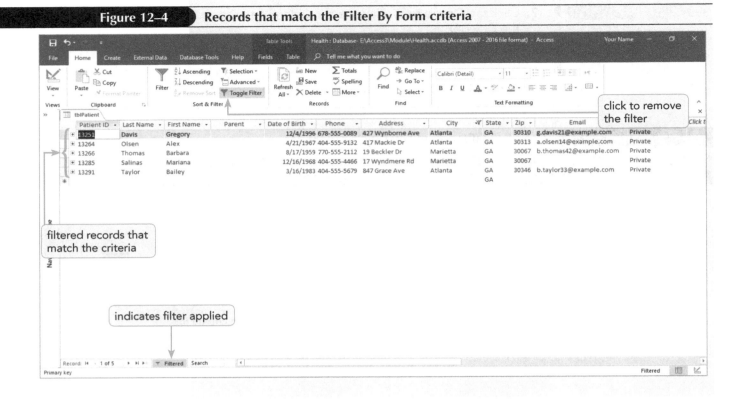

Now that you have defined the filter, you can save it as a query so that Donna can easily view the information in the future.

Saving a Filter as a Query

When you save a filter as a query, you can reuse the filter by opening the saved query.

REFERENCE

Saving a Filter as a Query

- Create a filter using Filter By Selection, Filter By Form, or Advanced Filter/Sort.
- If you applied the filter using Filter By Form, click the Advanced button, and then click Filter By Form.
- On the Home tab, in the Sort & Filter group, click the Advanced button, and then click Save As Query.
- Type the name for the query, and then press ENTER.

Next, you'll save the filter as a query named qryAtlantaMariettaPrivateFilter.

To save the filter as a query:

▶ **1.** On the Home tab, in the Sort & Filter group, click the **Advanced** button, and then click **Filter By Form**. The datasheet displays the selection criteria.

▶ **2.** In the Sort & Filter group, click the **Advanced** button, and then click **Save As Query**. The Save As Query dialog box opens.

▶ **3.** Type **qryAtlantaMariettaPrivateFilter** in the Query Name box, and then click **OK**. The filter is saved as a query in the Health database.

Now you can clear the selection criteria, close the Filter by Form tab, and return to Datasheet view.

▶ **4.** In the Sort & Filter group, click the **Advanced** button, and then click **Clear Grid** to remove the selection criteria from the filter datasheet.

▶ **5.** Close the tblPatient: Filter by Form tab to return to Datasheet view for the tblPatient table. The five filtered records are still displayed in the datasheet, and the filter is still applied.

▶ **6.** In the Sort & Filter group, click the **Toggle Filter** button, click the **Advanced** button, and then click **Clear All Filters**. Because no filters are applied, the table displays 52 records. Next, you'll leave the tblPatient table open while you open the qryAtlantaMariettaPrivateFilter query in Design view.

▶ **7.** Open the Navigation Pane, open the **qryAtlantaMariettaPrivateFilter** query, switch to Design view, and then close the Navigation Pane. In the design grid, the first And condition ("Atlanta" And "Private") appears in the Criteria row, and the second And condition ("Marietta" And "Marietta") appears in the or row. You can interpret these criteria as "the records that contain Atlanta and Private, or that contain Marietta and Private." See Figure 12–5.

| Figure 12–5 | Filter saved as a query in Design view |

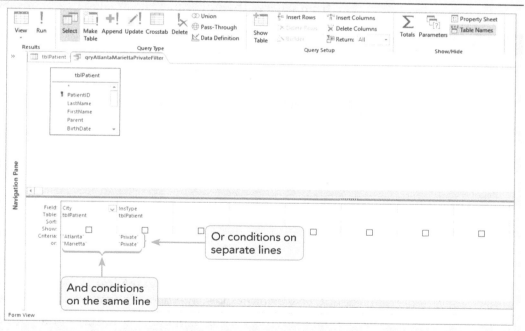

▶ **8.** Run the query to display the five records that satisfy the selection criteria, close the query, close the tblPatient table, and then click **No** in the dialog box that prompts you to save the table design changes. You don't want to save the filter with the table because you've already saved the filter as a separate query.

The next time Donna wants to view the records selected by the filter, she can run the qryAtlantaMariettaPrivateFilter query. She could also open the tblPatient table and apply the qryAtlantaMariettaPrivateFilter query as a filter.

Applying a Query as a Filter

- Open the table to which you want to apply the filter in Datasheet view.
- On the Home tab, in the Sort & Filter group, click the Advanced button, and then click Filter By Form.
- In the Sort & Filter group, click the Advanced button, and then click Load from Query.
- In the Applicable Filter dialog box, click the query you want to apply as a filter, and then click the OK button.
- On the Home tab, in the Sort & Filter group, click the Toggle Filter button to apply the filter.

To apply the qryAtlantaMariettaPrivateFilter query as a filter, you first need to open the tblPatient table.

To apply the query as a filter:

▶ **1.** Open the Navigation Pane, open the **tblPatient** table, and then close the Navigation Pane.

▶ **2.** In the Sort & Filter group, click the **Advanced** button, and then click **Filter By Form**. The blank Look for tab in the Filter By Form datasheet is displayed.

▶ **3.** In the Sort & Filter group, click the **Advanced** button, and then click **Load from Query**. The Applicable Filter dialog box opens. See Figure 12–6.

Figure 12–6	Applicable Filter dialog box

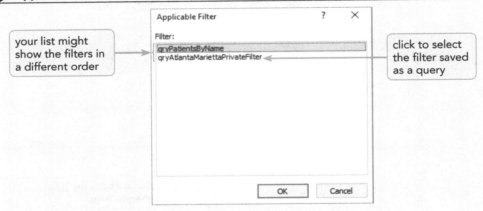

your list might show the filters in a different order

click to select the filter saved as a query

▶ **4.** Click **qryAtlantaMariettaPrivateFilter** in the Filter box if necessary to select it, and then click **OK**. The query is displayed in the Filter by Form window.

▶ **5.** In the Sort & Filter group, click the **Toggle Filter** button. The five filtered records are displayed in the datasheet.

▶ **6.** Click the **Advanced** button, click **Clear All Filters**, and then close the tblPatient table without saving your design changes.

Donna finds the qryAtlantaMariettaPrivateFilter useful, but she'd also like a list of the patients who have visited the clinic, and their visit information, for patients who live in either Atlanta or Marietta, and who have private health insurance. To generate this list, you can use the qryAtlantaMariettaPrivateFilter as a subquery within a query that searches for these patient visit records in the tblVisit table. You'll modify the qryAtlantaMariettaPrivateFilter query to use a subquery.

Creating a Subquery

When you create a query using a SQL SELECT statement, you can place a second SELECT statement inside it; this second query is called a **subquery**. The subquery is run first, and then the results of the subquery are used to run the outer query. A subquery is also known as an **inner query**. It runs inside another query, referred to as a **parent query**, which is simply a query that contains a subquery. A parent query can also be referred to as an **outer query**.

The records that result from the parent query are the only records that will be used as the dataset for the subquery. You can think of this arrangement as a query within a query. For instance, you might have a query that finds all patients from Atlanta and then use a subquery to find all patients within those records who visited the clinic in November. The subquery would be patients who visited in November, and the parent query would be patients whose city is Atlanta. This is a simple example, and you could certainly create one query that contains both the tblVisit and tblPatient tables, with criteria that set the city and visit date appropriately. However, in other situations you may be dealing with much more complex parent queries and subqueries. In these cases, rather than dealing with troubleshooting one very complex query, you could build two simpler queries and combine them in this manner. This can be a time-saving technique because you can create a very complex query by combining queries that are easier to understand.

To view the qryAtlantaMariettaPrivateFilter query in SQL view:

▶ 1. Open the Navigation Pane, open the **qryAtlantaMariettaPrivateFilter** query in Design view, and then close the Navigation Pane. In the design grid, the first And condition ("Atlanta" And "Private") appears in the Criteria row, the second And condition ("Marietta" And "Private") appears in the or row, and the Or condition combines the first And condition with the second And condition.

▶ 2. On the Query Tools Design tab, in the Results group, click the **View** arrow, click **SQL View**, and then click a blank area of the window to deselect the SQL SELECT statement. See Figure 12–7.

| Figure 12–7 | SQL statement for the qryAtlantaMariettaPrivateFilter query |

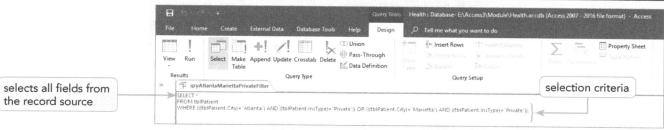

selects all fields from the record source

selection criteria

SELECT * FROM tblPatient selects all fields from the tblPatient table in the order in which they appear in the table. The WHERE clause specifies the selection criteria: records with a City field value of Atlanta and an InsType field value of Private, or records with a City field value of Marietta and an InsType field value of Private.

In the next set of steps, you'll add the following outer query to modify the query to use it as a subquery:

SELECT * FROM tblVisit WHERE PatientID IN (

This will perform a SELECT query to find all fields (*) in the tblVisit table. The IN function will contain the SQL code for the qryAtlantaMariettaPrivateFilter query, which becomes the subquery. You'll need to add a right parenthesis) before the final semicolon to end the subquery. The finished SQL statement is shown in Figure 12-8.

Figure 12-8   **SQL SELECT statement using a subquery**

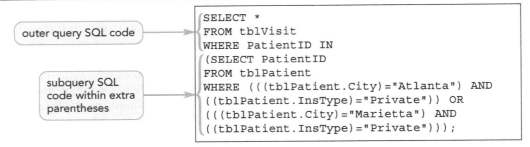

outer query SQL code

subquery SQL code within extra parentheses

```
SELECT *
FROM tblVisit
WHERE PatientID IN
(SELECT PatientID
FROM tblPatient
WHERE (((tblPatient.City)="Atlanta") AND
((tblPatient.InsType)="Private")) OR
(((tblPatient.City)="Marietta") AND
((tblPatient.InsType)="Private")));
```

To create this query, you'll copy the qryAtlantaMariettaPrivateFilter query and then add to this SQL code to form the query that uses this as a subquery.

To create the query that contains a subquery:

▶ **1.** Close the qryAtlantaMariettaPrivateFilter query, and then open the Navigation Pane.

▶ **2.** Right-click **qryAtlantaMariettaPrivateFilter**, and then on the shortcut menu, click **Copy**.

▶ **3.** On the Home tab, in the Clipboard group, click **Paste** to open the Paste As dialog box, and then save as the copy with the name **qryAtlantaMariettaPrivateFilterVisit**.

▶ **4.** Open the **qryAtlantaMariettaPrivateFilterVisit** query in Design view, and then close the Navigation Pane.

▶ **5.** On the Query Tools Design tab, in the Results group, click the **View arrow**, click **SQL View**, and then click a blank area of the window to deselect the SQL SELECT statement.

▶ **6.** Click to the left of the SELECT statement, press **ENTER** three times, and then click in the top blank line of the SQL window to position the insertion point.

▶ **7.** Type **SELECT ***, press **DOWN ARROW**, type **FROM tblVisit**, press **DOWN ARROW**, and then type **WHERE PatientID IN**

▶ **8.** Edit the next line to add **(** (an open parenthesis) to the left of SELECT, and then delete the asterisk (*) that comes after SELECT and replace it with **PatientID** so the statement is:

(SELECT PatientID

▶ **9.** Click to the left of the semicolon at the end of the SQL statement and type **)** (close parenthesis). See Figure 12-9.

Figure 12–9   **Modified SQL statement**

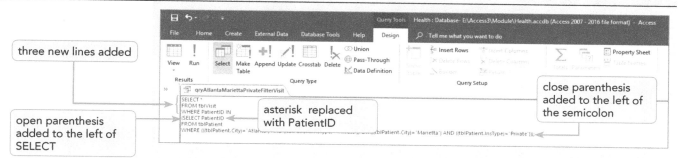

three new lines added

open parenthesis added to the left of SELECT

asterisk replaced with PatientID

close parenthesis added to the left of the semicolon

▶ **10.** Save your query design changes, and then run the query. The query returns eight records from the tblVisit table whose PatientID values are in the qryAtlantaMariettaPrivateFilter.

▶ **11.** Switch to Design view, and then click the first column's **Field** box to deselect all values. The value in the PatientID Criteria box is a subquery that selects Atlanta and Marietta patients who have Private health insurance. See Figure 12–10.

Figure 12–10   **Query using a subquery in the Design window**

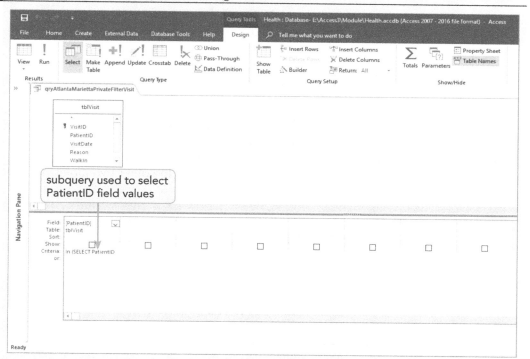

subquery used to select PatientID field values

It's unclear from looking at the column in the design grid that all fields are displayed from the tblVisit table.

▶ **12.** On the Query Tools Design tab, in the Show/Hide group, click the **Property Sheet** button to display the properties for the query. See Figure 12–11.

Figure 12–11   **Properties for the query**

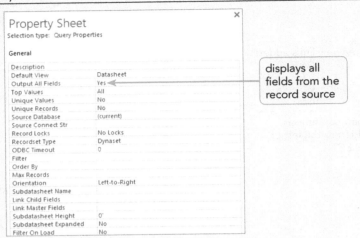

The Output All Fields property setting of Yes specifies that the query displays all fields from the record source, the tblVisit table, without these fields being added to the design grid.

▶ **13.** Close the Property Sheet, close the query, and then click **Yes** when prompted to save changes to the query design.

Donna wants to keep track of the degrees—such as associate's degree, bachelor's degree, and master's degree—earned by employees. Because each employee can earn more than one degree, and each degree can be earned by more than one employee, there's a many-to-many relationship between employees and degrees. To implement this many-to-many relationship, you could use the existing tblEmployee table, create a separate tblDegree table to store the Degree field values, and then create a third table to tie together the other two tables. You could also accomplish this using a multivalued field.

Using Multivalued Fields

A multivalued field is a lookup field that allows you to store more than one value. When you define a multivalued field in a table, the values are not actually stored in the field in that table. Instead, they are stored as hidden values in system tables that have a many-to-many relationship with the table. The values in these system tables are managed, manipulated, and displayed as if the data were stored in the multivalued field in the table.

Using a multivalued field, you can add a Degree field to the tblEmployee table and use the Lookup Wizard to enter the Degree field values and specify that you want to store multiple values in the Degree field. Donna and her staff can then select one or more Degree field values from the list of degrees.

INSIGHT

Using Multivalued Fields

Users with limited Access and database experience are the intended audience for multivalued fields because understanding the concepts of many-to-many relationships and creating them are difficult for beginning or casual database users. Experienced database users generally avoid multivalued fields and instead implement many-to-many relationships because that method provides total control over the data, rather than limiting options as working with multivalued fields does. One of the limitations of multivalued fields is that except in special circumstances, you can't sort records based on the values stored in a multivalued field in queries, forms, and reports. Also, multivalued fields do not convert properly to a database managed by a DBMS such as SQL Server or Oracle. If you need to convert an Access database using a multivalued field to another DBMS in the future, you'd have to change the multivalued field to many-to-many relationships, which is a change that's much more difficult at that point than if you had avoided using a multivalued field from the beginning. As a precaution, you should save a copy of the database file before you create a multivalued field.

You'll use the multivalued field feature without modifying the existing tables and relationships in the Health database, so Donna can decide whether you should keep the multivalued field or use a traditional many-to-many implementation. You'll make a copy of the tblEmployee table, and then you will add the multivalued field to the copied version of the table. This way, you can delete the copy of the tblEmployee table if Donna decides not to use a multivalued field. If Donna decides to keep it, she has the option to delete the original tblEmployee table and rename this new table as the tblEmployee table.

To create a copy of the tblEmployee table:

▶ 1. Open the Navigation Pane, right-click **tblEmployee**, and then on the shortcut menu, click **Copy**.

▶ 2. In the Clipboard group, on the Home tab, click the **Paste** button to open the Paste Table As dialog box, and then click the **Table Name** box to deselect the current name. See Figure 12–12.

Figure 12–12 Paste Table As dialog box

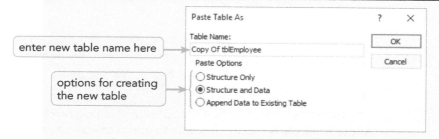

When you copy a table to create a new table, you can use the design of the table without copying its data (Structure Only), use the design and copy the data from the table (Structure and Data), or add the data to an existing table (Append Data to Existing Table).

You'll create the new table using the design and data from the tblEmployee table.

▶ **3.** Change the name in the Table Name box to **tblEmployeeCopy**, make sure the **Structure and Data** option button is selected, and then click **OK**. A new table named tblEmployeeCopy is created, and it contains the same structure and data as the tblEmployee table.

Now you can add the multivalued field to the tblEmployeeCopy table.

To add the multivalued field to the tblEmployeeCopy table:

▶ **1.** Open the **tblEmployeeCopy** table in Design view, and then close the Navigation Pane.

▶ **2.** In the blank row below the SupervisorID field, click the **Field Name** box, type **Degree**, press **TAB**, click the **Data Type** arrow, and then click **Lookup Wizard**. The first Lookup Wizard dialog box opens. You'll type the Degree field values instead of obtaining them from a table or query.

▶ **3.** Click the **I will type in the values that I want** option button, and then click **Next** to open the second Lookup Wizard dialog box, in which you'll type the Degree field values.

▶ **4.** Click the **Col1** box in the first row, type **Certificate**, press **TAB**, type **Associate**, press **TAB**, type **Bachelor**, press **TAB**, type **Master**, press **TAB**, and then type **Doctorate**. These are the five values that users can choose among for the Degree multivalued field. See Figure 12–13.

Figure 12–13	Values for the Degree multivalued field

▶ **5.** Click **Next** to open the last Lookup Wizard dialog box, and then click the **Allow Multiple Values** check box to add a checkmark to it, specifying that you want the Degree field to be a multivalued field. See Figure 12–14.

Figure 12-14   Specifying a multivalued field

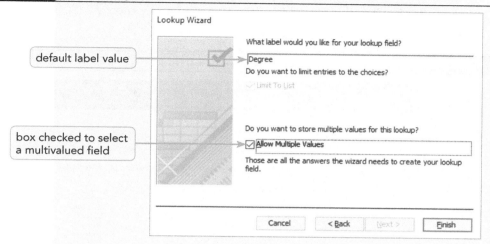

You'll accept the default label name of Degree for the field.

▶ **6.** Click **Finish** to complete the definition of the Degree field as a lookup field that allows multiple values, or a multivalued field.

▶ **7.** In the Field Properties pane, click the **Lookup** tab. The Degree field has its Row Source property set to the five values you typed in one of the Lookup Wizard dialog boxes, and the Allow Multiple Values property is set to Yes. See Figure 12-15.

Figure 12-15   Degree field as a multivalued field

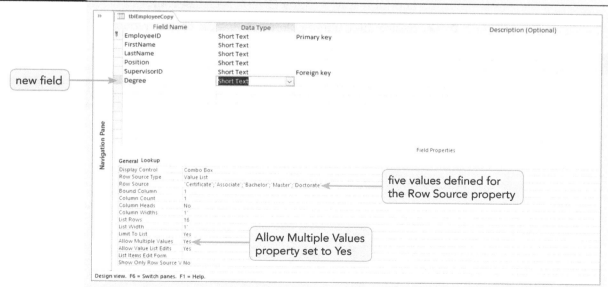

If you forget to select the Allow Multiple Values check box when you use the Lookup Wizard, you can switch to Design view and set the Allow Multiple Values property for the field to Yes to change a field to a multivalued field. If you need to add values in the future to the multivalued field, you can add them to the Row Source property.

▶ **8.** Save your table design changes, and then switch to Datasheet view.

▶ **9.** Click the right side of the **Degree** box for record 2 (Susan Wilder) to open the value list for the field. See Figure 12–16.

Figure 12–16   **Value list for the Degree multivalued field**

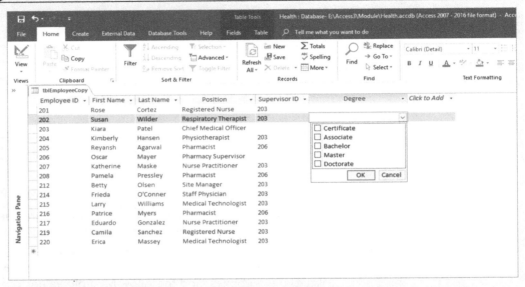

▶ **10.** Click the **Associate** check box, and then click **OK**.

▶ **11.** For record 4 (Kimberly Hansen), select **Bachelor**, **Master**, and **Doctorate**, and for record 9 (Betty Olsen), select **Bachelor**.

▶ **12.** Resize the Degree column to its best fit. See Figure 12–17.

Figure 12–17   **Values selected for the multivalued field**

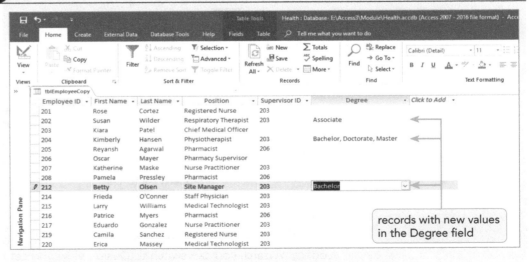

Next, you'll create queries to display all field values from the tblEmployeeCopy table to display the multivalued field values.

To create queries to display the Degree multivalued field:

▶ **1.** Save and close the tblEmployeeCopy table, click the **Create** tab, and then in the Queries group, click the **Query Wizard** button to open the New Query dialog box.

▶ **2.** Make sure the Simple Query Wizard option is selected, click **OK** to open the Simple Query Wizard dialog box, from the tblEmployeeCopy table select all fields, click the **Next** button, change the query title to **qryEmployeeCopy**, and then click **Finish**.

▶ **3.** Click the first row's **Employee ID** column value to deselect all values (if necessary), and then resize the Degree.Value column to best fit. The query results include 17 records. See Figure 12–18.

Figure 12–18	Query that displays the Degree multivalued field

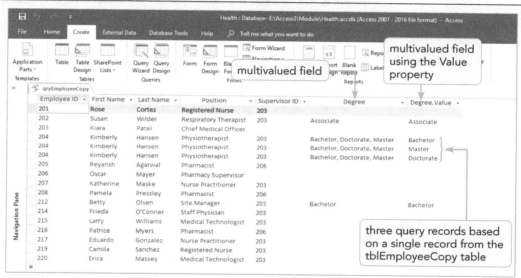

Trouble? The rightmost column heading on your screen might be the equivalent of tblEmployee-Copy.Degree.Value instead of Degree.Value, indicating the Degree field in the tblEmployeeCopy table. This difference does not affect the contents of the column.

The six fields from the tblEmployeeCopy table are displayed in seven columns in the query recordset because the Degree field is displayed in two columns: the Degree column and the Degree.Value column. The Degree column displays field values exactly as they appear in the tblEmployeeCopy table; all values for the Degree multivalued field, such as those for Kimberly Hansen, are displayed in one row in the query. The Degree.Value column displays the Degree multivalued field in expanded form so that each value appears in a separate row in the query. "Degree.Value" identifies the Degree field and the Value property for the Degree field.

In queries that contain a multivalued field, you should display the field in a single column, not in two columns, with values appearing as they are in the table or in expanded form. You can eliminate the extra column by deleting it, by clearing its Show check box in Design view, or by selecting just one of the two fields in the Simple Query Wizard when you select the fields for the query.

4. Click the **Home** tab, notice that the Ascending and Descending buttons in the Sort & Filter group are active, click the first row's **Degree** box, notice that the Ascending and Descending buttons are grayed out, and then click the first row's **Degree.Value** box. The Ascending and Descending buttons are active, and you can sort records in the query based on the values in the Degree.Value column.

Next, you'll review the query design.

5. Switch to Design view, and then resize the tblEmployeeCopy field list to display all the values in the list. See Figure 12–19.

Figure 12–19 Design of the query containing the Degree multivalued field

The Degree field in the tblEmployeeCopy field list has a collapse indicator to its left that you can click to hide the Degree.Value entry below it. The rightmost column in the design grid, [Degree].[Value], uses the Value property for the Degree field. Using the Value property with a multivalued field displays the multivalued field in expanded form so that each value is displayed in a separate row.

You'll delete the [Degree] column from the query design, retaining the [Degree].[Value] column and setting its Caption property, and then you'll save the query with a new name.

6. Right-click the **column selector bar** for the [Degree] column to select the column and open the shortcut menu, and then click **Cut**.

7. Click the **column selector bar** for the [Degree].[Value] column to select it, open the Property Sheet for the [Degree].[Value] column, set the Caption property to **Degree**, and then close the Property Sheet.

8. Click the **File** tab to open Backstage view, in the navigation bar, click **Save As**, click **Save Object As**, and then click the **Save As** button to open the Save As dialog box.

9. Change the query name to **qryEmployeeCopyValue**, click **OK**, click the **Home** tab, and then switch to Datasheet view. The datasheet appears, displaying 17 records in the query recordset.

▶ **10.** Close the query, open the Navigation Pane, open the **qryEmployeeCopy** query in Design view, and then close the Navigation Pane.

▶ **11.** Delete the **Degree.Value** column, save the query, and then run the query. The query returns 15 records from the tblEmployeeCopy table and displays the Degree multivalued field values in one row.

▶ **12.** Close the query, and then, if you are not continuing on to the next session, close the Health database.

Donna is pleased with your work and will review it as she decides whether to use the multivalued Degree field or a many-to-many relationship. In the next session, you'll add Attachment fields using the tblEmployeeCopy table and evaluate database performance and management options.

REVIEW

Session 12.1 Quick Check

1. Filter By ___ filters records that match multiple selection criteria using the same Access comparison operators used in queries.

2. You can save a filter as a(n) ___ and reuse the filter by opening the saved object.

3. What is a subquery?

4. What is a multivalued field?

5. You use the ___ property to display a multivalued field in expanded form so that each value is displayed in a separate row in a query.

Session 12.2 Visual Overview:

The Use Access Special Keys option enables or disables the F11 key (show/hide the Navigation Pane), CTRL+G (show/hide the Immediate window in VB editor), and ALT+F1 (start VB Editor).

The Application Title option value appears in the Access window title bar.

The Current Database option displays options that apply only to the currently open database.

The Display Form option specifies the form that opens automatically when you open the database.

The Enable design changes for tables in Datasheet view option allows you to change a table's design in Datasheet view.

The Display Navigation Pane option controls whether the Navigation Pane is available in the Access window.

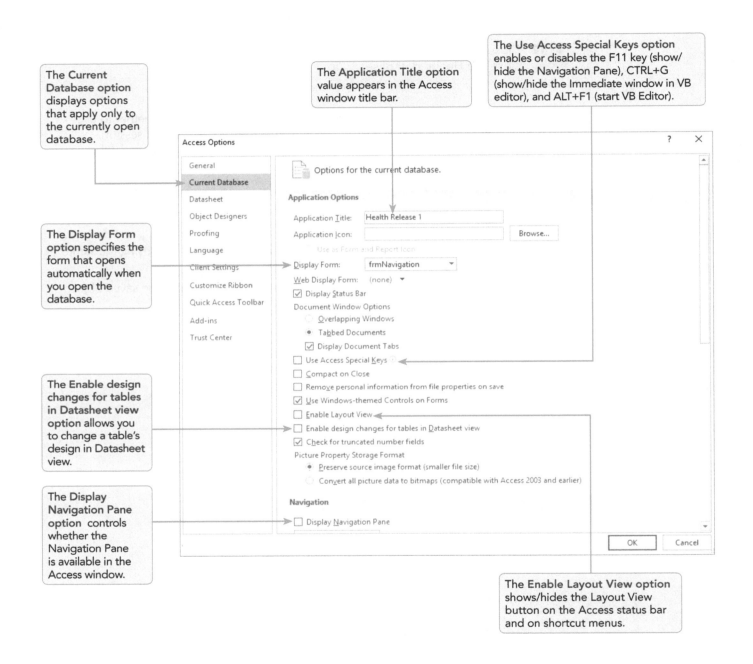

The Enable Layout View option shows/hides the Layout View button on the Access status bar and on shortcut menus.

Database Options

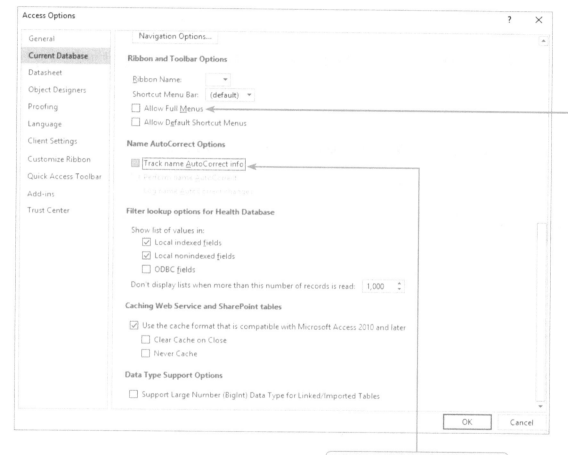

The Allow Full Menus option shows/hides all options on the ribbon. Uncheck to display only the File and Home tabs.

The Track name AutoCorrect info option stores information about changes to the names of fields, controls, and objects.

Creating an Attachment Field

In addition to storing data such as text, numbers, and dates in a database, you can attach external files such as Excel workbooks, Word documents, and images, similar to how you attach external files to email messages. You use the **Attachment data type** to attach one or more files to a table record. The attachments are stored as part of the database. An attachment data field can contain one or more file attachments in a table record.

Donna wants to be able to attach documents to the tblEmployeeCopy table that contain information about Kimberly Hansen's degrees and expenses. You'll add a field with the Attachment data type and use it to attach the documents to the table.

TIP

After you change a field type to Attachment, you can't change the field type again. Instead, you have to delete the field and re-create it with a new field type.

To add a new field with the Attachment data type to the tblEmployeeCopy table:

▶ **1.** If you took a break after the previous session, make sure that the Health database is open.

▶ **2.** Open the Navigation Pane (if necessary), open the **tblEmployeeCopy** table in Design view, and then close the Navigation Pane.

▶ **3.** Click the **Field Name** box for the blank row below the Degree field, type **AddedDocuments**, press **TAB**, type **at**, press **TAB** to select Attachment as the data type, press **F6** to navigate to the Caption box in the Field Properties pane, and then type **Added Documents**. The AddedDocuments field is added to the table. See Figure 12–20.

Figure 12–20 **New AddedDocuments field with the Attachment data type**

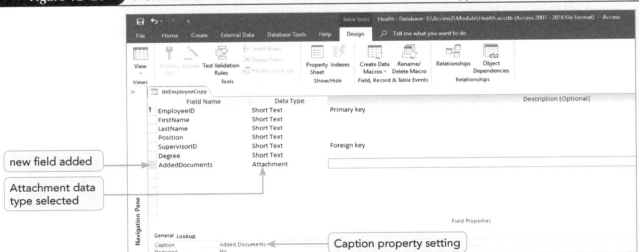

▶ **4.** Save your table design changes, switch to Datasheet view, resize the Added Documents column to its best fit, click the first row's **Employee ID** box to deselect all values, and then save your datasheet format changes. See Figure 12–21.

Figure 12–21 **Attachment field displayed in the table datasheet**

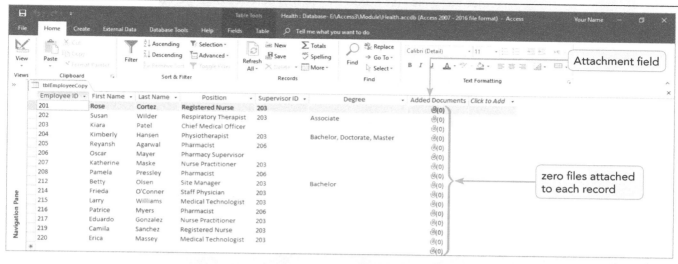

Each AddedDocuments field value displays an attachment icon in the shape of a paper clip followed by a number in parentheses that indicates the number of files attached in that field for the record. You haven't attached any files, so each record displays zero file attachments. Donna has some files from Kimberly Hansen that she would like you to attach to her record in the Added Documents column.

▶ **5.** In the row for Kimberly Hansen, right-click the **Added Documents** box to open the shortcut menu, and then click **Manage Attachments** to open the Attachments dialog box. You'll add all three of Kimberly's files as attachments to the AddedDocuments field for Kimberly Hansen.

▶ **6.** Click **Add** to open the Choose File dialog box, navigate to the **Access3 > Module** folder included with your Data Files, click **Support_AC_12_KimberlyHansenBachelorDegree.docx**, and then click **Open** to add the Support_AC_12_KimberlyHansenBachelorDegree.docx file to the Attachments dialog box.

▶ **7.** Click **Add** to open the Choose File dialog box, click **Support_AC_12_KimberlyHansenMasterDegree.pdf**, press and hold **CTRL**, click **Support_AC_12_KimberlyHansenExpenses.xlsx**, release **CTRL**, and then click **Open**. The three files you've added now appear in the Attachments dialog box. See Figure 12–22.

Figure 12–22 **Attachments dialog box**

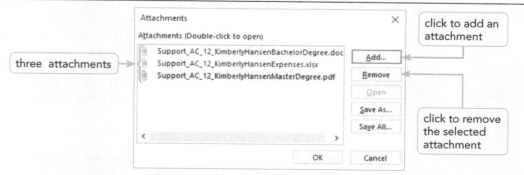

▶ **8.** Click **OK** to close the dialog box. The table datasheet now indicates that three files (as noted by the 3 in parentheses) are attached to the AddedDocuments field in the record for Kimberly Hansen.

Next, you'll open one of the files attached in the record for Kimberly Hansen, remove one of the attached files, and save an attached file.

To open, remove, and save files attached in a table field:

▶ **1.** In the row for Kimberly Hansen, right-click the **Added Documents** box, and then on the shortcut menu, click **Manage Attachments** to open the Attachments dialog box.

▶ **2.** Click **Support_AC_12_KimberlyHansenExpenses.xlsx** in the Attachments list, and then click **Open**. Excel starts and opens the Support_AC_12_ KimberlyHansenExpenses.xlsx workbook.

▶ **3.** Close Excel. You return to the Attachments dialog box open in the Access window.

> **TIP**
>
> The Support_AC_12_ KimberlyHansenBachelor-Degree.docx document remains in the Access3 > Module folder because detaching a file doesn't delete it.

▶ **4.** Click **Support_AC_12_KimberlyHansenBachelorDegree.docx** in the Attachments list, and then click **Remove**. The Support_AC_12_ KimberlyHansenBachelorDegree.docx document is removed from the Attachments list, and it no longer is attached to the AddedDocuments field for the Kimberly Hansen record.

▶ **5.** Click **Support_AC_12_KimberlyHansenMasterDegree.pdf** in the Attachments list, click **Save As** to open the Save Attachment dialog box, if necessary, navigate to the location where you are storing your Data Files, type **NP_AC_12_KimberlyHansenMasterDegreeDetach** in the File name box, and then click **Save**.

▶ **6.** Click **OK** to close the Attachments dialog box. Because you removed the Support_AC_12_KimberlyHansenBachelorDegree.docx file as an attachment, the AddedDocuments field for the Kimberly Hansen record now shows that it has two attachments.

Donna is considering adding an employee number for each employee that could be automatically generated when a new employee record is added. You can do this by adding an AutoNumber field to the tblEmployeeCopy table.

Using an AutoNumber Field

As you know, when you create a table in Datasheet view, the AutoNumber data type is assigned to the default ID primary key field because the AutoNumber data type automatically inserts a unique number in this field for every record in the table. Therefore, it can serve as the primary key for any table you create. When defining a field with the AutoNumber data type, you can specify sequential numbering or random numbering, either of which guarantees a unique field value for every record in the table.

You'll add an AutoNumber field to the tblEmployeeCopy table.

To add an AutoNumber field to the tblEmployeeCopy table:

▶ **1.** Switch to Design view, right-click the **row selector** for the EmployeeID field to open the shortcut menu, and then click **Insert Rows**. A blank row is inserted above the EmployeeID row. Next, you'll add the AutoNumber field to this new first row in the table design.

▶ **2.** Click the first row's **Field Name** box, type **EmployeeNum**, press **TAB**, type **a**, press **TAB** to accept AutoNumber as the data type, press **F6** to navigate to the Field Properties pane, press **TAB** three times to navigate to the Caption box, and then enter **Employee Num** in the Caption box. You've finished adding the EmployeeNum field to the table. See Figure 12–23.

Figure 12–23   **EmployeeNum field added with the AutoNumber data type**

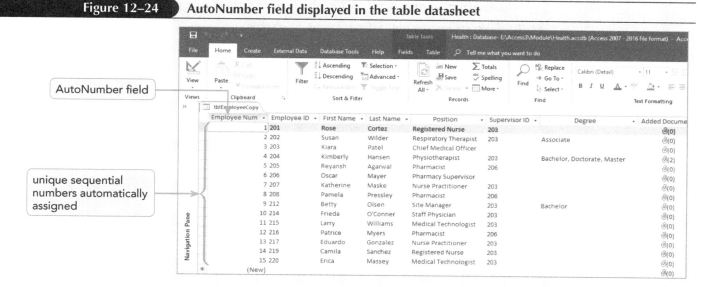

▶ **3.** Save your table design changes, switch to Datasheet view, resize the Employee Num column to its best fit, and then click the first row's **Employee Num** box to deselect all values. The new EmployeeNum field is displayed as the first column in the table, and unique incremental (sequential) numbers appear in the EmployeeNum field for the 15 records in the table. See Figure 12–24.

Figure 12–24   **AutoNumber field displayed in the table datasheet**

Employee Num	Employee ID	First Name	Last Name	Position	Supervisor ID	Degree	Added Docume
1	201	Rose	Cortez	Registered Nurse	203		ⓤ(0)
2	202	Susan	Wilder	Respiratory Therapist	203	Associate	ⓤ(0)
3	203	Kiara	Patel	Chief Medical Officer			ⓤ(0)
4	204	Kimberly	Hansen	Physiotherapist	203	Bachelor, Doctorate, Master	ⓤ(2)
5	205	Reyansh	Agarwal	Pharmacist	206		ⓤ(0)
6	206	Oscar	Mayer	Pharmacy Supervisor			ⓤ(0)
7	207	Katherine	Maske	Nurse Practitioner	203		ⓤ(0)
8	208	Pamela	Pressley	Pharmacist	206		ⓤ(0)
9	212	Betty	Olsen	Site Manager	203	Bachelor	ⓤ(0)
10	214	Frieda	O'Conner	Staff Physician	203		ⓤ(0)
11	215	Larry	Williams	Medical Technologist	203		ⓤ(0)
12	216	Patrice	Myers	Pharmacist	206		ⓤ(0)
13	217	Eduardo	Gonzalez	Nurse Practitioner	203		ⓤ(0)
14	219	Camila	Sanchez	Registered Nurse	203		ⓤ(0)
15	220	Erica	Massey	Medical Technologist	203		ⓤ(0)
*	(New)						ⓤ(0)

Next, you'll review the property settings for the Position field in the tblEmployeeCopy table to verify they are correct.

To view the property settings for the Position field:

▶ **1.** Switch to Design view, and then click the Field Name box for the Position field to display its properties. See Figure 12–25.

Figure 12–25 | **Property settings for the Position field**

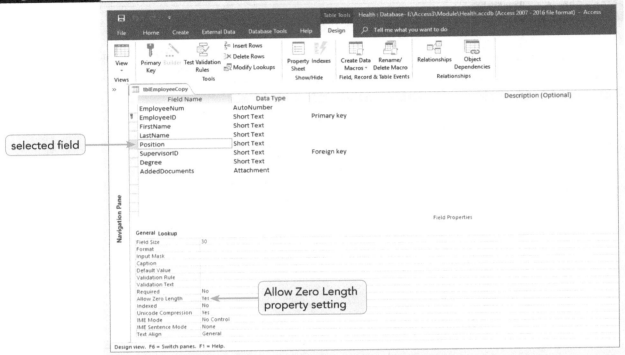

The Position field's Required property is set to No, which means field value entries are optional. The Allow Zero Length property is set to Yes, which is the default setting for Text fields and Memo fields. When a field's **Allow Zero Length property** is set to Yes, the field can store a zero length string value.

▶ **2.** Save and close the tblEmployeeCopy table.

INSIGHT

Setting the Allow Zero Length Property to No

For a Text or Memo field, there is a difference between how you specify a null field value and a zero length value and how the two values are interpreted. Recall that null means that the field does not contain any value at all and describes a text field or a numeric field that is empty. A numeric field that contains the number zero is not empty. Similarly, a text field that contains a zero length value is not empty. You specify a zero length value in a Text or a Memo field by typing two consecutive double quotation marks (""). (You used this method in the previous session.) You specify a null value in a Text or Memo field by entering a No value in the Allow Zero Length property. When you view a value for a Text or Memo field that has its Allow Zero Length property set to Yes, you can't determine if the field value has been set to null or has a zero length value because both field values look the same—the absence of a visible value.

However, the two values are treated differently. If you run a query to display all records in the table that have a null value in the field using the IsNull function, only the records with null field values appear in the query recordset; the records with zero length values in the field do not appear. And if you change the query to display all records that have a nonnull value, the records with zero length values in the field appear in the query recordset, which often raises questions from users about why those records are displayed. A typical user doesn't understand the distinction between a null value and a zero length value and doesn't need to make this distinction, so you should set the Allow Zero Length property to No for Text and Memo fields.

Donna has a previous version of Access on her home computer and wonders if she can open the Health database on that computer.

Saving an Access Database as a Previous Version

The default file format for databases you create in Access 2019 uses the .accdb filename extension and is referred to as the Access 2007 file format because it was introduced with Access 2007. None of the versions of Access prior to Access 2007 can open a database that has the .accdb filename extension. However, you can save an .accdb database to a format that is compatible with previous versions of Access—specifically, to a format compatible with Access 2000 or to a format compatible with Access 2002-2003; both have the .mdb filename extension. For people who don't have Access 2019, Access 2016, Access 2013, Access 2010, or Access 2007 but do have one of the previous versions of Access, saving the database to a previous version allows them to use the database. Unfortunately, when an Access 2007 file format database uses features such as multivalued and Attachment fields, you cannot save the database in a previous version.

To save an Access 2007 file format database as a previous version, you would complete the following steps (note that you will not actually save the database now):

1. Make sure that the database you want to save is open and all database objects are closed, and that the database does not contain any multivalued fields, Attachment fields, or any other features that are included only in Access 2007 file-formatted databases.
2. Click the File tab to open Backstage view, click Save As in the navigation bar, click Save Database As, and then click Access 2002-2003 Database or click Access 2000 Database, depending on which file format you want to use.
3. Click the Save As button. In the Save As dialog box, navigate to the folder where you want to save the file, enter a name for the database in the File name box, and then click the Save button.

Donna is glad to know it's possible for her to open the database on her home computer. Because the Health database currently uses multivalued and Attachment fields, she'll continue to work on the database only at the office, so you don't need to save it as a previous version now.

Next, Donna asks you to analyze the performance of the Health database.

Analyzing Database Performance with the Performance Analyzer

Donna wants the Health database to respond as quickly as possible to user requests, such as running queries and opening reports. You'll use the Performance Analyzer to check the performance of the Health database. The **Performance Analyzer** is an Access tool that you can use to optimize the performance of an Access database. You select the database objects you want to analyze for performance and then run the Performance Analyzer. You can select tables, queries, forms, reports, and macros either as a group or individually. The Performance Analyzer lists three types of analysis results: Recommendation, Suggestion, and Idea. You can use Access to perform the Recommendation and Suggestion optimizations for you, but you must implement the Idea optimizations. Analysis results include changes such as those related to the storage of fields and the creation of indexes and relationships.

REFERENCE

Using the Performance Analyzer

- Start Access, and open the database you want to analyze.
- On the Database Tools tab, in the Analyze group, click the Analyze Performance button.
- Select the object(s) you want to analyze, and then click OK.
- Select the analysis result(s) you want the Performance Analyzer to complete for you, and then click the Optimize button.
- Note the Idea optimizations, and perform those optimizations, as appropriate.
- Click Close.

You'll use the Performance Analyzer to optimize the performance of the Health database.

To use the Performance Analyzer to optimize the performance of the Health database:

▶ 1. Click the **Database Tools** tab, and then in the Analyze group, click the **Analyze Performance** button. The Performance Analyzer dialog box opens. See Figure 12–26.

Figure 12-26 Performance Analyzer dialog box

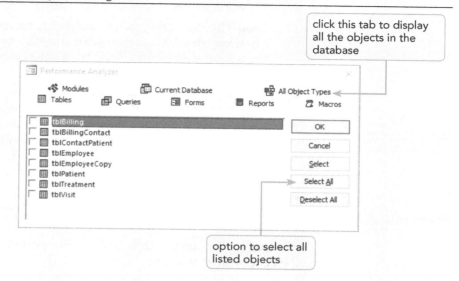

You'll analyze every object in the Health database.

▶ **2.** Click the **All Object Types** tab, and then click **Select All**. All objects in the Health database are listed on this tab, and all of them are now selected.

▶ **3.** Click **OK**. The Performance Analyzer analyzes all the objects in the Health database and, after a few moments, displays the analysis results. See Figure 12-27.

Figure 12-27 Performance Analyzer analysis results

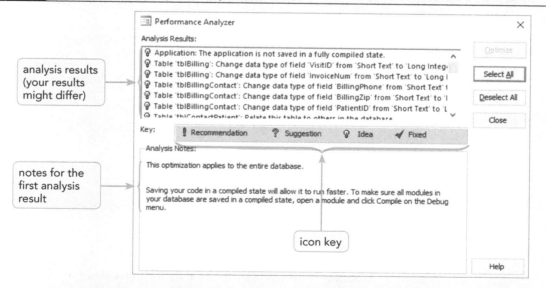

Trouble? The contents of the Analysis Results box on your screen might be different from those shown in Figure 12-27, depending on how you've completed the steps in the previous modules.

The icons that appear to the left of each result indicate the type of analysis result. Most of the analysis results are of the Idea type, which means that you have to implement them yourself. You should consider all the Idea type of analysis results, but more important now are the Recommendation and Suggestion types of analysis results, which the Performance Analyzer can complete for you automatically.

▶ **4.** Click several entries in the Analysis Results box, and read each entry and its analysis notes.

You'll let the Performance Analyzer automatically create a relationship between the tblEmployee table and itself because the table has a one-to-many relationship based on the EmployeeID field as the primary key and the SupervisorID field as the foreign key.

▶ **5.** Scroll the Analysis Results box as necessary, click the **Table 'tblEmployee': Relate to table 'tblEmployee'** analysis result (its icon is a green question mark, indicating it is a Suggestion type of analysis result) to select it, and then click the **Optimize** button. The Performance Analyzer creates a relationship between the tblEmployee table and itself, and the icon for the selected analysis result changes to a checkmark to indicate a "Fixed" status.

▶ **6.** Click **Close** to close the dialog box.

Next, you'll open the Relationships window to view the new relationship created by the Performance Analyzer.

To view the relationship created by the Performance Analyzer:

▶ **1.** Click the **Database Tools** tab, and then in the Relationships group, click the **Relationships** button to open the Relationships window. See Figure 12–28.

Figure 12–28   tblEmployee table one-to-many relationship

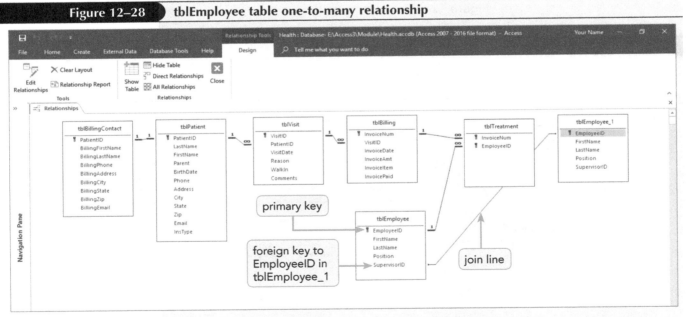

Trouble? The field lists in the Relationships window might be in different positions from those shown in Figure 12–28. This difference causes no problems.

The Performance Analyzer added a second copy of the tblEmployee table (named tblEmployee_1) and a join line between the tblEmployee and tblEmployee_1 tables to the Relationships window. The join line connects the primary table (tblEmployee_1) to the related table (tblEmployee) using the

EmployeeID field as the primary key and the SupervisorID field as the foreign key. You'll use the Edit Relationships dialog box to view the join properties for the relationship.

▶ **2.** Right-click the join line between the tblEmployee_1 and tblEmployee tables, and then click **Edit Relationship** on the shortcut menu to open the Edit Relationships dialog box. See Figure 12-29.

Figure 12-29   **Edit Relationships dialog box for the new relationship**

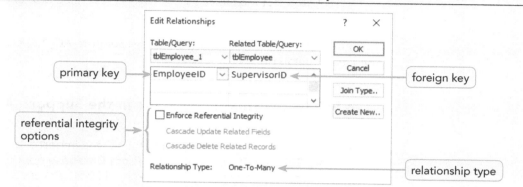

The referential integrity options are not selected, so you'll select them now for the new one-to-many relationship to show this as a one-to-many relationship in the Relationship window.

▶ **3.** Click the **Enforce Referential Integrity** check box, click the **Cascade Update Related Fields** check box, and then click **OK** to close the dialog box.

▶ **4.** Close the Relationships window, and then click **Yes**, if necessary, to save your changes.

Donna also has the responsibility at Lakewood Community Health Services for maintaining a separate database named Support_AC_12_Referral.accdb in which she stores information about patients who have been referred by other physicians but who have not yet contacted the Community Health Services. Donna wants to be able to retrieve the data in the tblReferral table in the Support_AC_12_Referral database from within the Health database. To provide Donna with access to this table, you'll create a link to the tblReferral table in the Health database.

Linking Tables between Databases

A **linked table** is a table that is stored in a separate database file from the open database and that can be updated from the open database. You can retrieve and update (add, change, and delete) records in a linked table, but you can't change its structure.

You'll provide Donna and other users of the Health database with access to the tblReferral table by using a linked table in the Health database. From the Health database, you'll be able to update the tblReferral table as a linked table, but you won't be able to change its structure. However, from the Support_AC_12_Referral database, Donna will be able to update the tblReferral table *and* change its structure.

REFERENCE

Linking to a Table in Another Access Database

- Click the External Data tab.
- In the Import & Link group, click the Access button to open the Get External Data - Access Database dialog box.
- Click the "Link to the data source by creating a linked table" option button.
- Click Browse to open the File Open dialog box, select the folder and file containing the linked data, and then click Open.
- Click OK, select the table(s) in the Link Tables dialog box, and then click OK.

You'll link to the tblReferral table in the Support_AC_12_Referral database from the Health database.

To link to the tblReferral table in the Support_AC_12_Referral database:

▶ **1.** Click the **External Data** tab, and then in the Import & Link group click the **New Data Source** button. Choose the **From Database** option, and then click the **Access** button to open the Get External Data - Access Database dialog box.

▶ **2.** Click the **Link to the data source by creating a linked table** option button, and then click the **Browse** button to open the File Open dialog box.

▶ **3.** Navigate to the **Access3 > Module** folder, click **Support_AC_12_Referral .accdb**, and then click **Open** to close the File Open dialog box and return to the Get External Data - Access Database dialog box. The path and file you selected now appear in the File name box.

▶ **4.** Click **OK**. The Link Tables dialog box opens. See Figure 12–30.

Figure 12–30   **Link Tables dialog box**

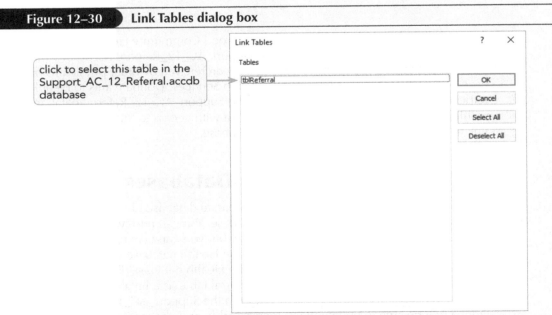

click to select this table in the Support_AC_12_Referral.accdb database

▶ **5.** Click **tblReferral** in the Tables box, and then click **OK**. The Link Tables dialog box closes, and you return to the Access window. A small blue arrow appears to the left of the tblReferral table icon in the Navigation Pane, identifying the tblReferral table as a linked table.

Donna will be reorganizing the company network folders soon and might move the Support_AC_12_Referral database to a different folder. She asks if moving the Support_AC_12_Referral database would cause a problem for the linked tblReferral table. You'll use the Linked Table Manager to handle this situation. The **Linked Table Manager** is an Access tool you use to change the filename or drive location for linked tables in an Access database. When you use Access to link to data in another file, the file's location (drive, folder, and filename) is stored in the database, and this stored location is used to connect to the linked data. If you change the file's location, you can use the Linked Table Manager to update the stored file location.

REFERENCE

Updating Linked Tables

- In the Navigation Pane, right-click the linked table name, and then click Linked Table Manager on the shortcut menu; or on the External Data tab, in the Import & Link group, click the Linked Table Manager button.
- In the Linked Table Manager dialog box, click the check box(es) for the linked table(s) you want to update, and then click OK.
- In the Select New Location dialog box, navigate to the linked table location, click the filename, and then click Open.
- Click OK, and then close the Linked Table Manager dialog box.

Next, you'll move the Support_AC_12_Referral database to a different folder, and then you'll use the Linked Table Manager to update the link to the tblReferral table in the Health database.

To move the Support_AC_12_Referral database and update the link to the tblReferral table:

1. Use Windows File Explorer to move the Support_AC_12_Referral.accdb database from the Access3 > Module folder to the Access3 folder, and then switch back to Access.

2. In the Navigation Pane, right-click **tblReferral** to open the shortcut menu, and then click **Linked Table Manager**. The Linked Table Manager dialog box opens. See Figure 12–31.

Figure 12–31   **Linked Table Manager dialog box**

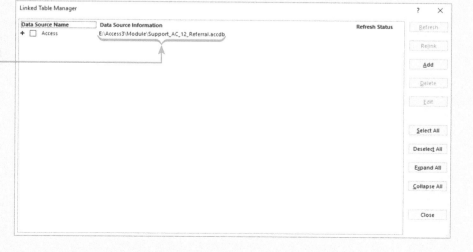

original location of the Support_AC_12_Referral.accdb database (your path may be different)

The tblReferral table is the only linked table, so it's the only table listed. The Access3 > Module folder provided with your Data Files, which is the original location of the Support_AC_12_Referral.accdb database, is listed as the current location for the tblReferral table.

▶ 3. Click **Select All**, and then click **Relink**. The Select New Location of Access dialog box opens.

▶ 4. Navigate to the **Access3** folder, click **Support_AC_12_Referral.accdb** in the file list, and then click **OK**.

▶ 5. A Relink tblReferral dialog box appears and asks for the name of the table you want to link. Since tblReferral is already highlighted, as it is the only table, click **OK** to close the dialog box. The Linked Table Manager dialog box now displays the Access3 folder as the current location of the linked tblReferral table.

▶ 6. Close the Linked Table Manager dialog box.

Next, you'll open the tblReferral table to update it as a linked table from the new location.

To update the tblReferral table and view its design in the Health database:

▶ 1. Open the **tblReferral** table in Datasheet view, and then close the Navigation Pane. The tblReferral table datasheet displays four records. First, you'll add a new record to the tblReferral table.

▶ 2. Click the **New (blank) record** button ▶ , type **15005** in the Patient ID column, press **TAB**, type **Suzanne** in the First Name column, press **TAB**, type **Miller** in the Last Name column, press **TAB**, type **470-555-1907** in the Phone column, press **TAB**, type **1234 Jasper Ct** in the Address column, press **TAB**, type **Atlanta** in the City column, press **TAB**, type **GA** in the State column, press **TAB**, type **30305** in the Zip column, press **TAB**, type **s.miller21@ example.com** in the Email Address column, and then press **TAB**.

Next, you'll switch to Design view to verify that you can't change the design of the tblReferral table from the Health database.

▶ 3. Switch to Design view. A dialog box appears informing you that the tblReferral table is a linked table whose design cannot be modified here, only from the source database. Click **Yes** to open the database anyway. The PatientID field is the current field, and the Help message in the Field Properties section indicates that you can't change the Field Name property value for linked tables. See Figure 12–32.

Figure 12–32   Linked table in Design view

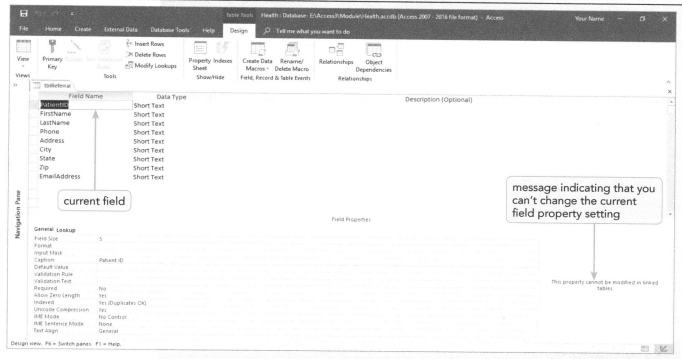

4. Press **F6** to select the Field Size property in the Field Properties pane. The Help message indicates that you can't change the Field Size property.

5. Press **TAB** to position the insertion point in the Format box. The standard Help message for the Format property appears, which means you can change this field property.

6. Close the table.

Now you'll open the Support_AC_12_Referral database to see the new record in the tblReferral table that you added from the Health database. Then you'll delete that record and view the table in Design view.

To update the tblReferral table and view its design in the Support_AC_12_Referral database:

1. Start another instance of Access, keeping the Health database open as well, and then open the Support_AC_12_Referral.accdb database located in the Access3 > Module folder provided with your Data Files.

   Trouble? If the security warning is displayed below the ribbon, click the Enable Content button.

2. Open the Navigation Pane (if necessary), open the **tblReferral** table in Datasheet view, and then click the **row selector** for record 5. The record for Suzanne Miller, which you added to the tblReferral linked table in the Health database, appears as record 5 in the tblReferral table in the Referral database.

3. On the Home tab, in the Records group, click **Delete**, and then click **Yes** in the message box that opens to delete record 5.

▶ **4.** Switch to Design view. Because the tblReferral table is not a linked table in the Support_AC_12_Referral database (its own database), the Help message in the Field Properties pane does not warn you that you can't change the Field Name property. You can make any design changes you want to the tblReferral table in the Support_AC_12_Referral database.

▶ **5.** Close the tblReferral table, and then close the Support_AC_12_Referral database. You return to the Health database.

Donna decides that she'd like to maintain the Support_AC_12_Referral database separately and asks you to delete the linked tblReferral table in the Health database. When you delete the linked tblReferral table in the Health database, you are deleting the *link* to the tblReferral table that exists in the Support_AC_12_Referral database; the tblReferral table will remain in the Support_AC_12_Referral database.

To delete the linked tblReferral table in the Health database:

▶ **1.** In the Health database, open the Navigation Pane, right-click **tblReferral** in the Navigation Pane to open the shortcut menu, and then click **Delete**. A dialog box asks if you want to remove the link to the tblReferral table. See Figure 12–33.

Figure 12–33 **Dialog box that opens when attempting to delete a linked table**

The dialog box confirms that you'll delete only the link to the tblReferral table but not the tblReferral table itself in the Referral database.

▶ **2.** Click **Yes**. The link to the tblReferral table is deleted, and the tblReferral table no longer appears in the Navigation Pane for the Health database.

Next, Donna wants to create several queries for the Health database, but she doesn't want the user interface for other users to be cluttered with queries they won't need to use. She asks if she can have a special user interface to access the data in the Health database. You can accomplish this by splitting the database.

Using the Database Splitter

TIP

Be sure to make a backup before splitting a database.

Users of a particular database might want to customize the user interface to create their own custom versions of the interface, while accessing the same central table data. The **Database Splitter** is an Access tool that splits an Access database into two files: one file contains the tables, and the other file contains the queries, forms, reports, and other database objects. Although a single master copy of the file containing the tables is stored and accessed, users can have their own copies of the other file and add their own queries, reports, and other objects to handle their unique processing needs. Each file created by the Database Splitter is an Access database. The database that contains the tables is called the **back-end database**, and the database that contains the other objects, including the user interface, is called the **front-end database**.

After you split a database, when users open a front-end database, the objects they open use data in the tables in the back-end database. Because the tables in the front-end database are linked tables that are stored in the back-end database, the front-end database contains the physical drive locations of the tables in the back-end database. You can move the front-end database to a different drive location without affecting the physical connections to the back-end database. However, if you move the back-end database to a different drive location, you'll need to use the Linked Table Manager to change the physical drive locations of the back-end database's tables in the front-end database.

People who develop databases and sell them to multiple companies usually split their databases. When a developer delivers a split database, the initial back-end database does not include the company's data, and the initial front-end database is complete as created by the developer. Companies use the front-end database to update their data in the back-end database, but they do not modify the front-end database in any way. Periodically, the database developer improves the front-end database by modifying and adding queries, reports, and other objects without changing the structure of the tables. In other words, the developer changes the front-end database but does not change the back-end database. The developer gives its client companies replacement front-end databases, which continue to work with the back-end database that contains the company's data.

Splitting a database also lets you place the files on different computers. You can place a copy of the front-end database on each user's computer and place the back-end database on a network server that users access through their front-end databases; this arrangement distributes the workload across the network. Finally, as a company grows, it might need a more powerful DBMS such as Oracle, SQL Server, DB2, or MySQL. You could retain the original Access front-end database and replace the Access back-end database with a new non-Access back-end database, which is an easier task than replacing all database objects.

Because splitting an Access database causes minimal disruption to a company's database processing as you periodically enhance the user interface, and because splitting provides greater flexibility for future growth, you should always develop your databases with splitting in mind. The entire process of splitting a database is illustrated in Figure 12–34.

Figure 12–34   **Split Access database**

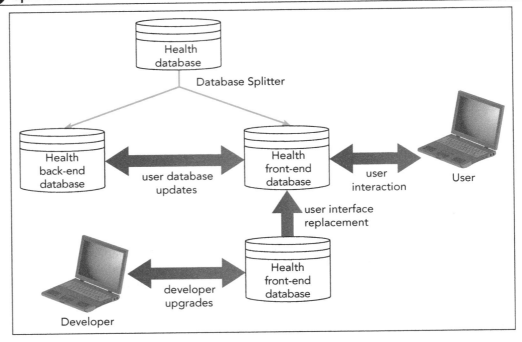

Using the Database Splitter

REFERENCE

- Make a backup copy of the database that you want to split.
- Start Access and open the database you want to split.
- Click the Database Tools tab, and then in the Move Data group, click the Access Database button to start the Database Splitter Wizard.
- Click the Split Database button, select the drive and folder for the back-end database, type a name for the database in the File name box, and then click the Split button.
- Click OK.

You'll use the Database Splitter to split the Health database into two files. You will make a backup copy of the database before you split the database.

To use the Database Splitter:

▶ **1.** Make a backup copy of the Health database.

▶ **2.** Click the **Database Tools** tab, and then in the Move Data group, click **Access Database**. The Database Splitter Wizard opens. See Figure 12–35.

Figure 12–35	Database Splitter Wizard

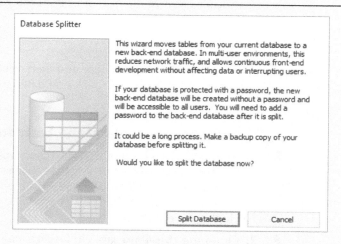

3. Click **Split Database**. The Create Back-end Database dialog box opens. The back-end database will contain the tables from the Health database. You'll use the default filename (Health_be with the .accdb extension) for the back-end database.

4. Navigate to the **Access3 > Module** folder (if necessary), and then click **Split**. After a few moments, a dialog box informs you that the database was successfully split.

5. Click **OK** to close the dialog boxes, and then scroll up to the top of the Navigation Pane, if necessary. See Figure 12–36.

Figure 12–36	Linked tables in the Health database

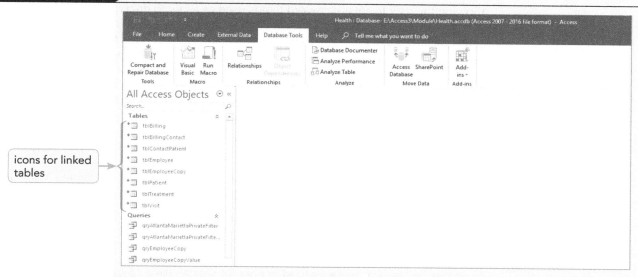

Each table in the Health database has a blue arrow next to its name indicating that it links to that table in another file. The tables are no longer stored in the Health database; they are stored in the Health_be database file you just created with the Database Splitter. You can use the linked tables as if they were stored in the Health database, except that you cannot change a table's design from the Health database. You have to close the Health database and open the Health_be database to change a table's design.

▶ **6.** Scroll down the Navigation Pane. The queries, forms, reports, macros, and modules you've created appear in the Navigation Pane and are still stored in the Health database.

You'll close the Health database and then open the Health_be database to verify which objects are stored in the back-end database.

To verify the contents of the back-end database:

▶ **1.** Close the Health database, and then open the **Health_be.accdb** database located in the Access3 > Module folder. The tables from the Health database appear in the Navigation Pane with their usual icons, indicating the tables are now stored in the Health_be database. No other objects exist in the Health_be database.

▶ **2.** Open the **tblBilling** table in Design view. You can modify the design of the tables in the Health_be database because they are stored in that database; they are not linked from another database as they are in the Health database.

▶ **3.** Close the tblBilling table, close the Health_be database, and then open the Health database.

Securing an Access Database

Security refers to the protection of a database against unauthorized access, either intentional or accidental. Access provides a unique approach to securing a database by allowing the user to set a password that is used as a key to encrypt the database.

Encryption translates the data in a database to a scrambled format that's indecipherable to another program and stores it in an encrypted format. If unauthorized users attempt to bypass Access and get to the data directly, they will see only the encrypted version of the data. However, users accessing the data using Access and who have the password will have no problem working with the data. When a user stores or modifies data in an encrypted database, Access encrypts the data before updating the database. Once you've encrypted a database, you can use Access to decrypt it. **Decrypting** a database reverses the encryption. Before a user retrieves encrypted data using Access, the data will be decrypted and presented to the user in the normal format.

To prevent access to a database by an unauthorized user through Access, you can assign a password to the database. A **password** is a string of characters assigned to a database that users must enter before they can open the database. As long as the password is known only to authorized users of the database, unauthorized access to the database is prevented. You should use a password that's easily remembered by authorized users but is not obvious or easily guessed by others.

Access provides a single method to encrypt a database and set a password at the same time.

PROSKILLS

Decision Making: Determining When to Encrypt Data Using a Password

You probably are familiar with setting a password and using it to unlock a cell phone or to sign into your email or another device or software application. In these cases, the password acts as an authorization for you to use the device or software. Some software applications use a password for more than simply opening a file. Access uses the password to actually encrypt the data. The password itself isn't stored anywhere. Instead, the password is used as part of a mathematical formula to encrypt the data. When a user tries to open an encrypted file, the user is prompted to provide a password, and attempts to open the file. If the entered password is correct, the password is used to decrypt the data and open the file. If the password is incorrect, the data is not readable, and, therefore, the file will not open.

Because the password itself isn't stored anywhere and the data is actually encrypted, the contents of the database cannot be recovered if a user forgets a password. This is a security feature and also a potential problem if you are concerned about losing the password. Unlike your cell phone, which can be reset and still used if the password is lost, an encrypted Access file cannot be used if the password is lost.

If the data isn't sensitive, it's not as important to encrypt the data with a password. An encrypted Access database provides security for data and should be considered when the data it contains is sensitive, such as credit card information or private health record information. If the database is accessible only from a desktop computer in a secured, locked office, that may be enough security, and it may not be necessary to add encryption.

If you've decided to set a password, therefore encrypting your database, keep in mind that passwords are more secure when they consist of a mixture of numbers, symbols, and both lowercase and uppercase letters.

Access has some built-in security so that users cannot accidentally change data. When you open a database from the Open dialog box in Access, the default setting is for **shared access**; that is, two or more users can open and use the same database at the same time. However, if you want to set a password for encrypting the database, you first need to open the database with exclusive access. You do this by clicking the Open arrow in the Open dialog box and selecting Open Exclusive on the menu that opens. When you open an Access database with **exclusive access**, you prevent multiple users from opening and using the database at the same time. You must open the database with exclusive access in order to set a password, so that you can guarantee that only one copy of the database is open when you set the password.

If you want someone to be able to view the data without changing it, you can open a database as a read-only file, by selecting the Open Read-Only option from the Open menu in the Open dialog box. **Open Read-Only** includes any database action that does not involve updating the database, such as running queries (but not action queries) and viewing table records. Actions that are prohibited when you open a database as read-only (because they involve updating the database) include changing the database design and updating table records. The other two open options on the Open menu open the selected database with exclusive access for reading and updating (Open Exclusive) or for reading only (Open Exclusive Read-Only).

When multiple users update the database at the same time, row-level locking is enabled so that one user can't change the row content while another user is viewing it. **Locking** denies access by other users to data while one user's updates are processed in the database. **Row-level locking** denies access by other users to the table rows one user is in the process of updating; other users can update the database simultaneously as long as the rows they need to update are not being updated by other users at the same time.

INSIGHT

Setting and Removing Password Encryption

In order to set a password, you first open an Access database file with exclusive access to ensure no other users are viewing or manipulating the data when you add or remove the password. After you open the file with exclusive access, you can open Backstage view to access the Encrypt with Password button. If you decide to apply encryption, you are prompted to type the password twice. This is a security feature to ensure that you did not make a mistake the first time you type the password. Both password entries must be identical in order to set the password encryption. To remove password encryption, you click the Decrypt Database button in Backstage view. Doing so cancels the password protection for the database and also decrypts the database.

Donna is pleased with the changes you have made. As a final enhancement to the user interface, she asks you to set Access to open the navigation form you created in a previous module automatically when a user opens the Health database.

Setting the Database Startup Options

TIP

To bypass the startup options that you set, press and hold SHIFT when you open the database or after entering the password in an encrypted database.

In Access you can specify certain actions, called **startup options**, that take place when a database opens. For example, you can specify the name that appears in the Access window title bar, prevent users from using the Navigation Pane, or specify a form that is automatically opened when a user opens a database.

Donna wants Access to automatically display the navigation form you created in a previous module when users open the Health database. Users can then avoid having to use the Navigation Pane to access the navigation form.

REFERENCE

Setting the Database Startup Options

- Open the database, and then click the File tab to open Backstage view.
- Click Options in the navigation bar to open the Access Options dialog box.
- In the left pane, click Current Database.
- Set the database startup options in the right pane, and then click OK to have these options take effect the next time the database is opened.

The Session 12.2 Visual Overview identifies the database startup options Donna wants you to set for the Health database. In addition, you'll disable the **Enable error checking option**, which checks for design errors in forms and reports and alerts you to errors by displaying the Error Checking Options button. Disabling the Enable error checking option will suppress the display of the triangle-shaped error indicators that appear in the upper-right or upper-left corner of a control when a potential error occurs. Unlike all the other options, which appear on the Current Database page in the Access Options dialog box, the Enable error checking option appears on the Object Designers page in the Access Options dialog box, and disabling this option will affect all databases you open.

You'll finish developing the Health database by setting the database startup options.

To set the database startup options in the Health database:

▶ **1.** Click the **File** tab to open Backstage view, and then in the navigation bar, click **Options** to open the Access Options dialog box.

▶ **2.** In the left pane of the dialog box, click **Current Database** to display the list of options for the current database.

▶ **3.** In the Application Title box, type **Health Release 1**, click the **Display Form** arrow, and then click **frmNavigation**. This sets the title in the Access title bar and sets the frmNavigation form as the initial form that loads when the Health database is opened.

▶ **4.** Scrolling as necessary, click the following check boxes to disable (uncheck) the options:

Use Access Special Keys

Enable Layout View

Enable design changes for tables in Datasheet view

Display Navigation Pane

Allow Full Menus

Allow Default Shortcut Menus

Track name AutoCorrect info

▶ **5.** Compare your Access Options dialog box to the Session 12.2 Visual Overview.

▶ **6.** In the left pane of the Access Options dialog box, click **Object Designers** to display the list of options for creating and modifying database objects, and then scroll to the bottom of the dialog box.

▶ **7.** If necessary, click the **Enable error checking** check box to clear it and disable all error checking options. See Figure 12–37.

Trouble? If the Error checking check box does not contain a checkmark, skip Step 7.

Figure 12–37 Error checking options in the Access Options dialog box

click to remove the checkmark and disable error checking

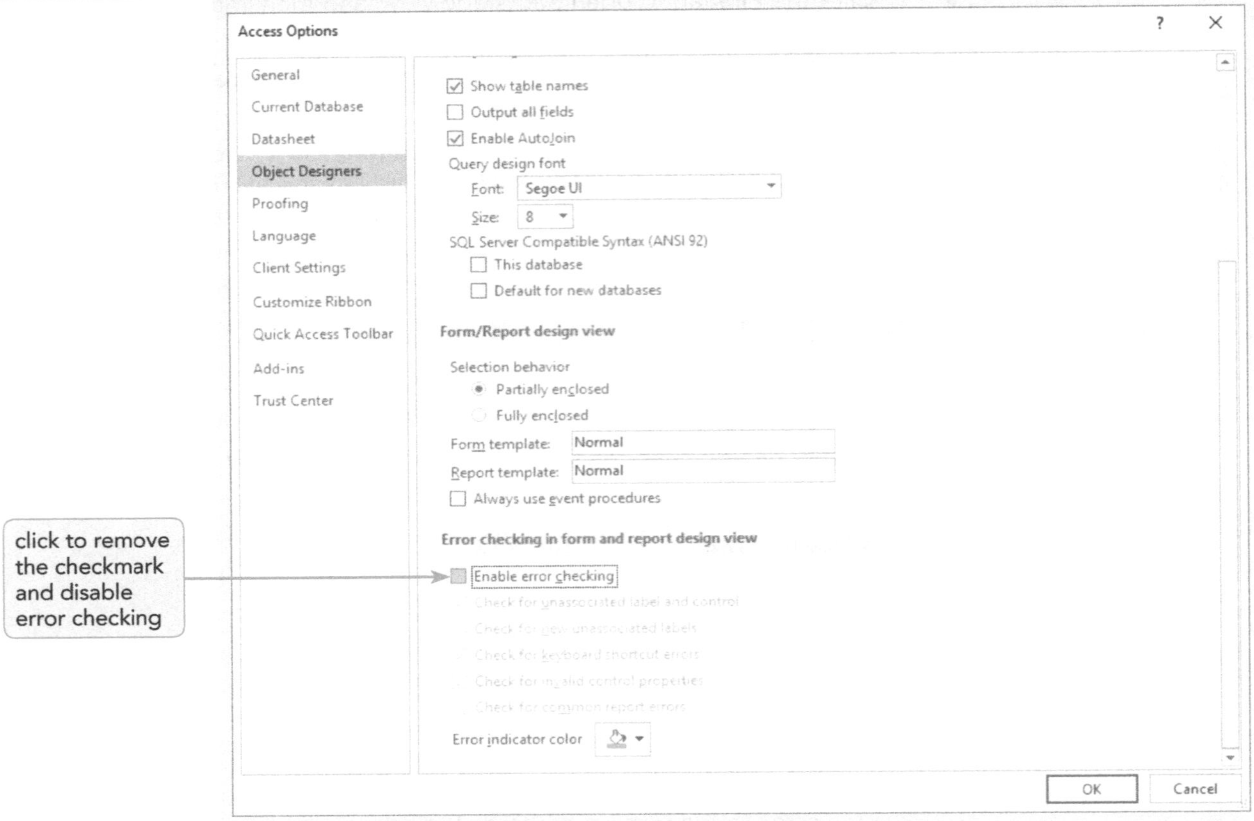

▶ **8.** Click **OK** to close the Access Options dialog box. A dialog box informs you that you must close and reopen the Health database for the options you selected to take effect.

▶ **9.** Click **OK** to close the dialog box.

To test the database startup options you have set, you need to close and reopen the Health database.

To test the database startup options:

▶ **1.** Click the **File** tab to open Backstage view, and then click **Close** in the navigation bar to close the Health database without exiting Access.

▶ **2.** Click the **File** tab to open Backstage view again, click **Open** in the navigation bar, and then in the Recent list, click **Health.accdb** to open the Health database. See Figure 12–38.

Figure 12–38   Health database user interface

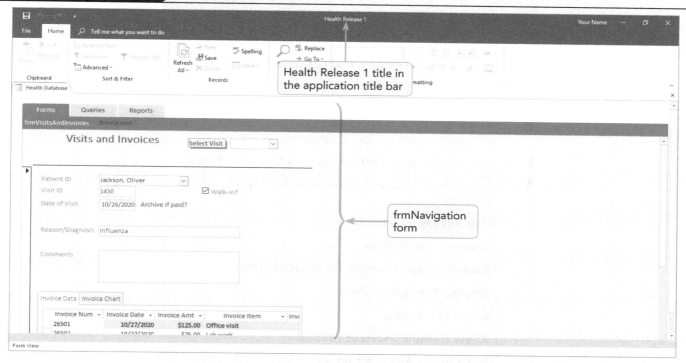

The Health database opens and displays the frmNavigation form. Notice the Navigation Pane is not available on the left side of the window, and the ribbon displays only the File and Home tabs. The name "Health Release 1" appears in the Access window title bar.

▶ **3.** Click each of the tabs in the navigation form to verify that all features work properly on the Health database user interface.

Donna likes the navigation startup setting but realizes that some of her staff will need access to the ribbon and database objects. One method her staff could use is to press and hold SHIFT when they open the database. You'll open the database using this method to bypass the startup options now.

To bypass the startup options when opening the database:

▶ **1.** Close the Health database. Doing so also closes Access.

▶ **2.** Start Access, and then press and hold **SHIFT** while you click **Health.accdb** in the Recent list.

The Health database opens without the startup options you set. For instance, the Navigation Pane is now accessible on the left side of the window, and you can now use the shortcut keys to close a table, which had been disabled previously in the startup options when Allow Default Shortcut Menus was disabled.

▶ **3.** Open the Navigation Pane, open the **tblEmployee** table in Datasheet view, and then right-click the **tblEmployee** tab to display the shortcut menu.

▶ **4.** Click **Close** on the shortcut menu to close the tblEmployee table.

Using SHIFT to open the file bypasses the startup options, but Donna thinks this method also defeats the purpose of having startup options. Instead, she would like you to change the database options to fully display the ribbon and enable the database objects again. You'll reset the database startup options.

To reset the database startup options in the Health database:

▶ **1.** Click the **File** tab to open Backstage view, and then in the navigation bar, click **Options** to open the Access Options dialog box.

▶ **2.** In the left pane of the dialog box, click **Current Database** to display the list of options for the current database.

▶ **3.** Click the **Display Form** arrow, and then click **(none)**.

▶ **4.** Scrolling as necessary, click the following check boxes to enable (check) the properties:

Use Access Special Keys

Enable Layout View

Enable design changes for tables in Datasheet view

Display Navigation Pane

Allow Full Menus

Allow Default Shortcut Menus

Track name AutoCorrect info

A dialog box opens that indicates the Track name AutoCorrect info option generates name maps for the database objects and may take several minutes.

▶ **5.** Click **OK** to accept and close the dialog box.

▶ **6.** In the left pane of the Access Options dialog box, click **Object Designers** to display the list of options for creating and modifying database objects, and then scroll to the bottom of the dialog box.

▶ **7.** Click the **Enable error checking** check box to select it and enable all error checking options.

▶ **8.** Click **OK** to close the Access Options dialog box. A dialog box may inform you that the Health database must close all objects and update dependency Information.

▶ **9.** Click **Yes** to close the dialog box (if necessary). A dialog box informs you that you must close and reopen the Health database for the changes to take effect.

▶ **10.** Click **OK** to close the dialog box, and then exit Access.

▶ **11.** Open the **Health.accdb** database again to verify the ribbon and database objects are displayed.

▶ **12.** Close the Health database and exit Access.

INSIGHT

Saving a Database as an ACCDE File

If a database contains VBA code, you can save an ACCDE file version of the database to prevent people from viewing or changing the VBA code. Saving an Access database as an **ACCDE file**, which has the .accde extension instead of the .accdb extension, compiles all VBA modules, removes all editable VBA source code, and compacts the resulting database. The database and its VBA code continue to run as normal, but users cannot view or edit the VBA code. Also, users can't view, modify, or create forms, reports, or modules in Design view, nor can they import or export forms, reports, or modules. Because an ACCDE file limits database design changes to tables and queries, saving a database as an ACCDE file is best suited to a front-end database. You should keep a backup copy of the complete front-end database in case you need to modify the database design. To save a database as an ACCDE file, follow these steps:

1. Open the database you want to save as an ACCDE file.
2. Click the File tab to open Backstage view, click Save As in the navigation bar, and then click Make ACCDE.
3. Click the Save As button to open the Save As dialog box.
4. Type the name for the file in the File name box, navigate to the location where you want to store the file, and then click the Save button.

Your work with the Health database is now complete. Donna is happy with your work and believes the database will fully satisfy the requirements of the clinic.

REVIEW

Session 12.2 Quick Check

1. You can specify sequential numbering or random numbering for a(n) ___ field.
2. What is the Performance Analyzer?
3. When do you use the Linked Table Manager?
4. What is the Database Splitter?
5. ___ refers to the protection of a database against unauthorized access, either intentional or accidental.
6. What is a startup option?

Review Assignments

PRACTICE

Data Files needed for the Review Assignments: Product.accdb *(cont. from previous module)*, **Support_AC_12_Ads.accdb, Support_AC_12_Autoclave_Specification_Sheet.pdf,** and **Support_AC_12_Autoclave.xlsx**

Donna asks you to complete your work with the user interface for the Product database. To meet this request, complete the following steps:

1. Open the **Product** database you worked with in the previous three modules.
2. Open the **tblProduct** table datasheet, use an AutoFilter to filter records using the TempControlled field for values of Yes and Sterile field for values of Yes, and then save and close the table.
3. Use Filter By Form with the tblSupplier table to select all records in which the state is FL or SC and the category is Supplies. Apply the filter, save the filter as a query named **qryStateSuppliesFilter**, clear all filters, and then close the table.
4. Create a query named **qryProductSubquery** that selects the SupplierID field from the tblProduct table for all products that weigh 50 pounds or more. (*Hint*: Do not show the Weight field.) Switch to SQL view, copy the SQL code, and save the qryProductSubquery query.
5. Create a new query in SQL view. Paste the SQL code that you copied in the previous step from qryProductSubquery, and add code that uses the existing code as a subquery and selects all fields from the tblInvoice table where the SupplierID is in the tblInvoice table. Run the query, save the query as **qryProductSubqueryInvoice**, and then close the query.
6. Add a multivalued field to the end of the **tblInvoice** table, defining permitted values of **Courier**, **Email**, **Fax**, and **USPS**, and naming the field **Transmitted**. Save the table, and then add the following values to the field in the table datasheet: for record 4—Email and USPS, for record 8—Courier, and for record 12—Fax and USPS. Close the table.
7. Use the Simple Query Wizard to create a query named **qryInvoiceValue** that displays all fields from the tblInvoice table; for the Transmitted field, display only the version of the field that uses the Value property, and change its Caption property setting to **Transmitted**. Save and close the query.
8. Add an Attachment field named **ProductFiles** to the end of the tblProduct table, using a Caption property setting of **Product Files**. Attach the files **Support_AC_12_Autoclave_Specification_Sheet.pdf** and **Support_AC_12_Autoclave.xlsx** to the ProductFiles field for record 3 (Product ID AU490 - Autoclave) in the tblProduct table, and then close the table.
9. Add an AutoNumber field named **ProductNum** to the beginning of the tblProductSpecialEnviron table, using a Caption property setting of **Product Num** and a New Values property setting of Random. View the table in Datasheet view to see the random numbers. Resize the Product Num column to its best fit. Save and close the table.
10. Use the Performance Analyzer to analyze the entire Product database, but do not implement any of the analysis results. How many analysis results of the Recommendation type did the Performance Analyzer find? Of the Suggestion type? Of the Idea type? If requested, record the answers in a Word document, and submit it to your instructor. Close the Performance Analyzer dialog box.
11. Use Windows File Explorer to move the **Support_AC_12_Ads.accdb** database from the Access3 > Review folder to the Access3 folder. In the Product database, link to the tblAd table, and then move the **Support_AC_12_Ads.accdb** database to the Access3 > Review folder. Use the Linked Table Manager to update the link to the tblAd table. Open the tblAd table in Datasheet view, and then add a new record to the table: Ad Num **7**, Ad Date **07/12/2020**, Ad Cost **$250.00**, and Placed **Web ad**.
12. Close the Product database without exiting Access, create a copy of the Product database in the Access3 > Review folder, and then rename the copy as **NP_AC_12_Sellers**. Open the **Product** database in the Access3 > Review folder, and then use the Database Splitter to split the Product database. Use the default name for the back-end database, and store it in the Access3 > Review folder.
13. Set the same database startup options for the Product database that you set in Module 12 for the Health database, using a value of **Vendor for Lakewood Community Health Services** for the Application Title option. Test the new startup options and then reset them as you did with the Health database; however, keep the new Application Title.
14. Compact and repair the database, exit Access, open the **Product** database, test all the navigation options, and then close the database.

Case Problem 1

APPLY

Data Files needed for this Case Problem: Instruction.accdb *(cont. from previous module),* **Support_AC_12_Allen.txt,** and **Support_AC_12_RoomOptions.accdb**

Great Giraffe   Jeremiah asks you to complete your work with the user interface for the Instruction database. To meet his request, complete the following steps:

1. Open the **Instruction** database you worked with in the previous three modules.
2. Open the tblStudent table datasheet, use an AutoFilter to filter records using the City field for values of Englewood and Littleton, and then save and close the table.
3. Use Filter By Form with the **qryStudentData** query to select all records in which the Last Name is Bailey or Brown. Apply the filter, save the filter as a query named **qryBaileyBrownFilter**, and then close the query.
4. Create a query named **qry40HoursSubquery** that selects the InstanceID field from the tblCourse table for all records that have a value of 40 for HoursPerWeek. (*Hint:* Do not show the HoursPerWeek field.) Switch to SQL view, copy the SQL code, and then save and close the qry40HoursSubquery query.
5. Create a new query in SQL view. Paste the SQL code you copied in the previous step from qry40HoursSubquery, add code that uses the current code as a subquery and selects all fields from the tblRegistration table where the InstanceID is in the tblRegistration table, and then run the query. Save the query as **qry40HoursSubquerySignupID**, and then save and close the query.
6. Add an Attachment field named **StudentAttachment** to the end of the tblStudent table, using a Caption property setting of **Student Attachment**. Cody Allen, one of the students at Great Giraffe, has written a note thanking them for their excellent instruction. The document is stored in the **Support_AC_12_Allen.txt** text file and is located in the Access3 > Case1 folder. Attach the document to the StudentAttachment field for record 2 (Cody Allen record) in the tblStudent table, resize the Student Attachment column to its best fit, and then save and close the table.
7. Add an AutoNumber field named **PlanNum** to the beginning of the tblCityPaymentPlan table, using a Caption property setting of **Plan Num** and a New Values property setting of Random. Specify the PlanNum field as the primary key. Resize the Plan Num column to its best fit in the datasheet, and then save and close the table.
8. Use the Performance Analyzer to analyze the entire Instruction database, but do not implement any of the analysis results. How many analysis results of the Recommendation type did the Performance Analyzer find? Of the Suggestion type? Of the Idea type? If requested, record the answers in a Word document, and submit it to your instructor. Close the Performance Analyzer dialog box.
9. Use Windows File Explorer to move the **Support_AC_12_RoomOptions.accdb** database from the Access3 > Case1 folder to the Access3 folder. Link to the tblRoomOptions table in the Support_AC_12_RoomOptions database located in the Access3 folder. Use Windows File Explorer to move the **Support_AC_12_RoomOptions.accdb** database to the Access3 > Case1 folder, and then use the Linked Table Manager to update the link to the tblRoomOptions table. Open the tblRoomOptions table in Datasheet view, and then add a new record to the table: Room ID **BIT 123A** and Capacity **35**. Save and close the tblRoomOptions table.
10. Close the Instruction database without exiting Access, create a copy of the Instruction database in the Access3 > Case1 folder, and then rename the copy as **NP_AC_12_InProgress**. Open the **Instruction** database in the Access3 > Case1 folder, and then use the Database Splitter to split the Instruction database. Use the default name for the back-end database, and store it in the Access3 > Case1 folder.
11. Set the same database startup options for the Instruction database that you set in Module 12 for the Health database, using a value of **Great Giraffe** for the Application Title option. Test the new startup options and then reset them as you did with the Health database; however, keep the new Application Title.
12. Compact and repair the database, exit Access, open the **Instruction** database, test all the navigation options, and then close the database.

CHALLENGE

Case Problem 2

Data Files needed for this Case Problem: CleanOut.accdb *(cont. from previous module)*, Support_AC_12_BEN36NE_111820.txt, and Support_AC_12_Trucks.accdb

Drain Adopter   Tandrea wants you to complete your work with the user interface for the CleanOut database. To meet her request, complete the following steps:

1. Open the **CleanOut** database you worked with in the previous three modules.

⊕ **Explore** 2. Open the tblSupply table datasheet, and then use an AutoFilter to filter records using the LastOrderDate field for values in the second quarter of a year. (*Hint*: In the Health database in the module, you filtered for November; here you will be filtering for Quarter 2 in the same fashion). Save and close the table.

⊕ **Explore** 3. Use Filter By Form with the **frmVolunteerMasterData** form to select all records in which the zip is 98225 and the volunteer has not been trained. (*Hint*: Review your options on how to select those volunteers that have not been trained since you do not have a list to choose from.) Apply the filter, save the filter as a query named **qry98225NotTrainedFilter**, and then close the form.

⊕ **Explore** 4. Create a query named **qrySpecialVolunteersSubquery** that selects the VolunteerID from the tblSpecialVolunteers table. Create a query named **qrySpecialVolunteersData** that contains all fields from the tblVolunteer table for records whose VolunteerID is in the subquery qrySpecialVolunteersSubquery. Use SQL view to create the qrySpecialVolunteersData query. The results should be sorted in descending order by VolunteerID. Save and close the query. (*Hint*: Create the qrySpecialVolunteersSubquery first, copy the SQL code from the subquery to create the new query qrySpecialVolunteersData, and then open the new qrySpecialVolunteersData in Design view to apply the sort order.)

5. Add a multivalued field to the end of the tblSupply table, defining permitted values of **Grounds**, **Roads**, and **Technician**, and naming the field **Areas**. Allow the user to choose more than one area. Save the table, and then add the following values to the field in the table datasheet: for record 1 (Broom01)—Grounds and Roads; for record 2 (Broom04)—Roads; and for record 4 (Gloves01)—Grounds, Roads, and Technician; for record 6 (Rake03)—Grounds. Resize the Areas column to its best fit, and then save and close the table.

6. Use the Simple Query Wizard to create a query named **qrySupplyMultivalued** that displays the SupplyID, Description, Cost, NumberOnHand, LastOrderDate, and Areas from the tblSupply table; for the Areas field, display only the version of the field that displays multiple values in a text box. Resize the Areas column to its best fit, and then save and close the query.

7. Add an Attachment field named **Notes** to the end of the tblDrain table, using a Caption property setting of **Special Notes**. This will be used to supply volunteers with extra information about drains. Attach a file named **Support_AC_12_BEN36NE_111820.txt** to the Notes field in the third record (BEN36NE). This document gives information about the cleaning of the BEN36NE drain on 11/18/2020. Resize the Special Notes column to its best fit, and then save and close the table.

⊕ **Explore** 8. Add an AutoNumber field named **SpecialNum** to the top of the tblSpecialVolunteers table, using a Caption property setting of **Special Num** and a New Values property setting of Increment. Specify the SpecialNum field as the primary key. Resize the Special Num column to its best fit in the datasheet, and then save and close the table.

9. Use the Performance Analyzer to analyze the entire CleanOut database. How many analysis results of the Recommendation type did the Performance Analyzer find? Of the Suggestion type? Of the Idea type? If requested, record the answers in a Word document, and submit it to your instructor. Notice the analyzer gives ideas that would have you change data types in various tables from the Short Text to Long Integer data type. Think about the consequences of performing this change, noting that when you created the relationships previously, you were careful to associate similar data types with each other. If changed now, you would have to ensure all the necessary data types would be updated to ensure integrity. You will not attempt any modifications at this juncture, so close the Performance Analyzer dialog box.

10. Use Windows File Explorer to move the **Support_AC_12_Trucks.accdb** database from the Access3 > Case2 folder to the Access3 folder. Link to the tblTrucks table in the Support_AC_12_ Trucks database located in the Access3 folder. Use Windows File Explorer to move the **Support_AC_12_Trucks.accdb** database to the Access3 > Case2 folder, and then use the Linked Table Manager to update the link to the tblTrucks table. Open the tblTrucks table in Datasheet view, and then add a new record to the table: Truck ID **Truck05**, Type **Standard pickup**, Year **2019**, and Color **Green**. Close the table.

⊕ **Explore** 11. Close the CleanOut database without exiting Access, create a copy of the CleanOut database in the Access3 > Case2 folder, and then rename the copy as **NP_AC_12_CleanStreets**. Open the **CleanOut** database in the Access3 > Case2 folder, and then use the Database Splitter to split the CleanOut database. Use the default name for the back-end database, and store it in the Access3 > Case2 folder.

⊕ **Explore** 12. Set the same database startup options for the CleanOut database that you set in Module 12 for the Health database, using a value of **Drain Adopter Program** for the Application Title property. Test the new startup options; however, do not reset the startup options as you did with the Health database. Close the CleanOut database and open it once again pressing and holding SHIFT to disable the startup options.

13. Compact and repair the database. Notice that once the database is compacted and repaired, the database is opened again and the startup options are again implemented. This will occur each time the database is opened unless you press and hold SHIFT when the database is being opened, or you change the startup options. Close the database.

POWERPOINT

Objectives

Session 5.1
- Import a Word outline
- Reset slides
- Reuse slides from another presentation
- Work in Outline view
- Create sections in a presentation
- Create section and summary zooms
- Insert icons
- Use the Effect Options dialog box to modify animations
- Move objects through layers on a slide

Session 5.2
- Embed a Word table
- Format a table with advanced options
- Embed an Excel worksheet
- Link an Excel chart
- Format a chart with advanced options
- Break links
- Annotate slides during a slide show
- Create handouts in Microsoft Word

Integrating PowerPoint with Other Programs

Creating a Presentation for a Rowing Convention

Case | South Bay College Rowing Team

Tyler Davis has been the head coach of the rowing team at South Bay College in Green Bay, Wisconsin, for the past 10 years. Although some coaches have a hard time attracting and retaining first-time rowers (called novices), Tyler consistently retains 90 percent of his novices. He has been asked to give a presentation describing his approach for coaching novices at an upcoming convention for rowing coaches.

In this module, you will import a Word outline to create slides and insert slides from another presentation. You will also divide a presentation into sections, create and use section and summary zooms, layer objects on a slide, apply advanced animation effects, and embed and link objects created in other programs. Finally, you will annotate slides during a slide show and create handouts in Microsoft Word.

Starting Data Files

PowerPoint5 →

Module

NP_PPT_5-1.pptx
Support_PPT_5_Fitness.xlsx
Support_PPT_5_Olivia.pptx
Support_PPT_5_Outline.docx
Support_PPT_5_Practice.docx

Review

NP_PPT_5-2.pptx
Support_PPT_5_Basics.pptx
Support_PPT_5_Erg.xlsx
Support_PPT_5_GPA.xlsx
Support_PPT_5_NovOutline.docx
Support_PPT_5_Races.docx

Case1

NP_PPT_5-3.pptx
Support_PPT_5_Budget.xlsx
Support_PPT_5_Hunger.pptx
Support_PPT_5_Plan.docx

Case2

NP_PPT_5-4.pptx
Support_PPT_5_Boys.jpg
Support_PPT_5_Data.xlsx
Support_PPT_5_ParentNotes.docx
Support_PPT_5_Slides.pptx

Session 5.1 Visual Overview:

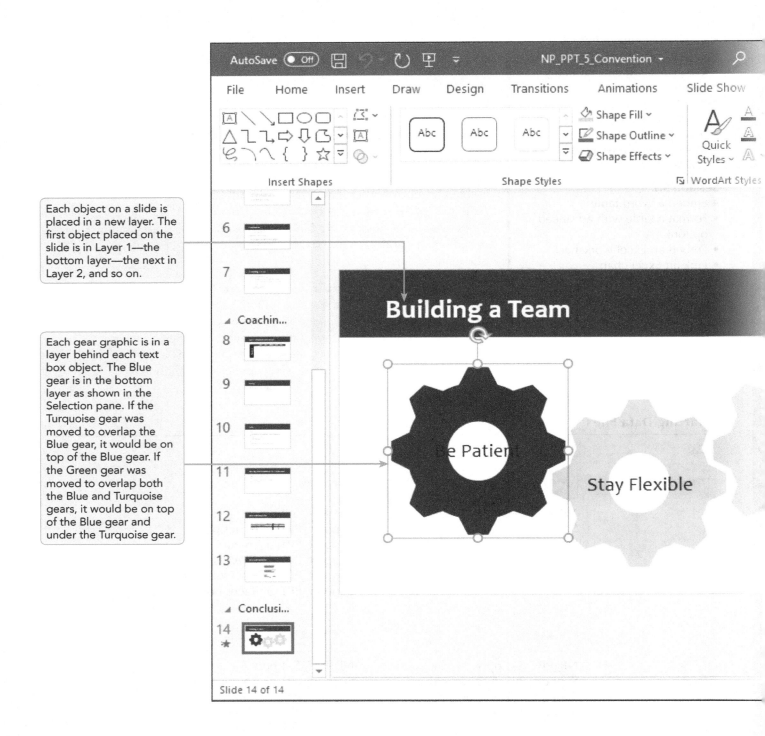

Each object on a slide is placed in a new layer. The first object placed on the slide is in Layer 1—the bottom layer—the next in Layer 2, and so on.

Each gear graphic is in a layer behind each text box object. The Blue gear is in the bottom layer as shown in the Selection pane. If the Turquoise gear was moved to overlap the Blue gear, it would be on top of the Blue gear. If the Green gear was moved to overlap both the Blue and Turquoise gears, it would be on top of the Blue gear and under the Turquoise gear.

Understanding Layers

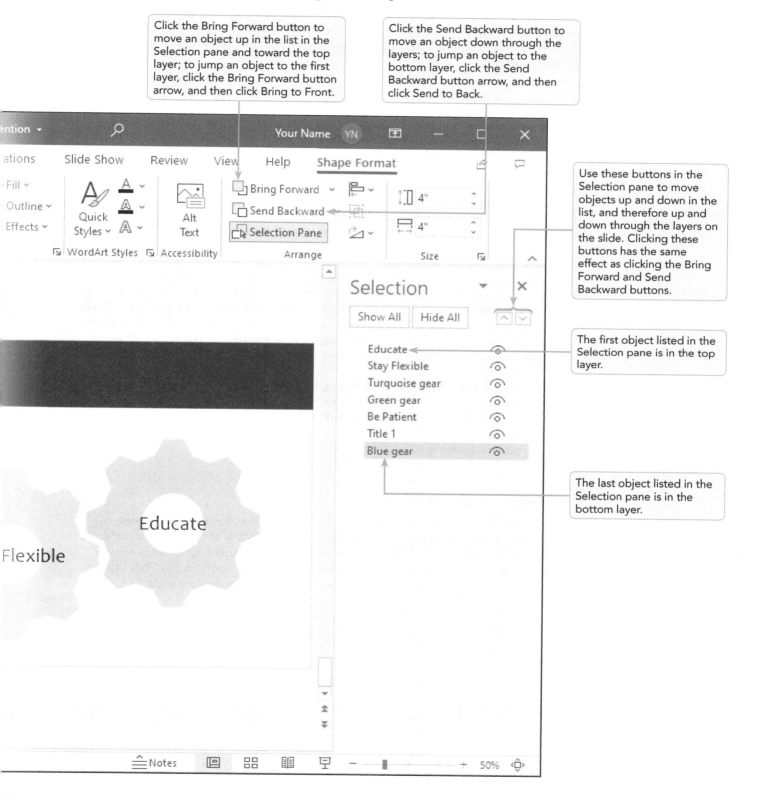

Click the Bring Forward button to move an object up in the list in the Selection pane and toward the top layer; to jump an object to the first layer, click the Bring Forward button arrow, and then click Bring to Front.

Click the Send Backward button to move an object down through the layers; to jump an object to the bottom layer, click the Send Backward button arrow, and then click Send to Back.

Use these buttons in the Selection pane to move objects up and down in the list, and therefore up and down through the layers on the slide. Clicking these buttons has the same effect as clicking the Bring Forward and Send Backward buttons.

The first object listed in the Selection pane is in the top layer.

The last object listed in the Selection pane is in the bottom layer.

Creating a Presentation by Importing Content

If content already exists in an outline in a Word document or in another presentation, you can reuse that content in your presentation instead of recreating it. If your content is in a Word document as an outline, when you import the outline, slides and bulleted lists are created. You can also reuse slides from one presentation in another presentation.

Creating a Presentation by Inserting a Word Outline

If your presentation contains quite a bit of text, it might be easier to create the outline of your presentation in Microsoft Word so that you can take advantage of the extensive text-editing features available in that program. Fortunately, if you create your presentation as an outline in a Word document and use the built-in heading styles, you can import it directly into a presentation.

In order to import a Word outline, the outline levels in the document need to be formatted with Heading styles. For example, the first-level items in the outline need to be formatted with the Heading 1 style, the second-level items need to be formatted with the Heading 2 style, and so on. In Word, you do this by clicking the style name in the Styles group on the Home tab.

When you import the formatted Word outline, each heading formatted with the Heading 1 style in Word (also called a level-one or first-level heading) becomes a slide title; each heading formatted with the Heading 2 style in Word (also called a level-two or second-level heading) becomes a first-level bulleted item; each heading formatted with the Heading 3 style in Word (also called a level-three or third-level heading) becomes a second-level bulleted item—that is, a subitem below the first-level bulleted items—and so on.

Tyler created a Word document outlining his best practices for successfully coaching novices. He applied heading styles to create an outline with text at various levels. He asks you to import his outline into a PowerPoint presentation that he created with a custom theme.

First, you will examine the outline in Word.

To examine the Word outline:

▶ 1. **sam** ⬇ Start Microsoft Word, and then open the document **Support_ PPT_5_Outline.docx**, located in the PowerPoint5 > Module folder included with your Data Files. The document contains an outline, and the insertion point is in the first line. On the Home tab on the ribbon, in the Styles group, the Heading 1 style is selected. This heading will become a slide title. See Figure 5–1.

Figure 5–1   **Outline in Word document**

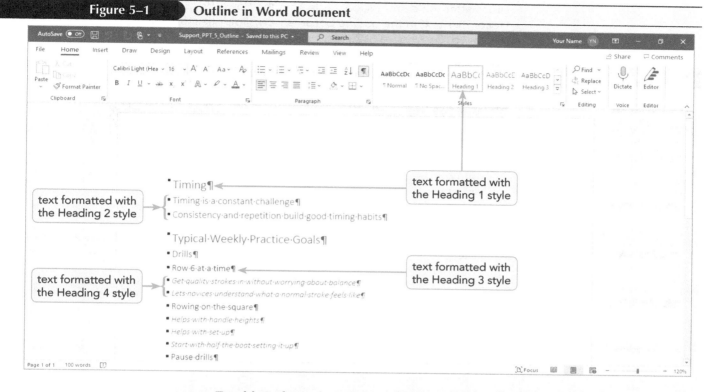

Trouble? If you don't see the dots to the left of each line and the paragraph marks at the end of each line, click the Show/Hide button ¶ in the Paragraph group on the Home tab. If the zoom percentage on your screen is not 120%, change it to 120%.

▶ **2.** Press **DOWN ARROW**. The insertion point moves down one line, and in the Styles group, the Heading 2 style is selected. This heading will become a first-level bullet on a slide.

▶ **3.** Press **DOWN ARROW** four times. The insertion point is in the line "Row 6 at a time". In the Styles group, the Heading 3 style is selected. This heading will become a second-level bullet on a slide.

▶ **4.** Close the document.

Now you will import the outline into PowerPoint. You do this using a command on the New Slide menu.

To import the Word outline into a presentation:

Tip

If imported content on a slide creates a bulleted list that is too long, use the Add or Remove Columns button in the Paragraph group on the Home tab to arrange text in multiple columns in a text box.

▶ **1.** Open the presentation **NP_PPT_5-1.pptx** from the PowerPoint5 > Module folder included with your Data Files, and then save it as **NP_PPT_5_Convention** to the location where you are saving your files. The presentation consists of two slides.

▶ **2.** On the Home tab, in the Slides group, click the **New Slide arrow**, and then click **Slides from Outline**. The Insert Outline dialog box opens.

▶ **3.** Navigate to the PowerPoint5 > Module folder, click **Support_PPT_5_ Outline.docx**, and then click **Insert**. The Word outline is inserted as new slides after the current slide, Slide 1, in the PowerPoint presentation. All the Heading 1 text in the outline became new slide titles. Slide 2 ("Timing") is displayed. See Figure 5–2.

Figure 5–2   **Presentation with slides created from the imported Word outline**

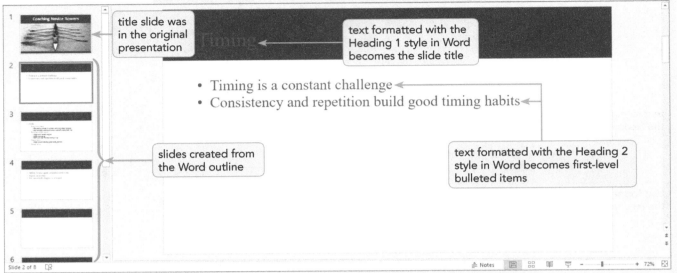

iStock.com/spepple22

Trouble? If Slide 2 is not selected, click the Slide 2 thumbnail in the pane on the left.

▶ **4.** In the Slides group, click the **Layout** button. Notice that a new layout, Title and Text, was created and applied. This layout was created when you imported the outline and it was applied to each slide created by importing the outline.

▶ **5.** Press **ESC** to close the Layout menu.

The text of the slides created by importing the outline retained the fonts and text colors of the outline document rather than picking up those of the presentation theme. You can fix this by resetting the slides. You can reset a slide any time that formatting is changed unexpectedly or isn't applied as you intended, or if placeholders are modified. When you reset slides, you reset every object on the selected slides, so you might need to reapply any formatting that you added.

You'll reset the slides created when you imported the Word outline.

To reset the imported slides:

▶ **1.** With the Slide 2 thumbnail selected, scroll down to the bottom of the pane containing the slide thumbnails, press and hold **SHIFT**, and then click the **Slide 7** thumbnail. The six slides that were created when you inserted the outline are selected.

▶ **2.** On the Home tab, in the Slides group, click the **Reset** button. The slide fonts now match the presentation theme. See Figure 5–3.

Figure 5–3   Slides reset to the presentation theme

Figure 5–3   Slides reset to the presentation theme

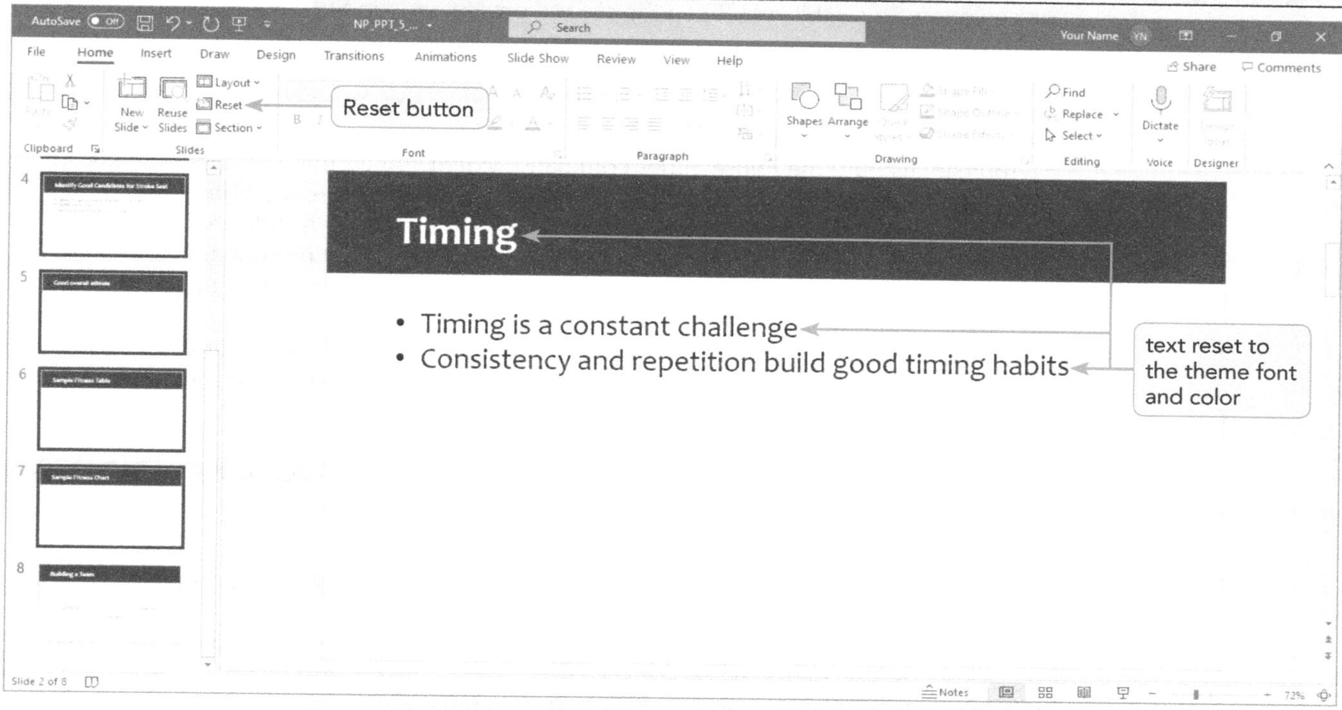

▶ **3.** Save the changes to the presentation.

The imported Word outline is now in the PowerPoint presentation with the custom theme of the NP_PPT_5_Convention presentation applied. Because you imported the outline, the text is now part of the PowerPoint file. Any changes you make to either the PowerPoint or the Word file will not be reflected in the other file.

Insight

Changing Slide Size and Orientation

The default for PowerPoint presentations is for slides to be sized for wide screen displays at an aspect ratio of 16 to 9. This is written as 16:9. To change the slide size, click the Slide Size button in the Customize group on the Design tab. To change the slide size to a 4:3 aspect ratio, click Standard (4:3) on the menu. To select other sizes or to create a custom size, click Custom Slide Size to open the Slide Size dialog box, and then select the size from the Slides sized for list.

Slides in a presentation can be in **landscape orientation**, which is wider than tall or **portrait orientation**, which is taller than wide. Handouts can also be formatted in either orientation. To change the orientation of slides or handouts, open the Slide Size dialog box. In the Orientation section of the dialog box, click the Portrait or Landscape option button in the Slides section or the Notes, Handouts, & Outline section.

Inserting Slides from Another Presentation

In addition to importing a Word outline, you can insert slides from another presentation. To do this, you open the second presentation in Slide Sorter view and then use the Copy command to copy a slide. In the presentation into which you want to paste the copied slide, switch to Slide Sorter view, click the location where you want to paste the copied slide, and then use the Paste command. You can paste the slide using the destination theme or the source formatting.

You can also use the Reuse Slides command. When you do this, you open the Reuse Slides pane, in which you can access the slides from another presentation or a slide library. Then you click the slides you want to insert. If the inserted slides have a theme different from the current presentation, the design of the current presentation will override the design of the inserted slides as long as the Use source formatting check box at the top of the Reuse Slides pane is selected.

Like an imported outline, after you insert slides from another presentation, there is no connection between the two files. Any changes you make to the imported slides appear only in the current presentation.

Reference

Reusing Slides from Another Presentation

- Display the slide you want to appear before the slides you insert from another presentation.
- On the Home tab, in the Slides group, click the New Slide arrow, and then click Reuse Slides to display the Reuse Slides pane.
- In the Reuse Slides pane, click Browse to open the Browse dialog box.
- Navigate to the location of the presentation that contains the slides you want to insert, click the file, and then click Choose Content.
- In the Reuse Slides pane, make sure the Use source formatting check box is not selected to have the inserted slides use the theme in the current presentation, or click the Use source formatting check box to retain the theme of the slides you want to import.
- In the Reuse Slides pane, click each slide that you want to insert into the current presentation.

Tyler asked his assistant coach, Olivia Connor, to create slides that describe the best practices to use when coaching novice rowers. You will insert the slides that she created into the NP_PPT_5_Convention presentation.

To insert slides from another presentation:

1. Display Slide 7 ("Sample Fitness Chart"). You want to insert slides from Olivia's presentation after Slide 7.

2. On the Home tab, in the Slides group, click the **New Slide arrow**, and then click **Reuse Slides**. The Reuse Slides pane opens.

3. In the Reuse Slides pane, click **Browse**. The Browse dialog box opens.

4. Navigate to the PowerPoint5 > Module folder, click **Support_PPT_5_ Olivia.pptx**, and then click **Choose Content**. Thumbnails of the five slides in the Support_PPT_5_Olivia presentation appear in the Reuse Slides pane. The theme applied to this presentation is different from the theme applied to the NP_PPT_5_Convention presentation. At the top of the pane, the Use source formatting check box is unchecked. See Figure 5–4.

| Figure 5-4 | Reuse Slides pane with slides from another presentation |

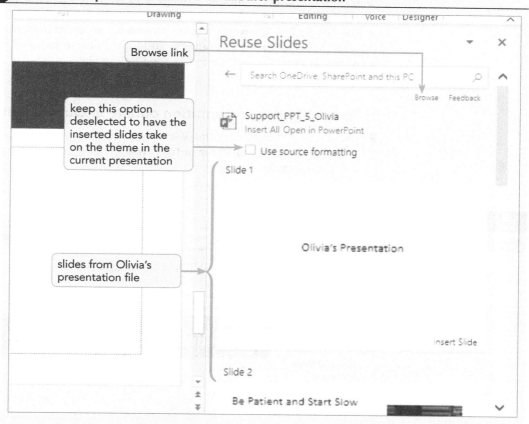

5. In the Reuse Slides pane, click the **Be Patient and Start Slow** thumbnail, which is the second slide. The slide is inserted into the NP_PPT_5_ Convention presentation after the current slide (Slide 7). Because the Use source formatting check box is not checked, the theme used in the NP_ PPT_5_Convention presentation is applied to the slide instead of the theme used in the Support_PPT_5_Olivia presentation.

6. In the Reuse Slides task pane, scroll down if necessary, click the **Educate and Explain** thumbnail, click the **Stay Flexible** thumbnail, and then click the **Scheduling Practice** thumbnail. The slides are added to the NP_PPT_5_ Convention presentation. (You do not need to insert the first slide, which is Olivia's title slide.)

7. Close the Reuse Slides pane.

8. Save the changes to the presentation.

The four slides you inserted from the Support_PPT_5_Olivia presentation are now Slides 8 through 11 in the NP_PPT_5_Convention presentation.

Working in Outline View

Outline view displays the outline of the presentation in the Outline pane, which appears in place of the pane that contains the slide thumbnails. In the Outline pane, presentation text is arranged as in an ordinary outline. Slide titles are the top levels in the outline, and the bulleted lists are indented below the slide titles.

You can use the Outline pane to see the outline of the entire presentation, move text around, and even change the order of slides. For example, you can move a bulleted item from one slide to another, change a subitem into a first-level item, or create a new slide by changing a bulleted item into a slide title.

The NP_PPT_5_Convention presentation has material from three sources: Tyler's original presentation, Tyler's outline, and Olivia's presentation. The presentation needs some organizing. You will do this in the Outline view.

To modify the presentation outline in Outline view:

▶ **1.** On the ribbon, click the **View** tab, and then in the Presentation Views group, click the **Outline View** button. The Outline pane, listing the outline of the presentation, replaces the pane containing the slide thumbnails. The Notes pane becomes visible as well. See Figure 5–5.

Figure 5–5   **Outline pane in Outline view**

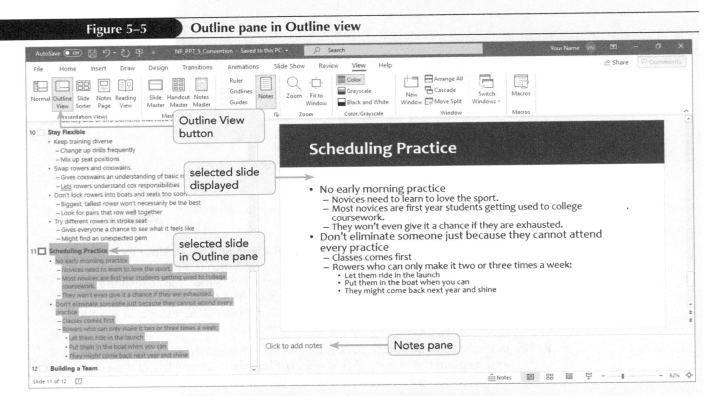

You need to change the first-level bulleted item "Drills" on Slide 3 ("Typical Weekly Practice Goals") so it becomes a slide title. You want the subitems below "Drills" to move with the "Drills" bulleted item so that they become bulleted items on the new Slide 4.

▶ **2.** Scroll up in the Outline pane, and then on Slide 3 ("Typical Weekly Practice Goals"), move the pointer on top of the bullet next to "Drills" so that the pointer changes to the four-headed arrow pointer ⊕.

▶ **3.** Click the bullet next to "Drills". The bulleted item "Drills" and all of its subitems are selected in the Outline pane.

▶ **4.** On the ribbon, click the **Home** tab, and then in the Paragraph group, click the **Decrease List Level** button ⊡. "Drills" becomes the title for a new Slide 4, and all of the bulleted items below it are moved up one level.

Next, you need to change the slide title on Slide 6 ("Good overall athlete") so it becomes a first-level bulleted item on Slide 5 ("Identify Good Candidates for Stroke Seat").

5. In the Outline pane, move the pointer on top of the **Slide 6** ("Good overall athlete") slide icon ☐ so that the pointer changes to the four-headed arrow pointer ✥, and then click the **Slide 6** slide icon ☐. Slide 6 is selected in the Outline pane and Slide 6 is displayed.

6. Press **TAB**. The selected text is demoted so that the slide title becomes the last first-level bullet on Slide 5. Now you need to move Slide 2 ("Timing") so it appears before Slide 4 ("Drills").

7. Move the pointer on top of the **Slide 2** ("Timing") slide icon ☐ so that the pointer changes to the four-headed arrow pointer ✥, press and hold the mouse button, and then drag the pointer down so that the horizontal line indicating the position of the item you are dragging appears above Slide 4, as shown in Figure 5–6.

Figure 5–6   **Dragging an item in the Outline pane**

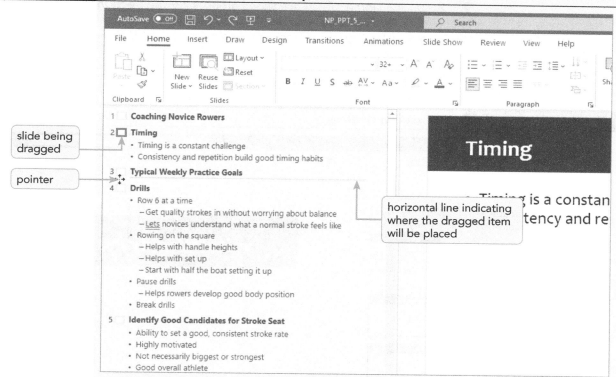

8. With the horizontal line positioned above Slide 4, release the mouse button. The "Timing" slide is now Slide 3. You are finished working in Outline view. On the status bar, the Normal button is selected, but you can click it anyway to return to Normal view.

9. On the status bar, click the **Normal** button 🔲. The presentation appears in Normal view, but the Notes pane is still visible.

10. On the status bar, click the **Notes** button. The Notes pane closes.

11. Save the changes to the presentation.

Organizing a Presentation Using Sections and Zooms

When you work with a long presentation, it can be helpful to divide it into sections. It can also be helpful to your audience if you create a summary slide from which you can link to each section.

Creating Sections in a Presentation

Tyler wants you to create a section that consists of the slides created from his outline. To do this, you need to first select the slide that will mark the beginning of the section. You can do this in Normal view or in Slide Sorter view.

To create sections in the presentation:

▶ **1.** In the pane containing the thumbnails, scroll up, and then click the **Slide 2** thumbnail. Slide 2 ("Typical Weekly Practice Goals") is displayed. This will be the first slide in the section you will create.

▶ **2.** On the Home tab, in the Slides group, click the **Section** button, and then click **Add Section**. The new section is created, and the Rename Section dialog box opens with the temporary name "Untitled Section" selected in the Section name box. In the pane containing the slide thumbnails, "Untitled Section" appears above the Slide 2 thumbnail and the Slide 2 thumbnail and all the slides after it are selected. See Figure 5–7.

Figure 5–7	New section created

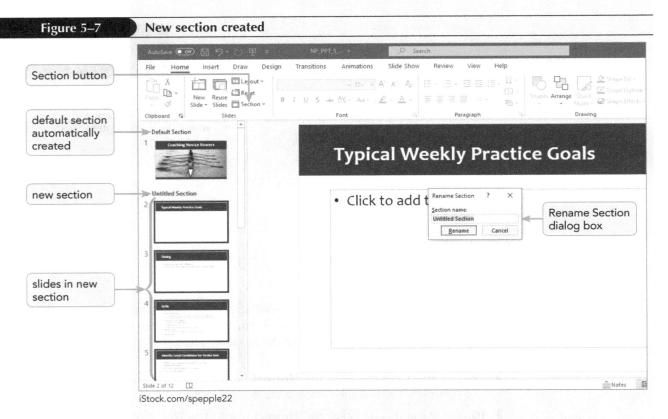

iStock.com/spepple22

▶ **3.** In the Section name box, type **Coaching Suggestions**, and then click **Rename**. The dialog box closes, and the section is renamed. At the top of the pane containing the thumbnails, the section name "Default Section" appears. When you create a section in a presentation that does not contain any other sections and you selected a slide other than Slide 1, all the slides before the new section are placed in a section as well. This first section is automatically titled "Default Section". Because you created a section that starts with Slide 2, the Default Section includes only Slide 1. You will rename this section.

▶ **4.** In the pane containing the thumbnails, click **Default Section**. The section name changes to orange, and the thumbnail in the section is selected.

▶ **5.** On the Home tab, in the Slides group, click the **Section** button, and then click **Rename Section**. The Rename Section dialog box opens.

▶ **6.** Type **Introduction**, and then click **Rename**. The section is renamed.

The Coaching Suggestions section that you created should include only the six slides that Tyler created. You need to create another section that includes the last five slides in the presentation.

▶ **7.** Create a new section named **Best Practices** with Slide 8 ("Be Patient and Start Slow") as the first slide in the section.

Creating Section Zooms and a Summary Zoom

You already learned how to create slide zooms on a slide. You can also add section zooms to a slide. A **section zoom** is a slide zoom linked to the first slide in a section that you click to display that slide followed by the rest of the slides in the section. When you use the Section Zoom command, only the first slide in each section appears in the dialog box for you to select.

Tyler wants you to add a slide containing section zooms to the presentation.

To create section zooms:

▶ **1.** Create a new Slide 2 in the Introduction section with the **Title Only** layout, and then add **Sections** as the slide title.

▶ **2.** On the ribbon, click the **Insert** tab, and then in the Links group, click the **Zoom** button. The Zoom menu opens.

▶ **3.** On the menu, click **Section Zoom**. The Insert Section Zoom dialog box opens. Unlike when you created slide zooms, only the three slides that are the first slides in the three sections appear in the dialog box.

▶ **4.** Click the **Section 1: Introduction** and **Section 2: Coaching Suggestions** check boxes, and then click **Insert**. The dialog box closes, and two section zooms are inserted on Slide 2.

▶ **5.** Click a blank area of the slide, click the top section zoom, and then drag it to the right so it is no longer on top of the other section zoom. The exact position doesn't matter.

Tyler tells you that the two sections that should have been added as section zooms are the Coaching Suggestions section and the Best Practices section.

▶ **6.** Click the **Introduction** section zoom ("Coaching Novice Rowers"), and then press **DELETE**.

▶ **7.** In the pane containing the slide thumbnails, scroll down until you can see the Best Practices section name, click the **Best Practices** section name but do not release the mouse button.

8. Drag the **Best Practices** section name onto Slide 2 somewhere to the left of the section zoom already on the slide. When you start dragging, the sections in the pane on the left collapse to show just the other two section names. See Figure 5–8.

Figure 5–8 Dragging a section name to create a section zoom

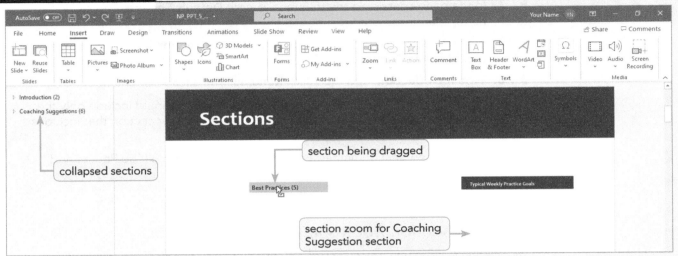

9. Release the mouse button. The section zoom for the Best Practices section is added to the slide and is selected.

10. Click the **Zoom** tab. See Figure 5–9.

Figure 5–9 Slide 2 with two section zooms

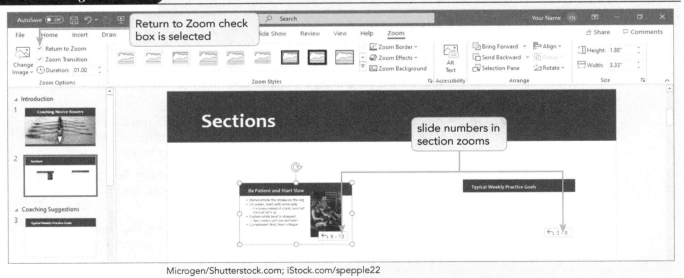

Microgen/Shutterstock.com; iStock.com/spepple22

Section zooms differ from slide zooms in three ways. First, when the Zoom tab is selected, a box on the section zoom lists the range of slide numbers included in that section. Second, the Return to Zoom check box is selected by default in the Zoom Options group on the Zoom tab. Finally, when you click a section zoom during a slide show, that slide appears with the Zoom transition (if you leave the Zoom Transition check box in the Zoom Options group selected), then each slide in the section appears using whatever transition is applied to it. After the last slide in the section appears, the slide that contains the section zooms reappears with the Zoom transition.

To align and use the section zooms on Slide 2:

▶ **1.** On Slide 2, click the "Be Patient and Start Slow" section zoom, press and hold **SHIFT**, click the "Typical Weekly Practice Goals" section zoom, and then release **SHIFT**.

▶ **2.** Click the **Zoom** tab if necessary, and then in the Arrange group, click the **Align** button. The Align menu opens. At the bottom of the menu, Align Selected Objects is selected. This means that commands you use on the Align menu will align the selected objects with each other.

▶ **3.** Click **Align Middle**. The menu closes, and the selected section zooms are vertically aligned with each other.

▶ **4.** In the Arrange group, click the **Align** button, click **Align to Slide**, and then click the **Align** button again. The Align menu opens. At the bottom of the menu, Align to Slide is now selected. Now commands you select on the Align menu will align selected objects with the slide.

▶ **5.** Click **Align Middle**. The two selected objects shift so that their middles are aligned with the middle of the slide.

▶ **6.** In the Arrange group, click the **Align** button, and then click **Distribute Horizontally**. The two selected section zooms are positioned so there is the same amount of space on either side of them and between them.

▶ **7.** On the status bar, click the **Slide Show** button ⬚. Slide 2 appears in Slide Show view.

▶ **8.** Click the **Be Patient and Start Slow** section zoom. That slide appears on the screen with the Zoom transition.

▶ **9.** Press **SPACEBAR** four times. The next four slides in the Best Practices section—Slides 10, 11, 12, and 13—appear on the screen.

▶ **10.** Press **SPACEBAR** once more. Slide 2—the slide that contains the section zoom—reappears with the Zoom transition.

▶ **11.** Press **ESC** to end the slide show.

You can also create a summary zoom. A **summary zoom** is a slide that contains section zooms, usually for all of the sections in the presentation. When you use the summary zoom command, the dialog box that appears contains all of the slides in the presentation. If the presentation contains sections, the first slide in each section is already selected in the dialog box. You can deselect any of these slides or select additional slides. If you select a slide that is not the first slide in a section, a new section is created with the slide you selected as the first slide in that section.

If you deselect a slide that is the first slide in a section, the section is not removed from the presentation when you create the summary zoom, but a section zoom for that section will not be created.

When you create a summary zoom, a new slide containing the section zooms is added before the first section you select. This slide is in a new section named "Summary Section".

To create a summary zoom:

▌ **1.** Click the **Insert** tab.

▌ **2.** In the Links group, click the **Zoom** button, and then click **Summary Zoom**. The Insert summary zoom dialog box opens. The first slide in each of the three sections is selected. See Figure 5–10.

Figure 5–10	Insert Summary Zoom dialog box

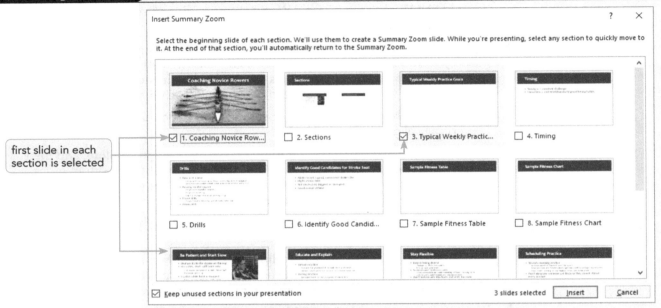

first slide in each section is selected

iStock.com/spepple22; Microgen/Shutterstock.com

Tyler wants Slides 7 and 8—the slides that will contain sample data—to be in their own section, and he wants Slide 13 to be in its own section.

▌ **3.** Click the **7. Sample Fitness Table** check box, scroll down in the dialog box, and then click the **13. Building a Team** check box. Slides 7 and 13 are now selected as well and each will become the first slide in a new section. The section created that begins with Slide 7 will contain Slides 7 and 8. Slide 9 is the first slide in the next section.

▌ **4.** Click **Insert**. A new Summary Section is created at the beginning of the presentation with a single summary zoom in it, and the Introduction section is now the second section. There are five section zooms on the summary zoom.

Tip

If you want to add or remove section slides from the summary zoom, click one of the section zooms, click the Zoom tab, and then in the Zoom Options group, click the Edit Summary button.

▌ **5.** In the pane containing the slide thumbnails, scroll down to the bottom. Slide 14 is in a new section titled "Building a Team", which is the same as the slide title of Slide 14.

▌ **6.** Scroll up until the section name above Slide 8 is visible in the pane that contains the slide thumbnails. Slides 8 and 9 are in a section titled "Sample Fitness Table". This is the slide title of the first slide in that section. See Figure 5–11.

| Figure 5–11 | Slides 8 and 9 in the new section |

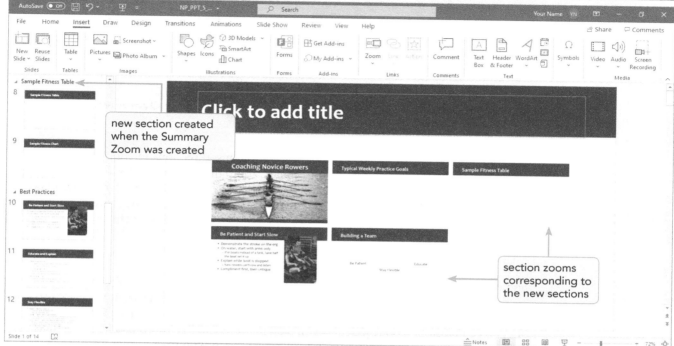

iStock.com/spepple22; Microgen/Shutterstock.com

▶ **7.** On Slide 1 (the summary zoom), click the **Building a Team** section zoom, and then click the **Zoom** tab. As with the section zooms you created on Slide 3, the slide numbers on each section zoom indicate the slides that are included in the section. In the Zoom Options group, there are two additional buttons that did not appear when you selected a slide zoom or the section zooms that you added to what is now Slide 3 ("Sections"). See Figure 5–12.

| Figure 5–12 | Zoom tab for a section zoom on a summary zoom |

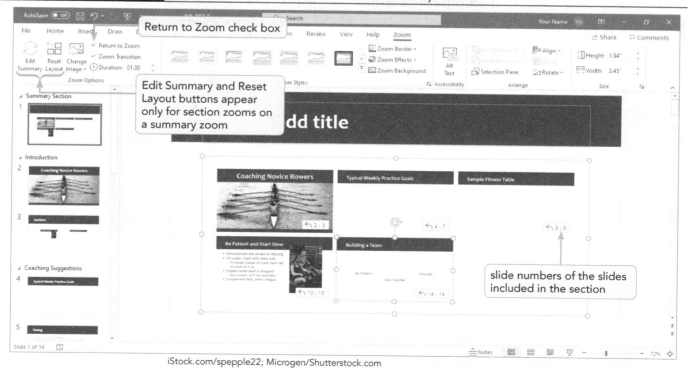

iStock.com/spepple22; Microgen/Shutterstock.com

Because the summary zoom contains section zooms, the Return to Zoom check box is selected for each section zoom. Tyler wants to end the slide show after displaying the Building a Team slide.

▶ **8.** In the Zoom Options group, click the **Return to Zoom** check box to deselect it. Now when the Building a Team slide is displayed and the slide show is advanced, the black slide that indicates the end of the slide show will appear instead of returning to Slide 2. You will add a title to the Summary Zoom.

▶ **9.** On Slide 1, click in the title placeholder, and then type **Overview**.

When you create a summary zoom, the "Keep unused sections in your presentation" check box at the bottom of the Insert summary zoom dialog box is selected. If you deselect a section in the dialog box and that check box is selected, the section that you deselected remains in the presentation. If you deselect that check box, the section is removed and the slides in that section become part of the previous section.

Manipulating Sections

Sometimes you need to manipulate sections. For example, Tyler wants the Introduction section to be the first section in the presentation, so you need to move it. You can also remove a section name and the slides in that section or remove just a section name. Sections can also be collapsed, allowing you to focus on one group of slides at a time. This is helpful when you are working on a presentation with many slides because you can collapse the sections containing slides you are not working on.

In addition to making the Introduction section the first section, Tyler wants the Best Practices section to appear before the Coaching Suggestions section. He also decided that he doesn't want the two slides in the Sample Fitness Table section to be in their own section and he wants you to make them part of the Coaching Suggestions section again. Finally, he wants you to rename the last section. You'll make these changes now.

To manipulate sections:

Tip

To delete a section and the slides in that section, right-click the section name, and then on the shortcut menu, click Remove Section & Slides.

▶ **1.** In the pane containing the slide thumbnails, scroll down, and then right-click the section heading **Sample Fitness Table**. A shortcut menu containing commands for working with sections opens. See Figure 5–13. You need to remove this section name.

Figure 5–13 | **Shortcut menu for a section name**

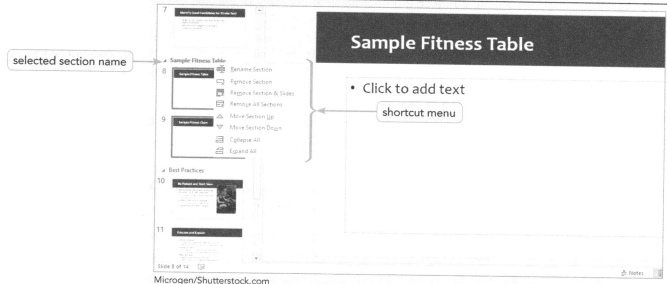

Microgen/Shutterstock.com

▶ **2.** On the shortcut menu, click **Remove Section**. The selected section name is deleted and Slides 8 and 9 are now part of the Coaching Suggestions section. Next, you will rename the last section.

▶ **3.** Scroll down, right-click the **Building a Team** section name, click **Rename Section**, type **Conclusion** in the Rename Section dialog box, and then click **Rename**. The section is renamed. You need to reorganize the sections.

▶ **4.** Scroll up, right-click the **Best Practices** section name, and then on the shortcut menu, click **Move Section Up**. The entire Best Practices section moves up above the Coaching Suggestions section. You can also drag a section to a new position.

▶ **5.** Scroll up, move the pointer on top of the **Introduction** section name, press and hold the mouse button, and then move the pointer up slightly. When you start dragging the section name, all of the sections collapse and the section you are dragging moves below the other four sections. See Figure 5–14.

Figure 5–14 | **Dragging a section to a new position**

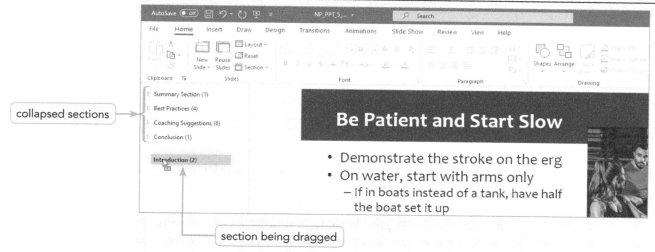

▶ **6.** Drag the **Introduction** section above the Summary Section, and then release the mouse button. The sections expand, and the entire Introduction section appears above the Summary Section.

▶ **7.** Next to the Introduction section name, click the **Collapse Section** arrow ◢. The section is collapsed, and the Collapse Section arrow ◢ changed to the Expand Section arrow ▷. (The arrows are orange because the Introduction section is selected.) The number 2 appears after the collapsed section name. This is the number of slides in the section.

▶ **8.** Right-click the **Best Practices** section name, and then on the shortcut menu, click **Collapse All**. All five sections collapse.

Now you will examine the summary zoom to see the effect of the changes you made when you renamed and reorganized the sections.

To examine and modify the section zooms on the summary zoom:

▶ **1.** Next to the Summary Section name, click the **Expand Section** arrow ▷. The Summary Section expands, and the Slide 3 thumbnail is visible.

▶ **2.** Click the **Slide 3** thumbnail, click one of the section zooms, and then click the **Zoom** tab. Because you reorganized the sections, the slide numbers on the Coaching Novice Rowers, Typical Weekly Practice Goals, and Be Patient and Start Slow section zooms have changed to reflect the new slide numbers in those sections. Also, because you deleted a section, there is a broken link symbol on one of the section zooms. See Figure 5–15.

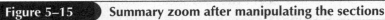

Figure 5–15   Summary zoom after manipulating the sections

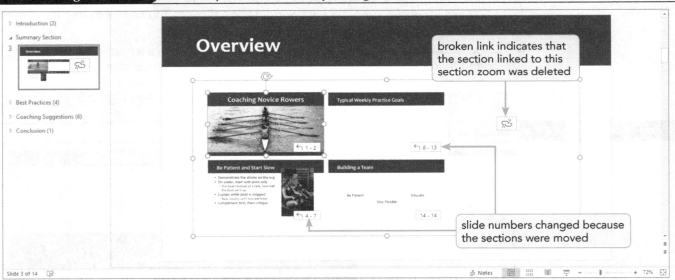

iStock.com/spepple22; Microgen/Shutterstock.com

You will swap the positions of the Typical Weekly Practice Goals and the Be Patient and Start Slow section zooms, and then use the Reset Layout command to align them correctly.

▶ **3.** Drag the **Typical Weekly Practice Goals** and the **Be Patient and Start Slow** section zooms to swap their positions. Don't worry about aligning them.

4. On the Zoom tab, in the Zoom Options group, click the **Reset Layout** button. The two section zooms you moved jump back to their original position. You need to recreate or edit the summary zoom.

5. In the Zoom Options group, click the **Edit Summary** button. The Edit Summary Zoom dialog box opens. Similar to the Insert Section Zoom dialog box, it contains only the first slide in each section. The only section not selected is the Summary Section. In the dialog box, the sections are listed in the order they appear in the pane containing the thumbnails. Before you update the summary zoom, Tyler wants you to remove the Introduction section from it.

6. Click the **Section 1: Introduction** check box to deselect it, and then click **Update**. The dialog box closes. On the summary zoom, the Introduction section zoom and the section zoom with the missing link are deleted and the three remaining section zooms are now in the correct order. You need to format the section zooms so that they stand out more on the slide. There is a selection box around all three section zooms.

7. Click a blank area inside the selection box around the section zooms.

8. On the Zoom tab, click the **Zoom Border arrow**, and then click the **Indigo, Text 2** color.

9. Drag the **Building a Team** section zoom to the right to center it below the other two section zooms. Now that you have created the summary zoom, you can hide Slide 2 with the section zooms.

10. Expand the Introduction section, click the **Slide 2** thumbnail, click the **Slide Show** tab, and then in the Set Up group, click the **Hide Slide** button.

11. Save the changes to the presentation.

Proskills

Problem Solving: Creating a Slide Show with Two Orientations

There may be times that the content of your presentation requires you to use a combination of portrait and landscape slide orientations. For example, suppose you are creating a presentation that contains some photos in portrait orientation and some in landscape orientation. In PowerPoint, you cannot create a single presentation file with slides in both orientations; rather, you need to create two presentations and create links between them. To do this, create one presentation using the default landscape orientation, create a second presentation and change the orientation to portrait, and then add the appropriate photos to each file. The primary file should be the presentation that you want to use at the start of your presentation. Then, decide the order in which you want the photos to appear. When you want to display a slide using the orientation used in the other presentation, insert a link on the slide that will appear prior to displaying the slide with the other orientation. To use the Link command, in the Insert Hyperlink dialog box, click Existing File or Web Page in the Link to list, click the file you want to link to, and then click the Bookmark button to open the Select Place in Document dialog box listing the slides in the presentation you selected. Click the slide you want to link to, and then click OK in the dialog boxes. If you need to, add a link in the second presentation back to the appropriate slide in the first presentation. You should store the two presentations in the same folder so that they will always be together.

Inserting Icons

In PowerPoint, icons are a type of graphic called a scalable vector graphic (SVG). SVGs are graphics created with drawing programs and do not lose quality when they are resized.

Icons share some characteristics with both pictures and shapes. For example, you can crop icons the same way you crop pictures. You can change the color of icons just as you can change the outline and fill color of shapes. And like both types of graphics, you can apply effects or styles to change the way an icon looks. If you want, you can convert an icon to shapes and then format each shape differently.

In PowerPoint, icons are sorted into categories, such as People, Education, Vehicles, Sports, and so on. To insert icons, click the Insert tab, and then in the Illustrations group, click the Icons button to open the Insert Icons dialog box. Click as many icons as you want to add to the slide, and then click Insert.

When you select an icon on a slide, the Graphics Format tab appears on the ribbon. Because icons share some characteristics with pictures and shapes, you can modify them in many of the same ways. Similar to the Shape Format tab, the Graphics Format tab contains buttons that let you change the fill color and the outline color, weight, and style of an icon. Like the Picture Format tab, the Graphics Format tab contains the Crop button. The Graphics Format tab contains commands to apply a style or effects, such as shadows or bevels, to the icon, and commands to align, group, rotate, and resize icons—all of which are available on both the Shape and Picture Format tabs.

Tip

To insert scalable vector graphics that are stored on your computer or network, use the Pictures button in the Images group on the Insert tab.

To insert an icon and modify it:

▶ 1. Expand the Conclusion section, display Slide 14 ("Building a Team"), and then click the **Insert** tab.

▶ 2. In the Illustrations group, click the **Icons** button. The Insert Icons window opens. The icons in the window are arranged into categories.

   Trouble? If a message appears telling you that you need to be online in order to use icons, click Cancel, connect to the Internet, and then repeat Step 2.

▶ 3. In the category list near the top, use the right arrow, if necessary, and then click **Analytics**. The window displays icons in the Analytics category. See Figure 5–16.

Figure 5–16 Insert Icons dialog box

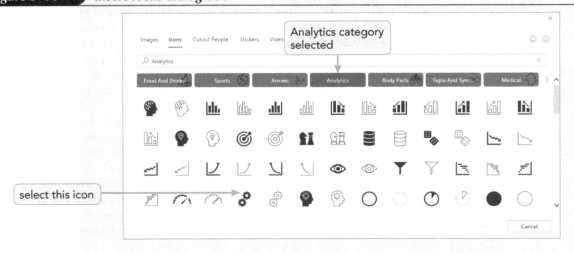

4. In the Analytics category, click the dark gray gears icon, as indicated in Figure 5–16. A box around the selected icon and a check mark in the upper-right corner appear. If you wanted, you could click more than one icon before clicking Insert.

5. Click **Insert**. The Insert Icons window closes and the icon of two gears is inserted on the slide. The icon is selected, and the Graphics Format contextual tab appears on the ribbon and is selected. You will resize the icon larger. Like pictures, icons also have their aspect ratios locked.

6. Resize the icon so it is six inches square, and then position it so that it is centered on the slide below the title. It will be on top of some of the text that is already on the slide.

7. On the Graphics Format tab, in the Graphics Styles group, click the **Graphics Fill arrow**, and then click the **Turquoise, Accent 2** color. Both gears are filled with the turquoise color.

If you want to recolor or manipulate different parts of the icon, you need convert it to shapes or ungroup it. To do this, select the icon, and then in the Change group on the Graphics Format tab, click the Convert to Shape button. Then you can click each shape that makes up the icon and format it any way you want using the tools on the Drawing Tools Format tab.

Tyler wants each gear to be a different color. You will convert the icon to shapes.

To convert an icon to shapes:

1. On the Graphics Format tab, in the Change group, click the **Convert to Shape** button. Although the icon does not look any different, the Graphics Format tab disappears, and the Shape Format tab appears instead. The selected object is now two grouped shapes instead of a single icon. The Home tab is selected, and there is still a selection box around the two grouped icons.

2. On the Home tab, in the Drawing group, click the **Arrange** button, and then in the Group Objects section of the menu, click **Ungroup**. The selection box around the two icons disappears and each gear has a selection box around it.

3. Change the height of the selected shapes to **4"**. Because the gears are now shapes instead of icons, their aspect ratios are not locked.

4. Change the width of the selected shapes to **4"**.

5. Click a blank area of the slide, click the top gear, and then change its fill color to the **Green, Accent 3** color.

6. Position the turquoise gear so it horizontally aligns with the center of the slide and so its middle vertically aligns with the middle of the "Stay Flexible" text box underneath it.

7. Duplicate the green gear, and then change the color of the duplicate to the **Indigo, Text 2** color.

8. Position the blue and green gears as shown in Figure 5–17. They should be middle-and center-aligned with the text boxes underneath them and their top and bottom edges should align with each other.

Figure 5–17   Gears positioned on Slide 13

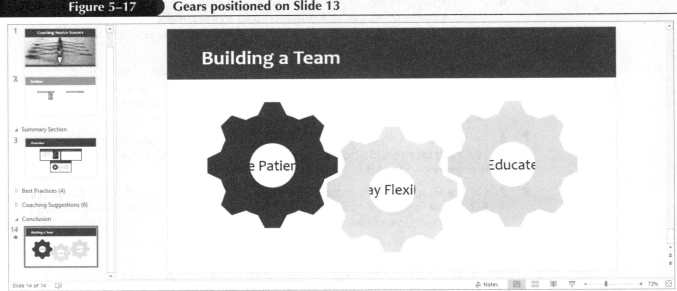

iStock.com/spepple22; Microgen/Shutterstock.com

▶ **9.** Open the Selection pane, click each Freeform object to figure out which name in the Selection pane corresponds to each shape, and then rename the three shapes as **Blue gear**, **Turquoise gear**, and **Green gear**.

▶ **10.** Close the Selection pane, and then save the changes to the presentation.

Using the Effect Options Dialog Box to Modify Animations

Tyler wants you to apply animations to Slide 14 ("Building a Team") so that the gears appear one at a time after the slide transitions, then change to a light color and rotate. Then he wants the text boxes to appear on top of the gears.

You could duplicate the gears, change the color of the duplicate gears to the lighter color, and then add exit animations to the original gears and entrance animations to the duplicate gears. Instead, you will modify the entrance animation that you will apply to the gears so that the gears change color when the slide show is advanced.

To modify an animation this way, you need to use the Effect Options dialog box. The exact title and contents of this dialog box vary depending on the selected animation, but it always contains an Effect tab and a Timing tab. For entrance, exit, and emphasis animations, the title of the dialog box matches the name of the animation. For most motion path animations, the title of the dialog box matches the selected direction effect.

The first thing you need to do to create the effect Tyler wants is to apply the Appear animation to the gears and then modify that animation so that the gears change to a lighter color when the slide show is advanced.

To change the fill color of shapes when the slide show advances:

▶ **1.** Click the blue gear, press and hold **SHIFT**, click the turquoise gear, click the green gear, and then release **SHIFT**.

▶ **2.** Apply the **Appear** entrance animation to the three selected objects. Tyler wants the gears to change to a lighter color when the slide show advances.

3. On the Animations tab, in the Animation group, click the **Dialog Box Launcher** ⬚. The Appear dialog box opens with the Effect tab selected. This is the Effect Options dialog box for the Appear animation. In the After animation box, Don't Dim appears. This means that nothing will happen to the selected objects when the slide show advances.

4. Click the **After animation** arrow. A menu opens listing options that will be applied to the selected objected once the slide show advances. See Figure 5–18.

Figure 5–18   Effect Options dialog box titled "Appear"

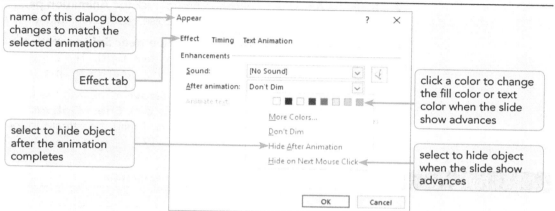

If you select either of the Hide options, the selected object will act as if the Disappear exit animation was applied to it when the slide show advances. If you select a color, the fill color of the shape will change to that color when the slide show advances. If the selected object was a text box, the font color would change to the selected color, and if the selected object was a shape with text in it, the fill color of the shape would change.

5. On the menu, click the third color square, which is light blue. The menu closes and the light blue color you selected appears in the After animation box.

6. Click **OK** to close the dialog box.

Now you need to add the Spin animation to the gears. You also need to modify this animation so that the gears keep spinning until the next slide appears.

To modify an animation so that it does not end until the next slide appears:

1. Select all three gears.

2. On the Animations tab, in the Advanced Animation group, click the **Add Animation** button, and then click the **Spin** emphasis animation. The Spin animation previews and the three gears spin in a clockwise direction. To make it look like the gears are operating together, you need to change the direction of the turquoise gear to counter-clockwise.

3. To the left of the turquoise gear, click the **2** animation sequence icon to select only the Spin animation applied to the turquoise gear. In the Animation group, the Spin animation is selected.

▶ **4.** In the Animation group, click the **Effect Options** button, click **Counterclockwise**, and then on the status bar, click the **Slide Show** button 🖵. Slide 14 appears in Slide Show view.

▶ **5.** Press the **SPACEBAR**. The three gears appear and are three different colors.

▶ **6.** Press the **SPACEBAR**. The gears all change to light blue and spin once. Now it looks like the gears are rotating so that each gear is making the gears touching it rotate.

▶ **7.** Press **ESC** to end the slide show. You need to modify the Spin animations so they continue until the slide is no longer on the screen.

▶ **8.** In the Advanced Animation group, click the **Animation pane** button. The Animation pane opens. The Turquoise gear Spin animation is selected in the pane.

▶ **9.** Press and hold **CTRL**, click the **Blue gear Spin** animation, click the **Green gear Spin** animation, and then release **CTRL**. The arrow appears next to the last selected animation, which is the Green gear Spin animation.

▶ **10.** In the Animation pane, click the **arrow** ▼ next to the Green gear Spin animation, and then on the menu, click **Effect Options**. The Spin dialog box opens with the Effect tab selected. This is the Effect Options dialog box for the Spin animation. See Figure 5–19.

| Figure 5–19 | Effect Options dialog box for the Spin animation |

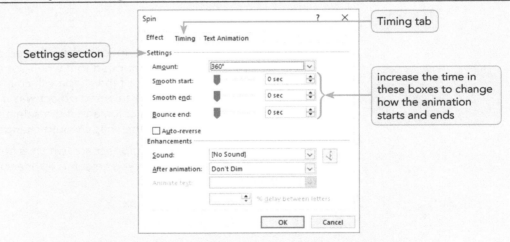

The Effect tab for the Spin animation contains a Settings section which was not in the Appear Effect Options dialog box. For the Spin animation, you can change how the animation starts and ends. If you increase the time in the Smooth start box, the animation will start more slowly and then increase to the appropriate speed. Likewise, if you increase the time in the Smooth end box, as the animation ends, it will slow down over the course of that time. And if you increase the time in the Bounce end box, the object will bounce in the direction of the animation at the end of the animation.

▶ **11.** Click the **Timing** tab, click the **Repeat** arrow, click **Until End of Slide**. Now the gears will continue to spin until the next slide is displayed. You also want to slow the animation down a little. You can change the Duration on the Animations tab or in this dialog box.

▶ **12.** Click the **Duration** arrow, click **5 seconds (Very Slow)**, and then click **OK**. The animation previews and the gears spin more slowly.

Tyler wants the text boxes that appear under the gears to appear on top of the gears after they start spinning, and he wants the characters in the text boxes to appear one letter at a time. He also wants a typewriter sound to play as each character appears. You will apply an animation to the text boxes.

To modify an animation applied to text so that the text appears one character at a time with a sound effect:

1. On Slide 14 ("Building a Team"), click the text in the center of the blue gear, press and hold **SHIFT**, click the text in the center of the turquoise gear, click the text in the center of the green gear, and then release **SHIFT**. The three text boxes are selected.

2. Apply the **Appear** entrance animation to the text boxes. The three Appear animations are added to the Animation pane and are selected.

3. In the Animation pane, click the **arrow** ▼ next to the Educate Appear animation, and then click **Effect Options**. The Appear Effect Options dialog box opens. Because the selected objects are text boxes, this dialog box now includes the Text Animation tab and an Animate text box on the Effects tab. In the Animate text box, All at once is selected.

4. On the Effect tab, click the **Animate text** arrow. The menu that opens contains two additional choices for the text: By word and By letter.

5. Click **By letter**.

6. Below the Animate text box, change the value in the box to **0.1**. This changes the pause between each letter appearing to 0.1 seconds.

7. At the top of the dialog box, click the **Sound** arrow, scroll down in the menu, click **Typewriter**, and then click **OK**.

8. On the status bar, click the **Slide Show** button 🖵. The slide appears in Slide Show view displaying only the slide title.

9. Press the **SPACEBAR**. The gears appear.

10. Press the **SPACEBAR**. The gears change to light blue and start spinning.

11. Press the **SPACEBAR**. The text in the three text boxes appears, one letter at a time, accompanied by a typewriter sound. You can't read the text because it is behind the gears.

    Trouble? Depending on your computer, the Typewriter sound might not play properly. Don't worry about this.

12. Press **ESC**, and then save the changes to the presentation.

Working with Layers

Every time you add an object to a slide, a new layer is created on the slide to hold that object. As illustrated in the Session 5.1 Visual Overview, you can send objects to the back (bottom) of the layers on a slide, or you can bring an object to the front (top) of the layers on a slide. To change an object's layer, you use commands in the Arrange group on the Format tab or on the Arrange menu in the Drawing group on the Home tab for whatever type of object is selected. You can also move objects through layers using the Selection pane.

You do not need to open the Selection pane to move an object through the layers on a slide, but if a slide contains many objects, it can be easier to work with them if you can see the complete list in the Selection pane.

You need to move the text boxes so that they are in layers on top of the gears.

To move objects through the layers on a slide:

▶ **1.** On Slide 14 ("Building a Team"), click the blue gear, click the **Shape Format** tab, and then in the Arrange group, click the **Selection Pane** button. The Blue gear object is the first item in the list in the Selection pane because it is in the top layer on the slide. The Title 1 object is the last item in the list, indicating it is in the bottom layer. See Figure 5–20.

Figure 5–20 Selection pane listing objects in layers

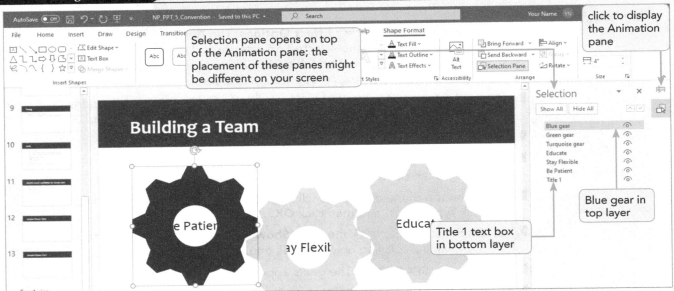

iStock.com/spepple22; Microgen/Shutterstock.com

▶ **2.** On the Shape Format tab, in the Arrange group, click the **Send Backward arrow**, and then click **Send to Back**. In the Selection pane, Blue gear moves to the bottom of the list, and on the slide, the blue gear is now behind the "Be Patient" text box.

▶ **3.** In the Selection pane, click the **Stay Flexible** object, and then in the Arrange group, click the **Bring Forward** button. On the slide, nothing appears to change, but in the Selection pane, the selected Stay Flexible object moved up one place in the list.

▶ **4.** At the top of the Selection pane, click the **Bring Forward** button twice. In the Selection pane, the selected object moves up two more positions so it is above the Turquoise gear object. On the slide, Stay Flexible text box now appears on top of the turquoise gear.

▶ **5.** In the Selection pane, click the **Educate** object.

▶ **6.** In the Arrange group, click the **Bring Forward arrow**, and then click **Bring to Front**. The Educate object moves to the top of the list in the Selection pane. On the slide, the Educate text box is now on top of the green gear.

During the slide show, Tyler wants the three gears to appear at the same time, one-half second after the slide transitions. After a one-second delay, he wants the gears to fade and start spinning and the text boxes to appear one at a time. You'll modify the start settings of the animations.

To modify the animations so that they start automatically:

▸ 1. Click the Animation Pane icon ⊞ to the right of the Selection pane to display the Animation pane, click the **Blue gear Appear** animation, click the **arrow** ▾ , and then click **Effect Options**.

▸ 2. In the Appear dialog box, click the **Timing** tab.

▸ 3. Click the **Start** arrow, and then click **After Previous**.

▸ 4. Change the value in the Delay box to **0.5** seconds, and then click **OK**. The start setting of the Turquoise gear and Green gear Appear animations is set to With Previous. In the Animation pane, you can see by the position of the green arrows that they will appear before the Blue gear appears. See Figure 5–21. You need to add the same delay to these animations.

Figure 5–21   **Animation pane showing the timing of the animations**

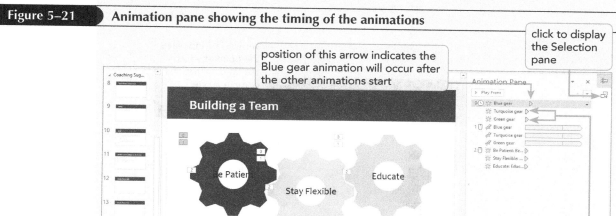

iStock.com/spepple22; Microgen/Shutterstock.com

▸ 5. In the Animation pane, select both the **Turquoise gear Appear** and **Green gear Appear** animations, click the **Animations** tab, and then in the Timing group, click the **Delay** up arrow twice. The green arrows now show that the three animations will occur at the same time.

▸ 6. Select the **Blue gear Spin** animation, change its Start setting to **After Previous**. The yellow bars for all three Spin animations shift right.

▸ 7. With the Blue gear Spin animation selected, change the Delay to **1.00** second. The yellow bar shifts right. This time, instead of adding the same delay to the other two Spin animations, you will reapply the With Previous start setting.

▸ 8. Select the **Turquoise gear Spin** animation and the **Green gear Spin** animation.

▸ 9. Next to the Green gear Spin animation, click the **arrow** ▾ . There is a check mark next to Start with Previous.

▸ 10. On the menu, click **Start with Previous** to reapply this start setting. The two yellow bars shift right so that they are aligned with the yellow bar of the Blue gear Spin animation.

Now you need to modify the Appear animations applied to the text boxes so that the first text box appears at the same time the gears start spinning, followed by the other two text boxes one at a time.

▶ **11.** In the Animation pane, select the three Appear animations applied to the text boxes, and then change their Start setting to **After Previous**. In the Animation pane, the green arrows shift right. The arrow indicating the Appear animation applied to the Be Patient text box is aligned with a vertical line through the three Spin animations. Even though the Appear animations are set to start After Previous, they can't start after the Spin animations end because the Spin animations are set to repeat until the end of the slide. The vertical line indicates the point at which the Spin animations complete one revolution. This shows that the Appear animations will start after the Spin animations complete one revolution. See Figure 5–22.

Figure 5–22	Animation pane showing the Appear animations shifted right

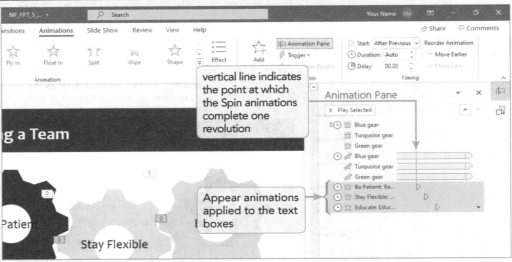

iStock.com/spepple22; Microgen/Shutterstock.com

▶ **12.** Select the **Stay Flexible Appear** animation, set a Delay of **0.50** seconds, and then do the same for the **Educate Appear** animation.

▶ **13.** On the status bar, click the **Slide Show** button. Slide 14 appears in Slide Show view. After one-half second, the three gears appear. After one second, the gears fade to blue and start spinning. Then there is a delay of six seconds, then the three text boxes appear, one after the other, with one-half second between each one. The reason the first text box appeared after a six-second delay is because the Spin animation was slowed down so that it takes five seconds to complete one full spin. Then you applied a one-second delay to the Appear animation applied to the text box. The six-second delay is too long.

▶ **14.** Press **ESC** to end the slide show. You will modify the Appear animation applied to the Be Patient text box so that it starts one second after the gears start spinning.

Tip

To zoom in or out on the animation time line in the Animation pane, click the Seconds button at the bottom of the Animation pane, and then click Zoom In or Zoom Out.

▶ **15.** Change the Start setting of the Be Patient Appear animation to **With Previous**, and change the Delay to **2.00** seconds. Remember that the Spin animations have a delay of one second applied to them. You need to set the delay of the Appear animation to two seconds because you want the text to appear one second after the spin animations start.

▶ **16.** Change the start setting of the Stay Flexible Appear and the Educate Appear animations to **With Previous**. Tyler wants a little more time between the text box animations.

▶ **17.** Change the Delay for the Stay Flexible animation to **3.50** seconds, change the Delay for the Educate Appear animation to **5.00** seconds, and then on the status bar, click the **Slide Show** button 🖵. The animations now appear as Tyler wants.

▶ **18.** Press **ESC** to end the slide show, close the Animation and Selection panes, and then save the changes to the presentation.

You have created a presentation by importing an outline and inserting slides from another presentation. You modified the presentation outline in Outline view, divided the presentation into sections, and created a summary zoom. You moved objects through layers and modified animation effects using the Effect Options dialog box. In the next session, you will insert and modify objects created in Excel and Word and format them. You will also annotate slides during a slide show and create handouts in Microsoft Word.

Review

Session 5.1 Quick Check

1. Describe how you use a Word outline to create slides in PowerPoint.

2. Describe how you insert slides from one presentation into another.

3. When you insert slides from one presentation into another, how do you apply the colors and other formatting from the destination presentation to the newly inserted slides?

4. What happens when you select a first-level bulleted item in the Outline pane in Outline view, and then click the Decrease List Level button?

5. Describe the two ways to create sections.

6. How are layers created on a slide?

7. How can you change the color of a shape or text to which an animation is applied when a slide show is advanced?

Session 5.2 Visual Overview:

source file (Word table)

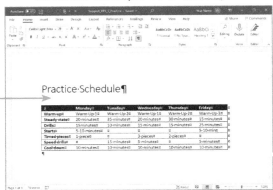

Practice·Schedule¶

The program used to create an object that you want to copy, embed, or link is called the source program; the file that initially contains the object is called the source file.

When you paste an object, a copy of an object created in a source program becomes part of the destination file; you can edit the object with the tools available in the destination program. There is no connection between the inserted object and its source file.

source file (Excel table)

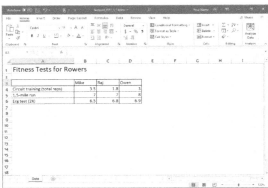

When you embed an object, a copy of the object along with a one-way connection to the source program become part of the destination file, and you can edit the object using the source program's commands. Changes made do not appear in the source file.

source program

You must have access to the source program to edit an embedded object; however, you do not need access to the source file.

source file (Excel chart)

When linking an object, you must have access to the source file if you want to make changes to the source object.

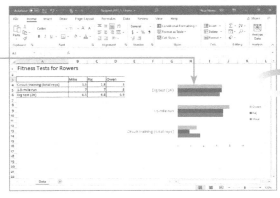

Importing, Embedding, and Linking

destination file
(PowerPoint presentation)

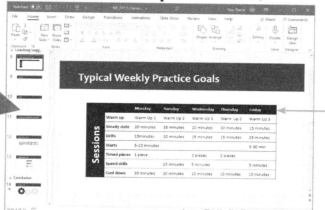

The program used to create the file into which you want to paste, embed, or link an object from a source file is called the **destination program**; the file in which you want to insert the object is called the **destination file**.

destination file
(PowerPoint presentation)

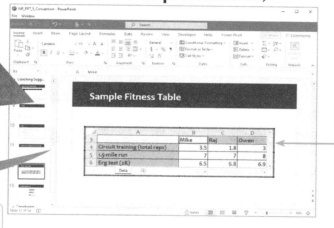

There is no connection between an embedded object and its source file; therefore, changes made to the object in the source file do not appear in the destination file.

When you link an object, a connection is created between the source and destination programs so that the object exists in only one place—the source file—but the link displays the object in the destination file as well.

destination file
(PowerPoint presentation)

If you edit a linked object in the source file, the link ensures that the changes appear in the destination file.

Inserting a Word Table

You know how to use PowerPoint commands to create a table on a slide, but what if you've already created a table in a Word document? You don't need to re-create it in PowerPoint. Instead, you can copy the table from the Word document and then paste it on a slide. Similar to importing a Word outline or inserting slides from another presentation, once you paste the table, the table becomes part of the PowerPoint file, and any changes you make to it will not affect the original table in the source file.

Tyler created a table in a Word document describing the weekly practice plan for his rowers. He wants you to include that table on Slide 8 in the NP_PPT_5_Convention presentation.

To insert a Word table on a slide:

▶ 1. If you took a break after the previous session, make sure the **NP_PPT_5_ Convention.pptx** presentation is open.

▶ 2. In the pane containing the slide thumbnails, collapse all of the sections, and then expand the Coaching Suggestions section.

▶ 3. Display Slide 8 ("Typical Weekly Practice Goals"), and then change the layout to **Title Only**.

▶ 4. Start Microsoft Word, and then open the document **Support_PPT_5_ Practice.docx**, located in the PowerPoint5 > Module folder included with your Data Files.

▶ 5. Move the pointer on top of the table so that the Table Select Handle ⊞ appears in the top-left corner, and then click the **Table Select handle** ⊞ to select the entire table. See Figure 5–23.

Figure 5–23 Selected table in Word document

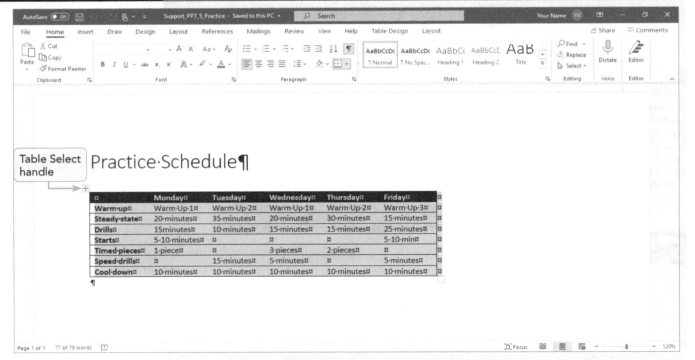

Tip

To insert an entire Word file on a slide, click the Object button in the Text group on the Insert tab, click the Create from file option button, browse to the Word file, and then click OK.

Make sure you change the values in the Height and Width boxes in the Table Size group, not the Cell Size group.

6. On the Home tab, in the Clipboard group, click the **Copy** button.

7. On the Windows taskbar, click the **NP_PPT_5_Convention – PowerPoint** button [P] to switch back to the NP_PPT_5_Convention presentation.

8. On the Home tab, in the Clipboard group, click the **Paste arrow**, and then click the **Keep Source Formatting** button. The table is pasted on the slide as a PowerPoint table with the formatting from the source file (the Word file). You need to make the table larger.

9. On the ribbon, click the **Layout** tab.

10. In the Table Size group, click in the **Height** box, type **4.2**, click in the **Width** box, type **9.5**, and then press **ENTER**.

11. Make sure the entire table is still selected, and then on the ribbon, click the **Home** tab.

12. In the Font group, click the **Font Size arrow**, and then click **18**. The font size of the text in the table increases to 18 points.

13. Point to the table border so that the pointer changes to the move pointer ⁺⁺, and then drag the table to position it so its center aligns with the center of the slide and so it is approximately vertically centered in the white area on the slide.

14. On the Windows taskbar, click the **Support_PPT_5_Practice – Word** button [W], and then close the document and exit Word. You return to the NP_PPT_5_Convention presentation.

Formatting Cells in Tables

Your previous work with tables focused on formatting and modifying a table's appearance and structure. You can also make formatting changes to individual cells. For example, you can merge cells, rotate text in cells, and change the width of borders.

When you merge cells, you combine two or more cells into one. You can merge cells in the same row, the same column, or the same rectangular block of rows and columns. Merging cells is especially useful when you need to enter large amounts of information into a single cell, or when you want to add a heading that spans more than one column. To merge cells, you use the Merge Cells button, which is located in the Merge group on the Layout tab.

Tyler recommends that practices be divided into seven sessions devoted to specific activities. You will create a new first column and merge the cells in that column to create one larger cell containing the label "Sessions".

To create a new first column and merge cells:

1. Click in any cell in the first column in the table, and then on the ribbon, click the **Layout** tab.

2. In the Rows & Columns group, click the **Insert Left** button. A new first column is added to the table.

3. Click in the second cell in the new column to position the insertion point, press and hold the mouse button, and then drag down to select the rest of the cells in the column.

4. On the Layout tab, in the Merge group, click the **Merge Cells** button. The seven selected cells are merged into one cell. See Figure 5–24.

Figure 5–24   Merged cell in imported table

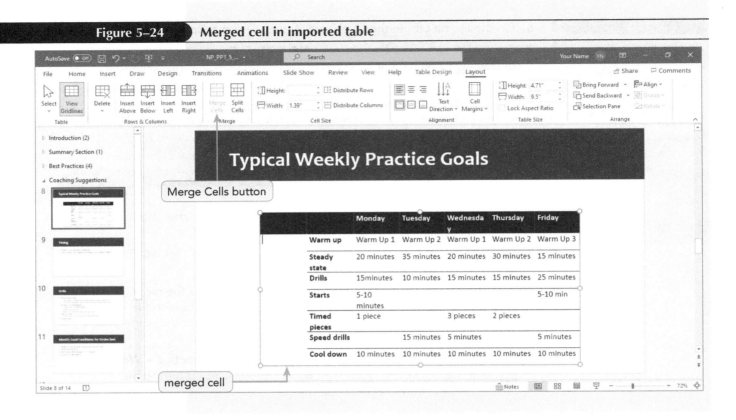

You can rotate text in a cell to read from the top to the bottom or from the bottom to the top. You will enter the label in the merged cell and then rotate it so it is read from bottom to top.

To enter, rotate, and format text in a cell:

▸ **1.** Click in the merged cell, if necessary, and then type **Sessions**.

▸ **2.** On the Layout tab, in the Alignment group, click the **Text Direction** button, and then click **Rotate all text 270°**. The text in the cell rotates so it reads sideways from the bottom up. See Figure 5–25.

Figure 5–25   **Text rotated in the merged cell**

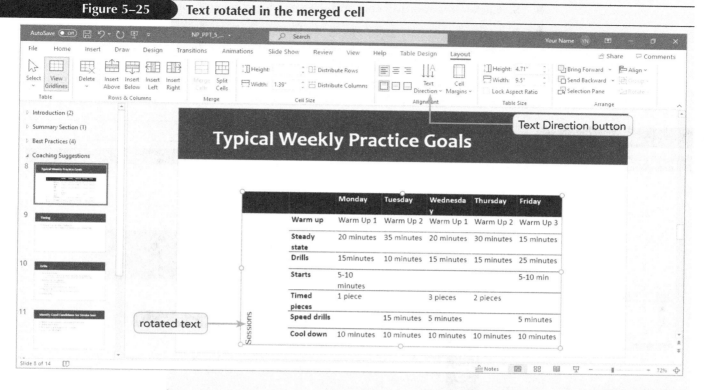

3. Double-click **Sessions** to select it, click the **Home** tab, and then in the Font group, click the **Bold** button B. The text is small and hard to read.

4. In the Font group, click the **Font Size arrow**, and then click **44**.

5. Click the **Table Design** tab.

6. In the WordArt Styles group, click the **Text Fill arrow** A ⌄ and then click the **White, Background 1** color.

7. In the Table Styles group, click the **Shading arrow**, and then click the **Black, Text 1** color.

To finish formatting the table, you'll adjust the width of the columns and align the cell contents so that the table elements are properly proportioned. Finally, you will center-align the text in the first column.

To resize columns and align the text in cells:

1. Click the **Layout** tab.

2. In the Table group, click the **Select** button, and then click **Select Table**.

3. In the Cell Size group, click in the **Width** box, type **1.56**, and then press **ENTER**. All the columns are resized to 1.56 inches wide.

   Trouble? If all of the columns resize so they are extremely narrow, click the Undo button on the Quick Access Toolbar. Then repeat Step 3, this time making sure you click in the Width box that is in the Cell Size group (not the Width box in the Table Size group).

4. In the Alignment group, click the **Center Vertically** button ▤. The content of each cell in the table is centered vertically.

> **5.** Click in the merged cell, and then change the width of this column to **1"**.

> **6.** In the Alignment group, click the **Center** button ▤. The text in the merged cell is now centered both vertically and horizontally.

> **7.** If necessary, reposition the table so its center aligns with the center of the slide and so it is approximately vertically centered in the white area on the slide. Compare your screen to Figure 5–26.

Figure 5–26   **Formatted and repositioned table**

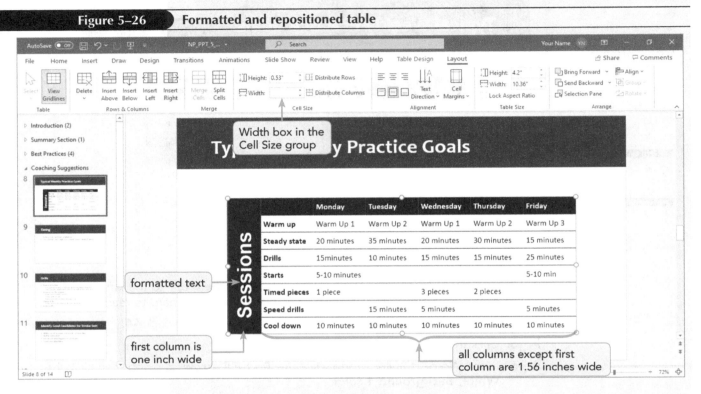

> **8.** Save the changes to the presentation.

Insight

Inserting Equations

If you need to add a complex mathematical equation to a slide, you can use the Equation button in the Symbols group on the Insert tab. Click the Equation button arrow, and then click one of the common equations on the menu to insert that equation. If the equation you want to enter is not listed in the menu, click the Equation button to insert an equation text box, and then type the equation, using the buttons in the Symbols group on the Equation tab to insert mathematical symbols, such as the square root sign ($\sqrt{}$). You can also click buttons in the Structures group on the Equation tab to insert mathematical structures such as fractions ($\frac{3}{4}$ or ¾) or the integral sign that is used in calculus ($\int$). You can also click the Ink Equation button in the Tools group on the Equation tab to open the Math Input Control window. Using a stylus or your finger if you have a touchscreen device or using the pointer, drag to write the equation in the window. When you are finished, click Insert to close the window and insert the equation you drew in the equation text box on the slide.

Inserting Excel Data and Objects

If you created a table or a chart in Excel, you can insert those Excel objects on slides instead of recreating them in PowerPoint. In addition to pasting an object from the Clipboard, you can embed or link it. Pasting, embedding, and linking all involve inserting an object from a source file into destination file. The difference is where the objects are stored and which program's commands are used to modify the object. Refer to the Session 5.2 Visual Overview for more information about the differences between pasting, embedding, and linking.

When you embed an object, you insert a link to the source program as well as the object itself, and this increases the file size. If you do not need to access the source program commands from within the destination file, pasting an object is probably a better choice than embedding it.

Embedding an Excel Worksheet

You can insert a worksheet created in Excel on a slide. When you do, you can choose to paste it as a table or a picture, embed it, or link it. To paste a worksheet as a table or a picture or to embed it, you use one of the buttons on the Paste menu. Note that when you paste Excel data as a picture, you cannot edit the data, but you can format the object using commands on the Picture Format tab. If you want to link the data in the worksheet, you need to click the Paste Special command on the Paste menu and then click the Paste link option button in the Paste Special dialog box that opens.

Tyler regularly has his rowers perform fitness tests. They are timed when they row two kilometers on a rowing machine called an ergometer (or erg, for short) and when they run one and a half miles. The number of times they complete a circuit of exercises is also counted. Tyler tracks this data in an Excel workbook. He uses this data to create charts that he posts so that the rowers are motivated to try to improve their numbers. Tyler asked you to embed sample data from the workbook into Slide 11 of the presentation.

Reference

Embedding an Excel Worksheet in a Slide

- Start Excel (the source program), open the file containing the worksheet you want to embed, and then select that worksheet's sheet tab.
- In the Excel worksheet, click and drag to select the cells you want to copy, and then on the Home tab, in the Clipboard group, click the Copy button.
- Switch to the PowerPoint presentation, and then display the slide in which you want to embed the copied cells.
- On the Home tab, in the Clipboard group, click the Paste arrow, and then click the Embed button, or click the Paste arrow, click Paste Special, make sure Microsoft Excel Worksheet Object is selected in the As list, and then click OK.

First, you will open the Excel workbook and then copy the cells containing the sample data to be embedded in Slide 11 of the NP_PPT_5_Convention presentation.

To embed Excel worksheet data in Slide 11:

1. Display Slide 12 ("Sample Fitness Table"), and then change the layout to **Title Only**.

2. Start Microsoft Excel, open the file **Support_PPT_5_Fitness.xlsx**, located in the PowerPoint5 > Module folder included with your Data Files, and then save the workbook as **NP_PPT_5_Fitness** to the location where you are storing your files. See Figure 5–27.

Figure 5-27   Data in Excel file

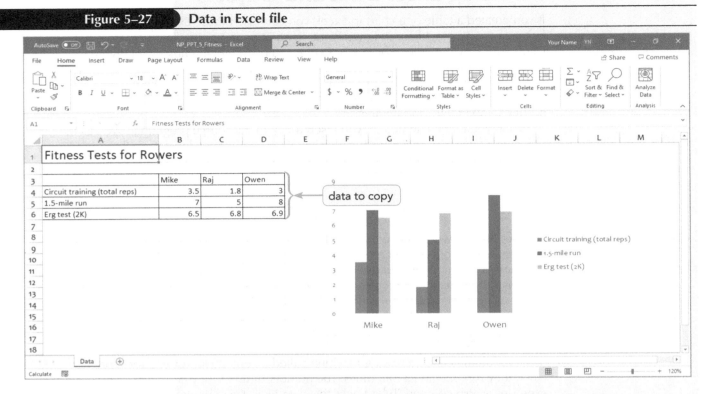

Trouble? If the worksheet is not at 120% zoom, use the Zoom slider on the right end of the status bar to change the zoom to 120%.

3. Move the pointer on top of cell **A3**, press and hold the mouse button, drag down to cell **D6**, and then release the mouse button. Cells A3 through D6 are selected.

4. On the Home tab, in the Clipboard group, click the **Copy** button.

5. On the Windows taskbar, click the **NP_PPT_5_Convention – PowerPoint** button to switch back to the NP_PPT_5_Convention presentation with Slide 12 displayed.

6. On the Home tab, in the Clipboard group, click the **Paste arrow**, and then click the **Embed** button. The worksheet is embedded in the slide with the presentation theme. Instead of the table contextual tabs, the Shape Format tab appears on the ribbon.

7. Resize the worksheet object so it is 2 inches high and 10.27 inches wide. (Change the measurements on the Shape Format tab in the Shape Height box in the Size group if necessary.)

8. Center align the embedded object on the slide and then drag it so it is approximately vertically centered in the white area on the slide.

Tip

To create an embedded Excel worksheet from within PowerPoint, click the Insert tab, click the Table button in the Tables group, and then click Excel Spreadsheet.

To modify an embedded worksheet, you double-click the selected worksheet object to display the Excel tabs and commands on the ribbon in the PowerPoint window. You can then change the data or format the table using the Excel commands on the ribbon.

Tyler wants you to fill the cells with color. He also wants the column and row labels to be bold. You'll make these changes now.

To modify the embedded worksheet:

▶ **1.** On Slide 12 ("Sample Fitness Table"), double-click the worksheet object. The ribbon changes to display the Excel tabs and commands, although the program title bar indicates you still are working in PowerPoint. Cells A3 through D6 in the worksheet are selected. See Figure 5–28.

Figure 5–28   **Embedded Excel object with Excel active**

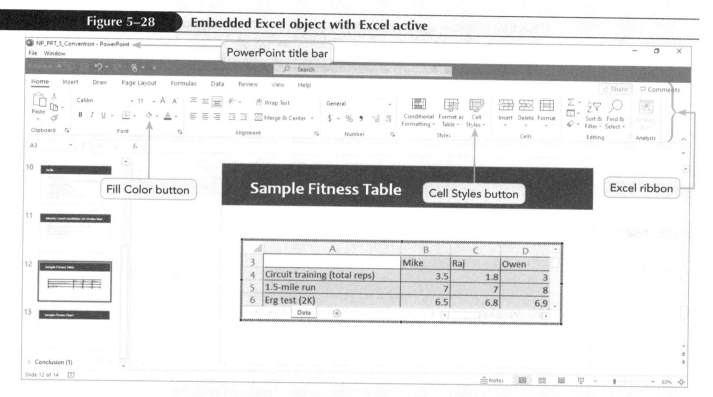

▶ **2.** On the Home tab, in the Font group, click the **Fill Color button arrow** ⬗ ⌄ , and then click the **Blue, Accent 1, Lighter 80%** color. The selected cells are filled with the light blue color.

▶ **3.** Move the pointer on top of cell **A4**, press and hold the mouse button, drag down to cell **A6**, and then release the mouse button. Cells A4 through A6 are selected.

▶ **4.** Press and hold **CTRL**, drag to select cells **B3** through **D3**, and then release the mouse button and **CTRL**. Cells A4 through A6 and cells B3 through D3 are selected.

▶ **5.** In the Styles group, click the **Cell Styles** button, and then click **Heading 4**. The selected cells are formatted with the Heading 4 style, which formats the text as bold and blue.

▶ **6.** Click a blank area of the slide. The ribbon changes back to the PowerPoint ribbon, and then the Excel window may become the active window.

▶ **7.** If necessary, on the Windows taskbar, click the **NP_PPT_5_Convention – PowerPoint** button 🄿 to switch back to the NP_PPT_5_Convention presentation with Slide 12 displayed. The embedded object is still selected.

▶ **8.** Click a blank area of the slide again to deselect the object. See Figure 5–29.

Figure 5–29 **Formatted data in the embedded Excel workbook**

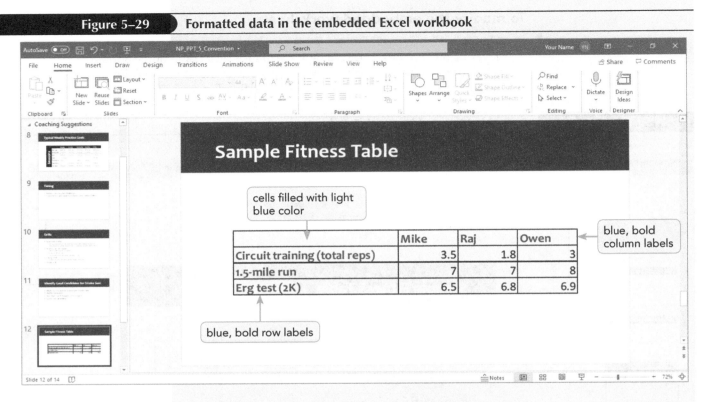

▶ **9.** Save the changes to the presentation.

Keep in mind that the changes you made to the embedded object did not change the original worksheet in the Excel workbook. Embedding maintains a connection only with the program that was used to create the object, not with the original object itself.

Linking an Excel Chart

If you need to include an Excel chart in your presentation that is based on data that might change, you can link the chart instead of embed it. For example, you might need to include a chart on a slide, but you know that the final data is not available yet or that the chart data will change over time. In this case, you should link the chart so that when the source file is updated, the linked chart in the destination file is updated and reflects the changes made to the source file.

There are two ways to link a chart from an Excel workbook to a presentation. After copying the chart, you can click the Paste arrow in PowerPoint and then click the Use Destination Theme & Link Data button or the Keep Source Formatting & Link Data button. Both of these options link the data of the chart, but not the chart itself. This means that if you change the way the chart looks in the Excel file, that change will not be reflected on the slide. Instead, when you click the chart on the slide, the chart tools contextual tabs appear on the PowerPoint ribbon and you can use the commands on those tabs to modify the chart.

If you want to link both the data and the chart, you need to use the Paste Special dialog box, which you open by clicking the Paste Special command on the Paste button menu. When you link a chart or data using the Paste Special dialog box, you do not have the option to use the style of the destination file, but any changes you make to the chart in the Excel file will be reflected in the PowerPoint file.

Reference

Linking Excel Chart Data and Format to a Slide

- Open the Excel file containing the chart to be linked, and then select the sheet tab that contains the chart.
- Point to the chart to display the ScreenTip "Chart Area", click the chart to select it, and then copy it to the Clipboard.
- Switch to the PowerPoint presentation, and display the slide to which you will link the chart.
- On the Home tab, in the Clipboard group, click the Paste arrow, click Paste Special to open the Paste Special dialog box, click the Paste link option button, and then click OK.

In the Excel workbook, Tyler created a column chart to illustrate the sample data. He wants you to link it to Slide 13 in the NP_PPT_5_Convention presentation.

To insert a chart linked to the Excel worksheet:

▶ **1.** Display Slide 13 ("Sample Fitness Chart"), and then change the layout to **Title Only**.

▶ **2.** On the taskbar, click the **NP_PPT_5_Fitness – Excel** button ![x] . The workbook appears with the Data worksheet selected. The column chart was created from the sample data.

▶ **3.** Move the pointer on top of the chart so that the ScreenTip "Chart Area" appears, and then click to select the chart.

   Trouble? If the ScreenTip displays something other than "Chart Area", move the pointer closer to the top or bottom edge of the chart.

▶ **4.** On the Home tab, in the Clipboard group, click the **Copy** button.

▶ **5.** On the taskbar, click the **NP_PPT_5_Convention – PowerPoint** button ![P] . The NP_PPT_5_Convention presentation appears with Slide 13 displayed.

▶ **6.** In the Clipboard group, click the **Paste arrow**, and then click **Paste Special**. The Paste Special dialog box opens. See Figure 5–30.

Figure 5–30   Paste Special dialog box

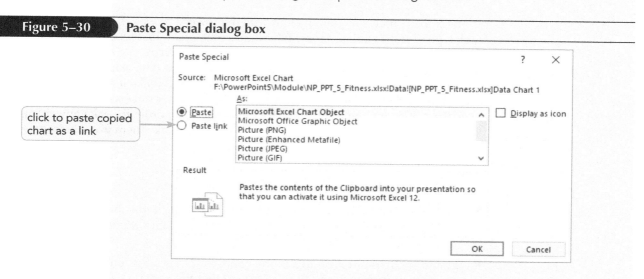

click to paste copied chart as a link

Tip

If you want to link worksheet cells, you must use the Paste Special dialog box.

7. In the dialog box, click the **Paste link** option button. The As list changes to include only one object, a Microsoft Excel Chart Object.

8. Click **OK**. The chart is linked to Slide 13 using the style of the source file. On the ribbon, the chart contextual tabs do not appear. Instead, the Shape Format tab appears.

9. On the ribbon, click the **Shape Format** tab, and then resize the chart so it is **5.3** inches high and about **9.84** inches wide, using the Shape Height and Shape Width boxes in the Size group on the Shape Format tab to help you.

10. Position the chart so its center aligns with the center of the slide and so it is approximately vertically centered in the white area on the slide.

Tyler wants to make some changes to the chart. First, he wants to change the sample data for Raj's time for the run so there is a greater difference in this data for the three rowers. He asks you to make the changes in the Excel worksheet and then make sure the changes are reflected in the PowerPoint presentation.

To modify the linked chart:

1. On Slide 13 ("Sample Fitness Chart"), double-click the linked chart. The NP_PPT_5_Fitness workbook becomes active.

   Trouble? If you store your files on the cloud, the workbook might open in the Excel 365 app in your browser. Your steps may differ slightly.

2. Click cell **C5**, type **5**, and then press **ENTER**. The column in the chart that shows Raj's time for the run changes to reflect the new data.

3. Switch to the NP_PPT_5_Convention presentation. The chart on Slide 13 has been updated to reflect the changed data.

   Trouble? If the chart on Slide 13 did not update, right-click the chart, and then on the shortcut menu, click Update Link.

The linked chart is a column chart with the rowers' names as the categories and each type of test as a data series. Tyler thinks that a bar chart would better illustrate the sample data he created, so he asks you to change the chart type to a bar chart. He also thinks that the data would be easier to understand if the data was plotted so that the types of tests are the categories. This representation will make it easier to compare how each rower did in each fitness test compared to the other rowers. Because you used the Paste Special command to link the chart to the slide, in order to make any changes to the chart, including formatting changes, you need to make them from the source file.

To change the chart type:

1. On Slide 13 ("Sample Fitness Chart"), right-click the chart, point to **Linked Worksheet Object**, and then click **Edit**. The Data worksheet in the Fitness workbook becomes active.

2. Move the pointer on top of the chart so that the ScreenTip "Chart Area" or "Chart" appears, and then click to select the chart.

3. Click the **Chart Design** or **Chart** tab, and then, in the Type group, click the **Change Chart Type** button. The Change Chart Type dialog box opens.

   Trouble? If you are using the Excel 365 app in your browser, click the **Change Chart Type arrow**, and then click **Clustered Bar** on the menu. Skip Step 4. In Step 5, click the **Switch Row/Column** button on the left of the ribbon.

4. In the navigation pane on the left, click **Bar**, and then click **OK**. The dialog box closes, and the chart is now a bar chart. Next you need to change how the rows and columns of source data are plotted on the chart.

Tip

You can also click the second option in the Change Chart Type dialog box to insert a chart with the rows and columns switched.

5. On the Chart Design tab, in the Data group, click the **Switch Row/Column** button. The chart changes so that the types of tests are the categories of data and each person's data is a data series. This means the legend identifying each bar color now contains the column labels Owen, Raj, and Mike, and the labels identifying the bars are now the row labels.

6. Save the changes to the Excel workbook, and then close the workbook and exit Excel. You return to the NP_PPT_5_Convention presentation. All the changes you made to the chart are shown in the chart on Slide 13. See Figure 5–31.

Figure 5–31 **Updated linked chart on Slide 13**

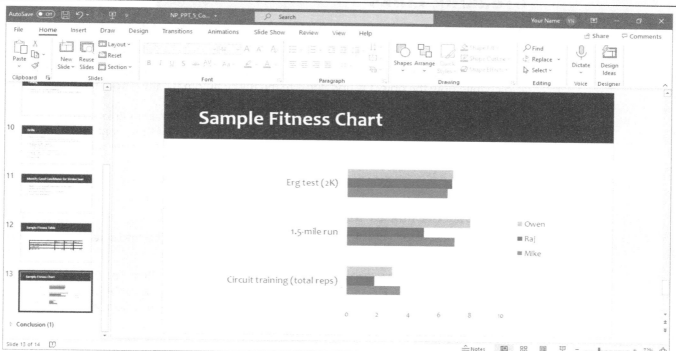

Trouble? If the changes were not applied to the chart on the slide, right-click the chart, and then on the shortcut menu, click Update Link.

7. Save the changes to the presentation.

You have now linked and edited an Excel chart in a PowerPoint presentation. Any additional changes made to the workbook will be reflected in the linked chart in the PowerPoint slide.

Proskills

Decision Making: Comparing Paste, Embed, and Linking Options

Each method of including objects from another file has advantages and disadvantages. The advantage of pasting or embedding an object instead of linking it is that the source file and the destination file can be stored separately. You can make changes to the object in the destination file, and the source file will be unaffected. The disadvantage of pasting or embedding an object is that you do not have access to the source program from within the destination file to modify the object. Another disadvantage of embedding an object is that the destination file size is somewhat larger than it would be if the object were simply imported as a picture or text or linked.

The advantage of linking an object instead of embedding it is that the object remains identical in the source and destination files, and the destination file size does not increase as much as if the object were embedded. The disadvantage is that the source and destination files must be stored together. When you need to copy information from one program to another, consider which option is the best choice for your needs.

Breaking Links

When you link an object to a slide, you need to keep the source file in its original location so that the link can be maintained. If you move the source file, you need to identify the new location from within the PowerPoint file. You do this by using the Links dialog box, which you can open from the Info screen in Backstage view. You can also change how the object is updated—manually or automatically—from the Links dialog box.

If you plan to send the presentation to others, you should break all links so that when they open the file, they don't see a message asking them if they want to update the links. You will break the link to the Excel data that was used to create the chart on Slide 13.

To break the link to the Excel workbook:

▶ 1. On the ribbon, click the **File** tab, and then click **Info**. The Info screen appears in Backstage view.

▶ 2. In the Related Documents section, click **Edit Links to Files**. The Links dialog box opens. See Figure 5–32. The filename of the object and the path appear in the Links list. Because it is selected, this information also appears below the Links box next to "Source".

Figure 5–32   **Links dialog box on the Info screen in Backstage view**

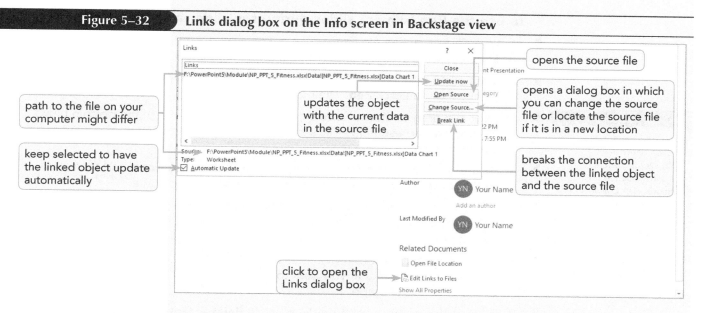

3. In the Links list, make sure the linked object is selected, and then click **Break Link**. The selected item in the list is removed. Now, if you change the data on which the chart is based in the Excel worksheet, the chart on Slide 13 will not reflect that change.

4. In the Links dialog box, click **Close**.

5. At the top of the navigation bar, click the **Back** button ⊕ to close Backstage view. On Slide 13, the chart is selected, and on the ribbon, the Picture Format tab appears. This happened because you broke the link to source file.

6. Save the changes to the presentation.

Annotating Slides During a Slide Show

During a slide show, you can annotate—add markup to—the slides to emphasize a point. To do this, you change the pointer to a pen, which allows you to draw lines on a slide during a slide show, or to a highlighter, which allows you to highlight something on a slide during a slide show. (As you saw when you recorded a slide show, you can also annotate a slide using the pen or highlighter while you are recording.) For example, you might use the Pen to underline a word or phrase that you want to emphasize or to circle a graphic that you want to point out. You can change the ink color of the Pen or Highlighter you select. You can also select the Eraser tool to remove Pen or Highlighter lines that you draw

After you go through a presentation and mark it, you have the choice of keeping the markings as drawn objects in the presentation or discarding them. If you keep them, you can convert them into text or shapes if you want.

To use the Pen to mark slides during the slide show:

1. With Slide 13 ("Sample Fitness Chart") displayed, on the status bar, click the **Slide Show** button 🖵. Slide 13 appears in Slide Show view.

2. Right-click anywhere on the screen, point to **Pointer Options** on the shortcut menu, and then click **Pen**. The mouse pointer changes to a small, red dot.

3. Click and drag to draw an arrow pointing to the right end of the bottom blue bar (the bar representing Mike's circuit training total reps). Next, you want to highlight Mike's name in the legend.

4. Right-click anywhere on the screen, point to **Pointer Options**, and then click **Highlighter**. The pointer changes to a small, yellow rectangle.

5. In the legend, click and drag across **Mike** and the blue square in the legend to highlight it with yellow. When the Pen or the Highlighter is active, you cannot advance the slide show by clicking the mouse button.

6. Press the **SPACEBAR** to move to Slide 14 ("Building a Team"). There is nothing on this slide that you want to annotate, so you'll change the pointer back to its normal shape.

7. Right-click anywhere on the slide, point to **Pointer Options**, and then click **Highlighter** to deselect it. The pointer changes to its normal shape. While you are changing the pointer options, the animations stop, and then restart when you are done.

8. Advance the slide show to display the black slide that indicates the end of the slide show, and then advance once more. A dialog box opens asking if you want to keep your ink annotations.

9. Click **Keep**, and then return to Slide 13 ("Sample Fitness Chart"), which displays the annotations you made during the slide show. See Figure 5–33.

Tip

To erase an annotation in Slide Show view, right-click anywhere on the slide, point to Pointer Options, click Eraser, and then click the annotation.

Figure 5–33   **Annotated Slide 13 in Normal view**

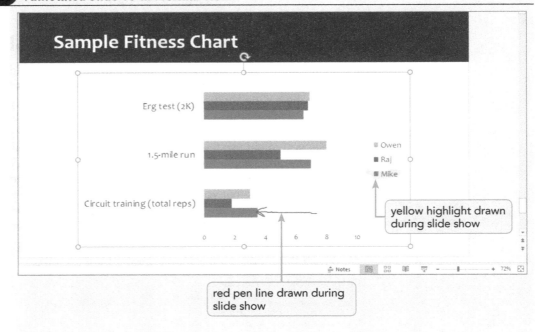

The marks you drew in Slide Show view can be manipulated or deleted just like any object on a slide. Annotations are treated as drawings, like shapes, so when you select an annotation on the slide, the Shape Format tab appears on the ribbon. You can change the color and width of annotations, as well as move them through layers, align and rotate them, and change their overall size. You can also convert annotations to text or shapes.

You will delete the highlight mark on Slide 13.

To delete an annotation mark on Slide 13:

Tip

To convert annotations to text or shapes, click the annotation to display the Convert Your Ink button on the slide, click it, then click the Text or Shape button.

Make sure you save the file now because you will be renaming it next.

1. On Slide 13 ("Sample Fitness Chart"), click the highlight mark in the legend that you drew during the slide show. The highlight mark is selected.

2. Press **DELETE**. The highlight is deleted.

3. In the pane containing the thumbnails, collapse the Conclusion and Coaching Suggestions sections, and then expand the Introduction section.

4. Display Slide 1 (the title slide), and then change the name in the subtitle to your name.

5. Save the changes to the presentation.

Insight

Using the Laser Pointer During a Slide Show

You can change the pointer into a red dot that looks like a laser pointer during a slide show so that you can point to objects or text on a slide during your presentation. To do this, right-click a slide during the slide show, point to Pointer Options on the shortcut menu, and then click Laser Pointer. As when you change the pointer to a Pen or Highlighter, you cannot click the mouse button to advance the slide show while the pointer is the Laser Pointer.

Creating Handouts by Exporting a Presentation to Word

You know how to print a presentation using the Handouts setting on the Print screen in Backstage view so that one or more slides are printed per page. Another way you can create handouts is to export your slides to a new Word document. When you do this, you can choose from the following options:

- **Notes next to slides**—lists the speaker notes next to each slide; the number of slides per page depends on how many lines of speaker notes are on each slide
- **Blank lines next to slides**—adds blank lines next to each slide, three slides per page
- **Notes below slides**—lists the speaker notes below each slide; one slide per page
- **Blank lines below slides**—adds blank lines below each slide, one slide per page
- **Outline only**—lists the outline of the presentation as a bulleted list with first-level bulleted items at the same level as slide titles and second-level bulleted items indented

Tyler wants you to export the presentation to Word to create handouts displaying thumbnails of the slides with lines for notes to the right of each thumbnail.

To create handouts by exporting the presentation to Word:

▶ **1.** On the ribbon, click the **File** tab to open Backstage view, and then in the navigation bar, click **Export**. The Export screen appears.

▶ **2.** Click **Create Handouts**. The screen changes to display a description of creating handouts in Microsoft Word and a button for doing this. See Figure 5–34.

Figure 5–34   Export screen in Backstage view with Create Handouts selected

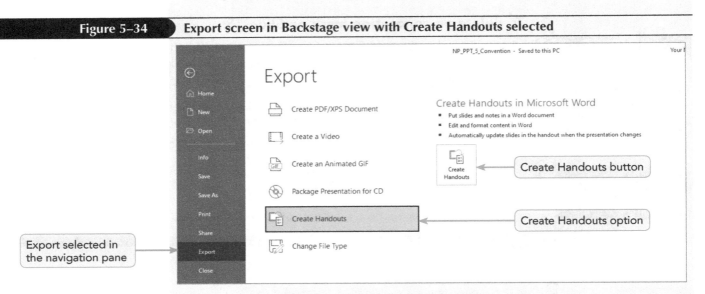

▶ **3.** Click the **Create Handouts** button. Backstage view closes, and the Send to Microsoft Word dialog box opens. You can choose from five options for creating handouts, and you can choose to link the slides instead of simply exporting them. If you choose to link the handouts, when you modify the presentation, the change will be reflected in the handouts. See Figure 5–35.

Figure 5–35   Send to Microsoft Word dialog box

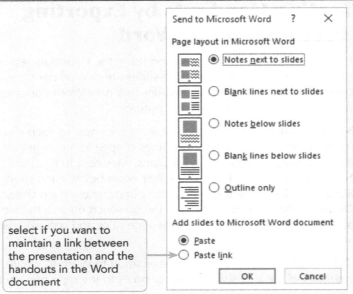

4. Click the **Outline only** option button, and then click **OK**. The dialog box closes, and a new Microsoft Word document is created. On the taskbar, a Microsoft Word button appears and starts blinking, indicating the document is being created. After the document is created, the button stops blinking. The time it takes for this to happen depends on the speed of your computer—it may take a minute or two.

5. On the taskbar, click the **Document1 – Compatibility Mode – Word** program button ▥. The handouts appear in a Word document with each slide title and first-level items in the bulleted lists in large font size (44 points in this case) and formatted as bold, and the sub-bullets in a smaller font size (18 points in this case).

   Trouble? If the pointer blinks and changes to a blue circle, the document is still being created. Wait until the pointer is no longer a circle before continuing.

6. Click the **File** tab, and then in the navigation bar, click **Save As** ▦. The Save As screen in Backstage view appears.

7. Click **Browse** to open the Save As dialog box, type **NP_PPT_5_Handouts** in the File name box, navigate to the location where you are storing your files, and then click **Save**. A dialog box appears telling you that the document will be upgraded to the newest file format.

   Trouble? If the dialog box telling you that the document will be upgraded to the newest file format doesn't appear, skip Step 8.

8. Click **OK**. The file is saved.

9. Close the NP_PPT_5_Handouts document and exit Word.

10. **sam** ⬆ Close the NP_PPT_5_Convention presentation.

In this session, you copied a table from a Word document and formatted the table in PowerPoint. You also inserted Excel objects by embedding them and linking them to their source files. Finally, you broke the links, annotated slides during a slide show, and then created handouts by exporting the presentation to a Word document. Tyler is satisfied with the presentation.

Review

Session 5.2 Quick Check

1. What does it mean to embed an object in a presentation?

2. If you modify the source file of a linked object, what happens to the linked object in the PowerPoint slide?

3. Why would you link an object instead of embed it?

4. If you link an Excel chart to a slide with one of the Paste Link buttons on the Paste menu, is the chart formatting linked as well?

5. How is an annotation that you created during a slide treated in Normal view?

6. Describe how to create handouts in Word.

Practice

Review Assignments

Data Files needed for the Review Assignments: NP_PPT_5-2.pptx, Support_PPT_5_Basics.pptx, Support_PPT_5_Erg.xlsx, Support_PPT_5_GPA.xlsx, Support_PPT_5_NovOutline.docx, Support_PPT_5_Races.docx

Tyler decided to create a presentation describing basic rules and procedures to new rowers at South Bay College. He prepared an outline of part of the presentation, and his assistant coach, Olivia, prepared slides describing basic terminology. He asked you to help create the final presentation. Complete the following steps:

1. Open the presentation **NP_PPT_5-2.pptx**, located in the PowerPoint5 > Review folder, add your name as the subtitle on Slide 1, and then save the file as **NP_PPT_5_Orientation** in the location where you are storing your files.

2. After Slide 1, create slides from the outline in the Word file **Support_PPT_5_NovOutline.docx**, located in the PowerPoint5 > Review folder. Reset the six slides you create.

3. After Slide 7 ("Average GPA"), insert Slides 1 through 3 from the **Support_PPT_5_Basics.pptx** presentation, located in the PowerPoint5 > Review folder, so they become Slides 8 through 10 in the NP_PPT_5_Orientation presentation.

4. In Outline view, on Slide 6 ("Average 5K Erg Test Scores in Minutes"), change the "Student Athlete" bulleted item into a new Slide 7 with its subitems as bulleted items on the new Slide 7. Then reorder the presentation by moving Slide 4 ("2021-2022 Race Schedule") so it becomes Slide 8, and moving Slide 12 ("If You Can't Make a Practice") so it becomes Slide 4.

5. Create four sections in the presentation and a summary zoom containing the four sections. One section should include Slide 1 (the title slide) and be named **Title**; another section should include Slide 2 ("Safety") and be named **Safety**; another section should include Slides 3 ("Typical Practice Schedule") through 9 ("2021-2022 Race Schedule") and be named **Routine and Expectations**, and the final section should include Slides 10 ("Terminology") through 12 ("Identifying the Rowers") and be named **Basics**.

6. Reorder the sections in the following order: Summary Section, Title, Basics, Safety, and Routine and Expectations. Add **Overview** as the slide title on the summary zoom, and then edit the summary zoom so that the section zooms appear in the correct order.

7. On Slide 8 ("If You Can't Make a Practice…"), insert two icons: in the Technology And Electronics category, a smartphone icon in the top row, and in the Communication category, the open envelope with the @ symbol on a piece of paper. Resize both icons so they are 3.5 inches high, and then duplicate the smartphone icon.

8. Position one of the smartphone icons above the text "Call" so its center aligns with the center of the "Call" text box. Position the other smartphone icon above the "Text" text box so its center aligns with the center of the slide. Position the envelope icon above the "Email" text box so its center aligns with the center of the "Email" text box.

9. Select all three icons, and then use the Align Middle command so that the middles of the three icons align with each other. With the three icons still selected, position them vertically so there is approximately one-half inch between the tops of the smartphone icons and tops of the green boxes and one-half inch between the bottom of the icons and the text below each icon.

10. Convert the Email icon to shapes. Ungroup the shapes, and then change the fill color of the @sign shape to Red, Accent 6, Darker 50%.

11. In the Selection pane, rename the two smartphone icon objects to **Call smartphone** and **Text smartphone**. Rename the envelope image to **Envelope** and the @ sign to **At sign**.

12. Open the Animation pane. Each green rectangle has the Collapse exit animation applied to it. The Left rectangle will animate when the slide show advances (On Click), and the animations applied to the other two rectangles will start after the previous action with a delay of one second.

13. Apply the Teeter emphasis animation to the Call smartphone object. Use the Teeter Effect Options dialog box to add the Chime sound to the animation. Change the order of this animation so it starts after the Left rectangle exit animation. Change the start setting so it starts after the previous animation.

14. Apply the Appear entrance animation to the Coach text box object (the text box that contains the message to the coach in the center of the smartphone icon on the middle green rectangle). (*Hint*: Use the Selection pane to select the Coach text box object.) Modify the animation using the Appear Effect Options dialog box by doing the following:

    a. Add the Typewriter sound to the animation.

    b. Change the color of the text when the slide show advances to the blue color that is fifth from the left on the menu.

    c. Change the animation of the text so that the letters appear one character at a time with 0.1 second delay between each letter.

15. Change the order of the Appear entrance animation applied to the Coach text box object so that the animation starts after the Middle rectangle exit animation, and then change its start setting to After Previous.

16. Apply the Blink emphasis animation to the At sign object. (*Hint*: Use the More Emphasis Effects command at the bottom of the Animations gallery.) Use the Timing tab in the Blink Effect Options dialog box to make the animation repeat three times and change the duration to 0.5 seconds. Make sure the Blink animation will occur after the Right rectangle exit animation, and then change the start setting to After Previous.

17. In the Selection pane, examine the layers on Slide 8. The green rectangles need to be on top of the icons so that Tyler can click them during the slide show to display the icons. Move the three green rectangles to the three top layers so that they are in layers on top of the icons and text boxes. Change the fill color of the rectangles to Blue, Accent 1, Darker 50%.

18. View Slide 8 in Slide Show view. Advance the slide show once to start the animations. End the slide show after the last animation.

19. Start Excel, open the **Support_PPT_5_GPA.xlsx** file located in the PowerPoint5 > Review folder, and then copy cells A3 through F5. In the NP_PPT_5_Orientation PowerPoint file, display Slide 12 ("Average GPA"), change the layout to Title Only, and then embed the cells you copied. Resize the embedded object so it is 1.5 inches high and 12.28 inches wide, and then position it so it is centered horizontally and vertically on the slide.

20. On Slide 12, fill cells A3 through F5 in the embedded workbook with the Gray, Accent 3, Lighter 80% color. Format cells A4 through A5 and cells B3 through F3 with the Heading 4 cell style, and then change the font size of the text in these cells to 14 points.

21. Open the Excel file **Support_PPT_5_Erg.xlsx**, located in the PowerPoint5 > Review folder, and then save it as **NP_PPT_5_Erg** in the location where you are saving your files. Copy the chart. Switch to the NP_PPT_5_Orientation presentation, display Slide 10 ("Average 5K Erg Test Scores in Minutes"), change the layout to Title Only, and then use the Paste Special command to link the copied chart to Slide 10. Use the Shape Height box in the Size group on the Shape Format tab to resize the linked chart so it is five inches high. Position the chart so its center aligns with the center of the slide and there is about one-quarter of an inch between the chart and the blue title rectangle.

22. Update the data on which the chart is based by typing **7:45** in cell B7 (indicating that the Novice Women's average score in Week 8 is 7:45 minutes), and then pressing ENTER. Change the chart type of the chart in the Excel workbook to Clustered Bar, and then switch the columns and the rows so that the team names are the categories. Save the changes to the NP_PPT_5_Erg workbook, and then close it. Close the Support_PPT_5_GPA workbook (do not save changes if asked) and exit Excel.

23. Break the link between the NP_PPT_5_Orientation presentation and the NP_PPT_5_Erg workbook.

24. On Slide 13 ("2021-2022 Race Schedule"), change the layout to Title Only. Copy the table in the Word file **Support_PPT_5_Races.docx**, located in the PowerPoint5 > Review folder, to Slide 13 using the source formatting. Close the Support_PPT_5_Races document and exit Word.

25. Resize the table so it is four inches high and 10.3 inches wide, and then change the font size of all the text in the table to 18 points.

26. Insert a new first column. In the new first column, merge the second through sixth cells, and then merge the seventh through eleventh cells. In the top merged cell, type **Fall**, and in the bottom merged cell type **Spring**.

27. Change the font size of the text in the merged cells to 36 points, and then rotate the text in the merged cells so it reads from the bottom of the cell up. Center the text in the merged cells both horizontally and vertically.

28. Resize the first column so it is 0.75 inches wide, resize the second column so it is 5.5 inches wide, and then resize the third column so that it is 3.8 inches wide. Position the table so its center aligns with the center of the slide and so there is approximately one inch between the table and the blue title rectangle.

29. Display Slide 6 ("Safety") in Slide Show view, circle the "Report all injuries" bulleted item using the red Pen, and then end the slide show, keeping the annotation.

30. Save the changes to the NP_PPT_5_Orientation presentation.

31. Create handouts in a Word document using the Outline only option. Save the Word document as **NP_PPT_5_NoviceHandouts** in the location where you are storing your files. Close the NP_PPT_5_NovicesHandouts file and exit Word.

32. Close the NP_PPT_5_Orientation presentation.

Apply

Case Problem 1

Data Files needed for this case Problem: NP_PPT_5-3.pptx, Support_PPT_5_Budget.xlsx, Support_PPT_5_Hunger.pptx, Support_PPT_5_Plan.docx

Community Kitchen Grace Kim works for Sullivan and Sanchez Consulting, a consulting firm that helps nonprofit organizations fundraise. Community Kitchen is a new nonprofit organization in Albuquerque, New Mexico, that was founded by local civic and religious groups to provide meals in a comfortable, welcoming atmosphere for people in need. Their goal is to provide family-style dining rather than a soup kitchen buffet line. They hired Sullivan and Sanchez Consulting to help them raise money to get started, and Grace was assigned to the project. Complete the following steps:

1. Open the presentation **NP_PPT_5-3.pptx**, located in the PowerPoint5 > Case1 folder included with your data files, replace the subtitle on Slide 1 with your name, and then save the file as **NP_PPT_5_Community** in the location where you are storing your files.

2. Create additional slides after Slide 4 from the outline contained in Word file **Support_PPT_5_Plan.docx**, located in the PowerPoint5 > Case1 folder. Reset the 11 newly created slides.

3. Demote all the text on Slide 6 ("Create partnerships") so "Create partnerships" becomes a first-level bulleted item on Slide 5 ("Building the Team").

4. Demote all the text on Slide 8 ("Equipment") so "Equipment" becomes a first-level bulleted item on Slide 7 ("Supplies"), and then move the "Equipment" bulleted item and its subitems up so the "Equipment" bulleted item is the second first-level bulleted item in the bulleted list on Slide 7.

5. On Slide 2 ("One Person in Six Is Hungry in New Mexico"), insert the filled icon of a person standing with arms down in the People category. Position the icon so its top aligns with the 2-inch mark on the vertical ruler and its left edge aligns with the left edge of the title text box.

6. Duplicate the icon, and then position the duplicate to the right of the original so that the two icons are horizontally aligned and there is about one-eighth of an inch between the "hands" of the two icons. Keep the icon selected.

7. Duplicate the selected icon. Another duplicate appears to the right of the second icon, positioned at the same distance from the second icon that the second icon is from the first icon. The third icon is selected.

8. Continue duplicating the selected icon nine more times so that there is a total of 12 icons in a row. (*Hint*: Press CTRL+D to execute the Duplicate command.)

9. Change the fill color of the sixth and the twelfth icon to Green, Accent 5.

10. Select all 12 icons. (*Hint*: On the Home tab, in the Editing group, click the Select button, click Select All, press and hold SHIFT, click the title text box border to deselect it, and then release SHIFT.) Apply the Appear entrance animation to the selected icons. Change the start setting to After Previous, and add a delay of 0.50 seconds.

11. Add the Blink emphasis animation to the green icons. (*Hint*: Make sure you use the Add Animation button and then use the More Emphasis Effects command at the bottom of the Animation gallery.) Change the duration of the Blink animations to 0.50 seconds. Modify the Blink animation applied to the green icons so that they repeat three times. Reorder each Blink animation so it occurs after the Appear animation applied to the same icon, and then change the start setting of the Blink animations to After Previous with a 0.25 second delay.

12. Change the delay applied to the seventh icon to 0.25 seconds. View Slide 2 in Slide Show view.

13. Insert Slide 2 and Slide 3 from the file **Support_PPT_5_Hunger.pptx**, located in the PowerPoint > Case1 folder, as Slides 3 and 4 in the NP_PPT_5_Community presentation. Apply the Morph transition to Slide 4.

14. Move Slide 2 so it becomes Slide 15, the last slide in the presentation. Create a new section named **Unused** that includes only Slide 15.

15. Start Excel, open the **Support_PPT_5_Budget.xlsx** workbook, located in the PowerPoint5 > Case1 folder, and then save it as **NP_PPT_5_Budget**.

16. In the NP_PPT_5_Budget workbook, copy the Projected Monthly Expenses column chart. Switch to the NP_PPT_5_Community presentation, display Slide 10 ("Monthly Expenses"), change the layout to Title Only, and then link the copied chart to Slide 10 using the Paste Special dialog box.

17. Edit the chart source file by changing the value in cell B8 to **-3500**, and then change the chart type in the source file to a pie chart.

18. On Slide 10, resize the chart so it is five inches high and 8.37 inches wide, and then center it in the space below the slide title.

19. Break the link between the NP_PPT_5_Community presentation and the NP_PPT_5_Budget workbook.

20. In the NP_PPT_5_Budget workbook, copy cells A17 through B33. Switch to the NP_PPT_5_Community presentation, display Slide 11 ("Annual Estimated Income"), and then change the layout to Title Only. Embed the copied data on Slide 11, resize the Excel object so it is five inches high and 5.31 inches wide, and then position it so it is centered in the blank area on the slide.

21. On Slide 11, double-click the embedded workbook, and then format cells A20 through B27 so that black border lines appear between all the cells. (*Hint*: Click the Borders arrow in the Font group on the Home tab, and then click More Borders. In the Format Cells dialog box, on the Border tab, click in the middle of the large box in the Border section to insert a horizontal line. If you accidentally add a line somewhere else, click it to remove it.) Save the NP_PPT_5_Budget workbook, and then close Excel.

22. In the presentation, create the following sections:
    - **Intro**, which includes Slides 1 through 4
    - **Organization**, which includes Slides 5 through 8
    - **Finances**, which includes Slides 9 through 11
    - **Menu & Operations**, which includes Slides 12 and 13
    - **Advertising**, which includes Slide 14

23. Create a summary zoom that contains section zooms for all of the sections except the Intro section and the Unused section. Leave the summary zoom as Slide 5. Change the layout of the summary zoom to Title Only. Select the four section zooms on the summary zoom, and then add a Red, Accent 1 border to the section zooms.

24. Create handouts in Word using the Outline only option. Save this file as **NP_PPT_5_ CommunityHandouts** in the location where you are saving your files, and then exit Word.

25. Save the changes to the NP_PPT_5_Community file, and then close it.

Troubleshoot

Case Problem 2

Data Files needed for this case Problem: NP_PPT_5-4.pptx, Support_PPT_5_Boys.jpg, Support_PPT_5_Data.xlsx, Support_PPT_5_ParentNotes.docx, Support_PPT_5_Slides.pptx

Northgate Counseling Center Donna Teton is a licensed social worker at Northgate Counseling Center in Idaho Falls, Idaho. Donna specializes in providing therapy to children. She has been hired by several school districts to talk to teachers, school support staff, and parents about ways they can identify and stop bullying. Complete the following steps:

1. Open the presentation **NP_PPT_5-4.pptx**, located in the PowerPoint5 > Case2 folder included with your data files, add your name in the subtitle on Slide 1, and then save the file as **NP_PPT_5_Bully** to the location where you are saving your files.

2. On Slide 1 (the title slide), select the six photos, and then group them together. (Each photo has a six-point black border.) Duplicate the grouped object, and then place the duplicate to the right of the original grouped object. Align the top and bottom edges of the two grouped objects. Position the left black border of the duplicated object directly on top of the right black border of the original grouped object. Finally, select both grouped objects and group them together.

3. Apply the Lines motion path animation to the grouped object, change its effect to Left, change its duration to 14 seconds, and change its start setting to With Previous. Click the motion path so that the red triangle that indicates the end of the motion path changes to a red circle. While pressing SHIFT to maintain a straight line, drag the red circle to the left until the images you are dragging are no longer blurry because they are directly on top of the original grouped object.

4. Open the Effect Options dialog box for the Lines animation (it will be titled "Left"). Change the Smooth start and end times to 0 seconds, and then have the animation repeat until the end of the slide. View Slide 1 in Slide Show view and watch until you see each image three times. If the transition between the end of the second set of images and the beginning of the third set of images is bumpy, repeat Step 3, and try to get the images exactly aligned on top of one another.

5. On Slide 2 ("What Is Bullying?"), insert the picture **Support_PPT_5_Boys.jpg**, located in the PowerPoint5 > Case2 folder.

6. Apply the Lines motion path animation to the picture of the boys. Drag the end point of the line up in a straight line to shorten the path so it is one and one-eighth inch long.

7. Add the Grow/Shrink emphasis animation to the picture of the boys. In the Grow/Shrink Effect Options dialog box, change the size to 73%. (*Hint*: Type the value in the Custom box on the menu.) Change the duration to 1.25 seconds.

8. Add the Fade exit animation to the picture of the boys.

9. Duplicate the picture of the boys. On the Picture Format tab, apply the Washout effect in the Recolor section of the Color menu. In the Selection pane, rename the picture with the washout effect applied to **Boys washout**. Rename the original picture **Boys**.

10. Resize the Boys washout picture so it is 5.5 inches high. Position it so its center aligns with the center of the slide and the center of the original picture of the boys and so its bottom edge aligns with the bottom edge of the slide. Remove the animations from the Boys washout picture.

11. Reorder the animations so that Lines animation applied to the Boys object occurs first, the Grow/Shrink animation applied to the Boys object occurs second, the Fade animation applied to the Boys object occurs third, the entrance animation applied to the title text box occurs fourth, and the entrance animation applied to the content placeholder occurs fifth.

12. Change the start setting of the Boys Grow/Shrink emphasis animation to With Previous and set a delay of 0.50 seconds. Set the Boys Fade exit animation to After Previous. Change the start setting of the Title Fade entrance animation to With Previous.

⚙ **Troubleshoot** 13. View Slide 2 in Slide Show view, pressing SPACEBAR to advance the slide show four times. Modify the slide as needed so that you see the Boys picture object at the beginning and the bulleted list on top of the Boys washout picture at the end.

14. Start Excel, and then open the file **Support_PPT_5_Data.xlsx**, located in the PowerPoint5 > Case2 folder, and then save it as **NP_PPT_5_Data**. Copy the column chart. In the PowerPoint file NP_PPT_5_Bully, link the chart to Slide 3 ("Bullying Behaviors Reported by Children 12-18") so that when the chart's format is changed in the Excel file, it will change in the PowerPoint file as well. Resize the chart so it is 5.25 inches high and 9.31 inches wide. Center it in the area below the slide title.

15. In the Excel file NP_PPT_5_Data, click cell C5, type **17**, and the press ENTER. Change the chart type to a clustered bar chart, keeping the types of behaviors as the categories. Save the file and exit Excel.

⚙ **Troubleshoot** 16. Donna sent the presentation to a colleague, and the colleague reported that every time she opens the file, she is asked if she wants to update the links. Modify the file so that this does not happen.

17. Reuse Slides 2 through 6 from the **Support_PPT_5_Slides.pptx** presentation file, located in the PowerPoint5 > Case2 folder by inserting them in order after Slide 3 in the NP_PPT_5_Bully file.

18. Insert slides from the outline **Support_PPT_5_ParentNotes.docx** after Slide 8.

⚙ **Troubleshoot** 19. The new Slides 9 and 10 don't look the same as the other slides. Change them so they match the look of the other slides.

20. Create a summary zoom by selecting Slides 2, 4, and 8 as the first slide in sections. Display the Zoom tab to see that the first section zoom contains Slides 3-4, the second section zoom in the first row contains Slides 5-8, and the section zoom in the bottom row contains Slides 9-11.

21. Rename the Default Section section to **Title**. Rename the What Is Bullying? section to **Introduction**. Rename the Behaviors to Look For section to **For Teachers**. Rename the Warning Signs section to **For Parents**.

22. Move the For Parents section so it comes before the For Teachers section.

⚙ **Troubleshoot** 23. Display Slide 2 (the summary zoom), and then display the Zoom tab. The slides are out of order. Fix this slide so that the first section is the section zoom that contains the picture of the boys, the second section zoom in the first row is the Warning Signs section zoom with Slides 5-7, and the Behaviors to Look For section zoom is in the third row on the left.

24. View Slide 9 ("Addressing Bullying Behaviors with Students") in Slide Show view. Draw a red line under the slide title, and then keep the annotation.

25. Create handouts in Word using the Outline only option. Save the Word document as **NP_PPT_5_BullyHandouts**. Exit Word.

26. Save the changes to the presentation, and then close it.

POWERPOINT

Objectives

Session 6.1
- Compare presentations, and accept or reject changes
- Add, reply to, and delete comments
- Modify the slide master
- Modify the style of lists
- Create and modify slide layouts
- Create custom theme fonts and colors
- Fill text and shapes with a color on the slide
- Save a presentation as a theme

Session 6.2
- Create a custom show
- Create and modify custom file properties
- Encrypt a presentation
- Mark a presentation as read-only
- Present a presentation online

Customizing Presentations and the PowerPoint Environment

Creating a Presentation for a City-Wide Green Challenge

Case | **Rockland, Missouri City Government**

The city council in Rockland, Missouri, issued a "Green Challenge" to the city department heads to come up with plans to make their departments more environmentally friendly. Each department head needs to present their ideas at the next city council meeting. Veronica Soto, the director of the Parks and Recreation department, created a plan to reduce the amount of trash collected at city parks and nature trails by placing recycling containers and dog waste receptacles next to all trash bins. She asks you to help her as she works on the presentation.

In this module, you will compare presentations and use comments. You will modify the slide master and layouts, and create a custom theme font set and color palette. You will fill shapes with a color from the slide. Then you will save the presentation as a theme. You will also create a custom show and create and modify custom file properties. Finally, you will encrypt a presentation, mark it as read-only, and then learn how to present the presentation online.

Starting Data Files

Module

NP_PPT_6-1.pptx
Support_PPT_6_Aiden.pptx
Support_PPT_6_Park.jpg
Support_PPT_6_Receptacle.jpg
Support_PPT_6_Recycle.png
Support_PPT_6_Tree.jpg

Review

NP_PPT_6-2.pptx
Support_PPT_6_Dan.pptx
Support_PPT_6_Night.jpg

Case1

NP_PPT_6-3.pptx
Support_PPT_6_Background.jpg
Support_PPT_6_Password.jpg
Support_PPT_6_Side.jpg

Case2

Support_PPT_6_Bullet.png
Support_PPT_6_Logo1.png
Support_PPT_6_Logo2.jpg

Session 6.1 Visual Overview:

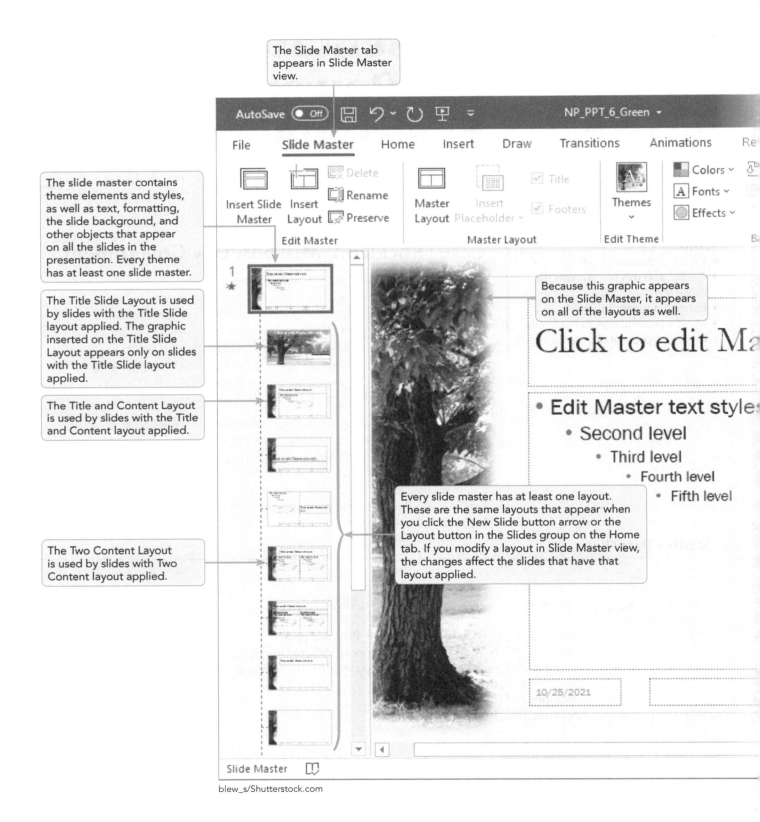

The Slide Master tab appears in Slide Master view.

The slide master contains theme elements and styles, as well as text, formatting, the slide background, and other objects that appear on all the slides in the presentation. Every theme has at least one slide master.

The Title Slide Layout is used by slides with the Title Slide layout applied. The graphic inserted on the Title Slide Layout appears only on slides with the Title Slide layout applied.

The Title and Content Layout is used by slides with the Title and Content layout applied.

The Two Content Layout is used by slides with Two Content layout applied.

Because this graphic appears on the Slide Master, it appears on all of the layouts as well.

Every slide master has at least one layout. These are the same layouts that appear when you click the New Slide button arrow or the Layout button in the Slides group on the Home tab. If you modify a layout in Slide Master view, the changes affect the slides that have that layout applied.

AutoSave ● Off

NP_PPT_6_Green

File   Slide Master   Home   Insert   Draw   Transitions   Animations

Insert Slide Master   Insert Layout   Delete   Rename   Preserve   Master Layout   Insert Placeholder   Title   Footers   Themes   Colors   Fonts   Effects

Edit Master   Master Layout   Edit Theme

Click to edit Ma

• Edit Master text style
  • Second level
    • Third level
      • Fourth level
        • Fifth level

10/25/2021

Slide Master

blew_s/Shutterstock.com

Slide Master View

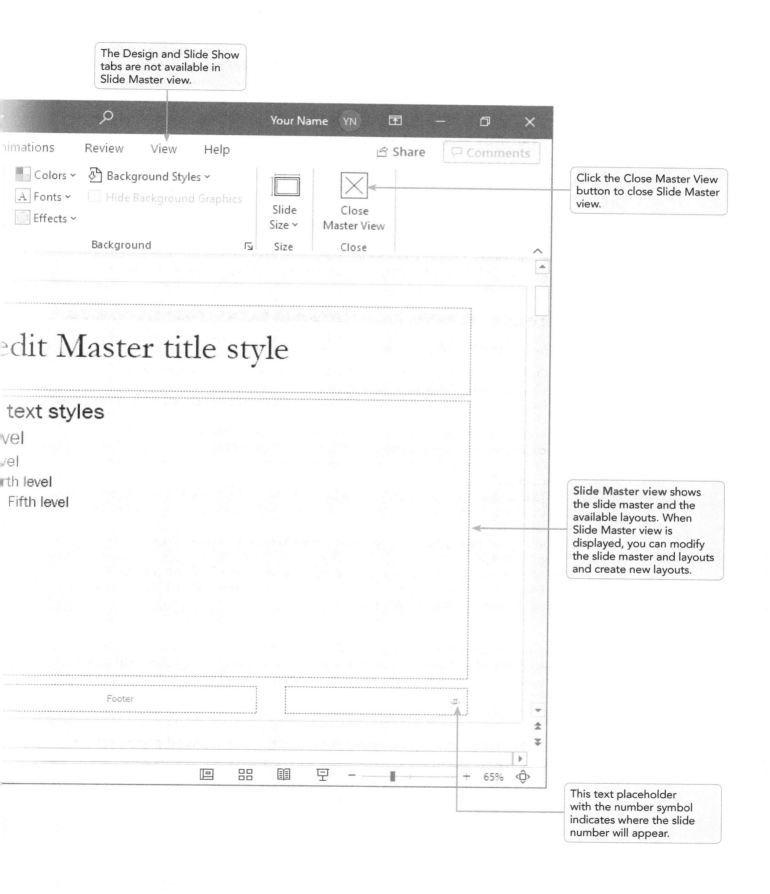

The Design and Slide Show tabs are not available in Slide Master view.

Click the Close Master View button to close Slide Master view.

Slide Master view shows the slide master and the available layouts. When Slide Master view is displayed, you can modify the slide master and layouts and create new layouts.

This text placeholder with the number symbol indicates where the slide number will appear.

Sharing and Collaborating with Others

It is a good idea to ask others to review your presentations before you finalize and present them. Another set of eyes can spot errors or inconsistencies that you might otherwise miss. When you send a presentation to colleagues for review, they can make changes and add comments. You then can compare the original and the reviewed versions of the presentation and accept the changes or ignore them. You also can add comments and reply to or delete existing comments in a presentation.

Comparing Presentations

To compare your original presentation to a version that a colleague has reviewed, use the Compare button in the Compare group on the Review tab. While you are comparing two presentations, the Revisions pane appears listing the changes, and change buttons 🔲 appear on the slide next to objects that have been changed. You can click a change button to see a description of the change made. Change buttons that appear in the pane containing the slide thumbnails indicate changes made at the presentation level. Change buttons that appear next to objects on the slide are changes that affect that object on that slide. You can view each change and decide whether to accept it or reject it.

Reference

Comparing Presentations

- On the Review tab, in the Compare group, click the Compare button to open the Choose File to Merge with Current Presentation dialog box.
- Navigate to the location containing the presentation with which you want to compare, click it, and then click Merge.
- In the Revisions pane, click each listed revision to open the box next to the corresponding change button; or, click each change button.
- In the box describing a change, click the check box to select it to see the change.
- To keep the change, keep the check box selected; to reject the change, click the check box to deselect it; or, click the Accept or Reject button in the Compare group on the Review tab.
- In the Compare group, click the Next button to display the next change in the presentation.
- After reviewing all the changes in the presentation, in the Compare group, click the End Review button, and then in the dialog box that opens asking if you are sure you want to end the review, click Yes.

Veronica created her presentation and then sent it to Aiden Callahan, the facilities manager, and asked him to review it. Aiden made a couple of changes and sent it back to Veronica. Veronica asks you to compare her original presentation with the reviewed presentation.

To compare the original presentation with the reviewed presentation:

▶ 1. **sam** ⬇ Open the presentation **NP_PPT_6-1.pptx**, located in the **PowerPoint6 > Module** folder included with your Data Files, and then save it as **NP_PPT_6_Green** in the location where you are storing your files.

▸ **2.** On the ribbon, click the **Review** tab, and then in the Compare group, click the **Compare** button. The Choose File to Merge with Current Presentation dialog box opens.

▸ **3.** Navigate to the **PowerPoint6 > Module** folder if necessary, click **Support_PPT_6_Aiden.pptx**, and then click **Merge**. The Revisions pane opens with the DETAILS tab selected. Slide 4 ("Recycling Program") is displayed. See Figure 6–1.

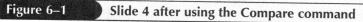

Figure 6–1   **Slide 4 after using the Compare command**

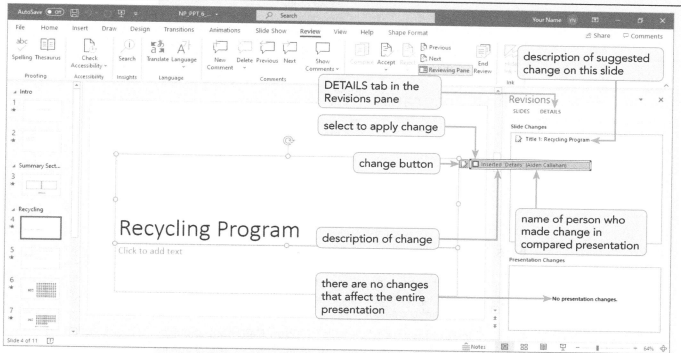

Changes that affect only the current slide are listed in the Slide Changes box at the top of the Revisions pane. Changes that affect the entire presentation would be listed in the Presentation Changes box at the bottom of the Revisions pane. The change button to the right of the title text box is selected and a description of the change is displayed. In this case, the description indicates that Aiden Callahan added the word "Details" to the text box.

▸ **4.** At the top of the Revisions pane, click **SLIDES**. The SLIDES tab appears. There is one change listed on this slide. See Figure 6–2.

Figure 6–2 **SLIDES tab in the Revisions pane listing a change on Slide 4**

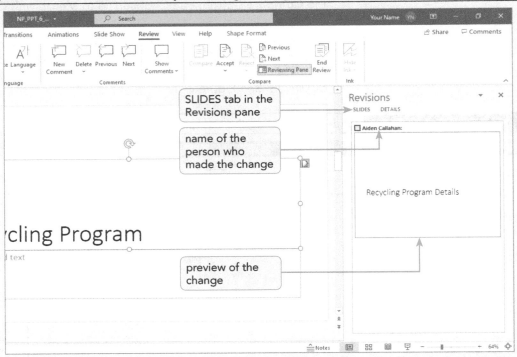

5. On the slide, click the **change** button to display details about the change, and then click the **Inserted "Details" (Aiden Callahan)** check box to select it. The change is applied to the title text box, and the title changes from "Recycling Program" to "Recycling Program Details." Veronica doesn't want you to make this change.

6. Click the **Inserted "Details" (Aiden Callahan)** check box to deselect it. The change is removed from the slide. The change is still listed in the Revisions pane because it is something that is different between the two presentations.

7. On the Review tab, in the Compare group, click the **Next** button. Slide 5 ("Reduce Amount of Trash Collected at Parks") appears with a change button and a description of the changes next to the content placeholder. The description says that "40" was inserted and "60" was deleted. On the slide, the last bulleted item ends with "60%." This is the original text. In the Revisions pane, on the SLIDES tab, the last bulleted item ends with "40%." This is Aiden's suggested change. He is correct—the expected percentage reduction of non-recyclable trash is 40%, not 60%. Veronica tells you to accept this change.

Trouble? If the Comments pane and a dialog box open, you clicked the Next button in the Comments group instead of in the Compare group. Click Cancel in the dialog box, close the Comments pane, and then repeat Step 7.

Trouble? If the description of the changes does not appear next to the change button on the slide, click the change button.

8. On the slide, click the **All changes to Content Placeholder 2** check box to select it. Check marks appear in all three check boxes, on the change button, and in the Aiden Callahan check box in the Revisions pane. On the slide, the last bulleted item now ends with "40%."

▶ **9.** On the Review tab, in the Compare group, click the **Next** button. A dialog box opens, telling you that was the last change in the presentation and asking if you want to continue reviewing from the beginning. Because Slide 1 was displayed when you clicked the Compare command, you don't need to continue from the beginning.

▶ **10.** Click **Cancel**. You are finished reviewing the merged changes. You need to end the review in order to accept the changes you selected, reject the changes you did not select, and remove the change buttons.

▶ **11.** In the Compare group, click the **End Review** button. A dialog box opens, asking if you are sure you want to end the review and warning that any unapplied changes will be discarded.

▶ **12.** Click **Yes**. The dialog box and the Revisions pane close, and the change button on Slide 5 disappears. On Slide 5, the last bulleted item now ends with "40%." This is the change you accepted.

▶ **13.** Display Slide 4 ("Recycling Program"). The word "Details" is not included in the slide title. That was the change you rejected.

The changes made to the presentation were recorded with Aiden's Microsoft username that he is signed into Office with. (The username is shown in the upper-right corner of the PowerPoint window.) If you are not signed into a Microsoft account when you use Office, when you save a file, the name in the User name box on the General tab in the PowerPoint Options dialog box is applied. You can change the username in the PowerPoint Options dialog box by clicking the File tab and then clicking Options in the navigation bar of Backstage view.

Working with Comments

When a colleague reviews a presentation, they can add comments to ask a question or make a suggestion. You can also add comments to direct others' attention to something on a slide or reply to a comment that someone else has placed on a slide.

If you are signed in to Office with a Microsoft account, when you insert a comment in a presentation, the comment is labeled with your Microsoft account username (in the upper-right corner of the PowerPoint window). If you are not signed in to Office with a Microsoft account, comments are labeled with the name in the User name box on the General tab in the PowerPoint Options dialog box. Signing in with your own name makes it obvious to the reviewer who made what changes. This is helpful when comparing revisions from multiple reviewers at once.

You will insert a comment labeled with your username.

To insert a comment on Slide 5:

▶ **1.** Display Slide 5 ("Reduce Amount of Trash Collected at Parks"), and then on the Review tab, in the Comments group, click the **New Comment** button. The Comments pane appears with a box labeled with your username, and on the Review tab, in the Comments group, the Show Comments button is selected. A comment balloon appears in the top-left corner of the slide. See Figure 6–3.

Figure 6–3 New comment added to Slide 5

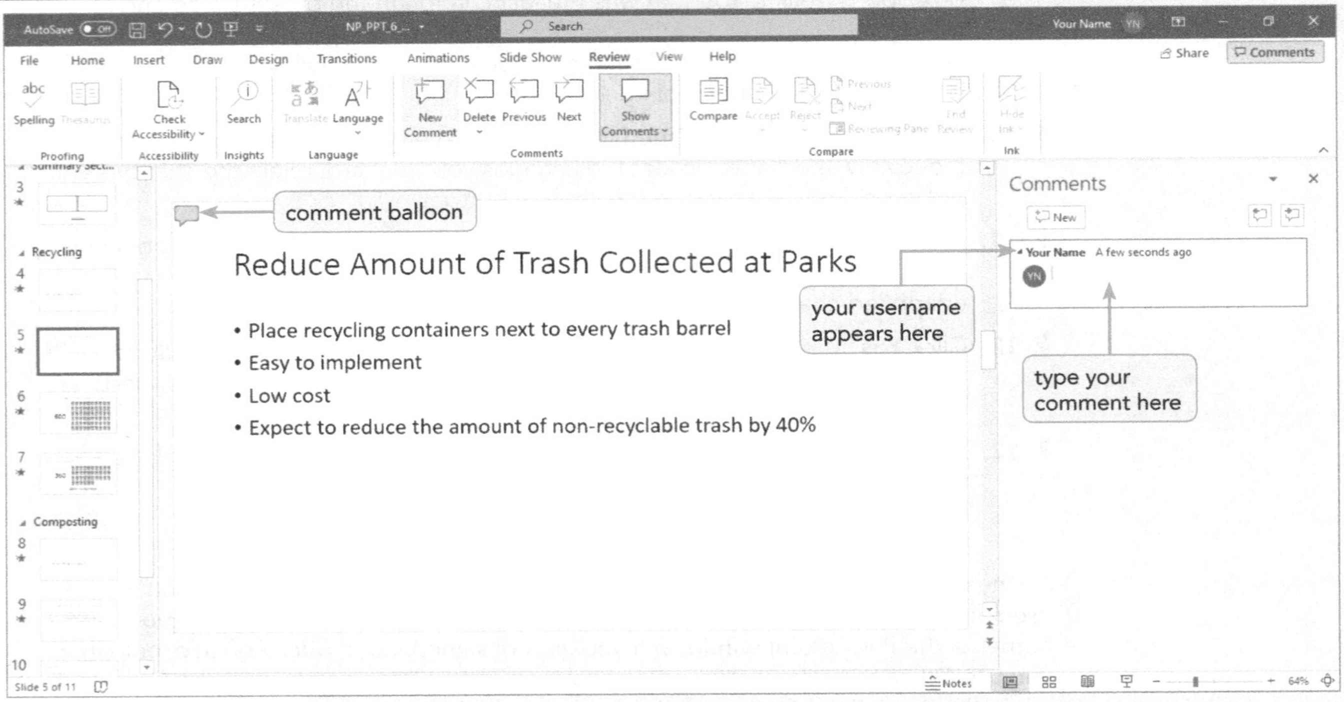

Tip

You can also click a comment balloon to open the Comments pane.

2. In the box in the Comments pane, type **In the third bullet, maybe add details about the cost per container.** (including the period).
3. On Slide 5, drag the comment balloon down to position it to the left of the "Low cost" item in the bulleted list.

If you need to change the username, click the File tab, click Options, and then in the User name box in the PowerPoint Options dialog box, type your name. To use this username instead of the username associated with your Microsoft Office account, click the "Always use these values regardless of sign in to Office." check box.

Veronica added a comment on Slide 2 ("The Challenge"). Instead of making the change the comment suggests, you will reply to her comment.

To reply to a comment:

Tip

To hide comments, click the Show Comments arrow in the Comments group on the Review tab, and then click Show Markup to deselect it.

1. On the Review tab, in the Comments group, click the **Next** button. A dialog box opens asking if you want to continue from the beginning of the presentation.
2. Click **Continue**. Slide 2 ("The Challenge") appears, and the comment that Veronica inserted appears in the Comments pane. A Reply box appears below the comment in the Comments pane.
3. Click in the **Reply** box, and then type **I agree.** (including the period).
4. Press **ENTER**. The reply is labeled with your username. On the slide, a second comment balloon appears on top of the first balloon. See Figure 6–4.

Figure 6–4   Reply to the comment on Slide 2

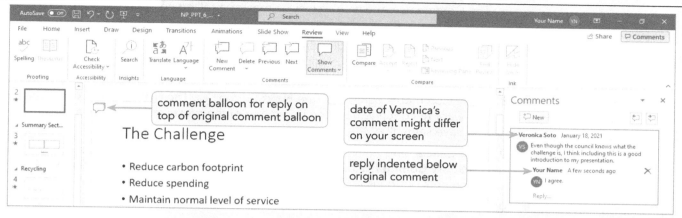

You need to check if there are any additional comments in the presentation. You can decide what to do based upon a comment, and then you can delete the comment when you are finished, if appropriate.

To review and delete a comment:

▶ 1. In the Comments pane, click the **Next** button. Veronica's comment on Slide 2 is selected.

▶ 2. In the Comments pane, click the **Next** button to select your reply, and then click the **Next** button again. Slide 3 (the summary zoom slide titled "Overview") appears, and another comment from Veronica appears in the Comments pane.

▶ 3. Read the comment in the Comments pane. Veronica added a title to the slide to keep the content accessible, but she thinks it shouldn't appear during a slide show. To hide the title, she asks if the slide title text should be the same color as the slide background.

▶ 4. On the slide, change the text color of **Overview** to **White, Background 1**, and then click the **Review** tab if necessary. Now that you've made the change, you can delete Veronica's comment.

▶ 5. In the Comments pane, move the pointer on top of Veronica Soto's comment. A border appears around the comment, and a Delete button appears. See Figure 6–5.

Figure 6–5   Delete button on the comment on Slide 3

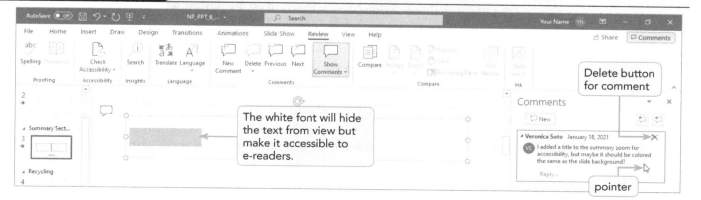

▶ **6.** In the Comments pane, click the **Delete** button ☒. The comment is deleted. The Comments pane now displays a message telling you that there are comments on other slides in this presentation.

▶ **7.** In the Comments pane, click the **Next** button ⮐. Slide 5 ("Reduce Amount of Trash Collected at Parks") appears. This is the slide to which you added a comment earlier.

▶ **8.** In the Comments pane, click the **Next** button ⮐. The dialog box asking if you want to continue from the beginning of the presentation appears again. You have seen all of the comments in the presentation.

▶ **9.** Click **Cancel**, and then on the Review tab, in the Comments group, click the **Show Comments** button. The Comments pane closes, and the Show Comments button is no longer selected.

▶ **10.** Save the changes to the presentation.

Proskills

Teamwork: Preparing Presentations for an International Audience

If you work for a company that conducts business internationally, you should evaluate your presentations to make sure they contain information that is appropriate for and clear to an international audience. For example, when a date is written using numbers in the United States, the first number is the month and the second number is the day of the month. In most of the rest of the world, the order is reversed—the first number is the day of the month and the second number is the month. For example, August 12, 2021 would be written as 8/12/2021 in the United States, and as 12/8/2021 in most of the rest of the world. Someone who lives in a country that uses the day first format could incorrectly interpret the United States format of 8/12/2021 as December 8, 2021. To avoid confusion, you should use a date format that includes the month name, such as August 12, 2021 if the presentation is intended for mostly audiences in the United States or 12 August 2021 if the presentation is intended for international audiences.

If you need to translate words in your presentation, you can use the Translate button in the Language group on the Review tab. Keep in mind that translations generated by PowerPoint are not always perfect. After you translate all or part of a presentation, you should have an expert in the language review the translation and make any necessary corrections.

If your presentation includes foreign words, the spell checker will flag those words as spelled incorrectly. This is because the proofing language for the presentation is set to English. To change the proofing language for a word, select the word, click the Language button in the Language group on the Review tab, click Set Proofing Language, and then click the language of the selected word.

Working in Slide Master View

Slide masters ensure that all the slides in the presentation have a similar appearance and contain the same elements. The layouts associated with slide masters pick up the formatting from the slide master. Then you can modify each layout as needed. Refer to the Session 6.1 Visual Overview for more information about slide masters.

You can modify a slide master and layouts in many ways. For example, you can change the size and style of text in the placeholders, add or delete graphics, change the slide background, and change the style of lists.

Changes you make to the slide master affect all of the slides in the presentation. For example, if you modify the font, font size, or font style of the title text or content placeholder on the slide master, or if you add an image or an animation to the slide master, it will appear on all the slides in the presentation. Changes you make to a layout in Slide Master view appear only on slides with that layout applied.

Modifying the Slide Master

Veronica wants you to make several changes to the appearance of the slides in the presentation. Because she wants the changes to be applied to all of the slides in the presentation, you will modify the slide master. First, you will switch to Slide Master view and examine the slide master and its layouts. All presentations contain at least one slide master and one layout. Most themes include multiple layouts.

To switch to Slide Master view:

Tip

You can also modify Handout and Notes masters. Click the appropriate button in the Master Views group on the View tab.

1. On the ribbon, click the **View** tab, and then in the Master Views group, click the **Slide Master** button. The view changes to Slide Master view. A new tab, the Slide Master tab, appears on the ribbon to the left of the Home tab. In place of the slide thumbnails in the pane on the left, the master layout thumbnails appear.

2. In the pane on the left, move the pointer on top of the selected layout thumbnail. The ScreenTip identifies this layout as the Title and Content Layout and indicates that it is used by Slides 2-3, 5, and 9-11. In addition to placeholders for the title and content, there are placeholders for the slide number, date, and footer.

3. Scroll to the top of the pane on the left, and then move the pointer on top of the top thumbnail, which is larger than the other thumbnails. This is the slide master, and it is named for the theme applied to the presentation—in this case, it is the Office Theme Slide Master because the theme applied to the presentation is the Office theme. The ScreenTip also indicates that it is used by slides 1-11, which are all the slides in the presentation.

4. Click the **Office Theme Slide Master** thumbnail. The slide contains the same elements as the Title and Content layout.

To begin creating the custom theme for Veronica, you will change the background color. She wants you to use a light shade of blue because the recycling bins she will put in the parks will be blue.

To change the fill color of the background of the slide master:

1. On the Slide Master tab, in the Background group, click the **Background Styles** button. The gallery of background styles opens. This is the same gallery that appears when you click this button on the Design tab in Normal view.

2. At the bottom of the gallery, click **Format Background**. The Format Background pane opens. The Solid fill option button is selected.

▶ 3. Click the **Color** button, and then click the **Blue, Accent 1, Lighter 80%** color. The blue color fills the background of the slide master and the background of all of the layouts as well. You didn't need to click Apply to All at the bottom of the Format Background pane because changes you make to the slide master appear on all of the layouts.

▶ 4. Close the Format Background pane.

Veronica wants a picture of a tree to appear along the left edge of the slides in the presentation. First, you need to adjust the placeholders on the slide master to make room for the picture.

To modify the size and position of the placeholders on the slide master:

▶ 1. On the slide master, change the width of the title text placeholder to **10"**, and then drag the title placeholder so its right edge aligns with the right edge of the content and slide number placeholders.

▶ 2. Change the width of the content placeholder to **10"**, and then drag it so its right edge aligns with the right edge of the title and slide number placeholders.

▶ 3. Change the width of the date placeholder to **1.5"**, and then drag it to the right so its left edge aligns with the left edge of the title and content placeholders.

▶ 4. Click the **Title and Content Layout** thumbnail. The changes you made to the slide master appear on this layout.

▶ 5. Click the **Title Slide Layout** thumbnail. The changes you made to the date placeholder appear on this layout, but the title and subtitle text placeholders did not change.

Now you will add Veronica's picture of a tree to the left side of the slide master. Then you will modify it by applying a soft edge effect so the edge blends into the background.

To add and format a picture to the slide master:

Tip

You can apply more than one theme to a presentation. To apply a theme to only one slide or to selected slides, right-click the theme in the Themes group on the Design tab, and then click Apply to Selected Slides.

▶ 1. Display the Office Theme Slide Master.

▶ 2. On the ribbon, click the **Insert** tab, in the Images group, click the **Pictures** button, and then click **This Device**.

▶ 3. Navigate to the **PowerPoint6 > Module** folder, click the **Support_PPT_6_Tree.jpg** file, and then click **Insert**. The picture is inserted on the slide master. In the pane containing the thumbnails, you can see that the picture also appears on all of the layout thumbnails.

▶ 4. On the Picture Format tab, in the Arrange group, click the **Align Objects** button, and then click **Align Left**. The picture is now aligned with the top, bottom, and left edges of the slide master. Veronica wants the right edge softened so it looks like it fades into the slide.

▶ **5.** On the Picture Format tab, in the Picture Styles group, click the **Picture Effects** button, point to **Soft Edges**, and then in the Soft Edge Variations section, click the **25 Point** style. A 25-point soft edge effect is applied to the picture. But now you can see blue around the top, left, and bottom edges of the picture.

▶ **6.** Change the height of the picture to **8.3"**. The height and width of the picture increased so that you can no longer see blue below the picture. You need to move the picture to the left and up off the slide a little so that you cannot see any blue on those edges. To do this, you will adjust the picture position to exactly match the figures in this text.

▶ **7.** Right-click the picture, and then on the shortcut menu, click **Format Picture**. The Format Picture pane opens.

▶ **8.** In the Format Picture pane, click the **Size & Properties** button , and then click **Position** to expand that section. The current horizontal and vertical position of the picture is zero inches from the top left corner. This means that the top of the selected object is aligned with the top of the slide and the left edge of the selected object is aligned with the left edge of the slide. See Figure 6–6.

Figure 6–6 ▶ **Position section in the Format Picture pane for the selected picture**

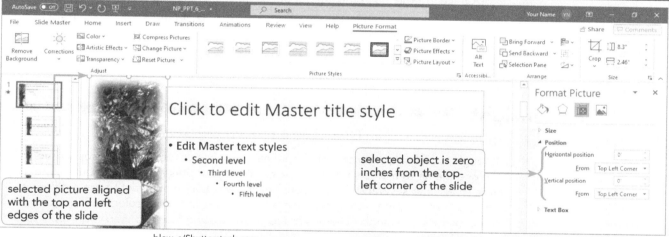

blew_s/Shutterstock.com

▶ **9.** Click the **Horizontal position** down arrow five times. The value in the Horizontal position box changes to -0.5" and the picture shifts one-half inch to the left of the edge of the slide. The value is negative because the left part of the object is off the slide by one-half inch.

▶ **10.** Click the **Vertical position** down arrow four times. The value in the Vertical position box changes to -0.4" and the picture shifts down. Now the edges of the picture hang off the edges of the slide and the blue background is no longer visible above, to the left, and below the picture.

When you make changes to the slide master, you should check the layouts you want to use to make sure the changes you made were applied.

▶ **11.** Click the **Title and Content Layout** thumbnail, and then click the picture of the tree on the slide. The picture is not selected. This is because the picture was not placed on this layout. You placed it on the slide master.

▶ **12.** In the pane containing the thumbnails, click the **Two Content Layout** thumbnail (the fourth small thumbnail). The picture appears on this layout, and the title text and date placeholders match the size and position of those placeholders on the slide master. The sizes of the two content placeholders need to be adjusted so they align with the title text and date placeholders. Veronica will modify this layout later if she needs to use it.

▶ **13.** Click the **Title Only Layout** thumbnail (the sixth small thumbnail). This layout looks fine.

▶ **14.** Close the Format Background pane.

Now that you have made changes to the slide master, you should rename it because it is no longer the Office Theme slide master.

To rename the slide master:

▶ **1.** In the pane containing the thumbnails, click the slide master.

▶ **2.** Click the Slide Master tab, and then in the Edit Master group, click the **Rename** button. The Rename Layout dialog box opens. The current name "Office Theme" is in the Layout name box.

▶ **3.** Replace the text in the Layout name box with **Rockland Parks**, click **Rename**, and then move the pointer on top of the slide master. The ScreenTip now shows the name Rockland Parks Slide Master.

Insight

Applying More Than One Theme to a Presentation

Although in general presentations should have a cohesive look, you can apply more than one theme to a presentation. For example, if your presentation is about different music styles, and several slides are about each style, you might want to use a different theme for each section. To apply a theme to only one slide or to selected slides, right-click the theme in the Themes group on the Design tab, and then click Apply to Selected Slides.

When multiple themes are applied to a presentation, each theme has a slide master and its associated layouts. You can see the additional themes in the pane containing the thumbnails in Slide Master view. The layouts for additional themes appear on the New Slide and Layout menus in Normal view.

Sometimes, if more than one slide master is applied to a presentation and no slides in the presentation use a layout connected to that slide master, the slide master is automatically deleted. To prevent that from happening, click the Preserve button in the Edit Master group on the Slide Master tab to select it.

Modifying the Style of Lists

Good presentation design dictates that list styles should be consistent across all slides in a presentation. You can modify the style of lists in many ways. For example, you can change the bullet symbol, size, and color or change the font used for numbers in a numbered list. If you modify the style of lists in a presentation, you should make these formatting changes to the slide master, ensuring that the changes appear on all layouts.

Reference

Modifying the Bullet Symbol

- To modify the bullet symbol for all the list levels, select the content text box. To modify the bullet symbol for only one list level, click in the placeholder text for that level.
- On the Home tab, in the Paragraph group, click the Bullets button arrow, and then click Bullets and Numbering to open the Bulleted tab in the Bullets and Numbering dialog box.
- To change the bullet symbol, click Customize to open the Symbol dialog box, click the new symbol, and then click OK; or, click Picture to open the Insert Pictures window, click the location of the picture you want to use as a bullet symbol, click the file, and then click OK.
- To change the size of the bullet symbol relative to the size of the text, adjust the percentage in the Size box.
- To change the color of the bullet symbol, click the Color button, and then click a color.
- Click OK.

Veronica would like you to change the color of the bullet symbols used in her presentation to a darker shade of the blue color used for the background of the slides. She also wants you to increase the size of the bullet symbols. You'll make this change on the slide master.

To modify the bullet character on the slide master:

Tip

To modify the bullet character of one level of bulleted items, place the insertion point in that level, and then click the Bullets arrow.

1. Display the Rockland Parks Slide Master if necessary, and then on the slide, click the border of the content placeholder. Now the change you make to the bullet symbol will affect all bullet levels.

2. Click the **Home** tab, and then in the Paragraph group, click the **Bullets arrow**. The Bullets gallery opens. See Figure 6–7. You can select one of the styles in the gallery or open a dialog box where you can customize your bullets.

| Figure 6–7 | Bullets gallery |

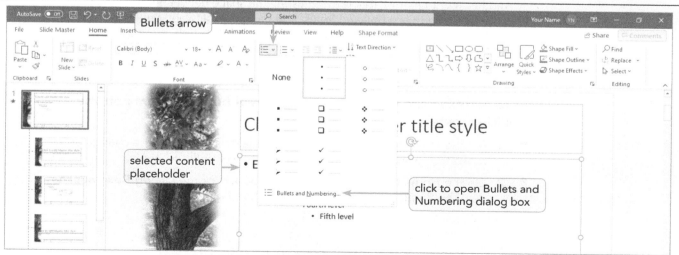

blew_s/Shutterstock.com

▶ 3. Click **Bullets and Numbering**. The Bullets and Numbering dialog box opens with the Bulleted tab selected. See Figure 6–8.

Figure 6–8   **Bulleted tab in the Bullets and Numbering dialog box**

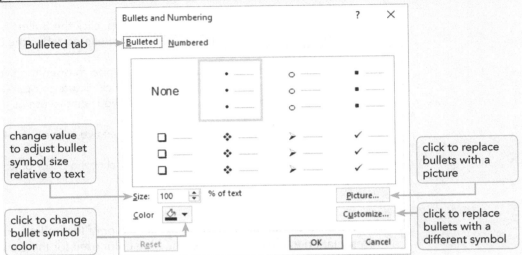

▶ 4. Click the **Color** button, and then click the **Blue, Accent 1, Darker 25%** color.

▶ 5. Select the value in the Size box, type **110**, and then click **OK**. The bullet symbols in the content placeholder change to the blue color you selected and are 10% bigger than they were.

You can customize the style of numbers in numbered lists in the same manner. To do that, you click the Numbering arrow in the Paragraph group on the Home tab. Then click one of the styles in the gallery, or click Bullets and Numbering to open the Bullets and Numbering dialog box with the Number tab selected. You can change the color and size of the numbers, and you can change the starting number if you want the list to start with a number other than 1.

Another way to modify lists is by adjusting the space between lines in a bulleted item, the space between bulleted items, and the space between bullets and the first character in a bulleted item. Veronica wants you to add a little more space before first-level bulleted items.

To increase the space above first-level bulleted items on the slide master:

▶ 1. On the slide master, click in the first bulleted item. Now the change you make to the spacing will affect only first-level bulleted items.

▶ 2. On the Home tab, in the Paragraph group, click the **Dialog Box Launcher** 🔲. The Paragraph dialog box opens. See Figure 6–9.

Figure 6–9   Paragraph dialog box

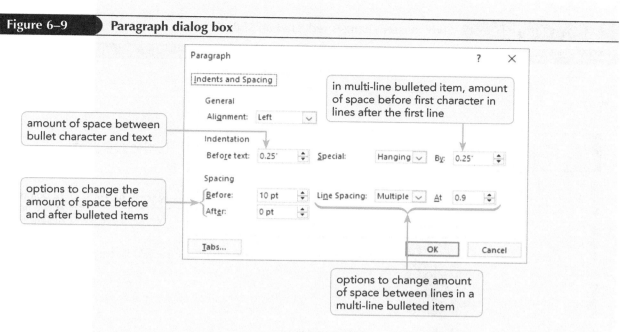

amount of space between bullet character and text

in multi-line bulleted item, amount of space before first character in lines after the first line

options to change the amount of space before and after bulleted items

options to change amount of space between lines in a multi-line bulleted item

3. In the Spacing section, click the **Before** up arrow. The value in the Before box changes to 12 pt, which means now there will be 12 points of space above each first-level bulleted item instead of 10 points. If you change the Line Spacing value, you would change the space between each line in a first-level bulleted item that contained more than one line.

4. Click **OK** to close the dialog box. On the slide master, the change is not apparent. You will see the change in Normal view.

Now you will examine the slides in Normal view to see the effect of the changes you made to the slide master.

To examine the changes made to the slide master in Normal view:

1. On the ribbon, click the **Slide Master** tab, and then in the Close group, click the **Close Master View** button, and then click the Slide 5 thumbnail if necessary. The Presentation appears in Normal view with Slide 5 ("Reduce Amount of Trash Collected at Parks") displayed. The slide background is light blue; the title text and content text boxes are not as wide as they were; the picture of the tree appears on the left side of the slide; the bullets are dark blue and a little larger than they were; and the space between the bulleted items increased by two points. These changes correspond to the changes you made to the slide master. See Figure 6–10.

Figure 6–10 Slide master changes reflected on Slide 5

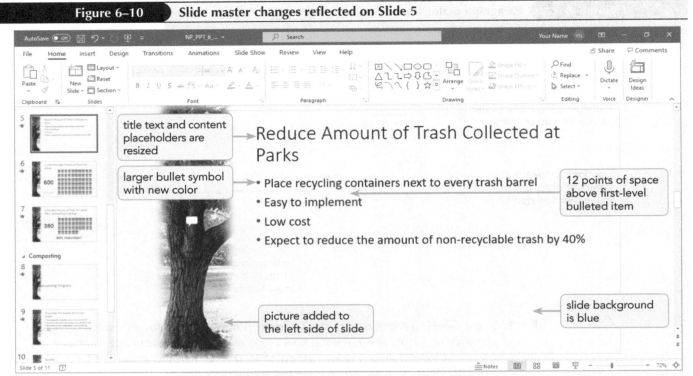

blew_s/Shutterstock.com

▶ **2.** Click the picture of the tree on the slide. Nothing happens. You cannot select or modify the picture because it is on the slide master.

▶ **3.** Click the title, and then change the width of the title text box to **5"**. This time, the change happens. For placeholders, the format of the placeholders is specified on the slide and layout masters, but you can override this with direct formatting on the slide.

▶ **4.** On the Quick Access Toolbar, click the **Undo** button ↶. The Comment balloon that you had positioned next to the "Low cost" bulleted item needs to be moved because the bulleted items moved.

▶ **5.** Drag the Comment balloon to the right and position it next to the "Low cost" bulleted item, and then close the Comments pane.

▶ **6.** Display Slide 3 (the summary zoom titled "Overview"). Because of the changes to the slide master, you need to modify the placement of the section zooms.

▶ **7.** Click one of the section zooms, and then drag the grouped object to the right so that the right edge of the grouped object aligns with the right edge of the slide. Visually, there is approximately the same amount of space between the section zoom on the right and the right edge of the slide as there is between the section zoom on the left and the picture of the tree. (The image of the slides on the section zooms contains text that runs into the tree. You will fix this in the next set of steps.)

▶ **8.** Click **Questions**, and then drag that text box to the right until a vertical smart guide indicates that the text box is centered below the space between the two section zooms.

Insight

Using the Font Dialog Box

Additional options for formatting text that are not included in the Font group on the Home tab are in the Font dialog box. To open this dialog box, click the Dialog Box Launcher in the Font group on the Home tab. The Font tab in the dialog box lets you change the underline style and color. You can also format text in the following ways:

- with a double strikethrough
- as superscript and subscript
- as all caps
- as small caps (where all the letters in a word are uppercase but when a letter is typed as a capital letter, that letter is somewhat larger than the rest of the letters)
- with equal character heights so that all the characters are the same height, even if they are a combination of upper and lowercase letters

On the Character Spacing tab, you can change the spacing between pairs of characters (called kerning). The default is for characters to be spaced normally, but when there is too much or too little space between characters with the normal spacing applied, the spacing will be adjusted to fix this problem, as long as the text is at least as large as the point size specified.

Creating Slide Layouts

If the theme you are using does not contain a layout that suits your needs, you can create a new layout. You do this in Slide Master view. After you create a new layout, it will be listed on the New Slide and Layout menus in the Slides group on the Home tab.

In Veronica's presentation, Slide 4 is the first slide in the Recycling section and Slide 8 is the first slide in the Composting section. Veronica applied the Section Header layout to these slides, but she wants to add a photo to each one. She wants you to create a custom section header layout. The custom layout will have a placeholder on the left side of the slide that can be used to add a picture to the slide.

To create a custom layout:

1. Switch to Slide Master view, and then in the Slides pane, click the **Section Header Layout** thumbnail (the third small thumbnail).

2. On the Slide Master tab, in the Edit Master group, click the **Insert Layout** button. A new layout is inserted below the Section Header Layout. The new layout contains the picture of the tree that is on the slide master. The new layout also includes placeholders for the slide title and the slide number, date, and footer. See Figure 6–11.

Figure 6–11 New layout added in Slide Master view

blew_s/Shutterstock.com

3. Change the width of the title text placeholder to **6.1"**, and then position it so its middle is vertically aligned with the middle of the slide and its right edge is approximately one-quarter of an inch from the right edge of the slide.

4. Click the Slide Master tab if necessary, and then in the Master Layout group, click the **Insert Placeholder arrow**. A gallery of placeholders opens. See Figure 6–12.

Figure 6–12 Placeholder gallery

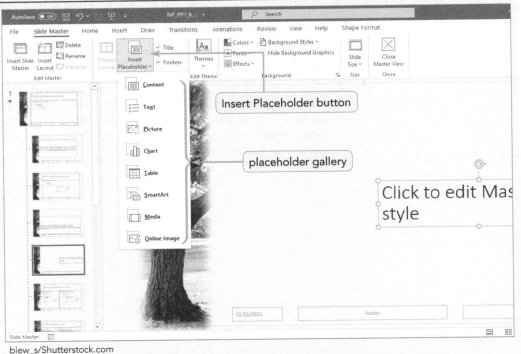

blew_s/Shutterstock.com

5. Click **Picture**. The pointer changes to the thin cross pointer ╋.

6. On the slide, click and drag to create a placeholder, and then resize it so that it is **7.5"** high and **6.5"** wide. The picture placeholder contains only one button—the Pictures button ▢.

7. On the Shape Format tab, in the Arrange group, click the **Align** button, and then click **Align Top**. The top and bottom edges of the placeholder align with the top and bottom of the slide.

8. In the Arrange group, click the **Align** button, and then click **Align Left**. The left edge of the placeholder aligns with the left edge of the slide. (Remember that the picture of the tree overlaps the top, left, and bottom edges of the slide.)

If you insert a picture that fills the placeholder, the tree will be covered. However, if you insert a picture with a transparent background, such as a logo, the tree will be visible. To fix this, you will hide the background graphics on this layout master.

9. Click the **Slide Master** tab, and then in the Background group, click the **Hide Background Graphics** check box. The check box is selected, and the picture of the tree is removed from this layout master. The blue fill in the background is not removed.

10. Reposition the title text placeholder so that there is the same amount of space between the left edge of the title text placeholder and the center of the slide as there is between the right edge of the picture placeholder and the center of the slide. See Figure 6–13.

Figure 6–13   Completed custom layout

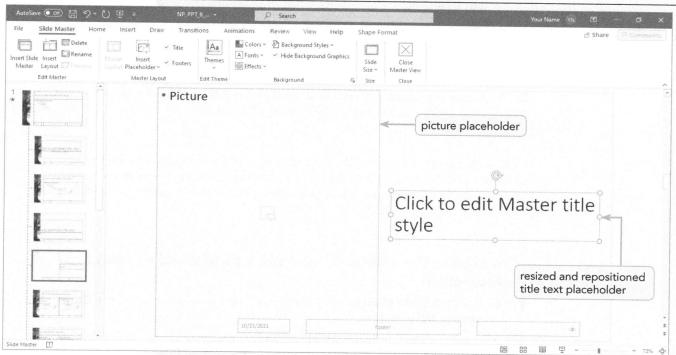

blew_s/Shutterstock.com

Now you need to rename the layout.

▶ **11.** Move the pointer on top of the new layout thumbnail that you created. The ScreenTip shows the name "Custom Layout Layout."

▶ **12.** On the Slide Master tab, in the Edit Master group, click the **Rename** button. The Rename Layout dialog box opens. The current name "Custom Layout" is in the Layout name box.

▶ **13.** Replace the text in the Layout name box with **Picture Section Header**, click **Rename**, and then move the pointer on top of the new layout. The ScreenTip now shows the name Picture Section Header Layout.

As you know, you can also insert a picture using a content placeholder. When you insert a picture using a *picture* placeholder, the picture fills the placeholder even if some of the picture needs to be cropped in order to make this happen. When you insert a picture using a *content* placeholder, the placeholder resizes to exactly fit the picture. To see the difference, you will create another custom section header layout, this time with a content placeholder. To do this, you will duplicate the Picture Section Header layout to create the new layout.

To duplicate and modify a layout:

▶ **1.** Right-click the **Picture Section Header Layout** thumbnail, and then on the shortcut menu, click **Duplicate Layout**.

▶ **2.** Rename the new layout as **Content Section Header**.

▶ **3.** Click the border of the picture placeholder to select it, and then press **DELETE**.

▶ **4.** On the Slide Master tab, in the Master Layout group, click the **Insert Placeholder arrow**, click **Content**, and then drag to draw a placeholder on the slide. The content placeholder looks like the content placeholder you have seen on the Title and Content layout in Normal view.

▶ **5.** Resize the content placeholder so that it is **7.5"** high and **6.5"** wide, and then align with the top and left sides of the slide.

Now that you have created the custom layout, you will decide which layout you want to use—the one with the picture placeholder or the one with the content placeholder. To make this decision, you will see how a picture looks using each layout in Normal view.

To explore the difference between a picture and a content placeholder:

▶ **1.** Click the **Slide Master** tab, and then in the Close group, click the **Close Master View** button.

▶ **2.** Display Slide 8 ("Composting Program"), and then on the Home tab, in the Slides group, click the **Layout** button. The Section Header layout is selected, indicating that it is applied to the slide. The two new layouts you created appear on the next line in the gallery.

3. In the gallery, click the **Picture Section Header** layout, then close any open task panes, if necessary. The layout is applied to Slide 8.

4. Duplicate Slide 8, and then apply the Content Section Header layout to the new Slide 9.

5. On Slide 9, click the **Pictures** button in the content placeholder, and then insert the picture **Support_PPT_6_Receptacle.jpg**, located in the PowerPoint6 > Module folder. The entire picture is visible and is as high as the content placeholder. The width of the content placeholder was reduced to five inches to just fit the picture. The picture *fits* inside the placeholder.

Tip

If you want to override the aspect ratio of a picture, open the Format Picture pane, display the Size & Properties tools, expand the Size section, and then deselect the Lock aspect ratio check box.

6. Display Slide 8, click the **Pictures** button in the picture placeholder, and then insert the picture **Support_PPT_6_ Receptacle.jpg**, located in the PowerPoint6 > Module folder. The picture completely fills the inside of the picture placeholder, but because the aspect ratio is locked, the top and bottom of the image are cut off so that the picture can be wide enough to fill the placeholder horizontally. The picture *fills* the placeholder.

7. On the status bar, click the **Zoom Out** button as many times as needed to change the zoom percentage to 50%.

8. With the picture on Slide 8 selected, click the **Picture Format** tab, and then in the Size group, click the **Crop** button. Crop marks appear around the picture, and you can see the top and bottom parts of the picture that were cropped off. See Figure 6–14.

| Figure 6–14 | Crop marks around a picture set to fill the placeholder |

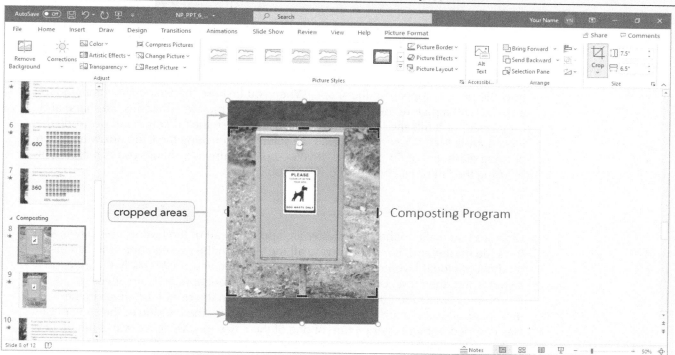

Rob kemp/Shutterstock.com; blew_s/Shutterstock.com

9. In the Size group, click the **Crop arrow**, and then click **Fit**. The entire picture now fits inside the placeholder, similar to the way it appears on Slide 9. However, the placeholder is still the same size.

▶ **10.** In the Size group, click the **Crop arrow**, and then click **Fill**. The picture fills the entire placeholder as it did when you inserted it, and the top and bottom of the image is again cut off. When the picture fills the placeholder, you can adjust the position of the picture in the placeholder.

▶ **11.** Within the crop marks, drag the picture down so that you can see the top of the receptacle, and then click a blank area of the slide.

▶ **12.** On the status bar, click the **Fit slide to current window** button ⟨⊕⟩, display Slide 9, click the picture to select it, and then display crop marks. The crop marks appear around the outer edges of the picture. None of the picture was cropped off to make the picture fit, and the placeholder was resized.

▶ **13.** Click the **Crop arrow**, and then click **Fill**. Nothing happens to the image. This is because the placeholder was resized to fit the picture exactly when you inserted it, so the picture already fills the placeholder.

▶ **14.** Click the **Crop** button to remove the crop marks, and then align the left edge of the picture with the left edge of the slide. Veronica wants you to use the layout with the content placeholder for the two section headers because she wants to be sure the entire picture will be displayed.

▶ **15.** Delete Slide 8, apply the Content Section Header layout to Slide 4 ("Recycling Program"), and then insert the picture **Support_PPT_6_ Recycle.png**, located in the PowerPoint6 > Module folder in the content placeholder on Slide 4. Now you need to delete the Picture Section Header layout.

▶ **16.** Switch to Slide Master view, click the **Picture Section Header Layout** thumbnail, and then in the Edit Master group, click the **Delete** button. The Picture Section Header layout is deleted.

If you fill a shape with a picture, you can use the Fill and Fit commands to adjust how the picture appears in the shape. When you first use the Shape Fill command to fill a shape with a picture, depending on the shape, the picture either fills the shape and is cropped, or it fills the shape but is distorted because the fill command overrode the locked aspect ratio. You can override the settings by clicking the Crop arrow and then clicking either Fill or Fit. Likewise, if you crop a picture to a shape, you can modify it by using the Fill or Fit command on the Crop menu.

Modifying a Slide Layout

Changes you make to the slide master are applied to all of the layouts associated with the slide master and, consequently, to all the slides in the presentation. You can also modify individual layouts in Slide Master view. When you do this, only the individual layout—and, therefore, only slides that have that layout applied—are affected.

Veronica wants the title slide to look different than the rest of the slides in the presentation. The picture of the tree that you placed on the left side of the slide master was cropped from a larger picture of one of the city parks. Veronica wants the picture of the park to appear as the background of the title slide. You will modify the Title Slide layout.

To modify an individual layout:

1. Display the Title Slide layout. You will fill the background of this layout with the picture of a park.

2. In the Background group, click the **Dialog Box Launcher** [⬜] to open the Format Background pane, and then click the **Picture or texture fill** option button. A texture is applied to the background of the Title Slide Layout. Notice that the picture of the tree on the left is on top of the texture. Even though you cannot select the picture of the tree on this slide because it is on the slide master, it is still in a layer on top of the slide background.

3. In the Format Background pane, click the **Hide background graphics** check box to select it. The tree is removed from the layout.

4. In the Format Background pane, click the **Insert** button, click **From a File**, click **Support_PPT_6_Park.jpg** located in the PowerPoint6 > Module folder, and then click **Insert**. The picture of the slide fills the background. Now you need to reposition and format the text placeholders so that they are readable.

5. Close the Format Background pane, and then resize the title text placeholder so it is **1.5"** high and **13.33"** wide.

6. Align the top of the title text placeholder with the top of the slide and align the left edge with the left edge of the slide.

7. Click the **Home** tab, and then change the color of the title text to the **White, Background 1** color and format it as bold. Next you will change the vertical alignment of the text in the title text placeholder.

8. In the Paragraph group, click the **Align Text** button. On the menu, Bottom is selected, and the text in the title text placeholder is vertically aligned at the bottom of the text box.

9. On the menu, click **Top**. The text in the text placeholder is now top-aligned.

10. Resize the subtitle text placeholder so it is **1"** high and **5"** wide, change the font size of the text in the subtitle text placeholder to **20** points, and then format the text as bold.

11. On the Home tab, in the Paragraph group, click the **Align Right** button [≡]. The horizontal alignment of the text changes to it is right-aligned in the text placeholder.

12. Align the right edge of the subtitle text placeholder with the right edge of the slide.

13. Right-click the subtitle text placeholder border, and then click **Format Shape**. The Format Shape pane opens.

    Trouble? If Format Shape is not on the shortcut menu, you didn't right-click directly on the border of the subtitle placeholder. Repeat Step 13, this time making sure that you right-click directly on the border of the subtitle placeholder.

14. In the Format Shape pane, click the **Shape Options** tab if necessary, click the **Size & Properties** button [▦], click **Position** if necessary to expand that section, and then change the value in the Vertical position box to **5.12"**. The placeholder text in the subtitle text placeholder is on top of the part of the grass that is very light. See Figure 6–15.

Figure 6–15   **Final Title Slide layout**

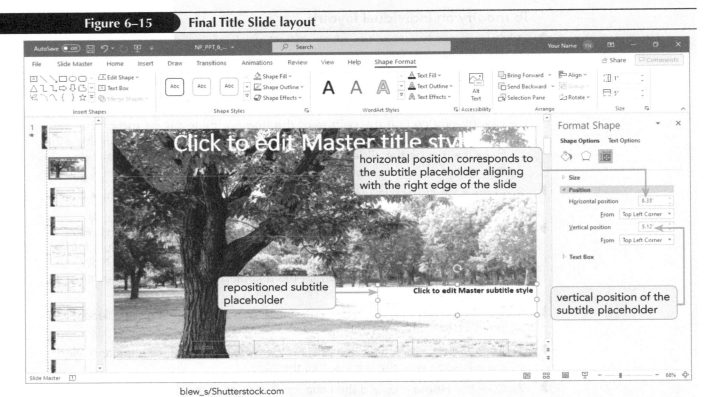

blew_s/Shutterstock.com

▶ **15.** Close the Format Shape pane, and then save the changes to the presentation.

Changing Theme Fonts and Colors

Recall that theme fonts are two coordinating fonts or font styles, one for the titles (or headings) and one for text in content placeholders and other text elements on a slide. You know that you can change the theme fonts and theme colors in Normal view. You can also change them in Slide Master view. If you don't like any of the built-in theme font sets, you can create a set of custom theme fonts. Likewise, you can create a custom theme palette.

To change the theme fonts:

▶ **1.** Click the **Slide Master** tab, and then in the Background group, click the **Fonts** button. The gallery of theme fonts opens.

Tip

To change the theme effects, click the Effects button in the Background group on the Slide Master tab.

▶ **2.** Scroll to the bottom of the list, and then click **Garamond-TrebuchetMs**. The font of the slide titles changes to Garamond, and the font of the lists changes to TrebuchetMs. Veronica likes the Garamond font for Headings, but she wants you to change the Body font to Franklin Gothic Book.

▶ **3.** In the Background group, click the **Fonts** button and then click **Customize Fonts**. The Create New Theme Fonts dialog box opens. See Figure 6–16.

Figure 6–16   Create New Theme Fonts dialog box

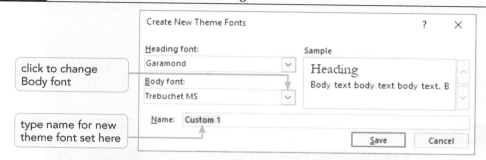

4. Click the **Body font** arrow, scroll up the alphabetical list, and then click **Franklin Gothic Book**.

5. Click in the **Name** box, delete the text in the box, type **Parks Dept Fonts**, and then click **Save**.

6. In the Background group, click the **Fonts** button. The new custom font set appears above the list of built-in font sets. See Figure 6–17.

Figure 6–17   Custom theme font set in the Fonts gallery

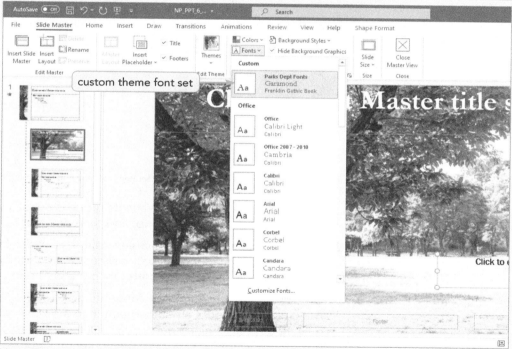

blew_s/Shutterstock.com

7. In the Close group, click the **Close Master View** button, and then in Normal view, click the **Design** tab.

8. In the Variants group, click the **More** button ⏷, and then point to **Fonts**. The custom font set you created appears at the top of this Fonts gallery as well.

Veronica used the default Office theme and color palette when she created her presentation. She asks you to apply a different color palette that has more green colors in it.

To change the theme colors:

▸ **1.** On the menu, point to **Colors**. The gallery of theme colors opens. See Figure 6–18. The Office color palette is selected.

| Figure 6–18 | **Colors menu displaying the gallery of color palettes** |

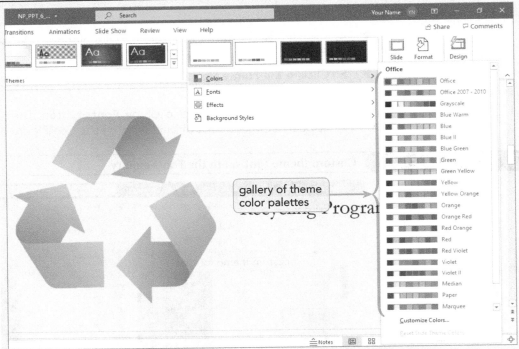

Kostenyukova Nataliya/Shutterstock.com; blew_s/Shutterstock.com; Rob kemp/Shutterstock.com

Trouble? If the menu in the Variants group is not still open, click the More button ▾ in the Variants group, and then do Step 1.

▸ **2.** Click the **Green** palette. The Green palette is applied to the presentation. The background color of all of the slides changed to light green. Veronica likes the green background better than the blue one you applied earlier.

▸ **3.** Display Slide 3 (the Summary Zoom titled "Overview"). The text link at the bottom of this slide is a darker green than the slide background, but is a little difficult to see. Veronica wants you to change the color of unfollowed links, but she wants followed links to be a different color. To accomplish this, you need to create a custom color palette.

▸ **4.** In the Variants group, click the **More** button ▾, point to **Colors**, and then click **Customize Colors**. The Create New Theme Colors dialog box opens listing the 12 colors included in the current color palette. At the bottom of the list, you can see that the Hyperlink color is green, and the Followed Hyperlink color is brown. See Figure 6–19.

Figure 6–19   Create New Theme Colors dialog box

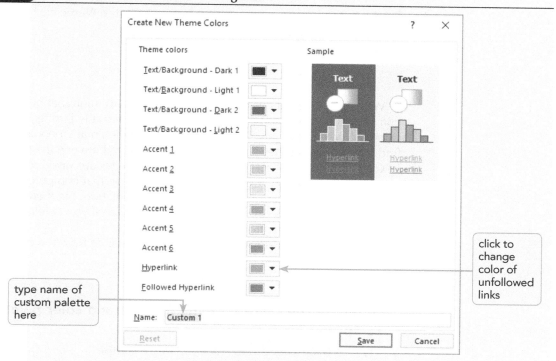

type name of custom palette here

click to change color of unfollowed links

5. Click the **Hyperlink** button. The current color palette appears with the theme color in the second to last column selected. You can select one of the colors in the palette or choose another color.

6. On the menu, click **More Colors**. The Colors dialog box opens with the Custom tab selected.

7. Click the **Standard** tab, and then click the red color as shown in Figure 6–20.

Figure 6–20   Standard tab in the Colors dialog box

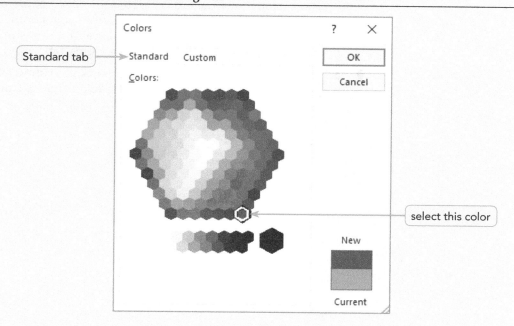

Standard tab

select this color

▶ **8.** Click **OK**. The Hyperlink color in the list is now the red color you selected.

▶ **9.** At the bottom of the dialog box, click in the **Name** box, delete the text, type **Parks Dept Colors**, and then click **Save**.

▶ **10.** Save the changes to the presentation.

When you create a custom color palette, keep in mind that not all colors are complementary, and some combinations can be visually jarring or illegible. Also avoid using red/green or blue/yellow combinations, which many people who are color-blind find hard to read as they have difficulty contrasting between the two colors.

Custom theme font sets and custom color palettes are saved to your computer, and you can apply them to any presentation opened on that computer. After you apply a custom theme font set or color palette to a presentation, the theme fonts or the color palette will still be applied to that presentation even if you delete the custom theme font set or color palette from the computer.

You'll delete the custom theme font set you created from the computer you are using.

To delete the custom theme font set and color palette from the computer:

▶ **1.** In the Variants group, click the **More** button ⊡, and then point to **Fonts**. The custom theme font set you created appears at the top of the menu.

▶ **2.** Right-click **Parks Dept Fonts** on the menu, and then on the shortcut menu, click **Delete**. A dialog box opens, asking if you want to delete these theme fonts.

▶ **3.** Click **Yes**.

▶ **4.** In the Variants group, click the **More** button ⊡, and then point to **Colors**. The custom theme font set you created appears at the top of the menu.

▶ **5.** Right-click **Parks Dept Colors** on the menu, click **Delete**, and then click **Yes**. The custom color palette is deleted from the computer. The custom font set and color palette were deleted only from your computer. They are both still part of the current presentation's theme. You can verify this by looking at the font list and Font color menu on the Home tab.

▶ **6.** Click in the title text box on Slide 3, click the **Home** tab, and then in the Font group, click the **Font arrow**. The Headings font is Garamond and the Body font is Franklin Gothic Book.

Proskills

Problem Solving: Should You Create Your Own Theme?

PowerPoint comes with professionally designed themes, theme colors, and theme fonts. You can also create a presentation based on a template stored on Office.com. If you decide you need to create a custom theme, you can start "from scratch" and assign every theme color and create your own combination of fonts. But unless you are a graphic designer, consider starting with a theme or theme colors that most closely match the colors you want to use, and then selectively customize some of the colors, fonts, or styles. By creating a theme this way, you can take advantage of the professional designs available in PowerPoint and on Office.com to create your own custom look.

Filling Text and Shapes with a Color Used on the Slide

To fill a shape with a color used on a slide, you click Eyedropper on the Shape Fill menu, and then click an area of the slide. The shape is then filled with the exact color that you clicked.

When you point to a color using the Eyedropper tool, a ScreenTip appears listing a general name for the color, such as Light Green, Gold, or Black, and the color's RGB values. RGB stands for Red, Green, and Blue. Every color is made up of some combination of these three colors on a scale of 0 through 255. For example, pure red has a Red value of 255 and Green and Blue values of 0, but a shade of orange has a Red value of 229, a Green value of 128, and a Blue value of 27.

Earlier, you changed the color of the title text on Slide 3 (the Summary Zoom titled "Overview") so that it would not be visible on the slide. You changed the text to white because the slide background was white. You need to change the color again now that the slide backgrounds are filled with green. The summary zoom has the Title and Content layout applied. Because many of the slides in the presentation have that layout applied, you will change the title text color on Slide 3, not on the Title and Content layout in Slide Master view.

To use the Eyedropper to select a fill color:

1. On Slide 3 (the Summary Zoom titled "Overview"), click **Overview**, and then click the border of the title text box. The entire text box is selected.

2. Click the **Home** tab if necessary, in the Font group, click the **Font Color** button $\boxed{A \cdot}$, and then click **Eyedropper**. The pointer changes to the eyedropper pointer ⌀.

3. Move the pointer on top of a green area of the slide. A box containing the color you are pointing to appears above the pointer, and a ScreenTip appears identifying the color as RGB(219,239,212) Light Green. See Figure 6–21.

Figure 6–21 Eyedropper showing the ScreenTip identifying a color on a slide

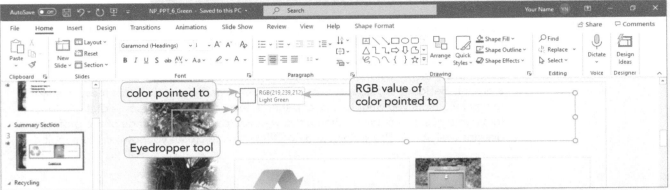

Kostenyukova Nataliya/Shutterstock.com; Rob kemp/Shutterstock.com; blew_s/Shutterstock.com

▶ **4.** Click the light green slide background. The text in the selected text box changes to the same color and is no longer visible.

On the title slide, the title text is hard to see on top of the picture. To fix this, you will try adjusting the transparency of the picture in the background. You will make this change in Slide Master view.

To change the transparency of a picture:

▶ **1.** Display Slide 1 (the title slide). The title "Green Challenge" is somewhat hard to read.

▶ **2.** Switch to Slide Master view to display the Title Slide layout, and then in the Background group, click the **Dialog Box Launcher**. The Format Background pane opens.

▶ **3.** In the Format Background pane, drag the **Transparency** slider to the right until the percentage in the Transparency box is 65%. The title is a little easier to read, but the picture looks washed out. Veronica doesn't like this effect.

▶ **4.** In the Transparency box, select **65%**, type **0**, and then press **ENTER**. The picture is again opaque—not transparent at all.

Making the picture transparent helped make the title text a little clearer, but it muted the colors in the picture too much. Instead, you will fill the title text box with a gradient of a color in the photo.

To use the Eyedropper to fill a text box with a gradient color:

▶ **1.** Click the title text placeholder, and then click the **Shape Format** tab. Because a shape (the title text placeholder) is selected, the pane changes to the Format Shape pane. The Shape Options tab and the Fill & Line button are selected, and the Fill section is expanded. The No fill option button is selected.

▶ **2.** On the Shape Format tab, in the Shape Styles group, click the **Shape Fill arrow**, and then click **Eyedropper**.

3. Move the pointer below the letters "a" and "s" in "Master." The rectangle that shows the color should be labeled Dark Green, and the ScreenTip should identify the color as something close to RGB(153,172,41). It's fine if your RGB values do not match this exactly.

4. When the pointer is positioned, click. The fill of the title text box changes to the color you clicked. In the Format Shape pane, the Solid fill option button is now selected, and the Color button has a green stripe.

Although you can now see the title text, it looks a little odd to have the green rectangle on top of the picture. To fix this, you will make the fill semi-transparent to see if that looks better. First, you will change the fill color so that it matches the color shown in the figures exactly.

To change the fill transparency of the title text box:

1. In the Format Shape pane, click the **Color** button. Below the Standard Colors row, a Recent Colors row appears. The green color you selected in the previous set of steps appears in the Recent Colors row. See Figure 6–22.

Figure 6–22	Color palette showing recently selected colors

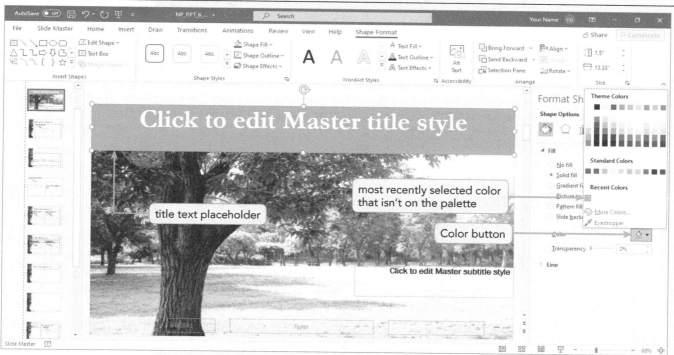

blew_s/Shutterstock.com

Trouble? If there is more than one color below the Recent Colors label, the most recently selected color—the green color you selected in the previous set of steps—is the first color in the row.

2. Click **More Colors**. The Colors dialog box opens with the Custom tab selected. See Figure 6–23.

Figure 6–23 **Custom tab in the Colors dialog box**

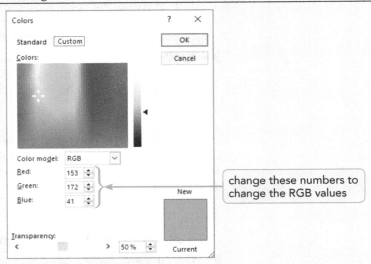

3. If necessary, change the value in the Red box to **153**, change the value in the Green box to **172**, change the value in the Blue box to **41**, and then click **OK**. Now you need to make the text box semi-transparent.

4. Drag the **Transparency** slider to the right until the value in the Transparency box is 50%.

You can now see the photo behind the title text box, but there is still a sharp distinction between the edges of the text box and the picture. To fix this, you will change the fill to a gradient of the green color and vary the transparency of the gradient stops from 100%—not transparent at all—to 0%—completely transparent. With this approach, you will be able to see the photo and read the text, and it won't be obvious that the title text box has a fill.

To change the fill to a gradient of transparencies:

1. In the Format Shape pane, click the **Gradient fill** option button. The title text box is filled with a gradient of a green color. In the Type box, Linear is selected.

2. Click the **Direction** button, and then click the **Linear Down** style. Now the options set for the first gradient stop will affect the top of shape, and the options set for the last gradient stop will affect the bottom of the shape. The first gradient stop on the slider is selected.

3. In the Format Shape pane, click the **Color** button, and then in the Recent Colors section of the palette, click the first color (the green color that you used to fill the title text placeholder shape).

4. Click the **Stop 2 of 4** tab, change its color to the same color as the Stop 1 of 4 tab, and then change its position to **50%**. You need to change the transparency of this gradient stop to 50%.

5. Scroll to the bottom of the Format Shape pane, and then drag the **Transparency** slider to the right until the Transparency box contains 50%.

6. Click the **Stop 4 of 4** tab, change its color to the same color as the Stop 1 of 4 and Stop 2 of 4 tabs, and then change the transparency to 100%.

> **7.** Click the **Stop 3 of 4** tab, and then click the **Remove gradient stop** button [⬚]. With the title text vertically aligned at the top of the text box, the text is clearer on the green background that is not transparent. See Figure 6–24.

| Figure 6–24 | Final gradient for the title text placeholder on the Title Slide layout |

blew_s/Shutterstock.com

The middle stop on the gradient slider is not necessary to create this effect. However, if you keep it, you can change its position from 50% to either extend or reduce the part of the text box that is not at all transparent.

> **8.** Close the Format Shape pane, and then switch to Normal view.

> **9.** **sam** ⬆ Save the changes to the presentation.

Make sure you save the changes to the presentation because you will be saving the file in another format in the next set of steps.

Insight

Creating a Photo Album

PowerPoint includes a built-in Photo Album command, which allows you to create a photo album with one, two, or four pictures per slide, and optionally, with titles and captions. The advantage of this feature is that you can insert a large number of photographs all at once into a presentation without needing to insert each picture individually. To create this type of photo album, you click the Insert tab, and then, in the Images group, click the Photo Album button to open the Photo Album dialog box. To add a photo, click the File/Disk button, select the photo or photos you want to add from the Insert New Pictures dialog box, and then click the Insert button. To modify a photo, click the check box next to it in the Pictures in album list, and then click one of the Rotate buttons to rotate the picture 90 degrees, and click one of the Brightness or Contrast buttons to make the image brighter or darker or to increase or decrease the contrast. To add text boxes below each photo for captions, click the Captions below ALL pictures check box.

To change the layout of the slides, click the Picture layout arrow, and then click a layout. Note that when you do this, you are not actually changing the layout of the slides. All of the options on the Picture layout menu that do not include a title place the slides on the Blank layout from the Office theme; all of the options that include a title place the slides on the Title Only layout from the Office theme. When you are finished setting up the photo album, click Create to create the photo album.

Saving a Presentation as a Custom Theme

Now that you have created a custom theme for Veronica, she asks you to save the theme so that she can apply it to other presentations. When you save a presentation as a theme, the changes are saved to the Document Themes folder. The Document Themes folder is created on the hard drive when Office is installed and is where the built-in themes are installed. If you save to this folder, the custom theme will appear in the Themes gallery on the Design tab. You can also save a theme to another folder, but then you will need to apply it in the same way you apply a theme that is used by another presentation.

When you save a presentation as a theme, it needs only one slide. The first thing you will do is delete all the slides except the title slide.

To save a presentation as a theme:

▶ **1.** Delete Slides 2 through 11. The section names are still listed.

▶ **2.** Right-click any section name, and then on the shortcut menu click **Remove All Sections**.

▶ **3.** Click the **File** tab, and then in the navigation pane, click **Save As** or **Save a Copy**. The Save As or Save a Copy screen in Backstage view appears.

▶ **4.** Click **Browse** to open the Save As dialog box. At the top of the dialog box, the path to the folder and the name of the folder containing the NP_PPT_6_ Green presentation appears. At the bottom of the dialog box, the name of the open file appears in the File name box. Below that, the file type appears in the Save as type box. The current file type is PowerPoint Presentation.

▶ **5.** Click the **Save as type** box. A list of file types appears.

▶ **6.** In the list, click **Office Theme**. At the top of the dialog box, the path changes to show the path to the folder Document Themes. See Figure 6–25.

| Figure 6–25 | Save As dialog box showing the Document Themes folder |

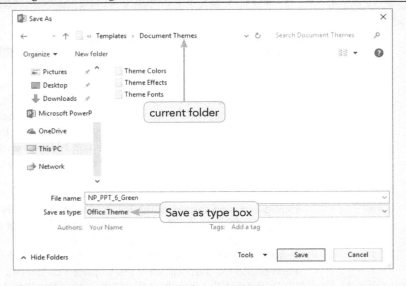

▶ **7.** In the File name box, change the file name to **NP_PPT_6_ParksTheme**, and then click **Save**. The dialog box closes, and the theme is saved. You could also click the More button ⮯ in the Themes group on the Design tab, and then click Save Current Theme to save the presentation as a theme.

▶ **8.** Click the **Design** tab, and then in the Themes group, click the **More** button ⮯. The custom theme appears in a new Custom section in the Themes gallery. See Figure 6–26.

Figure 6-26 **Custom theme in the Themes gallery**

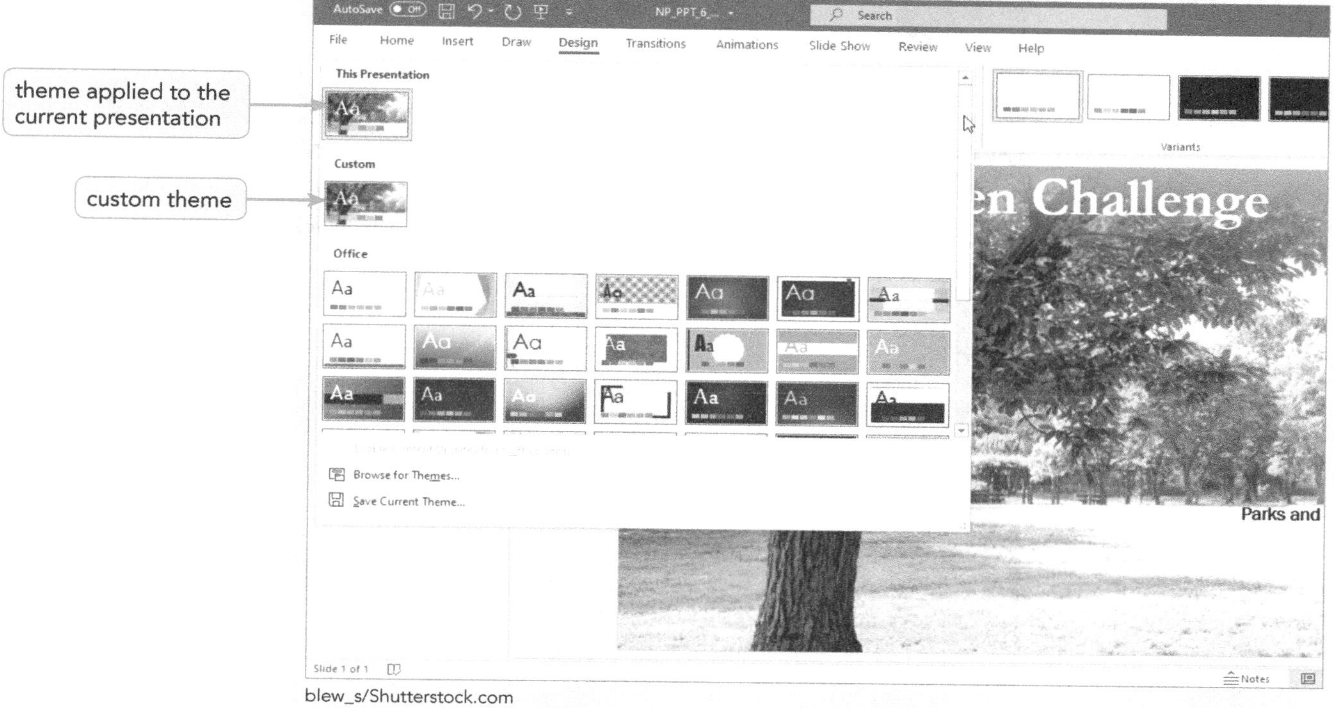

theme applied to the current presentation

custom theme

blew_s/Shutterstock.com

Recall that a template is a PowerPoint file that has a theme applied and also contains text, graphics, and placeholders that help a user create a final presentation. You can also save a presentation as a template if you want to preserve some of the content. To save a presentation as template, select PowerPoint Template in the list of file types on the Save As screen in Backstage view or in the Save as type box in the Save As dialog box. When you do this, the folder path you are saving to changes to the path to the Custom Office Templates folder.

Once you have saved a custom theme, there are several ways you can apply it to a presentation. If you saved it to the Document Themes folder, the theme will appear on the Design tab in the Themes group, and you can click the custom theme to apply it to the current presentation. Or when you are creating a new presentation, you can click Custom on the New screen in Backstage view, click the Document Themes folder, and then click the custom theme. You can also apply a custom theme to the current presentation using the same method you use to apply a theme from any presentation by clicking the More button ⯆ in the Themes group on the Design tab, and then clicking Browse for Themes.

To create a new presentation using a custom theme:

▶ 1. Click the **File** tab, and then in the navigation pane, click **New**. The New screen appears in Backstage view. The Office tab is selected. This tab contains all of the built-in themes. If you click one, a new presentation will be created with that theme applied. You can also click one of the Suggested searches links or type in the "Search for online templates and themes" to find templates that have a theme applied as well as placeholder content.

▶ 2. Click **Custom**. The New screen changes to show themes and templates stored in the Document Themes folder on your computer. See Figure 6-27.

Figure 6-27   Custom theme on the New screen in Backstage view

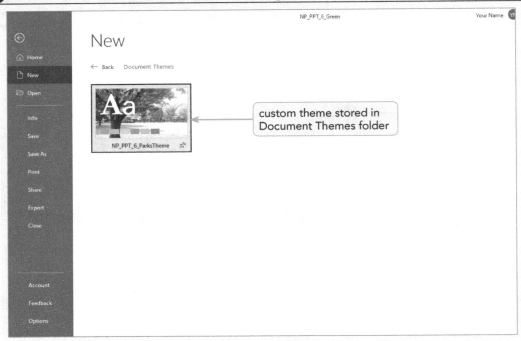

blew_s/Shutterstock.com

> **Trouble?** If folders appear instead of the custom theme, click the Document Themes folder.

> **3.** Click **NP_PPT_6_ParksTheme**. A window opens showing the Title layout of the selected theme. See Figure 6-28.

Figure 6-28   Window that appears when a theme is selected on the New screen

blew_s/Shutterstock.com

> **4.** Click the **Create** button. The window and Backstage view close and a new presentation is created with the custom theme you created applied.

> **5.** Add a new Slide 2 with the Title and Content layout.

Tip

If you have AutoSave enabled, click the Undo button on the Quick Access Toolbar as necessary to undo the deletion of Slides 2-11 and skip steps 7-9.

> **6.** Add your name as the title on the title slide, save the new presentation as **NP_PPT_6_ThemeTest** to the location where you are saving your files, and then close it. The NP_PPT_6_Green presentation is the active presentation again. It contains only the title slide. You saved the completed presentation before you saved the file as a theme, so you will close this version without saving changes, and then reopen the version you saved.

> **7.** Click the **File** tab, and then click **Close**. A dialog box opens asking if you want to save the changes to the presentation.

▶ **8.** Click **Don't Save**. The dialog box and the presentation close.

▶ **9.** Open the file **NP_PPT_6_Green** from the location where you are storing your files.

If you open a template from the New screen in Backstage view, a new presentation will be created based on that template. If you open a template from the Open screen in Backstage view, the template itself will open.

You'll delete the custom theme you created from the computer you are using.

To delete the custom theme from the computer:

▶ **1.** Click the **Design** tab. In the Themes group, the custom theme applied to the current presentation appears. The second theme is the custom theme you saved.

▶ **2.** Move the pointer on top of the first theme. The ScreenTip that appears says "Rockland Parks: used by all slides."

▶ **3.** Move the pointer on top of the second theme. The ScreenTip that appears says "NP_PPT_6_ParksTheme."

▶ **4.** In the Themes group, right-click the second theme with the ScreenTip "NP_PPT_6_ParksTheme." A shortcut menu opens.

▶ **5.** On the shortcut menu, click **Delete**. A dialog box opens, asking if you want to delete this theme.

▶ **6.** Click **Yes**. The custom theme is deleted from the computer.

In this session, you compared presentations and worked with comments. You also modified the slide master by changing the formatting and adding pictures on the slide master and on individual layouts, by changing the bullet style, by modifying a layout, and by creating a custom layout. You also created a custom theme font set and theme color palette. You used the Eyedropper tool to fill text and a shape with a color used on the slide, and you modified a title text box by making part of it transparent. Finally, you saved the custom theme. In the next session, you will create a custom show, modify and create advanced file properties, encrypt the presentation, and mark it as final.

Review

Session 6.1 Quick Check

1. What types of changes are listed when you compare presentations: changes to individual slides, changes to the entire presentation, or both?

2. What happens to the layouts when you modify the slide master?

3. What happens to Title and Content layout when you modify the Title Slide layout?

4. Describe how to create a new layout.

5. Describe how to add a placeholder to a layout.

6. If you delete a custom theme font set from your computer, does the presentation revert back to its original theme font set?

7. When describing a color, what do the letters R, G, and B stand for?

8. How do you get a custom theme to appear in the Themes gallery on the Design tab?

Session 6.2 Visual Overview:

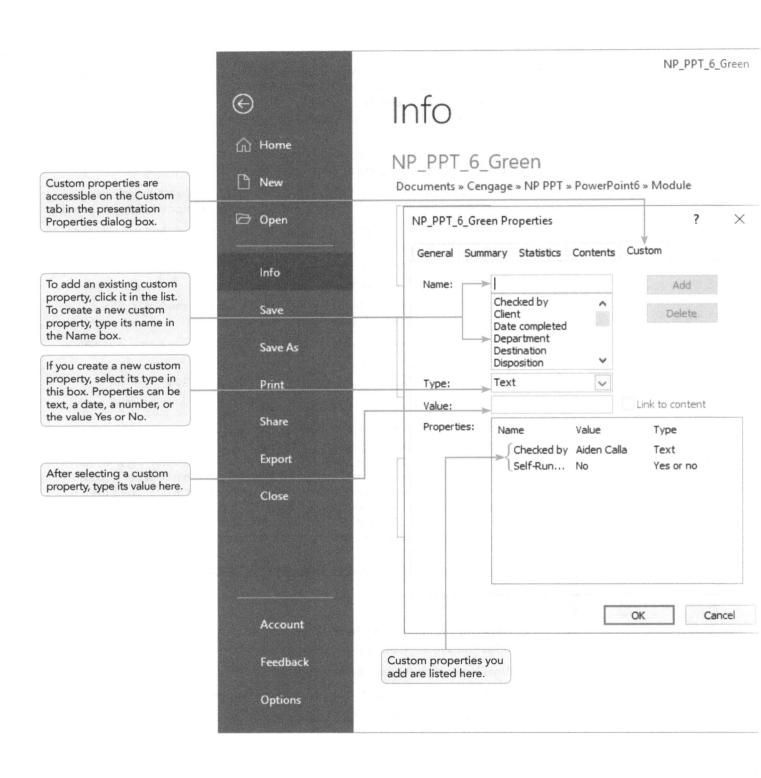

Custom properties are accessible on the Custom tab in the presentation Properties dialog box.

To add an existing custom property, click it in the list. To create a new custom property, type its name in the Name box.

If you create a new custom property, select its type in this box. Properties can be text, a date, a number, or the value Yes or No.

After selecting a custom property, type its value here.

Custom properties you add are listed here.

Advanced File Properties

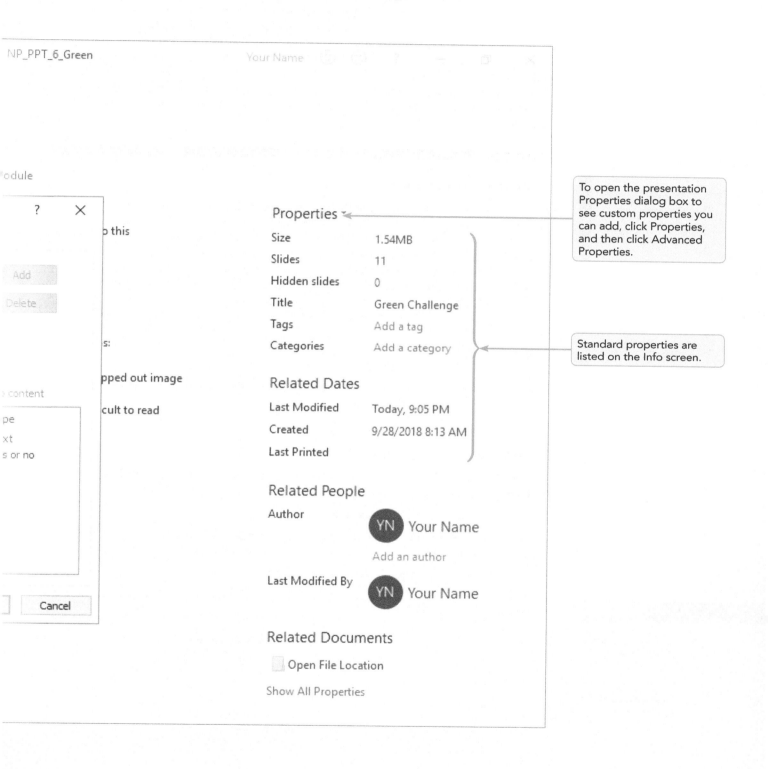

NP_PPT_6_Green   Your Name

odule

?   ✕   o this

Add

Delete

s:

pped out image

content

cult to read

pe

xt

s or no

Cancel

Properties ◄

Size	1.54MB
Slides	11
Hidden slides	0
Title	Green Challenge
Tags	Add a tag
Categories	Add a category

To open the presentation Properties dialog box to see custom properties you can add, click Properties, and then click Advanced Properties.

Standard properties are listed on the Info screen.

Related Dates

Last Modified	Today, 9:05 PM
Created	9/28/2018 8:13 AM
Last Printed	

Related People

Author   YN Your Name

Add an author

Last Modified By YN Your Name

Related Documents

Open File Location

Show All Properties

Creating a Custom Show

A **custom show** is a subset of slides in a presentation that can be reordered without changing the order of the slides in the original presentation. A custom show is saved as part of the presentation in which it is created. Custom slide shows are helpful if you need to quickly create a presentation for a specific audience or if you know you will be presenting to an audience that needs to see only some of the slides in a presentation or needs to see the slides in a different order. Custom slide shows are also useful if you will be using the same slide in multiple custom shows and you need to make a change to the slide. When you change a slide, the updated slide will appear in all the custom shows in which it is included.

Reference

Creating a Custom Show

- On the Slide Show tab, in the Start Slide Show group, click the Custom Slide Show button, and then click Custom Shows to open the Custom Shows dialog box.
- Click the New button to open the Define Custom Show dialog box.
- In the Slide show name box, type the name of the custom show.
- In the Slides in presentation box, click the check boxes next to the slides you want to add to the custom show, and then click the Add button to add those slides to the Slides in custom show box.
- To reorder slides in the custom show, select a slide in the Slides in custom show box, and then click the Up or Down arrow.
- Click OK, and then click Close.

Veronica asks you to create a custom show in the NP_PPT_6_Green presentation that contains only the four slides in the Recycling section.

To create a custom show:

▶ **1.** If you took a break after the previous session, make sure the **NP_PPT_6_ Green.pptx** presentation is open.

▶ **2.** On the ribbon, click the **Slide Show** tab.

▶ **3.** In the Start Slide Show group, click the **Custom Slide Show** button, and then click **Custom Shows**. The Custom Shows dialog box opens.

▶ **4.** Click **New**. The Define Custom Show dialog box opens. See Figure 6–29.

| Figure 6–29 | Define Custom Show dialog box |

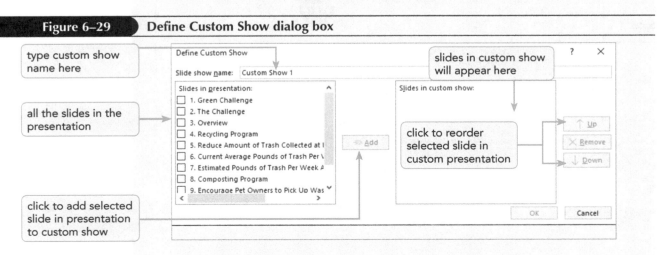

5. In the Slide show name box, delete the text, and then type **Recycling**. Next, you'll select the slides that you want to use in the custom show.

6. In the Slides in presentation box on the left, click the check boxes next to **4. Recycling Program**, **5. Reduce Amount of Trash Collected at Parks**, **6. Current Average Pounds of Trash Per Week**, and **7. Estimated Pounds of Trash Per Week After Adding Recycling Bins**.

7. Click **Add**. The selected slides on the left are added to the Slides in custom show box on the right and are renumbered 1-4 in the box on the right.

8. Click **OK**. The custom show you created is added to the list in the Custom Shows dialog box.

9. Click **Close** in the dialog box.

To run the custom show, you can click the Show button in the Custom Shows dialog box, or you can run it from Normal, Slide Show, or Presenter view.

To run a custom show:

1. On the Slide Show tab, in the Start Slide Show group, click the **Custom Slide Show** button. The menu now includes the custom show you created. See Figure 6–30.

Figure 6–30   **Custom Slide Show menu listing a custom show**

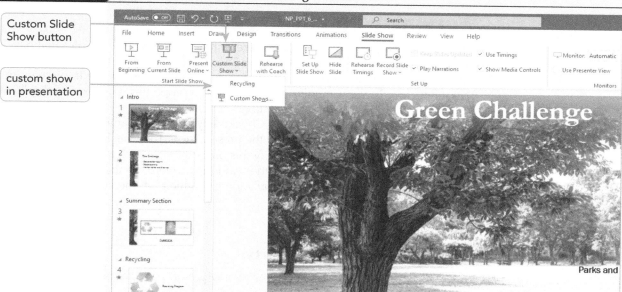

Custom Slide Show button

custom show in presentation

blew_s/Shutterstock.com; Kostenyukova Nataliya/Shutterstock.com; Rob kemp/Shutterstock.com

---

Tip

You can format text or an object on a slide as a link to a custom show. In the Insert a Hyperlink dialog box, click Place in This Document in the Link to list, and then click the custom show name.

2. Click **Recycling**. The first slide in the custom show, "Recycling Program", appears in Slide Show view.

3. Advance the slide show four times to display the remaining slides in the custom presentation and the black slide that indicates the end of a slide show, and then advance it once more to return to Normal view.

4. Save the changes to the presentation.

Insight

Working with 3D Models

You can insert 3D models on a slide. To do this, click the 3D Models arrow in the Illustrations group on the Insert tab. To insert a 3D model stored on your computer or network, click From a File. To insert a 3D model from an online library called Remix 3D, click Stock 3D Models. Remix 3D contains 3D models uploaded by members of the Remix community.

The 3D Model tab appears on the ribbon when a 3D model is selected. Like any other object on a slide, you can resize a 3D model by dragging a sizing handle or by changing the measurements in the Height and Width boxes in the Size group. In addition, you can click a view in the 3D Model Views group to rotate the model as indicated or you can drag the 3D control in the middle of the image to rotate the object in three dimensions. You can also click the Pan & Zoom button in the Size group to add a magnifying glass icon to the right of the model. If you drag the magnifying glass icon up or down, the model increases or decreases in size inside the object border.

You also have access to additional animations when a 3D model is selected. You can apply the 3D Arrive animation, which is an entrance animation for 3D models. You can also apply the 3D Turntable, Swing, and Jump & Turn animations, which are emphasis animations for 3D models. And you can apply the 3D Leave animation, an exit animation for 3D models. The Effect Options menus for all of the 3D animations contain options to change the direction and the rotation axis of the animation. Some of the animations allow you to change the intensity of the animations and some allow you to change amount of the animation.

Working with File Properties

You can use file properties to organize presentations or to search for files that have specific properties. Refer to the Session 6.2 Visual Overview for more information on file properties. To view or modify properties, you need to display the Info screen in Backstage view. To view, modify, or create custom properties, you need to display the Properties dialog box for the presentation.

Veronica wants you to modify the Checked by property so that you can list the names of people who have reviewed the presentation. The Checked by property is not listed on the Info screen. To modify this property, you need to open the Properties dialog box for the presentation, and then add the property on the Custom tab. Even after you modify a custom property by adding a value to it, the custom property will still not appear on the Info screen.

To add a custom file property:

▶ 1. Click the **File** tab, and then in the navigation pane, click **Info**. The Info screen in Backstage view appears.

▶ 2. At the top of the list of document properties, click the **Properties** button, and then click **Advanced Properties**. The NP_PPT_6_Green Properties dialog box opens.

▶ 3. Click the **Custom** tab. This tab lists additional properties you can add. See Figure 6–31.

Figure 6–31   Custom tab in the NP_PPT_6_Green Properties dialog box

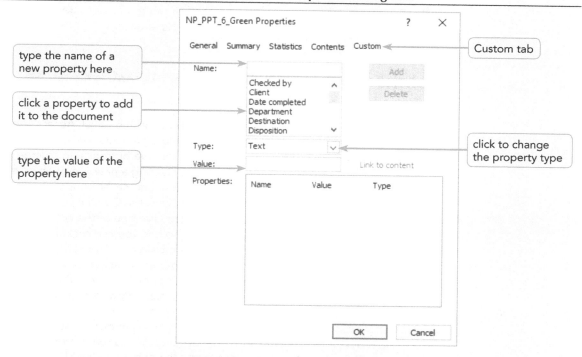

type the name of a new property here

click a property to add it to the document

type the value of the property here

Custom tab

click to change the property type

> **4.** In the Name list, click **Checked by**. "Checked by" appears in the Name box above the list.

> **5.** Click in the **Value** box, type **Aiden Callahan**, and then click **Add**. "Checked by" and the value you gave it appear in the Properties list below the Value box.

Properties are one of four types: Text, Date, Number, or Yes or no. All of the properties you have worked with so far are Text properties and contain text as their value. A property with the Date type can contain only a date as its value, and a Number type property can contain only a number. Yes or no type properties have the value Yes or No.

Veronica will use the NP_PPT_6_Green presentation when she speaks in front of the city council. The council wants the department heads to post self-running versions of their presentations on the city's website as well. Veronica plans to create another version of her presentation for the website that contains a little more explanatory text. She will also review the presentation for accessibility. To help her keep track of her presentations, she wants you to create a new custom Yes or no property named Self-Running. The current version of her presentation will have No as the Self-Running property. The version that she will post on the city's website will have Yes as the Self-Running property.

To create a new custom file property:

> **1.** In the NP_PPT_6_Green Properties dialog box, click in the **Name** box, and then type **Self-Running**.

> **2.** Click the **Type** arrow, and then click **Yes or no**. The Value box changes to show Yes and No option buttons.

> **3.** Click the **No** option button, and then click **Add**. "Self-Running" and the value you gave it appear below "Checked by" in the Properties list.

▶ **4.** Click **OK**. The dialog box closes.

▶ **5.** On the Info screen, in the navigation pane, click the **Back** button ⊙ to close Backstage view, and then save the presentation.

Insight

Customizing PowerPoint

In PowerPoint, you can customize the ribbon and the Quick Access Toolbar to suit your working style or your needs for creating a particular presentation. To customize the Quick Access Toolbar, you can add or remove buttons and change its location in the window. You customize the ribbon by creating a new group on an existing tab or creating a new tab with new groups and then adding buttons to the new groups.

To customize the Quick Access Toolbar, click the Customize Quick Access Toolbar arrow on the Quick Access Toolbar. You can click one of the commands on the menu that opens to add that command to the toolbar, you can click the command to move the Quick Access Toolbar below the ribbon below, or you can click More Commands to open the PowerPoint Options dialog box with Quick Access Toolbar selected in the pane on the left. To customize the ribbon, right-click one of the ribbon tabs, and then click Customize the Ribbon. This opens the same PowerPoint Options dialog box with Customize Ribbon selected in the pane on the left.

In both cases, the right side of the dialog box changes to show two lists. On the left is an alphabetical list of commands. On the right, the current buttons on the Quick Access Toolbar or the current tabs and groups on the ribbon are listed. The list of commands on the left are Popular Commands; to see all the commands in PowerPoint, click the Choose commands from arrow, and then click All Commands. To add a command to the Quick Access Toolbar or to the selected group on the ribbon, click the command in the list on the left, and then click Add. To add a command to the ribbon, you must create a new group first. Select the tab on which you want to create the new group (or click the New Tab button to create a new tab), and then click the New Group button.

Encrypting a Presentation

To **encrypt** a file is to modify it to make the information unreadable to anyone who does not have the password. When you encrypt a PowerPoint file, you assign a password to the file. The only way to open the file is by entering the password. When you create passwords, keep in mind that they are case sensitive; this means that "PASSWORD" is different from "password." Also, you must remember your password. This might seem obvious, but if you forget the password you assign to a file, you won't be able to open it.

Reference

Encrypting a Presentation

- On the ribbon, click the File tab, and then click Info to open the Info screen in Backstage view.
- Click the Protect Presentation button, and then click Encrypt with Password.
- In the Encrypt Document dialog box, type a password in the Password box, and then click the OK button to open the Confirm Password dialog box.
- Retype the password in the Reenter password box.
- Click OK.

Veronica wants you to encrypt the NP_PPT_6_Green file so that it can be opened only by people with whom she has shared the password.

To encrypt the presentation with a password:

1. On the ribbon, click the **File** tab, and then click **Info** to open the Info screen in Backstage view.

2. Click the **Protect Presentation** button. A menu opens listing options for protecting the presentation. See Figure 6–32.

Figure 6–32 **Protect Presentation menu on the Info screen**

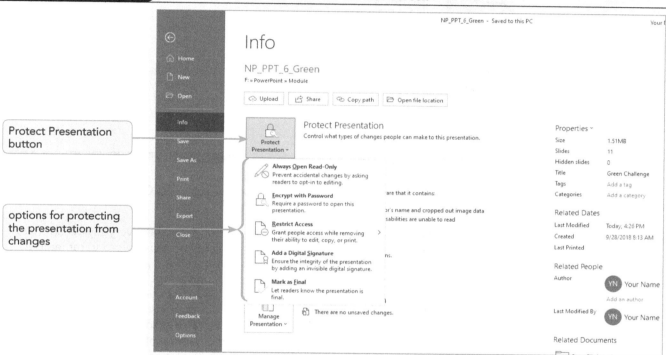

Protect Presentation button

options for protecting the presentation from changes

Tip

To remove the password, delete the password in the Encrypt Document dialog box, and then click the OK button.

3. Click **Encrypt with Password**. The Encrypt Document dialog box opens. Here you'll type a password.

4. Type **Green**. The characters you type appear as black dots to prevent anyone from reading the password over your shoulder.

5. Click **OK**. The dialog box changes to the Confirm Password dialog box.

6. Type **Green** again to verify the password, and then click **OK**. The Protect Presentation section heading and the Protect Presentation button are yellow to indicate that a protection has been set, and the message in the Protect Presentation section explains that a password is required to open the presentation. See Figure 6–33.

| Figure 6–33 | Info screen after encrypting a file |

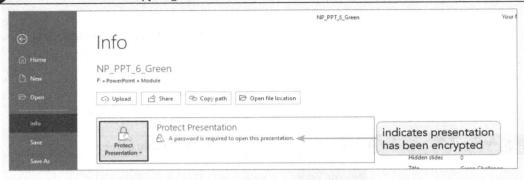

Now, when you save the file, it will be in an encrypted format so that it can't be opened except by someone who knows the password. (Normally, you would use a stronger password than "Green," but for the purpose here, you'll keep it simple and easy to remember.)

 Proskills

Decision Making: Creating Strong Passwords You Can Easily Remember

In a world where sharing digital information electronically is an everyday occurrence, a password used to encrypt a presentation is just one more password to remember. When deciding on a password, you should consider a strong password that consists of at least eight characters using a combination of uppercase and lowercase letters, numbers, and symbols. However, this type of password can be difficult to remember, especially if you have to remember multiple passwords. Some people use the same password for everything. This is not a good idea because if someone ever discovered your password, they would have access to all of the data or information protected by that password. Instead, you should come up with a plan for creating passwords. For example, you could choose a short word that you can easily remember for one part of the password. The second part of the password could be the name of the file, website, or account, but instead of typing it directly, type it backwards, or use the characters in the row above or below the characters that would spell out the name. Or you could split the name of the website and put your short word in the middle of the name. Other possibilities are to combine your standard short word and the website or account name, but replace certain letters with symbols—for example, replace every letter "E" with "#," or memorize a short phrase from a poem or story and use it with some of the substitutions described above. Establishing a process for creating a password means that you will be able to create strong passwords for all of your accounts that you can easily remember.

Making a Presentation Read-Only

You can make a presentation **read-only**, which means that others can read but cannot modify the presentation. There are two ways to make a presentation read-only. You can mark the presentation as final or you can set the presentation to always open as read-only. The next time you open a presentation marked as final, it will be read-only. If you turn off the read-only status, make changes, and then save and close the file, it will no longer be marked as final. If a presentation is set to always open as read-only and you turn off the read-only status to make changes, the next time you open that presentation, it will still be marked as read-only.

When Veronica posts her revised presentation on the city's website, she wants to make it read-only. She asks you to experiment with the two ways to do this and decide which method would be a better choice for this purpose.

To mark the presentation as final and as read-only:

▶ **1.** On the Info screen in Backstage view, click the **Protect Presentation** button, and then click **Mark as Final**. A dialog box opens stating that the presentation will be marked as final and then saved.

▶ **2.** Click **OK**. The dialog box and Backstage view close, and another dialog box opens telling you that the document has been marked as final.

   Trouble? If the dialog box stating that the document has been marked as final does not appear, a previous user clicked the Don't show this message again check box in that dialog box. Skip Step 3.

▶ **3.** Click **OK**. The ribbon is collapsed, a yellow MARKED AS FINAL bar appears below the collapsed ribbon, the Marked as Final icon appears in the status bar, and "Read-Only" appears in the title bar. See Figure 6–34.

Figure 6–34 **Presentation after marking a file as final**

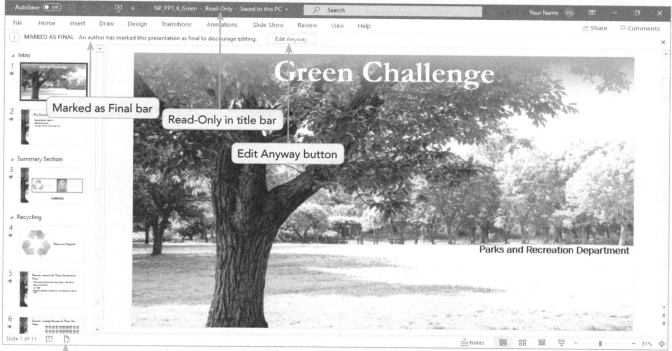

blew_s/Shutterstock.com; Kostenyukova Nataliya/Shutterstock.com; Rob kemp/Shutterstock.com

▶ **4.** Close the NP_PPT_6_Green file, and then reopen it. The Password dialog box appears.

▶ **5.** In the Password box, type **Green**, and then click **OK**. The presentation opens, and the yellow MARKED AS FINAL bar appears.

▶ **6.** In the MARKED AS FINAL bar, click **Edit Anyway**. The bar disappears and the ribbon is displayed.

▶ **7.** Save the presentation, close it, and then reopen it, typing **Green** in the Password box when asked. The yellow MARKED AS FINAL bar does not appear.

▶ **8.** Click the **File** tab, click **Info**, click the **Protect Presentation** button, and then click **Always Open Read-Only**. Additional text added below the Protect Presentation button name tells you that the presentation has been set to read-only.

▶ **9.** In the navigation pane, click **Save**.

▶ **10.** Close, and then reopen the presentation. The yellow bar appears again. This time, it is labeled READ-ONLY.

▶ **11.** In the READ-ONLY bar, click **Edit Anyway**, display Slide 1 (the title slide), click **Parks and Recreation Department** in the subtitle text box, move the insertion point to the end of the line, press **ENTER**, and then type your name.

▶ **12.** Save the presentation, close it, and then reopen it. The yellow READ-ONLY bar appears. If you want to remove the Always Open as Read-Only status, you need to click Edit Anyway in the READ-ONLY bar first.

▶ **13.** Close the presentation file.

Now if you want to modify the presentation, you must remove the editing restriction by clicking the Edit Anyway button in the yellow MARKED AS FINAL bar.

Insight

Adding a Digital Signature and Restricting Access

A **digital signature** is an electronic attachment not visible in the file that verifies the authenticity of the author or the version of the file by comparing the digital signature to a digital certificate. A **digital certificate** is a code attached to a file that verifies the identity of the creator of the file. When you digitally sign a document, the file is marked as read-only. If anyone removes the read-only status so that you can make changes to the document, the signature is marked as invalid because it is no longer the same document the signatory signed. You can obtain a digital certificate from a certification authority.

To add a digital signature to a file, click the Protect Presentation button on the Info screen in Backstage view, and then click Add a Digital Signature. If the Get a Digital ID dialog box opens indicating that you don't have a digital ID and asking if you would like to get one from a Microsoft Partner, that means no digital certificate is stored on the computer you are using. If you click Yes, your browser starts and a webpage opens, listing certificate authorities from whom you can purchase a digital certificate.

If you or your company has access to a Rights Management Server or you are using Office 365 with RMS Online, you can restrict access to a presentation so that others can read it but not make any changes to it or copy or print it. To do this, click the Protect Presentation button, and then use the Restrict Access command.

Presenting Online

You can run a slide show over the Internet so that anyone with a browser and the URL (the address for a webpage on the Internet) for the presentation can watch it while you present. When you present online, you send the presentation to a special Microsoft server that is made available for this purpose. (If you have access to a SharePoint server, you can send the presentation to that server instead.) A unique web address is created, and you can send this web address to anyone you choose. Then, while you run your presentation on your computer in Slide Show view, your remote audience members can view it on their computers in a web browser at the same time. Note that viewers will not be able to hear you unless you also set up a conference call.

In order to present online, you need a Microsoft account (or access to a SharePoint server), and you need to be connected to the Internet. If you don't have a Microsoft account, you can get one by clicking the Sign in link in the upper-right corner of the PowerPoint window or on the Microsoft webpage at microsoft.com. Once you have a Microsoft account, you can connect to the Microsoft server from within your PowerPoint presentation to create the unique web address for your presentation and start presenting online.

To present a slide show online, click the Slide Show tab, and then in the Start Slide Show group, click the Present Online button to open the Present Online dialog box, as shown in Figure 6–35.

Figure 6–35   Present Online dialog box

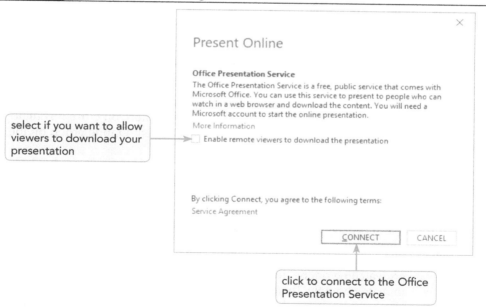

Click CONNECT. If you are signed into your Microsoft account in Office, the dialog box changes to display the link to your presentation on the Microsoft server and a new tab—the Present Online tab—appears on the ribbon, as shown in Figure 6–36. If you are not signed in to your Microsoft account, you will need to sign in before the link is created. (To present online, the file cannot be marked as file or set to always save as read-only, and it cannot have a password.)

Figure 6-36 Present Online dialog box after web address is created

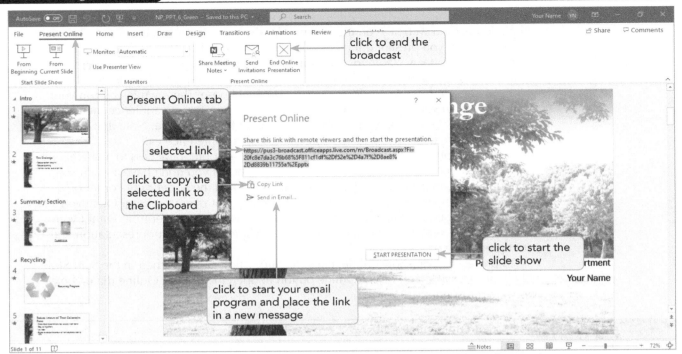

blew_s/Shutterstock.com; Kostenyukova Nataliya/Shutterstock.com; Rob kemp/Shutterstock.com

To invite people to watch your presentation, you need to send them the link. You can copy the link and send it to people via email, Facebook, or whichever your preferred method of communicating over the Internet is, or you can click Send in Email to open your email program and automatically include the link in the message. If you need to retrieve this link again after you close this dialog box, you can click the Send Invitations button in the Present Online group on the Present Online tab.

To start the online slide show, click START PRESENTATION in the Present Online dialog box, or click one of the buttons in the Start Slide Show group on the Present Online tab. The presentation appears in Slide Show view on your computer (although you can switch to Presenter view if you prefer). Anyone watching the presentation online will see the first slide in the browser window. You can advance through the slide show as you normally would, and viewers will see the slides on their screens. Note that no matter what transition you see in Slide Show or Presenter view on your computer, viewers watching online might see a different transition. In addition, not all animations will animate correctly. Therefore, if you plan to present online, you should preview the presentation in your own browser first and make sure the transitions and animations are acceptable.

To end the online slide show and disconnect from the Microsoft server, click the End Online Presentation button in the Present Online group on the Present Online tab. In the dialog box that opens warning you that everyone watching the online presentation will be disconnected, click the End Online Presentation button.

If you needed to sign into your Microsoft account in order to present online, you are now signed into that account in Office. To sign out, click your username in the upper-right corner of the PowerPoint window, and then click Account settings to open the Account screen in Backstage view. Below your username, click Sign out.

You have finished working on Veronica's presentation. She has the versions she needs to effectively share and collaborate with her staff to create consistent presentations to meet multiple purposes.

Review

Session 6.2 Quick Check

1. What is a custom show?

2. Can you modify custom properties on the Info screen in Backstage view?

3. What are the four types of properties?

4. What is an encrypted presentation?

5. What are the two ways to make a presentation read-only?

6. What happens when you present online?

Practice

Review Assignments

Data Files needed for the Review Assignments: NP_PPT_6-2.pptx, Support_PPT_6_Dan.pptx, Support_PPT_6_Night.jpg

Veronica Soto, the head of the Parks and Recreation department in Rockland, Missouri, researched another idea for meeting the Green Challenge issued by the city council. Currently, lights on walkways and in ball fields in city parks are on seven days a week from dusk until 11:00 p.m. She will present a plan to light certain fields only when a group has been issued a permit, but she wants to discuss the idea of leaving some fields lit for pick-up games. She gave a copy of her presentation to Dan Yost, the head of the department of public works. He reviewed it and returned it to her. She asks you to help her evaluate Dan's comments and complete her presentation. Complete the following steps:

1. Open the file **NP_PPT_6-2.pptx**, located in the PowerPoint6 > Review folder included with your Data Files. On Slide 1, add your name as the subtitle, and then save the file as **NP_PPT_6_Lights** in the location where you are saving your files.
2. Compare the NP_PPT_6_Lights presentation with the file **Support_PPT_6_Dan.pptx**, located in the PowerPoint6 > Review folder. Do not accept the change that says that Dan deleted your name on Slide 1 (the title slide), accept the change on Slide 2 ("Who Uses the Ball Fields?"), and then end the review.
3. On Slide 2 ("Who Uses the Ball Fields?"), read and then delete Dan's comment.
4. On Slide 7 ("Concerns"), read the comment from Dan, and then type the following as a reply: **That's a good idea. I'll look into the feasibility of that.** (including the period).
5. On Slide 4 ("New Lighting Plan"), insert the following as a new comment: **Maybe extend the time to 11:00 p.m. on weekend nights?**. Reposition the comment balloon to the left of the second bulleted item.
6. Apply the Parallax theme, and then choose the third variant. Change the theme fonts to the Consolas-Verdana theme font set, and then customize that theme font set so that Heading text uses the Arial font. Save the custom theme font set with the default name.
7. Delete the custom theme font set from the computer.
8. Modify the slide master by doing the following:
   a. Change the width of the title text placeholder to 10", and then align its right edge with the right edge of the content placeholder.
   b. Change the width of the content placeholder to 10", and then align its right edge with the right edge of the title text placeholder.
   c. Change the width of the footer placeholder by to 7.98", and then align its left edge with the left edge of the content placeholder.
   d. In the content placeholder, change the font size of the first-level items to 28 points, and change the font size of the second-level items to 24 points. Change the vertical alignment of the content placeholder to Top.
   e. Change the color of the bullet characters to Green, Accent 2, Darker 25%, and change their size to 150% of the text.
   f. Change the space before every bulleted item to 12 points.
   g. Ungroup the graphic on the left side of the slide master. Change the fill of the top green shape to Green, Accent 2, and then change the fill of the bottom green shape to Green, Accent 2, Darker 25%.
9. Duplicate the Title Slide Layout. Rename the new layout to **Title Slide Alternate**.
10. Delete the graphic on the Title Slide Alternate layout. Deselect the Footers check box in the Master Layout group on the Slide Master tab.
11. In the new layout, change the height of the title text placeholder to 1.8", change its width to 13.33", align its center to the center of the slide, and align its top to the top of the slide. Change the vertical alignment of the text in the title text placeholder to Top.

12. Change the width of the subtitle text placeholder to 7". Align its right edge with the right edge of the slide. Position it horizontally 6.33" from the top-left corner and vertically 4.88" from the top-left corner.

13. Fill the background of the Title Slide Alternate layout with the picture in **Support_PPT_6_Night.jpg**, located in the PowerPoint6 > Review folder.

14. Fill the title text placeholder shape with a gradient with three gradient stops, all three formatted with the color with the RGB value of 5,21,36. Position the first stop at 0% and format it so it is completely opaque (0% transparent). Position the second stop at 50% and format it so it is 50% transparent. Position the third stop at 100% and format it so it is 100% transparent.

15. Change the color of the text in the title text placeholder and the subtitle text placeholder to White, Background 1. Format the text in the title text placeholder as bold.

16. Rename the slide master to **Alt Parks Theme**.

17. In Normal view, change the layout of Slide 1 (the title slide) to the Title Slide Alternate layout. Then reset Slide 5.

18. Create a custom show named **New Plan** that contains Slide 4 ("New Lighting Plan"), Slide 5 ("Projected Reduction in Kilowatt Hours"), and Slide 6 ("Projected Reduction in Kilowatt Hours").

19. Add the custom property Editor with your name as the value of that property. Create a new custom property named **Draft** of the type Yes or no, and select Yes.

20. Save the changes to the presentation.

21. Make sure you saved the changes to the presentation, delete Slides 2 through 7, and then save the presentation as a theme named **NP_PPT_6_ParksTheme2** in the location where you are saving your files. (Make sure you change the folder to the folder where you are saving your files. Do not save the theme to the Document Themes folder.)

22. Undo the slide deletions from the NP_PPT_6_Lights presentation, and then save it.

23. Encrypt the presentation with the password **Lights**, and then mark the presentation as final.

Apply

Case Problem 1

Data Files needed for this Case Problem: NP_PPT_6-3.pptx, Support_PPT_6_Background.jpg, Support_PPT_6_Password.jpg, Support_PPT_6_Side.jpg

Pascal Cybersecurity Michael Petrakis was hired as an intern at Pascal Security in Minneapolis, Minnesota. When Pascal Security is hired by a new client, Michael's supervisor, Anjali Krishnamurthy, visits that client and presents an overview of the services that Pascal Cybersecurity will be providing. Anjali asked Michael to create a PowerPoint presentation to be used as a starting point for this talk. She also asked Michael to create a theme that others can use. Michael created a presentation with four sections: an Introduction section, a section about the importance of using strong passwords, a section about the new network policies that will be introduced, and a section about new policies for employees' mobile devices. Anjali will add the content to the last two sections when she reviews the presentation. Complete the following:

1. Open the file **NP_PPT_6-3.pptx**, located in the PowerPoint > Case1 folder included with your Data Files, add your name as the subtitle, and then save the file as **NP_PPT_6_Cyber** in the location where you are saving your files.

2. Change the color palette to Blue Warm.

3. Change the theme font set to a custom set that uses Gill Sans Nova for Headings and Garamond for Body text. Delete the custom font set from your computer.

4. On the slide master, change the width of the title text placeholder to 10.8", and then left-align it with the content placeholder, if necessary.

5. Change the width of the content placeholder to 10.8", and then left-align it with the title text placeholder, if necessary.

6. Change the width of the slide number placeholder to 2.3", and then right-align it with the content placeholder if necessary.

7. Change the color of the bullet characters in the bulleted list to Blue-Gray, Accent 1, Darker 50%, and change the size of the bullet characters to 110% of text.

8. Increase the space before first-level bulleted items to 12 points.

9. On the Title Slide layout, remove the date, slide number, and footer placeholders by using the appropriate command in the Master Layout group on the Slide Master tab.

10. On the Title Slide layout, change the width of both the title text placeholder and the subtitle text placeholder to 13.33". Change the height of the title text placeholder to 2", and change the height of the subtitle text placeholder to 0.6". Top- and left-align the title text placeholder with the top and left edges of the slide. Bottom- and left-align the subtitle text placeholder with the bottom and left edges of the slide.

11. Change the vertical alignment of the text in the title text placeholder so it is middle-aligned. Horizontally align the text in the subtitle text placeholder so it is right-aligned, and vertically align it so it is bottom-aligned.

12. Format the text in both placeholders as bold, and change the text color to White, Background 1.

13. On the slide master, insert the picture in **Support_PPT_6_Side.jpg**, located in the PowerPoint6 > Case1 folder. Resize it so it is 8" high and 1.52" wide, and then apply a 10-point soft edge to the picture. Position it so that it is horizontally 12.22" from the top-left corner of the slide and vertically -0.25" inches from the top-left corner of the slide.

14. On the Title Slide layout, hide the background graphics, and then fill the background of the Title Slide layout with the picture **Support_PPT_6_Background.jpg**, located in the PowerPoint6 > Case1 folder.

15. On the Title Slide layout, fill the title text placeholder with the dark blue color above the "le" in "style." Change the fill color to the color with an RGB value of 12,28,44, if necessary.

16. Change the fill of the title text placeholder to a gradient fill with five stops of type Linear and direction Linear Down. Set the positions of the five gradient stops to 0%, 20%, 50%, 80%, and 100%. Change the color of each stop to the recent blue color (with the RGB value of 12,28,44). Change the transparency of the stops at 0% and 100% to 100% transparency. Change the transparency of the stops at 20% and 80% to 50% transparency.

17. Insert a new layout named **Content Section Header** after the Section Header layout. Resize the title text placeholder so it is 1.45" high and 4.6" wide. Position it so that it is vertically centered in the middle of the slide and horizontally its position is 6.02" from the top-left corner of the slide.

18. Insert a content placeholder that is 5" high and 5.5" wide. Left-align it with the left edge of the slide. Vertically, align it with the middle of the slide.

19. Modify the Two Content layout by changing the width of the two content placeholders to 5.3". Align the content placeholder on the left so its left edge aligns with the left edge of the title text placeholder. Align the content placeholder on the right so its right edge aligns with the right edge of the title text placeholder.

20. Rename the slide master to **Cyber Theme**.

21. In Normal view, reset Slide 5, if necessary. Change the layout of Slide 4 to the Content Section Header layout, and then insert the picture **Support_PPT_6_Password.jpg**, located in the PowerPoint6 > Case1 folder, in the content placeholder.

22. Create a custom property named **Draft** of the type Yes or no. Set its value to Yes.

23. Encrypt the presentation with the password **Cyber**, and then set the presentation to always be read-only.

Create

Case Problem 2

Data Files needed for this Case Problem: Support_PPT_6_Bullet.png, Support_PPT_6_Logo1.png, Support_PPT_6_Logo2.jpg

Smith Harris Accounting   Victoria Hofbauer is an associate staff auditor at Smith Harris Accounting in Phoenix, Arizona. Her manager asked her to create a simple custom theme that the department will use for presentations. Refer to Figure 6–37 as you complete the following steps:

Figure 6–37   Slide master and Title Slide layout for the custom theme

Slide Master

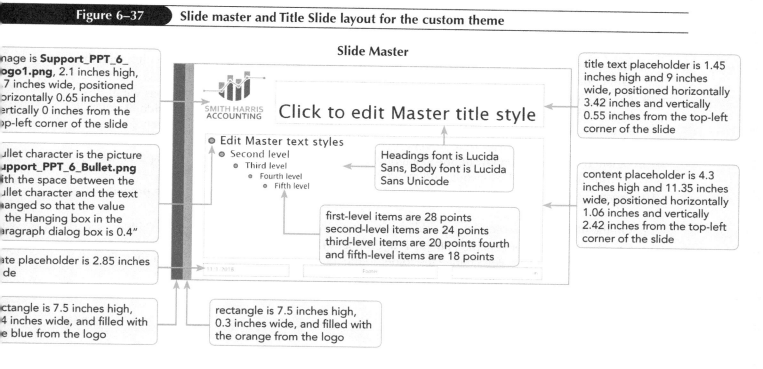

nage is **Support_PPT_6_ ogo1.png**, 2.1 inches high, 7 inches wide, positioned orizontally 0.65 inches and ertically 0 inches from the op-left corner of the slide

ullet character is the picture **upport_PPT_6_Bullet.png** ith the space between the ullet character and the text anged so that the value the Hanging box in the aragraph dialog box is 0.4"

ate placeholder is 2.85 inches de

ctangle is 7.5 inches high, 4 inches wide, and filled with e blue from the logo

rectangle is 7.5 inches high, 0.3 inches wide, and filled with the orange from the logo

title text placeholder is 1.45 inches high and 9 inches wide, positioned horizontally 3.42 inches and vertically 0.55 inches from the top-left corner of the slide

Headings font is Lucida Sans, Body font is Lucida Sans Unicode

first-level items are 28 points second-level items are 24 points third-level items are 20 points fourth and fifth-level items are 18 points

content placeholder is 4.3 inches high and 11.35 inches wide, positioned horizontally 1.06 inches and vertically 2.42 inches from the top-left corner of the slide

Title Slide Layout

xt is horizontally center-aligned d vertically top-aligned

ckground is filled with the cture **Support_PPT_6_ go2.jpg** set at 75% nsparency

xt is horizontally center-aligned d vertically middle-aligned

text is formatted as bold

title text placeholder is 2.3 inches high and 11.35 inches wide, positioned horizontally 0.99 inches and vertically 0.2 inches from the top-left corner of the slide

subtitle text placeholder is 1.81 inches high and 11.35 inches wide, positioned horizontally 0.99 inches and vertically 4 inches from the top-left corner of the slide

onep99/Shutterstock.com

1. Create a new, blank presentation, and then save the file as **NP_PPT_6_Company** in the location where you are saving your files.

2. Create the slide master and Title Slide layout as described in Figure 6–37. Rename the slide master to **Smith Harris**.

3. Delete the custom font set from your computer.

4. On the Two Content layout, resize the two content placeholders so that they are 4.3 inches high and 5.5 inches wide. Position the content placeholder on the left so that its left edge aligns with the left edge of the date placeholder, and position the content placeholder on the right so that its right edge aligns with the right edge of the title text placeholder. Change the vertical position of both content placeholders so they are 2.42 inches from the top-left corner of the slide.

5. On the Blank layout, hide the background graphics. Copy the blue and orange bar from the slide master, and then paste them on the Blank layout.

6. After the Title and Content layout, insert a new layout. Rename it to **Title and Table**.

7. On the new Title and Table layout, insert a rectangle two inches high and 2.4 inches wide. Align its top edge with the top of the slide, and then change its horizontal position to 0.75 inches from the top-left corner of the slide. Remove the shape outline of the rectangle, and then fill it with the White, Background 1 color. Move the rectangle to the bottom layer on the slide.

8. On the Title and Table layout, if necessary, resize the title placeholder to 11.35 inches wide. Insert a Table placeholder. Resize it so that it is 4.3 inches high and 11.35 inches wide. Position it so that its left and right edges align with the left and right edges of the title text placeholder, and then change its vertical position to 2.42 inches from the top-left corner of the slide.

9. Delete the Comparison layout, the Content with Caption layout, the Picture with Caption layout, the Title and Vertical Text layout, and the Vertical Title and Text layout.

10. Create a new custom property named **Theme** of the type Text. Add **SH Theme** as the property value.

11. On the title slide in Normal view, add your name as the title. Save the changes to the file.

12. Save the file as a theme named **NP_PPT_6_CompanyTheme** to the location where you are saving your files. (Make sure you change the folder to the folder where you are saving your files. Do not save the theme to the Document Themes folder.) Close the NP_PPT_6_Company file.

INDEX